Fifth Edition

THE EXPANDING FAMILY LIFE CYCLE: INDIVIDUAL, FAMILY, AND SOCIAL PERSPECTIVES

Monica McGoldrick
Director, Multicultural Family Institute,
Highland Park, New Jersey

Betty Carter
Emerita Director, Family Institute of Westchester

Nydia Garcia Preto
Associate Director, Multicultural Family Institute,
Highland Park, New Jersey

PEARSON

Boston Columbus Indianapolis New York San Francisco Hoboken
Amsterdam Cape Town Dubai London Madrid Milan Munich Paris Montreal Toronto
Delhi Mexico City Sao Paulo Sydney Hong Kong Seoul Singapore Taipei Tokyo

VP and Editorial Director: Jeffery W. Johnston
Acquisitions Editor: Julie Peters
Program Manager: Megan Moffo
Editorial Assistant: Andrea Hall
Executive Product Marketing Manager: Christopher Barry
Executive Field Marketing Manager: Krista Clark
Team Lead Project Management: JoEllen Gohr
Team Lead Program Management: Laura Weaver
Project Manager: Janet Portisch
Procurement Specialist: Deidra Skahill
Art Director: Diane Lorenzo
Art Director Cover: Diane Ernsberger
Cover Design: Cenveo® Publisher Services
Media Producer: Allison Longley
Editorial Production and Composition Service: Cenveo Publisher Services
Full-Service Project Manager: Harleen Chopra, Cenveo Publisher Services
Printer/Binder: LSC Communications
Cover Printer: LSC Communications
Text Font: Times LT Std

Credits and acknowledgments borrowed from other sources and reproduced, with permission, in this textbook appear on the appropriate page within text.

Library of Congress Cataloging-in-Publication Data

ISBN 10: 0-205-96806-6
ISBN 13: 978-0-205-96806-0

Betty Carter (1929–2012) was the bright star that guided the evolution of this book from its first edition in 1980. The brilliance and creativity of Betty's thinking is still at the center of our thinking about the life cycle and of this book. We still feel deeply her presence as our guardian angel as we move the ideas forward to address the dramatically changing life cycle of the twenty-first century. We hope we are continuing to live up to her highly collaborative and rigorous standards even without her physical presence. This book has been very much a continuation of her creative energy and we hope it is worthy of her.

CONTENTS

LIST OF FIGURES

LIST OF GENOGRAMS

PREFACE

WHAT IS NEW TO THIS EDITION

- Expanded delineation of individual and family life cycle tasks and phases in relation to the larger societal context
- New chapter on friendship over the life cycle
- New chapter on sexuality over the life cycle
- Expanded exploration of psychological and physical health and illness over the life cycle
- Completely revised discussion of men's issues through the life cycle, individually, in family life, and in the social context
- Revised discussion of the expanding phase between adolescence and adulthood, often referred to as "adultolescence," where young people are requiring more time for developing their ability to support themselves and a new generation of family
- Revised discussion of cultural and spiritual aspects of major diagnostic categories in the DSM5.
- Provides clinical example to demonstrate using the three-generational multicontextual framework for assessment and intervention.
- Expands discussion of the rapidly changing patterns of coupling and marriage through the life cycle.

FOR WHOM WE ARE WRITING

The Expanded Family Life Cycle is a book for professionals and students in all areas of health care, social service, and education: psychology, social work, family therapy, nursing, and sociology, and all fields of counseling, such as school, vocational, college, addictions, and pastoral counseling. Our aim has been to lay out a perspective that has broad applicability for understanding and working with individuals and families as they evolve through the life cycle in a social and cultural context. We have divided the book into three parts: Perspectives on the Evolving Family Life Cycle, Life Cycle Transitions and Phases, and Clinical Dilemmas and Interventions.

REDEFINING HUMAN DEVELOPMENT

The book bridges the traditionally separate spheres of individual development and the family life cycle in a way that transforms the traditional categories and proposes a new, more comprehensive way to think about human development and the life cycle within the larger context of cultural and social perspectives. Our expanded view of family actively includes the reciprocal impact of stresses at multiple levels of the human system: the individual, the immediate family household(s), the extended family, the community, the cultural group, and the larger society.

PUTTING THE INDIVIDUAL IN CONTEXT

Although social scientists give lip service to the notion of the individual's role in the system, there has been a tendency for mental health professionals to compartmentalize theorizing about families separately from theorizing about the individual. Theories of individual development, evolved in the field of human development, have espoused primarily psychodynamically oriented schemas, especially Erikson's modifications of Freudian theory, that ignore the gender, race, sexual orientation, and class norms of society that have produced deeply skewed models of "normal" child and adult development; such schemas make those who don't conform to dominant norms seem deficient. This thinking has been reinforced by the entire enterprise of diagnosis focused on universalizing individual pathology and ignoring systemic assessments as they influence human health and illness, strengths and resilience. Such splitting is not compatible with systemic thinking. It leads to divergent and inconsistent definitions of problems and their locus. Murray Bowen's family systems theory, like George Engel's bio-psycho-social model in medicine, is a notable exception to this tendency to split individual and family systems thinking. Bowen's theory places individual behavior and feelings squarely in the context of the family system, elaborating on the intricacies of the impact and the interaction between an individual and the family system of three or more generations. Bowen's theory also holds each adult individual responsible for creating change in the system. We have made a continuing effort in this edition to spell out a more comprehensive framework for individual development in the context of relationships and society (Chapter 1). The importance of situating individual development in context of the larger system is brought home by Steve Lerner in his expanded chapter (27) on the intersection between the therapist's life cycle issues and that of the family in treatment—a key dimension of the fit between therapist and family as the clinical process unfolds. As his chapter profoundly illustrates, this framework helps us locate the points at which the chronic background anxiety in a family is likely to coincide with the acute stress of navigating a current life cycle transition.

REDEFINING FAMILY: WIDENING OUR LENS

This edition celebrates the diversity of the twenty-first century. We refer not only to cultural diversity but also to the diversity of family forms. There are many ways to go through life in a caring, productive manner, and no specific family structure is ideal. Indeed, most life cycle theory has focused theoretical and research attention on the developmental stages of just one family form: the White, Anglo, middle class, nuclear families of a once-married heterosexual couple, their children, and (occasionally) their extended families. This book expands the definition of family in ways that attempt to include everyone in our society. We have widened our lens to deal more concretely in large and small ways with the fact that every family is a group of individuals embedded in communities and in the larger society whose impact is definitive and must be taken into account for interventions at the family level to succeed.

Our choice of language symbolizes our recognition of the vast changes in family structure that are taking place. We have replaced the limited term "nuclear family," which has come to refer only to a father and mother and their children in intact first families, with the term "immediate family," referring to all household members and other primary caretakers or siblings of children, whether in a heterosexual couple, single-parent, unmarried, remarried, gay, or lesbian household. We believe "commitment to each other" more than biological or legal status to be the basic bond that defines a family.

While it may be statistically accurate to outline the widely experienced stages of the family life cycle, focusing on marriage (Chapter 14), the birth and development of children and adolescents (Chapters 15 and 16), midlife and launching (Chapter 17), young adulthood (Chapter 13), aging (Chapter 18), and death (Chapter 19), no single list of life stages can be sufficiently inclusive. Throughout this edition, we have tried to recognize the vast number of people whose family life cycle varies in significant ways from the traditional stage outline. Individuals of different cultures and socioeconomic groups go through the stages at very different ages. A growing number of adults are choosing not to marry (Chapter 10) or, like gays and lesbians, are prevented from marrying (Chapter 7) or, like the poor (Chapter 5), find marriage almost impossible to afford. It thus becomes appropriate because of the increasing diversity of couples over the life cycle to speak of "couples therapy" rather than "marital therapy" (Chapter 14). Growing numbers of women are delaying childbearing or are choosing to remain childless. The prevalence of divorce and remarriage is requiring a large proportion of our society to manage additional life cycle stages and complete restructuring of their families as they move through life. There has been a dramatic increase in the percentage of permanent single-parent households created by divorce or single-parent adoption. For clinical interventions with families at these stages, we offer chapters on divorce (Chapter 20), single parents (Chapter 21), and families transformed by the divorce cycle: reconstituted, multinuclear, recoupled, and remarried families (Chapter 22).

Families that experience migration must also negotiate an additional life cycle stage of adjusting to a new culture (Chapter 12). Finally, vast differences in family life cycle patterns are caused by oppressive social forces: racism, sexism, homophobia, classism, ageism, cultural prejudices of all kinds, poverty, and immigration. We seek to include all of these dimensions in our thinking, while still providing clear and manageable clinical suggestions related to the family's place in its many contexts. Chapters that expand on these more inclusive perspectives include the chapters on women (Chapter 2) and on men (Chapter 3), on social class (Chapter 4), and on LGBT families (Chapter 7). Further expanding our view of family relationships, we have separate chapters on siblings through the life cycle (Chapter 9), spirituality (Chapter 8), sexuality (Chapter 6), chronic physical and mental illness (Chapter 23), alcohol problems (Chapter 24), domestic violence (Chapter 25), and on creating meaningful life cycle rituals (Chapter 26).

While family patterns are changing dramatically as we enter the twenty-first century, the importance of community and connection is no less important than ever, but we must shift our paradigm to understand people's experiences of community as they move through life. We have added a chapter on friendship through the life cycle (Chapter 11) to convey the centrality of these connections throughout our life cycle. Our identity is bound up in our interrelatedness to others. This is the essence of community—relationships that bridge the gap between private, personal, and family relationships, and the impersonal public sphere. We have a need for a spiritual sense of belonging to something larger than our own small, separate concerns. With our ever-greater involvement in work, time for anything "unnecessary" has been disappearing, leaving little time for church or synagogue, friends, family Sunday dinners, supporting children's school activities, political action, or advocacy. These activities often get lost in the scramble to survive, leaving little but the individual striving for power and money. We look at the concept of home as a place of self-definition and belonging, a place where people find resilience to deal with the injustices of society or even of their families, a place where they can develop and express their values. Home reflects our need to acknowledge the forces in our history that have made us strong, but it is also a concept that we remake at every phase of life, with family, with friends, with work, with nature, with smells and sounds and tastes that nurture us, because they give us a sense of safety and connection. Clinical intervention needs to acknowledge the importance of these spiritual, psychological, and physical places of belonging and safety at each life cycle phase. We see the concept of home as at the core of a meaningful life cycle assessment. We must assess clients with regard to their sense of belonging and connection to what is familiar. Having a sense of belonging is essential to well-being. Grasping where this sense of home is for a client is an essential part of any assessment and clinicians and policy makers who do not consider our deep-seated need for continuity and belonging as we go through life, especially through traumatic transitions and disruptions, will increase the trauma of the original experience.

THE SOCIAL PERSPECTIVE

In addition to focusing on the individual in the context of the family, this text expands our lens to the community and larger societal levels as they impact families and individuals. Our aim is to facilitate readers including in their clinical evaluations and treatment all the major forces that influence human beings as they move through life: race, class, sexual orientation, gender, ethnicity, spirituality, politics, work, time, community, values, beliefs, and dreams. We do not have separate chapters on culture, because we believe that consideration of culture, race, and ethnicity is so essential to every issue discussed in the book. All authors have worked to keep cultural considerations in the forefront of their clinical descriptions. As our awareness of societal patterns of domination and privilege has grown, we have expanded our analysis of the impact of social norms on families. We have also included throughout the book cases that reflect the social forces that impinge on individual and family functioning. It is our strong belief that this expanded family life cycle context is the best framework for clinical intervention because it deals with the development over time of individuals in their family relationships and within their communities as they struggle in this new millennium to define and implement life's meanings within a larger society that helps some more than others. To be lasting, change must encompass every level of our lives. We have summarized this multicontextual lifecycle framework in our opening chapter.

MONICA MCGOLDRICK'S ACKNOWLEDGMENTS

The 5th edition of *The Expanding Family Life Cycle* has been a labor of love with my dear friend and sister, Nydia Garcia Preto. I am extremely grateful that Nydia, who has been my collaborator in so many other efforts over four decades, has been at my side to develop this new edition. We have struggled together mightily to figure out how to transform this edition to include the rapidly changing patterns of families in the twenty-first century. I am so appreciative of her thoughtful efforts to make sense of the complex issues of the life cycle in this new century. I know I pressed her for more time than she had, and I am grateful for the many days we spent at our table trying to figure out how to express ourselves, organize our thoughts, understand the complex phenomena of the life cycle, and to deal with the numerous challenges of this many layered book for which we had a strong vision that demanded much rigor from our authors. This book has also been the fruition of my love for and debt to Betty Carter, with whom I shared so much for so many years. For three decades, she and I wrote together, taught together, and thought together more closely than I have ever done with anyone else. I have greatly missed her in working on this edition. Having to proceed without her enormous good humor, creativity, energy, and willingness to stretch me and herself and others has been hard indeed. I have missed her at every turn. I am thankful to Nydia's commitment and good thinking (just when I run out of steam!). I am extremely proud of what we have accomplished together. I am very grateful as well for the contributions from so many colleagues who have delivered the best papers ever for this edition! I know Betty would appreciate their efforts. This edition required a whole rethinking of the life cycle to fit the changing circumstances as we proceed in the new millennium. Nydia and I have worked hard to understand the increasing complexities of families as they move through the life cycle and deal with increasingly difficult global constraints. These complexities have made it very difficult to write in as straightforward a way as we would wish. Each time we would write a sentence, we would say, "On the other hand, there is this other factor that influences that phenomenon." Space constraints were especially challenging, and we were incredibly fortunate in the efforts of our authors to write meaningful chapters in their limited space.

I thank my wonderful friends for the support they give me every day, no matter where on the globe they are. In addition to Nydia, my appreciation goes to Nollaig Byrne, Froma Walsh,

John Folwarski, Imelda McCarthy, Jayne Mahboubi, Elaine Pinderhughes, Matthew Mock, Maria Root, Fernando Colon, Robert Jay Green, Michael Rohrbaugh, Doug Schoeninger, Glenn Wolff, Salome Raheim, Vanessa Jackson, Vanessa Mahmoud, Gyorgy Gaspar, Liz Nicolai, Kalli Adamides, Charlotte Danielson, Jane Sufian, Janey Hart Tollinger, John Dumas, Roberto Font, Barbara Petkov, and Sueli Petry. I also thank my friends, Evelyn Lee, Michael White, and Sandy Leiblum, and my dearest friend and sister, Carol Anderson, who lived through thick and thin with me for more than 40 years. Her brilliance and friendship inspire me every day. I miss Carol and my other friends greatly, and they live on in my heart every day. I hope I am doing them proud with this work.

My son has gotten married since our previous edition appeared, so I have gained a new daughter, Anna, and a wonderful new extended family in her parents, Renee Psiakis and Bill DePalma. How lucky is that! Sophocles has kept the home fires burning, as he has done for more than 45 years now, while I was preoccupied or off working to bring this book forth. I am very grateful for his love and steadiness through all. I thank my sisters, Morna and Neale, for being at my side for my life cycle journey, and my nephews, Guy and Hugh, for rooting for me from their place in the next generation. I celebrate the entrance of my grandnephew, Renzo Robert Livington, the first member of the next generation of our family, who is a complete love. Long may he thrive. I have always been fortunate to stand on the shoulders of my parents; my caretaker, Margaret Pfeifer Bush, my Aunt Mamie, and my godparents, Elliot and Marie Mottram, and Jack Mayer.

Finally, I thank my sister, soulmate, friend, and longtime collaborator Betty Carter for her friendship and intellectual stimulation over so many years. I am so grateful for her life force, her humor, her intelligence, her sticking power, and the warmth of her friendship for so many years.

NYDIA GARCIA PRETO'S ACKNOWLEDGMENTS

Working on this new edition of *The Expanding Family Life Cycle* with Monica McGoldrick has been an extraordinary experience. Monica's commitment and ability to stay focused and excited about these ideas have been inspirational for me. Although there were times when events in my own life cycle limited the time I could give to working on this book, the hours we spent thinking and sharing ideas, writing and rewriting, and then thinking again because changes were taking place faster than we thought were always rewarding. Taking part in this project has been challenging and transformative in more ways than I expected. I want to thank Monica for her friendship, encouragement, and generosity throughout the years we have worked together. Our personal histories and lives are very different, yet we seem to share a strong spiritual connection and a thirst for learning about and understanding the complexities of life, which for me has been essential. It has been a privilege to work with her, and to share the joys and pains in our personal and professional lives during all these years.

When she first asked me to co-edit the previous edition of this book, a book I have found to be fundamental in my learning about families, I was taken aback. Knowing how closely she and Betty had worked together, and how powerful and influential their thinking has been for so many of us who studied with them, I questioned the value of my contribution. My initial response was not to do it. But, in her wonderfully convincing way, Monica presented her reasons for asking me. We teach together, we stay up late trying to figure out how to continue on this journey of learning and teaching the concepts we love and find transformative. We love working with families, teaching about systems theory, strategizing about changing systems, mentoring students, building networks, and supporting each other when we are without answers. How could I not be part of rethinking and editing this wonderful book? I continue to be thankful for her trust, for our collaboration, and for the creativity that she brings to our work.

I am also especially thankful for the experience of working with all the authors in this book, whose amazing contributions and good will when we kept asking for rewrites made this edition possible. They are truly dedicated scholars and clinicians. I have learned so much from them! I also want to acknowledge the generous and invaluable support of my colleagues at MFI: Barbara Petkov, Roberto Font, and Sueli Petry, who were willing to read my writing and listen to my complaints, and my friends who understood my unavailability when I could not play with them. And, of course, I am especially grateful for the encouragement and support I received from the many members of my family, particularly my daughter Sara and son David. They have given me the opportunity to experience the complexities of being a mother raising children while also having a career. We have gone through adolescence, and now they are both at different stages of adulthood. I am learning about staying connected while letting go, and enjoying having two wonderful grandsons, Tahan (16) and David (5). We have survived my separation from their father and are adjusting to different configurations of family structure. I thank them for their lessons, their challenges, and their love. This year when Carl, their father, died after a battle with cancer, they showed an amazing ability to love and nurture as we took care of him, and helped him die with dignity. Through the years, Carl and I remained friends, for which I am grateful, and very thankful for his extended family's exceptional understanding, friendship, and support.

I have found strength in the memories of my life with my mother, Santa; father, Herminio; and brother, Luis, who are now gone, but living in my heart. And I especially want to acknowledge my partner in life, Conrad, whose generosity and caring keep me hopeful as I become older.

JOINT ACKNOWLEDGMENTS

We give heartfelt thanks to every author in this book. We know we have been, as Betty used to put it, "critical, hands-on, in-your-face editors, full of requirements and suggestions." It could not have been easy for you authors, but you came through with wonderful, thoughtful new material.

And those of you who answered our cries for help very late in the process—you know who you are—we'll never forget your rescue of several important chapters! And to those who did yet one more draft when you thought you weren't up to it—and you know who you are—we are grateful for your perseverance. We love you for it and we know the readers will as well. We are grateful to Tracey Laszloffy who put enormous effort into the extraordinarily challenging task of creating multiple-choice questions for psychological and cultural concepts as complex as those presented in this book. We also thank our friend and collaborator, Sueli Petry, for all the extra work she did in the development of this manuscript. We are so grateful for her quiet willingness, steadiness, and extraordinary competence in making complicated tasks doable. Our administrator, Georgeann Sorensen, and office manager, Roberto Font, supported our efforts on the book by keeping our office running smoothly, so that we could concentrate on the many tasks this book entailed. You helped us keep things in order, communicated with authors, and also protected us when we needed time alone to concentrate on the book.

We are very grateful that Pearson brought this 5th edition of our Life Cycle book to fruition. We thank all the people who worked diligently to make the book a reality, in these difficult times for book publishing and even while the organization was undergoing a major transition. Julie Peters oversaw the publication, with the help of many others. We thank also our previous Pearson editor, Ashley Dodge, who took our calls in the middle of the night and was a true friend in helping us wend our way through a complex system. Our Project Manager, Harleen Chopra went way beyond the call of duty to help us finish the production in as timely a fashion as possible. We thank you all.

ABOUT THE EDITORS

Monica McGoldrick, M.A., M.S.W., Ph.D. (h.c.), is the Director of the Multicultural Family Institute in Highland Park, New Jersey, and on the Psychiatry Faculty of the Robert Wood Johnson Medical School of Rutgers University. Her other books include *Ethnicity and Family Therapy*, Third Edition; *Genograms: Assessment and Intervention*, Third Edition; *Living Beyond Loss*, Second Edition; *Revisioning Family Therapy: Race, Culture, and Gender in Clinical Practice*, Second Edition; and *The Genogram Journey: Reconnecting with Your Family* published by W. W. Norton in 2011, which translates her ideas about family relationships for a popular audience, using examples such as Beethoven, Groucho Marx, Sigmund Freud, and the Kennedys. Her newest book *The Genogram Casebook: A Companion to Genograms: Assessment & Intervention* will be published in 2016.

She received her B.A. from Brown University, a Masters in Russian Studies from Yale University, and her M.S.W. and an Honorary Doctorate from Smith College School for Social Work. Dr. McGoldrick is known internationally for her writings and teaching on topics including culture, class, gender, loss, family patterns (genograms), remarried families, and sibling relationships. Her clinical videotape demonstrating the use of the life cycle perspective with a multicultural remarried family dealing with issues of unresolved mourning has become one of the most widely respected videotapes available in the field. Her new videotape, *Harnessing the Power of Genograms*, demonstrates an initial interview with a client exploring the connections between the presenting problem and the client's history and family relationship patterns.

Nydia Garcia Preto, M.S.W., is the Associate Director at the Multicultural Family Institute in Highland Park, New Jersey, where she also has a private practice. Ms. Garcia Preto was formerly a Visiting Professor at the Rutgers Graduate School of Social Work, and for many years the Director of the Adolescent Day Hospital at the University of Medicine and Dentistry of New Jersey. She received her M.S.W. from Rutgers Graduate School of Social Work and her B.A. in Sociology at Rider College. A highly respected family therapist, author, and teacher, and organizational trainer, she has publications in textbooks and journals on issues of cultural competence, Puerto Rican and Latino families, Latinas, immigration, ethnic intermarriage, and families with adolescents. She is coeditor of the most recent edition of *Ethnicity and Family Therapy*. Ms. Garcia Preto received the Frantz Fanon, M.D. Award from the Post Graduate Center for Mental Health for her work with Puerto Rican and Latino Adolescents and Families, and the Social Justice Award from the American Family Therapy Academy. She and her colleagues at MFI have developed many trainings for many years on multiculturalism in clinical work and organizational consulting on cultural competence.

Betty Carter, M.S.W., (1929–2012), was the founder and Director Emerita of the Family Institute of Westchester in White Plains, New York. She spent over 30 years as a family therapy clinician, supervisor, teacher, and director of a major training institute. She received awards from the American Family Therapy Academy, Hunter College School of Social Work, and the American Association for Marriage and Family Therapy Research and Education Foundation. With her colleagues Peggy Papp, Olga Silverstein, and Marianne Walters, she cofounded the Women's Project in Family Therapy, which promoted a feminist revisioning of family therapy and received awards from both the Family Therapy Academy and the AAMFT. Their work culminated in a book on gender-sensitive family therapy practice: *The Invisible Web: Gender Patterns in Family Therapy Relationships*.

In 1996 Betty Carter authored a trade book on couples, *Love, Honor and Negotiate: Building Partnerships That Last a Lifetime*. She published numerous professional book chapters and journal articles, along with educational videotapes produced by Steve Lerner for Guilford Press. Her husband of more than 50 years, Sam, was a musician. They had two sons and three grandchildren. She always said that of all her ideas she always loved the family life cycle framework most "because it contains all the other ideas and has room for more."

CONTRIBUTORS

Constance Ahrons, Ph.D., *Professor Emerita, University of Southern California and former Director of the Marriage and Family Therapy Doctoral Program, USC, LA. Private practice in San Diego, CA.*

Carol Anderson, M.S.W., Ph.D. (1939–2014), *Professor Emerita, University of Pittsburgh Medical School, Pittsburgh, PA.*

Maria Anderson, M.S.W., *is a therapist in the Adolescent Division of Addiction Medicine at the Western Psychiatric Institute and Clinic, Pittsburgh, PA.*

Kiran S. K. Arora, Ph.D., *is on the faculty of Long Island University, Brooklyn, New York.*

Deidre Ashton, M.S.S.W., L.C.S.W., *Individual, Couple and Family Therapist, Clinical Supervisor, Consultant, Private Practice, Philadelphia, PA; Associate faculty, Multicultural Family Inst., NJ.*

Timothy Baima, Ph.D., *Associate Professor at Palo Alto University and in private practice in San Mateo, CA.*

Kathy Berliner, L.C.S.W., *Marriage and Family Therapist. Former faculty, Family Institute of Westchester.*

Lynne Blacker, L.C.S.W., *is in private practice in New York City.*

Celia J. Falicov, Ph.D., *Clinical Professor, Department of Family Medicine and Public Health and of Psychiatry, Director of Mental Health Services, Medical Student-Run Free Clinic, University of California, San Diego.*

Richard H. Fulmer, Ph.D., *Private practice, New York, NY; Faculty, Child and Adolescent Program, National Institute for the Psychotherapies, New York, NY.*

Paulette Moore Hines, Ph.D., *Private practice, Training & Consultation; Founding faculty, Multicultural Family Institute; Executive Director, Emerita - Center for Healthy Schools, Families & Communities, Rutgers University Behaviorial Health Care (formerly University Behavioral HealthCare); Clinical Assistant Professor, Department of Psychiatry - Rutgers Robert Wood Johnson Medical School.*

Evan Imber-Black, Ed.D., *Program Director of the Marriage and Family Therapy Masters Degree at Mercy College, Dobbs Ferry, NY; and Director of the Center for Families and Health, Ackerman Institute for the Family.*

Demaris Jacobs, Ph.D., *Former faculty, Family Institute of Westchester.*

Jodie Kliman, Ph.D., *Core faculty, William James College (formerly Massachusetts School of Professional Psychology), Newton, MA; founding member of the Boston Institute for Culturally Affirming Practices.*

Tracey Laszloffy, Ph.D., *Private practice and Director of the Center for Relationship Healing, Norwich, CT.*

Steve Lerner, Ph.D., *Private practice, Lawrence, KS.*

Matthew Mock, Ph.D., *Professor of Psychology, J.F.K University; Private clinical and consulting practice, Berkeley, CA; Former Director CIMH Center for Multicultural Development; California Institute for Mental Health (CIMH) & Family, Youth, Children's & Multicultural Services, City of Berkeley, CA.*

Barbara Petkov, L.M.F.T., Ed.S., *Faculty of the Multicultural Family Institute, and in private practice in Highland Park, NJ.*

Sueli Petry, Ph.D., *Faculty of the Multicultural Family Institute, Psychologist, Rutgers University Behavioral Health Care, Newark, NJ, and in private practice, Highland Park, NJ.*

John Rolland, M.D., MPH., *Professor of Psychiatry & Behavioral Neurosciences; University of Chicago Pritzker School of Medicine; Executive Co-Director, Chicago Center for Family Health.*

Mary Anne Ross, B.A., *Coordinator of Training and Consultation, COPSA Institute for Alzheimer's Disease and Related Disorders, Rutgers University Behavioral Health Care, Piscataway UMDNJ.*

Natalie Schwartzberg, L.C.S.W., *Marriage and Family Therapist. Former faculty Family Institute of Westchester.*

Froma Walsh, M.S.W., Ph.D., *Firestone Professor Emerita, School of Social Service Administration and Department of Psychiatry, The University of Chicago, Co-Founder and Co-Director, Chicago Center for Family Health.*

Marlene F. Watson, Ph.D., *Associate Professor, Couple & Family Therapy Department, Drexel University in Philadelphia, PA.*

Chapter 1

The Life Cycle in Its Changing Context: Individual, Family, and Social Perspectives

Monica McGoldrick, Nydia Garcia Preto, Betty Carter

— **Learning Outcomes** —————————————————————

- Describe how generations within a family impact each other.
- List changes in family life cycle patterns that have occurred in recent decades.
- Describe the importance of belonging and friendship in healthy development.
- Define the individual, family, and social levels of the multi-contextual framework for clinical assessment, and describe the components of each level.
- List and describe the guidelines for a multi-contextual life cycle assessment.

"Life must be understood backward, but . . . it must be lived forward."

Soren Kierkegaard, 1843 (Kierkegaard, 2000, p. 12)

The Family Life Cycle: A System Moving Through Time

Human development takes shape as individuals evolve through the matrix of the family life cycle, embedded in the larger sociocultural context. All human experiences are framed by the interlocking nature of individual trajectories and kinship networks in the context of temporal motion, culture, and social change. An individual's life takes place in the context of the family and the social system's past, the present tasks it is trying to master, and the future to which it aspires. Thus, the family life cycle, embedded in the larger social context, is the natural framework within which to focus our understanding of human identity and development. This chapter and this book offer a multicontextual life cycle framework for understanding families in the United States in their cultural context over their life course. Statistics offered refer to the United States unless otherwise specified and are an effort to help clinicians appreciate individuals as they move through their lives, in the context of their families and the larger social system.

We are born into families. They are the foundation of our first experiences of the world, our first relationships, and our first sense of belonging to a group. We develop, grow, and hopefully die in the context of our families. Families comprise people who have a shared history and an implied shared future. They encompass the entire emotional system of at least three, and frequently four or even five, generations held together by blood, legal, emotional, and/or historical ties. Relationships with parents, siblings, and other family members go through transitions as they move through life. Boundaries shift, psychological distance among members changes, and roles within and between subsystems are constantly being redefined (Norris & Tindale, 1994; Cicirelli, 1995;

Tindale, 1999; Meinhold, 2006; McKay & Caverly, 2004; Connidis, 2001, 2008). It is extremely difficult to think of the family as a whole because of the complexity involved.

As a system moving through time, families are different from all other systems because they incorporate new members only by birth, adoption, commitment, or marriage, and members can leave only by death, if then. No other system is subject to these constraints. A business manager can fire members of his organization viewed as dysfunctional, and members can resign if the organization's structure and values are not to their liking. In families, by contrast, the pressures of membership with no exit available can, in the extreme, lead to severe dysfunction or even suicide. In nonfamily systems, the roles and functions are carried out in a more or less stable way, by functional replacement of those who leave for any reason, or else the group dissolves and people move on into other systems. Although families also have roles and functions, their main value is in the relationships, which are irreplaceable.

Until recently, therapists have paid little attention to the family life cycle and its impact on human development. Even now, psychological theories tend to prioritize individual development, relating at most to couples or parents and children in the nuclear family, ignoring the multigenerational context of family connections that pattern our lives. But our society's swiftly changing family patterns, which assume many configurations over the life span, are forcing us to take a broader view of both development and normalcy. Those milestones around which life cycle models have been oriented (birth, marriage, childbearing, and death) hold very different roles in the lives of families in the twenty-first century than they did in earlier times. Even in the three decades of this book's history, we have revised the definitions of life cycle phases and their meanings with each of our five editions to reflect our evolving understanding of this framework and the exciting and dramatically changing realities of the life cycle of families in the United States in our times.

The tremendous life-shaping impact of one generation on those following is hard to overestimate. For one thing, three, four, and sometimes now five different generations must adjust to life cycle transitions simultaneously. While one generation is moving toward old age, the next is contending with late middle age, caregiving, or the empty nest. The next generations cope with establishing careers and intimate peer adult relationships, having and raising children, and adolescents, while the youngest generations are focused on growing up as part of the system. Naturally, there is an intermingling of the generations, and events at one level have a powerful effect on relationships at each other level. The important impact of events and relationships in the grandparental generation is routinely overlooked by therapists who focus only on the nuclear family. Indeed, human beings are unique for the role grandparents and other adults play in parenting (Bateson, 2010). This supportive role is supremely important for our very survival as a species, as the extra caretaking provided by grandparents, aunts, uncles, and other adults is very protective for children's development.

The developmental literature has also largely ignored the powerful impact children have on adult development. Children's role in changing and "growing up" their parents, as parents respond to the unfolding of their children's lives, is lost in a unidirectional linear framework. It also ignores the powerful role grandchildren often play in promoting their grandparents' development, just as grandparents are often a major influence on their development (Mueller, Wilhelm, & Elder, 2002; Mueller & Elder, 2003). Children are actually a major impetus for growth for older generations. Indeed, there is suggestive evidence that having only daughters impacts fathers' feminist sympathies, and the more daughters they have, the more impacted they are (Washington, 2007). Just as parents, siblings, peers, and neighbors influence us (Bertrand, Luttmer, & Mullainathan, 2000; Fernandez, Fogli, & Olivetti, 2004), so do our children. Far from being the one-way street that most life cycle formulations have offered us, our lives continually spiral through multigenerational and contextual connections with those who come before us, those who go with us through life, and those who come after us.

In addition to what we have inherited from past generations and what we learn from our children, as we move through the family life cycle, there is also, of course, the impact of living in a given place at a given time. It is always important to consider the cohort to which family members belong, that is, the period in history when they grew up. The cohort to which people belong historically influences their worldview, their sense of possibility, and their beliefs about life cycle transitions. Each generation or cohort is different, as cultures evolve through time, influenced by the social, economic, and political history of their era, which makes their world view different from the views of those born in other times (Elder & Shanahan, 2006; Elder & Giele, 2009; Gladwell, 2008).

Cohorts born in different cultures and living through different periods vary, of course, in fertility, mortality, acceptable gender roles, migration patterns, education, attitudes toward child-rearing, couple relationships, family interrelationships, and aging. Those who lived through the Great Depression and World War II, those who experienced the Black migration to the North in the 1940s, the baby boomer generation that grew up in the 1950s, those who came of age during the Vietnam War in the 1960s, and cohorts who grew up during the Reagan years, will have profoundly different orientations to life, influenced by the times in which they have lived. For more references on cohorts, see Elder (1992, 1999); Elder and Shanahan (2006); Elder and Johnson (2002); Mueller and Elder (2003); Schaie and Elder (2005); Johnson, Foley, and Elder (2004); Neugarten (1979); Treas (2002); Shanahan and Elder (2002); Brown and Lesane-Brown (2006); Gladwell (2008).

And as Malcolm Gladwell (2008) points out, there are specifics of being at a certain key life cycle point when opportunities open up. For example, 19 percent of the wealthiest 75 people ever born anywhere in the world were born in the United States between 1830 and 1840. These people made their money in the industrial manufacturing era of the 1860s and 1870s, when Wall Street emerged, and the rules by which the economy had traditionally operated were transformed. Gladwell suggests that those born after the 1840s were too young to participate and those born before the 1830s were too old and fixed in their ways of doing things to become part of the new era. Thus, there is a certain life cycle trajectory that influences our creativity in particular ways, assuming that we have the family and community to support the endeavor.

A similar pattern occurred with the development of computers in the 1970s. Bill Gates, Steve Jobs, and a great many of the other key geniuses of the computer age were born smack in the mid-1950s and came of age at the first moment when anyone had the opportunity to work on the newly developed main frame computers. They grew up in communities and families that fostered their developing interests and allowed for their creative energy. Thus, if we want to understand what creates resilient, innovative, healthy citizens, we need to look at a multiplicity of factors including the historical era, the individual, the family and its social location (in terms of class, race, and ethnicity), and the community life in which they were embedded. Each group or cohort born at a given time in history and living through various sociocultural experiences at the same life cycle phase is, to an extent, marked by its members' experiences, particularly those that occur during their "coming of age" phase of the life cycle (late adolescence and early adulthood).

> Assess your comprehension of the family life cycle: a system moving through time by completing this quiz.

The Changing Patterns of the Family Life Cycle

Of course, the phases of the life cycle themselves are rather arbitrary breakdowns. The meaning of various phases is also changing in our time. For example, the phase of aging has changed dramatically in the past century, as people are living 30 years longer in the past century than they ever lived in human history. Even the phase of "retirement" has a completely different meaning in the past 50 years, as people are now in the same physical condition at 65 or 70 as they used to be in their early 50s or even younger (Bateson, 2010). The phase of midlife, some are calling it "Adulthood II" (Bateson, 2010), is also new, since there never before was a phase of active healthy adult life post child-rearing. Even the notion of childhood is not universal. It has been described as the invention of eighteenth-century

Western society and adolescence as the invention of the nineteenth century (Aries, 1962), related to the cultural, economic, and political contexts of those eras. The notion of young adulthood as an independent phase could be thought of as an invention of the twentieth century, due to society's technological needs. In recent times, it is even suggested that we need a new phase called "adultolesence" to describe the period that is expanding at both ends in between adolescence and independent adulthood (Kimmel, 2009). Adolescence has expanded downward by about 4 years in the past century to about 12 for girls and 14 for boys. Our society has created a huge dilemma with children who are physically the size of adults, and think they should be free to act like adults, but they are often unable to support themselves for as long as 20 years from age 12 into their 30s! Where it used to be possible for someone with a high school education to support a spouse and children, this is, for the most part, no longer the case. In general, the tasks of finishing one's education, leaving home, finding a spouse, and becoming a parent all used to occur within a short period of time in the early 20s. But within the past generation, these tasks have been spread out and changed so that the average marriage does not occur until people are in their late 20s, and education may continue until at least that late. So there may be an increasing phase of "preparation" for adulthood during which unlaunched children require ongoing parental support in a very changed life cycle process than has ever been the case before.

The inclusion of women as independent individuals could be said to be a construct of the late twentieth century. The lengthy phases of midlife, the empty nest, and older age have certainly been developments primarily of the late twentieth and early twenty-first centuries, brought about by the smaller number of children and the greatly increased life span of our times. Given the current changes in the family, the twenty-first century may become known for an even more expanded launching phase, influenced by the educational requirements of the postindustrial age. We are also certainly involved in a transformation in our concept of marriage and of nurturing/ caretaking relationships with both children and older family members. So we must be extremely cautious

about stereotyping people who do not fit into traditional norms for marriage, or having children, as if these were in themselves measures of maturity, which they are not. We must consider in our clinical assessment the critical life cycle challenges of individuals and families at each point in their lives, while being careful not to marginalize those whose life courses differ from the norms of the majority. As Johnnetta Cole (1996) put it: "No one family form— nuclear, extended, single-parent, matrilineal, patrilineal, fictive, residential, nonresidential—necessarily provides the ideal form for humans to live or raise children in" (p. 75).

And we must keep in mind that the family of the past, when the extended family reigned supreme, should not be romanticized as a time when mutual respect and satisfaction existed between the generations. The traditional, more stable multigenerational extended family was supported by patriarchy, sexism, classism, racism, and heterosexism. In those traditional family structures, respect for parents and obligations to care for elders typically went along with their control of resources, and was often reinforced by religious and secular sanctions against those who did not go along with the ideas of the dominant group. Now, with the increasing ability of younger family members to determine their own fate regarding marriage and work, the power of elders to demand filial piety is reduced.

Family life cycle patterns are changing dramatically in the past century. In 1900, the average life expectancy in the United States was 47 years; by the year 2000, dying before old age has become a rare event. About 75 percent of the population lives beyond their 65th birthday, whereas, in 1850, only 2 percent of people lived to this birthday (Skolnick, 2013)! Half of the longevity increase of all human history has taken place since 1900. At that time, half of all parents experienced the death of a child; by 1976, this rate was only 6 percent. In 1900, 25 percent of children had lost a parent by death before the age of 15; by 1976, only 5 percent of children experienced this. In 1900, one out of 62 children had lost both parents; by 1976, this was only 1 out of 1800 (Skolnick, 2013).

At the same time that we are living much longer and experiencing much less untimely loss than ever in history, our couple and parent–child patterns have been changing rapidly. One of the greatest changes in living patterns in the United States in recent years is the increase in single-person households. Since 1960, the percentage of people living alone has doubled. Today, 27 percent of all households consist of one person, the highest level in U.S. history (U.S. Census Bureau, 2010).

Overall changes in family life cycle patterns have escalated dramatically, in recent decades owing to many societal patterns as indicated in Figure 1.1.

Despite the fact that in our era nuclear families often live on their own and at great distance from extended-family members, they are still part of the larger multigenerational system, their past, present, and anticipated future relationships being intertwined. Family members have many more choices than they did in the past: whether or whom to marry; where to live; how many children to have, if any;

Figure 1.1 Recent societal changes influencing life cycle patterns.

- A lower birth rate
- Longer life expectancy
- The changing role of women
- The rise in unmarried motherhood
- The rise in unmarried couples
- Increasing single-parent adoptions
- Increasing LGBT couples and families
- Increasing longevity with the implications of caretaking needs at the end of life
- Greater physical distance among family members
- Increasing work time, especially for women
- High divorce and remarriage rates
- Increasing two-paycheck marriages to the point where they are now the norm
- Changing household composition: more single-person households than ever before

how to conduct relationships within the immediate and extended family; and how to allocate family tasks. Our society has moved from family ties that were obligatory to those that seem voluntary, with an accompanying increase in ambiguity of the norms for relationships. Relationships with siblings and parents are fairly often disrupted by occupational and geographic mobility as families move through the life cycle; even couples are increasingly managing long-distance relationships.

Another major change in life cycle patterns is that child-rearing, which used to occupy adults for their entire active life span, now generally occupies less than half of adult life prior to old age. Even women who choose primary roles as mother and homemaker now face an "empty nest" phase that is likely to be longer than the number of years they devote to child care. The meaning of family is thus changing drastically, and there are often no agreed-upon values, beyond child-rearing, by which families define their connectedness.

Indeed, the notion of the nuclear family seems to be an invention of the industrial age. Prior to that, families lived in community groups, but with mechanized transportation and the need for concentrated groups of workers for factories, the size of family groups became smaller. In traditional societies, when children were raised in large family groups, there were usually three or more caregiving adults for each child younger than six, and there was little privacy. Through most of history, families lived in clans of extended families of about 40 people (Perry, 2002). By 1500 in the west, the average household had decreased to 20 people, by 1850 to 10, and by 2000 to less than 3 in the United States with, as stated earlier, 27 percent living alone!

In our society, with three people or fewer in the average household, families often do not even eat family meals together, and spend a great percent of available family time watching TV or on the computer (Perry, 2002). Children, young adults, as well as parents who have launched their children, and the aging, tend to live in age-segregated cohorts. Age segregation is a big factor in the frequent isolation of family units, which is also a result of the high mobility of families and the frequent lack of stable, long-lasting community networks.

The changing role of women has been central in changing family living patterns. Almost half of the U.S. labor force is made up of women (U.S. Department of Labor, Bureau of Labor Statistics, 2011), which means they have less time to be social connectors within the family and within the community. Yet, our social institutions still operate mainly on the assumption that women in families will do all the caretaking society needs without compensation. And women are still, largely, trying to do this caretaking. The "typical" caregiver in the United States is a woman in her 40s, who works outside the home, and spends more than 20 hours a week providing unpaid care (Family Caregiver Alliance, 2009; Folbre, 2012). But, because our society does not reward attention to the needs of others, women, shockingly, have no Social Security benefits for any time they have spent caretaking! They often experience serious economic losses for the time they spend caring for others, including lost wages, health insurance and other job benefits, and lower retirement savings (Rivers & Barnett, 2013a).

There is also an increasing chasm between less fortunate children, who grow up in poverty with financially pressed, often single parents, and more advantaged children, who grow up in comfortable circumstances with highly educated dual-earner parents. While privileged children live lives with many scheduled activities and have little time for free play, children in poor families often have no access to resources that would support their development and education at all. These profound differences create a huge differential even in longevity between the rich and the poor. Education is, in fact, a powerful differential in the potential for a longer, healthier life (Kolata, 2007; Vaillant, 2012). In 1980, the differential was only 3 years, but that difference has increased to 10 years (Pear, 2008). At the age of 35, even a year of more education leads to as much as a year and a half longer life expectancy (Pear, 2008). Children, in general, might develop very differently if our society provided real equity in access to education and health care, most of all for our youngest citizens (Neuman & Celano, 2012; Friedman, 2012). If we as a society really believe in social justice, we owe it to our children to be accountable to them, rather than individualizing our response to child problems with punishment,

medication, and court sanctions. What if we required children to be accountable to the community in making up for their misdeeds? Speck and Attneave (1973) recommended such interventions decades ago. If we were accountable to our children, they could be accountable back to the community of those who care for them, and our world might begin to look very different (Perry, 2002).

Our social institutions must change to address the needs of families today. Hopefully, the more flexible upcoming generations will assist in this process and the universality of changes in families' structure will bring about new thinking on family and social policy and a new attention to the integrity of families in their community context.

> **Assess your comprehension of the changing patterns of the family life cycle by completing this quiz.**

Dimensions of Human Development in the Context of the Family and Society

This chapter and this book attempt to broaden traditional Euro-American formulations of human development, which have begun with the individual as a psychological being and generally defined development as growth in the human capacity for autonomous functioning. In African and Asian cultures by contrast, the very conception of human development begins with a definition of a person as a social being and defines development as the evolution of the human capacity for empathy and connection. It makes much more sense to think of human development always in the context of the family and society (Korin, McGoldrick, & Watson, 1996; Jordan, 1997). This framework defines maturity by our ability to live in respectful relation to others and to our complex and multifaceted world. Maturity requires us to appreciate our interconnectedness and interdependence on others and to behave in interpersonally respectful ways, controlling our impulses and acting on the basis of our beliefs and values, even if others do not share them. This view of maturity requires the ability to empathize, trust, communicate, collaborate, and respect others who are different and to negotiate our interdependence with our environment and with our friends, partners, families, communities, and society in ways that do not entail the exploitation of others.

Most previous theories of "normal" human development proposed supposedly inherent, age-related, developmental stages for the individual (Erikson, 1963, 1994; Levinson, 1986, 1996; Sheehy, 1977, 1995; Vaillant, 1977; and others). Even many feminist theorists have ignored the family system in their effort to move away from traditional notions of the family, and act as if the individual existed in society with no mediating family context.

Part of the pull, even for family therapists, to revert to psychodynamic thinking whenever the individual is under consideration, seems to come from the predominance of models of psychology built on Freud and Erikson's ideas of psychosocial development. Compared to Freud's narrow focus on human development evolving through different erogenous zones, Erikson's (1963, 1968) outline of eight stages of human development was an effort to highlight the interaction of the developing child with society. However, Erikson's stages actually emphasize not relational connectedness of the individual but the development of individual characteristics (mostly traits of autonomy) in response to the demands of social interaction (Erikson, 1963). Thus, trust, autonomy, industry, and the formation of an identity separate from his family are supposed to carry a child to young adulthood, at which point he is suddenly supposed to know how to "love," go through a middle age of "caring," and develop the "wisdom" of aging. This discontinuity—a childhood and adolescence focused on developing one's own individuality and autonomy—expresses exactly what we believe is wrong with developmental norms of male socialization even today; they devalue by neglect most of the major tasks of adulthood: collaboration, interdependence, intimacy, caring, teamwork, mentoring, and sharing one's wisdom.

We want to draw attention to the developmental transitions required as people move through life and to help clinicians think in terms of where people are in their life cycle development and what tasks they need to accomplish at this phase. We believe it is essential to embrace and affirm (with all their complexities) the importance of all levels of the human system: individual, familial, and social.

Although we do not believe life cycle stages are inherent or universal, we do believe that individuals and families transform, and need to transform, their relationships as they evolve, to adapt to changing circumstances over the life course. Moving to a new phase requires a change of the system itself. That is, family members must change their roles and rules of relating as they move to a new phase. Most of these phases pertain to entries and exits of family members or to changes in the nature of family members' relationships, role functioning, and status in relation to each other. Coupling and having children are, of course, the major life cycle phases of family member expansion, while launching and death are the major phases of contraction. The relationships and roles of family members with each other must also shift as parenting phases move from parents raising young children, to parents managing adolescents, to parents launching young adults, to parents welcoming their children's partners and their families, to midlife adults caring for aging parents. Each of these phases requires major change in how the family is organized and how it functions. All families must renegotiate their relationships with each other many times as they move through life. When families cannot adapt to individual and systemic changes as their life cycle phases require, they become stuck and their healthy development is subverted.

Our conceptualization of human development broadens the focus from discrete tasks and stages of accomplishment to an identity which evolves in the context of our families, and our social and cultural world, including dimensions of gender, class, race, spirituality, sexual orientation, and ethnicity. We believe that these dimensions of culture structure development in fundamental ways. Because our society so quickly assigns roles and expectations based on gender, culture, class, and race, children's competences are not milestones that they reach individually, but rather accomplishments that evolve within the complex web of these dimensions. Racial, religious, and other prejudices are generally learned emotionally in childhood and are very hard to eradicate later, even if one's intellectual beliefs change.

Children's acquisition of cognitive, communicative, physical, emotional, and social skills to succeed over the life course is circumscribed by the social context in which they grow up. Our evaluation of their abilities is meaningful only if these constraints are taken into account.

Developing a schema that examines human development by including milestones of emotional connectedness from earliest childhood has drawn us to the work of those whose perspectives have gone beyond White male development. These include Hale-Benson (1986), who explored the multiple intelligences and other developmental features she identified in African American children; Comer and Poussaint (1992), who factored racism and its effects into their blueprint for the development of healthy Black children; Ian Canino and Jeanne Spurlock (2000), who outlined many ways in which minority ethnic groups socialize their children; and Joan Borysenko (1996), whose descriptions of the stages of female development appear to have universal applicability for understanding interdependence, a concept that girls and children of color learn early, but that is ignored in traditional western theories of development.

Dilworth-Anderson, Burton, and Johnson (1993), and Burton, Winn, Stevenson, and Clark (2004), and their colleagues argue for the importance of a life cycle perspective because it is based on interdisciplinary ways of thinking, being a framework that emerged from the cross-fertilization of the sociology of aging, demographic cohort analysis, and the study of personal biography in social psychology and history. In their view, a life cycle perspective represents a dynamic approach to the study of human development by focusing on the interlocking nature of individual trajectories within kinship networks in the context of temporal motion, culture, and social change. They have highlighted the importance of a life cycle perspective for research, offering as it does the conceptual flexibility to design frameworks and studies that address families in their diverse contexts and structures (Dilworth-Anderson et al., 1993). This is a most compelling argument, and one that we highlight to encourage culturally meaningful research that includes diverse populations.

Coming from a very different context as a psychodynamically trained psychiatrist who inherited two large longitudinal research samples, George Vaillant has come to argue very similarly for the importance of a life cycle perspective based on multiple conceptualizations (1977, 1983, 1995, 2002, 2012). Vaillant, whose work has now gone on for more than 40 years, has indeed offered a magnificent developmental account of the evolution of his longitudinal research. He demonstrates the complex dynamics and interplay of his own life cycle and that of the other researchers, with the lives and theories of the men they have been studying.

Developing a self in context: Belonging

Healthy development requires establishing a solid sense of our cultural, spiritual, and psychological identity in the context of our connections to others. This context carries every child from birth and childhood through adulthood to death and defines his or her legacy for the next generation. As we have been stressing, gender, class, culture, race, sexual orientation, and spirituality structure, our developing beliefs, values, relationships, and ways of expressing emotion, prescribe each person's identity and ways of being emotionally connected to others.

This context involves the development of a sense of belonging or "home," as we go through life. Researchers on African Americans and others who have been marginalized in our society have written often about the need for "homeplace," for belonging, for rootedness, and connection to place and kin that is a crucible of affirmation for their sense of social and cultural identity (hooks, 1999). Homeplace involves multilayered, nuanced individual and family processes that are anchored in a physical space that elicits feelings of empowerment, belonging, commitment, rootedness, ownership, safety, and renewal. This includes the ability to develop relationships that provide us with a solid sense of social and cultural identity. In the long-term ethnographic and clinical research with African Americans of Burton and her colleagues, "homeplace" emerges as a pivotal force for individuals and families throughout their life course (Burton, Hurt, Eline, & Matthews,

2001; Stevenson, Winn, Coard, & Walker-Barnes, 2003; Burton, Winn, Stevenson, & Clark, 2004).

While the particulars of the meaning of home are likely to change over the life cycle, the need for a sense of belonging remains essential to our well-being throughout life. This sense of belonging is especially important for marginalized populations, who are denied a sense of belonging by the dominant culture, and for immigrant groups, who must find ways to recreate their sense of belonging in a new culture. Many people in the United States do not seem to have an evolving sense of themselves as community members or participants in the development of a U.S. identity or as evolving citizens of a global community.

A sense of home provides the security and safety to develop self-esteem, political consciousness, and also to resist the oppressive forces of our society (Burton et al., 2004). Of course, those who are gay, lesbian, bisexual, or transgender may need special adaptive strategies to find a place where they can feel at home, because the very place that others rely on fundamentally may become a place of greatest danger. This is often true as well for children whose families suffer from mental illness, violence, addictions, and other negative or disruptive forces.

Home may be a physical location, with physical associations, but it is also absolutely a spiritual location. Burton and her colleagues provide important clinical examples of the value of proactively attending to our clients' need for the continuity and belonging provided by the concept of "homeplace" (Burton et al., 2004). Transferring clients to a new therapist or a new home, or ignoring their important kin connections, even where there are serious dysfunctions, may only compound their distress. We see the concept of belonging, homeplace, and connection to what feels safe as being at the core of a meaningful life cycle assessment.

Grasping where this sense of home is for a client is an essential part of any assessment, and clinicians and policy makers who do not consider our deep-seated need for continuity and belonging as we go through life, especially through traumatic transitions and disruptions, will increase the trauma of the original experience. We can, through our clinical efforts, validate, empower, and strengthen family and community ties or, by ignoring them, perpetuate the invalidation, anomie, and disconnection of the dominant value structure of our society, which privileges individualism, autonomy, competition, and materialistic values, over connectedness to a whole network of kin with whom one is linked by history and hopefully by a shared future.

Friendship through the life cycle

As part of our sense of home and the importance of community, friendship is one of our most important resources through life. Indeed, dramatic research on women in the past few years has turned upside down five decades of stress research that focused on the fight-flight responses to stress, by demonstrating that women are more likely to "tend and befriend," that is, their tendency to turn to their friends when under stress throughout the life cycle is a major resource and protection (Taylor, Klein, Lewis, Gruenewald, Gurung, and Updegraff, 2000). It helps when marriages are in trouble, when a spouse has died, and it even contributes to longevity. While our society has a well-developed ideology about marriage and family, we have tended to relegate friendship to the cultural attic, which has blinded us to its importance throughout the life cycle (Rubin, 1993). Friends can be crucial supports from early childhood and through adolescence and young adulthood, mitigating family trauma and dysfunction and providing encouragement, socialization, and inspiration for our development. In the phases of adulthood, friends can again buffer stress, tell us the truth about ourselves, stimulate us to change our ways, and, in fact, keep us healthy. The loss of a close friend at any point in the life cycle can be a major stress. Friends should always be included on genograms and considered in our life cycle assessment and intervention. Indeed, Christakis and Fowler (2011), and others (Conniff, 2014) are suggesting through scientific research what we have always known, that our lives are majorly determined not just by nature and nurture, but by our social networks.

Developing a self in context: Gender

Although there has always been a "his" and "hers" version of development, until the late twentieth century, only the former was ever described in the literature (Dinnerstein, 1976; Gilligan, 1993; Miller, 1976). Most theoreticians tended to subsume female development under male development, which was taken as the standard for human functioning. Separation and autonomy were considered the primary values for male development, the values of caring, interdependence, relationship, and attention to context being considered primary only for female development. In general, developmental theories have failed to describe the progression of individuals in relationships toward a maturity of *interdependence*. Yet human identity is inextricably bound up with one's relationships to others, and the notion of complete autonomy is a delusion. Human beings cannot exist in isolation, and the most important aspects of human experience have always been relational.

Most developmental theorists, however, even feminist theorists, have espoused psychodynamic assumptions about autonomy and separation, overfocusing on relationships with mothers as the primary factor in human development.

Much of the feminist literature continued the overfocus on mothering, even while locating the mother–child dyad within a patriarchal system (Chodorow & Contratto, 1991; Dinnerstein, 1976). Most child development theories, even feminist theories (Chodorow, 1974; Gilligan, 1993), explain male development's focus on autonomy and independence as resulting from the child's need to separate from his mother by rejecting feminine qualities. Silverstein and Rashbaum (1994), Gilligan (1993), and Dooley and Fedele (2004) have effectively challenged the assumption that male development requires separating from one's mother. Gilligan (1993) critiqued Piaget's conception of morality as being tied to the understanding of rights and rules and suggested that for females, moral development centers on the understanding of responsibility and relationships, whereas Piaget's description fits traditional male socialization's focus on autonomy. Eleanor Maccoby (1990, 1999), the Stone Center at Wellesley (Jordan, Kaplan, Miller, Stiver, & Surrey, 1991; Jordan, Walker, & Hartling, 2004), and others (Barnett & Rivers, 2004; Michael Kimmel, 2009, 2012, 2013) have expanded our understanding of the power dimensions in the social context of development. Their

work suggests a broader conception of development for both males and females.

As women have come to insist upon the right to a personal identity, perhaps a feminist movement was inevitable. Having always had primary responsibility for home, family, and child care, women began to resist their burdens as they came to have more options for their own lives. Given their pivotal role in the family and their difficulty in maintaining concurrent functions outside the family, it is perhaps not surprising that they have been the most prone to symptom development at life cycle transitions. For men, the goals of career and family have been parallel. For women, these goals have generally presented a serious conflict. Surely, women's seeking help for family problems has much to do with their socialization, but it also reflects the special life cycle stresses on women, who have borne primary emotional responsibility for family relationships at every stage of the life cycle.

Men's roles in families are also changing. While men of color have long had more flexible family roles, White men and others are participating more in child care (Khazan, McHale, & Decourcey, 2008; Levine, Murphy, & Wilson, 1993) and housework (Byron, 2012; Barnett & Rivers, 1996; Bureau of Labor Statistics, 2007), and many are realizing, in their minds, if not always in action (Hochschild, 2012), that equity and partnership are a sensible ideal for couples (Sayer, Bianchi, & Robinson, 2004). Sociologist Michael Kimmel holds out the ideal of men cherishing and nurturing their family relationships and also reforming the norms of the public arena to increase everyone's potential to live in a way which honors family and community commitments (Kimmel, 2012). He welcomes feminism, gay liberation, and multiculturalism as blueprints for the reconstruction of masculinity. He believes that men's lives will be healed only when there is full equality for everyone (Kimmel, 2013).

Traditional norms of male development (Green, 1998; Kivel, 2010; Dolan Del Vecchio, 2008) have emphasized characteristics such as keeping emotional distance; striving for hierarchical dominance in family relationships; toughness; competition; avoidance of dependence on others; aggression as a means of conflict resolution; avoidance of closeness and affection with other males; suppression of feelings except anger; and avoidance of "feminine" behaviors such as nurturing, tenderness, and expressions of vulnerability. Such norms make it almost impossible for boys to achieve the sense of interdependence required for mature relationships through life. Given such distorted norms for healthy development, it is not surprising that men so often grow up with an impaired capacity for intimacy and connectedness. Our culture's distorted ideals for male development have made it hard for men to acknowledge their vulnerability, doubt, imperfection, role confusion, and desire for connection (Kimmel, 2013).

Female development was until relatively recently viewed from a male perspective that saw women as adaptive helpmates to foster male and child development. Values that were thought to be "feminine" were devalued by male theoreticians such as Erikson, Piaget, and Levinson, while values associated with men were equated with adult maturity. Concern about relationships was seen as a weakness of women (and men) rather than a human strength. George Vaillant (2002, 2012; Wolf, 2009), in the largest longitudinal study ever conducted, has come after many years to the conclusion that relationships are key to male development in the long run, a surprise to him and to many others!

In fact, women have always defined themselves in the context of their changing relationships over the life span. Erik Erikson's (1968, 1994) still widely taught eight stages of development ignored completely the evolution of our ability to communicate, "tend" or "befriend" (Taylor, 2002), characteristics that most distinguish us from all other animals. Sara Lawrence-Lightfoot, recent author of a wonderful book about creativity and learning in the "third chapter" of life, tries to use Erikson's scheme, but finally admits that his eighth-stage model "seems too linear and predictable to match the messier, more unruly stories people were telling me" (2009, p. 43). She has to admit as well that Erikson seems to have missed entirely the reciprocity that is such a powerful part of our "giving forward" in life. Identity is defined as having a sense of self *apart from* rather than *in relation to* one's family and says nothing about developing skill in

relating to one's family or to others. It suggests that human connectedness is part of the first stage of trust versus mistrust, during the first 2 years of life, but he discusses this as attachment primarily to the mother, as have so many since then. The developmental literature, strongly influenced by the psychoanalytic tradition, has focused almost exclusively on mothers, giving extraordinary importance to mother–child attachment in the earliest years of life, to the exclusion of all other relationships in the family or to later developmental phases. This focus has led to a psychological determinism that early child experiences with one's mother are responsible for whatever happens later in the life cycle. The complex nature of human attachments from earliest infancy has been grossly oversimplified in discussions of early attachment that focus primarily on mothers. All of Erikson's five stages from infancy to adulthood focus on individual rather than relational issues: autonomy versus shame and doubt, initiative versus guilt, industry versus inferiority, and identity versus role confusion.

Doubt, shame, guilt, inferiority, and role confusion are all defined as counter to a healthy identity. Yet these concepts all have great significance in our understanding of our interrelationship to other human beings and to nature. We have to recognize that we need to develop skills in listening and learning, admitting our doubts and mistakes. While Erikson's own personal life story may explain his skewed perspective (McGoldrick, Gerson & Petry, 2008; see www.multiculturalfamily.org for Erikson's genogram life story), but we must still challenge such perspectives on human development. In Erikson's scheme, even the concept of generativity is ignored during the time of greatest human creativity, bearing and raising children, and appears only at midlife!

Children's sense of security evolves through their connection and identification with those who care for them—mothers, fathers, siblings, nannies, babysitters, grandparents, aunts, uncles, teachers, and all the others who participate in raising them. Traditional formulations of child development have ignored this rich context and offered us a one-dimensional lens for viewing a child's development: through the mother–child relationship. In most cultures throughout history, mothers have not even been the primary caretakers of their children, usually being busy with other work. Older siblings, grandparents, and other elders were more often the primary caregivers of young children. When we focus so myopically on mothers, we not only project impossible expectations on them, but we are also blinded to the richness of the environments in which most children grow up.

Eleanor Maccoby, who has been writing for many years about gender differences in sex-role development, has repeatedly pointed out that while innate gender differences do not appear to be major, the social context constricts girls from earliest childhood, and gender segregation is pervasive. This seems to be influenced primarily by boys' orientation toward competition and dominance, to which girls seem to be averse, and girls' apparent minimal ability to influence boys when they are together (Maccoby, 1999). It seems natural that girls are averse to interacting with anyone who is unresponsive and that they begin to avoid such partners. But what is it in the social context that reinforces boys for being unresponsive to girls? And what can we do to change these patterns? Obviously, there is much that we need to do as adults to ensure that girls' opinions are validated and given space in social interactions, but we must change our socialization of boys to increase their sensitivity and responsiveness to others. This is something that must be worked on from earliest childhood, if girls are to achieve equity in relationships.

Women tend to enter into deeper levels of reciprocity with their children than men do and to communicate with them better. Extensive gender segregation continues in workplaces (Chugh & Brief, 2008; Alksnis, Desmarais, & Curtis, 2008) and in some social-class and ethnic groups in which leisure time is still spent largely with others of the same sex even after marriage.

Kagan and Moss (1962) a generation ago traced achievement-oriented adults back to their relationships with their mothers, but did not look at their relationships with their fathers. They found that achievement-oriented males had very close, loving relationships with their mothers in infancy, while the females had less intense closeness with their mothers than the average. Hoffman (1972) suggested that a daughter is more likely to become achievement oriented if she does not experience the training in dependence that has generally been prescribed for girls. It appears that a mother's education and success play a larger role in the success of at least their sons.

Like Maccoby (1990, 1999), Kimmel and Messner (2008), and many others, we doubt that children's development of distinct styles of interacting has much to do with the fact that they are parented primarily by women. Maccoby thinks that processes within the nuclear family have been given too much credit and blame for sex-typing. The larger society's attitudes about gender roles, conveyed especially through the peer group, appears most relevant as the setting where children discover their differential social power: boys discover the requirement of maintaining their status in the male hierarchy, and the gender of friends becomes paramount. Many of the apparent gender differences we observe are undoubtedly not gender differences at all, but differences resulting from being in different positions in society (Kimmel, 2012).

Parents expect and reinforce different behaviors in their sons than in their daughters (Mallers et al., 2010; Rivers & Barnett, 2013b). They treat boys and girls differently from earliest infancy. In general, they discuss emotions—with the exception of anger—more with their daughters than with their sons. They use more emotional words when talking to their daughters (Brody & Hall, 1993). Fathers tend to treat young boys and girls in a somewhat more gendered way than mothers do (Raley & Bianchi, 2006). The "appropriateness" of these behaviors is then validated by the media as well as by teachers, pediatricians, relatives, babysitters, and by parents' own observations of children's play groups. Meanwhile, science argues about whether these are inborn differences or self-fulfilling prophecies. Only if we expand our lens to children's full environment can we properly measure the characteristics that may help them to attain their full potential and see clearly the influences that limit it. Seo (2007), for example, found that a father's involvement with his young children had a long-term influence on their children's later-life satisfaction.

The connected self: Beyond autonomy and self-determination

Infants and toddlers begin early to develop trust in their immediate environment, which ideally supports their safety and development. As soon as they reach the point of leaving the safety of their home environment, however, developing trust depends on how their cultural group is positioned in the larger world. It takes greater maturity for children to be able to develop their sense of self in a nonaccepting environment in which they do not receive support, than in a context in which everyone in the outside world affirms their values. Members of the dominant groups of our society receive this affirmation daily, whereas many others do not. A gay or lesbian child, a disabled child, a girl, a child of color, or a poor child is often stigmatized and vilified, and is not the one depicted in books, TV programs, and movies as the "valued" child. Thus, a nonprivileged child who does manage to develop a strong self has accomplished a developmental feat beyond that of a child who has always been affirmed both at home and in the larger society (Kunjufu, 1995). Our theories of child development must take this into account.

Actually, because of the ways U.S. history is still mistaught to our children, emphasizing only the good of White domination and minimizing racial and gender inequities that have been so built into our nation's structure, we are still having to fight for them to receive liberty and justice for all. Some children may lack certain adaptive skills because they live in such an affirming, nonchallenging environment that they are sheltered from feeling "other" when messages are given about our heroes and our exploits from Columbus on down to current politics. The dominant versions of our history that are taught to children may keep them oblivious to the contributions of people of color to their lives, to our nation and to the development of civilization as a whole (Loewen, 2008, 2010). Children who have not had the experience of being "other" because of their race, gender, sexual orientation, or other reasons have a tendency to be oblivious to the experiences of those whose lives are not part of the dominant group in our society.

We must appreciate the adaptive and resilient strategies developed by families that are not part of the privileged group in our society. Children raised in poverty, of whom a much larger proportion are children of color, are incredibly disadvantaged in their development, having less access to a safe home and neighborhood environments, to adequate education and health care. They are less supported in every way by our society. Their families experience more illness, unemployment, incarceration, disruption, and untimely death than others, and their dreams tend to be short circuited throughout their lives. In addition, sometimes "children who cannot conceptualize a future for themselves, do not have the motivation to defer the gratification found in premature sexual activity or substance abuse" (Hale, 2001, p. 43). Their life cycle trajectories are stunted by their lack of support at every level: racism, class oppression, and growing up in physically and psychologically dangerous environments. Everything must be done to support their resilience and nurture their development as children. It is much more difficult to change their life course, if they are not supported in early childhood (Goldstein & Brooks, 2012).

Given the American focus on individualism and free enterprise, it is not surprising that autonomy and competitiveness have been considered desirable traits leading toward economic success in the marketplace, and qualities to be instilled in children (Dilworth-Anderson et al., 1993). While self-direction and self-motivation are excellent characteristics, they can be realized only in privileged individuals who have health and resources and are helped to do so by their families and by society. Development requires much more than intellectual performance, analytical reasoning ability, and a focus on one's own achievements, as if they resulted from completely autonomous efforts. The people with the most privilege in our society—especially those who are White and male and who have financial and social status—tend to be systematically kept unconscious of their dependence on others (Coontz, 1992, 1998, 2006). They remain unaware of the hidden ways in which our society supports their so-called autonomous functioning. Thus, many White men who benefited from the GI bill to attain their education now consider it a form of welfare to provide education to minorities of the current generation. Those who are privileged tend to develop connections amidst a web of dissociations. Their privilege generally maintains their buffered position and allows them the illusion of complete self-determination. When people of any class or culture are raised to deny their emotional dependence on others, they tend to experience a terrible awakening during divorce, illness, job loss, or other adversities of life. Indeed, the most challenging aspect of development involves our beliefs about, and interaction with, others who are different from ourselves. Our level of maturity on the crucial dimension of tolerance and openness to difference is strongly influenced by how our families of origin, communities, cultures of origin, and our society as a whole have dealt with difference.

We believe maturity depends on seeing past myths of autonomy and self-determination. The connected self is grounded in a recognition of human interdependence. It requires that we appreciate our basic dependence on each other and on nature as illustrated in Figure 1.2.

We believe that children are best able to develop their full potential, emotionally, intellectually, physically, and spiritually, when they are exposed in positive ways to diversity and encouraged to embrace it. Children who are least restricted by rigid gender, cultural, or class role constraints have the

greatest likelihood of developing an evolved sense of a connected self.

This framework requires us to learn to control our emotional reactivity so that, unlike other animals, we can control our behavior and think about how we want to respond, rather than being at the mercy of our fears, phobias, compulsions, instincts, and sexual and aggressive impulses. This kind of reactivity has nothing to do with authentic and appropriate emotional expressiveness. Daniel Goleman (2006) discusses this process of mind over emotional reactivity, attributing to Aristotle the original challenge to manage one's emotional life with one's intelligence: "Anyone can become angry. That is easy. But to be angry with the right person, to the right degree, at the right time, for the right purpose and in the right way—this is not easy" (cited in Goleman, 2006, p. ix). The question is, as Goleman says, "How can we bring intelligence to our emotions, civility to our streets and caring to our communal life?" (2006, p. xiv).

Our assessment of development must also take into account the societal obstacles to a person's accomplishing the tasks leading to mature functioning. Women and people of color have generally grown up with an oppressive socialization that actually forbids the assertive, self-directed thinking and behavior essential for this definition of maturity. Girls in this society are expected to put the needs of others before their own. People of color are expected to defer to the beliefs and behaviors of White people, and the poor are expected to perform as well as the privileged without the same resources. A White male will generally be responded to with respect for asserting his beliefs, while a woman or person of color may be sanctioned or even harmed or ostracized by the community. Our developmental model must take this uneven societal playing field into account. Over the past 50 years, our society has made many strides in rebalancing support for girls' development and acknowledgment of the developmental needs of children of color and others who are not part of the dominant group. But we still have far to go to defeat the destructive gender and racial stereotyping of our children and to promote the full individual and social development of all children in our society. We are indeed the most flexible species on earth because of

---

Figure 1.2 Skills for mature relating.

Skills of Mature Relating Include the Following Abilities:

1. To listen with an open heart, without attacking or becoming defensive. Relate with openness, curiosity, tolerance, empathy, and respect for people who are different from ourselves.

2. To collaborate with others generously at work, at home, at play and in community activities.

3. To accept one's self and maintain one's values and beliefs, even if others do not agree.

4. To engage in nurturing, mentoring, and caring for others and accepting their care in return.

5. To consider other people and future generations, when evaluating sociopolitical issues such as the environment and human rights.

our social brains, which enable us to coordinate our needs with those of people around us. Our success as a species, as Shelly Taylor says in *The Tending Instinct* (2002), has come entirely from this gregarious nature. We owe it to the next generation not to permit the current deterioration of relationship and of community life to continue. No goal is more important for our future than developmental connectedness.

> Assess your comprehension of dimensions of human development in the context of the family and society by completing this quiz.

A Multicontextual Life Cycle Framework for Understanding Human Development

We believe that individual development always takes place in the context of emotional relationships, the most significant of which are family relationships, whether by blood, adoption, marriage, or informal commitment. Families are always embedded in a social and cultural context. From this perspective, it is impossible to understand individuals without assessing their current and historical family and cultural contexts as they are evolving through time. The family is the most immediate focus for therapeutic intervention because of its primacy in mediating both individual and social forces, bridging the two.

Whatever affects one member of a family affects other members as well—siblings, aunts, uncles, nieces, nephews, friends, godparents, and godchildren. The question often is, how involved are they with each other and how involved are they willing to be? What happens to an individual also has community ramifications. A person's education, health care, and safety require various community resources throughout the life cycle. Access to resources for help with an alcohol problem, mental illness, a stroke or other disability will have profound implications for the whole family's negotiation of their individual and family life cycles.

From the 1960s at least, some theorists began looking beyond the individual to the life cycle of families as well, the brilliant pioneers Reuben Hill (1970) and Evelyn Duvall (1977) being preeminent

among them. Their organizing principles for thinking about family development were primarily focused on couples and children. However, as the family is no longer organized primarily around married heterosexual couples raising their children, but rather involves many different structures and organizing principles, identifying family stages and emotional tasks for various clusters of family members is complex. Yet, even within this diversity, there are some unifying principles that we use to define stages and tasks, such as the primary importance of addition and loss of family members for the family's emotional equilibrium through life's many transitions (Hadley, Jacob, Milliones, Caplan, & Spitz, 1974).

We offer the following map to help conceptualize the complexities of the life cycle, showing the individual (mind, body, spirit) in the context of the multigenerational family system (immediate family, and extended family and kinship system), both of which are always embedded in the larger social context (friends, community, culture, and the larger society), and all moving through time together (Figure 1.3).

Time, of course, never stands still, so we wish we could have a three-dimensional map to convey the motion of the entire system, which is always evolving. We have drawn the map with the three inner circles representing the spiritual self, the psychological or intrapsychic self or mind, and the body or physical self. The two middle circles represent the immediate family and extended family and informal kinship network. The four outer circles represent the sociocultural context, including the friendship and community systems, the culture, and the larger society.

All clinical assessment involves taking into account the individual, family, and social context in which people are living. We have outlined in Figure 1.4 the core dimensions of each level of the context. Whatever the presenting problem is, the three levels of individual, family, and social context should be carefully evaluated. Our discussion of the three levels begins with the outside level, the social context, to highlight its importance and because it is so often given short shrift in the assessment of clinical problems. This assessment guideline is a general framework with questions to be covered, not a guide for conducting an interview. We believe clients should be assessed on the dimensions we have outlined here.

Figure 1.3 Multicontextual Life Cycle Framework for Clinical Assessment.

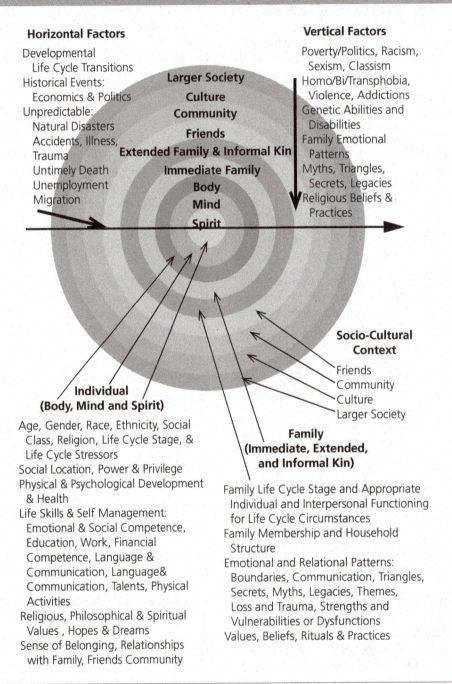

Horizontal Factors

Developmental
   Life Cycle Transitions
Historical Events:
   Economics & Politics
Unpredictable:
   Natural Disasters
   Accidents, Illness,
   Trauma
   Untimely Death
   Unemployment
   Migration

Vertical Factors

Poverty/Politics, Racism,
   Sexism, Classism
Homo/Bi/Transphobia,
   Violence, Addictions
Genetic Abilities and
   Disabilities
Family Emotional
   Patterns
Myths, Triangles,
   Secrets, Legacies
Religious Beliefs &
   Practices

Larger Society
Culture
Community
Friends
Extended Family & Informal Kin
Immediate Family
Body
Mind
Spirit

**Socio-Cultural
Context**
Friends
Community
Culture
Larger Society

**Individual
(Body, Mind and Spirit)**

Age, Gender, Race, Ethnicity, Social
   Class, Religion, Life Cycle Stage, &
   Life Cycle Stressors
Social Location, Power & Privilege
Physical & Psychological Development
   & Health
Life Skills & Self Management:
   Emotional & Social Competence,
   Education, Work, Financial
   Competence, Language &
   Communication, Language&
   Communication, Talents, Physical
   Activities
Religious, Philosophical & Spiritual
   Values , Hopes & Dreams
Sense of Belonging, Relationships
   with Family, Friends Community

**Family
(Immediate, Extended,
and Informal Kin)**

Family Life Cycle Stage and Appropriate
   Individual and Interpersonal Functioning
   for Life Cycle Circumstances
Family Membership and Household
   Structure
Emotional and Relational Patterns:
   Boundaries, Communication, Triangles,
   Secrets, Myths, Legacies, Themes,
   Loss and Trauma, Strengths and
   Vulnerabilities or Dysfunctions
Values, Beliefs, Rituals & Practices

Figure 1.4 Dimensions of Clinical Assessment: The Individual, Familial, and Sociocultural Contexts.

Individual (Body, Mind, and Spirit):

Age, Gender, Race, Ethnicity, Social Class, Religion, Life Cycle Stage & Life Cycle Stressors:

Take into account the basic demographics of each client and family member in terms of race, ethnicity, gender, religion, and social class. What is the sexual orientation and general attitude about gender roles of clients and how do their attitudes fit with those of family and community?

Have there been life cycle stressors such as births, loss of work, immigration or other moves, divorce, separation, a history of chronic physical or mental illness, genetic problems, trauma, untimely, unresolved or recent losses, physical or sexual abuse, war, or crime?

Social Location, Power and Privilege:

How do race, ethnicity, religion, life cycle stage, disability, gender, sexual orientation influenced clients' social location?

Do clients have a sense of psychological power, physical strength, and financial resources in relation to their life needs and the needs of family members or community?

Are there any indications of abuse or oppression at home, work, school, or in the community? How may the education, financial resources and social status of clients and their families be influencing the current situation? How may social class mobility have influenced family relationships, created subtle tensions or lead to isolation or loss for family members?

Physical and Psychological Development and Health:

Is there appropriate development of cognitive, physical, emotional and social functioning? Assess clients' assets, strengths, and disabilities: intelligence, self direction, learning abilities, developmental lag. Have symptoms developed such as sleep or mood disorders, behavioral disturbances, addictions to drugs, alcohol, food, sex, gambling, spending, etc? What temperaments do clients have? Are they shy, passive, outgoing, affiliative, aggressive, etc.?

Life Skills and Self Management:

Does the client have the ability to manage his or her life financially, emotionally, sexually, physically and spiritually? Do family members share these skills or not?

Emotional and Social Competence: Can clients function independently? Can they manage their emotions in relationships? Develop and maintain friendships? Can they nurture and care for others and accept care and nurturing from others.

Education: What is client's level of education, skill and development of his or her talents?

Work Patterns: What are the client's competencies, experiences, frustrations, and problems with work? Can they work collaboratively as well as independently? Do they view work as meaningful? What is the history of layoffs and hopelessness about finding meaningful work? Are they workaholics?

Financial Competence: What is client's yearly income and from what sources? How much control does client have over income? Are there child support payments? What is the level of debt? How many people does the client support? What are the savings, expected inheritance, or trust funds?

Language & Communication: Does the client have adequate language skills or language disabilities in the current context? Can client communicate ideas, feelings, needs and desires?

Talents: Musical, artistic, organizational, interpersonal, or other talents?

Physical Activities: Is client physically active or athletic.

(Continued)

Figure 1.4 Continued

Religious, Philosophical & Spiritual Values, Hopes and Dreams:

What are clients' beliefs about God and about the meaning of life, death, and life after death? What are their concerns about those who are less fortunate? Do they believe in something larger than themselves? Do clients belong to a faith community? Do they feel at home there? What are their hopes and dreams for themselves, their family, and community, and for future generations? To what degree do they pursue their fulfillment?

Sense of Belonging:

Do clients have a sense of "home" or of comfort and belonging in their families, communities, society and friendship networks, work system, etc.? What social networks, confidants, friends, connections to community organizations, and social groups do they have? Do clients initiate social contacts or share doubts and dreams with anyone?

Family Context: Immediate, Extended and Informal Kinship Network

Family Life Cycle Stage and Appropriate Individual & Interpersonal Functioning for Life Cycle Circumstances:

Assess whether family members are engaging in normative tasks of their specific life stage. Does the family have appropriate interdependence for their life cycle circumstances?

Family Membership and Household Structure:

Assess how multi-generational issues in the extended family may be influencing the immediate situation. Whether or not family members acknowledge it, and whether or not they are speaking to each other, all family, including extended family, are relevant to understanding of family's present emotional system. Pay attention to special pressures on single-parent families and on single adults and to clients' friendships and community connections, and to communication and relationships with ex-spouses and their families, especially if there are children.

Emotional and Relational Patterns: Boundaries, Communication, Triangles, Secrets, Myths, Legacies, Themes, Loss & Trauma, Strengths & Vulnerabilities or Dysfunctions:

What is the family's emotional climate: intimate, disorganized, unpredictable, tense, angry, cold, or distant. What triangles are operating? Are there secrets about births out of wedlock, suicides or affairs. Are there myths, legacies, taboos, or important themes in the family? Is there a history of chronic physical or mental illness, genetic problems, traumatic, untimely, unresolved, or recent losses, physical or sexual abuse, war, crime, immigration? Are there skills, talents, strengths, vulnerabilities, disabilities, or dysfunctions that are affecting family structure? How does the family set boundaries? Are there cut-offs, conflicts, or triangles in marital, parent-child, sibling, or other family relationships? Is there fusion or enmeshment in any family relationships? Assess communication patterns including decision-making (authoritarian, egalitarian, casual, or rigid)? Do family members have negotiation skills and ability to share intimately with each other? Do they show brilliance, artistic, musical, athletic talent, or talent for relationships or for transforming bad situations? Or, on the other hand, do they have learning, developmental and physical disabilities, addictions, violence, chronic illness and mental illness?

Values, Beliefs, Rituals & Practices:

What are the family's beliefs about the meaning of life and relationships? Do they believe, for example, that "Family is everything," "Upward mobility is essential," or " Money can get in the way of spiritual peace." Inquire in particular about beliefs and values related to the current symptoms. Are problems "God's punishment" or the result of someone being "a bad seed," or having a spell put on another?

Figure 1.4 Continued

Sociocultural Context

Friends:

Assess all clients for the strength of their friendship networks in terms of confidants they share personal problems with, "buddies" they hang out with, acquaintances they socialize with, etc. and for their ability to make and maintain friends over their life course.

Community:

Assess clients for their sense of comfort and belonging in their community and community changes they have experienced. Do they feel safe, accepted, and comfortable in their neighborhood? What political, social, professional, internet groups, fraternities or sororities, etc. do they belong to. Assess the community of clients' school and work systems. Do they feel accepted? Have they experienced bullying or mistreatment of any kind in work or community systems?

Culture:

Inquire about clients' ethnic and racial heritage and assess how identified are they with the various elements of this background. Assess how language, immigration and immigration status may be factors in their current situation.

Larger Society:

Assess clients' sense of power and privilege within the larger society. Do they feel at home or marginalized or oppressed in the society? How may their race, religion, social location, sexual orientation, disability, age, ethnicity, or immigration status contribute to their sense of well-being, belonging, or marginalization?

In Figure 1.3 we have represented historical, developmental, and unpredictable influences on individuals, families, and the social system schematically (Carter, 1978) along two dimensions that affect them as they evolve through life. The vertical axis of our chart shows how historical issues flowing down the family tree influence families as they go through life (biological heritage, genetic makeup, cultural, religious, psychological, and familial issues). The vertical axis includes cultural and societal history, patterns of power, social hierarchies, and beliefs that have been passed down through the generations. Andrew Solomon (2013) refers to this vertical axis as one's "vertical identity," referring to those aspects of who we are that are passed down from parent to child over the generations. It includes society's inherited norms of racial, gender, cultural, and religious prejudices, which limit the options of some and support the power of others. A group's history, in particular the legacy of trauma, will have an impact on families

and individuals as they go through life whether they were the oppressors or the oppressed. For example, legacies of the Holocaust affect both Jews and Germans; legacies of slavery affect both African and American countries that supported slavery; legacies of homophobia affect both homosexuals and heterosexuals; legacies of colonization affect both Native peoples and those who colonized their lands. The impact of these legacies is ever greater the more this history has been denied.

At a family level, the vertical axis includes the family's history and patterns of relating and functioning that have been transmitted down the generations, primarily through the mechanism of emotional triangling. It includes all the attitudes, taboos, expectations, labels, and loaded issues with which we grow up. At an individual level, this axis includes the genetic characteristics one inherits, including illnesses and abilities. These aspects of our lives make up the hand we are dealt. What to do with them is up to us.

The horizontal axis of the life cycle chart represents the developmental and unpredictable influences that are affecting families in the present as they go through life. Solomon (2013) refers to an individual's "horizontal identity" as acquired traits, foreign to one's parents, that become part of a child's self, and that transform his or her life trajectory, and that of the family. It describes how social influences affect families as they cope with the changes and transitions of their life course. Factors on this dimension include both predictable developmental life cycle phases and unpredictable events, the "slings and arrows of outrageous fortune," that may disrupt the life cycle process, such as untimely death, birth of a developmentally challenged or gifted child, gender non-conformity, chronic illness, or job loss. The horizontal axis relates to community connections, current events, and social policies that affect families. Of course, the current horizontal axis issues often become factors on the vertical axis for the next generations.

> Assess your comprehension of a multicontextual life cycle framework for understanding human development by completing this quiz.

Anxiety, symptom development, and healing

Individuals and families characteristically lack a time perspective when they are having problems. They tend to magnify the present moment, overwhelmed and immobilized by their immediate feelings. Or they become fixed on a moment in the past or the future that they dread or long for. Painful experiences such as illness and death are particularly difficult for families to integrate and are thus most likely to have a profound, long-range impact on relationships in the next generations. Families and individuals tend to lose the awareness that life always means motion from the past into the future with a continual transformation of familial relationships. As the sense of motion becomes lost or distorted, healing involves restoring a sense of life as a process and movement both from and toward.

Therapeutic interventions with a life cycle framework aim at helping families to reestablish their evolutionary momentum so that they can proceed forward to foster each member's unique development. Relevant life cycle questions include how family members are managing their same-generation and intergenerational relationships at each phase for the healthy evolution of the family. Are certain family members overfunctioning for others and are certain developmental or caretaking needs being neglected?

Individual and family stress are often greatest at transition points from one life cycle phase to another, as families must rebalance, redefine, and realign their relationships. Symptom onset has been correlated significantly with the normal family developmental process of addition and loss of family members such as birth, marriage, divorce, and death (Hadley et al., 1974). We found that a significant life cycle event, the death of a grandparent, when closely related in time to another life cycle event, the birth of a child, correlated with symptom development at a much later transition in the family life cycle, the launching of the next generation (Walsh, 1978; McGoldrick, 1977). Such research supports a clinical approach which tracks patterns through the family life cycle over several generations, focusing especially on nodal events and transition points to understand dysfunction at the present moment. The implication is that if emotional issues and developmental tasks are not dealt with at the appropriate time, they are likely to be carried along and act as hindrances in future transitions and relationships. For example, if young people do not resolve their issues with their parents, they will probably carry them into their young adult relationships and beyond. In life cycle terms, there is an expiration date on blaming your parents for your problems; at a certain point in life, maturity requires letting go of resenting your parents for what they did wrong or else you remain trapped in your family history.

Given enough stress on the horizontal, developmental axis, any individual family is likely to appear dysfunctional. On the other hand, even a small horizontal stress on a family in which the vertical axis is full of intense issues is likely to create great disruption in the system. The anxiety engendered on the vertical and horizontal axes is the key determinant of how well the family will manage its transitions through life. It becomes imperative, therefore, to assess not only the dimensions of the current life cycle stress but also their connections to family themes and triangles coming down in the family over historical time. Although all change is, to some degree, stressful, when the horizontal (developmental) stress intersects with a vertical (transgenerational) stress, there tends to be a quantum leap in anxiety in the system. To give a global example, if one's parents were basically pleased to be parents and handled the job without too much anxiety, the birth of the first child will produce just the normal stresses of a system expanding its boundaries. On the other hand, if parenting was a problem in the family of origin of one or both spouses, and has not been dealt with, the transition to parenthood may produce heightened anxiety for the couple. Even without any outstanding family of origin issues, the inclusion of a child could potentially tax a system, if there is a mismatch between the child's and the parents' temperaments. Or, if a child is conceived in a time of great political upheaval that forces the family to migrate, leaving its cultural roots for another country, ordinary stresses of the child's birth may be accompanied by extra stressors. The break in cultural and family continuity created by immigration will affect family relationships and family patterns throughout the life cycle for generations.

The sociocultural context of human development

Community represents multiple levels of the human system, from the small face-to-face neighborhood, group, or local community to the larger cultural group, to the nation, and then to our increasingly "global" society. All these levels have an enormous impact on the individuals and families under their sway. They offer protective safety and a sense of "home" and group identity or alienation, marginalization, and disaffection.

There is an African saying, "If I don't care for you, I don't care for myself," which expresses the sense that our identity is bound up in our interrelatedness to others. This is the essence of community defined as the level of interaction that bridges the gap between the private, personal, and familial, and the great impersonal public sphere. We have a need for a spiritual sense of belonging to something larger than our own small, separate concerns. With our

ever greater involvement in work, time for anything "unnecessary" has been disappearing, leaving little time for church or synagogue, friends, family Sunday dinners, supporting children's school activity, political action, or advocacy. These activities easily get lost in the scramble to survive in a tense, high-wired time that rewards nothing but the individual acquisition of power and money.

Many traditional communities (and families) have been repressive as well as secure and supportive of their members, but only as long as members conformed to family or community norms. Our social networks of friends and collective associations are no longer the given that they were in the past. We must find our own place in shifting social networks from neighborhoods to Internet communities. Community is one of the best antidotes to the violence and anomie of our society and our best hope of an alternative to consumerism as a way of life. And the focus on clients' having a sense of home is ever more important when the network of belonging is as rapidly changing as in our society. Shaffer and Amundson (1993) defined community as a dynamic whole that emerges when a group of people participate in common practices, depend on one another; make decisions together, identify themselves as part of something larger than the sum of their individual relationships, and commit themselves for the long term to their own, one another's, and the group's well-being. Choice is the operative idea here, not nostalgia.

With our increasingly global economy, our context has more and more become the entire earth, which makes finding a sense of belonging even more difficult. Clinicians have an important role to play in encouraging clients to think about the meaning of family and community to them and asking whether they are living according to their values and ideals. To do this, they must overcome training that has often advocated avoiding topics of spirituality or philosophy. In spite of thousands of years of holistic approaches to healing, our society has tended to keep physical, emotional, and spiritual healing separate.

We have also become one of the world's most class-stratified nations, with almost impenetrable walls between people of different status. The upper class lives in gated communities (where the emphasis is on security, not community), while the underclass lives behind prison bars, on the street, or in cell-like corners of the ghetto with almost no access to transportation to other parts of the community (Fullilove, 2004); and people in between are often confused about where they fit. The poor have tended not to vote, but as we are seeing in recent times, great political victories can be won with even a small percentage of eligible voters. If concerned citizens bring the poor into the system, things could change as politicians seek to respond to voters. What if we asked our clients if they planned to vote? What if we discussed social or political action with them? We have to remind ourselves and our clients that if we limit our efforts to just personal and family change, within an unchanged larger society, we are helping to preserve the status quo.

To keep family therapy relevant to today's families, we have to learn how and when to discuss the important issues that shape and determine our lives. We have to learn to reconnect family members with their dreams and their values and to discuss the inequalities in our society frankly—the racism, classism, sexism, and homophobia that are built into the system. We need to help clients join together within their families and networks to create change within themselves and then look outward to help bring change to their communities and to every level of the social system.

To counter society's privileging of particular skills for only certain people, we must challenge families on their role expectations and take into account crucial information on a family's social style and expectations, not just with culturally diverse families, but with all families (Canino & Spurlock, 2000; Le et al., 2008).

Issues we need to explore include the following:

- Is the family isolated or active in their community?
- Does their culture expect frequent and intense social interactions in an extended network or does it privilege privacy and a nuclear-family orientation?
- What kind of community is the family living in socially and culturally: a homogeneous community or a heterogeneous setting, a safe community, a community with resources?
- Who are the models and teachers of socialization skills in the community?
- Do the skills taught at home converge with those required at school, in the park, or on the playing field?

Much has been written about the impact of the norms and values of the larger society on the individuals and families within it. What is most important for the clinician to grasp is that race, class, gender, and sexual orientation are not simply differences; they are categories that are arranged hierarchically with power, validation, and maximum opportunity going to those at the top: Whites, the affluent, men, and heterosexuals. We must learn to be aware of and deal with these power differences as they operate (1) in the therapy system, in which they add to the already existing power differential between therapist and client; (2) within the family system, in which social stress easily becomes family conflict; and (3) between the family and society, in which they either limit or enhance the options available for change. Clinically, the therapist must be prepared to discuss explicitly how racism, sexism, classism, and homophobia may be behind the problems clients are taking out on each other. The goal is to help the family members to join together against the problems in society instead of letting these problems divide them. In order to facilitate growth toward the kind of maturity we are discussing, it is essential that therapists help clients discuss these societal issues so that clients are not left feeling they are causing their own problems. Explicit discussion and strategies are needed to overcome the obstacles to change, which unaware therapists may blame on the client's "resistance."

The diagnostic challenge is to make a clinical judgment as to whether a behavioral or emotional attribute or symptom "is a culturally syntonic way of manifesting distress, a behavior adopted to survive in a particular sociocultural milieu, or a universal symptom of psychiatric disorder. These judgments can be sound only if clinicians are knowledgeable about the culture of their patients" (Canino & Spurlock, 2000, p. 102).

Many guidelines and programs have been shown to be effective in fostering children's emotional competence in schools and other settings. We should do all that we can as mental health practitioners to support the establishment of such programs in clinics and schools in our communities. The most crucial factor in teaching emotional competence is timing, with infancy as the beginning point and childhood and adolescence as crucial windows of opportunity (McLaughlin, 2008; Salovey, 2007; Cohen & Sandy, 2007).

The family context of human development

We have used the concepts of stages and tasks to define the changing relationships, status, and membership in families at transition points over the life course that mark transformations of the system itself. When symptoms arise, they can be a signal that there is a life cycle transformation necessary and that the family has gotten stalled in trying to make first-order change (rearranging the parts of the system) when second-order change (transformation of the system itself) is what is necessary. Any assessment must explore where the family is in their life cycle process and whether current problems reflect the need for such a transformational process to get them back on track.

We offer a provisional schema for tracking individuals and families' motion through different phases of life (see Figure 1.5). This map considers the transformational nature of different stages of life, the emotional processes required to proceed developmentally, and the tasks that are necessary for families to continue their evolution through the life course. Of course, this is not a universal scheme. Many family members do not find partners or have children, but nevertheless, they are part of the generation caring for the next generation(s) and the previous generation(s) and moving through life generally with their cohort of peers, friends, and siblings, who together share the same generational and intergenerational tasks of the life cycle. Many families go through other transitions (divorce, remarriage, migration, disability, traumatic or untimely loss, etc.) that require them to pass through entire extra life cycle phases requiring shifts in their status, rules, roles, and relationships to each other. Furthermore, different segments of any family will always be going through different life cycle phases at the same time, some members of the family dealing with new couple formation, others with becoming parents, or with adolescence, yet others with launching, and still others with later-life caretaking and death.

We have begun our schema with the young adult phase of the life cycle because we see this as the pivotal and crucial phase for the grounding of the next generation of the family. The future depends on the young adult's development of self-management and new ways of relating to others as a responsible citizen. Key life issues such as work, partner relationships, caring relationships for older and younger generations, and social responsibility get determined at this phase.

The individual life cycle in context

At an individual level, human development involves the accomplishment of certain physical, intellectual, interpersonal, social, spiritual, and emotional life cycle tasks. Each person's individual life cycle intersects with the family life cycle at every point, causing at times conflicts of needs. A toddler's developmental needs may conflict with a grandmother's life plans, if she is the child's primary caretaker. When individual family members do not fit into normative expectations for development, there are repercussions for family as well as individual development. A family's adaptation to its tasks will likewise influence how individuals negotiate their development, and the cultural, socioeconomic, racial, and gender context of the family will influence all of these developmental transitions. (Quintana & McKown, 2008).

We offer here an outline of the tasks at each phase of the individual life cycle which, like our schema for family life cycle phases, is a rough and suggestive guideline, not a statement of true and fixed life cycle stages. People vary greatly in their pathways through life. There are serious limitations to any schematic life cycle framework, and this schema is meant to be suggestive, not exhaustive (see Figure 1.6). Furthermore, accomplishing

Figure 1.5 Phases of the family life cycle.

Family Life Cycle Phase	Emotional Process of Transition: Key Prerequisite Attitudes	Second-Order Tasks/Changes of the System to Proceed Developmentally
Emerging Young Adults	Accepting emotional and financial responsibility for self	a. Differentiation of self in relation to family of origin b. Development of intimate peer relationships c. Establishment of self in respect to work and financial independence d. Establishment of self in community and larger society e. Establishment of one's worldview, spirituality, religion, and relationship to nature f. Parents shifting to consultative role in young adult's relationships
Couple Formation: The Joining of Families	Commitment to new expanded system	a. Formation of couple system b. Expansion of family boundaries to include new partner and extended family c. Realignment of relationships among couple, parents and siblings, extended family, friends, and larger community
Families with Young Children	Accepting new members into the system	a. Adjustment of couple system to make space for children b. Collaboration in child-rearing and financial and housekeeping tasks c. Realignment of relationships with extended family to include parenting and grandparenting roles d. Realignment of relationships with community and larger social system to include new family structure and relationships
Families with Adolescents	Increasing flexibility of family boundaries to permit children's independence and grandparents' frailties	a. Shift of parent–child relationships to permit adolescent to have more independent activities and relationships and to move more flexibly into and out of system b. Families helping emerging adolescents negotiate relationships with community c. Refocus on midlife couple and career issues. d. Begin shift toward caring for older generation

Figure 1.5 Continued		
Family Life Cycle Phase	**Emotional Process of Transition: Key Prerequisite Attitudes**	**Second-Order Tasks/Changes of the System to Proceed Developmentally**
Launching Children and Moving On at Midlife	Accepting a multitude of exits from and entries into the system	a. Renegotiation of couple system as a dyad b. Development of adult-to-adult relationships between parents and grown-up children c. Realignment of relationships to include in-laws and grandchildren d. Realignment of relationships with community to include new constellation of family relationships e. Exploration of new interests/career, given the freedom from child care responsibilities f. Dealing with health needs, disabilities, and death of parents (grandparents)
Families in Late Middle Age	Accepting shifting generational roles	a. Maintaining or modifying own and/or couple and social functioning and interests in the face of physiological decline: exploration of new familial and social role options b. Supporting more central role of middle generations c. Making room in the system for the wisdom and experience of the elders d. Supporting older generation without overfunctioning for them
Families Nearing the End of Life	Accepting the realities of family members' limitations and death and the completion of one cycle of life	a. Dealing with loss of spouse, siblings, and other peers b. Making preparations for death and legacy c. Managing reversed roles in caretaking between middle and older generations d. Realignment of relationships with larger community and social system to acknowledge changing life cycle relationships

the individual tasks of a stage depends on resources available at family and social levels to help individuals develop their abilities. In addition, we must be open to considering life patterns that vary from the dominant norm and adjust our expectations for these variations. The larger social context will heavily influence how people go through various stages. For example, gay and lesbian adults are likely to be stressed at many life phases including the phase of young adulthood, because of the social stigma still attached to their partnering, parenting, and developing their spirituality, as well as by the frequent

Figure 1.6 Tasks of individual life cycle.

Infancy (Birth to About 2) Development of Autonomous Skills, Empathy and Emotional Attunement to Others

- Learn to communicate needs and have some sense of trust, comfort, and relationship with caretakers and with the world around them

- Caretakers must meet infant's needs consistently, so they can develop a sense of security and trust in others

- Learn to coordinate body, develop motor skills, begin to talk, play, walk, feed themselves

- Learn to overcome fears of new people and situations, to reognize themselves as separate and begin to develop empathy for others

Early Childhood (Approximate Ages 2 to 6) Increasing Autonomy and Self Management Skills, Emotional Competence and Ability to Relate to Others

- Develop language, communication, motor skills, more control of body, and the ability to relate to the world around

- Develop ability to take direction, cooperate, share, trust, explore, and be aware of self as different from others, including awareness of gender and racial differences and disabilities

- Develop ability to recognize someone else's pain as different from their own and to comfort others

- How discipline is handled at this phase influences development of emotional competence, shaming and physical punishment having deleterious effects

- Begin ability to form peer relationships

- Develop various cognitive skills with numbers, words, objects

Middle Childhood (About 6 to 12 or 13) Learning, Expanding Social World, Belonging, Awareness of Difference

- Many developmental leaps in cognitive, motor, and emotional relationship skills and in interdependent perceptiveness

- Expand social world in terms of ability to communicate and to handle relationships with an increasing range of adults and children beyond their families

- Focus on "belonging" and exclusion, competition, cooperation, awareness of self and "otherness" in terms of gender roles, race, culture, sexual orientation, class, and abilities/disabilities. Adults must mentor them to support cooperation or else competitiveness becomes a problem

- Increase access to knowledge through reading, TV, and internet, which fosters understanding of self in relation to family, peers, community, and knowledge about human beings and nature

- Increase in ability to be intimate and empathic and to express anger, fear, and pain in nondestructive ways

- Increasing intuition, tolerance for difference, sense of morality, and ability to challenge lack of fairness

Figure 1.6 Continued

Adolescence (from Puberty to about age 21). Finding One's Own Voice: Seeking Identity in Context of Societal, Parental, and Peer Pressures to Conform: Balance Between Self and Others

- Dramatic physical emotional, sexual, and spiritual changes, starting with puberty
- Refine physical, social and intellectual skills and learn about the world
- Renegotiation of identity with parents and increasing independent functioning
- Increased sense of morality about relationships, recognition of injustices and challenging values they have been given
- Begin to define who they want to become as adults
- Develop sexual, physical, spiritual and moral identity
- Increase discipline, emotional competence and self management for working individually and collaboratively,
- Increase understanding of self in relation to peers, family, and community in terms of gender, race, culture, sexual orientation and disabilities
- Increase ability to judge and handle complex social situations and relationships including intimate physical relationships

Young Adulthood (About 21 to early 30s) (New Phase in Human History) Establishing Oneself in the World: Love and Work. Development of Committed Mutual Relationships and Financial Independence

- Generativity in terms of partnering, work, establishing one's own place in communities of friends, social groups, and beginning to raise children
- Increase ability to manage their life financially, emotionally, sexually, and spiritually
- Increase discipline to develop physical and intellectual work and social relationships, and tolerance for delayed gratification to meet one's goals
- Learn to focus on long-range life goals regarding work, intimate relationships, family, and community
- Develop ability to nurture others physically, emotionally, and sexually
- Evolve further in ability to respect and advocate for others less fortunate than themselves or to help themselves if socially disadvantaged
- Develop ability to negotiate evolving relationships to parents, peers, children, and community, including work relationships

Middle Adulthood (Early 30s to mid 50s) Emergence into Authentic Power and Becoming More Aware of the Problems of Others

- Firm up and make solid all the tasks of early adulthood
- Nurture, support and deepen relationships with children, partners, family, friends, including caretaking of older family members

(Continued)

Figure 1.6 Continued

- Reassess one's work satisfaction, financial adequacy and consider possibility of reinventing oneself to achieve greater life balance

- Accept the choices that made some dreams and goals attainable, but precluded others

- Focus on using their authentic power to mentor the next generation; involve themselves in improving community and society, whether they are personally advantaged or disadvantaged

- Solidify their philosophy of life and spirituality

Late Middle Age (Mid 50s to 70s) Beginning Wisdom Years: Reclaiming the Wisdom of Interdependence

- Handle some declining physical and intellectual abilities

- Deal with menopause, decreasing sexual energies, and one's changing sexuality

- Come to terms with their failures and choices with accountability but without becoming bitter

- Plan and handle work transitions and finances

- Define one's grandparenting and other "senior" roles in work and community

- Take steps to pass the torch and attend to their connections and responsibilities to the next generation

- Accept their limitations and multiple caretaking responsibilities for those above and below

- Deal with death of parents and others of older generations

Aging (From 70s on) Grief, Loss, Resiliency, Retrospection, and Growth

- Respond to loss and change as opportunity to reevaluate life circumstances and create new fulfilling pathway

- Remain as physically, psychologically, intellectually, and spiritually active and as emotionally connected as possible

- Come to terms with death while focusing on what else one can still do for oneself and others

- Bring careful reflection, perspective, and balance to the task of life review

- Accept dependence on others and diminished control of one's life

- Affirm and work out their financial, spiritual, and emotional legacy to the next generation

- Accept death of spouse and need to create a new life

- Accept their own life and death

necessity to keep their true lives secret at work. These struggles, created by our society, have implications for negotiating the life course smoothly and for emotional development and well-being.

Those who do not form couple relationships at this phase will often feel marginalized in the larger social context. Clinicians must be careful not to participate in psychologizing clients' reactions to such marginalization, but rather to help them define a life course for themselves and not be constrained by society's definitions. With these caveats in mind, we offer the following tentative guidelines for conceptualizing the individual life cycle. Furthermore, even though we offer suggestive time periods for each phase, we are aware that these are always no more than statistical approximations. The age at which people reach various milestones such as secondary sexual characteristics or adult intimate relationships or disabilities of old age have been changing rapidly in the past several generations and in different cultural contexts and are likely to continue changing, so we must beware of seeing the norms as "true" or "real" or "necessary."

Our guidelines for individual and family development must be flexible and able to take account of changing circumstances. Traditional schemas have given priority to White children's style of communication: linear spoken language, minimal body language, a preference for written over verbal expression, and a tendency to view the world in discrete segments rather than holistically. This is reflected in the requirements that children learn to sit still for long periods of time; concentrate alone on impersonal learning stimuli; conform to rigorous time frames; and engage only in very controlled, restricted, and mostly individual learning experiences. Sommers (2013) gives us good indication of the problems these restricted learning environments create for boys' development, and proposes creating more developmentally appropriate learning contexts, including more opportunity for physical activity during the day, to maximize the likelihood that we give all our children a chance to succeed.

Peggy McIntosh (1985, 1989) long ago described in her article "On Feeling Like a Fraud" the ways women may end up feeling inadequate in academia, when they are offered intellectual approaches that emphasize a linear, hierarchical order rather than organic relationships among ideas. Catherine Bateson (1994) and Peter Senge (2006) likewise challenged the very ordering of education as a precursor to living life, suggesting instead that it makes more sense to thread education throughout our lives.

Our ability to maintain openness to learning throughout life (which also requires the ability to acknowledge our ignorance and need to learn!) is more essential than ever in our rapidly changing world. Thus, we have emphasized the learning tasks at each phase of the life cycle, which have not always been highly valued in our culture.

When political leaders hesitate, revise their views, or apologize for mistakes, we take it for weakness, not strength. The implications of this are evident. People of privilege can be at the greatest disadvantage because of the smugness and inflexibility of mainstream learning styles, which may leave them unable to acknowledge their ignorance or to place themselves in the position of learner. Many adults take on the challenge of new learning only when they are desperate. We need to modify our cultural norms, so that people do not feel humbled or threatened before they can open themselves to new learning, and so that there is affirmation and support for asking for help with something they cannot do. People need to become perpetual learners throughout their lives (Senge, 2006), so that they have the flexibility to change with new circumstances. In our rapidly changing technologically global environment, we must modify the rigid roles we have encouraged for males especially, without which they will not be able to succeed.

The richness of learning styles should be celebrated, and human beings should be encouraged throughout life to develop their unique styles and to appreciate others for their different ways of knowing and doing. Girls and women should be allowed and encouraged to develop their individual abilities without being viewed as selfish. They should be supported in developing leadership skills and in being comfortable with their accomplishments without fearing that their success hurts others, while boys and men should be encouraged to develop their relational and emotional selves, currently devalued in our theories and in the dominant society, which sees these styles as "unmanly." Psychological studies reveal that when fathers are involved in child-rearing in a major way, sons become more empathic than sons raised in the traditional ways (Miedzian, 2002; Meeker, 2008). A 26-year longitudinal study found that the single factor most linked to empathy was the level of paternal involvement in child care (Koestner, Franz, & Weinberger, 1990). The negative role modeling of a distant father on his children appears to be significant and should be taken into account clinically.

In the same way that we must expand our notions of educational development to be open to new learning throughout the life cycle, we need to expand traditional development theories that have conveyed that intelligence is one dimensional. The intellectual tasks that theorists such as Piaget have used as definers of maturity are extraordinarily narrow indicators and totally inadequate for understanding the rich possibilities of a child's intellectual development (Ogbu, 1990). Many other forms of intelligence have been described, including social and emotional intelligence; interpersonal and intrapersonal intelligence; graphic, musical, and other forms of artistic and spatial intelligence; linguistic intelligence; intelligence in understanding nature; and so on (Goleman, 2006, 2007; Hale, 2001; Gardner, 2006; Stavridou & Kakana, 2008; Sew, 2006).

In China, studying music is all about learning to play in harmony together. There is no concept of the musical virtuoso. So, the highest development involves the most accomplished ability to be in harmony with others. American Indians, as another example, raise their children to be keen observers of the world around them. Intelligence in this context involves being able to look and listen carefully to animals, birds, and trees in ways that are almost totally unknown to most other children in the United States.

Many values within African American communities are also at odds with the dominant priorities for human development. African Americans are exposed to a high degree of stimulation from expressive performers of music and the visual arts, which permeate the Black community. Their cultural style is organized in a circular fashion, in contrast to the linear organization of European/U.S. culture (Hale, 1986).

Nonverbal expression and highly physical expressiveness of emotions, such as moving close or touching others, are in general more characteristic of non-White cultures. Most non-Whites must master two cultures to succeed. Even though they are using complex thinking skills on the street, transferring these skills to the classroom remains a problem. Our current theories of intellectual development fail to make room for people of color to look any way but deficient and pathological (Quintana, 2008; Quintana & McKown, 2008).

Daniel Goleman (2006, 2007, 2011a, 2011b) has made clear the extreme importance of understanding and supporting the development of emotional and social intelligence. All the skills essential for academic success are related to emotional competence: curiosity, confidence, intentionality, self-control, relatedness, cooperativeness, and communication. School success is not predicted by a child's fund of facts or a precocious ability to read, but rather by emotional and social measures: being self-assured and interested; knowing what kind of behavior is expected and being able to rein in the impulse to misbehave; being able to wait, follow directions, and ask the teacher for help; and being able to express one's own needs in relationships with other children. Almost all children who do poorly in school lack one or more of these elements of emotional intelligence, regardless of other cognitive abilities or disabilities (Goleman, 2006). Social intelligence includes the ability to find solutions to social dilemmas such as how to deescalate a fight, how to make friends in a new situation, how to sense another's needs and feelings, how to defuse bullying, how to make others feel at ease, how to help rally support for a new idea, and how to deal with volatile people to calm a situation. All of these abilities are extremely important to our successful development as human beings. Without such interpersonal intelligence, we will end up isolated. Yet, our theories rarely emphasize the pervasive need for these abilities for adult functioning. The healthy value of emotional connectedness is evident from the fact that isolation is as significant a risk to health and mortality as are smoking, high blood pressure, high cholesterol, obesity, and lack of exercise. Empathy, the earliest emotion, is the root of all caring about others: intimacy, ethics, altruism, and morality itself.

Emotional and social incompetence and disconnection lead to the following:

1. Prejudice, lack of empathy, and the inability to direct adequate attention to the needs of others
2. Aggression, poor self-control, and antisocial behavior
3. Depression and poor academic performance
4. Addictions (attempts to calm and soothe oneself with drugs and other addictive behaviors

Goleman suggests that curing our current worldwide tendencies toward depression and crime will require helping families and schools to realize that a child's development and education must include developing essential human competencies such as self-awareness, self-control, empathy, and the arts of listening, resolving conflicts, and cooperation (Goleman, 2006, 2007; McLaughlin, 2008; Cohen & Sandy, 2007; Shinn & Yoshikawa, 2008). To change our world, we must focus on child development, the critical window of opportunity for setting down the essential emotional habits that will govern children's lives in adulthood. Later remedial learning and unlearning in adulthood are possible, but they are lengthy and hard. It should come as no surprise that our schema emphasizes the development of empathy and self-management as the primary skills for relating to others through life.

Multicontextual Assessment

Our outline for a multicontextual assessment aims to help clinicians think of assessment and intervention within both a cultural and a longitudinal framework. Clients generally lose their time perspective when in distress. They have generally lost sight of where they have come from and where they are going. While other cultures have attended much more to community in their models for healing, the dominant Western framework for therapeutic interventions involves "talking it out" in individualized therapy, which emphasizes confidentiality above connectedness.

Our framework aims, instead, to help clients expand their focus while at the same time making the complex information about lives and history manageable and clinically relevant. By broadening the context, we amplify clients' possibilities to recognize their own natural resources and strengths, which come from their history, social surroundings, and dreams for the future. We urge clinicians to go beyond their clients' presenting problems to discuss their values, dreams, strengths, and vulnerabilities in the context of their personal, familial, community, and cultural heritage.

Whether the clinician gathers information about their clients' lives and history in a structured interview or as it emerges over several sessions, it is obviously preferable to obtain it sooner rather than later. We advocate using a family genogram and a chronology or time line as basic tools for this assessment. The genogram (McGoldrick, Gerson, & Petry, 2008) is the basic and most important tool for mapping information, because it help clinicians to quickly locate individuals in context and to see their life cycle situation—which parts of the family are going through which phases—launching, adolescence, migration, separation or divorce, recoupling, retirement, or chronic illness. The genogram helps clinicians map the information essential to a multicontextual assessment in terms of their kinship network, culture, class, race, gender, religion, relationships, and history. Using the genogram to collect historical and contextual assessment information is, in itself, a collaborative, client-centered therapeutic intervention. By its nature, gathering genogram information involves the telling of stories and emphasizes respect for clients' perspectives, while bringing forth the multiple perspectives of different family members. A family chronology or time line lists the events of family history in chronological order, which is essential for tracking the evolution of family history over time. This enables the clinician to track stressors in relation to family life cycle events, particularly the entry, exit, and changes in functioning or relationships of family members. We have found that using this tool with individuals and families helps them remember events and make connections that clarify and change their perspective about the present situation, often in a positive way.

The framework we are presenting does not make for a simple neat case assessment, but we believe it is the best way to meaningfully conceptualize and respond to the problems clients present. The tasks and phases we have presented are, of course, oversimplifications. But, if we are honest, no case fits into a simple description. Life is complicated. The guidelines we offer will naturally have to be used flexibly, as individuals and families do not fit into neat packages.

Figure 1.7 offers guidelines for gathering information on clients' problems, although not necessarily in the order they will be collected.

Engaging with clients entails connecting first with what is most salient for them, but also in the initial engagement phase, we would hope to cover

---

Figure 1.7 Guidelines for a multicontextual life cycle assessment.

What?

What is your assessment of the problem?

What is the presenting problem, who is defining it, and who is being identified as the patient (Index Person or IP)?

How do others in the family or context view the problem? Does the IP share the definition? Does anyone not share the definition?

What solutions have already been tried? What solution do they want now?

What are the family's beliefs, values and cultural strengths for dealing with the problem related to the problem?

Who is making the referral and what is that person's relationship to the family and stake in the problem? Might any triangles develop with them?

What kind of relationship has the family had with professional helpers and self-help supports in the past?

Who?

Assess the membership, demographics, and structure of the family: names, ages, gender, class, race, sexual orientation, dates of birth, marriage, separation, divorce, illness, and death. The best format for tracking this information is a genogram along with a timeline for key family events.

When? Why Now? Vertical and Horizontal Stressors? Life Cycle Issues?

When did the problem begin and what has happened since that time to ameliorate or exacerbate it?

What may be precipitating horizontal and vertical stressors, such as anniversary reactions, moves, losses, or life cycle transitions?

What life cycle phase is the family in now? Are there life cycle tasks they have not realized they need to address? Are family members' relationships and behaviors appropriate for their current life phase? Have there been stresses in previous generations at this life cycle phase?

Individual and Family Relationships and Functioning:

Do clients have the ability to manage their lives?

Has there been appropriate development of cognitive, financial, emotional, sexual, physical, spiritual, and social functioning? Assess their education, work patterns, talents, skills, temperament, vulnerabilities, and dysfunctions.

Are there cut-offs, conflicts, triangles or enmeshment, sleep or mood disorders, behavioral disturbances, addictions to drugs, alcohol, food, sex, gambling, spending, etc., mental or physical illness? Assess the family's emotional climate, communication patterns, boundaries, themes, legacies, secrets, history of trauma and loss?

What multi-generational issues and patterns may be influencing the immediate situation?

Figure 1.7 Continued

Do they have a sense of "home" or of comfort and belonging in their family, community, friendship network, work system, etc.? Can they develop and maintain friendships? Can they nurture and care for others and accept care and nurturing from others.

What are the family's values, spiritual beliefs, dreams and sources of hope and resilience? Do they believe in something larger than themselves? Do they belong to a faith community?

Sociocultural Context:

What is clients' sense of their power, privilege, or oppression in society?

How may their race, religion, spiritual beliefs, languages spoken, social location, sexual orientation, disability, age, ethnicity, or immigration status contribute to their sense of well-being, belonging, or marginalization?

Are there differences in language skills and acculturation or social mobility within the family, which may have led to conflicts, power imbalances, and role reversals, especially where children are forced to translate for their parents?

---

the skeleton of the items described in this outline, as well as a basic genogram and family chronology (at least for the primary family members and problem situation).

Underlying our questions is the wish to help clients view themselves as belonging to history, to their present context, and to the future. Many would argue that clinicians do not need to do such an extensive inquiry into clients' circumstances. Assessing ethnicity and immigration, for example, is often avoided as being "impolite," but it is crucial for determining whether a family's dysfunction is a "normal" reaction to a high degree of cultural stress, or whether their reactions go beyond the bounds of transitional stress. We have offered questions to help clients and their families locate themselves in their cultural context, and to explore and identify values in their heritage that are sources of strength and resilience, and that can help them transform their lives, and their ability to work toward long-range goals that fit with their cultural values.

As we have said repeatedly, our assessment of families and our interventions must also attend to the unequal ways that families are situated in the larger context so that we do not become part of the problem by preserving the status quo. It is extremely important that we do not "psychologize" social problems by searching for the roots of every problem in the interior motivations and actions of the individual

and/or the family. Many clinical problems are directly connected to the social system.

CASE ILLUSTRATION

The Aiello-Lopez Family

The following case illustrates using a multicontextual life cycle framework for assessment.

Cindy Lopez, a 17-year-old high school junior of Puerto Rican and German/Irish/Italian background, was referred for family therapy with her mother and grandmother by a caseworker, Paula, who had been seeing her since she was referred for missing school and self-cutting 6 months earlier. A few months later, Cindy was hospitalized after the police were called in to a fight where she threatened to kill her mother, Karen. Cindy had been stealing from her grandmother and from local stores, encouraged by her lesbian girlfriend, April, who was using and selling drugs. The mother and grandmother had forbidden her to see the girlfriend, but she was insisting and there had been a number of family rows to which the police had been called. Cindy had been put on medication while in the hospital, and a psychiatrist was also prescribing medications for her mother for anxiety, and for the grandmother for depression and Parkinson's symptoms.

We met for a first session with Cindy; her mother Karen; Karen's mother, Helen, who over the years had functioned as Cindy's primary parent; and Cindy's younger brother, Joey, 13, who had been diagnosed with Attention Deficit Hyperactivity Disorder, and was on medication as well. The family indicated there were many issues they fought over, not just Cindy's girlfriend, April, but the car, finances, and issues with Helen's younger sister, Ginny, who had moved into the family home 3 years ago and reportedly had a serious drug problem.

During the first session, we tried to slow down the family's fighting, engaging them in developing a family play genogram, using miniature items to represent each other on a genogram, which we created with them. The task enabled them to join together and also allowed us to get the basic information

about the family, which they seemed too agitated to provide in conversation.

The genogram (see Genogram 1.1) indicated that there was indeed a lot going on in the family. Eight family members were living in the household: Cindy; Joey; Karen and her husband Joseph, an immigrant from Ecuador; Helen (the grandmother), her son Jimmy (from a previous relationship); Helen's younger sister Ginny; and their uncle Jackie who had been raised as their brother. In addition to the life cycle issues of the Identified Patient, Cindy, an adolescent beginning to launch, the family were dealing with at least three other life cycle transitions at the same time: the son, Joey, was entering adolescence, which appeared a bit problematic, as he was immature for his age and did not appear to have good control of his behavior. The mother, Karen, seemed

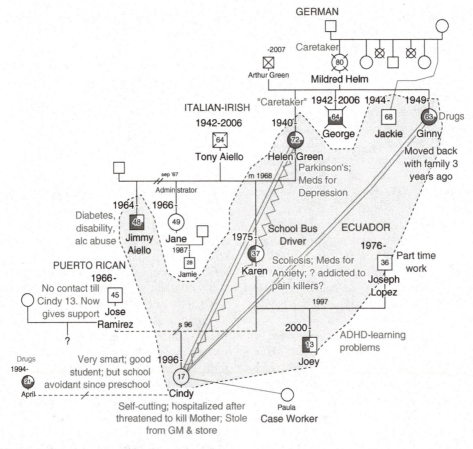

GENOGRAM 1.1 The Aiello-Lopez Family

to be having problems managing her children and her own life, both because her physical health was not good (she has scoliosis and "anxiety") and struggled financially. There was a question of whether she might be abusing drugs or alcohol. The grandmother's functioning also seemed to have deteriorated in the recent past and it was unclear if she had some cognitive deficit as well as problems with her physical health. In other words, the family was dealing with four life cycle phases at this time:

1. Adolescence–Launching: Cindy at 17, was beginning to drive, and soon would be finishing high school.
2. Adolescence: Joey, 13, was immature, had ADHD, and was soon to begin high school.
3. Middle adulthood: Karen, had health and anxiety problems, was possibly abusing pain killers, had difficulty mothering and supporting herself, she was more a daughter than a mother in the household. Karen's relationship with her husband, Joseph, also seemed problematic. He was living in the context of a family system to which he appeared not very connected and was suspicious of his wife's behavior with other men.
4. Aging: Helen, at 69, appeared to be losing functioning. As the major caretaker and support of household, she now needed care herself. The family thought she should not be driving, but she owned the only available car. Jimmy had a car, but no one had access to it but him. Jimmy had a physical disability and was reportedly abusing alcohol, although he was the only fully employed member of the household. Helen's younger siblings were also aging and, not having launched, appeared to be dependent on her and to have problems themselves. The grandmother seemed to be the major support for the rest of the family and it was unclear what they would do without her support.

The most immediate crisis in the family appeared to the grandmother's life cycle transition, rather than Cindy's. Cindy, as often happens when a child is the presenting problem, was possibly the most functional family member of all. Her symptoms were perhaps designed to mobilize needed supports in relation to the grandmother's crucial deterioration in functioning status, which seemed to be increasing the anxiety of the family.

In terms of the adolescence and launching of the two children, we were actually more worried about what would happen to Joey in the coming years. Cindy seemed highly capable of rallying supports for herself, even though she had missed a lot of school. She was a good student, who was still on time to graduate. Interestingly, she said her ambition was to become a social worker!

At the end of the first session, we summarized the problems the family seemed to be dealing with. All the adults living in the home except Joseph (Ginny, Jackie, Jimmy, Helen, and Karen) had physical or physiological problems and were not able to manage full adult responsibilities. Major immediate problems seemed to be Helen's health, Karen's health, the financial stress, Cindy's problems with school, behavior, and relationships, and Joey's behavior and development. We wanted to meet Joseph, but were told he did not like therapists and would not want to meet with us. We summarized from the family play genogram that daughter, mother, and grandmother all wanted to have better relationships with each other as the first and main goal. We pointed out the caring nature of the family as indicated by their very positive choices for each other in the family play genogram exercise, in spite of their conflicts. We talked to Karen separately about the need for her to slow her anxiety down so we could help her. She readily agreed her anxiety was a problem.

Our assessment continued for several sessions. Therapy always requires ongoing assessment and interventions themselves are always part of that ongoing assessment, giving important information about the family's readiness and commitment to change. For the second session, because Cindy was unable to attend, we saw the mother and grandmother together and separately, inquiring cautiously about their health. We gave them homework to meet together outside of the house to discuss how they would handle Cindy and to share some quiet time. This was intended to underline their shared "parenting" of Cindy, to reinforce their need to work together, and to foster their ability to take breaks from the fighting at home.

In the third session, we again saw the three generations of women: daughter, mother, and grandmother. All three of them now wanted a single goal—help getting the school to let Cindy back. We agreed to work with the caseworker to figure how to help Cindy get back to school.

We asked Cindy to bring in her biological father Jose to the fourth session. We were quite amazed meeting him that he was so motivated for Cindy to continue her schooling and to work out things with her other family members. He placed great emphasis on Cindy's need to realize she must not leave home right after high school to live on her own. He talked about the problems he had in life as a result of not finishing school and not taking his responsibilities as a father for many years. He said as well that he had made a mistake that led to jail when he was a young man and that his parents had pressed him many times to "do the right thing" and reconnect with his daughter, which he had not done until she was 13. Now he was paying toward her support, although he was struggling with his own employment but wanted to stay connected to her. He complained that Cindy often did not return his calls unless she needed money. We talked about Cindy not knowing her Puerto Rican grandparents and proposed that Jose take her to meet them and show them pictures of her life, as she said she had done the first time she met her father when she was 13. She expressed discomfort that she did not know Spanish and they did not know much English, but we reassured her that with her father's help they would all find ways to communicate. Jose assured us and his daughter that he would support her return to school in whatever ways he could.

The following session (fifth) had to be conducted on Skype with Cindy and her grandmother, because Karen was sick. Karen and her sister Jane had talked to their mother about her giving up driving, which had become dangerous. During this conversation, Helen talked about her own history. Her mother, Mildred, had also been a caretaker. As the oldest of five children whose mother had died in childbirth with the youngest, Jackie, Mildred had taken over caring for her younger siblings and raised Jackie as Helen's younger brother. Mildred had cared for all her younger siblings and then for her children until she died at the age of 80. Helen was now con-

tinuing the caretaking since her mother had died in 2000. Cindy was amazed to hear about Mildred, whom she had never known and proudly commented that she and her grandmother were both following in the footsteps of the caretaker great grandmother. The other side of this shared quality of caretaker, as we could see, was that for three generations there has been trouble at the launching phase of the life cycle and at the school completion phase.

Helen and all her siblings had dropped out of high school as did all her three children. Her daughter Jane left school because she was pregnant, but managed to learn enough on the job to rise from secretary to an office administrator. Jimmy, who also did not finish high school, was employed, but at the age of 49 has been living in his mother's house for many years, because of his health problems. Helen's sister Ginny also dropped out of school, and was unemployed. Uncle Jackie basically never left home and moved in with Helen when Mildred died.

So, while we might be right that Cindy's psychological problems are as serious as those of several other family members, there is a good precedent for her to get stuck at the launching phase, by either remaining as caretaker for others in the household or, as her father feared, by launching prematurely and making bad young adult choices, which would lead to a return home, like her uncle Jimmy and grand aunt Ginny.

We wanted to keep our thinking as broad as possible about the pathways she and others in the family who had gotten stuck in their life trajectories could find to manage their lives. We wanted to help them find ways to work together to do the caretaking required in this family in the next years and manage their own lives. In fact, in the fourth session, Karen mentioned, of her own accord, that she had realized she was dependent on pain killers and had determined to begin a program to get off them. Ginny took some initiative to participate in the family conversations, and we were hoping to engage Joseph, whom Cindy believed she could get to Skype with us from his computer, even if he would not come in.

Thinking about the Aiello-Lopez family from the perspective of individual, family, and social life cycle perspectives, there are a number of aspects for us to keep in mind beyond the individual strengths and vulnerabilities of each person and the conflicts and triangles that became problematic at a family level.

At a social level, the family imbeds the multicultural and multiracial dynamics that are an increasingly prominent aspect of our society. We can be sure that the Puerto Rican and the Ecuadorian sides of the family have experienced racism in the larger context. But as we began to work with them, they were sensitive to questions about culture, probably fearing our own attitudes as representatives of the dominant society. We learned that Helen had often used racial epithets in speaking of Joseph, which must have made it very difficult for him to live in her home. And it must have been hard for Karen, Joey, and perhaps Cindy, who felt connected to both the grandmother and to Joseph to experience her grandmother's racist remarks toward him. If Jose had become more involved, he would probably have been subject to similar disparagement. At a subtler level, we have wondered how such racist attitudes may have influenced family patterns over the generation in the past. We did not know the family well enough to learn how other cultural differences, between the German great grandparents and Helen's choosing a Polish partner and then an Italian immigrant husband, may have been influenced by subtle or overt prejudice, as happens very often when family members marry out of their group. Beyond this, the family appears to have been downwardly mobile in the past generation. Helen's father managed to buy his own two-family house, which Tony Aiello moved into with Helen when they married. He had a steady income and managed to support his daughter Karen and his wife's two children (Jimmy and Jane), who took his name. Later he supported his granddaughter, Cindy, and made it possible for Karen and Joseph to live in the home, when their finances were unstable. But since his death in 2006, the family has been struggling more and additional members of the extended family have moved in: Ginny and Jackie, Jimmy, and for several years his girlfriend, Angie, though she moved out last year. Another young girl, Jo, daughter of a friend of Karen's, came to live with the family from the time she was 5 because of her mother's drug addiction, until she

become pregnant at the age of 19 and moved out with her boyfriend.

Now the middle generation is increasingly needing support themselves. The grandfather is gone, and the grandmother is more in need of support than able to do for others physically or psychologically. Jane, who was always an outside support, is herself feeling stressed by the needs of her mother, her aunt and uncles, her sister, and her niece and nephew. The lack of educational and financial competence of many family members means that they are in considerable need of supports, but are not acknowledging these needs. We believe that the more stability the family can maintain, while they continue to raise and launch Cindy and Joey, the better long range future they will have. If Jose continues his support and if his family can contribute to the emotional well-being of the granddaughter, this can be a real plus for Cindy.

Another significant factor is the social stigma of homophobia that Cindy and the family will continue to have to deal with. In the short run, Karen has been a major support to her daughter in regard to her sexual orientation. Helen reportedly had great difficulty when granddaughter first came out a year before they came for treatment, but over that year apparently became much more accepting. If Cindy and, even better, her mother and other family members could connect to community social supports for LGBT family members, they might actually find extra resources to help them manage their lives.

What seems very clear is that, in spite of their many problems and symptoms, the family has a strong sense of loyalty and caring. We learned as we worked with them that they had a family rule that they would not fight on holidays. So we asked them to expand this and to try having a day a week free from conflicts. They laughed, but seemed to institute this. In addition, they transformed the homework rituals we gave them to better fit their needs. For example, we suggested that mother and grandmother spend 10 minutes away from others listening to music and not talking. They apparently talked it over, decided they did not like the same music and that they would prefer to go to a local diner for coffee—not to talk about problems but just to "chat." And somehow it worked, though they soon included Cindy in these outings, which led to it being a story-telling outing as both mother and grandmother agreed to tell Cindy stories about Mildred, Arthur, and others in the family's past history.

Facilitating the collaboration of the parents, aunts, and uncles in supporting the grandmother is another aspect of the life cycle oriented support we want to encourage. Can all the "next" generation contribute to helping the grandmother function at her maximum, while accepting that there is a level of control she will not have as she moves forward. She will need to accept others taking over some of the family functioning, as they have begun to do regarding driving. Actually several family members, including Jose and Joseph, have helped Cindy learn to drive. But at the same time, we want to ensure that Cindy does not just get drawn into becoming the next overfunctioning caretaker, replacing Helen and before that Mildred, while others in the family remain underfunctioners in terms of self-management and ability to maintain responsible interdependence in the family.

Summary of the Case Using the Guidelines for a Multicontextual Life Cycle Assessment

What? The Aiello-Lopez family was referred to us by a social worker, Paula Ruiz, who had been doing home-based therapy for the past 6 months with Cindy Lopez, a 17-year-old Puerto Rican-Italian-German high school junior. Cindy had had a brief psychiatric hospitalization for cutting, stealing, and truancy, which had led to the police being called, due to a family fight. Following the hospitalization, she had attended an intensive outpatient program, and was now planning to return to school. The school and the two hospitals where she had been treated believed Cindy was the problem. Paula, whom we had known for many years, thought the whole family had problems requiring intervention, with which we concurred.

Although Cindy, her mother Karen, and her grandmother Helen agreed during the initial session that their relationships were the problem, our assessment was that the biggest threat to the family's stability was the grandmother's diminishing functioning physically and mentally, as well as the financial instability of all family members and the drug problems of Karen,

Jimmy, and Ginny which were creating great volatility in the household. We were also worried about Joey, who, at the age of 13, appeared to have difficulty controlling his emotions during the session, though the others did not seem concerned about this. To us it seemed Cindy's behavior was more a message that "the house was on fire" because of her beloved grandmother's diminished functioning, which was escalating the already chaotic situation of the entire household.

Who? The "who" in this family is shown on the family's genogram (see Genogram 1.1).

When? Why now? Horizontal and vertical stressors? Life cycle issues? Cindy's cutting and stealing began in the year prior to her hospitalization, but her school avoidant behavior had been going on since grade school. She had come out to the family at the age of 15 and began a relationship with April, a 20-year-old, who had gotten her involved in stealing money to buy drugs. This led to the family fight that precipitated Cindy's hospitalization, after which she broke up with April, but was still angry that her phone calls were being monitored by her mother.

Precipitating horizontal stressors include the grandmother's deterioration in functioning; the mother's anxiety and addiction to pain killers; Joey's behavioral problems as he entered adolescence; and also Cindy's loss of the support of her aunt Ginny, who was abusing drugs more since moving into the household. She seemed to have gone from a resource to a liability for Cindy.

The family was dealing with multiple life cycle transitions: Cindy's adolescence: Joey was moving from childhood into adolescence and seemed to have problems adjusting socially, although the family did not see his rather disruptive behavior as a problem. Karen and Joseph were having marital and financial problems, which were compounded by Karen's drug use, which appeared to also limit her ability to parent either child.

But the greatest problem seemed to be the inability that every generation was having accepting that the necessary changes in their relationships were needed to support the aging and impaired grandmother. There appear to have been major vertical stressors as well. There have been launching problems in this family for three generations: in the grandparental generation, none of the grandmother's siblings Ginny, Jackie, or George launched successfully. In the parental generation, neither of Cindy's parents, Karen or Jose, nor her uncle Jimmy, appear to have launched successfully. And now in the third generation, Cindy is at risk of not launching successfully if she cannot finish school, and we worry for Joey, given his limitations and the family's apparent lack of attention to his needs. Along with the lack of ability to get launched is the vulnerability, especially for women, of becoming lifelong overfunctioning caretakers of children and siblings, who are in the reciprocal underfunctioning position in the relationships. The caretakers in this family have included the grandmother, Helen, and her own mother, Mildred, as well as her daughter, Jane, who seems to be the only one in her generation who could fall into that overfunctioning position, although so far she seems to be setting pretty good boundaries for herself. Cindy already thinks of herself as following in the caretaking footsteps of her grandmother and great grandmother. There also seem to have been parenting problems for Karen, Joseph, and Helen in raising Cindy; and Karen and Joseph clearly seemed to be having couple and midlife identity and functioning problems.

Individual and family relationships and functioning. The family has many dysfunctions, limitations, and conflicts (drug and alcohol problems, psychological, educational, financial, and employment dysfunction). But at the same time they have a great deal of caring for each other, and a rather impressive ability to keep functioning and relating even with their limitations. Cindy's father returned to Cindy's life in the past few years, which is a hopeful sign. Karen's willingness, after only a few sessions to embark upon giving up her addiction to painkillers and the great support offered by her husband, Joseph, are also hopeful signs. The family's ability to creatively give up fighting for holidays and to rework therapy homework assignments to make them more suitable to their situation are further indications of their resilience. The functioning of Jane, Helen's second child, is another sign of resilience. She seems to have the ability to pitch in to help the family, without becoming an overfunctioning caretaker who gives up her own needs for others. Even though Jane herself,

like the others, got pregnant and never finished high school, she managed to raise a well-functioning son, to have maintained stable, high-level employment, and a successful marriage for the past 30 years. Now she helps the family by managing the grandmother's finances and taking them to medical appointments, but she otherwise continues to stay in charge of her own life and relationships.

Sociocultural heritage. Cultural strengths of the Aiello-Lopez family include a strong commitment to family, the ability to pull together and agree at times not to fight, their ability to acknowledge each other's good points, and their caring, even when they were angry. An additional strength is the family's, especially the mother's, support for Cindy's sexual orientation. Even the grandmother, though initially disapproving, came around to accepting her granddaughter's sexual orientation relatively quickly. Vulnerabilities include their difficulty addressing the family's current health, emotional and financial problems, and working toward a greater stabilization of the system as a whole. The grandmother's background is primarily German. Her husband was Italian and Irish, and her daughter Karen's partners were Puerto Rican and Ecuadorian. The family seems to have experienced downward mobility, perhaps a function of the early maternal loss in the great-grandparental generation, which probably played a role in the next generation's difficulty launching (George, Jackie, and Ginny). Helen had the courage to end her first marriage to a man who was abusive to her and developed a very strong marriage with her second husband, Tony, who adopted her two children from her first marriage. Since his death, the family seems to have struggled increasingly financially and due to the addiction of several family members, who moved into the household. Racism has surely also played a role for both Joseph and Jose, but neither has brought that into the clinical discussions. We heard from the mother and daughter about the grandmother's racist comments to her son-in-law, Joseph, but have not yet had the opportunity to address that in therapy. The family lived in a mixed community but seemed uncomfortable talking about race. The family's background is Roman Catholic but religion did not appear to play a prominent role as a spiritual resource.

Power imbalances related to social location (finances, work stability, partner stability, and social class difference) appear to have caused continual conflicts between Jane and Karen, though they do seem, once again, to be able to put family first, especially when dealing with their mother. If Cindy finishes high school and goes to college, she will be first in the immediate family to do so. That would likely move her to different social location, which could create psychological distance from the rest of her family but would also probably strengthen the family's resources in other ways.

— Conclusion

The need for flexibility in our life cycle thinking in our time is urgent. We need multiple models to allow people to shape and reshape their lives to meet changing circumstances in our rapidly changing world (Bateson, 2001). Most of us will have to reinvent ourselves many times as we go through life, always in relation to those in our social and family network of belonging, and in our times especially each generation must be flexible in relation to changing rules and relationships as they go through life's transitions. The days of models that laid out fixed phases and tasks are long gone, if they were ever helpful.

What clinicians require is a framework that does not force clients to make molehills out of mountains by ignoring major aspects of their lives, and focusing clinical attention only on their individual thoughts, feelings, and behavior. At the same time, our family models need to articulate not a rigid, inequitable multigenerational patriarchal family model, but recognition of our connectedness in life—regardless of the particular family structure or culture—with those who went before us, those who go with us, and those who will follow after us. Exploring problems within this broad and flexible framework will help individuals and their families draw on the multiple resources of their actual kin arrangements for resilience, healing, support, and caretaking as they go through life.

Recall what you learned in this chapter by completing the Chapter Review.

— References

Alksnis, C., Desmarais, S., & Curtis, J. (2008). Workforce segregation and the gender wage gap: Is "women's" work valued as highly as "men's"? *Journal of Applied Social Psychology, 38*(6), 1416–1441.

Aries, P. (1962). *Centuries of childhood: A social history of family life.* New York: Vintage.

Barnett, R. C., & Rivers, C. (1996). *She works/he works: How two-income families are happier, healthier, and better-off.* San Francisco: Harper.

Barnett, R. C., & Rivers, C. (2004). *Same difference: How gender myths are hurting our relationships, our children, and our jobs.* New York: Basic Books.

Bateson, C. (2001). *Composing a life.* New York: Grove Press.

Bateson, M. C. (1994). *Peripheral visions.* New York: HarperCollins.

Bateson, M. C. (2010). *Composing a further life: The age of active wisdom.* New York: Vintage.

Bertrand, M., Luttmer, E., & Mullainathan, S. (2000). Network effects and welfare cultures. *Quarterly Journal of Economics, 115,*, 1019–1025.

Borysenko, J. (1996). *A woman's book of life: The biology, psychology and spirituality of the feminine life cycle.* New York: Riverhead Books.

Brody, L. R., & Hall, J. A. (1993). Gender and emotion. In M. Lewis & J. Haviland (Eds.), *Handbook of emotions* (pp. 442–460). New York: Guilford.

Brown, T. N., & Lesane-Brown, C. L. (2006). Race socialization messages across historical time. *Social Psychology Quarterly, 69*(2), 201–213.

Bureau of Labor Statistics. (2007). *American time use survey* (DC USDL 08-0859). Washington DC: U. S. Government Printing Office.

Burton, L. M., Hurt, T. R., Eline, C., & Matthews, S. (2001, October). *The yellow brick road: Neighbor-*

hoods, the homeplace, and life course development in economically disadvantaged families. Keynote address presented at the second biennial meeting of the Society for the Study of Human Development, Ann Arbor, MI.

Burton, L. M., Winn, D. M., Stevenson, H., & Clark, S. L. (2004). Working with African American clients: Considering the "homeplace" in marriage and family therapy practices. *Journal of Marital and Family Therapy, 30*(4), 397–410.

Byron, E. (2012). A truce in the chore wars. *Wall Street Journal,* Dec 7, 2012.

Canino, I., & Spurlock, J. (2000). *Culturally diverse children and adolescents: Assessment, diagnosis and treatment, 2nd ed..* New York: Guilford Press.

Carter, E. A. (1978). Transgenerational scripts and nuclear family stress: Theory and clinical implications. In R. R. Sager (Ed.), *Georgetown Family Symposium: Vol. 3, 1975–76.* Washington, DC: Georgetown University.

Chodorow, N. (1974). Family structure and feminine personality. In M. Z. Rosaldo & L. Lamphere (Eds.), *Woman, culture and society* (pp. 43–66). Stanford, CA.: Stanford University Press.

Chodorow, N., & Contratto, S. (1991). The fantasy of the perfect mother. In N. J. Chodorow: *Feminism and psychoanalytic theory* (pp. 79–96). New Haven: Yale University Press.

Christakis, N. A., & Fowler, J. H. (2011). *Connected: The surprising power of our social networks and how they shape our lives—How your friends' friends' friends affect everything you think, feel and do.* Boston: Back Bay Books.

Chugh, D., & Brief, A. P. (2008). 1964 was not that long ago: A story of gateways and pathways. In A. P. Brief (Ed.), *Diversity at work* (pp. 318–340). New York: Cambridge University Press.

Cicirelli, V. G. (1995). *Sibling relationships across the life span.* New York: Plenum Press.

Cohen, J., & Sandy, S. (2007). The social, emotional and education of children: Theories, goals, methods and assessments. In R. Bar-On, J. G. Maree & M. J. Elias (Eds.), *Educating people to be emotionally intelligent* (pp. 63–77). Westport, CN: Praeger.

Cole, J. B. (1996). Community, family and the healing power of responsibility. In E. Dinwiddie-Boyd (Ed.), *In our own words.* New York: Avon Books.

Comer, J. P., & Poussaint, A. F. (1992). *Raising Black children.* New York: Penguin.

Conniff, R. (2014). Nature, nuture, network. New Haven: Yale Alumni Magazine. Sept/Oct, 2014, pp 42-49. http://www.yalealumnimagazine.com/articles/3943/nicholas-christakis

Connidis, I. A. (2001). *Family ties and aging.* Thousand Oaks, CA: Sage.

Connidis, I. A. (2008). *Negotiating actual and anticipated parental support: multiple siblings voices in three generation families. Journal of Aging Studies,* 22(3), 229-238.

Coontz, S. (1992). *The way we never were.* New York: Basic Books.

Coontz, S. (1998). *The way we really are.* New York: Basic Books.

Coontz, S. (2006). *Marriage: A history.* New York: Viking.

Dilworth-Anderson, P., Burton, L., & Johnson, L. B. (1993). Reframing theories for understanding race, ethnicity and families. In P. G. Boss, W. J. Doherty, R. LaRossa, W. R. Schumm, & S. K. Steinmetz (Eds.), *Sourcebook of family theories and methods: A contextual approach* (pp. 627–646). New York: Plenum.

Dinnerstein, D. (1976). *The mermaid and the minotaur.* New York: Harper & Row.

Dolan Del Vecchio, K. (2008). Making love; Playing power. Berkeley, CA: Soft Skull Press.

Dooley, C., & Fedele, N. M. (2004). Mothers and sons: Raising relational boys. In J. V. Jordan, M. Walker & L. M. Hartling (Eds.), *The complexity of connection: Writings from the Stone Center's Jean Baker Miller Training Institute* (pp. 220–249). New York, Guilford.

Duvall, E. M. (1977). *Marriage and family development* (5th ed.). Philadelphia: Lippincott.

Elder, G. (1992). Life course. In E. Borgatta & M. Borgatta (Eds.), *Encyclopedia of sociology* (Vol. 3, pp. 1120–1130). New York: Macmillan.

Elder, G. (1999). *Children of the great depression: Social change in life experience* (25th anniversary ed.). Boulder, CO: Westview Press.

Elder, G. H., & Giele, J. Z. (Eds.). (2009). *The Craft of Life Course Research,* New York, Guilford Press.

Elder, G. H., & Johnson, M. M. (2002). Perspectives on human development in context. In C. von Hofsten & L. Backman (Eds.), *Psychology at the turn of the millennium* (Vol 2: Social, developmental and clinical perspectives, pp. 153–177). Florence, KY: Taylor & Frances/Routledge.

Elder, G. H., & Shanahan, M. J. (2006). The life course and human development. In R. M. Lerner & W. Damon (Eds.), *Handbook of child psychology* (Vol. 1, 6th ed., pp. 665–715). Hoboken, NJ: John Wiley & Sons.

Erikson, E. (1963). *Childhood and society* (2nd ed.). New York: W. W. Norton.

Erikson, E. (1968). *Identity: Youth and crisis.* New York: Norton.

Erikson, E. (1994). *Identity and the life cycle.* New York: W. W. Norton.

Family Caregiver Alliance (2009). Caregiving. Retrieved 5/28/13. http://www.caregiver.org/caregiver/jsp/content_node.jsp?nodeid=2313

Fernandez, R., Fogli, A., & Olivetti, C. (2004). Mothers and sons: Preference formation and female labor force dynamics. *Quarterly Journal of Economics*, *119*(4), 1249–1300.

Folbre, N. (2012). For love or money: Care provision in the United States. Thousand Oaks, CA: Russell Sage Foundation.

Friedman, H. S. (2012). The measure of a nation: How to regain America's competitive edge and boost our global standing. Amherst, NY: Prometheus Books.

Fullilove, M. (2004). *Root shock: How tearing up our neighborhoods hurts America and what we can do about it*. New York: Ballantine.

Gardner, H. (2006). *Multiple intelligences*. New York: Basic Books.

Gilligan, C. (1993). *In a different voice*. Cambridge, MA: Harvard University Press.

Gladwell, M (2008). Outliers: The story of success. Boston: Little Brown.

Goldstein, S., & Brooks, R. B. (Eds.). (2012). *Handbook of resilience in children*. New York: Kluwer Academic/Plenum Publishers.

Goleman, D. (2006). *Emotional intelligence, 10th Anniversary Edition, Why it can matter more than IQ*. New York: Bantam.

Goleman, D. (2007). *Social intelligence*. New York. Bantam.

Goleman, D. (2011a). Leadership: The power of emotional intelligence. Northampton, MA: More than sound.

Goleman, D. (2011b). The brain and emotional intelligence: New insights.

Green, R. J. (1998). Traditional norms of male development. In R. Almeida (Ed.), *Transforming gender and race* (pp. 81–84). New York: Harrington Park Press.

Hadley, T., Jacob, T., Milliones, J., Caplan, J., & Spitz, D. (1974). The relationship between family developmental crises and the appearance of symptoms in a family member. *Family Process, 13,* 207–214.

Hale-Benson, J. E. (1986). *Black children: Their roots, culture and learning styles*. Baltimore: Johns Hopkins University Press.

Hale, J. E (2001). *Learning while Black: Educational excellence for African American children*. Baltimore: Johns Hopkins University Press.

Hill, Reuben. (1970). *Family development in three generations*. Cambridge, MA: Schenckman Publishing Co.

Hochschild, A. (2012). *The second shift: Working parents and the revolution at home, Revised*. New York: Viking.

Hoffman, L. W. (1972). Early childhood experiences and women's achievement motives. *Journal of Social Issues 28*(2), 261–278.

hooks, b. (1999). *Yearning: Race, gender, and cultural politics*. Boston: South End Press.

Johnson, M. K., Foley, K. L. & Elder, G. H. (2004). Women's commiunity service. 1940-1960: Insights from a cohort of gifted American women. Sociological Quarterly, 45(1). Pp. 45–66.

Jordan, J. V. *(Ed.)*. (1997). *Women's growth in diversity: More writings from the Stone Center*. New York: Guilford Press.

Jordan, J. V., Kaplan, A. G., Miller, J. B., Stiver, I. P., & Surrey, J. L., Eds. (1991). *Women's growth in connection*. New York: Guilford.

Jordan, J. V., Walker, M., & Hartling, L. M. (Eds.). (2004). *The complexity of connection: Writings from the Stone Center's Jean Baker Miller Training Institute*. New York: Guilford.

Kagan, J., & Moss, H. (1962). *Birth to maturity*. New York: Wiley.

Khazan, I., McHale, P., & Decourcey W. (2008). Violated wishes about division of childcare labor predict coparenting process during stressful and non stressful family evaluation. *Infant Mental Health Journal, 29,* 343–361.

Kierkegaard, S. (2000). The essential Kierkegaard. Princeton, NJ: Princeton University Press.

Kimmel, M. S. (2012). *Manhood in America: A cultural history* (3rd ed.). New York: Free Press.

Kimmel, M. S. (2013). *The gendered society* (5th ed.). New York: Oxford University Press.

Kimmel, M. S. (2009). *Guyland: The perilous world where boys become men*. New York: Harper/Collins.

Kimmel, M. S., & Messner, M. A. (2008). *Men's lives* (8th ed.). Needham Heights: MA: Allyn & Bacon.

Kivel, P. (2010). The act-like-a-man box. In M. S. Kimmel & M. A. Messner (Eds.). Mens lives (pp. 83–85). Boston: Allyn & Bacon.

Koestner, R., Franz, C., & Weinberger, J. (1990). The family origins of empathic concern: A 26-year longitudinal study. *Journal of Personality and Social Psychology, 58*(4), 709–717.

Kolata, G. (2007, January 3). A surprising secret to a long life: Stay in school. *New York Times,* pp. 1, 29.

Korin, E., McGoldrick, M., & Watson, M. (1996). Individual and family life cycle. In M. Mengel & W. L. Holleman (Eds.), *Principles of clinical practice: Vol. 1,* Patient, doctor and society, (pp. 21–46). New York: Plenum.

Kunjufu, J. (1995). *Countering the conspiracy to destroy Black boys* (Vol. 4). Chicago: African American Images.

Lawrence-Lightfoot, S. (2009). *The third chapter: Passion, risk, and adventure in the 25 years past fifty.* New York: Farrar, Straus, & Giroux.

Le, H., Ceballo, R., Chao, R., Hill, N. E., Murry, V. M., & Pinderhughes, E. E. (2008). Excavating culture: Disentangling ethnic differences from contextual influences in parenting. *Applied Developmental Science, 12*(4), 163–175.

Levine, J., Murphy, D., & Wilson, S. (1993.) *Getting men involved: Strategies for early childhood programs.* New York: Scholastic.

Levinson, D. J. (1986). *The seasons of a man's life.* New York: Ballantine Books.

Levinson, D. J. (1996). *The seasons of a woman's life.* New York: Knopf.

Loewen, J. W. (2008). Lies my teacher told me: Everything your American history textbook got wrong, Revised and updated edition,

Loewen, J. W. (2010). Teaching what really happened: how to avoid the tyranny of textbooks and get students excited about doing history. New York: Teachers College Press, Columbia University.

Maccoby, E. E. (1990). Gender and relationships: A developmental account. *American Psychologist, 45,* (4), 513–520.

Maccoby, E. E. (1999). *The two sexes: Growing up apart: Coming together (The family and public policy).* Boston: Belknap Press.

Mallers, M. H. Charles, S. T., Neupert, S. D., & Almeida, D. M. (2010). Perceptions of childhood relationships with mother and father: Daily emotional and stressor experiences in adulthood. *Developmental Psychology,* November, 46(6): 1651-1661.

McGoldrick, M. (1977). Some data on death and cancer in schizophrenic families. Presentation at Georgetown Presymposium, Washington, DC.

McGoldrick, M., Gerson, R., & Petry, S. (2008). *Genograms: Assessment and intervention.* (3rd ed.). New York: W. W. Norton.

McIntosh, P. (1985). *On feeling like a fraud.* (Work in Progress Working Paper Series, 18). Wellesley, MA: The Stone Center.

McIntosh, P. (1989). *On feeling like a fraud,* (Part 2). (Work in Progress Working Paper Series, 37). Wellesley, MA: The Stone Center.

McKay, V., & Caverly, S. (2004). The nature of family relationships between and within generations: Relations between grandparents, grandchildren, and siblings in later life. In J. Nussbaum & J. Coupland (Eds.), *Handbook of communication and aging research* (2nd ed., pp. 251–272). Mahwah, NJ: Lawrence Erlbaum Associates Publishers.

McLaughlin, C. (2008). Emotional well-being and its relationship to schools and classroom: A critical reflection. *British Journal of Guidance and Counselling, 36*(4), 355–366.

Meeker, M. (2008). *Boys should be boys: 7 secrets to raising healthy sons.* Washington DC: Regnery Publishing.

Meinhold, J. (2006). The influence of life transition statuses on sibling intimacy and contact in early adulthood. (Doctoral dissertation, Oregon St. Univ., 2006). *Dissertation Abstracts International Section A: Humanities and Social Sciences, 67*(30), 1107.

Miedzian, M. (2002). *Boys will be boys: Breaking the link between masculinity and violence.* New York: Doubleday.

Miller, J. B. (1976) *Toward a new psychology of women.* Boston: Beacon.

Mueller, M. M., & Elder, G. H., Jr. (2003). Family contingencies across the generations. Grandparent-grandchild relationships in holistic perspective. *Journal of Marriage and the Family, 65* 2), 404–417.

Mueller, M. M., Wilhelm, B., & Elder, G. H. (2002). Variations in grandparenting. *Research on aging, 24*(3), 360–388.

Neugarten, B. (1979). Time, age and the life cycle. *American Journal of Psychiatry, 136,* 887–894.

Norris, J. E., & Tindale, J. A. (1994). *Among generations: The cycle of adult relationships.* New York: W. H. Freeman & Company.

Neuman, S., & Celano, D (2012) *Giving our children a fighting chance.* New York: Teachers College Press.

Ogbu, J. U. (1990). Cultural mores, identity, and literacy. In J. W. Stigler, R. A. Shweder, & G. H. Herdt (Eds.), *Cultural psychology: Essays on comparative human development* (pp. 520–541). New York: Cambridge University Press.

Pear, R. (2008, March 23). Gap in life expectancy widens for the nation. *New York Times,* p. 19.

Perry, B. D. (2002). Childhood experience and the expression of genetic potential: What childhood neglect tells us about nature and nurture. *Brain & Mind, 3*(1), 79–100.

Quintana, S. (2008). Racial perspective taking ability; Developmental, theoretical and empirical trends. In S. Quitana & C. McKowan (Eds.), *Handbook of race, racism and the developing child* (pp. 16–30). Hoboken, NJ: John Wiley.

Quintana, S., & McKown, C. (Eds.) (2008). Handbook of race, racism and the developing child. Hoboken, NJ: John Wiley.

Raley, S., & Bianchi, S. (2006). Sons, daughters, and Family procesesses: Does gender of children matter? *Annual Review of Sociology,* 32(1):401–421.

Rivers, C., & Barnett, R. C. (2013a). The new soft war on women: How the myth of female ascendance is hurting women, men and our economy. New York: Tarcher.

Rivers, C., & Barnett, R. C. (2013b). The truth about girls and boys. New York: Columbia University Press.

Rubin, L. (1993). *Just friends: The role of friendship in our lives.* New York: Harper Collins.

Salovey, P. (2007). Integrative summary. In R. Bar-On, J. G. Maree, & M. J. Elias (Eds.), *Educating people to be emotionally intelligent* (pp. 291–298). Westport, CT: Praeger / Greenwood Press.

Sayer, L., Bianchi. S., & Robinson, J. (2004). Are parents investing less in children? Trends in mother's and father's time with children. *American Journal of Sociology, 110,* 1–43.

Schaie, W., & Elder, G. (Eds.). (2005). Historical influences on lives and aging. In *Societal impact on aging series.* New York: Springer.

Senge, P. (2006). *The fifth discipline: The art and practice of the learning organization.* New York: Doubleday.

Seo, J. (2007). The long-term influence of father involvement on emerging adults' psychological well-being. *Dissertation Abstracts International Section A: Humanities and Social Sciences, 68*(5-A), 2191.

Sew, J. W. (2006). Review of multiple intelligences reconsidered. *Discourse and Society, 17*(4), 554–557.

Shaffer, C., & Amundsen, K. (1993). *Creating community anywhere: Finding support and connection in a fragmented world.* New York: Tarcher/Perigee Books.

Shanahan, M. J., & Elder, G. H. (2002). History, agency and the life course. In L. J. Crocket (Ed.), *Agency, motivation and the life course* (pp. 145–186). Lincoln, NE: University of Nebraska Press.

Sheehy, G. (1977). *Passages.* New York: Bantam.

Sheehy, G. (1995). *New passages.* New York: Ballantine Books.

Shinn, M., & Yoshikawa, H., Eds. (2008). *Toward positive youth development: Transforming schools and community programs.* New York: Oxford University Press.

Silverstein, O., & Rashbaum, B. (1994). *The courage to raise good men.* New York: Penguin Books.

Skolnick, A. (2013). The life course revolution. In A S. Skolnick & J. H. Skolnick (Eds.). *Family in transition* (17th ed., pp. 31–39). Boston: Pearson.

Solomon, A. (2013). *Far from the tree: Parents, children and the search for identity.* New York: Scribner.

Sommers, C. H. (2013). The boys at the back. New York Times, Feb 3, 2013, pp. Sunday Review, 1, 6–7.

Speck, R., & Attneave, C. (1973). Family Networks. New York: Pantheon Books.

Stavridou, F., & Kakana, D. (2008). Graphic abilities in relation to mathematical and scientific ability in adolescents. *Educational research, 50*(1), 75–93.

Stevenson, H., Winn, D-M., Coard, S., & Walker-Barnes, C. (2003, May). Towards a culturally relevant framework for interventions with African-American families. Presentation made at the Emerging Issues in African-American Family Life: Context, Adaptation, and Policy Conference, Duke University, Durham, NC.

Taylor, S. E. (2002). *The tending instinct.* New York: Henry Holt.

Taylor, S. E., Klein, L. C., Lewis, B. P., Gruenewald, T. L., Gurung, R. A. R., & Updegraff, J. A. (2000). Female responses to stress: Tend and befriend, not fight or flight. *Psychological Review, 107*(3), 41–429.

Tindale, J. (1999). Variance in the meaning of time by family cycle, period, social context, and ethnicity. In W. Pentland, A. Harvey, M. Lawton, & M. McCall (Eds.), *Time use research in the social sciences* (pp. 155–168). Dordrecht, Netherlands: Kluwer Academic Publishers.

Treas, J. (2002). How cohorts, education, and ideology shaped a new sexual revolution on American attitudes toward nonmarital sex, 1972–1998, *Sociological Perspectives, 45*(3), 267–283.

U.S. Census Bureau (2010). U.S. Census Bureau reports men and women wait longer to marry. Retrieved 5/28/13. http://www.census.gov/newsroom/releases/archives/families_households/cb10-174.html

U.S. Department of Labor, Bureau of Labor Statistics (2011). Employment and Earnings, Annual Averages. January.

Vaillant, G. (2002). *Aging well: Surprising guideposts to a happier life.* Boston: Little, Brown and Company.

Vaillant, G. (2012). *Triumphs of experience: The men of the Harvard study.* Cambridge, MA: Belknap.

Vaillant, G. E. (1977). *Adaptation to life.* Boston: Little, Brown and Company.

Vaillant, G. E. (1983). *The natural history of alcoholism.* Cambridge, MA: Harvard University Press.

Vaillant, G. E. (1995). *The natural history of alcoholism revisited: Causes, patterns, and paths to recovery.* Cambridge, MA: Harvard University Press.

Walsh, F. (1978). Concurrent grandparent death and birth of schizophrenic offspring: An intriguing finding. *Family Process, 17,* 457–463.

Washington, E. L. (2007). Female socialization: How daughters affect their legislator fathers' voting on women's issues. *American Economic Review, 86* 3), 425–441.

Wolf, S. J. (2009, June). What makes us happy. *Atlantic,* 8–16.

Chapter 2

Women and the Family Life Cycle

Monica McGoldrick

Learning Objectives

- Identify how women's life cycle roles have changed in recent decades.
- Describe how women's life cycle roles impact their education and experiences in academia.
- List the unique challenges that women face in the workplace.
- Discuss the changing roles women play in families.
- Describe how women are impacted by their roles as caregivers.
- Compare how men and women experience marriage.
- Identify and describe the stresses that accompany different life cycle stages for mothers.
- Discuss the challenges women face in the final phase of life.
- Describe the importance of friendship as a resource for women.
- Compare how women and men experience loss.

Introduction

Women have always played a central role in families, but the idea that they have a life cycle apart from their roles as wife and mother is relatively recent and is still not fully accepted. Traditionally, "human development" referred to male development. Women's development was defined by the men in their lives, and their role was defined by their position in the life cycle of their father, husband, or children. The expectation for women has been that they would care for others: first men, then children, then the elderly. Only recently has it been an option for them to have a life of their own.

Overall, women lead far more complex, varied, and unpredictable lives than men, reinventing themselves many times to meet different circumstances. While men's work life tends to follow a linear course, women's usually consists of starts, stops, meanders, interruptions, revisions, and detours as they accommodate the others in their lives. Clinical work involves helping both men and women appreciate women's courage, the odds they face, and to break down the patriarchal vision of women as sex objects and servers of others rather than human beings in their own right. And in spite of all the progress that has been made in the past two generations, gender inequities are still pronounced at every life cycle phase and for every group of women.

Economic independence for women, which has profound implications for traditional family structures, is crucial for women's protection from abuse, divorce, poverty, and powerlessness in old age. Women are 30 percent more likely to live in poverty than men at every age and the differences pertain to all races and cultures (Costello, Wight, & Stone, 2003; Bennetts, 2011). In old age, they are twice as likely to be poor (Bennetts, 2011) and this is true for all racial and ethnic groups (Cathome, 2008). Statistics show that about 25 percent of African American women and Latinas, and about 10 percent of White women live in poverty, a national catastrophe for our future, showing how little we as a nation care for our future citizens.

While couple relationships are becoming much less unequal in dual-worker families, the economic pressures on women remain a major issue throughout the life cycle. In spite of men's increasing participation in household chores, which has risen dramatically, even in working-class families, it still lags far behind the participation of women (Barnett & Rivers, 1996; Hochschild, 2012; Coontz, 2013a). But the biggest problem for women is our nation's refusal to support child care, as other advanced nations of the world have done, an essential obligation for a country that requires dual-worker families (Coontz, 2013a). Only five states in the United States offer any income replacement at all even for infant care (Sandberg, 2013). At the other end of the life cycle, elder care, again an issue left primarily to women, is also not supported by our society, leaving enormous numbers of women to fend for themselves without health care, or even social security to support them. On the positive side lurks the possibility that we are entering a new era when gender roles will be transformed between men and women so that both have work and relationship options. As Liza Mundy puts it, this will challenge some of the most basic and supposedly hard-wired ways men and women see each other: "It will alter how we mate, how and when we join together, how we procreate and raise children, and, to use the phrase of the founders, how we pursue happiness. It will reshape the landscape of the heart" (Mundy, 2012, p. 7).

Even as we acknowledge women's commonalities, we know their life cycle experiences differ greatly, depending where they are in the sociopolitical structure. Poor women, LGBT women, and women of color are especially likely to remain invisible, experiencing double and triple jeopardy for their multiple oppressions. We must pay attention to their adaptive strengths as we assert the traumatic inequities they experience. The struggles of these women are dramatically more complex and difficult than those of White heterosexual middle-class women. Audre Lorde long ago described a key difference between Black and White women boldly:

Some problems we share as women, some we do not. You fear your children will grow up to join the patriarchy and testify against you; we fear our children will be dragged from a car and shot down in the street, and you will turn your backs upon the reasons they are dying. (1984, p. 9)

African American and other marginalized women perceive their womanhood differently than White women and may at times not identify with gender oppression, seeing racism as such a dominant issue in their lives (Hall & Greene, 1994).

Women of color have had to struggle for centuries with the abuses of rape, sexual abuse starvation, loss of their children, of their land, of their history, and of their dreams for the future. We must learn from the multigenerational legacies of oppressed women who have been marginalized by oppression for centuries; the complexity of roles, strengths, and adaptive strategies of those who learned to care, teach, and support others to survive; to feed their children and nurse the sick and elderly, and to love their families and friends and communities. We must affirm their narratives and survival strengths, and encourage them to move their lives forward for their own sake and the next generations. Recognition of legacies of oppression, and of women's adaptive strategies is essential to our assessment and to intervention with women of all different backgrounds.

Women's Changing Life Cycle Roles

Women's lives have always required amazing improvisation. They were never about the trajectory toward success and achievement, which still seems the desired narrative for men of the dominant groups in our society. Women's lives have always involved, like making a quilt, trying to invent something coherent from all sorts of diverse elements.

Women's lives require weaving together of many strands, attending to multiple tasks, sounds, and images at once. They created the "nest" that was home for everyone else; they provided the food, the nurturance, and the care for all from the youngest to the oldest; they created the family rituals, bought the presents, and made birthdays and Thanksgivings happen. They nursed the sick, washed and mourned the dead, and attended to the needs of other mourners.

Women are exposed to higher rates of change and instability in their lives than men and are also more vulnerable to life cycle stresses, because of their greater emotional involvement in the lives of those around them. This means that they are doubly stressed, exposed to a wider network of people for whom they feel responsible, and more emotionally responsive to them. Their role overload leaves them further burdened when unpredictable stresses such as illness, divorce, or unemployment occur. Women are generally much more emotionally affected than men by deaths and by other events in their networks. Men respond less and even hear less about the distress in their caring networks of family, neighbors, and friends. People who need emotional support more often seek out women as confidants. Therefore, women have more demands for nurturance made on them. Daughters are more involved with their parents and visit them more than sons do. Grandmothers are twice as likely to have warm relationships with grandchildren as grandfathers. Indeed, grandfathers tend to be active with their grandchildren only if their wives are (Lott, 1994).

But women have until recently been systematically kept out of the public spheres of life—government, business, the world of power, money, and leadership—all of which had to change, for women to have a life cycle of their own. As Carolyn Heilbrun discussed in her classic analysis of women's biography, *Writing a Woman's Life*, women's right to her own story depends on her ability to act in the public domain. Heilbrun saw power as "the ability to take one's place in whatever discourse is essential to action and the right to have one's part matter" (1988, p. 18). Women's right to have their part matter in the public domain determines their possibilities also in the intimate, personal domain—from infant care to physical, psychological, spiritual, and financial security in old age, a phase of life that has always been primarily for women, but which even now is still controlled by a government run primarily by men, rather than by women themselves. The conundrum of responsibility without power has long characterized women's lives. Women had responsibility for clothing their children, but fashion and

advertising have been a man's world; women were the cooks at home, but not the chefs of record; they were the artistic creators of the home, but not the artists of record.

For centuries, women remained voiceless in the public sphere, having to stitch their lives together here and there as they could. This was a tragedy, but it has also given them an adaptive strength, making them able to weave lives out of many disparate strands. Even in the private sphere, in their homes, the pervasive private abuse, persecution, and humiliation of women have been an unacknowledged societal shame for centuries. Battering of women, date rape, marital rape, dehumanizing treatment of women as sex objects, psychological abuse, financial control, sexual harassment, and exploitation of women have only recently begun to be acknowledged as problems. Bill Clinton spoke publicly of the problem more than a decade ago:

> *If children aren't safe in their homes, if college women aren't safe in their dorms, if mothers can't raise their children in safety, then the American Dream will never be real for them. Domestic violence is now the number one health risk for women between the ages of 15 and 44 in our country. It is a bigger threat than cancer or car accidents.* (Clinton, 1995)

The exclusion of women from public spheres of education, lawmaking, business, the arts, money, and power is gradually changing. Women's roles have been changing dramatically in the past generation. But the issues remain. Instead of being passed from their fathers to their husbands, they are claiming an increasing span of time to define their own lives. They are delaying marriage (more than two-thirds under 25 are now unmarried), and many are experiencing a period of independent living and work before marriage (Coontz, 2006). The typical first-time bride in 2007 was 27, almost 4 years older than her counterpart of 1970. Childbearing has fallen below replacement levels, as women increasingly postpone childbearing. They are refusing to stay in stifling or abusive marriages. Almost half of marriages end in divorce and women with the most education and income who divorce are less likely to remarry, in contrast to men, the most wealthy and well educated of whom are the most likely to stay married or to remarry quickly. But women are also more likely to move down to poverty after divorce, while men's income actually rises after divorce (Lyle, 2012). The vast majority of the poor are women or children, most of who live in one-parent households. For the increasing number of teenaged unmarried mothers, their mothers and aunts are playing a major role in raising their children. For the first time, a fair number of women in their 30s and 40s are choosing to have and raise children without partners, a new phenomenon altogether. Lesbians, who are increasingly having children together, are expanding the concept of family and community to include their own special relationships with friends, extended family, and ex-lovers (Slater, 1995). And women are living longer and reinventing themselves well into their 80s and 90s (Heilbrun, 1997; Lawrence-Lightfoot, 2009; Bateson, 2011). Finally, the majority of people who live alone are women (11 million versus 6.8 million men), mostly widowed or divorced elderly whose numbers have increased dramatically since 1970.

> **Assess your comprehension of women's changing life cycle roles by completing this quiz.**

Women and Education

Education is a key to liberation. Women now make up 60 percent of college graduates (Fisher, 2013). Indeed there is strong evidence that the Ivy League and other prestigious colleges offer affirmative action for male students to keep the proportion of men close to 50 percent (Kivel, 2002; Britz, 2006; Pollitt, 2006). But it remains hard for women to achieve some of the positions in our society that education prepares them for (Sandberg, 2013). Male dominance among professors and researchers often make it difficult for women to find mentors, but even the dominant discourse often leaves women at the margins. Peggy McIntosh (1985, 1989) decades ago described the ways women can end up feeling inadequate in academia because of the absurd requirement to act as if all ideas fit in logical and hierarchical sequence.

Language is an invention . . . Life doesn't come in sentences, paragraphs or arguments. For me, the outline now joined the argumentative paper as a problematical form, requiring pretenses, such as subordinating all ideas to one "main" or governing idea. . . . For me the outline is . . . a fraudulent form. My genre . . . is the list . . . On a list everything matters; you need not rank, subordinate, and exclude. (1989, p. 2)

We must challenge the categories we have been offered to gain better perspective on the complex threads of a woman's life cycle. Clearly the battle for equal rights has not been won in academia even if women are receiving more degrees (Sandberg, 2013; Hochschild, 2012; Rivers & Barnett, 2013b). And whether we think women should do more to create the changes that are necessary or that society should do more, more needs to be done. McIntosh (1985, 1989) called for developing a "double vision" regarding a woman's sense of being a "fraud." On the one hand, we need to help women overcome their feelings of inadequacy and of not deserving a place to stand or speak out. We need to validate and appreciate women's acknowledgment that they do not know everything and their resistance to making pronouncements as if they held "the" truth, as men have done so often. It helps if we keep a broad perspective on the difficulties women face externally in being treated as invisible, and having internalized the dominant culture's perception that they are not as capable. Much of our therapy work with women relates to supporting them in expanding their lives in the public domain of work, school, governance, business, power, and money.

CASE ILLUSTRATION

Marta Powell

Marta Powell was a talented, highly educated artist of Irish and German background, who had attended private schools and an Ivy League university where she met her husband Robert, whose ancestors went back to the Mayflower. Both Marta and Robert completed masters in fine arts, but then he became a college professor and she became the "wife," continuing her artwork on the side and through cooking, sewing, gardening, and decorating their home. Nepotism rules prevented her from working in the university's art department, but eventually she got a job as an adjunct, teaching graphic design in the architecture department. By the time her sons left for college, Marta had become depressed and frustrated and wondered what had become of her own aspirations. When another professor fell ill, she had the opportunity to attend a summer Artists seminar. Once she was away, she realized how unhappy she had become in her marriage. She had sacrificed too much of herself for her husband's dreams and lost sight of her own. When her husband was negative about renegotiating their relationship, she told him she wanted a divorce. The divorce left her feeling amazingly free. She had not realized until then how much she had come to take responsibility for whatever went wrong in her husband's world. Now she no longer had to worry about his unhappiness and could, for the first time, concentrate on her own life. However, without her husband's income, she quickly moved toward the poverty level. She tried to figure out how to move ahead on the academic pathway, but continuously felt inadequate in preparing the required papers for presentation and publication because her thinking went in spirals and loops, and she could not make it go in a straight line. At this point, her depression and frustration led her to seek help. When she told her story, she was shocked by the therapist's response to her narrative. She had come to think of her life as a failure, but the therapist characterized her as a pioneer who had kept up her creativity through all sorts of endeavors during the years when by her station in life she had not formally pursued her career, and now she was getting ready, suggested the therapist, to break forth in a new incarnation, drawing on all the work she had been doing throughout her life. Of course, doing a linear outline was too constraining for someone as creative as she. And, of course, she was frustrated! How could she not be? With minimal coaching, Marta found her way to publishing and presenting in her own voice and moved to a new university where, within a few years, she was a highly respected member of the senior faculty. At the age of 60, she achieved tenure and at the age of 70 became an Emerita Professor at her university.

Marta required minimal therapeutic input. Had she seen a therapist who focused on her depression rather than her creativity and the life cycle dilemma of a woman in her situation, she might, of course, have had a very different life trajectory. The clinical input she received helped her see herself as a true pioneer among the women of her generation and to appreciate the accomplishments of her improvised life. Very often this is all that women need: help to empower themselves and realize how much they have accomplished already, to see themselves as women whose lives have been constrained by circumstance, and who need to gather strength from others who understand their situation. Marta had had good female friends throughout her life and close relationships with her three sisters, although these relationships had been sidelined during her marriage. At the point of her separation, she reconnected with these relationships and from that point on, her network of friends became her greatest resource as she developed herself over the next chapter of her life.

We must pay more attention to the family and community networks that women have always been responsible for maintaining, and that are crucial to their well-being (Taylor, 2002). We must also attend to the possibilities of equity, partnership, connection, and flexibility in couple relationships, friendships and intergenerational bonds through the life cycle. Women of color, of course, experience double jeopardy and lesbians of color, triple jeopardy, in adjusting to a world in which the institutions have been defined by others. They have had to try to learn in educational contexts that have no connection to their life experience whatsoever.

Many women, especially lesbians and women of color, have been thrown into experiences in which societal assumptions had absolutely no connection to their life experience and in which, in order to survive, they had to draw on their inner resources and make improvisatory connections and transformations to build bridges to what was relevant in their hearts.

Therapists have important work to do with women at every phase of the life cycle in encouraging their ideas, intuitions, and adaptive resourcefulness, helping them to realize that they are not frauds and validating their ways of knowing even while not buying into the by now disproven stereotypes that women are not capable of thinking as well as men (Rivers & Barnett, 2013b).

> Assess your comprehension of women and education by completing this quiz.

Women and Work

Women make up almost half (47 percent) of the labor force today, though they still earn less than men do for the same job, and they include 65 percent of mothers with children (Wang, Parker, & Taylor, 2013). This includes two-thirds of mothers of children younger than 3 years, 73 percent of whom work full time (Hochschild, 2012). But the continuing differential role of men and women in the larger context is illustrated by the fact that a large portion of women are still in sex-segregated, low-paying jobs such as secretary-administrative assistants, teaching, nursing, childcare, waitressing, and housekeeping (Glynn & Powers, 2012).

Several myths have been created about women and work. The first is that traditionally mothers did not work or worked only for extra money or selfish reasons, which is, of course, absurd. Women's work and income are essential for the survival and well-being of most families in the twenty-first century as has been true throughout human history. In traditional cultures, mothers always worked, and children were raised primarily by grandparents and older siblings.

Another myth is that maternal employment is bad for children. In fact, maternal employment tends to improve a mother's self esteem and well being (Coontz, 2013b).

Indeed, maternal depression, which is correlated with unemployment, does have a negative impact on children. Employed mothers have higher aspirations for their children, discuss and share school activities more, encourage independence skills more, have more parenting satisfaction, fewer family conflicts, and are more effective at limit setting; their children have fewer behavior problems, watch less TV, and experience greater family cohesion; in addition father involvement is significantly greater when mothers are employed, which is associated with a host of favorable affective and cognitive outcomes and with children's social adjustment (Gottfried & Gottfried, 2008). Of course, jobs with no flexibility, poor pay, no benefits, irregular schedules, and low control may jeopardize health, whereas having high-quality roles, even if they are numerous, may help to maintain or enhance health. But even with difficult jobs, the income and ability to provide for one's children is an asset. Women with more high-powered, high-status careers obviously have more advantages. Job-related social support has particularly beneficial effects on women's health. In any case, there is no evidence that children lose out when their mothers are employed and there are many advantages to maternal employment (Marcus-Newhall, Halpern, & Tan, 2008; Meers & Strober, 2009).

Achieving equal pay for equal work is a major issue for women in the United States, one-third of who earn more than half of their family's income. Indeed, two-fifths of working women are the sole heads of their households. Among African American women and other women of color, the undercompensation is even greater. Daughters appear to benefit most of all from having a working mother, being more self-confident, getting better grades, and being more likely to pursue careers themselves than children of non-employed mothers (Hoffman, 1989). For African American families, a mother's working has been shown to improve not only her self-esteem (Hoffman, 1989) but also her daughters' likelihood of staying in school (Wolfer & Moen, 1996). Furthermore, fascinating and little-publicized early findings suggested that the high achievement of mothers was even more predictive of high achievement of both their sons and their daughters than in the high achievement of fathers (Losoff, 1974; Padan, 1965).

In any case, very few families can afford to have children these days unless both husband and wife have paying jobs. Still, while family and work are seen as mutually supportive and complementary for men, for women work and family remain highly conflicting demands. Traditionally, the family has served to support and nurture the male worker for his performance on the job, whereas working women have been seen as depriving their families by working. In no sense is the family a refuge for women as it has been for men.

In spite of household and other strains, the more roles a woman occupies, the healthier she is likely to be. Employed married parents have the best health profile, whereas people with none of these roles have the worst profile. While, of course, it matters what kind of work people are doing, employed women are generally healthier than non-employed women, and lack of employment is a risk factor for women's health (Gannon, 1999; Dell'Antonia, 2012; Coontz, 2013b). Multiple roles may provide cognitive cushioning in the face of stress. There is a significant relationship between underemployment and decreased physical and mental health. While work seems to be a stress on men, indications are that paid work actually improves the health of women. Women who are homemakers end up with a lower sense of self-esteem and personal competence, even regarding their childcare and social skills, than do mothers in the paid workforce. Women who take any time off from full commitment to the paid workforce lose a great deal of ground in their power in their relationships, their work flexibility, and their financial options (Barnett & Rivers, 1996).

As more women have entered the workplace, they have become more aware of the external constraints on them in the labor force (e.g., pay and job discrimination and sexual harassment) and this awareness can be intensely stressful, even when it leads to change. The main clinical implication is that therapists need to be active educators in therapy, helping women realize that they are not alone, encouraging them to network to diminish their isolation, and empowering them to join forces to change the way society operates. Sexual harassment seems to be the major source of stress for working women. A woman who must bring a charge of sexual harassment against her boss by herself will have great difficulty. A class action suit is enormously easier to handle, and women are more likely to win when they operate together. Linking women to other women is one of the most important tools we clinicians have. The following case illustrates a remarkable instance of a woman who was able to label her work and financial problems as primary for herself rather than her marital relationship.

CASE ILLUSTRATION

Velma Jefferson

Velma Jefferson, a 55-year-old African American school administrator, came to the therapy with a very specific agenda: She had had a heart attack the previous summer, which she believed was caused by her marital distress. She was 7 years from retirement and wanted me to help her not have another heart attack over her husband, Carl, before then. At that point she figured she would have the resources to leave him if he did not change his ways, but until that time she could not afford to lose the share he gave to their income. She hoped he would change, but she did not want to waste her time with marital therapy. She thought if he wanted to work on himself that would be fine, but she wanted help to keep herself healthy and not be derailed by his lies and promises. The couple had been married in their early 20s but she had left him 5 years later because of his physical abuse, taking their little daughter to Chicago where she had family. Three years later, he followed her there, promised to turn over a new leaf and she remarried him. Since that time he had never been physically abusive, but she said he was a "high roller" full of lies about his relationships with other women, always letting her down financially with big promises and then gambling most of his money away or spending it on himself. She was tired of arguing with him about where he had been or with whom and about his excuses regarding money. Because of his financial problems, the house was in her name and if she could hold on for the next few years she would have her pension and the money from the house to retire to Georgia, which was her dream. I soon met the husband who was very keen for couple therapy to begin and could not understand why I was not trying to help them work out their "misunderstandings." We had a couple of joint sessions where Velma laid out that she was tired of arguing about money and would expect her husband to pay his share of the mortgage and his contribution to food and household expenses, but was no longer going to nag him about the money. He could just leave it on the table. He tried to bring up that she was always suspicious that he had a girlfriend. I asked if he did and he denied it but said she never believed what he said. She said she would not be asking about this again. When I met with Carl alone he was very frustrated that I was not doing more to help him connect with his wife who, he was sure, was angry with him. I questioned him further about a girlfriend because he had had some hesitation in her presence. He admitted he had been involved with someone for many years; he had been trying to end the relationship, but the girlfriend's son was mentally ill and she needed him. He said he did not have the heart to end the relationship. We discussed the limits his wife seemed to be establishing regarding the finances, even though she had not said she would do anything, if he did not come through with the expected money. He said she had been a wonderful wife and he wanted my help to win her back. We discussed his drinking and spending patterns and he said he had decided the previous week to cut down on his drinking because it was costing him a lot of money.

From that point on I coached the spouses separately to achieve their goals. Velma's goal was to stay healthy and follow through on her objective of not letting herself be derailed by anger and frustration with Carl, which had taken up too much space in her life. His aim was to win her back, which, he gradually realized, meant stopping his excessive drinking, spending, and involvement with other women. Over the next several years, Velma developed her network of friends, worked on herself physically to stay calm, and interpersonally to avoid getting into "useless" discussions with Carl about issues where he might lie. She had had a negative attitude about organized religion, having been pained by the hypocrisy of her abusive minister father's religiosity. She now found a spiritual community, which had meaning for her and in which she felt she could continue when she moved to Georgia.

For Carl, her behavior seemed like shock therapy. He gradually became committed to working on himself, perhaps because he sensed she had set herself a real bottom line, not now, when she could not manage a separation, but in the future when she was definite she would separate, if he did not change. At the time of Velma's retirement, their relationship was in a very different place. He had become a caring, thoughtful, and appreciative husband. He had reconnected with a daughter he had fathered but abandoned in his earlier adulthood, and was con-

necting now with his grandchildren. The couple had ended therapy several years before retirement but made a reunion appointment before moving together to Georgia. In that session, they reviewed the importance of Velma taking responsibility for keeping herself healthy and Carl for building the trusting and loving relationship he wanted with his wife.

Velma Jefferson did not think of her problems in gender terms. But my understanding was that her accommodation to her husband for so many years, going along with him to the point of jeopardizing her own health before taking a stand, are common behaviors for women, who have been raised to accommodate and think of their own needs as selfish. What was remarkable was her clarity about what she needed to do to survive and her ability to seek the resources she needed to get herself to a healthy place. Luckily I was able to support her in this journey. The main clinical point is not to pathologize women who are coming to an understanding of their oppression, but to support their efforts to empower themselves as Velma Jefferson did.

 Assess your comprehension of women and work by completing this quiz.

Women in Families

Being part of a family and the breaking up of a family have profoundly different implications for men and women. Women in less traditional marital relationships have better physical health, higher self-esteem, more autonomy, and better marital adjustment than women in less equal relationships. Indeed, being part of a family has been a serious danger for many women but rarely for men. Women are 10 times more likely than men to be abused by an intimate partner and 6 times more likely to be abused by an intimate partner than by a stranger. One-third of women murdered each year are killed by an intimate partner (on average three women per day in the United States according to The National Organization for Women, 2013).

Yet, as problematic as traditional patterns have been for women, changing the status quo has been extremely difficult. Rivers and Barnett (2013a) speak of the incomplete gender revolution. Even as women are rebelling against the burden of bearing full responsibility for making family relationships, holidays, and celebrations happen, they still feel guilty when they do not do what they have grown up expecting to do. When no one else moves in to fill the gap, they often feel blamed that family solidarity is breaking down and believe that it is their fault. Men's emotional and physical distance is still largely ignored in writings about the changing family. In earlier times, when community cohesion was greater, women often had at least a network of extended family and neighbors to help out. But nowadays extended families are often not easily accessible, and networks that traditionally eased the burdens of child-rearing by providing supplementary caretakers are generally not available. The importance of these invisible networks has rarely been acknowledged by society, which has espoused values that have regularly and intentionally uprooted families for jobs, military duty, or corporate needs. Thus, when women lack such supports, they are often unable to articulate what is wrong, as the need for community and family support has not been socially validated. Without such acknowledgment, women often blame themselves or are blamed by society for not holding things together. Conservative commentators talk about the selfishness of "parents," who are spending less time with their children, by whom they mean mothers, because they fail to refer to the fact that fathers have been absent from families for a long time already. Such backlash responses to the changes in women's roles in our times typically harks back nostalgically to that idiosyncratic period in the U.S. history: the 1950s for White middle-class families, when women, at higher rates than at any other time in history, were isolated in nuclear families as homemakers with their children. As Stephanie Coontz (2006) has pointed out, the "traditional" marriages of that generation created the most drug-oriented, rebellious children of the 1960s as well as the fastest-growing divorce rate in the world, so we should think twice about our reverence for that phase of the "good old days," not to mention the suppression of women entailed in that family arrangement.

Susan Faludi (1991) and many others since (Rivers & Barnett, 2013a) have challenged the conservative backlash response to the changing roles of women, which blamed women for destroying families by their selfishness in considering their own needs first (Sandberg, 2013).

Most household labor is still done by women, other family members still thinking of their role in chores as "helping her." And, as Blumstein and Schwartz (1983, 1991) found decades ago, money still buys power in marriage. It buys the privilege to make decisions—concerning whether to stay or leave, what the family will purchase, where to live, and how the children will be educated. In other words, money talks. In the years since this study, the patterns have not changed as much as they should have.

Women in the Middle: Women and Caretaking

Unfortunately, the well-being of both children and the elderly may be gained at the expense of the quality of life of the middle generation of women who are most burdened and *squeezed* by overwhelming demands of caretaking for both older and younger generations.

Sometimes referred to as "the sandwich generation," they are often caught in a dependency squeeze between their parents and their children and grandchildren. Older women are also often pressed to accept work their lives have not prepared them for, as they did not expect to have to seek employment after midlife. But current economics often require them to earn money well into their 70s. The realities of their financial future are increasingly hitting women at midlife. They are realizing how severely the inequalities of their position in the power structure limit their other options for the rest of their lives.

Traditionally, women have been held responsible for all family caretaking: for their husbands, their children, their parents, their husband's parents, and any other sick or dependent family members. Even now, almost one-fifth of women aged 55 to 59 are providing in-home care to an elderly relative. Over half of women with one surviving parent can expect to become that parent's caretaker. Usually one daughter or a daughter-in-law has the primary responsibility for the care of elderly women. Clearly, caring for the very old (who are mostly women) is primarily a woman's issue. But increasingly, younger women are in the labor force and thus unavailable for caretaking without extreme difficulty. Increasingly, with more and more four-generation families, the caregivers themselves are elderly and struggling with declining functioning. Twelve percent of caregivers are themselves older than 75 (Marks, 1996; Family Caregiver Alliance, 2009).

> **Assess your comprehension of women in the middle: women and caretaking by completing this quiz.**

Women's Exclusion from Power Under the Law and Societal Expectations

The overwhelming majority of lawmakers in our society are males. Their record on legislation in support of family caretaking is a travesty. This is a critical issue for divorced women, mothers of small children, women of color, the elderly, and others who do not have the power to make the laws and thus get doubly burdened: with the responsibility and without the power or resources to take care of their families. The laws regulating social services do not support women. Contrary to the claim that government services sap the strength of family supports, the failure to provide public services to families exacerbate marital and intergenerational conflicts, turning family members against each other. It is the well-being of those caretakers with the fewest financial resources that is most in jeopardy (Mundy, 2012).

We must move farther and faster to tackle the hard political tasks of restructuring home and work so that women who are married and have children can also earn money or have their own voice in the decision making of society. The guilt of less-than-perfect motherhood and less-than-perfect professional career performance are real, because it is not possible to "have it all," when jobs are still structured for men whose wives take care of the details of life, and education, transportation, and homes are still structured for women whose only responsibility is running their families (Barnett & Gareis, 2008). Unless we as

therapists acknowledge these inequities in the social structure in our clinical work with families, we contribute to the mystification of both women and men about the principles organizing families that support a seriously dysfunctional and inequitable system.

Even though more women than men now get college degrees, the pressure on them to lower their sights for educational or career opportunities is at times intense. They are presented with more obstacles at work and negative pressure from media, community, and family. Often, they have also internalized beliefs about their own limitations and women as secondary to men.

As for specific problems due to gender, women tend to feel at a disadvantage in mixed-sex interaction. Men are less influenced by the opinions of others in a group than are women and have more influence on group process than women do (Sandberg, 2013). Women are more likely to withdraw or take unilateral action to get their way in a dispute, a pattern that appears to reflect their greater difficulty in influencing a male partner through direct negotiation (Maccoby, 1999).

Clinically, it may be useful to help clients outline all the unrecognized work that their mothers and grandmothers did to raise their families and keep a household going. This emphasizes their courage, abilities, hard work, and strength as role models for positive identification, as women have typically been hidden from history. A major focus of clinical work is coaching women to transform their family relationships and redefine their own lives.

Women and Marriage

Marriage now plays a less comprehensive role in defining a woman's social and personal life than in the past. But "his" marriage is still very different from, and a great deal less problematic than, "her" marriage. Although men traditionally feared marriage as ensnarement, marriage has always been good for men's health, but only good marriages are healthy for women (DeNoon, 2003; Goleman, 1986; Heyn, 1997). Woman often gave up more to be married than men (her occupation, friends, residence, family, and name). She adjusted to his life. Although men are willing to spend time with women during courtship in ways that enhance the woman's sense of intimacy, after marriage, they tend to spend less time talking to their wives. Women are increasingly frustrated by the degree of relating that their husbands offer. While men and women's priorities in marriage differ (e.g., regarding the place of sex and of financial security), men tend to be less willing to admit their role in problems and tend to rate their marital communication, relationships with parents, and sexual relationships as good, while women are more likely to see them as problematic (Goleman, 1986; Gotta et al., 2011). Women often consider their husband's fidelity more important than men do and men are more likely to expect fidelity from their wives than from themselves.

As Jessie Bernard (1982) pointed out long ago: it is ironic that women, who are seen as dependent and less competent than men, have had to function without emotional support in their marriages—to be, indeed, almost totally emotionally self-sufficient. Women have typically had to bolster their husbands' sense of self-esteem but have been seen as nags when they sought emotional support for themselves. In clinical practice, men's marital complaints have typically centered on their wives' nagging and emotional demands, while wives' complaints are more about their husbands' lack of emotional responsiveness and under-responsibility for homecare and children. In any case, the general lack of political and social equality between marital partners still makes the myth of marital equality a dangerous mystification for most women. The transition to marriage is an important time for helping young women (and men) look beyond these inequitable, often dysfunctional couple roles. Patterns that get set at this point in the life cycle may have great importance later on. Many young women resist challenging the romantic myths about marriage until later stages, when real problems emerge. But it is a lot easier to change patterns in the early years than later, when they have become entrenched and when women's lack of power in the social domain is likely to increase with parenting responsibilities.

> **Assess your comprehension of women and marriage by completing this quiz.**

Mothers and Children

Although our society has been changing rapidly, normative expectations for men and women in families have lagged behind the realities of family life (Gotta et al., 2011). Mothers are particularly vulnerable to blame and guilt because of societal expectations and they bear primary responsibility for the care and well-being of homes, husbands, children, and aging parents. The traditional family not only encouraged, but even required, dysfunctional patterns such as the over-responsibility of mothers for their children and the complementary under-responsibility or disengagement of men. Daughters and daughters-in-law still tend to bear responsibilities for their own and their husbands' extended families. Now that most women are combining work and family responsibilities, they are increasingly overburdened.

Even for today's dual-career couples, the transition to parenthood tends to mark a reversion to a more traditional division of roles, with women doing the lion's share of household maintenance and childcare planning. Even so, having a child per se does not appear to cause women psychological distress, but leaving the labor force does (Barnett & Rivers, 1996). Our culture still leaves women with the primary responsibility for child-rearing and blames them when it goes wrong. It is clear that mothers are by no means receiving social support for the parenting tasks expected of them. The 2010 Census shows dramatic changes in mothers' lives in the United States in the past decades: mothers are the sole or primary source of family income for 40 percent of households with children younger than 18 years, a rise from only 11 percent in 1960. These "breadwinner" mothers seem to divide into two distinct groups: 37 percent are married mothers (mostly White and college educated) who earn more than their husbands; the other 73 percent are single mothers, mostly younger, are more likely to be Black or Hispanic, who lack a college degree and earn only about one-fourth of the other mothers earn!

Differences between males and females appear to be less based on biology than on socialization, which affects people so powerfully and so early (Carothers & Reis, 2013; Fine, 2011; Kimmel, 2013). We do know that females are more likely to survive the birth experience, less likely to have birth defects, and less vulnerable to disease throughout life. The major gender differences in early childhood are that girls develop language skills earlier, and boys tend to be more active (Maccoby, 1999). But because studies of infants show that parents talk and look more at girls and engage in more rough play with boys, we cannot say whether these gender differences are biological or social (Rivers & Barnett, 2013b). Moderate differences continue in performance on mathematical and spatial abilities, while sex differences in verbal abilities fade (Goleman, 2011). Most other aspects of intellectual performance continue to show gender equality (Rivers & Barnett, 2013b), but social behavior still orients boys to competition and girls to relationships. Preschool girls try to influence others by polite suggestions, and have less and less ability to influence boys, who are increasingly unresponsive to polite suggestions. Both boys and girls respond to a vocal prohibition by another boy. Maccoby (1999) concluded girls find it aversive to keep trying to interact with someone who is unresponsive and begin to avoid such partners.

Questions therapists can ask to challenge the gender role status quo include the following: Do both parents equally attend children's school plays and sports events? How are your children changing your perspective on the meaning of your life? Does the father get to spend time alone with each child? (It is almost impossible to develop intimacy if he does not.) Is the time spent fairly equally divided among the daughters and sons? How are domestic responsibilities divided? How is money handled and by whom? Who makes decisions about spending? What are each parent's hopes and expectations for each child in adulthood? How do you as parents try to counter societal preferential treatment of boys and show your daughters they are valuable?

Adolescence

Adolescence is a time when traditional deferential behaviors for girls come particularly to the fore. School sports, for example, unfortunately still too often highlight boys' competitive prowess, with girls cheerleading on the sidelines. Clinically, in working with adolescents and their families, it is important to question the chores, responsibilities, and roles each is asked to play in the family. Are girls spending too much time and money on their clothes and appearance in response to media messages that they

should concentrate on being sex objects? Are sons encouraged to develop social skills, or are parents focused primarily on their achievement and sports performance? Are daughters encouraged to have high academic aspirations? Are both sexes given equal responsibility and encouragement in education, athletics, aspirations for the future, extended family relationships, buying gifts, writing, calling, or caring for relatives, household chores? Do both sexes buy and clean their own clothes? Are daughters encouraged to learn about money, science, and other traditionally "masculine" subjects? Clinicians can help by asking questions about these patterns.

We also need to help families find more positive ways of defining for their daughters the changes of the menstrual and reproductive cycle so that they do not see themselves as "unclean" or "impure." For so long, if sex was even discussed in the family, daughters were not taught to appreciate their bodies but to think sexuality was dangerous and would reflect negatively on them. Sons, by contrast, were taught to view their bodies and sexuality as positive, powerful, and fulfilling aspects of their identity.

Adolescence is a key time in a young woman's life. It is the time when, traditionally, she was specifically inducted into the role of sex object and when, instead, she needs to be encouraged to form her own identity and life. Although acceptance of conventional gender values is at an all-time high during adolescence, it is also during this phase that crucial life-shaping decisions are made. It is extremely important for therapists to support and encourage parents to be proactive with their daughters, to counter discriminatory messages that girls receive within the culture, and to encourage them not to short circuit their dreams or submit to objectification in their relationships or work.

This phase may mark a time for conversion to a feminist position for fathers of daughters, as they want to support their daughters, having the same rights and privileges as men do. This awareness is important to capitalize on therapeutically. Mothers may be feeling a strain as their children pull away, particularly as they realize the limitations of their own options if they have devoted themselves primarily to child-rearing. On the other hand, mothers may feel a special sense of fulfillment in their daughters' going beyond the constrictions that limited their own lives. As Ruth Bader Ginsberg (1993) said when nominated for the supreme court: "I pray that I may be all that . . . [my mother] would have been had she lived in an age when women could aspire and achieve and daughters are cherished as much as sons."

Stepmothers

Remarried families offer a number of particularly trying situations for women. Most difficult of all family positions is undoubtedly the role of step-mother. Given our culture's high expectations of motherhood, the woman who is brought in to replace a "lost" mother enters a situation fraught with high expectations that even a saint could not meet. One of the major clinical interventions is to remove from the stepmother the burden of guilt for not being able to accomplish the impossible—taking over the parent-ing for children who are not her own. Our general guidelines involve putting the biological parent in charge of the children, however difficult that may be when the father works full time and feels that he has no experience with "mothering." The problem for the stepmother is especially poignant, as she is usually the one who is most sensitive to the needs of others, and it will be extremely difficult for her to take a back seat while her husband struggles awk-wardly with an uncomfortable situation. The fact is that she has no alternative. The major problem for women in remarried families is their tendency to take responsibility for family relationships, to believe that what goes wrong is their fault and that if they just try hard enough, things will work out, as the situation carries with it built-in structural ambiguities, loyalty conflicts, guilt, and membership problems.

Launching children and moving on

For women, this may be a time of special opportu-nity to reinvent themselves, but also a time of special stress, as women often feel very much behind the skills to deal with the outside world. Just when their children no longer need them and they are beginning to be defined by the male world as too old to be de-sirable, they must reinvent themselves. The initial steps are usually the hardest. Once they have begun to move in this arena, many women experience a new confidence and pleasure in their independence—able

to really claim their lives for themselves. Because of the social and management skills they have generally developed in the previous life cycle phases, women have remarkable resources for building a social net-work. Their lifelong skills in adapting to new situa-tions also serve them in good stead. But the world of work still does not recognize their efforts in a way that is commensurate with their contribution. Wom-en have generally been excluded from the financial world—and experience frequent discrimination in banks, legal and business institutions. In addition, they have typically not been socialized to expect or demand the recognition they deserve, whether they function as career women in business or are raising grandchildren at the age of 50 (Sandberg, 2013).

Of course, the divergence of interests for men and women, as well as the shift in focus of energies that is required at this phase, often creates marital tensions for parents, at times leading to divorce. Far from the stereotypes, the majority of midlife and older women who divorce find it is a catalyst for self-discovery, change, and growth (Anderson, Stewart, & Dimidjian 1994; Apter, 1995). They tend to develop new confidence and self-esteem, despite the staggering drop in their income after divorce. However, many of them still have little idea how to confront the financial realities of their lives. The financial empowerment of women deserves more clinical attention. Their options for remarriage are much more limited than men's and the likelihood of remarriage after a divorce at this phase is quite slim. In part, this is due to the skew in availability of part-ners, and, in part, older women's having less need to be married and thus, perhaps, being less willing to "settle," particularly for a traditional marriage, which could mean a return to extensive caretaking and sacrifice of their own needs and interests.

Obviously, women who have developed an identity primarily through intimacy and adapta-tion to men will be vulnerable in divorce during the launching phase, when they may feel that their very self is disintegrating. Women's risks at midlife due to their embeddedness in relationships, their orienta-tion toward interdependence, their subordination of achievement to care, and their conflicts over com-petitive success are a problem of our society more than a problem in women's development.

This life cycle phase has often been referred to as the "empty nest" and depicted as a time of depression for women. Menopause, which usually occurs in a woman's late 40s or early 50s, has generally been viewed negatively as a time of physical and psychological distress, especially for those whose whole lives have been devoted to home and family. However, this appears to be much more apparent than real (McQuaide, 1998). Typically, women are grateful and energized by recapturing free time and exploring new options for themselves. They are not nearly as sorry to see the child-rearing era end as has been assumed. For many women, it is a turning point that frees them sexually from worries about pregnancy and marks a new stabilization in their energies for pursuit of work and social activities.

Assess your comprehension of mothers and children by completing this quiz.

Older Families

The final phase of life might be considered "for women only," as women tend to live longer and, unlike men, are rarely (though increasingly more often!) paired with younger partners, making the statistics for this life cycle phase extremely imbalanced.

Women who need care and those who give it are statistically the poorest and have the least legislative power in our society. As mentioned earlier, legislators have given little consideration to services that support family caregivers. The immediate cause of nursing home admission is more likely to be the depletion of family resources than deterioration in the health of the older relative. While the increase in remarried families might mean that a wider kinship network is available for caregiving, the increasing divorce rate probably means that fewer family members will be willing or available to provide care for elderly parents. Caretaking stresses affect at least two generations of women, as both women and their caretakers will be increasingly stressed as time goes along. And since both those who give care and the recipients are generally women, the subject tends to escape public view. As therapists, we can counter this imbalance by redefin-

ing the dilemmas of both the elderly and their caretakers as serious, significant issues.

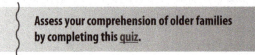
Assess your comprehension of older families by completing this quiz.

Women and Their Friendship Networks

Friendship is an extremely important resource for women throughout the life cycle. From earliest childhood, girls concentrate more energy on working out friendships than boys do. Girls assess activities in terms of their impact on relationships, whereas boys usually subordinate relationships to the games they are playing. Throughout life, women tend to have more close friends than men do, but the relationships that women have are often not validated by the larger society (Antonucci, 1994). Schydlowsky (1983) showed that the importance of women's close female friendships diminishes from adolescence through early adulthood, as they focus on a mate and coupling, and then increases throughout the rest of the life cycle. Marriage may actually isolate couples from friends in ways that can be problematic for their identity development and stability (Gerstel & Sarkisian, 2006). This can be a particular problem for women, whose close friendships are a major support in life, second only to good health in importance for satisfaction throughout the life cycle (Taylor, 2002).

A major UCLA study of women's friendships has turned upside down many decades of stress research primarily focused on men, which had concluded that under stress people's response is either fight or flight. On the contrary, under stress women are more likely to "tend and befriend"—that is, to nurture their children and seek out their friends (Taylor et al., 2000). Study after study has shown that social ties to friends reduces stress and health risk. Berkowitz (2002), for example, found that the more friends women had, the less likely they were to develop physical impairments as they aged and the more likely they were to be enjoying their lives.

We urge family members to respect and nurture friendship systems and challenge in therapy societal values that would allow a husband to block his wife's friendships or invalidate their importance. In traditional heterosexual couples, women were expected to make friends with their husbands' friends' wives to facilitate their husbands' social or business contacts, rather than to form their own friendships based on common needs and interests. In such traditional arrangements, women were expected to replace friends whenever they moved for their husbands' jobs. Such arrangements do not respect friendship as a basic support throughout the life cycle and show distorted prioritizing of career networking over friendship. On the other hand, in many situations, women have the primary responsibility for social arrangements, which may leave men not developing the closeness they themselves need to function at their best in life. So women may need to pull back and allow men the space, just as they need to do with children and aging parents, to develop intimate and caretaking relationships in their lives.

The expanded networks of many Lesbian communities can provide a corrective model, emphasizing the importance of friendship and neighborhood networks, even including ex-partners in a permanent extended community network. Lesbians' careful nurturing of their networks is an excellent adaptation to a society that has been unsupportive and invalidating of their life cycle rituals and transitions, leaving them one of the most invisible of minorities. This adaptive response is one, from which we can all learn.

> Assess your comprehension of women and their friendship networks by completing this quiz.

Women and Loss

Women are often left alone to deal with the sorrow of losses in a family. Men are more likely to withdraw, take refuge in their work, and to be uncomfortable with women's expressions of grief, not knowing how to respond and fearful of losing control of their own feelings. Women may perceive their husbands' emotional unavailability as a double loss—abandonment when they need comfort most. When husbands are expressive and actively involved in illness, death, and the family bereavement process, the quality of the marriage and family relationships can improve markedly.

Most commonly, when there is a loss, it is women who present themselves—or are sent by their husbands—for treatment of depression or other symptoms of distress concerning loss. Interventions need to be aimed at decreasing the gender-role split so that all family members can experience their grief and be supportive to one another in adapting to loss. Facilitating fuller involvement for men in the social and emotional tasks of the loss process will enrich their experience of family life as it lessens the disproportionate burden for women. A greater flexibility of allowable roles for both men and women will permit the full range of human experiences in bereavement as in other areas of family life.

The full participation of male and female family members in mourning rituals should be encouraged. One woman, at the death of her 100-year-old grandmother, expressed her desire to be a pallbearer at the funeral. A cousin replied that only males did that; another added that they had already picked six pallbearers (who all happened to be male grandchildren). She persisted, suggesting that they simply have more than six. In the end, all twelve grandchildren, including five women, shared that important experience.

—— Conclusion: Affirming Women Through the Life Cycle ——

Therapy requires re-contextualizing women's history, countering societal pressures for voicelessness and invisibility, and affirming women's own life stories. Traditional therapies have probably done more harm than good, failing as they did to acknowledge women's oppression and invalidation in the larger context and psychologizing social problems that made women think they were responsible for creating problems in which they were, in fact, trapped by the social structure. Thus, it is most important, in working with women of every age, to be a force for liberation, validating the ways in which women are different, and encouraging them to follow their dreams. A wise poet, Pat Parker (1985), illustrates the power of this multigenerational perspective—one that puts us within the context of "herstory," of not denying the problems that remain, but validating the power of the women who have come before, the connectedness they have to the present generation, and the mentoring of those who will come after. She draws strength and pride from her ancestors. And she wills her rage to future generations to take the necessary risks and become doers who will wage the necessary battles to change their future.

We aim toward a theory of family and individual development where both instrumental and relational aspects of each individual will be fostered. The "feminine" perspective has been so devalued that it needs to be highlighted. It is hoped that both men and women will be able to develop their potential without regard for the constraints of gender stereotyping that have so constricted human experience until now. Traditional marriage and family patterns are no longer working for women, if they ever did, and the statistics reveal women's refusal to accept the status quo. We need to work out a new equilibrium that is not based on the patriarchal family hierarchy. We need to understand and appreciate women's potential and dilemmas and consider all women together: Gay and straight, young and old, Black and White, and all the hues in between.

Recall what you learned in this chapter by completing the Chapter Review.

— References

Anderson, C. M., Stewart, S., & Dimidjian. S. (1994). *Flying solo*. New York: W. W. Norton.

Antonucci, T. C. (1994). A life span view of women's social relationships. In B. F. Turner & L. E. Troll (Eds.), *Women growing older* (pp. 239–269). Thousand Oaks, CA: Sage.

Apter, T. (1995) *Secret paths: Women in the new midlife*. New York: W. W. Norton.

Barnett, R. C., & Gareis, K. C. (2008). Community: the critical missing link in work-family research. In A. Marcus-Neuhall, D. F. Halpern, & S. J. Tan (Eds.), *The changing realities of work and family* (pp. 71–84). New York: Wiley-Blackwell.

Barnett, R. C., & Rivers, C. (1996). *She works/he works: How two-income families are happier, healthier, and better-off*. San Francisco, CA: Harper.

Bateson, C. (2011). *Composing a further life: The age of active wisdom*. New York: Vintage Press.

Bennetts, L. (2011). Women: The invisible poor. *The Daily Beast, September 14, 2011.*

Berkowitz, G. (2002). *UCLA study on friendship among women: An alternative to fight or flight*. Retrieved from (April 14, 2010) www.anapsid.org/cnd/gender/tendfend.html

Bernard, J. (1982). *The future of marriage*. New Haven, CT: Yale University Press.

Blumstein, P., & Schwartz, P. (1983). *American couples: Money, work and sex*. New York: William Morrow & Company.

Blumstein, P., & Schwartz, P. (1991). Money and ideology: Their impact on power and the division of household labor. In P. Blumberg & R. Lesser (Eds.), *Gender, family and economy: The triple overlap* (pp. 261–288). New York: Sage.

Britz, J. D. (2006, March 23). To all the girls I've rejected [Letter to the Editor]. *New York Times*, p. 23.

Carothers, B., & Reis, H. (2013). The tangle of the sexes. *New York Times*, April 21, 2013. P. SR9.

Cathome, A. (2008). *The straight facts on women in poverty*. Center for American Progress. Retrieved (April 20, 2013) from http://www.americanprogress.org/wp-content/uploads/issues/2008/10/pdf/women_poverty.pdf.

Clinton, W. (1995). 25 million in grants announced for the violence against women act (March). *Criminal Justice Newsletter*, 26(6), 6–7.

Coontz, S. (2013a). Why gender equality stalled. *New York Times*. February 16, 2013. Retrieved February 18, 2013.

Coontz, S. (2013b). The triumph of the working mother. *New York Times*, June 2, 2013, p. SR 11.

Coontz, S. (2006). *Marriage: A history*. New York: Viking.

Costello, C. B., Wight, V. R., & Stone, A. J. (2003). *The American woman: 2003–2004*. New York: Macmillan.

Dell'Antonia, K. J. 2012. Full-time work means better health for mothers. New York Times, August 23, 2012. Retrieved (May 26, 2013) from http://parenting.blogs.nytimes.com/2012/08/23/full-time-work-means-better-health-for-mothers/

DeNoon, D. (2003). Only happy marriage healthy for women. Retrieved (February 22, 2013) from http://www.webmd.com/balance/news/20030915/only-happy-marriage-is-healthy-for-women.

Faludi, S. (1991). *Backlash: The undeclared war against American women.* New York: Crown Publishers.

Family Caregiver Alliance (2009). Caregiving. Retrieved (May 28, 2013) from http://www.caregiver.org/caregiver/jsp/content_node.jsp?nodeid=2313

Fine, Cordelia (2011). *Delusions of gender: How our minds, society and neurosexism create difference.* New York: W. W. Norton.

Fisher, A. (2013). Boys vs. girls: What's behind the college grad gender gap? CNN Money. Retrieved (May 9, 2013) from http://management.fortune.cnn.com/2013/03/27/college-graduation-gender-salaries/

Gannon, L. R. (1999). *Women and aging.* Oxford, UK: Routledge.

Gerstel, N., & Sarkisian, N. (2006). Marriage, the good, the bad and the greedy. *Contexts, 5*(4), 16–21.

Ginsberg, R. B. (1993). Speech on being appointed to the Supreme Court. Retrieved (April 19, 2013) from http://www.nytimes.com/1993/06/15/us/supreme-court-transcript-president-s-announcement-judge-ginsburg-s-remarks.html?pagewanted=all&src=pm

Glynn, S. J., & Powers, A. (2012). The top 10 facts about the wage gap: Women are still earning less than men across the board. Center for American Progress, April 16. Retrieved (April 20, 2013) from http://www.americanprogress.org/issues/labor/news/2012/04/16/11391/the-top-10-facts-about-the-wage-gap/

Goleman, D. (1986, April 1). Two views of marriage explored: His and hers. *New York Times*, p. 19.

Goleman, D. (2011). The brain and emotional intelligence: New insights. Florence, MA: More Than Sound Publishers.

Gotta, G., Green, R.J., Rothblum, E., Solomon, S., Balsam, K., & Schwartz, P. (2011). Heterosexual, lesbian, and gay male relationships: A comparison of couples in 1975 and 2000. *Family Process, 50*(3), 353–376.

Gottfried, A. E., & Gottfried, A. W. (2008). The upside of maternal and dual-earner employment: A focus on positive family adaptations, home environments and child development in the Fullerton Longitudinal Study. In A. Marcus-Neuhall, D. F. Halpern, & S. J. Tan (Eds.), *The changing realities of work and family* (pp. 25–42). New York: Wiley-Blackwell.

Hall, R. L., & Greene, B. (1994). Cultural competence in feminist family therapy: An ethical mandate. *Journal of Feminist Family Therapy, 6*(3), 5–28.

Heilbrun, C. G. (1988). *Writing a woman's life.* New York: Norton.

Heilbrun, C. G. (1997). *The last gift of time: Life beyond sixty.* New York: Dial Press.

Heyn, D. (1997). *Marriage shock: The transformation of women into wives.* New York: Villard.

Hochschild, A. (2012). *The second shift: Working parents and the revolution at home.* New York: Viking.

Hoffman, L. W. (1989). Effects of maternal employment in the two-parent family. *American Psychologist, 44*, 283–292.

Kimmel, M. (2013). *The gendered society*, 5th edn. New York: Oxford University Press.

Kivel, P. (2002, February 10). Affirmative action for White men? *Motion Magazine*. Retrieved (February 27, 2010) from www.inmotionmagazine.com/pkivel4.html

Lawrence-Lightfoot, S. (2009). The third chapter: Passion, risk and adventure in the 25 years past fifty. New York: Farrar, Straus, & Giroux.

Lorde, A. (1984). *Sister outsider.* Freedom, CA: The Crossing Press.

Losoff, M. M. (1974). Fathers and autonomy in women. In R. B. Kundsin (Ed.), *Women and success: The anatomy of achievement* (pp. 103–109). New York: William Morrow.

Lott, B. (1994). *Women's lives* (2nd ed.). Pacific Grove, CA: Brooks/Cole.

Lyle, B. (2012). After divorce women rebound faster but stay in poverty longer. *Huffington Post.* October 22, 2012. Retrieved (May 6, 2013) from http://www.huffingtonpost.com/brendan-lyle/after-divorce-women-rebou_1_b_1970733.html

Marks, N. F. (1996). Caregiving across the lifespan. *Family Relations, 45*(1) 27–36.

Maccoby, E. E. (1999). *The two sexes: Growing up apart: Coming together (The family and public policy).* Boston, MA: Belknap Press.

Marcus-Newhall, A., Halpern, D. F., & Tan, S. J. (Eds.). (2008). *The changing realities of work and family.* New York: Wiley-Blackwell.

McIntosh, P. (1985). *On feeling like a fraud.* (Work in Progress Working Paper Series, 18). Wellesley, MA: The Stone Center.

McIntosh, P. (1989). *On feeling like a fraud,* (Part 2). (Work in Progress Working Paper Series, 37). Wellesley, MA: The Stone Center.

McQuaide, S. (1998). Women at midlife. *Social Work, 43*(1), 21–31.

Meers, S., & Strober, J. (2009). *How Working Couples can have it all by sharing it all: Getting to 50/50.* New York: Random House.

Mundy, L. (2012). The richer sex: How the new majority of female breadwinners is transforming sex, love, and family. New York: Simon & Schuster.

National Organization for Women (2013). Violence against women in the United states: Statistics. Retrieved (May 20, 2013) from http://www.now.org/issues/violence/stats.html.

Padan, D. (1965). *Intergenerational mobility of women: A two-step process of status mobility in a context of a value conflict.* Tel Aviv, Israel: Publication of Tel Aviv University.

Parker, P. (1985). *Jonestown & other madness.* Ithaca, NY: Firebrand Books.

Pollitt, K. (2006, March 23). Affirmative action for men. *The Nation,* Retrieved (June 28, 2010) from www.insidehighered.com/news/2006/03/27/admit.

Rivers, C., & Barnett, R. C. (2013a). The new soft war on women: How the myth of female ascendance is hurting women, men and our economy. New York: Tarcher.

Rivers, C., & Barnett, R. C. (2013b). The truth about girls and boys. New York: Columbia University Press.

Sandberg, S. (2013). *Lean in: Women, work, and the will to lead.* New York: Knopf.

Schydlowsky, B. M. (1983). *Friendships among women in midlife.* Unpublished doctoral dissertation, University of Michigan.

Slater, S. (1995). *The lesbian family life cycle.* New York: Free Press.

Taylor, S. E. (2002). *The tending instinct.* New York: Henry Holt.

Taylor, S. E., Klein, L. C., Lewis, B. P., Gruenewald, T. L., Gurung, R. A. R., & Updegraff, J. A. (2000). Female responses to stress: Tend and befriend, not fight or flight. *Psychological Review,* 107(3), 41–429.

Wang, W., Parker, K., & Taylor, P. (2013). Breadwinner moms. Pew Research Center. May 29, 2013. Retrieved (May 29, 2013) from http://www.pewsocialtrends.org/2013/05/29/breadwinner-moms/

Wolfer, L. T., & Moen, P. (1996). Staying in school: Maternal employment and the timing of Black and White daughters' school exit. *Journal of Family Issues,* 17(4), 540–560.

Chapter 3

Men and the Family Life Cycle

Matthew R. Mock & Timothy R. Baima

Learning Objectives

- Define patriarchy and male privilege.
- Describe ways in which patriarchy interferes with love, intimacy, and relational growth.
- List ways that men can resist patriarchal definitions of masculinity.
- Explain how gender expectations and socialization both support and interfere with boys' development.
- Identify and describe ways to nurture and support the healthy development of boys.
- Discuss the benefits and stresses of work that are unique to men.
- Describe how traditional views of masculinity impact how men experience marriage.
- List challenges men face during the transition to fatherhood.
- Describe the importance of men's continued growth in the last phase of life.

Introduction

The life cycle is rapidly changing for men. Role expectations for men and women are gradually becoming more egalitarian, with women often sharing in financial responsibilities and men sharing responsibilities for childcare and household work. As more women work and people live longer, men are more responsible to provide care for aging parents as well as children. As people marry later and divorce becomes more common, men spend more of their lives single. Single men are not able to rely on women to help maintain their relationships with family and friends. Communication skills are becoming increasingly important in the workplace, and in an age of globalization and social networking, men need to be lifelong learners in order to adapt and succeed. Many men welcome transforming gender roles. These men embrace opportunities to enjoy egalitarian relationships with partners, more involvement with children, and the ability to express emotions. Flexibility is at the heart of differentiation and is critical for boys and men to be able to adapt and thrive in the context of social change. However, flexibility is at odds with the deeply engrained patriarchal social values that have defined masculinity for centuries. In fact, it appears that even with the growing advancements in equality, inequality remains the status quo. While women have made strides in upper echelons, men continue to be overly represented in leadership roles in government and businesses worldwide (Rivers & Barnett, 2013). Even though men have significantly increased their involvement with their children, very few men are equally involved with the emotional development and nurturance of their children (Garfield, 2015). The underlying patriarchal value system of this society continues to unjustly privilege males and oppress females. What is less obvious is that patriarchy also impairs the mental, emotional, and relational health of boys and men.

The word "patriarchy" is often mischaracterized as anti-male sentiment, or mistakenly believed to refer to a social organization in which every man has power over every woman. Patriarchy is actually a value system that structures our society, constructs our view of gender, defines "natural" roles for men and women, and creates a sense of what is inherently feminine and masculine. In addition, patriarchy has been at the heart of shaping processes through which gender expectations are taught, including creating a variety of punitive consequences for those who do not conform. While not everyone conforms to patriarchal values, no one escapes patriarchy affecting their life in some way (hooks, 2004). Patriarchy plays such a tremendous role in shaping our sense of masculinity, it must be examined in order for therapists to understand the ways in which boys and men navigate relationships across the life cycle. When therapists understand some of the ways patriarchy and male privilege interfere with men's individual and relational development, they are in much better positions to support men in expanding possibilities for living richer, more fulfilling lives.

bell hooks (2004) defines patriarchy as "a political-social system that insists that males are inherently dominating, superior to everything and everyone deemed weak, especially females, and endowed with the right to dominate and rule over the weak and to maintain that dominance through various forms of psychological terrorism and violence" (p. 18). A social value that assumes males are inherently superior and entitled to dominate unjustly affords them unearned privilege and power. Some of the ways in which males are privileged include the following: Boys are encouraged to be more active and outgoing; men can rest assured co-workers and will not think they got their job solely because of their gender even if it is true; men are far less likely to face sexual harassment and if they do they are not likely to be blamed for inviting it by dressing seductively; and if a man chooses not to have children, his masculinity will not be called into question, while if he chooses to have children and a career, no one will think him selfish for choosing to work instead of stay at home to raise his children (Deutsch, 2010). Even less desirable male attributes are infused with privilege in a patriarchal society. For example, the notion that men have uncontrollable sexual urges may lead others to give them a pass, or even see them as victims, when they are accused of child molestation, sexual harassment, and rape. Likewise, the notion that men are inherently violent leads to downplaying the severity of intimate partner violence and child abuse, and boys and men are honored and respected for their immature use of violence at every level from schoolyard brawls to international conflicts. Men

who monopolize conversations in the classroom or the boardroom are likely to be viewed as passionate and assertive. Male privilege does not mean that men are always viewed as right and superior. It means that our dominant social values tend to lead people to attribute positive qualities to men, justify their actions even when they are hurtful toward others, afford them special advantages over women, and protect them from having their privilege challenged.

It is important to note that not all men are equally privileged. Other dimensions of culture such as race, ethnicity, social class, sexual orientation, religion, age, physical and mental abilities, and immigration status lead some men and women to be unjustly afforded privilege and power over other men. Therefore, while all men share social privilege on the basis of gender, many are marginalized and oppressed as well (Collins, 1998; Hardy & Laszloffy, 2002; Mock, 2008; Kimmel, 2008). The problem with male privilege is not men, but a value system that insists that some people are inherently superior and entitled to dominate others (Barnett & Rivers, 2004; hooks, 1984). However, as long as this value system is in place, inequality and injustice will continue to strain men's relationships.

Power and privilege come at a cost. Male privilege is based on the idea that males are inherently superior to females and patriarchal masculinity is based largely on domination and control of all that is feminine and weak. In order to become masculine, boys are taught to dampen, stifle, and disconnect from all parts of their humanity that could be considered feminine. Starting in infancy, they are taught not to cry, whine, show fear, need too many hugs, love too openly, move or dance in ways that look girlish, play games that model nurturing, be too emotionally supportive, or be too physically affectionate. Learning to be masculine seems far more about learning which parts of oneself to do away with than what parts of oneself to nurture. In fact, the first act of violence boys commit is likely to be against themselves, as they kill off any precious part of their humanity that would make them appear less masculine. This makes fragmentation and disconnection the very essence of patriarchal masculinity (hooks, 2004; Kimmel, 2013).

Patriarchy is deeply ingrained in our consciousness because its values are taught to us from the time we are born and continuously reinforced throughout our lives. Women teach children patriarchal values just as effectively as men, and the only instrument used to deliver its messages more than violence is shame (hooks, 2004). Parents, teachers, siblings, friends, and other adult mentors police boy's natural human expressions by mocking their vulnerabilities, expressions of affection, and need for love. Shame cannot nurture self-worth or love. It simply produces fear rooted in insecurity. This fear and insecurity is inseparably connected to men's enactment of domination and control. Men are often most susceptible to misusing and abusing power, not when they feel powerful, but when they feel insecure, vulnerable, or afraid. It is during these times that boys and men are most likely to feel that some form of disrespect, disobedience, or disagreement defies the deference they consider their entitlement from the patriarchal value system. Because their sense of masculinity has been created through shame and disconnection, there is little solid self to stand on when one feels challenged. Instead, shame nurtures reactivity. Consequently, boys and men often attempt to coerce others with the same kind of intimidation that was used to teach them to be more masculine, and that they used to disown parts of themselves. Men's use of control, intimidation, and violence cause many women and children to fear them, and as hooks (2004) points out, we cannot truly love someone we fear, which is why so many spiritual traditions teach that there is no fear in love. Many men are confused as to why their lives are void of love and authentic intimacy. They are mystified as to why relationships with partners, children, and friends feel so empty when they have followed all of patriarchy's rules (hooks, 2004; Kimmel, 2013). These men have often bought into patriarchy's biggest lie, which is that love is merely emotion and can therefore coexist with intimidation, domination, and abuse. However, when love is viewed as action, this simply cannot be the case (hooks, 2000; 2004). Men not only limit the amount of love in their lives by instilling fear in others but also limit their capacity for self-love by fearing what is in their own hearts and souls. The abuse they direct toward themselves to deny and repress any part of their humanity that does not fit with their ideas of patriarchal

masculinity stifles authentic self-love. Fear of one's emotions and vulnerabilities can easily grow into self-hatred over time. When men are not able to love themselves, intimacy with others cannot be based on true connection. Instead men may oscillate between acts that maintain dominance, and seeking partners to provide them with all of the love and acceptance they have been unable to give themselves. Since this is an impossible task, men who depend on others this way are bound to become disappointed and dissatisfied in their relationships.

Consequently, men are hurting and longing for deeper connections, while the whole of society seems to ask them not to talk about it. Even women who say they want men to be more emotionally expressive often grow uncomfortable when men start to open up. They may even be the first to indicate that they would prefer men to share less. This is not surprising, since women are socialized by patriarchy as well. When women are taught that they are inherently vulnerable and need to depend on men as a source of stability and strength, and when there are organized and institutionalized efforts to undermine women's strength and autonomy, women may feel that men's expressions of vulnerability threaten their own stability (hooks, 2000; 2004).

These are just a few examples of ways in which patriarchy interferes with love, intimacy, and relational growth. Even though patriarchy interferes with the love and connection so many men long for, living lives that resist patriarchy's rules for masculinity and relationships is very challenging. Ironically one of the hallmarks of privilege is being unaware that one has it. Men rarely feel privileged or powerful, so many men are unaware of ways in which unearned privilege impacts their relationships. Even men who are aware of male privilege, in general, are likely to find it difficult to identify ways they abuse or misuse power and privilege in their own relationships. It is hard to notice their own assertion of privilege, just as it may be hard for the spouse to notice how she is being steamrolled.

Over time, power and privilege breed a sense of entitlement in men. Patriarchy promises men an opportunity to compete for unlimited wealth, status, influence, and sexual fulfillment. Furthermore, it teaches them that a differential form of respect is their birthright and any real man will make sure he receives it. Men are often much more in touch with what patriarchy promises them than they are with the ways in which patriarchy cannot possibly deliver on its promises. Men who have not acquired all patriarchy promises are more likely to blame others for their predicament than to question patriarchy, and may be criticized for not fulfilling their masculine role. This is especially true for White straight men, who often assume their perceived entitlement to compete with other men means competing with other straight White men. As opportunities for women, people of color, immigrants, and Gay men increase, many of these men blame reduced income and career opportunities on others taking something away from them, not noticing or acknowledging the gross disparities in wealth distribution, an overall reduction in educational outcomes across the country, and an ever-increasing number of jobs being outsourced. As these men cry out that a woman or an immigrant stole *their* job, they reveal the sense of entitlement patriarchy instilled in them—that the job they wanted was somehow *theirs* to begin with. Straight White men who are enraged over efforts to increase equality and opportunities to those who have been historically marginalized in this society fail to recognize that they are the benefactors of the greatest affirmative action plan of all time, otherwise known as world history (Kimmel, 2013). But their failure to recognize this (and that of others who seek the same kind of power) is likely rooted in the fact that patriarchy requires men to disown so much of their humanity that they become largely dependent on privilege, success, and entitlement for self-definition. In a patriarchal society, men are defined by what they are able to provide, produce, and achieve (Kimmel, 2012) rather than being valued for their uniqueness and simply being (hooks, 2004). When a sense of self is based on entitlement and privilege, any loss of special privilege or advantage can be experienced as tantamount to a loss of self (Kimmel, 2013). In our society, we do not have another widely embraced value system that men can draw upon to guide their identity and relational development. Consequently, when others do not comply with the patriarchal requirement to defer to men, men may feel that their relationships are at odds with the foundation of their identity. Some men make an honest effort to reconcile their relationships with patriarchal-informed notions of masculinity and identity by becoming benevolent patriarchs. These men may become more gentle, emotionally expressive, and vulnerable in their relationships without compromising their sense of entitlement. It may be many years before these men realize that silencing others and exerting control through passivity, withdrawal, and benevolent blame have created barriers to connection and intimacy in their most valuable relationships (Garfield, 2015; hooks, 2004).

Other men actively resist compliance with patriarchy's definitions of masculinity and rules for relationships. Some are doing this intentionally, with unjust disparities of power and privilege in the forefront of their minds. Some have simply been disillusioned with patriarchy's rigidity and limitations and are seeking identities based on the fullness of their humanity and relationships characterized by mutuality, respect, humility, self-reflection, accountability, responsibility, vulnerability, intimacy, and love. These efforts are complicated by pressure to comply with societal expectations. However, men who resist patriarchy's requirements for identity and relationships are likely to be those in the best position to develop the flexibility needed to navigate life cycle stages that are rapidly becoming more complex. These men are likely to enjoy better mental, emotional, and relational health. The following are three themes that capture much of the essence of resisting patriarchal definitions of masculinity across the life cycle.

1. Establish and maintain a sense of masculinity that claims all parts of humanity, including vulnerability, emotions, and affection, allowing these and other parts of self to flourish while at the same time resisting patriarchal influences that erode core aspects of humanity.
2. Develop a sense of identity based on celebrating uniqueness and resisting privileged entitlement as well as compulsive status, power, or other forms of external validation to sustain a sense of self worth.
3. Value interdependence and honor connectedness with others across time, and cultivate

ongoing relationships based on mutuality, humility, responsibility, and authentic intimacy.

Males are in the best position to embrace these values when those with whom they are in relationships also resist patriarchy's rigid requirements and cherish the qualities listed above in men. The remainder of this chapter discusses ways in which these themes manifest themselves throughout the life cycle and illustrates how therapists can help men and boys navigate these issues to grow in relational maturity.

> Assess your comprehension of the introduction by completing this quiz.

Childhood and Adolescence

Gender expectations about boys' independence, adventurous spirits, and inherent leadership abilities provide many boys with a childhood full of wonderment, comradery, and personal fulfillment. Families, peers, schools, and religious and community organizations frequently nurture autonomy, competence, problem-solving skills, and teamwork in boys. While it is important to acknowledge the fun and freedom many boys enjoy, and the ways in which some of their developmental tasks may be well supported, it is essential for therapists to be familiar with the ways gender socialization interferes with development. Masculinity is frequently considered so important that parents and caretakers make nurturing masculinity a priority over nurturing other essential needs such as emotional intelligence, communication, and attachment. Erroneous ideas about gender often interfere with seeing what boys need most. All boys need permission to be fully human. All boys need the ability to have and express their emotions. All boys need and long for physical affection. They need and long for parents, compassionate adults, and friends who will listen as they share their inner worlds. Unfortunately, these are all too frequently the very things boys are required to disown in order to become more masculine.

Parents who attempt to raise their sons in ways that resist dominant gender expectations may find that outside of the family their sons' non-compliance with gender norms leads to ridicule and social isolation. These parents must continuously find ways to support their sons' social adjustment, while nurturing the values they want them to embrace. For example, parents who want to resist society's demands that boys embrace aggression may want to keep their sons from engaging in violent games. However, when all of their son's friends begin to play paintball or are offered free boxing lessons by a community outreach program, parents may determine that it would be more damaging to forbid their son to participate, than to allow him to join in with his friends. Ongoing dialogue that helps boys make meaning of their experiences without disowning valuable parts of themselves or embracing damaging social values may be more effective in nurturing values than attempting to shield boys from society (Kane, 2012). However, this type of vigilance and conversation takes time and energy. Society's increased understanding of the harmful effects of patriarchy and the complexity of raising boys comes at the same time that parents are commonly under a tremendous amount of stress. Increased wealth inequality means that many parents are working longer hours, or going back to school while working full time. In 2005, the child poverty rate in the United States remained at 19 percent overall with African American, and Latino children more than three times likely to be in poverty (Davis, Kilburn, & Schultz, 2009). Parents commonly feel weary from negotiating basic child care with various caregivers while also handling the emotional stress of managing rapidly changing couple relationships, or dealing with ex-partners or newly forming remarried families.

Childhood and adolescence can also be stressful and confusing times. Social media, millions of websites, and Internet pornography are always available and continuously advertise to boys who can often be confused and misdirected by the messages they receive online. In school, boys are commonly perceived as slower to read and write, and they tend to find it more challenging to sit quietly and listen to teachers. Their need for large-muscle activities is constrained in schools with reduced recess time. Boys are more likely than girls to have behavior problems and receive the majority of school suspensions. Boys are more likely to be placed in special education and to be diagnosed with attention-deficit hyperactivity disorder (ADHD) (Aulette, Wittner, & Blakely, 2009), conduct disorder, and spectrum disorders (Rao & Seaton, 2009). However, boys are seriously underdiagnosed for depression. Gay, Bisexual, and Transgendered boys, especially those of color, have a particularly high risk of depression, suicide, and addiction (Cannon & Marszalek, 2012). Adolescent boys are more likely to abuse alcohol and drugs than girls. African American and Latino boys are more likely to be involved with crime and violence on school property but less likely to be diagnosed with ADHD or to receive appropriate services. Boys of color are disproportionately charged with crimes and institutionalized at alarming rates (Davis et al., 2009). Once boys are in the judicial system, the downward spiral is often hard to break (Kerby, 2012).

In this time of increased complexity, stress, and confusion, even mythological perfect parents could not completely protect their sons from the influences of patriarchal socialization. We are all vulnerable to falling back on our earliest learnings when stressed, including inaccurate education about the needs and nature of boys. Therapists can support boys by reminding parents and other caretakers what their true needs are. Society's dominant process of socializing boys highlights many of their neglected needs.

In a patriarchal society, masculinity is valued at the expense of femininity. Teaching boys to be masculine frequently involves shaming them into rejecting all things associated with being feminine, including vulnerability, affection, and the expression of any emotions other than happiness and anger (Levant, 2005). By school age, the innumerable messages boys have received from multiple sources have taught them to suppress fear, sadness, loneliness, hurt, disappointment, and any form of neediness (Rao & Seaton, 2009). Boys are taught that they must be independent, self-reliant, stoic, tough, aggressive, cool, rambunctious, and obsessed with sports, cars, and sex. Boys learn very early in life that "real boys" seek high social status, are always ready for sex, and are never feminine or Gay (Levant, 2005). Boys are told to be strong and in control by being assertive or aggressive, not backing down or making mistakes. They are to take charge and be responsible.

With otherwise limited definitions and descriptions of masculinity, adolescent boys have a tendency to hold themselves in opposition to others: nonfemale, nonhomosexual, and anti-authority. For adolescent males, subtle and overt messages of what it means to be a man in American society are often experienced as expectations that constrain them from what they may really feel or want to be. When adolescent boys do not conform to what it means to be stereotypically a "man in the making," they may be taunted with names like wimp, fag, nerd, punk, bitch, sissy or mama's boy (Kivel, 2010). Consequently, boys learn that there are genuine parts of themselves that are at odds with being masculine, and that these parts are bad. They may attempt to disown these parts, or may even feel forced to do so. All too often, boys are highly successful at numbing themselves to their emotions and needs. However, no one is able to do this completely. Therefore, when boys internalize the message that some parts of themselves are unacceptable and find that they are unable to eradicate these parts of themselves entirely, they can become full of shame and self-loathing. This type of gender socialization also teaches boys that feminine and vulnerable characteristics are inherently inferior, which breeds a sense of entitlement and superiority over girls, women, Gay boys and men, and all males who do not reject qualities considered to be feminine or weak. This socialization impairs boys' abilities to form enduring relationships. The qualities they are taught to disown are qualities that help nurture intimate connection and navigate conflict. Furthermore, true intimacy cannot be achieved in any relationship when one person considers himself superior and more entitled than the other.

Fortunately the rejection of all that is considered feminine, vulnerable, and weak is neither immediate nor absolute. For example, while boys tend to practice less self-disclosure and emotional expression than girls, until mid-adolescence most boys consider emotional intimacy to be the most precious aspect of their friendships. It is not until around the age of 15 that boys begin to emotionally withdraw in their friendships with other boys out of fear that emotional intimacy will be associated with childishness, femininity, or homosexuality. However, boys continue to long for the emotional intimacy they had in their friendships when they were younger, long into adulthood (Garfield, 2015). Adolescent boys often turn to girlfriends to meet all of their emotional needs, and while this is an unrealistic expectation, it shows that boys remain connected to parts of their inner world. Interestingly, boys are more likely to maintain intimate friendships with other boys when their parents resist rigid gender socialization and nurture empathy and emotional intelligence in their sons (Way, 2011). Boys who enjoy warm nurturing relationships with their parents reap the benefits throughout their lives. Longitudinal studies indicate that warm nurturing childhoods predict the development of empathy, cultivating fulfilling relationships throughout adulthood, enjoying good physical and mental health, being satisfied with work, and even earning a higher income than men who grew up without a warm nurturing childhood (Vaillant, 2012).

Unfortunately, parents and other caring adults too frequently allow patriarchal assumptions, such as "boys are unemotional," "it's better for boys to figure things out on their own," and "too much affection will turn my son into a mama's boy," convince them that giving boys less care, less intimate conversation, and less affection is actually desired and needed. It is easy to assume that boys would simply ask for more care if they wanted it. Unfortunately, the more boys are conditioned to repress their emotions and needs for affection, the less likely they are to communicate their needs to others. In fact, out of an effort to both appear and to be strong, boys frequently deny their needs. Repression becomes habitual leading many boys to so thoroughly disconnect from their needs that they are seldom, if ever, aware of them. Just as warmth and nurturance predict many positive outcomes for boys, the use of repression as a coping mechanism is associated with a variety of negative health outcomes and impaired development throughout the life cycle (Vaillant, 2012). Even when boys are aware of their needs, dominant expectations of masculinity often inhibit them from seeking help (Vogel, Heimerdinger-Edwards, Hammer, & Hubbard, 2011). Adults who want to nurture emotional intelligence in boys need to tenaciously assume that boys need care, empathy, and affection because boys will seldom seek out this kind of intimate connection and may even overtly deny that it is important to them.

Finding ways to nurture boys without making them feel overly coddled or infantilized is a challenging task with no easy answers. However, it is a task all parents and caring adults must wrestle with if they want to raise boys to love, respect, and honor all parts of themselves and others. This task can be especially difficult for fathers who were denied this kind of nurturance when they were boys. Fathers who were raised in a time in which some deference to patriarchal authority was the norm might have difficulty seeing through adolescent boys' anger and defiance to their longing for guidance and love (Garfield, 2015; hooks, 2004). This task can be complicated for single mothers as well. Fearing that without a male role model in their sons' upbringing they will raise their sons to be overly feminine, many of these mothers become strict enforcers of patriarchal masculinity (hooks, 2004). Therapists can support healthy development of boys by helping parents and other adult caretakers examine the effects of rigid compliance with patriarchal rules in their own lives. They can help adults heal and reclaim disowned parts of their own humanity in order to increase their ability to cherish and nurture the fullness of humanity in the boys they care for. They can help adults see the cries of loneliness, pain, frustration, and despair that lie embedded in acts of destruction, rage, withdrawal, and violence. They can encourage participation in groups that support spiritual and emotional growth, teach boys to form meaningful connections across differences, and negotiate compromises. Therapists can relieve parents' guilt by reminding them that there are a multitude of forces socializing their sons. They can also help connect parents with organizations and support systems that will join with them in nurturing all parts of their sons. The following case demonstrates some of the ways themes of patriarchy manifested in an adolescent client and were addressed in therapy.

CASE ILLUSTRATION

DeShaun

DeShaun was a 17-year-old African American sophomore at an inner-city high school, referred to therapy by a school counselor. He was not passing his classes. His teachers described him as disruptive and at risk of expulsion for a recent fight with another student. Increased conflict with his foster parents jeopardized the stability of his placement. He smoked marijuana daily and his foster parents and teachers could not identify any indication that he cared about his life. His foster parents and some of his teachers knew that his brother had been killed a few years ago in gang violence and that his mother had died of cancer a year ago. While sympathetic to his past, his foster parents were burnt out and felt unappreciated, and his teachers tended to describe him as "trouble—just like his brother had been."

The therapist focused on building a connection with DeShaun during the first several sessions. DeShaun was willing to talk about casual things, especially his 8-month-old Rottweiler, Bear, that his foster parents gave him in an attempt to help him with his losses. DeShaun also told his therapist that he smoked marijuana every day, not to get high, but to get by. During the course of the first few sessions, DeShaun learned that his girlfriend was pregnant and said without any apparent emotion that he did not care whether or not she kept the baby. When the therapist shared that his teachers had said he did not seem to care about anything, he simply shrugged his shoulders and said, "Guess not." The therapist did not believe DeShaun did not care, but suspected he was trying to protect himself from a tremendous amount of pain the way patriarchal society had taught him—to stuff his emotions away. When the therapist attempted to reflect the emotions he suspected lay beneath DeShaun's apathetic presentation, his attempts were met with shrugs or distant gazes.

This type of exchange characterized several sessions until a reckless driver ran over Bear. DeShaun said that he was shocked to find himself standing over Bear watching him die, feeling no emotion at all. He insisted that people are supposed to feel something when things like this happen, and worried that he might be going crazy. This experience provided an opportunity to examine how DeShaun's methods of coping were costing him part of his humanity. He and the therapist began to explore his memories of stress and loss, searching for the last time he could remember feeling something. DeShaun identified numerous events in which he only remembered feeling mad or

apathetic. His clearest memory of pain was his brother's murder. The therapist then asked DeShaun how he felt when his mother died. This was the first time DeShaun outwardly showed emotion to the therapist. He tearfully explained that after his mother was diagnosed with cancer, the two of them had a big argument. DeShaun had told her that he hoped the cancer would kill her, and left the house. He lived with a friend after that and rarely talked with his mother. The cancer accelerated rapidly and his mother died before she and DeShaun had healed their relationship. When he learned of her death, DeShaun cursed her, did not go to the funeral, and cut off from her family. Eventually, he was placed in foster care.

Therapy began to focus on the social messages DeShaun had internalized about men expressing emotions, and being vulnerable and dependent on others. He and his therapist discussed ways in which young African American men who express emotion are feared by some and thought of as punks by others. They examined the notion that young men who are independent are somehow stronger and more competent than those who are connected and depend on others for support. Gradually, DeShaun started to acknowledge that he was using Marijuana, repression, and isolation to protect himself from his pain, and decided this was unfair to himself. The therapist took him and his girlfriend to visit his mother's grave for the first time. There he was able to tell his mother all the things he wished he could have told her when she was alive. He added that she was going to be a grandmother and promised to bring a picture of the baby when it was born. DeShaun had mixed feelings about becoming a father. He seemed to like the idea but resent the responsibility. He said that his father had never been there for him, so he did not see why he had to be there for his baby. Therapy began to help him weave characteristics such as responsibility and integrity into his concept of masculinity. The therapist encouraged him to write a letter to his father that held him accountable for not being there for him. DeShaun held on to the letter with the thought that he might send it to his father one day. The therapist also encouraged him to reconnect with one of his mother's sisters. Together they wrote a letter to this aunt that explained DeShaun's withdrawal and apparent apathy were simply attempts to protect himself from pain. He added that he would like her to be a part of his life. DeShaun seemed to be impacted most of all by getting involved in a basketball ministry at a local church. In this group, he learned to be more honest and emotionally connected to other young men. He felt part of a meaningful community for the first time in his life and began to feel that he had something of worth to offer others.

> Assess your comprehension of childhood and adolescence by completing this quiz.

Men and Work

Most people find value in some form of work. Developing mastery at a skill, contributing to a community effort, creating something that others find valuable, and earning money all help foster with sense of competence, worth, belonging, and personal fulfillment. The benefits of work enhance self-actualization and relational growth for men and women alike. However, for far too many people in our society, work becomes a burden, obsession, or escape that interferes with individual development and leaves little time and energy for relationships and love. In the current economy, jobs are scarce and finding work that is personally fulfilling and pays a livable wage is becoming a luxury. Young men who base their manliness on their money and achievement are increasingly challenged to define themselves as adults. Consequently, many young men find themselves in a limbo between adolescence and adulthood, living out a kind of "amorphous uncertainty." For many, college is used to delay taking on developmental tasks of young adulthood (Kimmel, 2008) while they search for some sort of meaning or rite of passage that will define them as real adults. Reduced opportunities in the current economy lead other men to despair. These men often draw upon the same patriarchal coping mechanisms that they were raised with and either become more emotionally shut down, or filled with rage they then direct toward women and immigrants who they believe are robbing them of opportunities (Kimmel, 2013). The interference of work with individual and relational development

is not unique to men. However, patriarchy socializes men to be particularly vulnerable to the ways in which work interferes with, rather than enhances, growth. Therapists who are familiar with the potential for problematic interactions between work and men's relationships will be best equipped to help them navigate life cycle tasks.

A central notion of patriarchy is that a man's worth is directly proportional to what he is able to achieve and produce. On the one hand, this notion has generated assumptions that men are naturally endowed with the ability to achieve and produce, leading them to be privileged in the workplace over women. On the other hand, this notion greatly restricts the range of ways in which the worth of men is defined. Men are prone to connect their self-worth to their work, and even look to their job and their income as their primary contribution to relationships. The notion that men ought to be providers for their families convinces many men that providing financially is their primary means of expressing loyalty and love. This notion is further exacerbated by the widely held belief that men are also naturally driven toward success and will make work and career their highest priority. Some men may feel their worth, as a man is threatened when their female partners also work, especially when this is out of financial necessity rather than seeking personal fulfillment. For other men, the notion that their worth in relationships is an outgrowth of what they are able to achieve and produce becomes so dominant that they rely on some form of work in order to relate to the people they love. These men seem to need a problem to solve, something to fix, or someone to teach in order to connect.

The time, energy, and focus work requires can become an escape from the emotional demands of life cycle tasks and the work of love and relationships for both women and men. The lure to escape into work is often particularly strong for men who are both trained to repress vulnerable emotions and socially rewarded for working. Men who rely on work this way are often more likely to be praised for being passionate, driven, loyal, and hard-working than identified as struggling to cultivate a more flexible and holistic sense of self-worth or to access the emotional strength necessary to do the work of relationships.

In order to be successful in challenging families to think critically about the potential harmful effects of work in men's lives, it is essential that therapists acknowledge and honor the value of work in men's lives as well. It is particularly important to keep cultural dimensions such as race, ethnicity, and social class in mind when discussing the ways in which work may interact with family relationships. For example, working class and poor men have long felt powerless, disrespected, and undervalued in the workplace. Similarly, men of color frequently hit up against invisible barriers to college and career advancements that our White supremacist society reinforces, while denying such barriers exist. Socially marginalized men often need to pour additional effort into work in order to get the appreciation and recognition given to socially privileged men. These men, and people who are in relationships with them, may be defensive against critiques that men work too much or use work as an escape, because they are very much attuned to their struggle to be respected and valued. In addition, when socially marginalized men say to their families, "I did it all for you," they are likely referring to enduring numerous experiences of devaluation as well as the work they did. Therapists cannot expand men's sense of worth by further devaluing the one thing that might give them a sense of pride. Instead, the significance of work must be valued and honored in order to open up space for cultivate worth and meaning in other aspects of their lives.

> **Assess your comprehension of men and work by completing this quiz.**

Men as Partners and Husbands

Men usually want to be a part of a romantic partnership in which they can find shared intimacy, mutual support, someone to go through life with, and a sense of purpose and meaning. However, boys are more frequently taught to compete and win than to compromise and care for others. As boys and young men repress parts of themselves associated with weakness and vulnerability, they frequently repress skills and personal qualities that support the formation and growth of romantic relationships. When tender emotion threatens masculinity and worth is equated with the ability to be dominant and in control of self and others, there is little space left for relational skills such as humility, self-reflection, admitting fault, self-disclosure, and expression of tender emotion and attachment needs. Creativity, commitment, and compromise are necessary relational skills that are at odds with patriarchy's narrow definitions of masculinity. The more narrowly a man defines himself, the less flexibility he will have to adapt to a variety of relational demands across the life cycle. The more masculinity is about winning, the more difficult it is for men to view negotiation as collaboration rather than competition. The more men's roles are defined by being strong for others, the more difficult it will be for them to get in touch with and express their vulnerability. The more men's worth is equated with what they can produce, the more challenging it is for them to simply listen to someone without trying to fix things for them. In addition, male privilege leads men to anticipate being accommodated. Consequently, it may not even occur to men to alter their personal goals, routines, or roles in the home, even when this would lead to increased happiness for themselves and their relationships.

By the time boys become young men, they have often developed an expectation that a relationship is something that will simply fulfill them rather than something they work on cultivating. Many straight men seeking a committed relationship are looking for a ready-made ideal women who will complete them, particularly those parts of themselves patriarchy has convinced them to repress and deny. For most men, sex is the primary vehicle through which they seek this fulfillment, perhaps because sex is the primary means through which men are permitted to experience and express disowned parts of themselves such as intimacy, closeness, tenderness, vulnerability, sensuality, and gentleness with their bodies (hooks, 2004). It is often easier for men to look for a source of external sexual fulfillment than to look inward to reclaim these parts of themselves. In addition, when men depend on sex to access the fullness of their humanity and affirm their masculinity and worth, it often becomes an obsession. However, sex cannot possibly fulfill all of these needs. Ironically, when sex inevitably disappoints men, they tend to become even more obsessed with it. Sexual obsessions are reinforced by myths that claim men must have sex or they will go crazy, and if men are denied they will eventually become sexual with anyone. These myths lead to the justification of and passivity toward all forms of male sexual violence (hooks, 2004). When men believe sex is the entitlement of any real man, they feel their masculinity is assaulted and diminished when they do not get as much sex as they crave (Kimmel, 2013). Single men who attempt to resist patriarchal dominance without questioning their sense of entitlement to sex may treat women kindly, but be furious if they find themselves in "the friend zone." Their anger suggests they believe their kindness obligates women to give them sex. When men perceive women's decision not to have sex with them as holding sexual power over them, they are prone to direct their sexual frustration toward women. This frustration is used to justify multiple forms of covert manipulation and overt coercion to get sex from women through any means necessary. Viewing sex as one's entitlement or a means through which one is completed and fulfilled by another fuels fusion. Men who are able to own all aspects of their humanity and look to their partners as someone to share in multiple aspects of connection, rather than to possess or dominate, are in a better position to increase differentiated intimacy in sex and all other aspects of their relationship.

Intimate relationships are often the primary vehicle through which men begin to reject patriarchy's narrow definitions of masculinity and embrace more of the fullness of their humanity. As men grow in this capacity, they are also more likely to take on more egalitarian roles in their relationships. However, men who resist traditional gender roles are likely to continue to have their actions interpreted through a patriarchal lens. Sometimes, men are teased for playing "Mister Mom," being a "good little wife," or other terms that seek to emasculate men by calling upon oppressive degrading ideas about women. Other times, they are praised for doing something above and beyond the call of duty in their roles as romantic partners and fathers. In our patriarchal society, it is rare that men who contribute to housework and take on roles that require them to be emotionally nurturing are simply viewed as doing something normal and expected.

Disparities often exist between a couple's values regarding gender roles and the ways in which they actually organize their relationships. Couples who value equality may continue to defer unconsciously to male entitlement and traditional gender roles. Men in these relationships may not recognize that skills that have always helped them assert themselves or get ahead in other contexts reinforce distance in their romantic relationships. Other couples may value traditional gender roles but actually have more equitable relationships. This is particularly true of working class and poor couples who may need to take on equitable roles out of necessity. While equality out of necessity may have certain advantages, it also presents a variety of challenges for couples. In a White supremacist society, people of color and immigrants' cultural norms are pervasively evaluated against a dominant White American norm and frequently characterized as incompetent, unstable, and dysfunctional. In many cultures, having a man as the head of the household and emotional anchor represents strength and stability for the entire family. Performing traditional gender roles may be a primary means through which men and women experience personal value in a broader society that pervasively devalues them. In cases such as these, assertions that equality in roles is a superior way to organize relationships can easily be experienced as further devaluation of cultural values (Sue & Sue, 2008). This offense can easily elicit defensiveness that may prevent men from examining ways in which patriarchy affects their lives and relationships from within their own cultural value system.

Therapists can help men grow in relationships by encouraging them to reclaim disowned parts of themselves that nurture relationships. Partners and other family members may need to examine their own assumptions about men and masculinity in order for this growth to be supported. Discussions of gender and gender roles are often framed as a competition between women and men. Therefore, therapists can support examination of gender in a couple's relationship by framing relationships as mutual endeavors that support one another's growth as well as the growth of the relationship. The following vignette illustrates some ways in which patriarchal norms were challenged in order to support greater intimacy and growth in a couple.

CASE ILLUSTRATION

Dave

At the age of 36, Dave seemed to have it made. He was fit, charming, and had a highly prestigious job at a tech company in the Silicon Valley. He came to therapy in a way that is common for many men, through the encouragement of his partner. He was living with his girlfriend, Molly, who was a 28-year-old law student. Molly originally sought individual therapy for herself. She had a history of experiencing waves of anxiety and depression that she believed stemmed from being raised by a passive mother and a rigidly controlling father, who sometimes went into fits of rage and made violent threats. As Molly neared the end of her graduate program, she began having episodes of anxiety about her future, followed by periods of despair. However, in her initial session, Molly primarily talked about her relationship with Dave. She had been going through a similar period of anxiety and depression when the two of them had met. She was filled with self-doubt at that time and Dave's cool demeanor and promising career made him seem like he had his life together. Dave had been very patient and gentle with her, which stood in stark contrast to her harsh, impatient father. Molly explained that when she felt like she was falling apart, Dave's gentleness comforted her and his lack of emotional reactivity reassured her. Now, however, this same kind of response seemed distant and superficial. Molly sought reassurance from Dave by talking about deepening the commitment in their relationship. This seemed to make Dave withdraw even more. The therapist proposed that since Molly's anxiety and depression were now connected to her relationship with Dave, it might be best to address them in couples therapy.

Dave agreed to join the therapy. He said that he loved Molly and wanted to do what he could to help her overcome her mood swings. He was relatively satisfied with her as a partner but found her need to discuss about the commitment of their relationship to be exhausting. He had ambivalent feelings about marriage and did not see any need to make promises that no one could know for sure they would be able to keep. Dave added that Molly had been asking him

about plans for a family, and what he would do if she were offered a position with a law firm in another location. Dave felt Molly's anxiety was driving her to ask questions for which he simply did not have answers. While at one time he was sexually passionate with Molly and enjoyed her company, he was now experiencing her as a drain on his energy.

The therapist was mindful that when there is distress in relationships between men and women, women often bear the most visible symptoms. He was hesitant to accept either Dave or Molly's assessment of the problem as something that existed solely within Molly. He asked how Dave typically responded to Molly's insistence to discuss their future. Dave said that at times he would try to talk with Molly. He would remind her that his stance on relationships had always been the same. He suspected she was projecting her feelings about her dad onto him and would ask her if there was something about him that was reminding her of her father. Other times he made suggestions about how she could ease her anxiety. Dave admitted that his attempts to help had not done any good, so lately he just checked out and let her vent. The therapist proposed that it sounded like Dave responded to Molly by trying to fix what he perceived to be a problem. With a sigh, Dave agreed adding that his role in relationships was often the fixer, "At work I fix bugs in programs and work out the bugs in the relationships between my employees. When my friends have a problem to solve, I'm the first person they call—and then there are my parents." With a little encouragement, Dave went on to share that as a child his parents had a highly contentious relationship. Each confided their frustrations with one another in him and sought his loyalty. Dave said at a very young age he realized that anytime he cried or got angry, it was likely to set his parents off fighting. Consequently, he learned that asking for things with a rational explanation usually got him what he wanted and helped keep peace in his home. Dave added that he longed to go back to peaceful times with Molly.

While the therapy continued to focus on both Molly and Dave, it was Dave who seemed most surprised by the benefits of couple therapy. He discovered that emotions had started feeling dangerous and unimportant to him in his relationship with his parents, but that in nearly every aspect of his life, any indication of vulnerability seemed to be quickly punished, while cool rational responses were rewarded. Consequently, as a young boy who longed for care and affection from his parents, he learned that he had to take care of himself. In every aspect of his life, the message that independence equaled maturity was reinforced. Dave had not had many life experiences that taught him how to depend on another person, or to feel comfort in vulnerability. He came to realize that focusing on other people's struggles distracted him from his own inner pain, and provided him with a sense of strength and competence. The thought of being vulnerable and depending on another person filled him with a sense of dread that he would be disappointed and let down. When asked where relying only on himself might lead him in the future, Dave tearfully replied that he would probably be as alone as he had always been. The therapist asked Dave to consider what he might gain if he were able to be more vulnerable and interdependent in his relationship with Molly. In reflecting on this, Dave realized that his life had begun to feel stagnant. It was a lack of trust in others that kept him from being able to be more passionate about Molly and about all aspects of his life. He gradually began to recognize that his cool rational demeanor and problem-solving nature were mere facades to mask his vulnerability to himself as well as others. With this awareness, he and Molly were able to create greater intimacy and passion in their relationship.

Assess your comprehension of men as partners and husbands by completing this quiz.

Fatherhood

For many men becoming a father is simultaneously the most frighteningly stressful and joyously wonderful life transition. This is perhaps more true than ever as fathers have become more involved with the raising of their children (Day, Lewis, O'Brien, & Lamb, 2004). The prospect of having a child increases pressure on men to perform traditional roles such as providing for the family. However, this life cycle transition requires a great deal of relational work as well. For example, men need to respond to the physical and emotional needs of their partners during pregnancy and after the birth of their child. The transition into parenthood tends to increase stress and decrease marital satisfaction. Several studies indicate that the more competent husbands are in their marital relationships, the more successful they are in adjusting to fatherhood. Additional studies indicate that expectant mothers' satisfaction with their partners has a positive impact on her experience as a parent (Habib, 2012). Fathers need to learn to provide emotional nurturance as well as physical care for their child. New fathers must also navigate increased contact from extended family that often accompanies the birth of a child. Expectant fathers tend to become more involved with their own parents, especially with their fathers (Habib, 2012). Seeking out connection with fathers may represent an increased understanding of the pressures on one's own father and an appreciation of his contributions to the family. Men who seek out connection with their fathers at this time may also be reminded of things their fathers did that they want to do differently with their own children. The more energy men have invested in learning to work on relationships prior to having children, the better equipped they will be to work through relational tasks with their partners and develop nurturing relationships with their children.

Vaillant's (2012) research suggests that a boy's closeness with his father remains meaningful in a variety of ways throughout his life. Men in this study who grew up with warm relationships with their fathers were better able to play and enjoy leisure time as adults. They seemed more likely to use humor to cope, and had lower anxiety and fewer physical and mental symptoms under stress in young adulthood. Men who grew up without good relationships with their fathers were more likely to call themselves pessimists, and had trouble letting others get close to them. They also seemed to be more likely to have unhappy marriages. Interestingly, growing up with poor relationships with their mothers was not correlated with having an unhappy marriage later in life. At the age of 75, men who grew up with good relationships with their fathers were more likely to report overall life satisfaction, but once again, this variable was not correlated with closeness to their mothers. Vaillant suspects that this correlation in later life is related to a more general finding that closeness with fathers seems to predict the ability of men to play and enjoy leisure time. This research indicates that warmth and nurturance from fathers has benefits that can remain with children throughout their lives. However, many fathers have had little practice with relational work and some have few or no examples of fathers who have done the work of relationships, love, and nurturance well.

Men may respond to the relational demands of fatherhood in a variety of ways. For many men, fatherhood is the most transformative of all life experiences. These men are likely to reexamine their priorities and sense of purpose in life, and respond to the relational tasks by becoming more emotionally present, nurturing, and mutually supportive in their relationship with their partner. For some men, the self-reflection and emotional intensity that naturally accompany this period of life may feel threatening to the emotional repression and self-certainty that has previously affirmed their sense of strength and stability. These men may feel inadequate in their abilities to provide nurturance and care and retreat into traditional gender roles, hiding their anxiety and other emotions behind business, humor, and irritability. These men may also respond to emotional and relational stress by placing more pressure on their partners to provide an idealized version of nurturance and care. This pressure often takes the form of enthusiastically praising his partner's parenting abilities while downplaying his own capacity to provide nurturance and care. Still other men may feel so inadequate in their role as a father, or so entitled to look out only for themselves, that they abandon their partner and children entirely. Gay fathers tend not to defer to traditional gender roles in raising children, partly because it is not an option (Erera, 2002). However, Gay fathers have typically grown up with the same socialization as other men and are equally challenged to grow in their abilities to provide nurturance and care.

When men take advantage of the relational and emotional demands of the transition into fatherhood, they may begin a trajectory of change and adaptability that serves them through various demands of parenting across the life cycle. Fathers who retreat even further into traditional gender roles are likely to find that emotional and relational work in fatherhood becomes increasingly difficult. For example, increased life expectancy and children staying at home longer all lead to men at midlife having more responsibilities to care for parents as well as children. As more women are in the workforce, men are no longer able to count on female partners and siblings to provide all the caregiving. In addition, launching children presents men with another loss and emotional transition. Fathers who have not learned to process emotions may become even more shut down. Furthermore, fathers who have depended on female partners to act as relational bridges between them and their children may find it difficult to maintain a meaningful connection with their children when they leave home. Men who are divorced or separated from their partners may become completely estranged from their children if they do not learn to reach out and be attuned and responsive in their relationships. Some of the most significant work therapists can do with men includes assisting them to understand their emotional life, and their relational needs and styles. Through supporting new ways of caring, taking risks by being more flexible and expansive in their parenting roles, men can be helped to be better fathers and partners (Kiselica & Englar-Carlson, 2010).

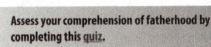

Assess your comprehension of fatherhood by completing this quiz.

Men in Later Life

Men's later years have been oversimplified as a mere continuation of midlife, a time that they develop wisdom, come to terms with not working, and prepare for death. However, longitudinal studies have revealed later life to be a time rich in possibilities and some of men's most joyful and fulfilling years (Vaillant, 2012). The happiest men in these studies were those that continued to develop and grow right up until their deaths, and relationships were central to the development and growth they experienced. They learned to mentor the next generation. They decreased rigid biases and developed wider perspectives and wisdom. They put their wisdom to work to preserve knowledge and culture in ways that would benefit society. Finally, they developed peace with the inevitability of death, believing their lives had been worth living right up to the end. Vaillant (2012) asserts that in old age, life becomes the sum of one's loves. The men in his study that experienced the most growth, joy, and fulfillment in later life were those whose lives were rich in love. Interestingly, this joy was not limited to men who had enjoyed loving relationships their whole lives. In fact, Vaillant's research powerfully testifies that when it comes to love, what goes right in men's lives is far more significant than what goes wrong. Even some men, who lingered in cold distant relationships into their 60s, were able to develop flourishing fulfilling relationships in their elder years. It is not uncommon for men to be more satisfied in their relationships in later life. Friendship and interdependence tend to increase in their marriages. Hormonal changes related to aging tend to help men become more emotionally attuned to their partners, and physical infirmities make it increasingly clear that mutual dependence is more of an advantage than a weakness. In Vaillant's (2012) study, some men deepened the intimacy in relationships with their partners, while others chose to leave unhappy relationships and found passionate intimate love for the first time in their lives.

Men in later life are often exciting to work with in therapy. In early adulthood and midlife, men are often attuned to patriarchy's false promises that prestige, financial success, and sexual conquests will fulfill them. These men are often hesitant to explore different ways of being in relationship with themselves and others. As men age, their bodies become weaker, they lose their sexual prowess, and find themselves more replaceable at work. Coping mechanisms that rely on independence, intimidation, and repression are more likely to stagnate personal growth and lead to isolation than to reap rewards. Consequently, many men in later life are more open to redefining themselves as men. They may find the power to forgive themselves and others, to open themselves to their emotions, take risks to pursue passions, depend on others, and love more freely and openly than ever before. The following case provides an example of some of the ways men in later life may embrace change.

CASE ILLUSTRATION

Jim

Jim was an 81-year-old Chinese American man referred by his physician. During his last exam, he had complained of lethargy, inability to sleep, and pervasive irritation. Jim and his wife had been married for over 50 years and had five grown children who were married and had children of their own.

Jim had always worked, even as a teenager. Six years prior to coming to therapy, he had retired from the same shipping company he had started working at to put himself through college. He described his job as his primary life activity. It was the primary means for him to socialize with others and gave him a sense of belonging. After a minor work-related injury at the age of 70, he was moved from working outside delivering packages to the office completing paperwork. At the age of 75, he decided to retire to "make way for the younger guys who were smarter." Jim continued to visit his old work place for a year but eventually stopped going. He simply no longer felt that he belonged. Shortly after this, he became more irritable and began declining to go out with his wife or visit his adult children and their families.

Jim's symptoms appeared to be related to difficulties adjusting to his stage in the life cycle. He had based much of his identity on his job and had relied on work to have a social life outside his family. He had also prided himself on being a father, particularly his ability to provide for his family. Now he was not sure what he had to offer his children and felt that they did not need him anymore. The therapist suspected that Jim would find many opportunities for happiness and fulfillment in his life if he were able to expand his notions about his roles as a man and his expectations of relationships. The therapist also suspected that as an immigrant Jim had already had to find ways to redefine himself at various points in his life. In order to invite Jim to reflect on his life in ways that might open up new possibilities for himself, the therapist asked questions such as, "What conversations have you been able to have with your children that you weren't able to have with your father?" and "What conversations do you hope your sons will be able to have with their children that they weren't able to have with you?" Jim was very moved by these questions. He remembered his father as distant, always emphasizing the importance of working hard, but not talking about important things such as the importance of family and Chinese culture. It was not until Jim came to the United States that he became aware of how important his Chinese heritage was to him. He struggled a great deal to carve out a life in San Francisco and to provide for his family. He was very grateful for the opportunities he had; however, those opportunities came at the cost of losing his connections to traditions, holidays, customs, language, foods—to much of his identity, to his home. The more firmly established he became in the United States, the more his interest in Chinese culture and the experience of Chinese immigrants grew. But Jim kept this interest to himself. He thought it best not to burden his family with his struggles and his longings for his home in China. Instead, he would teach his children about Chinese culture and remind them to, "never forget that you are Chinese, or your Chinese ancestors who sacrificed so much for you," but stopped short of sharing his own sacrifices. In this conversation, Jim wondered what he had experienced as his father's distance was actually his father's effort to protect him. Jim concluded that parents want to protect their children, but children want to know their parents. This conversation opened up similar conversations in therapy for Jim to explore sharing stories and experiences with his children that he had kept from them in the past. Together Jim and the

therapist discussed how meaningful it could be to Jim's children to hear his stories and how that might even help them develop a greater appreciation for the culture and history he worked so hard to impart to them. Jim's children were receptive to him wanting to share his stories. His oldest son Mark was particularly interested and Jim was delighted to learn that Mark had longed to hear his stories ever since he was a teenager. Mark arranged for a trip to Angel Island, the west coast port for early Chinese and Asian immigrants. He was so enthralled with going that Mark helped arrange for him to be a volunteer docent. Unable to traverse parts of the island physically, he asked his wife to accompany him, an invitation that she relished. Jim was proud to have an opportunity to continue to study Chinese American history, and share his knowledge and passion with others. As Jim felt more open with his children, he became more playful with his grandchildren as well. He remembered that as a young child, he would make kites, and taught his grandchildren how to make them as well. At the end of therapy, he was far from lethargic and irritable. He was excited about his relationship with his family and about how much there was for him to learn and to pass on to others.

Assess your comprehension of men in later life by completing this quiz.

— Conclusion

Today, men may have more opportunities than ever before to be pioneers in redefining masculinity. More men are discovering ways to embrace mutuality and interdependence in their relationships and the fullness of their humanity in themselves. Being a pioneer is challenging though, and when the unfamiliarity of this territory becomes threatening and painful, many potential pioneers long to return to patriarchy's old familiar home of repression, control, and rugged independence. As a society, we must be continuously involved in unpacking the boxes historically constructed for boys and men. Therapists can

be instrumental in helping men thrive in new territories. They can do this by helping men learn to love and accept all that they are, to see strength in vulnerability and the power of interdependence. Therapists can remind men that they have more to gain than to lose in doing this work, not only for themselves but also for future generations.

Recall what you learned in this chapter by completing the Chapter Review.

— References

Aulette, J., Wittner, J., & Blakely, K. (2009). *Gendered worlds*. New York: Oxford Press.

Barnett, R., & Rivers, C. (2004). *Same difference: How gender myths are hurting our relationships, our children, and our jobs*. New York: Tarcher Publishers.

Cannon, E., & Marszalek, J. (2012). Counseling gay and questioning boys and young men. In S. Degges-White & B. Colon (Eds.). *Counseling boys and young men*. New York: Springer Publishing Company.

Collins, P. H. (1998). *Fighting words: Black women and the search for justice*. Minneapolis, MN: University of Minnesota Press.

Davis, L., Kilburn, M., & Schultz, D. (2009). *Reparable harm: Assessing and addressing disparities faced by boys and men of color in California*. Retrieved (January 17, 2013) from www.rand.org/content/dam/rand/pubs/monographs/2009/RAND_MG745.1.1pdf.

Day, R. D., Lewis, C., O'Brien, M., & Lamb, M. (2004). Fatherhood and father involvement: Emerging constructs and theoretical orientations. In V. Bengsten, A. Acock, K. Allen, P. Dilworth-Anderson, & D. Klein (Eds.), *Sourcebook of family theory & research*. Thousand Oaks, CA: Sage Publishers.

Deutsch, B. (2010). The male privilege checklist. In M. S. Kimmel & M. A. Messner (Eds.). *Men's Lives*. Boston, MA: Allyn & Bacon.

Erera, P. I. (2002). *Family diversity: Continuity and change in the contemporary family*. Thousand Oaks, CA: Sage Publications.

Garfield, R. (2015). *Breaking the male code. Unlocking the power of friendship*. New York: Gotham Books.

Habib, C. (2012). The transition to fatherhood: A literature review exploring paternal involvement with identity theory. *Journal of Family Studies*,18 (2–3), 103–120.

Hardy, K. V., & Laszloffy, T. A. (2002). Couple therapy using a multicultural perspective. In A. S. Gurman & N. S. Jacobson (Eds.), *Clinical handbook of couple therapy (3rd ed.)* (pp. 569–559). New York, NY: Guilford Press.

hooks, b. (1984). *Feminist theory: From margin to center*. Cambridge, MA: South End Press.

hooks, b. (2000). *All about love: New visions*. New York: HarperCollins.

hooks, b. (2004). The will to change: Men, masculinity, and love. New York: Washington Square Press.

Kane, E. W. (2012). *The gender trap: Parents and the pitfalls of raising boys and girls*. New York University Press: New York.

Kerby, S. (2012). *The top 10 most startling facts about people of color and criminal justice in the United States: A look at the racial disparities inherent in our nation's criminal-justice system*. Center for American Progress. Retrieved from www.americanprogress.org January 13, 2013.

Kimmel, M. (2008). *Guyland: The perilous world where boys become men*. New York: HarperCollins.

Kimmel, M. (2012). *The gendered society*. New York: Oxford University Press.

Kimmel, M. (2013). *Angry white men: American masculinity at the end of an era*. New York: Nation Books.

Kiselica, M., & Carlson, M. (2010). Identifying, affirming, and building upon male strengths: The positive psychology/positive masculinity model of psychotherapy with boys and men. *Psychotherapy Theory, Research, Practice, Training*, 7, 276–287.

Kivel, P. (2010). The act-like-a-man box. In M.S. Kimmel & M.A. Messner (Eds.). *Men's lives*. Boston, MA: Allyn & Bacon.

Levant, R. F. (2005). The crisis of boyhood. In G. Good & G. Brooks (Eds.), *The new handbook of psychotherapy and counseling with men* (pp. 161–171). San Francisco, CA: Wiley & Sons.

Mock, M. (2008). Visioning social justice: Narratives of diversity, social location and personal compassion. In M. McGoldrick & K.V. Hardy (Eds.) *Re-Visioning family therapy: Race, culture and gender in clinical practice* (2nd edn.). New York: Guilford.

Rao, A., & Seaton, M. (2009). *The way of boys: Promoting the social and emotional development of young boys*. New York: Harper Collins.

Rivers, C., & Barnett, R. C. (2013). *The new soft war on women: How the myth of female ascendance is hurting women, man–and our economy*. New York: Penguin Group.

Sue, D. W., & Sue, D. (2008). *Counseling the culturally diverse: Theory and practice*. New Jersey: Wiley & Sons.

Vaillant, G. (2012). *Triumphs of experience*. Cambridge, MA: Harvard University Press.

Vogel, D., Heimderdinger-Edwards, S., Hammer, J., & Hubbard, A. (2011). "Boys don't cry": Examination of those links between endorsement of masculine norms, self-stigma, and help-seeking attitudes from men from diverse backgrounds. *Journal of Counseling Psychology*. 58, 368–382.

Way, N. (2011). *Deep secrets: Boy's friendships and the crisis of connection*. Cambridge: Harvard University Press.

Chapter 4

Social Class and the Life Cycle

Jodie Kliman

— Learning Outcomes —————————————————————————

- Describe the effects of downward mobility on families and effective strategies for managing the stress caused by financial hardship.
- Identify how factors such as race, culture, and gender intersect with social class.
- Define class position and describe how it differs from socioeconomic status.
- List and describe the four major social classes.
- Explain how internal class differences can affect families.
- Describe how social class influences what resources are available to families.
- Identify how social class affects the rights, responsibilities, and developmental tasks of older children and adolescents.
- Describe how social class influences the decisions young people make as they start their adult lives.
- Discuss the impact of social class on the final stage of life, including the age at which that stage occurs.
- Explain how the class history and class position of therapists can influence their cultural narratives about their clients.

Introduction

Four babies, Sophie, Daniel, Ta'esha, and Miguelito, were born into three families in three different class positions.[1] Because their families have unequal access to educational, work, and recreational opportunities and face related disparities in their health and longevity, these children have entered into divergent family life cycle patterns with different expectations for the duration and nature of intergenerational relationships. This chapter addresses the influences of social class on American family life cycle trajectories, how families understand those trajectories, and their implications for family therapy. The focus is on family life cycles in the United States, as class structures differ widely internationally. Throughout, this chapter illustrates how class position combines with other sources of privilege and marginalization, such as race, gender, marital status, sexual orientation,

religion, immigration history, and health, to shape family life through the life cycle.

Class position intensifies or softens crises' impact on families at each family life cycle stage. It influences whether family members receive higher education or life-saving surgery, whether they turn to paid helpers or unpaid relatives for help, and whether they immigrate together or separately. One member's serious illness, devastating in any family, can also cause job loss and even homelessness if working-class relatives lose work time to care for her. This chapter explores how families and their therapists see their lives through lenses formed by their class-based experiences, and the implications of those intersecting lenses for family therapy.

Social class shapes the developmental and meaning-making systems of all families and the relationships within and between families. It is therefore useful to explore the clinical and social implications of each member's individual social class history, trajectory, and current position and how these all

---

[1] All family descriptions in this chapter, except my own, are composites.

members' interpenetrating class histories, trajectories, and current positions shape their shared family life cycle. This chapter also explores how families make sense of their convergent and divergent journeys from cradle to grave, from ancestors to progeny, in their respective social contexts.

Downward mobility and obstacles to upward mobility

Despite a soaring wealth and opportunity gap between the richest and poorest (U.S. Census Bureau, 2013b; Yen, 2013), dominant U.S. discourse promotes mutually contradictory beliefs in a classless society (in which all, but the richest and the invisible poorest, are "middle-class") *and* in nearly universal intergenerational upward mobility (Kliman, 2010; Kliman & Madsen, 2005). These contradictory class narratives are challenged by current economic reality, as jobs and retirement funds disappear and downward mobility grows. Downwardly mobile baby boomers and generation x'ers and their families, who grew up expecting upward mobility but now face the sputtering remains of global economic crisis, may feel self-doubt, helplessness, and shame. How can family therapists help people consider the economy's contributions to the inadequacy of their incomes to their needs without contributing to these paralyzing feelings?

Downward mobility can be incremental or sudden. When housing, health care, childcare, and education costs climb incrementally or when a full-time service job is cut to part-time, families with stagnant or shrunken paychecks find themselves in trouble. People feeling ashamed of struggling financially more than their own parents had may not realize that their elders' housing and medical costs were a mere fraction of today's costs, or that the long-defunct post-World War II GI Bill paid for their fathers' educations and homes, or that a high school diploma once guaranteed steady factory or office work with benefits. Working-class parents with high school diplomas and even college-educated parents with "middle-class" jobs, now facing growing employment insecurity and declining real incomes, work for years to send children to college, only to find that even public colleges are now beyond reach.

Families can experience sudden downward mobility when a breadwinner is laid off, forced to work part-time, or disabled; when grandparents lose retirement funds; or a credit line is frozen during a health crisis. Many women must suddenly fully support children after divorce, abandonment, or their partners' disability or death—while making 80 percent of what men do, if they are able to work full-time (U.S. Census Bureau, 2013c). Because many mothers cannot work full-time, women as a group make only 62 percent of what men earn (U.S. Census Bureau, 2013c). Like slow downward mobility, sudden downturns can feel shaming. Families may turn inward, rather than toward community, as they wonder, "why was *I* (or my father) laid off and not someone else?" or "why couldn't we save more for a rainy day?" If there is a family history of economic struggle, such a crisis can confirm feelings of helplessness.

Families in immediate crisis or on unsure financial footing may reach desperately for risky solutions, as they struggle with big dilemmas: "Should we get married now, so he gets my health insurance?" "With our daughter's cancer treatment uncovered by insurance, we'll have to pay for chemo with a credit card, at 13.99 percent!" "With no credit to borrow against, I'll just have to give up college and work at Wal-Mart." "If I join the army, my family can have my salary—or at least my death benefits." For downwardly mobile, previously middle-income youth without access to enough college funding, college may seem essential enough to put on high-interest credit cards, ensuring great debt, but not graduation. Family therapists can help families manage the stress and relational reactivity caused by financial hardship.

Understanding societal contributions to downward mobility can reduce family members' experiences of shame, depression, and violence. Externalizing questions (White, 2007) can invite families to separate the impact of financial inequality from their relationships and shared identities so they can move forward. Externalizing questions can help families to appreciate and act on their values and to build on their relational resilience and resistance to internalizing shaming social narratives about economic struggle. Seeing their troubles in social context reduces shame; multiple family groups coping with unemployment, underemployment, or other economic crisis can also counter shame and build mutual support.

A recent Associated Press study (Yen, 2013) found that although census reports show that 12 percent of adults aged 25 to 60 live under the poverty line of $23,021 for a family of four, this figure is only a static snapshot representing the immediate moment. This snapshot hides the troubling finding that four in ten adults fall into poverty for at least a year (many while raising children), often cycling in and out of poverty, due to unemployment, underemployment, or some other crisis. These "invisible poor" may need food stamps, free emergency medical services, or disability income for long periods— or they may work now, but have a history of poverty. The invisible poor are increasingly White, not because families of color now earn more than before, but because more Whites have fallen into periodic poverty or near poverty (Yen, 2013).

Intersections of class and other factors

Families often have internally diverse class origins and trajectories. Families of different class backgrounds may find themselves related through marriage or coupling. One sibling may veer away from the class trajectories of siblings born into the same class position. She may lose class privilege through divorce, disability, mental illness, substance abuse, cutoff, or other tragedy, or gain it through education or marriage. In the latter instance, Renee, encouraged by a teacher, was the first in her African American working-class family to attend college, on a full scholarship. She married a graduate school classmate, Jason, the son of two British American professionals. When her sister, Marceline, a single mother, loses her job, she needs their help to avoid eviction, but feels both shame and resentment toward her more fortunate sister and anger at her brother-in-law, whom she sees as spoiled and snobbish. Jason is mystified by Renee's sense of obligation to divert their investments into a crisis he sees as not his own.

When her in-laws hear about her sister's potential eviction, Renee feels both angry at them and ashamed of her sister. Unfamiliar with the rigors of living paycheck to paycheck, Jason's parents disparage Marceline and accuse Renee of enabling her "irresponsibility." When Jason neither supports Renee's priorities nor defends her sister, marital tensions escalate. At the same time, Renee responds defensively when her own parents criticize her for not sharing more, forgetting "where she comes from," and acting "better" than her kin. Imagine the contradictory class (and racial) narratives Renee and Jason's children will metabolize as they grow up, as the biracial and class-mixed progeny of these two very different families.

Family therapists can help families address the strains exacerbated by internal class differences. Helping families deconstruct class (and other, intersecting social) narratives and class disparities can help families demystify the limits or possibilities of their choices, values, and possibilities. Doing so can help fraught family relationships, injured by class privilege or marginalization, to heal and grow. This in turn may help future generations of relatives to relate to each other with solidarity and mutual respect and caring, even across class divides.

It is important to address class's intersections with race, culture, and gender for the families of those we work with. Renee and Marceline grew up valuing collectivism; sharing resources is essential for survival in poor communities and in African American communities. Jason's family, steeped in individualist narratives of British Americans and privileged classes, saw Marceline's need as evidence of personal failure and Renee's desire to help as foolish.

Class, race, and gender, while distinct, intertwine to privilege some and disempower others. The median household income in 2011 was about $49,000 for non-Latino Whites but only $35,000 for African Americans and $31,000 for Latinos of all races (U.S. Census Bureau, 2013a). The poverty line is set at a sorely inadequate $21,000 for a family of four. While about 12 percent of all White households live under the poverty line, twice as many Black households and households with Latinos of all races live in these severe conditions (U.S. Census Bureau, 2013a). For families headed by single mothers, the figures are starker still: a third of White single mothers, 47 percent of Black single mothers, and 49 percent of all Latino single mothers raise their children in poverty.

Economically diverse communities of color have fewer medical services and fewer sources of healthy, affordable food; they also have lower quality education and more violence, with direct consequences for longevity and how long family members can expect to live together. Whites live longer than Blacks (Centers for Disease Control and Prevention, 2011) and wealthier Americans of all races live longer than their poor counterparts. Although federal data show that Latinos live longer than Whites, this finding needs further attention. Of note, immigrant Latinos tend to live longer and be healthier, even when they have low income and educational levels, than do U.S.-born Latinos with more economic and educational attainment. This "Latino Paradox" may be explained by the healthier diet and the family- and community-centered lifestyle of immigrant Latinos, as compared to their more acculturated U.S.-born counterparts (Lemare, 2012). Strikingly, Latinos are the only cultural group for whom higher levels of education and income do not ensure longer or healthier lives.

Immigration status also moderates income's effects on the family life cycle. Class position and understandings of class can change radically, for better or worse, on immigration, as family members leave one culture and economic system for another. The median household income for noncitizen householders is reported at 75 percent of U.S.-born householders (U.S. Census, 2012). This discrepancy might be still greater if all undocumented workers reported their earnings, which are often well below minimum wage. It is noteworthy, however, that well-educated immigrants who come for graduate education or professional careers, often becoming citizens, also skew this figure, as their income is slightly higher than the national median. As the government has tightened its own belt, immigrant families (documented and undocumented) lose health insurance and other forms of essential assistance, plunging more families into poverty. Since the National Affordable Health Care Act was passed, countervailing legislation has strived to reduce government assistance to poor working and unemployed families in the areas of health care, Head Start, and food assistance. As a result, the health burden on families only increases. As family health worsens, the health care system itself is further stressed, further worsening family health for the most vulnerable.

Children are most vulnerable to poverty; most households below or just above the poverty line have children (U.S. Census, 2013a). Greenstone, Looney, Patashnik, and Yu (2013), in their review of the impact of class position on children, report that families in the top income quintile spend seven times more a year on their children's educational activities than in the lowest quintile. Moreover, mothers with college degrees spend 4.5 hours more a week interacting with their children than do those with high school diplomas, and educated parents offer more enrichment activities. As a result, richer children hear a full 30 million more words by the age of 3 and have an education-enhancing vocabulary at 150 percent of their working-class peers and double that of their impoverished peers.

Schools in poor communities with the greatest educational and social needs have far fewer resources. Immigrant children miss school to translate for parents and return to classes they cannot easily follow. Poor children whose parents cannot afford younger siblings' daycare often miss school, as do children whose asthma is exacerbated by exposure to lead, bus fumes, and other toxins endemic in poor communities. Children with learning disabilities related to toxic exposure in utero and in early childhood are often undiagnosed and unsupported in overcrowded, underfunded schools. Family therapists can address such class-related issues with families, along with those related to higher exposure to trauma and violence, when schools, ignoring the social context in which children's difficulties emerge, label them as behavior problems or unmotivated.

Gender, marital status, and sexual orientation also moderate the effects of class on families (Kliman, 2005, 2010). Because women make less than men, Lesbian couples and single women, both Lesbian and straight, live with their children on less income than Gay or heterosexual couples. Many women stay in unhappy, and even abusive, relationships, to avoid extreme poverty. Burton and Cherlin's (2009) study of impoverished women found that poor women often have children by multiple men in serial nonmarital relationships—sometimes with men who abuse and exploit them, starting in their teens or early 20s, and learn early not to trust or count on men.

A family therapist may have trouble understanding how a mother could let her children experience or witness abuse unless he knows how hard it is to support children without education or job experience and how impoverished women may learn to expect such treatment. Exploring gender and economic constraints in the face of a mother's needing to feed her children can help therapists work respectfully and knowledgeably with a family in such distress.

> Assess your comprehension of the introduction by completing this quiz.

Understanding Social Class

Class position involves one's relationship to the economic structure, which varies between countries and regions. This relationship includes the nature and relative self-direction of one's labor (Ehrenreich, 1989, 2009). Class position relates not only to income but also, more importantly, to wealth (one's assets minus debts), and access to money, information, influence, privilege, and other resources. It is interwoven with educational level and to the intangibles of social standing in one's immediate and larger community (Kliman, 1998, 2005, 2010).

Class includes educational experience and related discourses about family, work, and community life, which vary greatly with educational level and intersect with race, ethnicity, and other factors. One self-defined "middle-class" family sends children to overnight camps, junior year abroad, volunteer internships, and professional schools, ensuring handsome future incomes. Children in another self-defined "middle-class" family's work full-time to help pay the family's rent, exhaustedly taking community college night classes; they can expect a considerably lower lifetime income (U.S. Census Bureau, 2013b) A third self-identified "middle-class" family of blue-collar and service workers cannot even dream of college because of poverty and/or immigration status; their children's high school diplomas produce far less future income.

Social class is often confused with *socioeconomic status* (SES). The latter, a decontextualized and hierarchical formula of educational and occupational levels, and income divides people into upper, middle, and lower SES, each of which is further subdivided. Yet most Americans place all but the wealthiest and the poorest in a vaguely defined middle class, and, in the wake of the Occupy Movement, place all but the richest one percent together in the "99 percent." This uniquely American conflation of class position and SES obscures how one's current and historical class positions influence workplace autonomy, access to resources, information, and the intangibles of influence, privilege, and power. It also obscures how wealth, education, and the intangibles of social standing matter more than income alone in how families live.

For example, Annie, an MBA student, reports that she took out student loans of $25,000 for tax advantage, but drives her attorney father's SUV, enjoys vacations abroad, lives rent free in the condo her parents bought and furnished for her, has a trust fund, and benefits daily from her family's wealth. In contrast, her business executive sister Laurel's undocumented nanny, Iris, supports her baby on $25,000, without health insurance, savings, or family money and is a paycheck away from homelessness. The two families' social, political, and informational resources differ as starkly as the expectations with which they raise their children.

A nonrelational, decontextualized concept of SES obscures how Iris's underpaid childcare work supports Laurel and her husband's highly paid work and separates Iris from her infant, who must stay with an aunt and cousins 10 to 12 hours a day. Class not only *affects* relationships, but it *is* a relationship between those in different class positions—and an unequal relationship at that (Kliman, 1998). Millionaires require low-wage earners. Families who employ household help may see their nannies as family members whom they treat generously, while the latter's kin rarely feel recognized, respected, or fairly treated by employer families.

Class position is constructed in relation to one's community, which may be economically homogeneous or mixed. Being employed, poor, working-class or professional class is experienced differently in different neighborhoods. For instance, the Jenkins's former neighbors, low income, largely Caribbean Islanders, and African Americans, saw the couple, a hospital orderly and a cafeteria worker, as "middle class" because they had two incomes. Since the area gentrified, their son, Greg, does not let the classmates whose beautifully rehabbed condos he visits see his shabby tenement apartment or his parents, who come home wearing work uniforms that mark his family as working class.

The Jenkins's family therapist needs to recognize how intergenerational class divergence shapes Greg's disrespect to and embarrassment about his parents, who sacrifice to give him an easier future, as he compares them to his classmates' parents. She must help Greg appreciate his parents' sacrifices, constraints, dignity, and commitments while helping his parents see how Greg's new expectations and priorities, nurtured in the shifting class context of his school, reflect their success in providing for Greg. How can she help this family find room for both realities? How can she avoid imposing her class-informed assumptions about parent–adolescent child relationships, or reactively over the family's assumptions about her class experience?

Social class influences family life cycle options subtly, in part through largely class-homogeneous social networks, as data from the Framingham Heart Study's (2008) longitudinal network analysis of obesity levels and smoking cessation suggest. Better-educated people are more influenced by acquaintances' quitting smoking and are more marginalizing of smokers than are less-educated peers, and so are less likely to smoke or be obese (thereby improving their longevity). The same likely applies to other family life cycle factors, such as when and if to have a first child, leave home, marry, get a degree, or binge drink.

Social class plays out differently in different countries and different economic systems. Western Europeans have higher taxes than Americans, which is outweighed by nearly free health care and higher education, subsidized daycare, and long, paid vacations that extend life, especially for the poor and working class. In many Latin American countries, professional and business-class families usually have live-in servants; on immigrating to the United States, these educated immigrant families may do more for themselves, feel more stress, and eat less healthily, while their former servants, on arriving here, perhaps without documents, struggle to survive on subsistence wages in a wealthy country, often sending most of their earnings home to families.

Class position is communicated in code, through dress, manners, language use, and leisure activities. Greg Jenkins's parents' clothing, furni-

ture, food, and grammar embarrass him; his friends' parents travel, eat, dress, speak, and decorate beautifully. His girlfriend, a classmate, teases him when he does not know cultural references that her family takes for granted and when he refuses family vacation invitations because he works during breaks, saving for the college she takes for granted. Greg's parents see his girlfriend as spoiled, entitled, and unproductive.

Class position and families

Class position shapes family structure and interactions and what family members expect of life and of each other. Class is a relationship. Great wealth requires the sacrifice of other people's resources and labor. The wealthiest—or ruling class—one percent are the families of top executives and some professionals and top entertainers, with mean incomes many times the mean U.S. income. The top tier of the one percent earns 540 times the national mean. More importantly, the top 1 percent owns 43 percent of the nation's wealth and the top 5 percent owns 72 percent of U.S. wealth (Dunn, 2012).

Work is optional for these wealthiest families; parents focus on philanthropy and board memberships, managing staffs that handle finances and multiple households, as well as on social functions, and sometimes work. Children, who are initially raised largely by servants, may leave home for boarding schools as early as latency age, returning only for vacations. If attachment bonds are strong first with servants and then at school, intimate bonds between parents and children and between siblings who do not live together will be attenuated. Intergenerational struggles between very wealthy youth and their parents and between the latter and their own aging parents, as well as conflicts between siblings, are not eased by the bonding and loyalties of a shared home life. Family ties may be based more on shared or competing financial interests, which do not enhance mutual devotion in times of emotional need, such as illness or loss. Untrained for earning a living, wealthy youth may not learn the basics of self-care and financial responsibilities required of most young people. They have staff for that. Therapists may be confused by these unfamiliar family patterns. They may also find themselves treated as employees, rather than as professionals, undercutting their effectiveness.

Families in the *professional-managerial class* have at least a college education and may identify as middle or upper-middle class. Their incomes can range from around $40,000 to $600,000, and their wealth varies similarly, yet they are often lumped together as if their economic and family experiences were similar and "in the middle" of a mythical bell curve distribution of income and wealth. Some have inheritances and parental help with mortgages and children's college, while others expect only limited family financial help, while still others have moved "up" from the working class and can get no such help. Families in this class expect moderate to high incomes and some autonomy and meaning at work, coupled with having to juggle expanding work hours and family responsibilities.

Parents are the primary caretakers through high school, but may have paid domestic help, which can range from live-in nannies and frequent housekeeping to part-time babysitters. Increasingly, such families have two earners or a working single parent, but are influenced by child-centered narratives valuing considerable time and attention to children. Historically, these families had the financial cushion to manage economic or health crises or divorce, but that cushion is disappearing for many in this group as pensions, savings, and jobs disappear or become increasingly "proletarianized" and as costs for health, education, and housing soar. Relational stress increases as parents lose income and the flexibility to have substantial time with family. Children are usually expected to leave home for college, but are often at least partly dependent on parents through college and even through advanced degrees. Marriage or coupling most often precedes childbirth, and usually happens after the college years. Parents in this group expect to have ongoing, close relationships with grown children and their families, although this class is so mobile that contact is increasingly virtual and only occasionally face to face.

Families in the *working class* are identified as "lower-middle-class" or as "working-poor," depending on their job and housing stability. Children in these families rarely go beyond high school, if that, and may live with family until marriage or coupling (or beyond) as a matter of economic necessity. Extended family ties often remain close, geographically and emotionally, over the generations, allowing emotional, financial, and other resources (such as childcare, house repair, or cars) to be shared.

Working-class high school and vocational school graduates once counted on job stability, but at the time of writing this book, with recovery from years of serious recession still sputtering, the working class is far more economically vulnerable than the groups discussed earlier. Previously, stable families have lost pensions, savings, and health insurance and full-time jobs have been "restructured" into part-time work without benefits—at the same time that costs have skyrocketed. Without the buffering of better-off relatives to shore them up in time of crisis, they can slide quickly into financial insecurity. Families that never had stability in the first place, like many immigrants with limited educations, or families with histories of periodic unemployment or underemployment, may slide into the underclass.

In the last decade, the working class has been increasingly "one paycheck away from homelessness." Homelessness has been on the rise, as has increasing food instability and reliance on food stamps, even for families with employed breadwinners. Working-class families' real-income level has declined significantly in 2011 dollars, in recent decades (U.S. Census Bureau, 2013b, 2013e), shattering any dreams of upward mobility for the majority of this group. While some gifted and particularly hardworking youth do get into college, it is usually without family financial support and without the earlier enrichment opportunities and family mentoring that the more privileged classes take for granted. Barring generous scholarships, finishing college in four years, and without crushing debt is a rarity.

Family therapists for working-class families should watch for signs of stress-related illness, shame, depression, substance abuse, family conflict, and violence, which family members may not connect with the impact of worsening financial hardship. Therapists from more privileged backgrounds must monitor their class-based assumptions about the necessity of higher education, when families may be unable to conceive of college as an option in their circumstances, and about the importance of independence for youth who may thrive only by staying embedded in kinship networks of mutual support, helping out as well as being helped throughout the life span.

The *underclass* includes families of the chronically unemployed, those on disability or welfare, runaway youth, and those working in the illegal drug, weapons, and sex trades (Ehrenreich, 1989), including human trafficking. Some are without homes, surviving in shelters, cars, and on the street. It also includes those immigrant and refugee workers who can only work in exploitative, extralegal conditions because of limited educations (and, for many, lack of documentation). Undocumented workers, often paid below minimum wage and off the books, may live with partners and children or may live in cheap and crowded group arrangements in order to send money to their children and other relatives in their home countries, who depend on their meager earnings for survival (Falicov, 2005). They are highly susceptible to exploitation, including trafficking, both domestically and internationally (Contreras & Bryant-Davis, 2012).

Most underclass families, with little to no education, have little hope of supporting themselves through legitimate (or any) work. Youth, not expecting to live long, are likely to have children very young, often without long-time partners. Teenaged mothers often raise their young children together with their own or their boyfriends' mothers, or leave the childrearing to their elders and may have several children before their mid-20s without a long-time partner (Burton & Cherlin, 2009). Increasingly, the poorest families struggle with inadequate or nonexistent housing. Most families rarely see a doctor, let alone family therapists. Many are invisible to the society around them. Those in therapy are often sent by child protective services, the judicial system, or schools. It is incumbent on family therapists to work collaboratively with underclass families, rather than as agents of social control, focusing on what the families themselves find useful (Fraenkel, 2006).

Invisible class differences

Family therapists often encounter couples and families with internally divergent class backgrounds who, not recognizing the impact of their class differences, run into contradictions and misunderstandings with each other. Therapists may notice unspoken but clashing expectations when, for instance, a (professional class) doctor's daughter and a (working-class) pipe fitter's daughter raising a family see themselves and each other as middle class. Words with multiple meanings in different class and cultural contexts, such as "responsibility," "support," "independence," or "respect" can get lost in translation, spawning arguments over saving versus spending versus sharing money with relatives, or over how to prioritize children's sports, enrichment classes, chores, family time, and what constitutes good manners. Helping families externalize the effects of class and explore its influence on meanings and expectations can move them from mutual judgment to mutual respect and understanding.

CASE ILLUSTRATION

Sophie and Daniel

We now return to the class-influenced family life cycle trajectories of four newborn babies mentioned at the start of this chapter. Twins Sophie and Daniel were delivered by caesarean section in a Boston teaching hospital after Daniel suffered fetal distress four weeks early. Their parents were Sarah, 39, a German-Jewish American lawyer, and Jeff, 44, a Scots-Irish American advertising executive. Insurance paid all hospital expenses and the couple easily managed their share of the high cost of Sarah's fertility treatments. Jeff's parents contributed to college funds for the twins and Jeff's older son, Max, yearly (see Genogram 4.1).

Twinship and prematurity both have cognitive and medical sequelae. Now four, Daniel has learning, sensory integration, and attentional difficulties, to his high-achieving family's disappointment—problems that might not have been noticed were the family's (and preschool's) expectations not been so high. Early intervention, weekly occupational therapy sessions, and private tutoring on pre-reading skills have helped. Sophie's sensory integration is mild and she learns easily, but her asthma and anxiety often flare on leaving home for preschool or play dates. Their parents, grandparents, and live-in nanny push the children to "live up to their potential like Max," despite their prematurity-related challenges; they get tears and tantrums in return.

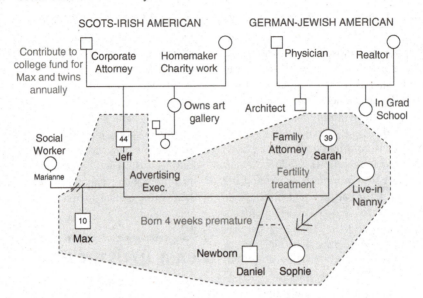

GENOGRAM 4.1 Sophie and Daniel's Genogram

Their private family therapist helps Daniel and his parents cope with his learning difficulties in a community that demands high achievement, while helping to plan for scaffolding to support his learning process when he starts kindergarten at a private school (which is not legally required to offer individualized education plans). He encourages Sophie to find self-soothing strategies—and encourages her family to allow her to develop socially a bit more slowly than her brothers. He encourages Sarah and Jeff to find extracurricular activities that pull for the children's areas of strength and strengthen areas of relative weakness, without overscheduling the twins, a hazard of life in wealthy suburban communities. These children, with every advantage of finances, family attention, schooling, and many paid helpers, are well prepared to manage their entry into elementary school and well beyond, despite their cognitive and medical challenges, without overwhelming their parents financially or emotionally.

CASE ILLUSTRATION

Ta'esha

Ta'esha was born 6 weeks premature, in a Baton Rouge, Louisiana public hospital, a few years after her family's displacement from New Orleans by Hurricane Katrina. Ta'esha's mother, Ronita, then 16, had started bleeding at 7 months and was hospitalized until delivery. In the absence of health insurance, a social worker helped Ronita (who could not reach her family, whose phone was disconnected) apply for much-needed free medical care. Ronita had wanted Ta'esha, whom she thought would always love her best. But holding a wrinkled, intubated, and un-cuddly four-pound preemie in the NICU scared her, and she started hoping her grandmother would take over the baby's care so she could return to school. She never considered adoption or, before that, abortion, as a more privileged girl might (see Genogram 4.2).

Ronita lives on her grandmother's disability insurance, received for her obesity, diabetes, and heart problems; Ronita's youngest brother, Donnell, has cerebral palsy and frequent seizures, uses a wheelchair, and also gets disability. Her mother and older brother, both high school dropouts, are chronically unemployed, like many of the poorest people displaced by Katrina (Henderson, 2009; Parks, 2009). Her father, a day laborer, had been murdered when she was 11.

Ronita had missed 2 years of school after Katrina, and had only been back for a year when she got

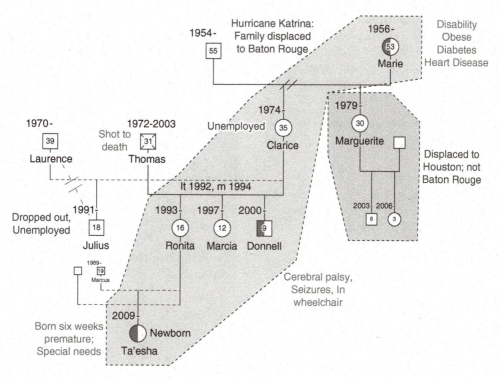

GENOGRAM 4.2 Ta'esha's Genogram

pregnant. The local schools, overwhelmed by thousands of children displaced from New Orleans (Rabina, 2009), had not welcomed more students—and besides, her help with her disabled youngest brother was needed at home. She had liked high school and had hoped to return to graduate, after having the baby. But her grandmother's diabetes worsened, and she was pregnant again, at 17, by a boy heading for trouble, but whose mother was happy to help with a grandchild. School had to take a back seat, and she settled in to taking care of her daughter, her brother, her grandmother, and her unborn baby (now that she had free prenatal care) while her mother looked for work and did her best to back Ronita up around the house.

A NICU nurse was concerned about the lack of family visitors and Ronita's tearful anxiety about having essential skin-to-skin contact with her newborn, fragile daughter. She alerted a hospital social worker, who contacted a visiting nurses' program and a home-based family therapy agency. The family's first therapist, a young and privileged social work

student, was overwhelmed by the challenges this multi-stressed family was facing. She did her best to support them—grandmother's worsening illness and the depression and household responsibilities burdening a teen mother. She worried when Ronita quickly became pregnant again, hoping that *this* baby would be easier to love. The therapist also needed to address the special needs of Donnell and Ta'esha, Clarice and Julius' unemployment, everyone's bereavement, and the perils of a high-crime housing project. She tried to ease the tension among three generations over authority and responsibility for the children, which comes with teen pregnancy—not an easy task for a childless youngest daughter in her mid-20s.

Getting this family early intervention to help Ta'esha develop cognitively and socially became the responsibility of the next intern therapist, as the original therapist had graduated by the time Ta'esha was eligible. A key task of the new therapist, another young, class-privileged White woman, was to appreciate how hard this overburdened family works to stay together and survive in terrible circumstances, rather than pathologizing or judging them (Madsen, 2007). That is essential if she is to help support two babies and Donnell, now a young adolescent, in their development and support Ronita in entering young adulthood as the mother of two and a key caregiver to the family.

CASE ILLUSTRATION

Miguelito

Miguelito was born during his father, Manny's, deployment to Iraq with the Reserves. Sonia, who had arrived from Mexico at the age of 2, gave birth in a community hospital with her sister Elena, who lives out of state, and her mother-in-law, Ana. Manny saw his big, healthy boy delivered, thanks to the Army's video hook-up.

The VA provided Manny only individual health care, so relatives emptied credit cards, Christmas accounts, and equity lines and arranged payment plans to cover Sonia's hospital costs (see Genogram 4.3).

Manny's parents, Puerto Rican migrants, had raised their children on military bases where his father, Miguel, served; fellow army families sustained the family during Miguel's peacetime deployments. Manny joined the Reserves after his father's death, to honor him and for the educational opportunity. As a Reservist, he and Sonia had lived far from a military community. Both their families felt that Sonia should not manage pregnancy and motherhood alone while dealing with Manny's combat deployments and increasingly difficult returns. Manny was more angry

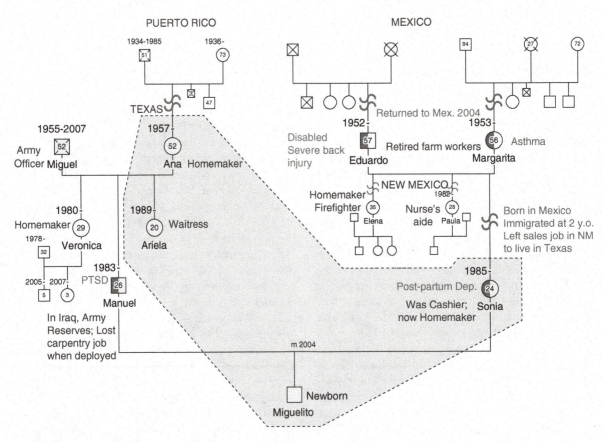

GENOGRAM 4.3 Miguelito's Genogram

and upset after each deployment (Gorbaty, 2008), and both families wanted to support the couple and their new son. Manny lost his carpentry job with this third deployment, so family income was limited. Sonia's parents, disabled former farm workers, were now back in Mexico, eking out a living. Her sisters could not take her in, so Sonia left her sales job in New Mexico to live in Texas with Manny's mother and sister.

Sonia's gynecologist suggested therapy for Sonia after diagnosing postpartum depression. The extended family decided on family therapy, since Ana (depressed since being widowed) and Sonia argued over Miguelito's care and what to tell Manny about Sonia's state of mind on his calls home. They found a bilingual family therapist, the brother of a career military officer, who understood the issues families face with military deployment, reunification, and combat-related stress. A father himself, he knew the challenges related to life with newborns, but not much about postpartum depression, or three-generation households, so he relied on the family's own experience and his supervisor to work constructively with this extended family.

He was seeing the family when Manny returned home with clear signs of heightened PTSD (post-traumatic stress disorder), to a 6-month old and a still-depressed and lonely wife. Family therapy with extended kin focused on integrating Manny back into his mother's household and on helping everyone understand and respond helpfully to Manny's hypervigilance and angry outbursts while ensuring that Sonia, Ana, and Ariela felt empowered to take care of themselves and the baby. A year later, Manuelito was thriving and Sonia's mood had lifted, but Manny was still struggling with PTSD.

> **Assess your comprehension of understanding social class by completing this quiz.**

Social Class and Families with Young Children

The birth of these four newborns shifted their respective families' developmental journeys, rerouting the ongoing, intersecting, multigenerational life courses of parents, siblings, and relatives. Each family's life cycle is shaped by social class location, which in turn influences the particulars of each child's birth, health, and options. That class location is influenced by the age, ethnicity, citizenship, health, and location of family members, and by the effects of disaster and war (which, in turn, affect members of different classes differently), among other factors.

Sophie, Daniel, and Ta'esha were all premature, but had different family life cycle outcomes. Twins, like Sophie and Daniel, are often premature, as are babies born, like Ta'esha, to African Americans, teenagers, smokers, and mothers with little or no prenatal care (Centers for Disease Control and Prevention, 2011), and those exposed to toxins common in inadequate housing. The families of Ta'esha, born into generations of poverty and of the twins, born into plenty, had medical, mental health, housing, and social support of radically different qualities.

The consequences of these differences are great; prematurity and low birth weight are major causes of infant mortality—the harshest family life cycle derailment. Premature infants who survive have high rates of attentional and other learning disabilities and chronic medical difficulties (National Library of Medicine & National Institutes of Health, n.d.). Many preemies who would have died decades ago survive today, but life-long chronic illnesses and learning disabilities can derail their family life cycles as well. The outcomes for prematurity and low birth weight are harshest for poor, young families. Poor, young parents like Ronita are less ready, both developmentally and financially, to care for chronically sick or disabled children, without the resources, information, or quality medical, educational, and psychological help that older affluent parents like Sarah and Jeff rely on to help their premature children thrive.

Ta'esha was born into generations of poor, Black teen mothers. Teen mothers and their families must spend a disproportionate amount of their limited time, energy, and money on their children's health needs; often giving up the very educations and jobs that improve economic circumstances. Furstenberg (2007) reports, however, that teen parenthood itself contributes less to the intergenerational transmission of poverty than does living in poor neighborhoods, without access to resources and information available elsewhere. Poverty and racism had already ravaged Ta'esha's family's neighborhood when Hurricane Katrina destroyed it, leaving schools, health centers, and social service agencies permanently boarded up, scattering neighbors nationwide.

School had to take a back seat for Ronita to taking her grandmother to the emergency room with angina, or attending to her brother's seizure, or caring for the respiratory infections common to preemies and babies in substandard housing. Ta'esha's mother and grandmother do not have enough education to support her thriving in the face of cognitive and medical challenges. Unlike Daniel and Sophie, Ta'esha will not get early intervention or much preventive medical care. Without such intervention, Ta'esha and her young Uncle Donnell may stay sick and do poorly in underperforming schools—until they drop out and start the cycle anew.

Miguelito started life as the healthiest of the newborns, but several factors counter that advantage. His father returned from deployment with an exacerbated PTSD (Gorbaty, 2008), ensuring a steady supply of stress hormones in Miguelito's own system when his father is home. If his father is killed in the next deployment, Sonia, a Mexican citizen, would lose the legal residency provided by 5+ years of marriage to an American citizen and the documentation for a job remunerative enough to support her son.

She and Ana do not have enough English or information to get adequate medical care or social services. His local school is substandard.

Miguelito is an only child, at least for now. Children in Ta'esha's family span 19 years and two generations, including her quasi-sibling mother, adolescent aunt and uncles, toddler Ta'esha, and the coming baby. Three generations of teen mothers' experience of raising children across this age range contrasts sharply with the twins' parents, whose greater privilege and more compressed 10-year span of children mean more manageable developmental needs.

Before antibiotics and modern obstetric and surgical practices, big sibling age ranges were common across classes. Many widowed parents remarried quickly to ensure their children's care and support, joining stepsiblings of varying ages, and children from the new union (Coontz, 1992). Before birth control was widely available, nuclear families also had wide ranges, and still do in some religious groups and in agrarian societies where children's labor is essential to family welfare and child mortality is high. The 14 siblings in my stepchildren's mother's underclass Black and Native American family were 28 years apart (see Genogram 4.4). As in most large families, older siblings cared for younger ones, as one parent could not care for so many children.

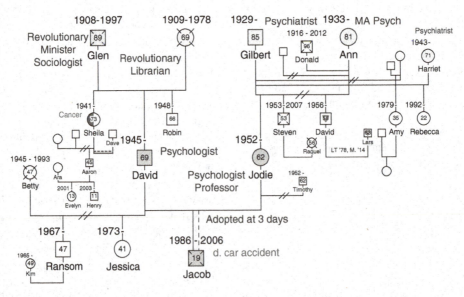

GENOGRAM 4.4 Author's Genogram

The next, mostly high school–educated next generation in her family had much smaller families; she herself had only two children. In the more privileged classes today, big age ranges result from divorce and remarriage more than death. My spouse and I (see Genogram 4.4) adopted our newborn when my older stepchild was nearly 20 and was in college. As great as the developmental and financial challenges were, as mature professionals, we had resources that were unavailable or unknown to Ronita and her mother—a grandmother in her 30s. Our higher income and help from family, friends, and paid sitters made a difference. In our baby's first year, our careers as psychologists allowed both of us to work half-time, which few parents can afford or arrange with employers. In contrast, our son's 22-year-old, divorced, working-class birth mother knew that keeping him, her second child, would mean losing her restaurant job and deep poverty for her family.

Since adoption and reproductive technology are so costly, social class affects whether single, Gay, Lesbian, and/or infertile, would-be parents can even start new generations (now that Gay and Lesbians can adopt and use reproductive technology in some states). Private adoption or non-kin surrogacy risk the development of exploitative relationships, with wealthier adoptive parents supporting and sometimes controlling younger, poorer women who bear them children. Children adopted domestically or internationally grow up in families with more class (and often more racial) privilege than their birth families, adding to identity challenges in adolescence.

> Assess your comprehension of social class and families with young children by completing this quiz.

Social Class and Families with Older Children and Adolescents

Class-specific narratives prevail in families' social networks regarding the rights, responsibilities, and developmental tasks of older children and adolescents. Is adolescence a time to explore one's options and identities, with family financial and emotional support, or to take on financial and domestic responsibility for one's family? Do teens attend college, work, join gangs, volunteer, enter the military, or take time to "find" themselves? In the more privileged classes, older children and teens are generally seen as needing guidance, care, and protection. In contrast, most working-class and underclass teens, and even older children, are often needed to help (or replace) parents with key domestic responsibilities such as Laundromat trips, cooking, childcare, and elder care. Some must navigate social systems for parents who speak little English or are disabled.

If youths in poor communities see few educated adults outside of school with legal, well-paid jobs, can they imagine and work toward a different future for themselves, which might mean leaving the only community they know? Or do they, like Ronita, become parents, hurtling away from education into premature responsibility and a grinding future for themselves and their children? Or do they give up altogether on the future, devaluing their own and others' lives, and entering gangs (Hardy & Laszloffy, 2005)?

Social Class and Families with Late Adolescents and Young Adults

How long do parents and children expect to live together? Do children leave home in their teens or 20s for college, work, military service, marriage, or prison, or do they never go? Do young single mothers with children live with their own parents or on their own? How much contact do they have with their parents? What determines adulthood? Is it the first "real" job, marriage, the first child, or high school graduation? Turning 18? Joining the army? Graduating from college or graduate school? Renting an apartment? Buying a home? Joining a gang?

Dominant U.S. cultural narratives normalize leaving home by the early 20s, although many ethnic groups prize collective family well-being over individual preferences. The more class privilege (and the more generations in the United States) a family has, the more they expect young adults (of any ethnicity) to live apart. Economic necessity requires poorer young people, regardless of ethnicity, to live at home and contribute to the household. Immigrants from developing nations may see teens as fully adult, without demarcating an extended adolescence.

The "American dream" for late adolescents involves leaving home for college. Even though most mental health professionals see higher education as the norm, only 30 percent of adults have bachelor's degrees—and that is a new high. Eighty-seven percent finish high school, though educational levels are lower for older adults and non-English speakers, especially Latinos (U.S. Census Bureau, 2013f). Many working-class youths who dream of college can only attend community college part-time, while working and living at home. One alternative, if dangerous, way for working-class youth to leave home is to join the military, especially in parts of the country with many military bases. Doing so in wartime, however, can prolong dependence on family (or government) because of war-related injuries (especially traumatic brain injuries) or PTSD—or cause early death.

Another dangerous choice is to become involved in gangs and/or in drug, guns, and sex trades—fast money for young men (and some young women) of all races in both urban and exurban communities with few legitimate well-paying jobs. In such communities, there is both more crime and a greater judicial readiness to arrest (sometimes violently), detain, and jail youth for behaviors that would get more youth more privileged by class (and, often, race) a stiff warning and a possible therapy referral. A prep school student who gets into a fight is expelled and gets a fresh start at a new private school; his poor counterpart of color is incarcerated for the same behavior.

The Department of Justice (2006) reports that in 2005, 12 percent of all African American men in their late 20s were incarcerated, as compared to 3.7 percent of Latino young men and only 1.7 percent of their White, non-Hispanic peers. The endemic nature of this violence should not be underestimated—young men who do not expect to survive into their 30s have little reason to rein in impulsive risk taking and violence, especially before their prefrontal cortexes have fully developed the capacity to stop and think through consequences.

Acting on what may or may not be experienced as a choice, in one's class context—to finish high school or beyond, or not; to get the seeming protection of a gang, or not; to have a child while still a child, or not—can have life-long consequences. Many teen parents must drop out of school to support their families. High school dropouts earn a median of about $21,000 a year, while a high school diploma gets half again as much. College graduates earn a median $59,000, while those with professional degrees earn a median $88,000—over four times more than dropouts (U.S. Census Bureau, 2013b). While college accrues high debt for most students, people with bachelors earn $1.3 million more than high school dropouts in a life time and have 4.4 percent unemployment, versus a staggering 18.7 percent for high school dropouts (Fitzgerald, 2012), and higher still for young men of color.

The children of college-educated parents are far more likely to enter and complete college, and do so in 4 years, not only because it is financially possible, but because exposure to cognitively enhancing environments makes it nearly inevitable (Yen, 2013), barring major mental illness or disability. These youth can leave home in name only, benefiting from a prolonged moratorium—time to "find themselves," exploring their options (Law or medicine? Sociology or neuroscience? Art or teaching or teaching art?) while still depending financially on parents, grandparents, or trust funds.

In contrast, underclass and many working-class youth, especially those of color, instead are too often separated from their families by parental incarceration, gangs, juvenile detention, or military service, while their professional-class peers are monitored and guided by parents, teachers, coaches, high school counselors specializing in college counseling, college advisors, and tutors. Wealthy youth may attend boarding schools, joining their families only for holidays and vacations. What are the implications of these differences for family therapists, who may tend to apply their class-informed experiences of their own or their children's adolescence?

What is the effect on the family life cycle when survival into adulthood is so uncertain, as it is in America's poorest zip codes, and in war zones everywhere? Family therapists whose class privilege buffers them against chronic danger must enter full-heartedly into the realities of families whose lives are so precarious, remembering that, "there but for the grace of God go I."

My own son, Jacob, died in a car accident at 19. His death stunned our family, friends, and colleagues.

People said, "It's not natural. Children are supposed to bury their parents; parents don't bury their children." Alas, parents do bury their children and always have, but since the advent of antibiotics and a volunteer military, and in a long hiatus from warfare inside our borders, class-privileged Americans no longer *expect* to lose their children. I certainly did not.

But poor families of color bury their children with heart-breaking regularity in urban neighborhoods best described as war zones, just one mile from my suburban home. Most inner-city Boston teens know at least one murder victim and many survivors and perpetrators of assault; their parents live in dread for them (Lazar, 2008). Families in war zones and disaster zones worldwide lose their young ones daily. And as every parent of color, of any class, knows, their son could easily become the next Trayvon Martin or Michael Brown (the Emmett Tills of our generation), simply because he is walking down the street. This violent rupture in the family life cycle was a shock in my family; it is no less agonizing, but is not a shock when it happens just two miles away, in a community ravaged by street violence.

Not expecting such abbreviated lives, college-bound youth usually delay having children until their late 20s, which avoids financial, childcare, and social challenges. But for poor youth whose neighbors and classmates die young of violence, addiction, preventable illness, or war and who see only their teachers and doctors with college degrees or stable careers, why wait for children? If your parents and other elders had their children young, that is simply, "the way it is."

> Assess your comprehension of social class and families with late adolescents and young adults by completing this quiz.

Social Class and Families with Adults in Mid- and Later Life

How long do people expect to live? How long do they expect parents, siblings, partners, and children to live? How do these expectations influence individual and family life cycles? Whether you expect to live a long life in good health or believe you may not live to see your 50th year will inform life-shaping decisions from early on. Do family members plan to work (or count on their relatives working) until their 60s? Do they foresee a comfortable retirement or scraping by on social security and Medicare? Or do they expect to work until they drop or until disability stops them, like Miguelito's grandfather, and Ta'esha's great-grandmother?

What do middle age and old age even mean, in class context? My father, 85, a psychiatrist, works full time, because he loves it *and* is paying his youngest child's (40 years my junior) college tuition (see Genogram 4.4). This obligation marks his upward mobility from his early childhood in the working class. He could afford to adopt as a grandfather at 62, and had reason to expect to see his youngest into adulthood, after surviving the death of his young grandson and middle-aged son. A downside of this class-specific parental age flexibility is that my sister, at my age, will surely have lost her parents and all her much-older siblings.

My father could choose a renewed parental status at his age because he could afford it and his labor is neither punishing nor life shortening, unlike Miguelito's maternal grandparents, who stooped over strawberries until disabled (see Genogram 4.3). Genes and disposition help too—my working, poor great-grandfather worked until 89, making paper pads in his basement. In contrast, my stepchildren's maternal grandfather, a poor African American/Native American father of 14, died before seeing most of his 40 grandchildren (see Genogram 4.4); my stepchildren's underclass, racially oppressed maternal grandparents led much harder lives than did their White, professional-class grandparents and step-grandparents.

Consider also the different experiences of grandparenthood for newborn Sophie and Dan's robust grandparents (ages 67–70), Miguelito's disabled maternal grandfather and caretaking paternal grandmother (ages 57 and 52), and Ta'esha's grandmother, age 30. What does it mean to be a grandparent at 70 or 30? What does it mean to have grandparents of those ages? Ta'esha's *great* grandmother, disabled at only 53 (see Genogram 4.2), is close in age to Sophie and Daniel's grandparents, while I, at 62, have no grandchildren. If infirmity can come in the 50s, having children young allows you to raise grandchildren while still vigorous (Stack & Burton, 1993), with older children filling in when your own energies flag.

An 80-year-old wealthy widow needing full-time nursing care can pay for home health aides or a lovely assisted living residence; her children comfortably delegate her care to staff. Her working-class counterpart enters an understaffed Medicare-funded nursing home, leaving her unemployed daughter and grandson, who had moved into her subsidized senior housing unit after fleeing domestic violence, homeless and unable to monitor her mediocre care. Ta'esha's underclass adolescent mother cares for her 50-something great-grandmother, among others.

As people live longer, elders increasingly serve as regular caretakers to grandchildren, ailing spouses and siblings, their own old parents, and/or ailing late middle-age children, sometimes simultaneously. Privileged families, whose members live longer, can meet this responsibility by coordinating paid help for loved ones. Working-class families, especially women, do the hard work of caretaking themselves, often at the expense to health and income.

Affluent families can afford to plan on getting old; their home equity, retirement plans, disability insurance, life, health, and long-term care insurance policies ensure that they and their loved ones will be well cared for. Less affluent families try to do at least some of the same, but often find they are already old and that growing housing, health care, childcare, and college costs and anemic pensions have eroded their hopes for a "good" retirement.

In contrast, Americans in the underclass, without any economic cushion, spend more than they earn, leaving little or nothing for old age. Many undocumented immigrant workers spend every extra penny on remittances to their families back home so their children and aging parents have enough to eat. These workers have often watched their elders die young and poor. Without the luxury to plan ahead, they work to the point of disabling injuries or chronic illness. Finally, in some violent urban neighborhoods, poor and working-class elders (and previously "middle-class" elders living in downwardly mobile communities and homes) may not see all their children or grandchildren, let alone retirement age (Stack & Burton, 1993).

Poorer, less educated people have shorter life spans. Access to health information, healthy food, safe exercise, and regular medical care correlates with neighborhoods' median income; thus, the poor are beset by high rates of chronic illnesses, some relating to factors like obesity and smoking. Poorer families are more vulnerable to work-related injuries, pollution, violence, and the damaging health consequences of worry about violence to self and family (Lazar, 2008). Even when medical care is available, significant health care delivery and outcome disparities exist based on income and education.

> **Assess your comprehension of social class and families with adults in mid- and later life by completing this quiz.**

— Conclusion: Implications for Family Therapy —————

The family life cycle of family therapists, like those of their client families, are shaped by class history and current class position. Their social locations influence their cultural narratives about a "healthy" family life cycle and about their clients. Lisa, a middle-aged family therapist and mother of two, was the first to attend college in her family. She works with a college student, Julia; her father, Will, a cardiologist; and her mother, Becca, a homemaker and volunteer. Will is

upset at Julia's "entitlement" and at Becca's enabling Julia's "profligate" spending.

Lisa finds herself siding with Will without knowing why until, exploring the family's class history, she finds that like her, Will had grown up financially struggling and put himself through college. He wants to spare his daughter his struggles, but also wants her to be grateful and wise with money. Becca takes comfort for granted. Had Lisa grown up privileged like Becca, especially if she were younger or childless, she might have seen Will as withholding and judgmental. That is, unless she explored his family class history and compared it to her own.

Of course, family therapists do best when they avoid judging or taking sides—this can be done by attending to how their assumptions about family life are informed by their own class and other social experiences, and attending to those of their client families (Kliman, 2005, 2010; McGoldrick & Hardy, 2008). This attention is especially important when clinicians are more class privileged than their client families. It is easy to pathologize class-bound life decisions and their impact on the family life cycle when therapists know nothing of the constricting realities of class oppression, or of the invisible benefits their own class privilege has bestowed on them.

> **Recall what you learned in this chapter by completing the Chapter Review.**

References

Burton, L., & Cherlin, A. (2009). "Trust is like Jell-o": Forms of trust in low-income mothers' romantic unions. *NCFR Reports: Family Focus on Poverty, 44.* Retrieved from https://orchid.hosts.jhmi.edu/wfp/files/09-11%20Trust%20is%20like%20Jell-O.pdf

Centers for Disease Control and Prevention. (2011). *Morbidity and mortality weekly report: Supplement, 60* (January 14). Retrieved from http://www.cdc.gov/mmwr/preview/ind2011_su.html

Contreras, P. M., & Bryant-Davis, T. (2012). *The psychology of modern-day slavery* (Film and discussion booklet). Washington, DC: Division 35, The American Psychological Association.

Coontz, S. (2000). *The way we never were: American families and the nostalgia trap.* New York: Basic Books.

Dunn, A. (2012, March 21). Average America vs. the one percent. *Forbes: Money Wise Women.* Retrieved from http://www.forbes.com/sites/moneywisewomen/2012/03/21/average-america-vs-the-one-percent/

Ehrenreich, B. (1989). *Fear of falling: The inner life of the middle class.* New York: Harper Collins.

Ehrenreich, B. (2009). *This land is their land: Reports from a divided nation.* New York: Henry Holt.

Falicov, C. (2005). Emotional transnationalism and family identities. *Family Process, 44*(4), 399–406.

Fitzgerald, J. (2013). College degree is costly, but it pays off over time. *Boston Globe,* (October 7). Retrieved from http://www.bostonglobe.com/business/2012/10/06/investment-higher-still-pays-today-economy/GV7iVC5847KP7g6zUvziEM/story.html

Fraenkel, P. (2006). Engaging families as experts: Collaborative family program development. *Family Process, 45*(2), 237–257.

Framingham Heart Study Press Releases. (2008). Smokers quit together and flock together: Social networks exert key influences on decisions to quit smoking. (May 21, 2008). Retrieved from http://www.framinghamheartstudy.org/participants/pr/08_0521.html

Furstenberg, F. (2007). *Destinies of the disadvantaged: The politics of teen childbearing.* New York: Russell Sage Foundation.

Gorbaty, L. (2008). *Family reintegration of reserve service members following a wartime deployment: A qualitative exploration of wives' experience.* Unpublished doctoral dissertation. Boston, MA: The Massachusetts School of Professional Psychology.

Greenstone, M., Looney, A., Patashnik, J., & Yu, M. (2013). Thirteen economic facts about social mobility and the role of education. Brookings Institute. Retrieved from http://www.brookings.edu/research/reports/2013/06/13-facts-higher-education

Hardy, K. V., & Laszloffy, T. (2005). *Teens who hurt: Clinical interventions to break the cycle of adolescent violence.* New York: Guilford Press.

Henderson, L. (2009). *Religious coping and subjective wellbeing: African Americans' experiences of surviving Hurricane Katrina.* Unpublished doctoral dissertation. Boston: The Massachusetts School of Professional Psychology.

Kliman, J. (Winter, 2010). Intersections of Social Privilege and Marginalization: A Visual Teaching Tool. *Expanding our social justice practices: Advances in theory and training* [special issue]. *AFTA Monograph Series: A Publication of the American Family Therapy Academy,* 39–48

Kliman, J. (2005). Many differences, many voices. In M. P. Mirkin, K. L. Suyemoto & B. F. Okun (Eds.) *Psychotherapy with women: Exploring diverse contexts and identities.* (pp. 42–63). New York: Guilford Press.

Kliman, J. (1998). Social class as a relationship: Implications for family therapy. In M. Mc-Goldrick (Ed.). *Revisioning family therapy: Race, culture, and gender in clinical practice.* (pp. 50–61). New York: Guilford Press.

Kliman, J., & Madsen, W. (2005) Social class and the family life cycle. In B. Carter & M. McGoldrick (Eds.). *The expanded family life cycle: Individual, family, and social perspectives* (3rd edition). (pp. 88–123). Boston, MA: Allyn & Bacon.

Lazar. (2008). Concern over safety soaring in Hub area: Study finds link between health, fear of violence. *The Boston Globe, Nov. 13, 2008).* Retrieved from http://www.boston.com/news/local/massachusetts/articles/2008/11/13/concern_over_safety_soaring_in_hub_area/?page=ful

Lemare, J. (2012). Latino life expectancy: Exploring the Hispanic paradox. *Hispanic Link News Service (News America Media),* (December 2). Retrieved from http://newamericamedia.org/2012/12/latino-life-expectancy-exploring-the-hispanic-paradox.php

Madsen, W. (2007). *Collaborative therapy with multi-stressed families* (2nd edn). New York: Guilford.

McGoldrick, M., & Hardy, K. V. (2008). *Re-visioning family therapy: Race, culture, and gender in clinical practice.* (2nd edn). New York: Guilford Press.

Institute of Medicine. (2007). Mortality and acute complications in preterm infants. Retrieved from http://www.ncbi.nlm.nih.gov/books/NBK11385/

National Library of Medicine and National Institutes of Health. (n.d.). *Medline Plus: Medical encyclopedia.* Retrieved from http://www.nlm.nih.gov/medlineplus/ency/article/001562.html

Parks, M. (2009). *Authentic happiness and religious coping for displaced African Americans three years after Hurricane Katrina.* Unpublished doctoral dissertation. Boston, MA: The Massachusetts School of Professional Psychology.

Rabina, T. (2009). *Disaster relief workers: Growth and meaning making after Hurricane Katrina.* Unpublished doctoral dissertation. Boston: The Massachusetts School of Professional Psychology.

Stack, C. &, Burton, L. (1993). Kinscripts. *Journal of Comparative Family Studies, 24* (2), 157–170.

United States Bureau of Labor Statistics. (2013). Earnings and unemployment rates by educational attainment. Retrieved from http://www.bls.gov/emp/ep_chart_001.htm

United States Bureau of Labor Statistics. (2010). Report 1025: Highlights of women's earnings in 2009. Retrieved from http://www.bls.gov/cps/cpswom2009.pdf

United States Census. (2012). Newsroom. Income, poverty and health insurance coverage in the United States: 2011. Retrieved from http://www.census.gov/newsroom/releases/archives/income_wealth/cb12-172.html#tablea.

United States Census Bureau. (2013a). Table 4. Poverty status of families, by type of family, presence of related children, race, and Hispanic origin. Retrieved from http://www.census.gov/hhes/www/poverty/data/historical/families.html

United States Census Bureau. (2013b). Table A-3. Mean earnings of workers 18 and over, by educational attainment, race, Hispanic origin, and sex: 1975-2011. Retrieved from http://www.census.gov/hhes/socdemo/education/data/cps/historical/index.html

United States Census Bureau. (2013c). Table P-2. Race and Hispanic origin of people by median income and sex: 1947 to 2011. Retrieved from http://www.census.gov/hhes/www/income/data/historical/people/

United States Census Bureau. (2013d). Table P-6. Regions of people by mean income and sex: 1967 to 2011. Retrieved from http://www.census.gov/hhes/www/income/data/historical/people/

United States Census Bureau (2013e). Table P-16. Educational attainment—People 25 and over by median income and sex: 1991-2011. Retrieved from http://www.census.gov/hhes/www/income/data/historical/people/

United States Census Bureau (2013f). 2012 *Statistical Abstract,* Table 229. Educational attainment by race and Hispanic origin. Retrieved from http://www.census.gov/compendia/statab/cats/education.html

United States Department of Health and Human Services/ Agency for Healthcare Research and Quality. (2007). *National healthcare disparities report.* Rockville, MD: Author. Retrieved from http://www.ahrq.gov/qual/nhdr07/nhdr07.pdf

United States Department of Justice-Bureau of Justice Statistics. (2006). Prison and jail inmates midyear 2005. Retrieved from http://www.ojp.usdoj.gov/bjs/abstract/pjim05.htm

White, M. (2007). *Maps of narrative practice.* New York: Norton.

Yen, H. (2013). Economic data show widening future struggle for Americans: 4 out of 5 have had problems. *Boston Globe* (July 29). Retrieved from http://www.bostonglobe.com/news/nation/2013/07/28/more-americans-see-economic-security-decline/naSHKupIkKBlV5k7qq6j3H/story.html

Chapter 5

The Life Cycle of Economically Fragile Families

Paulette Moore Hines

Learning Outcomes

- List and describe variables which impact the wellbeing of multistressed families throughout the family life cycle.
- Describe the effects poverty has on the family life cycle.
- Explain the developmental challenges faced by adolescents and emerging adults who are living in poverty.
- Identify effective intervention strategies for adolescents and emerging adults who are living in poverty.
- List and describe the challenges faced by couples that live within the context of poverty.
- Describe strategies for supporting parents and other caretakers in multistressed families.
- Identify the stressors that are unique to multistressed families in later life.
- Discuss treatment strategies for supporting families living in poverty during late life stages.
- List and describe the assessment and treatment tasks that therapists have when helping multistressed families.
- Describe strategies that therapists can use to avoid burnout when working with families who live in poverty.

Introduction

Poverty in the United States is usually defined in three different ways: the official census way, which uses a set of income thresholds that vary depending on family size and composition; an income-based method that factors in services that are available to families and children in need; and the third is a measure of what households actually spend (Edsall, 2013). Part of the problem in understanding poverty and its effects on families throughout life is that there is no single definition. In 2012, the U.S. Census found that more than 16 percent of the population in the United States lived in poverty, including about 22 percent of all children (U.S. Census, 2012). During the last decade, young families have been the most affected by high unemployment, loss of income, and increasing health costs. The normal developmental stress that families experience as they transition through the different phases of the life cycle will be exponentially complicated when poverty affects their lives.

These vulnerable families are diverse in race, ethnicity, education, work status, residence (i.e., metropolitan, rural, suburban, concentration of poverty), marital status, household composition, immigrant status, country of origin, and citizenship. They vary in coping styles, resilience, and other protective factors. Some live in single-family units; others share households with members of their kin network, friends, or others, and more than one third (36 percent) of families living below the poverty threshold with children are estimated to be homeless (National Center on Homelessness & Poverty, 2013). Some are downwardly mobile; others are slowly improving their economic status. For some, poverty is temporary, and others have struggled with poverty for multiple generations.

We use the terms "families living in poverty," "economically fragile families," and "multistressed families" (Madsen, 2013) interchangeably in this chapter. These families are challenged not only financially. Families living in poverty encounter innumerable, external barriers to "pulling themselves up by their bootstraps." Their efforts to move up the economic ladder are continually thwarted by the pernicious and pervasive effects of poverty and classism.

The media and professional literature construct and reinforce a negative identity and perpetuate the inaccurate notion that the poor are a homogenous population, doomed to be dysfunctional. The popular discourse is that these families are lazy, irresponsible, immoral, ignorant, and inadequate. This negative characterization leaves therapists vulnerable to blaming families living in poverty for their predicament, sometimes unaware of our classist assumptions, and apt to overlook the fact that living with an inadequate income will stretch the reserves of any family. Although contextual factors render low-income families vulnerable to adverse outcomes, being "poor" simply does not dictate family functioning. In fact, numerous factors mediate the effects of adverse economic, environmental, and social conditions on family outcomes. Relevant mediating factors include the number of generations families have been embedded in poverty; the level of a family's connection with their larger family systems, acculturation, legal status in this country, spirituality, religiosity, and the extent to which family members avoid self-defeating responses to opression (Escobar, Nervi, & Gara, 2000).

Over recent decades, a growing number of family theorists, researchers, and practitioners have countered deficit-focused perspectives about families living in poverty and have brought much-needed attention to their strengths. These include Akinyela (2008), Aponte (1994), Billingsley (1992), Boyd-Franklin (2003), Burton (1995, 1996a, 1996b), Hardy and Laszloffy (2008), Robert Hill (1999), Hines and Boyd-Franklin (2005), Hines (2008), McAdoo (2007), and Pinderhughes (1989). The common thread across this expanding body of work is that the lives of individuals living in ongoing, oppressive circumstances can best be understood and supported within a framework that acknowledges the far-reaching interactive effects of classism, racism, social, economic, and political disenfranchisement, and the residuals of these (e.g., internalized racism).

There are innumerous examples of economically challenged individuals and families from whom we can learn much about resilience. It is essential for therapists to focus on their resourcefulness and ability to survive and even thrive under oppressive circumstances throughout the history of this country. It is a true testament to the resilience of the human spirit that despite being born into the context of economic poverty and, for some, racism and cultural discrimination, countless uncelebrated individuals manage to keep their families healthy, safe, fed, housed, and go on to make significant gains in education, economics, politics, and many other arenas. Many others struggle economically throughout life, but are still distinguished by a defiant spirit of hope, an exceptional capacity for problem solving, and a commitment to transcending the odds (Hines, 2008).

Our purpose in this chapter is to dispel the notion that family therapy is a futile endeavor with families living in economic poverty, and to reinforce the value of working from a multicontextual life cycle framework that situates families within their cultural and life cycle context and links them with the rich resources and strengths of their heritage.

> **Assess your comprehension of the introduction by completing this quiz.**

Factors Affecting Economically Fragile Families Throughout the Life Cycle

Despite the racial and cultural diversity among poor families in this country, it is safe to say that they all face numerous barriers to transcending the oppressive circumstances under which they live every day of their lives. The specific stressors and level of anxiety generated by the demand for changes in family structure and relationships that families encounter at different stages in their life cycle might vary, but their marginal and precarious economic position puts them at higher risk for negative physical, emotional, and relational outcomes. Clearly, it is imperative to help families secure the resources critical to their health, safety, and basic well-being. As family therapists, our challenge is to resist blaming those who we easily label as resistant, apathetic, or inadequate and to foster hope and healing. Our call is to help families refuse the pulls to sabotage themselves, to strive to become their best no matter how tough and disappointing life may be, to pick themselves up when life knocks them down, and to actively take control of what is within their ability.

To be effective agents of hope and healing, therapists must expand the lens through which we understand the realities of living below the poverty threshold and translate our understanding into policies and practices that help rather than further wound those we seek to help. The following is a brief overview of several contextual variables which impact the well-being of multistressed families throughout the family life cycle and, therefore, must be factored into our efforts to engage, assess, and intervene with this population.

Racial/Cultural discrimination

Families struggling with poverty are a culturally diverse population of which the largest groups are non-Hispanic Whites. However, individuals from marginalized groups, because of race and ethnicity, are disproportionately represented among those living below the poverty threshold. In 2011, American Indians, Alaskan Natives, and Blacks or African Americans had a roughly equivalent national poverty rate of 28 percent (U.S. Census Bureau, 2012). Among Hispanics, the national poverty rate was just over 25 percent with variations based on country of origin. In contrast, the 2007–2011 national poverty rate for Whites was almost 10 percent (DeNavas-Walt, Proctor, & Smith, 2012). Racial differences persist even when education is held constant; Blacks are poorer than non-Hispanic Whites even when they have a high school or college degree (Simms, Fortuny, & Henderson, 2009). They must contend daily with institutionalized policies and practices that disconnect, invalidate, and crush their dreams.

Female-headed households

Families with children headed by single women are particularly vulnerable to poverty. The number of out-of-wedlock births in the United States has climbed to an all-time high regardless of race or ethnicity; however, the rate is highest among African Americans. In 2011, about 31 percent of single female-headed families were living in poverty, and their children were more than four times as likely to be living in poverty as children living in married couple families (DeNavas-Walt, Proctor, & Smith, 2012). Given a societal shift toward increasingly complex living arrangements, researchers have begun to distinguish between household composition and family structure. Using census data for 2000, Snyder, McLaughlin, and Findeis (2006) explored differences in poverty for four different cohorts: Women who have never been married, women who have separated or divorced, women who are cohabitating with partners, and a growing number of unmarried grandmothers. They found that the presence of multiple wage earners, including cohabitants, increased earnings and prevented families from falling below the poverty threshold.

High unemployment/underemployment

Counter to popular assumption, about 7 percent of workers aged 18 to 64 were living in poverty in 2011 (DeNavas-Walt, Proctor, & Smith, 2012). Even so, there is a gap between the income they earn and what is required for self-sufficiency (Simms, Fortuny, & Henderson, 2009). Technology changes have impacted the labor market and there are not enough jobs available even for the college educated. Workers with the least education and experience are most vulnerable to unemployment and underemployment, and are likely to lose job earnings at a time when their kin networks are also hard hit by rising costs and cuts in state and federal government assistance (U.S. Census Bureau, 2012). In 2010, poverty among the unemployed was more than twice the rate of those with employment (Nichols & Callan, 2013). Again, variations across gender and ethnic/racial groups are notable. In 2011, the unemployment rate was about 16 percent for African Americans, 12 percent for Hispanics, and 15 percent for Native American Indian and Alaska Natives compared to 7 percent for non-Hispanic Whites and 7 percent for Asians (Bureau of Labor Statistics, 2013). Some estimate that unemployment in some large inner cities is an appalling 40 to 50 percent for Black and Latino males. The picture is equally bleak for many of the estimated 11.5 million unauthorized immigrants living in the United States who fall within the childbearing range (Hoefer, Rytina, & Baker, 2011).

Some essentially drop out of the labor market out of frustration and hopelessness about finding employment or because they lack the means to negotiate work with child care, transportation, poor health, ill family members, and other barriers to working. They must also contend with the assumptions others make that they devalue work, are lazy, and have no ambition.

Reflective of how external stressors can impact at an individual level, there is strong evidence that once work disappears from a community and people grow up without even the hope of working, drug use and crime intensify dramatically, and the disorganization of the social community becomes overwhelming.

Uncertainty

Unrelenting stress is normative in low-income families and the potential exists for distress that can impact the quality of individual functioning and couple/family relationships. Their capacity to work around obstacles and to be hopeful about life is stretched continuously. It is tough to manage food, housing, health care, child care, heating, transportation, and other basic needs on their household budgets. They are unlikely to have savings and are very likely to have limited access to credit to manage unexpected expenditures. Ordinary problems—such as a dead car battery or a sick child—can easily become crises because of a lack of resources to solve them. When they borrow money, they are saddled with very high interest rates that impact their future resources. Credit ratings are affected by one's history of paying bills on time; the ability to pay is based on having an adequate income and eligibility for employment is negatively affected by poor credit ratings. When poor family members do have jobs, they are too often low level, part time, short term, and low paying. It is not uncommon for families to move one or more times a year, often meaning that children live in many different family constellations. A high rate of relocation and high rates of crime, particularly in urban neighborhoods, can hamper social connectedness, activity outside the house, and a sense of community. Neighbors may not know one another and, in these instances, lack the benefit of long-term and trusting relationships and the social support that might otherwise be afforded.

Persistent stress adversely affects their physical as well as spiritual and emotional health (Williams, Neighbors, & Jackson, 2003). Recent research suggests that adverse childhood experiences can have a deleterious impact into late adulthood (Nurius, Logan-Greene, & Green, 2012; Butterworth, Cherbuin, Sachdev, & Anstey, 2012) and that perceived injustice, not just exposure, is key to negative outcomes (Negi, 2013).

Toxic environments

Those who are economically poor are also usually politically disenfranchised. For far too many, the places where they live, work, attend school, and play are far from health enhancing. They are the most likely to work in conditions that are not regulated and potentially hazardous to health. Some live in environments that are blighted and that have inadequate green and open space. Too often, safe and affordable recreational resources are lacking. Housing is likely to be situated near known health threats (e.g., electrical stations) and they may live in or near high-crime areas. They are more likely than their middle-class counterparts to encounter community violence and a high volume of noise. Their children are disproportionately represented among those who attend schools that are inadequately resourced and low performing. Some live in communities that are densely populated by other low-income families; others live in higher income communities that are unwelcoming because of their addresses or low-income status. The message associated with any of these circumstances alone or in varying combinations is one of societal devaluation.

Ongoing trauma exposure, disruptions in attachments, and untimely losses

Frequently embedded in extended family networks, members of multistressed families are prone to experience multiple disruptions in emotional attachments and shifts in household composition throughout their life cycle. These complex, unresolved losses occur as a result of job loss, illness, separation or divorce, death, imprisonment, alcohol and drug addiction, child abuse, domestic violence, and the spiraling effects of these circumstances. The associated trauma is often given inadequate if any attention, thereby increasing the potential for reverberations across a lifetime and often multiple generations.

Reliance on institutional supports

An analysis of 2004 indicates that approximately 22 percent of mothers of childbearing age (15 to 44) in the United States participated in one or more government assistance programs (DeNavas-Walt, Proctor, & Smith, 2012). Many survive only because of the help they receive from their family, friends, churches, and community-based organizations when crises arise. Having to depend on government resources to meet basic needs means complying with numerous regulations, and facing continuous threats of cuts to resources which barely allow them to survive. At the same time, coping with stigma and demeaning treatment can push an already stressed system over the edge.

> Assess your comprehension of factors affecting economically fragile families throughout the life cycle by completing this quiz.

The Condensed Family Life Cycle: Assessment and Treatment

While there are variations based on ethnicity, race, and other factors, progression through the life cycle phases is generally more accelerated for those living in poverty than for their working- and middle-class counterparts. Individuals tend to have children and become grandparents at far earlier ages than their higher income counterparts (Burton, 1996a). When families have a condensed, overlapping intergenerational structure, family roles are chronologically and developmentally out of sync (Burton, 1996b). For example, the adolescent mother, by giving birth, is launched into young adult status (parenthood), and her young adult mother becomes a grandmother, often being forced to assume the responsibilities of surrogate parent. The potential for role overload in such life cycle patterns is tremendous. The abrupt assumption of new roles and responsibilities often means that individuals have inadequate time to resolve their developmental tasks. Facing so many

pressures, adults may be overwhelmed, inconsistent, or too busy to be responsive to individual needs, whether theirs or their children's. Outcomes depend on the extent to which transitions are anticipated, the level of support available from extended family, and the extent to which the development of caretakers is stalled (Burton, 1996a, 1996b).

Given the likelihood of an accelerated progression through the life cycle, low-income families can be described as spanning three basic life cycle stages. These stages usually overlap when family members are part of a multigenerational, extended family system. Economic challenge and its spiraling tentacles also influence family structure, household composition, role definitions, and the developmental tasks that family members face as they move through each phase. Thus, we highlight the developmental challenges at each stage and offer some key assessment and intervention considerations.

Stage 1: Adolescence and emerging adulthood

At every life cycle phase, families need to provide family members with a balance of independence and connection that will promote their success. Financial limitations, family obligations, and other realities of poverty exacerbate the general vulnerabilities of adolescence and young adulthood, and achieving this balance can be especially difficult for members of multistressed families to work out. In addition to the ordinary tasks of adolescence, teens have the added burden of developing a sense of efficacy in the face of persistent negativity about "youth culture" and class-related bias. Youth of color are in triple jeopardy; they face racism, classism, and prejudice because of their youth and inexperience. Their environment is full of minefields, and there is little room for error; actions such as dropping out of school or being argumentative when stopped by the police may have lifelong consequences.

The schism between societal expectations and the barriers to fulfilling these prescriptions puts these youths and young adults at high risk for depression, anxiety, physical problems, rage, and a host of other problems. Youth who are Gay, Lesbian, Bisexual, Transgendered, or Queer are at even higher risk for mental health problems and homelessness, as they also face bias and stress because of homophobia. While yearning for independence, acknowledgment, and respect, some youths from low-income families learn to protect themselves emotionally by tuning out the rules of the dominant society that devalues and excludes them and projecting an external demeanor that masks the disappointment, hopelessness, and helplessness that flow from their economic, racial, gender, and age-based oppression (Franklin, 2004). Staying connected with their dreams and not compromising their priorities require extreme determination.

It is challenging for parents to help their children approach school and the world of work with optimism. Indicative of this fact, teens with family incomes below $20,000 were two and half times as likely to be disconnected from the job market and education as those with family incomes of at least $100,000; young adults in the more disadvantaged family income group were three times as likely to be disconnected (Casey Foundation, 2012).

Far too many youths from low-income families graduate from schools that leave them ill prepared to compete in society. In a recent study, researchers found that of those who had lived in poverty for at least a year, 22 percent did not graduate, compared with only 6 percent of those who had never been poor (Casey Foundation, 2012). Further, a high school degree now carries little guarantee that a person will find work, and training beyond high school costs money that youths too often do not have and lack adequate guidance to pursue.

Even more than their elders, young adults need the skills to operate in a bicultural school and work context. Young adults of color encounter far more subtle racism than their parents and grandparents experienced growing up. Parents of color have the complex task of teaching their children to cope with racism without over-focusing or under-focusing on the issue, a challenge at any life cycle phase, but especially so at this time when regardless of the situation rebelliousness and the value teens place on the opinions of their peers interfere with their receptiveness to learning from their parents.

Pregnancy and related sexually transmitted diseases are usually high on parents/caretakers' worry list, especially for their adolescent daughters. For sons, parents fear for their safety and lives, knowing

that authorities in lower income communities are more quickly to arrest them for minor offenses, book, remand them for trials, and give them harsh dispositions (Bishop, 2005). Their neighborhoods are too often drug and crime ridden, and there are constant pulls to engage in illegal activity.

Many low-income young adults live in their parents' households, with extended family or friends, whatever inner and/or interpersonal conflict this living arrangement entails. Still, their income often remains inadequate. In 2011, for example, young adults, age 25 to 34 who lived with their parents, had an official poverty rate of 9 percent based on family income, but almost 44 percent had an income below the poverty threshold for a single person under age 65 (U.S. Census Bureau, September 12, 2012). Some youths try to fend for themselves in spite of their difficulties making financial ends meet; others get married and/or have children with the assumption that this new status will force others to acknowledge them as adults.

The best protection is having parents/caretakers and mentors, who help them anticipate and negotiate the harsh realities of their world, convey clear principles for living, maintain high expectations, monitor the youths' activities without being overprotective, and also hold them accountable for their choices, however limited.

KEY ASSESSMENT AND INTERVENTION CONSIDERATIONS. Therapists often need to conduct both separate and joint sessions with parents and youths to help them sort out their beliefs, feelings, and concerns. Therapists should assess whether there is a need to coach parents and caretakers to (1) communicate clear, specific conduct guidelines to their children; (2) acknowledge situations that are unfair and perhaps even oppressive; and (3) hold youths accountable to themselves, their families, and their community for whether they choose to use constructive or destructive strategies to cope with adversity.

Given the time and energy that are dedicated to surviving each day, we should not underestimate the value of simply creating a forum where family members allow each other to have a voice. Therapists must be able to sift through family members' expression of their pain, disillusionment, and rage while reminding them of the values they hold, which sometimes may not be reflected in the choices they are making daily. With clear sensitivity to the level of pathologizing that families living in poverty experience, therapists must also be willing to label destructive behaviors, even while acknowledging their positive intent. It may be useful to facilitate discussion between parents and adolescents about differences in the challenges that they have faced. Getting adults to tell relevant stories is an excellent strategy for (re)connecting everyone with the legacies that can serve as road maps for coping with current struggles. For recent immigrant groups helping them talk about their country of origin, and connecting with the strengths in their family stories of immigration, helps adolescents and young adults feel less disconnected from their support networks.

Parents may become immobilized in their ability to set limits on their children out of frustration or hopelessness about their children's chances of finding a meaningful place in society. Therapists can be of great help in getting parents and other caretakers to come up with a clear position or to at least avoid sabotaging each other in setting limits. Anxieties need to be channeled into activities that do not exacerbate the youth's inclination to invalidate parental feedback. Respected older male relatives and community members may be brought in to help young men reexamine their definitions of manhood and free themselves of the limitations that their peers and larger society may impose. The viewing of popular movie segments can serve as a powerful stimulus for conversations about courage and conduct and help family members make emotional as well as cognitive shifts that are critical to their well-being.

It is critical for the executives in families to impress on their adolescents the necessity of having a plan of action to achieve their dreams. Therapists should not assume that parents or adolescents possess the toolbox of life and social/emotional skills needed to negotiate the demands of life or the confidence to apply them.

Stage 2: Coupling and raising young children

Couples who live within the context of poverty face the challenge of developing and sustaining intimate relationships, realigning relationships with extended families, raising children, and negotiating multiple and sometimes conflicting demands with little or no respite from the stress of managing life with inadequate resources.

SUSTAINING INTIMATE RELATIONSHIPS. Even though adults living below the poverty line are generally aware of the social inequities affecting their ability to earn adequate and consistent income, the media provides a constant inducement for couples to idealize marriage and compare their lives and relationships to those whose resources are dramatically better than their own (Burton & Tucker, 2009).

The declining rates of marriage and the trend toward parenthood outside of marriage reflect not a cultural devaluation of marriage (Staples, 2007), but rather an adaptation to circumstances that limit the appraisal by both women and men that they and their families will fare better financially if married. The opportunity to generate adequate earnings is basic to the ability of adults to fulfill personal, familial, and societal expectations as intimate partners, parents, and family members who are concerned with the welfare of elderly relatives and young children. The growing number of households headed by single adults (largely women) and the increase in households with cohabiting adults over the last decade signal that even when low-income women retain high expectations of marriage and have a lack of trust that they can depend on their partners to fulfill their societal prescription as providers, they do not necessarily opt out of intimate relationships, and most still prefer to become mothers. In this context and, increasingly in the larger society, couples face the challenge of negotiating alternatives to traditional role definitions and relational scripts that work to the satisfaction of both partners (Burton, Cherlin, Winn, Estacion, & Holder-Taylor, 2009; Burton & Tucker, 2009; Eyre, Flythe, Hoffman, & Fraser, 2012).

TAKING ON PARENTAL ROLES. Birth rates for U.S. teens, aged 15 to 19, fell in 2011 to a record low of 31 per 1,000 women in this age group (Hamilton, Martin, & Ventura, 2011). However, when sexual involvement leads to pregnancy, young women frequently reject abortion and adoption, choosing to have and keep their babies. Particularly if their education is interrupted, their role can become constricted to that of caretaker. If they attempt to enter the job market, child care and transportation costs can be prohibitive. Their children are at high risk for growing up in poverty. Many are forced to obtain public assistance to ensure housing, food, and medical benefits (Dye, 2008; Kim, Shelley, & Loveless, 2012).

The role of young fathers with children born outside of marriage is often vaguely defined (Paschal, 2006). If they still identify with their adolescent peer group, they may be slow to accept shared responsibility for their children. They also may be reluctant to commit to a relationship with their children and their mothers when they have no way to meet their financial obligations. Mothers may consciously or unwittingly restrict fathers' involvement to protect their children from the possibility of broken promises. This protective stance is sometimes based on a narrative that is driven by unresolved issues with their own fathers. In time, children may expect their fathers' absence or limited involvement, though the disconnect can be a source of pain.

Parents of any age can easily become overburdened with too many responsibilities and too few resources and emotional reserves (Barnet, Liu, & DeVoe, 2008). Frequently, children are close in age, and it is not uncommon for children to span the range from infancy through adolescence. Older children may take on responsibility for helping to reduce the parental load, helping with child or elder care, household maintenance, or working to contribute to the family's meager cash resources. Parents tend to be authoritarian and use physical punishment to ensure that children quickly learn and abide by lessons that are intended to protect them from dangers in their harsh surroundings.

REALIGNING RELATIONSHIPS WITH EXTENDED FAMILY. The birth of children hastens couples' need to integrate new partners and often children from prior relationships as well as disabled, elderly or other dependent relatives into their extended-family networks. Household sharing, which according to the U.S. Census (2012) occurs in about 18 percent of all households regardless of income, is not unusual among lower income families. Sometimes households include relatives of one or both partners as well as non-family members, creating the challenge of fitting together disparate, sometimes tenuous and changing relationships. Younger mothers, in particular, may rely on their own mothers or older family members for help with child care. While the extended-family network may provide a much-needed cushion of emotional, if not financial, support, a high level of connection leaves room for some predictable problems. Couples may struggle with issues of loyalty between their newly created family and one or both extended-family systems.

Clinically, it is important to grasp that single-parent family structures are not inherently dysfunctional, but they are particularly vulnerable because of poverty and task overload. More relevant than the structure of the single-parent family are household composition, the availability of essential resources, and a family's patterns of functioning. When a family's adaptive strategies are pushed too far, its members become vulnerable for a host of negative outcomes. While earlier research suggests that children raised in married partner households have better physical and mental health outcomes, Gibb, Fergusson, and Horwood's (2011) 30-year, longitudinal study indicated that legal relationship status was not related to mental health once due allowance was made for relationship duration.

KEY ASSESSMENT AND INTERVENTION CONSIDERATIONS. Given the likelihood of role overload and isolation at this phase, helping parents and other caretakers to maintain supportive, reciprocal connections with family, fictive kin, friends, and community supports is extremely important. This is even more critical when aging grandparents assume parental responsibilities, especially when children have special needs stemming from parental drug addiction and AIDS. Sibling relationships should be validated and nurtured as an extremely important part of the relationship network (Watson, 1998). It may also be of value to help couples/families maximize the involvement of noncustodial fathers and the paternal-extended family, if these connections have not been developed. Parents and grandparents who are struggling to rear children without the financial and/or emotional support or involvement of the children's parent(s) may need coaching about when and what to communicate to children about their parents, as well as help managing their own feelings about the circumstances without triangling children into unresolved adult conflicts.

Many parents and caretakers require assistance to increase their focus on caring for self and reducing the level of their overfunctioning. For some, self-care will involve setting limits on relationships in which there has been little or no reciprocity in terms of emotional or concrete support. For others, it will involve reducing their role overload by negotiating to share family tasks. Therapists may need to structure discussions that help families to see the dangers of overdependence on one person.

Stage 3: Families in later life

Life for families living at or below the poverty threshold at this phase may involve deteriorating health and repeated loss. For some, this is due to the size of their kinship system, and for most it is because of the long-term impact of adverse socioeconomic and political realities. In addition, those without insurance are particularly prone to give inadequate attention to preventive care. Illness is too frequently disregarded by the elderly until their functioning is seriously impaired. Consequently, low-income elderly have a lower life expectancy than their counterparts who are better off financially (Waldron, 2007). For those who have immigrated to this country and left their extended families behind, mourning losses is particularly difficult, as economically they may not be able to travel, or legally they may be putting themselves at risk for deportation.

Given the cultural emphasis on being strong and the common interpretation that this means to "keep on keeping on," family members tend not to grant themselves time to rebound from physical and emotional depletion. Often the pursuit of interests and dreams they long ago set aside are never explored. In contrast to middle-class families, this phase of the life cycle does not signify retirement or a lessening of daily responsibilities. Many continue working to make ends meet in spite of poor health. Even when they do retire, they may neither anticipate nor have "empty nests." In 2000, over 14 percent of all female-headed households with children were headed by a grandmother (Snyder, McLaughlin, &

Findeis, 2006). For those struggling with poverty, even when they are not the sole caretakers for their grandchildren, they are often active members of expanding households and family networks, providing concrete and emotional assistance to grandchildren, adult children, parents, and other elderly kin (Kreider, 2007; Musil & Standing, 2006).

Elderly family members can be great sources of human wisdom and strength by virtue of their experience and survival. They serve as family advisors, mediators, and transmitters of the family history and culture. Grandparents often have relationships with their grandchildren who are as close as, if not are closer than their relationships with, their own adult children. They may spend more time nurturing their grandchildren, nieces, nephews, and other kin than they were able to devote to their own children. Their homes are usually the gathering place for the kin system.

KEY ASSESSMENT AND INTERVENTION CONSIDERATIONS. The assistance that aging family members are able to provide to others, particularly in later life, can help them retain a sense of purpose. However, an important question for clinical assessment is whether they can do so without compromising their own physical, financial, and emotional well-being.

Denial about a decline in functioning, illness, or ultimately death may result in delayed family communication around issues that are critical to maintaining family stability. Family members may benefit from coaching to confront an elderly family member about the need for medical treatment, restrictions on activity, or the need for institutionalized care. Elderly family members, themselves, may serve as the catalysts for gathering family members to address the need for a changing of the guard so that continuity of family functioning is maintained. When family members are ambivalent or opposed to therapy, appealing to their concern for their elderly family members can be helpful. They may be receptive to the idea of helping the elderly experience greater peace of mind from knowing that all is in order. In return, therapists can motivate the elderly to participate in sessions by emphasizing the need for family members to access the wisdom of their elders and to prepare themselves to fill the void when the elderly person can no longer participate in caretaking.

Older family members are sometimes ambivalent about discussing certain topics (e.g., drugs, illicit sex, or criminal behavior) with younger family members if they have not resolved their own guilt and/or confusion about choices made when they were younger. But their advice can be even more credible because of their life experience and it may be helpful for them to speak openly about information they may have long avoided or kept secret. Exploring individual and family legacies often results in reconnecting with stories, images, and the fortitude of ancestors and can mobilize family members to move forward with tasks they have magnified to the status of undoable.

> **Assess your comprehension of the condensed family life cycle: assessment and treatment by completing this quiz.**

Overarching Assessment and Treatment Considerations

Simply stated, therapists have several, interactive assessment and treatment tasks that are essential to helping families: (1) to understand the concerns that have led a family to therapy; (2) to promote an understanding of what has happened to stall the family's functioning in relation to the presenting concerns at this stage of their family life cycle; (3) to solicit their future vision for their lives, beyond their specific concerns; (4) to foster hope and connect/reconnect them with the values, strengths, talents, and resources available to support them in their life journey; and (5) to motivate and coach them to develop and implement a road map to get from where they are to where they want to go. The multicontextual family life cycle framework facilitates engagement as well as effective assessment and intervention with multistressed families. The approach counters the pervasive narrow, individualist focus that characterizes so much of the social science literature and that essentially blames the victim. It minimizes oversimplification and artificial categorization of people's lives and takes into account the reality that family functioning is affected by multiple, intersecting past and present influences, internal and external to the family. Assessment and treatment

guided by this framework can expand therapists' as well as families' vision of future possibilities.

However, as Madsen (2013) argues, the most important task for therapists is engaging or "joining" multistressed families. The need to attend to families' hope and motivation is continuous. These families have experienced innumerable barriers to meeting their most basic needs, not to mention barriers they have had to achieving their dreams. We urge therapists to consistently assume what Madsen calls an "anthropological stance" or genuine interest in learning from families at every juncture, rather than relying on generalizations about their lives. Simultaneously, we urge therapists to recognize families' potential vulnerability and, when needed, strengthen their ability to resist hopelessness, frustration, anger, depression, giving up, and "solutions" that sabotage their well-being.

Genograms are clearly a vehicle for exploring family values and traditions and connecting families to sources of hope and strength that are personally and culturally congruent as they confront the hills and valleys of daily life. Constructing genograms with multistressed families helps them see the big picture with all its complexities and lowers the potential for family members or therapists to feel flooded. Constructing a genogram with a family allows therapists to identify and keep track of who is who, establish their relationships, track differences in perspective about the problem and preferred solutions, solicit information about strengths and resources, as well as to make notations regarding numerous other facts of individual, family, and cultural functioning (McGoldrick, Gerson, & Petry, 2008). Actively involving other helping agents in a respectful, collaborative process can increase the chances for clients to benefit from coordinated, integrated planning and support.

It is important for therapists to be aware that constructing a genogram can evoke a variety of feelings. Being attentive to non-verbal cues that signal clients' discomfort is important. Genogram details should be gathered gradually as the family comes to trust that the process will help them move forward. For recent immigrants, telling their stories of immigration, and asking who remained behind, to what extent they maintain contact, and whether they financially help family members in their country of origin are important questions. Sending money to family is a very common source of stress for families already at the poverty line.

A growing number of theorists and practitioners have formulated culture-based prevention and treatment approaches (e.g., Phillips, 1990; Rowe & Grills, 1993; Nobles, 2004; Hines, 2008) that are undergirded by the premise that healthy functioning within an oppressive context is maximized through active resistance of negative messages about one's value and potential, and by consistent use of principles that define what one stands for and how one behaves. Another common premise undergirding culture-based approaches is that transformative healing involves resolving the problems of today by drawing upon helpful solutions of the past.

Drawing on these scholars' body of work and the seven principles of Kwanzaa, a celebration of African American heritage (Karenga, 1988), Hines and Sutton (1998) developed SANKOFA, an evidenced-based violence prevention approach that has universal application but particular resonance for those who have been marginalized in society due to class, race, and ethnic prejudice. The SANKOFA program helps youth reduce their risk for violence. It increases their awareness that choices always exist, however limited, and enhances their commitment to principles that can serve as guidelines for dealing with complex and challenging life circumstances. We have coined the term "The 7 Cs" to refer to key themes of the SANKOFA program:

1. *Consciousness* pertains to having a clear awareness of one's dreams, purpose, feelings, thoughts, beliefs, family and cultural heritage, and potential, as well as obstacles to self- and group actualization, including classism and racism.
2. *Connectedness* pertains to unity or sticking together, a sense of interrelationship with our family as well as with the larger kin network and community.
3. *Caring* pertains to the ability to nurture, protect, support, and show concern for the safety of one's family and the larger group and a belief in giving back.
4. *Competence toward one's purpose* pertains to self- and group actualization, developing ourselves to our fullest potential.

5. *Conduct* pertains to engaging in right behavior and to teaching others how to do so. It involves the ability to forgive and resolve past injustices with one another.
6. *Creativity* involves using originality, inventiveness, imagination, intuition, and artistic abilities to transform pain into meaning and hope.
7. *Courage* pertains to demonstrating the spiritual strength to withstand adversity and to achieve one's goals: to live up to the examples of one's ancestors.

In the clinical arena, as well, it can be valuable to motivate and support families in reconnecting with how their cultural roots and strengths can help keep them afloat in the midst of unrelenting challenges. While the assessment process involves an exploration of the specific problems that brought the family into therapy, a related aim is to convey the importance of pausing to broaden the lens through which clients understand the presenting concern(s) and potential solutions. Therapists are encouraged to explicitly acknowledge the need for families to collectively explore who they are, what they stand for, and what their dreams are in the midst of a world where there are a lot of pulls to let others define them and their life course.

Examples of additional question that can help families shift the narrative to one that highlights their strengths, deepens their motivation to build on their family and cultural legacies, and move from a position of hopelessness to hopefulness and power include the following:

- What happened to you? How does what happened to you affect you now? How, in spite of what happened, have you been able to triumph? What external factors have contributed to your wounding? What needs to be healed? What gifts have you been able to bring forth from this wounding experience? What lessons/wisdom can you share with others based on your experiences? What would life in full power look and feel like to you (Jackson, 2012; Akinyela, 2008)?

- What keeps you going in spite of ongoing adversity?

- Do you have a mission or calling something that you think you are meant to do?
- Are there sayings or stories passed down to you that have special meaning for you when you face challenges? How might you operationalize this resource in your life now?
- What wisdom would your ancestors pass on to you if they could consult with you regarding your current concerns?
- What rules do you believe are important for you and your family to follow in life?
- What must you do to avoid giving up your power and dreams?
- How is the choice you have made consistent with the principles you embrace?
- What behavior would reflect caring for yourself and the people you love?
- What images or words from the past do you need to call upon to help you accomplish this difficult but very worthwhile goal?
- Are there any cutoffs in your larger family? If so, what are the benefits of addressing these?

Family discussions about the values and principles that drive decision making in relation to major life challenges can be transformative in fostering the emotional shifts that are often prerequisites for behavioral change. The process of telling their story gives family members the opportunity to speak to the logic and positives that have driven their past behavioral and relational choices., In addition, it provides therapists the opportunity to assume a non-pathologizing stance and to convey positive regard for positive intentions (Hardy & Laszloffy, 2005), while neither romanticizing nor denying any dysfunction. Helping families distinguish the factors in their predicament that are influenced by external forces and those which are self-imposed and clearly within their control to change can be of huge benefit. In doing so, therapists can help family members take responsibility, individually and collectively, for moving toward their vision and discontinuing behavior that reinforces their own powerlessness. The integration of the 7 Cs and healing questions into the assessment and treatment processes can help families draw distinctions between the past,

present, and future. This allows them to punctuate the strengths and resources that have allowed current and past generations to resist oppression when faced with as traumatic or worse circumstances than those they currently confront. This process emphasizes the power that family members have, going forward, to make choices that will enhance their success and well-being, even in a context of seeming intractable barriers.

We strongly recommend incorporating and prescribing culturally congruent strategies to help families connect with their history, potential, and hope for overcoming their current challenges (Hines, 2008). These strategies include drawing on relevant videos, scriptures, meditations, teaching fables, and popular books based on the lives of people with whom they identify, and oral history interviewing of family and community members.

Certainly, the realities that accompany work with multistressed families compel therapists and agency administrators to think beyond the 45 to 60 minute hour and to use time flexibly (Goodman, Smyth, & Banyard, 2010). It goes without saying that institutional policies and practices, including those of insurance payers, must align in support of therapists' flexibility in delivering services. There is, of course, nothing sacred about time allotted for sessions. Half or full-day sessions can enable therapists to engage and mobilize key family members who may not otherwise be available for appointments. Extended sessions also make it easier to engage and mobilize families before they are distracted by new stresses (Hines, Richman, Hays, Maxim, 1989).

> Assess your comprehension of overarching assessment and treatment considerations by completing this quiz.

CASE ILLUSTRATION

The Long Family

The following case vignette illustrates the use of a multicontextual family life cycle framework with a family that had spiraled from working to nonworking poor. Their story exemplifies the reality that

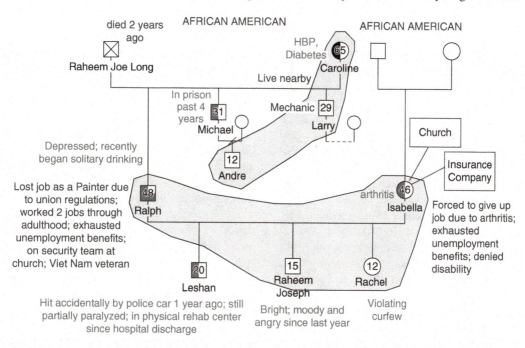

GENOGRAM 5.1 Long Family Genogram

resilience may be strained in the midst of living under fire. But neither poverty of spirit—loss of hope, dreams, and human potential—nor dysfunction is inevitable nor irreversible.

The Long family was referred for treatment by school personnel to address the excessive school absences and growing anger and moodiness of 15-year-old Raheem. The immediate family consisted of Raheem; his parents, Isabella (age 46) and Ralph (age 48); and a 13-year-old sister, Rachel (see Genogram 5.1). The previous year, Raheem's oldest brother, Lashan, at the age of 19 had been accidentally run over as he was walking to evening classes at a local college by a police car that had been chasing someone else. After a 2-month hospitalization spent in a medically induced coma, Lashan had been living at a nearby physical rehabilitation center. Ralph's mother, Caroline, age 65, lived nearby with her 29-year-old son, Larry, and her 12-year-old grandson, Andre, who had lived with her since he was a toddler. Andre's father (Caroline's son), Michael, age 31, had been incarcerated for the last 4 years. Larry worked as a mechanic and spent much of his free time with

his girlfriend. Caroline's health had begun to decline from diabetes and high blood pressure. Her husband, Raheem Joseph (known as Joe), had died from a stroke 2 years ago, while at his second evening job. Most of Raheem's maternal extended family lived in his mother's hometown, several states away. The Longs had regular telephone contact with them.

The therapist invited all family members except Lashan to the first session. Only Larry refused to attend. The therapist stressed that everyone's participation was welcome, since their input was critical to understanding and helping Raheem. Though family members seemed initially anxious and unsure about what was expected of them, they quickly agreed that Raheem's chance to realize his potential was at great risk.

Raheem's problematic behavior had begun after his brother's accident. Lashan had been the first in the family to attend college. While there was an experimental treatment that might reverse his partial paralysis, the company which insured the police car had persisted in their refusal to cover the recommended procedures. While Lashan seemed to quietly accept the delay, Raheem often became agitated when discussing the situation. Throughout Raheem's life, his father, Ralph, had worked two jobs to make ends meet. But shortly after Lashan's accident, he lost his primary job as a painter because new regulations blocked the employment of nonunion workers. Since then, Ralph could find only occasional odd jobs, without health benefits. Isabelle had been forced to give up her part-time school crossing guard job because of a painful arthritic condition. Both Ralph and Isabelle had exhausted their unemployment benefits. Isabella had been denied disability but was awaiting a decision on her appeal. Ralph had become noticeably less involved at church where he had formerly volunteered with the parking and security team, a group of men he had enjoyed. Isabella and Caroline suspected that Ralph was hiding the fact that he had begun to drink. Recently, Rachel had started to violate her curfew and angrily accused her mother of being overprotective of her but permissive with Raheem.

After constructing a genogram and creating a time line with the family, the therapist shared his hypothesis that the family had been pushed to their limit by the need to manage major, simultaneous challenges without the opportunity to renew their energy and spirits. The normal family life cycle stressors of various members moving through adolescence, young adulthood, middle age, and the end of life were exacerbated by the psychological fatigue of ongoing efforts to resist the negative messages from the larger social–political environment, the void left after the grandfather's death, the traumatic threat of losing Lashan, the injustices of the insurance company's decision to restrict Lashan's access to treatment, the dramatic decline in the family's meager financial underpinnings, and the deterioration of Isabella's and Caroline's health. The therapist created a visual of these as well as various other stressors that were impacting the family on a daily basis, including escalating crime in their neighborhood, negative peer pressure, and the inadequacy of their school system. The family members had been handling their legitimate feelings of grief, anger, anxiety about the future, hopelessness, and helplessness in their own ways, but had all been reluctant to acknowledge openly their struggle.

The therapist surmised that Raheem was so bright and talented that it was difficult for his parents to connect with the reality that he was still learning to regulate feelings of anger, anxiety, disappointment, and despair and his acting-out was evidence of the vulnerability that we all have to make self-defeating choices. He was named for his grandfather to whom he had been very close. The grandfather's unexpected death just after Lashan's accident left him without the level of warrior spirit and capacity to believe in himself, that is essential to navigating around one challenge after another. As Raheem approached his junior year, he increasingly feared that neither he nor Lashan would fulfill their family's expectations that they complete college and escape a life of financial hardship. The therapist validated Raheem's assessment that the road to success was full of potholes for him as a young man of color and normalized the need for family members to slow down, update their roadmap or navigator, and stay sufficiently refueled in the spirit to support him in his journey.

Isabelle and Ralph were connected in their concerns, emotional pain, and hope, but were divided about how to counter the circumstances that threatened their family. To *connect* the family with a sense of their potential to act on their own behalf, the therapist asked questions that shifted the narrative to focus on the family's strengths. He encouraged the grandmother, father, and mother to talk about their family history during a subsequent session with Raheem, Rachel, and Andre. They told stories of the extraordinary challenges that members of their family had overcome over the generations and the *creative* ways that their ancestors and elders had found to address their anger in the face of repeated injustices. Themes of family togetherness, faith, perseverance, and leadership were prominently threaded in these empowering memories. Returning to the list of stressors impacting the family, the therapist facilitated what grew into a lively conversation about which of the stressors were within the family's capacity to exert any influence.

In a separate session, the therapist met with Ralph, Isabelle, and Caroline to discuss their expectations and the messages they were giving to the children in the family (i.e., *conduct*). The therapist discussed with them how to hold the youths in the family as well as each other accountable and helped the parents and the grandmother define what shifts were necessary in their co-parenting to maximize their success in accomplishing their common child-rearing goals. At the therapist's urging, Ralph considered the potential benefits of promoting a *connection* between his son and nephew with his imprisoned brother, Michael, and subsequently took Raheem and Andre with him to visit Michael at the prison for the first time in 9 years. Michael was able to penetrate Raheem's armor and impressed upon him the inaccuracy of any glamorization of life behind bars. He spoke candidly to Raheem and Andre about the devastating ways in which his drug abuse had affected not only him but also his son and mother.

In subsequent individual sessions with Ralph, the therapist urged him to call upon the *courage* that had brought him through the Vietnam War and the wisdom passed on by his father to confront his feelings of being down and out, to address his children's need for a positive role model, and live up to his own desire to be responsible as a father and husband (*conduct*). Ralph was reluctant to attend AA meetings but finally agreed and initiated a supportive relationship with a man in his church group who was in recovery and an active member of a church-sponsored recovery group. Isabelle and Ralph were coached to communicate their concerns to one another without resorting to yelling and distancing behaviors. Ralph was able to articulate his disappointment that he had fallen short of being a good husband and father. Isabella acknowledged the contributions that Ralph had made and, more important, the contributions that he could continue to make to his wife and family in spite of his joblessness. The therapist coached the couple to renegotiate their roles in their home. Similarly, Raheem and Rachel rehearsed ways to negotiate for privileges with their parents. Ralph began to take a more active role in the family and coordinated meetings to help Raheem reestablish his academic standing.

The therapist then turned his attention to the grandmother's health. Caroline spoke to her family about her belief in not giving in to her aches and pains. Discussion ensued about how she could acknowledge her illness by taking her medication and continue to support herself and her grandchild but give up the overtime cleaning and home health care jobs she regularly accepted. In turn, she insisted that the family join her in attending church services on Lashan's birthday, which all anticipated would be a difficult day for the family. The family was pleased to have the church community surround them with a special prayer during the service. Acknowledging the innumerable demands and circumstances that impeded their social activity, the therapist asked the parents and grandmother to explore the down side of allowing themselves to become totally depleted.

The therapist acknowledged the family's unspoken concern that these efforts, without new opportunities, would still fall short of helping the family reduce their dependence on government assistance. With the coaching of the therapist, Ralph made a connection with a cousin who owned a small business and was able to secure a part-time position, which had the potential of becoming full time. The therapist devoted one session with Ralph and Isabella to discuss his impression that Ralph was struggling with depression. He patiently explored their ambivalence about medication and enlisted them in a conversation about the warning signs that they should heed if Ralph's efforts to overcome his depression proved more difficult than Ralph envisioned. The therapist encouraged the family to heed the cultural belief that "it takes a village to raise a child" and to utilize the resources available at their church, which included mentoring and tutoring for Andre and cultural and social opportunities that the three teens could more actively explore. Isabella and Ralph, acknowledging that they needed all the support they could get for themselves and their children, given the multiple stressors that besieged them, decided that making a road trip to Isabella's upcoming family reunion at her parent's birthplace (i.e., *reconnecting*) was a financially difficult but important therapeutic step to take.

> **Asess your comprehension of the case illustration: the long family by completing this quiz.**

Avoiding Therapist Burnout

Work with families who live in poverty requires significant time, creativity, energy, clarity, passion, and investment in self-care. These are families whose daily experiences include ongoing challenges in terms of concrete resources and related emotional, relational, spiritual, and physical health concerns. Most therapists who work with families living in poverty have a genuine commitment to assisting the population but often ignore the need to retreat and replenish their own energy.

Our capacity as therapists to refuel our own tanks requires staying connected with our respective wellsprings of energy and spiritual renewal. Additionally, it is helpful to be mindful of the pitfalls of operating as though our assumptions represent truths, to explore where we fall on the continuum of privilege, and to assess our personal beliefs about poverty and coping with adversity. Clearly, therapists who work with low-income families must embrace the task of linking families to concrete resources when the need is evident. At the same time, it is helpful to stay in regular, active consultation with colleagues who can help us stay out of the minefield of guilt or "do-gooder" behavior that does not benefit our clients or ourselves. Our commitment to humility and collaboration must extend to an openness to learn from our clients and to facilitate their motivation and capacity to take control of what is within their ability to change and not sabotage themselves.

Also vital to the capacity of front-line practitioners to stay the challenging but rewarding course of working with multistressed families is active collaboration with policymakers, funders, and the leadership of service agencies to improve the policies and practices that restrict access to services and too often sabotage therapists' engagement and effectiveness.

> **Assess your comprehension of avoiding therapist burnout by completing this quiz.**

— Conclusion

Stress in the lives of those living below the poverty threshold is unrelenting. A growing body of research speaks to the reality that living in poverty is an adverse consequence with potentially long-lasting consequences at the individual, family, and societal levels. There is much that could be done, given sufficient public and political will, to reduce if not prevent the intersecting health, social, and economic disparities. Family therapy is by no means a panacea. However, we have argued in this chapter that multicontext family therapy can help economically fragile families to navigate the predictable challenges associated with poverty and each stage of the family life cycle. The road to engaging and effectively working with this population requires acknowledging their ingenuity and tenacity in the face of obstacles that make it difficult for them to escape poverty and hold on to their dreams. As agents of hope, healing, prevention, and health promotion, we must encourage them to make the healthiest choices their circumstances afford and to be active, unrelenting advocates for social justice.

While most attention has been given in the literature to families living in economic poverty who succumb to individual and family dysfunction, our field would do well to turn more of our attention to families who might be described as "bruised but not broken." It is families who are well functioning even within the context of inadequate income and resources who remind each other and therapists that innumerable families living in economic poverty evidence tremendous strength. It is they who remind us that economic poverty does not necessarily dictate "poverty of spirit" (hopelessness). It is they who remind us that people are not defined by the situations they confront but by how they respond to the situation. They remind us of the huge benefits that can arise when we confront adverse life circumstances with a focus on consciousness (of our purpose), conduct, choices, courage, creativity, competence, caring, and connection.

> **Recall what you learned in this chapter by completing the Chapter Review.**

— References —

Akinyela, M. (2008). Once they come: Testimony therapy and healing questions for African American couples. In M. McGoldrick & K. Hardy (Eds.), *Revisioning family therapy* (2nd edn.). New York: Guilford.

Aponte, H. (1994). *Bread and spirit: Therapy with the new poor.* New York: W. W. Norton.

Barnet, B., Liu, J., & DeVoe, M. (2008). Double jeopardy: Depressive symptoms and rapid subsequent pregnancy in adolescent mothers. *Archives of Pediatrics & Adolescent Medicine, 162*(3), 246–252.

Billingsley, A. (1992). *Climbing Jacob's ladder: The enduring legacy of African-American families.* New York: Simon & Schuster.

Bishop, D. (2005). The role of race and ethnicity in juvenile justice processing. In D. F. Hawkins & K. Kempf-Leonard, Eds. *Our children, their children: Confronting racial and ethnic differences in American Juvenile Justice.* Chicago, IL: University of Chicago Press.

Boyd-Franklin, N. (2003). *Black families in therapy: Understanding the African American experience* (2nd edn.). New York: The Guilford Press.

Bureau of Labor Statistics, U.S. Department of Labor. (2012). The Editor's Desk, Racial and ethnic characteristics of the U.S. labor force, 2011. Retrieved from http://www.bls.gov/opub/ted/2012/ed_201209905.htm

Burton, L. M. (1995). Intergenerational patterns of providing care in African-American families with teenage childbearers: Emergent patterns in an ethnographic study. In V. L. Bengston, K. W. Schale, & L. M. Burton (Eds.), *Adult intergenerational relations: Effects of societal change,* (pp. 79–125). New York: Springer.

Burton, L. M. (1996a). Age norms, the timing of family role transitions and intergenerational caregiving among aging African American women. *Gerontologist, April 36*(2), 199–208.

Burton, L. M. (1996b). The timing of childbearing, family structure and the role responsibilities of aging Black women. In E. M. Hetherington & E. A. Blechman (Eds.), *Stress, coping and resiliency in children and families* (pp. 155–172). Mahwah, NJ: Lawrence Erlbaum Associates.

Burton, L., & Tucker, B. (2009). Romantic unions in an era of uncertainty: A post-Moynihan perspective on African American women and marriage. *The Annals of the American Academy of Political and Social Science,* 621, 132.

Burton, L., Cherlin, A., Winn, D., Estacion, A., & Holder-Taylor, C. (December 2009). The role of trust in low-income mothers' intimate unions. *Journal of Marriage and Family,* 71, 1107–1124.

Butterworth, P., Cherbuin, N., Sachdev, P., & Anstey, K. J. (June 2012). The association between financial hardship and amygdala and hippocampal volumes: Results from the PATH Through Life project. *Social Cognition Affect Neuroscience,* 7(5): 548–556.

Casey Foundation. (2012). *Youth and work: Restoring teen and young adult connections to opportunity.* Annie E. Casey Foundation Press Release, December 12, 2012. Retrieved from www.accf.org/kidscount/youthwork

DeNavas-Wait, C., Proctor, B., & Smith, J. (2012). U.S. Census Bureau, Current Population Reports. *Income, Poverty, and Health Insurance Coverage in the United States: 2011.* (pp. 60–243). U.S. Government Printing Office, Washington, DC.

Dye, J. L. (2008). Participation of mothers in government assistance programs: 2004. Current population reports, pp. 70–116. U.S. Census Bureau, Washington, DC.

Edsall, T. (2013, March 13). Who is poor? *The New York Times, Opinion Pages.*

Escobar, J., Nervi, C., & Gara, M. (2000). Immigration and mental health: Mexican Americans in the United States. *Harvard Review of Psychiatry,* 8(2), 64–72.

Eyre, S. L., Flythe, M., Hoffman, V., & Fraser, A. E. (June 2012). Primary relationship scripts among lower-income, African American young adults. *Family Process,* 51(2), 234–249.

Franklin, A. J. (2004). *From brotherhood to manhood: How black men rescue their dreams and relationships from the invisibility syndrome.* Hoboken, NJ: Wiley.

Gibb, S. J., Fergusson, D. M., & Horwood, L. J. (January 2011). Relationship duration and mental health outcomes: Findings from a 30-year longitudinal study. *British Journal of Psychiatry,* 1, 24–30.

Goodman, L. A., Smyth, K. F., & Banyard, V. (January 2010). Beyond the 50-minute hour: increasing control, choice, and connections in the lives of low-income women. *American Journal of Orthopsychiatry,* 80(1), 3–11.

Hamilton, B. E. K., Martin, J. C., & Ventura, S. J. (2011). Births: Preliminary data for 2010. National *Vital Statistics Reports,* 60(2), Table S-2.

Hardy, K. V., & Laszloffy, T. A. (2008). The dynamics of a pro-racist ideology: Implications for training family therapists. In M. McGoldrick & K. Hardy (Eds.), *Revisioning family therapy: Race, culture and gender in clinical practice* (2nd edn). New York: The Guilford Press.

Hardy, K. V., & Laszloffy, T. A. (2005). *Teens who hurt: Clinical interventions to break the cycle of adolescent violence.* New York: Guilford Press.

Hill, R. B. (1999). *The strengths of Black families: Twenty-five years later.* Lanham, MD: University Press of America.

Hines, P., (2008). Climbing up the rough side of the mountain. In M. McGoldrick & K. Hardy (Eds.), *Revisioning family therapy: Race, culture and gender in clinical practice* (2nd edn.). New York: The Guilford Press.

Hines, P., & Boyd-Franklin, N. (2005). African American families. In M. McGoldrick, J. Giordano, & N. Garcia-Preto (Eds.), *Ethnicity and Family Therapy* (2nd edn.), New York: The Guilford Press.

Hines, P., Richman, D., Hays, H., & Maxim, K. (1989). Multi-impact family therapy: An approach to working with multi-problem families. *Journal of Psychotherapy and the Family, 6,* 161–175.

Hines, P., & Sutton, C. (1998). SANKOFA: A violence prevention curriculum. Piscataway: University of Medicine and Dentistry of New Jersey.

Hoefer, M., Rytina, N., & Baker, B. (2011). Estimates of the Unauthorized Immigrant Population Residing in the United States: January 2011. Office of Immigration Statistics, Policy Directorate, U.S. Department of Homeland Security. Retrieved from http://www.dhs.gov/xlibrary/assets/statistics/publications

Jackson, V. (2012). *Transforming powerlessness into power.* (Available from Microtraining: Alexander St. Press at: http://vstr.beta.alexanderstreet.com/index.php?a=filmDetail&filmID=4038.)

Karenga, M. (1988). *The African American holiday of Kwanzaa: A celebration of family, community and culture.* Los Angeles: University of Sankore Press.

Kim, J., Shelley, K., & Loveless, T. (2012). Dynamics of economic well-being: Participation in government programs, 2004 to 2007 and 2009: Who Gets Assistance? *Current Population Reports,* pp. 70–131. Washington, DC: U.S. Census Bureau.

Kreider, R. (2007). Living arrangements of children: 2004. *Current Population Reports,* pp. 70–114. Washington, DC: U.S. Census Bureau.

Madsen, William C. (2013). *Collaborative therapy with multi-stressed families* (2nd Ed.). New York: The Guilford Press.

McAdoo, H. (2007). *Black families.* Thousand Oaks, CA: Sage Publications.

McGoldrick, M., Gerson, R., & Petry, S. (2008). *Genograms: Assessment and intervention* (3rd edn.). New York: W.W. Norton.

Musil, C., & Standing, T. (2006). Grandmothers' diaries: A glimpse at daily lives. In B. Hayslip Jr., & J. Hicks Patrick (Eds.) *Custodial Grandparenting: Individual, cultural, and ethnic diversity.* New York: Springer Publishing Company, pp. 89–104.

National Center on Homelessness & Poverty. (2013). Homelessness. *Almanac of Policy Issues.* Retrieved from www.policyalmanac.org/social_welfare/homeless.html

Negi, N. J. (2013) Battling discrimination and social isolation: Psychological distress among Latino day laborers. *American Journal of Community Psychology, 51* (1–2), 164–174.

Nichols, A., & Callan, T. (2013). *Unemployment and poverty.* Urban Institute. Retrieved from http://www.urban.org/publications/412400/html

Nobles, W. W. (2004). African philosophy: Foundations for black psychology. In R. Jones (Ed.), *Black Psychology* (4th ed.). New York: Harper & Row.

Nurius, P.S., Logan-Greene, P., Green, S. (2012). Adverse childhood experiences (ACE) within a social disadvantage framework: Distinguishing unique, cumulative, and moderated contributions to adult mental health. *Journal of Preventive Intervention Community, 40*(4), 278–290.

Paschal, A. (2006). *Voices of African-American teen fathers: "I'm doing what I got to do".* New York: Haworth Press.

Phillips, F. B. (1990). N. T. U. psychotherapy: An Afrocentric approach. *The Journal of Black Psychology, 71*(1), 55–74.

Pinderhughes, E. (1989). *Race, ethnicity and power.* New York: The Free Press.

Rowe, D., & Grills, C. (1993). African centered drug treatment: An alternative conceptual paradigm for drug counseling with African-American clients. *Journal of Psychoactive Drugs, 25*(1), 21–33.

Simms, M., Fortuny, K., & Henderson, E. (August, 2009). Racial and ethnic disparities among low-income families. The Urban Institute LIWF Fact Sheet.

Snyder, A., McLaughlin, D., & Findeis, J. (2006). Household composition and poverty among female-headed households with children: Differences by race and residence. *Rural Sociology, 71* (4), 597–624.

Staples, R. (2007). In search of love and commitment: Dealing with the challenging odds of finding romance. In H. McAdoo (ed.) *Black families.* Thousand Oaks, CA: Sage Publications.

U.S. Census Bureau (2012, Sept. 12). Income, poverty and health insurance coverage in the United States: 2011. Retrieved from http://www.census.gov/newroom/releases/archives/income_wealth/cb12_172.html

U.S. Census Bureau (2012). Current Population Survey, 2011 Annual Social and Economic Supplement. Retrieved from http://www.census.gov/hhes/www/poverty/data/

Waldron, H. 2007. *Trends in mortality differentials and life expectancy for male social security-covered workers, by socioeconomic status.* Social Security Administration.

Watson, M. (1998). African American siblings. In M. Mc-Goldrick (Ed.), *Revisioning family therapy* (1st ed., pp. 282–294). New York: The Guilford Press.

Williams, D. R., Neighbors, H. W., & Jackson, J. S. (2003). Racial/ethnic discrimination and health: Findings from community studies. *American Journal of Public Health*, 903, 200–208.

Chapter 6

Sexuality and the Family Life Cycle

Tracey Laszloffy

— Learning Outcomes

- Define the terms sex, gender, gender assignment, gender identity, transgendered, gender roles, and sexual orientation.
- List and describe five factors that influence individual and family development with respect to sexuality.
- Describe common messages about gender and sexuality and the corresponding feelings and behaviors that stem from them.
- Explain how a family's cultural norms, including religious affiliation, social class, ethnicity, migration and racial background, influence development with respect to sexuality.
- Examine how some of the principles that organize U.S. society shape our relationship with sexuality.
- List and describe factors that inhibit or impair sexual satisfaction in couple relationships.
- Describe changes in a couple's sexuality during pregnancy and when a family has young children.
- List and describe challenges associated with sexual development during adolescence.
- Explain changes in sexuality that occur during midlife and later life.
- Describe how sexuality relates to an understanding of the family life cycle.

Introduction

Sex is elemental. Without sex, the continuation of our species would be impossible. At the same time, it is one of the most complex aspects of human experience. It consists of a synergistic interplay of biological, psychological, familial, spiritual, cultural, and societal forces that are exceedingly difficult to unravel.

An exploration of human sexuality must begin by untangling the confusion created by the language we use to discuss issues of gender and sexuality (Lev, 2004). For example, the terms *sex* and *gender* are often used interchangeably, but they refer to two different, although highly interrelated, concepts. *Sex* is a biological phenomenon that is determined by five factors, including chromosomes (e.g., the presence or absence of a Y chromosome), sex hormones, gonads (ovaries or testes), the internal reproductive anatomy (uterus or testicles), and external genitalia (vulva or penis). Most human beings are born with either a male or a female sex, although sometimes a person is

born with ambiguous sex organs and is thus considered intersexed (World Health Organization, 2010).

Gender on the other hand is a cultural phenomenon. It is a socially constructed experience that societies overlay onto the biology of sex. Most societies have constructed and therefore only recognize two possible genders that correspond with the two biological sexes, male and female. However, just as the biology of sex is not absolutely binary, and despite the strong bias that exists toward a binary system of gender, many people experience gender in ways that extend beyond the simple either/or duality of male and female.

There are several dimensions of gender that must be considered. The first is *gender assignment* that occurs at birth and is determined by a newborn's biological sex. *Gender identity* is an internal experience. It refers to the gender that persons feel themselves to be. While in most cases this corresponds with the gender that is assigned at birth based on one's biological sex, this is not always the case. Transgendered individuals experience an internal conflict between the gender they feel themselves to be and their biological sex/gender assignment. In fact, it is important to clarify the meaning of the frequently cited term *Transgendered*. This is an umbrella term that refers to a wide range of gender experiences and presentations. And finally, the issue of gender presentation is tied to the term *gender roles* that are behaviors that individuals engage in and communicate their gender outwardly to others.

Gender is a social construction and as such, each culture has its own particular way of constructing gender categories and the behaviors that are appropriate to each. However, there is a high degree of similarity across cultures to the extent that most societies are organized around patriarchal norms. Gender systems that are constructed in accordance with patriarchal norms confer men with greater access to social power, resources, opportunities, and rewards than women. Even in modernized Western cultures where there has been a strong shift toward more egalitarian ways of enacting what it is to be "male" and "female," patriarchal assumptions continue to influence how people think and behave as men and women.

Sexual orientation refers to the gender(s) that one is attracted to in relation to the gender that one is. For example, persons who are attracted to members of their opposite gender are considered heterosexual, while those who are attracted to members of their own gender are deemed homosexual, and those who are attracted to people of both genders are regarded as bisexual. Sex researchers now understand that sexual orientation (like gender) is not as dichotomous as once believed and instead it is defined by a continuum. Conceptualized in this way, many people probably are neither exclusively heterosexual nor homosexual, but instead lean more heavily (though not purely) in one direction versus the other. Variation between people is more likely a matter of the degree to which one leans toward one end of the continuum or the other.

Most studies on human sexuality approach this subject from an individual perspective. They focus on the process of biological maturation and how this leads to adult sexual development and experience. This framework is a necessary component of understanding human sexuality, but it fails to capture the wider and more complex landscape of human sexual experience. Human sexuality is a relational phenomenon and as such it is important to consider it within a social context. This focus on the socially constructed and symbolic interactionist dimensions of sexuality is consistent with the perspective that was first advanced by John Gagnon and William Simon beginning in the 1960s. Their work posed a dramatic counterpoint to the biologically based paradigm that had previously dominated gender and sexuality research. They argued that a complex set of culturally shaped meanings and symbols organize human sexual experience and the subjective understandings individuals have of their gender and sexuality (Kimmel, 2007). This perspective heavily informs our approach to the study of human sexuality by locating it within a family context, and specifically, within a family life cycle framework. Moreover, we will examine how human sexuality develops, is experienced, and is expressed over time and from one generation to the next within the interlocking contexts of family, culture, and society.

> **Assess your comprehension of the introduction by completing this <u>quiz</u>.**

Sexuality: Individual and Family Development

Individual and family development with respect to sexuality is influenced by many factors. This chapter considers five factors: (1) family boundaries; (2) family beliefs and messages about gender and sexuality, and the feelings and behavior patterns that stem from these; (3) intergenerational patterns related to gender and sex; (4) cultural norms; and (5) societal organizing principles.

Boundaries

Boundaries in families regulate how a family system functions. They regulate who is responsible for what, and how family members relate to and interact, both with each other and with people outside the family. Boundaries define where one person ends and another person begins. Boundaries in families exist along a continuum from rigid to loose. The more deeply a system's boundaries lean in either extreme, the less functional the system is. Healthy families have clear boundaries that fall somewhere in the mid-range between rigid and loose. Such systems allow some kinds of information and contact to flow freely while simultaneously buffering against the flow of other kinds of information and contact.

Families that have clear boundaries also have adaptable boundaries that change as the family evolves through its life cycle. Boundaries become firmer or more flexible to support the developmental demands of individuals and the family over time. For example, in families with young children there is a need for a firmer boundary around how sexual issues are addressed. Some information is shared but tailored to the developmental limits of young children. This might mean that parents focus on teaching their children the difference between "good touch and bad touch." Moreover, because even very young children sometimes fondle their genitals, in families with clear boundaries parents do not react with shock or shaming. Instead they normalize the pleasure that comes from self-touching while also teaching children when, where, and under what circumstances such touching is appropriate. In families with adolescents, boundaries need to soften to allow for a greater flow of information related to sexuality. Parents of adolescents need to allow more direct and explicit discussion of and education about sexual issues.

Family systems with rigid boundaries enforce extreme separation between family members and prohibit open, direct discussion of sexual issues or expression of even the most limited sexual behavior. When a family's boundaries are too rigid, children receive minimal sexual information from their parents, and minimal permission to ask questions or raise issues for discussion. When sexual issues do come up, they tend to arouse disapproval and shame, thereby forcing sexual thoughts, feelings, and behaviors underground. As a result, young people enter puberty with little preparation for the changes they are about to undergo, or they are armed with information they obtained from peers, the media, and the Internet which may prove more harmful than having no information at all.

CASE ILLUSTRATION

The Bergens—A Case of Rigid Boundaries

The Bergen family was characterized by extremely rigid boundaries such that family members had minimal interaction and shared very little about themselves with each other. Dirk, the oldest son of four boys, had been a boy scout from the time he was very young, and was very close to his scout leader, Mr. Frankel. Because there was so much distance in Dirk's family, he was hungry for attention and connection and Mr. Frankel was like a surrogate father in many ways, guiding and nurturing Dirk. However, when Dirk was 12, Mr. Frankel's attention crossed the line and he began molesting Dirk sexually. Dirk was conflicted because he did not like Mr. Frankel's sexual advances, although he hungered for the attention and affirmation he received. Confused and ashamed Dirk grew increasingly depressed, but neither of his parents noticed. The rigid boundaries in the family helped make Dirk vulnerable to Mr. Frankel's exploitation. These boundaries also fostered a climate where Dirk did not feel permission or safety to open up to his parents about what was happening, nor did his parents notice their son's increasing sullenness and depression.

Conversely, families with loose boundaries are defined by extreme closeness between family members to the extent that individuals have a hard time perceiving the distinction between their own thoughts, feelings, and needs; and the thoughts, feelings, and needs of other family members. Such families are defined by a great deal of emotional and psychological overlapping. In terms of sexuality, families with loose boundaries do not establish adequate limits and they lack appropriate prohibitions. Consequently, there is too much exposure and access to sexual content and activity, and too much permission to act out in sexually irresponsible ways. Families with loose boundaries fail to recognize or uphold age-appropriate parameters around sexual material and activity that can be damaging for children. Children raised in such families are not taught how to set limits with other people about what is comfortable or appropriate; hence, they are more vulnerable to experiences around intrusion and violation.

CASE ILLUSTRATION

The Mishras—A Case of Loose Boundaries

The Mishra family was characterized by extremely loose boundaries. Because the family of five lived in two-bedroom house, the middle child, Reena, slept on the couch in the living room between the ages of 4 and 16. This in and of itself was a reflection of the family's economic status, not a boundary issue. However, it was not uncommon for Mr. Mishra to awaken in the middle of the night and come into the living room to watch television, sometimes watching pornography. Reena was disturbed by her father's behavior but felt powerless to address it. Most of the time, she pretended she was still asleep and tried to not hear the television. This behavior reflects how loose the boundaries were in the Mishra family. Moreover, there were several occasions when the family was on vacation when they all shared a single hotel room. Again, the single room was not an issue, but the fact that Mr. Mishra sometimes pressured his wife to have sex with him while his children were presumably asleep in the next bed further reflected their loose boundary and a disregard for how exposure to sexual issues affected the children. The loose boundaries in the Mishra family left Reena doubting her ability to hold onto herself and set and maintain limits with others. Consequently, she avoided intimacy and by the age of 30 she was still a virgin and had never had a serious romantic relationship.

Sexual beliefs/messages and resulting feelings/behaviors

All families are governed by particular beliefs and messages about gender and sexuality and these dictate how family members' feel, behave, and interact. These beliefs and messages can be overt and covert, but either way, they organize how people conduct themselves and how a family functions. Figure 6.1 presents some examples of common beliefs and messages about aspects of gender and sexuality and the corresponding feelings and behaviors that stem from these.

Intergenerational patterns related to sex and gender

Families evolve through time and across generations. Hence, much of what occurs in a given family at a given moment in time is heavily influenced by what has been inherited from previous generations. The sexual genogram by Hof and Berman (1986), which is highly compatible with a family life cycle perspective, is a tool for conducting a multigenerational assessment of a family that focuses on identifying how a family's sexual legacy over several generations may be affecting its current development. Recently, Belous, Timm, Chee, and Whitehead (2012) have updated the sexual genogram to more fully reflect diverse experiences and contemporary issues. Informed by a Queer-Critical theory lens, they have argued that traditional approaches to genogram construction are inherently heteronormative and use discriminatory symbology. "Particularly, the use of different symbols to distinguish differences in gender, sexual orientation, and relationship status intrinsically privilege one group over another; labeling groups of people as 'different' and requiring separate symbols and construction methods. It is due to this that the changes to the general construction and interpretation of the sexual genogram are proposed, including gender, sexual orientation and attraction, relationship lines, sexual communication and sexual environment" (p. 284).

Following along with the idea that the sexual genogram is a vital tool that can aid in the process of gathering information that focuses on issues of gender, sexuality, intimacy, and power in a family system, below are a series of questions that were adapted from Hof and Berman (1986):

- What are the overt and covert messages in the family regarding sexuality, intimacy, your body, and masculinity, and femininity?

- How have the family's boundaries encouraged or discouraged expressions of sexuality and intimacy?

- What family members were the most comfortable with issues of sexuality and how was that expressed? Who was the most uncomfortable with issues of sexuality and how was their discomfort expressed?

Figure 6.1 Beliefs/messages.

Beliefs/Messages	Resulting Feelings/Behaviors
It is okay for men to have multiple sexual partners—doing so makes a man a stud or a player. In contrast, it is not okay for a woman to do the same—women who have multiple sexual partners are promiscuous, immoral, ungodly, and need to be sanctioned.	Men feel permission to have multiple sexual partners and flaunt it with pride. Women feel conflicted about having multiple sexual partners and they either limit their activity or try to downplay or hide their behavior. Women who are open about having multiple sexual partners are more likely to feel shame than men who behave similarly.
Bodies that do not confirm to societal ideals (which most do not) are shameful and embarrassing.	Those whose bodies do not conform to the societal ideal feel ashamed and try to hide their bodies.
Sex is dangerous, bad, and shameful.	People often feel shame in response to sexual thoughts, desires, and behaviors, and many people avoid openly acknowledging or discussing their sexual thoughts, feelings, and/or behaviors.
Women who wear sexually provocative clothing are asking to be raped.	Women who are raped are often directly or indirectly blamed, especially if they were wearing sexually provocative clothing. As a result, women who are raped often feel shame and end up blaming themselves for their violation.
It is immoral for children to be born out of wedlock.	Unmarried women who get pregnant often feel shame and when an unplanned pregnancy occurs outside of marriage, it can pressure people to marry when they otherwise would not choose to do so.
Homosexuality is bad, wrong, or sinful.	People who are not heterosexual often feel shame and internal conflict about their sexual orientation. As a result, some may deny their true sexuality to themselves and/or others.

- What were the relationships between power, sexuality, and gender in your family?
- How do you think your family's cultural background has influenced how it has handled issues of sexuality, intimacy, gender, and power?
- What attitudes were expressed in your family about sexual violence? If there has been/is sexual violence in your family, how is this handled and addressed?
- Were there issues related to sex and intimacy that generated shame and guilt? For whom?
- Were there family "secrets" regarding sexuality and intimacy (e.g., incest, unwanted pregnancies, abortions, affairs)?
- How do you perceive your sexuality? How does your partner perceive his/her sexuality?

- What questions have you had about sex or intimacy in your family that you never asked? If you were to ask, who would you most likely ask?
- Are there ways you wish your family system were different with respect to issues of sexuality/intimacy, gender, and power?
- How do you imagine other family members would answer these questions?

Cultural norms

Families have unique cultural identities that influence their development, composed of various factors including religious affiliation, social class, ethnicity, migration, and racial background.

RELIGION, SEX, AND SIN. Of all the dimensions that comprise a family's cultural background, religion is one of the most influential with respect to how a family experiences sexuality. All religions communicate specific notions about gender, sex, and power that influence family development, even in families that do not necessarily have a strong religious sense.

Most religions convey a great deal of negativity about sex that creates a context of shame and guilt. Virtually anyone who was raised in a family where religion was a facet of their upbringing has been subjected to, and has internalized, some degree of sexual shame and guilt stemming from the belief that sexual desire, activity, and pleasure are bad, and much more so for women than for men.

Many religions also teach that sex is only permissible when it occurs between a man and woman, within the confines of marriage, and most specifically, for the purposes of procreation. This further contributes to shame and guilt for those who elect to engage in pre-marital or extra-marital sex.

As ecofeminist scholars have pointed out, many pre-agricultural and pre-industrial societies were organized around earth-based religions where the feminine principle, fertility goddesses, and nature symbolism were preeminent. But eventually, these earth-based religions were crushed under the weight of the patriarchal, militaristic sky-gods of Judaism, Christianity, and Islam (Merchant, 1980). These religions are inherently dualistic and thus they divide the world into opposites and assign differential value to these opposites such that one is valued and one is devalued (e.g., good/evil, light/dark, male/female, and spirit/flesh). In this way, maleness is associated with the "higher order" realms of mind, spirit, and culture/technology, while femaleness is associated with the "lower order" realms of the body, the flesh, and the earth/nature. From this perspective, sexuality is deemed bad, sinful, and dangerous to the extent that it operates at the level of the flesh, and thus is inherently a lower-order function associated with femaleness. Hence, the sin that is found in sex is rendered inherently female (Warren, 2000).

While most religions discourage sexual feelings and activity unless it occurs within marriage for procreation, female sexuality tends to be more heavily restricted, censored, and shamed than male sexuality. In this context, boys are raised to believe their sexual feelings and impulses are normal, "manly," and healthy, while girls are taught to deny theirs or to be ashamed of whatever desire they may understand themselves to be feeling. The effect this has on couple relationships is that men are more likely to be comfortable with their bodies and in expressing themselves sexually, while women are more likely to struggle, which contributes to tensions related to how often and in what ways couples are sexual.

Within patriarchal religions, women are stripped of the power to control their own sexuality and to act authoritatively on behalf of their own needs and desires. The proliferation of pornography and the sexual abuse of women is the logical extension of these underlying dynamics, all of which have their roots in patriarchal religious principles.

SOCIAL CLASS. Social class is another factor that shapes sexual attitudes, behaviors, and experiences. For example, middle-income teens tend to delay first intercourse longer than low-income teens. One possible reason for this difference may be that low-income adolescents have greater pressures to grow up quickly and assume adult roles earlier than their middle-income counterparts. Moreover, while girls and women of all social class groups have unintended pregnancies that lead to childbirth, middle-income teens have fewer than low-income teens. Furthermore, while abortion rates overall have dropped in the last decade, they have risen about 25 percent among low-income girls and women (Jones, Finer, & Singh, 2010).

The intersection between social class and power also shapes how sexuality is experienced, viewed, and treated. The social marginalization and devaluation that poor and working-class people are subjected to infiltrates sexuality throughout the life cycle. Given the extent to which violence against women is tolerated by society, poor and working-class women are especially vulnerable. They are sexually assaulted at higher rates than their middle- and upper-income counterparts, and are treated as less credible victims when they report their victimization. Class bias contributes to assumptions that the sexual violation of poor and working-class women is somehow "natural" to their social class because their poverty renders them slightly "less human" (e.g., wild animal nature) and therefore as somehow deserving of, and even enjoying their victimization.

In her work on sexual violence, Phipps (2009) has pointed out that to have one's sexual violation taken seriously in a patriarchal society, a woman has to be viewed as respectable and this is often based on how well she performs stereotypical femininity, which is undeniably linked to class standing. The influence of class on how sexual violence is treated also affects men. Although there are no significant class differences in the rate with which men commit acts of sexual violence, poor and working-class men are more often arrested, prosecuted, convicted, and subjected to harsher sentences than men from higher income groups (Phipps, 2009).

ETHNIC/RACIAL BACKGROUND. Ethnic and racial groups each have their own set of values, attitudes, and beliefs about sex that regulate behavior. For cultures that have strong religious influences, there is a tendency toward more conservative sexual attitudes that include viewing sex as dangerous and threatening. Because families are embedded within their ethnic and racial cultures, they absorb these ideas that organize family interactions and relationships over time.

For ethnic and racial minorities, experiences with social marginalization and devaluation influence how their sexuality is viewed and treated. The dehumanization that often occurs of ethnic and racial minorities contributes to perceptions that they are more "animalistic," and therefore, more sexual and more prone to sexual misconduct as part of their "nature." This makes women of color in particular more vulnerable both to sexual violence and the secondary violence of having their violation made invisible in the courts and in the society.

Societal organizing principles

An examination of some of the principles that organize U.S. society and shape our relationship with sexuality must begin with an acknowledgment of the highly conflicted relationship our society has with sex. On one hand, deeply embedded Judeo-Christian values contribute to a view of sex as sinful and shameful. On the other hand, a media-driven, consumer culture pushes sex incessantly, using it to sell everything from movies to automobiles to food. These mixed messages about sex are confusing and reflect a deep underlying ambivalence about sexuality as something to be both reviled and revered.

Societal ambivalence about sex creates a context where there is excessive exposure to sex, but this exposure is narrow and incomplete. On one hand, sex is everywhere. Yet what we really know and understand about the depth and complexity of sex is greatly limited. Individual and family development occurs against the backdrop of this societal ambivalence. Whatever sexual issues and dynamics families are contending with, they do so within a social context that floods them with sexual imagery and content, and yet only offers the most meager consideration of the deeper, more complex aspects of human sexual experience.

MONOGAMY. One of our society's most deeply embedded organizing principles is a conviction in the sanctity of monogamy. Mainstream U.S. society regards monogamy as the only truly acceptable way to have a long-term relationship. In many ways, it is regarded as the foundation of our social order. Because our society places such a high value on monogamy, when extra-marital (or extra-relationship) sex occurs, it morally frowned upon and tends to arouse tremendous hurt, guilt, shame, anger, and disillusionment. Yet, as much as monogamy is socially valued and as much as infidelity is shunned, the reality is that over the course of married life in the United States, infidelity occurs in roughly 25 percent of relationships (Whisman & Snyder, 2007).

CAPITALISM AND PATRIARCHY. Two organizing principles of U.S. society that powerfully shape how sex is viewed and treated are capitalism and patriarchy. Capitalism turns sex into a commodity that can either be sold directly or used to sell other goods and services. There are entire industries, both legal and illegal, organized around selling sex. On the legal side, pharmaceutical companies sell sexual enhancement drugs such as Viagra and Cialis; manufacturers and retailers sell sexual aids and toys; movie producers and distributors make and sell pornographic videos and magazines; and even an assortment of professionals including doctors, therapists, and sexual surrogates make money by helping people to have more or more satisfying sex. On the illegal side, prostitution and the sex trade all profit from the sale of sex, and often in ways that involve extreme exploitation and abuse of women and children. Additionally, capitalism uses sex as a vehicle to sell other products and services.

Patriarchy establishes and reinforces male dominance over women and children. Under patriarchy, attitudes toward sex vary depending on whether the participants are male or female. Since men are valued and empowered within a patriarchal system, male sexuality is deemed positive and is encouraged and admired. Conversely, since patriarchy devalues and subjugates women, their sexuality is portrayed as dangerous (and therefore as something that must be controlled by men), and as bad and shameful (and therefore as something that must be repressed and denied). There have been periods in human history (e.g., the Han Dynasty of ancient China, preconquest Mexico) when female sexual desire has been recognized, honored, and treated with sacredness. However, patriarchy has been an organizing principle of most societies across time; hence, female sexuality has been degraded and punished throughout much of recorded human history.

Because of the differential valuation attached to femaleness and maleness, boys develop greater comfort with their bodies and their sexuality earlier on than do females. The mere fact that boys start to masturbate on a regular basis around ages 8 or 9, while girls typically do not begin until at least mid-adolescence reveals the differential level of comfort they have with their bodies and their sexuality. The differences between boys and girls with regard to early awareness and expressions of sexuality have implications for how men and women experience and express their sexual desire during adulthood. In general, men feel far greater latitude to acknowledge and act upon their sexual desire than do women, who generally internalize the prohibitions and negativity about their desire.

Recently, the sexual revolution has heightened women's freedom to express themselves sexually and experience deeper levels of physical fulfillment. Nevertheless, female sexual desire is still regarded as dangerous and shameful and in countless ways, expressions of liberated female sexual desire are punished. For example, if a woman has the audacity to pursue and express her sexual desire without apology, she is likely to be labeled a slut. To survive this, Wolf (1997) explained that most girls learn early on that they must split their sexuality off from "legitimate" identity. This involves joining with boys to condemn other girls who have dared to act upon their sexual desire. They learn to target the girl who most embodies their sexuality, thereby making those girls the scapegoat for all of the badness that society attaches to female sexuality.

The interaction of patriarchy and capitalism objectifies women's bodies and their sexuality, thereby fostering a climate that leads to sexual violence against women and children. Despite progress in the area of gender equality and increased public awareness of sexual violence, women are routinely abused sexually. Nearly one in five women reports being raped at least once in their lifetime (National Center for Injury Prevention and Control, 2012) with most victims knowing their attackers (Centers for Disease Control and Prevention, 2010). Moreover, it is estimated that at least 60 percent of rapes are never reported. Among female rape victims, 42 percent were raped before the age of 18 with 93 percent of juvenile sexual assault victims knowing their attackers (Bureau of Justice Statistics, 2000). It is estimated that one out of four girls and one in six boys will be sexually assaulted by the time they are 8 years old (Truman, 2011).

Adding insult to the injury of sexual assault, patriarchy contributes to a perception that when women are sexually abused, somehow, they are responsible for their victimization. Recently, for example, in response to complaints filed by students, several prominent universities, including the University of North Carolina at Chapel Hill, Occidental, Swarthmore, Dartmouth, Yale, and the University of Colorado at Boulder have become the target of federal investigations for failing to adequately address reported sexual assaults (Kingkade, 2013). At Occidental University, when a student went to a Department of Public Safety (DPS) officer to report a sexual assault at a fraternity, the officer told her "women shouldn't go out, get drunk and expect to not get raped." In other cases, where investigations found the perpetrators to be guilty of rape they received minimal punishments such as being assigned book reports and brief suspensions (Baker, 2013).

Assess your comprehension of sexuality: individual and family development by completing this quiz.

Sexuality Over the Family Life Cycle

There are a variety of factors that influence how human beings experience, understand, express and/or repress, and generally relate their sexuality. This section focuses on examining how familial and cultural patterns and dynamics intersect with individual and family life cycle stages to shape human sexual development and experience.

Couplehood

The coupling experience is greatly influenced by what we learned in our families about sex while growing up, and hence the sexual thoughts, beliefs, and feelings we internalized. For example, growing up in a family that has repressive ideas about sexuality or growing up in a family with indiscriminately open sexual attitudes can complicate the process of dating, mate selection, and the formation and maintenance of an intimate couple relationship.

The majority of Americans become sexually active at some point during adolescence, although most people do not marry until later in life. In 1970, the average age for first marriage was 22, but by 2010 it had increased to 27 (U.S. Census Bureau, 2011). In fact, fewer people marry now than in the past with fewer than half of U.S. households comprised married couples. Since the idea that sex must be saved for marriage has less power now than it once did, many young adults have multiple sexual partners prior to coupling or marriage, and unmarried coupling occurs much more frequently than in previous generations.

Sexuality within a couple relationship may serve various functions including procreation, to satisfy physical desires, to achieve emotional closeness and intimacy, or as an abuse of power. Conventional wisdom implies that sex is natural and therefore should come naturally in couple relationships. There are a number of factors, however, that tend to inhibit or impair sexual satisfaction in couple relationships. First, despite the proliferation of sexual imagery and information available in today's society, what most people know about sex is limited to the technical aspects. While most adolescents get some kind of sex education in school and an informal sex education from peers and the media, few are exposed to more in-depth information about the emotional and relational aspects of sexuality (Shoveller, Johnson, Langille, & Mitchell, 2004). Hence, many adults find themselves limited when it comes to how to identify, express, and experience sexuality in ways that address its more complex psychological and relational dimensions. Second, many women have internalized negative views about their bodies and their sexuality and this makes it exceedingly difficult to have a healthy sexual connection with a partner. Additionally, the widespread sexual abuse of girls and of some boys imposes another complication on healthy sexual functioning in adulthood. Yet, perhaps one of the greatest impediments to a healthy couple sex life is that few people enter relationships understanding how to participate in ways that promote real intimacy and connection. Sex in a relationship over time is only as good as the quality of the couple's intimacy.

Noted couples and sex therapist David Schnarch (2010) has done extensive research demonstrating that many of the sexual problems that couples experience are rooted in the struggles they have establishing and building intimacy. While popular notions of intimacy portray it as a state of excessive connection and fusion, in fact, real intimacy is reflected in the capacity to balance connection and belonging on one hand, with autonomy and separateness on the other. Unfortunately, there are few places in today's society where we teach this principle. As a result, most adults have a very limited view of what constitutes intimacy and how this relates to healthy, satisfying sexual functioning. The result is that many couples struggle with some kind of sexual dissatisfaction, at least at some point in their relationship.

For many people, the typical "solution" to frustrations in their couple relationship is to have an affair. While it is more common for men to stray outside of their relationship in response to sexual frustration or dissatisfaction, infidelity for both men and women is very often a response to unmet intimacy needs. The difference is that many men process their intimacy needs in sexual terms, but when time is taken to unpeel what is driving their sense of dissatisfaction, like women, most men find that they are struggling with how to be intimately connected in a meaningful way.

In a similar vein, couples and sex therapist Esther Perel, author of *Mating in Captivity* (2007), has argued that contrary to popular wisdom, too much connection and "we-ness" undermines desire and sexual satisfaction. She has explained that love may require closeness, but desire requires distance, transgression, surprise, and play. Couples who are able to maintain some autonomy and respect for each partner's unique individuality, and who are able to remain open to novelty, curiosity, experimentation, and exploration, are better able to nurture passion and eroticism in long-term relationships. With respect to affairs, Perel noted in an interview with Polly Vernon that, "When you have an affair, this is rebellion! This is not a mild act! We have affairs to beat back the sense of deadness. We have affairs not because we are looking for another person, but because we are looking for another version of ourselves. It's not our partner we seek to leave with the affair, it's ourselves. It's what I've become that I don't like. It's how I've truncated myself. That there are parts of me that I have been so out of touch with, for decades" (Vernon, 2010). Perel has explained that there are many different ways partners can strive to balance connection with separation, and in so doing, keep themselves and their eroticism alive. One such way involves consensual non-monogamy. "Perel sees non-monogamy by consensual agreement becoming more acceptable and integrated into marriage in the future, much as pre-marital sex has become an accepted norm and monogamy now means having one sexual partner at a time rather than one for life" (Booth, 2013, p. 92).

Among gay and lesbian couples, well-known couples researchers like Pepper Schwartz (1998) and John Gottman (2003) have demonstrated that LGBT couples are similar to heterosexuals with respect to the relationship challenges they face and the pathways they follow to achieve intimacy and satisfaction. One way in which differences have been observed is with respect to rates of sexual frequency. Specifically, there is some evidence that gay male couples have the highest sexual frequency, while lesbian couples have the lowest, often referred to as "lesbian bed death" which is the tendency among lesbians to have virtually no sex after several years of being together. There is no clearly demonstrated reason for these differences. One of the most popular explanations is that rates of sexual frequency are tied to gender differences. Since men tend to initiate sex more often than women, the rate of sexual activity is likely to be higher where both partners are men and lower when both partners are women (Peplau, Fingerhut, & Beals, 2004). Additionally, gay and lesbian couples also have to negotiate their relationship and their sexuality within a social context that is devaluing and marginalizing, which creates an added layer of stress that heterosexual couples do not have to face.

Pregnancy

We live in an age when women are having babies across a wide spectrum of the life cycle. In some cases, pregnancy occurs during adolescence. In most cases, this means sex came first and what followed was an unexpected pregnancy, which involves high degrees of anxiety and distress. In terms of planned pregnancies, women delay childbearing longer now than any time before, with the average age of a first birth occurring around 25, and a growing number of women having children into their late 40s (Mathews & Hamilton, 2009). In these cases, sex is secondary to pregnancy. It serves as a means to an end and in some cases sex is entirely removed from the equation, as with in vitro fertilization. A common complaint when couples are trying to get pregnant and having difficulties is that sex often feels contrived and robotic, like something they are being asked to perform on a schedule and therefore resent.

During pregnancy, couples can continue to experience a normal sex life. It is only in the latest stages of pregnancy that sex is discouraged primarily because it becomes uncomfortable for women.

Following pregnancy, most women are physically able to resume normal sexual activity within several weeks after giving birth. However, the massive hormonal changes their bodies have undergone, coupled with the psychological and emotional shifting that refocuses their energy onto their newborn child, tend to result in diminished sexual activity. It is not uncommon for men to feel slighted during this period of time, missing sex with their partners and feeling secondary to the needs of their children.

Young children and families

After the baby's first year, it is common for couples to resume more regular sexual activity, unless the woman becomes pregnant again. With the inclusion of children, the challenge many couples face is how to create time for their relationship. The trap many fall into is that they relate primarily as parents and not as a couple, or in worst case scenarios, women assume virtually all parenting responsibilities and men gravitate deeply into the world of work. When this occurs, couple relating, which includes sex, becomes extremely limited.

The quality of their parents' sexual life influences what children learn and come to feel about sex in general, and specifically about their own sexuality. Whether parents are coupled (either with each other, or with other partners) or single, how they feel about their bodies, how often they have sex, and their overall degree of sexual satisfaction affect their mood and disposition. How parents think and feel about sex in general and their sexuality specifically influences how they raise their children and this in turn influences how their children come to think and feel about sexual issues and themselves as sexual beings.

CASE ILLUSTRATION

Selena

Selena grew up with a single mother, Rosetta. Her father left the family when Selena was 2 and never contacted her after that. Her mother was an attractive, successful professional woman who dated frequently and had had a series of relationships with men that never lasted long. As early as age 5, Selena remembered overhearing her mother having sex and the enjoyment this seemed to bring her. Yet she also observed her mother's intense discomfort with her body, to the point Rosetta refused to be seen in the summer in a bathing suit. This exposure to her mother's body image issues and sexual practices greatly influenced Selena from an early age. By the time she was a young adult, her view of her body and sexuality had been greatly shaped

by this early socialization. Upon seeing a therapist for the first time, Selena explained that her mother was an enigma to her. She was aware of her body image struggles and yet she also observed the ease with which her mother was sexual with a variety of men. Selena explained that she had internalized her mother's body image anxiety, so much so that she refused to allow anyone to see her naked. She also disliked the number of men her mother had dated and had vowed that she would never do that herself. Now that Selena was finally in a relationship with a man she deeply loved, she was struggling with how to be sexual with him since she could not tolerate the thought of him seeing her naked.

The therapist pointed out that there were two different issues relative to her mother that Selena disliked: (1) the ease with which her mother engaged in multiple casual sexual relationships and (2) her mother's negative feelings about her body. The therapist also pointed out that Selena had chosen to reject the first of these for own life, yet she had adopted the second one. The therapist suggested that the most powerful way to be true to herself would be to continue to choose to be sexual only within the context of committed relationships and to choose to embrace her body and share it freely with someone she loved. Doing both of these things would disrupt the legacy from her mother that she feared and disliked. That was a new way for Selena to think about her situation and it helped her to free herself of the anxiety she had held from her mother's history.

Adolescents and families

Adolescence, by its very nature, is characterized by identity confusion, uncertainty, questioning, and experimentation. It is normative for adolescents to have questions about who they are and how they fit into the world. Hopefully, this stage of uncertainty occurs in a family system that provides young people with the space to be confused, to question, and to experiment, while simultaneously holding them accountable through the application of clear and consistent boundaries and rules. However, because many families manifest some underlying anxiety about sexuality, there are often unstated prohibitions against openly discussing sex or engaging in sexual behavior. As a result, many teens struggle to explore sexual issues with minimal parental guidance, nurturance, or support.

A study conducted by the U.S. Centers for Disease Control and Prevention revealed that approximately 35 percent of high school students are sexually active and almost half of them have engaged in sexual intercourse (Doyle, 2007). The average age of first intercourse is 16.9 years for males and 17. 4 years for females. Age of first intercourse varies by race and social class. The average age for White teens is 16.6, 15.8 for African American teens, 17.0 for Hispanic teens, and 18.1 for Asian Americans teens (Smith, 2006). For low-income families, the age of first intercourse is much earlier at about age 14.

The process of adolescent sexual exploration and discovery is complicated by two common risk factors: unplanned pregnancy and contracting a sexually transmitted disease (STD). The human brain develops from back to front and hence the last region to fully mature is the prefrontal cortex. This is the part of the brain that controls executive functions including foreseeing and weighing the consequences of behavior, impulse control, delaying gratification, inhibiting inappropriate behaviors, modulating intense emotions, and processing multiple sources of information when faced with complex situations (Casey, Jones, & Hare, 2008). Because most adolescents lack the brain maturation that is required to use good judgment when faced with potentially risky situations, they are more apt to engage in high-risk behaviors even when they have been informed of the potential consequences.

Given their limited brain maturation, despite being educated with the facts, many teens fail to employ protective measures to prevent unplanned pregnancies and STDs. Every year, an estimated one in four sexually active teens contracts an STD (a quarter of all new cases of sexually transmitted infections) (Doyle, 2007). Yet teen pregnancy rates have dropped 25 percent for teens between the ages of 15 and 19 between 2007 and 2011, and since 1991 the rates have been cut in half (National Center for Health Statistics, 2012). Nevertheless, one in three girls who have sex before the age of 20 gets pregnant (Martin, 2011).

Often, the prospect of having to tell one's parents greatly compounds the stress of unplanned teenage pregnancy. For teens whose families have a strong religious orientation, a confession of this nature can be especially stressful. An admission of pregnancy also exposes the fact that one was engaged in sexual activity outside of marriage. Teens who fear the reactions that such an admission might provoke may choose to terminate a pregnancy to avoid parental anger, disapproval, and shaming. It is estimated that about one third of teens who get pregnant have abortions and in most of these cases, their parents are not aware (Guttmacher Institute, 2013; Jones & Boonstra, 2004). For teens who choose to carry their babies to full term and either raise them or give them up for adoption, their lives and the lives of their families are nevertheless altered forever.

For adolescents who may not be exclusively heterosexual, questions about their sexual orientation are often a source of stress. The process of trying to define one's self sexually is complicated by the extent to which the surrounding environment assumes heterosexuality. As a result, most sexual minority youth must struggle to understand themselves sexually, while living in a society and in families that may not offer the kind of openness, support, and encouragement they need for healthy identity experimentation and development (Stone Fish & Harvey, 19).

Andrew Solomon (2013) explained that families often struggle to provide appropriate support to sexual minority youth who are trying to understand and define their sexual identity. Solomon views families as having both vertical and horizontal dimensions of identity. The vertical dimensions consist of attributes and values that are passed down from parent to child across the generations, both through strands of DNA and also through shared familial and cultural norms. The horizontal aspects involve traits that are not inherited from our families. He says that being gay, lesbian, or bisexual are often horizontal identities because most sexual minority children are born to straight parents and have to learn what it means to be who they are from places outside their families. This is also the case with being transgendered, having a disability, being a genius, and so forth.

Heterosexual adolescents also engage in a process of exploring and experimenting with their sexuality, but they do in the context of messages from society and their families that are consistent with their sexual orientation. Hence, they have the opportunity to explore their sexuality without having to struggle with outside questioning and disapproval of their sexual orientation.

Midlife

Some midlife families have delayed childbearing and are contending with raising young children in middle age, while others are launching or have launched children and are faced with rediscovering who they are independent of their parenting role. Still, for those adults who have never had children, there is less of a dramatic shift in focus in the middle years, although they must still contend with anxieties that commonly arise with each passing year and the corresponding decline in once taken-for granted capacities (e.g., decreased eyesight, a slower metabolism, more "aches and pains").

As the population at large lives longer, and with lifestyle improvements related to nutrition and fitness, sexuality remains an important component of living a quality life for most people.

For women, menopause can be both a blessing and a stressor. While many women are relieved not to have to contend with their periods, it can be a challenging process to redefine oneself as a woman who can no longer reproduce. Also for many women at menopause, intercourse becomes painful physically, since the reduction in estrogen causes vaginal dryness.

For men, sexual arousal begins slowly declining after early adulthood and by midlife, men often have more difficulty achieving and sustaining an erection. Forty percent of men experience some type of erectile dysfunction by midlife (Keesling, 2006). While this can contribute to feelings of inadequacy, with the increased use of medications such as Viagra and Cialis, many more men are able to manage erectile issues more effectively.

Families with older family members

Human beings are fully capable of remaining sexual well into their old age. Depending on their physical health and energy level, older people can desire and experience sex as a regular part of their lives. It is not uncommon for sexual activity to become less focused around intercourse and more around kissing, touching, and caressing each other.

The extent to which older adults are able to experience and enjoy sex in their later years is affected by the family's overall openness toward sexuality, and at the same time, the extent to which older adults express and participate in being sexual also shapes the family.

> Assess your comprehension of sexuality over the family life cycle by completing this quiz.

CASE ILLUSTRATION

The Mahoney-Corelli Family

The Mahoney-Corelli family highlights the importance of viewing cases within the context of a multigenerational framework. This case progresses through several phases of the family life cycle tracking how the family's boundaries, their sexual rules and messages, the legacy that was inherited from previous generations, and the influence of societal and cultural norms have interacted to shape individual and family development in terms of sexuality.

The Presenting Issue and Assessment. The Mahoney family consisted of Angela and Patrick, married for 19 years, and their two children—Frank, age 17, and Patsy, age 15. Angela initiated therapy because she was concerned about Frank who had been caught with a group of friends drinking on school property and was suspended. Moreover, Frank had grown increasingly angry leading to several outbursts against his father and a male teacher at school. Angela was less concerned about Frank's drinking which she attributed to typical teenage behavior, and was more worried about his increased anger. Patrick was less worried and more irritated with his son, whom he described as disrespectful and suggested that what he most needed was someone to "knock some sense into him." This comment provoked Frank and angry words were exchanged between the father and son. Patrick told his son he needed to learn how to behave and Frank lashed back telling his father "You're one to talk about how to behave. Since when is cheating on your wife behaving right?"

Frank's outburst exposed the fact that slightly less than a year ago Angela started to suspect that Patrick was having an affair. After confronting him repeatedly, he eventually confessed. It was also revealed that Frank knew of his father's infidelity because his mother had confided it in him. And finally, it made clear that Frank's recent attitude and behavior issues were a reaction to the distress in the parents' marriage.

The therapist maneuvered to loosen the rigid boundary that divided the spouses while firming up the boundaries between mother and children. She did this by asking to meet alone with Patrick and Angela, thereby employing a classic structural technique for reconfiguring subsystem boundaries and restructuring interactions. Now the couple had to face each other without the children to triangulate.

During the first session alone with the couple, they revealed that they had struggled sexually for many years. Angela experienced low sexual desire, saying that she had very negative feelings about sex and rarely wanted to be sexual. Patrick, on the occasions they attempted to be sexual, struggled to maintain an erection. Patrick said he did not understand his erectile difficulties because he was attracted to his wife, and did not have this problem with the other woman. It was apparent to the therapist that Angela and Patrick were deeply disconnected from each other and each struggled with feeling unwanted and undesired by the other.

Gathering data and constructing a genogram

Guided by the assumption that the couple's dynamics were rooted in intergenerational patterns involving boundaries, sexual rules and messages, and the influence of cultural and societal norms, the therapist gathered information about their histories and worked with the couple to construct a genogram (see Genogram 6.1). Through this process, she learned the following about their histories.

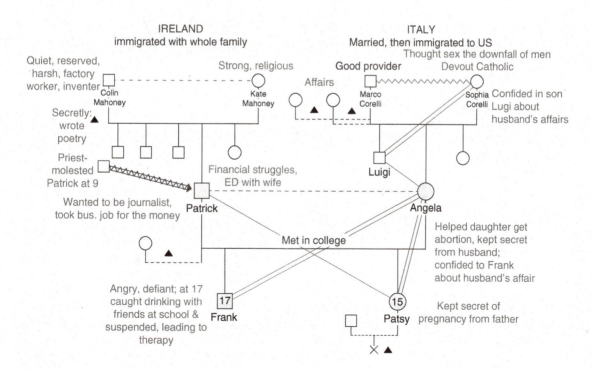

GENOGRAM 6.1 Mahoney/Corelli Family Genogram

Patrick's family of origin

Patrick Mahoney grew up in an Irish American family in Boston, the fourth of five children. His parents, Colin and Kate Mahoney, were Irish immigrants who met in the United States when they were 21 and were married 6 months later. Patrick described his mother as a strong woman who was guided by her religious devotion. He described his father as a quiet, reserved man who operated according to a strict moral code and could be a harsh disciplinarian.

Colin had no formal education but was a gifted mechanical designer and invented many ingenious parts for the company that employed him. Unfortunately, he was not a savvy businessman and as a result, his company made a fortune on his designs, but he himself struggled financially throughout his life. Because his sense of pride was largely tied to his ability to provide for his family, he was further humiliated by the fact that Kate, a skilled seamstress, earned a supplemental income for the family with her small sewing business.

The Mahoney family was defined by rigid boundaries and emotional disengagement. Because Patrick knew little of his parents' emotional reality, he was shocked later in life when he found a hidden collection of poetry his father had written. When he asked his mother about it, she admitted that Colin's secret aspiration was to be a poet, but he had forsaken his desire out of his sense of responsibility to provide for his family. Only then did Patrick realize how much loss his father must have felt around the sacrifices he had made to care for his family.

Because of the family's rigid boundaries and emotional distance, Patrick's parents never realized that when he was 9, he was molested by a parish priest, while serving as an altar boy. They never recognized that he had become sullen and withdrawn, although they did notice a decline in his grades that they responded to punitively.

Angela's family of origin

Angela Corelli was raised in an immigrant Italian family in Lowell, Massachusetts. Her parents, Sophia and Marco, grew up in rural Italy and a year after marrying emigrated to the United States with their firstborn child, Luigi. Marco worked in a mill

and Sophia stayed home to care for and raise the three children they eventually had. She was a devout Catholic and believed it was her duty to serve God, her family, and her community. Marco was also devoted to his family, working long hours to provide for them. At the same time, he had numerous extramarital relationships.

Angela's family was characterized by loose boundaries between family members and a high degree of closeness. Angela grew up learning that it was important to sacrifice her own needs to take care of others. The blurred boundaries and intense emotional closeness were reflected in Sophia's reliance on her son Luigi for emotional support. Because she made him her confidant she told him about his father's infidelities and allowed him to witness the pain this caused her. Luigi in turn shared this information with Angela.

Angela perceived her mother as asexual, saying she had gained weight early in the marriage, often wore dark, drab clothing, and spoke harshly of women in the neighborhood who flaunted their sexuality. Her mother taught her that sex was the downfall of men. Angela had a conflicted relationship with her father. She respected him greatly for his strong work ethic and how he provided for his family, but she also resented him for hurting her mother.

Becoming a couple and raising their children

Patrick and Angela met as sophomores at Boston University and they married shortly after graduating. Patrick wanted to be a writer, but he turned down a job with a small newspaper in favor of a higher paying sales position with a gas company. Angela worked as a teacher until the birth of their first child when she decided to become a stay-at-home mother.

Through the years, the dynamics that evolved in the family were characterized by a rigid boundary between Angela and Patrick and a loose boundary between Angela and the children, Frank and Patsy. Angela functioned as the primary caretaker of the children and had an intense emotional connection with them. Patrick was emotionally distant from his family, although he had a soft spot for Patsy whom he idealized. As a function of the loose boundary between Angela and the children, she shared secrets with each of them. When Patsy was 15, she got pregnant which she confided in her mother but never wanted her father to know. Angela agreed to keep Patsy's confidence and even helped her to have an abortion. With Frank, Angela confided Patrick's infidelities to him and she shared the anger and hurt she felt. Her husband's transgression reminded her of her father's infidelities and the pain that this had caused her mother.

An additional stressor in the family was related to financial pressures. Several years earlier, Patrick had taken a new job with another company with the understanding the pay would be better. It turned out to be a poor move because the company was unstable and after only a few months he was laid off. For the next year, Patrick was unemployed and the family struggled. While he eventually found a new job, the humiliation of not being able to provide for his family was hard on Patrick.

Interventions

Having gathered a great deal of information as part of constructing their genogram, the therapist guided the couple to identify the intergenerational patterns that had been transmitted over the generations and how these were shaping the current issues in the family. With minimal prompting, Angela and Patrick identified the theme around male infidelity, emotional and sexual distance between spouses, women devoting themselves to home and family such that there was an intense emotional closeness between mothers and children, and men working excessively and being largely disengaged from their children and wives. Following their lead, the therapist emphasized the pattern of men defining their worth in terms of economic success and making sacrifices to be good providers. That led Angela to share that she had just realized that both Patrick and his father had abandoned aspirations that involved writing so they could focus on providing for their families. Seeing this for the first time, Angela was able to access and convey compassion toward Patrick, including thanking him for the sacrifices he had made and the loss he had suffered. Patrick was visibly moved by her expression.

Another notable pattern the therapist highlighted involved women avoiding or feeling negatively about sex. Angela had clearly observed that in her mother,

and she guessed that her mother had learned that from her own mother. She could see how she had internalized the negativity that her family and her culture had communicated. The therapist guided her in a deeper exploration of the family, cultural, and societal norms and values that had shaped Angela's beliefs and feelings about sex in general and her sexuality specifically. Angela admitted that she did not feel like she was a sexual person and deep down, she disliked that about herself. She had always wondered what was wrong with her, although now she was starting to understand her feelings about sexuality as they related to the experiences in her family and even in her culture.

The therapist shared with the couple that most families have secrets that often reside at the center of the dysfunctions that haunt family members. She explained that fear and shame are usually what compel people to hold secrets. She cautioned that unless family members were willing to risk truth telling, no real intimacy or healthy relating would be possible. She asked each partner to think about what secrets they might possibly be holding and invited them to consider sharing these in the next session in the spirit of healing themselves, their marriage, and their family. It was this prompt that eventually led Patrick to admit the sexual abuse he had suffered as a child. In speaking this truth for the first time, he admitted he felt a relief he had never known before. It was an unburdening that he had craved his whole life but never felt the freedom to choose for himself. In therapy, with guidance from the therapist, Angela was able to respond with the comfort and reassurance that Patrick desperately needed to hear.

While it brought her great trepidation to do so, Angela admitted that she was harboring a secret that was a source of deep inner conflict because it involved one of their children. She required Patrick's promise that he would not become enraged and lash out in some way that would be hurtful to anyone involved. Eventually, Angela told him the truth about their daughter's sexual activity that resulted in pregnancy and abortion. Patrick was mortified. This information devastated the view he had of his daughter and it enraged him that his wife had conspired to help her get an abortion behind his back. With the therapist's guidance, he eventually was able to acknowledge feeling hurt that his daughter had not trusted him with something so serious, but he also had to admit that he could understand how scary and painful it would have been for her to risk "falling from grace" in this eyes. Angela pointed out that the abortion was harder on her, as an observant Catholic, than on him, because he did not adhere to religion. Nevertheless, against her own values, she supported Patsy because she realized that given their daughter's age and emotional state, having the child would have been devastating for her. This was something Patrick could relate to, and eventually, after his initial rage had been vented and dissipated, he was able to express his sadness that his daughter had endured this ordeal and his guilt that he had not helped her to feel safe in coming to him. He also was able to acknowledge the generational repeat that he had not felt able to tell his parents of his sexual abuse and now his daughter had not been able to tell him of her sexual indiscretion.

A critical component of Angela's disclosure to Patrick was that it strengthened the alliance between them while disrupting the parent–child coalition. The therapist explained that they had stopped functioning as a team a long time ago and each had found other ways to direct their energy and to get their needs met.

Angela had become overly involved with her children as reflected in Patsy's seeking support only from her mother in her time of need. Angela's closeness with Frank was another manifestation of energy that had been diverted out of the marital subsystem. The therapist referred back to the relationship Angela's mother, Sophia, had had with her brother Luigi. She asked if she saw the similarity and what she made of it. Angela could not deny that she, like her mother, had come to rely on closeness with her son as a substitute for unmet emotional needs in her marriage. This disclosure opened space for Angela to talk about how lonely and neglected she had felt over the years and, with the therapist's guidance, Patrick was able to hear and validate her feelings and acknowledge his inattentiveness. He admitted he had poured himself in to his work out of desperation to establish his sense of worth as a man and as result he had neglected the people he loved most.

Patrick's admission triggered Angela's anger because, as she pointed out, work had not been his only source of diversion. At that point, the therapist

had to take steps to address and help them heal the damage that had been inflicted by the affair. While healing from the trauma of infidelity takes a long time, it begins with the person who was unfaithful taking full responsibility, genuinely apologizing, and seeking the other partner's forgiveness. Because of the steps the couple had started to make together, it was easier for Patrick to respond non-defensively to Angela's anger. With the therapist's guidance, he admitted his wrongdoing. He explained that he had felt like a failure in so many ways and the affair had been an escape from those feelings. He admitted that until these therapy sessions, he felt like his wife did not value or respect him. He acknowledged that this did not excuse his behavior. It was explanation not justification, and as badly as he may have been feeling, nothing could excuse his affair. At that point, he broke down and expressed extreme remorse saying that he was ashamed for all these ways he had failed his family and he begged for his wife's forgiveness. Seeing his vulnerability so openly displayed softened Angela. While she still felt anger and would for a long time to come, his admission and acknowledgment, and his genuine show of feeling moved her. It helped her to respond with reassurance that she wanted them to heal and to reconnect, and she believed that was possible.

Gradually, the therapy process was helping to reconfigure the boundaries in the family system. The couple was more engaged than they had been in years and to further strengthen their connection, and to reinforce the de-triangulation of the children, especially Frank, the therapist held a session with just Patrick and Frank. In that session, Frank expressed a lot of anger toward his father. Having been prepped by the therapist, Patrick was able to avoid reacting to his son's anger and instead he validated his feelings. He also took responsibility for the fact that he had not been present enough in the family and he explained that this was going to change. He shared with Frank that he grew up in a family where his father worked all the time and he learned that to be a good man meant making enough money to provide for your family. He was only now starting to see that was not true and he did not want to teach his son the same wrong message. He told Frank that being a good man meant treating the people you love with respect and giving them your time and attention and that he planned to do that from here onward. While Frank refused to admit in the session that he believed his dad or was comforted by what he had shared, not surprisingly, his behavior and his disposition began to change for the better. His anger faded away and he started doing better in school.

The final issue the therapist addressed with the couple had to do with their sexual relationship. The couple was taking important steps to challenge family legacies, to confront cultural and societal norms that had not served them well, and to refocus their energy between them without diverting it elsewhere. With this foundation, their sexual relationship started to improve. Because Patrick was not harboring pent up feelings of inadequacy that he felt were reflected in his wife's eyes, eventually he was able to maintain an erection with her. That in turn was affirming to Angela who had felt sexually rejected in response to his erectile difficulties. His ability to sustain an erection, coupled with the vulnerability he had shared with her, and steps he had taken to be accountable for his transgressions helped her to feel close to and cared for by her husband. Moreover, she was challenging deeply held beliefs about sexuality and herself as a sexual being which was helping her to access desire for him that she had cut herself off from long ago.

> **Assess your comprehension of the case illustration: the mahoney-corelli family by completing this quiz.**

— Conclusion

Sexuality is a fundamental and inherently relational aspect of human experience. Any effort to understand human development; the family life cycle; and how individuals, families, and relationships of all kinds grow and change over time must include a focus on sexuality. This chapter has approached the study of sexuality across the family life cycle by considering how a family's boundaries, its beliefs and messages about gender and sexuality, the intergenerational patterns that have been transmitted about gender and sexuality, cultural norms, and societal organizing principles pursuant to gender and sexuality all interact to shape individual and family development over time. Even when a person or a family is not experiencing sexual problems per say, sex is always a part of the context and their experience. Therefore, any effort to study or understand the family life cycle must consider how human sexuality develops, is experienced, and is expressed over time and from one generation to the next within the interlocking contexts of family, culture, and society.

> **Recall what you learned in this chapter by completing the Chapter Review.**

— References

Baker, K. J. M. (2013, May 9). That was quick: Feds to investigate Occidental for sexual assault. *Jezebel*. Retrieved from http://jezebel.com/that-was-quick-feds-to-investigate-occidental-for-sexu-498482653

Belous, C. K., Timm, T. M., Chee, G., & Whitehead, M. R. (2012). Revisiting the sexual genogram. *The American Journal of Family Therapy, 40*(4), 281–296.

Booth, M. (2013, September). Lets talk about sex therapy: A special report. *Psychologies Magazine*, 89–93.

Casey B. J., Jones R. M., & Hare T. A. (2008). The adolescent brain. *Annual New York Academy of Science, 1124*, 11–26.

Centers for Disease Control and Prevention (2010). *National intimate partner and sexual violence survey (NISVS) 2010 summary report*. Retrieved from http://www.cdc.gov/violenceprevention/pdf/cdc_nisvs_overview_insert_final-a.pdf

Doyle, R. (2007, January). By the numbers: Teen sex in America. *Scientific American Magazine*.

Gottman, J. M., Levenson, R. W., Swanson, C., Swanson, K., Tyson, R., & Yoshimoto, D. (2003). Observing gay, lesbian and heterosexual couples' relationships: Mathematical modeling of conflict interactions. *Journal of Homosexuality, 45*(1), 65–91.

Guttmacher Institute (2013, June). *Facts on American teens' sexual and reproductive health: In brief, fact sheet.* Retrieved from http://www.guttmacher.org/pubs/FB-ATSRH.html

Hof, L., & Berman, E. (1986). The sexual genogram. *Journal of Marital and Family Therapy, 12*(1), 39–47.

Jones R. K., Finer, L. B., & Singh, S. (2010). *Characteristics of U.S. abortion patients.* New York: Guttmacher Institute.

Jones R. K., & Boonstra, H. (2004). Confidential reproductive health services for minors: The potential impact of mandated parental involvement for contraception. *Perspectives on Sexual and Reproductive Health, 36*(5), 182–191.

Keesling, B. (2006). *Sexual healing: The complete guide to overcoming common sexual problems,* 3rd edn. Alameda, CA: House Hunter.

Kimmel, M. (Ed.). (2007). *The sexual self: The construction of sexual scripts.* Nashville, TN: Vanderbilt University Press.

Kingkade, T. (2013, May 23). Sexual assaults mishandled at Dartmouth, Swarthmore, USC, complaints say. *Huffington Post.* Retrieved from http://www.huffingtonpost.com/2013/07/11/college-sexual-assault-complaints_n_3536004.html

Knox, D., & Schacht, C. (2011). *Choices in relationships: An Introduction to marriage and the family,* 11th edn. Independence, KY: Cengage Learning.

Lev, A. I. (2004). *Transgender emergence: Therapeutic guidelines for working With gender-variant people and their families.* Haworth Clinical Practice Press. Binghamton, NY.

Martin, T. W. (2011). Birth rate continues to slide among teens. *Wall Street Journal.* Retrieved June 21, 2013.

Mathews, T. J., & Hamilton, B. E. (2009). Delayed childbearing: More women are having their first child later in life. *NCHS Data Brief, 21.* Retrieved from http://www.cdc.gov/nchs/data/databriefs/db21.pdf

Merchant, C. (1980). *The death of nature: Women, ecology and the scientific revolution.* San Francisco: Harper San Francisco.

National Center for Health Statistics. (2012). *Provisional monthly and 12-month ending number of live births, deaths, and infant deaths and rates: United States, January 2011–December 2012.* National Center for Health Statistics.

National Center for Injury Prevention and Control (2012). *Sexual violence fact sheet, 2012* [Data file]. Retrieved from http://www.cdc.gov/ViolencePrevention/pdf/sv-datasheet-a.pdf)

Peplau, L. A., Fingerhut, A., & Beals, K. P. (2004). Sexuality in the relationships of lesbians and gay men. In J. H. Harvey, A. Wenzel, & S. Sprecher (Eds.). *Handbook of Sexuality in Close Relationships* (pp. 349–369). Mahwah, NJ: Lawrence Erlbaum Associates.

Perel, E. (2007). *Mating in captivity: Reconciling the erotic and the domestic.* New York: Harper Collins.

Phipps, A. (2009). Rape and respectability: Ideas about sexual violence and social class. *Sociology, 43*(4), 667–683.

Schnarch, D. (2010). *Intimacy and desire.* New York: Beaufort Books.

Schwartz, P., & Rutter, V. (1998). *The gender of sexuality: Exploring sexual possibilities.* Walnut Creek, CA: Alta Mira Press.

Shoveller, J. A., Johnson, J. L., Langille, D. B., & Mitchell, T. (2004). Socio-cultural influences on young people's sexual development. *Social Science & Medicine, 59,* 473–487.

Smith, T. W. (2006). American sexual behavior: Trends, socio-demographic differences and risk behavior. *National Opinion Research Council.* Chicago, IL: University of Chicago Press.

Stone Fish, L., & Harvey, R. (2005). *Nurturing queer youth.* New York: Guilford Press.

Solomon, A. (2013). *Far from the tree: Parents, children and the search for identity.* New York: Scribner.

Truman, J. L. (2011). *Criminal victimization, 2010, national crime victimization survey.* Bureau of Justice Statistics [Data file]. Retrieved from http://www.bjs.gov/content/pub/pdf/cv09.pdf

U.S. Bureau of Justice Statistics (2000). *Sexual assault of young children as reported to law enforcement, 2000.* U.S. Bureau of Justice Statistics.

U.S. Census Bureau (2011). *Table MS-2. Estimated median age at first marriage, by sex: 1890 to the present.* Release date: May 2011.

Vernon, P. (2010). Is anyone faithful anymore: Infidelity in the 21st century. *The Guardian,* March 6, 2010. Retrieved from http://www.theguardian.com/theobserver/2010/mar/07/polly-vernon-infidelity-betrayal-help-relationships

Warren, K. J. (2000). *Ecofeminist philosophy: A western perspective on what it is and why it matters.* Landham, MD: Rowman & Littlefield.

Whisman, M. A., & Snyder, D. K. (2007). Sexual infidelity in a national survey of American women: Differences in prevalence and correlates as a function of method of assessment. *Journal of Family Psychology, 21,* 147–154.

Wolf, N. (1997). *Promiscuities. The secret struggle for womanhood.* New York: Ballantine Publishing.

World Health Organization (2010). *What do you mean by "sex" and "gender"?* [Data file]. Retreived from http://www.who.int/gender/whatisgender/en/

Chapter 7

Lesbian, Gay, Bisexual, and Transgender Individuals and the Family Life Cycle

Deidre Ashton

— Learning Objectives —

- Define the acronym LGBT and explain why LGBT people are discussed as one group in the family life cycle.
- Describe legal impediments LGBT people face when coupling or growing a family.
- Explain how the intersection of cultural identity with sexual orientation and gender identity can intensify identity development tasks and add more complexity to the processes of the family life cycle.
- Recognize the importance of familiarity with LGBT identity development models when working with LGBT communities.
- Discuss how coming out as lesbian, gay, bisexual, or transgendered impacts individuals and families.
- List and describe challenges and opportunities unique to the development of LGBT people and their families as they become young adults.
- Describe the challenges and opportunities that LGBT people experience during the coupling stage.
- Discuss how deciding to become parents impacts an LGBT couple and their families.
- Identify how developmental tasks differ during adolescence when a family includes an LGBT person.
- Explain the challenges and opportunities that LGBT people and their families experience during later life.

Introduction

Lesbian, Gay, Bisexual, and Transgender (LGBT) people have been members of families of origin, families of choice, and families of creation across cultures and nations throughout history (Blando, 2012). Prior to the spread of homophobia through Western colonialism, same-sex relationships were socially accepted and well integrated into family structures in many cultures throughout the world (Williams, 1998). The contemporary LGBT civil rights movement marked by the Stonewall rebellion of 1969 has vigorously fought for the legal rights of LGBT people as individuals entitled to fair and just treatment in all areas of life including employment, housing, education, health care, marriage, and family formation. Prior to Stonewall, LGBT people were frequently portrayed as single adults, ostracized from their families of origin, incapable of establishing lasting partnerships, unfit to raise children, and relegated to the "gay ghettos" of major urban cities. Although there is still much work to be done, the LGBT civil rights movement has made significant strides in establishing and protecting the rights of LGBT people to couple, have children, and be recognized as healthy, productive, moral, and lawful members of families, communities, and society.

This chapter focuses on how LGBT people move through the family life cycle. It builds on the framework of Tom Johnson and Pat Colucci's chapter "Lesbians, Gay Men, and the Family Life Cycle" in earlier editions of this book. The reader will be oriented to the life cycle discussion through clarification of terminology, a review of the current legal status of LGBT families, conceptualization of LGBT individuals and families as multicultural people, and a review of models of LGBT identity formation.

The need for clarification of language is related to the generally accepted, erroneous construction of gender and sexual identity as biologically determined. The dominant culture maintains that biological sex determines gender identity, gender identity determines gender role, and gender role determines sexual orientation (Lev, 2004). The terms LGB are categories of sexual orientation or identity (Lev, 2004; Mallon, 2008a; Savin-Williams, 1996). LGB may be the self-selected terms that represent the individual's sexual orientation, the direction of sexual, affectional, and emotional attraction (Lev, 2004; Mallon, 2008a; Savin-Williams, 1996). Thus, individuals of LGB orientation may have various sexual identities, gender identities, or gender role expressions. For others, LGB may also be the self-selected terms that reflect sexual identity or the individual's sense of sexuality that integrates biological sex, gender identity, gender role expression, and sexual orientation (Lev, 2004). Among heterosexual and LGB individuals, there may be variation in biological sex, gender identity, and gender role expression. Transgender or gender-expansive (Baum et al., 2012) may be the self-selected terms that reflect experiences of gender identity that fall outside of the dominant culture's biologically determined, bipolar gender system (Lev, 2004). Among Transgender or gender-expansive individuals, there may be variation in sexual orientation, sexual identity, and gender role expression. In this chapter, the terms lesbian, gay, and bisexual reflect sexual orientation or identity and the terms gender-expansive transgender reflect gender identity.

If "LGB" references sexual identity/orientation, and "T" references gender identity, it may seem that we are conflating aspects of identity that are simultaneously related and different by discussing LGBT people as one group in the family life cycle. The reasons for doing so are fourfold: (1) although separate constructs, sexual identity, sexual orientation, gender identity, and gender role are interrelated; (2) LGBT people share in common the experience of transcending the limiting dominant social construction of sexuality and gender identity and thus share histories of marginalization; (3) LGBT people have all been marginalized in the discussion of families; and (4) Bisexual and Transgender people are often made invisible in the literature and in LGBT

communities. However, it is critical to acknowledge that while similarities exist, the experiences of these four groups are not identical, and thus there will be variations in family life cycle issues. This chapter overviews LGBT experiences in the family life cycle. The reader is encouraged to study each group separately to cultivate a more nuanced understanding of LGBT people and their families.

> **Assess your comprehension of the introduction by completing this quiz.**

Current Status of LGBT Families in the United States

Understanding the laws regulating coupling and family growth is essential to working with LGBT-headed families. The LGBT civil rights movement has made great strides in legitimizing the created families of LGBT communities by pursuing the legalization of Gay marriage and adoption of children by LG individuals and couples.

Access to marriage

The 2013 repeal of section 3 of the Defense of Marriage Act (defining marriage as a legal union between one man and one woman [DOMA, 1996]) by the Supreme Court of the United States was a watershed moment in the movement to grant full marriage equality to same-sex couples. The ruling provides same-sex couples access to some of the over 1,000 federal benefits granted to opposite-sex married couples (American Civil Liberties Union [ALCU] et. al., 2013). The ruling is limited as some federal agencies may base marriage recognition on the laws of the state of residence instead of the state of marriage (ACLU et. al., 2013). The ruling also left section 2 of DOMA in tact allowing each state to regulate coupling (United States v. Windsor et. al., 2013) rendering many couples and families invisible and unprotected. However, at the time of writing this book numerous states and the District of Columbia have granted full marriage equality to same-sex couples (Human Rights Campaign [HRC] 2015, National LGBTQ Task Force [NLGBTQTF], 2014). It is expected that by the summer of 2015 the Supreme Court of the United States will determine the constitutionality of state prohibitions of same-sex marriage (Beam, Loller, Sewell, & White, 2015).

The Transgender community remains more vulnerable than the LGB community. A preexisting marriage of an individual who transitions from one sex to another remains valid (American Civil Liberties Union 2013). In some states, access to marriage is based on the postsurgical sex of the transitioning partner, while in others it is based on the natal sex of each partner. Transgender couples may experience difficulties accessing benefits granted by marriage because of transphobia, heteronormativity, and cis-normativity.

The movement toward marriage equality for all continues as activists pursue passage of the Respect for Marriage Act that would ensure federal recognition of all marriages (ACLU et al., 2013).

Family growth

LGBT individuals and couples grow their families biologically, through formal and informal adoption, foster care, and by blending families. In states with marriage equality or other forms of same-sex unions, both partners are presumed to be the parents of a child born to them (National Center for Lesbian Rights [NCLR], 2014). In states prohibiting same-sex unions, the non-blood-related parent must establish parental rights through adoption or parentage judgment (NCLR, 2014). Several states prohibit second-parent adoptions by LGB partners, and adoption by same-sex couples, or leave adoption decisions to local jurisdictions (NCLR, 2014). The federal government appears more protective of parent–child relationships than couple relationships as federal law mandates that all states and jurisdictions recognize adoptions regardless of local law (NCLR, 2014).

Currently, there are no legal protections for gender-expansive parents (ACLU-NCTE, 2013) and courts have ruled against these parents regarding custody because of their Transgender identity (ACLU, 2013). Although some courts recognize that Transgender identity is not harmful to child development, they fall short of acknowledging that gender identity is not relevant to child development as evidenced by emerging research (Mallon, 2008b).

Advocacy of LGBT civil rights leaders, organizations, and shifts in public opinion are rapidly changing regulation of coupling and parenting. On a daily basis, LGBT individuals, families, and communities demonstrate their resilience in the face of legally sanctioned oppression and defy myth and rhetoric that they are antithetical to family values. Anyone working with LGBT families should consult the laws of their jurisdiction to understand the specific context of that family.

> Assess your comprehension of current status of LGBT families in the united states by completing this quiz.

Diversity Among LGBT Families

LG individuals have been characterized as bicultural because they have been raised in the heterocentrism of the dominant culture (Laird, 1993; Lukes & Land, 1990), but, in fact, LGBT individuals are multicultural as they are also members of various racial, ethnic, religious groups, and social classes, and occupy a range of locations along the continua of gender and sexuality. The diverse experiences, worldviews, and values of LGBT individuals and families are shaped by the intersection of these social locations and are particularly salient as we live in a world that is organized and ranked by these dimensions (Cole, 2009; Moore, 2011; Moore & Brainer, 2012; Singh & Harper, 2012). The intersection of multiple identities is a source of strength, and simultaneously results in the powerful interactive effects of multiple forms of oppression (Bowleg, 2008; Walters & Old Person, 2008, Moore, 2011, Moore & Brainer, 2012). Multiculturalism and intersectionality are the lenses through which LGBT people in the family life cycle are viewed.

A national survey of multiracial, Latino/a, Black, Asian, and Pacific Islander LGB individuals revealed that both racial and queer identity were valued by the majority of the over 5000 participants (Battle, Pastrana, & Daniels, 2013a, 2013b, 2013c). Although integration of multiple aspects of identity and active participation in each reference group may be optimal, many LGBT people of color are challenged to choose allegiance to the White, eurocentric LGBT community, or their heterocentric racial/

ethnic community. They must choose to seek protection from the heterosexism and homo-, trans-, and biphobia or sanctuary from racism. Choosing allegiance to the White LGBT community could result in the loss of support of the ethnic/racial community that has been present throughout the life course. Choosing allegiance to the ethnic/racial community could result in the loss of burgeoning support of the White LGBT communities. The racism of White LGBT communities goes further in maintaining white skin, heterosexual, and male privilege, and the heterosexism of communities of color is understood as a survival strategy, as homosexuality can be mistakenly seen as a challenge to the survival of the race (Greene, 1998; Walters & Old Person, 2008). Bisexuality and Transgenderism are viewed similarly within communities of color. These loyalty binds can intensify identity development tasks and add more complexity to the processes of the family life cycle.

> Assess your comprehension of diversity among LGBT families by completing this quiz.

Models of LGBT Identity Development

Familiarity with LGBT identity development models is beneficial to a discussion of the family life cycle, as the family is the context in which identity development takes place and the tasks and processes of LGBT identity development interact with those of the family life cycle. LGBT identity development can begin at any stage of development. It occurs along with, or in the context of, other aspects of identity development such as race/ethnicity (Bowleg, Burkholder, Teti, & Craig, 2008; Lev, 2004; Walters & Old Person, 2008). Some people become aware of their LGBT identity early; for others, awareness emerges at later life stages (Connolly, 2004a; Herdt & Beeler, 1998; Sanders & Kroll, 2000). Regardless of when LGBT identity development begins, experiences vary. People move around and through the stages at various rates and times, in varying order, and sometimes skip stages without indicating pathology or arrested development (Lev, 2004; Savin-Williams, 1996; Walters & Old Person, 2008).

Models have been developed to explicate the processes by which individuals discover, reveal, and develop a sense of pride in a subjugated sexual or gender identity in a heteronormative world. Each model highlights processes in which individuals move from self-awareness, to disclosure, to identity integration (Cass, 1979; Cass, 1998; Lev, 2004; Weinberg, Williams, & Pryor, 1994). Scholars have criticized the LGB models for being developed largely based on the experiences of White, Western middle-class people, equating behavior with identity, and failing to integrate cultural and historical contexts (Lev, 2004; Moore & Brainer, 2012). In many non-Western cultures and communities of color, identity is not based on the object of sexual attraction (Moore & Brainer, 2012). An individual may love a person of the same sex, be sexually involved, raise children, share a life and not identify as LGB. Savin-Williams (2005) proposes a differential developmental trajectory in which queer youth go through a process that is both like and unlike that of heterosexual youth and also like and unlike other queer youth accounting for within group variation, and multiple pathways into LG identity. The reader is encouraged to become familiar with these models as a starting place for working with the LGBT community, but is reminded to always privilege the pathways to LGBT identity presented by the individuals with whom they are working.

> Assess your comprehension of the models of LGBT identity development by completing this quiz.

Identity Management and Coming Out

Just as identity development begins at any stage of the life cycle, so can disclosure or coming out (Mallon, 2008a). Disclosure is an individual and relational process in which LGBT individuals become aware of their sexual identity or orientation or their gender variance and inform others. Many people conceptualize coming out as a one-time event, but because the world is heteronormative, coming out is a lifelong process (Mallon, 2008a) that is better conceptualized as identity management (Connolly, 2012). All of the previously referenced identity models include coming out as part of the identity formation process, as these are recursive processes in that disclosure "redefines" self and self-labeling "drives" disclosure (Savin-Williams, 1996).

Disclosure may vary according to familial and cultural norms. Methods of disclosure include both verbal and nonverbal expressions that can be voluntary or involuntary. Today's youth may not take on an identity label constructed by the dominant LGBT culture, or engage in conventional disclosure (Savin-Williams, 2005). Among people of color, nonverbal signifiers may be privileged over verbal disclosure (Walters & Old Person, 2008) and thus silence may not be an indicator of pathology but is likely culturally appropriate (Singh & Harper, 2012). The absence of explicit dialog does not connote secrecy as Battle et al. (2013a, 2013b, 2013c) found that the majority of people of color in a nationwide survey were out to friends and family. Salience of identity may be related to the coming-out processes for LGBT people of color. Black Lesbians and Bisexual women who find their sexual identity more salient are more likely to be out than those who find their racial identity to be more salient (Bowleg et al., 2008). Moore (2011) challenges conventional coming out constructs, identity development models, and labels as representing only one pathway into LGB identity and suggests that coming to Lesbian identity for Black women is a more complex process shaped by sex, gender, race, and class that she prefers to reference in the more culturally congruent language of "coming into the life."

Families of LGBT individuals also go through a coming-out process shaped by their values, beliefs, existing dynamics, quality of relationships, coping strategies, and oppressive forces (Connolly, 2004a; LaSala, 2010; Savin-Williams, 1996). LaSala (2010) frames coming out during adolescence as a relational process in which the family moves from awareness of the child's differentness to disclosure/ discovery, in which the child may experience relief from anxiety and parents assume the anxiety to acceptance and celebration. Lev (2004) outlines a process for families of Transgender individuals in which families move from a sense of betrayal and confusion to integration of the family member back into the system. Like individual coming out, the family process is not a one-time event, but will be repeated across the life span and in the context of the family life cycle.

> **Assess your comprehension of identity management and coming out by completing this quiz.**

The Family Life Cycle

The family life cycle discussion will focus on the ways multigenerational LGBT families complete the tasks and processes of each stage in the context of multicultural identities, sexual and gender identity development, coming out, heterosexism, heteronormativity, and a biologically determined binary gender identity system. The unique challenges and opportunities of being "other" at each stage will be examined with the understanding that these challenges are not related to sexual or gender identity but rather to the experiences of marginalization and multiple oppressions (Lev, 2004; Mallon, 2008a; Walters & Old Person, 2008). Although the following discussion will address voluntary coming out for the individual and family, it is acknowledged that an involuntary or unplanned discovery can heighten stress and anxiety for the individual and the family.

Regardless of life cycle stage, there are challenges LGBT families will commonly experience, including the cumulative effects of heterosexism, heteronormativity, and gender oppression from the larger society resulting in minority stress-generated mental health concerns (Giammattei & Green, 2012). Minority stress is amplified for those who occupy multiple marginalized statuses. The initial response to coming-out is often unpredictable and stressful as relationships can be at risk. Disclosure of an LGBT identity by any family member at any stage may delay completion of tasks, or for adolescents and young adults, it may accelerate launching (Lev & Sennot, 2012). Because of heteronormativity, biological determinism, and the lack of accurate information, families must integrate the sexual or gender identity of the LGBT member into the system, and cope with the family's shifting identity. Families grieve their expectations and assumptions about the LGBT family member and determine to whom to disclose, how, and when (Connolly, 2004a; Lev, 2004; Mallon, 2008a). LGBT individuals raised in heterosexual families, where all members are gender conforming and adherent to conventional gender roles, lack role models to inform sexual and gender identity formation, the coming-out process, and the development of survival strategies in the face of sexual and gender oppression (Connolly, 2004a). Families that have experienced racial oppression may see the individual's LGBT status in opposition to strategies taught to combat racism (Greene, 1998; Walters & Old Person, 2008) and may fail to see these strategies as helpful in combating heterosexism. Families of color may worry that the young adult now has another layer of oppression with which to cope. Dominant culture families who are unaware of experiences of oppression may feel unprepared to help their child cope with the newly declared devalued status. Both dominant culture and marginalized families may support and operate from heterosexist, homo-, bi-, and transphobic ideologies, and therefore may unintentionally participate in oppressive systems that harm and dehumanize their family members (Connolly, 2004a). They will have to come to terms with their attitudes and beliefs about homosexuality, bisexuality, and gender variance. Even the most accepting families that embrace LGBT friends must face their internalized oppression.

Along with challenges come benefits, or at least opportunities, at all stages of the life cycle. Queer youth raised by LGBT parents have role models within the family, and have likely learned LGBT culture, history, norms, and rituals within their families of origin (Luvalanka, 2012). Individuals who lack role models in their families of origin have unique opportunities to name themselves and to create family structure and roles based on needs and preferences instead of existing prescriptions. Similar to communities of color that define family in a broad manner including both blood and non-blood kin in varying functional roles (Boyd-Franklin, 2003; Watts-Jones, 1997; Walters & Old Person, 2008), LGBT communities have adopted this practice forming families of choice (Weston, 1991). In doing so, LGBT communities are finding ways to provide instrumental

and emotional support in the face of adversity and a mechanism for transmitting values, norms, knowledge, rituals, and survival skills. Although some LGBT families choose to adopt gender roles rooted in heteronormativity, many families transcend traditional roles and define them based on equality, interests, and talents (Mallon, 2008b). For example, research suggests that among LG couples, family responsibilities and chores tend to be more evenly distributed between partners (Gotta et al., 2011). LGBT families and communities have the opportunity to create rituals helpful in transitioning through the life cycle (Imber-Black & Roberts, 1998).

Throughout the discussion of life cycle stages, there is an implicit assumption that every adult wants to couple and raise children. Many healthy, well-adjusted individuals may not partner or parent by choice or circumstance. Remaining single or childless does not represent pathology or exclude individuals from the life cycle process. Single adults, and those who do not parent, have membership, roles, tasks, and meaningful relationships within the contexts of their families of origin and choice, and communities.

Leaving home and staying connected: adulthood

Launching reflects exiting from one's family of origin, but young adulthood also reflects entry into a life that is simultaneously independent and connected to the family of origin. Tasks focus on accepting movement in and out of the family system, shifts and renegotiations in the parental (couple) system, forming adult-to-adult relationships between older generations and the young adult, adjusting to changing abilities, health issues, and eventual loss of the older generation. For the single adult, tasks include starting career/work life, cultivating intimate relationships with peers, and assuming financial and emotional responsibility for self.

When young adults come out as LGBT to their families at this stage, the process can feel risky, as they may be early in their independence and still experience a heightened need for the support of their families of origin. Yet, queer young adults are not as vulnerable as adolescents and children because they are no longer fully dependent on their families.

Furthermore, LGBT young adults may be aware that family of origin support can be replaced or augmented by a developing family of choice or peer network. If the young adult has not come out to the family of origin, being single may allow the system to assume heterosexuality and gender conformance. If the young adult has come out, then being single may allow the family to view the nonheterosexual or nonconforming gender identity as a phase to be grown out of upon meeting the "right" person. The family of the bisexual single adult child may see bisexuality as a phase and push for opposite-sex dating in an effort to promote heterosexuality.

Because entry into single adulthood is a time of restructuring in the family of origin, the young person and the family may struggle with the role and place of the LGBT person in the family as the member may be failing to meet family expectations. When a family member comes out while the young adult is launching, the family may shift attention from launching the single young adult to coming to terms with the newly announced identity of the family member. Young adults may neglect their own tasks to support the newly out member, or to help the family cope with conflict.

As young adults establish their work lives and strengthen their peer support networks, they must constantly decide to whom they can safely disclose (Connolly, 2012), and that may impact their relationships and careers. As at other stages, some young adults may choose to lead double lives participating in LGBT communities while presenting as heterosexual or gender conforming in the rest of their lives. The challenges of dating may be further complicated by variation in stage of development regarding sexual and gender identity development (Connolly, 2012) as well as other identity statuses (e.g., race), adding another layer of complexity to this life cycle stage.

At first glance, it may appear that an LGBT identity is burdensome to young adults and their families. However, this perceived burden affords the family the opportunity to consciously examine its values, beliefs, and ways of being and relating to one another, as well as the opportunity to create a stronger, more open, and communicative family structure. Some families may break apart, but many families successfully complete this life cycle stage and continue to move forward

(Benshorn, 2008; Cramer & Roach, 1988; Griffin, Wirth, & Wirth, 1986; Johnson, 1992; Robinson, Walters, & Skeen, 1989).

CASE ILLUSTRATION

Randy

Randy, a 23-year-old African American man who is close to his multigenerational family of origin was raised in and remains a member of a historically Black, fundamentalist Christian church in a predominantly African American urban, northeast community. While growing up, his family viewed Randy as "soft" and "girly." Throughout high school, he found himself drawn to activities traditionally reserved for girls and experienced himself as neither man nor woman but transgendered. Randy's family saw his behavior as sinful and pushed him to repent through prayer and worship. Randy found his family's urgings intolerable and longed to openly explore his gender freely, to date men, and strengthen his connection to LGBT communities of color. Despite limited income, Randy moved out of the family home, into an LGBT neighborhood, and started dating a new acquaintance. After 3 weeks, Randy invited his new acquaintance to move in with him because he could not afford rent on his own. The acquaintance sold stolen property out of the apartment to earn his share of the rent. The two were caught, arrested, and convicted. Because it was Randy's first offense, and the court viewed transgenderism as pathological, Randy was referred for mental health treatment. The agency worker supported Randy to explore his gender and to identify and negotiate the conflicts he felt regarding his gender identity, religious beliefs, and family norms. The worker helped Randy to connect to an LGBT affirming faith community that had its roots in African American spirituality and traditions. Randy and the worker also met several times with his family of origin. Although the family held that Randy's behavior was sinful, they were willing to provide emotional support and guidance so that he could successfully live on his own with the understanding that they would silently pray for him and that Randy would refrain from discussing his gender identity in their presence. Randy accepted these terms for now, and invited his family to continue to participate in the therapeutic process. Living independently and connecting to an affirming, culturally relevant faith community allowed him to grow in his identity as an African American, Christian, gender-expansive man who is authentically connected to his family of origin.

Coupling

During the coupling stage, two adults form a committed union while blending their respective families and realigning their relationships with families of origin and choice, and friends. The formation of a healthy committed union may also include multiple partners. Partners in polyamorous unions face additional challenges while living in a heteronormative context that often pathologizes these relationships including challenges related to lack of social and legal relationship recognition.

Identifying a partner can be challenging particularly in conservative communities, even when aided by technology (Giammattei & Green, 2012; Lev & Sennott, 2012). The primary tasks of coupling are to solidify intimate bonds with a desired emotional and sexual companion, build a shared life, pursue common goals, support the individual goals of each partner, and formalize the status of the relationship as committed. Coupling may have several unintended or intended outcomes for LGBT people. Coupling may serve as a declaration of sexuality particularly in cultures where nonverbal cues are valued over verbal declarations. Same-sex coupling may also be a signal to the family that being LGB is not just a phase. If a bisexual person couples with a person of the opposite sex, the family may continue its heterocentric assumptions, causing conflict and frustration for the bisexual person (Weber & Heffern, 2008).

Most individuals develop their ideas about coupling from familial observations, popular culture, and media. From these sources, they learn values, norms, create the definition of a couple, and develop expectations. Some LGB couples will apply a heterosexual paradigm to their relationship and seek to live by these norms and roles. Others create their own way of enacting couplehood.

Tunnell (2012) describes three basic tasks of all couples: (1) creating a couple identity and bound-

ary around the unit, (2) regulating closeness and separateness, and (3) accommodating difference. These tasks can be complex for heterosexual couples but are further complicated by heterosexual privilege and traditional gender role socialization for LGBT couples. Identity and boundary formation are interactive processes involving the couple, their families, communities, and society. There is a recursive relationship among couple recognition, couple identity, and boundary formation. Recognition strengthens identity and boundary formation, and couple identity and boundary formation drive the desire for social recognition (Tunnell, 2012). Families of origin and creation, as well as society in general, serve as sources of recognition. Social recognition includes legal protections and helps to draw the boundary around the couple as a subsystem functioning within larger contexts. Despite the expansion of marriage equality, in some states the second-class domestic partnership or civil union remains the only option for same-sex couples. Failure to validate the couple may hamper identity formation resulting in stress and conflict for the couple. LGBT couples may choose to physically and or emotionally move away from invalidating sources and move toward affirming sources such as the family of choice. Sexual monogamy is often a presumed boundary marker for heterosexual, dominant culture couples. This is not necessarily the case for queer couples. Thus, an additional task in boundary formation may be decision making regarding sexual exclusivity (Tunnell, 2012).

Regulation of closeness and distance within their relationship may be more difficult for same-sex couples because of socialization (Tunnell, 2012). In U.S. culture, men tend to be socialized to be independent and to seek separateness and are often shamed for desiring connection. Women are generally socialized to be interdependent and to seek emotional connection and may be shamed for displays of independence and separateness. Contemporary feminist-informed clinical literature suggests that Lesbian couples desire more intimacy and closeness and do not report what may be seen as fusion as problematic. In fact, Lesbian couples may actually find what is described as enmeshment to be self-affirming, satisfying relational needs, and providing protection against homophobia, heterosexism, and sexism (Connolly, 2012). To their same-sex relationships, men may bring greater expertise in creating separateness, while women may bring greater expertise in creating closeness. Each same-sex couple will need to find a way to cultivate expertise in both areas, and each individual will have to give up participation in socially sanctioned shaming in response to out-of-conventional-gender-role behaviors.

Just as closeness may be a protective factor in same-sex relationships, difference may be a threat. In addition, gender role socialization contributes to this threat perception as men have likely been trained in competition and dominance and women in accommodation. Therefore, when difference emerges, men may address it through competition and combat while women may minimize difference by silencing their own opinions and needs. In same-sex unions, partners may have to work harder at accommodating difference or asserting separateness by relinquishing gendered expectations (Connolly, 2012; Tunnell, 2012).

The process of joining respective families and gaining familial support will be influenced by whether or not the couple is out. For couples who are out, the degree of familial support may be informed by whether or not the individuals are accepted within their families of origin, whether or not the couple expresses their status in a culturally acceptable manner, the individual family's attitudes toward gender variance and nonconforming sexuality, and the effects of internalized, intersecting oppressions. In order to join, each family must be willing to come out, among themselves and to the partner's family.

Additional challenges faced by LGBT couples include legal costs. Despite the partial defeat of DOMA, couples may still need attorneys to develop contracts establishing many of the rights automatically granted to heterosexual married couples. These legal contracts are costly and given the variation across states, cannot grant all of the benefits bestowed upon married heterosexual couples. LGBT couples who are members of the dominant racial/ethnic group will have to cope with the effects of heterosexism and homophobia on their relationship (Connolly, 2004b), while LGBT couples of color will face the interactive effects of multiple forms of oppression. Couples may be affected by, and will need to work through, their own internalized homo-, bi-, transphobia, and

heterosexism (Connolly, 2004b). Family members who seem supportive may engage in unintentional invalidating actions such as introducing the partner as a friend, expecting the adult child to privilege the family of origin over the partner, providing separate sleeping accommodations when visiting, or failing to recognize the couple's anniversary.

Couples in which one or both partners are bisexual may have additional challenges. First, because the dominant culture frequently understands sexuality and sexual orientation as binary, sexuality is assumed to be either hetero- or homosexual, so bisexual individuals must decide whether or not to disclose their sexual identity to their partner (Bradford, 2012). If they choose to come out to their partners, the couple may deal with the relational fallout, which may include mistrust, a sense of betrayal, and an erroneous assumption that the bisexual partner will be unfaithful (Bradford, 2012). Often bisexuality is not accepted as complete identity and so both same-sex and opposite-sex partners may be waiting for the bisexual partner to clarify his or her identity (Bradford, 2012). Each partner must explore and understand the meaning of bisexuality, how bisexuality will inform sexual behavior, and if choosing to operate outside of heteronormative constructs of coupling, the couple must make disclosure decisions (Bradford, 2012). Finally, when partnered with an opposite-sex person, the bisexual partner may experience invisibility while also benefitting from heterosexual privilege, generating feelings of shame and guilt (Weber & Heffner, 2008).

When Transgender individuals disclose their gender variance as a member of an existing Lesbian, Gay, or heterosexual couple, it may be falsely assumed that the individual wants to terminate the relationship (Israel, 2004). Coming out may send the committed relationship into a crisis, as partners often feel betrayed and experience the disclosure in ways that are similar to learning of infidelity or illness (Lev, 2004). As the couple faces the crisis and moves through the emergence process, both people will address relationship viability, negotiate relationship rules, and address couple sexual identity (Lev, 2004; Malpas, 2012). Like bisexual individuals, gender-expansive people must determine when and if to come out to a partner or potential partner. Many couples in which there is a gender-expansive partner find ways of negotiating this transition, relinquishing their fear, shame, and ignorance about the gender spectrum, and are able to move forward in their lives with the transgender member fully integrated into the family system (Lev, 2004).

Some of the benefits and opportunities for LGBT couples are freedom from traditional gender role, to create unique ways of being a couple, and to define the terms of their relationship including who will work, money management, decision making, and addressing issues of sexual exclusivity. LGBT couples may turn to their families of choice to determine how to be a couple borrowing that which is appealing and abandoning what is unappealing.

CASE ILLUSTRATION

Deborah and Sabrina

After 3 years of dating, and cohabitating for 2 years, Deborah who is Jewish American, and Sabrina, who is Irish American, decided to marry. Their families of choice instantly celebrated the decision. Sabrina wanted to include their families of origin in the ceremony, while Deborah did not want to include her family of origin because she was not out to them. Sabrina believed the ceremony presented the opportunity to tell Deborah's family that they were not just roommates. This difference erupted into intense conflict that prompted the couple to postpone the ceremony and seek therapy. During the course of LGBT affirming therapy, it became apparent that each partner was at a different stage of identity development, and there were differences concerning their expectations regarding family of origin involvement in their lives. Sabrina and Deborah worked to resolve their differences by clarifying and working through relationship expectations. The couple came to a mutual understanding regarding the role of Deborah's family in their relationship and Sabrina came to respect the boundary that Deborah had already created. The couple resumed planning their ceremony, which they created by borrowing from their respective cultural traditions. Sabrina's family of origin was prominently featured throughout the ceremony and a small private dinner was held for Deborah's family. The

couple recently celebrated their seventh anniversary and continues to thrive, in part, due to the continued support of their families of choice and Sabrina's family of origin, and the couple's clarification and negotiation of their relational expectations.

Parenting: families with young children

The primary process of families with young children is integrating new members into the family system. Couples assume responsibility for their children while maintaining responsibility for, and to, each other, and making space for the child. Additionally, familial relationships change and couples help their families adjust to their new roles as grandparents, aunts, etc.

Deciding to become a parent brings a host of questions to be addressed. The decision itself is one that is a significantly more conscious process for LGBT couples and individuals. They must determine the method by which they will become parents including donor insemination using a known or anonymous sperm donor, surrogacy, shared custody of children from a prior relationship or encounter, adoption, or formal or informal fostering. Some Lesbian and Gay couples opt to conceive a child together, acting as donors or surrogates for one another, and may choose to parent together. If a known donor or surrogacy is chosen, couples must decide if the donor or surrogate will be in the child's life, whether the child will have knowledge of that individual's status, and at what age such information will be shared. Lesbian couples choosing to birth biological children must decide which partner, or if both partners, will become pregnant. Gay men must decide which partner's sperm or if both will be used in surrogacy. Couples becoming parents through adoption may face obstacles because of heteronormative agency workers. LGBT individuals and their partners may experience difficulties in gaining custody and visitation of biological children from prior relationships. Once the method of having children has been selected, parental rights must be established. While married couples are automatically granted parental rights, LGB couples who do not have access to marriage equality must establish the legal connection of both parents to the child. Decisions regarding becoming parents and protecting parental rights may be class informed, as those with the greatest access to financial resources, medical care, community and familial support have a greater range of options from which to choose (Lev & Sennott, 2012; Mezey, 2012; Moore, 2011). Decisions may also be informed by racial and ethnic norms, for example, more working-class couples of color parent children from prior relationships, or from extended blood and fictive family networks (Moore, 2011).

Once these decisions are made and the couple engages in the process of becoming parents, they must also determine what and when to disclose to the families of origin. Regardless of the existing degree of acceptance in the families of origin, having a grandchild, niece, or nephew, etc., not only increases the visibility of the LGBT individual, but also increases the visibility of the families of origin. Conflict may arise within LGBT families where silence or invisibility is the term for acceptance of an LGBT identity. If a couple has been presenting to their families of origin as friends or roommates, or if the family has been denying the true nature of the relationship, having a child may push the couple to disclose or the family out of denial.

LGBT couples must make adjustments in their own relationships to integrate children into the family system. They must renegotiate the boundaries that define their identity as a couple, their roles, responsibilities, expectations regarding closeness and distance, and connections to friends and work. Additionally, the parenting couple must develop or refine their decision-making system as they collaborate to raise their children. New parents must reorganize priorities, making the care and nurturing of their children paramount. Existing couple and family of origin issues may intensify (Mallon, 2008b). LGBT couples must help integrate their new child into their families of origin. They may follow family of origin norms regarding the relationships between the child and other family members or they may create their own standards. The way that family members respond to new children and integrate them into the family may be informed by heterosexism or homo-, trans-, and biphobia, and thus families of choice may take up that life cycle task either in place of, or in addition to, the families of origin.

Individuals who come out after becoming parents have additional tasks. They must negotiate being

their authentic selves while maintaining family ties and bonds with children and current or former partners with whom they may co-parent. Co-parents, children, and other family members may react with shock. Of course, negotiation of the parent's identity and transition process become additional tasks for the family (Mallon, 2008b; Malpas, 2012). The co-parent may be confused about the past and present meaning of the couple relationship in the context of the partner's newly disclosed identity. How children respond may be related to their stage of development. For young children, the disclosure may be meaningless, but for adolescents it can be unsettling as they are dealing with their own emerging sexuality. LGBT parents may feel concerned about how the disclosure will affect their legal rights related to custody and or visitation (Mallon, 2008b). Although it is a complex and often painful process, being true to self and disclosing provides children with a model for how to be one's authentic self in the face of challenges (Mallon, 2008b).

Literature about Transgender parents and the effects of growing up with a gender-expansive parent is extremely limited (Lev, 2004; Mallon, 2008b). Despite the lack of evidence supporting that being raised by an LGBT parent increases the likelihood of nonconforming gender or sexual identities or struggles in these areas, concerns run rampant about the impact of the parent's gender identity on the gender or sexual identity of their children. Although it is recognized that children raised in families where a parent is transitioning may have difficulty, the expectation is that they will cope in a manner similar to other normative life cycle transitions (Lev, 2004).

Families with young children who express gender nonconformity will have the additional tasks of developing coping and advocacy skills to respond to their other children, relatives, friends, schools, and other social institutions, and for incorporating the needs of the gender-expansive child into family life (Lev, 2004). Some young children grow up feeling different but are unable to name the nature of the difference. During adolescence, or later in life, they may come to understand that difference as being related to their emerging sexual identity, orientation, or gender identity (Lev, 2004; Savin-Williams, 1996). It is the role of the family to provide nurturance, unconditional support, and acceptance as their children discover who they are in the world, and how to name and present themselves.

LGBT parents experience unique challenges related to their own sexual or gender identity or related to the nonconforming sexual and gender identities of their young children. Once they become parents, they must learn to cope with the stress related to witnessing their child's experience of heterosexism, homo-, trans-, and biphobia, and they must teach their children to cope with oppression. Parents must resist the influence of internalized heterosexism that activates in them the hope that their children will be heterosexual or gender conforming (Lev, 2010). They may worry about their children being teased either about their parents' sexual or gender identity, or about the child's gender nonconformance. However, the same skills used to cope with bullying for other reasons, or in response to other forms of oppression, are applicable to these situations (Mallon, 2008a, 2008b). Parents must provide their children with language for talking about their family in a manner that is comfortable for the child (Lev & Sennott, 2012). Additionally, the provision of a nurturing, supportive, and loving home is a powerful buffer against all types of bullying and oppression.

LGBT families with young children also experience unique opportunities that include transcending the limitations of gender roles and the opportunity to create alternative family structures that are more consistent with the concept that "it takes a village" to raise a child. LGBT families of color may be particularly adept at taking advantage of the support offered by families of choice due to a cultural tendency to define family broadly. There is a significant body of research demonstrating that relationships among family members and the quality of care provided by parents are much more critical and important to the healthy development of children than the sexual or gender identity of parents or family structure (Mallon, 2008b).

CASE ILLUSTRATION

Esther and Julia

When Esther, a Korean American woman, and Julia, a Jamaican woman, celebrated their 10th anniversary,

they decided to have a child. They elected to use an anonymous donor and decided that Esther, who was older, would be the first to carry and deliver their child, and in a few years Julia would become pregnant using the same donor. After locating a fertility clinic that would service a Lesbian couple, the two proceeded with their plan. They had a healthy baby girl named Ayana. The baby suffered from severe colic prompting Julia's mother to stay with the couple for several months to help out. Sleep deprivation, worries about Ayana, lack of privacy, and concerns about their ability to parent disrupted the plan to have a second child and created tension between them. Esther and the baby went to stay with a close friend. Although supportive on the surface, Julia's mother told her that she was not surprised by their failure, as everyone in their family agreed that these two women needed a man to make a family. Julia sent her mother home and asked that she and other family members think about how they could be a supportive kinship network to Ayana. She pleaded with Esther to return home, sought the support of their family of choice, and suggested that they begin couple's therapy. Esther agreed, Ayana's colic improved, the couple adjusted to their parenting roles, renegotiated their relationship, confronted the heterosexism in Julia's family, and had their second child 4 years later.

Parenting: families with adolescent children

Families raising adolescents are focused on revising boundaries to allow increased independence of children, the increasing frailty of the older generation, and movement in and out of the family system. During this stage, the adolescent is separating from the family, individuating, and identifying more with the peer group. Parents are refocusing attention on themselves as a couple (or for single parents dating/partnering), their own life's work, friendships, and caring for the older generation.

An additional task for the family includes integrating the LGBT family member into the system regardless of whether it is the parent or child who is LGBT identified.

During adolescence, coming out to oneself and others is often a complex process that can be filled with joy, excitement, pain, fear, loneliness, conflict, acceptance, and rejection. Becoming aware of one's sexual identity or orientation at this stage may be helpful to the young person, as it may clarify feelings of differentness or feelings that previously may have been confusing (Savin-Williams, 1996). This clarification of misunderstood feelings may also hold true for gender-expansive youth. While teens are often seeking independence from parents, disclosure to the family of origin may be motivated by a desire to be closer to family, to be one's authentic self, and to enlist support (Savin-Williams, 1996; LaSala, 2010). The closer the young person is to the family, the higher the stakes are for gaining or losing familial support (Stone Fish & Harvey, 2012). If a parent is LGBT or comes out, the social stigma of having an LGBT parent may increase stress and anxiety as the adolescent strives to integrate the parent's identity with his or her own and to fit in with peer groups (Welsh, 2008). Separation from parents motivated by negative feelings about the parent's sexual identity or gender variance may result in family conflict. As youth become increasingly aware of negative social attitudes toward homosexuality, bisexuality, and gender variance, concern for the well-being of the family, fear of oppression, and conflicted feelings about wanting to pass as a heterosexual family may emerge (Welsh, 2008). It is imperative that parents support adolescents to cope with these feelings, or locate a trusted adult, mutual support group, or helping professional to do so.

LGBT youth who become aware of their attraction to both sexes or the same sex, or are aware of their gender variance, have a much more tumultuous journey than their heterosexual, gender conforming peers (Hunter & Mallon, 2000; Lev, 2004; Lev & Sennott, 2012). The development of positive sexual or gender identities may be the most challenging tasks for LGBT youth when they live in heteronormative or openly hostile families, schools, and communities. Youth raised in LGBT-headed families may worry that their own queer identities will reinforce the heterosexist myth that queer parents cause their children to be queer, thereby pathologizing the entire family and invalidating the adolescent's authentic knowledge of self (Luvalanka, 2012). They may also feel pressure to be heterosexual or gender conforming in response to parental internalized heterosexism. LGBT parents worry that their children will experience the same oppression that they did and children may delay coming out for the same reason.

Although there is a dearth of research concerning the experiences of LGBT youth of color, a few speculations can be made. LGBT youth of color are more likely to be members of collectivist ethnicities; the family is more likely to be inclusive of blood and non-blood kin, community members, and ancestors (Boyd-Franklin, 2003; Walters & Old Person, 2008; Watts-Jones, 1997). Thus, coming out to the family and community becomes a more complex process, as the adolescent considers cultural norms and the range of responses of a broader, more complex family network that has played a pivotal role in protecting and supporting the youth in a world that is organized by white-skin privilege. Sadly, it can be expected that LGBT youth of color will contend with intersecting oppressions resulting in conflicting allegiances at a time when they most need to locate reference groups in which they feel welcomed, validated, and at home.

Parents, especially, are in a position to shape the lives of their LGBT adolescents in a positive way, as studies have demonstrated that parental acceptance has positive impact on self-acceptance among LGBT youth, and that family acceptance significantly enhances self-esteem, social support, general wellness, and protects against substance abuse, depression, and suicidality (Ryan, Russell, Huebner, Diaz, & Sanchez, 2010; Savin-Williams, 1996). As more families, schools, and communities become LGBT affirmative, social and psychological outcomes for adolescents will be enhanced.

CASE ILLUSTRATION

Sonia

Sonia's parents were called to school by her high school counselor. The counselor had been seeing Sonia for a few weeks out of concern for her declining grades, her withdrawal from school activities, and her overall sadness. On this day, Sonia told the counselor that she thought that her family would be better off if she were dead. The parents, a Latino couple that had been married for 20 years, arrived to the school angry with Sonia because they had to take time from work in response to what they described as a ridiculous statement. Sonia was taken to the local hospital where she was diagnosed with major depressive disorder and referred for psychotherapy. The therapist began meeting with Sonia individually and at times with the entire family. The therapist worked with the family to make room for Sonia's feelings, to understand the changes in her behavior, and to explore how processes in the family system related to Sonia's behaviors. During an individual meeting with the therapist, Sonia shared her attraction to both boys and girls and asked the therapist to refrain from disclosing this information to the rest of the family because she feared rejection. The therapist agreed, and as they continued talking the therapist sought to understand Sonia's concerns while listening for potential sources of support within Sonia's life. During a family meeting, it was discovered that Sonia's 19-year-old brother, Roberto, had many Gay male friends and that Roberto saw nonconforming sexual and gender identities as normative. When meeting alone with the therapist, Sonia began to consider sharing her bisexuality with Roberto and eventually, with the support of the therapist, did so. Roberto initially responded with surprise, and then offered his unconditional love and support to Sonia while agreeing to keep her confidence. As the sibling alliance strengthened, Sonia enlisted Roberto's help in coping with other family issues. Although she chose not to discuss her sexuality with her parents, Sonia was able to address other concerns with her parents. Subsequently, her mood and grades improved, and Sonia was able to use the therapy to explore her emerging sexuality and to decide when and how to come out to her parents.

Families in later life

During this stage, families adjust to shifting generational roles. The middle generation may be caring for and supporting the fullest functioning of the older generation, while also benefitting from their wisdom and experience. Tasks for older family members include supporting the middle generation, maintaining their highest level of functioning, cultivating their own interests, nurturing their couple relationship, coping with the loss of loved ones, partners, siblings, peers, etc., and preparing for death.

Because of the advances made by the LGBT civil rights movement, LGBT families in later life may now be constituted in a variety of ways, headed by an LGBT single adult, couple, or multiple partners with or without LGBT or heterosexual children, or may be headed by a heterosexual single person, couple, or multiple partners with LGBT children or adult children (Blando, 2012). There may be variation in tasks, challenges, and benefits depending on type of family formation.

Individuals, who come out after raising families or coupling, will have to contend with the responses of partners, adult children, grandchildren, and families of origin, as they work to integrate the new found identity into a life that has been lived longer (Blando, 2012). Individuals who come out later in life may also experience additional oppression in the form of ageism (Blando, 2012). However, they may find the process less stressful, as they are often wiser, more experienced, better resourced, more financially stable, and more independent than those who come out earlier in life (Blando, 2012). Older adults who are less financially independent, or whose health is failing, may face similar challenges as adolescents when disclosing because of their dependence on family support.

Prior to the contemporary LGBT civil rights movement and the depathologizing of sexual and gender nonconformance, it was riskier and dangerous to disclose an LGBT identity to anyone. Thus, prior to the 1969 Stonewall rebellion, individuals were less likely to live as out LGBT individuals and more likely to lead double lives. Some LGBT individuals, who came out to their families, found acceptance (Herdt & Beeler, 1998), while others were rejected or chose to disconnect from their families in order to live more authentically. In situations involving cutoffs, the family of choice may have emerged as more salient and relevant. The family of choice may have been established over the life course, thereby playing a significant role in providing material or emotional support (Friend, 1991; Kehoe, 1989; Kimmel & Sang, 1995; Reid 1995; Tully, 1989). Thus, among LGBT people, the tasks and processes of later life may occur in the context of the families of choice, either in addition to or in place of families of origin.

Many LGBT individuals will assume the tasks of the elder generation, such as forming adult relationships with adult children, grandparenting, and focusing on their relationships with partners with ease, while others will contend with disapproval and rejection. Some assume the roles of mentors and elders in their families of choice and in return receive needed care. In LGBT-headed families, by this stage, the sexual or gender identity may be a nonissue, as the younger generations have been raised in this context. As LGBT couples and individuals grow older, they may require care or assistance from their own children, siblings, or other family of origin members. If there have been cutoffs in family of origin relationships, old conflicts may resurface causing older LGBT adults to seek out families of choice for assistance. If the family of origin never recognized a partner, children, or family of choice, they may become concerned that the older LGBT relative may be isolated and not have a community to care for them. As LGBT couples age, they may also contend with illness and the loss of a partner and face challenges from systems of care that do not accommodate same-sex couples or invisiblize the sexuality of elders (Giammattei & Green, 2012). If families of origin or creation did not accept the relationships, there may be a lack of support in obtaining care, for grieving, and rebuilding life as bereft partners. Finally, if wills and other legal documents were not created, a partner may be denied the right to make health care and other end-of-life decisions, or the right to claim their partner's belongings or shared property.

During later life, LGBT adults and their families have the opportunity to act as models for disclosure, living authentically, and thriving and surviving in the face of oppression for younger generations of LGBT individuals and families. Older adults may also act as mentors, parents, grandparents, etc., to members of their families of creation and their families of choice.

CASE ILLUSTRATION

Janice and Marva

Janice and Marva met while working together as nurses. They were both married to men and were raising young families. Although they were already best friends, when Marva's husband died suddenly, the friendship between her and Janice deepened and the two families became inseparable. As time passed, Janice and Marva grew to understand their relationship as more than friendship. They were soul mates who were deeply in love with one another. However, because they feared that their children would reject them, and Janice did not want to hurt her husband, they continued to represent themselves as friends over the next 20 years. When Marva's adult children moved out of state, she went with them to be closer to her grandchildren. Janice could not tolerate the separation, so she divorced her husband and relocated to be near Marva. Marva and Janice created a life together without formally coming out to their families. Their adult children and their grandchildren liked and respected both of them and viewed each woman as their "other" mother/grandmother. This living arrangement worked until Marva became gravely ill. When Marva's adult children attempted to exclude Janice from participating in health care and other decisions about Marva's future, the two women disclosed the full nature of their relationship to their families. Both families were distressed. Janice's family distanced themselves and blamed the relationship with Marva for their parent's divorce. After initial upset, Marva's family came to accept and respect Marva and Janice as a couple and helped them establish legal documents to protect their rights as a couple. Janice and Marva's children cared for Marva together until her death 5 years later.

> **Assess your comprehension of the family life cycle by completing this quiz.**

— Conclusion

LGBT individuals have always been members of families and always will be. The commitment to family bonds and lasting relationships is evidenced by the fierceness, innovativeness, and creativity with which LGBT individuals create and expand their families. The United States is slowly recognizing and legitimizing LGBT families and creating structures that will nurture their survival, but there is still a long way to go before all LGBT-headed families are afforded the rights and benefits that are identical to those granted to heterosexual-headed families. LGBT individuals and their families face many of the same life cycle processes and tasks as dominant culture families and draw from their experiences as multicultural people to transact these processes and complete these tasks. The additional tasks and challenges that emerge for LGBT individuals and their families do not emerge because there is something

wrong with being LGBT. They emerge because of heterosexism, homo-, bi-, and transphobia, rigid adherence to a biologically determined binary gender system, and the interactive effects of multiple forms of subjugation. LGBT individuals and their families are resourceful in negotiating these additional tasks and often turn challenges into opportunities for self-determination. We must focus on the unique aspects of LGBT families and the diversity of the many family forms that exist globally to promote the well-being of LGBT families, and to expand our understanding (Giammattei & Green, 2012; Lev & Sennott, 2012; Moore & Brainer, 2012).

> **Recall what you learned in this chapter by completing the Chapter Review.**

— References

American Civil Liberties Union. (2013). *Know your rights—Transgender people and the law*. Retrieved March 18, 2015, from www.aclu.org/lgbt-rights/know-your-rights-transgender-people-and-law

American Civil Liberties Union, Center for American Progress, Family Equality Council, Freedom to Marry, Gay and Lesbian Advocates and Defenders, Human Rights Campaign, Immigration Equality, Lambda Legal, National Center for Lesbian Rights, National Gay and Lesbian Task Force, Out-Serve-LSDN (2013). LGBT Organizations fact sheet series: After DOMA what it means for you. Retrieved July 1, 2013 from http://www.nclrights.org/site/DocServer/Post-DOMA_General-Overview.pdf

American Civil Liberties Union & National Center for Transgender Equality (2013). Protecting the rights of transgender parents and their children: A guide for parents & lawyers. Retrieved July 1, 2013, from http://www.aclu.org/files/assets/aclu-tg_parenting_guide.pdf

Battle, J., Pastrana, Jr., A., & Daniels, J. (2013a). *Social Justice Sexuality Survey: The executive summary for the Asian & Pacific Islander population*. Retrieved July 31, 2013, from www.socialjusticesexuality.com

Battle, J., Pastrana, Jr., A., & Daniels, J. (2013b). *Social Justice Sexuality Survey: The executive summary for*

the Black population. Retrieved July 31, 2013, from www.socialjusticesexuality.com

Battle, J., Pastrana, Jr., A., & Daniels, J. (2013c). *Social Justice Sexuality Survey: The executive summary for the Latina/o population*. Retrieved July 31, 2013, from www.socialjusticesexuality.com

Baum, J., Brill, S., Brown, J., Delpercio, A., Kahn, E., Kenny, L., & Nicoll, A. (2012). *Supporting and caring for our gender-expansive youth*. Retrieved March 18, 2015, from www.hrc.org/youth-report/supporting-and-caring-for-our-gender-expansive-youth.VRMEgmYtrHk

Beam, A., Loller, T., Sewell, D., & White, E. (2015). *Gay Marriage: High Court sets stage for historic ruling. New York Times*. Retrieved March 18, 2015, from www.nytimes.com.aponline/2015/01/16/us/politics/ap-us-supreme-court-gay-marriage.html

Benshorn, S. (2008). A qualitative examination of the ecological systems that promote sexual identity comfort among European American and African American lesbian youths. (Doctoral dissertation, DePaul University, 2008). Ann Arbor, MI: Proust, LLC.

Blando, J. A. (2012). Counseling lesbian and gay individuals, couples and families in late life. In J. Bigner & J. Wetchler (Eds.) *Handbook of LGBT-affirmative couple and family therapy* (pp. 249–261). New York: Routledge.

Bowleg, L. (2008). When Black + lesbian + woman Black lesbian woman: The methodological challenges of qualitative and quantitative intersectionality research. *Sex Roles, 59,* 312–325.

Bowleg, L., Burkholder, G., Teti, M., & Craig, M. L. (2008). The complexities of outness: Psychosocial predictors of coming out to others among Black lesbian and bisexual women. *Journal of LGBT Health Research, 4*(4), 153–166.

Boyd-Franklin, N. (2003). *Black families in therapy: Understanding the African American experience* (2nd ed.). New York: Guilford Press.

Bradford, M. (2012). Affirmative bisexual couple therapy. In J. Bigner & J. Wetchler (Eds.) *Handbook of LGBT-affirmative couple and family therapy* (pp 57–68). New York: Routledge.

Cass, V. C. (1979). Homosexual identity formation: A theoretical model. *Journal of Homosexuality, 4*(3), 219–237.

Cass, V. C. (1998). Sexual orientation identity formation: A Western phenomenon. In R. J. Cabal & T. S. Stein (Eds.), *Textbook of homosexuality and mental health* (pp. 227–251). Washington, DC: APA.

Cole, E. (2009). Intersectionality and research in psychology. *American Psychologist, 64*(3), 170–180.

Connolly, C. M. (2004a). A process of change. *Journal of GLBT Family Studies, 1*(1), 5–20.

Connolly, C. M. (2004b). Clinical issues with same-sex couples: A review of the literature. In J. J. Bigner & J. L. Wetchler (Eds.), *Relationship therapy with same-sex couples* (pp. 3–12). New York: Haworth Press.

Connolly, C. M. (2012) Lesbian couple therapy. In J. Bigner & J. Wetchler (Eds.) *Handbook of LGBT-affirmative couple and family therapy* (pp 1–22). New York: Routledge.

Cramer, D. W., & Roach, A. J. (1988). Coming out to mom and dad: A study of gay males and their relationship with their parents. *Journal of Homosexuality, 15*(3/4), 79–91.

Defense of Marriage Act, 1 U.S.C. Chapter 1, 28 U.S.C. Chapter 15 (1996).

Friend, R. (1991). Older lesbian and gay people: A theory of successful aging. In J. A. Lee (Ed.), *Gay midlife and maturity* (pp. 99–118). New York: Haworth Press.

Giammattei, S. V. & Green, R. (2012). LGBTQ couple and family therapy: History and future directions. In J. Bigner & J. Wetchler (Eds.) *Handbook of LGBT-affirmative couple and family therapy* (pp 1–22). New York: Routledge.

Gotta, G. Green, R., Rothblum, E., Solomon, S. Balsam, K., & Schwartz, P. (2011). Heterosexual, Lesbian, and Gay Male relationships: A comparison of couples in 1975 and 2000. *Family Process, 50* (3), 353–376.

Greene, B. (1998). Family, ethnic identity and sexual orientation: African American lesbians and gay men. In C. J. Patterson & A. R. D'Augelli (Eds.), *Lesbian, gay, and bisexual identities in families: Psychological perspectives* (pp. 40–52). New York: Oxford University Press.

Griffin, C. W., Wirth, M. J., & Wirth, A. G. (1986). *Beyond acceptance: Parents of lesbians and gays talk about their experiences.* Englewood Cliffs, NJ: Prentice-Hall.

Herdt, G., & Beeler, J. (1998). Older gay men and lesbians in families. In C. J. Patterson & A. R. D'Augelli (Eds.), *Lesbian, gay, and bisexual identities in families: Psychological perspectives* (pp. 177–196). New York: Oxford University Press.

Human Right Campaign (2015). *Marriage Center.* Retrieved March 18, 2015, www.hrc.org/campaigns/marriage-center

Hunter, J., & Mallon, G. P. (2000). Lesbian, gay, and bisexual adolescent development. In B. Green and G. L. Croom (Eds.), *Education, research, and practice in lesbian, gay, bisexual, and transgendered psychology—A research manual. Psychological perspectives on lesbian and gay issues* (Vol. 5, pp. 226–243). Thousand Oaks; CA: Sage Publication.

Israel, G., (2004). Supporting transgender and sex reassignment issues: Couple and family dynamics. In J. J. Bigner & J. L. Wetchler (Eds.), *Relationship therapy with same-sex couples* (pp. 53–64). New York: Haworth Press.

Imber-Black, E., & Roberts, J. (1998). *Rituals for our times: Celebrating, healing and changing our lives and our relationships.* New York: Jason Aronson.

Johnson, T. W. (1992). Predicting parental response to a son or daughter's homosexuality (Doctoral dissertation, Rutgers University, 1992). *Dissertation Abstracts International,* 54 (9-B) 4901. New Jersey: Rutgers University Press.

Kehoe, M. (1989). *Lesbians over sixty speak for themselves.* New York: Haworth Press.

Kimmel, D. C., & Sang, B. E. (1995). Lesbians and gay men in midlife. In A. R. D'Augelli & C. J. Patterson (Eds.), *Lesbian, gay, and bisexual identities over the lifespan: Psychological perspectives* (pp. 190–214). New York: Oxford University Press.

Laird, J. (1993). Lesbian and gay families. In F. Walsh (Ed.), *Normal family processes* (4th ed., pp. 282–328). New York: Guilford Press.

LaSala, M. (2010). *Coming out, coming home*. New York: Columbia University Press.

Lev, A. I. (2004). *Transgender emergence: Therapeutic guidelines for working with gender-variant people and their families*. New York: Haworth Press.

Lev, A. I. (2010). How queer! The development of gender identity and sexual orientation in LGBTQ headed-families. *Family Process 49*, (3) pp. 268–290.

Lev. A. I. & Sennott, S. L. (2012). Clinical work with LGBTQ parents and prospective. In A. Goldberg & K. Allen (Eds.) *LGBT-parent families: Innovations in research & implications for practice* (pp. 241–260). New York: Springer.

Lukes, C. A., & Land, H. (1990). Biculturality and homosexuality. *Social Work, 35,* 155–161.

Luvalanka, K. (2012). The second generation: LGBTQ youth with LGBTQ parents. In A. Goldberg & K. Allen (Eds.) *LGBT-parent families: Innovations in research & implications for practice* (pp. 163–176). New York: Springer.

Mallon, G. P. (2008a). Social work practice with lesbian, gay, bisexual, and transgender people within families. In G. Mallon (Ed.), *Social work practice with lesbian, gay, bisexual, and transgender people* (2nd ed., pp. 241–268).

Mallon, G. P. (2008b). Social work practice with LGBT parents. In G. Mallon (Ed.), *Social work practice with lesbian, gay, bisexual, and transgender people* (2nd ed., pp. 269–312). New York: Routledge.

Malpas, J. (2012). Can couples change gender? Couple therapy with Transgender people. In J. Bigner & J. Wetchler (Eds.) *Handbook of LGBT-affirmative couple and family therapy* (pp. 69–88). New York: Routledge.

Mezcy, N. J. (2012). How Lesbians and Gay men become parents or remain childfree. In A. Goldberg & K. R. Allen (Eds.), *LGBT-parent families: Innovations in research & implications for practice,* (pp. 59–70). New York: Springer Science.

Moore, M. R., & Brainer, A. (2012). Race and Ethnicity in the lives of sexual minority parents and their children. In A. Goldberg & K. R. Allen (Eds.), *LGBT-parent families: Innovations in research & implications for practice,* (pp. 133–148). New York: Springer Science.

Moore, M. R. (2011). *Invisible families: Gay identities, relationships, and motherhood among Black women*. Berkeley, CA: University of California Press.

National Center for Lesbian Rights (2014). Legal recognition of LGBT families. Retrieved March 18, 2015, from www.nclrights.org/wp-content/uploads/2013/07/legal_recognition_of_LGBT_families.pdf

National LGBTQ Task Force (2014a). Relationship Recognition for same sex couples in the United Sates. Retrieved July 1, 2013, from http://thetaskforce.org/downloads/reports/issue_maps/rel_recog_6_26_13_color.pdf

National Gay and Lesbian Task Force (2013b). State laws prohibiting recognition of same sex relationships. Retrieved July 1, 2013, from http://thetaskforce.org/downloads/reports/issue_maps/samesex_relationships_5_15_13.pdf

Reid, J. D. (1995). Development in late life: Older lesbian and gay lives. In A. R. D'Augeli & C. J. Patterson (Eds.), *Lesbian, gay and bisexual identities over the lifespan: Psychological perspectives* (pp. 215–242). New York: Oxford University Press.

Robinson, B. E., Walters, L. H., & Skeen, P. (1989). Response to learning that their child is homosexual and concern over AIDS: A national study. In F. W. Bozett (Ed.), *Homosexuality and the family* (pp. 59–80). Binghamton, NY: Harrington Park Press.

Ryan, C., Russell, S. T, Huebner, D., Diaz, R. & Sanchez, J. (2010). Family Acceptance in Adolescence and the Health of LGBT young adults. *Journal of Child and Adolescent Psychiatric Nursing, 23* (4), 205–213.

Sanders, G. L., & Kroll, I. T. (2000). Generating stories of resilience: Helping gay and lesbian youth and their families. *Journal of Marital and Family Therapy, 26*(4), 433–442.

Savin-Williams, R. C. (1996). Self-labeling and disclosure among gay, lesbian, and bisexual youths. In J. Laird & R.-J. Green (Eds.), *Lesbians and gays in couples and families: A handbook for therapists* (pp. 153–182). San Francisco: Jossey-Bass.

Savin-Williams, R. C. (2005). *The new gay teenager*. Cambridge, MA: Harvard.

Singh A. A. & Harper, A. (2012). Intercultural issues in LGBTQQ couple and family therapy. In J. Bigner & J. Wetchler (Eds.) *Handbook of LGBT-affirmative couple and family therapy* (pp. 283–298). New York: Routledge.

Stone Fish, L. & Harvey, R. G. (2012). Raising Lesbian, Gay, or Bisexual youth: An affirmative family therapy. In J. Bigner & J. Wetchler (Eds.) *Handbook of LGBT-affirmative couple and family therapy* (pp. 183–198). New York: Routledge.

Tully, C. T. (1989). Caregiving: What do midlife lesbians view as important? *Journal of Gay and Lesbian Psychotherapy, 1,* 87–103.

Tunnell, G. (2012) Gay Couple Therapy. In J. Bigner & J. Wetchler (Eds.) *Handbook of LGBT-affirmative couple and family therapy* (pp. 25–42). New York: Routledge.

United States v. Edith Schlain Windsor, in her capacity as executor of the estate of The Clara Spyer, et al., 570 U.S.___2013.

Walters, K. L., & Old Person, R. L., Jr. (2008). Lesbians, gays, bisexuals and transgender people of color: Reconciling divided selves and communities. In G. Mallon (Ed.), *Social work practice with lesbian, gay, bisexual, and transgender people* (2nd ed., pp. 41–68). New York: Routledge.

Weber, G., & Heffern, K. T. (2008). Social work practice with bisexual people. In G. Mallon (Ed.), *Social work practice with lesbian, gay, bisexual, and transgender people,* (2nd ed., pp. 69–82). New York: Routledge

Welsh, M. (2008). *A phenomenological exploration of adolescents raised by same-sex parents.* Unpublished doctoral dissertation, Massachusetts School of Professional Psychology, Boston, MA.

Watts-Jones, D. (1997) Toward an African American genogram. *Family Process, 36,* 375–383.

Weinberg, M. S., Williams, C. J., & Pryor, D. W. (1994). *Dual attraction: Understanding bisexuality.* New York: Oxford University Press.

Weston, K. (1991). *Families we choose: Lesbians, gays, kinship.* New York: Columbia University Press.

Williams, W. L. (1998). Social acceptance of same-sex relationships in families: Models from other cultures. In C. J. Patterson & A. R. D'Augelli (Eds.), *Lesbian, gay, and bisexual identities in families: Psychological perspectives* (pp. 53–74). New York: Oxford University Press.

Chapter 8

Spirituality and the Family Life Cycle

Sueli Petry

— Learning Objectives

- Describe ways that spirituality may be used in therapy as a resource throughout the family life cycle.
- Examine spirituality's significance when facing times of stress.
- Discuss the implications of using spirituality for treatment.
- List and describe tools clinicians can use to track the ways in which spiritual beliefs may change over time and as families encounter different experiences.
- Explain how to do a systemic assessment that takes into account spiritual resources and family strengths across the life cycle.
- Discuss the benefits and challenges of spirituality for children.
- Explain the role spirituality can play in identity development during adolescence.
- Describe the impact of spirituality on the lives of young adults.
- Express the importance of spirituality during midlife.
- Discuss the relationship between spirituality and the developmental tasks of late life.

Introduction

Our spirituality as human beings is a fundamental resource throughout the life cycle. Spirituality has been a healing force through countless generations, embedded in culture and religious traditions. Spiritual beliefs can be a powerful resource for people who have lost their way, are feeling despair, or are suffering from oppression, racism, poverty, and trauma (Aponte, 1994, 2009; Barrett, 2009; Boyd-Franklin, 2003a; Cruz, 2013; Hines, 2008; Kamya, 2005, 2009; Walsh, 2008, 2009). It can be a resource in all phases of the life cycle and may become even more important in later age as a means of reviewing one's accomplishments, life's meaning, and coming to terms with the end of life.

Yet, very few mental health professionals explore spirituality as a source of strength, although there have been attempts to remedy this situation. The Joint Commission on the Accreditation of Healthcare Organizations requires that a spiritual assessment be conducted with mental health and substance abuse patients (JCAHO, 2008), and the Professional Codes of Ethics for social workers and psychologists direct professionals to respect religious diversity (NASW, 2008; APA, 2010). Fortunately, psychiatry expanded the category of "religious or spiritual problem" in the *Diagnostic and Statistical Manual of Mental Disorders, Fifth Edition (DSM-5)* (American Psychiatric Association, 2013) informed by research on the spiritual and religious aspects of the major diagnostic categories (Peteet, Lu, & Narrow, 2011), and recommends that religion and spirituality be considered as a matter of course within a cultural formulation.

In this chapter, we address spirituality in clinical work, within the religious diversity present in the United States, exploring the ways spirituality may be used in therapy as a resource throughout the family life cycle. We offer guidelines for including spirituality in any clinical assessment and discuss implications for treatment. Various models have been proposed for assessing spirituality (Birkenmaier, Behrman, & Berg-Weger, 2005; Hodge, 2004; McGoldrick, Gerson, & Petry, 2008), exploring spirituality over the life cycle (Kelcourse, 2004), and exploring the influence of cultural experiences on spirituality using a genogram or ecomap (Hodge, 2004). Here, we provide a framework for a systemic assessment, which places the presenting problem in the context of spiritual development, culture, and life cycle stage, using genograms and family chronologies. Understanding context provides alternative views of why a problem exists and helps clinicians and clients see opportunities for new ways of being and relating. Genograms help the clinician and the client to consider family members' spiritual beliefs, how the family has survived and dealt with problems in the past, and to identify people in the family network who might be available as resources for spiritual and emotional support. Family chronologies used in conjunction with genograms facilitate tracking family patterns through time and space (McGoldrick, Gerson, & Petry, 2008). Together, these tools help clinicians track the ways in which spiritual beliefs may change over time and as families encounter different experiences. The emphasis on fluidity and change over time and space creates a sense of hope and helps people to see the various ways their families have transformed suffering and adapted to difficult circumstances, through understanding, forgiveness, and growth.

Assess your comprehension of the introduction by completing this quiz.

Spirituality and Religion in America

Although accurate statistics on spiritual and religious practices are difficult to confirm, recent polls suggest that 60 percent of Americans describe themselves as "very" or "moderately" religious, while only 16 percent endorse "no religious preference" (Gallup, 2012). In recent years, the Internet has created opportunities for "virtual faith communities," where people may communicate with each other and find inspiration. A Google© search of the word "spirituality" resulted in dozens of spiritual Web sites, one of the largest, "Beliefnet" (www .beliefnet.org), offers a variety of spiritual resources including message boards and prayer circles for multiple faiths. The religions represented in the United States have changed significantly in the last three

decades. Although Christianity has remained dominant, the non-Christian population has been increasing steadily. Islamic centers or mosques, and Hindu and Buddhist centers, can be found in nearly every major city in the United States. Americans identify as Jewish, Muslim, Hindu, Buddhist, Baha'i, Jain, Pagan, Zoroastrianist, and more (Pew Forum on Religion and Public Life, 2008). This suggests that therapist and client may have differing views or experiences regarding spirituality, which can affect the way they relate to each other. Understanding how to proceed with a spiritual assessment and how to integrate it into treatment will help therapists raise the topic confidently.

Assess your comprehension of spirituality and religion in america by completing this quiz.

The Family Life Cycle and Spirituality

Children and spirituality

In the first stages of life, until adolescence (infancy, early childhood, middle childhood, and pubescence), children are dependent on their parents and are the beneficiaries of their parents' spiritual beliefs. They learn values and social behavior and conform to expectations guided by the family's spiritual or religious practices. Often, they derive comfort from religious rituals and beliefs. For instance, a prayer before bedtime can allay a child's anxiety about the darkness or sleeping alone and can help the child feel safe when he or she believes that God, Spirit, or some higher power loves and cares for him or her. Moreover, children develop and grow spiritually just as they do physically and emotionally (Roehlkepartain, King, Wagener, & Benson, 2006). They develop increasing spiritual capacities and experiences as they mature, and their innate sense of wonder leads to exploration and speculation about spirituality (Hart, 2006). When working with traumatized children of varying cultures and religions, asking about spiritual beliefs will likely open up avenues to help them to transform pain and to heal (Kamya, 2009). For those who have lost a parent or sibling, spiritual beliefs can help them to grieve, as all religions have rituals or beliefs for dealing with death and bereavement. Spirituality can be a tremendous resource in working with children, just as it is in later stages of the life cycle.

Yet, spiritual beliefs may cause children discomfort when they believe they have not lived up to what is expected of them. Parents may not be aware that their children are agonizing over some small infraction that is inflated in their minds. Children may worry about what will happen to a family member, friend, or others who do not conform to the spiritual practices they have been taught or who do not follow a prescribed code of behavior. In clinical work with children, assessing a child's spiritual beliefs in the context of their family's beliefs may uncover areas of concern for the child. Exploring children's spiritual beliefs is relevant also in working with children in foster care, families struggling with substance abuse, children who have been sexually abused, and even children with less severe problems such as impulsivity and behavioral difficulties. Some children believe God is watching them and will punish them for their bad behavior. Understanding the child's beliefs, as well as the family and cultural beliefs, will allow the clinician to address areas of concern for the child and parent and will provide a means to draw on those beliefs to foster healing.

CASE ILLUSTRATION

Anthony and Angelina—Children's Spiritual Beliefs May Comfort or Cause Anxiety

This case illustrates how a spiritual assessment helped the parents in this Brazilian American evangelical family to comfort and support their children, and fostered the family's healing. At this stage of families with young children, Anthony (10 years old) and Angelina (8 years old) were the recipients of their parents' beliefs. The children feared that God would punish their mother when she relapsed in substance abuse, but with clinical intervention the parents had the power to allay the children's fears.

Anthony and Angelina were living with their father (Hugo) after their parents separated and at the time of separation, their mother (Mariza) was abusing drugs. When they started therapy, Mariza was in treatment for substance abuse and had weekly supervised visits with the children. To assess this family, it was important to meet each parent separately and the children alone to allow everyone to speak frankly, and to limit the children's exposure to any of the parents' negative reports about the other. Although children are often exposed to parents' arguments at home, it is best to protect children from such scenes in the therapeutic setting.

In the parent sessions, both Hugo and Mariza said they had drifted away from their religious beliefs and experimented with drugs before getting married. Later they stopped using drugs and returned to their religious practice in the evangelical Church. The couple remained active in the Church until their separation; Hugo and the children continued their religious practices, but Mariza stopped attending services. The reason for the parents' separation seemed to be related to Mariza's substance abuse, but would need further exploration.

When I met Anthony, alone, I asked him about his spiritual beliefs, and he hesitantly said that using drugs was a sin and he worried that God would punish his mother because she had used drugs. His loyalty to his mother prevented him from discussing this with his father or anyone else. In a later session with both children, I asked if they had any fears about God and learned they were afraid that God would punish them because they were sometimes angry with their mother. The children's spiritual beliefs caused them feelings of anxiety and guilt. However, as I continued with the spiritual assessment, I discovered that their spirituality gave this family something to believe in that was larger than themselves, a belief that could be drawn on to comfort the children and help them to heal.

In separate sessions with each parent, Hugo said he believed in the guidelines of his religion, but having lived through many experiences including abusing drugs himself, he concluded that God was forgiving and provided guidance rather than punishment. Mariza was ambivalent about her beliefs. She believed God would help her find the strength to overcome her addiction and be reunited with her children, but she was struggling with feelings of anxiety and guilt over her behavior, and anger because she felt judged by some members of her congregation. It was clear that Mariza could not be helpful in allaying the children's fears until she resolved her own mixed emotions. Hugo, on the other hand, was in a better position to do so. After coaching him on how to encourage his children to share their feelings and fears, he comforted them and told them that God loved them and their mother. He told his children that God would look after their family and would help them to get through their troubles.

Hugo's spiritual belief gave the children hope. If he had taken a different position, it would have been harder for the children to reconcile their feelings of anxiety. Anthony, because he was older, would be more likely to begin to question his parents' beliefs at this age and to start to form his own views in order to reconcile his religious beliefs with his love for his mother. However, at this stage of the life cycle, both children would have been vulnerable to increasing feelings of anxiety, had it not been for their father's reassurance. If Hugo had not been able to reassure his children, I may have sought help from his pastor.

When parents have stricter religious views, it may be more difficult for children to reconcile religious beliefs when they or their loved ones do not live up to prescribed codes of behavior or when they encounter people with different beliefs. In that scenario, spirituality and religion can become a source of struggle, rather than strength. At such times, the clinician will need to accept the parents' beliefs and look to other avenues for intervention.

Often children feel guilty when they misbehave. Once they are aware of the problem, parents can usually figure out a way to help their children reconcile their spiritual beliefs with the realities of the world. Parents want their children to feel safe and loved. We as clinicians can help by respecting the parents' beliefs and coaching them to talk to their children in a way that invites children to ask questions, rather than to suffer silently. Children in families who practice a religion that is marginalized in our society are vulnerable to teasing and prejudice from other children or even adults. Clinicians can intervene by inquiring about experiences of prejudice and coaching parents so that they can in turn raise the issue with their children. Children feel protected and buffered from the cruelty of the outside world when families provide such a safe haven.

When treating children whose parents have left, died, or are otherwise not available, asking about children's beliefs and enlarging the genogram to include beliefs of family, friends, relatives, teachers, and mentors will help children to draw on spiritual strengths. We should not overlook this resource just because a client is young. Children of all ages have the capacity for spiritual thoughts and beliefs, and very often their spirituality can help them to heal.

Assess your comprehension of the family life cycle and spirituality by completing this quiz.

Adolescence: Identity Development and Spirituality

As children enter adolescence, they can be more autonomous, seek out experiences on their own, and challenge the system as they search for meaning and form their own opinions about their family's spiritual beliefs. This is the stage when young people are searching for an identity and voicing authentic opinions and feelings in the context of societal, parental, and peer pressure to conform to age, gender, and racial stereotypes. Some adolescents will question their families' spiritual beliefs as they try to develop an independent sense of identity. While others, particularly those in marginalized groups, may embrace their families' beliefs as they try to affirm their sense of identity within a dominant culture that marginalizes them, such as Muslim teens growing up in a predominantly Christian community (Chaudhury & Miller, 2008). African American adolescents tend to draw on spiritual strengths to foster a positive racial identity and to overcome the insults of living in a racist society (Moore-Thomas & Day-Vines, 2008), and are often better adjusted in communities where spirituality is emphasized because it increases their sense of belonging, pride, and self-worth (Aponte, 1994; Boyd-Franklin, 2003a; Marsiglia, Parsai, Kulis, & Nieri, 2005; Roehlkepartain, King, Wagener, & Benson, 2006). Still some adolescents in nondominant religious groups may rebel against their family's traditions in order to "fit" with the dominant group.

Given all that we know about spirituality as a resource for helping adolescents in therapy, clinicians need to ask questions about adolescents' beliefs.

However, adolescents with a religious affiliation different from the clinician's, or no religion, may be uncomfortable with this topic. First acknowledging that you have different religious beliefs and then asking an open-ended question such as "Will you tell me about your belief?" is one way to communicate that you are comfortable with your differences and that you honor the adolescents' beliefs.

CASE ILLUSTRATION

Joshua—Adolescents Challenge

Family Beliefs

The following case illustrates how an adolescent may shake up the family system and challenge adult beliefs, leading adults to reconsider their own views on religion and spirituality. The case evolved over many months and the treatment is reported here in four phases.

Joshua (18) and his parents Michael (56) and Marcy (53) sought family therapy when Joshua stopped attending high school in his senior year. The crisis occurred when Joshua told his parents he was gay. Joshua felt accepted in his circle of friends, and he wanted the same acceptance from his family. Michael and Marcy were anguished by their son's coming out and their religious belief that homosexuality was a sin, as it is considered in nearly all organized religions due to the rigid constructs of sexuality created by patriarchy.

Phase 1: The genogram (see Genogram 8.1) set the context for examining the challenges to spiritual beliefs.

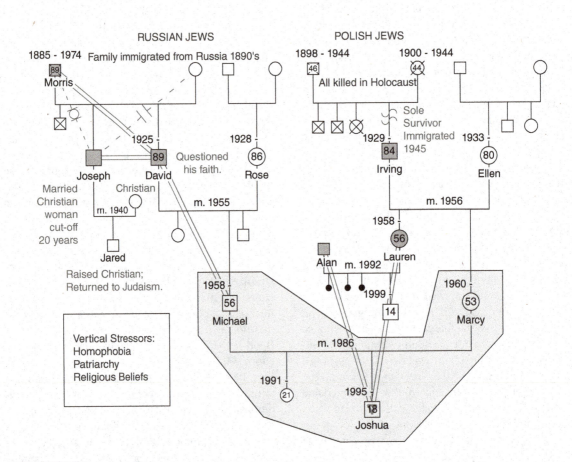

GENOGRAM 8.1 Joshua's Genogram

In the initial stage of treatment, we explored what Joshua's coming out meant for the family. I asked the parents to meet alone first to allow them to speak freely without hurting their son. I met Joshua alone once, and later we moved to sessions including all of them, with short meetings with each of them to check on how they were feeling. As shown on the genogram, both Michael and Marcy came from religious families where homosexuality was not accepted, and both had suffered family losses related to religious beliefs.

Phase 2: The chronology (see Figure 8.1) highlighted how earlier generations either turned away from religion or turned toward religion in response to loss, and ultimately transformed the pain of loss and found ways to remain connected through their beliefs.

I asked about the family's history of religious beliefs and practices and wrote down the dates of various events they reported. Michael's uncle Joseph was cut off from his family in 1940 when he married a Christian woman; this was a difficult loss for Michael's father, David, who had been very close to Joseph.

Figure 8.1 Chronology for the case of Joshua.

1940	Michael's uncle, Joseph, married a Christian woman, left Jewish faith, and was cut off from family for 20 years.
1940	Michael's father, David, was very close to Joseph and the brothers secretly remained in contact through letters.
1945	Marcy's paternal grandparents' family was killed in the Holocaust, her father was the sole survivor. He immigrated to New York in 1945 and joined a Jewish community.
1960	Joseph's son, Jared, returned to study Jewish religion and the cutoff between Joseph and Morris was repaired.
1992	Marcy's sister and her husband (Lauren and Alan) suffered several miscarriages. They consoled themselves through their faith, and by doting on Joshua.
2009	Family sought therapy when Joshua told his parents that he was gay.

The brothers remained connected through correspondence. The cutoff lasted 20 years and was repaired when David's son, Jared, returned to the Jewish religion in his adolescence. As we tracked these dates related to the challenges to the family's religious beliefs and created a chronology of the family history, a pattern of loss of family, loss of faith, and return to faith emerged. Michael saw that his family had survived challenges of faith and family cutoffs in the past. The family became hopeful that they would survive this new challenge.

Marcy's paternal grandparents, uncles, and aunt were all killed in the Holocaust in 1944, a tragic loss for her father, Irving, who was the sole survivor. In 1945, Irving moved to New York, found a Jewish community where he felt welcomed, and began to heal from the loss of his family. From 1992 through 1999, Marcy's sister Lauren suffered several miscarriages and was very distraught. Her faith carried her through those difficult years, and when she celebrated the birth of her son, in 1999, the religious ceremony was especially meaningful for the family. Tracking these events and writing them down on the chronology reinforced for Marcy that her family had already suffered too many losses, and that being Jewish was very important for her. She could neither lose her son nor her religion.

Phase 3: Therapy enlarged the context to explore religious beliefs about homosexuality within the societal constructs of patriarchy and oppression.

We discussed the implications of Joshua's coming out in light of patriarchy, homophobia, and society's constructs about love and marriage. Enlarging the context brought to light how rigid constructs of sexuality were created by patriarchy and oppression so that nearly all of the world's major religions and governments colluded in dictating sexual behavior and marginalizing homosexuality. These conversations helped to alleviate feelings of shame and opened up multiple possibilities for spirituality, religion, and sexuality. As a result, the family moved to a more liberal congregation that allowed gay and lesbian rabbis. Joshua had challenged his parents' beliefs. Their determination to remain connected to their son made them reconsider their own views on religion and find an alternative they could live with.

Phase 4: The genogram identified family members who would be good sources of support for the family in coming out to their extended family and friends.

Using the genogram, we identified Marcy's sister and her husband, Lauren and Alan, as "good resources" who would be supportive. They chose to tell them first and then to gradually tell the others. The systemic spiritual assessment enlarged the context and created a space where Joshua felt like a fully accepted member of his nuclear family, which they then extended to their relatives and larger community.

This treatment evolved over many months and many families do not have such a successful outcome. However, this family was very committed to each other, as they realized all the more through the exploration of their struggles with religion and spirituality over several generations.

Assess your comprehension of adolescence: identity development and spirituality by completing this quiz.

Early Adulthood: Time to Explore and Make Choices About Spiritual Beliefs

As young adults differentiate from their families of origin, they may move away from their religion, especially as they come in contact with a wider social network in our diverse society and go to college or enter the workforce. They may become less involved in their family's religious practices and many explore other spiritual paths. Some may wish to distance from practices they felt were oppressive; however, more often this is simply a result of exposure to others' beliefs intersecting with the developmental task of differentiation. Young adults who grew up with no religion may become more religious or may engage in "shopping" for religion or searching for a community. Young people are more likely to engage in varying religious practices and alternative spiritual beliefs (Pew Forum on Religion and Public Life, 2009). Others may need to let go of religion, and say they do not believe, in order to feel freer.

At some point, individuals have to make a choice about where they stand in relation to their family's beliefs. Often this happens when they move away from home or when they engage in intimate relationships. For many, a crucial time when they need to take a position about their beliefs occurs as they form relationships and make decisions about marriage ceremonies.

Approximately one fourth of American adults who are married or living with a partner are in religiously mixed relationships, and the number would be much higher if families with different Protestant denominations were included (Pew Forum on Religion and Public Life, 2008). Jewish communities in particular are concerned about the high rate of intermarriage, and Jewish families may react with disappointment or disapproval (Walsh, 2009). Historically, many religions prohibited interfaith marriages, but as society has become more open, interfaith marriages have become more prevalent. This is a relevant issue in marriage and family therapy. Spouses with similar beliefs and religious practices report greater personal well-being, more relationship satisfaction, and lower likelihood of divorce (Myers, 2006). Some questions that are helpful in gathering data for the spiritual genogram when working with couples are as follows: What are their spiritual beliefs? What is the history of their family's religious beliefs and practices, including changes in belief? What has been the impact of intra-family religious differences or those between the family and the surrounding community? Have any family members changed religion? How did other family members react to this change? (McGoldrick et al., 2008). These questions will help the clinician immediately assess the complexities of the spiritual resources available to the couple.

CASE ILLUSTRATION

Lorraine and Richard—Interfaith Couple's Counseling

Lorraine sought couple's counseling before marriage. One major point of contention was that Richard had not told his family that they did not want a religious wedding ceremony. Lorraine felt that Richard

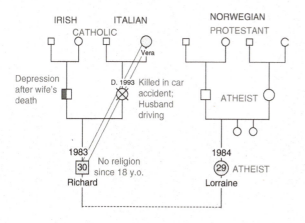

GENOGRAM 8.2 Lorraine and Richard's Genogram

through the use of the genogram helped Richard realize that he was more religious than he thought.

In future sessions, I encouraged Lorraine and Richard to consider how they would raise their children, celebrate holidays, and commemorate other occasions in the future. They were thoughtful young people who loved and respected each other. They had a lot to talk about, now that Richard was finally talking.

was behaving in a cowardly manner. She wondered whether this was going to be a pattern in their relationship and wanted to address it before they married.

Getting the family and spiritual history for the genogram helped me to learn that Lorraine was an atheist, she was the eldest of three girls, and her ethnicity was Norwegian (see Genogram 8.2). Her grandparents were Protestant but not very religious and her parents were atheists. Richard was Catholic but had not attended services since he moved away from home in his first year of college. He was the only son of an Irish-Catholic father and Italian-Catholic mother. When he was 10 years old, his mother died in a car accident. The father was driving and afterwards went into a depression and never remarried. All four grandparents helped raise Richard after his mother died.

I asked the couple to tell me more about their spiritual beliefs. Lorraine said she believed in science, nature, and charity and she had high moral values. She felt that Richard should be proud of her. Instead he was behaving as if he were ashamed of her and afraid of his family.

Richard said he was not religious but he was not sure what he believed. I wondered if his indecision was related to loss and asked Richard how his family had grieved the death of his mother. Richard said that he and his grandmother lit a candle in church every day for his mother for many years. He said that thinking about it now, he still envisioned his mother in Heaven. Encouraging the couple to talk about their spiritual beliefs in the context of their family history

Even when couples of different faiths have made the adjustments with their families and each other, spiritual and religious beliefs may become a source of conflict as they decide how they wish to raise their children. Often couples who viewed religion as unimportant find that the birth of a child changes their perspective and they feel strongly in providing religious instruction for their children (Walsh, 2009). As young adults move from coupling to starting a family, they consider what they want their children to learn and believe about religion and spirituality. This may become a source of conflict, as couples try to decide how they wish to raise their children, as illustrated in the case of Ana and Luis. In this case, questions about their spiritual beliefs, in conjunction with the genogram, quickly identified complex issues related to spirituality, class, gender, and oppression.

CASE ILLUSTRATION

Ana and Luis—Spirituality Overcomes Oppression

Ana called for an appointment for marriage counseling—she said she was feeling sad and lonely because Luis spent many hours out of the home working and studying while she stayed home with young children. She felt they had been growing apart lately. The initial genogram questions revealed that Ana and Luis were married in 2004, they immigrated from Peru 3 years later and they had two children, Miguel (age 5) and Anita (age 2) (see Genogram 8.3). In response to questions about their spiritual beliefs, Ana and Luis said their family was Catholic. This was a vague answer and it gave me a hint that there might be a problem in this area. I asked, "Your family is

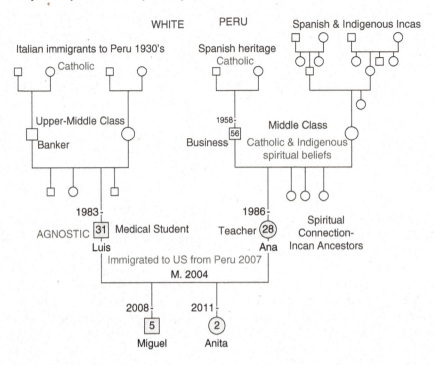

GENOGRAM 8.3 Ana and Luis' Genogram

Catholic, but what is *your* belief?" Luis said he was agnostic and uncertain about religion. He disagreed with many of the conservative tenets of Catholicism and he did not want to teach his children such conservative beliefs. Ana said she believed in God, and before the birth of their children she had not given much thought to religion, but now felt strongly that she wanted her children to be baptized. She said that since she and her husband disagreed, they had put off making a decision about baptizing their children rather than arguing about it. My hypothesis that they had a problem regarding spiritual beliefs was confirmed. Clinicians may feel uncomfortable pushing for an answer in this area, but probing gently often reveals important clinical information.

I suspected that Ana was feeling lonely because in their effort to avoid conflict, she and Luis did not talk to each other about their differences of opinion. I wondered whether gender role expectations made it difficult for her to be assertive with Luis regarding her religious beliefs, and I asked her to tell me about her feelings about baptizing her children. She said she was embarrassed to say that she worried

that the children might suffer harm if they were not baptized. She said she knew that she was just being superstitious, but at times she thought that her children would be vulnerable to an "evil eye," or kept out of Heaven if they died without the sacrament of Baptism. This generated further hypotheses that their differences in spiritual beliefs were related to social class status. Luis's upper-middle-class family was likely less tolerant of indigenous beliefs deemed to be superstitious than Ana's family who had risen from poor to middle class and had indigenous ancestry. Also, Ana's description of her beliefs as "superstitious" marginalized them, and I speculated that her embarrassment was a result of internalized oppression.

We tracked family history and religious beliefs, and related them to social class, power, and oppression. Luis' family immigrated to Peru in the 1930s from Italy where Catholicism had a 2000-year history, and the family continued to practice Catholicism in much the same way they had in Italy. Ana's family had been in Peru for a long time; she did not know when her Spanish ancestors first arrived. Their spiritual beliefs were a mixture of Roman Catholic and indigenous beliefs. I asked about the timing and changes in spiritual practices and tracked them on the chronology (see Figure 8.2).

> **Figure 8.2** Chronology for the case of Ana and Luis.

Relevant historical context relating to spiritual beliefs: Religion in Peru was influenced by the Spanish conquest in the sixteenth century and currently more than 75 percent of the population is Catholic. Historically, Catholicism was mixed with expressions of the indigenous and African religions.

Pre-1800s   Ana did not know when her White ancestors arrived in Peru. Her family was mixed racially: White from Spain and the indigenous Incas. Religion was a mixture of Catholicism and indigenous beliefs.

1930s   Luis' family migrated to Peru from Italy. They were White and Catholic.

1983   Luis was born in Peru, third of four children—family was of upper-middle-class socioeconomic status; they practiced traditional Catholic beliefs.

1986   Ana was born, first of four children. Her family was poor but moved up in status to middle class through her father's education. They were Catholic and practiced a modified version of their ancestors' spiritual beliefs, such as respect for nature and honoring a "huaca" (holy space), along with the Catholic rituals.

1987   Ana's father was promoted and the family moved to Lima. Family began to attend Catholic Church in Lima, where most parishioners were upper-middle class.

2004   Luis and Ana married.

2007   Luis and Ana immigrated to the United States from Peru (the only ones in family to travel to the United States). Luis was a medical student in New Jersey and Ana was a teacher by profession, but did not work in the United States.

February 15, 2008   Son, Miguel, was born.

May 1, 2011   Daughter, Anita, was born.

July 2012   The couple sought marriage counseling.

I also recorded the context of class, race, culture, and spiritual beliefs on the genogram, which I showed to the couple. It helped Luis and Ana to see the influence of class and colonization on their beliefs. The upper social classes in Peru were less likely to include indigenous people, and indigenous beliefs were devalued as a consequence of the oppression of colonization. Ana's family moved in socioeconomic status from poor to middle class through her father's education and employment, and they had combined Catholic and Incan rituals for many years. But her parents abandoned those rituals when they moved from their village to the capital city of Lima.

I talked about the concept of internalized oppression and asked Ana whether she believed it had influenced her parents' decision to abandon the indigenous rituals in order to be accepted among their new cosmopolitan friends in the corporate world of Lima. The question enlarged the context for Ana and Luis. Ana thought her family felt slightly ashamed of their indigenous ways. She wondered whether her mother had felt as lonely after they moved to Lima as she herself was feeling now. Luis began to consider whether his disillusionment with Catholicism was in response to subtle but similar societal pressures he might be feeling to fit into the scientific community, as a medical student in the United States.

The changes in spiritual beliefs over time were tracked through the chronology, and genogram questions facilitated discussions of the contexts of ethnicity, social class, gender role expectations, power, and oppression. Ana and Luis saw their marital problems in a larger context. They knew that spiritual beliefs had sustained their ancestors. They began to see the loss of spiritual beliefs in their family as a result of internalized oppression and disconnection from their community. They recognized the benefits of spiritual beliefs and community as protective factors and wanted them for their children and themselves. They made plans to join a church and to visit Peru more often.

Spirituality can be a source of strength as well as difficulty for couples. Luis and Ana were alone and far from their home and family. As young adults who were busy working and establishing a career and family in a new country, they had not been overly concerned about spiritual matters. The birth of their children brought spirituality to the forefront, and it became a source of conflict. Ana avoided the conflict and became sad and lonely as a result. Talking about the historical, political, and familial context of their spiritual beliefs helped the couple draw on their spiritual resources and the strength of their community to reconnect with each other.

> Assess your comprehension of early adulthood: time to explore and make choices about spiritual beliefs by completing this quiz.

Middle Age: Beliefs Reaffirmed

As in any stage of the life cycle, under particularly difficult circumstances, middle-aged people will draw on their spiritual beliefs to sustain them. However, for most, middle age is not a time of deep spiritual change because generally people have already made decisions about their spiritual beliefs earlier in life, usually in early adulthood. Midlife is roughly between ages 45 and 65—the age of launching children and/or caring for elderly parents or aging relatives, in some cultures more than others. By this age, most people have had a number of losses and other negative experiences. Some people may turn deeper into spirituality or renew their faith in their religion to make meaning of their losses and disappointments (Wink & Dillon, 2002), or as they deal with other challenging issues. For example, adult children caring for their aging parents with chronic illness may experience a deeper intimacy and spiritual bond with them (Walsh, 2009), and they may find that spiritual resources are especially important at this time (Smith & Harkness, 2002). The importance of spirituality may increase as middle-age adults become older, or have health problems, and face their own mortality. People who had put aside spiritual beliefs may find a need to reconsider their beliefs especially as they try to make sense of loss, trauma, disillusionment, and lost dreams.

CASE ILLUSTRATION

Lucy—Spirituality, Spirits, and Resiliency in the face of Untimely Loss

This case illustrates the need for clinicians to be open to multiple possibilities regarding spiritual beliefs. It is not enough to be sensitive to other beliefs. We must be ready to embrace spiritual and cultural resources we may not understand and that may make us uncomfortable, in order to provide good clinical care.

Lucy, a 53-year-old Cuban American woman, who had been diagnosed with chronic major depressive disorder with psychotic features, was grieving the recent death of her 33-year-old daughter from brain cancer (see Genogram 8.4). After her daughter died, Lucy became withdrawn, tearful, restless, and unable to sleep. Although spirituality can be a resource in many circumstances, it is particularly appropriate for bereavement issues because all religions have rituals or beliefs for dealing with death, and this comforts many people. When asked about her spiritual belief, Lucy said she converted to Catholicism when she married into a very religious Catholic family. I asked about her spiritual belief before marriage, and she hesitantly told me that her own family of origin had practiced *espiritismo* (the belief in spirits), not unusual in Cuba and other Latino cultures (Petry, 2004; Korin & Petry, 2005). She seemed conflicted about her belief in spirits and needed encouragement. I acknowledged that I was aware of the practice of *espiritismo* and said I would like to know more about her belief. Still hesitant, Lucy told me that she saw her daughter's spirit.

I suspected Lucy was having a psychotic hallucination and asked about conversations she may have had with her daughter to assess for psychosis and suicidal ideation. Other than telling me she saw her daughter's spirit, all of Lucy's answers, as well as her mood and affect, were appropriate. She denied suicidal ideation. She was tearful but said she felt comforted by her daughter's presence and that she needed to be well to help raise her grandchildren. Although my hypothesis needed more testing, I felt reasonably sure that she was safe at this point, and Lucy seemed to be more at ease. I felt I had established rapport with her.

At the end of our first session, Lucy asked me if she might take the risk of telling me something. I nodded and said, "Yes, certainly." She told me the spirit of a man named Francisco was standing near and guarding me. She caught me off-guard and I was visibly surprised. Lucy said, "I know you recognize his name by the look on your face," and she described his

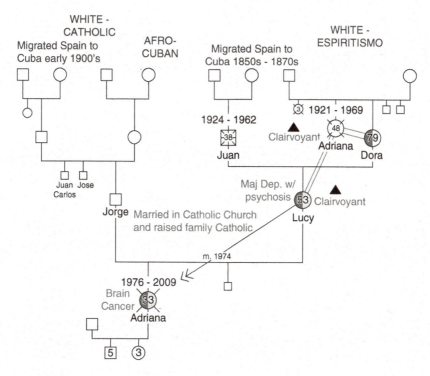

GENOGRAM 8.4 Lucy's Genogram

appearance, a White man with gray hair and a receding hairline descending in a V-shaped point known as a widow's peak. She was describing my grandfather, Francisco Separovich, who died in 1973. This was the first time I met Lucy; she could not have known about my grandfather. Lucy had the ability to see the dead. She saw my grandfather. Now I had to reconsider my hypothesis. Was Lucy clairvoyant? Was her long-term depression caused by a lifetime of being misunderstood? I had joined with Lucy and encouraged her to talk to me about her belief by telling her I knew of *espiritismo*. Yet, I had not expected this. I had tried to be sensitive to Lucy's beliefs, but I had not believed in her. Now I had to accept that Lucy had abilities I did not understand! And I had to be comfortable with not understanding in order to do a better assessment.

In subsequent sessions, we worked on her genogram and discussed her family's spiritual beliefs. Lucy spoke about a family myth that her Aunt Adriana was clairvoyant and that she had inherited her

aunt's abilities. As a child, Lucy had been close to this aunt, but as a young adult she distanced from her family and from her belief in *espiritismo* when she met her husband. Even though many people in Cuba believed in *espiritismo*, it was nonetheless an unconventional belief. Lucy described a typical progression of spiritual development over the life cycle: she questioned her spiritual beliefs as a young adult and then abandoned her old beliefs and adopted Catholicism, which she thought was a more acceptable religion. Having struggled with her beliefs in young adulthood and having made her choice, Lucy probably would not have given too much thought to her spiritual beliefs in middle age. However, the loss of her daughter compelled her to reconsider her decision. She derived little comfort from her adopted religion, and perhaps her chronic depression was caused, at least in part, by the denial of her earlier beliefs and her abilities.

Using the genogram to explore spiritual, cultural, and family themes helped Lucy to reconnect with her family's history and beliefs. She began to feel better as she acknowledged that she had felt lost when she denied her belief to practice a more conventional religion. She decided that she could indeed hold both beliefs. She could be Catholic and also believe in spirits. Eventually, she told me that her daughter's spirit had gone on its journey, which she understood to mean that her daughter was at peace. From a clinical perspective, I understood this as progress in the process of grief, and believed that Lucy was feeling stronger and therefore could let her daughter go.

My systemic assessment brought out Lucy's strengths, derived from her spirituality and culture. Spiritual beliefs that had been denied because they were unconventional were revived, and they transformed pain and suffering for Lucy. She was still reluctant to talk about her belief in spirits outside of our therapy sessions, but remembering her Aunt Adriana and talking about her spiritual beliefs and childhood experiences in Cuba helped Lucy to find a more inclusive spirituality. Feeling that her spiritual beliefs were validated helped Lucy begin to heal.

No doubt, I was more comfortable than others may have been with Lucy's story because we have similar cultural backgrounds, and her beliefs were familiar to me. However, clinicians can be prepared to hear about uncommon spiritual beliefs by doing the work of self-exploration, which leaves one centered and better able to listen. Sometimes, we do not need to understand or share the belief. Simply listening, with an open heart, can be validating and empowering for the client.

Assess your comprehension of middle age: beliefs reaffirmed by completing this quiz.

Older Adults: Aging and Facing Mortality

The developmental task at this stage of the life cycle, reviewing a lifetime's relationships and accomplishments and coming to terms with aging and mortality, is spiritual. People who are lucky enough to reach old age in relatively good health and have the time and energy to contemplate death usually want to prepare to dispense of worldly goods, repair relationships, and review their life's work. People do not necessarily become more religious or spiritual as they age, but the process of making sense of life is spiritual. Those who are religious may turn toward the rituals and community of their religious practice to accomplish this task. Those who are not particularly religious or spiritual nonetheless often engage in this spiritual process as they approach the end of life. We all want to believe that our life has meaning and love. This is the essence of spirituality.

Spirituality can be a powerful resource especially for the elderly who are poor, disadvantaged, and disempowered. Poverty and oppression leave people with diminished power over their destiny. It contributes to the loss of a sense of identity and self-worth, making the task of reviewing one's life particularly painful. Spirituality can give meaning to people's struggles and help them transcend the deprivation of poverty and oppression (Aponte, 2009; Boyd-Franklin & Lockwood, 2009). It can be the light that gives purpose and value to life.

CASE ILLUSTRATION

Pearl—Spirituality Promotes Dignity in the Face of Poverty and Oppression

Pearl was a 76-year-old African American great-grandmother raising her 15-year-old great-grandson, Jerome. Pearl was diagnosed with terminal cancer and was referred by her primary care physician for therapy. I began with the family history using the genogram and asked Pearl about her spiritual belief. Pearl told me that her faith in God and her church community had always pulled her through. She said she had struggled all her life, but she was a survivor. She had raised three children and helped to raise nine grandchildren. She had no fear of dying as she was at peace with God, but she wanted to work on a plan for someone to care for Jerome after she died.

Pearl had had more than her share of troubles. She had endured the stresses of poverty and discrimination, but she did not feel defeated. She drew strength from her faith. She was facing a terminal illness and nearing the end of her life, but her spiritual beliefs gave her strength to carry on with dignity and grace.

Unfortunately, medical advances and our Western beliefs have made acceptance of death more difficult with the emphasis on mastery over destiny. Some older adults believe that good health and the belief that one is in control of one's life is more important than spirituality (Lewis et al., 2009), but as physical health declines, a focus on psychological and spiritual well-being will help older adults deal with losses related to health issues, diminishing physical stamina and productivity, deaths of loved ones, and their own mortality. Therapists can encourage the elderly to share their life story and assess for spiritual resources to help them avoid depression, disillusionment, or fear of illness and death.

At the same time, while spirituality can be a significant source of strength, unresolved spiritual struggles, such as conflicts over religious beliefs, can cause difficulties leading to declines in health, stress, anxiety, depression, and even death (Ano & Vasconcelles, 2005; McConnell, Pargament, Ellison, & Flanell, 2006). A systemic assessment will help clinicians probe beyond the surface and evaluate for spiritual resources as well as areas for concern.

Good questions that can be asked at this stage of the life cycle are as follows: Have your beliefs changed over the years? Do your beliefs bring you comfort? Do you consider spirituality to be a source of strength? Whether the answer is "yes" or "no," follow up each question by asking, How? and Why? or Why not? and Are you at peace?

CASE ILLUSTRATION

Eleanor—Unresolved Spiritual Issues and Depression

This case illustrates how unresolved struggles with religious beliefs made it difficult for Eleanor to find peace. In order for her to move forward, the therapy had to address her spiritual conflict.

Eleanor, an 86-year-old widow of Polish descent, was referred for treatment of depression. She had completed treatment for colon cancer, which was in remission, yet she was sad, withdrawn, and isolated. Before this illness, Eleanor had been perky and energetic. After retiring from her position as a secretary in a manufacturing company, she had remained active for many years. Until recently she had volunteered at a hospital, taken classes at the local community college, and taken care of herself and her apartment. Now she had to force herself to get out of bed before noon; she had lost interest in everything, and she was afraid to leave home.

In exploring her history, Eleanor told me she was Polish Catholic, the eldest of four children, but had not attended church for many years. I asked if her beliefs had changed over the years, and she told me that she did believe in God but was disillusioned with the Catholic Church a few years ago when she learned that a priest had sexually abused her brothers when they were boys. Eleanor had been married to Joe, who was also Polish Catholic, and they had raised their children in the Catholic religion.

She said that she was afraid to die. She enjoyed good relationships with family members, and was especially close to her sister, but she could not talk to them about her fear of dying. As Eleanor spoke about her family history, I wondered whether her unresolved issues with the Catholic Church were exacerbating her stress, anxiety, and depression. At this stage in the life cycle, Eleanor's developmental tasks included dealing with chronic illness and making meaning of her life. My hypothesis was that she needed to resolve her conflicts with the Catholic religion in order to manage those tasks and be at peace.

I encouraged her to bring her sister, Caroline, to therapy because they were close. I asked about their belief in God and afterlife. Eleanor's conversations with Caroline helped her realize that she could believe in God and pray at home. She concluded that her decision not to attend church was the right one for her, but she could still honor her spiritual and religious beliefs in her own way.

The systemic assessment including questions about spirituality helped Eleanor to see her problem in the context of her family's history with the Catholic religion. She found spiritual peace by speaking directly to God and sharing her thoughts with her family. Finding peace allowed her to work on her life cycle tasks of dealing with chronic illness and facing death.

> Assess your comprehension of older adults: aging and facing mortality by completing this quiz.

Conclusion

Throughout history and across cultures, people around the world have relied on religion and spirituality to promote emotional well-being during times of celebration and times of loss or trauma. Our positive emotions made us spiritual (Vaillant, 2008). Spiritual awareness and growth are possible throughout all life cycle stages, and spirituality becomes especially significant when facing times of stress. The case illustrations presented highlight how to do a systemic assessment that takes into account spiritual resources and family strengths across the life cycle, tracking changes over time and looking for opportunities to enlarge the context in order to transform pain into healing.

> Recall what you learned in this chapter by completing the Chapter Review.

References

American Psychiatric Association. (2013). *Diagnostic and statistical manual of mental disorders* (5th ed.). Washington, DC: American Psychiatric Publishing.

American Psychological Association. (2010). *Ethical principles of psychologists and code of conduct, including 2010 amendments.* Retrieved June 21, 2013, from http://www.apa.org/ethics/code/index.aspx

Ano, G. G., & Vasconcelles, E. B. (2005). Religious coping and psychological adjustment to stress: A meta-analysis. *Journal of Clinical Psychology, 61,* 461–480.

Aponte, H. J. (1994). *Bread and spirit: Therapy with the new poor.* New York: W. W. Norton.

Aponte, H. J. (2009). The stresses of poverty and the comfort of spirituality. In F. Walsh (Ed.), *Spiritual resources in family therapy* (2nd ed., pp. 125–140). New York: Guilford.

Barrett, M. J. (2009). Healing from relational trauma: The quest for spirituality. In F. Walsh (Ed.), *Spiritual resources in family therapy* (2nd ed., pp. 267–285). New York: Guilford.

Birkenmaier, J., Behrman, G., & Berg-Weger, M. (2005). Integrating curriculum and practice with students and their field supervisors: Reflections on spirituality and the aging (ROSA) model. *Educational Gerontology, 31,* 745–763.

Boyd-Franklin, N. (2003a). *Black families in therapy: Understanding the African American experience* (2nd ed.). New York: Guilford Press.

Boyd-Franklin, N., & Lockwood, T. (2009). Spirituality and religion: Implications for psychotherapy with African American families. In F. Walsh (Ed.), *Spiritual resources in family therapy* (2nd ed., pp. 141–155). New York: Guilford.

Chaudhury, S. R., & Miller, L. (2008). Religions identify formation among Bangladeshi American Muslim adolescents. *Journal of Adolescent Research, 23*(4), 383–410.

Cruz, S. (Ed.). (2013). *Christianity and culture in the city: A postcolonial approach.* Lanham, MD: Lexington Books.

Gallup (2012). State of the states. Retrieved May 17, 2013, from http://www.gallup.com/poll/125066/State-States.aspx?ref=interactive

Hart, T. (2006). Spiritual capacities of children and youth. In E. C. Roehlkepartain, P. E. King, L. Wagener, & P. L. Benson, *The Handbook of Spiritual Development in Childhood and Adolescence.* Thousand Oaks, CA: Sage Publications, Inc.

Hines, P. (2008). Climbing up the rough side of the mountain. In M. McGoldrick & K. V. Hardy (Eds.), *Revisioning family therapy: Race, culture and gender in clinical practice* (2nd ed., pp. 367–377). New York: Guilford Press.

Hodge, D. R. (2004). *Spiritual assessment: Handbook for helping professionals.* North American Association of Christian Social Workers.

Joint Commission on Accreditation of Healthcare Organizations. (2008). Retrieved May 18, 2013, from www.jointcommission.org

Kamya, H. (2005). African immigrant families. In M. McGoldrick, J. Giordano, & N. Garcia Preto (Eds.), *Ethnicity and family therapy* (3rd ed., pp. 101–116). New York: Guilford.

Kamya, H. (2009). Healing from refugee trauma: The significance of spiritual beliefs, faith community and faith-based services. In F. Walsh (Ed.) *Spiritual resources in family therapy* (2nd ed., pp. 286–300). New York: Guilford.

Kelcourse, F. B. (2004). *Human development and faith: Life-cycle stages of body, mind, and soul.* St. Louis, MI: Chalice Press.

Korin, E. C., & Petry, S. S. (2005). Brazilian families. In M. McGoldrick, J. Giordano, & N. Garcia Preto (Eds.), *Ethnicity and family therapy* (3rd ed., pp. 166–177). New York: Guilford Press.

Lewis, M. J., Edwards, A. C., & Burton, M. (2009). Coping with retirement: Well-being, health, and religion. *The Journal of Psychology, 143*(4), 427–448.

Marsiglia, F. F., Parsai, M., Kulis, S., & Nieri, T. (2005). God forbid! Substance use among religious and non-religious youth. *American Journal of Orthopsychiatry, 75*(4), 585–598.

McConnell, K. M., Pargament, K., Ellison, C. G., & Flanell, K. J. (2006). Examining the links between spiritual struggles and symptoms of psychopathology in a national sample. *Journal of Clinical Psychology, 62*(12), 1469–1484.

McGoldrick, M., Gerson, R., & Petry, S. (2008). *Genograms: Assessment and intervention.* (3rd ed.). New York: W. W. Norton.

Moore-Thomas, C., & Day-Vines, N. L. (2008). Culturally competent counseling for religious and spiritual African American adolescents. *Professional School Counseling, 11,* 159–165.

Myers, S. (2006). Religious homogamy and marital quality: Historical and generational patterns. *Journal of Marriage and the Family, 68*(2), 292–304.

NASW (2008). *Code of ethics of the National Association of Social Workers.* Retrieved May 18, 2013, from www.socialworkers.org/pubs/code/code.asp

Peteet, J. R., Lu, F. G., & Narrow, W. E. (Eds.). (2011). *Religious and spiritual issues in psychiatric diagnosis: A research agenda for DSM-V.* Arlington, VA: American Psychiatric Publishing.

Petry, S. S. (2004). Bereavement customs of Brazil—Mourning in different cultures. In F. Walsh & M. McGoldrick (Eds.). *Living beyond loss: Death and the family* (2nd ed., pp. 119–160). New York: W. W. Norton.

Pew Forum on Religion and Public Life (2008, February). *U.S. religious landscape survey: Religious affiliation diverse and dynamic.* Retrieved May 18, 2013, from religions.pewforum.org/pdf/report-religious-landscape-study-full.pdf

Pew Forum on Religion and Public Life (2009, December). *Many Americans mix multiple faiths: Eastern, new age beliefs widespread.* Retrieved May 18, 2013, from http://www.pewforum.org/Other-Beliefs-and-Practices/Many-Americans-Mix-Multiple-Faiths.aspx#1

Roehlkepartain, E. C., King, P. E., Wagener, L., & Benson, P. L. (2006). *The handbook of spiritual development in childhood and adolescence.* Thousand Oaks, CA: Sage Publications, Inc.

Smith, A. L., & Harkness, J. (2002). Spirituality and meaning: A qualitative inquiry with caregivers of Alzheimer's disease. *Journal of Family Psychotherapy, 13*(1–2), 87–108.

Vaillant, G. E. (2008). *Spiritual evolution: How we are wired for faith, hope, and love.* New York: Broadway Books.

Walsh, F. (2008). Spirituality, healing and resilience. In M. McGoldrick & K. V. Hardy (Eds.), *Re-Visioning family therapy: Race, culture and gender in clinical practice* (2nd ed., pp. 61–75). New York: Guilford.

Walsh, F. (Ed.). (2009). *Spiritual resources in family therapy* (2nd ed.). New York: Guilford Press.

Wink, P., & Dillon, M. (2002). Spiritual development across the adult life course: Findings from a longitudinal study. *Journal of Adult Development, 9*(1), 79–94.

Chapter 9

Siblings and the Life Cycle

Monica McGoldrick & Marlene F. Watson

— Learning Objectives —

- Explain the significance of sibling relationships through the family life cycle.
- Describe the effects that age spacing has on sibling relationships.
- Examine how gender roles influence sibling patterns in understanding a family.
- Discuss how class, culture, and race impact sibling patterns.
- List and describe the characteristics associated with a person's birth order.
- Describe how a disabled sibling impacts family dynamics through the family life cycle.
- Identify and describe patterns that sibling relationships follow during young adulthood.
- Examine how sibling relationships impact couple relationships.
- Discuss the challenges to sibling relationships during midlife and after the death of parents.
- List and describe rules for dealing with sibling relationships through the family life cycle.

My dearest friend and bitterest rival, my mirror and opposite, my confidante and betrayer, my student and teacher, my reference point and counterpoint, my support and dependent, my daughter and mother, my subordinate, my superior and scariest still, my equal.

Elizabeth Fishel (1979, p. 16)

The Importance of Sibling Relationships Through the Life Cycle

Sibling relationships are the longest that most of us have in life. Indeed, from a life cycle perspective, the sibling bond may be second only to the parent–child bond in importance. In our modern world, spouses may come and go, parents die, and children grow up and leave, but if we are lucky, siblings are always there. During the middle phases of the life cycle, siblings may be preoccupied with partners, children, and work, but as people move through the life cycle, sibling relationships show increasing prominence (Cicirelli, 1994, 1995, 2002; White & Riedman, 1992a; Meinhold, 2006; McKay & Caverly, 2004; Friedman, 2003). Our parents usually die a generation before we do, and our children live on for a generation after us. It is rare that our spouses are closely acquainted with our first 20 or 30 years or for friendships to last from earliest childhood until the end of our lives. Our siblings thus share more of our lives genetically and contextually than anyone else, particularly sisters, since sisters tend to be emotionally more connected and are likely to live longer than brothers. In fact, we can divorce a spouse much more finally than a sibling (McGoldrick, 1989b).

Yet sibling relationships have been largely neglected in the family therapy literature and in the mental health field in general. Children generally spend more of their out-of-school time in childhood with siblings than with anyone else in their lives (McHale & Crouter, 2005) and are more likely to grow up in households with siblings than with fathers. In later life, once parents are gone, the sibling bond can become our primary attachment, though at that point sibling relationships also become optional and may break apart (Gold, 1987, 1989; Norris & Tindale, 1994). Especially in recent times as parents are living longer and often need long-term caretaking, conflicts among siblings can become painfully intensified in late middle age (Friedman, 2003; Connidis & Kemp, 2008; Walker, Allen & Connidis, 2005). It is a great mystery why family scholars and developmental psychologists so often overlook this area of study, given the primary reciprocity of siblings to well-being throughout life (McHale & Crouter, 2005).

Apart from Adler's (1959, 1979) early formulations, followed up by Walter Toman's Family Constellation (1976), hardly any attention has been paid to siblings in the psychological literature. Luckily, a number of excellent works in the past few years have begun to counter this neglect. For more psychological literature on siblings, see Bank and Kahn's *The Sibling Bond* (2008), Kahn and Lewis's *Siblings in Therapy* (1988), Barbara Mathias's *Between Sisters* (1992), Marianne Sandmaier's *Original Kin* (1994), Susan Scarf Merrell's *The Accidental Bond* (1995), Frank Sulloway's *Born to Rebel* (1996), Victor Cicirelli's *Sibling Relationships across the Life Span* (1995), and George Howe Colt's *Brothers* (2012).

In our view, the neglect of siblings in the literature reflects cultural attitudes that overvalue the individual and nuclear family experience and neglect the lifelong connections that we have to our extended family members throughout the life cycle.

We hope that this chapter will encourage therapists to affirm the importance of sibling connections through the life cycle in all clinical assessments, and validate sibling relationships through therapeutic interventions that support and strengthen these bonds and to hold specific sibling sessions when appropriate.

Perhaps our therapies would be facilitated if we worked on the basic assumption of including siblings unless there is a reason not to. That is, in doing an assessment, we could start with the question "Why not have a sibling session to understand or help clients in this situation?" rather than starting with the negative and including siblings only if there is a specific sibling conflict, as is the assumption of most clinical guidelines.

In some families, relationships with siblings remain the most important throughout life. In others, sibling rivalry and conflict cause families to break apart. Siblings are models for future relationships with friends, lovers, and other contemporaries, and for a significant portion of the population, their strongest and most intimate relationships.

In today's world of frequent divorce and remarriage, there may be a combination of siblings, stepsiblings, and half-siblings who live in different households and come together only on special occasions. There are more multi-racial and multi-ethnic siblings and families with siblings of different backgrounds, with the potential for greater cultural richness, and also for sibling resentments and conflicts around skin color, race, or ethnicity, which are important to address. Additionally, adoption may result in multi-racial/multi-ethnic siblings with the same potential for increased cultural enrichment as well as possible resentment and conflict in adulthood. There are also more only children, whose closest sibling-like relationships will be with their friends or cousins. There are more two-child families as well, in which the relationship between the children tends to be more intense for the lack of other siblings, especially if their parents divorce or if they are close in age. Thus, sibling relationships may become more salient for the current generation because of all the factors that are diminishing the size of the family and community network. Clearly, the more time siblings spend with one another and the fewer siblings there are, the more intense their relationships are likely to be. Furthermore, siblings who have little contact with outsiders grow to rely on each other, especially when parents are absent, unavailable, or inadequate.

Though there has been extremely little research on longitudinal aspects of sibling relationships, siblings generally seem to have a commitment to maintaining their relationships throughout life, and it is rare for them to break off their relationship or lose touch with each other completely (Cicirelli, 1985, 2002). Among the few findings that we have are data showing that siblings of the disabled, especially sisters, are particularly likely to become drawn into emotional caretaking demands from their families. Involving siblings in planning and treatment obviously benefits the whole family. Yet very few programs for the disabled include work with siblings (whether children or adults) as a focus of their intervention.

The evidence is that sibling relationships matter a great deal. According to one important longitudinal study of successful, well-educated men (the Harvard classes of 1938–1944), the single best predictor of emotional health at the age of 65 was having had a close relationship with one's sibling in college. This was more predictive than childhood closeness to parents, emotional problems in childhood, or parental divorce, more predictive even than having had a successful marriage or career (Vaillant, 1977).

Myers (2011) found that most adults maintain their sibling relationships over their lives. Thus, given the significance of sibling relationships and their longevity, it seems important for therapists to address conflicts, resentments, and cutoffs whenever possible. Techniques that promote understanding and forgiveness are important for addressing sibling rifts. Forgiveness may have a crucial role in all intimate relationships (Bright, Cameron, & Caza, 2006; Cameron & Caza, 2002; Fincham, Jackson, & Beach, 2006; Waldron & Kelley, 2008), but especially because siblings hold each other's history and are important to the fabric of life, we should take every opportunity to assist siblings in developing authentic and meaningful connections and to build trust and attachment (Lawler et al., 2005). We must be attentive to enlarging our focus in family therapy to include siblings in order to prevent or heal sibling fractures and facilitate supportive sibling alliances. Even where a sibling is not yet able to maintain a healthy relationship, we can coach clients to open their hearts to possibilities for when the sibling may reach the point of readiness to engage and repair a broken relationship (McGoldrick, 2011; Wade, 2010).

> **Assess your comprehension of the importance of sibling relationships through the life cycle by completing this quiz.**

Age Spacing

Sibling experiences vary greatly. An important factor is the amount of time brothers and sisters spend together when they are young. Two children who are close in age, particularly if they are of the same gender, generally spend a lot of time together, must share their parents' attention, and are usually raised under similar conditions. Siblings who are born far apart spend less time with each other, growing up

at different points in the family's evolution and are likely to have fewer shared experiences; they are in many ways more like only children.

Sulloway (1996) maintains that children who are closest in age have the greatest competition and rivalry for their parents' care; therefore, the second sibling has the greatest need to differentiate from the older to find a niche for him or herself. The ultimate shared sibling experience is that of identical twins. They have a special relationship that is exclusive of the rest of the family. Twins have been known to develop their own language and maintain an uncanny, almost telepathic sense of each other. Even fraternal twins often have remarkable similarities because of their shared life experiences. The major challenge for twins is to develop individual identities. Since they do not have their own unique sibling position, there is a tendency to lump twins together. This becomes a problem especially when, as adolescents, they are trying to develop their separate identities. Sometimes twins have to go to extremes to distinguish themselves from each other.

Gender Differences

Sister pairs tend to have the closest relationships. Sisters generally have been treated differently from brothers in families, given the pivotal caretaking role that sisters typically have in a family. Both brothers and sisters report feeling more positive about sisters (Troll & Smith, 1976) and indicate that a sister was the sibling to whom they felt closest (Cicirelli, 1982, 1995; White & Riedman, 1992a). According to a survey by Cicirelli (1983), the more sisters a man has, the happier he is and the less worried about family, job, or money matters. Sisters seem to provide a basic feeling of emotional security. And the more sisters he has, the more time he will spend raising his own children and the more generous he will be to others (Grant, 2013). The more sisters a woman has, the more she is concerned with keeping up social relationships and helping others (Cicirelli, 1985). Siblings can provide role models for successful aging, widowhood, bereavement, and retirement. They act as caretakers and exert pressures on each other to maintain values.

With rare exceptions, fewer expectations for intellectual and worldly achievement are placed on, or allowed to, sisters than brothers. It is interesting that in Hennig and Jardin's classic study (1977) of highly successful women in business, not a single woman in the sample had had a brother. Research indicates that while the preference for sons is diminishing (Washington, 2007), there is still a greater likelihood that a family with only female children will continue to try for a boy. We have come a long way from the infanticide that other cultures have resorted to when they had daughters instead of sons, but the remnants of those attitudes still exist. Families are more likely to divorce if they have only daughters, and divorced fathers are more likely to lose contact with children if they are daughters, and women pregnant with girls are less likely to marry (Dahl & Moretti, 2008). On the other hand, recent research has shown that parenting daughters increases feminist sympathies. Fathers of daughters vote significantly more liberally than fathers who have only sons, and the more daughters a father has, the higher his propensity to vote liberally, particularly on reproductive rights issues (Washington, 2007).

Unlike oldest sons, who typically have a clear feeling of entitlement, oldest daughters often have feelings of ambivalence and guilt about the responsibilities of their role. Whatever they do, they feel that it is not quite enough, and they can never let up in their efforts to take care of people and make the family work right. They are the ones who maintain the networks; who make Thanksgiving, Christmas, and Passover happen; who care for the sick; and who carry on the primary mourning when family members die. They are central in family process, more often taking responsibility for maintaining family relationships than their brothers. Sisters not only do the majority of the caretaking, but they also tend to share more intimacy and have more intense relationships than brothers, although they typically get less glory than brothers do. From childhood on, most sibling caretaking is delegated to older sisters, with brothers freed for play or other tasks (Cicirelli, 1985). Brother-to-brother relationships appear to be characterized by more rivalry, competitiveness, ambivalence, and jealousy (Adams, 1968; Cicirelli, 1985), while sister relationships are characterized by more

support and caretaking. However, societal and intra-family racism based on skin color as a measure of beauty induce rivalry, competitiveness, and ambivalence among sisters and clinicians need to be sensitive to reframing such conflicts as created by the social context rather than by psychological aspects of the family (Watson, 2013).

Sister relationships, like those of women friends, are more often devalued than peer relationships involving men. A woman who wants to avoid a move for her husband's job to be near her sister is considered strange indeed. She will probably be labeled "enmeshed" or "undifferentiated." Yet it is the sister who was there at the beginning, before the husband, and who will most likely be there at the end, after he is gone. A strong sense of sisterhood seems to strengthen a woman's sense of self (Cicirelli, 1982, 1985).

With the best of intentions, parents may convey very different messages to their sons than to their daughters. In certain cultures, such as Italian and Latino, daughters are more likely to be raised to take care of others, including their brothers. Some cultural groups, such as Irish and African American families, may, for various historical reasons, overprotect sons and underprotect daughters (McGoldrick, 1989a; McGoldrick, Giordano, & Garcia Preto, 2005). Other cultural groups have less specific expectations. Anglos, for example, are more likely to believe in brothers and sisters having equal chores. But, in general, it is important to notice how gender roles influence sibling patterns in understanding a family (McGoldrick, 1989b).

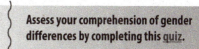

Assess your comprehension of gender differences by completing this quiz.

Culture, Class, Race, and Ethnicity

In addition to early parental loss, temperament, the child's physical attributes, family traumas, and major life changes related to politics, economics, and emotional factors affecting families, class, culture, and race also powerfully influence sibling patterns. Cultures and classes differ in the expected roles and relationships of siblings (Leder, 1991; McGoldrick et al., 2005; Nuckolls, 1993; Sandmeier, 1994; Sulloway, 1996; Zukow, 1989).

A family's ethnic identity may determine whether siblings are close, distant, or created equal (Leder, 1991) and the meaning of the siblinghood. Some ethnic groups, such as Asians, may show a greater preference for male children; some, such as African Americans, value the family unit over individual members; others, such as Anglos, give priority to autonomy and self-reliance. Even the concept of sibling rivalry is culture bound, being largely a Western phenomenon that stems from a focus on individual achievement, competition, and status. In contrast, a huge segment of the world's population dissuades children from assuming the stance of sibling as rival by instilling in them a sense of "we-ness" rather than "I" (Sandmeier, 1994). In cultures that train their children to view each other as necessary, siblings are more likely to have lifelong, enduring ties.

In some oppressed cultures, the closely knit sibling bond is also influenced by historical needs for survival. Family members rely on mutual support and aid to fulfill basic material and emotional needs. In African American families, the tradition of tightly woven sibships that was passed down from African culture is combined with the family's need to function as a unit to deal with the forces of racism (Watson, 1998). Thus, strong sibling bonds may be more necessary for African Americans than for people in cultures that are not affected by oppression and in which siblings can live independently of each other. In cultures in which sibling caretaking is a major form of caretaking, as it is for African Americans, strong emotional attachment, positive or negative, may have a profound effect on siblinghood throughout the life cycle (Watson, 1998). Although large sibships such as those that may be found in Irish Catholic families may also produce older sibling caretakers, this role will probably end with childhood. Among African Americans, however, sibling caretakers tend to continue their role into adulthood. Childhood sibling caretaking helps to prepare them for their lifelong role as each other's keeper (Watson, 1998). Hence, the expectations of African American siblings have implications for individual and family development throughout the life cycle.

Some cultures use the term "brother" or "sister" to convey the depth of a cherished relationship. The Vietnamese, for example, address lovers and spouses as "big brother" or "little sister," and African Americans may greet one another with the term "Brother" or "Sister" to convey their sense of kinship (Sandmaier, 1994). Such terms of endearment express the particular culture's valuing of sibling relationships.

The family's emotional map is governed by its cultural roots. Families of Northern European and Anglo backgrounds may discourage strong displays of feeling or affection and will probably view themselves, their siblings, and their parents as a related collection of individuals. German brothers and sisters also may be likely to refrain from showing strong or open affection toward one another because of the cultural prescription to maintain a stiff upper lip (Sandmaier, 1994). In Italian culture, in which the family supersedes the individual, sibling relationships tend to be close, especially between same-sex pairs. In a study conducted by Colleen Leahy Johnson (1982), 63 percent of middle-aged Italian women saw a sibling daily, in contrast to 12 percent of their Anglo counterparts. Among college-educated older Americans, African American siblings were three times as likely as Whites to focus on themes of loyalty, solidarity, and enduring affection. Hence, the cultural message that African Americans receive to stay together and help each other does not disappear as family members move up the class ladder or move toward old age.

In Greek and Jewish cultures, conflicting messages about family loyalty and individual success and competition may add to sibling tensions. Siblings may be fierce rivals at the same time that family cohesion is expected (Sandmaier, 1994). Irish siblings may have deeply ambivalent feelings toward one another. Irish culture's emphasis on dichotomies and labels may spark sibling rivalry, while simultaneously inducing guilt in the sibling for having bad thoughts. Thus, buried resentments that enable siblings to appear connected while the parents are alive may lead to sibling cutoffs in the wake of parental death.

Culturally influenced family rules and scripts set the stage for sibling relationships (Sandmaier,

1994; Watson, 1998). As more Americans face longer lives without partners or children, sibling relationships must be revisited. Our brothers and sisters are potentially emotional and physical resources at all points of the life cycle, but individual needs for attachment and belonging are apt to be more critical at later junctures of the life cycle.

In cultures that prize individuality over family unity, siblings' life cycle patterns may remain distinct and separate as brothers and sisters keep their families of procreation apart. In cultures that demand family cohesion or enmeshment, siblings' life cycle patterns may become fused, making it difficult for families of procreation to establish their own traditions and ways of relating.

Understanding the cultural context of sibling relationships provides a larger framework for addressing individual issues of self-esteem and identity, unresolved issues of childhood, and sibling relationships through the life cycle. A sister from a culture that prefers sons may stop blaming her brother and have greater compassion for her parents once she realizes the cultural script in which they all played a part.

Class differences are likely to have a major impact on adult siblings from oppressed cultures or poor families. Unacknowledged or overt resentments may characterize adult sibling relationships for siblings who end up in different socioeconomic groups. Lower-class African American siblings may hold their resentment of middle-class or professional brothers and sisters in check because of cultural expectations of familyhood and their need for physical support. Middle-class brothers and sisters may resent lower-class siblings for relying on them but not feel free to express such resentment because of the sense of family obligation.

In Jewish families, sibling resentment or cutoffs may result from intense feelings around the success or lack of success of one's brother or sister. Parental reactions to successful and non-successful children may exacerbate sibling fissures related to class differences. The need to prove oneself intellectually superior and successful for Jewish siblings may be related to their cultural history and oppression. Class differences between Jewish siblings might adversely affect their relationships, especially

if one perceives the other as having had an unfair advantage.

Class differences in Anglo families may result in sibling antagonism, but the cultural pattern of individuality and autonomy may obscure such resentments or conflicts. Since these siblings tend not to mingle except for formal family occasions, sibling tensions would go virtually unnoticed and would probably not be dealt with by the siblings themselves. Lower-class family members at family events may be treated like poor relations, or they may be closed out of family events altogether. Although lower-class family members could be treated negatively by middle-class African Americans, it would not go unnoticed, and the mother would probably intervene on behalf of the lower-class sibling. Regardless of the ethnic or cultural group, class tensions are likely to surface when aging or ill parents require care from children.

Class may influence the way rebellion intersects with sibling position. Just as oldest sisters may be more rebellious than oldest brothers because the gender inequities impinge on an oldest sister's "right" to be the leader, oldest siblings in minority families may become more rebellious than oldest siblings from the dominant groups because of the interaction of social privilege and status with sibling status. Sibling position may exaggerate the class effects of oppression, which lead people to resist the status quo (e.g., making a younger sibling of a poor family even more rebellious).

Sulloway (1996) found that, as with the interaction of gender and birth order, the oldest child in a poor family may use a strategy of rebellion against the status quo as the best way to achieve eminence. Radical reformers have tended to come from racial minorities and lower classes, and to be later-borns. In Sulloway's research, abolitionism attracted the highest proportion of later-borns of any reform movement he surveyed. Still, because Sulloway's research focused primarily on Europeans who became involved in scientific revolutions, we need further research on culture, class, gender, and sibling patterns from other countries where lives include other spheres of activity and interest. Sulloway suggests that the early parental loss in the upper classes diminishes sibling differences based on birth order, as nannies and other caretakers come in to replace the lost parent, and siblings become more supportive of each other as they share their loss. In middle- and lower-class families, the opposite may happen. The oldest child may be drawn into the burden of parenting younger siblings and becomes even more conservative, leading the younger siblings to become even more rebellious than otherwise. Large sibships reinforce the first-born's duties as surrogate parent.

Racial/Ethnic identity of siblings

Racial and ethnic identity can seriously influence relationships for better or worse, particularly if siblings identify with different racial/ethnic groups or are of different racial or ethnic groups through remarriage or adoption, as the following case illustrates.

CASE ILLUSTRATION

Robert and His Family

A White family sought treatment for their adolescent son's school failure and acting out. Both the mother and father were White, but Robert, the identified patient, the oldest of the three siblings, was slightly darker in skin color. The siblings seemed to taunt him with negative stares and sarcastic remarks. In recounting the family's history, both the mother and father denied that there were any prior marriages. It was not until the second session that the mother finally admitted to my (MW) probing, that Robert was her son from a prior relationship. At the third session, I specifically asked about Robert's experience of being darker than his siblings. It was only then that the mother admitted that his father was Black. With my (MW) help in a family session, Robert described being called the N-word by his siblings and the lack of protection and support that he felt from both parents and siblings. He was struggling with his racial/ethnic identity both at home and at school, which contributed to his school failure and acting out. I engaged the family in a discussion of racism, including corollary White privilege, and its impact on self-identity and development. The siblings, who were younger in age, were modeling the negative behavior of extended family members and of the father

who resented his wife's relationship with a Black man. Like many families, Robert's family downplayed his siblings' name calling as "normal" sibling behavior. After hearing Robert's pain and feelings of not being accepted at home or school, the parents agreed to work on new rules for sibling behavior and to be more open about Robert being biracial. Also, the parents realized the need for them to work on their relationship rather than allow marital resentments to spill over into their parenting.

If left unattended, sibling conflicts related to racial and ethnic identity may become entrenched, leading to resentments or cutoffs in adulthood. Parents may be unaware or unable to acknowledge racism in their own homes or its impact on sibling relationships. However, the experience of difference among siblings can impact sibling development and rob siblings of support in adulthood. Racial and ethnic differences in siblings, just like gender, sexual orientation, and abilities can transform these potentially lifelong beneficial relationships into disconnection, distrust, and disharmony unless the differences are acknowledged and dealt with by parents who have the courage to face racism and White privilege and other of society's oppressive systems.

 Assess your comprehension of culture, class, race, and ethnicity by completing this quiz.

Birth-Order Effects on Sibling Relationships

Although birth order can profoundly influence later experiences with spouses, friends, and colleagues, many other factors also influence sibling roles, such as temperament, disability, class, culture, looks, intelligence, talent, gender, and the timing of each birth in relation to other family experiences—deaths, moves, illnesses, changes in financial status, and so on.

Parents may have a particular agenda for a specific child, such as expecting him or her to be the responsible one or the baby, regardless of that child's position in the family. Children who resemble a certain family member may be expected to be like that person or to take on that person's role. Children's temperaments may also be at odds with their sibling position. This may explain why some children struggle so valiantly against family expectations—the oldest who refuses to take on the responsibility of the caretaker or family standard bearer or the youngest who strives to be a leader. In some families, it will be the child who is most comfortable with the responsibility—not necessarily the oldest child—who becomes the leader. Parents' own sibling experiences will affect their children as well. But certain typical patterns often occur that reflect each child's birth order.

In general, oldest children are likely to be the over-responsible and conscientious ones in the family. They make good leaders, because they have experienced authority over and responsibility for younger siblings. Often serious in disposition, they may believe that they have a mission in life. In identifying with their parents and being especially favored by them, oldest children tend to be conservative even while leading others into new worlds; and though they may be self-critical, they do not necessarily handle criticism from others well.

The oldest daughter often has the same sense of responsibility, conscientiousness, and ability to care for and lead others as her male counterpart. However, daughters generally do not receive the same privileges; nor are there generally the same expectations for them to excel. Thus, they may be saddled with the responsibilities of the oldest child without the privileges or enhanced self-esteem.

The middle child in a family is in between, having neither the position of the first as the standard bearer nor the last as the baby. Middle children thus run the risk of getting lost in the family, especially if all the siblings are of the same gender. On the other hand, middle children may develop into the best negotiators, more even-tempered and mellow than their more driven older siblings and less self-indulgent than the youngest. They may even relish their invisibility.

Frank Sulloway (1996) argues on the basis of a large sample of historical figures that later-born children, both middle and youngest children, are very much more likely to be rebels than are oldest or only children because of the Darwinian imperative for survival. The niche of following in the parental footsteps has already been taken by the oldest, and

they need to find a different niche to survive. They therefore tend to be less parent-identified, less conscientious, and more sociable. Traditionally, in many European cultures, younger children, sons in particular, had to be disposed of, since the oldest took over the family farm or business from the father; younger sons tended to become warriors or priests or fulfilled other less conventional roles in society.

A middle sister is generally under less pressure to take responsibility, but she may feel the need to try harder to make her mark because she has no special role. She remembers running to catch up with the older sister from childhood and running frantically from the younger one, who seemed to be gaining on her every minute (Fishel, 1979).

The youngest child often has a sense of specialness that allows self-indulgence without the overburdening sense of responsibility of oldest children. This pattern may increase in intensity with the number of siblings there are in a family. The younger of two children probably has more a sense of pairing and twinship—unless there is a considerable age differential—than the youngest of 10. Freed from convention and determined to do things his or her own way, the youngest child can sometimes make remarkable creative leaps leading to inventions and innovations.

Youngest children can also be spoiled and self-absorbed, and their sense of entitlement may lead at times to frustration and disappointment. In addition, the youngest often has a period as an only child after the older siblings have left home. This can be an opportunity to enjoy the sole attention of parents but can also lead to feelings of abandonment by the siblings.

A younger sister tends to be protected, showered with affection, and handed a blueprint for life. She may either be spoiled (especially if there are older brothers) and have special privileges or, if she is from a large family, she may feel frustrated by always having to wait her turn. Her parents may have run out of energy with her. She may feel resentful about being bossed around and never quite taken seriously. If she is the only girl, the youngest may be more like the princess, yet the servant to elders, becoming, perhaps, the confidante of her brothers in adult life and the one to replace the parents in holding the family together at later life cycle phases.

Like middle children, only children show characteristics of both oldest and youngest children. In fact, they may show the extremes of both at the same time. They may have the seriousness and sense of responsibility of the oldest and the conviction of specialness and entitlement of the youngest. Not having siblings, only children tend to be more oriented toward adults, seeking their love and approval and in return expecting their undivided attention. The major challenge for only children is to learn how to get along with others their own age. Only children often maintain very close attachments to their parents throughout their lives but find it more difficult to relate to friends and spouses. Although there are many stereotypes about only children as more selfish and lonely and less able to share, the research does not bear this out. They appear as good at sharing, collaborating, and connecting as other siblings (Sandler, 2013).

The number of children in a family is also a determining factor in siblings' life course. The more siblings there are, the less likely success appears to be, as a function of having to compete for resources (Conley, 2005).

> Assess your comprehension of birth-order effects on sibling relationships by completing this quiz.

Life Cycle Issues in Families With Disabled Siblings

We need to plan therapeutically for the lifelong implications that a handicapped child has for all family members, especially for the adjustment and caretaking responsibilities of the siblings. Siblings respond not only to the disabled child but also to parents' distress and/or preoccupation with the needs of the disabled child. Parents also may shift their hopes and dreams onto their other children, which can create burden and sibling strains (Cicirelli, 1995). Older children tend to make a better adjustment to disability than do younger ones because older children are better able to put the situation in perspective. Relative birth order is also important. A younger sibling may have difficulties associated with needing to assume the role of functional older caretaker sibling (Boyce & Barnett, 1993). Siblings become especially stressed when parents expect them either to be preoccupied with the needs of the disabled sibling or to treat him or her as "normal." During adolescence, siblings may feel particular embarrassment about a disabled sibling. On the other hand, if they have developed greater maturity through sibling caretaking experiences, they may feel out of step with peers (Cicirelli, 1995).

Oldest sisters of disabled siblings are at greatest risk because of increased parental demands on them. Brothers of the disabled tend to spend more time away from the family (Cicirelli, 1995). This is something that clinicians can help families to change. We must gently question parental expectations and encourage parents to include brothers in caretaking and prevent sisters from becoming overburdened. Otherwise, in later life, brothers may become completely disengaged from the disabled sibling, while sisters are left with total responsibility for them.

Small families tend to experience more pressure when there is a disabled child because there are fewer siblings to share the responsibility. The pressure seems increased when the disabled sibling is a brother, probably because of parents,' especially fathers,' reactions of personal hurt to pride in having a disabled son. Sisters seem more ready to accept the role of caretaker for a brother and to have more sibling rivalry or competition with a disabled sister. In a study of siblings of children with intellectual disabilities, older sisters were more affected than older brothers, because they generally got the lion's share of the caretaking responsibility for the sibling (Cicirelli, 1995). Their career and family decisions were also the most influenced by the disabled sibling. Sisters tended to be closer to the impaired child than brothers, to be given more responsibilities as well as more information about the sibling's disability than brothers were. Older sisters were found to enter the helping professions more often than other siblings.

The following is an illustration of the life cycle implications of the imbalance in caretaking responsibilities between an older sister and younger brothers in providing care for a disabled brother. It provides a classic portrayal of the findings in the literature.

CASE ILLUSTRATION

The Donnelly Family

The Donnelly family is of Irish-German and Roman Catholic background. Both parents had died in the past few years of chronic illnesses, leaving behind an oldest daughter, Mary Ann; a younger brother, Jim; and youngest fraternal twin brothers, Michael and Charles. Charles had been born with cerebral palsy. Mary Ann had been reared for a caretaker's role since childhood; she also had taken care of her chronically ill father for 2 years before his death. And then she cared for her chronically ill mother until her death 2 years later. Although she had attended college and had a successful career as a computer analyst, she was never free to take even an overnight vacation from her brother.

When her other brothers distanced themselves from her and Charles in the wake of the mother's death, Mary Ann began to have unexplained stomach pains, and her family physician referred the family for therapy. The family therapist initially addressed the family's problems as unresolved mourning and attempted to involve the reluctant brothers in taking some responsibility for the disabled brother in an attempt to reconnect the family by helping them to mourn the death of their mother. Many attempts were made to assemble all family members together.

Charles's twin brother Michael was easier to involve in therapy than the older brother, Jim. Michael had almost cut off from the family when he married his Italian wife, Lucia, of whom the family disapproved. The marriage had occurred shortly after the father had died, and the mother had felt doubly bereft by the loss of her husband and her son, who, she said, chose to leave the family in their time of need. Michael almost seemed to have been waiting for the chance to sort out issues he had with the family. Within 2 months, he sought help for his own marital problems and continued working hard on his connections to his brother and sister.

The older brother, Jim, was much harder to involve in the therapy. He made one excuse after another for not attending sessions and then said that his wife's feelings were hurt because Mary Ann had not attended his daughter's christening. He assumed unquestioningly that it was the sister's responsibility to care for Charles, a role Mary Ann herself seemed to accept as hers alone. She presented as guilt ridden and depressed, having pledged undying loyalty to her mother's dying wish that she care for Charles, despite the fact that her personal and social life had been sacrificed by this commitment.

To understand this better, we inquired about the sibling relationships of both parents and discovered that the father, also named Jim, also an oldest son, had been virtually cut off from his sole sister, who had cared for their widowed mother, who was wheelchair bound with multiple sclerosis for many years. We were able to explore with the other siblings the father's longstanding depression, which they believed resulted from his own unhappy cutoff from his parents. We discovered that the sibling overfunctioning and underfunctioning in the current generation and the imminent cutoffs reflected similar imbalances in both parents' families that had led to sibling cutoffs at midlife. Mary Ann and Charles initially wanted to ignore Jim and his family, but the therapist challenged them to try to overcome the family legacy of sibling cutoff. The therapist also challenged Mary Ann and the others with her "duty" and the long-held family and cultural beliefs about sisters' obligations in caretaking. She has recently been successful in asserting herself with Charles's doctors regarding their assumptions about Charles's need for her continual monitoring. She took her first vacation in many years, while Charles went to stay with Michael and his wife.

> Assess your comprehension of life cycle issues in families with disabled siblings by completing this quiz.

Sibling Positions and Parenting

If you have struggled in your own sibling position, as a parent you may overidentify with a child of the same gender and sibling position as yourself. One father who was an oldest of five felt that he had been burdened with too much responsibility, while his younger brothers and sister "got away with murder." When his own children came along, he spoiled the oldest and tried to make the younger ones toe the line. A mother may find it difficult to sympathize with a youngest daughter if she always felt envious of her younger sister. Parents may also identify with one particular child because of a resemblance to another family member. Whether these identifications are conscious or unconscious, they are normal. It is a myth that parents can feel the same toward all their children. Problems develop when a parent's need for the child to play a certain role interferes with the child's abilities or with two siblings' relationship to each other or to outsiders. A parent's identification with a child may be so strong that he or she perpetuates old family patterns in the next generation. On the other hand, if their own experience has been different, parents may misread their own children. A parent who was an only child may assume that normal sibling fights are an indication of trouble.

Siblings and Adolescent Relationships

At least by adolescence, siblings provide important models and alter egos. One sibling may begin to live out a life path for the other, so that they become alternate selves. Sisters in particular also often share secrets, clothes, and sensitivities about their parents' problems.

Gay and lesbian adolescents may have a particularly difficult time at this phase of their budding sexuality, in dealing with peers, parents, and institutions. Having a supportive sibling network can be an extremely important cushion against these rejections, while the lack of sibling support can add to the sense of isolation and rejection children can feel at this time.

Obviously, not all siblings are close. Childhood rivalries and hurts carry over into adolescence and adulthood. At family get-togethers, everyone tries, at least at first, to be friendly and cordial, but beneath the surface old conflicts may simmer. By adolescence, sibling dysfunction may require one child to grieve the loss of dreams for another and for their relationship, if the other is seriously dysfunctional, suffering from autism, mental illness, or addiction.

Sibling Relationships in Young Adulthood

Closeness to siblings has been found to be strong just before they leave their parental home (Bowerman & Dobash, 1974; Troll, 1994). This closeness tends to be followed by a distancing during the early and middle years of adulthood, but at later life cycle phases people rate affectional closeness with siblings higher and conflict lower than do middle-aged siblings (Brady & Noberini, 1987). As they reach young adulthood, sisters often grow farther apart, each focusing on their own friends, work, and relationships and on developing their own family. Siblings may get together during holidays at the parental home, but often the focus is primarily on the relationship of each to the parents or spouses rather than on their relationships with each other. Support may be weakest at this phase, and competition may be strongest: Who went to the better school? Whose husband or children are more successful? Whose life is happier? The images that each develops of the other are often colored less by their personal interchanges than by the rivalries carried over from childhood or the parental images, transmitted by parents about the other's life. A younger sister who felt dominated or abused by her older brother may feel uncomfortable even sitting at the same table with him. All the unpleasant memories flood back. Two brothers who spent their childhoods competing in sports, in school, and for parental attention may find themselves subtly competing in the holiday dinner table conversation. Even if there are no major flare-ups, family members may leave the dinner feeling bored or vaguely dissatisfied, glad that such occasions occur only a few times a year.

Whether deliberately or inadvertently, parents can perpetuate such old sibling patterns. A mother may compare one child with another, perhaps chiding one for not calling as often as another does. A father might talk repeatedly about how proud he is of his son, not realizing that he is ignoring his daughter. A parent may elicit the support of one sibling in an effort to "shape up" another. Clinically, therapists can do much to challenge such values on behalf of all siblings.

It is also at this phase that sisters may move into different social classes as they marry and move, according to the culture's expectations, to adapt to their husband's socioeconomic context. They themselves are often not able to define this context, which has traditionally been defined by the husband's education, work, and financial status. Although some cultures, such as African American and Irish, emphasize friendship between siblings more than other groups, such as Scandinavian or Jewish culture (Woehrer, 1982), the sister bond is generally continued through a mutual sense of shared understanding and responsibility for the family, more than through common interests, especially when class differences between the sisters have developed.

> Assess your comprehension of sibling relationships in young adulthood by completing this quiz.

Sibling Positions and Marital Relationships

Sibling relationships can often pave the way for couple relationships—for sharing, interdependence, and mutuality—just as they can predispose partners to jealousy, power struggles, and rivalry. Since siblings are generally our earliest peer relationships, we are likely to be most comfortable in other relationships that reproduce the familiar sibling patterns of birth order and gender. In general, marriage seems easiest for partners who fit their original sibling pattern, for example, if an oldest marries a youngest, rather than two oldest marrying each other. If a wife has grown up as the oldest of many siblings and the caretaker, she might be attracted to a dominant oldest, who offers to take over management of responsibilities. But as time goes along, she may come to resent his assertion of authority, because, by experience, she is more comfortable making decisions for herself.

All things being equal (and they seldom are in life!), the ideal marriage based on sibling position would be a complementary one in which, for example, the husband was the older brother of a younger sister and the wife was the younger sister of an older brother. However, the complementarity of caretaker and someone who needs caretaking or leader and follower does not guarantee intimacy or a happy marriage.

In addition to complementary birth order, it seems to help in marriage if one has had siblings of the opposite sex. The most difficult pairing might be that of the youngest sister of many sisters who marries the youngest brother of many brothers, since neither would have much experience of the opposite sex in a close way, and they might both play the spoiled child waiting for a caretaker.

There are, of course, many other possible sibling pairings in marriage. The marriage of two only children might be particularly difficult because neither has the experience of the intimate sharing that one does with a brother or sister. Middle children may be the most flexible, since they have experiences with a number of different roles.

Coupling and marriage tend to increase the distance between siblings. Sisters may be pressured by their spouses to decrease their intimacy with each other, and that pressure may create sibling distance that lasts until later life. Maya Angelou (1981) once described the efforts siblings must make to remain connected in spite of spousal pressure. They must work at maintaining their sibling relationships throughout the life cycle. Even if a spouse does not want you to remain connected, you must go when your sister calls.

> Assess your comprehension of sibling positions and marital relationships by completing this quiz.

In-Laws, Step- and Half-Siblings

The relationship of half- and stepsiblings through life depends on many factors including the distance in age, gender, presence of full siblings in the household, gender of stepparent and continuity of stepparent experience, length of time living together during childhood, marital status, race, social class, religion, parental divorce, proximity and emotional closeness to parents and to each other, and the overall cultural values of family connectedness (White & Riedman, 1992b). In general, they are not as close as full siblings except where circumstances have drawn them into special connection as where a parent or another sibling has been impaired or lost. Nevertheless, people generally define step- and half-siblings as "real" kin, even though the connections are overall weaker than for full siblings.

In similar ways, sister-in-law and brother-in-law relationships can have some of the positives of sibling relationships without the tensions, but things only sometimes work out this way. Sisters-in-law share a future but not a biological or childhood history.

The interesting aspect of in-law patterns is the extent to which the structure of the family tends to determine in-law relationships, even though family members are so often sure that it is just personality characteristics they are reacting against in rejecting an in-law.

Sisters-in-law who marry into families that have only brothers probably have the greatest likelihood of developing positive connections to the new family. The wife of a youngest brother of older sisters is probably in the most difficult position, since this brother may have been treated like a prince. He may be resented though protected by his sisters, whom he probably tried to avoid for their "bossiness." When he finds a wife, his choice is likely to reflect in part his need for some protection against other powerful females, and his wife may then become the villain, supposedly keeping him from having a closer relationship with his sisters. Nevertheless, family relationships of those who have been raised as kin and peers, such as half- or step-siblings and often also cousins or those who live through adulthood as kin and peers such as sisters- and brothers-in-law have real clinical importance. They may be significant resources and supports to family connectedness. On the other hand, when their connections are negative, they can be a source of great difficulty.

Sibling Relationships in Midlife

Often, it is not until midlife that siblings reconnect with each other, through the shared experiences of caring for a failing or dying parent, a divorce in the family, or perhaps a personal health problem, which inspires them to clarify their priorities and to redefine which relationships in life really matter to them. Sometimes, at this point, relationships that have been maintained at a superficial level may break under the strain of caretaking or under the pain of the

distance that has grown between them. On the other hand, siblings may now be brought closer to each other. Their relationships may solidify through the realization that their parents will not always be there and that they themselves must begin to put the effort into maintaining their own relationship.

In our culture, sisters are generally the caretakers of parents and other unattached older relatives or the managers who have responsibility to arrange for their caretaking. In other cultures, such as in Japan, this role goes to the wife of the oldest son. In our culture, if sisters do not do the primary caretaking, they often feel guilty about it, because the cultural pressure on them by others to do caretaking is so strong.

Sibling relationships can be a most important connection in adult life, especially in the later years. However, if negative feelings persist, the care of an aging parent may bring on particular difficulty. While the final caretaking of parents may increase a child's commitment and closeness to them (Bass & Bowman, 1990), it may either draw siblings together or arouse conflicts over who did more and who felt loved less. If there are unresolved problematic issues in a family, they are likely to surface at this time in conflicts over the final caretaking, the funeral, or the will. At such a time, siblings may have been apart for years. They may have to work together in new and unfamiliar ways. The child who has remained closest to the parents, usually a daughter, often gets most of these caretaking responsibilities, which may cause long-buried jealousies and resentments to surface. Or perhaps sisters may end up in conflict over how to do the caretaking, while brothers remain on the sidelines, offering at times financial support, but less often their time or emotional support for the caretaking. Because it is women who tend to be central in maintaining the emotional relationships in a family, sisters may focus their disappointments on each other or on their sisters-in-law more than on their brothers, who are often treated with kid gloves and not expected to give much in the way of emotional or physical support when caretaking is required.

It is at the death of the last parent that sibling relationships become voluntary for the first time in life. While parents are alive, siblings may have contact with and hear news about each other primarily as a function of their relationships with their parents. Once the parents die, siblings must decide for the first time whether to maintain contact with each other.

> **Assess your comprehension of sibling relationships in midlife by completing this quiz.**

Sibling Relationships After the Death of Parents

Once both parents have died, sibling relationships become truly independent for the first time. From here on, whether they see each other will be their own choice. This is the time when estrangement can become complete, particularly if old rivalries continue. The focus may be on concrete disagreements: Who should have helped in the care of their ailing parent? Who took all the responsibility? Who was more loved? Strong feelings can be fueled by old unresolved issues. In general, the better relationships siblings have, the less likely it is that later traumatic family events will lead to parting of the ways.

At the end of the life cycle, sisters are especially likely to be a major support for each other or even to live together. Older women are especially likely to rely on their sisters, as well as their daughters and even their nieces for support (Anderson, 1984; Lopata, 1979; Townsend, 1957). Anderson (1984) found that sisters were the ones whom older widows most often turned to, more often than to children, even though they were not more available geographically. She speculated that the reasons might include sisters' shared history of experiences and life transitions. She concludes that siblings, especially sisters, take on added significance as confidants and emotional resources for women after they have been widowed.

Because siblings share a unique history, reminiscing about earlier times together is an activity in which they engage at many points in the life cycle. Such reminiscing tends to become even more important late in life. It helps all siblings to validate and

clarify events and relationships that took place in earlier years and to place them in a mature perspective. It can become an important source of pride and comfort (Cicirelli, 1985). This seems especially meaningful for sisters who tend anyway to define themselves more in terms of context and to place a high value on the quality of human relationships. Cicirelli (1982) found that having a relationship with a sister stimulates elderly women to remain socially engaged with others as well. Although the relationships of sisters, like all female relationships, tend to be invisible in the value structure of the culture at large, sisters tend to sustain one another in time of need throughout life. In old age, they become indispensable. They often become each other's closest companions, sharing not only a lifetime of memories of home and family, but also even similar housekeeping styles, recipes, and prejudices about how things should be done. The details do matter as we age. Especially as we grow older, it is the details—of our memories, or of our housekeeping, or of our relationships with each other's children—that may hold us together.

Rules of Thumb for Sibling Relationships Through the Life Cycle

1. Take a proactive stance about including siblings in assessment, whatever the presenting problem. Say to yourself, "Why not have a sibling session?" rather than thinking of including a sibling only when the client presents a sibling problem directly.
2. When one sibling is bearing the weight of sibling caretaking for a parent or a disabled sibling, work to improve the balance of sibling relationships so that the siblings can be more collaborative.
3. Assess and carefully challenge inequities in family roles and emotional and caretaking functioning of brothers and sisters. In general, sisters tend to be seriously overburdened and brothers to seriously underfunction in terms of meeting the emotional needs of the broader family.
4. Validate the importance of sibling relationships and encourage resolution of sibling conflicts whenever possible.

We are coming to appreciate more the importance of adult sibling relationships as researchers have observed that family support for caregivers correlates with the presence of siblings (Bedford, 1989, 2005). As we age, some sibling relationships lose the competitive quality of childhood and become more like friendships (McGhee, 1985; Norris & Tindale, 1994). As personal resources may become overtaxed by the demands of frail or demented aging parents, sibling bonds may either become overtaxed or provide the extra energy for caretaking. Sibling relationships may also become closer with aging, as activities and preoccupations of earlier life cycle phases diminish. The loss of a spouse who may have interfered with sibling closeness leaves siblings with more time and need for the comfort and sharing of the sibling bond. Cicirelli (1989) found that attachment is more likely to characterize sibling ties when sisters are involved. It does appear that sibling rivalries generally diminish in later life. Generational solidarity increases and sibling bonds appear to have greater salience for siblings as they age (Norris & Tindale, 1994).

— Conclusion

Throughout the family life cycle, relationships are constantly changing. Our relationships with our parents are the first and, perhaps, foremost in reminding us of our family lineage—where we come from. Without knowledge of our uncles, aunts, grandparents, and great-grandparents, how can we know who we are? Just as important in shaping our personality development are our relationships with our siblings (Adler, 1959, 1979; Sulloway, 1996; Sutton-Smith & Rosenberg, 1970).

Unlike our relationships with our parents, friends, and spouses, sibling relationships are lifelong. However, the gender differences are pronounced in sibling relationships. Sibships of sisters tend to differ from sibships of brothers. Whereas brother relationships often are more competitive and superficial, sisters tend to be more connected and deeply involved in each other's lives and the lives of other family members throughout the family life cycle. Although less honored or glorified, sisters are often the designated caretakers of disabled family members. They are confidantes and healers of the family. Their lifelong friendships become even more significant and stronger after parents die and as they themselves enter old age. Given the importance of these bonds, which are always present in the family therapy context, therapists should become more aware of their influence, initiate more clinical research, and integrate these observations in their interventions. Including siblings in therapy at any point of the life cycle can validate the importance of their relationships; help them to resolve their conflicts, whether recent or deep seated from unresolved childhood conflicts; and strengthen them for their future.

Sibling sessions can unlock a client's stuckness, provide richness to an understanding of a client's history, and provide relief for dealing with current stresses. A single sibling session may become a pivotal experience in an adult's therapy. One isolated research scientist who sought therapy because of his wife's frustration with his emotional distance held a session with his three brothers who came from all over the country for the meeting. All three brothers, who were in their 40s, discussed their different responses to their mother's mental illness in their childhood and learned that each had become isolated in his own way. Each brother thought his problems were unique and individual, but they discovered as they reviewed their life experiences how profoundly connected they had always been and would always be. This session shifted the client's basic relationship with his wife. He now saw himself as a man among brothers going through life together, and felt strengthened in his ability to be open with his wife. As was described earlier, sibling sessions can encourage under-involved siblings to share caretaking burdens, modify gender imbalances, resolve longstanding conflicts, and increase collaboration.

> **Recall what you learned in this chapter by completing the Chapter Review.**

References

Adams, B. N. (1968). *Kinship in an urban setting.* Chicago, IL: Markham.

Adler, A. (1959). *The practice and theory of individual psychology.* Patterson, NJ: Littlefield, Adams.

Adler, A. (1979). *Superiority and social interest.* New York: W. W. Norton.

Akhtar, S., & Kramer, S. (Eds.) (1999). *Brothers and sisters: Developmental, dynamic and aspects of the sibling relationship.* New York: Jason Aronson.

Anderson, T. (1984). Widowhood as a life transition: Its impact on kinship ties. *Journal of Marriage and the Family, 46*(1), 105–114.

Angelou, M. (1981). *The heart of a woman.* New York: Random House.

Bank, S. P., & Kahn, M. D. (2008). *The sibling bond.* New York: Basic Books.

Bass, D. M., & Bowman, K. (1990). Transition from caregiving to bereavement: The relationship of care-related strain and adjustment to death. *The Gerontologist, 30,* 135–142.

Bedford, V. H. (1989). Understanding the value of siblings in old age. *American Behavioral Scientist, 33,* 33–44.

Bedford, V. H. (2005). Theorizing about sibling relationships when parents become frail. In V. L. Bengston, A. C. Acock, K. R. Allen, P. Dilworth-Anderson, & D. M. Klein (Eds.), *Sourcebook of family theory & research* (pp. 173–174). Thousand Oaks, CA: Sage Publications.

Bowerman, C. E., & Dobash, R. M. (1974). Structural variations in inter-sibling affect. *Journal of Marriage and the Family, 36,* 48–54.

Boyce, G. C., & Barnett, W. S. (1993). Siblings of persons with mental retardation: A historical perspective and recent findings. In Z. Stoneman & P. W. Berman (Eds.), *The effects of mental retardation, disability, and illness on sibling relationships: Research issues and challenges (pp. 145–184).* Baltimore, MD: Paul H. Brookes.

Brady, E. M., & Noberini, M. R. (1987, August). *Sibling support in the context of a model of sibling solidarity.* Paper presented at the annual meeting of the American Psychological Association, New York, NY.

Bright, D. S., Cameron, K. S., & Caza, A. (2006). The amplifying and buffering effects of virtuousness in downsized organizations. *Journal of Business Ethics, 64,* 249–269.

Cameron, K. S., & Caza, A. (2002). Organizational and leadership virtues and the role of forgiveness. *Journal of Leadership and Organizational Studies, 9,* 33–48.

Cicirelli, V. G. (1982). Sibling influence throughout the life span. In M. E. Lamb & B. Sutton-Smith (Eds.), *Sibling relationships: Their nature and significance across the lifespan* (pp. 267–284). Hillsdale, NJ: Lawrence Erlbaum Associates.

Cicirelli, V. G. (1983). Adult children's attachment and helping behavior to elderly parents: A path model. *Journal of Marriage and the Family, 45,* 815–825.

Cicirelli, V. G. (1985). Sibling relationships throughout the life cycle. In L. L'Abate (Ed.), *The handbook of family psychology and therapy* (pp. 177–214). Homewood, IL: Dorsey Press.

Cicirelli, V. G. (1989). Feelings of attachment to siblings and well-being in later life. *Psychology and Aging, 4,* 211–216.

Cicirelli, V. G. (1994). The longest bond: The sibling life cycle. In L. L'Abate (Ed.), *Handbook of developmental family psychology and psychopathology* (pp. 27–43). New York: Wiley.

Cicirelli, V. G. (1995). *Sibling relationships across the life span.* New York: Plenum Press.

Cicirelli, V. G. (2006). *Older adults' views of death.* New York: Springer.

Conley, D. (2005). *The pecking order.* New York: Vintage.

Connidis, I. A., & Kemp, C. (2008). Negotiating actual and anticipated parental support: Multiple sibling voices in three-generation families. *Journal of Aging Studies, 22*(3), 220–238.

Dahl, G. B., & Moretti, E. (2008). The demand for sons. *Review of Economic Studies, 75,* 1085–1120.

Fincham, F. D., Jackson, H., & Beach, S. R. H. (2006). Transgression severity and forgiveness: Different moderators for objective and subjective severity. *Journal of Social and Clinical Psychology, 24,* 860–875.

Fishel, E. (1979). *Sisters: Love and rivalry inside the family and beyond.* New York: William Morrow.

Friedman, F. B. (2003, April). Siblings of a certain age: The impact of aging parents on adult sibling relationships. *Dissertation Abstracts: 2003-95007-127. International Section A: Humanities & Social Sciences, 63*(10-A), 3727.

Gold, D. T. (1987). Siblings in old age. Something special. *Canadian Journal on Aging, 6,* 199–215.

Gold, D. T. (1989). Sibling relationships in old age: A typology. *International Journal of Aging and Human Development, 28,* 37–51.

Hennig, M., & Jardim, A. (1977). *The managerial woman.* Garden City: Anchor/Doubleday.

Grant, A. (July 20, 2013). Why men need women. *New York Times*. Retrieved July 23, 2013, from http://www.nytimes.com/2013/07/21/opinion/sunday/why-men-need-women.html?pagewanted=all&_r=0&pagewanted=print

Howe Colt, G. (2012). *Brothers*. New York: Scribner.

Johnson, C. L. (1982). Sibling solidarity: Its origin and functioning in Italian-American families. *Journal of Marriage and the Family, 44,* 155–67.

Kahn, M. D., & Lewis, K. G. (Eds.) (1988). *Siblings in therapy. Life span and clinical issues.* New York: Norton.

Lawler, K. A., Younger, J. W., Piferi, R. L., Jobe, R. L., Edmondson, K. A., & Jones, W. H. (2005). The unique effects of forgiveness on health: An exploration of pathways. *Journal of Behavioral Medicine*, 28, 157–167. doi:10.1007/s10865-005-3665-2

Leder, J. M. (1991). *Brothers and sisters: How they stage our lives.* New York: Ballantine.

Lopata, H. Z. (1979). *Women as widows: Support systems.* New York: Elsevier.

Mathias, B. (1992). *Between sisters: Secret rivals, intimate friends.* New York: Delacorte Press.

McGhee, J. L. (1985). The effects of siblings on the life satisfaction of the rural elderly. *Journal of Marriage and the Family, 41,* 703–714.

McGoldrick, M. (1989a). Irish women. In M. McGoldrick, C. Anderson, & F. Walsh (Eds.) Women in families. New York: W. W. Norton.

McGoldrick, M. (1989b). Sisters. In M. McGoldrick, C. Anderson, & F. Walsh (Eds.), Women in families. New York: Norton.

McGoldrick, M. (2011). The genogram journey. *You can go home again: Reconnecting with your family* (1st ed.). New York: Norton.

McGoldrick, M., Giordano, J., & Garcia Preto, N. (2005). *Ethnicity and family therapy* (3rd ed.). New York: Guilford Press.

McHale, S. M., & Crouter, C. A. (2005). Sibling relationships in childhood: Implications for life-course study. In V. L. Bengston, A. C. Acock, K. R. Allen, P. Dilworth-Anderson, & D. M. Klein (Eds.), *Sourcebook of family theory & research* (pp. 184–190). Thousand Oaks, CA: Sage Publications.

McKay, V. C., & Caverly, R. S. (2004). The nature of family relationships between and within generations: Relations between grandparents, grandchildren, and siblings in later life. In J. Nussbaum & J. Coupland (Eds.), *Handbook of communication and aging research* (2nd ed., pp. 251–272). Mahwah, NJ: Lawrence Erlbaum Associates Publishers.

Meinhold, J. (2006). The influence of life transition statuses on sibling intimacy and contact in early adulthood. (Doctoral dissertation, Oregon St. Univ., 2006). *Dissertation Abstracts International Section A: Humanities and Social Sciences, 67*(30), 1107.

Merrell, S. S. (1995). *The accidental bond: The power of sibling relationships.* New York: Times Books.

Merrill, D. M. (1996). Conflict and cooperation among adult siblings during transition to the role of filial caregiver. *Journal of Social and Personal Relationships, 13*(3), 339–413.

Myers, S. A. (2011). "I have to love her, even if sometimes I may not like her": The reasons why adults maintain their sibling relationships. *North American Journal of Psychology*, 13, 51–62.

Noberini, M. R., Brady, E. M., & Mosatche, H. S. (1983). A Retrospective Lifespan Study of the Closest Sibling Relationship. *The Journal of Psychology*, 113, 231–243.

Norris, J. E., & Tindale, J. A. (1994). *Among generations: The cycle of adult relationships.* New York: W. H. Freeman & Company.

Nuckolls, C. W. (1993). *Siblings in South Asia: Brothers and sisters in cultural context.* New York: Guilford Press.

Sandler, L. (June 8, 2013). Only children: Lonely and selfish? *New York Times*, Retrieved June 15, 2013, from http://www.nytimes.com/2013/06/09/opinion/sunday/only-children-lonely-and-selfish.html?_r=0

Sandmaier, M. (1994). *Original kin: The search for connection among adult sisters and brothers.* New York: Plume.

Shanas, E., & Streib, G. F. (1965). *Social structure and the family.* Englewood Cliffs, NJ: Prentice-Hall.

Shufro, C. (2008). Findings: The daughter effect. *Yale Alumni Magazine, LXXI*(6), 30.

Sulloway, F. J. (1996). *Born to rebel: Birth order, family dynamics, and creative lives.* New York: Pantheon Books.

Sutton-Smith, B., & Rosenberg, B. G. (1970). *The sibling.* New York: Holt, Rinehart & Winston.

Toman, W. (1976). *Family constellation* (3rd ed.). New York: Springer.

Townsend, P. (1957). *The family life of older people.* London: Routledge and Kegan Paul.

Troll, L. (1994). Family connectedness of old women: Attachments in later life. In B. F. Turner, & L. E. Troll (Eds.), *Women growing older* (pp. 169–201). Thousand Oaks, CA: Sage.

Troll, L. E., & Smith, J. (1976). Attachment through the life span: Some questions about dyadic bonds among adults. *Human Development, 19,* 156–170.

Vadasy, P. F., Fewell, R. R., Meyer, D. J., & Schell, G. (1984). Siblings of handicapped children: A developmental perspective on family interactions. *Family Relations, 33*(1), 155–167.

Vaillant, G. E. (1977). *Adaptation to life.* Boston, MA: Little, Brown and Company.

Wade, N. G. (2010). Introduction to the special issue on forgiveness in therapy. *Journal of Mental Health Counseling, 32*, 1–4.

Waldron, V. L., & Kelley, D. L. (2008). *Communicating forgiveness.* Thousand Oaks, CA: Sage Publications, Inc.

Walker, A. J., Allen, K. R., & Connidis, I. A. (2005). Theorizing and studying sibling ties in adulthood. In V. L. Bengston, A. C. Acock, K. R. Allen, P. Dilworth-Anderson, & D. M. Klein (Eds.), *Sourcebook of family theory and research* (pp. 167–173). Thousand Oaks, CA: Sage Publications.

Washington, E. L. (2007). Female socialization: How daughters affect their legislator fathers' voting on women's issues. *American Economic Review, 86*(3), 425–441.

Watson, M. F. (2013). Facing the black shadow. E-Book.

Watson, M. (1998). African American siblings. In M. Mc-Goldrick (Ed.), *Re-visioning family therapy* (1st ed., pp. 282–294). New York: Guilford Press.

Wellman, B. L. (1979). The community question: The intimate networks of East Yorkers. *American Journal of Sociology, 84*(5), 1201–1231.

White, L. K., & Riedman, A. (1992a). Ties among siblings. *Social Forces, 71*(1), 85–102.

White, L. K., & Riedman, A. (1992b). When the Brady Bunch grows up: Step/half-and full-sibling relationships in adulthood. *Journal of Marriage and the family, 54*, 197–208.

Woehrer, C. (1982). The influence of ethnic families on intergenerational relationships and later life transitions. *Annals of American Academy, 464*, 65–78.

Zukow, P. G. (Ed.). (1989). *Sibling interaction across cultures.* New York: Springer-Verlag.

Chapter 10

Single Adults and the Life Cycle

Kathy Berliner, Demaris Jacob, & Natalie Schwartzberg

Learning Objectives

- Describe challenges that are unique to single, heterosexual adults.
- Discuss the social implications of marriage.
- List the functions of marriage in the family structure.
- Explain how multigenerational marital events can impact family views of marriage and singlehood.
- Describe how class and culture impact a single person's view of single life.
- List and describe tasks single people must achieve at each phase of adulthood.
- Examine the developmental tasks single people undertake in their twenties.
- Describe the unique challenges that single people face during their thirties.
- Discuss ways that single adults can experience an authentic life.
- List and describe the tasks of single people in later life.

Introduction

Although most people marry at some point in their lives, the numbers of those who are single are increasing. In 1970 in the United States, 19 percent of men and 14 percent of women older than 18 years had never been married. By 2006, 33 percent of men and 26 percent of women had not married. Factors such as delayed marriages, increased options for single parenthood, a 40 to 50 percent divorce rate, and longer life expectancy mean that more people than ever will live single during the course of their lives. In the recent 2010 census, 44 percent of the population, (102 million) or 18 and older, were single (U.S. Census Data).

It is thus much more common to be single in the twenty-first century. As more people decide to live alone, societal tolerance has broadened to include many more "acceptable" forms in which adults may live, increasing the options for adult life. There has been a mushrooming of singles' organizations, advocacy groups, and blogs not aimed at achieving marriage but at addressing the needs of the unmarried. At the same time, our society continues to have a bias toward marriage and toward nuclear families of two married parents and children that no longer represents the norm. In 2008, the U.S. Government launched a $5 million media campaign aimed at 18 to 30 year olds extolling the benefits of marriage, just like health campaigns to stop smoking or wear seat belts (Jayson, 2007). The research on the benefits of marriage is as yet inconclusive with some studies indicating married people are healthier and some indicating no difference between married people and singles on measures of emotional maturity and physical health (DePaulo, 2006). What is not surprising is that being in a troubled marriage has been found to be more detrimental to health than single status. The presumed health advantage also disappears for divorced and widowed compared to those single throughout their entire lives (Parker-Pope, 2010).

Apart from the institution of marriage, what research does show is that affiliation reduces stress (Taylor et al., 2000), and marriage has been the traditional way to be socially engaged, particularly for men. While marriage may be less of a requirement of adulthood, it still represents for many the desired, if not idealized, state. This ambivalent relationship with the institution of marriage is reflected in a 2010 Pew Research survey where four in ten Americans characterized marriage as obsolete. In the same study, most of those who were not married

(61 percent) responded that they hoped to marry at some point (Pew Social Trends, 2011).

We know that single people are likely to experience strong feelings about their single status. Our therapeutic focus is to help the single person view the single life as an authentic way to live, even in the context of societal messages that denigrate them or relegate them to the margins of the "mainstream" culture. At the same time, it is important to recognize that singlehood presents practical challenges and an authentic life does not occur in the abstract. In addition to managing social and familial stigma, the single person must address the human need to seek and maintain emotional ties to others. This includes the pursuit of romantic relationships and the expression of sexuality as well as the maintenance of friendships so that they endure within continual shifts in mutual emotional availability. It also often means connecting to other forms of "family," whether religious, political, or other. Without the organizational structure of marriage, these tasks can feel daunting and fuel a discontent with single life.

Because singleness has been regarded as simply a transitional period between families, when prolonged it is often seen as a sign of failure to achieve an essential adult task. While marriage is one of life's big milestones, problems arise when people regard marriage as *the* next step necessary for the unfolding of adult life. The single person may become frozen, waiting for marriage, not moving forward with the business of life. We all will, in all likelihood, spend some part of our adult life singly. This chapter describes the issues and the pressures contributing to emotional and developmental growth in the single person's life cycle, without marriage and children as the driving factors.

We have tried to grasp the experience of living life singly, without children or a live-in romantic partner, and to validate the experiences of those who may marry in the future, those who choose to be single, those who may rear children without partners, and those who simply happen to find themselves single at a time in their lives when they had not imagined they would be. Much of the material in this chapter is derived from our book *Single in a Married World* (Schwartzberg, Berliner, & Jacob, 1995), which contains a more comprehensive dis-

cussion of the clinical issues and the context (ethnic, class and cultural, and sexual orientation and identity) of the single person. While some of what we present is relevant to gay and lesbian single people, the experience of living in the intense homophobia of our society, and the denial of the legal sanction of marriage, until recently, wields a profound impact. Additional issues overlay those that heterosexual single people deal with and are beyond the scope of this chapter.

> **Assess your comprehension of the introduction by completing this quiz.**

Setting the Clinical Stage

Clients often come to therapy distressed about their single status, and in working with these clients, therapists must recognize the impact of messages from the culture, and the family that imply that single people are not mature adults. The therapist, not immune to these messages, must be careful to avoid replicating them by focusing on dating issues rather than helping to encourage the developing self. The therapist needs to understand the meanings *each individual client* has taken from (1) the larger society, (2) multigenerational themes in the family, (3) class and culture, and (4) gender.

Marriage as social empowerment

Marriage is an empowering institution that creates an automatic status change for both men and women in the family of origin, in religious and societal organizations, and in the perception of self. It provides public acknowledgment of movement to responsible adulthood and participation in the ongoing history of family and society. As one 50-year-old divorced Jewish woman put it, "I became a second-class citizen overnight."

The importance of marriage, and conversely societal discomfort with singlehood, varies with political climate. The emotional power of the code phrase "family values" gives the clear message that those who live outside a heterosexual marriage are outside the accepted fabric of American life itself. The struggle in the gay community to be able to achieve the status of "married" may well be taken as evidence of the sense of empowerment and legitimacy that marriage provides (Cherlin, 2005). We have not changed all that much; this is reminiscent of life in the 1950s, when the postwar culture also elevated marriage, the family, and family consumerism (Coontz, 1992).

Furthermore, community and religious life is structured to a great degree around passages of life created by marriage and parenthood. A christening, a bar or bat mitzvah, confirmation, and graduation are the events that are celebrated. Single people participate, but the main story is always about someone else's children.

Marriage and the family of origin

Marriage has important functions in the structure of the family of origin. It is the way to perpetuate names, rituals, and family lineage. In the ongoing life of the family, marriage often initiates the realignment of relationships between parent and child. It can signal a "successful" end to the rearing of children and defines new boundaries between generations. When marriage does not occur in the expected time frame, a gridlock can occur in the unfolding of family life, leaving parents and the single adult struggling to find other ways to mark adulthood. This process has historically been more difficult for daughters who only recently are being raised to have an adult role outside of marriage.

Multigenerational themes

The meaning of marriage and singlehood in each family is best viewed from the perspective of at least three generations. The highly conflictual or abusive marriage of an emotionally important ancestor, for example, may continue to ripple its "marriage meaning" through time. Marital events such as divorce are also pertinent. Parents may worry that their divorce is influencing their child's ability to wed, or unresolved issues from the divorce may perpetuate a reactivity that either romanticizes or damns marriage. The view of single people in the family will also be an influence. Identifying role models who have led satisfying single lives may provide a counterpoint to the importance of marriage.

Class and culture

The single client's vision of the roadmap of a single life and the alternatives available, are highly impacted by class (the amount of money available) and culture (the converging threads of religious, racial, ethnic, and immigration history). As therapists, we tend to make fewer inquiries about money than we do about emotional and multigenerational legacies; this omission does a disservice to all families, but especially to lower-income people. Economic status not only impacts alternatives such as the viability of establishing a residence outside the parental home but also the issue of "marriageability" itself (particularly for men). The decline in blue collar jobs since the 1970s, for example, has made men without a college education less desirable as marriage partners (Cherlin, 2012). In the American Black community, societal changes, both cultural and structural, have had a significant impact on marital status. Racism, high mortality and incarceration rates, and economic disadvantage in obtaining skills necessary for upward mobility have all served to decrease the pool of marriageable men (Lane et al., 2004). At the same time, as the rate of Black women entering college and graduate school has increased, the disparity in achievement has made it harder for Black women to find equal status partners; high achieving Black women have a lower marriage rate than their White counterparts (Nitsche & Brueckner, 2009). According to the 2010 census, the age of first marriage for both Black men and women has steadily increased and surpassed White men and women from 1980 to the 2010 as well as the number of never married by the age of 45 (U.S. Census Data, 2010), representing a drastic change in the Black community's historical embrace of marriage (Heiss, 1988). While not as dramatic, the rate of marriage has also declined for Hispanics as well as Asians (Pew Social Trends, 2011).

Living in a time of economic fluctuation or depression can also seriously disrupt people's vision of what they "should" be doing to be successful as single adults. There are wide cultural variations in patterns of launching young adults into the world beyond family of origin. For example, those of Anglo American heritage traditionally expect their children to establish independence early and with less parental involvement than those of Italian or Brazilian heritage

(McGoldrick, Giordano, & Garcia Preto, 2005). In times of economic growth, the expected early launching can be accomplished; in hard economic times, single adults and their parents may feel they have failed and have no well-known pathways of incorporating independent adults into daily family life.

A deep ethnic thread impacting "acceptable" alternatives for single people is the experience of genocide in the family multigenerational religious or ethnic history (Rosen & Weltman, 2005). Jews and Armenians, among others in our recent past, have been people whose liquidation has been systematically attempted. Thus, the emotional imperative to procreate is strong, with marriage the prescribed precursor. Choosing to remain single in this context becomes not just an individual decision; it impacts the continuance of the entire culture.

There are also wide cultural variations in who is considered "family" and in the presence (or absence) of valued roles available to the single person throughout the life cycle within family, religious, and cultural contexts. Family may mean just immediate relatives, several generations as in Italian families, or one's ancestors as in Asian families. In working with single clients, it is important to gain as complete a picture as possible of their understanding of what singlehood means in their own context. For example, many Black Americans have grown up within an expansive notion of family, including blood and non-blood kin, which makes more room for valued functional roles for single people than do cultures that place emphasis on nuclear family units (Boyd-Franklin, 2006). The Irish have had a greater tolerance for singlehood than almost any other group (McGoldrick, 2005). Marriage was viewed not as a framework for self-fulfillment but rather for parenting, often bringing economic hardship in the wake of increasing numbers of children (Diner, 1983). For women, the church—not the family—had historically been the center of community life (McGoldrick, 2005).

These provide only a few examples of the complexity of the interweaving of cultural and class threads that impact single clients. Understanding these legacies is essential so that therapists will be less likely to impose their own cultural biases, and clients can approach family of origin issues in new ways. Clients who are fixated on marriage may see

these explorations as digressions; therapeutic finesse lies in respecting clients' perceptions while making the larger context relevant.

 Assess your comprehension of setting the clinical stage by completing this quiz.

The Single Person's Life Cycle

Single people often have difficulty locating themselves in the flow of "normal life"; they and their families are unclear what the next step is when marriage and/or childbirth do not occur. Our life cycle phases and tasks have been based on life's chronological milestones as well as other drivers of adult development.

At each phase of adulthood, single people still need to confront the expectation of marriage, cope with having an unrealized goal if marriage is desired, and understand the impact of living a life that is different from the expected norm. While we have broken the life cycle into phases, we recognize that there will be considerable variation as to when issues emerge as well as overlap from stage to stage. What is consistent is the ongoing need for emotional support and attachments. Creating support systems and accommodating their ebb and flow over the life span demands more effort and thought for single people, whereas married people, especially with children, can fall back on those social structures that accompany marriage. Single people should therefore, not neglect this work even if they anticipate marriage. At the same time, it is easy to idealize the amount of support, nurturance, and affiliation that marriage provides.

Although the stages of the single adult life cycle form a progression through nodal points of the aging process (which trigger the need for growth), the specific ages associated with each life cycle stage are meant to be viewed as relatively elastic guidelines.

The 20s: Establishing adulthood

Tasks for the 20s
- Restructuring interaction and boundaries with family from a dependent to an independent orientation
- Finding a place for oneself in the world outside the family—in work, friendships, and love

The complex emotional work of the young adult is launching from the family of origin and finding a place for herself or himself in the world. During the past two decades, with the trend toward marrying later, this stage may include a period of living on one's own or with a partner (Cherlin, 2005), with early marriage playing less of a role in defining boundaries and bestowing adult status. Anxiety about single status for most will be at its lowest in the 20s, when developing a career or job skills for men and women is at the forefront. The backdrop for the 20s, however, continues to be the assumption that coupling will eventually take place and that finding a mate is part of the "work." The young adult's gender, class, ethnicity, and sexual orientation will shape the vision each young adult has of how and when this will be accomplished. For LGBT singles, negotiating this transition is also frequently accompanied and complicated by whatever stage they may be with regard to gender identity and disclosure of that identity to family.

When the central emphasis of the young adult period is preparing for a career and developing a sense of self, concern about finding a mate will be lower. In cultures in which universal and early marriage is expected, however, or when career opportunities are limited and/or young people do not have the money for prolonged career preparation, a focus on marriage or childrearing as the next step will arise earlier.

GENDER DIFFERENCES. While both men and women of all educational levels are postponing marriage, there are gender differences in the perception of the impact of achievement on marriageability. It passes for common wisdom that men increase their status through education and earning power while for women achievement may diminish their chances for marriage. The perception is that men also have more time to become marriageable while women's marriageability decreases with age. Over the last decade, however, better educated and achieving women are marrying in greater numbers than less educated women, and two-income couples are the largest growing demographic of married people (Zernike, 2007). Yet, popular culture portrays higher achieving single women at best as missing

their moment to find a mate or at worst lacking in the ability to form relationships. The pressure on men to achieve and accept responsibility, perhaps in the face of high achieving women and uncertain economic times, has spawned what has been coined the "bro" culture for middle-class White young men described by Kimmel in his book *Guyland*, in which 18- to 26-year-old men are embracing a prolonged adolescence and buddy substitute family that is both homophobic and anti-woman, in the service of avoiding adult responsibility (Kimmel, 2009). It is important for the therapist to inquire about the impact of these cultural stereotypes and help the client challenge outmoded beliefs that reinforce the "marriage gradient" in which men should marry women of equal or less economic status and women should marry equal or up.

Black women may feel less in a bind; while White parents (especially working-class ones) have viewed marriage for daughters as a route to financial stability, Black parents have placed much more emphasis on preparing daughters to work (Higginbotham & Weber, 1995) and tend not to see marriage as a replacement for the need to earn money (Staples & Johnson, 1993). Currently, never married Black women, living alone, are the fastest growing cohort to achieve middle-class status suggesting that marriage does not necessarily provide an income benefit (Marsh, Darity, Cohen, Casper, & Salters, 2007).

MARRIAGE AS A PREMATURE SOLUTION. Although less frequently than in previous generations, young adults may enter marriage as a premature solution to the central emotional work of negotiating an adult self within the family of origin or as a way to escape intense intergenerational conflict in the home. When children cannot afford to leave and establish their own territory, or when parents expect their children to live at home until marriage, the conflict between generations can escalate greatly.

Therapy may involve helping the young client and his or her family to postpone a precipitous marriage that would only detour or triangulate the emotional work of negotiating an adult self. Renegotiating new boundaries without marriage is a difficult task, however, when positions are rigid and conflict is intense.

ESTABLISHING RELATIONSHIPS OUTSIDE THE FAMILY. Friendships and love relationships outside the family supply the emotional foundation for emerging independence and the development of an adult self. When friendships are taken seriously, as they should be, and not viewed as transitional to marriage, there is less of a tendency to invest all of one's emotional energy in finding "Mr(s). Right." LGBT young adults often more readily take this step as a necessity when families have not been supportive. While therapists need to inquire about the meaning, depth, and extent of friendships in all people's lives, it can be particularly helpful in working with single people. Finding a path that places equal emphasis on the development of work skills and the capacity for close relationships is important for the healthy growth of both sexes. The treatment of Bob illustrates the problems a man may have with investing in friendships.

CASE ILLUSTRATION

Bob

Bob, a White, middle-class, 28-year-old man of British, Dutch, and German background, entered therapy depressed and demoralized because he had been unable to find a new girlfriend after the breakup of a 3-year relationship. Bob was very successful at work but was lonely and isolated. He had trouble making friends on his own and counted on girlfriends to provide emotional anchorage. His neediness was pushing women away.

Rather than focusing exclusively on his difficulties in romantic relationships, the therapy addressed the crucial task of creating social networks. For Bob, looking at multigenerational themes was particularly relevant. He came from a Midwestern Protestant family. The older of two boys, he described his mother as emotionally distant and his father as warm but weak. His mother, to whom he looked for the moral leadership of the family, had never sought friends. She thought the need for friends indicated a weakness of character. When Bob was coached to find out more about his mother's family, it emerged that her own mother had been orphaned at birth. Although Bob's grandmother had been raised

by a caring relative, she had feared becoming emotionally attached. The lesson she taught her daughter, Bob's mother, was that one should act as if one does not need people.

Tracking the generational messages about the meaning of friends was key for Bob in opening up awareness of his needs for affiliation. Having friends would make for a more enjoyable life and take the intensity off finding a mate. Bob's work in exploring his parents' history allowed him to approach his family differently. He now began to have more personally revealing conversations with his mother, broaching previously taboo subjects such as her "self-sufficiency" compared to his own neediness.

If the young adult can keep anxiety about finding a spouse low enough, the process of dating can be helpful in learning about the self in relationships and in experimenting with adult gender and social roles. Dating that is fraught with intensity about latching onto a mate can only become draining and painful.

Owning an adult self also includes finding ways to validate one's sexuality. This means either dealing with the complexities of being sexual outside of marriage (including the specter of AIDS in each encounter) or, if celibacy is valued, acknowledging the absence of sex as a healthy choice. For the LGBT single, embracing the adult self may have the additional impact of announcing a difference in sexuality to family and friends.

The 30s: The single crisis

> Tasks for the 30s
> - Facing and accepting single status as a healthy life course
> - Expanding life goals to embrace possibilities in addition to marriage, including childrearing

During the 30s, the experience of singlehood can begin to change even for those who have used the 20s to develop and enjoy the capacity to live alone, investing in work and friendships. As more peers marry and start families, the template for the "real" business of life begins to shift and single people can begin to feel out of sync. As a result, the task of looking for a partner can intensify, often eclipsing the development of an independent self. Women usually experience this "singlehood panic" at a younger age than men, partly because of the pressure of the biological clock and partly because of the societal judgment that says that men may choose to remain single, but women do so only involuntarily (Klinenberg, 2012).

This increased anxiety means that requests for therapy often focus on enhancing marriageability. Rather than trying to move clients off this goal, it is better to stay relevant to the client's vision of the purpose of treatment, since the desire to be married is an important adult goal. Getting married is a legitimate—but incomplete—frame for therapy. An initial dilemma is how to honor a client's desire for marriage and still address issues in a context that does not make marriage the end product of successful treatment. Moving ahead with work on the developmental tasks of this phase can lower anxiety and increase self-respect. But moving too exclusively— not acknowledging the validity of a desire for marriage or the real problems a single client might have with intimacy—can be experienced by the client as the therapist's judgment that the client really *is* "unmarriageable."

To remain open to the possibilities for marriage yet not be taken over by this pursuit, the single person and his or her family need to make a major shift: attaining the belief that there is more than one way to lead a healthy life. This shift is fundamental to the emotional work of this period and sets the stage for later years, should the client remain single.

Working on life cycle tasks does not rule out marriage but simply facilitates the experience of growing as an adult. It takes into account the reality that the client is now single, whatever the future brings. Coming to grips with singlehood means looking at the ways the single person may be putting his or her life on hold, such as postponing financial planning, setting up a home, even buying kitchen utensils. Not doing these things helps maintain the presumption that important aspects of life proceed only after marriage.

What are put on hold are usually the things that the institution of marriage has typically assigned to a heterosexual mate. Traditional gender training does not lend itself well to single status, and members of each sex need to develop skills in areas that are assumed to be the province of the other. For a woman, this means that work has to be taken seriously to provide both financial stability and a sense of identity—something that women (particularly lower-middle-class White women) have not been socialized to consider. For a man, it means learning how to develop networks and friendships (Kimmel, 2012; Meth & Pasick, 1990). For both, it means making one's home feel like a home.

Friendships need to accommodate what Peter Stein (1981) called their "patchwork" quality. This is a time when friends move into and out of romantic relationships or marry and therefore are not consistently available. A large circle of friends to share celebrations and life together can help decrease the sense of abandonment when good friends shift their primary emotional loyalty to another.

Helping single clients to articulate aspects of an adult self in the family of origin is a key aspect of coaching in this phase. Acknowledging sexual maturity outside marriage can be one of the most anxiety-provoking areas for both client and parents.

CASE ILLUSTRATION

Young Soon

Young Soon, a Korean American woman in her mid-30s, was the youngest of seven children and the only single person in the family. Though she had a very successful career in television industry, she had never considered moving out of the parental home. She felt a strong obligation to her widowed mother and, in the context of her Korean cultural heritage, took meaning and validation in fulfilling what was a necessary and important "job" in not leaving her mother to live alone. Her single status was not a major concern for her, but she did feel restricted in terms of her activities away from home. She also wanted more privacy when at home, to have "alone time," and also have friends over.

Being a single woman and still achieving independence while living at home was not a common pathway in her culture, and she was at a loss about how to manage these adult needs without previous role models. People may feel there is something lacking or wrong with them when they experience needs and feelings that have little place for expression in traditional cultural models, particularly when two cultures "collide" such as the Korean model with the American emphasis on individual achievement and fulfillment. It takes a delicate therapeutic touch to validate these "disloyal" needs and feelings while at the same time respecting the client's attachment to the values with which they have been raised and which they believe. Young Soon decided that a first step would be to establish one room in their home as "hers" and, being artistic, was able to create a space that felt to her as a Parisian boudoir would, in which she could feel herself. Her own decoration, it goes without saying, was very different from the rest of the home. After feeling more comfortable with the whole spectrum of her feelings, Young Soon next spoke to her siblings about needing their cooperation so that she could go out on her own and sometimes stay away from home. The siblings were amenable and agreed to spend more time at their mother's house, which allowed Young Soon the opportunity to stay away a few days on her own and at the same time know that her mother was cared for in the traditional family way.

In Korean families, each relationship involves reciprocal obligations and responsibilities (Kim & Ryu, 2005). Young Soon was being responsive to what she saw as her cultural role of caring for her mother. At the same time, she found a way to lead a more satisfying life as a single person without eliminating the contexts of family and culture that gave meaning to her life.

Toward their mid-30s, most women and some men and their families experience heightened concern over potential childlessness. The thought of missing out on one of life's most profound experiences surfaces and may keep reverberating for years. When combined with parental distress over not having grandchildren, this sadness can develop into a dense web of reactivity. It is important to truly hear this concern without trying to change or fix it.

The painful intensity of these feelings can lead to closing off discussion about marriage or childlessness to maintain pseudo-calm in the family. When family colludes to deny important realities, however, relationships and personal growth suffer.

CASE ILLUSTRATION

Susan

Susan, a 39-year-old Jewish woman, and an only child, no longer discusses her childlessness with her parents. When she had divorced 10 years ago, she had apologized to her mother about not giving her a grandchild. Her mother then had been very reassuring, telling her that parenthood was not all it was cracked up to be and not to worry. She was totally taken aback when, now 10 years later, her mother relayed an anecdote of meeting a friend who had recently become a grandmother. Susan asked the name of the baby, to which her mother replied, "I didn't ask. It made my heart ache."

Susan's own pain about her lack of children, which she had hidden from her family, and her high reactivity to her mother's similar feelings, led her to close off this toxic issue, thereby freezing the development of their mother–daughter relationship. While the realization that there will be no future generation is generally painful for any family and family member, there are occasions when familial, racial, and religious themes form a dense web of emotional reactivity that is very difficult to work with. In Susan's case, her relationship with her mother had always been characterized by a mutual unspoken protection agreement: Susan was not to cause her mother pain but was to achieve and be happy. Susan's mother, on the other hand, was to remove any pain that Susan was experiencing so as to "make her happy." In the context of the Jewish race, with the recent history of the Holocaust, not producing children to ensure the overall survival of its people took on not only a familial but an entire cultural sadness and guilt. Susan's age made apparent to both mother and daughter that children would probably not be coming. Susan, therefore, was causing her mother pain and her mother had difficulty pretending it did not matter. They had developed no way for negotiating this "betrayal" to each other. "Failing" family, race, and religion, all core cornerstones of defining who we are, created, of course, deep and difficult feelings.

Exploring these familial, racial, and religious themes is often helpful in lowering the intensity of emotional reactivity, so that people can widen their view beyond their own feelings of guilt, failure, and anger. Susan no doubt would have benefited from examining the intersection of her unique family dynamics with the cultural and religious issues as well as her own sense of loss. She might then have been able to make a more sympathetic bridge to her mother, allowing the relationship to evolve.

Midlife: Developing alternative scripts

Tasks for Midlife:
- Addressing the "ideal family" fantasy to accept the possibility of never marrying and the probability of never having biological children
- Redefining the meaning of work
- Defining an authentic life that can be established within single status
- Establishing an adult role within the family of origin

A 40th birthday ushers in the realization that time is running out. The emotional weight of closing options falls most heavily on women. Women have a procreative time limit and usually continue to feel social and personal pressure to marry "up" (taller, richer, and older). Men can have children much later in life and many continue to have a wide range of acceptable partners from which to choose. However, for both men and women at this age, there is the probability of never achieving the family they might have expected to have. If marriage does happen, it will likely be with a divorced or widowed spouse. If childrearing is in the picture, it will likely be with someone else's children or as a single parent.

A drift toward segregation between single and married people, begun in earlier years, is typically firmly in place by midlife. There are powerful reasons for this divide, among them differing demands for time and commitment, stereotypical perceptions of single people as a threat to married life, and what might feel like an onslaught of rituals and celebrations of married and child focused life. This segregation can contribute greatly to feelings of isolation from "mainstream life" as well as to idealized fantasies of married life. Work on diminishing this gap can help a great deal.

Helping clients to disentangle the main loss—spouse, child, or "package"—is important. It opens up consideration of alternatives. Those whose primary distress centers on childrearing, for example, can explore other options for bringing children into their lives, including the difficult step of single parenthood, rather than remaining mired, awaiting a spouse. The pain of these losses around expected family and particularly around childlessness may wax and wane throughout life, getting retriggered by changes in circumstance and priorities.

GENDER DIFFERENCES Connecting with a viable social network becomes increasingly difficult yet more important for single men as they get older. By the end of the 40s, unmarried men's health status deteriorates much faster than that of married men (Schoenborn, 2004), with the difference long attributed to the positive benefits of marriage and having a wife. At the same time, never married men fare better than those who are widowed or divorced, suggesting that marriage may insulate men from learning to care for themselves. Interestingly, the health gap between married and single has been closing according to recent reports, raising the question as to whether it is marriage that makes the difference or access to social resources and support, historically found in a spouse, now developing to service a growing single population (Liu & Umberson, 2008).

Not surprisingly, never married women have reportedly less difficulty accessing and maintaining a social network, as it is a skill long developed and valued in women. According to The General Social Survey (GSS), the largest study of social behavior in America, single and divorced women over the age of 35 use this skill even more than their married counterparts and have more frequent contact with friends and neighbors (Klinenberg, 2012). Anderson, Stewart, and Dimidjian (1994) in their book *Flying Solo* recount the stories of midlife women who feel happy about their lives in part because they have worked on their social networks as well as taken care with their economic lives. Based on in-depth interviews of 90 women—unmarried, divorced, and/

or single mothers—these stories reflect the sense of competence, satisfaction, and pleasure in life that these women feel.

DEFINING AN AUTHENTIC LIFE AS A SINGLE ADULT. Societal emphasis placed on marriage and children as the primary vehicles for mature love may leave some single adults feeling that their relationships and loves are less valuable. If love and the need for connection can be framed as part of the normal drive for adult attachment, it need not be entangled with the institution of marriage. Then the single person's loving experiences, whatever their form, are legitmized and not disparged as substiutes for the real thing.

Disentangling love from marriage allows single people to legitimize their loving experiences, whatever their form, and not feel that they are substitutes for the real thing.

Another aspect of feeling authentic involves forging a connection with future generations. This connection helps people to feel a sense of continuity with history and meaning beyond individual achievement and personal satisfaction. Single people will need to create their own connections; they are not automatically provided by marriage and the family package. Single people often do not realize that connection to the future is important. One woman who chose to become a Big Sister said, "I don't know why I waited so long to bring a child into my life."

Feeling authentic also means accepting that friends are family, not a poor substitute. Being aware of the quality and breadth of these friendships circles is critical to clinical work because feeling attached to others provides stability and satisfaction in the lives of single people. Strong friendships, according to several recent studies, are positively correlated with longevity and healthier living (Parker-Pope, 2009). The availability of friendships may vary throughout the life cycle for single people as it does for everyone. People can move in and out of relationships; they may move to different areas of the country, or may become ill and die. Therefore, single people have to be aware that they need to work at keeping an emotional support system alive. Women may have an easier

time of this because they have been socialized to express the need for connection to others that we all have (Taylor et al., 2000). If single men have not worked at this in earlier stages, they are at more of a disadvantage by this age as their single cohort is vastly diminished.

REDEFINING THE MEANING OF WORK. The workplace is usually the central organizing hub of daily life for single people, and the connection of work life to personal satisfaction cannot be overestimated. Work is more than earning money; skills and talents must be used in a meaningful way in one's job or in other arenas. Clients themselves may not realize the importance of work to their feelings, continuing to view their job as a means to pay the rent while waiting for their "real" life to begin. For Lorraine, however, the needed redefinition revolved around the meaning of the fruits of her labor.

CASE ILLUSTRATION

Lorraine Sampson

Lorraine Sampson, a 48-year-old Black American woman, came for a consultation around recent feelings of apathy and emptiness about her life. Usually, she had a "zest for life" and took pride and pleasure in her work (she was partner in a law firm), her family, and her friends. Lorraine had relationships with men on and off all her adult life, but "men have never been the center" of her life.

Lorraine came from South Carolina and was a middle child of four. Her family, of working-class background, was well known and respected in their town, having lived there for three generations. She had two sisters, both of whom were married with children, and a brother who had died in his 20s of a drug overdose. When Lorraine thought of family, however, it included more than just her nuclear family. In keeping with the African American notion of family, Lorraine kept in close touch with not only aunts, uncles, and grandparents but also with many members of her church who had been with her in growing up.

With her expanded notion of family came an enhanced sense of responsibility and interconnectedness.

She had benefited from this family sense as a young woman, when the "family" had sacrificed considerably to send her—the "studious one"—to college and law school. As soon as Lorraine got her first job, she began helping the next generation. First, she sent money home to be used for education, and later she had nieces, nephews, and cousins live with her while they attended college.

She had been "mothering" in this way for over 20 years, and now she believed the younger generation was at the point where they could take over. Lorraine had been looking forward to using her money on deferred personal pleasure, when her sister, together with her two grandchildren, came north to live. Again Lorraine felt she had to take Alva and the children under her wing, as they were strangers to the city. This was the beginning of her depression.

Lorraine, while single, had an integral place in her extended family, as well as opportunities and obligations to be a close, involved, active aunt and second mother to the younger generation. Childlessness or lack of a legitimate role was not an issue for her in her singleness. In addition, her success was highly valued by the family. However, because she had neither nuclear family nor children of her own, and was financially self-reliant, the implied reciprocity in the mutual support system (Boyd-Franklin, 2006) was not enacted. Her desire to lead a more "selfish" life put her at odds with her family's expectations of her.

For many Black families, as well as others with limited economic resources, the answer to the question "When does the caretaking stop?" may be "Never." It is particularly important that therapists coming from different backgrounds respect the resiliency and the interconnections of extended family networks, and not view Lorraine's dilemma, for example, as a lack of differentiation or as a problem in learning how to disappoint others; that is, just say "No." Lorraine, an intelligent person, readily grasped the value of exploring the issue of what being selfish meant in her family, of the fates and lives of other "selfish" women, of the women who had "turned their back" on their family. In the course of these conversations,

Lorraine was able to more deeply connect with the women in her family, and to find that none viewed the issue (self versus family) in the unilateral way in which Lorraine was seeing it (i.e., you cannot quit until someone else takes over from you).

Taking work seriously goes hand in hand with taking responsibility for one's financial future. This is a necessity in the 40s and 50s. Men may have anxiety about how they are managing their money, but they do not usually doubt their need to do it. Women, on the other hand, may have been brought up to believe that this is man's territory and might also need to learn about finance along with the therapy. This endeavor can be filled with anxiety; many women associate it with giving up on the possibility of ever being taken care of through marriage.

FAMILY WORK. Feelings of anxiety or failure as parents can resurface at this time, as it sinks in that their "child" really may never marry or have the "ideal" family form. When parental emotionality meshes with the single person's reactivity around the same issues, the potential for misunderstanding and possible cutoff is high, decreasing the chances of either parents or the single person talking openly about the challenges much less the benefits of being single. Openness about one's life at this phase as well as invitations into the single person's world furthers the establishment of an adult self. This might include hosting events rather than being the perennial guest both with siblings and parents. It can also involve building separate relationships with nieces and nephews. Seeing one's life as legitimate and having parents and siblings do so as well will help if and when parents become infirmed and need caretaking. Too often, the unmarried sibling, particularly if female, is presumed to have more time and less responsibilities.

Later years: Putting it all together

Tasks for Later Years:
- Maintaining connectedness
- Consolidating decisions in work life
- Acknowledging and planning for the future diminishment of physical abilities
- Enjoying the freedom and autonomy of singlehood

This phase may extend two decades or more, encompassing "second life" goals and plans, job shifts, retirement, and the death of parents, until failed health signals the last years. Two factors that greatly impact the single person's perspective during this time are economic class and health status. If money is limited so then are the choices of life style; people may envision having to live with a relative or a friend, thereby limiting the independence to which they may have been accustomed. Likewise, early brushes with disability, disease, or illness will shape what choices are seen as emotionally and physically viable. A large number of single people in these later years, however, will have enough income and be in good enough health to be emotionally positioned to reap the fruits of single status: freedom and autonomy. Less encumbered by financial and/or emotional responsibility toward adult children than their married counterparts, single people can devote more time and energy to shaping personally meaningful work, "second life" goals and plans, job shifts, and retirement.

Later years signal an increasingly greater gender difference in overall health indices between single men and women with the health of men who are unmarried deteriorating much faster. Indeed, men who never married were more than twice as likely to die early than those who had been in a stable marriage throughout their adult life. Being single, or losing a partner without replacement, increased the risk of early death during middle age and reduced the likelihood that one would survive to be elderly (Siegler et al., 2013). Additionally, The National Center for Health Statistics (Gorina et al., 2005) found that elderly White men (65 years and older) have a suicide rate triple that of the overall U.S. rate, and are eight times more likely to kill themselves than women of their same age. The suicide rate for divorced White men in particular, according to a study done in 2000, was twice that of married or single White men (Kpowsoa, 2000). Marriage apparently continues to serve an integrative and supportive function, particularly for men. While there has been very little research on older single gay men and the impact of social networks, the process of developing "chosen families" at earlier stages may provide a form of health protection for gay men (Shippy et al., 2004). For the health of women, however, the protective benefit of marriage is more likely related to the greater economic security that comes with marriage as women have less difficulty cultivating social support in or out of the context of marriage (Roelfs et al., 2011).

By age the age of 65, only 42 percent of women are living with a spouse, compared to 72 percent of men (U.S. Census Data 2010). Unmarried women moving through the later years, then, find themselves to be less statistically deviant than do unmarried men, when the great majority of single men's peers are still married.

MAINTAINING CONNECTEDNESS. According to Siegel (1999), attachments to others are crucial not only for emotional well-being but also for the continued development of the brain overall. "...emotionally meaningful events can enable continued learning from experience throughout the lifespan." The continued growth and complexity of neural connections, Siegel suggests, may well be the foundation of the "development of wisdom with age . . . the capacity to see patterns over time and across situations." (pp. 307–308). "Emotionally meaningful" to Siegel is being grounded in social connectedness and interactions with other people.

Maintaining connectedness becomes increasingly difficult as people move through their later years: Friends and family members die or move away to retirement communities or easier climates; the arrival of retirement (even when sought) may present a serious disruption on one's network; and the onset of waning physical strength makes it harder for people to travel distances to visit friends and family. People at all life phases may not recognize the long-term impact of shifts and losses in their network, but careful inquiry needs to be made about losses at this phase, when the extent is usually greater than at any prior time.

Family relationships often need realignment as parents age and become infirm. Parental anxiety around single status may resurface after years of dormancy as parents struggle to feel their child is "settled" before they die. Family of origin work with parents is particularly poignant now, since this may be the last opportunity for the adult child to resolve feelings about single life and communicate some reassurance to aged parents.

The need to care for aged parents often puts strains on sibling relationships, which may have stayed frozen in time at the point when each child left home. Research done on marriage and social ties has shown that the unmarried siblings are more apt to care for aging parents than their married siblings (Gerstel & Sarkisian, 2007a) and that unmarried women are called upon to be primary caretakers significantly more often than widowed daughters (Connidis, 2001). Implicit in this selection is the judgment that the lives of single women are more flexible than those of people with children. Family of origin work with siblings is made more difficult when there is little emotional glue other than the connection to the aging parents. The cost of non-resolution, however, may be the dissolution of family connections after the parents' death.

CONSOLIDATING DECISIONS ABOUT MONEY AND WORK—PLANNING FOR THE FUTURE. Emotional intensity about using one's life fully tends to increase as that inner voice says, "If I don't do it now, I never will." Single people may have an advantage in making major shifts because they do not have to adjust plans around spouses and children. Exploring options for even partial realization of goals and dreams that have been put on the shelf is always useful. Even if money is limited and jobs cannot be changed, life can include these dreams. One 55-year-old woman who worked on a factory assembly line saved for 10 years for a trip to a distant country. Accomplishing this enabled her to feel like an adventurous woman instead of a factory drudge.

Planning for the future is critical at this juncture. It includes thinking about a home base that feels financially and physically secure (and may mean considering joining forces with others to pool resources). If a client strongly resists addressing these issues, examining multigenerational themes may help.

CASE ILLUSTRATION

Lauren

Lauren, a 54-year-old never-married Jewish woman, had derived a lot of satisfaction from her work and great enjoyment in her life. Both her brothers had married and had children, and Lauren enjoyed being auntie to them. Unusual for a Jewish woman, Lauren had not been too bothered by either her single status or her childlessness. She was a cherished only daughter who was raised to feel she was indeed very special in her talents and intelligence. She felt that developing her talents was exactly what her parents would have wanted for her. Now, however, she found herself almost paralyzed with anxiety about her future. She had kept no money aside and was frightened about the coming years. At the same time, she strongly resisted saving money. She hosted expensive dinners and took lavish vacations, which only increased her panic.

When multigenerational themes were explored, it emerged that both her mother and grandmother had died before the age of 60. Both had had lives of hard work and little luxury. Her paralysis about planning for a future was fueled by her unconscious belief that she was not going to have one. Her vision of life cycle included death within the next 5 years. Bringing this powerful template into conscious awareness was crucial in freeing Lauren from her "inexplicable" terror.

For some, establishing security may mean considering joining forces with others to pool resources, even looking for alternative living situations that decrease social isolation. At the same time, as our life span increases, more and more people are choosing to live alone. Sweden, frequently at the cutting edge of social change, has taken active steps to accommodate this trend and created small-scale developments with small apartments that allow people to live on their own but have common space to support interaction and community (Klinenberg, 2012).

A final piece of planning is the making of one's will. This is more than a duty; it is a profound emotional experience. Looking at possessions and deciding how and with whom you want them to be valued after your death can change a client's entire perspective. People retrieve memories that have been pushed aside and rediscover priorities and attachments that have faded. Communicating decisions directly to the people involved can shift relationships in one's current life.

CASE ILLUSTRATION

John

John, who was raised in a working-class Italian Catholic family, had always had an affectionate and fun-filled relationship with his nieces; he was the one who took them to concerts, the theater, and dinner. When John decided to tell them about their inheritance from him, his lawyers and his own family tried to talk him out of it. They felt he might "make them lazy" and not feel they needed to get education or get a job. He decided to tell them anyway. He went ahead, on the grounds that his nieces should have this information in planning their own futures. For the first time, his nieces realized the depth of his love for them and came to see him as a second parent.

ENJOYING THE FREEDOM. Personal freedom is one of the great benefits of singlehood, and using it well gives richness to the single experience. We all experience life differently as we age, married or single. Some like King Lear rant and rage against the inequities, others like Prospero accept changes with grace, while others like Woody Allen and Clint Eastwood continue on with their work life (Scott, 2009). Most older people will likely experience a mix of these feelings and the significance of marital status may recede to be only one among many factors in adaptation. What is critical for all of us is a supportive network. Researchers are now coming to realize that friendship has a bigger impact on the sense of well-being than family relationships and finding that good friendships can make the difference between sickness and health (Parker-Pope, 2009). Successful aging, married or single, lies in maintaining friendships and emotional connections for as long as possible.

> Assess your comprehension of the single person's life cycle by completing this quiz.

> Recall what you learned in this chapter by completing the Chapter Review.

— References

Allen, K. R. (1989). *Single women/ family ties: life histories of older women* Newbury Park, CA: Sage.

Anderson, C. M., Stewart, S., & Dimidjian, S. (1994). *Flying solo*. New York: Norton.

Boyd-Franklin, N. (2006). *Black families in therapy: Understanding the African American experience* (2nd ed.). New York: Guilford Press.

Cherlin, A. (December 25, 2012). Do unmarried poor have bad values or bad jobs. Retrieved May 13, 2013, from http://www.bloomberg.com/news/print/2012-12-25/do-unmarried-poor-have-bad-values-or-bad-jobs-.html

Cherlin, A. J. (2005). American marriage in the early twenty-first century. *The Future of Children, 15*(2) 33–55.

Connidis, I. A. (2001). *Family ties and aging*. Thousand Oaks, CA: Sage.

Coontz, S. (1992). *The way we never were: American families and the nostalgia trap*. New York: Basic Books.

DePaulo, B. (2006). *Singled out: How singles are stereotyped, stigmatized, and ignored, and still live happily ever after*. New York: St. Martins' Press.

Diner, H. (1983). *Erin's daughters in America: Immigrant women in the 19th century*. Baltimore, MD: Johns Hopkins Press.

Franklin, J. H. (1988). A historical note on Black families. In H. P. McAdoo (Ed.), *Black families* (2nd ed., pp. 23–26). Newbury Park, CA: Sage.

Gerstel, N., & Sarkisian, N. (2007a). Marriage reduces social ties. Discussion paper for the *Council on Contemporary Families*. Retrieved April 14, 2010, from www.prospects.org/cs/articles

Gorina, Y., Hoyert, D., Lentzner, H., Goulding, M. (2005). Trends in causes of deaths in older persons in the United States. *National Center for Health Statistics*. Retrieved from www.cdc.gov.

Heiss, J. (1988). Women's values regarding marriage and the family. In H. P. McAdoo (Ed.), *Black Families* (2nd ed., pp. 201–214). Newbury Park, CA: Sage.

Higginbotham, E., & Weber, L. (1995). Moving up with kin and community: Upward social mobility for Black and White women. In M. L. Anderson & P. H. Collins

(Eds.), *Race, class & gender: An anthology* (2nd ed., pp. 134–147). Belmont, CA: Wadsworth.

Holland, B. (1992). *One's company.* New York: Ballantine.

Jayson, S. (2007). Free as a bird and loving it: Being single has its benefits. *USA Today.com.*

Lane, S. D., Keefe, R. H., Rubinstein, R. A., Levandowski, B. A., Freedman, M., Rosenthal, A. Cibula, D. A., & Czerwinski, M. (2004). Marriage promotion and missing men: African American women in a demographic double bind? *Medical Anthropology Quarterly, New Series, 18*(4), 405–428.

Liu, H., & Umberson, D. J. (2008). The times they are a changin': Marital status and health differentials from 1972 to 2003. *Journal of Health and Social Behavior, 49*(3), 239–253.

Kim, Bok-Lim, C. & Ryu, E. (2005). Korean families. In M. McGoldrick, J. Giordano, & N. Garcia Preto (Eds.), *Ethnicity and family therapy* (3rd ed., pp. 349–362). New York: Guilford Press.

Kimmel, M. S. (2009). *Guyland: The perilous world where boys become men.* New York: Harper/Collins.

Kimmel, M. S. (2012). *The gendered society* (5th ed.). New York: Oxford University Press.

Klinenberg, E. (2012). *Going solo: The extraordinary rise and surprising appeal of living alone.* New York: The Penguin Press.

Kposowa, A. (2000). Marital status and suicide in the national longitudinal study. *Journal of Epidemiology and Community Health, 54,* 254–261.

Marsh, K., Darity, W. Jr., Cohen, P., Casper, L., & Salters, D. (2007). The emerging Black middle class: Single and living alone. *Social Forces,* 86 (2), 735–762.

McGoldrick, M. (2005). Irish families. In M. McGoldrick, J. Giordano, & N. Garcia Preto (Eds.), *Ethnicity and family therapy* (3rd ed., pp. 544–566). New York: Guilford Press.

McGoldrick, M., Giordano, J., & Garcia Preto, N. (Eds.) (2005). *Ethnicity and family therapy* (3rd ed.). New York: Guilford Press.

Meth, R., & Pasick, R. (1990). *Men in therapy: The challenge of change.* New York: Guilford Press.

Nitsche, N., & Brueckner, H. (2009, August). *Opting out of the family? Social change in racial inequality in family formation patterns and marriage outcomes among highly educated women.* Paper presented at the American Sociological Association 104th Annual Meeting, San Francisco.

Parker-Pope, T. (April 20, 2009). What are friends for? A longer life. *New York Times,* Section D.

Parker-Pope, T. (April 14, 2010). Is marriage good for your health? *New York Times.*

Pew Research Social and Demographic Trends (2011, December). *Marriage rate declines and marriage age rises.* Retrieved from http://www.pewsocialtrends .org/2011/12/14/marriage-rate-declines-and-marriage-age-rises/

Rosen, E., & Weltman, S. F. (2005). Jewish families: An overview. In M. McGoldrick, J. Giordano, & N. Garcia Preto (Eds.), *Ethnicity and family therapy* (3rd ed., pp. 667–679). New York: Guilford Press.

Roelfs, D. J., Shor, E., Kalish, R., & Yogev, T. (2011). The rising relative risk of mortality for singles: Meta-analysis and meta-regression. *American Journal of Epidemiology, 174(4)*, 379–389.

Schoenborn, C. A. (2004). Marital Status and Health: United States, 1992-2002. *Advance Data from Vital and Health Statistics,* number 351.

Schwartzberg, N., Berliner, K., & Jacob, D. (1995). *Single in a married world.* New York: W. W. Norton.

Scott, A. O. (2009, April 15). Directors in their magic hour. *New York Times,* p. AR1.

Siegler, I. C., Brummett, B. H., Martin, P., Helms, M. J. (2013). Consistency and timing of marital transitions and survival during midlife: The role of personality and health risk behaviours. *Annals of Behavioral Medicine, 45*(3), 338–347.

Shippy, R. A., Cantor, M. H., & Brennan, M. (2004). Social networks of aging gay men. *Journal of Men's Studies, 13*(1), 107–120.

Siegel, D. J. (1999). *The developing mind: How relationships and the brain interact to shape who we are.* New York: Guilford Press.

Staples, R., & Johnson, L. B. (1993). *Black families at the crossroad: Challenges and prospects.* San Francisco, CA: Jossey-Bass.

Stein, P. (1981). Understanding single adulthood. In P. Stein (Ed.), *Single life: Unmarried adults in social contexts* (pp. 9–20). New York: St. Martin's Press.

Taylor, S. E., Klein, L. C., Lewis, B. P., Gruenewald, T. L., Gurung, R. A. R., & Updegraff, J. A. (2000). Female responses to stress: Tend and befriend, not fight or flight. *Psychological Review, 107*(3), 411–429.

U.S. Census Bureau (2010). *America's Families and living arrangements.* Retrieved December 2, 2010, from www.census.gov

U.S. Census Bureau (2008). *Families and living arrangements.* Retrieved April 14, 2010, from www.census.gov

Zernike, K. (2007, January 21). Why are there so many single Americans. *New York Times,* p. D2.

Chapter 11

Friendship Across the Life Cycle

Kiran S. K. Arora & Timothy R. Baima[1]

Learning Objectives

- List and describe the benefits of friendship.
- Describe the relationship between childhood friendships and family relationships.
- Explain the effects friendships have on development during childhood and adolescence.
- Identify the roles that socio-cultural factors play in children's friendships.
- Discuss how gender impacts friendships of heterosexual adults.
- Examine how adult romantic relationships and friendships affect each other.
- Describe the role that friendship plays in later life.
- Compare the role that friendship plays in the lives of LGBT people versus heterosexual people.

Introduction

Friendships are among our deepest, most meaningful and longest-lasting relationships we have in life (Fehr, 1996). Friends enrich our lives with intimacy, companionship, laughter, and joy. They validate our beliefs, bear witness to our emotions, and challenge us to grow. The ability to *be a friend* to others, increases the meaning and purpose in our lives. In fact, simply knowing that we matter to our friends is associated with overall happiness (Demir et al., 2011). In the presence of friends, some people find freedom to be their most whole and authentic selves. Friends may naturally draw important characteristics out of one another that are difficult to access and express in other relationships. Friends also help us transcend the boundaries of our own existence by acting as windows into perspectives and experiences that resonate with us, but are not our own. We honor particularly close friends by referring to them as family, and when we share a special bond with a family member, we call them our friend (Rawlins, 2009). In some cultures, friends may take on roles of family during rituals and ceremonies when family members are absent or deceased.

It is probably impossible to measure the full emotional and psychological benefits of friendship. Studies have shown that supportive friendships increase self-esteem and buffer against the psychological impact of life cycle transitions, stress, and family difficulties (Bagwell & Schmidt, 2011; Sherman, Lansford, & Volling, 2006). Friendship reduces the risk of loneliness and depression and increases overall physical and mental health (Monsour, 2002; Way, 2011). Our perceptions of challenging situations can even be altered through friendship. In one study, college students were asked to stand at the bottom of a hill carrying heavy backpacks and estimate the steepness of the hill. Students who stood next to close friends believed the hill was significantly less steep than those who stood next to acquaintances, strangers or alone (Schnall, Harber, Stefanucci, & Proffitt, 2008). With friends by our side, life's obstacles seem more manageable. We are empowered to overcome struggles and encouraged to take on challenges that may otherwise have appeared insurmountable.

This chapter has been coauthored by a straight South Asian Sikh woman and a straight white Christian man who have been friends for many years. Our hope is that this chapter generates critical thinking and rich dialogue about the significance of friendship in the context of a family life cycle framework for therapeutic assessment and intervention.

---

[1] Both authors contributed equally to this chapter.

Trends Across the Life Cycle

Friendships usually form around similarities in social class, race, sexual orientation, gender, religiosity, education level, and marital status (Fehr, 1996). While these similarities play a significant role in initiating a relationship, friends will not usually become close unless they also share similar values. Intimate friendship bonds grow out of having fun and relaxing together, providing reciprocal support, and sharing personal details of one another's lives (Fehr, 2000). Interestingly, it seems that spending time together and talking on a regular basis are the most important factors in maintaining a friendship. Since friendships are not bound by formal commitments or honored with rituals, regular interactions may dignify the existence of the relationship and acknowledge its importance (Duck, 1994). People commonly expect friendship to offer enjoyment, respite from stress, and support for other significant relationships. Many people do not expect to have to work on their friendships as they do with romantic and family relationships. However, as friends become closer and the benefits of the relationship increase, they also tend to experience more anger and conflict with one another. Betrayals in friendships are relatively common, exceeded only by betrayals between romantic partners, and can easily lead to the severing of the relationship. Typical betrayals include emotional or sexual involvement with a friend's partner, and failure to come to the defense of a friend who is being criticized by others. The most common response to conflict and betrayals in friendship is passive avoidance. Working through difficulties directly is the least common strategy used by friends, even though it tends to produce the most satisfactory outcomes. The most pervasive threat to friendship seems to be changes in people's lives that reduce their ability to interact on a regular basis. However, friends who "drift apart" are more likely to later restore their friendship than friends who end their relationship due to conflict or betrayal (Fehr, 2000).

Friendships and family relationships interact and affect each other significantly throughout the life cycle. The quality and stability of our friendships seem to be connected to the quality of relationships in our families of origin (Karen, 1998), and family relationships are nurtured by the support of friends (Collins & Madsen, 2006; Guiaux, van Tilburg, & van Groenou, 2007; Milevsky, 2005; Sherman, et al., 2006; van Aken & Asendorpf, 1997). When family relationships are strained, we may bring friends with us on visits to help neutralize tension. Additionally, friends can offer outside perspectives on our family members, which may help us resolve conflicts or deepen empathy and intimacy in these relationships. Friends can meet needs that are not fulfilled by family (van Aken & Asendorpf, 1997), and if we lack high-quality friendships, we may unreasonably burden our partners, children, parents, siblings, and other family member with expectations to meet all of our needs.

Friends frequently play special roles in rites of passage and can be irreplaceable sources of support through life cycle transitions. In rites of passage such as weddings, close friends often fill the roles of maid of honor and best man. Asking a friend to fill these roles simultaneously honors the specialness of the friendship, and requests a special level of support. During life cycle transitions, such as adjusting to a new baby, friends may act as essential support systems. A new mother who is breastfeeding may find far more support, encouragement, and relief from a friend who is or has gone through a similar experience than she would from a host of professionals or family members.

The Internet and social media are reshaping the ways we connect with friends and give and receive support when we cannot be together in person. Some have speculated that this technology is changing the concept of friendship and causing people to lose essential social skills (Wang & Wellman, 2010). However, most studies suggest that as the Internet changes the way friends interact, the essential characteristics and expectations of friendships stay the same. Social media and instant messaging have even been shown to enhance intimacy, trust, communication, and commitment between friends (Amichai-Hamburger, Kingsbury, & Schneider, 2013; Reich, Subrahmanyam, & Espinozo, 2012), and increase the likelihood that friends will spend time together in person (Reich et al., 2012; Wang & Wellman, 2010). Additionally, online communication may be used to initiate difficult conversations. For example, adolescents may discuss significant developmental themes such as sexuality online (Reich, et al., 2012) and LGBT people may come out online or post hints about their sexual orientation (DeHaan, Kuper, Magee, Bigelow, & Mustanski, 2013). While it may seem easier to initiate conversation online, communicating through social media also increases misunderstandings and people tend to find it less satisfying than face-to-face interactions (Thompson & Lougheed, 2012).

Most people tend to use online media to enhance existing friendships; however, marginalized groups, such as LGBT people, may find the Internet to be a safer context to find new friends or learn about events such as rallies and parties (DeHaan et al., 2013). Others may go to dating sites looking for romantic partners and find friendship as well as romance (Holt et al., 2012). Usually, meeting online does not replace face-to-face connection, but simply makes meeting in person easier (DeHaan et al., 2013). When friends with key similarities are scarce, people may use the Internet as a primary medium to maintain as well as initiate friendships. For example, Hunyady (2008) writes about friendships that are formed and maintained on a blog for lesbian nuns. Therapists can support clients in using the Internet and social media to escape isolation, initiate friendships, and maintain meaningful connections. Sites such as www.meetup.com provide a forum for people with common interests to meet and join each other in shared activities.

> **Assess your comprehension of trends across the life cycle by completing this quiz.**

Friendship in Childhood and Adolescence

Children of all ages speak passionately about the importance of their friends (Bagwell & Schmidt, 2011). Unfortunately, adults sometimes believe children to be less capable of deep and complex emotions and minimize the significance of childhood friendship (Doka, 2002). In an effort to discourage cliques and bullying, some schools and summer camps are even discouraging elementary and middle school-aged children from having a best friend (Stout, 2010). Well-meaning efforts such as this one fail to take into account decades of research supporting the benefits of close intimate friendships (Bagwell & Schmidt, 2011; Way, 2011). In friendships, children create extra-familial safe havens that validate their worth and provide them with opportunities to try out various forms of self-expression and relationship building (Rubin, Fredstrom, & Bowker, 2008). Friendship supports children through life transitions and promotes empathy, leadership skills, and pro-social behavior (Bagwell & Schmidt, 2011). High-quality friendships reduce the risk of depression, drug use, gang membership, early pregnancy, and suicide (Way, 2011) and may buffer against the negative effects of bullying from peers and rejection or lack of understanding from parents (Bagwell & Schmidt, 2011; Rubin et al., 2008). Close supportive friendships have even been associated with better outcomes for children in therapy (Baker & Hudson, 2013).

Interaction of childhood friendships and family relationships

The benefits of childhood friendship are undeniable. Some theorists have even proposed that childhood friends support development in ways family relationships cannot (Sullivan, 1953). However, the research to date suggests that instead of playing a unique role in childhood development, friendships complement the role of family relationships (Bagwell & Schmidt, 2011). For example, an ongoing task of childhood development is to understand the interpersonal dynamics of emotions and emotional expression. Families and childhood friendships frequently have different rules and expectations for acceptable emotional expression. Consequently, family relationships and friendships complement development as children learn to discern which relational contexts are best suited for the expression and validation of various emotions. Influences from parents and friends also tend to complement one another. Children's choice of friends tends to reflect the core values of their parents (Youniss & Haynie, 1992), and adolescents tend to be more influenced by parents than friends when making decisions with long-term consequences (Bengtson, Biblarz, & Roberts,

2002). Attachment-based research suggests that every aspect of friendship is intimately connected to the quality of relationships between parents and children (Bagwell & Schmidt, 2011; Karen, 1998). Children's relationships with their primary caregivers teach them what to expect from other relationships. Nothing is more effective in teaching children essential relational skills such as empathy, communication, and supportive responsiveness than treating children with empathy, engaging them in communication, and supportively meeting their needs. Whether children tend to feel safe and supported or anxious and uncared for in relationships is closely connected to how well they are understood and cared for in their families (Karen, 1998). While friendship has been shown to buffer against internalizing negative effects of parental rejection (Bagwell & Schmidt, 2011), attachment research has consistently shown that children who have not experienced a securely attached relationship to a caregiver find forming and maintaining high-quality intimate friendships much more challenging than children who are securely attached. Children who have a securely attached relationship to their parent tend to make friends more easily and be more empathetic in their friendships. They read social cues and modify their behaviors in order to form and maintain connections with other children. Children with anxious attachment styles seem less adept at reading social cues and modifying their behaviors. When their attempts to connect irritate other children, they often persist with the same irritating behaviors rather than modify them. Children with an anxious ambivalent attachment style also tend to express more jealousy when their friends want to spend time with other friends. Children with avoidant attachment styles have the most difficulty forming friendships. Adolescents with an avoidant attachment style often isolate themselves or bully other children (Karen, 1998). Children who do not have a secure attachment are as likely to have a friend as securely attached children, but are more likely to have unrealistic expectations of their friends (Selman & Schultz, 1990). They seem to have more difficulty negotiating common tasks of friendships, such as determining roles and resolving conflict (Karen, 1998) and their friendships tend to be less satisfying, less intimate, and less stable (Fredstrom

et al., 2012.; Way, 2011). Children who experience satisfying communication with their parents are also more likely to have high-quality friendships as adults (Schwarz, Stutz, & Ledermann, 2012; Way, 2011). One longitudinal study on adolescent girls found that good communication with mothers and perceiving that parents were happy in their marriage predicted having a high-quality friendship in adulthood. Surprisingly, having a high-quality friendship in adolescence was not associated with whether these girls had a high-quality friendship as an adult (Baril, Julien, Chartrand, & Dubé, 2009).

Developmental characteristics of friendship in childhood and adolescence

Childhood friendships are clearly distinct from other peer relationships. Children experience friendships as more fun than other peer relationships and friends perceive each other as more likeable than non-friends (Bagwell & Schmidt, 2011). Friends enjoy more positive engagement with one another, and more feelings of equality, closeness, and loyalty. They tend to be better at resolving conflicts between themselves and will even perform better on task-related activities than non-friends (Newcomb & Bagwell, 1995).

Characteristics of friendships evolve as children progress through developmental stages. Toddlers may simply show a strong preference for particular peers. They are affectionate with their friends, clearly enjoy their companionship, and respond to their distress. They may even create rituals such as sitting next to one another during story time. Toddlers also engage in more imaginary play with their friends than they do with other peers. This may be an expression of intimacy since young children use symbolic imaginative play to express their inner worlds (Bagwell & Schmidt, 2011).

Companionship, common interests, and play characterize friendships in preschool and the earliest years of elementary school. Children begin to understand that their behavior matters to their friends. Communication, collaboration, and compromise become increasingly important as children develop an understanding of the connections between their behaviors and the quality of their relationships.

Around the age of 9, boys and girls begin to place increased value on loyalty, genuineness, and sharing similar values in their friendships. Children at this age identify closeness, caring, and self-disclosure as the most precious qualities of their friendships (Bagwell & Schmidt, 2011; Way, 2011). Intimacy begins to form, and while behavioral expressions of intimacy change with age and vary across gender, culture, and social class, feeling intimately connected to one's friends remains important through every subsequent stage of development (Selman & Shultz, 1990). As children enter preadolescence, status, popularity, and a sense of belonging become increasingly important. Consequently, while most pre-adolescents use pro-social behaviors to stabilize their friendships, popular children are often able to make and maintain friends by the status and visibility they offer through association (Poorthuis, Thomaes, Denissen, van Aken, & de Castro, 2012). Popularity increases a sense of belonging in school, but does not prevent loneliness when popular children lack close friends. High-quality friendships buffer against loneliness, but do not give children a sense of belonging (Bukowski, Hoza, & Boivin, 1993). Increased social pressure to gain and maintain status may complicate efforts to build and nurture intimacy in friendships adding to the complexity and emotional intensity of this developmental period.

Adolescence is commonly thought of as the developmental stage in which friendship changes dramatically. However, expectations of friendships in adolescence represent more of an evolution of earlier expectations than the formation of something entirely new. The self-disclosure that began to take shape in preadolescent friendships continues to increase and deepen as children progress through adolescence. This sharing builds intimacy and provides more opportunities to demonstrate mutual support and commitment (Bagwell & Schmidt, 2011). Intimate friendships support healthy identity development for adolescents. The voluntary nature of friendships gives adolescents a sense that their interests, ideas, feelings, and personal characteristics truly matter to others (Cotterell, 2007). Adolescents often feel they are able to be their most authentic selves when they are with their friends (Youniss & Smollar, 1985).

Sociocultural factors and friendship in childhood and adolescence

Sociocultural factors play critical roles in children's friendships. Dominant notions that unjustly attribute special worth to some people and devalue others impact children's perceptions of who to be friends with and how to behave in a friendship (Way, 2011). Sociocultural and demographic factors may also be associated with the perception or actual existence of similar interests, values, and experiences that facilitate the formation of friendship bonds. Children and adolescents tend to select friends who are demographically similar to themselves (Rubin et al., 2008), and similarities are associated with friendship closeness and stability (Poulin & Chan, 2010). Children as young as 4 years prefer friends of the same race, and as they get older they are less likely to have an interracial friendship (Aboud & Janani, 2007; Kawabata & Crick, 2011). Children of color tend to have more interracial friends and more positive perceptions of these friendships than their white counterparts. Interestingly, advanced social skills and leadership qualities are associated with having cross-ethnic friendships, while higher levels of aggression are associated with fewer cross-ethnic friendships (Pica-Smith, 2011). Other studies suggest that half of middle school aged children would prefer to not go to school with an LGBT child (Poteat, & Espelage, 2009), and that most children prefer to be friends with a thin child rather than an overweight child (Palmer & Rutland, 2011).

Both boys and girls prefer friends of the same gender with girls showing a stronger preference than boys (Bagwell & Schmidt, 2011). Because girls tend to be better at social skills that stabilize friendships, such as self-disclosure, pro-social behaviors, and conflict resolution, it seems their friendships would be more stable. However, some studies suggest that in fact girls have less stable friendships than boys (Benenson & Christakos, 2003). While girls and boys have the same kinds of expectations from friends, girls may have higher standards for how these expectations ought to be fulfilled and be more sensitive to interpersonal stress and friendship transgressions (MacEvoy & Asher, 2012).

While boys tend to bond around activities (Rose & Rudolph, 2006), the notion that boys desire less intimacy in their friendships is incorrect. Way's, 2011 longitudinal research revealed that the thing 10- to 15-year-old boys value most in their friendships with other boys is having someone with whom they can share their inner most feelings and secrets. Boys in Way's research frequently reported that this is not only something they value but also something that "keeps them sane." However, between the ages of 16 and 18, boys' friendships become highly unstable. At this age, internalized patriarchal and homophobic definitions of mature masculinity begin to interfere with boys' ability to cultivate intimacy in their friendships with each other. They come to think of self disclosure and intimacy between boys as immature, girlish, or gay. As expressing emotions and the need for support becomes the anathema, the "antithesis of manliness," boys begin to feel that they must choose between intimacy and masculinity. By late adolescence these cultural rules lead most boys to a sense of deep alienation (Way, 2011).

As boys grow into men, they continue to long for the intimacy and emotional support they enjoyed in their male friendships when they were younger. Sadly, most boys and men find it too challenging to reconcile patriarchal notions of manliness with their truest desires. However, those who resist patriarchal notions of masculinity are most likely to continue to have emotionally supportive and intimate friendships (Garfield, 2015; Way, 2011).

> Assess your comprehension of friendship in childhood and adolescence by completing this quiz.

Adult Friendships

In adulthood, friends continue to enrich life with fun, companionship, support, and intimacy. They offer a range of perspectives on experiences and provide advice and support on other relationships and critical life decisions.

Friends help one another laugh at their shortcomings, empower one another to face their fears, and remind one another of their abilities and worth. Important life events and rituals such as weddings, births of children, and funerals are often made complete by the presence of friends. During these significant life events, people commonly honor the special role a friend has played in their life, and express a hope that this special connection will continue, by asking friends to fulfill special roles, such as a godparent. Sharing significant and intimate life events weaves friends together in the fabric of one another's lives. Long-term friends may be particularly special to people for this reason.

Friends and resiliency

Despite the significance of friendships, they are not always the highest priority relationship in adults' lives. Friends may interact less when they are investing energy into developing careers or relationships with romantic partners. Therefore, friendships are more stable when friends are flexible with one another. Flexibility also increases the sense that friendships are relationships in which people can find respite. Friendship between well-adjusted individuals can be drawn on at times when life becomes arduous. However, friendships between ill-adjusted individuals may lack reciprocal support, create distress, and even impair development (Hartup & Stevens, 1999).

Supportive friendships provide companionship and increase self-esteem and happiness, while an absence of quality friendships is correlated to negative effects such as poor physical health and loneliness (Rowe & Kahn, 1998; Weiss, 1974). Supportive friendships can reduce the psychological impact of stress, including stressful situations connected to one's family. Friends may even make up for support that is missing from family members due to illness, death, or an emotional or physical absence (Collins & Madsen, 2006; Guiaux et al., 2007; Milevsky, 2005). Family fragmentation is a common consequence of oppression (Hardy & Lazsloffy, 2005). A resilient quality of oppressed groups such as African Americans and LGBT people is an ability to replace more traditional family support systems with strong friendship networks (Ellison, 1990; Malley & Tasker, 2007).

Gender and adult heterosexual friendships

Gender remains a centrally organizing factor in adult friendships. Women are commonly characterized as building intimate friendships through conversation, self-disclosure, and nurturing emotional support, while men are characterized as building friendships around activities and common interests (Fehr, 1996; Muraco, 2012). Although these broad characterizations capture common qualities of same sex heterosexual friendships, they may reflect compliance with dominant sex-role scripts more than inherent qualities of men and women. Furthermore, they do not capture the nuances and feelings beneath observable surface patterns measured by quantitative research. Throughout their lives, girls and women tend to be encouraged and rewarded for sharing feelings, providing emotional support, and acting in ways that stabilize relationships. Because of this, women can weave meaningful conversation and self-disclosure into their interactions even when they are engaged in activities. Women tend to experience more frequency of self-disclosure (Aries & Johnson, 1983) and more depth in their conversations (Farrell, 1985). Friendships between women have also been found to contain more reciprocal support and to be more secure than friendships between men (Voss, Markiewicz, & Doyle, 1999). However, some studies suggest that friendships between women can be competitive (Werking, 1997), and some women may find female friends to be too sensitive and dramatic at times (Rawlins, 2009).

Men tend to build friendships around shared activities (Wright & Scalon, 1991). In addition to being fun and gratifying in their own right, activities may serve as a way for men to build emotional intimacy over time (Fehr, 1996; Muraco, 2012). Friendships between men tend to contain less self-disclosure and emotional support. However, men place a high value on emotional closeness in their friendships with other men, and long for more, but dominant sex-scripts about manliness make men hesitant to initiate this type of intimate exchange with other men. Men who have friendships rich in self-disclosure and emotional support are still not as likely to have as many of these friendships as women (Fehr, 1996; Muraco, 2012).

Can women and men be friends? For decades, this has been the theme of countless films, television shows, and novels, which usually answer the question with a resounding, "No!" When the question

was famously asked in the film *When Harry Met Sally*, the story unfolded to suggest Sally's notion that men and women could be friends was naive, and affirm Harry's assertion that sex will always get in the way. Even the cast of *Friends* could not remain "just friends." Despite the stories told in popular culture, numerous studies indicate that friendships between men and women are common (Fehr, 1996; Monsour, 2002; Rawlins, 2009). In fact, cross-sex friendships often provide men and women opportunities to stretch the boundaries of rigid gender scripts. Men commonly report being more satisfied with the emotional support they receive from female friends and women enjoy the laidback nature of male friends. Cross-sex friends offer validation about one another's attractiveness and desirability. Men and women also provide one another with an insider's perspective into the other gender, which friends find particularly useful for their romantic relationships (Monsour, 2002; Rawlins, 2009).

The media portrayal of difficulties with cross-sex friendships is not entirely unfounded though. Rather than asking whether men and women can be friends, it seems a more useful question is how potential sexual attraction and power inequalities challenge these friendships (Fehr, 1996; O'Meara, 1989). Even though it is unreasonable to assume sexual attraction between men and women is inevitable, our society generally lacks a way to make sense of close emotional bonds between men and women that do not involve sexual attraction. Instead compulsory sexuality is assumed whenever emotional intimacy is created across gender (Monsour, 2002; Muraco, 2012). While this dominant discourse denies the emotional experiences of all queer people and many cross-sex friendships, it does describe the ideological context in which cross-sex friendships exist. Consequently, men and women have few non-romantic models of closeness to help them make sense of the emotional bonds they form with one another (O'Meara, 1989; Muraco, 2012). Men are particularly prone to misinterpret friendliness as flirtation (Fehr, 1996). If this is not confusing enough, friends and family of close cross-sex friends often pressure them to become a couple or simply hook up to see what happens. Partners of these friends frequently struggle to accept that there are not romantic or sexual undertones to the friendship, which easily leads to jealousy (Fehr, 1996; Monsour, 2002).

Sexual and romantic attraction does sometimes emerge in cross-sex friendships. It is commonly believed that friendship ends when romance begins. According to this belief, romance either ruins friendship or transforms it into something that can no longer be considered a friendship. However, it seems that this is not necessarily the case. Many cross-sex friendships are maintained despite unreciprocated or mutual attraction. Some friends may have sex and then decide to end a sexual relationship and maintain a platonic friendship, while others may incorporate sex into their friendship without any expectations of love or commitment. If attraction or sex becomes a part of a friendship, friends need to find ways to negotiate boundaries and expectations on an ongoing basis. Attraction and sex are, however, commonly reported as undermining cross-sex friendships (Monsour, 2002). Difficulty negotiating boundaries and expectations is undoubtedly part of the undoing of these friendships; however, it seems reasonable to assume that emotions such as love, desire, betrayal, and jealously make it difficult to maintain friendships regardless of how well boundaries and expectations have been defined.

Equality is a definitive characteristic of friendship. Therefore, some have argued that as long as social inequality between men and women exist, true friendships between them cannot be achieved (O'Meara, 1989). Some studies suggest that disparities of power and privilege manifest in cross-sex friendships in a number of subtle ways. Women tend to defer to the relational style of men in cross-sex friendships (Fehr, 1996). A number of studies also suggest that men tend to avoid the discomfort of seeking emotional support from other men, and instead rely on female friends to follow dominant social expectations and be their emotional caretakers (Monsour, 2002; Muraco, 2012; Rawlins, 2009; Way, 2011). Additionally, there are countless ways our society privileges male ways of being by defining them as strong, secure, mature, and rational and devalues female ways of being by defining them as weak, emotional, dramatic, and dependent. It is impossible to estimate how much these dominant social messages impact the ability of women to fully

express themselves in their friendships with men. Additionally, men are likely to act out of privilege in these friendships, denying or redefining ways in which women experience the friendship as restrictive and devaluing. Similarly women are likely to silence their own voice in these friendships and deny their own experiences in order to ensure the comfort of men (Hardy & Laszloffy, 2002). Power inequalities certainly challenge cross-sex friendships and the degree to which both friends can be authentic with one another. However, Hardy and Laszloffy, 2002 assert that all relationships contain some disparities of power and privilege, and that greater levels of authentic intimate connection may be achieved by addressing these inequalities.

Heterosexual couples and friendships

Romantic relationships frequently present challenges to friendships. The formation of a couple involves more than a partnership between two people. Couples must find a way to integrate other aspects of their lives, including friends they had when they were single. Some of these friends may integrate easily into the new relationship while others may not get along with their friend's partner or have difficulty accepting the relationship. Friendships that were not very close or were based on activities that do not fit the couple's relationship may be lost at this time (Johnson & Leslie, 1982). Activities that couples enjoy together often lead to the formation of new friendships, and couples may gravitate toward spending time with other couples because of common experiences. The formation of new friends and the loss of others during this life cycle transition appears to be informed by gender dynamics. Women tend to change their conversational style to accommodate their male partners and their friends much more than men. Women also tend to experience less emotional intimacy in their friendships with other couples than they do in their individual friendships, while men experience about the same level of emotional intimacy (Greif & Deal, 2012a).

Friendships also support the stability of couple relationships. Couples with shared friendships tend to be happier and have longer-lasting friendships. As a couple's relationship becomes more established, interacting with other couples becomes a way to rekindle some excitement and novelty (Slatcher, 2010). Friends are a crucial component in the lives and well-being of couples. They provide a platform where not only general family problems can be discussed but also a place where marital distress may be shared (Allgood, Crane, & Agee, 1997). Being able to process one's romantic relationship with friends often supports much of the work of that relationship and plays a critical role in the growth of a couple (Helms, Crouter, & McHale, 2003).

Friendships and divorce

Divorced couples experience the pain of emotional, financial, social, and relational losses. When couples divorce, their shared network of friends is often threatened. Friends may take sides with one member of the divorcing couple or distance themselves or cut off completely in an effort to avoid getting caught in the middle of the couple's conflict. As a couple divorces, each partner may distance themselves from friends who are connected to their partner or their deteriorating marriage, and seek out new friends instead. (Greif & Deal, 2012b). Studies that investigated the impact of divorce on friendships have found that approximately half of the people who go through divorce lose some, if not all, of their friends in the process (Greif & Deal, 2012b; Rands, 1988). When friendships are preserved, it is usually with long-time friends , or with the same-sex partner of couples who had been friends of the divorcing couple (Greif & Deal, 2012b). While one's overall social network may wane during and after divorce, this does not necessarily translate to a lack of relational intimacy in one's friendships. The friendships one does maintain are frequently reservoirs of support for divorcing couples (Wang & Amato, 2000).

Little research has been conducted on friendships between former spouses. The prominent view is that romantic relationships end because they are dysfunctional and the best solution to healing is to sever all ties. However, a variety of relational possibilities exist between former spouses, including close friendship (Stacey, 1990). Some former partners are able to transcend "broken" relationships, confirm one another's growth, and create strong friendships (Masheter, 1998). These friends may

continue to provide assistance in roles they once took in their marriages, such as cooking meals or doing repairs around the house (Ahrons, 1994). Other former partners may develop a friendship that focuses on the well-being of their children (Masheter, 1998).

When working with individuals who are ending intimate relationships, therapists should emphasize the importance of investing in old and new friendships. Friends can provide special gifts such as providing a supportive ear, offering different perspectives on how to live one's life, and sharing valuable information on parenting as a new single parent. Therapists can also encourage clients to bring their friends to therapy. In therapy, friends can develop an intimate understanding on the significance of the loss and therefore be better equipped to nurture the friendship.

Friendships in Later Life

Friends are a valuable resource in later life as they continue to offer companionship and functional support (Rook & Ituarte, 1999). Lifelong friends can provide validation of one's life experiences to one another as they transition into later life (Hartup & Stevens, 1997; Sias & Bartoo, 2007). Friends in later life can serve as confidants, assist in day-to-day living, and provide emotional support. Despite the importance and vitality of these relationships, there is a decline in friendships with increasing age (Shaw, Krause, Liang, & Bennet, 2007; Stevens & van Tilburg, 2011). This can be attributed to loss such as limited mobility, abilities, or illness. Older individuals may also become selective in their interactions due to their awareness of potential death (Carstensen, 1992). With age, tangential friendships seem to become increasingly unimportant, and close relationships that offer greater relational intimacy become centralized.

It is not uncommon for men to rely on one female partner to meet most, if not all, of their emotional needs in young adulthood and midlife. In later life, these men may not have sufficiently developed the skills to form other supportive friendships, and are particularly prone to isolation and loneliness if their partner becomes ill or dies (Wall, Pickert, & Paradise, 1984). Women have a longer life expectancy than men, which has several implications for their friendships in later life. As women age, they are likely to lose male partners, family members, and friends. Consequently, they are at greater risk for loneness in later life (Knipscheer et al., 1995). Close friendships may increasingly become some of the most central relationships for elderly women, especially if they have lost their partners and are distant from other family. Physical condition, social circumstances, and the extent to which family members are present influence the degree to which older women socialize with friends (Powers, 1996). Due in part to the greater life expectancy for women, they tend to have more same-sex friendships and fewer cross-sex friendships as they age (Stevens & van Tilburg, 2011).

Simply having friends, however, is not enough to protect the elderly from loneliness. Just as anyone else, they need a network of friends who can meet a variety of needs (Stevens & van Tilburg, 2000). Some elderly people who have not developed skills to initiate and solidify friendships earlier in life may be particularly prone to isolation and loneliness. Places of worship, political and community organizations, charities, and clubs have long provided them with ways to connect in meaningful communities. Additionally, social programs designed to provide common platforms for the elderly to come together and share their common and unique experiences may be instrumental in helping them form strong supportive friendship networks (Roberto, 1996). The following vignette highlights themes of friendship in later life while also touching on the significance of friendship at other stages of the life cycle.

CASE ILLUSTRATION

Jyoti

Jyoti (68 years old) recently lost her husband, Baltej, to cancer. In the past 2 years, she along with her two sons, Dev and Raj, and daughters-in-law, Meena and Jennifer, had cared for Balraj over the course of his illness, providing palliative care. The children, who live in different cities, set up a schedule so that someone would be with Jyoti at all times. Jyoti and Baltej's core group of friends who had been through the ups and downs of life with them have also been

instrumental in the daily care and support of the family during this difficult time. These friends had a special place in Baltej and Jyoti's life. The common theme that brought this group of friends together was that they all immigrated from India to the United States decades ago, leaving parents and siblings behind. They became one another's family of choice.

The transition into widowhood has been highly stressful for Jyoti. She has withdrawn from people and activities that once gave her joy and struggles with accepting that she will not have physical access to Baltej anymore. While she continues to grieve over the loss of her husband, she is faced with several decisions that require her attention. Jyoti's children would like her to change cities and move in with one of them, selling the home she and Baltej once shared. Jyoti and Baltej's friends would like her to continue living in her own home and adjust to a new life without Baltej. In addition, Jyoti's dream of moving back to her birthplace, India, seems much more attainable now that she can take charge of her own life as a single person.

The therapist assisted Jyoti in her transition to widowhood by encouraging her to express her grief. While these experiences are typical of those who have lost loved ones, so is the initial realignment of the family. Encouraging the family to share their concerns about the reality of daily living for Jyoti is paramount. For Jyoti, her friends have had a significant role in her life. They are a part of her family. Inviting friends to the family's therapy sessions was highly beneficial. Jyoti's friends provided assurance that they will continue to care for her as she moves through and beyond this transition. They also provided insight and reflection on Jyoti's life prior to her loss. This insider's knowledge spoke to the dreams and values that Jyoti holds for her life, informing her children of what their mother has valued, and reminding Jyoti of her interests and resiliency. Her friends also benefitted from facing their own feelings of loss during this difficult time. In therapy, Dev and Raj were reminded of the importance of friendship and discussed how disconnected they felt from their friends lately. The illness of their father and their worry for their mother had taken over their lives. The therapist facilitated a process by which Dev and Raj could invite their friends back into their lives. Reentry into life without Baltej is also difficult for Jyoti. Whatever decision she makes about her living situation, reaffirming the role of her friends in her life as a widow is critical to her well-being.

Friendships among lesbian, gay, and bisexual people

Lesbian, gay, bisexual, and transgendered people are immersed in societies that demonize them, question the validity of their truest identities and the worthiness of their love, and deny them hundreds of rights afforded to heterosexuals. For generations, queer people have been cultivating friendships that nurture their identities and self-worth in a pervasive context of dehumanization. They have committed themselves to friendships that are as, if not more, meaningful, intimate, and supportive than family relationships. These friendships may be the most stable and long-lasting relationships in their lives. Queer people commonly create families of choice that may consist of friends, family, mentors, partners, and past partners and lovers (Malley & Tasker, 2007). Families of choice, which may be formed at any point during the life cycle, support members through various developmental challenges, and celebrate important milestones and rites of passage. Rituals such as monthly gatherings and retreats are often created to solidify bonds. For some members, the family of choice might serve as a primary family, while other members may have a partner, children, and strong ties to their family of origin as well (Ariel, 2008). In either case, families of choice nurture self-worth and competence and offer members wisdom and guidance in the context of safe and secure relationships (Mitchell, 2008).

While there is a great deal of variance in whom queer people befriend, and how they cultivate intimacy, being familiar with some trends can help prevent therapists from judging queer friendships through a heteronormative lens. Lesbians, gay men, and bisexuals commonly have more friends than heterosexuals and tend to receive more support from friends than they do from their families of origin. Friendships between lesbians are often rich with emotional expression and support (Galupo, 2007a). The emotional closeness in lesbian friendships sometimes leads to attraction, sex, and romantic relationships. When romantic relationships between lesbians end, it is fairly common for them to work on preserving emotionally intimate friendships. These friendships can generate jealousy and suspicion for new romantic partners (Degges-White, 2012). Friendships between gay men sometimes start off as casual sexual relationships that gradually grow in emotional intimacy. These friendships may be preserved whether a sexual relationship ends or continues to be a part of their friendship. Some gay men find sex to rapidly increase emotional intimacy, but most find sex to be damaging to their friendships. Emotional intimacy tends to be highly valued in close friendships between gay men, and friends are commonly viewed as the most consistent and reliable people in their lives (Nardi, 1999). However, gay men may be most satisfied with the emotional support they receive from women (Galupo, 2007a; Shippy et al., 2004), and at least one study has suggested that older gay men do not receive as much emotional support as they desire (Shippy et al., 2004).

In general, queer people tend to be most satisfied with the support they receive from people who embrace their sexual orientation. Perhaps, it is for this reason that bisexuals tend to have the most difficulty creating networks of support. Bisexuals are less likely than lesbians and gay men to have friends of the same sexual orientation, and less likely to have friends and family who accept their sexual orientation. They tend to have more straight friends than their gay and lesbian counterparts. In order to preserve friendships with straight friends, they often refrain from discussing sex and dating same-sex partners. When they do discuss same-sex partners with straight friends, it is not uncommon for straight friends to distance themselves (Galupo, 2007b). A similar trend has been found in friendships between gay and straight men. While these friendships can be close and supportive, when gay men do not conform to heteronormative expectations, there is a much greater chance of the straight friend distancing himself (Barrett, 2013).

Friendships across both gender and sexual orientation have been associated with a variety of benefits. An understanding that these friendships will not become sexual facilitates increased trust and intimacy between male and female friends. Straight men and women commonly place a high value on the liberty they feel to step outside rigid gender scripts in the contexts of these friendships, which also provide an opportunity to increase insight and awareness into one another's experiences. Queer friends find it beneficial to have windows into the lives and relationships of their straight friends. Cross-gender friendships can also facilitate greater understanding and sensitivity to the experiences of men and women. Men in these friendships commonly report an increased awareness of male privilege and greater respect for women, while women commonly report an increased ability to trust men. Cross-orientation friendships usually help straight people develop greater empathy and understanding into the experiences of gay and lesbian friends, normalize same sex relationships, and increase insight into the oppression and injustices queer people endure (Muraco, 2012).

However, friendship across differences in and of itself is not enough to eradicate the internalization of stereotypical and devaluing social discourses about gender and sexual orientation. Friendships across gender and sexual orientation differences are formed in a heteronormative context that equates emotional intimacy between men and women with romance and sexual passion. Women and men in these friendships often find themselves struggling to convince others that their friendship is both platonic and valuable. Women may want a gay friend to be in their wedding, which challenges heteronormative traditions. Gay male friends often experience anticipatory grief when their straight female friends plan for marriage, and rightly so. These friendships tend to become much more distant after straight friends marry. Friends also commonly act out of sexist and heteronormative socialization, which may directly or indirectly devalue the self-worth of their friends. Straight men tend to expect advice on dating women and emotional support from lesbian friends, even though lesbians are more likely to receive emotional support from their female friends (Muraco, 2012). Straight women often enjoy affirmation on physical appearance and positive validation from men that does not contain sexual overtones, but this affirmation reinforces dominant expectations about physical appearance being directly proportional to a woman's worth (Muraco, 2012). Straight women may express homophobia or reinforce stereotypical notions that gay men are hypersexual, while gay men may express sexist beliefs (Muraco, 2012; Rumens, 2008).

Just as friends continue to be important even when queer people have supportive families, family remains important even when queer people have strong friendship networks. Many queer people identify family members as friends, and find family members to be among the most important people in their support networks. Support and acceptance from family has been associated with significant mental health benefits and reduced risk of self-harming behaviors (Ryan, Russell, Huebner, Diaz, & Sanchez, 2010). The support LGBT people receive from friends and family may benefit them in distinctly unique ways. For example, one study of young adults in Israel found that support from friends was closely linked with the likelihood that a queer person would come out, while support from family was more closely linked with self-acceptance. While these possible distinctions are interesting, the importance of acceptance and support from both family and friends cannot be overemphasized. Acceptance from both friends and family is associated with less internalized homophobia and binegativity, greater self-worth, less high-risk and negative coping behaviors, more hopefulness for the future, and greater overall life satisfaction (Ryan et al., 2010; Sheets & Mohr, 2009). The following case provides a clinical application for many of the themes discussed throughout this chapter.

CASE ILLUSTRATION

Greg

Greg (37) and Kevin (46) met at a club shortly after Kevin had moved to the Silicon Valley from Los Angeles. At that time, Greg had a wife and a son, Jason. Greg and Kevin had an affair that rapidly became serious. Eventually, Greg left his wife and moved in with Kevin. Greg wrestled with a great deal of shame related to his upbringing that taught him being gay was sinful and gross, and feeling that he had ruined his wife and son's lives. It was extremely difficult for Greg to accept himself and to come out to the people who mattered most to him. Kevin was the only gay man Greg was close with, and he leaned exclusively on him for support. Kevin was raised by his white mother and had very little contact with his African American father. Embracing both his mixed ethnicity and sexual orientation was extremely challenging for Kevin. As a child his mother would tell him that "it didn't matter" that he was Black. When he came out to her, she simply told him that she loved him anyway, but it was probably best for him not to tell his grandparents. Kevin learned to love and accept himself in a community of queer people of color in Los Angeles. One friend, Julian, was the first person with whom Kevin felt that he could be both African American and gay. Kevin had grown more distant from these friends due to investing so much energy into his job and his relationship with Greg. He grew weary of providing Greg with so much support while feeling like he was getting very little in return. Kevin felt isolated and overlooked at his new job and suspected his race had a lot to do with it. He had not talked about it much with Greg, because he was not sure Greg would understand and did not want the added stress of educating Greg about racism.

As the couple worked to increase mutual understanding and support in their relationship, they began to recognize that they needed friendship support to complement the support they gave one another. Greg realized that his dependence on Kevin

placed an unfair burden on him. He decided to seek out more gay friends and mentors. Therapy also helped Greg be a witness to Kevin's experiences of racism and exclusion at work. Kevin was grateful for Greg's increased empathy, but realized that as a white man Greg simply could not give him the same feeling of belonging and understanding he had with his community of friends in Los Angeles. Kevin reached out to these friends again and established an annual dinner to ensure they maintained their relationships. The therapist encouraged Kevin and Greg to deepen friendships with other couples who could provide understanding and support for their relationship. Kevin invited a friend from work over for dinner, an African American woman whose Christian parents had not approved of her marrying an Islamic Persian man. The couples shared stories of ways they had learned to rely on friends to celebrate milestones and hold joy for their relationship when family was unable to. Greg was also concerned that his 15-year-old son was growing isolated. Jason joined a few sessions and shared that he was unsure how his friends would react if they knew his dad was gay. Consequently, Jason had said very little about his dad or his parents' divorce. The therapist got permission to meet Jason and two of his closest friends at school. Jason's friends were very accepting. The conversation inspired one friend to share that his mother had bipolar disorder, which he had not told anyone before this session. The three friends made a pact to be honest with each other, and to always provide each other support.

> **Assess your comprehension of friendships in later life by completing this quiz.**

— Conclusion

This chapter has summarized general themes found in the current literature related to friendship. It may be obvious to many that friendships are extremely significant throughout the life cycle. However, lack of emphasis on friendships in the family therapy literature, training, and supervision may lead beginning therapists to neglect them in their clinical work. We invite readers to consider the potential

of exploring themes of friendship with their clients. How might friends be able to complement the roles of family members as clients work through life cycle tasks? How might therapy help people work through relational difficulties in friendships and work toward greater levels of intimacy and mutual support? When clients talk about distancing themselves from friends, how might therapists investigate underlying fusion that may play a role in conflicts and tension? We believe therapy will be richer and more effective when therapists keep these questions and others like them in mind.

> **Recall what you learned in this chapter by completing the Chapter Review.**

References

Aboud, F. E., & Janani, S. (2007). Friendship and identity in a language-integrated school. *International Journal of Behavioral Development, 31*(5), 445–453. doi: 10.1177/0165025407081469

Ahrons, C. (1994). *The good divorce*. Harper Collins.

Allgood, S. M., Crane, D., & Agee, L. (1997). Social support: Distinguishing clinical and volunteer couples. *American Journal of Family Therapy, 25*(2), 111–119. doi:10.1080/01926189708251060

Amichai-Hamburger, Y., Kingsbury, M., & Schneider, B. H. (2013). Friendship: An old concept with a new meaning? *Computers in Human Behavior, 29*(1), 33–39.

Ariel, J. (2008). Women aging together in community. *Journal of Lesbian Studies, 12*(2/3), 283–292.

Aries, E. J., & Johnson, F. L. (1983). Close friendship in adulthood: Conversational content between same-sex friends. *Sex Roles, 9*(12), 1183–1196. doi:10.1007/BF00303101

Bagwell, C. L., & Schmidt, M. E. (2011). *Friendships in childhood & adolescence*. New York: Guilford.

Baker, J. R., & Hudson, J. L. (2013). Friendship quality predicts treatment outcome in children with anxiety disorders. *Behaviour Research and Therapy, 51*(1), 31–36. doi: 10.1016/j.brat.2012.10.005

Baril, H., Julien, D., Chartrand, É., & Dubé, M. (2009). Females' quality of relationships in adolescence and friendship support in adulthood. *Canadian Journal of Behavioural Science, 41*(3), 161–168. doi: 10.1037/a0015313

Barrett, T. (2013). Friendships between men across sexual orientation: The importance of (others) being intolerant. *The Journal of Men's Studies, 21*(1), 62–77. doi: 10.3149/jms.2101.62

Benenson, J. F., & Christakos, A. (2003). The greater fragility of females' versus males' closest same-sex friendships. *Child Development, 74*(4), 1123–1129.

Bengtson, V. L., Biblarz, T. J., & Roberts, R. E. L. (2002). *How Families still matter: A longitudinal study of youth in two generations*. New York: Cambridge University Press.

Bukowski, W. M., Hoza, B., & Boivin, M. (1993). Popularity, friendship, and emotional adjustment during adolescence. In B. Laursen (Ed.), *Close friendships in adolescence: New Directions for Child Development* (pp. 23–37). San Francisco: Jossey-Bass.

Carstensen, L. L. (1992). Social and emotional patterns in adulthood: Support for socioemotional selectivity theory. *Psychology and Aging, 7*(3), 331–338. doi:10.1037/0882-7974.7.3.331

Collins, W., & Madsen, S. D. (2006). Personal relationships in adolescence and early adulthood. In A. L. Vangelisti & D. Perlman (Eds.), *The Cambridge handbook of personal relationships* (pp. 191–209). New York, NY: Cambridge University Press.

Cotterell, J. (2007). *Social networks in youth and adolescence* (2nd ed.). New York: Routledge

Degges-White, S. (2012). Lesbian friendships: An exploration of lesbian social support networks. *Adultspan Journal, 11*(1), 16–26.

DeHaan, S., Kuper, L. E., Magee, J. C., Bigelow, L., & Mustanski, B. S. (2013). The interplay between online and offline explorations of identity, relationships, and sex: A mixed-methods study with LGBT youth. *Journal of Sex Research, 50*(5), 421–434. doi: 10.1080/00224499.2012.661489

Demir, M., Özen, A., Doğan, A., Bilyk, N. A., Tyrell, F. A. (2011). I matter to my friend, therefore I am happy: Friendship, mattering, and happiness. *Journal of Happiness Studies, 12*(6), 983–1005. doi: 10.1007/s10902-010-9240-8

Doka, K. J. (2002). *Disenfranchised grief: New directions, challenges, and strategies for practice*. Champaign, IL: Research Press

Duck, S. (1994). Steady as (s)he goes: Relational maintenance as a shared meaning system. In D. J. Canary & L. Stafford (Eds.), *Communication and relational maintenance* (pp. 45–60). New York: Academic Press.

Ellison, C. G. (1990). Family ties, friendships, and subjective well-being among Black Americans. *Journal of Marriage and the Family, 52*(2), 298–310. doi:10.2307/353027

Farrell, M. P. (1985). Friendship between men. *Marriage & Family Review, 9*(3–4), 163–197. doi:10.1300/J002v09n03_12

Fehr, B. (1996). *Friendship processes*. Thousand Oaks, CA: Sage.

Fehr, B. (2000). The life cycle of friendship. In C. Hendrick, & S. S. Hendrick (Eds.), *Close relationships: A sourcebook* (pp. 71–82). Thousand Oaks, CA: Sage.

Fredstrom, B. K., Rose-Krasnor, L., Campbell, K., Rubin, K. H., Booth-LaForce, C., & Burgess, K. B. (2012). Brief report: How anxiously withdrawn preadolescents think about friendship. *Journal of Adolescence, 35*(2), 451–454.

Galupo, M. P. (2007a). Friendship patterns of sexual minority individuals in adulthood. *Journal of Social and Personal Relationships, 24*(1), 139–151.

Galupo, M. P. (2007b). Women's close friendships across sexual orientation: A comparative analysis of lesbian-heterosexual and bisexual-heterosexual women's friendships. *Sex Roles 56*(7-8), 473–482. doi: 10.1007/s11199-007-9186-4

Garfield, R. (2015). *Breaking the male code. Unlocking the power of friendship.* New York: Gotham Books.

Greif, G. L., & Deal, K. (2012a). The impact of divorce on friendships with couples and individuals. *Journal of Divorce & Remarriage, 53*(6), 421–435. doi:10.1080/10502556.2012.682894

Greif, G. L., & Deal, K. (2012b). *Two plus two: Couples and their couple friendships.* New York, NY: Routledge/Taylor & Francis Group.

Guiaux, M., van Tilburg, T., & van Groenou, M. (2007). Changes in contact and support exchange in personal networks after widowhood. *Personal Relationships, 14*(3), 457–473. doi:10.1111/j.1475-6811.2007.00165.x

Hardy, K. V., & Laszloffy, T. A. (2002). Couple therapy using a multicultural perspective. In A. S. Gurman & N. S. Jacobson (Eds.), *Clinical handbook of couple therapy* (3rd ed., pp. 569–593). New York, NY: Guilford Press.

Hardy, K. V., & Laszloffy, T. A. (2005). *Teens who hurt: Clinical interventions to break the cycle of adolescent violence.* New York: Guilford Press.

Hartup, W. W., & Stevens, N. (1997). Friendships and adaptation in the life course. *Psychological Bulletin, 121*(3), 355–370. doi:10.1037/0033-2909.121.3.355

Hartup, W. W., & Stevens, N. (1999). Friendships and adaptation across the life span. *Current Directions in Psychological Science, 8*(3), 76–79. doi:10.1111/1467-8721.00018

Helms, H. M., Crouter, A. C., & McHale, S. M. (2003). Marital quality and spouses' marriage work with close friends and each other. *Journal of Marriage and Family, 65*(4), 963–977. doi:10.1111/j.1741-3737.2003.00963.x

Holt, M., Rawstorne, P., Wilkinson, J., Worth, H., Bittman, M., Kippax, S. (2012). HIV testing, gay community involvement and internet use: social and behavioural correlates of HIV testing among Australian men who have sex with men. *AIDS and Behavior, 13*(1), 13–22. doi: 10.1007/s10461-010-9872-z

Hunyady, M. K. (2008). We are family: I got all my sisters with me! *Journal of Lesbian Studies, 12*(2–3), 293–300. doi: 10.1080/10894160802161489

Johnson, M. P., & Leslie, L. (1982). Couple involvement and network structure: A test of the dyadic withdrawal hypothesis. *Social Psychology Quarterly, 45*(1), 34–43. doi:10.2307/3033672

Karen, R. (1998). *Becoming attached: First relationships and how they shape our capacity to love.* New York: Oxford University Press.

Kawabata, Y., & Crick, N. R. (2011). The antecedents of friendships in moderately diverse classrooms: *Social preference, social impact, and social behavior. International Journal of Behavioral Development, 35*(1), 48–57. doi: 10.1177/0165025410368946

Knipscheer, C. P. M., de Jong Gierveld, J., van Tilburg, T. G., & Dykstra, P. A. (Eds.). (1995). *Living arrangements and social networks of older adults.* Amsterdam: Free University Press.

MacEvoy, J. P., & Asher, S. R. (2012). When friends disappoint: Boys' and girls' responses to transgressions of friendship expectations. *Child Development, 83*(1), 104–119. doi: 10.1111/j.1467-8624.2011.01685.x

Malley, M., & Tasker, F. (2007). 'The difference that makes a difference': What matters to lesbians and gay men in psychotherapy. *Journal of Gay and Lesbian Psychotherapy 11*(1–2), 93–109. doi: 10.1300/J236v11n01_07

Masheter, C. (1998). Friendships between former spouses: Lessons in doing case-study research. *Journal of Divorce & Remarriage, 28*(3-4), 73–96. doi:10.1300/J087v28n03_04

Milevsky, A. (2005). Compensatory patterns of sibling support in emerging adulthood: Variations in loneliness, self-esteem, depression and life satisfaction. *Journal of Social and Personal Relationships, 22*(6), 743–755. doi:10.1177/0265407505056447

Mitchell, V. (2008). Choosing family: Meaning and membership in the lesbian family of choice. *Journal of Lesbian Studies, 12*(2-3), 301–313. doi: 10.1080/10894160802161497

Monsour, M. (2002). *Women and men as friends: Relationships across the life span in the 21st century.* Mahwah, NJ: Lawrence Erlbaum Associates.

Muraco, A. (2012). *Odd couples: Friendship at the intersection of gender and sexual orientation.* London: Duke University Press.

Nardi, P. M. (1999). *Gay men's friendships: Invincible communities.* Chicago, IL: University of Chicago Press.

Newcomb, A. F., & Bagwell, C. L. (1995). Children's friendship relations: A meta-analytic review. *Psychological Bulletin, 117*, 306–347.

O'Meara, J. D. (1989). Cross-sex friendship: Four basic challenges of an ignored relationship. *Sex Roles, 21* (7–8), 525–543. doi: 10.1007/BF00289102

Palmer, S., Rutland, A. (2011). Do children want skinny friends? The role of 'weight' in children's friendship preferences and inter-group attitudes. *Anales de Psicologia, 27*(3), 698–707.

Pica-Smith, C. (2011). Children's perceptions of interethnic and interracial friendships in a multiethnic school context. *Journal of Research in Childhood Education 25*(2), 119–132. doi: 10.1080/02568543.2011.555495

Poorthuis, A. M. G., Thomaes, S., Denissen, J. J. A., van Aken, M. A. G., Orobio de Castro, B. (2012). Prosocial tendencies predict friendship quality, but not for popular children. *Journal of Experimental Child Psychology, 112*(4), 378–388. doi: 10.1016/j.jecp.2012.04.002

Poteat, V. P., & Espelage, D. L. (2009). Willingness to remain friends and attend school with lesbian and gay peers: Relational expressions of prejudice among heterosexual youth. *Journal of Youth and Adolescence, 38*(7), 952–962. doi: 10.1007/s10964-009-9416-x

Poulin, F., & Chan, A. (2010). Friendship stability and change in childhood and adolescence. *Developmental Review, 30*(3), 257–272. doi: 10.1016/j.dr.2009.01.001

Powers, B. A. (1996). Relationships among older women living in a nursing home. *Journal of women & aging, 8*(3/4), 179–198. doi: 10.1300/J074v08n03_12

Rands, M. (1988). Changes in social networks following marital separation and divorce. In R. M. Milardo (Ed.), *Families and social networks* (pp. 127–146). Thousand Oaks, CA: Sage Publications, Inc.

Rawlins, W. K. (2009). *The compass of friendship: Narratives, identities, and dialogues.* Los Angeles: Sage.

Reich, S. M., Subrahmanyam, K., & Espinoza, G. (2012). Friending, IMing, and hanging out face-to-face: Overlap in adolescents' online and offline social networks. *Developmental Psychology, 48*(2), 356–368.

Roberto, K. A. (1996). Friendships between older women: Interactions and reactions. *Journal of women and aging, 8*(3/4), 55–73. doi: 10.1300/J074v08n03_05

Rook, K. S., & Ituarte, P. H. G. (1999). Social control, social support, and companionship in older adults' family relationships and friendships. *Personal Relationships, 6*(2), 199–211. doi: 10.1111/j.1475-6811.1999.tb00187.x

Rose, A. J., & Rudolph, K. D. (2006). A review of sex differences in peer relationship processes: Potential trade-offs for the emotional and behavioral development of girls and boys. *Psychological Bulletin, 132*, 98–131.

Rowe, J. W., & Kahn, R. L. (1998). *Successful aging.* New York: Pantheon.

Rubin, K., Fredstrom, B., & Bowker, J. (2008). Future directions in . . . Friendship in childhood and early adolescence. *Social Development, 17*(4), 1085–1096. doi: 10.1111/j.1467-9507.2007.00445.x

Rumens, N. (2008). Working at intimacy: Gay men's workplace friendships. *Gender, work, and organization, 15*(1), 9–30. doi: 10.1111/j.1468-0432.2007.00364.x

Ryan, C., Russell, S. T., Huebner, D., Diaz, R., & Sanchez, J. (2010). Family acceptance in adolescence and the health of LGBT young adults. *Journal of Child and Adolescent Psychiatric Nursing, 23*(4), 205–213.

Schnall, S., Harber, K. D., Stefanucci, J. K., & Proffitt, D. R. (2008). Social support and the perception of geographical slant. *Journal of Experimental Social Psychology 44*(5), 1246–1255.

Schwarz, B., Stutz, M., & Ledermann, T. (2012). Perceived interparental conflict and early adolescents' friendships: the role of attachment security and emotion regulation. *Journal of Youth and Adolescence, 41*(9), 1240–1252. doi: 10.1007/s10964-012-9769-4

Selman, R. L., & Schultz, L. H. (1990). *Making a friend in youth: Developmental theory and pair therapy.* Chicago, IL: University of Chicago Press.

Shaw, B. A., Krause, N., Liang, J., & Bennett, J. (2007). Tracking changes in social relations throughout late life. *The Journals of Gerontology: Series B: Psychological Sciences and Social Sciences, 62B*(2), S90–S99. doi:10.1093/geronb/62.2.S90

Sheets, R. L. Jr., & Mohr, J. J. (2009). Perceived social support from friends and family and psychosocial functioning in bisexual young adult college students. *Journal of Counseling Psychology, 56*(1), 152–163. doi: 10.1037/0022-0167.56.1.152

Sherman, A. M., Lansford, J. E., & Volling, B. L. (2006). Sibling relationships and best friendships in young adulthood: Warmth, conflict, and well-being. *Personal Relationships, 13*(2), 151–165. doi:10.1111/j.1475-6811.2006.00110.x

Shippy, R. A., Cantor, M H., Brennan, M. (2004). Social networks of aging gay men. *Journal of Men's Studies 13*(1), 107–120.

Sias, P. M., & Bartoo, H. (2007). Friendship, social support, and health. In L. L'Abate (Ed.), *Low-cost approaches to promote physical and mental health: Theory, research, and practice* (pp. 455–472). New York, NY: Springer Science + Business Media. doi:10.1007/0-387-36899-X_23

Slatcher, R. B. (2010). When Harry and Sally met Dick and Jane: Creating closeness between couples. *Personal Relationships, 17*(2), 279–297. doi:10.1111/j.1475-6811.2010.01276.x

Stacey, J. (1990). *Brave new families: Stories of domestic upheaval in late twentieth century America.* New York: Basic Books.

Stevens, N., & van Tilburg, T. (2000). Stimulating friendship in later life: A strategy for reducing loneliness among older women. *Educational Gerontology, 26*(1), 15–35. doi:10.1080/036012700267376

Stevens, N. L., & van Tilburg, T. G. (2011). Cohort differences in having and retaining friends in personal networks in later life. *Journal of Social and Personal Relationships, 28*(1), 24–43. doi:10.1177/0265407510386191

Stout, H. (June 16, 2010). A best friend? You must be kidding. *New York Times.*

Sullivan, H. S. (1953). *The interpersonal theory of psychiatry.* New York: Norton.

Thompson, S. H., & Lougheed, E. (2012). Frazzled by Facebook? An exploratory study of gender differences in social network communication among undergraduate men and women. *College Student Journal, 46(1),* 88–98.

van Aken, M. G., & Asendorpf, J. B. (1997). Support by parents, classmates, friends and siblings in preadolescence: Covariation and compensation across relationships. *Journal of Social and Personal Relationships, 14*(1), 79–93. doi:10.1177/0265407597141004

Voss, K., Markiewiczk, D., & Doyle, A. (1999). Friendship, marriage and self-esteem. *Journal of Social and Personal Relationships, 16(1), 103–122.*

Wall, S. M., Pickert, S. M., & Paradise, L. V. (1984). American men's friendships: Self-reports on meaning and changes. *Journal of Psychology: Interdisciplinary and Applied, 116*(2), 179–186. doi:10.1080/00223980.1984.9923635

Wang, H., & Amato, P. R. (2000). Predictors of divorce adjustment: Stressors, resources, and definitions. *Journal of Marriage and the Family, 62*(3), 655–668. doi:10.1111/j.1741-3737.2000.00655.x

Wang, H., & Wellman, B. (2010). Social Connectivity in America: Changes in Adult Friendship Network Size From 2002 to 2007. *American Behavioral Scientist, 53*(8), 1148–1169.

Way, N. (2011). *Deep secrets: Boy's friendships and the crisis of connection.* Cambridge: Harvard University Press.

Weiss, R. S. (1974). The provisions of social relationships. In Z. Rubin (Ed.), *Doing unto others* (pp. 17–26). Englewood Cliffs, NJ: Prentice-Hall.

Werking, K. (1997). *We're just good friends: Women and men in nonromantic relationships.* New York: Guilford.

Wright, P. H., & Scanlon, M. B. (1991). Gender role orientations and friendship: Some attenuation, but gender differences abound. *Sex Roles, 24*(9-10), 551–566. doi:10.1007/BF00288413

Youniss, J., & Haynie, D. L. (1992). Friendship in adolescence. Developmental and *Behavioral Pediatrics 13*(1), 59–66.

Youniss, J. & Smollar, J. (1985). *Adolescent relations with mothers, fathers, and friends.* Chicago, IL: University of Chicago Press.

Chapter 12

Migration and the Family Life Cycle

Celia J. Falicov

— Learning Objectives —

- Define MECA.
- Examine the benefits and challenges of migration and acculturation.
- List and describe contextual stressors that impact immigrants.
- Describe how migration affects family organization.
- Identify how gender and gender roles cause tension in immigrant families.
- Explain how migration impacts the life cycle stages of a family.
- Explore the importance of rituals and religion in immigrant families.
- Describe the impact of migration on generations that come after the immigrant generation.

Introduction

The heart of the family life cycle construct is the notion that members of a family will most likely navigate interconnected life cycle events together. The experiences of migration pull exactly in the opposite direction by making it difficult to share these life cycle experiences. Indeed, most immigrants cannot plan a stable or predictable common future that involves family members, their communities, and cultures. Migration alters in multiple ways how expected and unexpected life cycle events are lived. Immigrants endure, for better or worse, the accumulation of several expected and unexpected transitions in the midst of a changed physical, social, family, and cultural landscape. Migration may be analogous to unexpected life events such as the adoption of children, divorce, remarriage, or early widowhood. The possibility of these events occurring was scarcely ever imagined in the immigrant's original life projections, as his or her identity was being shaped from mid-childhood onwards. For non-normative events of this sort, there is little preparation, no celebratory rituals, few social frameworks for navigation, and only a few imagined new scenarios for development

that could replace the old imagined maps of the future (Falicov, 2014a).

This chapter focuses on how migration intersects with the life cycle of families. The multidimensional, ecological, and comparative approach (MECA) provides an orientation to the conceptual and practice topics involved in understanding continuities and changes in the life cycle of immigrant families. The issues outlined and illustrated in this chapter help therapists understand and frame life cycle issues when they engage in conversations with immigrant families. A focus on cultural and contextual variability of the life cycle afforded by MECA requires first a brief historical social critique of the life cycle construct in family therapy.

> **Assess your comprehension of the introduction by completing this quiz.**

A Social Constructionist View of the Life Cycle

The life cycle framework was first developed by family sociologists in the 1950s (Duvall, 1957). At that time, functionalist and universalistic ideals, informed by Talcott Parsons' model (1951) of traditional family roles in the nuclear family, were the prevailing models of family life and family development.

A serious shortcoming of this foundational life cycle paradigm was the lack of attention to how life cycle experiences are inextricably tied to cultural diversity and to social justice issues. Another shortcoming was that life cycle stages were regarded as predictable, normative, universal, and cumulative. Little room was made for the range of individual responses; the impact of racial, social class, gender and gender orientation oppression, the cultural diverse values (religion, family forms); and the unpredictable immigrant adaptations that we increasingly need to acknowledge today.

A social constructionist viewpoint can potentially portray a more accurate picture of the family life cycle by acknowledging the impact of age and stage, cultural variation, social inequities, and individual uniqueness within a complex reality of multiple family forms (Erickson, 1998; Falicov, 2006, 2011). The need for a more complex and fluid perspective of the life cycle is patently clear when discussing immigrant experiences, given that clinicians must always include cultural diversity, migration processes, and contextual stressors for purposes of assessment, intervention, or prevention.

> **Assess your comprehension of a social constructionist view of the life cycle by completing this quiz.**

MECA for Migration and Life Cycle Processes

MECA (multidimensional, ecological, and comparative approach) (Falicov, 1995, 1998, 2012, 2014a, 2014b, in press) provides a framework for understanding how the experiences of migration and acculturation, which inevitably bring about changed ecological contexts and gradual transformations in family organization, have an inevitable impact on the life cycle of immigrants. The topics encompassed by the four MECA domains describe how continuity and change take place due to migration/acculturation

and ecological context, as domains that require a *social justice lens* in clinical practice. Continuity and change processes also take place in family organization and family life cycle, domains that require taking a *cultural diversity lens* into account for clinical purposes. The contents of these four domains are summarized in Figure 12.1. Continuities and changes in these domains need to be assessed in terms of the risks and relational resilience (Walsh, 2006) manifested by each family.

> **Assess your comprehension of the MECA for migration and life cycle processes by completing this quiz.**

MECA: Migration/Acculturation

Migration is a massive individual and family transition in time and space. It begins before the act of relocation and goes on for a long time, affecting the descendants of immigrants for several generations. Even when freely chosen, the transition of migration is replete with loss and disarray—there is loss of language; the separation from loved ones; the intangible emotional vacuum left in the space where "home" used to be; the loss of community; and the lack of understanding of how jobs, schools, banks, or hospitals work. Immigrants are rendered vulnerable, isolated, and susceptible to individual and family distress.

Yet, not all is dislocation, trauma, and crisis. Migration can also be an adventure that opens possibilities of living a better life and provides an opportunity to prove oneself capable of resilient survival and hardiness. Immigrants may learn a new language, find new work, or acquire a better education. They may learn to form new bonds while constructing new lives and partially reinventing themselves. Indeed, the study of the immigrant experience offers fertile ground to consider and identify what helps people rebound from crisis and maintain hope, as well as what risks may challenge their resolve (see Figure 12.1).

Migration as a developmental process

It is possible to construct migration as a developmental process in itself, a process with its own stages and

Figure 12.1 Multidimensional ecological comparative approach (MECA) cultural diversity and social justice processes.

Transformations: Continuity and Change

Migration and Acculturation
- As a developmental process
- As ambiguous losses and gains
- Trauma pre-, during, postmigration
- Type of migration (e.g., undocumented)
- Composition of migration (e.g., father alone)
- Lack of transitional ritual
- Transnationalism and technologies of communication
- Psychological or virtual family

Ecological Context
- Linguistic and cultural dissonance
- Poverty
- Host country anti-immigrant reception
- Racism and double consciousness
- Community insertions
- Isolation
- Protection of ethnic community insertion
- Virtual community
- Neighborhood dangers (drugs, violence, gangs)
- Contextual protections (language, social network)

Family Organization
- Reorganizations in interdependence and hierarchies
- Relational stresses
  - Generational tensions and reorganizations
  - CEFSA: culture, ecological fears and separation anxiety
  - Gender role reorganizations in couples
  - Biculturalism
- Separations and reunifications
- Long-distance connections: transnational triangles
- Transnational therapies

Family Life Cycle
- Socially constructed: cultural ideals, meanings, timings vary with age, stage, gender
- Rites and rituals (spontaneous, religious, therapeutic)
- Pileup of stressful transitions
- Absences at crucial transitions
- Second-generation transnational exposure
- The immigrant's paradox

Social Justice

Cultural Diversity

transitions, ranging from a preparatory stage (which usually also involves developmental steps) moving through periods of overcompensation or decompensation and ending with transgenerational impact (Sluzki, 1979). If migration itself is an evolutionary process, it follows that migration stages and transitions intersect with how other expected life cycle stages and transitions are experienced.

Migration as ambiguous loss and gain

Another distinctive feature of migration is the lifelong experience of ambiguous loss that most immigrants need to learn to live with (Boss, 1999). The ambiguity does not only involve the possibility of return but it also involves a balance or imbalance of losses and gains that characterizes immigrant life (Falicov, 2002, 2012, 2014b). To this already complex set of challenges, we must add the fact that immigrants, like non-immigrants, cannot escape the eventuality of other unexpected transitions such as illness or premature death, and the occurrence of other ambiguous losses such as divorce. Yet, not all migration challenges are sad and bleak, as there are gains to be enjoyed. The experience can bring a sense of adventure and excitement, of hope and new dreams, possible greater economic stability and prosperity over time, and increased human and civil rights.

Variations in the experience of traumatic migration

Migration outcomes are contingent on a number of pre-migration experiences such as the type of migration (undocumented, permanent visa, etc.) or the composition of the migrating group (extended family, solo immigrant) that shape, constrain, and have long-lasting influences on how postmigration adaptations unfold.

The possibility of migration-related trauma must be considered, as it may have a long-lasting effect on how the life cycle events unfold. Documented, undocumented, refugee or asylum seeker status creates vastly different physical, social, emotional, and cultural contexts for immigrants. Unlike the fairly predictable, albeit lengthy, situation that accrues for the immigrant that can obtain a legal visa or a work permit and trust the process of becoming a permanent resident or U.S. citizen, the undocumented immigrant and the asylum seeker often risk many potential harms. These dangers range from a perilous border passage that can result in death, robbery, or rape by the smuggler to slavery or prostitution inflicted by an employer after entering the United States. Many psychological stresses also result from living "in the dark" because of fear of detention that often culminates in deportation. Asylum seekers live with the painful ambiguity of having escaped a terrible situation, but have no assurance of a safe future. Their fate is uncertain, always awaiting a decision as to whether they will be granted legal status to stay or sent back to their old country where their lives will be at risk or their freedom curtailed.

Family composition at migration

Whether members of the family unit migrate together as a couple, family or extended group, or in sequential stages, the family composition before and after migration (from extended three- and four-generation families to two-generation nuclear arrangements, single parent or individual alone)—has important implications for family connections and disconnections that affect outcomes and coping with the stresses of separation, reunifications, or adaptation to the host culture.

Lack of transitional rituals

It is perhaps because of its ambiguous, inconclusive, and fragmented quality that migration as a life transition is devoid of clear rituals or rites of passage. The preparations that precede the actual departure may bear some similarities to rituals, but practices such as packing symbolic, meaningful objects (e.g., photographs or other mementos, including a small cache of native soil) are random and idiosyncratic, and do not usually involve family members or friends. There is no formal structure, no designated place or time, no cultural collective celebration that allows people to come together to mark the transition, try to transcend it, and provide a container for the strong emotions everybody is feeling. Thus, migration is similar to other transitions that lack cultural rituals: a miscarriage represents a future life that was cutoff; a divorce leaves partners feeling that what could have been is no longer possible. Even the term "adopted country," like an adopted child not raised by its biological parents, suggests that there was a "homeland," a map of a possible territory that could have been inhabited but is not now accessible.

Transnationalism and technologies of communication

Today, many immigrants are transnationals, that is, they are able to remain in contact with their places and families of origin through a variety of means from jet travel to Skype. New technologies of communication facilitate connections. They may send money home in order to support the family who did not migrate or to contribute to a community cause (Falicov, 2007, 2008, 2014a). Rather than living with a broken heart like immigrants did in the past when they gradually lost connections with their countries and families, new immigrants can live with two hearts, one here and one there. We may then speak of a psychological or virtual family. Mothers or fathers may migrate alone, hoping that their sacrifice will provide a better life for their children whom they leave under the protection of good family care, but nevertheless the relational costs may be very high as we will discuss later. The vicissitudes of migration in the areas of ecological contexts and the changes in family organization create additional disruptions that alter family life cycle experiences.

> Assess your comprehension of MECA: Migration/ Acculturation by completing this quiz.

MECA: Ecological Context

Contextual stressors are part and parcel of immigrant life in ways that impact how life cycle experiences are timed, lived, and coped with. Some of these stressors and the resilience with which they are faced are addressed here.

Linguistic and cultural dissonance

When a family moves to a different country, they face linguistic and cultural dissonance with the new society. This incongruence has been described as a lack of reciprocity or lack of "fit" between the dominant society's expectations and the immigrant family's ways (Falicov, 1988b). Patterns that are adaptive for individuals and families in a rural village in Sudan do not function effectively in a Philadelphia urban ghetto. The values, norms, and behaviors learned in the home country may become a source of acculturative stress when the family comes in contact with the institutions of the new culture. The immigrant parents' model of child-rearing and the developmental expectations may be "out of phase" with the dominant culture's model, as represented in the school, the peer group, or the health system. Normal developmental stresses are thus intensified by external cultural dissonance.

Host country receptions and community insertions

Negative or ambivalent receptions and shortage of adequate economic and social opportunities because of race and/or class discrimination alter radically the ability to absorb the losses of migration and the adaptations to optimize success. Isolation is an endemic problem of many immigrants as community social supports vary widely depending on the opportunities for reconstructing ruptured social networks and recreating cultural spaces in ethnic neighborhoods or in work settings. Without the contextual protections of language and familiar social network, isolation may contribute to a host of bio-psychosocial consequences such as depression or somatizations at any age, or drug abuse, alcohol consumption, violence, and gang joining in adolescence. Virtual communities made possible through new technologies of communication may be an important part of immigrant long distance connection with their original ecological settings (Falicov, 2008).

The stresses of racism

Ecological stressors often transform immigrants into the disadvantaged position of being members of a racial, cultural, socioeconomic, and citizenship minority that is often discriminated against. Even when they were people of color in their own country, they were not "others" in terms of culture and language. They were legitimate citizens of their nations. The stresses of racism are deleterious to health outcomes, intellectual performance, overall behavior, and family stability at all stages of the life cycle.

Double consciousness as a resilient response

Many immigrant families are aware of the risks that racism inflicts on their family members. Therapists need to be aware of possible complex responses families develop with the hope to protect their members from the long-term consequents of racism. The following case illustrates a situation where the family elects to absorb the injustice for the sake of larger goals of family survival and advancement.

CASE ILLUSTRATION

A OAXACAN Family

A family consisting of mother, father, and six children who had arrived in Southern California from Oaxaca, Mexico, 6 years before was referred to therapy because a White upper-class neighbor had accused their 9-year-old son of "molesting" her 4-year-old daughter while the children played in the fields. The Oaxacan family had lived for 6 years in a home on the grounds of an estate belonging to their wealthy American employers. The father was employed as a ranch hand and the mother helped with household chores. As their story unfolded and I interviewed members individually, I began to suspect that the situation could easily be normalized within developmental limits. The little girl, the 9-year-old "alleged perpetrator," and her 6-year-old brother had been playing together outdoors. The three children agreed that the girl was wiggling and crossing her legs because she needed to urinate. The older Mexican boy pulled the girl's panties down, told her to spread her legs, and held her in the upright position because the toilet was too far to walk to make it on time. As the boy attempted to help the girl with her predicament, she got scared and started to scream. She then ran home to her mother, crying all the way. The agitated young mother took the girl to the pediatrician but a medical exam showed no evidence of genital bruising.

Racism was undoubtedly part of the negative interpretation of the boy's behavior. But it is also important to note that the White and economically privileged 32-year-old mother of the 4-year-old girl had just been diagnosed with a recurrence of leukemia. In her high state of emotional distress, fears about potential dangers to her daughter and worries that she might no longer be present to protect her rose to the fore. Certainly, this young mother was in the throes of an unexpected tragic turn of her own life cycle expectations. Through this and other similar experiences, I have come to believe that racism rears its ugly head even more intensely during times of stressful transitions than during stable times.

When I met the Mexican family, I offered my explanations for why the events may have been misinterpreted. The father, who had very dark skin and striking Mayan features, was usually a silent man. Although uneducated, when he talked, a deep intelligence was revealed. He said, "I thank you very much for your efforts. We want to please ask you to do us a favor very important for us. We want you to tell "them" that in these sessions you have worked with our son and you think he is "cured" of

whatever problems he had, and that in your professional opinion, no sexual transgressions will ever happen again." Surprised and dismayed, I asked why he wanted me to go along with the accusation, and he said: "Because, when they look at us, they think: these Mexicans are good people because they work hard, 'le hacen la lucha' (they struggle hard), but if something goes wrong they suddenly see the faces that they believe we're hiding under the surface, the faces of rapists and abusers."

I thought that his explanation was one of the best I had ever heard about "double consciousness" (Du Bois, 1903). This father knew who he was and how he was seen by others. He was painfully aware of the gross, racist preconceptions about Latino immigrants held by Whites.

He continued "and you cannot change that, or if you yourself want to take on that struggle, we will be hurt and we will lose what we gained so far. We miss our town very much but we can raise our family much better here. My wife has found a church for us, my oldest daughter may be able to go to medical school, my employer is buying a computer for my youngest boy who is very smart . . . you see . . . I will keep an eye on this boy, I promise you, but please do not question their story, 'no vale la pena' (it is not worth the sorrow). It could cost us everything we worked for."

I think he was asking me not to rescue his family, because in doing so, I might be, like so many well-intentioned helping professionals, isolating elements of a complex social ecology without asking themselves or the families they treat if interventions meant to help at one level might cause problems at another. Perhaps this father's request would allow him to exercise some measure of protection for the collective life cycle needs of his large family (going to school, graduating, and getting a good career and livelihood). Choosing the greater good for the family at the expense of the individual could be understood as a cultural strategy of a collectivistic setting, where so many interconnected people could lose a chance to a better future for the sake of defending one individual who is wrongly accused. The African American mother in the play *Doubt* (Shanley, 2007) elects to downplay or doubt the plausible sexual abuse of her son to avoid further stigmatization and hamper his already limited chances to succeed in life. Likewise, the Oaxacan father, in my example, was electing to ignore or downplay the abuse being committed toward his own child because the consequences of defending him or pressing charges could be much more dire than accepting the injustice being perpetrated.

Fortunately for all involved, the accusing mother withdrew her complaint and the White employer collaborated with my view of the situation. I intervened also by asking the school to allow the boy to stay in an afternoon program that gave him more age-appropriate activities than playing with and rescuing younger children.

In this family, we can see the ambiguity of gains, losses, and dual visions of immigrants. Striving for the dream of stability in a new land is riddled with pressures to assimilate the dominant culture's story, which negatively judges dark-skinned, poor immigrants and deprives them of legal resources to fight unfair accusations. The social climate of structural exclusion and psychological violence suffered by immigrants and their children is not only detrimental to their participation in the opportunity structure, but it also affects the immigrant children's sense of self, through a process that Suárez-Orozco and Suárez-Orozco (2002) aptly call "social mirroring."

Silence, poverty, undocumented status, and empowerment

Although unspoken by this family and many others, another common burden that silences standing up for one's rights is the lack of legal residence documents. Many families are plagued with having to accept ignominies for the sake of continuous undercover residence, a situation that causes daily stress in the workplace and the neighborhood.

Most immigrants and their children are aware of the hostilities and prejudice toward them and their barriers to full societal participation. From a psychological viewpoint, this awareness may be debilitating when internalized or denied, but it may be empowering when it helps stimulate strategic social justice activism. Proponents of critical pedagogy emphasize that awareness of one's own marginal status is the first step toward empowerment (Trueba, 1999). Therapists must be able to discuss the impact of ecological stressors on their life cycle to the extent that immigrant families are comfortable with these conversations and have developed trust in the therapists' understanding of their complex predicaments.

Assess your comprehension of the MECA: ecological context by completing this quiz.

MECA: Family Organization

Family organization is a fundamental domain of developmental analysis for several reasons. Normal expectable life cycle processes (e.g., the growth of children) universally entail changes in family organization, such as changes in interdependence and in hierarchies among family members (Minuchin, 1974) and immigrants, of course, undergo expectable life cycle stages and transitions. Migration and acculturation impose additional reorganizations in the same areas to cope with changed circumstances. For example, there may be an increased dependence of parents on more acculturated offspring along with parental loss of authority.

Additional reasons for immigrant family reorganization may be tied to cultural diversity given that many immigrant ethnic groups come from collectivistic and rural settings that uphold different values about family relationships than individualistic and urban ones. These differences may generate family conflict and alter intergenerational and gender relationships in terms of interdependence and autonomy and in terms of power hierarchies from authoritarian to democratic. Separations and reunifications among family members also change the equation of closeness–distance and interdependence and impinge on established hierarchies (see Figure 12.1). In the sections that follow, I elaborate on these topics related to family organization.

Family reorganizations due to migration changes

Migration precipitates family reorganization to cope with changed circumstances. Family organization is altered relative to interdependence and hierarchy because some family members compensate for the physical or emotional absence of others by assuming new roles and functions. These new makeshift family roles may precipitate or slow down the pace at which life cycle transitions, such as leaving home or getting married, occur. This situation may also intersect and be intensified by collectivistic cultural preferences such as family interdependence and respect for parental authority.

The phenomena of the oldest child as the "family helper and cultural intermediary"—between parents and institutions, and even between parents and the younger children—has been widely reported in immigrant families. From an individualistic point of view, the family helper may be regarded as overburdened and losing his or her chance to be free from responsibility in adolescence. However, he or she can also be regarded as performing a valuable family function that helps him or her to learn mature behaviors and increases self-esteem. Nevertheless, with increased age and acculturation, the burdens of parentified status may begin to accrue, particularly when they interfere with new culturally patterned life cycle requirements. In these situations, we may observe that the process of migration may have reversed generational hierarchies. The intersection of gender and migration also plays a significant role in the reorganization of roles and functions of family members, since girls may be assumed to be natural caretakers of family needs as the following case illustrates.

CASE ILLUSTRATION

Mary Gonzales

Mary Gonzales, a 32-year-old social worker of Mexican origin, came to therapy with her parents and her siblings. She wanted to help them find a better way to deal with discipline issues they were encountering with their youngest daughter, Gladys, who was 14 years old and defied her parents' authority. Twenty years ago, when the family arrived in California from Mexico bringing with them three children born there, the oldest child and only girl, Mary, became the translator and intermediary between the parents and

the institutions of the new country. Gladys, one of three other children born in the United States, considers Mary to be the only person in the family who understood American culture and English well. Indeed, Mary had been the indefatigable translator of language and culture for her parents and her younger siblings.

Mary's first attempt to obtain more autonomy from her role as parentified daughter and sister took place when she married an American man of Scottish descent. However, in spite of this built-in cultural and language distance, she moved with her husband in the lower floor of the apartment building where her parents and siblings lived and continued to perform the same social and family intermediary role.

The second attempt toward greater autonomy from her family of origin appeared during tragic circumstances when Mary anticipated her likely permanent absence from her family. The latter may be seen as the real motive for the clinical consultation although the ostensible reason was Gladys's misbehavior. Recently, at the age of 32, Mary received a diagnosis of fatal ovarian cancer. In the face of this unexpected life cycle tragedy, the rigid family organization that developed as an adaptation to migration must change to free Mary from parentified tasks and to prepare her parents to take over those responsibilities. The therapeutic conversation was used to clarify that before the migration, the parents had been very capable parents who had raised three successful children, but had become debilitated in their authority toward their younger, American children because of the stresses of language and culture change (Falicov, 1997).

Generational tensions and family reorganizations

The developmental issues of adolescence involve fairly universally a striving toward greater personal autonomy, and this often implies testing parental limits. This process can be difficult in the face of high-risk ecological conditions brought about by migration, poverty, and neighborhood dangers such as drugs, sex, and crime. Many immigrant parents exert their authority to protect their children from these dangers. Although generational tensions may be a natural occurrence in all families, migration often complicates the situation. Parents who might otherwise work out a gradual separation from their teens find the task especially difficult through anxiety over losing their children to an unknown society and their sociocultural need to define family as "life together." Parents also fear the many ecological dangers that minority adolescents encounter in the streets. These factors may contribute to children of immigrant parents having less individual freedoms than their American counterparts, while they may also manage more responsibilities toward parents, grandparents, and younger siblings.

CEFSA: Cultural differences, ecological fears, and separation anxiety

Three possible explanations can be entertained by a clinician when trying to understand parent–adolescent tensions in immigrant families: (1) differences in language and cultural values between "old-fashioned" parents and "liberated" youth; (2) ecological dangers and parental fears; and (3) separation anxiety and fear of losing family interconnectedness. In order to explore these three areas when interviewing families, I devised the acronym CEFSA: cultural differences, ecological fears, and separation anxiety (Falicov, 2014a). It is necessary for clinicians to explore these issues with families to establish a focus for collaborative practice.

Gender and parental control

Freedoms can differ significantly for boys and girls within the same family. Many Latino parents will not let girls go out because of fear that they will get pregnant, and parents have biological arguments that designate girls as the "weaker sex."

CASE ILLUSTRATION

A Colombian Family

A Colombian family in therapy for depression of the 19-year-old daughter, Consuelo, related that both the mother and the father controlled her behavior by having her boyfriend visit her in the home and sit and watch TV without touching even the side of their arms, because in their estimation the most minimal physical contact stimulated their temptations. In contrast, Consuelo's 18-year-old brother was allowed to come home late at night after drinking, going to dances, and spending time in the back of cars with girls. To add to the controls, this younger brother was entrusted to supervise her activities in the street when boys were around. When Consuelo would express her emotional upset to her parents over the "double standard" implied, she would get a few slaps in the face for her disobedience and intimations that she was on the brink of becoming a woman of ill repute for wanting to go out alone with her boyfriend.

Family therapy sessions focused on helping Consuelo articulate to the parents how her depression was precipitated by her natural wishes to grow up, have a peer group and a boyfriend, all in the context of "being good" and please her parents simultaneously. Parents were helped to review recollections of their wishes and experiences at a similar age and the different family and social contexts that provided a family support system for their growth. Up to this point, the parents had only rigidly focused on the cultural gender expectations without any perspective about the contextual differences in their lives, the need to discuss more clearly their ecological fears, and even their anxieties about losing their daughter to an unknown world. These conversations helped create an empathic field of understanding between parents and daughter whereby each side was able to increase their flexibility and ability to compromise to include the needs of the other. It is possible that the parents' motivation for a move toward a more bicultural approach to both gender and generational expectations stemmed from witnessing their daughter's depression and understanding how cultural differences, ecological fears, and separation anxiety were fueling a more rigid attitude than they would have had otherwise. The daughter's motivation to comply with her parents' wishes for greater knowledge of her activities stemmed from a more mature understanding of her parents as vulnerable and suffering the stresses of immigration and culture change.

Zayas (2011) has constructed a clinically useful model of why so many Latina teens became depressed and attempted suicide, a model based on the notion that different cultural ideals of relatedness create internal conflicts for the immigrant family. The suicide attempt is seen as representing a major developmental internal conflict between the adolescent's need for autonomy and her deep respect for family unity and obedience that originated in her cultural socialization. These hypotheses seem applicable to other collectivistic ethnic immigrant groups that struggle with developmental dilemmas of autonomy and family loyalty.

Clinicians must be cognizant of these dilemmas and not encourage cultural solutions that favor one generation over the other. New studies strongly suggest that families that embrace nonlinear acculturation such as "biculturalism" (i.e., adolescents who attempt to maintain strong ties to their parents' cultures and have parents who reach out to learn the skills of the new culture) perform better academically, face less anxiety, and adjust more easily socially (Smokowski & Bacallao, 2011).

Gender role reorganizations in couple relationships

Tensions between tradition and modernity also affect relationships between husbands and wives. The economic opportunities open for women who migrate, the more liberal attitudes toward the control of fertility, and the legal protections against domestic violence that immigrant women encounter in the United States facilitate a desire for a more companionate, egalitarian model of marital relationships than the one lived prior to the migration. Thus, immigrant women strive to develop a more modern type of marriage based on greater trust, intimacy, and sexual love. Marital conflict or marital growth may ensue, with men having a variety of reactions to these strivings, ranging from feeling threatened to sharing the dream of a different kind of intimacy (Hirsch, 2003). Of course, many couples around the world deal with similar issues due to the advent of women's liberation, but migration may intensify the conflict and precipitate divorce without the containing backdrop of extended family

and community. These reorganizations intensified by migration have very real consequences for the life cycle development of men and women and for the cultural role models they pass on to the next generation.

Family separations and reunifications

Migration always involves *family separation* of one kind or another. Physical relocation separates individuals from the extended family or the nuclear family and at a minimum from the community and friends. Separations deprive immigrants from the possibility to continue to build shared life cycle narratives with loved ones.

Separations add two new transitions to the expectable life cycle. One is the separation and the other is the reunification. Themes connected to the separation need to be integrated in therapy with immigrant families, as these significant stressors alter many normative expectations about family life (Mitrani, Muir, & Santisteban, 2004; Suárez-Orozco, Todorova, & Louie, 2002; Falicov, 2007, 2014a).

The players in the drama of separation also vary. Separations and subsequent reunifications may take place between nuclear and extended family members when the nuclear family migrates together or between spouses or between a parent and the rest of the family when a man or a woman comes first with the thought of later reunification. Children who are left temporarily under kin care may be separated not only from parents but also from departing siblings. Of course, another separation will take place when the children leave the caretaker to be reunited with parents, causing difficult adaptations for all involved.

The most substantive ruptures of migration are those that involve primary systems of care. Among these, the most disruptive ruptures involve separations between parents and children, in particular those between mothers and children. Increasingly, women, as well as men, leave their children with family caretakers to embark on a journey that could presumably remedy economic injustice.

The family consequences of the usually desperate decisions to separate vary depending on many factors (Falicov, 2014a). One factor is the preexistence of cultures of migration that legitimize leaving children behind and provide role models for these decisions in the history of the community. Other important elements are the quality of the long distance connection between caregiver and the biological parent, which influences the nature of transnational triangles involving children. The ages of the children and possibly the length of the separation itself shape the life cycle outcomes for the families involved (Suárez-Orozco et al., 2002; Suárez-Orozco, Suárez-Orozco, & Todorova, 2008).

The outcomes of these alterations also depend on the attributions of meaning made by those who left and those who stayed. A child can feel abandoned and neglected by a parent's absence or can regard the parent as a hero or heroine that has sacrificed his or her own comfort for the well-being of his or her children, depending on the family narratives that develop around the migration (Artico, 2003). Therapists must inquire about the meanings that each family member attributes to the separation.

Current research about maternal depression after reunification reveals that encouraging communication about past experiences related to the separation has healing family effects (D'Angelo et al., 2009). Parent–child attachments are affected by separations and adolescents manifest behavior problems, drug involvement, anxiety, and depression in clinical populations (Garcia-Coll & Magnuson, 1997; Santisteban & Mena, 2009). School difficulties are also more frequent in children who have suffered migration related separations from their parents (Suárez-Orozco et al., 2008).

TRUTH OR LIES. The estrangement that often accompanies separations among family members is compounded by the tendency of those who left and those who stayed to alter the truth of their experiences in an effort to protect the listener from being exposed to difficult news such as unemployment, health issues, depression, or family conflicts that the listener cannot remedy or do anything about. Denial may play a further role in acknowledging the difficult realization that the sacrifices of migration may not have been worthwhile. This lack of transparency in long-distance immigrant communication may contribute to further emotional distance.

Therapeutic techniques designed to share knowledge of life cycle events that took place in the lives of various family members, such as "catching-up life narratives," are helpful at the time of reunification (Falicov, 2002, 2014a).

CASE ILLUSTRATION

Isabel

Isabel, a 33-year-old mother, an immigrant from Manila, Philippines, was referred by a physician for multiple somatic complaints: aches and pains that traveled from place to place in her body (headaches, joints, heart palpitations) for which no medical cause could be found. Less than two years before this consultation, Isabel had reunited with her now 13-year-old daughter, Violeta, from whom she had separated at the age of one and a half. The daughter had remained with the maternal grandmother for a decade with only one visit from her biological mother. The mother's plan to live together in the host country did not materialize into the expected panacea. Violeta was initially morose and uninterested in work or play and was doing poorly in school. The teenager became more energized only when she began to hang around with the "wrong crowd." Isabel had no authority over her, as the girl disrespected curfews and any directions that came from the mother. It was as though strangers reunited with no shared history and the mother had no place at all in the family hierarchy. It is not uncommon for parents and children to have idealized the thought of an eventual reunion only to find out that the harsh reality of the many relational losses incurred is very different than the fantasy everyone had imagined. Isabel had handled the ambiguities of migration, the separation, and her loss of physical and psychological home by postponing her grief, in the hopes of recovering a deep sense of home later, when she could reunite with her daughter. Now she awakened from her dream with a harsh reality of many losses. The daughter, of course, was experiencing multiple losses herself including the deep attachments to her grandmother, extended family, and peer group. She was now faced with her new marginal status as an immigrant in the United States and had become depressed.

Furthermore, during the years of separation and superficial contact between mother and daughter, much of reality had not been shared. The mother protected the daughter from hearing about her loneliness and sadness and the employment instability and the many economic sacrifices she had to make to send money home. The daughter protected the mother by not sharing any of her feelings of being abandoned and not having a mother around when other children did. She did not tell her either about the teasing and exploitative behaviors she endured at the hands of her uncle and cousins who lived in the same household.

A "catching-up life narrative" technique was utilized in therapy. Both mother and daughter were asked to describe to each other the trajectory of their separated lives, including the homes they lived in, the school and work experiences, the joys and disappointments in friendships, the celebrations that stood out, the times when they missed each other and wanted to be together. The therapist took notes and asked them to bring photos, objects, and mementos that symbolized those times in concrete and subjective ways. The notes and the objects were put inside a white cardboard box that was given to them with the project of decorating the box together. To the next session, Isabel and Violeta proudly brought the box that they had labeled as the "treasure box." Their first truly bonding experience had been to spend the weekend decorating top, bottom, and sides as a collage of cutouts of colorful magazine photos topped with paper flowers.

The reverberations of the experience of separation may be painfully revisited at various life cycle stages for the main protagonists. Even in the case of older people, it is important to explore the history of separations and reunifications during migration. The power of the past in the lives of immigrants may appear in full force and unexpectedly in older age.

CASE ILLUSTRATION

Antonio

Antonio, a moderately successful 65-year-old farmer who had arrived in California from Mexico at the age of 16 requested psychotherapy for agitated depression. The focus of his ruminations was a debt of gratitude toward his long-deceased grandmother. Since his recent retirement, he had for the first time spontaneously reconnected with memories of those people in his past who demonstrated love and devotion toward him. At the top of his list was the gratitude he will never be able to express toward his grandmother.

Compounding his sense of loss was his current estranged and somewhat disrespectful attitude of his five grown children toward him. They do not value the many sacrifices he had made to provide an education for them. For example, the two younger children bitterly complain that he never went to their soccer games the way American fathers do.

In the therapy, two goals were outlined. One was to create bridges with the community his grandmother belonged to and explore concrete ways to honor her memory. The other goal was to spend time with his children and grandchildren to share his migration story including the culture and class contexts in which he grew up. This therapeutic approach is consonant with the lifelong need of many immigrants to keep alive past memories along with present experiences.

TRANSNATIONAL THERAPIES. Since many families today have become virtual or psychological families rather than being families that interact face to face, this situation can be capitalized on for therapeutic purposes. Clinicians can incorporate technologies of communication either in the office or the home setting. Videoconferencing, Skype, cell phones, and emails make possible for separated families to remain connected and updated. These connections allow for conducting therapy during the separation period rather than waiting until reunification to repair family bonds, thus insuring some prevention of future suffering. For an extensive discussion of this topic and clinical illustrations, see Falicov (2007, 2008, 2014a) and Bacigalupe and Lambe (2011).

Assess your comprehension of the MECA: family organization by completing this quiz.

MECA: Family Life Cycle

Every family's life cycle is affected by *cultural changes* in one way or another, but cultural change is a theme that dominates the internal and external life of immigrants. Each society conditions the family to transmit rules that are adaptive to broad societal requirements (see Figure 12.1). In turn, each family prepares its members to live in their own society and to speak the language of its people. I have written before about the importance of taking into account cultural variations as social constructions in the conception and practices of the life cycle (Falicov & Karrer, 1980; Falicov, 1988a, 1997). Life cycle specifications about timing, markers, processes, and age and gender expectations are culturally and socially constructed and passed on through generations. A deep challenge for immigrants is how to fit into and conduct life cycle transitions in a different language and with different cultural ideals and norms than those acquired in the culture of origin.

Normal developmental stresses may be intensified by cultural contrasts, contradictions, and dilemmas. A new developmental task may be to reconcile two different cultural codes and optimally find pathways toward biculturalism.

Awareness by the clinician of cultural variations in the family life cycle and the cultural dissonances that immigrants often suffer in terms of how to navigate life cycle stages and transitions has implications relevant and even crucial to the treatment process, such as recognizing family crisis points, differentiating functional from dysfunctional behavior, and selecting treatment goals and interventions that are either culturally appropriate or take into account how to resolve cultural conflicts.

Age and life stage implications for migration

The developmental stages in the process of leaving one's home country begin with a prologue of thinking, planning, talking, and making concrete inquiries and moves. The time span for this prologue may vary from an impulsive individual decision to a prolonged mutual deliberation, but it always involves a powerful motivation full of doubts and certainties, hopes and regrets, choice points about who is to come, when, why, where, and what for, followed by interpersonal attributions of responsibility and most importantly the experience of ruptured attachments among family members.

There are multiple subjective consequences of these decisions upon the family that migrates and for those family members who remain behind. These consequences vary depending on the ages and life cycle stages and also the gender of those who are planning to leave and those who are staying. Migration is vastly different for women and men; infants, children, or adolescents; and young adults or aged persons. Developmental issues such as language acquisition, socialization, internalization of cultural codes, and a formed or unformed sense of national identity figure into the ease or difficulty of departure and adaptation. Emotional symptoms are also part of the passages. Depression is a common symptom among those who have left their home countries, regardless of their age (Falicov, 2003). There may also be a significant increase in anxiety about the safety and adaptation of the immigrants on the part of younger and older family members who have stayed in the country of origin.

Migration is processed differently at the cognitive, emotional, and behavioral levels at different ages. During the first years of life, separation from the multiple caretakers that may have been present in the extended family may be a major loss. In middle childhood, the separation from the original school setting can be very confusing, even emotionally traumatic. The confusion may be accentuated by the differences in expectations between the culture of the old school and that of the new one.

In adolescence, separation from attachment to a country and a national identity may be dislocating both at the cognitive and the emotional levels. Young adulthood may offer the felicitous coincidence of a need for an autonomous beginning in work or education and the openness to learning new language and customs. Growing old and anticipating death may alter an immigrant's view of the original wish to migrate and rekindle longings for a return to the homeland.

In sum, the level of flexibility to adaptation, the ability to learn a new language, the willingness to absorb new cultural values, the aim to obtain reasonable balances of continuity and change, and the ability to process transnational relationships will depend, to some extent, on one's age and life cycle stage at the time of migration. Even the possibility of raising the next generation to develop a bicultural identity will depend, to some extent, on the age and the flexibility of the immigrant generations at the time of migration.

Rites and rituals

Many societies mark life cycle transitions with rituals of celebration and rites of passage that emphasize change and continuity over generations. Immigrant families may come from ethnicities that adhere to rituals and believe in their communal value.

SPONTANEOUS RITUALS. I have described elsewhere (Falicov, 2002, 2012, 2014a) a number of remembrance-oriented behaviors that acquire characteristics similar to rituals and that are inextricably connected to the processes of migration. Many immigrants create bridges to their families and hometowns by visiting and sending messages and remittances. They also recreate ethnic spaces in their current homes and neighborhoods that evoke the music, the sights, and flavors of their cultures. It is usual to preserve cultural rituals tied to the life cycle, such as birthdays, weddings, and funerals.

The application of rituals in therapy has been described extensively by Imber-Black et al. (2003). The healing potential offered by the cultural continuity of rituals in the lives of immigrants needs to be considered in therapeutic interventions. An exploration of these rituals in therapy may give indications as to how culturally immersed or disengaged a family is and also provide possible potential therapeutic tools.

RELIGION AND SPIRITUALITY. During cultural, developmental, and other life cycle transitions, immigrant families turn more intensely to the comfort and continuity of past traditions, such as prayer and local cures. Religion and spirituality have a powerful role in the navigation and demarcation of life cycle transitions through the performance of religious rituals. For immigrants, the practices of religion are the most transportable of all assets (Falicov, 2009).

This draw toward one's primary ethnicity can be used as a therapeutic resource to help immigrant families utilize practices that enhance continuity and belonging while propelling life forward. Even acculturated immigrants, who may have become disdainful or dismissive of indigenous practices or magical beliefs, may tend to tap into their ancestors' core beliefs when times are especially stressful.

Pileup of life cycle transitions in transnational contexts

The life cycle of families may present a pileup of stressors when the transitions undergone by some members in one country may affect or be affected by transitions that other family members are undergoing in another country. Events that cannot be shared by those who left and those who stayed, such as growing old, illness, or death of a close relative, intensify the ambiguities caused by the losses and gains of migration. Absences at crucial transitions tax immigrants already burdened with their own difficult ecological, organizational, or life cycle issues.

Perhaps aided by the access to new technologies of communication, many new immigrants believe that there will be time in the future to visit their home countries, renew old connections, and fulfill responsibilities to family. However, when these fantasized continuities come to a brutal halt with a discontinuous fatality, the emotional flooding can be overwhelming.

CASE ILLUSTRATION

Ana Luisa

Ana Luisa, a 42-year-old woman, had been married for 15 years and living in San Diego with her European American husband and their two daughters when she entered a marital crisis. She heard that her father has died suddenly in Honduras. Her husband did not understand the depth of her grief and was upset about her threats of divorce. He knew that she followed him back to America because she had fallen in love with him when he had met her in her country. For the first time, she blamed him for her separation from her family. When she was inconsolable, her two young daughters and her husband could provide little comfort and sharing of memories because they hardly knew her father. Her own grief had become frozen and she was experiencing a great deal of confusion as to which family and which country she really belonged.

Therapeutic interventions included at-home and long-distance rituals that allowed for more collective participation in the life cycle transition. In therapy, the husband and children were asked if they would help mom mourn her father and make preparations for a pretend wake or a funeral ceremony for her father. At their request, Ana Luisa's mother visited. She brought photos, records of her husband's favorite music, and some personal items of grandpa's such as a 1940s fedora hat that had made him look dapper. The five of them shared nightly family meals and fireside chats with grandfather's music in the background. They made a little altar over a small round table with these items, a photo, and candles. Sharing the threads of healing memories and stories never told before, they began to weave a collective tapestry that enveloped those who left and those who stayed with a common, transnational love. Ana Luisa reflected on her feelings of guilt and her realization that many years had passed when she was busy working and raising children, all the time counting that there would be a future time to reconnect more deeply with her father again, a truncated illusion that needs to be reckoned with now.

Periods of grief and mourning may be capitalized on as an opportunity for renewal of the continuity of those family and social connections that are still possible to maintain with the communities of origin.

SECOND-GENERATION TRANSNATIONAL EXPOSURE. A new cultural scenario for the immigrant second generation is brought about by global communication technologies that allow for transnational exposures to their parents' countries and long-distance family relationships (Stone, Gomez, Hotzoglou, & Lipnitsky, 2005; Falicov, 2005, 2007, 2014a). A comparative study of adolescence in New York and in Ticuani, a small town in Puebla, Mexico, uncovers interesting aspects of adolescence in transnational contexts (Smith, 2006). In New York, adolescent girls are locked down, parental controls are intense, and adolescence is experienced as a very constraining life stage. However, when the adolescents, girls and boys, go to Ticuani, their parents' hometown, for summer visits, parents and grandparents granted them a lot more freedom. In Ticuani, the adults trust a greater safety and familiarity than in New York, because there is a richer community of relatives and acquaintances of the same language and culture to keep an eye on youth. So paradoxically, in their parents' country, adolescents have more personal freedoms and more caring from adults than in the United States.

These findings confirm the concept of CEFSA described earlier in this chapter, namely, that cultural differences, ecological dangers, and separation anxiety contribute to parents' needs to exert stricter controls over adolescents than they would in their own countries. This leaves second-generation adolescents with having to find ways to integrate these two sets of parental directives, complicating their life cycle predicaments between dependency and autonomy. Nevertheless, this new transnational scenario paves the way to increase resilient biculturalism for both generations rather than the proverbial cultural dissonance between parents and children in immigrant families.

The immigrant's paradox

The matter of cultural continuity and change in the life cycle is revisited again in recent studies reporting that the generation of foreign-born immigrants has better physical and mental health than their children who are born and raised in this country. It appears that the higher the acculturation to American society in terms of language, citizenship, and self-identification, the poorer the mental health as expressed in depression or drug and alcohol abuse. Likewise, higher acculturation has been linked to health problems such as high blood pressure and diabetes and a variety of psychosomatic symptoms in several but not all immigrants groups. This finding of decreasing physical and mental health with increased acculturation over the generations has been dubbed "the immigrant's paradox" (Vega et al., 1998; Organista, 2007; Alegria et al., 2008).

Among Mexicans, the immigrant generation seems to have better overall physical and mental health, less depression, and better school performance than the subsequent generations raised in the United States. Flexible maintenance of traditions and cultural rituals creates a protective sense of "home" with a mix of the old and the new.

Nevertheless, adherence to traditional culture is not always protective. Among foreign-born Asian youth, the rate of completed suicide is higher than among U.S.-born Asian American youth. This may suggest that rapid family acculturation is more protective of depression and suicidality for Asians than for Latino adolescents. One of the theories for this finding is that acculturated youth have more support from their peer group. For the Asian families less acculturated to the U.S. life style, intergenerational conflict may either threaten the very basis of their hierarchical value system or may isolate the adolescent without the supportive benefits of a peer group (Lau, Jernewall, Zane, & Myers, 2002).

Thus, it may depend on the ethnic group and their circumstances whether it works better to have a low or high level of family acculturation. These ethnic-specific findings suggest that therapists need to adopt a careful and inquisitive stance in matters of acculturation and intergenerational conflict. At times, they could support families' wishes to retain their language and cultures. In other instances, they may have to gently become agents of acculturation, depending on each family's wishes and needs and their particular blend of cultural continuity and cultural change.

> Assess your comprehension of the MECA: family life cycle by completing this quiz.

Conclusion

Migration alters how expected and unexpected life cycle transformations evolve. MECA is used in this chapter to understand the various ways in which migration experiences affect the life cycle course of families. It deals with how migration and acculturation experiences, ecological context stressors, and transformations in family organization change the shape and meaning of life cycle events.

The dislocation of migration adds complexity and stresses to the developmental course. The successful adaptation to the multiple stresses and opportunities involved will depend on favorable external circumstances and the family's flexibility and ability to adapt to new requirements while retaining important aspects of their cultural heritage. As migration increases everywhere, family adaptation to the inevitable life cycle progression will be greatly aided by the attention to cultural diversity and the social justice extended to immigrants by institutions, communities, and individuals in the receiving country.

> Recall what you learned in this chapter by completing the Chapter Review.

References

Alegria, M., Canino, G., Shrout, P., Wee, M., Duan, N., Vila, D., et al. (2008). Prevalence of mental illness in immigrant and non-immigrant groups. *Am. Journal of Psychiatry 165*, 359–369.

Artico, C. I. (2003). *Latino Families Broken By Immigration: The Adolescents' Perceptions*. New York, NY: LFB Scholarly Publishing LLC.

Imber-Black, E., Roberts, J., & Whiting, R. A. (2003). *Rituals in families and family therapy*. New York: Norton & Company, Inc.

Bacigalupe, G., & Lambe, S. (2011). Virtualizing intimacy: Information communication technologies and transnational families in therapy. *Family Process, 50,* 12–26.

Boss, P. (1999). *Ambiguous loss*. Cambridge, MA: Harvard University Press.

D'Angelo, E., Llerena-Quinn, R., Colon, F., Shapiro, R., Rodriguez, P., Gallagher, K., et al. (2009). Adaptation of the preventive intervention program for depression for use with Latino families. *Family Process, 48* (2), 269–291.

Du Bois, W. E. B. (1903). *The souls of black folk*. Chicago, IL: McClurg.

Duvall, E. (1957). *Family Development*. Philadelphia, PA: Lippincott.

Erickson, M. (1998). Re-visioning the family life cycle theory and paradigm in marriage and family therapy. *American Journal of Family Therapy, 26*, 4, 341–353.

Falicov, C. J., & Karrer, B. M. (1980). Cultural variations in the family life cycle: the Mexican American family. In E. Carter & M. McGoldrick (Eds.). *The family life cycle: A framework for family therapy*. New York: Gardner Press.

Falicov, C. J. (1988a). Family sociology and family therapy contributions to the family development framework: a comparative analysis and thoughts on future trends. In C. J. Falicov (Ed.), *Family transitions: Continuity and change over the life cycle* (pp. 3–51). New York: Guilford Press.

Falicov, C. J. (1988b). Learning to think culturally in family therapy training. In H. Liddle, D. Breunlin, & D. Schwartz (Eds.), *Handbook of family therapy training and supervision*. New York: Guilford Press.

Falicov, C. J. (1997). So they don't need me anymore: weaving migration, illness and coping. In S. Daniel, J. Hepworth, & W. Doherty (Eds.) *The shared experience of illness: Stories about patients, families and their therapists* (pp. 48–57). New York: Basic Books.

Falicov, C. J. (2002). Ambiguous loss: risk and resilience in Latino families. In M. Suarez-Orozco & M. Paez (Eds.), *Latinos: Remaking America* (pp. 274–288). Berkeley, CA: University of California Press.

Falicov, C. J. (2005a). The Latino family life cycle. In B. Carter & M. McGoldrick (Eds.), *The expanded family life cycle: Individual, family and social perspectives* (Chapter 8, pp. 141–150). New York: Allyn and Bacon.

Falicov, C. J. (2005b). Emotional transnationalism and family identities. Commentary to Stone el al. *Family Process 44*, 399–406.

Falicov, C. J. (2006). El Ciclo de Vida Familiar: Un esquema para la psicoterapia de familia. In A. Roizblatt (ed.), *Terapia Familiar y de Pareja*. Chile: Edit. Mediterraneo.

Falicov, C. J. (2007). Working with transnational immigrants: Expanding meanings of family, community and culture. *Family Process, 46*, 157–172.

Falicov, C. J. (2008). Transnational Journeys. In M. McGoldrick & K. Hardy (Eds.), *Revisioning culture, race and class in family therapy*. New York: Guilford Press.

Falicov, C. J. (2009). Religion and spiritual traditions immigrant families: Significance for Latino health and mental health. In F. Walsh (Ed.), *Spiritual resources in family therapy* (pp. 156–173). New York: Guilford Press.

Falicov, C. J. (2011). Migration and the family life cycle. In M. McGoldrick, N. Garcia-Preto, & B. Carter (Eds.), *The expanded family life cycle: Individual, family and social perspectives* (Chapter 22, 4th ed., pp. 336–347). Massachusetts: Allyn & Bacon.

Falicov, C. J. (2012). Immigrant family processes. In F. Walsh (Ed.), *Normal family processes* (pp. 297–323). New York: Guilford Press.

Falicov, C. J. (2014a). *Latino families in therapy* (2nd ed.). New York: Guilford Press.

Falicov, C. J. (2014b). Psychotherapy and supervision as cultural encounters: The MECA framework. In C. Falender, E. Shafrankske, & C. J. Falicov (Eds.), *Multiculturalism and diversity in clinical supervision: A competency-based approach* (Chapter 2). Washington, DC: APA.

Falicov, C.J. (2014c). Immigrant clients, supervisees, and supervision. In C.A. Falender, E.P. Shafranske, & C.J. Falicov (Eds.), *Multiculturalism and diversity in clinical supervision: A competency-based approach*. (Chapter 5, pp 111–144). Washington, DC: American Psychological Association.

Falicov, C. J. (2014c). The multiculturalism and diversity of families. In T. Sexton & J. Lebow (Eds.), *Handbook of family therapy: Theory, research and practice*.

Falicov, C.J. (in press). The multiculturalism and diversity of families. In T. Sexton & J. Lebow (Eds.), *Handbook of family therapy: Theory, research and practice*. New York: Brunner-Routledge.

Garcia- Coll, C. and Magnuson, K. (1997). The psychological experience of immigration: a developmental perspective. In A. Booth, A. C. Crouter, & N. Landale (Eds.), *Immigration and the family: Research and policy on U.S. immigrants*. Mahwah, NJ: Lawrence Erlbaum Associates, Inc.

Hirsch, J. (2003). *A courtship after marriage: Sexuality and love in Mexican transnational families*. Los Angeles, CA: University of California Press.

Lau, A. S., Jernewall, N. M., Zane, N., & Myers, H. F. (2002). Correlates of suicidal behaviors among Asian-American outpatient youths. *Cultural Diversity and Ethnic Minority Psychology, 8*, 199–213.

Minuchin, S. (1974). *Families and family therapy*. Cambridge: Harvard University Press.

Mitrani, V. B., Muir, J. A., & Santisteban, D. A. (2004). Addressing immigration-related separations in Hispanic families with a behavior-problem adolescent. *American Journal of Orthopsychiatry, 74*(3), 219–229.

Organista, K. (2007). *Solving Latino psychosocial and health problems: Theory, practice and populations.* New York: John Wiley and Sons.

Parsons, T. (1951). *The social system.* Glencoe, IL: Free Press.

Santisteban, D. A., & Mena, M. P. (2009). Culturally informed family therapy for adolescents: A tailored and integrative treatment for Hispanic youth. *Family Process, 48*(2): 253–268.

Shanley, J. P. (2007). *Doubt: A parable.* New York: Dramatist Play Service, Inc.

Sluzki, C. E. (1979). Migration and family conflict. *Family Process, 18*(1), 379–392.

Smith, R. C. (2006). *Mexican New York: Transnational lives of new immigrants.* Berkeley, CA: University of California Press.

Smokowski, P. R., & Bacallao, M. (2011). *Becoming bicultural: Risk, resilience and Latino youth.* New York: New York University Press.

Stone, E., Gomez, E., Hotzoglou, D., & Lipnitsky, J. Y. (2005). Transnationalism as a motif in family stories. *Family Process, 44,* 381–398.

Suárez-Orozco, C., Todorova, I., & Louie, J. (2002). Making up for lost time: The experience of separation and reunification among immigrant families. *Family Process 41*(4), 625–644.

Suárez-Orozco, C. E., & Suárez-Orozco, M. M. (2002). *Children of immigration.* Cambridge, MA: Harvard University Press.

Suárez-Orozco, C., Suárez-Orozco, M., & Todorova, I. (2008). *Learning a new land: Immigrant students in American society.* Cambridge, MA: Harvard University Press.

Trueba, E. T. (1999). *Latinos Unidos: From cultural diversity to the politics of solidarity.* Lanham, MD: Rowman & Littlefield.

Vega, W. A., Kolody, B., Aguilar-Gaxiola, S., Alderete, E., Catalano, R., & Caraveo-Anduaga, J. (1998). Lifetime prevalence of DSM-III-R psychiatric disorders among urban and rural Mexican American in California. *Archives of General Psychiatry, 55,* 771–782.

Walsh, F. (2006). *Strengthening family resilience* (2nd ed). New York: Guilford Press.

Zayas, L. H. (2011). *Latinas attempting suicide: When cultures, families and daughters collide.* New York: Oxford University Press.

Chapter 13

Becoming an Adult: Learning to Love and Work

Richard H. Fulmer

Learning Objectives

- Describe how the young adulthood life cycle stage has changed for the most recent generation and the potential causes of these changes.
- Identify the developmental tasks of both early and late young adulthood.
- Compare how the developmental task of work is handled in early and late young adulthood.
- Examine how the developmental task of love changes as a person transitions from early to late young adulthood.
- Explore shifts that occur between early and late adulthood related to outlook, family dynamics, and the use of alcohol and drugs.
- Describe unique challenges posed by young adulthood for individuals with same-sex attractions.
- What are the effects of social class and gender on family formation during later young adulthood.
- Discuss effects of child-rearing and child care for women of all social classes.

Introduction

Young adulthood is the developmental period in which one family is succeeded by another. The grown children develop authority, learn to love strangers as they do family, and begin to support themselves. Parents assist this succession by providing a home base, relinquishing control, taking pride, offering assistance, and reassuring themselves. They inspire by providing examples of mature love and satisfaction from work. Parental happiness, or at least parental satisfaction with their own responses to the demands of life, is a bulwark against the grown child's discouragement, cynicism, or despair.

Young Adulthood(s) in the New Century

Although the beginning of this phase is still marked by older adolescents leaving home after graduating from high school (Furstenberg, Kennedy, McCloyd, Rumbaut, & Settersten 2003), today's young adults are reaching the dominant culture's markers

of full adulthood—completing their education, living financially independently from parents, marrying and having children—much later in life. According to Arnett (2007); Arnett & Fishel (2013), the length of this life cycle stage has been expanding, now stretching from 18 to 29 or even longer, especially for White, middle-class families in the United States.

Some commentators see the lengthening of this developmental period as driven by the drastic economic changes in our society. Others see it as caused by the values of baby boomer parents, who wish their children to pursue interests that are personally fulfilling rather than just becoming financially independent. Both younger and older generations have been disparaged as "boomerang kids" and "helicopter parents." Some see the expansion of this period as necessary for self-discovery and identity development (Arnett, 2007), while others fear the prolongation as a developmental arrest or a self-indulgent refusal to accept the responsibilities of adulthood (Jay, 2013; Twenge, Freeman, & Campbell, 2012; Kimmel, 2008).

How family therapists regard this period will certainly influence how we treat it: as an artifact of difficult financial conditions, as an opportunity for creative maturation for both the parental and young adult generations, or as a potentially malignant interaction of parental over-involvement and adult child overdependence. This family tension (for the children, between being free of parental control and prematurely losing parental support; for the parents, between offering protective guidance and overindulging a developmental delay) is often still the central clinical problem of treating families in this stage.

The ways families accomplish the tasks of this stage in their lives vary with gender, socioeconomic status, race, culture, sexual orientation, and time in history. It is misleading to see any one path as "normal" and all others as "deviant." This chapter proposes a developmental model that is meant to describe some themes and tasks for the period and then suggests how environmental conditions create diverse young adulthoods for different groups in society. It will also divide young adulthood into two phases, early and late, which entail different developmental tasks and objectives. In most of the cases I see at this developmental phase, it is usually parents who seek help. I usually see them alone first to get their view of the problem and to begin to shape a genogram. I next see the emerging adult alone. I often have several meetings of parents and grown children separately until I clarify for myself how they are negotiating the tasks of the period. This chapter will focus on the normal developmental vicissitudes of emerging adulthood, not on the several major mental illnesses—major depressive disorder, schizophrenia, and bipolar disorder, for example—that characteristically and coincidentally have their onset during it but are not caused by it. If I encounter a client who is suffering from one of these disorders during this assessment phase, I recommend a combination of family psychoeducation, medication, and, if necessary, inpatient hospitalization, but I will not describe these techniques here. I tell the grown children that I will not tell the parents things they tell me unless I think they are putting themselves or others in danger. I tell both parents and children that I think it is better if they ask and tell important things directly to each other and I will work toward that. When I get each side to frame their important questions or statements, I start to get the whole family together

to facilitate non-accusatory declarations of what they want and do not want from each other. I use empathy to communicate or correct my understanding of each and interrupt them during sessions to coach them on effective expression. In a setting in which I see only the young adult, as in a college counseling service, I make the same statement about confidentiality to the student. In the rest of this chapter, I will try to describe to clinicians the practical and emotional experiences I think are important for both generations during emerging adulthood. I hope that these descriptions will help clinicians find an empathic stance with all members of the family. I will occasionally offer brief technical suggestions, but my main goal is to help the therapist make the patients feel understood.

> Assess your comprehension of young adulthood(s) in the new century by completing this quiz.

Early Young Adulthood: Developmental Tasks

Erik Erikson (1963) wrote that Sigmund Freud's goal for therapy was to enable patients to work and to love. The young adult must negotiate a path between these activities. For the middle and upper classes, one path focuses on the development of a highly valued profession. Ideally, this work expresses a personal meaning, and, for that reason, may be pursued with a virtually religious intensity. The young worker may endure lengthy and costly training, sacrifice social pleasures, move to inconvenient or unfamiliar venues, and/or delay economic compensation, even subordinating relationships to work. In later emerging adulthood, this path divides into two. The second path finds very important meaning in human relationships in addition to work, eventually resulting in the building of a new family. Both roles are essential to society. Religious, political, and military leaders, as well as artists, scientists, and cultural innovators, all continue to find such primary meaning in their work that they may not develop a strongly invested family life. A larger number find as much or more meaning in relationships and become "household-ers," physically reproducing society.

Work tasks: Preparation without pay or earning out of necessity

Young adults of all social classes hope to depend on their families of origin for tangible and emotional support as they pursue financial independence through work. The way in which this independence can be earned has changed a great deal in recent decades. Industrial jobs have declined and union influence has diminished with them. The jobs that have replaced them are in providing service, often require technological skills and are less stable, obtained and lost through ongoing competition (Kamenetz, 2007). This job market requires skills acquired through some form of postsecondary education. Today nearly 75 percent of high school graduates enroll in some type of college after high school (Draut, 2007). The middle-class culture grants a moratorium on cash-producing work during this period, but only to those able to pay (or borrow enough) for such delay. For lower-income groups, the need to support oneself or family without interruption makes even a brief break in wage earning extremely difficult or impossible, and borrowing may be out of the question.

The average rate of freshmen graduating from public high school in 4 years in our 50 largest cities is 53 percent, compared with 71 percent in the middle-class suburbs (Dillon, 2009), so a very substantial proportion of our population does not enjoy this moratorium. "Postsecondary education" for dropouts consists of unskilled labor, temporary jobs, on-the-job training by employers, or "training" in criminal activities on the street or during temporary incarceration.

Relationship tasks: Trying to find love in lust

In the realm of relationships, the young adults must not only loosen ties with their families of origin but also expand and transfer their deep family attachments to others of both sexes. The quality of the intimate relationships that young adults form will be influenced by the parental, marital, and sibling relationships they have experienced.

To correct the usual split between concern for autonomy in male development and emotional connectedness in female development, I emphasize the importance of relatedness in male development and the need for a period of self-focus and separateness during young adulthood in female development.

For both sexes, early young adulthood is a period when the development of work skill and, if possible, professional identity take precedence over the development of relationships. Arnett (2006); Arnett & Fishel (2013) calls this "the self-focused age" and contends that it is "normal, healthy, and temporary." If relationship and work opportunities conflict (such as admission to a desirable college that does not offer a spot to a romantic partner), the middle-class young adult will usually choose in favor of work. These priorities tend to change in later emerging adulthood. For lower-income groups, however, when college or some other extended educational preparation is not available, family relationships (including a new baby) may become (or remain) a much more important source of meaning and satisfaction than a job.

> **Assess your comprehension of early young adulthood: developmental tasks by completing this quiz.**

Early Young Adulthood: Learning to Work

Learning to work: Blending meaning with remuneration

Young men have been expected to work at cash-producing jobs to support first themselves and then their families. Since the 1960s, however, women of all social classes feel more entitled to find meaning in work and many want to increase their future independence from men. They also realize that real wages have declined so much since the 1960s that it is only the most affluent families that can survive on the husband's income alone. Women have been very successful in joining the work force. Since 2005, they have become more numerous (58 percent) than men as postsecondary students at every level (Lewin, 2006). For every 100 women who achieve a Bachelor's degree, only 73 men now do so. (Doty, 2009). Many colleges practice "affirmative action" toward men by admitting some males with lower SAT scores and grades than some females to keep the proportion of men on campus from falling too low (Delahunty-Britz, 2006).

Learning to love and "Hooking up"

Kathleen Bogle (2008) observed that college students pair-date much less often, but are more likely to "hook up" in casual sexual encounters that do not necessarily imply an ongoing relationship. Fielder et al. (2013), however, surveyed 483 first year college females and found that while hookups have become prevalent, only 7 to 18 percent had a sexual hookup each month, while 25 to 38 percent had sex in the context of relationships each month. This recent finding may reflect a return to relationships or may indicate a hesitation to report the (perhaps for women) still less-socially-approved hookup. It has been thought for some years that the hookup culture was driven by men, but Hamilton and Armstrong (2009) contend that middle and upper-middle class college women pursue a "self -development imperative" that makes hookups more desirable than deeper relationships that are too demanding and distracting. Kimmel (2008) agrees that neither male nor female students tend to stay in monogamous relationships for very long while they are in college.

Clinicians may ask both men and women about the quality of these experiences. Are they having fun? Would they prefer something else? Do they ever happen when they are not drunk or high? What is that like? Have they ever had "unprotected" sex? Have they ever had sex out of "obligation" or performance expectations rather than desire? The answers to these questions may lead to a discussion of how sexual activity fits into the young person's identity. Although "hooking up" seems to have brought increased extramarital sexual activity for some decades now, neither Bogle nor Kimmel report higher rates of out-of-wedlock pregnancies or abortions for the college women they describe. College students practice rigorous birth control, including, since June 2013, an over-the-counter morning-after pill. Worried parents might be able to comfort themselves with Kimmel's eventual reassurance about "hooking up" as a time-limited developmental stage, not a new lifestyle.

For low-income young adults, a similar pattern of nonpermanent, nonexclusive, pleasure-oriented sexual relationships is reported, but with less effort to avoid pregnancy. Nathan Fosse (2010) interviewed 38 African American men from poor urban neighborhoods, 20 of whom reported being "faithful" to their current partners, while 18 practiced nonmonogamy. These men distinguished between women they considered casual partners for mutually recreational sex and those to whom they were more socially and emotionally connected. Fosse reports that many of his respondents considered these more serious relationships to be of greater importance to them, and yearned to consider them reliable, thus suggesting affiliative needs even in these notoriously (by their own proclamation) "single" men. Pregnancies, unplanned but not truly unexpected, help to cement the interpersonal bond and raise the status of both mother and father without marriage (Fosse, 2010; LeBlanc, 2004; Edin & Kefalas, 2005; Edin & Nelson, 2013).

Idealism

Not having much life experience, many young adults try to use values to guide themselves. They feel that problems can be solved by living in accordance with ideals rather than by acting in their own immediate self-interest. They are also often grandiose, feeling they can easily avoid the mistakes their elders have made. Although not fully mature, this arrogance may still be a necessary maturational stage on the way to developing true personal authority.

Young adults' consciously (and sometimes righteously) held values often differ, at least superficially, from those of their parents. If they are still accepting their parents' financial support, they may have to tolerate the moral dilemma of holding a benefactor in contempt. This may pose conflicts with parents, depending on how they handle the disrespect of grown children. Therapists might sympathize with parents and praise them for their emotional tolerance.

Alcohol and drugs

Early young adulthood is the period when consciousness-altering drugs—such as alcohol, marijuana, the neuro-enhancers Ritalin or Adderall, hallucinogens, cocaine, and heroin—are most enthusiastically used. There must be multiple reasons for this—the exercise of freedom from parental supervision, a social lubricant for the many anxiety-filled social contacts of the period, or an aid to ecstatic, sometimes sexual, celebration at parties. While most will grow out of this phase eventually, often in later emerging adulthood, young people whose family members are or have been addicted to substances are at serious risk of becoming entangled in a similar addiction. After hearing of the first blackout, clinicians might ask "Was it fun"? They might learn about when it was fun and how it stopped being so. After two blackouts, they might ask "If you saw a friend doing what you were doing, would you be scared for him or her?" Be glad the patients are telling you their experience and encourage them to treat themselves with kindness and concern for their own safety. Drinking is supposed to be fun. If they can keep it so (a life's work), they are probably OK. If they cannot, I would consider (after consultation with colleagues) telling the student you will call his or her parents and do so, urging a family conference.

Poor urban young adults of color have easier access to "hard drugs" in their neighborhoods than do college students. They are also more susceptible to being recruited to sell, and much more likely to be arrested for selling (with heavier penalties than possession) than white college students, who are treated more leniently by police and can hire more effective lawyers. Some poor families are financially supported by their young adults who are dealers (Venkatesh, 2006). These young adults run a higher risk of developing serious addictions or, if selling, they may suffer incarceration or death. Drug use that might be "recreational" for a college student could be lethal for a poor young person.

Parents and college

Few young adults present for family therapy, but their parents do. If their children have gone to college, some psychoeducation about the ordinary vicissitudes of college life (the need for the organization of time, uncertainty about choosing an academic focus, sexual freedom, and substance use) may

diminish parental anxiety (Arnett & Fishel, 2013). I also ask parents how, when they were in this developmental period themselves, they renegotiated their relationship with *their* parents, and how they want their relationships with their own children to change. Coaching parents to use a light touch focused on inquiry and problem solving rather than reprimand and exhortation can be useful, as is coaching parental follow-through.

While normalizing such change and some of the shocking parts of college life, clinicians must also name the red flags that should command the parents' attention. These may include missing classes, failing to turn in work, academic dishonesty, or debilitating use of drugs or alcohol. Any grades of C or below deserve a careful inquiry, and more than one such grade requires a conference between parents and student, perhaps face to face. This is assuming, of course, that the student permits the parents to view his or her transcript. One middle-class family I saw told me that their bright son, who had declared his learning disabilities to his highly-respected college, had done well in a special, structured program which ended after his first 2 years. In the middle of his junior year, they were surprised to receive a letter from the administration that, because of several failing grades, his enrollment was being suspended. It emerged that when the student was no longer offered the structured program, he began to flounder and soon became overwhelmed. To conceal his failures, he had used his considerable talents to hack into the university's computer-based grade reporting system and improved the grades to which his parents had access. Teased by the media and colleges themselves for being "helicopter parents," the astounded couple felt they had not "hovered their helicopter" low enough or long enough to protect their son. His college certainly had not been vigilant about his deterioration and he was still too ashamed of his disabilities to reveal his plight. These conscientious parents were no longer embarrassed by their vigilance, an attitude I strongly reinforced.

Learning disabilities

Changes in environmental demands and increases in emotional maturity during young adulthood may have an ameliorating effect on learning disabilities during young adulthood. While success in high school requires good performance in many different academic tasks, the specialization of a college "major" or a first job permits students and employees to concentrate on their strengths. As young adults mature, they may accept their disabilities more and feel less shame, resiliently working their way around their difficulties.

These advantages allow them to manage the ill effects of disabilities, but the structure of college (less class time, more homework) also introduces some dangers. One of these is the loss of organizational support provided by parents and a structured school day, especially in the management of time. Clinicians should be alert to diagnosed and undiagnosed disabilities and help parents replace their direct supervision by engaging college services (securing and funding the necessary testing to certify the disability, for instance) to replace such structure. Students with disabilities need much more aggressive academic advice than those without. Schools rarely provide it unless asked, and students usually will not ask, either out of ignorance or shame, or both. Unaware of "drop" deadlines, for example, students may not withdraw in time from courses in which they are hopelessly behind. One or two "F's" in their freshman year can devastate their cumulative GPA (grade point average), even in subsequent years. Students who are struggling can petition to take a lower course load and graduate in 5 years instead of four. Devastatingly low grades can be expunged and effectively done over at a slower pace or with tutoring. Such solutions can permit a comeback, but they may require additional funds, strong parental support, and occasionally parents' direct intervention with college officers. Clinicians can recommend and discuss possible parental or student resistance to such actions without thinking they are encouraging "helicoptering" or dependence.

Low-income young adults with learning disabilities who do not attend college (probably the majority) are on their own in finding adult services, counseling about rights and what economic assistance may be available (Marshak, Seligman, & Prezant, 1999). Clinicians may be able to help secure adult services for these clients, but finding such assistance in the adult world after formal schooling is uncharted territory.

CASE ILLUSTRATION

Arlene, Ray, and Judy

It may be necessary to coach parents through launching their young adult child when learning problems require extra adult supports at this phase. Arlene and Ray (both successful lawyers) worried about their daughter Judy, a bright high school senior. Her intellectual processing was slow and she had been diagnosed with mild attention deficit disorder. It was only with considerable tutorial structure that she was able to finish high school with good grades and high enough Scholastic Aptitude Test (SAT) scores to be accepted at several good colleges.

However, her difficulty in working independently on subjects for which she was not motivated made her parents think she needed an extra year before college, and I agreed. She enrolled at a postsecondary school for learning disabled students and with some fits and starts managed fairly well until the spring she turned 19. Although she liked the school, Judy had difficulties with the organizational aspects of college. She slept late, missed classes, and (most maddeningly) did not turn in work she had finished.

At that point, she dropped out, and the parents brought her into sessions for the first time. With Judy sitting between them, first one parent would remonstrate, then the other. I could see that her slow processing (combined, of course, with her guilt and anxiety) interfered with her ability to respond. Judy would fall behind in listening to her loving, anxious, emphatic parents, becoming ever more silent. I made the rule that if one parent addressed Judy, the second parent could not add anything until Judy had responded to the first. The parents, having been frustrated by Judy's increasing silence, and Judy, feeling she had lost her voice, all accepted this very willingly. The parents began to pause, and Judy began to fill the silences with her own ideas, albeit haltingly.

After her shaky beginning, the parents decided to again defer Judy's admission to a mainstream college and reenrolled her at the learning disability postsecondary school. Continued coaching and several family sessions to help parents and daughter work on the boundaries of their support and her initiative enabled Judy to complete the preparatory learning disability college. Judy and her parents learned that while she could be overwhelmed by a large volume of work, she could do very well by taking a lighter load and a slower pace.

She enrolled in a mainstream college that would permit this part-time course load. Living away from home the first semester, Judy could structure her work for one, but not both of the courses she took. She did well enough to remain in the school, but had to agree to repeat one course. Judy, however, was happy to still be in school and proud to be working toward a B average in a mainstream college. I reassured the parents about their efforts. Arlene criticized herself for over-involvement and vowed (with Ray's strong agreement) that she would never work this hard with Judy again. Judy now acknowledged her own passivity: "If mom takes control, I sit back. I need less push from her. I learned two things: First: I need someone to help me work. Second: It can't be Mom." This discriminating insight was accepted by all. Judy had finally developed a realistic idea of just how much help she needed, and, for the first time, actively asked for it.

I saw Judy's problems as compounded by the pressures of a popular attitude, which sees disability as a result of low motivation and feels parents should adopt a "sink or swim" strategy (Levine, 2003). I reassured them that it was due, in large part, to their active intervention that their daughter was moving along well. They recruited the same tutor that had been successful with Judy in high school to meet with her weekly in college. She moved into her parent's basement with two classmates. They visited me only once or twice a year. Judy's insight into her own limitations and her unfailing patience and determination contributed greatly to her success, as did her parents' combination of strong support and increasing self-restraint. At a later follow-up, the family was very proud to tell me that Judy had graduated from the mainstream college, receiving a Bachelor's degree with a B+ average.

Mentors

While this is a time of more or less polite contempt toward parents and their allies, the moral simplicity of young adults permits them to idealize a mentor who can serve as a bridge between immersion in family and greater self-definition. This worshipful relationship holds dangers, however, if either participant uses the relationship in an exploitive way. College students may venerate upperclassmen, teaching assistants, or teachers. Lower-income youth who are not in college may accept guidance from members of their extended family, employers, superiors in the armed forces, athletic coaches, senior street acquaintances, gang leaders, or, if incarcerated, older prisoners. Clinicians may wish to inquire about what patients are learning from their mentors that their parents did not offer. A curious, nonjudgmental approach may encourage patients to also share misgivings, if they have any. If the patient can articulate his or her ambivalence and assess the mentor in a discriminating way, the client can gain from the mentor without having to emulate him or her.

The same-sex peer group affects love

An exclusive group of peers (in college or neighborhood) can form an important transition for the young adult between the family of origin and the pair-bond that is sometimes the basis for the family of procreation. A feeling of belonging, the structure of shared rules, hierarchy, mutual caring, and loyalty in gangs bridges the lonely gap between family of origin and family of procreation for both sexes (Taffel & Blau, 2001). At the beginning of young adulthood, it can enable separation by creating an alternative home place. It may be especially important for gay men and lesbians who sometimes "come out" to peers before they do to their families (Chandler, 1997).

A few years later, however, the emerging adult may find the gang has a conservative aspect, pulling against further progress into the erotic/romantic couple that forms the nucleus for a new family. Many young people yearn for such close relationships, but the anxiety they provoke inspires young people to seek security in their peer groups. This group-versus-pair conflict of the same-sex group can be seen at every socioeconomic level, for both men and women.

Kimmel (2008) describes fraternity boys enforcing homophobic and sexist norms as standards for masculinity. In his *Code of the Street*, Elijah Anderson (2000) sees it in young, poor African American mothers who become more bonded to other young mothers than to the fathers of their children. African American male rap singers (and the middle-class young White men who feel represented by their songs) look to their "Dawgs" for cautionary tales about faithless women who would ensnare them, using mottos like "Bros before Hos" (Fulmer, 2008). Powerful middle-class sisterhoods make unflattering comparisons between men and their own sex with remarks such as "Do you notice how a really great guy would only be an ordinary girlfriend?" and (in remarkable "agreement" with the rappers) "Men are dogs!"

The same-sex peer group affects work

The gang also influences the work of young adults. Military leaders and athletic coaches customarily use loyalty to buddies to inspire compatriots to risk life and limb for the success of the group. Leaving this intense context of team-related meaning can be difficult when, later in young adulthood, individual initiative becomes necessary for success in work. Often a new work group can be found, but this is a perilous transition. Sometimes, adults try to retain their membership in the old group. The risks of entrepreneurship that might permit exit from poverty, like the risks of love in the couple bond, may be discouraged by the group. Some individuals may resist this old tie and become independently successful, while others may find their motivation diminished by gang judgment.

How could it be that the same buddies who supported them when they were young would, only a few years later, now hold them back? Clinicians can recognize and help put into words their patients' conflicts between loyalty and their changing needs as they enter later young adulthood, permitting them a deliberate, thoughtful choice.

> **Assess your comprehension of early young adulthood: ages 18 to 22: learning to work by completing this quiz.**

Later Young Adulthood: Trying to Consolidate Work and Family

Learning to love: Beginning to form a pair bond

Bogle (2008) reports that as college students graduate and begin the transition to late young adulthood, they return to a pair-dating culture. The loss of the relatively familiar population of fellow students and the relative physical safety of the college campus make women more cautious about the male strangers they are meeting. A second major reason for beginning to date is that both men and women may begin to think about more serious, permanent relationships. Again, clinicians can help patients articulate the difference between someone who is a fun date and thinking of someone as spouse material.

"Perfect" love

Individuals from all social classes and sexual orientations begin to seek relationships with a new ambition: finding a relationship that is exclusive, intimate both erotically and emotionally, and expressive of deeply held personal values and ideas about the self. Eventually, this becomes a search for a life partner, but it often takes an early form as a search for a perfect love. This search for perfection in relationship is often an important transaction between the young adult and his or her family of origin. It is a heady experience to be discovered by someone whose love is not based on role obligations and who is different in some important way from one's parents.

Learning to love: From self-involvement to beginning to think like a householder

The grandiosity and asceticism of early young adulthood is gradually replaced by a more realistic view of what can be accomplished: a more complex, situation-based morality; disillusionment; a focusing of work interests; and a wish for a home. Interest shifts from the difficult task of definition of the self to the more complex project of defining family and self-in-a-family. As realism replaces grandiosity, young adults may enjoy actually making some of their dreams come true. They may also have a sense of disappointment in that the fantasy of many possibilities is reduced to just a few realities. A supportive therapist may be especially important as the passage of time and real achievements inevitably narrow alternatives.

Mentors–disillusionment

Late young adulthood may be a time when individuals become disillusioned with their mentors. This experience can be depressing, however, as the heady feeling of "having the answer" begins to erode. Young adults may feel that their mentors have deceived them and end their relationships in a storm of bitter disappointment. Or they may simply grow away from the mentors, losing interest in their charisma.

Alcohol and drugs in later young adulthood

By their mid-20s, many individuals gradually back away from intense drug and alcohol use as social anxieties lessen and adult obligations increase. The exceptions, of course, are people who have become addicted. In later emerging adulthood, substance abuse can be seen more clearly as a compulsion and addressed as such clinically. Clinicians may inquire about substance abuse in previous generations of the family.

These experiences—the acquisition of real satisfactions, the ability to consider the needs of others as well as one's own, the realization that many fantasies cannot be pursued, sobriety itself—are the beginnings of the householder identity.

Family dynamics

If the departing young adult is first-born, parents may turn their attention more fully to younger siblings who remain at home. Those children may grow into the space vacated by the older brother or sister with mixed consequences. A formerly crowded living situation may be relieved if a sibling can move into the now-empty bedroom. The older child may feel dispossessed, however, and that he or she has lost a home base, demanding full reinstatement when returning for holidays.

Older children may return for other reasons, such as in the case of a lower-income family in which an 8-year-old boy had become depressed and had recently begun sleeping with his mother. We wondered if he was regressing into an earlier dependency until we learned that his emerging adult sister had returned home to recover from a crack episode and had reclaimed the couch the boy usually slept on, which had been hers as an adolescent. While taking a genogram, clinicians should also inquire about the current emotional and physical well-being of every other member of the family and pursue the implications of this information for the identified patient.

Parents' relationship

As children move on, parents may turn back to each other as a couple. If reviving the couple relationship is successful, it can fill the loss of day-to-day parental activities and contact with children. If, however, parental activities were a welcome distraction from marital discord, the couple's problems may reemerge with disruptive effect. If a marriage that was held together for the sake of childrearing is dissolved, young adults may feel that their loyalties must be divided, and the continuity of their family is interrupted, leaving them to fend for themselves.

In a lower-income family, where parents never lived together as a couple, the executive pair may have been grandmother and mother. If the young adult moves out, the grandmother may get a welcome rest, and the mother may be free to pursue postsecondary training to improve her employment opportunities. It is also possible, however, that mother's now teenage daughter will feel the urge (and be unconsciously encouraged by her mother) to fill the house with new life and mother (now a grandmother) will take care of the newborn while daughter (now a young adult mother) tries to finish high school, enroll in college, or enter the labor force. The therapist should try to proactively stay ahead of this pattern. The mother may bring the daughter in, complaining of intractable conflict and trying hard to restrain her with negative judgments. Daughter consequently fears that to mature is to lose her mother's love, but also wants to be free of her control. She may surprise everyone by trying to solve this conflict with a suicide attempt. If the attempt is unsuccessful, a pregnancy may soon follow, and everyone buckles down to a new role, but another family without a well-educated breadwinner has begun. The therapist might head this off by interpreting the daughter's fear of losing her relationship to her mother if she grows up into, say, a job outside the home. However, the clinician must also get the mother to reassure daughter that she will continue to love her and really does not want her to start a family until a substantially later time.

How financial support affects the relationship between parents and adult children

In recent years, a depressed economy has caused the costs of college to rise much faster than inflation. Student loans are more costly, and Pell grants, which covered three fourths of college costs in the 1970s, now cover less than one third. Students graduate with higher debt (The Project on Student Debt, 2013) and often the best solution to defray expenses after graduation is to temporarily live with parents. One in four young adults will return at least once, and clinicians can reassure parents that such returns should be considered adaptive until proven otherwise (Arnett & Fishel, 2013; Pew Research Center, 2013; Parker, 2012; Weissmann, 2013). If the young adult still lives at home or has been to college and returned, parents usually present with some conflict with children wanting adult status while living under their roof. The young adult may expect no curfew, freedom to sleep elsewhere without parental inquiry, or to sleep at home with a girlfriend or boyfriend without explanation. Parents may feel obliged to enact some stereotype of thwarting dependency. They may want to continue a high school tradition of respectful gestures toward the parent, and to secure the safety of their home by monitoring guests. Clinicians may frame these good faith but contradictory goals as developmentally appropriate for both generations, and help negotiate adjustments that acknowledge the family's new needs. Young adults can demonstrate maturity by working (school or job) outside the home and being considerate (rather than entitled) in their behavior. Contributing some of their earned money to the support of the household can make them more welcome. Parents can aid growth by increasingly

recognizing their children's rights and responsibilities as adults.

Low-income families heroically make their boundaries permeable according to need (Venkatesh, 2006). Because of their willingness to "double up," poor families are our country's greatest single bulwark against homelessness. Permeability and the consequent shifting membership of the family challenge the need for order and hierarchy, particularly young adults who are developmentally programmed to resist authority and who may not be emotionally attached to the "chain of command" of the family. Sometimes, returning young adults can add stability as a new authority and model for self-improvement, but sometimes they may undermine established rules and increase disorder. Clinicians might want to keep tabs on the shifting membership of families, and ask how boundaries are managed with each change. It may help to coach mothers of all social classes to have discussions with their teenage daughters about dressing more modestly when a brother's young adult male friend is staying for a while. According to Le Blanc (2004), low-income mothers make an effort to prevent the sexual abuse of young females by never leaving their young girls in the apartment with a man who is not a blood relative. Middle-class parents whose college students' friends are home with younger siblings should be equally alert. It is important for clinicians to assist mothers to enforce this rule. It comes under extra pressure when friends of brothers are in and out, and it is sometimes effective to support mothers in their vigilance and planning for backup from an adult female neighbor or an adult babysitter when they are out and the young men are there.

Whitbeck (2009) describes a more difficult developmental path through emerging adulthood for the truly homeless young. In his longitudinal, 3-year study, he shows that children who unilaterally exit or are kicked out of their homes are often in intractable conflict with their parents. While this conflict is itself a traumatic loss, being homeless further "deforms" their journey to attain the markers of full adulthood. For instance, he shows the malignant effects of lack of parental support during these years when he describes homeless teens who are first diagnosed with conduct disorder and often follow a deteriorating path to antisocial personality disorder and major depressive disorder. Whitbeck's work certainly makes clear the importance of parental support and guidance throughout emerging adulthood by documenting the negative consequences for young adults when it is absent. Clinicians should do their best to encourage families to find alternatives to homelessness—living with relatives, finding temporary residential placements, or locating church or other not-for-profit organizations to shelter ejected children until they can find jobs that enable them to support themselves legally.

Special Challenges of Young Adulthood for Lesbians, Gays, and Bisexuals

Tolerance of same-sex relationships has increased markedly in some locations and cultures in the United States over the last decade. Same-sex marriage was legalized in Massachusetts in 2003 and in 12 other states since. Where such acceptance has increased, it has changed the shape of gay young adulthood. Savin-Williams (2005) finds the new generation of gay youth to be far less suicidal, to feel less rejected by society, and even to be less likely to define themselves by their gayness. As recently as a decade ago, gays feared both family and high school community disapproval and so waited until they had left home to "come out." Now the mean age of gays "coming out" to others has decreased from age 23 (D'Augelli, Hershberger, & Pilkington, 2001) to 18 (Savin-Williams, 2005) or even 16 (D'Augelli, Grossman, & Starks, 2006), an age when they are still living in their childhood households. This earlier time for self-disclosure suggests less fear of negative family response, more community support for the families, more cohesion within families, and more support for the gay member from the family (Denizet-Lewis, 2009).

But considerable intolerance remains. At this writing, thirty-five states prohibit same-sex marriage in their constitutions and/or state laws (NCSL, 2013). In 2011, the FBI reported decreases in hate crimes committed because of race, religion, and national origin, while anti-gay hate crimes continued to increase (LA Times, 2012; FBI, 2011). Clinicians

may help LGB young adults and their families with a developmental goal (one that heterosexuals do not have to face) to reduce their internalized homophobia (Rosario, Scrimshaw, Hunter, & Braun, 2006).

In line with the differences within the population just reported, Diamond and Butterworth (2008) conclude that when family rejection does occur, it remains a powerful negative force in gay young adulthood. They found that White and Latino LGB (their research does not include transgendered) youth who reported high levels of family rejection were far more likely to be depressed, to use illegal drugs, and to attempt suicide. Non-Latino White women reported the lowest levels of family rejection, while Latino men reported the highest (Ryan, Huebner, Diaz, & Sanchez, 2009). Clinicians should note that some researchers question whether disclosure to family is always beneficial as a therapeutic goal. They suggest that therapists working with LGBT clients contemplating disclosure should make a case-by-case judgment whether any particular family has enough flexibility and good will to accept the difficult news without estrangement (Diamond & Butterworth, 2008). A vivid *The New Yorker* article (Aviv, 2012) tells of gay teenagers rejected by their families who become homeless and have no way to get enough income to establish an address that would permit them to apply for a job that would allow self-support. A tart response to the article in a subsequent letter to the editor emphasizes that the recent advances in legal recognition of gay marriage benefit only the middle class and are irrelevant to this estranged underclass whose needs are so much more basic.

LaSala (2010) interviewed 65 gay and lesbian youth and their parents, discovering a family adjustment process in reaction to gay children coming out to their parents. This study is especially useful to clinicians in that it does not describe gay self-acceptance as a solely individual process but as a reciprocal pattern of parent–child interaction. While LaSala considers the news that a child is gay to be an "earthquake," he also notes that all the families attracted to his study had recovered at least somewhat from that news. His work emphasizes the mechanisms of adjustment that are possible, but cautions that his sample did not include families who did not recover or were persistently estranged.

Researchers differentiate some of the unique stresses of young adulthood for lesbians. Rosario, Scrimshaw, and Hunter (2008) report that within the lesbian population, those with a more "masculine" self-presentation experience more homophobia and "gay-related stressors" than lesbians with a "femme" presentation. Young gay men may not be driven by the same anxiety about "proving" their masculinity, nor are they responsible for nearly the amount of crime as straight men. But Pachankis (2009) makes it clear that gay men measure themselves (as do straight men) by the standards of "precarious manhood," often leading to an experience of deep inauthenticity. For instance, boys who show behavior described as "effeminate" (not all of whom who eventually identify as gay men) often still receive negative reactions to those gender nonconforming styles from peers and parents, particularly fathers. Gay males may internalize this disapproval and the years of internalized societal censure may be associated with attachment difficulties and depressive symptoms in young adult life (Josephson & Whiffen, 2007).

If leaving the home town after high school for a more gay-friendly environment increases the social opportunities for gay young adults, the "hookup" culture of college described earlier for heterosexuals may be a natural fit for college-aged gay men. At this writing, it is too early to cite research, but perhaps with greater opportunities for marriage, gay men might tend more toward relationship-oriented scripts (as straight couples do) after leaving the culture of college.

> Assess your comprehension of special challenges of young adulthood for lesbians, gays, and bisexuals by completing this quiz.

Some Effects of Social Class and Gender on Family Formation during Later Young Adulthood

Many writers (Badinter, 1996; Gilmore, 1990) believe that heterosexual manhood must be achieved or proven, leaving masculine identity in doubt until it is. Vandello et al. (2008) refer to this phenomenon as "precarious manhood." Michael Kimmel deplored this pressure in *Manhood in America* (2011) when he asserted that heterosexual manhood is negatively defined in three main ways: that a true man does not show immaturity or vulnerability, does not display any "feminine" characteristics, and does not show any "gay" personal style. The narrowness of adult male heterosexual sex-role expectations may make men feel that they can never gain adult status without renouncing important parts of themselves (Kilmartin, 1994).

In his book, *Guyland* (2008), Kimmel sees this narrow definition of heterosexual masculinity as stimulated by homophobia, enforced by the same-sex gang, and permitted by parents who abdicate responsibility for guiding the middle-class young men he is describing when they enter college.

To some degree, men are expected to eventually prove love by work, that is, by financially supporting those they love, their families. The anticipation of being able to do this permits the proud, anti-authoritarian young middle-class man to accept the ordinary humiliations of learning a skill, temporarily enduring financial deprivation, or of having to do a low-status job to gain access to a higher-status one. Young men must prove themselves in love and work, but what if there is no work? In lower-income neighborhoods, even entry-level jobs are not available. Because of racism, young men often cannot see the senior men of the neighborhood ascending through and beyond such jobs. Consequently, they have little reason to expect to prove themselves or gain status or attract and support a wife through work (Franklin, 2004).

Joblessness makes crime seem like a reasonable alternative to such men, often leading to incarceration: 60 percent of Black male high school dropouts risk imprisonment, thus making incarceration a normative experience during emerging adulthood for that group (Western, 2006).

Not surprisingly, straight young adult men of all races are the age group and sex that commit the largest number of violent crimes. Of persons arrested for murder and manslaughter, 90 percent are males and 40 percent are between the ages of 18 and 24 (U.S. Department of Justice, 2006). Being responsible for such a disproportionate share of violent crime, straight young men are understandably the most feared group in any society. Every culture must struggle with the problem of what to do with this highly energetic, highly dangerous group. One strategy is to imprison them, which our society does increasingly every year with a huge bias toward poor men of color. Another strategy is to harness their idealism and daring by giving them the opportunity to kill and be killed in war.

Precariously employed men of color may despair of filling the provider role in families

Young adult men of all races and socioeconomic classes engage in risky behaviors, exposing themselves to serious, sometimes lethal dangers. The leading cause of death for young White men is accidents (Center for Disease Control, 2009). For young Black men, it is murder (Center for Disease Control, 2009). Nearly every poor young Black man knows peers who are incarcerated; have died of a drug overdose; were beaten up badly by peers, strangers, or police; or were killed. They may think of their young adulthoods as their only adulthoods, that is, they see a much shorter life horizon than more affluent males. In LeBlanc's (2004) *Random Family*, as the young men grow older (ages 21 to 25), they also wish to impregnate particular women to whom they are emotionally attached, and are especially eager to have sons. These young women also begin to wish for children and expect to be valued more highly (and for a longer time) if they can bear a man his first son. Perhaps these strong wishes for sons are also an artifact of the young men's anticipated short life horizon—that they do not expect (or perhaps even want) to live long, but they do want a son to be a legacy. Understanding these powerful motivations for early pregnancy may help middle-class clinicians empathize with their low-income, unskilled, unwed patients. The few employment opportunities for lower-income young adults may have created a culture in which the extensive training now necessary for employment seems out of reach. It may seem like early pregnancy is the most viable source for meaning and enjoyment in life. Clinicians may be able to elicit other dreams, however, if they ask their young patients, "What would be your ideal life?" If their patients can articulate these yearnings, therapists

may be able to help them build a series of difficult but realistic steps toward employability. Stories of others who have walked such a path may inspire and learning to celebrate incremental progress will be important. The genogram of the extended family may be used to identify family members who could help or offer connections.

Barriers to affiliation for low income men

Although Wilson (2009) strongly emphasizes that structural causes are the most important determinants of Black male unemployment, he believes that such unemployment is also abetted by a poor job referral network among Black men in the culture. He reports a study by Sandra Smith (2007) that found that lack of trust among themselves caused lower-income Black men to not use informal personal referrals from friends and relatives to seek work as other ethnic groups often do. They consequently develop a defensive, individualistic, "go-it-alone" value system. Wilson emphasizes that this culture is not a "Black" culture, but that it is a characteristic of the Black lower class and quite different from the Black middle class in which church groups, fraternities, and clubs generate prosocial bonds.

While mistrust within the population of lower-income Black men may contribute to the extreme unemployment seen there, it also seems to extend into the other domain in which a young man might prove himself—the realm of love. Wilson also notes the lack of trust between men and women in the poor Black population (Wilson, 2009). He reports that men protest that women are attracted to material resources that their meager employment prospects cannot supply. Such mistrust is hardly confined to lower-income Black males, however. In their song *Girls Don't Like Boys*, the White, male, very middle-class rock group, Good Charlotte (2002), sings that women do not really feel affection for men, but only tolerate them for their ability to supply cars and money. This is a classic plaint stimulated by all young males' fears of inadequacy and consequent rejection by females, but in the case of low-income men, it is also literally true that they lack material resources, whatever the attitudes of women are. Clinicians who are able to engage these young men may wish to plot their informal job referral networks, just as they would do a genogram, beginning by asking if they know anyone who has a job. If we heed Smith, however, we would be very attentive to a defensive hesitation to use these connections because of his go-it-alone philosophy. He might be helped in this reticence if the clinician can find a job holder who would testify to being helped himself in securing his own employment, but the clinician should be aware that asking for assistance may be especially dangerous to self-esteem in this culture.

Precariously employed fathers may strive for affiliation with their children in an "uncle" role

Young Black fathers have been criticized by eminent figures (Bill Cosby, Barack Obama) in recent years for not being responsible for their children's welfare. Two new studies have put forward strong evidence that economic conditions and young Black men's consequently lower achievement in education and employment have made marriage an unlikely or fragile institution for them. They are actually very motivated to be active and enduring fathers, but the fact that they cannot become or remain husbands, not that they allegedly lack appropriate paternal values, is the reason they may become estranged from their children.

Ralph Richard Banks (2012) portrays young Black males' yearning to have and be good fathers and their lack of trust for the institution of marriage in a telling anecdote. Some Black boys ask their teacher how to be good fathers. The teacher offers to bring some married couples in to class to speak about childrearing. They protest, saying they are not interested in studying marriage, but only about how to be good *fathers*. To emphasize their distance from the idea of marriage, one boy contends that marriage is only "for white people". Banks conducted 100 interviews with middle-class Black women and men. He focuses on how Black male unemployment and relatively (to Black females) low achievement in educational and vocational realms has made them less appealing as marriage partners. The educated men's relative scarcity has, however, made them more appealing to the majority of educated Black women who prefer not to marry out of their race. Their scarcity, argues Banks, has given educated Black men the market power to avoid the fidelity expectations of marriage and require Black women to tolerate extramarital sex and conception, divorce, "sharing" of Black men, childlessness, or involuntary celibacy. The "marriage decline" in all social classes has left Black Americans the least married group in our nation. Banks emphasizes, however, that the same disparity between the sexes in achievement (and increase in market power for the scarce men) is happening for White people, because the same marriage decline is occurring for them. Banks states that the father's relationship to his children is mediated through his relationship with the children's mother. This relationship is vulnerable to the bitterness between parents that may accompany separation. He thus explains absence of father or delinquency not as a product of fathers' deficient values, or not caring about their children, but of the overall decline of marriage itself. It follows that family therapists may still bend their efforts to preserve or repair the parental (rather than the marital) relationship in middle-class never-married or divorced families.

Edin and Nelson (2013) present a study of 110 unwed, low-income fathers whom they interviewed in depth over a number of years about their fathering attitudes and practices. They found that the couple relationships that resulted in progeny were often impulsive, brief, casual, and not heavily invested with emotion. The men were often very pleased that they were responsible for the pregnancy. They readily acknowledged their fatherhood, even though it exposed them to child support claims, and even though they had poor prospects for employment to support such children. The men fully expected the women to be the primary breadwinners as well as the ones to provide the bulk of the child care. They were proud to be able to support themselves. They often enacted a relationship with their children like a benign uncle, bringing presents and playing with them rather than struggling with their discipline. They did not want to give money to the mother because they feared the mother would spend it on herself. This detail is exemplary of the lack of trust in the couple relationship in this population that other workers (Wilson, 2009; Fosse, 2010; Banks, 2012) have cited. When this fragile couple relationship fails, the father's access to his children is often compromised by the mother's (understandable) wish to control visitation regulations. He then seeks another couple relationship from which he can try again to enact not a marriage, but an in-person fathering experience. Edin and Nelson (2013) argue that these less-than-perfect fathers are not being irresponsible by their lights and that they should be treated as a resource, not judged. Can the mothers of their children expect them to be reliable in this reduced role?

Edin and Nelson's radical, positive framing of the *fathering* (as distinct from *husbanding*) impulses of these unwed, unemployed men may help clinicians discover ways to encourage the emotional and behavioral support they may be able to contribute to their offspring. I have found it worthwhile to recruit fathers (with mother's permission) to come in to therapy sessions. Recruiting is successful only if I talk to them directly rather than asking mother to bring them. Even then, I have only sometimes been successful. I must get across to both the father and the mother that I am focusing on them as a parental subsystem, not trying to reunite them as a marital couple. I keep in mind that the men expect to be shamed and so try to focus on what they do as fathers rather than what they fail to do. If they seem open at all, I ask what their own fathers were like and how they would like to be the same or different. I ask how they developed their ideals for being a good father and what those ideals are. If I manage a meeting or two with such a father, I might ask if he could come in with his child or children. If they do, I talk with them about the positive and negative aspects of their relationship. Sometimes, a plan can develop that helps the child. For instance, Edin and Nelson tell of an unwed father who stopped lecturing his misbehaving son but instead went to school and sat in his classroom for several days to support his attendance. His presence had a good effect on his son's school participation.

Assess your comprehension of some effects of social class and gender on family formation during later young adulthood by completing this quiz.

Child-Rearing and Child Care as a Source of Meaning for Women of all Social Classes

Women's lives have been lived more in relationship than men's at every stage. For many decades, women married out of one household and into another. In recent years, however, middle- and upper-middle class women, like men, often leave home and live alone before marrying. For this reason, young adulthood for these women can be the era of their lives that is least centered on relationships.

Young adult women have not been expected to be as financially independent as men, or to live in a domicile separate from their parents. They are also not expected to prove their adult gender identity. They are permitted and expected to maintain relatedness, sometimes being drafted into child care or elder care to their extended families. Even if such service is not requested, they are more subject to a feeling of continued obligation to family and friends.

Young women are generally more thoughtful about the timing of their giving birth and subsequent child care than are young men. Aspiring professional women once anticipated that they could "have it all," by using a strategy of developing their careers first and adding a husband and children later. Some women who are currently middle aged look back at these expectations when they were young adults and now consider them naive, particularly if they were disappointed by age-related infertility.

Edin and Kefalas (2005) interviewed a group of 162 poor single mothers who were equally divided among Whites, Latinas, and African Americans to understand why low-income women tend to have children before they marry, thus reversing the middle-class sequence. Their participants considered marriage an excellent aspiration, seeing it as a luxury that they might never be able to afford. The women felt that children, however, were an absolutely necessary source of meaning and identity. They reported that lower-income women often feel they should be able to support themselves and their children completely before they consider marriage. The mothers fear losing control to an authoritarian husband. The authors feel that socioeconomic class (more than race) drives the cultural differences in timing of pregnancy during young adulthood between these women and those in the middle class.

Young adult mothers have a more clearly defined role in their extended families (as caregivers to their children) than do jobless young men. By entering this economy of mutual obligation, they gain adult status and respect, but they are rarely free to pursue solitary postsecondary education that would permit an exit from poverty and allow financial self-sufficiency. Physical separation or even financial self-sufficiency may not be a realistic or even desirable goal for young adult mothers. Because of the variety and changing nature of these family structures, discovering the executive subsystem is not always a straightforward task. A very useful question for young adult mothers is "Who helps you?" The answer begins to reveal whom she can or must count on. A follow-up question that addresses the emotional climate of this network is "Who gets to express his/ her opinion on how you are raising your kids?" This group may include some additional individuals who do not supply care directly, but who affect the morale of the mother with their criticisms. This therapist has found it useful to inquire carefully about the mothers of the fathers of all the mother's children, even if the fathers are estranged, incarcerated or dead. These paternal grandmothers are sometimes active critics of the mother's child-rearing practices, but also sometimes do important backup child care for their son's children. Whatever their role, they are often involved in the family in an important way but may not be mentioned unless the therapist asks.

> **Assess your comprehension of child-rearing and child care as a source of meaning for women of all social classes by completing this quiz.**

— Conclusion: Young Adulthood As a Transition for The Family —

As this is the developmental period when family members are meant to be least in relationship with each other, seeing individuals or coaching subsystems is often a necessity and sometimes the first choice of therapies. Although emerging adulthood provides very different challenges for different parts of our society, some of its characteristics are experienced by all. Young adults attempt to develop a distinct identity, form powerful emotional bonds with strangers, take over their own material support, and prepare to create a new family. Parents continue to be vital sources of identification, support, and guidance. They become powerful examples of what to eschew or what to aspire to as their children form their own lives. Most grown children still want to make their parents proud, and most parents still hope their children will admire them. I encourage family therapists to make use of both systemic and developmental approaches when dealing with the vicissitudes of this exciting and productive phase of life.

> **Recall what you learned in this chapter by completing the Chapter Review.**

— References

Anderson, E. (2000). *Code of the street: Decency, violence, and the moral life of the inner city.* New York: W.W. Norton.

Arnett, J. J. (2000). Emerging adulthood: A theory of development from the late teens through the twenties. *American Psychologist*, 55(5), 469–480.

Arnett, J. J. (2006). *Emerging adulthood: The winding road from the late teens through the twenties.* New York: Oxford.

Arnett, J. J. (2007). The long and leisurely route: Coming of age in Europe today. *Current History*, 136–142.

Arnett, J., & Fishel, E. (2013). *When will my grown-up kid grow up? Loving and understanding your young adult.* New York: Workman.

Aviv, R. (December 10, 2012). "Netherland". *The New Yorker*, p. 60.

Banks, R. R. (2012). *Is marriage for White people? How the African American marriage decline affects everyone.* New York: Dutton.

Barker, G. T. (2005). *Dying to be men: Youth, masculinity and social exclusion*. New York: Routledge, Taylor & Francis.

Badinter, E. (1996). *XY. On masculine identity*. New York: Columbia University Press.

Benjamin. J. (1988). *The bonds of love: Psychoanalysis, feminism, and the problem of domination*. New York: Pantheon.

Bergman, S. (1991) (Ed.). Men's psychological development: A relational perspective. In *Work in Progress* (Vol. 48). Wellesley, MA: Stone Center.

Bogle, K. A. (2008). *Hooking up: Sex, dating and relationships on campus*. New York: New York University.

Brooks, D. (October 10, 2007). The Odyssey years. *Op-Ed. New York Times*.

Canada, G. (1998). *Reaching up for manhood: Transforming the lives of boys in America*. Boston, MA: Beacon.

Centers for Disease Control and Prevention. (2009). Leading causes of death by age group, Black Males—United States, 2009. Retrieved from: http://www.cdc.gov/men/lcod/2009/LCODBlackmales2009.pdf

Centers for Disease Control and Prevention. (2009). Leading causes of death by age group, White Males—United States, 2009. Retrieved from: http://www.cdc.gov/men/lcod/2009/LCOD_whitemen2009.pdf

Chandler, K. (1997). *Passages of pride: True stories of lesbian and gay teenagers*. Los Angeles: Alyson Books.

Cole, D. (July 2, 2009). The same-sex future *The New York Review of Books*. pp. 12–16.

Collinge, A. (2010). *The student loan scam: The most oppressive debt in U.S. history and how we can fight back*. Boston, MA: Beacon Press.

Coontz, S. (1992). *The way we never were: American families and the nostalgia trap*. New York: Basic.

Cote, J. (2000). *Arrested adulthood: The changing nature of maturity and identity*. New York: New York University.

D'Augelli, A. R., Hershberger, S. L., & Pilkington, N. W. (2001). Suicidality patterns and sexual orientation-related factors among lesbian, gay and bisexual youths. *Suicide and Life-Threatening Behavior, 31*, 250–265.

D'Augelli, A. R., Grossman, A. H., & Starks, M. T. (2006). Childhood gender atypicality, victimization, and PTSD among lesbian, gay, and bisexual youth. *Journal of Interpersonal Violence, 21*, 1462–1482.

Delahunty-Britz, J. (March 23, 2006). To all the girls I've rejected. Op-Ed. *The New York Times*.

Denizet-Lewis, B. (September 27, 2009). "Junior High: Coming Out in Middle School". *The New York Times Magazine*, p. 36.

Diamond, L., & Butterworth, M. (2008). The close relationships of sexual minorities: partners, friends and family (pp. 348–375). In M. C. Smith & T. G. Reio (Eds.), *Handbook of research on adult development and learning*. Mahwah NJ: Lawrence Erlbaum.

Dillon, S. (April 22, 2009). Large urban-suburban gap seen in graduation rates. *The New York Times*.

Doty, C. (October 23, 2009). Addressing the gender gap in college aspirations. *The New York Times*. Retrieved from: http://thechoice.blogs.nytimes.com/2009/10/23/addressing-the-gender-gap-in-colleges/

Draut, T. (2007). *Strapped: Why America's 20-and-30-somethings can't get ahead*. New York: Anchor.

Edin, K. & Kefalas, M. (2005). *Promises I can keep: Why poor women put motherhood before marriage*. Berkeley: University of California.

Edin, K. & Nelson, T. (2013). *Doing the best I can: Fatherhood in the inner city*. Berkeley: University of California.

Erikson, E. (1963). *Childhood and Society* (2nd ed.). New York: Norton.

Falicov, C. (2009). Commentary: On the wisdom and challenges of culturally attuned treatments for Latinos. *Family Process, 48*(2).

FBI (2011). Hate Crime Statistics. Table 1: Incidents, Offenses, Victims and Known Offenders. Retrieved from: http://www.fbi.gov/about-us/cjis/ucr/hate-crime/2011/tables/table-1

Fielder, R. L. Carey, K. B., Carey, M. P. (2013). Are hookups replacing romantic relationships? A longitudinal study of first-year female college students. *Journal of Adolescence Health*, 52, 657–659.

Fosse, N. (2010). Doubt, duty, destiny: The cultural logics of infidelity among the urban poor. *The Annals of the American Academy of Political and Social Science*, 626–630.

Franklin, A. J. (2004). *From brotherhood to manhood: How black men rescue their relationships and dreams from the invisibility syndrome*. Hoboken, NJ: John Wiley and Sons.

Fulmer, R. H. (2006). From law to love: Young adulthood in Milton's Paradise Lost. *American Imago*, 63(1), 25–56.

Fulmer, R. H. (2008). 'Don't Save Her'-Sigmund Freud meets Project Pat: The rescue motif in hip-hop. *The International Journal of Psychoanalysis*, 89 (4) 727–742.

Furstenberg, F. F. Jr., Kennedy, S., McCloyd, V., Rumbaut, R., & Settersten, R. Jr. (2003). Between adolescence and adulthood: Expectations about the timing of adulthood. *Network on Transitions to Adulthood and Public Policy, Research Network Working Paper*. 1, July 29. Retrieved from http://www.transad.pop.upenn.edu/news/between.pdf

Gilmore, D. (1990). *Manhood in the making: Cultural concepts of masculinity.* New Haven: Yale University Press.

Good Charlotte (2002). Girls and Boys. *The Young and the Hopeless.* Epic Records.

Haley, J. (1980). *Leaving home: The therapy of disturbed young people.* New York: McGraw-Hill.

Hamilton, L. & Armstrong, E. A. (2009). Gendered sexuality in young adulthood: Double binds and flawed options. *Gender & Society, 23*(5), 589–616. doi: 10.1177/0891243209345829

Hewlett, S. A. (2002). *Creating a life: Professional women and the quest for children.* New York: Talk Miramax Books.

Jay, M. (2013). *The defining decade: Why your twenties matter—And how to make the most of them now.* New York: Twelve/Hachette Book Group.

Josephson, G., & Whiffen, V. E. (2007). An integrated model of depressive symptoms in gay men. *American Journal of Men's Health, 1,* 60–72.

Kamenetz, A. (2007). *Generation debt: How our future was sold out for student loans, credit cards, bad jobs, no benefits, and tax cuts for rich geezers—and how to fight back.* New York: Riverhead.

Kelley, M., L., & Fitzsimons, V. M. (2000). *Understanding cultural diversity* (p. 292). Sudbury, MA: Jones and Bartlett Learning.

Kerr, B. (1994). *Smart girls: A new psychology of girls, women and giftedness* (Rev. Ed.). Scottsdale, AZ: Gifted Psychology Press.

Kilmartin, C. (1994). *The masculine self.* New York: Macmillan.

Kimmel, M. (2011). *Manhood in America* (3rd ed.). New York: Oxford.

Kimmel, M. (2008). *Guyland: The perilous world where boys become men.* New York: Harper Collins.

LaSala, M.C. (2010). *Coming out, coming home: How families adjust to a gay or lesbian child.* New York: Columbia University Press.

LeBlanc, A. (2004). *Random family: Love, drugs, trouble, and coming of age in the Bronx.* New York: Scribner.

Levine, M. (2003). *The myth of laziness.* New York: Simon and Schuster.

Lewin, T. (July 9, 2006). The new gender divide: At colleges, women are leaving men in the Dust. *The New York Times.*

Marshak, L., Seligman, M., & Prezant, F. (Eds.) (1999). *Disability and the family life cycle: Recognizing and treating developmental challenges.* New York: Basic Books.

National Conference of State Legislatures (NCSL). (2013). U.S. Supreme Court Declines Jurisdiction on Appeal of California Law Prohibiting Same-Sex Marriage. Retrieved from: http://www.ncsl.org/issues-research/human-services/same-sex-marriage-overview.aspx

Pachankis, J. (2009). The use of cognitive behavioral therapy to promote authenticity. *Pragmatic Case Studies in Psychotherapy, 5* (4) 28–38.

Parker, K. (2012). The Boomerang Generation: feeling okay about living with mom and dad. Pew Research Center. Retrieved from: http://www.pewsocialtrends.org/files/2012/03/PewSocialTrends-2012-BoomerangGeneration.pdf

Pew Research Center. (2013). Retrieved from: http://www.pewsocialtrends.org/files/2013/02/Financial_Milestones_of_Young_Adults_FINAL_2-19.pdf

Project on Student Debt. (2012). The Class of 2011. Retrieved from: http://projectonstudentdebt.org/files/pub/classof2011.pdf

Rosario, M., Scrimshaw, E., & Hunter, J. (2004). Ethnic/racial differences in the coming-out process of lesbian, gay and bisexual youths: A comparison of sexual identity development over time. *Cultural Diversity and Ethnic Minority Psychology*, 10 (3) 215–228.

Rosario, M., Scrimshaw, E., Hunter, J., & Braun, L. (2006). Sexual identity development among lesbian, gay, and bisexual youths: Consistency and change over time. *The Journal of Sex Research, 43* (1) 46–58.

Rosario, M., Scrimshaw, E., & Hunter, J. (2008). Butch/femme differences in substance use and abuse among young lesbian and bisexual women: Examination and potential explanations. *Substance Use & Misuse, 43*(8), 1002–1015.

Rotheram-Borus, M. J. (1997). *Passages of pride: True stories of lesbian and gay teenagers* (p. 130; quoted in Chandler, K., 1997). Los Angeles: Alyson.

Ryan, C., Huebner, D., Diaz, R., & Sanchez, J. (2009). Family rejection as a predictor of negative health outcomes in White and Latino lesbian, gay and bisexual young adults. *Pediatrics, 123,* 346–352.

Ryan, D. (2012, December 10). Hate crimes down in 2011, but anti-gay violence up, FBI says. *Los Angeles Times.*

Savin-Williams, R. C. (2005). *The new gay teenager.* Cambridge MA: Harvard.

Smith, S. (2007). *Lone pursuit: Distrust and defensive individualism among the black poor.* New York: Sage Foundation.

Taffel, R., & Blau, M. (2001). *The second family: How adolescent power is challenging the American family.* New York: St. Martin's Press.

The Project on Student Debt. (2009). Retrieved from http://www.projectonstudentdebt.org/.

Twenge, J. M., Freeman, E. C., & Campbell, W. K. (2012). Generational differences in young adults' life goals, concern for others, and civic orientation, 1966–2009. *Journal of Personality and Social Psychology 2012*(102),1045–1062.

U.S. Department of Justice. (2006). Bureau of Justice Statistics. Retrieved from: http://www.ojp.usdoj.gov/bjs/crimoff.htm

Vandello, J., Bosson, J., Cohen, D., Burnaford, R., & Weaver, J. (2008). Precarious manhood. *Journal of Personality and Social Psychology 95*(6), 1325–1339.

Venkatesh, S. (2006). *Off the books: The underground economy of the urban poor*. Cambridge, MA: Harvard University Press.

Weissmann, J. (February 26, 2013). Here's exactly how many college graduates live back at home. *The Atlantic*. Retrieved from: http://www.theatlantic.com/business/archive/2013/02/heres-exactly-how-many-college-graduates-live-back-at-home/273529/

Western, B. (2006). *Punishment and inequality in America*. New York: Sage Foundation.

Whitbeck, L. (2009). *Mental health and emerging adulthood among homeless young people*. New York: Psychology Press, Taylor & Francis Group.

Wilson, W. J. (2009). *More than just race: Being black and poor in the inner city*. New York: W. W. Norton.

Chapter 14

Becoming a Couple: The Joining of Families

Monica McGoldrick

Learning Outcomes

- Explore how the key dimensions of couple relationships have evolved and changed to form today's meaning of marriage.
- List and describe factors that influence marital adjustment.
- Define and compare intimacy and fusion.
- Examine how the life cycle stage of becoming a couple is unique for gay and lesbian couples.
- Discuss the impact that weddings have on couples and their families.
- Explain the role of sexuality in couple relationships.
- Describe the dynamics of triangles that can form between couples and members of their families of origin.
- Discuss the impact that cultural differences can have on couple relationships.

I've been married three times. . . and each time I married the right person.

—Margaret Mead

For most of history it was inconceivable that people would choose their mates on the basis of something as fragile and irrational as love and then focus all their sexual, intimate, and altruistic desires on the resulting marriage.

—Stephanie Coontz (2005, p. 15)

Marriage in our Times[1]

Of all dilemmas of the life cycle, the existential dilemma of coupling is probably the most difficult interpersonally. Marriage is the only family relationship we swear is both exclusive and forever, and it is the family relationship least likely to be either.

Couples come in many varieties: gay and straight, married and unmarried, ambitious tall wives and short, nurturing homebody husbands, in spite of stereotypes of the husband as stronger, taller, smarter, with more earning power, and the wife as the physically attractive "helpmeet." The ideal itself costs us all a tremendous amount in terms of our ability to be ourselves, find harmony in our relationships, and support the tasks of family life. Indeed, a major role for therapists is to normalize the patterns of those who do not fit into traditional stereotypes and to educate couples about the pitfalls of those mythical images (Lerner, 2012).

Liza Mundy (2012) thinks we are entering an era when gender roles are changing dramatically in terms of who will be the provider and who will do the caretaking, which she thinks will alter

---

[1] This chapter will not consider arranged marriages because the author has not had experience with them. The parameters for arranged marriage seem so different from the general U.S. cultural arrangements for marriage that it would require quite a different chapter to discuss. I apologize for my ignorance on this topic, but it is not one where book learning seems adequate for understanding.

how we mate, how we procreate, and how we raise our children. "It will reshape the landscape of the heart" (Mundy, 2012, p. 7). The meaning of marriage in our time is profoundly different from its meaning throughout all previous human history, when it was tightly embedded in the economic and social fabric of society, and often more about getting good in-laws, increasing the family labor force, and solidifying political and economic power in the community than about finding a life companion (Coontz, 2005). The changing role of women and the dramatic effects of widely available contraceptives, along with our increasing longevity and the mobility of our culture, have contributed to a major redefinition of marriage in our society. While at its best marriage has become more fair and fulfilling for both couples and their children than ever before, when marriage depends on love, flexibility, and equity it becomes more fragile and optional than ever before (Coontz, 2005).

The role of marriage in the life cycle has also been changing dramatically (Cherlin, 2013; Hymowitz, Carroll, Wilcox, Bradford, & Kaye). Men and women are having sex earlier, but marrying later and less often than ever before. Of course, the economy is playing a major role here, making it almost impossible for working-class men and even for the middle class to afford marriage. Where marriage used to be thought of primarily as a business and cultural arrangement between families and as the gateway or foundation for adulthood, it is now being thought of more as the capstone or celebration of adult achievement, after the couple have completely worked out their financial independence and career goals, which only really seems to work for the upper middle class (Douthat, 2013; Klein, 2013). Marriage has become a choice or even a status symbol for self-sufficient individuals who no longer require a spouse for survival (Cherlin, 2012, 2013). Indeed, if a man is not able to be "the good provider" and has not moved toward equitable partnership in the administrative and relationship tasks of a family, women often think marriage is not worth undertaking. More people are living together before marriage, living with several partners before deciding to marry, or not marrying at all. Only about 48 percent of U.S. households include married couples, down from 78 percent of households in

1950 (Tavernise, 2011). Marriage rates are decreasing dramatically (33 percent of men and 26 percent of women never marry) and the age of marriage has been increasing dramatically, from age 20 to age 26 for women and from age 23 to age 28 for men in the last 50 years (Bolick, 2011). One of the biggest factors in whether people marry is economic, as demonstrated by their education. Of those with a college education or more, 88 percent of women aged 33 to 44 are married and their divorce rate in the first 10 years is only 17 percent. Meanwhile, of those with less than a high school diploma, only 79 percent have been married and the divorce rate within the first 10 years is 50 percent (Cherlin, 2013). While the overall U.S. rate of marriage declined by 17 percent since 1970, it has declined 34 percent for African Americans and others who are questioning the value of marriage unless the husband is a real partner (Jones, 2006). A large study of poor women found that about two thirds of them had experienced physical or sexual abuse, and these women, when they had options, were much more reluctant to marry (Cherlin, Burton, Hurt, & Purvin, 2004). They advise that if we want to encourage more marriage among the poor, we need to take measures to directly respond to the high levels of abuse these women bear. It is also interesting that a wife's being employed lowers the couple's risk of divorce (Coontz, 2013).

Couples are also marrying increasingly for health benefits, which are becoming expensive and hard to hold on to (Sack, 2008). There are, of course, also societal constraints on who can marry whom. Gays and lesbians still struggle to get legal and religious recognition of their relationships. Interracial marriages have also only been legal since the Supreme Court decision in Loving vs. Virginia in 1967. Prior to that, interracial couples could be sent to prison. Those with a college education are most likely to marry others of the same social location and less likely to marry up or down. As the category of couples "married and raising their own children" has become the exception rather than the rule, this group is increasingly the province of the college educated and affluent (Harden, 2007).

Andrew Cherlin, for years one of the premier trackers of U.S. marriage patterns, says that as a nation we still seem to believe in marriage more than other Western societies, and the overwhelming majority of people in the United States do eventually marry. And yet we have the highest divorce rate in the Western world and the greatest number of cohabiting relationships that break up more rapidly than those in other Western countries (Cherlin, 2009b, 2012). Cherlin attributes this paradoxical pattern of believing in marriage while practicing divorce to reflect our conflicting values about marriage. We view it as a cultural ideal, but it conflicts with our belief in free choice, which becomes reflected in our high rate of marital breakups. It is also a paradox that we have been creating governmental programs to promote marriage, which they do not seem able to do (Cherlin, 2012). Yet we have fought same-sex marriage more than other countries (Cherlin, 2009a). Cherlin points out that these patterns create great turbulence in American family life, where the coming and going of partners occurs more than elsewhere and is difficult for children, particularly because it is accompanied by a lack of stable community networks. Unfortunately, as Cherlin (2012) makes clear, these patterns often relegate the poor to having children in brittle cohabiting relationships, which are relatively unstable and not the best environment for raising children.

While marriage is used to symbolize the transition to parenthood; now it often reflects a greater continuity with the phase of young adulthood, since childbearing, especially for the middle and upper classes, is increasingly postponed for a number of years after marriage. And indeed, increasing numbers of women (20 percent as of 2006) are not having children, double the percent of only 30 years ago (Zezima, 2008).

As a multigenerational, communal event, marriage symbolizes a change in status among all family members and generations and requires that the couple negotiate new relationships as a twosome with many other subsystems: parents, siblings, grandparents, nieces, nephews, employers, and friends. In fact, the status changes of marriage may not be fully appreciated by the family until the next phase, the transition to parenthood, which challenges traditional gender roles and multigenerational family patterns even more. Increasingly, women want to have their own careers and are resistant to having the

primary responsibility for the household and child care, nor are they satisfied with husbands who are absent from family life. Men's participation in child care is increasing, but more slowly.

In traditional societies, to talk of the choice to marry or not would be about as relevant as to talk of the choice to grow old or not; it was considered the only route to full adult status. To marry was simply part of the "natural" progression through life, unless catastrophe intervened. Only recently have society's norms on this been modified, as more of the population do not fit into traditional patterns and raise questions about their viability.

Another paradox is the stereotype that men are polygamous and women are monogamous. If this were so, it is strange indeed that there has been so much effort throughout history to control women's sexuality with censure, veils, genital mutilation, etc. (Barnett & Rivers, 2004).

A major problem for our understanding of coupling is that patriarchal rules for male domination in marriage get obfuscated and mystified by the mythology of coupling as a love story of two equals. The patriarchal courtship ideal of Cinderella and Prince Charming gets mystified with a myth of two lovers whose souls and bodies mingle, such that they will think and act as one in a partnership that lasts until death. The contradiction in these two propositions makes marriage a problem for both men and women, but especially for women, a fact which has only recently begun to come to national and international consciousness. When women have options and resources, traditional marriage, where the woman is the "helpmeet," is increasingly viewed as a bad bargain.

 Assess your comprehension of marriage in our times by completing this quiz.

Marriage: Sex, Love, Power, Money, and Administration

The emotional and sexual dimensions are the ones given priority in the dominant framework, and the issues of power are subtly kept invisible.

Key Dimensions of Couple Relationships:

- **Economics** (a continuum from family support and finances controlled by one to equally earned and shared)
- **Emotional Connection** (a continuum from communication and intimacy to mind control and dependence)
- **Power** (a continuum from male privilege, dominance, intimidation, and abuse to partnership, equity, and respect for each partner)
- **Boundaries** (a continuum in relation to all other connections: friends, extended family, work, children, and religion—may be tight and controlled by one partner, or flexible in each area)
- **Sexuality** (a continuum from sexual intimacy to sexual objectification, rape, and exploitation)
- **Childrearing** (a continuum from shared parenting to women's sole responsibility)
- **Administration of Chores and Leisure Activities** (a continuum from dominance to shared decision making regarding tasks and arrangements for home care, food preparation, health care, education, work, transportation, vacation, and leisure time)

The complexity of these dimensions conveys how difficult this life cycle phase is. However, along with the transition to parenthood, which marriage has long symbolized, society has skewed us toward a romanticized view of this transition as the easiest and most joyous, which adds greatly to its difficulty, since everyone—from the couple to the family and friends—wants to see only its happiness. The problems entailed in forming a couple may thus be obscured and pushed underground, only to intensify and surface later on.

Furthermore, as Michael Lerner has pointed out, finding a partner, which used to be a community affair, has become an individual decision often made in terms of what the partner can do to satisfy our needs:

In the past relationships were embedded in larger communities of meaning and purpose. The relationship was not about itself, but about some larger shared goal. But today, with those communities of meaning in decline, people increasingly look to their primary sexual relationship to become a compensation for the meaninglessness surrounding them. Yet judged against such standards, very few relationships feel adequate (Lerner, 1995, p. 10).

More than any other life transition, marriage is viewed as the solution to life's problems of loneliness, work and career uncertainty, or extended-family difficulties.

The joke that there are six in the marital bed is really an understatement. It has been said that what distinguishes human beings from all other animals is the fact of having in-laws. In the animal kingdom, mating involves only the two partners, who, usually mature, separate from their families, and mate on their own. For humans, it is the joining of two enormously complex systems. If couples could fully appreciate the emotional complexity of negotiating marriage from the start, they might not dare to undertake it.

Marriage requires that two people renegotiate a great many issues they have previously defined individually or through their culture and family of origin, such as money, space, time, and when and how to eat, sleep, talk, have sex, fight, work, and relax. The power aspect of negotiating these dimensions often remains invisible, since power inequities in most heterosexual couples are highly likely to be obscured by the couple, the extended family, and the accepted rules of society (Carter & Peters, 1996). Decisions must be made about which family traditions and rituals to retain from each side of the family and which ones partners will develop for themselves. Partners have to renegotiate relationships with parents, siblings, friends, extended family, and co-workers once they marry; it is extremely important, especially for women, that they not curtail these relationships, which are an important life-sustaining force and which would leave them vulnerable to isolation and too frequently to abuse in the marriage.

Contrary to the widespread cultural stereotypes that marriage is something men should dread and fear, the research supports the opposite—marriage improves men's mental health, sex lives, and financial success and leads them to lower rates of drug and alcohol abuse and depression (Barnett & Rivers, 2004; Mundy, 2012).

Overall, of course, the real question is not whether marriage is good for people but what is the quality of the marriage. A stressful marriage is not good for anyone's health, more particularly for women (Parker-Pope, 2010; Gallo, Troxel, Matthews, & Kuller, 2003; DeNoon, 2003). And on the other side, a good marriage can provide social support, increase in well-being, self-esteem, etc. But given the long-term power that patriarchal values and arrangements still have on marriage, women often subtly lose power when they marry, making decisions that are not good for their long-range financial security or self-esteem when they move out of the paid work force and into more of the new family's caretaking responsibilities. These are not couple issues only. They are the result of our society's failure to provide social supports that allow couples to spend time caring for others without jeopardizing their own future.

Contrary to the stereotypes of the frustrated old maid and the free unencumbered bachelor, so-called spinsters may do better than bachelors, although bachelors are doing better than they used to, perhaps because they are increasingly finding ways to have a meaningful social network.

As more and more couples are passing through a stage of living with one or several partners before marriage, the transition to marriage has become much less of a turning point in the family life cycle than it was in the past. Obviously, the meaning of a wedding changes when a couple has been living together for several years and participating jointly in extended-family experiences. Nevertheless, the transition to marriage can create great turmoil, more so if the partners have not yet dealt with their extended family as a couple. Indeed, the parents may have been hoping the couple would break up and now have to acknowledge the centrality of their child's relationship. It places no small stress on a family to open itself to an outsider who is now an official member of its inner circle, often the first new member added to the system for many years. Parents must now deal with their child and the partner as a twosome, which can radically change the interactional dynamics. The tendency of members to polarize and see villains and victims under the stress of these changes can be very strong and becomes a key issue for intervention to prevent long-term conflict or estrangement.

In any case, there seems to be a timing to the phase of coupling. Many people who marry before 20, as we have seen, tend to have more difficulty adjusting to the tasks of coupling and are much more likely to divorce. Those who marry later are less likely to divorce, and marrying later is becoming more the norm than marrying early. Early marriage may reflect cultural patterns (e.g., Latinos) or class norms (e.g., working-class couples), but those who marry early may also be running away from their families of origin or seeking a family they never had. They may leave home by fusing with a mate in an attempt to gain strength from each other. They may have more difficulties later on as a result of their failure to develop an independent identity first. Women who marry late may be ambivalent about losing their independence and identity in marriage, while men who hesitate may be avoiding commitment. Some of those who marry late have seen a negative image of marriage at home; others have been enmeshed in their families and find it hard to leave home, form outside relationships, or develop a secure work situation.

In spite of the trend toward delaying marriage and pregnancy, a majority of people do marry and have children before the age of 35. Naturally those who have children shortly after marriage have relatively little time to adjust to the status changes of marriage and its accompanying stresses before moving on.

The timing of marital decisions often appears to be influenced by events in the extended family, although most couples are unaware of the correlation of these events or the process that underlies their decision to marry. People often seem to meet or make the decision to marry shortly after the retirement, illness, move, or even untimely death of a parent or after another traumatic loss. What is amazing, considering the long-range implications of marriage, is that so many couples spend so little time thinking about the decision. The sense of loss or loneliness can be a strong contributing factor in the desire to build a close relationship. A person in need of being "completed" may be blind to the less-than-ideal aspects of a prospective spouse. This desire for completion is likely to lead to difficulty accepting the spouse's differentness in the course of the relationship.

> Assess your comprehension of marriage: sex, love, power, money, and administration by completing this quiz.

What Makes Marital Adjustment More Difficult?

Many factors influence marriage and marital adjustment. At an individual level, it is influenced by the developmental trajectory of both spouses: their level of self-management, emotional, financial, educational and interpersonal competence, the values and beliefs they have about marriage, about the acceptable roles of men and women, and about equity in relationships. One of the most important factors influencing marital adjustment over the entire life cycle is addiction (Vaillant, 2012). Mental illness of a partner and early trauma can also, of course, have profound impact on marital adjustment. While the saying is that "opposites attract," it appears that the more differences spouses have between them, the harder their marital adjustment is likely to be: differences in life cycle phase, social location, age, ethnicity, race, religion, sibling constellation, and sibling position. An only child marrying 1 of 10 siblings would likely have a harder adjustment than spouses who are both from 2 sibling families. A 25-year-old who has never been married and a 50-year-old with three teenage children are likely to have a difficult adjustment. Cultural differences can also contribute to couple problems over the life cycle (Rastogi & Thomas, 2009). If you marry someone from a similar culture (Italian-Puerto Rican), it may be easier than if you marry someone from an extremely different culture (Korean–Jewish). In general, if either partner remembers his or her childhood or adolescence as unhappy, it is also likely to make marital adjustment more difficult.

At a family level, marital adjustment will be influenced by the relationship partners have with their extended families. In general, couples do best when the extended family is supportive, but it is a question whether a cutoff from the family is better than an extended family that is engaged but conflictual, many suggesting that the latter is healthier—at least the family is struggling to stay connected. Overall the greater the distance each partner has from his or her extended family in social class, education, religious beliefs, and other dimensions, the harder it will be to fit the disparate pieces of the systems together.

At a social level, there are again many factors influencing marital adjustment, beginning with the availability of economic and health cushions to support the couple, and also whether their community provides a sense of validation or "home" to ease their adjustment. Indeed indications are that marriage actually tends to isolate partners from other people in ways that pose potential long-term problems. They have fewer ties to relatives, fewer intimate talks with others, are less likely to care for aging parents, and less likely to socialize with friends during the couple formation period (Sarkisian & Gerstel, 2008). This can be a particular problem for women, whose close friendships are a major support in life. Close female friendships appear to be second only to good health in importance for satisfaction throughout the life cycle. The following list suggests possible adjustment issues we have found relevant in our clinical experience and through our exploration of the literature over the past decades. Many aspects of a marriage are hard to research. Evidence of marital adjustment is difficult to ascertain, since marriage is so complex to study. For example, just staying married is not necessarily a positive measure of a marriage. The quality of marriages is difficult to show, as Vaillant's longitudinal research over more than 50 years makes very clear. Many individuals in his study did not tell the truth until they were in their 80s, though they had been participating in interviews since they were adolescents (Vaillant, 2012). People do not easily tell all the truth about crucial aspects of their lives. Furthermore, researchers almost never explore extended-family relationships over any meaningful period of time, if at all, because they are so difficult to study. Hopefully, computerized health care records will soon make meaningful longitudinal research on family systems more possible. This would be the only way we could answer the complex questions about marriage and family relationships across the life cycle (Figure 14.1).

Assess your comprehension of what makes marital adjustment more difficult by completing this quiz.

Fusion and Intimacy

A basic dilemma in coupling, once one acknowledges the hidden dimension of power in all relationships, is the confusion of intimacy with fusion. There is a profound difference between forming an intimate relationship and using a couple relationship to complete one's self. Poets have long talked about the difference. To paraphrase Rainier Maria Rilke: Real love does not mean merging, giving up self,

Figure 14.1 Issues that tend to make marital adjustment more difficult.

Contextual factors

- Couple do not have jobs or resources to support themselves adequately.
- The wedding occurs without family or friends present.
- Either spouse started but did not complete either high school or college.

Timing of the relationship

- The couple meets or marries shortly after a significant loss.
- The couple marries early (before age 20) or late (after age 40).
- The couple marries after an acquaintanceship of less than 6 months or more than 5 years of engagement.
- The wife becomes pregnant before or within the first year of marriage.

Partners differ in

- Religious, racial, ethnic, or class background.
- Financial power, socioeconomic status, education, career options, or skills.

The husband believes that men's rights, needs, or privilege should predominate in marriage and that women should serve the needs of others over their own needs. The danger increases if he tries to

- Dominate the wife.
- Isolate her from work, friends, or family.
- Control her financially or intimidate her physically.

Family of origin issues

- Either partner has a different level of success or social location from his or her own parents, especially a lower success and social location than his/her parents, or the couple comes from a disrupted family.
- The couple resides either extremely close to or at a great distance from either family of origin.
- The couple are from incompatible sibling constellations.
- Either spouse has a poor relationship with siblings or parents, or the parents had poor or unstable relationships themselves.
- Either spouse considers his or her childhood or adolescence to have been an unhappy time.

and uniting with another. What would a relationship be with someone unclarified, undeveloped and undefined. Love is an inducement to both partners to ripen. . . It is a great exacting claim. (Rilke, 1954, p. 54).

There are, of course, sex differences in the way fusion is experienced, since women have traditionally been raised to consider "giving themselves" in a relationship as normal, and men have generally been raised to see the vulnerabilities of intimacy as "unmanly." Thus, men more often express their fusion by maintaining a pseudo-differentiated distant position in relationships, or by jealousy and possessive demands that their partners conform to their wishes, and women by giving up their dreams, their opinions, and even their identity in the relationship. The romantic mythology about couples has led to much confusion in notions of closeness, enmeshment, and fusion, on one side and differentiation, autonomy, disengagement, and distance on the other. The categories offered by Green and Werner (1996) as shown in Figure 14.2 have provided a useful and demystifying framework for understanding the individual and collaborative aspects of intimate couple relationships.

Gottman (1993) and his colleagues (Carstensen, Gottman, & Levenson, 1995) found that the expression of negativity was as necessary as positivity in a marriage, though the ratio between the two needed to be about 4 to 1:4 positive messages to 1 negative message for the relationship to be successful!

In addition, we must keep in mind that relationships of heterosexual couples tend to be defined along power and status lines. That is, the partner who makes more money and has more status (usually the man) tends to control the relationship decisions, right down to where they will go on vacation and who will clean the toilet. There have been indications that lesbian couples had more flexibility to define their roles and relationships on a basis other than money, power, and status (Blumstein & Schwartz, 1983). Both lesbian and gay couples appear to have more intimate, cohesive relationships than do heterosexual couples, lesbians the most so, possibly because there is so much they must overcome in the larger social context to have their relationship at all (Gotta et al., 2011).

Others may expect a couple to fuse and view the wife as somehow joined to the identity of her husband, increasing the difficulties for a woman in maintaining her separate identity. Men's fear of intimacy and the social expectations of his "independence" along with women's adaptiveness tend to inhibit men from developing intimacy in relationships, which requires them to learn a new model of human development, within which they can allow

Figure 14.2 Characteristics of intimate relationships.

Closeness-Caregiving: made up of warmth, time together, nurturance, physical intimacy, and consistency

Openness of Communication: made up of openness, self-disclosure, and the ability to face conflict and differences without avoidance

Lack of Intrusiveness made up of:

1. Lack of separation anxiety, possessiveness or jealousy
2. Respecting the other's need for privacy and time & space alone
3. Lack of emotional over-reactivity to the other's life problems
4. Lack of mindreading of the other—thinking one knows the other's thoughts or wishes better than he or she does
5. Lack of aggressive criticism, hurtful attacks, attempts to diminish the other or dominate the other in Disagreements

themselves interdependence in their relationships (Dolan Del Vecchio, 2008; Kimmel, 2013).

The tendency to seek fusion with a partner is related to a person's lack of maturity in relation to his/her family of origin. In other words, couples seek to complete themselves in each other to the degree that they have failed to resolve their relationships with their parents, which would enable them to build new relationships based on each person's freedom to be himself or herself and to appreciate the other as he or she is. When people seek to enhance their self-esteem in marriage, they deny their "differentness" from their spouse and may develop severe distortions in communication to maintain the myth of agreement. As one woman put it:

> *My husband and I have always been afraid of the stranger in each other. We keep wanting to believe that the other thought the same as we thought they were thinking. We just couldn't appreciate that here was a new and different person, with his or her own thoughts and feelings, who would make life more interesting.*

During courtship, couples are usually most aware of the romantic aspects of their relationship. Marriage shifts the relationship from a private coupling to a formal joining of two families. Issues that the partners have not resolved with their own families tend to be factors in marital choice and are likely to interfere with establishing a workable marital balance.

Our beliefs about romantic love may be largely determined by our experiences in our family of origin. From this perspective, Romeo and Juliet may have felt intensely attracted to each other precisely because their families prohibited their relationship. Such obstacles may lead to an idealization of the forbidden person. Like so many romantic heroes, Romeo and Juliet were conveniently spared a deeper view of their relationship by their untimely deaths, preserving the romance and perhaps obscuring the more pedestrian underlying family dramas that probably fostered their attraction in the first place. In everyday life, the outcome of such love affairs is often not so romantic, as the following case illustrates.

CASE ILLUSTRATION

Susan and Joe

Susan, the older of two children of a middle-class Jewish family, met her future husband, Joe, in the summer of her first year of college. Her parents had been unhappily married and had invested all their energies in their children's success.

Susan planned to go away to college as did her "computer genius" younger brother, Jon. A month after her high school graduation, Susan's lawyer father had a stroke. Her mother, who had always been anxious, had been hospitalized for depression when Susan was 10. Ever since the mother was viewed as fragile and now seemed quite close to the edge, criticizing her husband continuously, now that he was so dependent. Susan gave up her plans for going away to college and enrolled in a local college. Over the next year, her father recovered, but then he had a second stroke and had to stop work. Shortly afterward Susan began dating Joe, a machinist whom she met at her summer job as a secretary. Joe was an only child from a working-class Puerto Rican family. Joe hoped to improve his situation by marrying Susan, whose family represented social and financial stability for him. These issues were important to him because of his own experience of racism as a Puerto Rican in New York City and his family's poverty, related to his father's disability from a work accident when Joe was a child. Joe's mother had cared for her husband, as well as for her own mother. Joe had always felt responsible for his parents but powerless to make them happy. He was delighted when Susan gave up college and began pushing to marry him. He had felt threatened by her college pursuits anyway. For Susan he represented the only way she knew to get away from her family's expectations. She had been conflicted about school, having felt inadequate in comparison to her brother, whose accomplishments were so much the focus of family attention. She had received mixed messages from her family about continuing her education. She had grown up not believing she was really smart and had felt under great pressure about schoolwork. Joe would free her from this pressure, and would not push her to achieve. He accepted her as she was. He had a steady income, which would mean she would not have to worry about her inability to concentrate on her fears of failure. She could be Joe's wife, raise a family, and her worries about her own identity would be over.

Joe and Susan were attracted to each other and felt better in their relationship than either remembered ever feeling before. Joe's parents disapproved of Susan's not being Catholic and suggested strongly that they wait. Susan's parents disapproved of her marrying someone without a college education and thought she should finish school herself first. They also disapproved of her marrying someone who was not Jewish, though the family was not religious. In quiet moments, Susan herself wondered if she might want someone more educated, but her parents' disapproval pushed her to defend her choice and to reject their "snobbery."

Prior to marriage, Susan and Joe had little chance to be alone together. What ever time they did have was filled with wedding arrangements and discussion of the families' pressures on them. But after the wedding, Susan felt restless. Things within her family had quieted down; they had no more reason to protest. Susan quickly became bored and began to pressure Joe to get a better job. Joe felt guilty for having "abandoned" his parents, something he had not let surface during courtship. To improve their financial situation and to deal with his guilt, he suggested they move into his parents' apartment, while the parents would move to a smaller apartment upstairs. It would save on expenses and be a good investment. Susan agreed, because it meant they would have much nicer living quarters. Almost immediately she began to feel pressure from Joe's parents to socialize with them and to have children for them.

Having married to escape her own parents, she now felt saddled with Joe's parents, with the added burden of not knowing them well, and often not understanding their conversations, because they spoke Spanish and she did not. Suddenly Joe's personality irritated her. Where initially she had liked him for his easy-going style and his acceptance of her, she now saw him as lacking ambition. She was embarrassed to have him spend time with her friends, because of his manners, grammar, and lack of education, so she began to avoid her friends, which left her even more isolated. She tried pressuring Joe to fulfill her dreams and satisfy all her relationship needs. He felt increasingly inadequate and unable to respond to her pressure. She felt he was a good lover but began to be more attracted to other men at work and to turn him away. His sense of inadequacy led him to retreat further and he took to going out in the evening with his own friends, with whom he felt more accepted.

Susan's resistance to parental expectations had now been transferred into the marriage. Joe's hopes for moving beyond his parents' disappointing lives had now been transformed into pressure from Susan for him to succeed, and he resented it. Neither partner had worked out individually what they each wanted in life. Each had turned to the other to fulfill unmet needs and now each was disappointed.

What began to happen between Susan and Joe is what happens to many couples when the hope that the partner will solve their problems proves unrealistic. There is a tendency to personalize stress and place blame for what goes wrong on the spouse. Given enough stress, couples tend to define their problems solely within the relationship.

Once this personalizing process begins, it is difficult to keep the relationship open. Susan began to blame her disappointments in life on Joe, and he saw himself as responsible for her unhappiness. One major factor that tightens couple relationships over time is their tendency to interpret more and more facets of life within the marriage. This is often promoted also by the wider social context, which supports this narrow focus on one's partner. During courtship, if one partner becomes depressed, the other is not likely to take it too personally, knowing that there are many reasons to get depressed and this may have nothing to do with him or her. The assumption that one is not responsible for the other's feelings permits an empathic response. After several years of marriage, however, partners have a greater tendency to view the other's emotional reactions as a reflection of their input and to feel responsible for getting the partner out of the depression. Once a partner begins taking responsibility for the other's feelings, more and more areas in the relationship may become tension filled. The more one spouse defines him or herself by the other, the less flexibility there will be in the relationship and the more their communication will become constricted in areas that are emotionally charged.

These responses are profoundly "gendered" as well. Because women have long been socialized to take responsibility for others' lives, feelings, and behavior and to consider it selfish to have a life of their own, they are more likely to internalize their problems and feel overresponsible for the marriage. Because men are socialized to define themselves primarily by their ability to provide for their families financially, perform sexually, and handle their emotions without overt emotional dependence, these dimensions will tend to organize their feelings of success. Beyond this they may externalize blame when things go wrong. As Anna Quindlen (2012) has pointed out, in any marriage where two hearts beat as one, that one is likely to be his, not because he is a tyrant, but because realistically that is the way the gender socialization of patriarchy operates.

In the case of Susan and Joe, neither of them probably had any awareness that she was bringing into the relationship a lifetime of feeling like a second-class citizen in relation to her brother. Nor did she realize that her mother's depression, anxiety, and frustration may have related to her having lived a life that disallowed any personal fulfillment, while she was supposed to devote herself to caring for others: her husband, her children, and her extended family. Her mother had been a brilliant student herself and had wanted to go to medical school, but she had been told by her parents that this was an inappropriate goal for a woman and would mean she would "never find a man." So she found a man, but probably lost herself in the process. Now Susan was perhaps repeating her mother's mistake, having absorbed her mother's feelings of being a second-class citizen in childhood.

Joe could not see that the very "life force" that attracted him to Susan soon became the rub. He felt "inadequate" in relation to her intelligence and drive. If he had not had to measure himself by a yardstick that said men should be smarter and more successful, he could have enjoyed her strength and intensity. Instead he saw it as a measure of his failure and tried to stifle or avoid it. Had Susan felt freer from the gender inequities and constraints of our society, she might have appreciated Joe for his sweetness and commitment to his family and used the marriage as a

base from which to evolve her own life and develop her confidence and skills.

Courtship is probably the least likely time of all phases of the life cycle for couples to seek therapy. This is not because coupling is so easy, but rather because of the tendency to idealize each other and not to want to look at how difficult it is to establish a lasting intimate relationship. While the first years of marriage are the time of greatest overall marital satisfaction for many, they are also a time of likely divorce. The degree of mutual disappointment will usually match the degree of idealization of the relationship during courtship, as in the case of Susan and Joe. The pull during courtship to ignore potential difficulties means they are avoided until further down the road.

On the one hand, most spouses have their closest and most open relationship during this period. It is common for living-together relationships to be harmonious and for symptoms of fusion not to develop until after marriage. The fusion may not become problematic as long as there is still a relatively flexible option to terminate the relationship. The commitment and boundaries of marriage may tighten a relationship, especially if a pattern of pseudomutuality developed earlier where partners felt pressured to pretend they liked everything about each other and wanted to share all their free time together, keeping all differences hidden.

In fact, Susan and Joe did not seek therapy until she became depressed in the wake of a miscarriage and began to look at what had happened to her in the marriage and before. Initally she sought therapy alone, but as she explored her own issues, Joe became motivated to deal with the marital problems. Over the course of exploring their very unformed relationship, Susan decided to return to college and Joe, after a period of anger and resentment, began to accommodate to her wishes and work his schedule around hers, which allowed her to finish school. Although there were many ups and downs, the couple did not separate during the period of therapy but rather found ways to deepen their connection and accept their cultural and educational differences.

It is not uncommon for two people who have been living happily together to find that things change when they marry, because they and society have now added to the situation the burdensome definitions of "husband" and "wife." These concepts often bring with them a heavy responsibility *for* rather than *to* each other, which living together did not engender, compounded by the feeling of no exit imposed by most religions. There may also be the burden of having passed definitively beyond youth into "serious" adulthood. Couples may also have the misperception that marriage will automatically fulfill them, regardless of other aspects of their lives. Of course, this is an even greater problem in our era when it is so difficult for those without a college education to support a family, and increasingly even for those with a college education. Family attitudes and social myths about marriage filter down from generation to generation, making such transitions smoother or more difficult.

Couples can become bound in a web of evasiveness and ambiguity, neither daring to be honest with the other for fear of hurting the other's feelings, if their families of origin had tenuous or negative relationships. Communication may become more and more covert, the more they define their own worth by the relationship. The concept of "marriage" may have taken on a meaning far beyond the fact of two people sharing their lives with each other. Couples may fall into stereotypical roles where she can think of nothing but getting married, the one thing he cannot think about. These patterns reflect the gendered opposite sides of the same lack of differentiation from their families of origin. Men who are not comfortable with their level of differentiation typically fear commitment, whereas women typically fear being alone. Recently, women want the freedom to develop their own lives and relationships while men may want them to stay at their side (Rosin, 2012).

> **Assess your comprehension of fusion and intimacy by completing this quiz.**

Gay and Lesbian Couples

The patterns described here for heterosexual couples may be both simpler and more difficult for gay and lesbian couples (Green & Mitchell, 2008; Gotta et al., 2011). It appears to be an advantage for gays and lesbians that they are less bound by the constricting rigidities of traditional gender roles, which may leave them freer to develop intimate relationships (Green et al., 1996). Both partners being of the same gender may increase the couple's understanding of each other. Although some therapists have thought that being of the same gender might increase the likelihood of fusion, research indicates both gay and lesbian couples seem to have more cohesive relationships than heterosexual couples, lesbians tending to have the greatest level of closeness (Green et al., 1996; Gotta et al., 2011). On the other hand, the lack of acceptance that many gay couples experience from their families and from society at large throughout the life cycle is a serious issue and one clinicians are often in a position to help families modify. The price of the secrecy forced on many gay and lesbian couples by society's disapproval is one we must change. The stigmatizing of homosexual couples by our society means that their relationships are still often not validated by their families or communities and they must cope with prejudice on a daily basis. The AIDS crisis produced a terrible trauma for the gay community, and its impact on a whole generation of gay men at the point of forming couple relationships must not be underestimated. Clinicians can help couples and their families counter familial and societal negativity by developing life cycle rituals to celebrate and affirm their relationships. Special effort is often required on the couple's part to receive adequate recognition of their relationship transitions.

CASE ILLUSTRATION

Katherine Moore and Rita Hidalgo

Katherine Moore, a 27-year-old journalist, and Rita Hidalgo, a 30-year-old graphic artist, had been living together for almost 2 years when they sought help for their relationship problems. Katherine was not sleeping, and Rita was concerned that she was depressed, anxious, and drinking too much. Katherine had been withdrawing from Rita, feeling she was becoming intrusive and bossy. Katherine had struggled since her midteens with her lesbianism. In college she dated men occasionally, hoping this would release her from her homosexual feelings and the disruption she believed a homosexual lifestyle would create for her and her family of origin. In fact, after college she kept a great distance from her parents, with whom she had always had a stormy relationship. She had been known in her family as the problem child since elementary school.

Her conservative Anglo-Irish family operated on the basis of keeping up appearances. Her older sister was the "good girl" and never went beyond the limits accepted by the family. Katherine was the outspoken rebel. She argued politics with her father, and when she became involved in women's rights he became particularly incensed. Katherine felt that her mother covertly sided with her at times but never dared to disagree openly with her father. After she became involved in women's rights, Katherine had several lesbian relationships, but Rita was her first live-in partner. Four months earlier, they had decided to commit to their relationship permanently, at which point Katherine's symptoms increased.

Rita, who came from a Puerto Rican family, had known clearly since high school that she was a lesbian and had socialized with a gay social group from the time she began college. She had not seen her father for years but felt close to her mother and sister. She had never directly spoken of her sexual orientation at home, but she had occasionally brought home female friends and sensed that her mother, who had never remarried after divorcing her father when Rita was 7, might be lesbian herself without knowing it. She suspected that a paternal aunt who had lived for years with another woman was lesbian too.

What precipitated Katherine's turmoil was her announcement to her parents during a visit, which she always made without Rita, that she was lesbian. She had decided to tell her parents about this because she was tired of keeping her life a secret. The resolution to have a commitment ceremony was part of this decision. Her mother initially seemed not unsupportive, but her father became extremely angry and told her this was just the last in a series of her "bad judgments" over many years. In several phone calls to her parents over the next weeks, she was greeted with stony silence by both parents. Rita tried to be supportive, but she had disapproved of Katherine's

telling her parents about her homosexuality, believing that "parents never understand and there's no point getting into all that." Katherine's symptoms had begun just after this. Rita became increasingly resentful of Katherine's preoccupation with her parents, feeling it was destroying their relationship. Katherine had spoken to a number of her lesbian friends who also advised her to forget about her parents, because her father sounded like "an insensitive redneck" and why bother.

As Katherine described her relationship with her parents, it became clear that she was seeking not only greater closeness with them but also their approval for her lesbian choice. Rita had trouble appreciating that she had to let Katherine work out her own relationship with her parents, whatever happened, but after a few discussions she agreed to back off and let Katherine figure things out for herself.

The initial therapy sessions focused on helping Katherine sort out her feelings and desires. She struggled to distinguish between her wish that her parents would approve of her lesbianism, her desire to be closer to them in general, and her wish for their approval of her behavior in particular. How could she remain connected to her parents even if they disapproved of her lesbianism, and how could she let go of her need for their approval? She was coached to write a series of letters to each parent about her years of distancing and rebellion, her criticism of them (for which she now apologized), and her appreciation of how difficult her lesbian choice must be for them. She spoke of her earlier fears that they would cut her off completely and her relief that they had not.

Katherine's letters helped her clarify for herself that her lesbianism was not a matter for her parents' approval or disapproval. She came to see that discussing her lifestyle with them came from a deep need to solidify her identity as an adult and end the secrecy of her life that had kept her distant from them. Luckily, through her motivation to understand herself and her respect for her parents' limitations, she was able to keep her couplehood with Rita from being overburdened by her hurt. After 6 months of therapy, Rita decided it was time to speak directly with her own mother, realizing through Katherine's efforts, how much could be gained by ending the secrecy, even when, as with Katherine, the response had not been particularly positive. Rita's mother said she had known for years and was just waiting for Rita to feel comfortable telling her. When, a few months later, they had their marriage ceremony, Rita's mother, sister, and paternal aunt came (though the aunt left her partner at home), but only Katherine's sister attended from her family. While this was not what they both had hoped for, Katherine felt reassured that her "good girl" sister had come. Perhaps in the future, when they planned to have a baby, Katherine's sister would be able to assist the parents in moving toward more acceptance, now that the "sisterhood" was solidified.

As can be seen from this example, the systemic problems around couple formation are generally similar, regardless of the content of the problems. However, certain patterns are quite predictable for gay and lesbian couples, as they are for religious, social class, ethnic, or racial intermarriages. When the extended family is extremely negative toward the couple, for whatever reason, we encourage couples to take a long view, not trying to turn the acceptance of their relationship into a yes-or-no event, but working gradually over time to build bridges for family closeness. Other life cycle transitions, particularly births and deaths, often create shifts in family equilibrium that may allow the couple to further redefine their family status.

> Assess your comprehension of gay and lesbian couples by completing this quiz.

The Wedding

The wedding is often seen as the end of a process: "And they lived happily ever after." But it is really just the beginning. Whether weddings involve jumping the broom, as in African American tradition; standing under a huppa and crushing a wine glass, as in Jewish tradition; feasting for many days, as in Polish tradition; or other customs, they are among the most interesting family rituals to observe and among the best times for preventive intervention in family process. Even now with marriage rates going down

and divorce rates high, weddings are becoming ever more expensive and elaborate, even for those who cannot afford them, perhaps reflecting the ongoing idealization of marriage in a world where marital relationships are relatively fragile.

As family events, weddings are generally the largest ceremonies organized by families themselves. The organization of the wedding, who makes which arrangements, who gets invited, who comes, who pays, how much emotional energy goes into the preparations, who gets upset and over which issues, are all highly reflective of family process. In general, when couples marry in unconventional ways, in civil ceremonies, or without family or friends present, there are reasons, such as the inability or unwillingness of the parents to meet the costs of the wedding; family disapproval because of race, religion, class, money, or ethnicity; premarital pregnancy; an impulsive decision to marry; and a previous divorce. From a clinical point of view, the emotional charge of such situations, when they lead to downplaying the marriage as a family event, may well indicate that family members are unable to make the status changes required to adapt to this new life cycle phase that requires an expansion of family boundaries to include the new spouse and his or her family, culture, life style, etc. Families that have difficulty making this transition are likely have difficulty at future phases. As rituals, weddings are meant to facilitate family transition to a new constellation. As such, they can be extremely important in helping families mark the change in status, relationships, and organization of the family.

Some families overfocus on the wedding, putting all their energy into the event, spending more than they can afford, and losing sight of the marriage as a process of joining two families. The average wedding (not including the ring or honeymoon) exceeds the median U.S. income (Safdar, 2012). Such spending appears to reflect distorted social mythology that makes it difficult for couples and families to focus on the true meaning of marriage. With changing mores, this focus on the wedding may become less intense, but there is still a large overlap of myth associated with marital bliss, which can get displaced onto wedding celebrations in counterproductive ways. Marriage may indeed become a toxic issue for families because of their particular history.

CASE ILLUSTRATION

Ted and Andrea

Ted and Andrea had toxic issues on both sides of their extended family and sought consultation to see if there was anything they could do to improve their situation. Through premarital coaching, they were able to field stormy reactions in their families and probably prevent years of simmering conflicts that had hampered both extended families over several generations. When they sought help they said they were planning to marry in their apartment with only a few friends present, unless they could bring their families around to accepting them as they were. Andrea's parents had eloped after her grandparents opposed their marriage because of religious differences and they had hardly seen their families since. Ted's paternal grandfather had had a heart attack at his son's (Ted's father's) wedding reception and died the next day. Thus, weddings had become dreaded events for both extended families.

Ted and Andrea began their work by contacting extended-family members to invite them personally to their wedding. They used these conversations to mention in a casual way the pain of the wedding history for the family. For example, Ted phoned his paternal grandmother, who was 85, and who his parents had assured him would never come to the wedding. He told her that his parents were sure she could not make it, but that it would mean a great deal to him to have her there, since he feared his father might have a heart attack and he would need her support. The grandmother not only made her own arrangements to have a cousin fly with her but also arranged to stay with her son, Ted's father, for the week after the wedding. At the reception, both bride and groom made toasts in verse to their families, in which they ticked off the charged issues with humor and sensitivity and made a special point of spending time with family members.

Surprisingly, few couples seek premarital counseling, in spite of the obvious difficulties in negotiating this transition, and in spite of the fact that preventive intervention in relation to the extended families might be much easier than dealing with issues down the road. The most that can be said is that it is extremely useful if one has access to any member of a family at the time of a wedding to encourage him or her to facilitate the resolution of family relationships through this nodal event. For example, it is often fruitful to convey to the couple that in-law struggles are predictable and need not be taken too personally. It is important for couples to recognize that the heightened parental tension probably relates to their sense of loss regarding the marriage. They generally fear they are losing their child rather than gaining another.

When families argue about wedding arrangements, the conflicts often cover up underlying systemic issues. Family members often view others as capable of "ruining" the event. A useful guideline is for each person to take his or her own responsibility for having a good time at the wedding. It is also useful for the couple to recognize that marriage is a family event and not just for the two of them. From this perspective, parents' feelings about the service need to be taken into consideration in whatever meaningful ways are possible. The more responsibility a couple can take for arranging a wedding that reflects their shifting position in their families and the joining of the two systems, the more auspicious for their future relationship.

CASE ILLUSTRATION

Jim and Joan

Jim Marcus spent 6 months in "coaching" for his wedding, at which he wanted the participation of his actively alcoholic mother and the three other mothering figures who had been important in his life. His parents had divorced when he was 5. His father remarried for 6 years when Jim was 8 and again when he was 15. He had grown up in his father's custody, with a family housekeeper-caretaker involved during and between his father's marriages. Jim had distanced himself from his alcoholic mother and from both stepmothers. Through coaching, he was able to reverse the process of cutoff in his arrangements for the wedding. He called his stepmothers and his childhood housekeeper to invite them specially to the wedding, discussing with each her importance in his life and how much it would mean to him to have her present at his wedding celebration. He wrote to his own mother and similarly reviewed the moments in their lives that were most meaningful to him. He arranged with his older brother to be on duty on the day of the wedding and escort the mother out if that became necessary.

The next problem was the parents of his fiancée, Joan, who were planning an elaborate celebration and wanted everything to go according to the book. This would have made Jim's less affluent family very uncomfortable. Initially, Joan became quite reactive to her mother's fancy plans and her way of making decisions without discussion. At the therapist's suggestion, she arranged to spend a day with her mother, during which time she could discuss her feelings about her upcoming marriage and approach her mother as a resource on how to handle things. She discovered for the first time that her mother had been married in a small civil wedding, because her Catholic parents disapproved of her marriage to a Jewish immigrant with no college education. Joan learned how her mother had yearned for a "proper wedding." She realized that her mother's wishes to do everything in a fancy way had grown out of her own unrealized dreams and were an attempt to give Joan something she had missed. With this realization, Joan could share her own wish for a simple celebration to make Jim feel comfortable, especially because of all the problems in his family, which she had never mentioned to her mother before. She asked her mother for advice on how to handle the situation. She told her how uncomfortable she was about the divorces in Jim's family and her fears that her own relatives would disapprove of him, especially if all his mothering figures attended the wedding. Suddenly her mother's attitude changed from dictating how things had to be done to a helpful and much more casual attitude. A week later, Joan's mother told Jim that if there was any way she could facilitate things with his mother, stepmothers, or other guests, she would be glad to do it.

It frequently happens that friendship systems and extended-family relationships change after the wedding. Many couples have difficulty maintaining individual friendships and move, at least in the first years, toward having only "couple friends." We encourage spouses to keep their individual friendship networks as well, since "couple friends" typically reinforce fusion and may not allow the spouses their individual interests and preferences, which are so important to their lifelong well-being.

 Assess your comprehension of the wedding by completing this quiz.

Sexuality

Our society has almost no images that would help us in developing sexually gratifying partnership relationships (Carter & Peters, 1996). Working with couples means helping them to become pioneers in their sexual relationships, just as it does in other aspects of forming a partnership, as opposed to the traditional couple relationship of a powerful, dominant male and a submissive, responsive female. Helping couples establish flexible and intimate sexual relationships involves freeing them from the gender stereotypes that are part of their familial and cultural heritage (Schnarch, 2010).

From early childhood, boys are encouraged to feel positive about their bodies sexually, whereas girls have rarely been encouraged even to be familiar with their genitalia, let alone to enjoy their sexuality. Boys typically begin to masturbate from early childhood, girls not till mid-adolescence, if then. Women generally have to bear the burden of the repercussions of sexuality in terms of contraception, and in many groups they are prohibited from using contraception or refusing sex, subjecting them to all the consequences of sexuality, from pregnancy to sexually transmitted diseases, but not to being proud of being sexual or even knowing how their bodies work. What is surprising is not that sex so often becomes a problem for a couple, but that it works out as often as it does.

The current generation has much more sexual experience and knowledge than previous generations. Unlike the increasng age at marriage, the age at sexual maturation and first intercourse have decreased.

Males and especially females are having sex with more partners at younger ages than ever before. The vast majority of young adults (approximately 90 percent) are sexually experienced, and most have sex regularly. At the same time, anxieties about AIDS, herpes, and other sexual transmitted diseases are active concerns for young couples today.

In the past, if a husband lost interest in sex, we assumed he was having an affair. Now we ask about recent changes in the wife's income and status, since sexuality seems so clearly linked with power issues in marriage for both partners. Even where a woman develops a flirtation or affair, as in the case of Susan and Joe, we explore whether her behavior might be an attempt (however misguided) to empower herself through a sexual relationship, because as a woman she has felt disempowered overall in the relationship. Our experience is that techniques to enhance sexual enjoyment are only a small part of dealing with a couple's sexual problems. It is important to consider the power dimension in a couple's relationship when the partners are experiencing sexual difficulty. Sex is at the heart of expressions of intimacy, and the inability to express intimacy is very likely to be related to familial and cultural factors that have made intimacy in this form and most forms are very difficult for men and women in our society. In addition to exploring sexuality in the extended family in order to understand the specific messages that partners have been given about their bodies, their own sexuality, and their expectations about what is "sexy" with a partner, therapists need to take into account the larger cultural dimensions within which our sexual relationships evolve (Schnarch, 2010). We must pay attention to the implicit power dimensions influencing this aspect and all other aspects of a couple's relationship. Given the very high levels of violence against wives in marriage and the trouble our nation still has acknowledging marital rape, we must be very careful not to limit our work with a couple to the interior of their intimate relationship without taking account of the power dimensions that operate in all couple relationships.

One of the most interesting, and usually forgotten, aspects of human sexuality is that unlike most other animals whose sexuality is limited to times when they can reproduce, human sexuality operates

regardless of fertility, which may suggest it is an adaptive development to help maintain joie de vivre, affection and caretaking in human relationships over the long haul of couples' lives (Bateson, 2010).

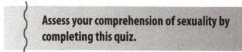

Assess your comprehension of sexuality by completing this quiz.

Patterns with Extended Family

Women tend to move closer to their families of origin after marriage, while men may become more distant, shifting their primary tie to the new nuclear family. In any case, spouses' ways of dealing with their families may differ. Many find marriage the only way to separate from their families of origin, but their underlying enmeshment in the family continues even after marriage. Patterns of guilt, intrusiveness, and unclear boundaries are typical of such systems. Other couples may cut off their families emotionally even before marriage, some going to the extreme of not inviting them to the wedding. Sometimes parents are seen as withholding and rejecting and the couple decides to do without them. Others push ongoing conflicts or tension under the rug. In such families, there is usually involvement of the extended family in the marriage plans, but often with fights, hurt feelings, and "scenes" around the wedding. This pattern of conflicts indicates that the family is at least struggling over the transition and is not forcing the feelings underground as in enmeshed or cutoff families. The ideal situation is where the partners have become independent of their families before marriage and at the same time maintain close, caring ties. In such instances, the wedding can serve for all the family as a sharing celebration of the new couple's shift in status.

Where couples cut off family relationships, their restrictive couple patterns may work until later life transitions destabilize them. Where conflicts are submerged, marriage may be an excellent opportunity to reopen closed relationships, for example, inviting to the wedding relatives with whom parents are out of touch. It is a good chance to detoxify emotional issues, reviewing marital and family ties over several generations as part of redefining the system. Otherwise underlying tensions may surface in emotional scenes or arguments around wedding plans, only to go underground again as family members try to act happy and friendly so as not to "create unpleasantness." The attempt to smooth things over in itself may increase the likelihood of future relationship eruptions. The fact is that all change disrupts the system and needs to be dealt with if the developmental processes are to proceed. It may be easier for the family to move on if they are in touch with their sense of loss at the time of the wedding and confused and uneasy about how to manage the new relationships. Whatever the patterns of difficulty with extended family—conflict, enmeshment, distance, or cutoff—the lack of resolution of these relationships is the major problem in negotiating this phase of the family life cycle. The more the triangles in the extended family are dealt with by an emotional cutoff, the greater the likelihood that the spouse will come to represent more than who he or she is. If the husband's relationship with his wife is his only meaningful relationship, he is likely be so sensitive to her every reaction, and especially to any hint of rejection, that he may overreact to signs of differentness by pulling her to agree with him or blaming her for not accepting him. In time, the intensity may make the relationship untenable, jamming the circuits. Our culture's social mobility and over-focus on the nuclear family to the neglect of all other relationships contributes to this tendency to place more emotional demand on a marriage than it can bear. Indeed the indications are that marriage actually tends to isolate partners from other people in ways that pose potential long-term problems (Sarkisian & Gerstel, 2008). Once a spouse becomes overly involved in the other's response, both can become bound up in a web of fusion and unable to function for themselves.

Some couples transfer parental struggles to the spouse directly. Others choose a spouse who handles the family for them. A man may choose a wife totally unacceptable to his parents and then let her fight his battles with his parents, while he becomes the "innocent bystander." The price everyone pays in such situations is the failure to achieve any real connection, since issues can never be resolved when other members are brought in to handle one's relationships. Similar problems arise when a person has

served a central function in his or her parents' lives or in the preservation of the parents' marital balance and does not feel entitled to marry.

In-laws

Among the problematic triangles for the couple, the one involving husband, wife, and mother-in-law is probably the most obvious. In-laws are easy scapegoats for family tensions. It is always easier to hate your daughter-in-law for keeping your son from showing his love than to admit that your son does not respond to you the way you wish he would. It may be easier for a daughter-in-law to hate her mother-in-law for "intrusiveness" than to confront her husband directly for not speaking up to define the necessary boundaries for their relationship with his parents. In-law relationships are a natural arena for displacing tensions in the couple or in the family of origin of each spouse. The converse of this is the spouse who has cut off his or her own family and seeks to adopt the spouse's family, forming a warm, enmeshed fusion with the in-laws, based on defining his or her own family as cold, rejecting, uninteresting, and so on.

Our society generally focuses blame on the mother-in-law rather than on the father-in-law, who is usually seen as playing a more benign role. Just as mothers get blamed for what goes wrong in families because they are given primary responsibility for family relationships, so do mothers-in-law get primary blame by extension. Many factors contribute to this process. Just as wives are often given responsibility for handling a husband's emotional problems, they tend to be put in the position of expressing issues for all other family members and then blamed when things go wrong.

Sibling issues in couple formation

Siblings may also displace their problems in dealing with each other onto the new spouse. Predictable triangles are especially likely between a husband and his wife's brothers or between the wife and her husband's sisters. Sisters may see their brother's wife as having "no taste," infusing the brother with superficial values, and so forth. What is missed by the system in such instances is that the brother probably chose his wife as a protection from his sisters, perhaps to set the limits he never dared set alone or to allow him to distance without the guilt of doing so directly. Often the brother will get his wife to take over dealing with his family altogether, which usually succeeds only in escalating the tension.

Good clues about a couple can be found in the marital relationships of each partner's parents, the primary models for what their marriage is about. The other basic model for spouses is their relationship with their siblings, generally their earliest and closest peers. Couples who marry mates from complementary sibling positions tend to enjoy the greatest marital stability (Toman, 1976). In other words, the older brother of a younger sister will tend to get along best with a younger sister of an older brother. They are likely to have fewer power conflicts, since he will be comfortable as the leader and she as the follower. In addition, they will tend to be comfortable with the opposite sex, since they have grown up with opposite-sexed siblings as well. Those who marry spouses not from non-complementary sibling positions may have more marital adjustments to make in this regard. An extreme case would be the oldest of many brothers who marries the oldest of many sisters. Both would expect to be the leader and would probably be less comfortable with the opposite sex, having grown up in strongly single-sexed environments.

Cultural differences

Another arena that becomes problematic in a marriage under stress is the cultural or family style difference. This may be more of a problem in the United States where people from so many diverse cultural backgrounds marry and find themselves in conflict because each starts out with such different basic assumptions (McGoldrick & Preto, 1984; McGoldrick, Giordano, & Garcia Preto, 2005; Karis & Killian, 2011).

CASE ILLUSTRATION

Jack and Maria

Jack and Maria applied for therapy after a year of marriage because Maria said she was convinced

Jack did not love her and that he had changed after they got married. The wife was the fifth of seven children from a Brooklyn family whose grandparents had immigrated from Italy. She had met her husband in college and was extremely attracted to his quiet strength and strong life ambitions. He was from a midwestern Protestant family of British, German, and Dutch heritage where, as an only child, he was strongly encouraged by his parents to work hard and have a morally upright life. Jack had found Maria vivacious and charming and had also been attracted to her family, because of their open affection and because, in contrast to his own "uptight" parents, they always seemed to have a good time.

Under stress, the couple found that the very qualities that had attracted them to each other became the problem. Jack became for Maria "an unfeeling stone." She complained: "He doesn't care about my feelings at all and ignores me completely." For Jack, Maria's vivaciousness now became "hysteria" and he found her "nagging, emotional outbursts, and screaming" unbearable.

As we discussed in therapy, their very different family styles of coping with stress and their opposing assumptions became obvious. In Jack's family, the rule was that you should keep your problems to yourself and think them out: With enough effort and thought, most problems could be worked out. Maria's family dealt with stress by getting together and venting. The family related intensely at all times, but especially when they were upset. These styles had been turned inward in the marriage and were tightening things even more. The more isolated Maria felt and the more she needed contact, the louder she sought attention and the more Jack withdrew to remain calm and maintain his balance. The more he withdrew, the more frustrated and alone Maria felt. Both had turned their differences, initially the source of attraction, into the problem and saw the other's behavior as a sure sign of not caring. Neither could see that their family styles were just different. They were compounding the difficulty by blaming each other for the other's response.

Once the family patterns could be clarified in the context of the extended family and ethnic backgrounds,

Maria and Jack were able to temper their responses and to see their differences as neutral, rather than as signs of psychopathology or rejection.

Assess your comprehension of patterns with extended family by completing this quiz.

Conclusion

Marriage in the twenty-first century is being profoundly affected by the diversity of marriage partners, the changing definitions of marriage, the increasing physical distance from families of origin, the changing role of women, the increase in unmarried couples living together, the frequency of changing partners, and the diminishing role of community in supporting families. Couples are increasingly isolated and expected to manage their lives and families without the community supports that in the past were a primary resource in raising children and meeting family needs. Couples are less bound by family traditions and are freer than ever before to develop male–female relationships unlike those of earlier members of their families of origin. Couples are required to think out for themselves many things that in the past would have been taken for granted. This applies also to the enormous gap that often exists between parents and children in education and social status. Although these differences can cause strain, we also live at a time when the possibilities for couples to have creative and equitable partnerships are great. The cultural differences can add flexibility to the system and stretch the family to become adaptive over the life cycle in new ways. The marriage cycle of couples choosing to marry in the twenty-first century will surely require this creative adaptation, and we have probably only begun to imagine how couple relationships in the future may evolve.

Recall what you learned in this chapter by completing the **Chapter Review**.

References

Barnett, R. C., & Rivers, C. (2004). *Same difference: How gender myths are hurting our relationships, our children, and our jobs.* New York: Basic Books.

Bateson, M. C. (2010). *Composing a further life: The age of active wisdom.* New York: Vintage.

Bolick, K. (2011). All the single ladies. The Atlantic. Retrieved February 20, 2013, from http://www.theatlantic.com/magazine/print/2011/11/all-the-single-ladies/308654/

Blumstein, P., & Schwartz, P. (1983). *American couples: Money, work and sex.* New York: William Morrow & Company.

Carstensen, L. L., Gottman, J. M., & Levenson, R. W. (1995). Emotional behavior in long-term marriage. *Psychology and Aging, 10*(1), 140–149.

Carter, B., & Peters, J. (1996). *Love, honor and negotiate: Building partnerships that last a lifetime.* New York: Pocket Books.

Cherlin, A. J. (2013). In the season of marriage, a question. Why bother? *New York Times*, April 28, 2013, p. SR 7.

Cherlin, A. J. (2012). Do unmarried poor have bad values or bad jobs. *Bloomberg News*, December 25, 2012. Retrieved December 28, 2012, from http://www.bloomberg.com/news/print/2012-12-25/do-unmarried-poor-have-bad-values-or-bad-jobs-.html.

Cherlin, A. J. (2009a). America n marriage in the early twenty-first century. In A. S. Skolnick & J. H. Skolnick (Eds.). *Families in transition,* (pp. 171–191). Boston, MA: Allyn & Bacon.

Cherlin, A. J. (2009b). *The marriage-go-round: The state of marriage and family in America today.* New York: Knopf.

Cherlin, A., Burton, L. M., Hurt, T., & Purvin, D. (2004). The influence of physical and sexual abuse on marriage and cohabitation. American Sociological Review, 69, 768–789.

Coontz, S., (2013). The triumph of the working mother. *New York Times*, June 2, 2013, p. SR 11.

Coontz, S. (2005). *Marriage: A history.* New York: Viking.

DeNoon, D. (2003). Only happy marriage healthy for women. Retrieved February 22, 2013, from http://www.webmd.com/balance/news/20030915/only-happy-marriage-is-healthy-for-women.

Dolan Del Vecchio (2008). *Making love, playing power: Men, women and the rewards of intimate justice*. New York: Soft Skull Press.

Douthat, R. (2013). Marriage looks different now. *New York Times*. March 30, 2013. A p. 22.

Gallo, L. C. Troxel, W. M., Matthews, K. A., & Kuller, L. H. (2003). Marital status and quality in middle-aged women: Associations with levels and trajectories of cardiovascular risk factors, *Health Psychology, 22*, (5), 453–463.

Gotta, G., Green, R. J., Rothblum, E., Solomon, S., Balsam, K., & Schwartz, P. *(2011)*. Heterosexual, lesbian, and gay male relationships: A comparison of couples in 1975 and 2000. *Family Process, 50*(3), 353–376.

Gottman, J. (1993). The roles of conflict engagement, escalation, and avoidance in marital interaction: A longitudinal view of five types of couples. *Journal of Counseling and Clinical Psychology, 61*(1), 6–15.

Green, R. J., & Mitchell, V. (2008). *Gay and lesbian couples in therapy: Homophobia, relational ambiguity and social support*. In A. S. Gurman & N. S. Jacobson (Eds.), *Clinical handbook of couple therapy* (4th ed., pp. 662–680). New York: Guilford.

Green, R. J. & Werner, P. D. (1996). Intrusiveness and closeness-caregiving: Rethinking the concept of family "enmeshment." *Family Process*, 35, 115–136.

Green, R. J., Bettinger, M., & Zacks, E. (1996). Are lesbian couples fused and gay male couples disengaged? Questioning gender straitjackets. In J. Laird & R.-J. Green (Eds.), *Lesbians and gays in couples and families: A handbook for therapists* (pp. 185–230). San Francisco: Jossey-Bass.

Harden, B. (2007, March 4). Numbers drop for the married with children; institution becoming the choice of the educated, affluent. *Washingtonpost.com*. Retrieved (April 14, 2010) from www/washingtonpost.com/wp-dyn/content/article/2007/03/03/Ar2007030300841.html

Hymowitz, K., Carroll, J. S., Wilcox, W., Bradford, & Kaye, K. (2013). Knot yet: The benefits and costs of delayed marriage in America. National arriage Project, University of Virginia and National Campaign to Prevent Teen and Unplanned Pregnancy. Retrieved October 11, 2013, from www.marriage@virginia.edu.

Jones, J. V. (2006, March 26). Marriage is for White people. *Washington Post*, p. B 1.

Karis, T., & Killian, K. (Eds.). (2011). *Intercultural couples*. New York: Haworth Press.

Kimmel, M. S. (2013). *The gendered society* (5th ed.). New York: Oxford University Press.

Klein, E. (2013, March 25*)*. *9 facts about marriage and childbirth in the United States*. Washington Post. Retrieved March 31, 2013, from http://www.washingtonpost.com/blogs/wonkblog/wp/2013/03/25/nine-facts-about-marriage-and-childbirth-in-the-united-states/

Lerner, H. (2013). *Marriage rules: A manual for the married and coupled up*. Gotham Books: New York.

Lerner, M. (1995, November/December). The oppression of singles. *Tikkun, 10*(6), pp. 9–11.

McGoldrick, M., Giordano, J., & Garcia Preto, N. (2005). *Ethnicity and family therapy* (3rd ed.). New York: Guilford Press.

McGoldrick, M. & Preto, N. G. (1984). Ethnic intermarriage: Implications for therapy. *Family Process, 23*(3), 347–363.

Mundy, L. (2012). *The richer sex: How the new majority of female breadwinners is transforming sex, love, and family*. New York: Simon & Schuster.

Parker-Pope. (2010). Is marriage good for your health. *New York Times*. April 14. p. C1, 4.

Quindlen, A. (2012*)*. *Lots of candles, plenty of cake: A memoir*. New York: Random House.

Rastogi, M., & Thomas, V. (2009). Multicultural couple therapy. Thousand Oaks, CA: Sage.

Rilke, R. M. (1954). *Letters to a Young Poet*. Translated by D. M. Hester, New York: W. W. Norton.

Rosin, H. (2012). *The end of men*. New York: Riverhead Books.

Sack, K. (2008, August 13). Health benefits inspire rush to marry or divorce. *New York Times*, p. A1.

Safdar, Kahdah (2012). Average wedding cost exceeds median income in U.S. May 21, 2012. Huffington Post. Retrieved February 23, 2013, from http://www.huffingtonpost.com/2012/05/21/cost-wedding-27000_n_1533464.html

Sarkisian, N. & Gerstel, N . (2008). Till marriage do us part: Adult children's relationships with their parents. *Journal of Marriage and Family, 70*(2), 260–376.

Schnarch, D. (2010). *Intimacy and desire*. New York: Beaufort Books.

Tavernise, S. (2011). Married couples are no longer a majority, census finds. *New York Times*. May 26, 2011, p. 1.

Toman, W. (1976). *Family constellation* (3rd ed.). New York: Springer.

Vaillant, G. (2012). *Triumphs of experience: The men of the Harvard study*. Cambridge, MA: Belknap.

Zezima, K. (2008, August 20). More women than ever are childless, census finds. *New York Times*, p. A12.

Chapter 15

Becoming Parents: The Family With Children

Monica McGoldrick, Barbara Petkov, Betty Carter

Learning Outcomes

- List and describe the changes that have occurred in the last generation in the timing and patterns of the life cycle phase of becoming parents.
- Discuss the impact a new baby has on its extended family system.
- Explore the stresses that the parenthood life cycle phase puts on couples and responses that can help alleviate these stresses.
- Describe the importance of quality child care to both children and families.
- List and describe developmental tasks that are important for families with young children.
- Examine important issues that should be addressed by parents and other care takers during early childhood.
- Discuss how single parenting, teenage parenting, infertility, adoption, and having children with disabilities affect child rearing tasks.
- Explore the clinical guidelines for working with a family presenting at the phase of parents with young children.

Making the decision to have a child—it's momentous. It is to decide forever to have your heart walking around outside your body.

—Elizabeth Stone

Nobody has ever before asked the nuclear family to live all by itself in a box the way we do. With no relatives, no support, we've put it in an impossible situation.

—Margaret Mead (en.wikiquote.org)

The Transition to Parenthood

Becoming a parent is one of the most definitive transitions in life, a crossing of the Rubicon. Life will never be the same again. It is lucky that most parents fall passionately in love with their new babies and consider them fascinating, because this helps carry them through the many difficulties in store for them. The roller coaster of the early months and years of parenthood come as a shock to most new parents: sleep deprivation, shredded schedules, endless chores, worry about the baby's development or one's own competence, and the need for ceaseless vigilance. The sudden threat of chaos puts enormous stress on new parents and on their relationship, since no amount of doing ever seems enough to get the job done before it needs to be done again.

The timing and patterns of this life cycle phase have changed dramatically within the past generation. Precipitated by the availability of birth control and shifts toward more equitable relationships between men and women, having a child has become a more or less conscious choice for the first time in history. Families are having fewer children, less than 2 per couple, down from 3.2 in 1976, and this will profoundly influence families throughout life cycle for future generations. The percent of women who do not have children has also doubled since 1970 from 10 to 20 percent. Educated professional women are even more likely to remain childless (27 percent) (Zezima, 2008). Since 1950, the percent of births taking place outside of marriage has also gone from 4 to 41 percent, but the rate is 53 percent for children born to women younger than 30 years (DeParle & Tavernise, 2012), although this includes a fair percentage same-sex and other non-married couples (Cherlin, 2009). In the same time period, the percent of households made up of married couples with children has shrunk from 43 to 25 percent (Tavernise, 2011). Overall about 60 percent of parents are couples where the husband is the primary breadwinner. Of the other 40 percent, 15 percent are married women who are the primary earners of their families and the final 25 percent are single parents, almost all mothers, who are raising one third of all our children (Anderson, 2013; Wang, Parker, & Taylor, 2013). The finances of parenting also reflect a most unfortunate imbalance. When a woman has a child (and the more children, the worse), her salary goes down. When a man has a child, his salary goes up! And this is when we control for type of job, education, experience, spousal income, and job hours (Miller, 2014; Budig & England, 2001).

The tasks of the parenting phase flow from the adjustment of the couple system to make space for children physically, psychologically, and spiritually. Making space requires collaboration in child-rearing, financial and housekeeping tasks, and realigning relationships with grandparents and other extended family, the community, and larger social system.

Each family brings to the transition to parenthood its own cultural history about intergenerational relationships, gender roles, and expectations for child–parent, grandparent, and aunt and uncle behavior, just as each person brings his or her own legacy from childhood. A person who remembers a happy childhood and good parents may want to repeat that experience, while someone escaping a terrible childhood wants to do it differently. There is no way to understand parenting without looking at this past, the cultural surround, and at families' expectations for their future.

The family demographics and patterns of childrearing demonstrate our society's increasing diversity of family forms. The parenting cycle now extends from early teen years to as late as age 50 for women and 60+ for men, and couple and parenting arrangements are diverse as well.

> ### Changing trends in American families for childrearing include the following:
>
> - At least one half of all children in the next generation will live in female-headed households (Webb, 2005), and most mothers are in the work force, making child care an increasing issue for families in the United States (Coontz, 2013).
> - An increasing proportion of U.S. families raising children are people of color, multiracial families, adoptive families (often with multiracial children), and multicultural families often speaking two primary languages for at least two generations.
> - An increasing proportion of families involve sexually variant parents and/or other close relatives.
> - Economic conditions affecting employment and the rising costs of child care, health care, and education are an ever-increasing factor in how well families can negotiate the stage of parenting children (Leonhardt, 2011; Reardon, 2013). These stressors create much more severe hardships for families at the margins: those who are poor, of color, immigrants, or whose children or other family members have special needs or experience social stigma.

What children need for their development

INFANCY TO ABOUT AGE TWO. The earliest tasks of infancy and early childhood involve skills of autonomy, empathy, and emotional attunement to others. Children learn from their earliest infancy to communicate their needs and to have a sense of trust, comfort, and relationship with their caretakers and with the world around them. They begin to develop body coordination and motor skills. They also begin to talk, play, walk, and to feed themselves. They learn to overcome fears of new people and situations, to recognize themselves as separate, and begin to develop empathy for others.

What parents, other guardians, and caretakers must do to support this growth is to meet children's needs consistently, so they can develop trust in others and a sense of security.

EARLY CHILDHOOD TO ELEMENTARY SCHOOL.
From the time children begin to walk until they enter primary school, their major tasks involve increasing the same skills of autonomy, self-management, emotional competence, and the ability to relate to others. They are developing language, communication, motor skills, control of their bodies, cognitive skills with numbers, words and objects, the ability to take direction, to cooperate, to share, to trust, to form peer relationships, and to explore the world around them. Children begin to recognize other's pain as separate from their own and to comfort them. They begin to become aware of themselves as different from others on many dimensions including gender, race, and ability level.

As children enter school, parents, guardians, and other caretakers must develop supportive parenting skills, especially in the area of discipline and rule setting. How this is handled will greatly influence a child's identity and emotional competence. Shaming and physical punishment have deleterious effects, whereas support and consistent nurturing and mentoring promote childrens' ability to stretch themselves in their learning and confidence.

CHILDREN THROUGH ELEMENTARY SCHOOL. The years of elementary school are a time when children make many developmental leaps in cognitive, motor, and emotional relationship skills and in perceptiveness of the interdependence of all relationships. Children are expanding their social worlds and learning about belonging and "otherness,"—inclusion and exclusion. They learn to communicate and to handle relationships with an increasing range of adults and children beyond their families. Their concerns often focus on competition, cooperation, expanded awareness of gender roles, race, culture, sexual orientation, class, and level of abilities. Children at this phase have increasing access to knowledge through reading, TV, the internet, and social media. Skills children need to work on at this phase include their ability to be intimate and empathic; and to express anger, fear, and pain in nondestructive ways, which increases their sense of morality and fairness, as well as their tolerance for differences.

Children need their parents' and caretakers' active involvement in mentoring them to support cooperation, non-violence, and respect for others, or else competitiveness can become a serious problem. They need their parents' support in not engaging in bullying behavior. Parents and other adults have a major role to play in teaching children to respect and support others in their social network and community.

Children may play adults off against each other to get what they want because they do not yet know how to confront adults to let them know when they feel neglected, rejected, or ignored (Comer & Poussaint, 1992). The quality of a child's relationships with adults is more important than the gender of the adults, for both male and female children. Children are aware of unfairness and hypocrisy of adults and authorities. It is important for adults to help them understand adult failings and to model responses to unfairness so that they do not feel powerless and cynical. Abused or neglected children may become aggressive—picking fights out of frustration, disconnection, and hopelessness.

As children grow in their cognitive, motor, and emotional relationship skills and interdependent perceptiveness, they expand their social world in terms of their ability to communicate and handle relationships with an increasing range of adults and children beyond their families. From quite an early age, they begin to understand their identity in terms of gender, race, culture, and sexual orientation and to differentiate themselves from others (Quintana, 2008; Bennett, 2007; Coll & Szalacha, 2004; Robbins, Szapocznik, Mayorga, Dillon, Burns, & Feaster, 2007). They also hopefully improve in their ability to follow directions, tolerate frustration, work independently, and cooperate with others. If they are not supported in developing these abilities for self-management, they may develop physical, emotional, or social symptoms—fears, anxieties, and withdrawn or aggressive behaviors.

Through elementary school years, children often spend a lot of time discussing, arguing, and changing the rules of games. As their independence–dependence struggle intensifies, it is important to teach them to do chores and meet responsibilities for their own sake, rather than because they are told, to encourage them to establish their own standards. Doing chores teaches them that their contribution to the family is valuable. Family rituals and celebrations are important to children, who start learning how to plan and organize events if their parents do this well. It matters a great deal whether children get the message "I can" or "I can't" from their school and family experiences.

We know a lot about what children need throughout their childhood for their psychological, spiritual, physical and social development. They need, first of all, continuity of nurturance and trust to develop a sense of a safe "home base," so they can learn discipline and self-management, the core of a solid identity, in order to function in their social world. They need to develop a sense of trust in order to communicate their needs, feelings and thoughts; to support their confidence in meeting new people; handling new situations and venturing out toward new learning; new connections; and new ways of communicating.

One of the least constructive ways to raise children, as Kohn (2014) points out, is with "conditional regard," that is, when parents offer children affection only based on their achievements and good behavior. Such attitudes promote children's developing a fragile and unstable sense of self (Assor, Kanat-Maymon, & Roth, 2014; Assor, Roth, & Deci, 2004). Children need to learn to accept themselves even when others do not accept them, and eventually to trust their own judgment and values in order to form their own solid sense of self, rather than feeling they have to accept unquestioningly the values of others. Children need adult support and modeling to learn empathy. For children to learn to manage their interdependence with others—their caretakers, their peers, and relationships with those who are both more and less powerful than they are, they require increasingly sophisticated negotiation skills. They need support from the adults in their lives to develop a sense of social justice.

For children's development in all these ways, they need parents and other supportive adults who have the energy to nurture and support them. But when parents are overstressed by work, poverty, racism, sexism, or heterosexism, they may be unable to give their children these essential supports.

Early in the transition to parenthood sleep is one of the most important requirements for parental functioning, and especially for parental patience.

Sleep deprivation compromises a person's behavior as much as excessive alcohol or drugs (Senior, 2014). They more easily become irritable and to yell, which is likely to make them feel bad about themselves and can become a vicious downward spiral.

Another major difficulty for parents is that children do not speak our language and they require constant monitoring. While children live in the present, parents must live in the future, taking precautions for children's behavior and making plans for the child's nurturance and care, since children cannot perceive future consequences. Meanwhile, because children live primarily in the present and their brains are not equipped to think about the future, they create chaos, messes, out of control situations, and are constantly testing the boundaries, whereas adults almost always like things to be predictable and in control.

So children are a tremendous challenge to our preferred ways of being (Senior, 2014). It is as if everyone is moving at the same speed but children are moving with their eyes closed and adults are the ones who have to steer (Gilbert, 2007). One of the reasons parenting a young child may be boring (one of the hardest things for most parents to admit!), in addition to reading the same story or watching the same video over and over, may be the amount of time parents basically have to spend nagging their children, that is, teaching them the boring rules of civilization, "clean up your mess, go get your coat," etc.

Among the other major problems that interfere with children's support is their parents' not being present or not being able to demonstrate their caring. As African American journalist Charles Blow (2014), advises: "Sometimes men don't see that masculinity is as much about tenderness as about toughness. Sometimes they don't know how to manage emotions. Sometimes the world has so beaten them and so hardened them that expressing any vulnerability feels like providing an opening for an enemy. Blow movingly describes the life cycle impact of this: "When there is an empty space where a father should be, sorrow often grows" (Blow, 2014). We therapists have a job to do: As a society we must change the way we raise boys to teach them tenderness along with toughness. And we must encourage all parents and other adults who participate in the development of children's lives—educators, uncles, aunts, grandparents, neighbors, health care providers—to nurture children becoming all that they can be, as they are our future.

Expectations versus Reality

Until the 1960s, the basic assumption was that motherhood and, by extension, parenthood meant an automatic leap ahead in fulfillment, joy, and status. But in the past decades and especially since the start of the new century, having children is increasingly being delayed, because women feel they have a choice when and whether to become mothers. There are educational and career goals to consider along with the difficulty of supporting a family.

Those who enter parenthood with fewer romantic expectations are more likely to emerge from the transition happier about their marriages and their spouses than those who believe they can somehow abide by the traditional gender rules of parenting (Belsky & Kelly, 1994). But more myths and romantic fantasies than realistic expectations are still attached to the transition to parenthood. Most of the mythology paints a glowing picture, especially of the mother and child, a central icon in cultures and religions from time immemorial. Women are still often vulnerable to the belief that a childless woman is not a "real" woman. For both sexes, parenthood seems to provide the final ticket for acceptance into adulthood: the woman mothering, and the man "providing." But in real life, the rewards of parenthood, expressed in all cultures across the ages, can often seem largely theoretical in the face of the difficult realities of raising and supporting children, especially in a society that still does not support parenthood as a societal benefit (Friedman, 2012). But the deeply held personal and intergenerational expectations and dreams of most families conflict with our society's astounding nonsupport for families with children.

The nuclear family made up of good provider father and homemaker mother characterizes a very small percentage of families in the United States, and yet it is the group the entire educational and work structures of our society are still organized to accommodate. Only 14 percent of children have stay-at-home mothers (Saad, 2012) and 86 percent of families must therefore arrange child care. Mothers who do stay home tend to be younger, foreign born, and specifically Latinas (Edwards, U.S. Census Bureau, 2009). Child care is the number 1 practical problem at this phase of the life cycle. The United States is the only industrialized nation in the world that leaves it to individual families to arrange and pay for child care themselves.

Poor children in the United States are worse off than poor children in all other industrialized Western nations (Friedman, 2012). The United States is one of only four countries in the entire world that do not have paid maternity leave, the others being Lesotho, Swaziland, and Papua New Guinea (Hall & Spurlock, 2013). U.S. support for health and education for children under 6, which is key to children's future well-being, is only two thirds of what the other major developed countries pay for these supports (CBS News, 2009). Child poverty rates in the United States are nearly double the average of the OECD, the leading organization of 34 major industrialized democratic nations around the world! Of the many risks for children in postindustrial societies, poverty puts children more at risk than any other single factor. The families most likely to live in poverty are single mothers, 40 percent of whom live in poverty, raising 50 percent of the poor children in this country, bringing the poverty rate for children to 22 percent of the child population (Bennetts, 2011). Among the most forgotten children of all are the children in foster care, almost half a million at any time (U.S. Department of Health and Human Services, 2013a). Many of these children would not need foster care if our government provided more social supports for families, schools, and communities. Children placed in foster care and those who become homeless are among the most stressed, their numbers having increased in recent decades (National Coalition for the Homeless, 2009). When children lose their homes, they also tend to lose the continuity of their schools and communities as well as their families. The more we as a nation can do to strengthen families, schools, and communities, the more we will be supporting our own future well-being. The dreadful statistics on our nation's lack of support for our most vulnerable children show how little we as a society care for our future citizens, a national catastrophe for our future.

There is also still lack of accommodation and wide societal disapproval for nontraditional couples, women who choose or need to go to work, spouses with children who believe that divorce is their best or only option, the poor, the multistressed, and single parents. These families often experience double jeopardy: the same or more economic difficulties than other families compounded by the disparagement and nonacceptance of their place in society.

The extended family

The new baby enters an extended family system that must now make emotional and relationship shifts to accommodate him or her. Many families celebrate the event with a religious ritual: a christening, Bris, or naming ceremony, usually followed by a party for family and friends. When children are adopted, families tend to celebrate the baby's or child's arrival date. As with other family transition rituals, issues about how and where the event is celebrated and who gets invited reflect the ongoing extended-family process. Whether or not there is a ritual or party, the new member of the system is greeted with many differing emotional reactions, depending on its sex, its health, how it is named, how long it was awaited, what kind of relationship its parents have with other family members, whether grandparents approved of the marriage, and whether they are all doing their part to shift to relationships in the parent and grandparent generations.

A first grandchild also creates new grandparents, who often jump into their new role without much planning or discussion with their children, not realizing that there are as many ways to grandparent as to parent. No way is "right," but some ways fit their lives and their children's lives better than others, and it is best when the issue is discussed early on. Complaints about intrusive or indifferent grandparents, or demanding or neglectful adult children, are signs of the need for such discussion.

Whether parents maintain close or distant extended family relationships, they can expect to inherit any unresolved extended family issues and patterns—triangles, ghosts, and taboo issues that are best examined and dealt with at this time, lest they engulf the new family in emotional problems later

on. This is a good stage to engage parents in family of origin work, even if they have previously resisted it. Parents will do many things for their children that they would not do for themselves, and this fact provides therapeutic leverage. It is also a good time for grandparents to give up old grievances and make new efforts to relate to their adult children and the children's spouses. Grandparents may need reminding that in a society with such a high divorce rate, it is wise to be good friends with your daughter-in-law.

Assess your comprehension of the transition to parenthood by completing this quiz.

Couple Relationships and Traditional Roles in the Parenthood Phase

Conventional wisdom used to be that becoming a parent was the best route to a happy marriage (Coontz, 2009). But as many observers have realized, "three's a crowd," when it comes to marital satisfaction at the parenting phase of the life cycle. Once a child arrives, lack of paid parental leave often leads the wife to quit her job and the husband to work more, which is likely to produce discontent on both sides. Marital quality tends to drop, often quite steeply, after the transition to parenthood, especially because parents so often backslide into more traditional gender roles, which they experience as less satisfying. The wife may resent her husband's lack of involvement in child care and housework. The husband may resent his wife's ingratitude for the long hours he works to support the family (Coontz, 2005).

Parents of young children must often relegate their own needs as individuals and as couples to the "back burner," while they cope with the many pressures of a helpless and demanding infant, one or two jobs outside the family, and all the tasks of an increasingly complex household. Time now becomes a rare commodity, with financial pressures, child care, home, and work demands. Establishing shared time is an important intervention to keep couples in balance during this task-overloaded phase of the life cycle. Nevertheless, parents today spend much more time with their children than they did 40 years ago. Married mothers spend 20 percent more time with their children than they did in 1985 and married fathers spend more than twice as much time as they used to, though still not nearly as much as mothers (Coontz, 2005).

In light of the severe role conflict and socioeconomic squeeze on families with young children, it is not surprising that this is the phase with the highest divorce rate and that poorer couples have twice the divorce rate of those who are financially comfortable (Ford & Van Dyk, 2009). Money pressure, time squeeze, couple isolation, sexual dissatisfaction, and unequal distribution of chores often increase with the couple's power shift toward traditional roles (Ault-Riche, 1994; Carter & Peters, 1997). These complaints often resound in therapy sessions, tempting clinicians to focus on practical solutions to specific issues instead of on the power imbalance itself, which, when righted, will enable the couple to negotiate fair resolutions of their own. Of course, many individual and marital problems have their roots in power inequities that existed long before the baby arrived.

The sexual problems that appear at this stage, often arguments over frequency, may be a result of the new mother's exhaustion, especially if she is nursing, and also may become an arena in which to conduct their power struggle. The first is transient and will pass; the second is an ominous threat to the couple's relationship and, if not dealt with, is likely to corrode their subsequent life together.

Arlie Hochschild's landmark study (1997, 2012), two decades ago, drew family therapists attention to the unfair share of housework and child care done by women even when both parents worked outside the home. Both men and women are still socialized to believe that mothers have special inborn or intuitive skills related to child care and that all young children need a mother as primary parent. In spite of the actual changes in our lives and in our beliefs, the two sacred cows—a "real" man's career and a "real" woman's mothering—maintain a stubborn hold on our emotions. Even when the wife earns more money than her husband, she tends to minimize or deny the importance of her earnings and often continues to manage most of the housework (Mundy, 2012). The consequences of this are that mothers often remain central

but overburdened and fathers often feel one-down, somewhat defensive and more on the periphery. When children have grown up viewing their mothers as the "real" parent expert, they are likely to pass along this paradigm unwittingly to the next generation.

The idea of shared parenting is not new (Belkin, 2008). Society is increasingly realizing that fathers should be active, hands-on parents, fully participating in the tasks of parenthood. Men in this generation are much more involved in household work and child care than ever before. Henneck (2003) says they average 16 hours weekly, though a report from the Bureau of Labor Statistics indicates it is more like 16 minutes per day compared to 52 minutes a day for women (Byron, 2012). Hochschild (2012) indicates that working women still do 5 to 7 hours a week more than their spouses.

But traditional definitions of male success (career achievement, money, and power) still hold sway in most men's lives. Many factors impede men from giving up the "good provider" role. Is his wife fully committed to being a co-provider for life, or will she suddenly decide that she will stay home with the children? Will he be penalized at work if he curtails his overtime or travel or takes family leave? In addition, male socialization has often left men cut off from their deepest feelings and somewhat fearful of intimacy. So most men still think of themselves as "helping" at home, even when their wives are employed full time. It still tends to be assumed in the workplace and by the couple themselves that the dilemma of juggling work and family is primarily the responsibility of the mother (Sandberg, 2013). Depending largely on their economic situation and the mother's career aspirations, she may quit work altogether, cut back to part time, or make whatever child care arrangements she can to keep working full time. If these alternatives are not what she expected to face or do not work out satisfactorily, she may become increasingly resentful and exhausted, blaming her husband and envying his single-track pursuit of work. Often it is only when mothers are away that fathers take on the parenting, perpetuating the stereotype that caring for children and home is women's work (Barnett & Gareis, 2008; Hochschild, 2012). But when men's capacity for nurturing is activated early in their children's lives, they tend to become deeply involved with their children (Pruett, 2001; Gerson, 1993; Barnett & Rivers, 2004). Caretaking their homes and children is not only good for their own health and stress levels, and improves their relationships with their children, but it increases their children's ability to express the full range of emotions, for girls to be assertive and boys to express more interpersonal affiliation and warmth (Barnett & Rivers, 2004; Brody & Hall, 1993). And two-income couples tend to be healthier and happier in every way, in spite of long work hours and the still unequal division of their labor in the "second shift" (Barnett & Rivers, 1996).

The highly charged debate about whether working mothers are detrimental for their children is misguided at many levels. Of course, competent child care is essential to children's development. But assuming one has quality child care, research makes very clear that the responsive and positive relationship of parents to each other and toward their children, encouraging their emotional, physical, and spiritual competence, is vastly more important in child development than any particular form of child care (Sandberg, 2013; Meers & Strober, 2009). Furthermore, parents in our era cannot support their families without working. In addition, work is extremely beneficial for mothers' mental health and well-being (Coontz, 2013). Thus, public funding that supports parents in caring for their children and guarantees that *all* American children receive high-quality child care is essential to our nation. The most important move that clinicians can make regarding this issue is to ensure that it is discussed as a *societal problem*, not a *mothering* problem.

> Assess your comprehension of couple relationships and traditional roles in the parenthood phase by completing this quiz.

Child Care and the Work–Family Dilemma

Because the two-paycheck family is now the U.S. norm, parental adjustment in work schedules is necessary when children are born. Seventy percent of U.S. women of working age are currently in the full-time workforce, including 65 percent of mothers with children under the age of 6 (Lavery, 2013). The U.S. government devotes almost nine times as much to defense as it does to education (Chantrill, 2013) and families are left to bear the burden of paying for child care. As a nation, we are not providing quality care and education for our children. Even in the first year of life, a baby's intellectual development depends on being spoken to regularly by attentive, engaged adults. Even the affluent, who can afford expensive live-in nannies, are not free from worry about what actually transpires in their absence. This, of course, has more serious implications for poor and working-class families, who miss out most when our society fails to provide adequate educational opportunities, including early education for *all* families. The poor, who need to rely on child care by relatives, have little or no other choice when early education and child care are not available. And poor families spend almost three times as much as middle-class families on child care, even though much of their care is done by relatives. The steady stream of media reports decrying the poor quality of U.S. child care fuels mothers' guilt about leaving their children. Clinically, family therapists should educate families about this and, again, relieve from their anxiety that it is their fault. Social class is a primary determinant of children's well-being and developmental options (Reardon, 2013). Economic distress contributes to couple and family instability, inadequate health care, a high degree of mobility, and elevated levels of stress and depression (Mintz, 2010). The proportion of children living with both parents varies greatly by cultural group: 82 percent of Asian children, 74 percent of Whites, 59 percent of Latinos, and 33 percent of African Americans are raised by both parents (Wang et al., 2013). Meanwhile, research has generally shown that the presence of a grandparent, mostly the maternal grandmother, can have a major positive impact on family well-being and children's life prospects, especially in struggling families (Angier, 2002; U.S. Department of Health and Human Services, 2013b).

> Assess your comprehension of child care and the work–family dilemma by completing this quiz.

Childrearing

The minute a child is born and often before, the nuclear family triangle (parents and child) is ready for activation. One of the biggest surprises for new parents may be the degree to which they discover passionate feelings about childrearing, a subject to which they may have given little previous thought. However, the imprint of their own childhoods, their levels of maturity, and their internalized ideas about their roles as parents make this a potentially hot issue for many couples. Gender socialization, leading to unequal participation in child care, only makes matters worse. Fathers are often cast as "idealists," responsible for preparing the child for the outside world, and mothers as "pragmatists," doing whatever works to get them and the children through each day. These prescribed roles can unwittingly lead to many destructive triangles of family life, especially those which polarize the parents in "too strict" or "too lenient" positions. "Father knows best," "angry mommy," and "the naughty kids" are familiar, unhappy scenarios of family life in which one parent can come to treat the other like one of the children.

What is clear is that societal prejudice about the abilities of girls and children of color need to be challenged by parents and teachers at every turn. The myth that girls are not as good as boys at science, technology, engineering, and math (STEM), or that they have a natural gift for reading emotions that boys lack, have been shown in repeated studies to be untrue (Rivers & Barnett, 2013). What is true is that when girls are told they are not as good as boys, they do less well (Rivers & Barnett, 2013). This is also true for children of color, who similarly internalize messages of inferiority (Watson, 2013) that need to be countered by the adults in their lives or they become self-fulfilling prophesies. Penner and Paret (2008) found in a longitudinal study of gender differences in math education that where boys and girls start out equal, even highly educated parents tend to continue the gender segregation in math and science by their gendered attitudes. Parents' responses are very important.

Because children tend to develop a great passion to belong in middle childhood, they often exclude others so that they can feel "in." They must be taught about oppression because they will be exposed to bullying whether as perpetrator, victim, or bystander. Parents have an important role to play in teaching their children to manage such situations, becoming role models demonstrating courage to challenge stereotypes and stand up for those who cannot always stand up for themselves (Comer & Poussaint, 1992; Comer, Joyner, & Ben-Savie, 2004; Quintana & McKown, 2008; Neblett et al., 2008; Suizo, Robinson, & Pahlke, 2008; Rivers & Barnett, 2013).

Children learn competitiveness and cooperation to the degree their parents, caretakers, or teachers teach them. Competitiveness will remain a problem unless they are taught models of collaboration. They should learn the truth about the inequalities embedded in U.S. history: slavery, colonialism, war, and oppression, in order to understand what the ideals of "liberty and justice for all" really mean at a social and community level. As they start to read, watch television, and play video games independently, they should also be monitored by parents, especially for exposure to racist, sexist, homophobic, and violent content, which can have a profound influence on them. Rap music, for example, has been particularly filled with perverted sexualized messages about girls and women, and Internet sites, at least 25 percent of which are pornographic, are explored by most children at least once (Rivers & Barnett, 2013). Children as they grow are deeply affected by parental and school definitions of "normal." They learn to imitate racist, sexist, homophobic, and other discriminatory words and actions (Thompson, Goodvin, & Meyer, 2006; Thompson, 2006). Although White children often express discriminatory behavior toward children of color, such responses diminish when antiracist norms have been established in the community (Monteiro, de Franca, & Rodrigues, 2009) and children raised in nonauthoritarian homes are much more likely to become antiracist as adults (Flouri, 2004).

Sex segregation increases greatly during grade school years, influenced by the fact that boys' behavior, unless checked, comes to be characterized by competition and dominance. Girls have such difficulty influencing in play with boys that they tend to avoid them (Maccoby, 1999). Boys tend to play more roughly in larger groups, and girls are more likely to form close friendships with one or two other girls. Studies have indicated that 50 percent of 3-year-olds, 20 percent of the 5-year-olds, and virtually no 7-year-olds, have friends of the opposite sex (Liu, 2006).

Children also segregate themselves by race, discovering that skin color is a code denoting rank and even fate (Comer & Poussaint, 1992; Ogbu, 1990; Bullard, 1997). Given their gendered socialization, girls become adept at reading verbal and nonverbal emotional signals and at expressing and communicating their feelings. Boys are taught to minimize emotions connected to vulnerability, guilt, fear, and hurt (Goleman, 2006). Without specific intervention, these unfortunate patterns will persist into adulthood. Boys especially, in their efforts to establish their own gender identity, may focus on their dislike of girls, which have been a longstanding part of the socialization toward masculinity (Kimmel, 2013); boys need adult validation of the girls' interests and feelings to avoid internalizing negative stereotypes about them. As children begin to develop a sense of right and wrong, they may tattle on wrongdoers, and are concerned about fairness, rules, and rule breaking, the foundation of their morals (Kochanska & Aksan, 2007). If they are continuously put down, they will lose faith in others; if they are not admonished for selfish or unfair acts, they will grow up with a false sense of privilege. In the dominant culture, boys grow up with a desensitization to violence and mistreating others (Kimmel, 2013). It is essential for parents to socialize their children about the larger societal structures that inhibit the full development of either sons or daughters. Clinicians play an important role whenever they are in the position of inquiring about children's behavior and parenting patterns to help them explore their deeper values and challenge the dominance/oppression structures of our society.

Much has been said about the dangers of mothers being too close to their sons (Dooley & Fedele, 2004). A much larger problem is fathers being too distant from all their children. All development occurs in the context of relationships, and it is essential for both parents to stay connected to their children. Clinicians should routinely encourage fathers' involvement with their children. The therapist must take a non-blaming stance in talking with men frankly about their fear of incompetence, angry reactions, jeopardizing their careers, and the general sense that they lack the requisite access to their own emotions. Men must be expected and encouraged to participate in family life.

The whole subject of cultural differences usually needs to be raised by the therapist, since White parents tend to be oblivious to their privilege and may not realize that they need to act early to prevent a later scenario of confusion, disorder, or even violence in relation to racism, homophobia, or sexism with their children. Parents can help their children by not pretending that discrimination does not exist, choosing children's schools carefully to ensure diversity, expanding their circle of playmates to include children of other races and cultures.

Minority parents are generally all too aware of the potential harm to their children of being part of a socially stigmatized group such as people of color and gay and lesbian families. Therapists should acknowledge parents' concerns; pay close attention to the child's level of self-esteem, feelings of competence, and positive group identification; and encourage families to join with others in their communities both for support and to counteract the negative effects of being stigmatized and alienated from the larger society. Therapists should, in other words, inform themselves about the impact of the social context on children and encourage parents to do the same.

Parental support is essential for helping children cope with peer pressure and distinguish their own values and attitudes from those of their peer group. It is a generally last chance for parents to influence a child's choice of peers and to widen the child's social circle by encouraging diversity. Parents need to affirm their support of their children's competence and abilities before teen struggles for independence begin. When children are preoccupied with prepubertal body changes and extremely sensitive to unkind remarks from others, they may not always cooperate or want to be affiliated with others who are "different." But it is important for them to see parents actively handling social problems in constructive ways. Their identification with the causes, problems, and privileges of groups they belong to provides direction, and motivation to think and act in contructive ways. As their ability to experience empathy deepens, they learn to appreciate distress beyond an immediate situation and to feel for the plight of an entire group, such as the poor, oppressed, or outcast (Goleman, 2006). Children need resources and support to contend with discrimination, bullying, racism, sexism, homophobia, and a general lack of safety in their communities and in their efforts to contend with the pressures of the dominant culture against them (Coll & Szalacha, 2004; Robbins et al., 2007).

Children who are shy need encouragement from adults to participate. They may be very sensitive to racial attitudes and may hide behind race or other "differences" to excuse poor performance, so adults should be careful not to permit children's outrage to become an excuse for poor performance. Self-esteem is precarious in grade school years and pride in gender, race, and sexual orientation is crucial to self-esteem. Without safe learning environments that offer anti-harrassment and anti-discrimination policies that include LGBT identity and gender expression, children are reliant on parents and other close adults to support their development and protect them from bullying and other oppressive behaviors (Comer & Poussaint, 1992; Murry & Brody, 2002; Neblett et al., 2008; Rivers & Barnett, 2013; Ryan, 2013).

Discipline

Many parental arguments about disciplining children spill over into therapists' offices, where we are called upon to say who is "right." This is the time to have reading material for parents, or to recommend a book for them, rather than to step into that triangle ourselves. Harriet Lerner's *The Mother Dance* (1998) is particularly effective against the pitfalls that precipitate discipline problems: parental guilt, anxiety, over-responsibility, and uncertainty. Family therapists should help parents agree on age-appropriate, practical approaches to discipline. If they cannot agree, we should help them to negotiate ways not to interfere with each other's methods, assuming, of course, that they are not harsh or harmful. Unless there is actual danger, one parent should not intervene when the other is disciplining a child. If they disagree, they should discuss the issue in private and either agree to disagree or shift parental responsibilities so that the parent who cares more about an issue (e.g., table manners) assumes responsibility for dealing with it. If the issue has already become toxic for parent and child, it will generally be helpful to shift responsibility to the less concerned parent. The suggestion of shifting responsibility will usually unmask an underlying problem of the parents' unequal involvement in parenting. Clinical approaches that do not address this imbalance will usually not end disputes over childrearing and discipline.

We must also remember that ethnicity and social class are key determinants of what parents have learned is appropriate discipline, and we should ask clients about their experience and ideas. Comer and Poussaint (1992) remind us that Black parents have often been strict disciplinarians because they felt that they had to force their children to obey so that they would not violate racial rules and come to harm. While agreeing with many Black parents who find White middle-class parents too permissive, therapists need to be clear about the negative impact of spanking or shaming and provide parents with practical alternatives.

Conflicts over discipline often reflect underlying marital problems. If parents are engaged in intense power struggles in other areas of their relationship, these will probably spill over into their approaches to childrearing. Parents may triangulate with a particular child because of the child's physical or behavioral problems, which arouse parental anxiety. Such cases are usually referred to in the literature as "child-focused families" and are not generally about discipline or even about the child, but rather about family of origin or problems in the marital relationship that have created a triangle that then displaces the anxiety onto discipline concerns.

This is not to suggest that all or even most child-rearing arguments are a sign of basic marital problems or that such arguments will disappear automatically if parents work on their relationship. Even when marital or family problems are primary, it is necessary to address the problem that brought the family to therapy first. As the couple work on the childrearing or discipline problems, it will usually become clear whether work on the marital relationship or the families of origin is necessary to change the presenting problem.

Protection against high-risk behaviors

Ron Taffel (2009) considers this generation of children to be the freest generation because of Internet exposure, the media, and our fast-paced world. However, he thinks children are also "freer from the constraints of history—the stories of generations past are missing. . . . (Children) feel less guilt and connection to the everyday job or career sacrifices of their parents" (pp. 12–13). Children's new freedoms bring with them anxiety, infused by endless access to adult media. They get to make very early decisions about high-risk behavior. Parents are left with fear and frustration about their children's safety. Children know parents feel helpless, and lose confidence in adults' ability to contain and protect them. What is desperately needed is for families to spend time together and parents to give undivided personal attention to their children to reconnect, engage, and share their personal journeys and their family and cultural history, which are essential to creating deeper tolerance, empathy, and a solid sense of self (Taffel, 2009).

It is the essence of a parent's job to teach their children what they themselves have learned about how to live a meaningful life. If parents do not think about and articulate their own values, children will infer them from the way their parents live. It is better for us to think about what we want to teach. Children need to develop personal, social, and spiritual values and a sense of idealism such as the importance of kindliness, loyalty, and helping others. It helps to see their parents involved at school, in the community, and in the political process if they are to learn to care about others.

Therapists can help parents look hard at how they are living and ask themselves about their real goals. In the scramble to make enough money, raise children, and pursue their own careers, parents often fall into one accommodation or another without meaning to. Because of the complexity of family life at this stage and the paucity of meaningful societal support, parents deserve the opportunity in family therapy to explore all options and possibilities for a more meaningful family life. Such discussions may

lead them to redesign their own relationships to better suit themselves.

Single parenting

Single parenthood is a growing world phenomenon, mostly involving mothers, and we need to develop helpful attitudes toward it. Although there is much general condemnation of single-parent families, it is important to realize that the structure itself is not the problem. Single-parent families range from highly functional to highly dysfunctional, depending on economics and emotional, family, and community connectedness. Too often, problems resulting from poverty or emotional and social isolation are attributed to family structure. To counter this tendency, therapists should assess a single mother's financial, familial, friendship, and social resources, which are her greatest protection against the stresses of parenthood. Financial stress is a major factor for many single parents, compounding all of the usual problems parents have, and causing many additional problems. Clearly, the children of a financially stable, emotionally connected mother can thrive whether she is married or not. But because single parents do not have partners to share responsibility, the support of family, friends, and community becomes all the more important.

Teenage parenting

In our society, a teenager is, by definition, not ready to be a parent. In any social or economic bracket, a teenager is a child, regardless of intelligence, sophistication, or street smarts. Currently about 10 percent of births in the United States are to unmarried teenagers (U.S. Census Bureau, 2012). Fortunately, these rates have shown a dramatic drop in the past decade with particularly strong decline for Latinas and African Americans, who together account for 57 percent of teenage births (CDC, 2011). These early births are costly in additional health care and foster care needs of children of teen mothers and in the lower educational attainment of the fathers and the mothers, only 50 percent of who complete high school, compared to 90 percent of their peers (CDC, 2011).

Any teenage child/parent needs further time to develop emotionally and intellectually before taking on the adult tasks of parenting and earning a living. Family therapy in this crisis should be aimed at protecting the young mother's development, as well as the baby's. Plans should be made to continue the teenager's education and, if the decision is to keep the baby, for housing with mature family members who can provide assistance with baby care. Involvement of the baby's father, of course, depends on his functioning, ability to provide financial and other support, and whether the parents plan to remain a couple. Tragically, up to 80 percent of fathers of children born to teenage mothers do not marry or support the mother or children (Brein & Willis, 1997), and children raised apart from their fathers are five times more likely to grow up poor than children with two parents at home (Horn & Sylvester, 2002).

Since a solid majority of American teenagers have had sex by the time they graduate from high school, it is important for the therapist to investigate the level of sex education attained by the teenage mother. The dissemination of birth control and disease control information to teenagers is a sensitive area with some families, and therapists need to approach this discussion diplomatically.

Infertility

A client once said: "The only thing worse than having a child with problems is not being able to have a child at all." The trauma of infertility generates grief and mourning, reactivated with every attempt and failure to conceive, whether through natural means or infertility treatments. The intensity of the experience is often overlooked by the couple's family, friends, and even therapists. This creates the danger that the couple will feel damaged, stigmatized, isolated, and depressed. This is especially likely for couples of religious or cultural groups that expect all couples to produce many children. Some cultural groups even accept infertility as a premise for divorce. About one out of eight married couples in the United States is infertile, one third attributed to the woman, one third attributed to the man, and one third attributed to a combination of reasons (Resolve, 2013). However, women are more often blamed for infertility, regardless

of cause, and exhibit greater emotional distress, probably because of their socialization to become mothers and also because most medical procedures for infertility involve the woman. Although White professional couples are the largest consumers of infertility services, which are extremely expensive and rarely covered by insurance, poor people of color with little formal education are more likely to be infertile (Meyers et al., 1995). Poor women on Medicaid have little access to infertility treatment, as few states have programs that cover infertility diagnosis or treatment (Hendler, Kennelly, & Peacock, 2011). Almost invisible among infertility sufferers are lesbian women who may try endless cycles of alternative insemination before giving up the cherished goals of pregnancy and giving birth.

Fertility treatments can also raise the agonizing dilemmas of multiple births following fertility drugs: "selective reduction" (abortion of some fetuses to save the others) or risks of serious birth defects that are much higher in multiple births. Obviously, all protracted fertility treatments place enormous stress on the couple. Family therapists need to keep informed of the developments and problems of fertility treatments so that we can help couples to determine when it is time to stop such treatments and seek other ways of becoming parents.

Adoption

The high cost of fertility treatments has kept this new technology from replacing the age-old alternative method of attaining parenthood: adoption. About 120,000 children are adopted each year in the United States, growing numbers of which are transracial or international. While the numbers have decreased by about one third since the 1970s, about 2.5 percent of all children under 18 are adopted (Adoption History Project, 2013), which means that a great many individuals and families (parents, siblings, grandparents, and extended family members) are touched by adoption. But the process and the prospects have become more complicated in recent years, due partially to the scarcity of White infants because of contraception and legal abortion and partially to the fact that more single mothers now feel free to raise their own children.

Recently, open adoption has become more common, where birth parents and adoptive parents meet one another, share identifying and genetic information, and communicate directly over the years. Some may get together regularly and view each other as extended kin; others have written or mediated communication until the adoptees are in their late teens. While advocates list many obvious advantages in direct contact, which can break the negative power of the adoption triangle with its cutoffs, fantasies, and loyalty conflicts, critics fear an invasion of adoptive family boundaries and the possibility that birth parents may be inconsistent or even drop out of children's lives. It is important for family therapists to pay close attention to the individual situation of each family to help clients think through which route they choose and then help them with its particular challenges. Most studies indicate that adoption outcomes are overwhelmingly positive (Groza, 2013).

Until there is greater flexibility in the adoption-approval process and more understanding and respect for alternative family structures, single parents who adopt children will tend to be viewed from a deficit perspective. It is extremely important for family therapists to keep an open mind about the strengths of adoptive families, whether trans-racial, single-parent, or gay and lesbian. An important right still being fought for is the right to adopt one's unmarried partner's child. This bestows legal parental rights on unmarried heterosexual partners and gay and lesbian partners.

Informal adoption is especially common among families of color, reflecting the reciprocity among kin that has been one of the most important survival mechanisms of African Americans (Boyd-Franklin, 2003). This sharing has produced permeable boundaries around Black family households that contrast sharply with the rigid boundaries of most White nuclear families. These flexible boundaries have been an integral part of Black community life since the days of slavery, permitting adult relatives or friends of the family to take in children whose parents are unable to care for them for whatever reason. Since adoption agencies were not originally designed to meet the needs of Black children, this informal network provides unofficial social services to poor Black families and children. Since Black clients understand all too well how their family structure may be judged by White therapists, they may be extremely uneasy if White clinicians do formal genograms early in treatment. It is probably wise for the clinician to be cautious about prying and let information emerge naturally in conversation.

Prospective parents need to be committed to teaching the child about his or her history and culture. Toward this goal, adoptive parents often join adoptive organizations, which offer support and affiliation with other families with similar intercultural relationships. Domestic interracial adoptions also require parental commitment to teaching children about their history and culture and develop a positive identity in both the birth and adoptive cultures (Zuniga, 1991). Comer and Poussaint (1992) emphasize also the importance of White adoptive parents' examining their motives carefully and protecting their children from racism by acknowledging and discussing racial and social class differences along with the adoption story frequently as children develop.

CASE ILLUSTRATION

Jerome, Karen, and Susan

Jerome and Karen, a white professional couple sought consultation about the acting out of their 10-year-old daughter, Susan, African American and adopted in infancy. The parents were idealists, who were puzzled by Susan's growing rebelliousness and recent behavioral and academic problems in school. She had previously done excellent schoolwork, was cooperative at home, and had many friends. The parents had lost touch with Black friends they had known previously and had not found new ones in their white suburb. Susan's friends were all white and were now starting to talk about the boys, clothes, and romance. Although she did not want to discuss it, Susan seemed afraid of what her standing would be, once dating commenced. The therapist told the parents the problem seemed to be that they were raising Susan as if she were white, or as if it did not matter that she was Black.

The parents were encouraged to locate activities both for themselves and for Susan in adjoining towns where there was ethnic, religious, class, and racial diversity. After a short period of defensiveness, they took on the task enthusiastically, joining a bicycling club and volunteering as parent chaperones at the neighboring town's school events. Susan joined after-school sports and recreation groups at the neighboring town's YWCA. Her difficulties at her own school diminished as she socialized with the new group of friends. The parents reported enjoying breaking out of their own self-imposed segregation. After 6 months, the mother announced that they had decided to move to the next town so they could pursue their new friendships and activities "without all the driving back and forth." They joked that this was "the community cure," and it was.

Gay and lesbian parenting

Gay and lesbian couples are both similar to and different from heterosexual couples and from each other. The variables that predict a positive transition to parenthood for lesbian and gay couples are the same as those for heterosexual couples: realistic expectations, good couple communication, partner adaptability, and the ability to tolerate chaos, noise, sleep deprivation, and a lack of solitude. Only accurate personal information will help us to avoid overgeneralizing about their parenting issues. The single most important factor in the development of a happy, healthy, and well-adjusted child in LGBT families as in all families is the nurturing relationship between parent and child (Perrin, Siegel, & Committee on Psychosocial Aspects of Child and Family Health, 2013).

In the past five decades, there has been a dramatic increase in lesbian and gay couples raising families with biological, step, adopted, and foster children. In spite of the discrimination that keeps many gay parents from acknowledging their sexual orientation in surveys, almost 50 percent of lesbians and 20 percent of gay men of childbearing age are raising children, compared to 70 percent of comparable heterosexuals (Gates, 2013). These percentages are increasing rapidly. LGBT parents struggle with issues of childrearing as do heterosexual couples, but they also contend with oppression, stigmatization, and economic disadvantages because of their sexual orientation (Gates, 2013). In addition, they are more likely to be racial or ethnic minorities and to be raising foster or adopted children, even more of whom are racial and ethnic minority children (Gates, 2013).

Another challenge is that gay and lesbian couples have few role models of specifically gay families. This necessitates important ground breaking decisions such as the very decision to become a parent, the conscious evolution of support networks to counteract social stigma, the creation of family rituals to celebrate family life cycle transitions, and the division of chores, child care, and arrangements in case of death or breakup of the relationship, which is even more important because these relationships are not as protected by law as they are for heterosexual couples (Bigner & Wetchler, 2012).

In clinical work with LGBT families, clinicians should stay informed about the social policy context these families face: they are excluded from the U.S. Census Bureau's definition of family (U.S. Department of Commerce, 2013); their civil rights are not protected in every state; their sexual contact is criminalized in over 20 states, though luckily no longer in the U.S. military; and in spite of many recent efforts to change state laws, they still lack the overall legal protection our government grants to heterosexuals by marriage, divorce, custody, and inheritance laws, including Medicaid and Social Security (Kuvalanka, McClintock-Comeaux, & Leslie, 2004; Hartman, 1996).

The pitfalls in the parental triangle are the same as with heterosexual parents; first is the possibility that parents may compete for who is the real parent: one parent may be closer as the primary caretaker, and the other parent may feel left out. This can be exacerbated if the primary parent is also the biological parent. Lesbian couples are often especially careful to divide child care, housework, and paid employment more evenly than do heterosexual couples (Tasker & Malley, 2012). Both partners seem to make equal sacrifices in exchange for this equality, working shorter hours or have turned down career opportunities to be more available at home. Stress and conflict may instead show up in competitiveness concerning bonding and childrearing. The birth mother who breast feeds may feel possessive toward her child and assume more nurturing roles, leaving the co-mother feeling excluded. She may become the preferred parent for rough and tumble play. This can become a source of tension between the parents (Bigner & Wetchler, 2012).

Gay and lesbian parents may be somewhat less vulnerable than heterosexual parents to children's "divide and conquer" strategies, because both have received the same gender programming about parenting and are more likely to see eye to eye on childrearing.

Gartrell, Bos, and Goldberg (2011) found that children raised by lesbian mothers, whether single or partnered, showed evidence of great confidence and self-esteem, which they attributed to the mothers' active engagement in their children's lives, fostering good communication, involving themselves in their children's schools and extracurricular activities. They found that an environment of acceptance and love and a sense of community were among the most positive aspects for growing up in a lesbian family. The children not only felt unconditionally loved by their parents but being raised in a lesbian family required the families to develop a wider definition of family (Gartrell et al., 2011).

What is not the same is the level of stress caused by social stigma and lack of social, and sometimes familial, support. While contact with a child may soften negative attitudes in the family of origin toward gay or lesbian offspring, the news of an impending child also brings all the coming-out issues to the fore again and may bring forth a new level of homophobia, as parents who have privately accepted their child's sexual orientation feel threatened by how public a grandchild will be. It is also important for family therapists to remember that although many families reject their gay and lesbian children, most do not (Laird, 1996). When treating LGBT couples and families, it is essential to address issues of relationships and family history as well as the behavioral norms of the systems that surround them (Goldberg & Allen, 2013; Bigner & Wetchler, 2012). Questions from family and others may center on fears that a child will be hurt psychologically by the social stigma and/or by having parents of only one gender. Many studies have demonstrated that children's well-being is affected much more by their relationships with their parents, their parents' sense of competence and security, and the presence of social and economic support for the family than by the gender or the sexual orientation of their parents (Barlow, 2013).

Children with disabilities

When children have disabilities, parents have additional childrearing tasks to deal with and the child, siblings, and extended family will have additional complications in their relationships to provide extra support and to deal with the loss that disability entails of hopes and dreams that may be curtailed (Solomon, 2013). It is important for the clinician to help the parents share their grief and sadness with each other and with other family members and friends. Their perceived need to "stay strong" for each other may make them fearful of letting the child or each other down. It is also essential that very specific plans be made to give respite and encourage other activities for the chief caregiver, usually the mother. The gender imbalances so common at this life cycle phase tend to be greatly exacerbated by having a child with disabilities. The reversion to more traditional gender roles may be intensified, as fathers may back away and mothers may become overly centralized. Mothers may need help to give themselves permission to go to work, go on vacation, or just pursue interests and hobbies. Probably it is both the burden of caretaking and the emotional stress that contribute to this problem, but it is worth a great deal to try to engage fathers and keep parents on the same page in managing their child and their family. Later in the life cycle, siblings will undoubtedly inherit the responsibilities of the disabled sibling, all of which should be taken into account from early on, including the direct impact on siblings of the disability.

When parents express worry over a young child's functioning, a good first question is whether the child's caregiver, school, or teacher has brought any problem to the parents' attention. Teachers and professional caregivers are generally quick to spot deviations from the norm. Spotting an apparent deviation and correctly diagnosing it, however, are two different things, and family therapists need to watch out for the "diagnosis of the year," defined for children and then found everywhere: ADD (Attention Deficit Disorder), ADHD (Attention Deficit Hyperactivity Disorder), MBD, unspecified "learning disabilities," and general "hyperactivity" are common examples (Thakkar, 2013). Since most, if not all, such disabilities of children now come with recommended medications, it is important to help the parents obtain a good assessment. Once a diagnosis and treatment plans have been made, possibly including special education, therapists can help parents not slip into an adversarial relationship with the school. Such a triangle, fueled by parents' anxiety, will severely complicate the school's work with the child.

Child abuse

This is a problem at every socioeconomic level in our society, and because so many of the assaults on children are perpetrated by their parents, relatives, caretakers, and family friends, they are all the more shocking. Therapists should be as alert to the signs of child abuse as they are to indications of wife battering. Any suggestion of child abuse is a reason to stop therapy as usual and explore in minutest detail the child's level of risk.

In most states, it is now possible to have the suspected perpetrator (rather than the child) removed from the home and denied access to the child. However, vigilant follow-up by the therapist is often necessary. Under no circumstances should a known child-abusing parent be included in family sessions until he or she has acknowledged the problem, agreed to whatever treatment and medication are recommended, and is able to be accountable in a meaningful way to the abused child and other family members. It should never be assumed that abuse will cease as a result of couple or family therapy alone.

> Assess your comprehension of childrearing by completing this quiz.

Clinical Guidelines

Whatever the presenting problem is at this life cycle phase, the entire three- or four-generational family system should be assessed carefully at an individual, family and sociocultural context level.

The following case describes the assessment and overview of a family presenting at the phase of Parents with Young Children.

CASE ILLUSTRATION

Sharon and Gary

Sharon sought therapy because of her anger toward her husband Gary's long work hours and his distant fathering style. Gary, a lawyer, commuted 2 hours a day, and worked 65 to 70 hours, 6 days a week. He was rarely home before 8:00 or 9:00 P.M. and brought work home for Sunday. He felt the necessity to work these long hours to pay for the families' high expenses. The family lived in an affluent suburb, employed a live-in nanny, and contributed to the support of Sharon's parents in Florida. Gary also felt the necessity to work these hours because his career goal was to become a partner in his law firm. Sharon was a social worker with a small private practice. She worked about 20 hours a week spread over 4 half-days and 2 evenings. Gary saw their two young children, Danielle, aged 6, and Sophie, aged 4, briefly in the mornings and tried to spend Sunday afternoons with Sharon and the kids. As a couple, they had "no time" (see Genogram 15.1).

The evaluation

1. **EACH INDIVIDUAL**
   All four immediate family members appeared to be physically healthy and functioning satisfactorily. Inquiry about the extended family did not indicate any major physical or psychological problems. Emotionally, Gary talked about work in a somewhat compulsive, distant way, and Sharon sometimes sounded more like the parent, than daughter or sibling, in her family of origin.

2. **THE FAMILY**
   The Couple: The couple spent almost no time together and sex was infrequent. They said in

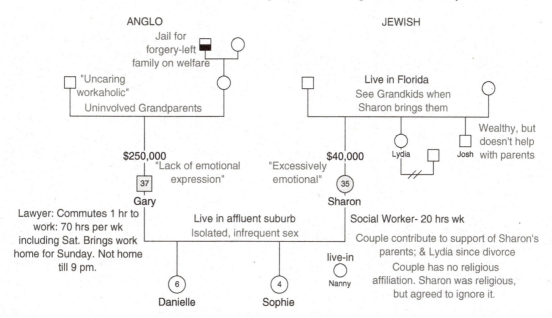

GENOGRAM 15.1 Genogram of Gary and Sharon's Family.

the early years together they had a more balanced and open relationship and shared dreams. Now Gary was ignoring or vetoing Sharon's suggestions. They had no effective method of discussing or negotiating differences. Family tasks were polarized, with Sharon doing or supervising all domestic tasks and Gary earning most of the income. She complained of his lack of emotional expressiveness, and he, of her excessive emotionality, which seemed to correspond to their gender and ethnic backgrounds: she was more emotionally expressive and he was more self-contained and understated. Gary was completely uninvolved in the household schedules and tasks; Sharon was the only hands-on parent.

The Family Emotional System: In the nuclear family, father and children spent little time together. The main triangle was that Sharon and the children were close and Gary distant.

Families of Origin: Relationships with the families of origin were either distant and unsupportive or overinvolved.

Gary's Family: Gary was extremely distant from his parents, who hardly ever saw him or Sharon. The paternal grandparents were minimally involved with the children. Gary called his father "an uncaring workaholic" but was shocked that Sharon saw him as just like his father. Gary's mother had never complained about the father's work focus and, in fact, had delivered emotionally laden messages to him about the importance of work.

Sharon's Family: Sharon was a typical overresponsible oldest daughter who felt obligated to take care of everyone in her family of origin. She contributed money to her sister so that she would not have to move after her divorce; she shrugged off her affluent younger brother's refusal to contribute financially to their parents; and she never objected to family members' impositions on her time or money. When Sharon's parents or sister insisted, Sharon took the children to visit them, but Gary rarely came.

Intergenerational Triangles: There were significant family-of-origin triangles on every level: Gary with his parents, Sharon, with her parents and her siblings, and with the children.

Emotional Issues: The major emotional issues were time, work, money, fathering, lack of intimacy, lack of negotiating skills, and not living according to their values.

Major Emotional Threats:

1. Growing distance and resentment between the couple
2. Emotional and physical distance between father and children

3. THE SOCIOCULTURAL CONTEXT

Community and Friends: This family was extremely isolated. Gary and Sharon's schedules had no time for involvement in any community organization at all. Both spouses had rejected their parents' religion—his Protestant, hers Jewish. Gary felt no interest in religious involvement and had elicited an early agreement from Sharon to leave religious affiliation out of their lives. For Sharon, this had become a problem. She had thought about joining a synagogue, but Gary always reminded her of their earlier agreement.

The Family's Place in the Larger Social System: This White, heterosexual, affluent, educated, professional couple belongs by these qualities to the most powerful portion of our society. Thus, if they can get psychologically free enough to avail themselves of their options, they have more power to change their situation than any others have. The norms of the social system that militate against their getting psychologically free enough to use their options might include the following:

- The socially approved male focus on career and money, reinforced by Gary's parents' example and messages about the "work ethic."
- Gary and Sharon's affluent, consumerist, time-starved life-style, called "success," and envied by their peers.
- The rigidity of the fast-track career path for corporate lawyers.

- Sharon's belief, socially approved and ethnically reinforced, that it is a daughter's "duty" to respond to the wishes and needs of her family of origin, regardless of the strain it puts on her own emotional and financial resources.
- Gary's belief, consistent with decades of social practice, that young children are fine as long as their mother is available, and fathers need only "provide."

The therapy

In therapy, Gary and Sharon accomplished the following:

- Gary agreed to come home "early" (by 7:00 P.M.) at least one night a week.
- Sharon stopped giving her sister money, while still maintaining a close connection.
- Sharon worked to restore a relationship with her brother and eventually requested that he start contributing his share of support to their parents. He agreed and resumed regular contact with them.
- Gary's talks with his mother revealed a secret about the issue of work: his maternal grandfather had been an alcoholic with a checkered work history who had once spent several years in jail for forgery, leaving his family on welfare. This had led Gary's mother to preach the value of working hard ever after. Now Gary could see the emotionally programmed aspects of his own work habits. He agreed to come home before 7:00 P.M. two nights a week.
- Gary had difficult, but useful, talks with his father about work. His father finally acknowledged that he regretted missing Gary's youth. Gary urged him not to miss his grandchildren's youth as well. The number of visits to and from Gary's parents increased from once a year to four times, interspersed with calls and gifts. During their visits, Gary took off time from work to be with the whole family.
- Gary and Sharon spent many weeks going over their budget. Sharon said that she would agree to sell their vacation house if Gary would get a less-demanding job. He said that he would

think about it, and he eventually did, moving to a slower-paced suburban firm at a lower salary.

- Sharon joined a synagogue after a long discussion of their religious and ethnic differences. She participated in the temple's discussion groups and in a social program to help the homeless and Gary even joined the men's group.
- After much discussion of "mother guilt," Sharon cut out one evening of work so that she and Gary could parent together and then spend a quiet evening as a couple.
- Through their work in therapy, they were able to see how their early dreams, values, and ideals contrasted with the reality of what their life had become and vowed to continue their work downshift and relationship expansion.
- Gary and Sharon joined a group that met monthly for dinner and theater.
- Gary said that as "daddy time" with his kids got more frequent, it got more enjoyable. "Like sex with Sharon," he added with a smile.

Gary and Sharon had three major advantages for making the many profound changes that they did: They had an earlier strong, passionate bond and dreams to return to; their families of origin, although problematic in many ways, were essentially free of major dysfunctional patterns; and their privileged positions in the social hierarchies gave them maximum flexibility for change once they decided to go for it. (Of course, their privilege might have kept them from seeing relationship values that are not so esteemed by the dominant culture.)

Shifting focus among levels of the system

Our clinical work does not lend itself to moving in an orderly way from one level of the system to the next, any more than real life does. So although therapy usually begins with the presenting problem—at this phase, often a child problem—the therapist's work will need to address the marriage, the family of origin, the community, and the constraints of the larger social system in any given session. To get a sustained focus and eventual resolution of key issues, it is important to keep mental track of the issues at each level. Be aware of a client's repeated shift away from

an uncomfortable area—maybe the marriage—back to a more "comfortable" problem—maybe the child. It is important to address the parents' preferred focus before shifting with some question about the marriage. Or one might work on the marriage indirectly through discussions of parenting roles.

Similarly, if a task to change behavior with a grandparent gets followed in the next session with a child or marital crisis, as sometimes happened with Gary and Sharon, it is important to make mental note of this, even if the opportunity to ask about the grandparent is postponed until later. The important point is that the therapist should track the process.

On the macro level, it is important to help a couple achieve some small initial resolution of their presenting problems before introducing the idea of actual work in the family of origin. The first move with Gary and Sharon was to get Gary to agree to come home early one evening a week. However, in any session, one might openly refer to extended family information gathered in the evaluation and connect it to the presenting problem to show that family of origin is a relevant focus. Thus, questions about Gary's parents and work made it clear that this was an intergenerational issue as well as a couple problem.

Questions and comments about community and the rules and norms of the larger social system are usually quite easy to introduce into the discussion, since there is often not as much resistance to talking about these areas as there is to personal and family issues. Of course, it is all connected in the end, as Gary and Sharon discovered when questions about community led to their deeply personal exchange about their religious and ethnic differences. There is still debate in family therapy about when or whether to include young children in sessions. We believe that changes in children up to adolescence depend primarily on parental intervention on their behalf or on changes in parental attitudes and behaviors. Also, children are too powerless to change the system, but sometimes feel responsible if included in problem-focused discussion and complaints. We want to see them for assessment purposes and to see how family members relate together and separately. And even when we do not work with them directly because in our view the power to change the situation rests primarily with the parents, we always ask detailed questions about their development. When we do work with them, it is always and only in the context of work with their families.

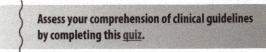

Assess your comprehension of clinical guidelines by completing this quiz.

Conclusion

In spite of all the complexities and difficulties of contemporary family life, we have never actually met any parent who regretted being a parent. Whenever we have done life cycle exercises with trainees, grouping people by life cycle stage and having them discuss the issues, one of the childless participants always says something like: "It's too hard. Why does anyone have children?" At this point, the parents laugh in astonishment trying to describe the joys, pleasures, and transcendence of parenthood. Maybe it is like talking about sex to a virgin—the problematic aspects of it may be clear, but it is almost impossible to fully articulate the physical, sensory, intellectual, emotional, and spiritual experience of connectedness to one's child through love.

Recall what you learned in this chapter by completing the Chapter Review.

References

Adoption History Project. (2013). Adoption Statistics. Department of History, University of Oregon. Retrieved April 28, 2013, from http://pages.uoregon.edu/adoption/topics/adoptionstatistics.htm.

Anderson, K. (2013). The number of US children living in single-parent homes has nearly doubled in 50 years: Census data. LifeSiteNews.com. Retrieved May 22, 2013, from http://www.lifesitenews.com/news/the-number-of-children-living-in-single-parent-homes-has-nearly-doubled-in/.

Assor, A., Kanat-Maymon, Y. & Roth, G. (2014). Parental conditional regard: Psychological costs and antecedents. In Weinstein, N. (Ed.). *Human motivation and interpersonal relationships: Theory, research and applications.* New York: Springer.

Assor, A., Roth, G., & Deci, E. L. (2004). The emotional costs of parents' conditional regard: A self-determination theory analysis. *Journal of Personality.* 72(1), 47-88, February.

Angier, N. (2002, November 5). Weighing the grandma factor. *New York Times,* pp. S1, S4.

Ault-Riche, M. (1994). Sex, money and laundry: Sharing responsibilities in intimate relationships. *Journal of Feminist Family Therapy, 6*(1), 69–87.

Barlow, R (2013). Gay parents as good as straight ones. Retrieved June 17, 2013, from http://www.bu.edu/today/2013/gay-parents-as-good-as-straight-ones/.

Barnett, R. C., & Gareis, K. C. (2008). Community: the critical missing link in work-family research. In A. Marcus-Neuhall, D. F. Halpern, & S. J. Tan (Eds.). *The changing realities of work and family* (pp. 71–84). New York: Wiley-Blackwell.

Barnett, R. C., & Rivers, C. (1996). *She works/he works: How two-income families are happier, healthier, and better-off.* San Francisco: Harper.

Barnett, R. C., & Rivers, C. (2004). *Same difference: How gender myths are hurting our relationships, our children, and our jobs.* New York: Basic Books.

Belkin, L. (2008, September 8). When mom and dad share it all: Adventures in equal parenting. *New York Times,* p. 4.

Belsky, J., & Kelly, J. (1994). *The transition to parenthood.* New York: Dell.

Bennett, M. D. (2007). Racial socialization and ethnic identity: Do they offer protection against problem behaviors for African American youth? *Journal of Human Behavior in the Social Environment, 15*(2–3), 137–161.

Bennetts, L. (2011). Women: The invisible poor. *The Daily Beast,* September 14, 2011.

Bigner, J. J. & Wetchler, J. L. (2012). Handbook of LGBT-affirmative couple and family therapy. New York: Routledge.

Blow, C. M. (2014). Fire shut up in my bones. Boston: Houghton Mifflin Harcourt.

Boyd-Franklin, N. (2003). *Black families in therapy: Understanding the African American experience* (2nd ed.). New York: Guilford Press.

Brody, L. R., & Hall, J. A. (1993). Gender and emotion. In M. Lewis & J. Haviland (Eds.), *Handbook of emotions* (pp. 442–460). New York: Guilford.

Brein, M. J. & Willis, R. J. (1997). Costs and consequences for fathers. In R. Maynard (Ed.), *Kids having kids: Economic and social consequences of teen pregnancy* (pp. 95–143). Washington, DC: The Urban Institute Press.

Budig, M. J. & England, P. (*2001*). The wage penalty for motherhood. *American Sociological Review*, Vol. 66/ April, pp. 204–226.

Bullard, S. (1997*). Teaching tolerance.* St. Charles, MO: Main Street Books.

Byron, E. (2012). A truce in the chore wars. *Wall Street Journal*, December 7, 2012. Retrieved May 15, 2013, from http://online.wsj.com/article/SB10001424127887 323401904578157500316162398.html.

Carter, B., & Peters, J. (1997). *Love, honor and negotiate: Building partnerships that last a lifetime.* New York: Pocket Books.

CBS News (2009). *Survey: U.S. spends but child welfare lags.* Retrieved from www.cbsnews.com/ stories/2009/09/01/national/main5280103.shtml.

CDC (Centers for Disease Control and Prevention. (2011). About teen pregnancy. Retrieved September 25, 2013, from http://www.cdc.gov/teenpregnancy/aboutteenpreg.htm.

Chantrill, C. (2013). US Education Spending. Retrieved May 14, 2013, from http//www.usgovernmentspending.com/us_eucation_spending_20.html.

Cherlin, A. J. (2009). *The marriage-go-round: The state of marriage and family in America today.* New York: Knopf.

Coll, C. G., & Szalacha, L. A. (2004). The multiple contexts of middle childhood. *The Future of Children, 14*(2), 81–97.

Comer, J. P., Joyner, E. T., & Ben-Avie, M. (2004). *Six pathways to healthy child development and academic success: Field guide to Comer schools in action.* Thousand Oaks, CA: Corwin Press.

Comer, J. P., & Poussaint, A. F. (1992). *Raising Black children.* New York: Penguin.

Coontz, S., (2013). The triumph of the working mother. *New York Times*, June 2, 2013, p. SR 11.

Coontz, S. (2009, February 5). Till children do us part. *New York Times,* p. A 31.

Coontz, S. (2005). *Marriage: A history.* New York: Viking.

DeParle, J. & Tavernise, S. (2012). For women under 30 most births occur outside marriage. *New York Times*, February 17, 2012. Retrieved May 22, 2013, from http://www.nytimes.com/2012/02/18/us/forwomen-under-30-most-births-occur-outside-marriage. html?pagewanted=all.

Dooley, C., & Fedele, N. M. (2004). Mothers and sons: Raising relational boys. In J. V. Jordan, M. Walker, & L. M. Hartling (Eds.), *The complexity of connection: Writings from the Stone Center's Jean Baker Miller Training Institute* (pp. 220–249). New York: Guilford.

Edwards, T. (2009, October 1). Stay-at-home moms are more likely younger, Hispanic and foreign-born than other mothers. *U.S. Census Bureau News,* pp. CB09–132.

Flouri, E. (2004, September). Mothers' nonauthoritarian child-rearing attitudes in early childhood and children's adult values. *European Psychologist, 9*(3), 154–162.

Ford, A., & Van Dyk, D. (2009, October 16). Then & now: A statistical look back from the 1970s to today. *Time Magazine, 174*(16), p. 27.

Friedman, H.S. (2012). *The measure of a nation: How to regain America's competitive edge and boost our global standing.* Amherst, New York: Prometheus Books.

Gartrell, N. K., Bos, H. M. W., Goldberg, N. G. (2011). Adolescents of the U. S. National Longitudinal Lesbian family study: Sexual orientation, sexual behavior and sexual risk exposure. *Archives of Sexual Behavior,* December 40(6): 1199–1209.

Gates, G. (2013) LGBT Parenting in the United States. Retreived June 4, 2013, from www.law.ucla.edu/ williamsinstitute.

Gerson, K. (1993). *No man's land: Men's changing commitments to family and work.* New York: Basic Books.

Gilbert, D. (2007). *Stumbling on happiness.* New York: Alfred A. Knopf.

Goldberg, A. E. & Allen, K. R. (2013). *LGBT-parent families: Innovations in research and implications for practice.* New York: Springer.

Goleman, D. (2006). *Emotional intelligence, 10th Anniversary Edition, Why it can matter more than IQ.* New York: Bantam.

Groza, V. (2013). Successful adoptions. Comeunity. com. Interview of Allison Martin with Victor Groza. Retrieved May 29, 2013, from http://www.comeunity .com/adoption/Groza.html

Hall, K., & Spurlock, C. (2013). Paid parental leave: U.S. vs. the world (INFOGRAPHIC). Huffington Post. February 21, 2013. Retrieved May 22, 2013, from http:// www.huffingtonpost.com/2013/02/04/maternity-leavepaid-parental-leave-_n_2617284.html

Hartman, A. (1996). Social policy as a context for lesbian and gay families: The political is personal. In J. Laird

& R.-J. Green (Eds.), *Lesbians and gays in couples and families* (pp. 69–86). San Francisco: Jossey-Bass.

Hendler, A., Kennelly, J. & Peacock, N. (2011). Reducing racial/ethnic disparities in reproductive and perinatal outcomes. New York: Springer.

Henneck, R. (2003). Family policy in U.S., Japan, Germany, Italy and France: Parental leave, child benefits/family allowances, child care, marriage/cohabitation and divorce. Contemporary Families. Retrieved May 6, 2013, from http://www.contemporaryfamilies.org/work-family/fampolicy.html.

Hochschild, A. (2012). *The second shift: Working parents and the revolution at home.* New York: Viking.

Hochschild, A. (1997). *Time binds: When work becomes home and home becomes work.* New York: Metropolitan Books.

Horn, W. F., & Sylvester, T. (2002). Father facts (4th edn.). National Fatherhood Initiative: Gaithersburg, MD.

Kimmel, M. S. (2013). *The gendered society* (5th edn.). New York: Oxford University Press.

Kochanska, G., & Aksan, N. (2007). Conscience in childhood: Past, present, and future. In G. W. Ladd (Ed.), *Appraising the human developmental sciences: Essays in honor of Merrill-Palmer quarterly* (pp. 238–249). Detroit, MI: Wayne State University Press.

Kohn, A. (2014). Do our kids get off too easy? *New York Times*, May 3, 2014. Retrieved 5/8/14: http://nyti.ms/1iSX7Md.

Kuvalanka, K. A., McClintock-Comeaux, M., & Leslie, L. A. (2004). Children with lesbian, gay, bisexual, and transgender parents: Current research, legislation, and resources available for family professionals. In P. Amato & N. Gonzalez (Eds.). *Vision 2004: What is the future of marriage* (Vol. 3, pp. 53–59). Minneapolis, MN: National Council on Family Relations.

Laird, J. (1996). Invisible ties: Lesbians and their families of origin. In J. Laird & R. J. Green (Eds.), *Lesbians and gays in couples and families: A handbook for therapists* (pp. 89–122). New York: Jossey-Bass.

Lavery, D. (2013). More mothers of young children in paid work force. Population Reference Bureau. Retrieved May 8, 2013, from http://www.prb.org/Articles/2012/us-working-mothers-with-children.aspx.

Leonhardt, D. (2011). How health insurance affects health. *New York Times*, July 7, 2011, p. B1.

Lerner, H. (1998). *The mother dance: What children do to your life.* New York: Harper Collins.

Liu, F. (2006). School culture and gender. In C. Skelton, B. Francis, & L. Smulyan (Eds.), *The Sage handbook of gender and education* (pp. 425–438). Thousand Oaks: CA: Sage.

Maccoby, E. E. (1999). *The two sexes: Growing up apart: Coming together (The family and public policy).* Boston, MA: Belknap Press.

Meers, S. & Strober, J. (2009). *How Working Couples can have it all by sharing it all: Getting to 50/50.* New York: Random House.

Meyers, M., Diamond, R., Kezur, D., Scharf, C., Weinshel, M., & Rait, D. (1995). An infertility primer for family therapists: Medical, social and psychological dimensions. *Family Process, 34,* 219–229.

Miller, C. C. (2014). For working mothers, a price to pay. New York Times, 9/7/2014, p. B. 6.

Mintz, S. (2010). American childhood as a social and cultural construct. In B. J. Risman (Ed.), *Families as they really are* (pp. 48–62). New York: W. W. Norton.

Monteiro, M. B., de Franca, D. X., & Rodrigues, R. (2009). The development of intergroup bias in childhood: How social norms can shape children's racial behaviors. *International Journal of Psychology, 44*(1), 29–39.

Mundy, L. (2012). The richer sex: How the new majority of female breadwinners is transforming sex, love, and famiy. New York: Simon & Schuster.

Murry, V. M., & Brody, G. H. (2002). Racial socialization processes in single-mother families. Linking maternal racial identity, parenting and racial socialization in rural, single-mother families with child self-worth and self-regulation. In H. P. McAdoo (Ed.), *Black children: Social, educational and parental environments* (2nd ed., pp. 97–115). Thousand Oaks, CA: Sage Publications.

National Coalition for the Homeless. (2009). *Who is homeless.* Retrieved May 22, 2013, from http://www.nationalhomeless.org/factsheets/who.html

Neblett, E. W., Jr., White, R. L., Ford, K. R., Philip, C. L., Nguyen, N., Hoa X., & Sellers, R. M. (2008). Patterns of racial socialization and psychological adjustment: Can parental communications about race reduce the impact of racial discrimination? *Journal of Research on Adolescence, 8*(3), 477–515.

Ogbu, J. U. (1990). Cultural mores, identity, and literacy. In J. W. Stigler, R. A. Shweder, & G. H. Herdt (Eds.), *Cultural psychology: Essays on comparative human development* (pp. 520–541). New York: Cambridge University Press.

Penner, A. M., Paret, M. (2008). Gender differences in mathematics achievement: Exploring the early grades and extremes. *Social Science Research, 37* (1), 239–263.

Perrin, C. P., Siegel, B. S. & Committee on Psychosocial Aspects of Child and Family Health. (2013). Promoting the well-being of children whose parents are gay or lesbian. American Academy of Pediatrics. Retrieved May 25, 2013, from http://pediatrics.aappublications.

org/content/early/2013/03/18/peds.2013-0377.full.pdf+html

Pruett, K. (2001). *Father need: Why father care is as essential as mother care for your child*. New York: Broadway.

Quintana, S. (2008). Racial perspective taking ability; Developmental, theoretical and empirical trends. In S. Quintana & C. McKowan (Eds.), *Handbook of race, racism and the developing child* (pp. 16–30). Hoboken, NJ: John Wiley.

Quintana S. & McKowan, C.(Eds.). (2008). *Handbook of race, racism and the developing child* (pp. 16–30). Hoboken, NJ: John Wiley.

Reardon, S. F. (2013). No rich child left behind. *New York Times,* April 28, p. SR 1, 4.

Resolve. (2013). Fast facts about infertility. National Invertility Association. Retrieved May 24, 2013, from http://www.resolve.org/about/fast-facts-about-fertility.html

Rivers, C., & Barnett, R. C (2013). The turth about girls and boys. New York: Columbia University Press.

Robbins, M. S., Szapocznik, J., Mayorga, C. C., Dillon, F. R., Burns, M., & Feaster, D. J. (2007). The impact of family functioning on family racial socialization processes. *Cultural diversity and ethnic minority psychology, 13*(4), 313–320.

Ryan, C. (2013). The real-life costs of anti-LGBT bullying. Huffington Post. Retrieved May 24, 2013, from http://www.huffingtonpost.com/caitlin-ryan/the-real-life-costs-of-ant_b_866253.html

Saad, L. (2012). *Stay-at-Home moms in U.S. lean independent, lower income*. Retrieved April 15, 2013, from . http://www.gallup.com/poll/153995/stay-home-moms-lean-independent-lower-income.aspx

Sandberg, S. (2013). *Lean in: Women, work, and the will to lead*. New York: Knopf.

Senior, J. (2014). All joy and no fun: The paradox of modern parenthood. New York: Harper Collins.

Solomon, A. (2013). *Far from the tree: Parents, children and the search for identity*. New York: Scribner.

Suizo, M. N., Robinson, C., & Pahlke, E. M., (2008). African American mothers' socialization, beliefs, and goals with young children: themes of history, education, and collective independence. *Journal of Family Issues 29*(3), 287–316.

Taffel, R. (2009). *Childhood unbound: Saving our kids' best selves-Confident parenting in a world of change*. New York: Free Press.

Tasker, F., & Malley, M. (2012). Working with LGBT parents. In J. J. Bigner & J. L. Wetchler (Eds.), Handbook of LGBT-affirmative couple and family therapy. New York: Routledge.

Tavernise, S. (2011). Married couples are no longer a majority, census finds. *New York Times*, May 26, 2011, p. 1.

Thakkar, V. G. (2013). Diagnosing the wrong deficit. *New York Times*. April 28, 2013, p. SR 1, 6.

Thompson, R. A. (2006). Nurturing developing brains, minds, and hearts. In R. Lally & P. Mangione (Eds.), *Concepts of care: 20 essays on infant/toddler development and learning* (pp. 47–52). Sausalito, CA: WestEnd.

Thompson, R. A., Goodvin, R., & Meyer, S. (2006). Social development: Psychological understanding, self-understanding, and relationships. In J. Luby (Ed.), *Handbook of preschool mental health: Development, disorders and treatment* (pp. 3–22). New York: Guilford.

U.S. Census Bureau (2012). Statistical Abstract of the United States. Table 86. Percentage of births to teens, unmarried mothers, and births with low birth weight: 1990 to 2008. Retrieved May 24, 2013, from www.cnn.com/2009/HEALTH/05/19/latinas.pregnancy.rate/index.html

U.S. Department of Commerce (2013). Current Population Survey(CPS)-Definitions. Retrieved May 18, 2013, from http://www.census.gov/cps/about/cpsdef.html

U. S. Department of Health and Human Services (2013a). Child welfare information gateway. Foster care statistics 2011. Children's Bureau. Retrieved May 22, 2013, from https://www.childwelfare.gov/pubs/factsheets/foster.pdf#Page=0&view=Key%20Findings.

U. S. Department of Health and Human Services (2013b). Time with your kids; A special family bond—Grandparents. Retrieved May 24, 2013, from http://www.bblocks.samhsa.gov/family/Time/grandparents.aspx

Wang, W., Parker, K., & Taylor, P. (2013). Breadwinner moms. Pew Research Center. May 29, 2013. Retrieved May 29, 2013, from http://www.pewsocialtrends.org/2013/05/29/breadwinner-moms/

Watson, M. F. (2013). *Facing the black shadow*. E-Book.

Webb, F. J. (2005). The new demographics of families. In V. Bengston, A. C. Acock, K. R. Allen, P. Dilworth-Anderson, & D. M. Klein (Eds.), *Sourcebook of family therapy and Research* (p. 101). Thousand Oaks, CA: Sage.

Zezima, K. (2008, August 20). More women than ever are childless, census finds. *New York Times,* p. A12.

Zuniga, M. (1991). Transracial adoption: Educating the parents. *Journal of Multicultural Social Work, 1*(2), 17–31.

Chapter 16

The Transformation of the Family System During Adolescence

Nydia Garcia Preto

Learning Outcomes

- Describe how families must transform to accomplish the developmental tasks of adolescence.
- List and describe risk factors for adolescents and preventative actions parents can take against these risks.
- Identify challenges faced by adolescent males as they define their identity.
- Identify challenges faced by adolescent females as they define their identity.
- Examine the impact that sexual orientation has on identity formation during adolescence.
- Examine the impact that racial and ethnic identity have on identity formation during adolescence.
- Explain the structural shifts and renegotiation of roles that occur in families during the life cycle stage of adolescence.
- Explore ways to support families who seek help during the life cycle stage of adolescence.

Introduction

The transformation families must make during adolescence is so profound that it requires a metamorphosis from a family that protects and nurtures children to a family that is the launching pad for the adult world of responsibilities and commitments. This is a time of great physical, emotional, sexual, and intellectual growth and it is usually marked by the onset of puberty, starting typically at 11 or 12 for girls, and 12 or 14 for boys. Boys shoot up in height, facial hair grows, and their voices deepen, cracking at the most crucial and embarrassing moments. Girls begin to menstruate, their breasts get bigger, they get more hairy, and their hips widen.

Most adolescents are uncomfortable and self-conscious about these changes, and feel that people are looking at them differently. And it is true, people are looking at them differently, especially their parents who are often shocked to watch their children suddenly turn into adult-looking people. Trying to keep up with the growth spurts, parents constantly have to buy new clothes and shoes with mixed feelings of excitement, sadness, and panic

about the expense. These changes make adolescents eat more and sleep longer, and have spurts of physical energy followed by periods of lethargy. They become cranky, moody, shut down, and challenging at home. They do not want to listen to limits or consequences. Parents become nags in their eyes, and children become inconsiderate, lazy, and disobedient in the eyes of parents.

This transformation happens so quickly that adolescents themselves have difficulty integrating the changes. Their sense of self is in flux, and finding who they are, or want to be, becomes their main focus. They try on different personalities, challenge values, norms, and try desperately to fit in with their peers. They feel intensely compelled to turn away from their childish ways and move toward independence, while at the same time wanting their parents to take care of them. The title of Anthony Wolf's (2002) book about adolescents *"Get out of my life but first could you drive me and Cheryl to the mall?"* depicts succinctly the dilemma in which parents and adolescents find themselves at this stage of life. Parents, who may have felt confident about their parenting skills, suddenly find themselves feeling anxious and insecure about how to keep their adolescents safe.

It is helpful for parents to understand that although adolescents might look like adults, the part of their brain that increases their ability to reason and to control impulses has not yet matured (Yurgelun-Todd & Killgore, 2006; Jetha & Segalowitz, 2012). Normalizing some of the behavior they experience as erratic and a necessary part of growing up tends to lessen their anxiety, and their feelings of inadequacy as parents. It is very important to validate their alarm and to support their wishes to protect their children from danger. Adolescents are more prone to take risks than adults because the hormones that signal seeking pleasure are at their height of intensity. The lag between physical, sexual, and mental development explains some of the erratic behavior and poor judgment that characterize many adolescents and that frighten adults.

Families must be strong and yet be able to make their boundaries more flexible. Most families, after a certain degree of confusion and disruption are able to change the rules and limits and reorganize themselves to allow adolescents more autonomy and independence. However, stressors such as disciplinary problems at home and at school, interpersonal losses, family violence, sexual orientation confusion, physical and sexual abuse, and bullying can result in the development of symptoms in the adolescent or in other family members. This is usually easier with each successive child, but is particularly difficult when parents do not support each other because they differ and argue about values and rules, whether they are together, separated, or divorced.

One of the most difficult tasks for parents over the life cycle is helping their teenagers be more thoughtful and less impulsive at a time when they are intensely focused on gaining more independence. Adolescents want more autonomy to make decisions about friends, clothes, and how to spend their free time, and parents have to provide the support and space they need to grow and develop. They also need parental guidance and supervision to learn and stay safe, especially when their wish for excitement can so easily lead to risky behaviors. A shift in the balance of authority and power in the relationship between parents and children is crucial, but for parents giving up control is often rightfully frightening. Engaging their adolescents in conversations about gaining privileges for responsible behavior, rather than imposing limits and expectations, can begin to make that shift.

Involving adolescents in the process of negotiating clear limits and expectations helps them take responsibility and be more accountable for their behavior. If they are responsible they earn privileges, such as having a phone, access to Internet, social networks, going out with friends, learning to drive, and using or getting a car. Time outs and grounding no longer work as well at this stage, since adolescents tend to experience those as punishments for children, rather than as consequences for their behavior. Getting into power struggles with them is also not useful, especially any physical restraining can become dangerous since by now they are as big, or stronger than parents. The more teens feel controlled by their parents, the more turbulent this process will be. The less accepted and connected they feel to parents, the more important validation from peers becomes. For a period of time peers become a "second family" (Taffel & Blau, 2001), a community in which adolescents can begin to act maturely and responsibly, while at home they are often under responsible, which leads parents to fall into over functioning. This pattern tends to stop growth and development, and it should be a signal for parents to stop and notice positive behavior. Acknowledging to adolescents that they are growing up and maturing when they behave responsibly goes a long way.

This chapter focuses on the overall transformation that families experience as they try to master the tasks of adolescence, keeping in mind that perceptions about adolescent roles and behaviors vary depending on socioeconomic and cultural context. Case examples will illustrate some of the issues that families are likely to bring to therapy during this phase, and therapeutic interventions that may be helpful.

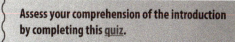

Assess your comprehension of the introduction by completing this quiz.

Risk Behaviors and Prevention

Today, in the United States, families are more challenged than ever by the risks of living in an increasingly endangered environment, in a society where, largely for economic reasons, parents choose or are forced to work longer and longer hours, limiting the time they can spend at home with their adolescents. The pressure is worse if they do not have the support of extended family or a supportive community for teaching and setting limits on their adolescents, and are forced to become more dependent on external systems. At the same time, teenagers are turning more and more to their social networks for emotional support, to music, TV, and especially the Internet for values and ideas about life. As a result, the family's function as an emotional support system is threatened. The threat is greater for families that are economically disadvantaged and living in poor urban and rural neighborhoods.

As adolescents begin to demand more freedom, parents can no longer protect or supervise them in the same way as when they were younger. Parents have good reasons to worry, since with greater opportunity to engage in risky behaviors and not yet developed ability to consider future consequences, adolescents are extremely vulnerable to danger.

> Read about the three adolescent risk behaviors with long range impact according to the world health organization.
> http://www.who.int/maternal_child_adolescent/topics/adolescence/dev/en/

Car accidents, violence, and suicide are among the highest causes of death for teenagers (Centers for Disease Control, 2013). Alcohol and drugs are strongly linked to risky behaviors. Although teen birth rates have been declining for two decades, they are still higher than those of other developed countries. Teens who become parents are at multiple risks for poor life outcomes: failing to finish high school, unstable couple relationships, and adult poverty (Hoffman & Maynard, 2008). Their children face particular challenges: they are more likely to have poorer educational, behavioral, and health outcomes throughout their lives, compared to children born to older parents.

Adolescents account for about one quarter of all sexually transmitted diseases (STDs) diagnosed every year, and four in ten sexually active teen girls have had an STD that can cause infertility and even death (Forhan et al., 2009). Teen males make up more than two thirds of HIV diagnoses, one of the leading causes of death in adolescents (Centers for Disease Control, 2010).

A recent study of substance abuse showed that 40 percent of high school seniors drank alcohol, 15 percent abused marijuana, and 13 percent smoked cigarettes (Johnston, O'Malley, Bachman, & Schulenberg, 2010).

Although mood swings are common during adolescence, warning signs of serious psychological problems are not always obvious. Some common symptoms include persistent irritability, anger, or social withdrawal, as well as major changes in appetite or sleep (Burland, 2001). One out of five adolescents has a diagnosable mental health disorder, and one in four shows at least mild symptoms of depression (Schwarz, 2009; Child Trends, 2010). Mental health disorders can disrupt school performance, harm relationships, and lead to suicide, which is the third leading cause of death among adolescents. Yet less than half of the adolescents who need mental health care receive it. Those least likely to receive services are homeless youth, those served by state child welfare and juvenile justice systems, and lesbian, gay, bisexual, and/or transgender youth (National Institute for Health Care Management, 2009).

The best prevention for these risk factors is for parents to stay connected with their children. Thus, the most important clinical intervention we can make with families during the adolescent phase of the life cycle is to help them stay connected. Living in a society where the dominant culture reinforces the idea that to be independent one must separate from parents does not make the work easy. Yet, we all need encouragement to hang in there, listen differently, confront our own limits, and take the necessary measures to earn our child's trust (Taffel, 2009).

Recent studies demonstrate that teens who feel close to their families were the least likely to engage in risk behaviors, and that high expectations from parents for their school performance were nearly as important (Davalos, Chavez, & Guardiola, 2005; Willoughby & Hamza, 2010). The research of Caitlin Ryan (2013) reinforces the positives of parental connection for LGBT youth exposed to bullying at school. Working with families toward acceptance and support of their children is clearly one of the most effective interventions to lower the risk of suicidal and other risk behaviors.

Assess your comprehension of risk behaviors and prevention by completing this quiz.

Evolving One's Identity: The Balance Between Self and Other

Finding one's own voice in a context of societal, parental, and peer pressures to conform is one of the most challenging tasks for adolescents. With maturity our sense of identity becomes clearer, and as we age it continues to change, but at no stage of development do we change as rapidly and as intensely as during adolescence. Finding a balance between themselves and others as they develop sexual, physical, spiritual, and moral identities involves having to increase their capacity for discipline, self-management, and emotional competence. These skills are essential for them to be able to work individually and collaboratively with others, and for building relationships with peers, family, and community.

Understanding who they are in relation to gender, race, culture, sexual orientation, and abilities is increasingly important in a society that is diverse and multicultural. Some of the questions that often run through an adolescent's mind are as follows: Who am I? Who do I want to be? Who does my family want me to be? Who do my friends think I am? It is not that they have not developed some sense of self by this time, since by the age of 2 they can distinguish boys from girls, and by the age of 4 they begin to learn that boys and girls are expected to behave differently.

Gender socialization happens at home, at school, through their interaction with peers, and from their exposure to mass media. The reason why the need for self-definition becomes so urgent during adolescence is that their brain undergoes major changes that charge them emotionally with intense energy and passion for exploration. It is as if their brains are programmed to make them pull away from their parents and toward their peers. They yearn for emotional and social engagement with peers. They want to explore the world with their friends, rather than with their parents.

The pressure to fit into the rigid patriarchal conception of what it means to be masculine or feminine in this culture is a major stressor. The focus on binary constructions of gender does not take into account the variations in gender identity and sexual orientation that pervade our society, and gives little acknowledgment to the fluid and constant intersections of gender identity with race, social class, and culture. During adolescence, the pressure to conform to this binary definition is at its highest point, while simultaneously adolescents experience an urgent need to challenge social conventions in an effort to form a genuine identity.

Their brains are developing increased capacity for abstract thinking, and for complex questioning, which enables them to challenge values, attitudes, and spiritual beliefs they have learned from their families, and from their social context. They have an uncanny ability to notice vulnerabilities in adults and to challenge inconsistencies in their behavior. They become more aware of how their social location defines their position in life, and begin to recognize injustices and take moral stands. This is a good time for parents and other adults in the family, for teachers, and other mentors in religious or community organizations to engage them in conversations about moral issues, and social judgment. Although they feel great pressure to fit with their peers, their emotional connection to parents and other adults in their lives is significant. They need role models who can teach them how to manage their emotions and behavior.

Adolescent males

For males, the social pressure to act as "real men" is pervasive. Those who are slight and short may develop insecurities because our society values being physically strong and athletic. Those with physical and developmental disabilities may have a particularly difficult time and are often the target of bullying at school. Fitting into the expectations of patriarchal masculinity means having to reject everything "feminine." Unfortunately, for them, this concept of femininity sometimes includes behavior that is connected with doing well in school, or showing interest in intellectual pursuits. Getting good grades may not be cool! They may begin to lag behind in building intellectual skills, and in learning about the larger world that surrounds them.

Those who do not conform with these rules take the risk of losing status, friends, and of being labeled a "fag," a term that does not necessarily describe homosexual behavior, but that strips them of their masculinity (Kimmel, 2013). Adolescents who are bullied and called "fag" by peers at school, on Facebook, or other social media suffer mercilessly. The cruelty of bullying often causes them to be so ashamed that they may become depressed, or suicidal. In some cases, feelings of pain and aggression can lead them to attempt suicide or commit violent acts. These reactions are more likely when they do not have support at home. When abuse at home is directed toward them, the risk for self-damaging behavior and violence becomes even more likely.

Being a man ultimately means giving up the freedom to express feelings, especially as adolescents move toward early adulthood and into the stage that Kimmel (2009) describes as *Guyland*, a culture that normalizes a lack of connection with their emotions and a restrictive expression of feeling. Distance from parents, especially from mothers, is encouraged as part of becoming independent. Many parents, particularly mothers, react to this change in the relationship by feeling rejected and pulling away from their sons. Unfortunately, the more adolescents become disconnected from their feelings, the less opportunity they have to learn how to balance relationships with others. This emotional disconnection makes it more difficult for them to cope with such emotions as fear, loss, and stress in life (Lombardi, 2011). They are at greater risk for acting-out behavior such as drinking and drugs, when they do not feel free to talk about problems and conflicts (Dooley & Fedele, 2004).

If they come to therapy, it is crucial to involve parents and caretakers in treatment with the goal of strengthening their emotional connections. Doing a three generational family genogram with them, and focusing on patterns of relationships between men and women, as well as how men connect with their children can help them talk about what is going on in the present. Questions such as "What needs to change for them to feel closer as a family? What fears or hurts get in the way? What are their hopes for the future?" can open possibilities for change.

Adolescent females

For adolescent girls, the pressure to be beautiful is enormous. They become more concerned with how women are "supposed to behave" and with their physical and sexual attractiveness. When their physical appearance does not match what their peer culture perceives as beautiful, their confidence drops. They become more anxious, and vulnerable emotionally, which increases the probability of becoming targets of bullying. Their weight, height, skin color, race, religion, sexuality, and sexual orientation become reasons for ridicule, and bullying. Bullying, sexual harassment, rape, or any abusive behavior has grave consequences for them. They are more likely than males to suffer from depression, low self-esteem, dissatisfaction with their bodies, eating disorders, and to attempt suicide (APA, 2014).

Regardless of the advances that this society has made toward gender equality, double standards for females remain pervasive. Females who are competitive are perceived as aggressive and unattractive, rather than as competent and successful, while males who are ambitious are seen as leaders. Those who try to break out and be more like one of the guys often find themselves in a bind. Females may want to be smart and pretty, and feminine and successful, but the pressure to conform to opposing standards simultaneously can be oppressive, especially because complaining in this patriarchal society means failure. They know that although they may be achieving educationally more than adolescent boys, when they look at who is at the top of businesses they see mostly males (Sandberg, 2013). There is also the dilemma that in our culture being beautiful also has negative connotations, as demonstrated by the jokes and caricatures about the "dumb blonde."

One of the major causes of stress for adolescent girls is that in the dominant culture in this country, physical attractiveness means being thin, and at an age when their bodies are changing and getting softer and fuller, they may begin to see themselves as fat. For many, dieting becomes a way to control weight. Eating disorders, more common in females, frequently appear in adolescence and affect all socioeconomic levels and all races. Girls' wish to be thin starts as early as 9 or 10 and more than 90 percent of those who have eating disorders are women between the ages of 12 and 25. Up to 10 million females and 1 million males struggle with eating disorders (NIMH, 2009). Between 1 and 5 percent of adolescent women meet the criteria for an eating disorder diagnosis. Females with anorexia nervosa have a suicide rate 10 times higher than those with any other mental health disorder (Hudson, Hiripi, Pope, & Kessler, 2007).

The high risk of suicide in this population often brings adolescents and their families to therapy. Working with them and their parents to enhance the adolescent's self-esteem, specifically about their bodies, has been found to be effective in protecting them from risk factors such as physical and sexual abuse (APA, 2014). Acceptance and support at home and in their community helps to increase resiliency against unhealthy eating patterns. Cultural contexts that promote acceptance of a broad range of appearances provide support for individuality and healthy development.

Sexual orientation

For those whose gender identity is nonconforming to patriarchal standards, and who are conflicted about their sexual orientation, the onset of puberty can exacerbate their sense of awkwardness. However, the changes that have taken place during the past decade in the way LGBT people and their lives are portrayed in society have made it possible for adolescents to feel freer about coming out earlier to themselves, their peers, and their parents. That is not to say that gay teenagers do not still suffer harassment at school or rejection at home. Parents'

reactions vary depending on their own constructions of gender and sexual identity and on their homophobia. Actually, the more gay youth are perceived as not conforming to gender norms, the more at risk they are for harassment and physical abuse. Girls who come out as bisexual but are still considered "feminine" seem to be less prone to harassment, as are some gay boys, who come out but are still perceived as "masculine."

Overall, the increasingly accurate and positive portrayals of gays and lesbians in popular culture have lessened the fears for adolescents and their families that they will never find happiness. The ability to communicate online has broken through the isolation that had been so detrimental to LGBT youth and has allowed gay teenagers to find information to refute what their families or churches sometimes may still tell them. In *The New Gay Teenager*, Savin-Williams (2005) writes that being young and gay is no longer an automatic prescription for a traumatic childhood. He also says that this is the first generation of gay adolescents who have the great joy of being able to argue with their parents about dating, just like their straight peers do.

Although there seems to be more openness about gender variance and sexual orientation, heterosexual parents, teachers, and counselors are likely to question adolescents about the validity of their feelings when they come out. The younger they are, the more we ask questions about their same-sex attractions in ways that we would never question straight youth when they talk about attractions to the opposite sex. Most of us working with adolescents have been trained to caution youth who identify as LGBT that sexual identity is a fluid process and that they should wait until they are older to determine how they really feel and what they want to do about it. We also coach parents not to be too reactive and to wait to see what happens as their children mature. The down side of this approach is that we deny their feelings and miss opportunities for connection and to encourage healthy sexual behavior.

Lack of support at home, at school, or from other adults in their community puts LGBT youth at greater risk for emotional problems, including suicide. Generally, gay and lesbian adolescents are more likely to disclose to mothers, fearing the reaction from fathers. Sometimes, the reaction at home is dangerous and violent, yet most LGBT adolescents want to be open with their parents.

CASE ILLUSTRATION

Horace

Horace is a 16-year-old white male of German ancestry. His situation at school and home led to suicidal behavior. During therapy, he talked about the loneliness and fear that he experienced. "My attraction to men is not something I chose. I tried for the longest time to push it out of my mind and do all the things that boys are supposed to do, but I can't change myself. Sometimes I get scared, especially when I hear about gay bashings, and bullying that goes on at school. I feel bad for my parents. They love me but don't understand why this is happening and are ashamed of me. They also fear for my life. No one else in the family knows, and I hate pretending in front of my grandparents. At school I'm constantly on the lookout, worried that they'll find me out."

Lesbian, gay, bisexual, transgender, and questioning youth are up to four times more likely to attempt suicide than their heterosexual peers (Massachusetts Youth Risk Survey, 2006). And, if rejected by their families for being LGBT, they are eight times more likely to attempt suicide (Ryan et al., 2009). One of the most alarming findings of Ryan's research is that Latino males reported the highest number of negative family reactions to their sexual orientation in adolescence. Such a response is often related to religious beliefs that connect being gay with sinful behavior, or a belief that their child's homosexuality is a medical or psychological condition that can be cured. On a more hopeful note, Savin-Williams (2005) and La Sala (2010) point out that most families of LGBT adolescents eventually move toward acceptance after a period of anxiety and sometimes rejection. The more acceptance they receive from their parents and caretakers, and other adults in the community, the more positive they will feel about their lives (Ryan, 2013).

There is also increasing support to ban therapies that are considered "reparative." California banned that type of treatment for adolescents in 2012, and there are movements to similar legislation in other states, such as in New Jersey (Gay and Lesbian Connection Monthly, 2012). The psycho educational materials that the Family Acceptance Project has put together are great resources to use with families and adolescents (Ryan, Russell, Huebner, Diaz, & Sanchez, 2010).

 Learn more about the family acceptance project here. http://familyproject.sfsu.edu/home

Working toward building connection, support, and acceptance in families is probably the most preventive and hopeful intervention we can make clinically.

Racial and ethnic identity

Forming a positive ethnic and racial identity is another antidote to risk behaviors. It is crucial for all adolescents, and even more so when they belong to groups that are marginalized in the dominant culture. It is particularly difficult when parents and families are themselves struggling to make it, and feeling oppressed by the social institutions that affect their lives. A positive, cultural identity is necessary to feel whole, to belong, and to have a feeling of home place (McGoldrick & Hardy, 2008; McGoldrick, Giordano, & Garcia Preto, 2005; Burton, Lawson, Obeidallah, & Allison, 1996). Many adolescents in this country live in two worlds. They live with their families in communities that are ethnic enclaves where immigrants settle to support each other or at least to feel connected to their motherlands. They may eat different food, listen to different music, and dress and behave according to their culture's expectations. They also have to negotiate living in a dominant culture that is patriarchal and racist, where they are seen as, and feel, different and marginal. They often feel powerless in the larger society, isolated, uncomfortable, and afraid that they will not be accepted for who they are.

When cultural differences interfere with their increased need to fit in with peers, some adolescents reject their own culture and disconnect from their families. The schism between societal expectations and what they are able to achieve puts these youths at high risk for depression, anxiety, rage, and a host of other problems. For example, although the number of Latina adolescents getting pregnant has decreased in the last few years, they continue to have twice the number of births as white girls (The Center for Latino Adolescence and Family Health, 2013), as well as an alarming rate of attempted suicide (Zayas & Pilat, 2008; Zayas, 2011).

Finding legacies of hope and of spiritual strength that have been passed down by their ancestors through history is crucial for the survival of many groups. Engaging families and adolescents in conversations about their histories, stories of immigration, and people who have overcome the forces of oppression can be empowering. Staying connected with their dreams and not compromising their priorities require extreme determination.

For African Americans, Latino/as, Asians, and other adolescents of color, forming an identity goes beyond values and beliefs about gender, since they have first to cope with how society defines, marginalizes, and oppresses them. For African Americans, forming a positive identity in a racist society in which being Black has been demeaned for centuries poses a grave challenge for adolescents and their parents. (Hardy & Laszloffy, 2005; Boyd-Franklin & Franklin, 2000). Black adolescents need to view themselves as valued to form a positive identity. Living among Whites and facing daily situations where they are demeaned for their skin color is hurtful and humiliating. The darker their skin, the more difficult it is. Although the visibility and influence of African Americans in politics and the popular culture have increased, even more so since Barak Obama became president, the insidious effects of racism on the everyday lives of Blacks in this country has not gone away.

For African American parents, the fears about the welfare and future of their children go well beyond worrying that their adolescents will not have good judgment and will put themselves in dangerous situations by abusing substances, having unprotected sex, or that predators will abuse them. They have to worry about the effects that racism will have on them, especially when they are poor and have little access to resources. It is a big reason for our country to worry, if we consider that the jobless rate of Black teenagers age 16 to 19 increased from 35.2 percent to 42.6 percent between May 2012 and May 2013 (U.S. Department of Labor, 2013), as compared to 22.1 to 21.6 for white teens. They fear especially for their sons' safety and lives, knowing that authorities are quicker to arrest them for minor offenses, book and remand them for trials, and give them harsh dispositions (U.S. Census Bureau, 2006–2008). Black males were incarcerated at a rate more than six times higher than white males and 2.4 times higher than Hispanic males (Drake, 2013). Living in neighborhoods where drugs and crime are rampant, they are constantly at risk of being pulled into the world of illegal activity and by the alluring experience of feeling powerful that making fast money can bring. Carrying weapons for self-defense is not uncommon for adolescents in these situations. In fact, homicide continues to be leading cause of death for African American males (Travis, 2013). Considering these statistics, it is no wonder many African American parents fear that their sons will be killed, and young men do not have the expectation to live a long, prosperous life.

Pregnancy is usually high on parents' worry list for their adolescent daughters, regardless of race or ethnicity, but as a group, Black girls have always been at higher risk. Recently, the overall rate of teen pregnancy across race and ethnicity has been declining, and though this is true for African American girls, as a group they are still a higher risk (Martin et al., 2012; Hamilton, Martin, & Ventura, 2010; Hamilton & Ventura, 2010). Also, of great concern for African American parents has been the high rate of HIV infection among Blacks, and especially for females. As with teen pregnancy, there has been a recent decline in the number of new cases reported of females infected with HIV, but African Americans continue to be far more affected than any of those belonging to other races and ethnicities, accounting for over 60 percent of all new infections (Centers for Disease Control, 2013).

Assess your comprehension of evolving one's identity: the balance between self and other by completing this quiz.

A Multicontextual Three-Generational View

The adolescent's demands for greater independence tend to precipitate structural shifts and renegotiation of roles in the family at a time when parents are usually redefining their marital relationship, and answering calls from grandparents. Parents may be called upon to be their own parents' caretakers, or to assist them in integrating the losses of old age and at the same time they feel taxed in supporting their now often ornery adolescents. Renegotiating relationships with grandparents as they face issues of retirement, moves, illness, and death may reactivate unresolved issues in that generation. Conflict between parents and grandparents may intensify the parents' marital problems, and in turn exacerbate the normal stress that adolescence generates between parents and teenagers. Or a conflict between parents and adolescents may add to the stress in the marital relationship, and ultimately force changes in the relationships between parents, grandparents, and siblings. When the normal stress and tension generated by adolescence intersect and reactivate unresolved emotional issues in previous generations, the family might have difficulty offering the support and connection that adolescents need to make a safe journey into adulthood.

In therapy, we often observe that parents who have made a conscious effort to raise their children differently by avoiding the "mistakes" their parents made are often surprised when children reach adolescence and observe similarities in personality between their children and their own parents. They may also find themselves repeating patterns of interaction they had with their parents during their adolescence. Paying attention to the triangles that operated in the parents' families of origin and coaching them to work with their own parents can lessen their reactivity enabling them to listen better to their children.

CASE ILLUSTRATION

Clara

Clara, 15, lived with her mother, Wanda, a 39-year-old Puerto Rican professional, and Wanda's paternal aunt, Marta. Wanda, since her divorce, had focused her energy on her work and on being a good mother. Clara, who had always been very close to her mother, had begun to pull away, stay out late, and show interest in boys. Wanda, afraid of the dangers in the street and worried that Clara would become pregnant, restricted her outings. The more Clara challenged the limits, the stricter her mother became. Clara threatened to run away. She spoke to a teacher at school, who referred the family for therapy. Wanda appeared angry and unwilling to listen to Clara's criticisms. She felt rejected by her daughter, for whom she had sacrificed so much. Clara felt bad about hurting her mother, but felt she was being unfair. I began by supporting Wanda's wish to protect Clara, validating the dangers girls are exposed to in this society, which made it easier for her to begin to listen to Clara's position. I invited Wanda to bring her aunt Marta to therapy, which clarified how Clara's adolescence had activated a triangle from the mother's own adolescence a generation before. When Wanda was an adolescent, she had been close to her aunt, her father's youngest sister, who lived with the family, and in a triangle with her own mother over rules and discipline. Once again Wanda and Marta were allied, but this time Clara was the one who felt isolated from her mother and aunt.

I was able to help shift the triangle by telling them that Clara needed support from both of them but primarily from her mother. I suggested that Clara was as confused as they by the different ways in which the two cultures dealt with adolescence. Asking them to identify which Puerto Rican values were creating the greatest conflict at home led them to thinking about a compromise. They agreed that dating was the greatest source of conflict, since in Puerto Rico this practice has very different rules and connotations. Dating used to start much later, and it usually took place in the company of family or friends. I pointed out that for Clara to live in this culture and feel comfortable with her peers, they needed to adapt to some of the values of this culture. As a compromise, they agreed to let Clara go on double dates, but only with people they knew, and to negotiate a curfew with Clara's input.

To make additional changes in the relationship between Clara and her mother, work had to be done with Wanda and her mother, who still lived in Puerto Rico. Coaching Wanda to share some of her conflicts with her mother through letters and on a visit to Puerto Rico and to ask her advice about disciplining Clara was a way to lessen the emotional distance between them. Wanda became more accepting of her mother's limitations and began to appreciate the attention she gave. This helped her to listen more attentively to her daughter.

In retrospect, I could have further helped strengthen the connections between Clara, her mother, and great-aunt by exploring with them intergenerational values about gender role socialization and expression that may have been contributing to their problem, asking questions such as: How was your mother's gender role different from your grandmother's? Why do you think grandmothers may be more permissive than mothers? How have expectations, freedoms, and obligations toward family members changed over time in your country of origin? How do you think immigration to this country has affected your expectations, freedoms, or obligations as women? How do the extended family, community, culture, and society create pressure to conform to certain rules for boys and girls? Do you think it is fair for boys to have so much more freedom in dating than girls? What did you think of the rules for freedom and the chores for girls and boys when you were a teenager? What do you think of mothers having so much more responsibility for parenting than fathers?

Another issue that this case raises is the considerable impact that the lack of extended family or other supports has on how families manage adolescence. Puerto Ricans and other ethnic groups tend to rely heavily on extended family members to help with the discipline of adolescents and the clarification of boundaries. It is common for Puerto Rican parents to send a rebellious adolescent to live with an uncle or godparent who can be more objective about

setting limits. This move also provides time for parents and adolescents to cool down when conflicts are intense, and obtain enough emotional distance from each other to regain control and reestablish a more balanced relationship. Relying solely on the nuclear family to provide control, support, and guidance for adolescents can overload the circuits and escalate conflicts.

For example, most parents with adolescents in the dominant culture are at midlife. They may be reevaluating their marriages and careers. The marriage emerging from the heavy caretaking responsibilities of young children may be threatened as parents review personal satisfaction. For many women, this may actually be the first opportunity to work outside the home without the restrictions they faced when the children were young. For many men, this is a time when they might be feeling stuck in a dead end job, or fearful of losing their work altogether.

Adolescents need nurturing, clear expectations, and appreciation, as well as a feeling of belonging from both parents (Taffel, 2005). Parents benefit when they recognize that their own personal dissatisfactions about work, marriage, or failed relationships with partners, family, or friends may be affecting their ability to connect with their children and guide them through this stage. When parents disagree and engage in explosive fights with each other, or become silent enemies whether in the same house or in separate homes, the risk increases for adolescents to engage in dangerous behavior. It is also important for parents to resist the impulse to focus entirely on the adolescent's problems and ignore their own needs (Cummings & Davis, 2010). When one parent becomes involved in an alliance with the children against the other, the problems presented by adolescents are likely to escalate.

These patterns may differ depending on factors such as race, class, and ethnicity. For instance, Burton et al. (1996) conducted a study of poor inner-city African American teens and found that in many of the families, there was a narrow age difference between the generations. The blurring of intergenerational boundaries in these age-condensed families affected the authority that parents had over children as well as the adolescents' perceptions of appropriate behavior. Consider, for example, a family where a 15-year-old daughter becomes a mother, her 29-year-old mother becomes a grandmother, and the 43-year-old grandmother becomes a great grandmother. The adolescent is suddenly launched into the young adult stage of life, as the result of having a child, yet developmentally is still an adolescent. Her mother, a young adult woman, fills a role usually held by someone in late middle age, or early old age. And her grandmother, who is in middle age, is now a great grandmother, a position usually held by older age women.

In families with such generational closeness in age, chronological and developmental challenges often do not fit generational roles. Parents and children may behave more like siblings, making discipline hard to carry out. Families may also have difficulty identifying adolescence as a specific life stage. Individual development, however, demands large changes during adolescence, and with them come anxiety and stress. Adolescents need acceptance, support, and guidance from their parents and caretakers to negotiate life cycle tasks, and to manage the normal anxiety and stress of their rapid developmental changes.

> Assess your comprehension of a multicontextual three-generational view by completing this quiz.

Clinical Assessment

Families with adolescents usually seek therapy when parents have reached a point of desperation about not being able to control their child's behavior. Whether they seek help on their own, are mandated by the courts, or referred by schools, hospitals, or other agencies, they feel angry and frightened by their children's behavior. Most parents are overworked, overcommitted, and tired, with few resources and little outside support, especially single parents who in most cases are mothers (U.S. Census, 2012). By the time we see them in therapy, parents often feel inadequate, and in response to their children's rebellion may have distanced emotionally.

In most cases, unless there are issues that may put adolescents at risk, meeting with them and their parents jointly for the first session provides the best opportunity for assessment. It is important to include in the session other caretakers in the home, such as grandparents who are often very involved in providing discipline and support. Engaging them in constructing a three-generational genogram of their family is the best way to gather historical and contextual information for clinical assessment. Asking each person to offer stories about the family history brings in different voices and perspectives about important events and transitions in the family.

Involving them in doing a time line, or chronology of events in their family, is essential for tracking vertical or horizontal stressors that may be interfering with their ability to accomplish the tasks of adolescence. Asking parents about their own adolescence, and to describe how their families managed during that stage of life, often reveals similar relationship patterns and triangles as in previous generations. Sometimes, they notice that the way they try to resolve conflicts with their adolescents follows the same pattern as in their families when they were adolescents. As families remember events in the past, they begin to make connections that clarify and that helps them view the present in a more positive light.

CASE ILLUSTRATION

Lois and Mark

Lois (60) and Mark (67), a Jewish, middle-class, professional couple, came to therapy with their 15-year-old, adopted daughter, Rachel. They were worried, and frustrated by her behavior. They had been concerned when Rachel's grades began fluctuating in junior high, but had attributed it to her having to adjust to a new school, and a new group of kids. Their alarm increased this year when her grades dropped significantly. She was having problems getting to school on time, completing assignments, and was retreating from activities she had previously enjoyed such as dance, working at the temple, and going out with friends.

At home she was withdrawn and did not listen to them. They feared that she was depressed, but whenever they tried talking with her, she got angry and pushed them away. Mark and Lois felt that the fighting at home had become intolerable and did not know what to do. Not only were they fighting with Rachel but also with each other about how to intervene. Rachel was angry with her parents, especially with Lois, whom she described as "psycho." She complained, "She yells all the time, and gives me no space. My parents are so negative and critical, and I feel that I am a disappointment to them."

The first step in engaging them in therapy was doing a family genogram to learn about their history, and to track the onset of the problem. They were very active in giving information, checking with each other, and telling stories. As they became involved in providing the history, they relaxed.

Mark was 47 and Lois was 40 when they met, and married after a year of dating. Initially, he hesitated because she wanted to have a child, and he already had two from his previous marriage, but eventually agreed to have another child with her. They decided to adopt when they could not get pregnant, but their age made this difficult. Adopting a toddler from Russia was a lot easier, and although expensive they decided to do it. Rachel was adopted when she was 15 months. They were very happy with her, and she seemed to adjust well. However, their decision to marry and adopt had created much conflict between Mark and his two older children, Helen (43) and Jonathan (40).

Mark had married Lois 2 years after his first wife died of ovarian cancer, and when his two children were getting launched. They had disapproved of the marriage, and resented Lois, feeling that she had pressured their father into marrying her and having a child. Helen and Jonathan, who were now married and had children, had continued to resent him, feeling that he favored his new family, and was not interested in his grandchildren. Mark was very hurt, and in turn had distanced from them emotionally. This conflict had been a major stressor for the family, and had escalated in the past year.

Mark had been hospitalized 5 years ago when he was severely depressed, and at that time was diagnosed with bipolar disorder and placed on medication. As a result, he had to leave his full-time job as a financial adviser, a change that affected the family's

finances and his role in the family. He avoided getting into arguments with Rachel for fear that he would lose control. This caused Lois to feel more overwhelmed and to resent him for adding to her stress. The year before coming to therapy he had been seriously ill with pneumonia and had to be hospitalized. The family had feared his death, and Jonathan and Helen had been very angry with Lois, feeling that she had not included them in decisions about his health. Lois had always tried to understand and avoided getting into arguments with them, but this time already overwhelmed by stress at home, and afraid about the future she did not hold back. The fight had further strained their relationship with Mark.

Having individual sessions with Lois, Mark, and Rachel gave each an opportunity to talk more openly about their feelings and views about the problem, and to further assess for other factors that may have been contributing to the family's situation. Meeting alone with Rachel gave more saliency to her problems. Rachel had been terrified when her father was so sick, and anxious about what would happen to the family if he died. The arguments between Lois, Helen, and Jonathan had frightened her, and she became more aware of how much resentment they felt toward her mother. She was sad that she had such little connection with them and their families. She felt very alone, was questioning her role in the family, and thinking much more about her adoption. She wanted to know more about her family in Russia, and about why she was given up.

She was struggling to find an identity at a time when her family was falling apart. Questions and feelings about her adoption had become more intense at this point in her life, and although her parents had shared whatever they knew, they were not able to answer questions like: Why me and not my other siblings? What are their lives like? Do I look like them? How would my life be if I had not been adopted? She wanted to know where she came from, and felt angry that Mark and Lois had taken her away from her home, but also loved them, and did not want to hurt them by talking about how she felt. She was having problems concentrating at school, and felt that her friends could not understand her because none of them were adopted, or had parents who were so old.

In following sessions asking Mark and Lois how their families had managed during their own adolescence helped them notice relationship patterns and triangles that were repeating in the present. As they continued to make connections between the past and the present, they began to understand how Rachel's adolescence, especially her pulling away and challenging behavior, was reactivating unresolved issues of loss and resentments that each had experienced during adolescence.

Lois had lost her mother when she was 3, and her father when she was 11. She was raised by her stepmother, Mildred, who she remembered as non supportive, critical, and abusive. Prior to her father's death, there had been a triangle in her family involving Mildred, her father, and Lois. Mildred would set limits and Lois responded by yelling and pushing her away, her father would excuse her behavior by explaining how devastated Lois had been when her mother died, and Mildred would be angry that he protected Lois and did not support her as a parent. The conflict between Lois and Mildred had escalated after her father died. However, she had stayed connected with her brother who was born shortly before her father died.

As Lois related the story she saw how the same pattern was repeating in the present. She wanted to be the accepting and loving mother she did not have, but as Rachel entered adolescence and began pulling away, Lois felt angry and rejected. She was hurt that Rachel was not appreciative of her efforts to help her. She called her ungrateful, and was getting into the same fights that she had with Mildred when she was Rachel's age. She was angry with Mark for not supporting her during these fights. Rachel felt that Lois was critical, negative, and abusive, but she did not have her father's protection.

Mark had been distant from his father and had resented him for not being a good provider, who squandered money on gambling and alcohol. As an adolescent, he went to his father's work on paydays, to get money for the family before he could spend it on alcohol. He was his mother's protector, especially after his older sister left home. When he was first married, he worked very hard to be a good provider, but this kept him away from home, and not very involved with his children. His wife's illness was very stressful for the family emotionally and financially. He worked longer hours to pay the bills, and spent less time at home. When Helen left for college, Jonathan, who was still in high school, assumed more responsibility at home, and became very close with his mother before she died. He understood the reason for Mark's absence, but resented not having his father's emotional support during his adolescence when he was alone with his mother.

Mark saw how he and Jonathan had been in similar triangles during adolescence. Both took care of their mothers and resented their fathers for not supporting them emotionally when they were adolescents. Mark had tried to change this pattern in his present family by being more involved with Rachel, but his over reaction to her challenges instead of supporting her had escalated the conflicts in the family. Learning about his illness five years ago had explained some of his erratic moods, and the medication had helped, but he felt more insecure as a husband, as a father, and hesitant as a grandfather. Last year when he was close to death, the conflict between his adult children and Lois had surfaced the pain and regrets he felt about not having been there when they probably needed him the most. He did not remember having problems with Jonathan and Helen during their adolescence, but knew that he had not been emotionally present to notice.

With help, Lois and Mark were able to make several shifts that opened possibilities for the family to get back on track. With coaching, Mark and Lois were able to listen to Rachel's struggles with an open heart, and without rushing to make her feel better. In the past, she felt that what she said was too painful for them to hear, or that they did not believe her. In response, she had shut down emotionally and pushed them back. She told them how ashamed she had felt telling her friends about Mark's mental illness, and how angry she was that as a result they had no money to have fun. It was difficult for them to hear that last year when she was afraid to lose Mark, she had also feared being left alone with Lois. Rachel also told them she wanted to know more about where she came from and about her family in Russia, and that she wished they could be closer to Jonathan and Helen and their children.

Lois told her they would be willing to take her to Russia and look for her family, but Rachel wondered if this was realistic since they were always fighting about money. With help, they were able to talk with her about the family's finances, and about Mark's health issues in more detail. Her wish to be closer to Helen and Jonathan had a very emotional effect on Mark, who was feeling an urgency to repair his relationship with them, and to get to know his grandchildren. He was open to the suggestion that writing letters to them could be a start. He wrote letters to each of them telling them how much he missed them, and the regret he felt about not having been there for them, and how sad he felt about not being there now. This was the beginning of a long process, but he was determined to pursue them and to listen with an open heart.

The more attention Mark and Lois paid to their emotional reactions when Rachel challenged them and pulled away, the easier it became for them to not feel personally attacked, or to distance emotionally. Asking about how they had managed to get through their adolescence engaged them in talking about positive connections with other adults, and to think about ways in which their parents had tried to support them. Encouraging them to talk about their parents' history, their story of migration and social context expanded their view and sparked their curiosity about stressors and factors that were being transferred down the generations. They were coached to learn more by asking relatives for information.

Lois, who was trying very hard to not replicate the relationship she had with Mildred, agreed that learning more about her stepmother would help feel less reactive with Rachel. She was able to reconnect with some of Mildred's cousins who remembered how challenging she had been at 15. They also talked about how difficult it had been for Mildred to raise a teenager and a toddler alone, after her husband died. The stories helped Lois think of Mildred more as a woman than as the "mean stepmother," and to feel compassion for her, knowing how overwhelming it must have been to raise and adolescent daughter as a single mother.

Rachel was very interested in the stories, but as she was able to tell her parents, she felt sad knowing that she might never be able to learn about her biological family's history. Rachel continued to struggle academically, and her parents continued to worry, but as Lois and Mark worked on learning more about their family of origin, they felt stronger, and more connected emotionally as a family. They were able to give Rachel more space, and not over function for her, and to be more available and involved in her life.

Assess your comprehension of clinical assessment by completing this quiz.

— Conclusion —

We live in a world that is changing rapidly, where personal and emotional connections are not a priority. Most of us are always rushing, and rarely have time to share stories with our children that connect our present to our past. When parents come home after working all day, they usually have little time to sit and listen. Jennifer Senior (2014) brilliantly describes in *All Joy and No Fun: The Paradox of Present Parenthood*, how parents in this country, especially in the middle class, driven by anxiety about an uncertain future, over schedule their children with activities to give them an edge. The paradox is that

often their fears about the future take away from enjoying the present.

Adolescents need direction, and engaging them in positive activities is helpful, but most of all they need to feel emotionally connected to those who love them. Every study about adolescents points to the importance of connection, acceptance, and support for them to stay healthy, and to have productive lives. When there is trouble in their lives and they come to us, we can make a difference by helping their families restore their hope and confidence.

"It takes a village to raise a child" may sound trite, but it is a concept that has deep meaning for any parent who experiences the loneliness and fear of raising adolescents who are troubled. Connecting parents with natural support systems to lessen the isolation that most of us experience in our present-day communities is necessary. Interventions that take into account the sociopolitical context in which we live and the effect on families with adolescents are critical. Adolescents are our future. They are resilient, creative, and passionate, and we must help those who love them keep them strong and healthy.

> **Recall what you learned in this chapter by completing the Chapter Review.**

— References

American Psychological Association. (2014). *A new look at adolescent girls: Body image concerns and disordered eating.* Washington, DC.

Boyd Franklin, N., & Franklin, A. J. (2000). *Boys into men: Raising our African American teenage sons.* New York: Penguin Books.

Burland, J. (2001). *Parents and teachers as allies: Recognizing early-onset mental illness in children and adolescents.* Arlington, VA: National Alliance for the Mentally Ill.

Burton, L., Obeidallah, D. A., & Allison, K. (1996). Ethnographic insights on social context and adolescent development among inner-city African-American teens. In R. Jessor, A. Colby, & R. Shweder (Eds.), *Essays on ethnography and human development.* Chicago, IL: University of Chicago Press.

Burton, L. M., Winn, B, D. M., Stevenson, H., & Lawson Clark, S. (2004). Working with African American Clients: Considering the "Homeplace" in marriage and family therapy practices. *Journal of Marital and Family Therapy, 30*(4), 397–410.

Burton L. M. (2007). Childhood adultification in economically disadvantaged families: A conceptual model, *Family Relations, 56*(4), 329–345.

Centers for Disease and Control. (2013). Youth Risk Behavior Surveillance System: Adolescent and School Health.

Centers for Disease and Prevention: (2013). HIV among African American women.

Centers for Disease Control and Prevention. (2010). *Slideshow: HIV surveillance in adolescents and young adults.* Retrieved February 14, 2011, from http://www.cdc.gov/hiv/topics/surveillance/resources/slides/adolescents/slides/Adolescents.pdf

Child Trends. (2010). *Child Trends Databank: Adolescents who feel sad or hopeless.* Retrieved February 15, 2011, from http://www.childtrendsdatabank.org/alphalist?q=node/126

Cummings, E. M., Davis, P. T. (2010). *Marital conflict and children: An emotional security perspective.* Guilford Press: New York.

Davalos, D. B., Chavez, E. L., & Guardiola, R. J. (2005). Effects of perceived parental school support and family communication on delinquent behaviors in Latinos and White Non-Latinos. *Cultural Diversity and Ethnic Minority Psychology, 11*(1), 57–68.

Dooley, C., & Fedele, N. M. (2004). Mothers and sons: Raising relational boys. In J. V. Jordan, M. Walker, & L. M. Hartling (Eds.). *The complexity of connection: Writings from the Stone Center's Jean Baker Miller Training Institute* (pp. 220–249). New York: Guilford.

Drake, B. (2013). *Incarceration rate widens between black and white men.* Pew Research Center, Washington, D.C.

Forhan, S. E., Gottlieb, S. L., Sternberg, M. R., Xu, F., Datta, S. D., McQuillan, G. M., et al. (2009). Prevalence of sexually transmitted infections among female adolescents aged 14 to 19 in the United States. *Pediatrics, 124*(6), 1505–1512.

Gay and Lesbian Connection (2012). Californians Bans "Reparative Therapies" for Minors. Administration. www.gayandlesbianconnection.com.

Hamilton, B. E., Martin, J. A., & Ventura, S. J. (2010). *Births: Preliminary data for 2009.* National Vital Statistics Reports 59(3): Hyattsville, MD: National Center for Health Statistics. Retrieved January 4, 2011, from http://www.cdc.gov/nchs/data/nvsr59/nvsr59_03.pdf

Hamilton, B. E., Ventura, S. J. (2010). Birth rates for U.S. teenagers reach historic lows for all age and ethnic groups. NCHS data brief, no 89. Hyattsville, MD: National Center for Health Statistics.

Hardy, K., & Laszloffy, T. (2005). *Teens who hurt*. New York: Guilford.

Hoffman, S. D., & Maynard, R. A. (Eds.). (2008). *Kids having kids: Economic costs and social consequences of teen pregnancy* (2nd ed.). Washington, DC: Urban Institute Press.

Hudson J. I., Hiripi, E., Pope, H. G., Kessler, R. C. (2007). The prevalence and correlates of eating disorders in the National Comorbidity Survey Replication. *Biological Psychiatry, 61*(3), 348–358.

Johnston, L. D., O'Malley, P. M., Bachman, J. G., & Schulenberg, J. E. (2010). *Monitoring the Future: National results on adolescent drug use: Overview of key findings, 2010. National Institute on Drug Abuse*. Retrieved February 16, 2011, from http://www.monitoringthefuture.org/pubs/monographs/mtf-overview2010.pdf

Kimmel, M. S. (2009). *Guyland: The perilous world where boys become men*. New York: Harper Collins.

Kimmel, M. S. (2013). *The gendered society*, 5th ed. New York: Oxford University Press.

La Sala, M. (2010). *Coming out, coming home: Helping Families adjust*. New York: Columbia Press.

Lombardi, K. S. (2011). *The mama's boy myth: Why keeping our sons close makes them stronger*. New York: Penguin Group.

Martin, J. A., Hamilton, B. E., Ventura, S. J., Osterman, M. J. K., Wilson, E. C., Mathews, T. J., (2012). Births: Final data for 2010. *National Vital Statistics Reports* June 20;62(1)1-69,72.

Massachusetts Youth Risk Behavior Survey, (2006). Massachusetts Department of Education

McGoldrick, M., & Hardy, K. V. (2008). *Revisioning family therapy: Race, culture and gender in clinical practice*. New York: The Guilford Press.

McGoldrick, M., Giordano, J., & Garcia-Preto, N. (Eds.). (2005). *Ethnicity and family therapy*. New York: The Guilford Press.

National Institute of Mental Health. (2009). *The numbers count: Mental disorders in America*.

National Institute of Mental Health. (2009). *Suicide in the U.S.: Statistics and Prevention*.

National Institute for Health Care Management. (2009). *Strategies to support the integration of mental health into pediatric primary care*. Retrieved February 16, 2011, from http://nihcm.org/pdf/PediatricMH-FINAL.pdf

Ryan, C. (2013). *The real-life costs of anti-LGBT bullying*. Huffington Post. Retrieved May 24, 2013, from http://www.huffingtonpost.com/caitlin-ryan/the-reallife-costs-of-ant_b_866253.html.

Ryan C., Huebner, D., Diaz R. M., Sanchez, J. (2009). Family rejection as a predictor of negative health outcomes in White and Latino Lesbian, Gay, and Bisexual young adults. *Pediatrics, 123* (1) 2007–3524.

Ryan, C., Russell, S. T., Huebner, D., Diaz, R., & Sanchez J. (2010). Family acceptance in adolescence and the health of LGBT young adults. *Journal of Child and Adolescent Psychiatric Nursing, 23*(4), 205–213.

Sandberg, S. (2013). *Lean in: Women, work, and the will to lead*. New York: Knopf.

Savin-Williams, R. C. (2005). *The new gay teenager*. Cambridge, MA. Harvard University Press.

Schwarz, S. W. (2009). *Adolescent mental health in the United States: Facts for Policymakers* Retrieved February 16, 2011, from http://nccp.org/publications/pdf/text_878.pdf

Senior, J. (2014). *All joy and no fun: The paradox of modern parenthood*. New York: Harper Collins.

Taffel, R. (2005). *Breaking through to teens: A new psychotherapist for the new adolescent*. New York, Gilford Press.

Taffel, R. (2009). *Childhood Unbound: Saving our kids best selves-confident parenting in a world of change*. New York. Free Press.

Taffel, R., & Blau, M. (2001). *The second family: How adolescent power is challenging the American family*. New York: St. Martin's Press.

The Center for Latino Adolescent and Family Health. (2013). *Silver School of Social Work*. New York University. New York.

Travis, S. (2013). *FAU Study: Homicide, top cause of death for Black men*. Sun Sentinel.

U.S. Bureau of Labor. (2009). *Employment rates for African Americans*.

U.S. Department of Labor Statistics. (2013). *Employment and unemployment among youth summary*.

U.S. Census Bureau. (2012). *America's families and living arrangements*.

U.S. Census Bureau. (2006–2008). *American Community Survey*.

Willoughby, T., Hamza, C. A. (2010). *A longitudinal examination of the bidirectional associations among perceived parenting behaviors, adolescent disclosure and problem behavior across the high school years. Journal of Youth and Adolescence, 60* (2), 463–478.

Wolf, A. E. (2002). *Get out of my life but first could you drive me and Cheryl to the mall?* New York: The Noonday Press.

World Health Organization, (2002). *The world health report: Reducing risks, promoting healthy life.* Geneva, Switzerland.

Yurgelun-Todd, D. A. & Killgore, W. D. S. (2006). Fear-related activity in the prefrontal cortex increases with age during adolescence: A preliminary MRI study. *Neuroscience Letters*, 406, 194–199.

Zayas, L. H., & Pilat, A. M. (2008). Suicidal behavior in Latinas: Explanatory cultural factors and implications for intervention. *Suicide and Life-Threatening Behavior, 38,* 334–342.

Zayas, L. H., (2011). *Latinas attempting suicide: when families, culture, and daughters collide.* New York: Oxford Press.

Chapter 17

Families at Midlife: Launching Children and Moving On

Nydia Garcia Preto & Lynn Blacker

— Learning Outcomes

- List and describe the developmental tasks associated with midlife.
- Compare today's midlife experience with the midlife experience of previous generations.
- Describe common misconceptions about midlife.
- Explain how men and women experience the challenges of midlife differently.
- Identify the unique challenges to launching children in today's world.
- Discuss how family members can transition from parent–child relationships to adult-to-adult personal relationships.
- Examine the challenges of renegotiating family relationships during midlife.
- Describe how the nature of couple relationships changes during midlife.
- Explain the reasons for increased divorce rates for couples in midlife.
- List and describe the developmental tasks related to losing a parent at midlife.

Introduction

Midlife, the longest phase of the life cycle, is a time of major family restructuring. The family shrinks when children are launched or when grandparents die. Additionally, many families experience loss through midlife divorce or the death of a spouse. Women may also "leave" voluntarily by joining the workforce or other outside involvement, while midlife men may suddenly experience the loss of employment when their work is restructured. On the other hand, the family expands through the marriage of adult children and the birth of grandchildren. Families may also expand when launched children return home, some with their own children, or if aged parents join the household. Any one of these events is a stress point that may motivate families to seek help.

In 1900, when the average life span was about 47 years (Skolnick, 2009), the phase of midlife barely existed. Life cycle tasks were compressed: launching and marrying one's children, burying parents, becoming grandparents, and losing partners commonly occurred concurrently within one decade.

Now midlife is generally the longest phase of life, lasting at times from the mid-30s (especially for working-class men and women) until the late 60s (for healthy middle-class families). If people thought of midlife at all a generation ago, the stereotypes about it were as a time of depression, "the empty nest," or the "midlife crisis"—that point of awareness that we are coming to the second half of life, where we begin to measure our lives by the time left rather than the time since birth, as Bernice Neugarten (1968) said long ago. It is a time to consider unrealized dreams and correct one's life trajectory—to re-think any aspect of our lives that has not been worked out yet and consider reinventing ourselves. But in general, midlife is less a crisis than a time of great potential. Margaret Mead spoke of midlife for women as that era of "postmenopausal zest" (Bateson, 2001, p. 28). It is a time when both men and women are freed up from the tasks of childrearing and creativity and energy are released.

Nowadays, the structures and patterns of families at midlife are very diverse: men and women can be single, never married, in committed relationships, divorced, remarried, widowed, or separated. A significant number of people are beginning new or second families at midlife rather than launching them, and many are not having children either by choice or other circumstances. So the diversity of family constellations and situations at this phase is one of its primary characteristics. And, because of better health and increasing longevity for a majority of the population, the length of the phase has greatly expanded and it may lengthen even more in the future.

Midlife does generally involve the launching of children (nephews and nieces if not one's own), and also a realignment of other family roles, such as becoming a couple again, for parents who are still married or in committed relationships; developing adult-to-adult relationships with children; accepting new family members through marriage, cohabitation, and birth; and resolving issues with, providing care for, and finally burying parents. This is also a time to reassess work choices, nurture friendships, and, for some, to have the opportunity to "come out" and give expression to aspects of their gender or sexual identity that they had felt forced to keep secret at earlier stages of life.

Women and Men at Midlife

Although every generation must go through approximately the same life cycle transitions and accomplish the same tasks, each cohort has a unique historical experience. Men and women who are now at midlife are the last of the baby boomers. They are a more racially and culturally diverse group than the generation before them, who were raised in the 1950s and 1960s. Many immigrated as children from Asia, Latin America, and other countries and have acculturated in different ways to the dominant culture in this country. They grew up during the Reagan years and experienced economic and social changes that have tended to move this country toward a more conservative political climate. Many grew up with traditional values and gender role expectations, namely, to be heterosexual, find a spouse, marry early, and, if female, stay home and take care of the children. Male entitlement strongly permeated their socialization. At the same time, men and women were exposed to a changing social climate, as the earlier baby boomers transitioned from postwar traditional values to more liberal and tolerant attitudes that were largely spearheaded by the Women's Movement, the Civil Rights Movement, and the Gay Liberation Movement.

Since 1960, many more women attended college, entered the full-time workforce, and got divorced. Today, more than ever before, women at midlife have pursued and achieved successful careers, and are living independent, fulfilling lives (Sandberg, 2013). Many earn enough money to support themselves and their families (often earning more than their male partners), and have felt freer to choose whether or not to marry, or be in a committed relationship. These changes in women's lives have had a remarkable effect on men's social roles. However, men have not adapted as rapidly as women to the social and economic changes taking place, and redefining their role in families and at work has become increasingly challenging for men (Rosin, 2012). This is particularly problematic for men who lose their jobs at midlife, especially if their identity has been defined by their work, and their life's worth measured by their ability to "provide" for their families.

Although the liberal social changes that began in the late twentieth century have led couples to seek more egalitarian marriages, gender role expectations determined by patriarchy continue to pose enormous challenges (Arnett & Fishel, 2013; Kimmel, 2013). Midlife is a time when men and women who have struggled for years to keep their relationships going may react very strongly to the urgent call of, "it's now or never." Feeling stressed and confused about what to do, they may seek help. In therapy, they often present a deep dissatisfaction with their lives, feeling that they have given up too much of themselves, and compromised too many values to preserve their relationship. They resent their partners, and feel blamed by them. Doing a family genogram and a time line of significant events in their lives can help them widen their lens and gain perspective as to how their social location, family values, and gender role expectations passed down through generations have influenced their life choices. Often when they realize the emotional cost that not having taken responsibility for their personal needs has had on their relationship, they are more open to considering changes necessary to create a more fulfilling relationship.

Facing Aging

A key developmental task at midlife is coming to terms with aging. Facing mortality precipitates a process of reassessment in a person's life, a review of accomplishments, dreams, regrets, losses, and the realization that time is running out. A popular view has been that this process of re-evaluation provokes a "midlife crisis" in both men and women. A common stereotype has been that when men get in touch with mortality, panic sets in, and fearing that they have squandered their lives, they suddenly quit their jobs, dash out of their marriages, and go on a spending spree on high-ticket items to bolster up their self-image. A typical assumption for women has been that menopause causes them to be hysterical, and panicked about having an empty nest, or being alone, or with a partner who does not understand their needs.

These misconceptions have given midlife a negative connotation, when in reality most women and men reevaluate their lives without catastrophe, and make changes that enable them to continue to have meaningful, productive lives. They may feel some sadness when their children leave home, but more often they defy the stereotypes of women's depression and disorientation and are pleased with the job they have done and feel freer than ever to explore and take on new challenges (Hunter, Sundel, & Sundel, 2002; Norsigian, 2011). Most women at midlife feel grounded, competent, and satisfied with their accomplishments, and the majority do not report significant anger, anxiety, depression, or self-consciousness related to menopause (Woods & Mitchell, 2006).

Similarly, research on men at midlife indicates that the overwhelming majority accomplish the developmental tasks of reevaluation through a long, introspective process rather than an acute acting-out crisis. Although they make adjustments in their relationships and work lives, relatively few men experience the process as catastrophic (Kimmel, 2013).

The impact of social location

But, as in every life stage, men and women experience the challenges of midlife differently, depending on their social location. For poor men and women midlife comes earlier. Those who are ill or without support may feel older and have a bleaker outlook on life than those who have more resources. Working-class and poor women typically anticipate being both homemakers and employees (in non-fulfilling jobs) throughout their adult lives. Midlife can be a most tumultuous time of life for low-income African American women (Hunter et al., 2002). Like Latinas, they are likely to be poorer than men, and in comparison to white women, they are twice as likely to be poor (Quigley, 2012). Working-class men, who often depend on physical strength for their jobs, are often considered middle aged in their 30s, and with poor access to health care, they may not expect to live much beyond retirement. This is particularly true of African American men, who have high mortality rates from heart disease, diabetes, and other chronic illnesses. When midlife adults have little economic autonomy, the tasks of reevaluating their life course and developing new plans and dreams may not seem realistic. It is essential to help families living under such adversity, to connect with the strengths of their heritage, their resourcefulness, and with those abilities that have enabled them to survive, and at times even thrive under oppressive circumstances throughout their lives.

The impact of developmental changes

For some, the normal stress associated with the challenges of midlife can escalate depending on their ability to make the required developmental changes and adjustments needed at this phase. Some women, for example, do experience serious menopausal symptoms, such as hot flashes, sleep problems, vaginal dryness, weight gain, osteoporosis, and cognitive changes. Providing psychoeducational information about the natural aspects of these changes and encouraging consultation with their physicians about possible treatment alternatives is crucial when women present with these symptoms. The psychological effects of menopause have been found to be culture bound (Hunter et al., 2002).

For many women in our society, particularly in the dominant culture, where beauty equals youth, aging means that they no longer feel desirable or valuable. Especially single women may lose hope of finding a partner and fear aging alone. It is important to help women reassess their lives, their accomplishments, and what they still want to do, whether starting a new career or a new creative passion, rather than buying into the negative stereotypes associated with this stage of life.

CASE ILLUSTRATION

Gail

Gail, a 49-year-old African American single parent, came to therapy because she was feeling extremely anxious and depressed since her daughter, Cheryl, 18 years old, had left for college. She was having difficulty doing her job as an LPN at a hospital where she had worked for years, calling and texting her daughter frequently during the day. She worried about Cheryl not waking up early enough to go to class, not eating properly, drinking, and putting herself at risk with boys. In other words, she feared that Cheryl could not be responsible without her mother to guide her. She also worried about not having enough money to pay the college expenses and still meet her own needs. As a solution, she was not spending money on herself, and she had stopped going out with friends. She stayed home, crying frequently, and sometimes drank too much.

In therapy, we spoke about her dreams for her daughter and for herself, and about other women in her family, especially her mother. We spoke about her own launching and the differences in how she left home and how Cheryl was leaving now. Looking at how proud she felt that her daughter, unlike herself, was going to college, which she as a single mother had been able to accomplish what her parents could not do for her, was a changing point in the treatment. She began to get in touch with her sense of competence again, acknowledge her confidence, and think about her daughter's strengths. She agreed to set some limits on her calling and texting Cheryl, who later related that the reduced communication had been a big relief.

Gail's financial situation continued to be very burdensome, but in therapy we noted that it did not have to prevent her from seeking companionship and support from family and friends. Sharing food with friends or family at home provided her with some of the social connection she needed. Gail was adept at relationships, and she responded well to this intervention. She also found keeping a journal to be a useful tool for identifying neglected and new interests, not to be used as time fillers but as expressions of her own authentic self, which she now had the freedom to explore.

The experience for midlife lesbians may be somewhat different, since they are much less prone to equate desirability and beauty with youth, thinness, or any of the other usual male criteria of female beauty (Hunter, 2005; Cole & Rothblum, 1990). And, since women generally tend to focus more on the emotional than the physical aspects of intimacy, lesbians may experience this transition in sexuality with less apprehension. However, the cessation of fertility may compound the experience of loss for lesbians who feel that their attempt to have children through insemination or adoption was prevented by social prejudice (Slater, 1995).

Men also experience gradual physical changes as they approach midlife, not necessarily bringing them below their maximal level of functioning; but these changes are significant enough to notice, such as baldness, weight gain, wrinkles, and less sexual prowess. Their physical stamina may continue to diminish, and certain types of work may no longer be possible, putting their livelihood in question. It is disconcerting, especially for heterosexual men, suddenly to feel marginal at work, or to lose their jobs altogether. As one client expressed in great distress, "I went to the journalist's circle at the Giants Stadium and suddenly realized that no one was greeting me by my name, and that I didn't know their names either." He felt that his social status had changed in that arena, and that his future career was in question. Helping him look at his identity in terms of his relationship with his children and partner led him to think about a different type of social status, one where he could have a more lasting influence.

Men may find themselves revising their values at midlife. Their work may take a different priority in their lives. They may be feeling especially regretful about having missed opportunities to get to know their children better as they try to renegotiate more adult relationships with them, while at the same time renegotiating relationships with their parents, and their partners. It is not that the questions they ask are so different from women's, but they tend to do their thinking alone, a consequence of their socialization. A family life cycle approach can help them normalize their anxiety and depression, as they realize that most men at this stage of life experience similar issues.

CASE ILLUSTRATION

Jerry

Jerry, a 55-year-old, a professor of Dutch ancestry, came to therapy feeling very depressed about not being able to concentrate enough to prepare lectures and teach his courses or to contribute to a research project that he had initiated with other colleagues in his department. He had been divorced for 3 years and thought he was adjusting well to single life. However, he now saw his absence as a father as the cause of his 19-year-old son's recent decision not to go to college and to marry an older woman. Jerry's work had always been a priority for him, which he believed had caused the end of his marriage. He now felt anxious about his son's life and about losing the connection with him. In therapy, Jerry began to review his early life in a Midwest farming community and to see how his values about masculinity had been heavily influenced by Dutch culture and religious beliefs. He had learned from the men in his family a fierce determination to work hard and to succeed which had prevented him from being the type of partner and father he wanted to be.

Helping him see that there was a present and future in the relationship with his son, and that making time for the two of them to enjoy common interests or meals might begin to change the relationship, gave him hope. In time, they established rituals for spending time fishing, which they both loved, which led to getting to know each other not only as father and son but also as men. As their relationship grew closer, they were able to joke about how in the future Jerry could take his grandchildren fishing.

Among gay men, concern about body image is particularly strong, as they fear that signs of aging will mean that they are less sexually desirable. The critical midlife task of accepting one's own mortality is also drastically heightened among gay men. A large proportion of men living with HIV/AIDS are now in midlife; some of these men have been HIV-positive for 10 years or more. In addition to their acute personal awareness of mortality, gay men have buried and grieved for numerous friends and partners. Therefore, rather than just beginning to confront mortality at midlife as heterosexuals typically do, gay men have been living with a heightened awareness of death on a daily basis for many years.

 Assess your comprehension of facing aging by completing this quiz.

Launching Children and Redefining Relationships with Them

Most midlife adults in this country who have raised children, especially in the white middle class, look forward to a less-pressured life as their children become independent and leave home. Many are bewildered when they are confronted with the unexpected reality that in today's world, launching is very different from what they experienced at that stage in their own lives. The patterns of launching to independent living with one's new created family that parents experienced a generation ago are changing dramatically. These patterns never did apply to families at the margins. The poor always needed their children's resources for ongoing support and the disabled have always needed their families for support. It was always more common in working-class and poor families for married children and their new families to move back with parents for financial reasons, but now this is also increasingly common for middle- and upper-class families.

The tasks of launching and renegotiating relationships between parents and adult children at midlife are becoming more complex as adult children have increasing struggles getting launched. While more than half of late adolescents are still leaving home for college or other training, many have difficulty making enough money to live independently, and remain at home or return after college (Arnett & Fishel, 2013; Kimmel, 2008). A Pew Report (2013) found that in the United States, about 40 percent of 18 to 24 year-olds are living at home with parents, and more than half of 18 to 24 year-olds have moved back home at least once, or have never moved out. Changes in the global economy and rising health costs are drastically limiting the choices that young adults can make about their own futures. Financial concerns, lengthened years of education, delayed marriage plans, or marital breakups may all lead to this boomerang effect.

The return of adult children home is a source of stress for most parents, especially for middle-class parents who usually anticipate the freedom that comes after children leave. Both young adults and their parents may find the leaving and returning home very difficult, and often question their competence. Parents fear they have failed to help their children become independent, and children feel they have let their parents down. How parents cope with this stress has much to do with how they interpret the children's presence. Parents may view the situation more negatively if their children are unemployed or move back after a marital breakup, than if children remain home while working or going to school and have never married.

In contrast, parents who are less acculturated to the dominant culture may experience their more acculturated children's wish to leave home as a failure on their part, and as their children's lack of loyalty. Cultures differ in how young people are expected to reach adulthood (Arnett & Galambos, 2003). Youths from ethnic minority groups are more likely than Whites to view adulthood as requiring "becoming capable of supporting a family financially, keeping a family physically safe, and caring for children" (p. 71). In some cultures, parents may expect young adults to live at home and contribute financially to the family until they marry, an expectation that may lead to problems when their more acculturated adult children want to live independently, and without economic responsibilities to their parents. Parents may react by feeling that their children are not being loyal, or grateful, and threaten to cut them off. If the family seeks help, conversations with parents and the young adult that help to clarify their differences, while focusing on their connection and love they have for each other can help the family move to a more positive position.

For African Americans, Latino/as, and for many other cultural groups, a high value has always been placed on interconnectedness between family members and there may actually never be an "empty nest," since the elderly are likely to remain active in the family's household way past midlife (McGoldrick, Giordano, & Garcia-Preto, 2005). Especially in families where illness, addictions, and AIDS have led to parents being unable to take care of their children, grandparents may also continue as caretakers way past midlife. These social and culturally transmitted influences contribute to the family's ease or difficulty in moving through this phase. Awareness of how our own cultural context and trajectory in life inform our clinical views and interventions is crucial when working with families negotiating impasses at this stage of life, since our views of independence, launching, family interdependence, and interconnectedness may be different from theirs.

In most families, however, the more responsible and less dependent their children are, whether living at home or not, the easier it is for parents to relate to them as adults, and support their efforts for more independence. In these families, parents usually continue living their lives, planning their futures, and feeling confident that their children are moving toward increased autonomy. But this shift can become extremely difficult, for example, when young adults return home after failing college, or because they were emotionally unable to be away from home, or when parents disagree about their children's ability to fulfill adult responsibilities. Increasingly, such families come to therapy, and need help in assessing their situation not from a perspective of failure but, as with other life cycle oriented interventions, taking account that the patterns of launching that applied in the past are not working today.

When they come to therapy, it helps to engage parents and their adult children in clarifying expectations for living together, and to make constructive plans for the future with the goal of increasing the young adult's self-sufficiency. This fosters hope and lessens feelings of stuckness. It is also important to explore with parents how their own launching was handled by their own parents. Are there any emotional patterns, or triangles that may be repeating in this generation and that may be preventing the family's ability to move on? We usually meet with the young adult alone, with parents alone, and then with them together to encourage more adult to adult relationships.

CASE ILLUSTRATION

Bert and May

Bert (60) and May (59) came to therapy because they were at their wits end with their daughter Sue Ann (22) who had returned home after one semester away in college, and was apparently acting out of control at home, fighting, lying, threatening to hurt May, and to break everything in the house. They felt like hostages at home, especially May who was frightened by Sue Ann's threats. Every time she had a fight with Sue Ann, she called Bert to come home. May was angry with him because he sometimes agreed with Sue Ann's complaints about her unrealistic expectations and criticism. Bert was resentful that May was not more tolerant with Sue Ann, and also very confused about what to do to help the situation. They wanted her to get a job, or go to school, and be more independent. Bert and May were caught in a triangle where the two were so focused on their daughter that they did not attend to their relationship. They had put on hold their plans to sell their house after Sue Ann went to college, and move to North Carolina, where May's sister and her family had moved recently. They were sad, angry, and frightened about the future.

Bert (German Catholic) and May (Irish Catholic) had adopted Sue Ann as an infant after trying to have children for several years. They had little information about her biological parents, except that the mother was African American and the father was probably Puerto Rican. According to them, Sue Ann had been a happy child until adolescence when she began to defy them and have difficulties at school. They had gone to family therapy for a short time, and the problems had subsided enough for her to go away to college. However, her adjustment at college became problematic, and during the second semester she became depressed and unable to function. She saw a counselor at college and was referred to a psychiatrist who diagnosed her as bipolar, prescribed medication, and recommended testing for learning disabilities. Her parents brought her home, followed up with psychiatric care, and had her tested. She did have special needs and was able to get the needed supports at a local college, but she continued to have difficulties at school, and problems at home were escalating.

In therapy, several issues surfaced that contributed to the family's turmoil and stuckness. Bert and May were disappointed and frustrated, and felt responsible for what they described as their daughter's failure to move on in life. Sue Ann expressed hurt and anger toward her parents, and thought they did not understand her. "I am a Black woman with White parents who don't understand what it's like for me out there. They don't like my Black friends and think they are 'low lifes,' and I hate the fact that I have to take medicine and that because of my learning problems, I might not be able to make it in school and take care of myself." Sue Ann felt stuck at home with parents who did not understand what it was like to be a woman of color in the world, with no money, no car, and working only a few hours a week. Bert and Mary felt that she was using excuses and that they could not trust her. They saw no end to their burden as parents.

Meeting alone with Bert and May, they were encouraged to talk about the adoption, their positive feelings and their disappointments, and about their struggles in raising Sue Ann and trying to help her cope with the challenges that a woman of color, with a psychiatric label, is likely to encounter. Asking about their family histories, their journey as a couple, their values, and particularly their memories of raising a Black daughter in a racist world began a process of understanding how their White middle class experiences of privilege did not equip them to help Sue Ann cope with her problems. In joint sessions with Sue Ann, they began to listen to her struggles without telling her how to fix them. The more they validated her experience, the less angry and out-of-control Sue Ann's reactions became. The more they focused on her strengths, and supported her adult behavior, the more responsibility she took in exploring options for work and school.

As the conflict at home lessened, what surfaced for Bert and May was that over the years they had distanced emotionally as a couple, and that the problems with Sue Ann had kept them from looking at their relationship. After the adoption, May had given up her career as a teacher to devote herself to being a mother and homemaker. Her connection with friends and colleagues tapered, and she mostly depended on her older sister, who lived close by, for support and companionship. Another factor that contributed to her world becoming smaller was that for years she struggled with rheumatoid arthritis, and recently her ability to be physically active was diminishing. In contrast, Bert, a successful businessman, had a very active life, and a large social network that kept him busy outside the home. He felt sorry for May and missed having a more active life with her, physically and sexually. May's loneliness had increased since her sister's move to North Carolina which happened around the same time Sue Ann returned from college. Without other supports nearby, her dependency on Bert had increased. She called him home from work whenever she had a fight with Sue Ann. Bert was afraid to leave them alone, but worried about his business suffering if he was absent.

As they reviewed their life together, the plans they had made as a couple, their dreams, and their present resources, they became more engaged with each other as spouses. They began to support each other differently by planning brief vacations, at first separately, until they were able to trust Sue Ann enough to leave her at home alone. May was excited about this plan, and went to visit her sister alone for a long weekend. While she was away, Bert and Sue Ann took the opportunity to visit some of the places they used to enjoy when she was a young girl. Father and daughter felt very positive about the time they had spent together, and reflected on how they had enjoyed relating more as adults. May had enjoyed the time with her sister, and felt encouraged that no catastrophe had taken place at home, and that instead Sue Ann and Bert had a positive experience.

Bert and May began to go out as a couple more frequently, and eventually took short trips to North Carolina where they spent time with family and looked for a retirement home. The more comfortable they felt with each other, the easier it became to share their plans with Sue Ann. She felt more accepted by them, and in turn became more open about her friends, her work, and about her African American boyfriend. She had been afraid to tell them about him because he drove a truck and came from a poor family, not college educated like them. Bert and May, with some coaching in therapy, were able to stay open, and to invite him for dinner. In a family session, Bert reminded May and Sue Ann that he came from a poor family, and had done all kinds of manual jobs to put himself through college. May remembered how her upper-middle-class parents had not been so happy about her relationship with Bert. As they shared these stories as a family, they began to relate more as adults with each other. Sue Ann was learning and realizing that her parents had their own lives and stories, separate from hers, and in turn May and Bert saw her as separate from them.

It is one thing to have children move out of the home. It is another to view them as adults and relate to them accordingly, and still another for young adults to see their parents as people with a history, life, and concerns of their own. Usually, parents and children stay closely connected after launching, often speaking several times a week (Arnett & Fishel, 2013). This eases the process of launching and validates their connection for both parents and children. When they see their children becoming more and more independent as young adults both inside and outside the family, parents feel that their job was well done and are able to relinquish some of their parental oversight. Unless there are major unresolved issues, or cut offs in their relationships at this stage, parents and children are increasingly able to interact on an adult, mutually supportive basis. In fact, parent–child relationships have been found to become more affectionate and close after children leave home (Arnett, 2004), and parents often come to view their children as close friends, especially after they marry and have children of their own (Lott, 2013).

Redefining parent–child relationships as adult-to-adult personal relationships does not happen automatically when grown children leave home or even when they marry and have children. It is quite common for unresolved emotional issues or differences to create situations of polite, dutiful distance instead of a warm and eager sharing of lives between generations. Resolving old issues is the central emotional task of the younger generation, but parents can help or hinder the process. Their shift from hands-on direction of adolescents to on-call consultant to young adults may not be easy. Some parents also find it difficult to be more open and personal with children whom they have always shielded from "adult" problems.

> Assess your comprehension of launching children and redefining relationships with them by completing this quiz.

Renegotiating Relationships with Other Family Members and Friends

Relationships with siblings and other family members as well as with friends take on new importance at midlife. Midlife siblings tend to draw together as aunts and uncles, parents, and grandparents become ill and die, leaving them to assume their place as the older generation. They especially face the stressor of arranging and providing care to their aging parents. After a parent's death, the primary caregiver may feel resentment toward her siblings for their lesser involvement. There may be other issues that have been chronic sources of conflict through other life phases. After the parents' deaths, siblings may distance or cut each other off rather than work at resolving these conflicts, unless they receive help, which they too rarely do. If the discord persists, the siblings risk losing a significant source of practical and emotional support that they may need in later life.

During the child-raising years, friendships are often diluted by the omnipresence of children at most social gatherings, but at midlife, they matter again in a profound and personal way. Midlifers are reinventing themselves. Their families look different. They may be suddenly single or come out as LGBT. For all the special concerns of midlife, long-term friends are there to provide a sense of belonging and continuity, while new friends are needed to address new interests and realities. With their heightened awareness of life's fragility, they consciously value and appreciate their friends. This is especially true for those who remained single, and have no children.

Accepting the expansion of the family through marriage and grandchildren

Midlife is a period of family contraction because of the launching of children and the illness or death of aged parents, and also a time of expansion and regeneration through marriage and the birth of grandchildren. Families must change their relationships with their grown children and incorporate their children's new spouses and families. Although some families experience antagonism with in-laws, parents often form close relationships with sons-in-laws and daughters-in-law (Apter, 2009). This process is facilitated if children have chosen spouses who are compatible with their parents' ethnic, class, and religious values or, alternately, if the family is flexible and open to differences. Family of origin traditions and beliefs regarding the appropriate degree of inclusion of in-laws also govern the melding process. If, on the other hand, the choice of a marriage partner is seen as a reactive challenge or way to distance from the parents, the blending of the two families will be more problematic.

Conflicts may develop around such issues as holiday plans or acceptable terms of address, with parental disapproval deepest about religion, race, or sexual orientation. In our experience, true cutoffs by parents are rare, though disapproval can go on for decades. Adult children are more likely, in our experience, to cut parents off for what they perceive as parental disapproval.

In general, these difficulties are actually displacements for unresolved family issues that are reenacted through the children's marriage. Because women are typically assigned the responsibility for the family's emotional life, the most difficult of these problems usually involve the women in the family: sisters-in-law, mothers with their sons or daughters, and mothers-in-law with daughters-in-law.

Betty Carter and Joan Peters (1996) note that the target of mother-in-law jokes is invariably the husband's mother. In this drama, the son is caught in the middle as family history is repeated. Mothers tend to fear losing their connection to their sons, regardless of who they marry, more than losing their connection to their daughters. The relationship between mother-in-law and daughter-in-law is usually the hot side of the triangle. If the son is distant and unavailable and, for instance, chooses to celebrate holidays and birthdays with his wife's family, the conflict is likely to increase, and often other triangles form especially with sisters-in-law. Fathers tend to remain distant, but are easily pulled into a triangle with mother and son. A triangle that has probably been there before the daughter-in-law joined the family, and that has to do with unresolved issues between fathers and sons, as well as between the parents. In this type of situation, we have found that meeting with the parents alone, if they are living together, to clarify the issues they think are creating the conflict with their son and his wife helps strengthen the parental bond and eases the conflict between mother, son, and daughter-in-law. The goal here is to help the parents talk with their son about their wishes for continued connection and willingness to create opportunities for sharing life with him and his wife. As Carter and Peters advise, the players who are responsible for handling the problem are the family members, not the in-laws.

Expansion of the family during this stage of life is increasingly happening through remarriage, or coupling with new partners. Stepchildren and stepparents have to negotiate new boundaries and adjust to different cultural and social differences, as families are becoming more diverse. For young adults, the tasks of launching and redefining their relationships with their parents often become problematic, as their connections have been compromised by the parents' divorce or separation. Conflicts between stepparents and stepchildren at this stage can be especially difficult because they do not have the bonding to keep from getting into triangles. Stepchildren have a high rate of leaving home prematurely, feeling a lack of support from their parents, or rejection and resentment toward new stepparents or stepchildren who are joining their family. Helping the couple demarcate boundaries that strengthen the bonds between parents and their own children can lessen the disconnection that young adults feel, and can promote more collaboration and inclusiveness as the family reconstructs.

One of the supreme rewards of midlife is grandparenthood. Grandparents say that the pleasure of seeing their own children parent the next generation is a joy that defies description. Family identity is solidified as the family reenacts meaningful life cycle rituals and ceremonies. Grandparents have an opportunity to revisit and perhaps redo their experience as parents without the day-to-day responsibility of child care.

Relationships may also be expanded through joining organizations as volunteers, starting new business ventures, or joining clubs or take classes for fun, where adults at midlife meet new people. For women, especially, this is a time when they may finally feel free to advance a career, or return to school. These activities become opportunities to develop new relationships with colleagues who can be enriching and supportive at this stage of life.

Renegotiating couple relationships

Most midlife couples have found that launching their children is good for their marriages and for each partner's general feeling of well-being. In fact, the presence of children in the home has not been found to correlate with marital happiness in any age group (Kimmel, 2013; Arnett & Fishel, 2013). The removal of stress and the simplification of household routines are certainly key factors in improved relationships at launching. Partners are no longer so focused on their children and can spend more energy on their marriages; with a heightened awareness that time is moving on, partners often expect more from their relationships. By midlife, the very nature of marriage tends to change. Relationships are increasingly characterized by friendship, companionship, equality, tolerance, and shared interests (Cordova, 2009). For many, this renewed focus on the relationship enhances their sexuality, although it is also common for sexual activity to decrease as couples move through midlife.

As with heterosexuals, LGBT couples are often more companionable and less passionate at this phase. Both Gays and lesbians report that, while they remain sexually active, sex does not have the urgency it had in their youth. This is particularly true of lesbians, who are typically less sexually active, though not less affectionate or expressive, than either gay male or heterosexual couples (Green, Bettinger, & Zacks, 1996; Lieblum, 2007). However, while sex may be less frequent, gays and lesbians report sex to be more satisfying in midlife (Nichols, 2005). Johnson and Keren (1996) noted that Gay couples were much less likely than heterosexual couples to view infrequent sex with their partners as an indicator of a relationship problem.

Launching children, however, does not always lead to greater marital happiness. Often marital issues and conflicts are buried during the tumult of the childrearing years and resurface after the children leave. Parents sadly become aware that through the years they have grown apart, and that their interests have changed. They find themselves moving past each other like ships in the night—in different directions and at different paces. As women develop autonomy and move toward outside commitments, careers, or school, men often want more time for leisure and travel and expect their wives to be free to join them (Carter & Peters, 1996). These gender disparities are often confusing and unsettling for the couple and may lead to significant shifts in the marriage, including a redefinition of what constitutes a "good" husband or wife. As women become more independent, there may be a change in the balance of power in the marriage and a renegotiation of marital expectations, plans, and dreams—or in the viability of the marriage itself.

Many couples seek help at this juncture. We have found that doing a three-generational family genogram with couples early in therapy engages them in telling their life stories, not just in relation to the present, but also about their lives before they met and decided to get together. Exploring how their parents and grandparents related to each other at this stage in their life often inspires them to look at similarities and differences. Good questions to ask are "What happened to your parents' relationship after you left home?" and "How were you affected by decisions your parents made about their relationships at that time?" Considering how intergenerational patterns may be influencing their present situation may open a door to new possibilities, and free the couple to make choices toward a more collaborative relationship. A review of their goals and dreams for the future as a couple frequently helps them view their differences in a broader perspective which may or may not be reason to end their marriage. It is always a useful intervention to help them get in touch with the bottom line in their lives, which is knowing that you can live without your partner if necessary (Lerner, 2012).

The shift in expectations between men and women at this phase may be primarily a white middle- and upper-class pattern. Economic and cultural factors, as well as the stresses of immigration, may not allow for much change in gender role expectations in more marginalized groups. However, conflict and difficulties may arise when one spouse begins to adapt and integrate to dominant culture values more rapidly than the other. That spouse may want more independence and autonomy, while the other spouse resists and feels threatened, leading to power struggles. If they come to therapy, in addition to exploring multigenerational family patterns, asking about their mutual expectations, hopes, dreams, their stories of immigration, changes in support systems, and daily experiences of social injustices at work, and in their community helps them gain perspective on the effect these factors may be having on their relationship. This added view may help them be more compassionate, tolerant, and respectful of each other's personal needs and goals.

Divorce at midlife

Sometimes, women or men come to the painful realization that the marriage is empty and make a decision to divorce. While divorce is prevalent in all age groups, it is particularly noticeable at midlife. Actually, the divorce rate in the general population has been lowering since the 1990s, but has doubled for those over 50 (Brown, 2012). In some cases, the empty nest does not lead to the solidification of the marriage. After many years of not dealing with differences, burying feeling and distancing from each other, or turning elsewhere, couples may realize that what is empty is the marriage. Some marriages simply cannot survive without the children present. Some hold onto their children as buffers; others decide to divorce. Two significant factors contribute to the timing of midlife divorces. First, there is a change in the structure of the family and a freedom that comes with the end of the day-to-day responsibility for children. The couple has a newly available time, finances, and emotional focus, which provides the opportunity and resources for change. Second, one or both of the spouses is motivated to seek a divorce by the unpleasant prospect of being left alone with a stranger or an adversary for the remainder of life. Both of these factors are magnified by the realization that time is running out for making such a dramatic life change.

Interestingly, more divorces at midlife are initiated by women (Apter, 1995; Walsh, 2007). Because women today are better educated than they were in the past, they are more marketable for employment. Sometimes, as women begin to experience their independence and develop their competence, they are less willing to remain in a relationship that they recognize as dead. The sense of empowerment that comes with making the decision to end an unsatisfying relationship helps enhance women's self-confidence and their capacity for assertiveness. Though some women may be terrified of being alone and of handling finances, the emotion that most often accompanies the decision to divorce is relief (Apter, 1995). Despite their fears, women rarely regret their decision to divorce (AARP, 2004).

When women turn outward and make a decision to separate, men are often surprised. They may experience a sense of confusion, vulnerability, and abandonment. Some men, as they go through the midlife process of reassessment, develop a renewed appreciation for their marital relationship, or at least they decide that remaining in the marriage is preferable to leaving, while others respond to the questioning of an unhappy marriage by seeking a new, exciting romance. Their developing awareness of mortality and a desire for that last chance for happiness may fuel this decision. However, a decision to end a long marriage is usually a protracted and painful one. Most people, regardless of ethnic or religious background, are likely to experience divorce as a personal failure. This is especially true for women, since they tend to assume it is their responsibility to make relationships work.

CASE ILLUSTRATION

Tina and ED

After 25 years of marriage, Tina (47) and Ed (49), both Jewish and upper-middle-class, launched their second child from the home. Tina had returned to graduate school and was deeply absorbed in her studies, while Ed was focused on his legal career. Despite these distractions, Tina found the silence between them to be a painful indicator of their long-term estrangement. She told Ed that if they did not enter marital therapy, she did not want to remain in the marriage. Ed agreed to enter treatment. After completing the initial assessment, the couple's therapist suggested a 9-month plan: Both Tina and Ed would agree to put their maximum effort into being the best partners they could be for the next 9 months; after that, they would reevaluate their relationship. During that period, in addition to couples work, both partners were individually coached to strengthen their own support systems and to identify and pursue their individual interests and needs. Despite this work, Ed and Tina remained disconnected. After 5 months, Ed disclosed that he was involved in a longstanding affair. With what she described as relief, Tina stated that she had had enough—the marriage was over. Both Tina and Ed agreed to remain in treatment for 3 months to handle the separation process as constructively as possible. They were given the names of local divorce mediators so that the separation and divorce process would be collaborative rather than adversarial. Individual therapeutic work with Tina focused primarily on her learning to manage her finances, while work with Ed primarily addressed developing plans to maintain contact with his children. Tina returned to treatment several months later to address the feelings of loss and failure that followed the initial sense of relief and hopeful expectation. Exploring with

Tina how her traditional Jewish cultural values that emphasize keeping the family together had influenced her avoidance of divorce for so long helped her see how those cultural legacies were contributing to her difficulty in moving on with her life.

Midlife is also a time when many men and women who have kept their sexual orientation secret choose to leave their marriages to live openly as homosexuals. Many LGBT parents wait to come out until their children reach young adulthood, thinking that the children will then be more able to accept their sexual orientation. However, delaying such a decision also has much to do with the ongoing homophobia that exists in the court system and the possibility of losing visitation rights with their children during divorce proceedings (Oswald & Holman, 2013; Bigner, 1996). Although there have been recent changes in some states to protect the civil rights of LGBT individuals, deciding to come out at midlife continues to mean losing the privileges that heterosexuals have in this society, especially when they are married.

CASE ILLUSTRATION

Karen and Stan

Karen, 46, of mixed European ancestry had been married for 18 years to Stan, 49, a successful businessman of similar ancestry, and had a daughter Jill (17) who was starting to plan for college. Karen had given up a teaching career to be a stay-at-home mother and was involved in several volunteer activities in her upper-middle-class community. Before her marriage, she had experienced romantic feelings for women but never acted on them. When she married Stan, she immersed herself in her roles as wife and mother and put those feelings out of mind. Then, after 15 years of marriage, she met Elaine (age 42) at a tennis game and felt drawn to her. The two women developed a close friendship and eventually became romantically involved. Because of Stan's frequent business trips, Karen was able to keep the relationship a secret. As devoted as she came to feel to Elaine, Karen felt equally committed to her family's stability and could not leave her marriage. Feeling torn between two lives and becoming increasingly

depressed about her struggle to maintain the pretense of stability, she entered therapy. Karen stated that she had no intention of leaving her family, but she needed help with her depression. Treatment initially addressed the stress of managing the logistics of her situation, but as she became more engaged she began to look at how her own homophobia was contributing to her feelings of shame and the need to keep her relationship with Elaine secret. Karen was then encouraged to look at her social network to identify those friends who would accept her as a gay woman. She was coached to firm up those relationships and then to slowly share her dilemma. She was also assisted in moving closer to her daughter, as that relationship was most important to her. Eventually, with much coaching, she was able to come out to her daughter and her husband. The road has not been easy, but with the help of therapy Karen continues to develop more honest relationships with her family, friends, and community.

Making the three major life cycle transitions of launching children, divorce, and coming out at the same point is phenomenally difficult. Any one of these life cycle transitions is extremely complex in itself, each requiring major role shifts and life style changes, with feelings that range from liberation to loss. When undertaken simultaneously, the complexity is multiplied.

While engaged in developing more adult-to-adult relationships with their children, LGBT parents are also dealing with their own developmental lag. Bigner (1996) notes that Gay men who come out at midlife may feel out of sync in terms of their development of a stable, positive homosexual identity compared with Gays who come out earlier in life. These men may prematurely seek to replicate the exclusive, committed relationship model of heterosexual marriages, which may complicate their integration into Gay culture.

Renegotiating relationships with parents

Contrary to the image of aging parents being packed off to the nursing home, many elderly people are financially stable and healthy enough to live independently throughout their lives. Unfortunately, we are also seeing that living longer means poorer health among people aging into their senior years (Center for Chronic Disease Control Prevention and Health Promotion, 2013). Those who develop infirmities or illness have been, for the most part, taken care of by their children, especially their daughters and daughters-in-law (Rubin, 2011). This pattern has been changing since more women are working and not able to provide home care to their parents. Families are not always living in the same neighborhood, which means less availability for checking on parents daily, taking them to doctors, or making hospital visits. The situation is drastically changing, but the arrangements that need to be made when parents do become ill are still expected to be made by the adult children. Hospitals and rehabilitation centers still discharge to family, unless the patient is institutionalized. Depending on the family's financial resources, long-term health insurance benefits, and on their knowledge and eligibility for home care and nursing home services paid by government programs such as Medicare and Medicaid, the pressure on the family to provide the care is very high. Working-class families, and especially undocumented immigrants who do not qualify for these services, end up assuming responsibility for the care at home.

Typically, the caregivers have been midlife daughters and daughters-in-law, not sons. Women tend to provide the day-to-day care for their aging parents and sometimes their in-laws, while their husbands and brothers provide financial support and supervise property and other assets. It is not that men do not care, but rather that the tasks of caregiving have traditionally been given to women. This has led to enormous inequities, especially for women in the workforce. Working full-time jobs while care taking for family members can become overwhelming, especially for poor women who lack access to resources. Feeling pressured, they often leave their jobs to do full-time caretaking. These breaks from work can also have serious financial consequences for women, because they often limit their ability to advance and their earning potential, as well as their social security benefits in the future.

Because people are living longer, the age at which adults are providing care for aging parents has moved from the 40s to the 50s. Also, because childbearing has been delayed and children are older when they leave home, people at this stage of life may be caring simultaneously for aging parents and young adults—and perhaps for returning children and grandchildren as well. Midlife adults caught in this competition of roles have been called the "sandwich generation."

Fortunately, this system overload usually occurs when adults are at their peak of competence, control, and ability to handle stress. If the family views caregiving as normal rather than burdensome, the phase will be less stressful. These caregiving expectations are strongly influenced by ethnic values. For example, Latino, Asian American, African American, and Native American families tend to normalize the caregiving role, while Irish and Czech families are less likely to do so. Anglo Americans, who value independence and self-sufficiency to the extreme, tend to find provision of care to the elderly particularly problematic for both generations (McGoldrick et al., 2005). However, even in families where caregiving is culturally supported, women caregivers are at high risk for stress-related illnesses and are sometimes called the hidden patients in the health care system. Sometimes, it is only when their physicians diagnose depression that they seek therapy.

CASE ILLUSTRATION

Delia

Delia, 48, a recently divorced Dominican woman, came to therapy with symptoms of depression and anxiety. She had decided to end the relationship with her husband after 30 years of an unhappy and unsatisfactory marriage, and after learning that he was being unfaithful. Her husband had left and she had stayed home with her two younger daughters who were living with her and commuting to college. The oldest daughter was 24 and had married after graduating from college. Delia had been ridden with guilt and confusion about her decision to separate, but after the divorce she felt a sense of liberation and was enjoying having control of her life. Then her father came to visit from Florida and asked to live with her. She did not want to give up her freedom now that her daughters were almost launched, but as his daughter she felt obligated to take care of him. After a few months, she began to feel resentful, trapped, and angry at her family, especially because her father began to complain that he felt lonely during the day when she was out working. He missed his community in Florida and regretted the decision to come to New Jersey.

Delia's father had been living alone in Florida for several years after her mother's death but in close proximity to his other three daughters. He had enjoyed his independence, but prior to his visit to New Jersey had begun to question his living alone. They worried about him and were relieved when he asked Delia to live with her. They agreed that because Delia was divorced and her daughters were more independent, she would be freer to take on the obligation. There was also a cultural assumption that as the oldest she would assume the responsibility of caretaker for her parents.

In therapy, Delia was able to talk about her conflict. She was feeling very pressured by her family's expectations and caught in a cultural dilemma. Although she felt close to her culture, unlike her siblings she had gone to college, had a graduate degree in social work, and had become more acculturated to the dominant culture. She wanted to be a good Dominican daughter but did not want to give up her freedom at this point in her life. With coaching, she was able to engage her sisters in creating a different plan, one that took into account her personal needs, rather than simply going along with their cultural assumptions that as a single woman and oldest daughter she would be the caretaker. She was also able to talk to her father about his needs and she and her sisters found an assisted living situation in Florida where he felt more connected to a community. They all took turns visiting him, and he visited them.

As a result of these pressures and the potential for burnout, caregivers may need assistance with identifying their own needs and setting appropriate limits. This is particularly true for single midlife women, who are frequently the most isolated members of the family, but who are assumed to be free of other responsibilities and are therefore the most likely to become overwhelmed. More resilient caregivers are able to view this period as an opportunity to resolve old issues with parents. For those who had managed their intergenerational issues as they occurred and moved more smoothly through earlier life cycle transitions, the postlaunching phase provides an opportunity for both generations to continue to adjust their relationship in ways that are mutually satisfying.

Just as people at this stage of life have the opportunity to redefine their relationships with their parents, they may also feel able to establish a more comfortable relationship with in-laws if they are not caught up in old conflicts with them. Recognizing their own mortality, they may now see themselves as peers with in-laws. Feeling on a more equal footing, the constraints of surface politeness or resentment may drop away, and they might be better able to express their own wishes.

> Assess your comprehension of renegotiating relationships with other family members and friends by completing this quiz.

The Death of Parents

Dealing with the death of parents is a normative task of midlife. However, normative does not mean easy. The death of a parent at any time is a major loss, but at midlife there are special developmental tasks that are related to, and may have an impact on, the resolution of their grief. As described by Scharlach and Fredricksen (1993), these tasks include the following.

Acceptance of one's own mortality

This is seen as the critical task of this life cycle phase. People are aware that they are now the executive generation and can no longer look to their parents for guidance. They may become more attentive to their own health, draft their wills, and make their own funeral arrangements. Along with freedom from child care, this awareness of mortality is a prime trigger for the life reassessment process.

Redefinition of family roles and responsibilities

They are now the heads of the family. The role of maintaining family contacts, continuing family rituals and values, and guiding the next generation now falls to them. This redefinition also includes attending to unresolved issues with siblings without the impetus of the older generation to prod them.

Change in self-perception

Those who experience the death of a parent may become more self-reliant and autonomous and at the same time more responsible toward others. This flowering of autonomy and emotional connectedness is often viewed as an indicator of midlife maturity.

Unresolved grief following the death of a parent is usually related to longstanding unresolved issues, such as feelings of dependency, criticism, guilt, or ambivalence. For immigrants, especially if they are undocumented or have few resources, not being able to return to their countries of origin when their parents die often results in unresolved grief. In therapy, helping clients talk about their experience of the death, and encouraging them to engage in mourning rituals, may provide an opportunity to work through some of these issues, even after the parents' death. As with all unresolved issues, if they are not addressed now, they are likely to resurface later in life.

> **Assess your comprehension of the death of parents by completing this quiz.**

— Conclusion

As people live longer, and are more actively engaged in creating new opportunities in their lives, the stage of midlife will continue to expand. Families will need to adjust to the realignments and redefinitions of roles that result from the restructurings at this phase of life. While women typically lead the way toward change, men frequently join the process by being jolted into an awareness that they are at risk of losing relationships they had taken for granted. And they have a good reason to worry. While the overall rate of divorce has decreased in this country in the past decade, it has almost doubled at midlife, and it is being initiated by women over 50! The patriarchal structure by which relationships in this society have been defined and upheld is not working as it did in the past. It is still there, but it is being challenged by social and economic shifts that limit opportunities for men, and move toward the need for more collaborative relationships. Collaboration generates feelings of connection which is essential for men and women to sustain families. For midlife adults, the decision about working on or ending unsatisfying relationships is largely based on whether or not they feel emotionally connected. Renegotiating and redefining relationships are core tasks at this stage of life, but accomplishing these shifts is becoming increasingly complex and difficult as the patterns for launching, and the definition of adulthood change.

Families at this stage are likely to seek therapy when they are having problems launching adult children, if the marriage is not working, when there are financial problems, loss of jobs, illnesses, death of older relatives, cutoffs with family members, or many other disconnections that might become urgent. A Multicontextual Family Life Cycle Framework for assessment and evaluation of these situations will be very helpful in engaging families in treatment. The urgency that people bring at this stage, knowing that it is "now or never," helps them be more open to possibilities, such as reexamining and altering the rigid role definitions that have defined their relationships during the childrearing years. They may be more accessible to clinical interventions than at earlier stages in their life. Thus, rather than being a time of winding down, midlife is a long life cycle stage that can be a fertile time for new options, growth, and change.

> **Recall what you learned in this chapter by completing the Chapter Review.**

References

AARP. (2004). The divorce experience: A study of divorce at midlife and beyond. Executive Summary. Washington, D.C.

Apter, T. (2009). *It's all relative*. The Observer. Retrieved from http://www.guardian.co.uk/lifeandstyle. Accessed 3rd March, 2015.

Apter, T. (1995). *Secret paths: Women in the new midlife*. New York: W. W. Norton.

Arnett, J. J., & Fishel, E. (2013). *When will my grown-up children grow up? Loving and understanding your emerging adult*. New York: Workman Publishing Co. Inc.

Arnett, J. J. (2004). *Emerging adulthood: The winding road from the late teens through the twenties*. New York: Oxford University Press.

Arnett J. J., & Galambos, N. J. (2003). Conceptions of the transition to adulthood among emerging adults in American ethnic groups. In: *Exploring cultural conceptions of the transition to adulthood. New directions for child and adolescent development*, 100, 63–75, Summer 2003, San Francisco, CA: Jossey-Bass.

Bateson, M. C. (2001). *Composing a life* (p. 28). New York: Atlantic Monthly Press.

Bigner, J. (1996). Working with gay fathers: Developmental, post divorce parenting, and therapeutic issues. In J. Laird & R. J. Green (Eds.), *Lesbians and gays in couples and families: A handbook for therapists*, (pp. 370–403). San Francisco, CA: Jossey-Bass.

Brown, S ., (2012). The gray divorce revolution: rising divorce among middle-aged and older adults, 1990–2009. Institute for Population Research.

Carter, B., & Peters, J. K. (1996). *Love, honor and negotiate: Making your marriage work*. New York: Pocket Books.

Center for Chronic Disease Control Prevention and Health Promotion: (2013). *The State of Aging and Health in America*. Atlanta, Georgia.

Cole, E., & Rothblum, E. (1990). Commentary on "Sexuality and the midlife woman." *Psychology of Women Quarterly, 14,* 509–512.

Cordova, J. (2009). *The marriage checkup: A scientific program for sustaining and strengthening*. Maryland: Jason Aronson

Green, R. J., Bettinger, M., & Zacks, E. (1996). Are lesbian couples fused and gay male couples disengaged? Questioning gender straitjackets. In J. Laird and R.-J. Green (Eds.), *Lesbians and gays in couples and families: A handbook for therapists*, (pp. 185-230). San Francisco: Jossey-Bass.

Hunter, S., Sundel, S., & Sundel, M. *(2002). Women at midlife: Life experience and implications for the helping professions*. Washington, DC: National Association of Social Workers.

Hunter, S., (2005). *Midlife and older LGBT adults: Knowledge and affirmative practice for the social services*. New York: Routledge.

Johnson, T. W., & Keren, M. S. (1996). Creating and maintaining boundaries in male couples. In J. Laird & R.-J. Green (Eds.), *Lesbians and gays in couples and families: A handbook for therapists,* (pp. 231–250). San Francisco, CA: Jossey-Bass.

Kimmel, M. (2013). *The gendered society*. New York: Oxford University Press.

Kimmel, M. (2008). *Guyland: The perilous world where boys become men. Understanding the critical years between 16 and 20*. New York: Harper Collins.

Leiblum, S. (2003). *Getting the sex you want: a woman's guide to becoming proud, passionate, and pleased in bed*. New York: ASJA Press.

Lerner, H. (2012). *Marriage rules: A manual for the married and the coupled up*. New York: Gotham Books.

Lott, T. (2013). When adult children become your friends. The Guardian. Retrieved from www.theguardian.com. Accessed 3rd March, 2015.

McGoldrick, M., Giordano, J., & Garcia Preto, N. (Eds.) (2005). *Ethnicity and family therapy*. New York: The Guilford Press.

Neugarten, B. (1968). The awareness of middle age. In B. Neugarten (Ed.), *Middle age and aging: A reader in social psychology* (pp. 93–98). Chicago, IL: University of Chicago Press.

Nichols, M. (2005). Sexual function in lesbians and lesbian relationship. In I. Goldstein, C. Meston, S. Davis, & A. Traish (Eds.), *Women's sexual function and dysfunction: Stud , diagnosis, and treatment*. London, England: Taylor & Francis.

Norsigian, J . *(2011) Our bodies, ourselves*. Boston's Women's Health Book Collective.

Oswald, R. F., & Holman, E. G. (2013). Place Matters: LGB families in Community Context. In A. E. Goldberg & K. R. Allen (Eds.), *LGBT-Parent Families*. New York: Springer.

Pew Research Center. (2013). *Social and demographic trends: A rising share of young adults live in their parents' home*. Washington, DC.

Quigley, B. (2012). *Working and poor in the USA*. Center for Constitutional Rights. Truthout.

Rosin, H. (2012). *The end of men.* New York: Penguin Press.

Rubin, L. (2011). *The dilemma of taking care of elderly parents.* Salon.

Sandberg, S. (2013). *Lean in: Women, work, and the will to lead.* New York: Knopf.

Scharlach, A. E., & Fredricksen, K. (1993). Reactions to the death of a parent during midlife. *Omega, 27,* 307–319.

Skolnick, A. (2009). The life course revolution. In A. S. Skolnick & J. H. Skolnick (Eds.), *Family in transition* (15th ed., pp. 31–39). Boston, MA: Allyn & Bacon.

Slater, S. (1995). *The lesbian family life cycle.* New York: The Free Press.

Walsh, J. (2007, November 28). *Are women initiating divorce?* Retrieved December 29, 2009, from http://ezinearticles.com/?Are-Women-Initiating-Divorce?&id=855366

Woods, N. , and Mitchell E. (2006) Depressed mood symptoms during the menopausal transition: observations from the Seattle Midlife Women's Health Study. *American Sociological Review, 55,* 235–242.

Chapter 18

Families in Later Life: Challenges, Opportunities, and Resilience

Froma Walsh

Learning Outcomes

- Describe how older populations and the family life course are changing in today's world.
- Examine the challenges and opportunities that retirement presents to individuals and families.
- Explain the impact that financial security, or lack thereof, has on later life.
- Identify and describe the benefits of grandparenthood for each generation in a family.
- Describe the challenges posed by chronic illness for both individuals and families.
- Discuss challenges faced by caregivers during later life.
- Describe how later-life challenges of parents interact with developmental issues of their children at their concurrent life phases.

For age is opportunity no less than youth itself, though in another dress, and as the evening twilight fades away, the sky is filled with stars invisible by day.

—Longfellow

Our elders never became senile because they were needed right to the end. Aunts and uncles taught you the philosophies and principles that you lived and worked by.

—Lavina White—Haida Nation, Alaska.

Introduction

This chapter examines the challenges, opportunities, and resilience of individuals, couples, and families in later life. Increasingly, older adults with prospects of greater longevity and years of good health are re-visioning possibilities for meaning and satisfaction. Salient issues in this phase concern retirement and financial security, grandparenthood, chronic illness and caregiving, end-of-life issues, and the loss of loved ones. Clinical guidelines and case illustrations are offered to address common problems and to encourage the potential for personal and relational integrity and positive growth in intimate, companionate, and intergenerational bonds.

The Graying of the Family

Declining birth rates, health care advances, and increasing longevity are contributing to the unprecedented rise in the number and proportion of older people in societies worldwide (Kinsella & He, 2009). In the United States, average life expectancy has increased from 47 years in 1900 to over 78 years by 2010, with women outliving men by 4 to 5 years (National Center on Health Statistics, 2012). Our aging population is also becoming more racially and ethnically diverse. However, health care disparities in prevention and treatment take a heavy toll on low-income families, especially in blighted communities. Life expectancy for African Americans is significantly lower than for Whites particularly for Black men. Of note, among persons who survive to age 65—and eligibility for Medicare—the differences in remaining life expectancy diminish, and even more so at the age of 75. Hispanics have the highest life expectancy, attributable at least, in part, to their strong kinship support networks.

The baby boom generation will soon swell the over-65 population to record levels: up from 8 percent in 1950 to 20 percent by 2030. With medical advances and healthier lifestyles, increasing numbers are living into their 80s, 90s, and past 100. For most Americans, older adulthood is being redefined as two life periods: persons aged 65 to 84 who are mostly healthy and vibrant and the very old, over 85, the fastest-growing segment of the older population and the group most vulnerable to serious illness and disabling conditions. Although research and clinical approaches tend to be individually oriented, family bonds are central in later life.

> Assess your comprehension of the graying of the family by completing this quiz.

The Varying and Extended-Family Life Course

The family life course is becoming ever more lengthened and varied (Walsh, 2012b). Four- and five-generation families add both opportunity and complexity in balancing members' needs and family resources (Bengtson, 2001; Bengtson & Lowenstein, 2003). Increasingly, adult children past retirement, with limited resources, are involved in caring for their elders. Multigenerational relational networks are becoming smaller and top-heavy, with a declining proportion of younger people. Greater insecurity and intergenerational tensions are likely, with global economic downturns and uncertainty in employment and benefits affecting both young and old. The trend toward having few or no children will leave aging persons with fewer intergenerational connections and strain family resources for financial and caretaking support.

Pathways through middle and later life are increasingly varied. With greater life expectancy, couples raising children may have 30 to 40 years ahead after launching them. It is challenging for one relationship to meet changing developmental priorities of both partners over a lengthened life course. While divorce rates are in the spotlight, it is perhaps more remarkable that over 50 percent of first marriages last a lifetime. Increasingly, couples are celebrating 50 and 60 years of marriage. Also, many single, divorced, and widowed older adults are finding happiness in new relationships. As one woman in her 70s remarked, "If I could count all three of my husbands, I've been married for over 40 years!"

Over a long lifetime, two or three marriages, with periods of cohabitation and single living, are becoming increasingly common, creating complex kin networks in later life (Walsh, 2012b). Single older adults and couples who are unmarried or without children forge a variety of significant bonds with siblings, cousins, nephews and nieces, godchildren, close friends, and social networks. In our mobile world, many relationships are carried on at a distance and sustained through frequent cellphone and Internet contact: Grandparents unable to be present for a wedding, birth, family gathering, or other milestone now joyfully witness and even participate in the event.

The family and social time clocks associated with aging are also more fluid. As many become grandparents and great-grandparents, others are beginning or extending parenthood. With various assisted reproductive strategies, adults in middle age, both gay and straight, are having children. With remarriage, come new stepparent relationships. Men, who commonly remarry younger women, often raise second families in later years.

The dramatic societal transformations over recent decades have increased intergenerational differences between traditional and contemporary roles and relationships. For instance, elders may expect daughters, but not sons, to be readily available to provide care when most women at midlife are now in the workforce, with stressful conflicting demands (Brody, 2004). Tensions are particularly likely between older immigrants, who carry more traditional values from their cultures of origin, and younger generations raised in our society. For instance, traditional Eastern Asian families value harmony and filial piety and expect that elders will be honored and obeyed. Cultural dissonance arises when younger generations depart from those norms.

Family therapy can facilitate family harmony with new mutual understanding by empowering family members to draw on personal strengths, recognizing, negotiating, and incorporating multiple worldviews and values (Lee & Mjelde-Mossey, 2004).

Aging gay men and lesbian women meet needs for meaning and intimacy in varied ways, influenced by their past experiences, present life circumstances, and social environment (Cohler & Galatzer-Levy, 2000; Neustifter, 2008). Those who built life structures with their sexual orientation closeted before the gay rights movement often find greater authenticity and freedom of expression in open committed relationships and possibilities for marriage in later years. Many older gay men, who survived the HIV/AIDS epidemic that ravaged the gay community, confronted both their mortality and tragic loss of partners and friends earlier in life passage.

To be responsive to the growing diversity of relationships and households in society, our view of "family" must be expanded to fit the lengthened and varied life course. Therapeutic objectives must be attuned to the challenges and preferences that make each individual, couple, and family unique. We will need to learn how to help family members live successfully in complex and changing relationship systems, buffer stressful transitions, and make the most of their later-life experiences.

> Assess your comprehension of the varying and extended-family life course by completing this quiz.

From Ageism and Gerophobia to a Larger Vision of Later Life

Our society has not readily confronted the challenges of later life or seen the opportunities that can come with maturity. Our gerophobic culture has held a fearful, pessimistic view of aging as decay, with the elderly stereotyped as old-fashioned, rigid, boring, useless, demented, and burdensome. Institutionalized forms of ageism perpetuate workplace discrimination. Adults older than 50 years have disproportionately lost jobs in the recent economic recession and are least likely to be rehired. With social media glorifying youth, many cling to youth and strive to recapture it, facing aging with dread or denial.

A grim picture of aging has been portrayed in the trajectory view of progressive deterioration, decline, and loss, ending in death. Biomedical and mental health fields have tended to pathologize later life, focusing on disorders and disability and discounting functional difficulties as an irreversible part of aging. Negative stereotypes of older persons have fostered pessimistic assumptions by clinicians that they are less interesting than younger clients, a poor investment for therapy, and too resistant to change. They are too often treated custodially, with a pat on the hand and a medication refill.

A larger vision of later life is required, recognizing the potential change, growth, and new learning that can occur. Scholars are reformulating conceptions of later years. Some propose three distinct periods: extended middle age (to age 75); old age (to 85); and very old age (85 and over). Senior scholars joke that their own definition of old age is a few years older than their current age. Extended middle age is a dynamic, new cultural shift for most people in their 60s and early 70s, who are healthy, active, and productive. Lawrence-Lightfoot (2009) calls this period "the third chapter" of adulthood, when traditional norms, rules, and rituals of careers seem less encompassing and restrictive; when many women and men embrace new challenges and search for greater meaning in life. In her interviews, individuals across races and social classes related stories involving loss and liberation, vulnerability and resilience, looking back and giving forward to others. Their vital engagement in life, while appreciating its unpredictable course, involves the need for grieving losses and reinventing themselves and their future, the need for new structure, purpose, and leisure for new learning and experimentation in uncharted post-career years. As assisted living and more extended care are needed, new possibilities for living arrangements and community involvement are being envisioned for more satisfying and meaningful later years.

The vital importance of family bonds

Stereotypes of American families have held that adult children do not care about their elders; have infrequent, obligatory contact; and dump them in institutions. Many presume that older adults are too set in their ways to change longstanding interaction patterns. In fact, family bonds and intergenerational relations for most Americans are mutually beneficial, dynamic, and coevolving throughout adult life (Bengtson, 2001). Families provide most social interaction, caregiving assistance, and psychological support for elderly loved ones. The vast majority of older adults live independently or with children or other relatives, including siblings and very aged parents.

Most couples who weather the inevitable storms in long lasting relationships and childrearing report high relationship satisfaction in their post-launching years, with more time and resources for individual and shared pursuits. Priorities for companionship and caregiving come to the fore. Although sexual contact may be less frequent, intimacy can deepen with a sense of shared history. New satisfactions are found in shared activities, such as travel, and in bonds with grandchildren.

The importance of sibling relationships commonly increases over adulthood (Cicirelli, 1995). The centenarian Delany sisters, born into a southern African American family, pursued careers and lived together most of their lives, crediting their remarkable resilience to their enduring bond. They shared enjoyment in conversation and laughter, watched over each other, and saw their differences as balancing each other out (Delany & Delany, 1993).

Most older Americans in good health prefer to maintain a separate household from children, yet they sustain frequent contact, reciprocal emotional ties, and mutual support in a pattern aptly termed "intimacy at a distance" (Blenkner, 1965). The proximity of family members and contact by phone and the Internet are especially important to those who live alone. Adult children and grandchildren also benefit in many ways from frequent contact with elders. However, in our mobile society, uprooting for jobs or retirement can strain the ability to provide direct caregiving and support in times of crisis.

In an ageist social context and a clinical focus on family childrearing phases, the family literature has given scant attention to the family in later life, other than caregiving challenges, and has rarely addressed the priorities and assets of older adult members. A life course perspective on family development and aging is required, emphasizing both continuity and change.

Later-life transitions and challenges

The family as a system, along with its elder members, confronts major adaptational challenges in later life. Changes with retirement, grandparenthood, illness, death, and widowhood alter complex relationship patterns, often requiring family support, adjustment to loss, reorientation, and reorganization. Many disturbances are associated with difficulties in family adaptation. Yet such challenges also present opportunities for relational transformation and growth.

A family's approach to later-life challenges evolves from its earlier patterns, life experiences, and cultural worldview. Systemic processes that develop over the years influence the ability of family members to adapt to losses and flexibly meet new demands. Certain established patterns, once functional, may no longer fit changing priorities and constraints. For families who have raised children, their launching from home sets the stage for relationships in later life. With the structural contraction of the family from a two-generational household to the couple or single parent, relationships with young adult children are redefined and parental involvement typically refocuses on individual and couple life pursuits. Most parents adjust well to this "empty nest" transition and welcome their increased freedom from childrearing responsibilities (Neugarten, 1996). Yet, many parents continue to provide financial and emotional support through college and beyond, and many adult children, for economic reasons, return to the nest.

> **Assess your comprehension of from ageism and gerophobia to a larger vision of later life by completing this quiz.**

Retirement

Retirement represents a significant milestone and adjustment for individuals and couples. Those who are healthy and financially secure are reinventing later life, from the stereotyped retreat in a comfortable rocking chair to new structure and purpose, with time for leisure, learning, and new pursuits. Family therapist Lorraine Wright has relabeled retirement as "preferment," a transition offering the opportunity to refocus energies to fit emerging needs and preferences. Many take on meaningful projects or new careers; some start riding Harleys and join motorcycle clubs.

For most, retirement involves the loss of job roles, status, and productivity, valued as our culture's (male) standards for identity, success, and self-esteem in adult life. Whether retirement was desired or forced will affect adjustment. Even when early retirement or a job layoff is due to the economy or a company's relocation, self-doubts can linger, as well as anxiety and bitterness at the loss of benefits and security. Loss of income and one's role as financial provider can significantly strain relationships. Residential change, common after launching children or retirement, can add further dislocation and loss of connections with nearby family and social networks, as well as familiar services and trusted health care providers. Losses are felt in giving up a home in which children were raised and many milestones experienced.

A successful transition involves a reorientation of values and goals and a redirection of energies and relationships. The trend for older adults to move away to age-segregated retirement developments has been shifting to a preference to remain in or near their communities. Many downsize from suburban homes to apartments close to shopping, restaurants, cultural opportunities, and young people. Many parents wait for adult children to settle, planning to move to be near them and their grandchildren. With job mobility so common, some elders experience subsequent uprooting to follow their children yet again. Often, adult children live in different regions, and grandparents shuttle around to spend time with all.

Retirement can be financially devastating for those who lack retirement savings and benefits. In the current economic downturn, many must continue working long past retirement age. Those who have lost jobs and benefits must find new work, but face age discrimination. Such pressures force a major

shift in expectations and later-life plans. Because of the stigma of dependency in our dominant culture, with its ethos of self-reliance, most older adults are reluctant to ask for or accept financial assistance from their adult children; issues of pride and shame keep many from even telling their children that they are financially strapped. A family consultation is helpful to enable discussion of sensitive issues, contextualize the situation, and find respectful ways to be of assistance.

In traditional homemaker/breadwinner marriages, couples may have difficulty with the husband's retirement, accompanied by losses of his job-related status and social network, especially if they have been uprooted from kin and social networks to accommodate career moves. Another challenge involves a retired husband's incorporation inside the home, with changes in role expectations, time together, and the quality of interaction. If he feels that he has earned full leisure yet expects his wife to continue to shoulder household responsibilities, her resentment likely will build. Dual-earner couples may get out of sync if one continues working past the other's retirement. For successful adaptation, couples need to renegotiate their relationship to achieve a new balance. With priorities and concerns shared through open communication, relational resilience can be strengthened as partners pull together to reshape their lives, plan financial security, and explore new interests to provide meaning and satisfaction (Walsh, 2015).

When a child has filled a void in a marriage, it can complicate a couple's subsequent adjustment to retirement.

CASE ILLUSTRATION

Maria, Luis, and Raul

Maria, 63, brought her husband Luis, 67, for treatment of alcohol abuse since his retirement. Living with the couple was their 42-year-old son Raul, who had returned home after a divorce. Longstanding close attachment between the mother and son had stabilized a chronically conflictual marriage over the years, when Luis had worked long hours outside the home. Retirement shifted the balance, as Luis, now home all day, felt like an unwanted intruder. Lacking job and breadwinning status as sources of self-esteem, he felt like an unworthy rival to his son for his wife's affection at a time in his life when he longed for more companionship with her. Competitive struggles fueled Luis's drinking, erupting into angry confrontations, as Maria sided protectively with their son.

In Latino families, as in many ethnic groups, parent–child bonds are commonly stronger than the marital dyad (see Falicov, Chapter 12). However, in this family, a pattern that had functioned over many years became a highly conflictual triangle when retirement disrupted the relationship system.

> **Assess your comprehension of retirement by completing this quiz.**

Grandparenthood

As people live longer, growing numbers become grandparents and great-grandparents (Drew & Silverstein, 2004). The experience can hold great significance, as Margaret Mead (1972), on becoming a grandparent, described "the extraordinary sense of having been transformed not by any act of one's own but by the act of one's child" (p. 302). Grandparenthood can offer a new lease on life in numerous ways. First, it fulfills needs for generativity through one's descendants, easing the acceptance of mortality. As Mead experienced, "In the presence of grandparent and grandchild, past and future merge in the present" (p. 311). Grandparenthood also stimulates reminiscence of one's own earlier childrearing and childhood experiences. Such perspectives can be valuable in gaining appreciation of one's life and parenting satisfactions despite regrets one may have.

Grandparenthood is a systemic transition that alters intergenerational relationships (Spark, 1974). When adult children become parents, it presents an opportunity for reconnection and healing of old intergenerational wounds, as they begin to identify with the challenges inherent in childrearing and develop more empathy for their parents' best intentions. Grandparents and great-grandparents, with knowledge of five or more generations, are in a unique position to connect the younger generations with those that came before them through their personal recollections and stories. Grandparents and grandchildren may enjoy a special bond that is not complicated by the responsibilities, obligations, and conflicts in the parent–child relationship (Mueller & Elder, 2003). It is often said that grandparents and grandchildren get along so well because they have a common enemy. Such an alliance can be problematic if a grandchild is triangulated in a parent–grandparent conflict.

CASE ILLUSTRATION

Sharleen

After the death of her father, Sharleen, age 32, a single parent, and her son Shaun, age 6, moved in with her mother to consolidate limited resources. Shaun's misbehavior and disrespect toward Sharleen brought the family to therapy. At the first session, Shaun went to his grandmother for help in taking off his boots. She quickly took over the discussion while Sharleen shrank back. Shaun, sitting between them, glanced frequently to his grandmother for cues. Each time Sharleen and her mother started to argue, Shawn drew attention to himself. He ignored Sharleen's attempts to quiet him, but responded immediately to his grandmother.

The grandmother complained that she was overburdened by having to take care of "both children." Sharleen felt that her mother undercut her efforts to take more responsibility by criticizing everything she did as "not right," meaning not her way. We explored the impact of the grandfather's recent death from a heart attack. The grandmother was devastated by the loss and uncertain how to go on with her life. Taking charge to help her daughter raise Shaun filled the void. Feeling ashamed of her financial needs, it also gave her a sense of value. We considered the loss and changes for all three generations and then directed attention to realigning relationships so that Sharleen could be a more effective mother with her son while honoring the grandmother's valuable contribution and her role as head of the household. Sharleen agreed to respect her mother's wishes about how she wanted her home kept as her mother agreed to respect Sharleen's ways of childrearing and to support her parental leadership.

In poor communities with high rates of early pregnancy, grandparenting commonly occurs early. Grandmothers, often in middle age, commonly provide childcare, especially when single parents must work. In kinship care, many grandparents are assuming the primary role in raising their grandchildren, either through legal guardianship or informal arrangements, when parents are unable to assume responsibility, as in cases of disability, substance abuse, or incarceration (Engstrom, 2012). While this meets a crucial need for the youngsters, it often takes a toll on grandparents' health, especially when they are on a limited income and have other heavy responsibilities. A family council meeting can involve others, such as aunts and uncles, in supportive roles and provide respite for the grandparent. Grandfathers are often hidden resources; even those who may not have been involved in raising their children may welcome the opportunity to play a mentoring role for grandchildren.

For many older adults, foster grandparenting can enrich later life, serve as a resource for single and working parents, and provide connectedness across the generations, especially where more informal contacts are lacking in age-segregated living arrangements. Seniors can also be encouraged to volunteer in childcare centers and after-school tutoring and mentoring programs, contributing their knowledge and interest, helping children learn, and enhancing their development.

> **Assess your comprehension of grandparenthood by completing this quiz.**

Chronic Illness and Family Caregiving

As our society ages, the number of people with chronic conditions is increasing and those impaired are living longer than ever before (Aldwin & Gilbert, 2013). Even for those in good health, fears of loss of physical and mental functioning, chronic pain, and

progressively degenerative conditions are common. Health problems and severity vary greatly. Among seniors aged 65 to 84, arthritis, high blood pressure, and heart disease are most prevalent. By the age of 85 or older, the risks of cancer and extensive disabilities increase, combined with cognitive, visual, and hearing impairment. Physical and mental declines contribute to, and are exacerbated by, depression and anxiety. Suicide rates also increase with age, particularly for older White men.

Because our society lacks a coherent approach to care for people with disabling chronic conditions, too many live with poor health and lack access to quality services. Families in poverty, largely in minority groups, are most vulnerable to environmental conditions that heighten the risk of serious illnesses, disabilities, and caregiver strain, as well as early mortality. Diseases such as asthma, diabetes, high blood pressure, and heart disease are most prevalent among the poor.

Family caregiving for the growing numbers of frail elderly is a major concern (Qualls & Zarit, 2009). By 2020, it is expected that 14 million persons will need long-term care. As average family size decreases, fewer children are available for caregiving and sibling support. In 1970, there were 21 potential caregivers for each person 85 or older; by 2030, there are expected to be only 6 potential caregivers, severely straining intergenerational resources. Recent findings that 20 percent of women aged 40 to 44 had no biological children intensify concern about the provision of care as this group reaches advanced age (Kinsella & He, 2009).

With later childbearing, many at midlife—the so-called sandwich generation—are caring simultaneously for their children and for aging parents, grandparents, and other relatives. Finances can be drained as children's college expenses collide with medical expenses for elders. Increasingly, adult children past retirement, with their own declining health and resources, assume care for their parents. The average age of caregivers is 57, but 25 percent are 65 to 74, and 10 percent are over 75. The role of primary caregiver has traditionally been assigned to women; currently, nearly three in four are wives, daughters, or daughters-in-law. Now that the vast majority of women are in the workforce, earning essential family income, a juggling of work and family roles can be exhausting (Brody, 2004).

Elders with chronic conditions increasingly receive care at home, often requiring costly treatments and medications, frequent hospitalizations, and intensive home-based care for daily functioning. Family and friends are the front lines of support. Nearly three quarters of disabled people rely exclusively on these informal caregivers (Qualls & Zarit, 2009). Prolonged caregiving takes a heavy toll. Eighty percent of caregivers provide help 7 days a week, averaging 4 hours daily. In addition to housekeeping, shopping, and meal preparation, two thirds assist with feeding, bathing, toilet, and dressing. The lack of useful management guidelines by most medical specialists adds to confusion and frustration. Some aspects of chronic illness are especially disruptive for families, such as sleep disturbance, incontinence, delusional ideas, and aggressive behavior. One symptom and consequence of family distress is elder abuse, which can occur in overwhelmed families, stretched beyond their means and tolerance, or in families with a history of substance abuse and violence.

Dementia: The long goodbye

Progressive brain disorders are among the most difficult conditions for families. Alzheimer's disease and other dementias affect 1 in 10 people older than 65 years—and nearly half of persons older than 85 years. Alzheimer's disease has been aptly called "the long goodbye" because of the progressive losses of functioning, identity, family roles, and relationships. These ambiguous losses complicate caregiving and mourning processes (Boss, 1999). The irreversible course of this devastating disease can last from a few years to more than 20 years, becoming an agonizing psychosocial and financial dilemma for families. Over time, mental and physical capacities are stripped away in gradual memory loss, disorientation, impaired judgment, and loss of control over bodily functions. In early stages, family members, not understanding the disorder, often become frustrated when the individual repeatedly asks the same questions, forgets earlier answers, or prepares a meal and forgets to serve it. With impaired memory, judg-

ment, and "sundowning," they may wander off, get lost, and forget who they are and where they live. They may make disastrous financial decisions. As the illness progresses, it is most painful for loved ones when they are not even recognized or are confused with others, even with those long deceased. Gentle humor can ease such situations, as in one case: At a weekly dinner with his parents, as David's mother cleared the table and went into the kitchen, his father leaned over to him and said: "Did you see that woman there? If I wasn't a married man I could really go for her!" David replied, "Dad, you are the luckiest man on earth because you ARE married to her—she's your wife!" They laughed together and his mother enjoyed the compliment.

With limited medical interventions for Alzheimer's disease, treatment primarily addresses symptom management and custodial care. Most families try to keep their loved one at home as long as possible, yet it is particularly difficult when caregivers live at a distance and must travel back and forth frequently. Part-time or full-time nurses or paid caregivers, extended family, and social support networks are crucial in coping with stresses, providing respite, and dealing with crisis situations. Adult daycare programs offer a therapeutic milieu, contact with others, and pleasurable activities for the impaired person as they relieve caregiver strain. Family psychoeducation provides useful illness-related information and management guidelines over the course of an illness, reduces caregiver anxiety and depression, and addresses functional and relational losses (Rolland, 2012).

Family intervention issues and priorities

With all elder caregiving, family intervention priorities include (1) stress reduction; (2) information about the medical condition, functional abilities, limitations, and prognosis; (3) useful guidelines for sustaining care, problem solving, and optimal functioning; and (4) links to supplementary services to support family efforts. Communities need to support families through a range of services, from day programs to affordable assisted living, as well as commitment to active participation of elders, including those with disabilities, in community life.

Family dynamics may require attention. For couples, chronic illness and disability can skew the relationship between the impaired partner and caregiving spouse over time. It can deplete financial savings and dash plans for the golden years. Couple therapy can help partners to gain mutual empathy; address such issues as blame, shame, and guilt; and rebalance their relationship to live and love as fully as possible (Rolland, 2012).

Intergenerational issues around autonomy and dependency come to the fore as aging parents lose functioning and control over their bodies and their lives. Meeting their increasing needs should not be seen as a parent–child role reversal, which can be infantilizing and shaming. Even when adult children give financial, practical, and emotional support to aging parents, they do not become parents to their parents. Despite frailties or childlike functioning, aged parents have had many decades of adult life experience and deserve respect as elders. Family therapists can facilitate conversations about dependency issues with sensitivity and a realistic appraisal of strengths and limitations. Many elders worry about being a burden on loved ones. Giving children the power of attorney also involves a loss of self-determination. In many cases, adult children have to challenge a parent's judgment and take control of risky behavior. In our mobile society, driving a car is a symbol of independence and freedom. Older adults, especially men, often refuse to give up driving, even with seriously impaired vision, reflexes, and judgment, and may be unwilling to admit the danger. In one family, the sons had to take away the father's keys, only to find he had driven again using other keys hidden away. Next, they removed the car's battery; the crafty father called a service station to install a new one. With caring, firmness, and humor, rather than angry rebuke, they appreciated the father's cleverness while taking further precautions.

In some cases, an aging parent, losing control and functioning, may become overly dependent on adult children. While one adult child may become overly responsible through anxiety or prior role functioning, others may distance themselves. A vicious cycle may ensue, with escalating neediness, burden, and resentment.

CASE ILLUSTRATION

The Zambrano family

Mrs. Zambrano, an 82-year-old widow, was hospitalized with multiple somatic problems and secondary symptoms of disorientation and confusion. She complained that her two sons, Vince, age 46, and Tony, 43, did not care whether she lived or died. The sons reluctantly came for a family interview. Tony believed that his mother's hospitalization was merely a ploy for sympathy, to make him feel guilty for not being at her beck and call as Vince was. He said that he had learned to keep his distance. Vince became increasingly frustrated: The more he did for his mother, the more helpless and critical she became. He felt drained by her neediness and complaints and was resentful toward Tony. This repeated a pattern in childhood: With the father often away on business, the mother had turned to Vince to meet her needs. The brothers were helped to realign their relationship to share responsibilities and to gain appreciation of their mother's losses, loneliness, and anxiety that her life was slipping out of her control. Raised to be "doers" and problem solvers, they felt helpless in the face of decline, death, and loss, no matter how much they did for her. They were encouraged to take turns visiting her and simply to be more fully present, sharing stories and reminiscences, which eased her anxiety, improved her functioning, and reassured her of their love.

From designated caregiver to caregiving team

In approaching all serious illness, we need to expand the traditional narrow focus on one individual who is designated as the caregiver to a collaborative approach to caregiving, involving all family members as a *caregiving team*. Most often, one adult child becomes overburdened and siblings are on the sidelines, unsure how to be supportive (Bedford, 2005; Siblings and the Life Cycle, Chapter 10). The sharing of responsibilities and challenges can become an opportunity to strengthen bonds and heal strained relationships. In families torn by past grievances, conflict, or estrangement, caregiving is likely to be more complicated. Life-and-death decisions can be emotionally fraught.

CASE ILLUSTRATION

JoEllen

JoEllen, 38 years old, was deeply conflicted when her father, hospitalized for complications from chronic alcohol abuse, asked her to donate a kidney to save his life. She felt enraged to be asked to give up something so important when he had not been there for her as a father over the years. He had been a mean drunk, often absent and many times violent. She was also angry that he had brought on his deteriorated condition by his drinking and had refused to heed his family's repeated pleas to stop. Yet, a dutiful daughter and a compassionate Christian woman, she did not want her father to die because she denied him her kidney.

I broadened the dilemma to include her siblings, suggesting that she discuss it with them, but JoEllen dismissed the idea, saying they were estranged and rarely in contact. I then encouraged her to talk with her mother, who informed her that the father had also asked her siblings for the kidney donation. JoEllen was furious that old rivalries would be stirred up: who would be seen as the good giving child or the bad selfish ones. She now took initiative to get the siblings together. When they met, old rivalries melted as they began to grapple with the dilemma.

I widened the focus forward, suggesting that they begin to envision how they might collaborate, proactively, to meet future challenges that might arise in caring for *both* aging parents. With this conversation, the eldest brother volunteered his kidney for their father. He was less conflicted because he remembered good times with the father before his problem with drinking. The others offered to support him and agreed to keep in contact and to contribute to their parents' future well-being, forging a new solidarity.

Placement planning

The point at which failing health requires consideration of extended-care placement can be a crisis for the whole family. Placement is usually turned to only as a last resort, when resources are stretched to the limit, and in later stages of mental or physical decline. Still, feelings of guilt and abandonment and stereotypes of institutionalization can make a placement decision highly stressful.

CASE ILLUSTRATION

The Gupta Family

Mrs. Gupta called for help, stating that she "felt helpless to control" her teenage son and feared that he "needed to be institutionalized." A family assessment revealed an escalating cycle—his defiance of her attempts to control his every activity—over the past 8 months, since Mrs. Gupta's mother had been brought to live in their home. She wept as she described her mother's deteriorating Parkinson's condition, feeling unable to provide round-the-clock care. She couldn't sleep at night after finding her mother on the floor one morning. Her control struggles with her son deflected her heightened concern: that her mother's condition was beyond her control and institutionalization might be needed. This provoked a crisis for her: At her father's deathbed, a year earlier, he had asked her to promise that she would always care for her mother. She had also heard stories that in regions of India, widowed women were banished from their homes and communities. She could not bear to abandon her mother. She felt alone with her dilemma, as her husband had distanced, preoccupied by his work.

This case underscores the importance of inquiry about elderly family members even when problems are presented elsewhere in the family system. It is also crucial to explore a spouse's distancing and lack of support. In this case, the husband revealed that he was trying to avoid his own hidden guilt over having left the care of his dying mother to his sisters. This crisis now became an opportunity for both of them to explore ways together to provide the best care in this situation, both in-home and in a care facility, without abandoning their loved one—or each other.

Family sessions, best done proactively, can enable members to assess needs and both kin and community resources and to share feelings, concerns, and mutual support in reaching a decision. Often, new solutions emerge that can support the elder's remaining in the community, with part-time or full-time in-home nursing care or in assisted living. Respite for caregivers is crucial to their well-being. When extended-care placement is needed, therapists can help families view it as the most viable way to provide adequate care and support their efforts in navigating the maze of options and coverage.

The importance of prevention for healthy and satisfying later years cannot be overstressed (Weil, 2005). Efforts are needed to lower risk factors that diminish life expectancy and well-being: the rampant increase of obesity, fast foods, sedentary life styles, and the loss of family ties, community participation, and productive employment or activity. We must also revision chronic care beyond the narrow focus on medical services and nursing homes. A report commissioned by the Robert Wood Johnson Foundation nearly two decades ago (Institute for Health and Aging, 1996) advanced a broader view to address chronic care challenges for the twenty-first century. The report envisioned a system of care: a spectrum of integrated services—medical, personal, social, and rehabilitative—to assist people with chronic conditions to live fuller lives. A continuum of care is needed to ensure that individuals and their families receive the level and type of care to fit their condition and changing needs over time and to support independent living, optimal functioning, social connections, and well-being.

> Assess your comprehension of chronic illness and family caregiving by completing this quiz.

End-of-Life Challenges and Loss of Loved Ones

Dealing with terminal illness is among families' most painful challenges, complicated by agonizing end-of-life decisions. Most people hope for a natural death, but what is a natural death in our times? Most elderly persons die after a long, progressively worsening illness and disability. Medical technologies prolonging life and the dying process pose unprecedented family challenges. It is crucial to address elders' needs for dignity and control in their own dying process as well as palliative care for comfort and pain alleviation. Clinicians need to work with families to reduce suffering, discuss important end-of-life decisions, and make the most of precious time together (Rolland, 2012; Walsh, 2015).

Later life is a season of cumulative losses of loved ones, friends, and peers. Family adaptation to loss involves shared grieving and a reorganization of the family relationship system (Walsh & McGoldrick, 2004). Avoidance, silence, and secrecy complicate mourning. When patient and family hide knowledge of a terminal illness to protect one another's feelings, communication barriers create distance and misunderstanding, prevent preparatory grief, and deny opportunities to say goodbyes. Therapists can assist family members with feelings of helplessness, anger, loss of control, or guilt that they could not do more. It is usually easier for younger family members to accept the loss of elders whose time has come, than for elders to accept the loss—and their own survival—of siblings or their own children or grandchildren who die first. The death of the last member of the older generation is a family milestone, signifying that the next generation is now the oldest and the next to face death. It is important, also, to address the impact of an elder's death for grandchildren, often their first experience with death and loss.

Spousal bereavement can be a highly stressful transition, with a wide range of responses in adaptation. Women, with a longer life expectancy than men, and tending to be younger than their husbands, are more likely to be widowed, with many years of life ahead. Women tend to anticipate the prospect of widowhood (Neugarten, 1996). Men tend to be less prepared: The initial sense of loss, disorientation, and loneliness contributes to an increase in death and suicide rates in the first 2 years. Social contact is often more disrupted for men, since wives tend to link their husbands to family and social networks, especially after retirement. Yet the long-term hardships are greater for widowed women with more limited financial resources.

The psychosocial tasks in the transition to widowhood involve grief over the loss and reinvestment in future functioning. Despite profound initial grief and challenges in daily living, most surviving spouses are quite resilient over time (Butler, 2008). Most report becoming more competent and independent, and take pride in coping well; only a few view the changes entirely negatively. A realignment of relationships in the family system also occurs (Walsh & McGoldrick, 2004). Family adaptational tasks involve shared acknowledgment of death and mutual support through the grief process, transforming shared experiences and physical presence into continuing bonds through spiritual connection, memories, stories, and deeds. Attention must also turn to the reality demands of daily functioning and self-support. Wherever possible, clinicians and adult children should help both partners to anticipate and prepare for widowhood. Many need to acquire new skills for independent living. The initial adjustment to being physically alone, in itself, is difficult. Within 1 to 2 years, most bereaved spouses regain interest in others and new activities. Further dislocation may occur if the family home is given up or if financial problems or illness block independent functioning. In such cases, many widows move in with adult children, siblings, or a very aged parent.

Remarriage is common for men but less so for women. Not only are there fewer available men but also many prefer not to remarry, especially if they have had heavy spousal caregiving responsibilities and are reluctant to take on that role again. Economic and legal issues, such as bequests for children, lead some older couples to live together—or separately—as committed companions without formal marriage. Critical to the success of remarriage is the relationship with adult children and their approval of the union. Problems can arise when a child views remarriage as disloyal to the deceased parent. Adult children may be shocked by an aged parent's intimacy with a new partner—especially when they cannot conceive of the elderly as attractive or sexually active. Some assume that a new mate is interested only in money. Conflict over a will frequently arises, particularly if children view inheritance as compensation for earlier

disappointments or as evidence that they are valued more than the new partner. Burial can be a contentious issue: whether with the deceased spouse and parent of children or with the new partner. Family therapists can facilitate important discussions and planning to avert later conflict.

> Assess your comprehension of end-of-life challenges and loss of loved ones by completing this quiz.

Cross-Generational Interplay of Life Cycle Issues

In every family, the later-life challenges of parents interact with salient developmental issues of their children at their concurrent life phases. With increasing diversity in family patterns and the tendency toward later marriage and childrearing, different pressures and conflicts may arise. The issues that come to the fore between an older adult parent and young adult child will likely differ from those that arise between a parent and a middle-aged child. Tensions are heightened when developmental strivings are incompatible.

CASE ILLUSTRATION

Julia

Julia, in her mid-20s, was beginning a social work career and engaged to be married when her 63-year-old mother, who lived 2,000 miles away, was diagnosed with congestive heart failure. Julia felt torn. Her love and sense of obligation were countered by reluctance to put her new job and marriage plans on hold indefinitely. The situation was complicated by issues of separation and identity, which are normative in early adulthood. Julia had always been close to her mother and relied on her direction and support. Her geographic distance from home in the life that she had established bolstered her self-reliance. Now as she was on the threshold of adult commitments, her mother needed her most and Julia feared losing her.

Phone contact became increasingly strained. Julia's mother saw her failure to return home as uncaring and selfish. Julia made a brief visit, feeling guilty and upset. The uncertain course of the illness made it difficult to know how long her mother would live or when to plan trips. Julia sent her mother gifts. One, picked with special care and affection, was a leather-bound book for her memoirs. On her next visit, Julia discovered the book, unopened, on a closet shelf. Deeply hurt, she screamed at her mother to explain. Her mother replied, "If I wrote my memoirs, I'd have to say how much you've let me down." Julia, very hurt, cut her visit short. Meanwhile, conflict escalated with her fiance, and the wedding plans were canceled. Deeply upset by the breakup, Julia phoned her parents for consolation. Her mother expressed her own disappointment at the canceled plans, saying that she now had nothing to live for. A few hours later, she had a stroke. Julia, too angry to respond, put off a trip home. Her mother died 2 weeks later. Julia scarcely grieved, throwing herself into her work and a new relationship. When that relationship broke up, delayed grief and remorse surfaced, bringing her for therapy. In learning more about her mother's life and losses, Julia found out that her mother's own mother had expressed disappointment in *her* as she was dying. In gaining compassion for her mother, she also reached out to her father, to know and appreciate him better while there was time.

In this case, the mother's developmental needs at the end of life occurred "off-time" from the perspective of the daughter's developmental readiness and out of sync with her age peers. Terminally ill, the mother needed to draw her family close and to feel that she had successfully fulfilled her role as a mother. The young adult daughter was threatened by the closeness and dependency at a time of impending loss, when she was not yet secure in her own life and felt her culture's pressure for autonomy. A transgenerational anniversary reaction complicated the situation as unresolved issues from the mother's estranged relationship with her own mother before her death were revived, adding fuel to the conflict, disappointment, and estrangement at her own life's end.

In our culture, young adults are emerging from the search for identity into issues of commitment and preoccupation with making initial choices, such as a life partner, career, and residence, choices that define one's place in the adult world. Responding to caregiving needs and threatened loss of aging parents at this life stage may be fraught with conflict. Clinicians need to help young adults offset the cultural push for family disconnection and prioritize relationships with their elders approaching the end of life.

Successful Aging: Meaning and Connection

Abundant research, including recent neuroscience findings, reveals that the aging process is much more variable and malleable than was long believed (Butler, 2008; Cozolino, 2008). Elders can enhance their own development by actively approaching their challenges and making the most of their strengths and options (Baltes & Baltes, 1990). Studies of normal adult development and family functioning find that a variety of adaptive processes, rather than one single pattern, contribute to successful later-life adjustment (Birren & Schaie, 2006). This diversity reflects differences in family structures, individual personality styles, gender roles, and ethnic, social class, rural versus urban, and larger cultural influences. The development of new modes of response and aspects of life that were earlier constrained enables a greater role flexibility and adaptation that contribute to life satisfaction.

Betty Friedan's (1993) analysis of international studies on aging suggests that older adults may actually integrate problems at a higher level than the young, particularly in attending to ethical and contextual issues. From studies of different populations, Friedan noted that many women who were the most vital in later life had experienced profound change and discontinuity. Those who were most frustrated, angry, and depressed had held on rigidly to earlier constraining roles or had repeated them. What distinguished women who were vital was not which roles they played in earlier adulthood, but rather whether they had developed a sense of purpose and structure for making life choices and decisions.

In contrast to the redefinition of self that many women experience with menopause, launching of children, widowhood, or divorce, Valliant (2002) found that many aging men's identities continue to be heavily invested in career success and sexual potency. Such culturally based "proofs" of masculinity generate anxiety, a sense of deficiency, and a void as these powers diminish. Notably, Vaillant (2012) found that meaningful relationships were the most important factor in men's successful aging. Love and intimacy might take many forms, deepening over time. It is important to challenge constraining views and explore possibilities for personal and relational fulfillment.

Similarly, successful family functioning in later life requires strong relational connections and flexibility in structure, roles, and responses to new developmental priorities and challenges (Walsh, 2012a, 2015). As patterns that may have been functional in earlier life phases no longer fit, new options can be explored. With the loss of functioning and death of significant family members, others are called upon to assume new roles, responsibilities, and meaningful connections. In doing so, they develop new competencies and enhanced sense of worth. Therapists can invite couples and families to reflect on the choices they have made in life and now wish to make for their remaining time, seeing their alternatives as both limited and extended by personal belief systems, gender, ethnic, and cultural identity, and social and economic position. These choices are never simple; most often they are complex and intertwined with the needs and decisions of others.

As Lightfoot-Lawrence (2009) found, many older people from varied walks of life approach maturity with celebration, finding possibilities in aging for enrichment and unexpected pleasures. For her, the greatest reward of parenting has been delight in her fully-grown progeny, considering them to be friends with an extra dimension of affection. She finds it powerfully reassuring at this time to think of life, and each day, as time to be fully savored. Many find it to be the best time of life, feeling freer to be themselves, reporting less conflict and more balance; better able to know and use their strengths; and surer of what matters in their lives.

> Assess your comprehension of successful aging: meaning and connection by completing this quiz.

The Wisdom and Spirit of the Elders

There is growing recognition that later years and relationships have a significance of their own. In Erikson's theory of human development, old age was seen as a critical period, when individuals review earlier life experiences and their meaning in the quest to achieve integration and overcome despair at the end of life's journey. In this process, new adaptive strengths and wisdom can be gained. The task of achieving integration is challenging, as older adults face the finiteness of life and awareness of past deficiencies, hurts, and disappointments. Vital involvement in the present is essential. Some look for models of aging in parents or grandparents; others look to friends, community members, and even iconic figures, from the Rolling Stones, B.B. King, and Georgia O'Keefe to Nelson Mandela and the Dalai Lama. Such attributes as humor, compassion, curiosity, and commitment contribute to a sense of integrity. Interviews with octogenarians reveal many pathways for integration and reconciliation of earlier life issues (Erikson, Erikson, & Kivnick, 1986). For the most resilient aged people, past trauma and inescapable missteps are put into perspective. Even those who do not achieve integration are actively involved in meaning-making efforts to reach some acceptance of their lives.

A common thread in successful aging is the dynamic process as older people come to see themselves not as victims of life forces, or defined by their limitations, but rather as resilient, with the capacity and initiative to shape as well as be shaped by events (Walsh, 2012a). Overcoming life's adversities involves the courage to reach out, seeing aging as a personal, relational, and spiritual evolution, seeking new horizons for learning, change, and growth. A priority for clinicians is to recognize and draw out sources of meaning and fulfillment and to facilitate efforts by older adults and families to integrate the varied experiences of a lifetime into a coherent sense of self, relational integrity, and life's worth.

King and Wynne (2004) proposed the concept of *family integrity* as the achievement of older adults' developmental striving toward meaning, connection, and continuity within their multigenerational family system. It involves three competencies: (1) dynamic transformation of relationships over time responsive to members' changing life cycle needs; (2) resolution or acceptance of past conflicts and losses; and (3) shared creation of meaning by passing on individual and family legacies across generations. Gaining family integrity generates a deep and abiding sense of peace and satisfaction with past, present, and future family relationships.

Notable in this life phase is the search for life's transcendent meaning. Spiritual beliefs and practices, whether within organized religion or not, come to the fore with aging, sustaining resilience for most elderly people (Schaie & Krouse, 2004; Walsh, 2009c). Research documents the power of personal faith and contemplative practices, such as prayer, meditation, and rituals, to strengthen well-being and healing by triggering positive emotions and brain activity and by strengthening immune and cardiovascular systems. For instance, a study of elderly patients after open-heart surgery found that those who were able to find hope, solace, and comfort in their religious outlook had a survival rate three times higher than those who did not. What matters most is the ability to draw on the power of faith to give meaning to precarious life challenges and to life itself. Belief in a spiritual afterlife, and reunion with loved ones and ancestors, offers solace and comfort.

The search for identity and meaning is a lifelong process. Individuals and their families organize, interpret, and connect experiences in many ways. We must be sensitive to the culture and time in which families and their members have lived and the contribution of critical events and structural sources of meaning. For some, religion is most salient; for others, it might be humanistic values, ethnic heritage, or their education that enabled them to rise out of poverty. Many elders show enormous potential for continual self-renewal as they forge new meaning and purpose in their later years. Emerging research suggests that older adults with a greater purpose in life have a reduced risk of Alzheimer's disease and mild cognitive impairment (Boyle, et al., 2010).

The Significance of Relational Connections

We are relational beings. A family systems orientation considers the broad network of relationships, identifying and recruiting potential resources for resilience in the immediate and extended family, including informal kin. Even in troubled families, "relational lifelines" for resilience can be found. Some individuals are good listeners and are emotionally supportive; others may be good problem solvers or bring good cheer and needed laughter. In fostering the resilience of aging family members, positive contributions might be made by siblings, adult children and godchildren, nephews, nieces, and grandchildren, friends, and even former spouses. One woman, aged 81, hospitalized with a life-threatening illness, greeted two visitors. To one, an acquaintance, she introduced the other, her former husband, saying "We were married in the past, but now we're close friends."

Companionate bonds, social ties, and community connections become increasingly valued with age (Sluzki, 2000). Research finds a strong link between social contact, support, and longevity. Elders who visit often with friends and family and maintain a thick network of diverse relationships are likely to live longer than those with few kin and social resources (Litwin, 1996). Baby boomers are creating "villages" of interdependence, so that they and their elders can live independently for as long as possible with community interaction, stimulating involvement, and access to needed services. Faith communities play an increasingly important role with aging, from shared communal values and rituals, involvement in congregational activities and community service, to practical, emotional, and spiritual support in times of need.

Longtime and childhood friends become increasingly valued; many reconnect at reunions and through Internet social networks. Old flames are sometimes rekindled in later life. Old friends connect us to our younger selves and offer perspective on our emerging lives. A woman in her mid-60s, anxious that her forgetfulness was an early sign of Alzheimer's disease, found humor and relief after her college roommate reminded her that she had always been absent minded.

Companion animals play a vital role for the well-being and resilience of many elderly (Baun, Johnson, & McCabe, 2006; Walsh, 2009a), especially those living alone. As one woman related, "My cats have been my constant companions and support—through marriage, divorce, remarriage and widowhood." Studies in nursing homes and dementia units find that animal-assisted therapy and weekly visits by volunteers with their pets significantly brighten mood, increase social interaction and appetite, and enhance the overall well-being of residents (Filan & Llewellyn-Jones, 2006). Clinicians should explore the meaning and significance of animal companions and their loss. Bereavement can be profound with the death of a cherished pet or with forced relinquishment when moving to a senior residence or nursing home that does not allow pets (Walsh, 2009b).

> Assess your comprehension of the significance of relational connections by completing this quiz.

Clinical Challenges and Opportunities: A Resilience-Oriented Approach

A resilience-oriented approach to practice (Walsh, 2003, 2012a) engages elders collaboratively, affirms their personhood, and focuses on their strengths, resources, and potential. We show interest in their life journey, with compassion for their struggles, suffering, and losses, and with affirmation of their courage and endurance. We encourage their efforts for meaning, purpose, joy, and connections, with conviction in their potential for personal and relational growth. We see their value in the lives of others and draw on kin and social networks to support their optimal functioning and well-being. In contrast, the traditional clinical focus on later life decline and deficits too often leads professionals to objectify the elderly, become unduly pessimistic, underestimate their resourcefulness, and make plans for them based on what professionals think best.

CASE ILLUSTRATION

Rita

Rita, a 78-year-old widow, was admitted to a psychiatric unit, diagnosed with a confusional state and acute paranoia after an incident in which she accused her landlord of plotting to get rid of her. Rita's increasing visual impairment was making independent living more difficult and hazardous. Her apartment was in disarray. She was socially isolated, stubbornly refusing assistance from "strangers." Her only surviving family member, a sister, lived in another state. The hospital staff, doubting that Rita could continue to function independently, planned a nursing home placement for her. Rita vehemently objected, insisting on returning to her own apartment. Hospitalization was extended "to deal with her resistance."

A family therapist's strength-based interviews with Rita led to a new appreciation of her as a capable person and to a more collaborative plan. Asked what she valued about living alone, she replied, "I'm not alone; I live with my books and my birds." The therapist expressed interest in hearing more about her life. Rita had been a teacher, happily married without children until her husband's death 10 years earlier. Her beloved father died the following year. After those painful losses, she withdrew, determined never to become dependent on anyone again. Rita centered her life on her work; she was known as a "tough cookie," respected by colleagues for her perseverance with challenging students. Since retirement, she had immersed herself in her books, a vital source of her resilience, enhancing her cognitive functioning and pleasure, and transporting her beyond her immediate circumstances. Many books held special meaning, inherited from her father, a scholar. They revived her close childhood relationship with him, when he had spent countless hours reading to her. Now Rita's loss of vision was most distressing, cutting her off from her valued connections. She enjoyed the chattering and singing of her birds and did not want to give them up with a move.

Rita's strong identification with her father involved intense pride in his part-Native American heritage, a hardiness in adversity, and a will to survive and adapt. The therapist's visit to Rita's apartment revealed these strengths. At first glance, all appeared chaotic: piles of books, clothing, and food containers everywhere. However, at closer inspection, Rita had organized her environment in a system that made sense to adapt to her visual impairment. She had color-coded food containers with a magic marker; arranged clothes by function; and stacked books by subject, easily locating what she needed.

Rita's stubborn "resistance" had been viewed as pathological denial of dependency needs. Yet self-reliance had served Rita well over many years. It was the failing of her primary mode of adaptation—her vision—that brought confusion and anxiety. Her reluctance to become dependent made her reject any aid with one exception: She agreed to contact a religious organization that sent Brothers to read to her whenever she called. She could allow help when she took initiative and had some control in the relational boundaries. This positive experience became a model for building a resource network to support Rita's objective of independent living. With encouragement, she agreed to contact trusted neighbors and shopkeepers for occasional assistance. She initiated weekly phone contact with her sister, which led to enjoyable visits with her niece, who loved hearing stories of her grandfather—Rita's beloved father.

Applying the concept of resilience to the family as a functional unit, a family-resilience approach affirms the potential in couples and families for healing and growth over the life course, tapping into their strengths and building resources as they confront later-life challenges (Walsh, 2003, 2012a, 2015). Caregiving and end-of-life challenges also hold potential benefits, deepening and enriching relationships, if family members are encouraged to make the most of precious time. Because unresolved conflicts and cutoffs may accompany children and grandchildren into their future relationships (Bowen, 1978), it is important to avert the fallout of hurt, misunderstanding, anger, alienation, sense of failure, and guilt. Strains can be prevented and repaired by helping family members to redefine and reintegrate their roles and relationships as they age and mature (King & Wynne, 2004).

A conjoint family life review expands the benefits of individual life-review sessions (Lewis & Butler, 1974) found to assist in the integration of earlier life stages, facilitating acceptance of one's life and approaching death. Sharing reminiscences can be a valuable experience for couples and family members, incorporating multiple perspectives and subjective experiences of their shared life over time. The process of sharing the varied perceptions of hopes and dreams, satisfactions, and disappointments enlarges the family story, builds mutual empathy, and can heal old wounds. Earlier conflicts or hurts that led to cutoffs or frozen images and expectations can be reconsidered from new vantage points (Fishbane, 2009). Misunderstandings and faulty assumptions about one another can be clarified. Successive life phases can be reviewed as relationships are brought up to date. Individuals in later life are often able to be more open and honest about earlier transgressions or shame-laden family secrets. Past mistakes and hurts can be more readily acknowledged, opening possibilities for forgiveness (Hargrave & Hanna, 1997). At life's end, the simple words, "I'm truly sorry" and "I love you" mean more than ever. Family photos, scrapbooks, genealogies, reunions, and pilgrimages can assist this work. Stories of family history and precious end-of-life conversations can be videotaped and preserved. The transmission of family history to younger generations can be an additional bonus of such work.

Looking ahead

Families should be encouraged to be proactive in considering and preparing for such challenges as transitional living arrangements and end-of-life decisions, discussions that are commonly avoided. Future-oriented questions can also open up new possibilities for later life fulfillment. One son worried about how each of his parents would manage alone on the family farm if widowed, but he dreaded talking with them about their death. Finally, on a home visit, he gathered up his courage. First he asked his mother, tentatively, whether she had ever thought about what she might do if dad were the first to go. She replied, "Sure, I know exactly what I'd do: I'd sell the farm and move to Texas to be near our grandkids." Her husband shook his head and replied,

"Well if that isn't the darnedest thing! I've thought a lot about it too, and if your mother weren't here, I'd sell the farm and move to Texas!" This conversation led the couple to sell the farm and move to Texas, where they enjoyed many happy years with their children and grandchildren.

Expanding Our Developmental Lens

Clinical literature and training programs tend to emphasize early developmental phases: young couples and families raising children. At launching of the young adults, attention follows the younger generation into their own life course and family formation, relegating the parent generation to the margins, as extended kin. The term "postparental" is unfortunate, as parents never cease to be parents, with lifelong concern for the well-being of their children—and any grandchildren. The term "family of origin" connotes an older generation left behind, with clinical inquiry about past influence. Because more people are living healthier and longer lives than in the past, we lack role models for later-life family relations, just as we lack appropriate labels and role definitions. We need to expand our developmental lens to the full life course, addressing the assets, needs, and concerns of individuals, couples, and families in their later years. I once assigned a group of medical students to interview an older couple about their life course. The (male) students looked stunned. One acknowledged that he had never had a real conversation with an older person, including his parents, and he had never considered what his own aging would look like. This led us to a valuable discussion of age segregation in our society and professional ageism stemming largely from our culture's preoccupation with youth and avoidance of the reality of aging, losses, and death.

As clinicians, we need to deepen awareness of our own apprehensions and biases and enlarge our perspective on the whole life course. We need to gain appreciation for what it is like to mature and become old, for relationships to evolve and grow stronger or be lost, and for new ones to develop, meeting emerging priorities. Our own painful issues with our aging family members—and denial of our own aging process—may contribute to anxiety, avoidance, over-responsibility, or empathic difficulties. As we better appreciate the elders in our own families, attend to our own losses and grievances, and explore our own growing maturity, therapeutic work with individuals, couples, and families in later life will take on deeper meaning and possibilities for growth.

The complexity and diversity of family networks in later life require careful clinical assessment. Given the prevalent pattern of intimacy at a distance, we must look beyond the sharing of a household to identify significant relationships and potential bonds. Drawing a genogram with an elder can be useful in identifying those who are significant and could be drawn upon for support and/or companionship, such as a godchild (McGoldrick, Gerson, & Petry, 2008). Problems involving family relationships with elderly members are often hidden behind complaints of marital distress or child-focused symptoms. Older adults are more likely to present somatic complaints than emotional or relational problems. Family relationships can exacerbate or alleviate their suffering. The stressful impact of chronic illness on loved ones requires attention to family needs for support, information, caregiving guidelines, respite, and linkage to community resources. Families are our most valuable resources in providing not only caregiving but also a sense of worth, lasting emotional ties, and human dignity in later years and in approaching life's end. We can strengthen their resilience by understanding their challenges and supporting them in our social policies and provision of health care.

Developmental models for understanding growth and change in later life need to include wisdom and integrative understanding of the values and meanings that are salient to elders. Clinical services must be flexible to fit the diversity of older people and their significant relationships and to support optimal functioning and integration in the community. It is important to engage in lifelong learning, keep active in meaningful pursuits, strengthen kinship bonds, rekindle old friendships, and make new ones.

Ecological models are also required to develop policies, programs, and living arrangements that fit the emerging needs and preferences of older adults and foster their optimal well-being (Aldwin & Gilbert, 2013). The importance of community—

reflecting location, a sense of shared connection or neighborhood cohesion, and feelings of belonging—is instrumental to positive mental health in later life. The World Health Organization (2007) has stressed the need to redesign the social and built environments for today's aging population, with "aging in place" a priority: near family, friends, neighbors, services, shopping, entertainment, and other amenities. The WHO's "Age-Friendly Cities" initiative encourages communities to become more inclusive of older adults, emphasizing enablement rather than disability, and friendly for all ages, encouraging interaction of residents young and old.

This expansion of later life has been called the "aging revolution." What will we do with this gift of long life? How can we contribute to people's ability to live and to love with vitality into advanced old age? Important in the resilience of our society is a sense of pride in age, the value of history and life experience, and the capacity to adapt courageously to change. Elders can be encouraged to draw on their rich experience to inform both continuity and innovation, as society's historians and futurists. The wisdom of our elders, linked with the energy and new knowledge of the young, can be the basis for rich interchange and planning for the future.

Assess your comprehension of expanding our developmental lens by completing this quiz.

Recall what you learned in this chapter by completing the Chapter Review.

References

Aldwin, C. & Gilbert, D. (2013). *Health, illness and optimal aging. 2nd ed.).* New York: Springer.

Baltes, P. B., & Baltes, M. M. (1990). Psychological perspectives on successful aging: The model of selective optimization with compensation. In P. B. Baltes & M. M. Baltes (Eds.), *Successful aging: Perspectives from the behavioral sciences* (pp. 1–34). New York: Cambridge University Press.

Baun, M., Johnson, R., & McCabe, B. (2006). Human-animal interaction and successful aging. In A. Fine (Ed.), *Handbook on animal-assisted therapy* (2nd ed., pp. 287–302). San Diego, CA: Academic Press.

Bedford, V. H. (2005). Theorizing about sibling relationships when parents become frail. In V. L. Bengston, A. C. Acock, K. R. Allen, P. Dilworth-Anderson, & D. M. Klein (Eds.), *Sourcebook of family theory & research* (pp. 173–174). Thousand Oaks, CA: Sage Publications.

Bengtson, V. (2001). Beyond the nuclear family: The increasing importance of multigenerational bonds. *Journal of Marriage and the Family, 64*(1), 7–17.

Bengtson, V., & Lowenstein, A. (Eds.). (2003). *Global aging and challenges to families.* New York: Aldine de Gruyter.

Blenkner, M. (1965). Social work and family relationships in later life with some thoughts on filial maturity. In E. Shanas & G. Strieb (Eds.), *Social structure and the family: Generational relations* (pp. 46–59). Englewood Cliffs, NJ: Prentice-Hall.

Boss, P. (2004). Ambiguous loss. In F. Walsh & M. McGoldrick (Eds.), *Living beyond loss* (2nd ed., pp. 237–246). New York: Norton.

Bowen, M. (1978). *Family therapy in clinical practice.* New York: Aronson.

Boyle, P. A., Buchman, A. S., Barnes, L. L., & Bennett, D. A. (2010). Effect of a purpose in life on risk of incident Alzheimer disease and mild cognitive impairment in community-dwelling older persons. *Archives of General Psychiatry, 67*(3), 304–310.

Brody, E. (1985). Parent care as normative family stress. *Gerontologist, 25,* 19–29.

Brody, E. (2004). *Women in the middle: Their parent-care years.* New York: Springer.

Butler, R. (2008). *The longevity revolution: The benefits and challenges of living a long life.* New York: Perseus Books.

Cicirelli, V. G. (1995). *Sibling relationships across the life span.* New York: Plenum Press.

Cicirelli, V. G. (2006). *Older adults' views of death.* New York: Springer.

Cohler, B. J., & R. Galatzer-Levy, R. (2000). *The course of gay and lesbian lives: Social and psychoanalytic perspectives.* Chicago, IL: The University of Chicago.

Cozolino, L. (2008). *The healthy aging brain: Sustaining attachment, attaining wisdom.* New York: Norton.

Delany, S., & Delany A. E. (1993). *Having our say: The Delany sisters' first 100 years.* New York: Dell.

Drew, L. M., & Silverstein, M. (2004). Intergenerational role investments of great-grandparents: Consequences for psychological well-being. *Ageing and Society, 24(1),* 95–111.

Engstrom, M. (2012). Kinship care families. In F. Walsh (Ed.), *Normal family processes* (4th ed., pp. 196–221). New York: Guilford Press.

Erikson, E. H., Erikson, J. M., & Kivnick, H. (1986). *Vital involvement in old age: The experience of old age in our time.* New York: Norton.

Filan, S., & Llewellyn-Jones, R. (2006). Animal assisted therapy for dementia: A review of the literature. *International Psychogeriatrics, 18*(4), 597–611.

Fishbane, M. D. (2009). Honor your father and your mother: Intergenerational values and Jewish tradition. In F. Walsh (Ed.), *Spiritual resources in family therapy* (2nd ed., pp. 174–193). New York: Guilford.

Friedan, B. (1993). *The fountain of age.* New York: Simon & Schuster.

Giles, H., Noels, K. A., Williams, A., Ota, H., Lim, T. S., & Ng, S. H., (2003). Intergenerational communication across cultures: Young peoples' perceptions of conversations with family elders, non-family elders, and same-age peers. *Journal of Cross-cultural Gerontology, 18*(1), 1–32.

Hargrave, T. D., & Hanna, S. M. (1997). *The aging family: New visions of theory, practice, and reality.* New York: Brunner/Mazel.

Institute for Health & Aging, University of California, San Francisco. (1996). *Chronic care in America: A 21st century challenge.* Princeton, NJ: Robert Wood Johnson Foundation.

King, D. A., & Wynne, L. C. (2004). The emergence of "family integrity" in later life. *Family Process, 43*(1), 7–21.

Kinsella, K., & He, W. (2009). *An aging world: 2008. International Population reports.* U.S. Census Bureau. Washington, DC: US Government Printing Office. Retrieved (6/16/10) from www.census.gov/prod/2009pubs/p95-09-1.pdf

Lawrence-Lightfoot, S. (2009). *The third chapter: Passion, risk, and adventure in the 25 years past fifty.* New York: Farrar, Straus, & Giroux.

Lee, M. Y., & Mjelde-Mossey, L. (2004). Cultural dissonance among generations: A solution-focused approach among elders and their families. *Journal of Marital & Family Therapy, 30*(4), 497–513.

Lewis, M. I., & Butler, R. N. (1974). Life review therapy. *Geriatrics, 29,* 165–173.

Litwin, H. (1996). *The social networks of older people: A cross-national analysis.* Greenwood, CT: Praeger.

McGoldrick, M., Gerson, R., & Petry, S. (2008). *Genograms: Assessment and intervention* (3rd ed.). New York: Norton.

Mead, M. (1972). *Blackberry winter.* New York: William Morrow.

Mueller, M. M., & Elder, G. H. Jr. (2003). Family contingencies across the generations. Grandparent-grandchild relationships in holistic perspective. *Journal of Marriage and the Family, 65*(2), 404–417.

Myerhoff, B. (1992). *Remembered lives: The work of ritual, storytelling, and growing older.* Ann Arbor, MI: University of Michigan Press.

National Center on Health Statistics (2012). Health, United States, 2012. Washington, DC: U.S. Department of Health and Human Services. Retrieved July 27, 2013, from http://www.cdc.gov/nchs/data/hus/hus12.pdf#018 .

Neugarten, B. (Ed.). (1996). *The meanings of age: Selected papers of Bernice L. Neugarten.* Chicago, IL: University of Chicago Press.

Neustifter, R. (2008). Common concerns faced by lesbian elders: An essential context for couple's therapy. *Journal of Feminist Family Therapy, 20*(3), 251–267.

Qualls, S. H., & Zarit, S. H., Eds. (2009). *Aging families and caregiving.* New York: Wiley.

Rolland, J. S. (1994). *Families, illness, and disability.* New York: Basic Books.

Rolland, J. S. (2012). Mastering the challenges of illness, disability, and genetic conditions. In F. Walsh (Ed.) *Normal family processes: Growing Diversity and Complexity.* New York: Guilford Press. (4th ed., pp. 452–482).

Schaie, K. W., & Willis, S. (Eds.). (2012). *Handbook of the psychology of aging* (7th ed.). San Diego, CA: Academic Press.

Schaie, K. W., & Krouse, N. (Eds.). (2004). *Religious influences on health and well-being in the elderly.* New York: Springer.

Sluzki, C. (2000). Social networks and the elderly: Conceptual and clinical issues, and a family consultation. *Family Process, 39*(3), 271–284.

Spark, G. (1974). Grandparents and intergenerational family therapy. *Family Process, 13,* 225–238.

Spark, G., & Brody, E. M. (1970). The aged are family members. *Family Process, 9,* 195–210.

Vaillant, G. (2002). *Aging well.* New York: Little, Brown.

Vaillant, G. (2012). *Triumphs of experience.* Cambridge, MA: Harvard University Press.

Walsh, F. (2003). Family resilience: A framework for clinical practice. *Family Process, 35,* 261–281.

Walsh, F. (2009a). Human–animal bonds: I. The relational significance of companion animals. Special section, *Family Process, 48*(4), 462–480.

Walsh, F. (2009b). Human–animal bonds: The role of pets in family systems and family therapy. *Family Process, 48*(4), 481–499.

Walsh, F. (Ed.). (2009c). *Spiritual resources in family therapy* (2nd ed.). New York: Guilford Press.

Walsh, F. (2012a). Successful aging and family resilience. In B. Haslip & G. Smith (Eds.) *Emerging Perspectives on Resilience in Adulthood and Later Life. Annual Review of Gerontology and Geriatrics, 32,* 153–172. New York: Springer.

Walsh, F. (2012b). The "new normal": Diversity and complexity in 21st century families. In F. Walsh (Ed.), *Normal family processes* (4th ed., pp. 4–27). New York: Guilford Press.

Walsh, F. (2015). *Strengthening family resilience* (3rd ed.). New York: Guilford Press.

Walsh, F., & McGoldrick, M. (2004). *Living beyond loss: Death in the family* (2nd ed.). New York: Norton.

Weil, A. (2005). *Healthy aging.* New York: Alfred A. Knopf.

World Health Organization (2007). *Global age-friendly cities: A guide.* Retrieved May 10, 2013, from http://www.who.int/aging/publications.

Chapter 19

Death, Loss, and the Family Life Cycle

Monica McGoldrick & Froma Walsh

Learning Outcomes

- Identify factors that impact the meaning and consequences of loss.
- List and describe family tasks that promote immediate and long-term adaptation for family members after a loss.
- Discuss tools that clinicians can use to assess a loss in the life cycle perspective.
- Examine factors that heighten the risk of maladaptive adaptation to loss.
- Describe the challenges faced by young couples when loss occurs.
- Explain the impact of different types of loss on a family with young children.
- Identify how the developmental issues of adolescents complicate how a family handles a loss.
- Discuss the challenges faced by families when loss occurs during midlife and late life.
- Identify hidden or stigmatized losses that offer unique challenges for grieving individuals or families.
- Describe the importance of incorporating cultural traditions and spiritual orientation when helping families face loss.

Introduction

Death and loss are the most profound challenges families confront. They are transactional processes involving those who die and their survivors in a shared life cycle that acknowledges both the finality of death and the continuity of life. Yet, the dominant Anglo American culture has long fostered a tendency to deny death and to minimize the profound impact of loss (Becker, 1973). Indeed, the medical profession tended to treat death as a failure. More recently, developments in palliative care and hospice ease suffering and provide support and comfort to patients and families facing end-of-life challenges. We have transformed the funeral into a celebration of life alongside the sorrow of loss, with more active involvement of significant family members and others in sharing memories, stories, and grief and providing mutual support.

Still, insufficient attention has been given to the ramifications of loss for the family system and the immediate and long-term effects of death for siblings, parents, children, and extended kin. Legacies of loss touch all survivors' relationships, rippling throughout the family network, influencing many who have never even known the person who died. The meaning and consequences of loss vary depending on many factors, including the state of relationships, family functioning, and the particular phase of the life cycle at the time of loss (Walsh & McGoldrick, 2004, 2013). Whatever our therapeutic approach, a family life cycle perspective enables us to facilitate adaptation, which strengthens the whole family for future life passage.

Family Adaptation to Loss

Death poses shared adaptational challenges, involving both immediate and long-term family reorganization and changes in a family's identity and purpose (Shapiro, 1994). The ability to accept loss is at the heart of all strengths in healthy family functioning

(Walsh, 2014, 2015). Adaptation does not mean resolution, but rather finding ways to put the loss in perspective and to move ahead with life. The multiple meanings of each death are transformed throughout the life cycle, as they are integrated with other life experiences, especially losses.

We must consider the tremendous diversity in cultural norms, religious traditions, and gender roles in approaching death, in funeral and burial or cremation rites, and in prescribed as well as proscribed mourning processes (Martin & Doka, 2000; Gamino & Ritter, 2009; Parkes, 2009; McGoldrick et al., 2004; Rosenblatt, 2008; Walsh, 2009b).

We also need to be mindful of the varied family structures and complex bonds in contemporary society and carefully assess the importance of relationships within and beyond a household (Walsh, 2012). For instance, the loss of grandparents, generally expected in later life, can have profound meaning if the grandparents have played a central childrearing role, as is common in many African American, immigrant, and single-parent families and in kinship care placements in cases of parental substance abuse, incarceration, child abuse, or neglect. More complicated emotional ramifications are likely to flow down the system if the parent and grandparent had a troubled relationship, which remained unresolved at the time of the grandparent's death.

The bereavement field has matured from early expectations of fixed stages, sequences, or schedules in a presumed "normal" mourning process to recognize the wide variation, complexity, and diversity of family and individual coping styles and pacing in grief (Wortman & Silver, 1989). Survivors commonly oscillate between preoccupation with grief and adaptive challenges ahead, reengaging in a world forever transformed by loss (Stroebe & Schut, 2010; Stroebe, Schut, & Boerner, 2010). When profound loss is suffered, we should not expect resolution in the sense of some complete, "once-and-for-all" getting over it. Resilience should not be seen as simply "bouncing back," readily getting "closure" on the experience, and moving on (Walsh, 2003). Recovery is a gradual process over time, usually lessening in intensity, yet often lasting a lifetime. Various facets of grief may reemerge with unexpected intensity, particularly with anniversaries and other nodal events. In traditional psychiatric approaches to grief work, mourning was thought to require letting go of lost attachments. Adaptive mourning seems best facilitated by transformation from physical presence of the loved one to continuing bonds through spiritual connections, memories, stories, deeds, and legacies to honor the life lost (Walsh & McGoldrick, 2004). Coming to terms with a significant loss involves making meaning of the loss, putting it in perspective, and weaving the experience of loss and recovery into the fabric of individual and collective identity and life passage from the past, through the present and into the future.

While we must be mindful of the varied approaches to loss, there are crucial family adaptational challenges that, if not dealt with, can heighten risk for individual and family dysfunction. Systemic interventions with distressed families can flexibly use or combine individual, couple, and family sessions (e.g., Kissane, Lichtenthal, & Zaider, 2007), as well as multi-family groups, to address presenting problems and strengthen the family to meet varied adaptive challenges in their journey ahead. We address four general family tasks to promote immediate and long-term adaptation for family members and to strengthen the family as a functional unit.

1. **Shared acknowledgment of the death and loss.** This is facilitated by direct contact with the dying person when possible and by clear information and open communication about end-of-life issues and the facts and circumstances of the death. Those unable to accept the reality of death tend to avoid contact or become angry with others who are grieving and moving on with life.

2. **Shared experience of loss.** Funeral rituals and visits to the grave or memorial site provide opportunity to pay respects, to share grief, and to receive comfort. A climate of trust, empathic support, and tolerance for varied pathways in healing is crucial. Intense emotions can fuel reactivity, longstanding conflicts, and cutoffs. Family efforts to make meaning of their loss experience involve gaining a meaningful perspective that fosters a sense of continuity with their belief system and life course, including

future implications of the loss (Nadeau, 2008; Walsh, 2015).

3. **Reorganization of family system.** Recovery from the disruptive impact of loss involves a realignment of relationships, redistribution of role functions to compensate for the loss, and restabilization in patterns of living, in order to promote adaptive cohesion and flexibility in the family system.

4. **Reinvestment in other relationships and life pursuits.** As time passes, survivors need to transform their lives and relationships to move forward, constructing new hopes and dreams, and revising life plans and aspirations.

> Assess your comprehension of family adaptation to loss by completing this quiz.

Assessing Loss in Life Cycle Perspective

The particular timing of a loss in the multigenerational family life cycle may increase the risk for dysfunction. In family assessment, a genogram and timeline are essential tools in tracking sequences and concurrences of nodal events over time in the multigenerational family system (McGoldrick, Gerson, & Petry, 2008; McGoldrick, 2011). When an individual in a family is symptomatic, we pay particular attention to unresolved past losses as well as recent and threatened losses. Availability of extended kin and social support are crucial and should be carefully assessed (McGoldrick & Walsh, 1983). A number of factors heighten the risk of maladaptation to loss.

Timing: When in the family's life cycle the death occurred

Untimely deaths, death on holidays, anniversaries, at the time of other key life transitions, and when there is a pileup of other events are especially stressful.

Untimely deaths that are premature in terms of chronological or social expectations, such as early widowhood, early parent loss, or death of a child, tend to be more painful for families. Many families struggle to find some meaning for a loss that seems unjust. Prolonged mourning is common. Survivor guilt can block life pursuits or satisfaction for spouses, siblings, and parents. The death of a child, which reverses the natural order of life, is the most painful loss of all.

When there has been a pileup of losses or the concurrence of loss with other life cycle transitions, developmental milestones, or major stress events, it may overload a family, posing incompatible demands. We pay particular attention to the concurrence of death with the birth of a child, since preoccupation with grief may interfere with parenting. If grief is blocked, a child born at that time may assume a special replacement function, which can be the impetus for high achievement or dysfunction. Similarly, a precipitous marriage in the immediate wake of loss may interfere with bereavement and/or investment in the new relationship in its own right. If a death that occurs on a significant holiday, birthday, or at the time of another major life transition, such as a wedding or childbirth, its difficulty can be increased by the anniversary association of the two events. So looking back is important, as well as looking at current stressors. But it is also important to look forward. Especially with traumatic deaths, intense feelings are often cut off and may go underground, becoming encoded in covert family scripts that are enacted years later with dire consequences (Byng-Hall, 2004). When a child reaches the age at which a parent experienced a traumatic death, it is important to assess a risk of suicide or destructive behavior (Walsh & McGoldrick, 2013).

Study of such transgenerational anniversary patterns with traumatic loss is needed to more fully understand such systemic transmission processes. Clinical interventions should aim to help family members gain awareness of covert patterns and to differentiate present relationships from the past so that history need not repeat itself.

Role and relationships with the deceased

The more important the person was in family life and the more central in family functioning (e.g., primary breadwinner or caregiver), the greater the loss. Especially difficult may be the death of an essential breadwinner, caretaker, or favorite child. The death of an only child, or the only son or daughter, leaves a particular void. The death of a family member with difficult history of substance abuse or relational trauma is likely to hold complications. Where relationships have been very conflicted, guilt and blame are often strong features of the experience.

The socioeconomic, ethnic, gender, religious, political, and historical context of the death

It is important to inquire about how the management of deaths is gendered by a family and to gently help them raise questions about highly gender-segregated roles in care of the dying or bereaved and in the arrangement of funerals and burial rituals.

Poverty, cultural isolation, and political or historical circumstances may intensify the impact of the loss—where deaths occur in a socially stigmatized situation such as when an undocumented immigrant dies, may have a large and complex social overlay that may make the death hard to deal with in personally and socially meaningful ways. The social context of the death is essential to assess.

The manner of death

Traumatic, violent (murder, suicide), ambiguous (disappearance or dementia), sudden or drawn out, or death where there are recriminations or others feel guilty can be especially complex. Research reveals that most survivors of traumatic deaths are resilient in recovery after the initial deep distress (Bonnano, 2004; Walsh, 2007). However, 15 to 30 percent of survivors may suffer long-term symptoms of PTSD, depression, anxiety, substance abuse, relational conflict, and estrangement. Massive trauma and loss of hope and positive vision can fuel transmission of negative intergenerational patterns (Danieli, 1985), affecting those not yet born. Survivors blocked from healing may perpetuate suffering through self-destructive behavior or revenge and harm toward others. With murder, atrocities, and injustice, the impetus for retaliation to restore a sense of family or community honor can lead to cycles of mutual destruction. Family therapy, community support, and pastoral counseling can be valuable in facilitating possibilities for forgiveness, reconciliation, healing, and resilience (Walsh, 2007, 2009b).

Violent deaths (murder and suicide) have a devastating impact. A senseless tragedy is especially hard to bear, such as a suicide or a death resulting from deliberate harm or negligence, as in drunk driving. Clinicians should sensitively inquire about past traumatic loss, particularly in refugee experiences; in military service; and in communities impacted by high crime, drugs, and gangs. The witnessing of atrocities and the taking and loss of lives may haunt survivors for years to come. Body deformity or dismemberment may be a recurring image. Posttraumatic stress symptoms affect all family relationships (Figley, 1998). *Suicides* are the most anguishing deaths for families to come to terms with, as family members struggle to comprehend the self-destructive act and whether they might have made a difference (Jordan & McIntosh, 2010).

Sudden death deprives family members of time to anticipate and prepare for the loss, to deal with unfinished business, or even to say their good-byes. A prolonged dying process can deplete family caregiving and financial resources and put needs of other members on hold. Relief at ending patient suffering and family strain is often guilt-laden (Ellison & Bradshaw, 2009). Moreover, with medical technology, families are increasingly confronted with excruciating end-of-life dilemmas over whether, and how long, to maintain life support efforts.

Ambiguity surrounding a loss can block mourning and produce anxiety and depression in family members (Boss, 2004). A loved one may be physically absent but psychologically present, such as an abducted child or a soldier missing in action. Uncertain about whether they are dead or alive, families may become consumed by desperate searches and attempts to get information to confirm the fate of their loved one. Serious conflict often arises as some family members hold out hope when others have given up and are ready to move on with life. The inability to recover a body complicates grieving.

The family's history of loss

Unresolved mourning of previous losses is especially difficult. Transgenerational patterns of traumatic or untimely loss are essential to note. Family patterns are often replicated in the next generation when a child reaches the same age or nodal point as the parent at the time of death or traumatic loss. One husband's extreme anger over his wife's desire to have a second child was only understood when genogram exploration revealed that his mother had died giving birth to his younger sister. He had not realized his own catastrophic fears of losing his spouse.

Family's relationships and resources at the time of death

Family flexibility, mutual support, and open communication are crucial dimensions for positive adaptation to loss (Walsh, 2003). It is important to identify and mobilize extended family and community resources to provide emotional support for immediate family members, address financial and practical concerns, meet spiritual needs, and fill in for lost role functions (e.g. care of young children or disabled family members).

Where the death follows a lingering or draining illness or accident, it can have wreaked havoc on family's financial or caretaking resources. This is likely to occur with dementia, which increasingly wears out both- the financial and caretaking resources of the family. But in addition it may have worn out the family's psychological and spiritual resources where the person has become hostile or difficult to deal with or has lost awareness of who family members are.

A death in highly conflictual or estranged relationships may be unexpectedly traumatic because it is too late to repair bonds. It is important to help families draw on their kin and social network to fill crucial role functions and to avoid precipitous replacement, such as a new partner or baby, sacrificing that individual's own needs and complicating that relationship.

> Assess your comprehension of assessing loss in life cycle perspective by completing this quiz.

Loss at Various Family Life Cycle Stages

Over the past century, the average life expectancy in the United States has increased dramatically from 47 years to nearly 80 years. Women die, on average, 5 years later than men, and Whites die, on average, 5 years later than African Americans (Hitti, 2010). Older Americans tend to die of chronic conditions in hospitals or nursing homes, although there is a growing impetus to enable individuals to die in their own homes. Most deaths before middle age result from accidents, homicide, or suicide, and with firearms, a major factor in death of adolescents and young adults. The expectable causes of death as well as the mourning process vary, depending on the phase of the family life cycle, the family context, and the nature of the death.

While this book begins a new life cycle with the young adult phase, since it is the beginning of a new life trajectory, we begin this chapter with the young couple because in dealing with death, it makes sense to consider losses at the young adult phase in relation to the launching phase of the family of origin, with parents in mid- and later life. Thus, we begin our discussion of loss at the new couple phase.

New couples

Losses that occur at this phase are likely to be experienced as untimely. Early widowhood complicates bereavement enormously for the spouse and for the entire extended family (Parkes & Weiss, 1983; Parkes, 2009). It can be a shocking and isolating experience without emotional preparation or social supports (Parkes 2001; Kastenbaum, 1998). Young widow(er)s, coping with spousal loss and the loss of shared dreams for the future, often find that peers distance to avoid confronting their own mortality or possible widowhood. Widowed men are less likely to have intimate male friends for emotional sharing. Some confuse sexual intimacy with needs for comfort and dependency. Relationships with in-laws, strained at this time, often break off as the survivor moves on to another relationship. Men tend to do so more rapidly, expecting a new partner to be sympathetic toward their situation. Those who run precipitously into a new relationship to avoid the pain of loss often carry along unaddressed mourning, which may surface painfully later. When couples present serious relational problems, we inquire about losses that occurred at the start of the relationship, as well as losses coinciding with problem onset.

Parental illness or death may propel an individual into marriage, embedding residuals of unaddressed mourning in the new couple relationship, as mentioned earlier. When couples are focused on establishing their own lives, the sense of responsibility to parents may produce conflicts between loyalty to the family of origin and to the marriage. Increased attention, caregiving, or financial support to the dying or surviving parent or absorption in the grief process can strain the couple relationship, especially if the grieving partner feels unsupported or the other partner feels neglected over an extended period of time. Loss may disrupt the intimate/sexual relationship (Paul & Paul, 1989). In cross-cultural marriages, a spouse expecting the marriage to come first may not understand that a partner, from a Latino culture, for example, may be expected to place intergenerational bonds and obligations over spousal investment (Falicov, 2013). Encouraging mutual understanding and support facilitates mourning and strengthens relational resilience (Walsh, 2015).

Changes in adult sibling relationships are often brought on by the death of a parent. Sisters are more likely to be stressed by the cultural expectation for daughters to be primary parental caregivers. Brothers tend to shoulder more of the financial responsibilities but less often the day-to-day caregiving. Old sibling rivalries may erupt into conflict over who was more favored at the end, more burdened, or more neglectful of the dying parent. Competitive struggles may ensue over succession issues where a family business is involved. On the other hand, siblings' relationships may at times improve after parental death. Two brothers who had competed for their father's approval since childhood found their relationship freed from old rivalries after his death.

For couples wishing to have children, infertility is often a hidden loss, involving the loss of hopes and dreams (Werner & Moro, 2004), for the extended family as well. The impact of loss becomes more painful as each monthly cycle passes and as menopause approaches, especially with repeated failure of arduous medical interventions. When out of step with siblings and friends who are excited over their own pregnancies or newborns, couples may avoid contact and discussion of their own situation. The incidence of infertility has been rising, associated, in part, with postponement of childbearing. Women who have pursued careers before starting a family are especially vulnerable to criticism and self-blame. It is crucial for clinicians to assuage feelings that adults have not progressed "normally" in the family life cycle without children. Moreover, more adults are choosing not to have children of their own. They are instead opting for surrogacy or adoption, and assuming valuable roles in children's upbringing as aunts, uncles, and godparents; many find fulfilling generativity through their careers.

Stillbirths, miscarriages, and abortion are often hidden, unacknowledged, or minimized by others, rendering the experience more painful and isolated (Doka, 2002; Werner & Moro, 2004). A decision for abortion is not easily made and can be fraught with moral, religious, and legal concerns. With perinatal losses, disappointment and sorrow in the loss of a desired child may be accompanied by the fear of future pregnancy complications. Well-intentioned relatives or friends may encourage couples to try immediately to conceive another child. Where there is social stigma or a lack of resources, partners may turn in on themselves, in a "two against the world" stance, or to withdrawal and mutual blame for the inability to make up for each other's sense of loss. Since the loss of a child places a couple's relationship at risk, brief couples' intervention can facilitate the mourning process and mutual support (Oliver, 1999). It is crucial to help partners share their grief. Mothers more often attend perinatal loss groups for parents than fathers, who should also be encouraged to participate. Grief may be facilitated by encouraging parents to name, have contact with a newborn, take a photo or keepsake, or to hold simple memorial and burial or cremation rites.

Families with young children

The loss of a mate at this life phase is complicated by financial and childrearing obligations, which can interfere with the tasks of mourning. Children may cover their own grief and distract the bereaved parent from grieving out of anxiety about losing their only surviving parent (Fulmer, 1983). Support from extended family members and friends is essential to permit the surviving parent to grieve. Yet, well-intentioned individuals sometimes encourage a survivor to rush into a new relationship, often to fill a missing parental role for children, which risks complicating their shared grief experience and children's acceptance of a new stepparent.

The death of a child is the most tragic of all untimely losses, reversing generational expectations (Worden, 2001). It is often said that, "When your parent dies, you have lost your past. When your child dies, you have lost your future." The sense of injustice in the death of a child can lead family members to profound questioning of the meaning of life, with the loss of parents' hopes and dreams. Families commonly turn toward their faith for comfort and new purpose in their lives (Walsh, 2009b). Some turn away, such as one father, who cried out, "I'm angry at God! How could a loving God take the life of an innocent child?" It was important to understand the tremendous significance of this child for the entire kin network: He was the firstborn son of a Greek orthodox extended family.

Of all losses, it is hardest not to idealize a child who has died. Grief tends to persist and may even intensify at nodal points, such as the graduation of the child's peers (Rando, 1986). A number of studies have documented the high distress of bereaved parents on such indicators as depression, anxiety, somatic symptoms, self-esteem, and sense of control in life. Particularly difficult can be the death of the firstborn, an only child, the only son or daughter, a gifted child, or one with special needs. Because small children are so utterly dependent on parents for their safety and survival, parental blame and guilt tend to be especially strong in accidental or ambiguous deaths, such as SIDS (sudden infant death syndrome). Blame is particularly likely to fall on mothers, who still tend to carry the primary responsibility for a child's well-being, even where paternal abuse or neglect are implicated. Parental difficulties with the loss of a child may be presented through symptomatic behavior of a sibling.

CASE ILLUSTRATION

The Lamb Family

The Lamb family came to therapy when their 4-year-old son, Danny, refused to go to nursery school. In taking a family history, the therapist learned that an older brother, Michael, had died suddenly at the same age, 3 years earlier, after developing a high fever from a virus he had picked up at nursery school. Mr. Lamb and his extended family blamed the mother for the death and had treated her coldly ever since. Isolated in her grief, she kept Michael's room intact and continued to celebrate his birthdays with Danny, each year making a birthday cake with candles for the age he would have been.

The marital relationship is particularly vulnerable after a child's death. Although early studies reported increased risk of divorce, there is evidence that most couples weather the tragedy and many report that their mutual support through the ordeal actually strengthened their bonds (Hagenmeister & Rosenblatt, 1997; Oliver, 1999). Bereavement is eased when both parents have participated in taking care of a sick child prior to death and when they share a philosophy of life or strong religious beliefs that offer meaning and comfort (Walsh, 2009b). Multifamily groups can provide a valuable supportive network for dealing with the painful experience of child loss. Strengthening their relationship is crucial at this vulnerable time (Walsh, 2015).

The needs of siblings and other family members are too often neglected around the death of a child. Siblings may suffer silently on the sidelines. Along with their sibling's death, they may experience secondary parent loss through their preoccupation with the dying process, funeral arrangements, and their own grieving. Some parents withdraw from surviving children to avoid being vulnerable to loss again, whereas others may become overprotective.

Normal sibling rivalry may contribute to survival guilt that can block developmental strivings well into adulthood. A sibling may also be inducted into a replacement role for the family. Such response is not necessarily pathogenic.

Investing energy in surviving children facilitates positive adjustment over time for parents (Videka-Sherman, 1982). However, our clinical experience suggests that if the child's own needs and unique attributes are not affirmed, later attempts at separation and individuation may be thwarted and disrupt the family equilibrium, precipitating intense grief responses in parents (McGoldrick & Walsh, 1983).

Children who lose a parent may suffer long-term effects, including illness, depression, and other emotional disturbances, as well as trouble forming intimate attachments or catastrophic fears of separation and abandonment (Boyd-Webb, 2002; Osterweis et al., 1984; Worden, 2008; Cook & Oltjenbruns, 1998). In our clinical experience, we have also seen many cases where a crisis erupts decades later when a child of a bereaved person reaches the same age as the parental loss.

CASE ILLUSTRATION

Phil and Stacey Kronek

Phil and Stacey Kronek had a stable, if unhappy, marriage for many years, both parents focusing their energies on their only daughter, Lisa. Stacey initiated couples therapy because Lisa, just turning 15, was reacting to the tension between the parents. In the first session, Phil (who had had many affairs over the years) announced that he wanted a separation. Within a month, he introduced his daughter to his new girlfriend, Marti, whom he planned to marry, insisting she call her "mom," although he was not even divorced. It was important to slow him down to explore the feelings behind his precipitous life changes. Lisa at the age of 15 was the same age as he had been when his own mother, also named Marti, had died of a sudden heart attack. His headlong rush to reconfigure his life seemed triggered by anxiety about his own adolescent loss, which he still found intolerable to discuss.

Children's reactions to death will depend on their stage of emotional and cognitive development,

on the way adults deal with them around the death, and on the degree of care they have lost. But children who lose a parent are not doomed to future difficulties. Longitudinal research makes clear that their later resilience and recovery depend largely on the caretaking they receive by surviving family members (Walsh & McGoldrick, 2004) and on what happens as their lives proceed after the loss (Vaillant, 2012). It is important for adults to recognize the limitations of a child's ability to understand what is happening and not to be alarmed by seemingly unemotional or "inappropriate" responses. It is also important to keep communication open to the many conversations over time that will facilitate growing understanding and acceptance. A small child seeks support and understanding through observing the reactions of others (Osterweis et al., 1984). It is crucial for adults not to exclude children from the shared experience of loss, hoping thus to spare them pain (Bowen, 2004). Involvement of extended family members is crucial to assume role functions of the lost parent and the bereaved spouse so there is not a vacuum in caregiving. If children are sent temporarily to live with relatives, it is important to keep siblings together so that they do not also lose this vital bond. Overall, a child's handling of parent loss depends largely on the emotional state of the surviving parent, the availability of other reliable caregivers, and the level of cooperation and support among family members and community after the death.

The loss of a grandparent is often a child's first experience in learning how to deal with the death. Children will be reassured by seeing that parents can cope with the loss. If the grandparent has suffered a prolonged illness with major caregiving demands, the parent will be stressed by pulls in two directions: toward the heavy responsibilities of caring for young children and toward filial obligations for the dying and surviving parent. In families where the grandmother had served a primary childrearing role, her loss is more profound, because of both the emotional bond for children and the function she served in the family. Other major losses, which often go unrecognized for children, include loss of a nanny, housekeeper, godparent, or a cherished pet (Walsh, 2009a).

Families with adolescents

Death at this phase can be complicated by adolescents' developmental issues. Tasks of separation and autonomy may conflict with their ability to acknowledge the significance of the lost bond and to give and receive emotional support. With life-threatening illnesses such as cancer, adolescent defiance often affects compliance with treatments, sparking battles with parents and heightening lethal risks. The most common adolescent deaths are from accidents—often complicated by impulsive, risk-taking, or self-destructive behavior, such as substance abuse and reckless driving—and from suicide and homicide (McIntosh, 1999). Family members commonly carry intense anger, frustration, sadness, and despair about the senseless loss of a young life. Lethal firearms have contributed to an alarming increase in homicides, particularly in neighborhoods where violence and drugs take a tragic toll of young lives. As Burton's (1995) research has shown, poor, minority adolescents in dangerous and blighted communities commonly have a foreshortened expectation of their life cycle and a sense of hopelessness about their future. The high risk of early violent death, especially for young males, fuels doubts about even reaching adulthood and contributes to a focus on immediate gratification, early sex and parenthood, and self-destructive drug abuse.

Any number of problems in living, fueled by the strong peer and media influences, contribute to an adolescent's self-destructive behavior, such as substance abuse, eating disorders, cutting, or an actual decision to commit suicide. When a suicide attempt occurs, the whole family should be convened, helped to understand and reconstruct meanings surrounding the experience, and to repair any family fragmentation from earlier adversities (Dunne & Dunne-Maxim, 2004). It is crucial to explore possible connections to other traumatic losses in the family system (Walsh & McGoldrick, 2004), especially suicides.

CASE ILLUSTRATION

David

David, age 13, was hospitalized following an attempted suicide. He and his family were at a loss to explain the episode and made no mention of an older brother, who had died shortly before David's birth. This event only came out in doing the family genogram. In exploring this, David revealed that to relieve his parents' sadness, he had grown up attempting to take his brother's place, wearing his hand-me-down clothes and combing his hair to resemble photos of the brother he had never known. Now that he was turning 14, and changing physically, he did not know how to be anymore, so he decided to join his brother in heaven. Family therapy focused on enabling David and his parents to relinquish his surrogate position and to encourage his own development.

Adolescents frequently retreat from family interaction following a death, may rebuff parents' initial attempts to engage them, and may talk to no one about the experience. Yet, studies find that most adolescents want to discuss core issues concerning the meaning of life, suggesting the importance of conversations that help them clarify their beliefs and feelings about death and loss (Walsh, 2009b). Such discussions will, of course, be attuned to each family's cultural and spiritual background and prior experience with loss.

Because our dominant culture encourages adolescents to push away from parental closeness, influence, and control, the death of a parent is likely to be complicated by mixed feelings and minimization of the significance of the loss. If the deceased parent is idealized by the family or community, a youth who experienced high conflict, abuse, or neglect may well feel disqualified and become alienated from the family, as in the case of Jack, described below.

Adolescents who may have wished to be rid of parental control may feel considerable guilt when a parent actually dies. Such a loss at this phase is likely to be complicated by the pull of peer models, of acting-out behavior to escape pain, through stealing, drinking, drugs, sexual activity, fighting, or they may withdraw socially. Girls may develop eating disorders, become sexually active or pregnant, or seek intimacy to comfort themselves and replace their loss. Adolescent's acting-out behavior, in turn, stresses the family, and may involve school or juvenile authorities. Such larger systems tend to focus narrowly on the child's problem behavior. It is crucial to assess the context of behavior problems routinely and, where there are recent or impending losses, to assist the family, not only the symptomatic child, in addressing them. Weingarten (1996), drawing on her positive experience in sharing her battle with a life-threatening illness with her own teenage children, argues that maturity, relational connectedness, and empathy are fostered if adolescents are encouraged to stay connected to their parents and to understand their life struggles. Since adolescents may not approach parents, it is crucial for parents to encourage them to voice their concerns and to keep the door open as other concerns surface over time.

CASE ILLUSTRATION

Letter to Camp Counselor

A single parent called after finding her 13-year-old daughter's letter to her camp counselor saying she wanted to die. The mother, who had been battling breast cancer for several years, had recently learned the cancer had spread and was no longer treatable. Trying to be cheerful, she kept the daughter busy with activities and avoided discussion of her terminal condition. The daughter, not wanting to burden her mother, showed no sign of distress and got straight A's at school. The therapist helped the mother share the reality of her condition and anticipate her loss, so that she and the daughter could prepare for the challenges ahead and make the most of the precious time they had left together.

Teenagers, as well as younger children, do worry about their own future. The daughter in this family, with heightened concern about her developing body at puberty, worried that she too would get breast cancer and die. With a heritable disease, offspring do carry risk of illness and death, and may suffer anticipatory loss.

Adolescents are often less ambivalent and more openly expressive of sadness about the loss of a grandparent. Naturally, a parent can feel conflicted when having to cope simultaneously with the grandparent's death and the adolescent's separation. This experience may be intensified if the parent's own adolescence was troublesome and old relational conflicts are unresolved. Teens are frequently the barometer of family feelings, expressing the unspeakable and drawing needed attention to family problems. If parents cannot deal with their own emotional loss issues, an adolescent will often pick up parental feelings and, not knowing a better way to help, will draw fire by misbehavior. Mourning is likely to be complicated by longstanding intergenerational triangles, in which problems between parent and grandparent a generation earlier led to a coalition between grandparent and grandchild, with the parent viewed as the common enemy.

Launching and moving on: Young adults and parents at midlife

Because of societal expectations for young adults to become independent from their families, the significance of loss may not be recognized, complicating mourning at this phase. At launching, the family renegotiates intergenerational relationships to a more equal balance as adults to adults. Where relationships have been uncomfortably close or intensely conflictual, young adults may seek distance through physical or emotional cutoff. Such pseudo-autonomy tends to disintegrate upon contact with the family and can lead to distancing in other relationships.

The death of a young adult is a tragedy for the entire family and may produce long-lasting grief (Rando, 1986, 1993). Many experience a sense of injustice in the ending of a life they have nurtured before it has reached its prime. Survivor guilt may block parents and siblings from continuing their own pursuits. Siblings may be expected to carry the torch and yet be blocked from realizing their own potential by prior sibling rivalry, survivor guilt, and conflicting family injunctions to replace, but not surpass, the lost child (Worden, 2008; McGoldrick, 2011).

CASE ILLUSTRATION

Brian

Brian, age 29, sought therapy for a repeated cycle of setting grandiose career goals that he pursued at a fevered pitch, only to undermine himself each time he was on the brink of success. He felt extreme discomfort whenever he returned home, which his parents had made into a "shrine" to his older brother, who had been killed in military service at the age of 21. Pictures, medals, and plaques covered the walls. Brian felt a strong expectation from his parents to fulfill their dreams for their firstborn son—yet he sensed a counter injunction that it would be disloyal to surpass his brother. Therapy focused on shifting his triangulated position, helping him and his parents to unknot his bind.

The impact of parent loss on young adults may be seriously underestimated by them, their families, friends, and even therapists. A parent's terminal illness is particularly difficult for those who have moved away and are invested in launching career or relationship commitments and feel torn between their own life pursuits and parental needs for care. Those who are not yet secure on their own may be threatened by dependence or fears that they cannot make their way without a parent's support. If the impact of parental loss is not acknowledged and dealt with, a young adult's launching may become forestalled or s/he may distance from the family and seek emotional replacement in a romantic involvement or in having a baby.

In some cases, newly initiated adult life pursuits may need to be abandoned or put on hold. The oldest son—or daughter—may be expected to become the head of the family or carry on a family business. Daughters are more likely expected to assume primary caregiving functions for the surviving parent, younger siblings, and aged grandparents. An adult child may need to move back home or take in a widowed parent.

CASE ILLUSTRATION

Jack

Jack, the youngest son with three older sisters from an Irish family, had lost his mother to a progressive brain cancer when he was 16, the year before he left home for college. All three sisters had already left home and then married within a year of the mother's death, in what seemed an effort to distance from her difficult last years. While in college, Jack sought therapy where, with coaching, he tried to talk to his father about those agonizing years. (His sisters refused to discuss the mother with him, blaming him for dredging up bad memories.). The father agreed to talk, but claimed he remembered nothing negative and said "God would forgive" Jack for what he was saying about his mother's rages in her last years. To Jack's surprise, the father went on a date the next week, the first time in the 3 years since the mother's death. After Jack's graduation, he returned home to live with his father, to whom he had become more attached during his college years, and who was now suffering from a heart condition. His career moved along, but Jack felt stalled in finding a relationship "that worked" until his father died, 20 years later! It was only at that point, at age 42, that he fell in love for the first time, again sought therapy, and was able to focus on starting his own family. It is interesting that the partner he chose was a woman who had herself returned home at the age of 19, when her sister suffered brain damage in a skiing accident and became paraplegic, cared for at home by their parents.

Caregiving responsibilities, guilt, and loyalty issues can complicate life cycle passage for years. The family at launching experiences a major transitional upheaval as children leave and the household must be reorganized without them—although in hard economic times, adult children often return home, confusing relational expectations.

Widowhood at midlife, like earlier widowhood, is much more difficult than in later life because it is untimely and less commonly experienced by peers. At launching, most couples reinvest energy in the marriage and make plans for their future together, with the anticipation of sharing activities that have been postponed while childrearing consumed attention and financial resources. With the death of a partner, these dreams of a shared future are lost. Friends and other couples who are unready to confront their own mortality and survivorship may distance. The bereaved spouse may also be reluctant to burden recently launched children who are not yet established. We encourage widowed women and men to put their own lives in perspective: to consider how they will manage on their own, to develop meaningful pursuits, and to build a supportive social network for the years ahead.

Parents at launching are typically confronting losses on both sides: As their children are leaving home, their aging parents may be declining in health or dying. Most adults in their middle years are prepared to assume increased caregiving responsibilities for aging parents and to accept their deaths as a natural, inevitable occurrence in the life cycle. Nevertheless, clinicians should be attentive to issues of caretaker burnout and resentments that may build up among siblings regarding caretaking. Interventions should focus on promoting collaboration among siblings as a caregiving team.

Caregiving and mourning processes are more complicated for the entire family if intergenerational tensions or cutoffs have been longstanding. Clinically, we move, wherever possible, to bridge cutoffs and promote reconciliation, to strengthen the family in coping with loss and finding positive benefits through shared efforts. A conjoint family life review can be valuable in structuring the sharing of memories to gain a more balanced, evolutionary perspective on family relationships over time. Family members may have mellowed about past grievances, viewing them differently, with new opportunity for repair, or at least a more empathic understanding of differences and disappointments.

Families in later life

With the death of aging parents, adult children at midlife typically confront their own mortality and think more about the time that remains ahead of them. The death of the last surviving family member of the older generation brings awareness that they are now the oldest generation and the next to die. Having—or anticipating—grandchildren commonly eases the acceptance of mortality, so there may be pressure on the recently launched generation to marry and start a family.

With expanded life expectancy, four- and five-generation families are becoming more common. The central life cycle task of old age—accepting one's own mortality—becomes quite real with the deaths of siblings, spouses, and peers. With so many losses common in later life, some older people withdraw and avoid funerals, so as not to face yet another painful loss and their own approaching death. Surviving the death of an adult child is especially painful. As the Chinese say, "White hair should never follow black [in death]." Increasingly, adult children in their later years, with declining health and resources, are needed to care for their very old frail and widowed parents, whose deaths occur most often after chronic illness and disability (Qualls & Zarit, 2009). Intergenerational family conflicts may erupt over issues of caregiving, dependency, and loss of functioning and control as health declines.

For couples, one partner will most likely die before the other. Since most wives outlive their husbands, more women over 65 are widowed, whereas most older men are married, and tend to remarry younger partners. Many widowed women prefer not to remarry, with gendered role expectations to take care of another husband. If the prior marriage was deeply valued, many older widow(er)s may also prefer not to remarry. Widows from more traditional marriages often find themselves unprepared for the financial burdens and lack of adequate retirement benefits of their own. Important areas for preventive intervention are to help men to attend to their own emotional process, and to help women become knowledgeable and empowered regarding their own economic security.

Adaptation to widowhood in older couples is influenced by the nature of the relationship and by the nature of the death, which most often occurs after prolonged challenges of chronic illness and disability (Carr & Jeffreys, 2010). Men are at especially high risk of illness, death, and suicide in the first year of widowhood, with the initial sense of loss, disorientation, and loneliness and the loss of a wife's caretaking. While women generally have a higher rate of depression, men's risk of depression after spousal death is higher (Stroebe, Hansonn, Henk, & Stroebe, 2008). For widowed men and women, feelings of loneliness tend to predominate, even more than for other losses (Parkes, 2009). Husbands' vulnerability to loss may be greater because men are socialized to deny their dependency on their spouse.

The psychosocial tasks for widowhood, as for other losses, are twofold: to grieve the loss of the spouse and to reinvest in future functioning. Common tasks include loosening bonds to the spouse and acknowledging the fact of the death, transforming shared daily experiences into memories. Open expression of grief and loss is important as well as attention to the demands of daily functioning, self-support, household management, and adjustment to being physically and emotionally alone. The challenge of widowhood is often compounded by other dislocations, particularly when the family home and social community are given up or when financial loss or illness reduce independent functioning.

Sibling relationships tend to become increasingly important over adult life, with expectations of "going the distance" together, so the death of a sibling can bring intense grief. Bereavement is complicated because losses reverberate up and down the generations and include the married family system of the sibling as well as the shared family of origin (Marshall & Davies, 2010).

Death in divorced and remarried families

With current high rates of divorce, remarriage, and redivorce expected to continue, clinical inquiry must extend beyond the immediate household to the broader network of family relationships and not overlook deaths in prior marriages, stepfamilies, and committed partnerships. The death of a former spouse may bring a surprisingly strong grief reaction, even if the marriage ended years earlier.

Children's losses of kin or step-relations who have been important to them at some phase in their development should also be attended to. The death of the biological parent leaves a stepparent or co parent who is not the legal guardian of children raised together with no rights to continue their relationship with the children, even where they have formed a strong attachment and assumed financial and other responsibilities. In cases of remarriage where loyalty conflicts are strong, biological children may vehemently contest a will that favors a stepparent and/or stepchildren. Another consideration concerns decisions about burial or comingling of ashes: with which spouse and family? Old wishes may be rekindled by children who wish to reunite their parents for eternity.

If the parents are divorced, the loss of the custodial parent may also set up problematic conflicts over who will take over raising the child. The loss of the noncustodial parent may be problematic because of residual feelings from the divorce, the child's lack of connection with the lost parent, and complex feelings between the custodial parent and the lost parent's extended family.

Assess your comprehension of loss at various family life cycle stages by completing this quiz.

Varied Life Course Challenges: Hidden and Stigmatized Losses

Since most lives today do not fit neatly into the categories and succession of stages, but rather have varied pathways through life, significant losses may be unrecognized. The loss of a committed partner may be felt as deeply as a marital spouse. With remarriage in later years, the death of a newly-wed spouse, although chronologically expectable, may, as in young couples, involve a shattering loss of hopes and dreams, without a shared history and memories to hold onto. Single individuals or couples, both gay and straight, who have chosen not to have children may be assumed erroneously to be suffering, as in the label "childless," or compensating for loss if they prefer to live with companion animals. Indeed, the loss of a cherished pet is one of the most underappreciated losses. Too often the bond is belittled and bereavement is disqualified by others, who say "It's only an animal; you can get another one" (Walsh, 2009b). Meaningful rituals can be valuable in acknowledging and supporting the grief process.

Societal and religious attitudes and laws regarding sexual orientation complicate all losses in gay and lesbian relationships. For couples lacking the legal standing of marriage, the right to be at the hospital bedside of a dying partner may be denied, as well as death benefits. A death may be grieved in isolation when the relationship has been a secret or has been disapproved of by the family or faith community. In states where same-sex marriage is not recognized and a couple is raising children, the nonbiological parent must gain legal status through formal adoption or guardianship for parental rights after the death of the partner who is the biological parent. In such cases, custody may be granted to relatives of the deceased biological parent, who may or may not provide the child access to the surviving partner/parent. The epidemic of AIDS, which initially devastated the gay community, has increasingly affected heterosexual men, women, and their children in poor communities worldwide, with multiple losses throughout relationship networks. While treatment advances have brought new hope for many, tragically the high cost of drug regimens limits availability.

> Assess your comprehension of varied life course challenges: hidden and stigmatized losses by completing this quiz.

Diverse Cultural and Spiritual Beliefs and Practices

Helping family members face death and loss requires respect for their particular cultural traditions and spiritual orientation, which are intertwined (McGoldrick, Giordano, & Garcia Preto, 2005; McGoldrick et al., 2004; Walsh, 2009b). Religion and spirituality come to the fore with death and dying, from existential questions about the meaning of life to convictions about proper final rites and the mystery of afterlife. In Eastern and native American spiritual belief systems, although death ends a life and brings sorrow for loved ones, it is seen as part of a larger life cycle, connecting all living beings. It is crucial to explore ways that core beliefs may offer comfort, such as belief in reunion in heaven, or may exacerbate suffering, such as the belief that infertility was God's punishment for the sin of infidelity. It is important to explore potential spiritual resources that fit client preferences. Research clearly documents the healing power of spiritual beliefs and practices: They offer transcendent values, meaning, and purpose and can provide solace and comfort through faith, prayer or meditation, congregational support, and connectedness to all of life (Walsh, 2009b).

> Assess your comprehension of diverse cultural and spiritual beliefs and practices by completing this quiz.

— Conclusion

At times of death, without mutual support the pain of loss is that much worse for those who grieve alone or not at all. When we foster relational connectedness in the face of loss, families and their members emerge strengthened and more resourceful in meeting future life challenges. It is most important to help the dying person and significant family members to take active charge of the experience of death and dying and make the most of precious time together. Clinicians can facilitate their discussion and crucial decision making, such as, where possible palliative care in a terminal illness phase, hospice care, advance directives, funeral arrangements, wills, disposition of belongings, and care for survivors.

The uniqueness of each life course in its context needs to be appreciated in every assessment of the multigenerational family life cycle and in our understanding of the many meanings of loss. Our own personal, cultural, and spiritual beliefs and experiences surrounding loss need to be examined as they constrain or facilitate our efforts to help grieving families. By coming to accept death as part of life, we discover new possibilities for growth.

> Recall what you learned in this chapter by completing the Chapter Review.

— References —

Becker, E. (1973). *The denial of death.* New York: Free Press.

Bonanno, G. A. (2004). Loss, trauma, and human resilience. *American Psychologist, 59,* 20–28.

Boss, P. (2004). Ambiguous loss. In F. Walsh & M. McGoldrick (Eds.), *Living beyond loss* (2nd ed., pp. 237–246). New York: Norton.

Bowen, M. (2004). Family reaction to death. In F. Walsh & M. McGoldrick, (Eds.), *Living beyond loss* (pp. 79–92). New York: W. W. Norton.

Boyd-Webb, N. (Ed.). (2002). *Helping bereaved children: A handbook for practitioners* (2nd ed.). New York: Guilford Press.

Burton, L. M. (1995). Intergenerational patterns of providing care in African-American families with teenage childbearers: Emergent patterns in an ethnographic study. In V. L. Bengtson, K. W. Schale, & L. M. Burton (Eds.), *Adult intergenerational relations: Effects of societal change,* (pp. 79–125). New York: Springer.

Byng-Hall, J. (2004). Loss and family scripts. In F. Walsh & M. McGoldrick (Eds.), *Living beyond loss* (pp. 85–98). New York: Norton.

Carr, D. & Jeffreys, J. F. (2010). Spousal bereavement in later life. In R. Neimeyer, D. Harris, H. Winokuer, & G. Thornton (Eds.), *Grief and bereavement in contemporary society: Bridging research and practice.* (pp. 81–92). New York: Routledge.

Cook, A. S., & Oltjenbruns, K. A. (1998). *Dying and grieving: Life cycle and family perspectives.* Orlando, FL: Harcourt, Brace & Co.

Danieli, Y. (1985). The treatment and prevention of long-term effects and intergenerational transmission of victimization: A lesson from Holocaust survivors and their children. In C. R. Figley (Ed.), *Trauma and its wake* (pp. 295–313). New York: Bruner/Mazel.

Doka, K. (2002). *Disenfranchised grief.* Champaign, IL: Research Press.

Dunne, E., & Dunne-Maxim, K. (2004). The aftermath of suicide. In F. Walsh & M. McGoldrick (Eds.), *Living beyond loss* (2nd ed., pp. 272–284). New York: Norton.

Ellison, C., & Bradshaw, M. (2009). Religious beliefs, sociopolitical ideology, and attitudes toward corporal punishment. *Journal of Family Issues, 30*(3), 320–340.

Falicov, C. (2013). *Latino families in therapy.* (2nd ed.) New York: Guilford Press.

Figley, C. (1998*). The traumatology of grieving.* San Francisco: Jossey-Bass.

Fulmer, R. H. (1983). A structural approach to unresolved mourning in single parent family systems. *Journal of Marital and Family Therapy, 9*(3), 259–270.

Gamino, L. A., & Ritter, R. H. (2009). *Ethical practice in grief counseling.* New York: Springer.

Hagenmeister, A., & Rosenblatt, P. (1997). Grief and the sexual relationship of couples who have experienced a child's death. *Death Studies, 21,* 231–252.

Hitti, M. (2010). New record for U. S. life expectancy. WebMD Health News. Retrieved April 9, 2010, from www.webmd.com/healthy-aging/news/20060419/record-us-life-expectancy

Jordan, J. R. & McIntosh, J. L. (Eds.). (2010). *Grief after suicide: Understanding the consequences and caring for the survivors.* New York: Routledge.

Kastenbaum, R. J. (1998). Death, society and human experience (6th ed.). Boston: Allyn & Bacon.

Kissane, D. & Lichtenthal, W. G., & Zaider, T. (2007). Family care before and after bereavement. *Omega, 56,* 21–32.

Marshall, B. & Davies, B. (2010). *Bereavement in children and adults following the death of a sibling.* In R. Neimeyer, D. Harris, H. Winokuer, & G. Thornton (Eds.), *Grief and bereavement in contemporary society: Bridging research and practice.* (pp. 107–116). New York: Routledge.

Martin, T. L., & Doka, K. J. (2000). *Men don't cry . . . women do: Transcending gender stereotypes of grief.* New York: Brunner/Mazel.

McGoldrick, M. (2011). *The genogram journey.* New York: Norton. (1st ed: *You can go home again: Reconnecting with your family.* New York: Norton.)

McGoldrick, M., Giordano, J., & Garcia Preto, N. (2005). *Ethnicity and family therapy* (3rd ed.). New York: Guilford Press.

McGoldrick, M., & Walsh, F. (1983). A systemic view of family history and loss. In M. Aronson & D. Wolberg (Eds.), *Group and family therapy 1983* (pp. 252–272). New York: Brunner/Mazel.

McGoldrick, M., Gerson, R., & Petry, S. (2008). *Genograms: Assessment and intervention.* (3rd ed.). New York: W. W. Norton.

McGoldrick, M., Schlesinger, J. M., Hines. P. M., Lee, E., Chan, J., Almeida, R., Petkov, B. et al. (2004). Mourning in different cultures: English, Irish, African American, Chinese, Asian Indian, Jewish, Latino, and Brazilian. In F. Walsh & M. McGoldrick (Eds.), *Living beyond loss: Death in the family* (2nd ed., pp. 119–160). New York: Norton.

McIntosh, J. L. (1999). Death and dying across the life span. In T. L. Whitman, T. V. Merluzzi (Ed.), *Life-span perspectives on health and illness* (pp. 249–274), London: Psychology Press.

Nadeau, J. W. (2008). Meaning-making in bereaved families: Assessment, intervention, and future research. In M. Stroebe, R. Hansson, H. Schut, & W. Stroebe (Eds.), *Handbook of bereavement research: 21st century perspectives* (pp. 511–530). Washington, DC: American Psychological Association.

Oliver, L. E. (1999). Effects of a child's death on the marital relationship. A review. *Omega, 39*(3), 197–227.

Osterweis, M., Solomon, F., & Green, M. (Eds.). (1984). *Bereavement: Reactions, consequences, and care.* Washington, DC: National Academy Press.

Parkes, C. M. (2001). *Bereavement: Studies of grief in adult life.* London, Routledge.

Parkes, C. M. (2009). *Love and loss: The roots of grief and its complications.* New York: Routledge.

Parkes, C. M., & Weiss, R. S. (1983) *Recovery from bereavement.* New York: Basic Books.

Paul, N., & Paul, B. (1989). *A marital puzzle.* New York: Norton.

Qualls, S. & Zarit, S. (Eds.). (2009). *Aging families and caregiving.* New York: Wiley.

Rando, T. (1993). *Treatment of complicated mourning.* Champaign, IL: Research Press.

Rando, T., Ed. (1986). *The parental loss of a child.* Champaign, IL.: Research Press.

Shapiro, E. (1994). *Grief as a family process.* New York: Guilford.

Stroebe, M., Hansonn, R., & Henk, S. & Stroebe, W. (2008). *Handbook of bereavement research and practice: Advances in theory and intervention.* Washington, DC: American Psychological Association.

Stroebe, M., & Schut, H. (2010). The Dual Process Model of coping and bereavement: A decade on. *Omega: Journal of Death and Dying, 61*(4), 273–289.

Stroebe, M., Schut, H., & Boerner, K. (2010). Continuing bonds in adaptation to bereavement: Toward theoretical integration. *Clinical Psychology Review, 30*(2), 259–268.

Vaillant, G. (2012). *Triumphs of experience: The men of the Harvard study.* Cambridge, MA: Belknap.

Videka-Sherman, L. (1982). Coping with the death of a child: A study over time. *American Journal of Orthopsychiatry, 52,* 688–698.

Walsh, F. (2003). Family resilience: A framework for clinical practice. *Family Process 42,* 1–18.

Walsh, F. (2007). Traumatic loss and major disasters: Strengthening family and community resilience. *Family Process, 46,* 207–227.

Walsh, F. (2009a). Human–animal bonds: II. The role of pets in family systems and family therapy, *Family Process, 48*(4), 481–499.

Walsh, F. (Ed.). (2009b). Spiritual resources in adaptation to death and loss. In F. Walsh (Ed.) *Spiritual resources in family therapy* (2nd ed., pp. 81–102). New York: Guilford Press.

Walsh, F. (2012). The "new normal:" Diversity and complexity in 21st century families. In F. Walsh (Ed.), *Normal family processes* (4th ed., pp. 4–27). New York: Guilford Press.

Walsh, F. (2014). Conceptual framework for family bereavement care: Strengthening resilience. In D. Kissane (Ed.) *Bereavement care for families.* (p. 17–29). New York: Routledge.

Walsh, F. (2015). *Strengthening family resilience* (3rd ed.). New York: Guilford Press.

Walsh, F., & McGoldrick, M. (2004). *Living beyond loss: Death in the family* (2nd ed.). New York: Norton.

Walsh, F. & McGoldrick, M. (2013). Bereavement: A family life cycle perspective. *Family Science, 4,* 20–27.

Weingarten, K. (1996). The mother's voice: Strengthening intimacy in families. New York: Guilford Press.

Werner, L. A., & Moro, T. (2004). Unacknowledged and stigmatized losses. In F. Walsh & M. McGoldrick (Eds.), *Living beyond loss* (pp. 247–271). New York: Norton.

Worden, J. W. (2001). *Children and grief: When a parent dies.* New York: Guilford.

Worden, J. W. (2008). *Grief counseling and grief therapy* (4th ed). New York: Springer.

Wortman, C., & Silver, R. (1989). The myths of coping with loss. *Journal of Counseling and Clinical Psychology, 57,* 349–357.

Chapter 20

Divorce: An Unscheduled Family Transition

Constance R. Ahrons

Learning Outcomes

- Describe how divorce alters a family's developmental life course.
- Examine divorce from historical, legal, and demographic perspectives.
- Explore how the issues and decisions of divorce depend on the placement of the divorce in the family's developmental life cycle.
- Discuss how divorce is a multidimensional process of family change.
- Identify sociocultural factors that alter how divorce affects a family.
- List and describe the transitions of the divorce process.
- Identify and describe the objectives of a healthy divorce.
- Identify strategies to help families reorganize as healthy systems.

Introduction

Although divorce is common in family life today, our culture clings to the view that it is deviant and the cause of many of society's social problems. In spite of greater social acceptance, divorce is still viewed as an abnormality that will go away only if we can find out how to make it do so. The reality is that divorce is a social institution in the same way that marriage is, and, as long as we continue to marry, we will continue to offer divorce as an optional safety valve for unsatisfactory marriages.

In this chapter, divorce will be examined from a normative perspective, and the process will be discussed as a multidimensional series of predictable transitions that affect families intergenerationally. It is an *unscheduled* life transition that affects large numbers of families and alters their developmental life course. Although all divorces have some common denominators, the placement of divorce in the developmental life cycle will result in differential effects on family members. For example, parents who divorce when their children are young will face different issues and decisions, such as custody and

living arrangements for children, than parents who divorce after their children are grown.

How divorce affects the family is also altered by diverse sociocultural factors. Ethnic and religious groups may differ in the way they perceive divorce, and these different perceptions influence how a family copes. In order to help families reorganize as healthy systems, clinicians need to understand the nature of the divorce process, the family's developmental stage, and the sociocultural background of the family.

 Assess your comprehension of the introduction by completing this quiz.

The Context of Divorce: Historical and Legal Perspectives

In the past three centuries, divorce rates reached their peak in the late 1970s. Between 1965 and 1980—the prosperous years—divorce rates more than doubled. However, in the 1980s, the economy dipped, and the divorce rate declined slightly. Since then the overall rate has leveled off and has remained steady.

It is interesting to note that the first recorded divorce in America happened back in 1639, in a Puritan court in Massachusetts, when James Luxford's wife asked for a divorce because her husband already had a wife. The divorce was granted. Public and legal debates about the high divorce rates occurred as early as the late 1700s. These early debates were very similar in tone and content to the discussions we hear these days about whether we should make divorce laws more or less difficult. The pattern of liberalizing divorce laws and then tightening them, seesawing from honoring the individual to honoring the society and back again, is one that we have seen throughout Europe and the United States.

The latter part of the twentieth century was marked by major reforms. In 1969 to 1970, California became the first state to change divorce from an adversarial to a nonadversarial process. Other states followed and, although there is considerable variability in divorce laws from state to state, by 1985 every state had adopted some form of no-fault divorce law. As this less punitive approach to divorce evolved, waiting periods became shorter, and reconciliation counseling was no longer mandatory in most jurisdictions. Referred to as "the divorce revolution," this important symbolic shift continues to be a source of major debate in the United States, and controversy exists about its impact on divorce rates and societal family values (Adams & Coltrane, 2007).

Demographics and the Probability of Divorce

The probability of divorce is associated with a number of demographic factors. Age is the strongest predictor. Couples who are 20 years of age or younger when they marry have the highest likelihood of divorce. In general, people with less income and education tend to divorce more than those with higher education and incomes. There are gender differences in divorce as well: women initiate nearly two thirds of divorces.

Geographically, there are some differences as well. People in the western part of the United States have higher divorce rates than those in the northeast. This may be due partly to the fact that the average marriage age is lower in the west. Also,

there is a higher concentration of Catholics in the northeast.

There are also significant racial and ethnic differences. Divorce rates for the African American population are two times those of Whites or Hispanics. Although the explanations for the higher divorce rate among African Americans vary, socioeconomic differences seem to play a part. On the average, African Americans are less educated, poorer, and more often unemployed than European Americans. Latinos have a lower divorce rate; however, they appear to have higher rates of separation than other racial–ethnic groups. Asian Americans have the lowest rates of any racial–ethnic group (Demo & Fine, 2009).

Religion also plays a part. Catholics and Jews have a lower divorce rate than Protestants. Since Catholicism is the religion of traditional Hispanics, part of the explanation for the racial differences in divorce rates may be attributed to religious affiliation. Although Catholics have a lower divorce rate, their rates have risen just as rapidly as those of the general divorce population (Ahlburg & DeVita, 1992).

Cohabitation is increasingly accepted as an alternative to marriage, and this has affected both marriage and divorce rates. In some European countries, a recent decline in divorce rates can be attributed to the increase in informal cohabitation arrangements. In Sweden, for example, this increase in cohabitation has decreased the marriage rate as well as the divorce rate. Breakups of these informal unions, of course, are not included in the calculation of divorce rates.

At present, it is estimated that approximately 40 percent of first marriages in the United States end in divorce (Demo & Fine, 2009). Demographic trends suggest that the current divorce rates in the United States are now fairly stable. Demographers predict that 40 to 60 percent of all current marriages will eventually end in divorce. Those who predict the lower rates say that the divorce rate will decline as the baby boomers age; that boomers who wish to divorce have already done so, and those who have not are past the stage of life when the odds of divorce are the highest (Glick, 1990). Those who predict an increase, whether large or small, say that women and men's roles will continue to change. That change, plus the increasing financial independence of women—historically the less satisfied party in marriage—will continue to push the rates upward (Bumpass, 1990).

Ethnic, Gender, and Life Cycle Variations

Although more studies are emerging on ethnic and racial populations, a serious weakness of the current state of divorce research is that most of the research is still based on White, middle-class samples. Our interest in divorce has been focused mainly on its effects on children, and most of the research has focused on young children and their mothers (Lamb et al., 1997). A growing body of research based on information collected from both parents, using court records rather than clinical data, is gradually beginning to provide important data on the entire family system (Ahrons, 1994; Hetherington, 1993; Maccoby & Mnookin, 1992; Stewart, et al., 1997). These studies tend to be small, in-depth studies based on in-person interviews, often conducted at two or three different time periods in the divorced family life cycle.

Larger studies, utilizing national samples, provide comparative information on divorced and married families. These studies usually focus on school-age children and their primary parent, most frequently the mother. These studies are often part of a larger study, and although they contribute greatly to our general knowledge of the effects of divorce, they provide less family interaction data than do the smaller, more intensive studies.

There is also a paucity of research on divorce in midlife and later life and on the effects on older children and young adults. Although the overall current divorce rates have leveled off, the divorce rate among those married 20 years or longer has actually doubled in the past decade. Because research is lacking, we can only hypothesize about the reasons for this increase. In these longer marriages, children may be in the process of leaving home or have already moved out of the family home. This "empty nest" transition usually occurs when the parents are in a midlife transition, and the convergence of these two transitions often creates a divorce crisis. Another possibility is that many couples in unhappy marriages put off separation until the children are grown.

The effects of a parental divorce on young adult children have not received attention from researchers until recently. Young adult children suffer the effects of their parents' divorce differently than younger children. They often feel they have to take care of one parent and/or become a confidant of a parent. For some, financial support from parents diminishes as their parents need to establish two separate households. Young adult children who are in college may feel the loss of their home and confusion or loyalty conflicts about where to spend the holidays.

The most confusing and complex situations in divorce are related to the LBG (lesbian, gay, and bisexual) populations. Although same-sex couples have been breaking up for years, only recently have they had the opportunity to legally marry in some states, and thus legal divorce is now a consideration. However, with a few exceptions, couples can divorce only in jurisdictions that recognize same-sex marriages, and the majority of states do not provide legal guidelines to govern separations of same-sex couples, many of whom are co-parents. This patchwork of laws in the United States leads to complex difficulties, such as how to get divorced in a state that does not recognize same-sex marriage (Lyness, 2012). This ambiguity extends to child custody issues, especially in those states that do not recognize same-sex marriages. Decisions made by the courts during a custody dispute bring in to debate the rights of biological parents.,

Most of what is presented in this chapter is based on the existing research, with particular emphasis on the author's own longitudinal study. When information is available in the literature on ethnic, gender, and life cycle variations, then findings will be noted.

The Social Context

Divorce is usually thought to be symptomatic of family instability and synonymous with family dissolution.

This view is reflected in the terms used to describe the divorced family: "broken home," "disorganized," "fractured," and "incomplete." Most research has been designed to search for problems created by divorce and often relies on clinical or problem-identified populations. Not only is divorce viewed that way in the professional literature, but it is also quite common to find divorce labeled in the media as the cause of all sorts of social problems, such as drugs, delinquency, and family violence.

The media is a powerful tool in defining how we view social issues. Unfortunately, the media leans toward short, sound-bite answers, even to the most complex social questions. These sound-bites become polarized, and divorce is positioned as either good or bad; children are either doomed or saved. One day we hear divorce dooms children to lifelong problems; the next day we hear children are doing well. These extreme positions—of divorce as disaster and divorce as inconsequential—oversimplify the realities of our complex lives.

This view has given rise to a distorted perception of divorce, leading investigators and practitioners to focus primarily on pathology. For example, the term "single-parent family" implies that a family contains only one parent; however, in most divorced families, although mothers are usually the primary caregivers, both parents continue to function in parental roles (Stewart et al., 1997). Divorce creates new households with single parents, but it results in a single-parent family only when one of the parents, usually the father, has no further contact with the family and does not continue to perform a parental function. More appropriate terminology would distinguish between these two circumstances and would describe the former as a "one-parent household" (Ahrons, 1980a, 1980b).

Although the loss of the father–child relationship is an all too common outcome for many children in divorced families, innovative custody arrangements—such as joint custody and the increased involvement of fathers in child-rearing roles—have also created postdivorce family arrangements in which the children continue to be reared by both parents (Ahrons & Tanner, 2003). The majority of postdivorce families have evolved continuing and well-functioning relationships that do not appear

to be at all pathological (Kelly, 2005; Lamb et al., 1997). In such cases, divorce has not terminated family relationships; rather, it has been a process whereby the form of these relationships has changed.

Divorce as a Multidimensional Process

From a legal and social status perspective, divorce is an event; it moves individuals from the condition of being legally married to that of being legally divorced. When the divorce decree is final, the partners are free to remarry. However, looked at from a family dynamics standpoint and not a legal standpoint, divorce is best regarded as a multidimensional process of family change. It has roots somewhere in the past, before the legal act transpired, and carries with it effects that extend into the future. Each family member will be profoundly affected by it; as members of a postdivorce family, individuals will be forced to learn new ways of coping and of relating to the society at large, as well as to each other.

The Binuclear Family

The process of divorcing culminates in a complex redefinition of relationships within the family. Although the structure of postdivorce families varies, some basic tasks must be accomplished in all separations. Once a family has established the ground rules for living separately (e.g., where the children will reside or how visitation will be arranged), the family needs to clarify rules for relating within and across the various subsystems within the family system, for example, the parental subsystem or the parent–child subsystem.

Dual-household binuclear families

The multidimensional divorce process can be viewed as a series of transitions that mark the family's change from married to divorced status. This process involves disorganizing the nuclear family and reorganizing it into a binuclear family. The binuclear family consists of two households or subsystems, maternal and paternal, which then form the nuclei of the child's family of orientation (Ahrons, 1979, 1980a).

Binuclear families are similar to extended kin or quasi-kin relationships. In many families, for example, the marriage of a child marks the beginning of a quasi-kin relationship between the families of the newly married couple. In this quasi-kin structure, two families are bonded through the marriage of their children. Jewish families have institutionalized this nonblood familial relationship. The Yiddish term *machetunim* means "relatives through marriage," referring specifically to the relationship between the family of the bride and the family of the groom (Rosten, 1989). Many Jewish families frequently spend holidays and special events with their "machatunim." These two families may or may not like each other, but amicability is not the primary reason for their gathering. They gather not as intimates, but as "blood" relations.

The bonds created by families joined through marriage are similar to the bonds of the divorced family. In both types of families, a child gives rise to the continuing bond. In the family joined through marriage, the relationship between the two sets of in-laws usually determines the interrelationships within the extended-family system. The style of relationship within the divorced family is usually based on the nature of the relationship between the divorced spouses.

Transitions of the Divorce Process

Transitions are turning points, uncomfortable periods that mark the beginning of something new while signifying the ending of something familiar. Although the changes may be anticipated with puzzlement and foreboding, they may also be approached with exhilaration. During transitional periods, families are more personally vulnerable, but paradoxically these are also the times when personal growth is most likely to occur.

Usually, when we think of transitions, we think in terms of the biological developmental clock: adolescence, midlife, or aging. In defining biological developmental transitions, in outlining typical themes, common feelings, and experiences, we normalize situations that otherwise would feel, and appear to be, abnormal. When people know what to expect, it does not take away all the upheaval, but it does help them to cope better with the difficult changes that the transition inevitably brings. People experience great relief when they can place themselves within a natural progression that has a beginning and an end. Although we usually define transitions within developmental frameworks (e.g., birth of a first child, retirement), some life transitions are unrelated to developmental or social time clocks.

Unlike other transitions that occur more or less on predictable chronological timetables, divorce can occur at any time during the family life cycle. Unlike expected transitions in the life cycle, divorce has a greater potential to cause disequilibrium that can result in debilitating crises. And, unlike family crises of sudden onset, the divorce process begins long before the actual decision to obtain a legal divorce. Divorce is an internal crisis of relationship, a deliberate dissolution of the primary bond in the family, and the family's identity appears to be shattered. For most people, ending a marriage is the most traumatic decision of their lives. The usual ways of coping are unlikely to work. People often act in ways that no one around them can make sense of. Abigail Trafford (1982) refers to this period as "crazy time."

Stress, crisis, and adaptation are three concepts that are often used in understanding how families cope with life's distressful events, such as chronic illness, death of a loved one, and unemployment (Boss, 1987, 2006; Rodgers, 1986). Stress occurs when there is an imbalance (perceived or actual) between what is actually happening—the stressors—and what family members feel capable of handling. Crisis occurs when stress exceeds the ability of individuals in the family to effectively handle the stressors. All families have different levels of tolerance—breaking points—beyond which they are no longer able to cope with the situation. When too many things hit all at once, when stressors pile up, system overload sets in. When the family's reservoir of coping behaviors becomes depleted or outmoded and they do not know what to do, they are in a crisis.

Divorce is ranked at the top of the list of stressful life events. Many stressors overlap in the divorce transitions. All of the normal coping abilities are taxed by complex personal and familial changes. Add the lack of adequate role models of good divorces, the absence of clear-cut rules or rituals for managing this new and unfamiliar stage of life, and the lack of external resources, such as community support and positive social sanctions, and crisis is certainly a predictable outcome.

Ambiguity is a big contributor to stress (Boss, 1983). For divorcing parents and their children, the knowledge that their family will continue to be a family, restructuring from a nuclear to a binuclear form, reduces some of the debilitating ambiguity associated with divorce. Understanding that divorce is a process with predictable transitions of disorganization followed by structured transitions of reorganization helps at least reduce the intensity and duration of the crisis. When families have knowledge of what to expect with adequate role models to assist them, they can better identify which decisions need to be made—and when—and can then decide what kind of new rules need to be established. The knowledge and ability to plan facilitate their capacity to cope more effectively during the crisis and manage the mass of overwhelming feelings. In effect, they move the divorce process toward "normality."

The lack of adequate norms, knowledge, and role models has been detrimental for divorcing families. Clinicians working with them have also lacked the knowledge and skills to help these families move through the transitions and emerge as healthy binuclear families. New strategies for assisting families through the divorce process that incorporate normative models, such as mediation, psychoeducational workshops, co-parenting seminars, and collaborative law, are emerging and creating healthier outcomes for families.

 Assess your comprehension of transitions of the divorce process by completing this quiz.

The Transitions Framework

Breaking down the very complex process of divorce into transitions—common developmental steps—allows us to explore the ways people adapt at each of the stages. Developed from my longitudinal research on divorcing families, five overlapping transitions, each with distinct role changes and tasks, were identified (Ahrons, 1980a, 1994; Ahrons &

Rodgers, 1987). The first three transitions—individual cognition, family metacognition, and systemic separation—form the core of the disorganizing emotional separation process. The last two transitions—systemic reorganization and systemic redefinition—form the family reorganization process.

Although they are presented sequentially in their ideal developmental order, the transitions usually overlap. Each transition includes social role transitions encompassing a complex interaction of overlapping experiences. There is no neat rule for when a particular transition will occur in a particular person or couple or for how long the transition will last. What we do know, from studies in the United States and from cross-national studies, regardless of cultural or national differences, is that it takes most people between one and a half and three years after the initial separation to stabilize their feelings (Cseh-Szombathy, et al., 1985). Each transition is heralded by increased stress. At the end of the transition, the stress tends to plateau or to decrease.

Individual Cognition: The Decision

The decision to end a marriage is usually far more difficult and prolonged than the decision to marry. The dread of negative repercussions, an uncertain future, and painful losses all combine to make the transition a wrenching and internally violent one. The first step toward divorce is rarely mutual. It begins within one person, often starting as a small, amorphous, nagging feeling of dissatisfaction. The feeling grows in spurts, sometimes gaining strength, sometimes retreating, flaring up, and again moving forward. For some people, this private simmering of unhappiness goes on for years. For others, a few months of depression may be more than they can bear. The hallmark of this transition is ambivalence, accompanied by obsession, vacillation, and anguish. It is not uncommon for the individual in the throes of this process to have an affair and/or seek out a therapist.

When an individual begins to seriously question feelings for his or her mate, a passage of emotional leave taking takes place. This "erosion of love" starts slowly and may be barely noticeable at first. Behaviors that were acceptable for years become annoying; habits that were tolerated become intolerable. More and more "evidence" is collected as a case is built to justify the decision to leave.

Characteristic of the coping mechanisms in this transition is the denial of marital problems. Spouses also resort to blaming to obtain respite from a situation that is perceived as intolerable. Marital conflicts usually escalate the search for fault in the other spouse and often result in his or her being labeled the culprit. This time can be a highly stressful one, especially for the children, who often become pawns in the marital strife. Conflict-habituated marriages are less threatening to some families than the uncertainty and change that accompany separation and divorce. In other families, instead of open conflict, there are a distancing and withdrawal of emotional investment, in the marriage and often in the family. In families with dependent children, it is not uncommon to make a decision—albeit often not adhered to—to stay in the marriage until the children are grown. The dissatisfied partner may decide to invest emotional energy in extramarital interests while attempting to maintain the facade of an intact family. These patterns usually result in family dysfunction. When marital relationships are highly conflictual or cold and distant, it is not unusual for a child living in that household to develop symptoms, which in turn may prompt the family to seek therapy. In this way, the "secret" may become exposed.

Another very common pattern that clinicians see is the couple who come in for therapy with two different—but not openly stated—agendas. Although both may come in for marriage counseling, one partner has already emotionally disengaged from the relationship and comes to therapy as a way to relieve his or her guilt. She or he can then say, "I've tried everything to make this marriage work, even marriage counseling." Or the disengaged partner, fearful of the other partner's reaction to the planned leave taking, may seek out a therapist who can become the caretaker/rescuer of the soon-to-be left partner. In both cases, the therapist has the difficult task of trying to help the couple honestly face their issues before any treatment contract can be arrived at.

Although a divorce often ends up being a mutual decision, at the early stages there is one person (the initiator or leaver) who harbors the secret desire to leave and one person who is initially unaware of that desire (the opposer or the left). In some cases, both partners may have had similar fantasies, but one person usually takes the first step and begins the process.

Leavers and lefts have very different feelings at the outset. The leaver has had the advantage early on of wrestling with his or her emotions, has already started grieving, and has already detached to some degree. The person being left is perceived to be the victim. This person's immediate reactions range from disbelief and shock to outrage and despair. The partners have unequal power at this point. The person being left is more vulnerable. Having had no time to prepare—to adapt to the overwhelming threat—the one being left is more likely to experience crisis at this point.

Who takes the role of leaver and who takes the role of left often relate to gender. In the United States and most European countries, it is estimated that two thirds to three quarters of all divorces are initiated by women. One of the biggest factors leading to this statistic is the increase in women's economic independence. It is not that women used to be happier in marriage than they are today, but they often believed that they could not survive outside of marriage without their husband's money. Even today, the lowest divorce rate occurs in traditional marriages with breadwinner husbands and full-time homemaker wives. Not only have women's economic opportunities expanded, so have their social opportunities. Even though we still live in a very coupled society, it is much easier today than it was even 20 years ago to live a full life as a single woman. Even so, many women say that they left because they had no choice. Stories of years of abuse, betrayal, or absenteeism by their husband are common.

Family Metacognition: The Announcement

Proclaiming one's desire to separate from one's partner is no easy task. But for some couples, the announcement is as far as their marital crisis will go. Sometimes, the moment of confrontation creates an opportunity to actually improve a marriage. For other couples, the announcement is the first step in a tangled escalating series of confrontations and reconciliations. For still others, one day they are married and the next day they are not; the announcement can also be a clear, direct, and sometimes almost instant path to separation and divorce.

Denial often follows any major shock. One common reaction is for the spouse to call the leaving partner's reasons frivolous. It is not uncommon, in the early phase right after the announcement occurs, to think that a few minor changes—becoming more attentive or more attractive—will help what seems to be an anomalous outburst to blow over. Although it is rare, sometimes a new wardrobe, flowers, extra telephone calls, and other efforts do help temporarily, especially when the potential leaver is still very ambivalent.

Leavers almost always portray a long, painful process of leave taking. The one being left is coping not only with rejection but also with having to develop an account after the fact. In the first two phases of the process, the leaver commonly feels guilty; the left feels angry. Rarely is the process symmetrical, let alone rational or mutual.

In many cases, the announcement seems spontaneous, as much a dreadful surprise to the leaver as to the left. In these cases, the discomfort is often so severe that the leaver (either consciously or unconsciously) resorts to setting up a situation that will bring the issue into the open without anyone having to accept responsibility. The leaver may get forgetful and leave a lover's letter on the dresser, stay out all night, or arrive home with the proverbial lipstick on the collar. Once discovered, the objects or events provoke a crisis, and it is over. Creating a crisis makes it possible to shift the blame. The couple can then fight about whatever issue got raised in the crisis, rather than dealing with the long-term issues of their distressing marital relationship.

BETRAYAL AND BLAME. Statistics on extramarital affairs are very varied and highly unreliable, owing to the unwillingness of many people to disclose them (Brown, 1991; Spring, 1996), but they are quite common to marital separations. What is worse than the affair itself—more difficult to cope with—is the protective web of lies. As each lie gets uncovered or explodes during a battle about the affair, the

betrayed spouse begins to question the entire history of the relationship. The betrayed person questions the betrayer closely, even obsessively, trying to separate truth from fiction. The betrayer and the betrayed rarely see eye to eye on how much talking is needed.

For a myriad of reasons, it is difficult for the betrayer to be truthful. Perhaps he or she wants to hold onto both the spouse and lover, wants to protect against possible legal ramifications, or does not want to inflict more pain. The betrayed senses that there is more and keeps pressing, trying to get to the bottom of things. The betrayer may comply for a while, then usually grows impatient with the constant focus and repetition. The betrayer thinks that the betrayed spouse is "carrying this too far." Blame then shifts to the betrayed spouse for not letting go (Brown, 1991; Lerner, 1993). This common and very predictable pattern, unfortunately, lays the groundwork for a highly acrimonious and destructive divorce process. If a clinician is brought into this process at this transition, she or he may be able to help the couple to sort out the issues and to understand the power struggle that pervades this process. However, all too often, the betrayer is unwilling to commit to therapy, and the issue of "the affair" pervades the rest of the divorce transitions. Although divorce is legally no-fault and adultery is no longer needed to show cause, blame often plays a big role in the emotional divorce process.

Rage, prejudicial myth making, depression, and impulsive desires to retaliate are normal reactions for the partner who is being left. Anger plays an important role when there is a bad blow to the ego. It temporarily shields the betrayed spouse from facing devastating emotions: grief, rejection, and even self-hatred. If, over the course of the marriage, mutual anger has been buried, the anger can easily erupt in this transition. All the past injustices that were not confronted are replayed. Both the earlier denial and the current anger help the one who has been left to cope with a life that is swinging out of control.

LOSS. Divorce is marked by severe losses. Not only are the losses related to the present life style, but there are also losses of future plans and fantasies. Even for the couple in the early stages of marriage, there are powerful feelings of loss. Their whole dream of married life may be shattered; the children they had planned for and the house they were going to buy remain unrealized dreams. Couples with young children have to face that their future plans will never materialize: the wonderful skiing vacations they were planning to take in a couple of years or the camping trip to the Grand Canyon. The midlife couple who divorces after a long marriage may have had retirement plans that will never come to fruition: the long awaited trip to Europe after the children were grown or that secluded house at the lake.

Unresolved grieving for losses is a major deterrent to making a healthy adaptation to divorce. Clinicians need to be aware that when anger is the major coping mechanism of a divorcing spouse, uncovering the grief may need to be a very slow process. Otherwise, the depression may be so overwhelming that the spouse, especially if she or he is the primary parent, may not be able to function in the parental role.

This transition is key to the rest of the transitions. Family therapy at this time can be very productive. Sometimes, even a few sessions can help to clarify how to deescalate the anger whenever it occurs during the divorce process. Additional sessions can help both children and adults to defuse their terror about the major changes that divorce brings; they can start to plan. To avert a serious crisis requires that both partners show considerable patience, maturity, and honesty. Leavers need to understand their partner's angry reaction and give him or her time to deal with it. Being able to talk about some of the changes that can be expected during the next transitions as the marriage is being dismantled is important, as frustrating and difficult as such talk may be. The more responsibly couples plan for a timely separation, the less likely it is to break down into debilitating crisis. For couples, being rational during such emotional times is often impossible without the help of a therapist.

Systemic Separation: Dismantling the Nuclear Family

Most people remember the day they separated— not the day their divorce was legally awarded—as the day their divorce began. Separation day is one of those marker events that divorced people never forget. For children, this is when they realize the enormity of what is going on, even though they may have suspected or feared the prospect for some time.

Some couples and children feel a great sense of relief at the separation transition, especially when the marriage had become highly stressful. Other families are overwhelmed with fear and anxiety. Still for others, it is the worst crisis point of all. Everyone experiences this transition as a time of major disorganization, when the routines of daily life go up in smoke. It is a time of anomie—normlessness. Old roles disappear; new ones have yet to form. The future of the family is unknown.

There are no clear-cut rules for separating. Who moves out? How often should spouses continue to see one another? When (and what) should they tell family and friends? Who will attend the school conferences next week? Who will get the season tickets for the theater? Who will attend the wedding of a mutual friend next month? These types of questions, seemingly trivial but deeply resonant, plague newly separated people at all stages of the family life cycle.

ORDERLY AND DISORDERLY SEPARATIONS. Separations fall on a continuum from orderly to disorderly, from the anticipated to the utterly shocking. Orderly separations are the least destructive. They are most likely to occur if there has been time for some preparation and planning before the actual physical separation. Disorderly separations usually occur when the earlier crisis points have not been worked through. Separation involves major life changes, and it requires careful planning, especially when there are children. Children have the right to know what is going on, and they need to have adequate time to process it with both parents. Even couples with grown children need to prepare their adult offspring—and grandchildren—for the changes that separation entails.

Abrupt departures usually create severe crises for those left behind. It is the ultimate rejection— abandonment. The abandonment leaves one feeling totally helpless and frequently culminates in a severe debilitating family crisis, such as a suicide attempt by one partner or a major clinical depression requiring hospitalization. Abandoned children regress, get depressed, or act out. The rejection is too great and too sudden to cope with.

Orderly separations have two common factors: good management and firm relationship boundaries. Good management requires knowing about and preparing for the transitions of divorce, averting crises by defusing tension at marker points, and giving the process enough time for everyone to adjust.

Boundaries are simply rules for how separated spouses will interact—and not interact. To construct good boundaries, spouses need to recognize how their roles have changed. To keep the boundaries firm, new rules and rituals need to be developed.

For women in particular, the two roles of wife and mother traditionally provide a central core of identity. Often, the two roles become enmeshed. It is not unusual to hear an ex-wife say, "He left *us*." The more a woman's identity is tied to a combined wife/mother role, the more likely she is to experience this stress of role loss.

Men's role loss after divorce may seem less pronounced than women's. Even though gender roles are shifting, men are still more likely than women to define themselves by work and to define their roles as spouses more narrowly. The more demanding and compelling his work, the more a man can throw himself into it to fill his time and thoughts, thereby anesthetizing the pain of the separation.

Even for the couple who divorces in the early stages of marriage, the discomfort of role loss is felt. Losing the role of being coupled and returning to singleness are fraught with feelings of failure and loss of status. For couples married longer, the extent of the role losses is more complex and severe. Their lives have usually been defined by their married status: friends, neighbors, community, and family all view them as a couple. Returning to a single existence that they have not experienced for 20 or 30 years requires a totally new self-definition.

Rules are needed for any system to function. When one household becomes two, many of the rules that are built into the marital system become instantly obsolete. New rules will be needed to define a new relationship. Separated couples need to find ways to reduce the intimacy and appropriately increase their distance. Until the actual separation, a couple is usually unaware of how interdependent their lives have become. Trial and error may be necessary until they establish a new comfort level.

Rituals mark important transitions and events. They solidify, solemnize, and publicize our values. They also quell our anxiety by showing us how to behave in the face of the unknown (Imber-Black & Roberts, 1992). Although many rituals exist that help people to enter a marriage, welcome a newborn, start a new job, or retire from one, there are no socially accepted rituals to mark the end of a marriage, the announcement of a divorce, the construction of a binuclear family, or the acceptance of new and sometimes instant members into a family of remarriage. No rites of passage exist to help mourn the losses, to help healing, or to help solidify newly acquired roles. Unlike other important transitions, divorce lies in a zone of ritual ambiguity.

While leaving its participants in a void with respect to public rituals, divorce also affects the private rituals that are so central to family life. Daily rituals such as opening the mail together over coffee or walking together to get the newspaper are seamlessly woven into the texture of family life; the more elaborate rituals that many families construct around birthdays and holidays will also disappear or change, leaving gaping wounds. When the nuclear family is dismantled in the wake of divorce, it is also necessary to dismantle what seemed like a permanent point of view of a portion of the past, present, and future.

What roles, rules, and rituals each family chooses to establish will vary depending on individual preferences, sometimes on ethnic background, and certainly on the particular life stage of the family.

Reconciliations are common during the separation transition. The pain of separating, the continuing bonds of attachment, the distress of children and extended family, and the realities of divorce can cause couples to reunite. When the reconciliation is based on these reasons and not on a basic understanding and correction of the marital problems, it is likely to be brief. In some families, parents separate and reconcile briefly, perhaps several times, increasing and prolonging the stress of the separation. In the most common divorced family form, the mother and children remain as one unit, while the father moves out and functions as a separate unit. The mother-headed household faces a dilemma: Should it reorganize and fill roles that had been enacted by the physically absent father, or should it maintain his psychological presence in the system by not reorganizing? If the mother–child subsystem tries to reassign roles, the father's return will be met with resistance. On the other hand, if they deal with him as psychologically present, they perpetuate family disequilibrium and stress. These children face a difficult and very stressful transition with the family in a constant state of disequilibrium characterized by boundary ambiguity (Boss, 1987) created by the father's intermittent exit and return. This "on again, off again" marital relationship often continues for years as the spouses resolve their ambivalence and make the transition to reorganization. This type of cyclical pattern is evidenced more in highly dysfunctional families, and family violence tends to be more prevalent in them.

As the marital separation is shared with extended family, friends, and the community, the tasks of the economic and legal processes begin. These mediating factors can help or hinder the transitional process. The couple usually encounters the legal system at this time and faces additional stress as they confront economic hardship and child-focused realities. This may escalate the crisis, since spouses now need to divide what they had previously shared.

LEGAL ISSUES. Although no-fault divorce legislation reflects changing social attitudes, for the most part the legal system still operates on an adversarial model. Based on a win–lose game, the legal divorce frequently escalates the spousal power struggle, adding additional stress to the already disorganized system. Today couples choosing to divorce have a variety of alternatives to address their differences in a less adversarial way. They may choose a *"pro se"* process in which they have no legal representation and write their own agreements.

In recent years, models of divorce that are not adversarial and do not rely on the court system are gaining popularity. Couple may now choose mediation, a process that employs a neutral legal or mental health professional to help them resolve their differences in a nonadversarial manner (Katz, 2007). The newest model is collaborative divorce, a team approach that originated in 1990 and has steadily grown in societal acceptance. This "no-court model" requires that divorcing couples agree not to pursue litigation to resolve the issues (Webb & Ousky, 2007). The couples, with the help of a team of professionals

(legal, mental health, and financial), sign a stipulation in which they pledge not to go to court to resolve their differences. The process includes a strong incentive to resolve their differences at the "collaborative table." Should they not be able to resolve their differences in the collaborative setting, they will have to engage new lawyers to represent them, which will increase their financial costs and emotional energy (Mosten, 2009). These alternative models encourage couples to be responsible for their own family decisions and teach the couple problem-solving techniques that will be useful throughout their postdivorce family life.

These first three turbulent transitions form the core of the emotional divorce process. The lingering feelings of attachment, ambivalence, and the ambiguity of the future combine in complex ways to make this a time of deep soul searching, anxious discomfort, and vacillating but intense desires. For couples with children, whether young or older, it is a process of letting go while still holding on. They have to begin the most difficult task of terminating their marital relationship while redefining their parental one.

Systemic Reorganization: The Binuclear Family

The presence of children, at any stage in the family life cycle process, requires that divorced parents restructure their lives in ways that allow children to continue their relationships with both parents. The nuclear family is now dissolved, and the highly complex and varied process of reorganizing needs to begin.

How a family reorganizes is crucial to the health and well-being of its members. Research clearly identifies several major factors that contribute to the healthy adjustment of children:

1. Children need to have their basic economic and psychological needs met.
2. They need support for maintaining the familial relationships in their lives that were important and meaningful to them before the divorce. That usually means not only parents but also extended family, such as grandparents.

3. They benefit when the relationship between their parents (whether married or divorced) is generally supportive and cooperative.

The reorganization into a binuclear family in which these three major factors are present provides children with the opportunity to survive divorce without long-term psychological damage (Ahrons, 2004, 2007). In most binuclear families, the children divide their living time—in a wide range of patterns—between two households. Some children divide their time fairly equally, either splitting the week or spending one week or longer in each household. Other children spend a majority of their time in one household, and still others alternate between households on a flexible, irregular pattern. College-age children need to decide how and where they will spend their vacation time. The importance of the binuclear family model is that the family remains a family, although the structure is very different than it was before the divorce. Giving divorced families a name that acknowledges that families continue to be families even after divorce encourages the development of new, more functional role models for divorcing families. It also gives them a legitimate status and removes from them the stigma of social deviancy.

THE FORMER SPOUSE RELATIONSHIP. To maximize the potential for these three factors requires a major transformation in the former spouse relationship. Each parent must find new ways of relating independently with the child while simultaneously developing new rules and behaviors with each other. This co-parenting relationship is central to the functioning of the binuclear family in much the same way as the relationship between married spouses is central to the function of the nuclear family.

In the past, there was some disbelief that divorced partners could have an amicable relationship. The lack of language to describe the former spousal relationship, except in terms of a past relationship (e.g., "ex" or "former"), is an indication of the lack of acceptance of it as a viable form. The general distrust of a continuing relationship after divorce is reflected in the prevailing stereotype that former spouses must, of necessity, be antagonists; otherwise, why would they divorce? This stereotype is reinforced by a bias in the available clinical material. Clinicians tend to see only difficult or problematic former spousal relationships, while well-functioning divorced families are less apt to seek professional intervention.

Unlike the popular stereotype that former spouses are, of necessity, mortal enemies, the realities are that there is as much complexity and variation in these relationships as there is in married spouses' relationships. Former spouse relationships form a continuum with the very angry and hostile relationships at one end and the very friendly at the other. There are many relationship variations between the two extremes (Ahrons, 1981, 1994; Ahrons & Wallisch, 1986).

CO-PARENTING RELATIONSHIPS. In analyzing the relationships between former spouses in the binuclear family study, five typologies emerged: perfect pals, cooperative colleagues, angry associates, fiery foes, and dissolved duos. Perfect pals are a small group of divorced spouses who remain close friends. If they have children, they are almost always joint custody parents who, equitably sharing child-rearing responsibilities, are good problem solvers with few conflicts.

The cooperative colleagues are a larger group who would not call each other friends but who manage for the most part to have an amicable relationship. They are child focused, and although they have conflicts, they are able to separate their marital from their parental roles, not allowing the former to contaminate the latter. When they are unable to resolve a conflict, they are likely to choose a mediator or therapist to help them rather than to resort to litigation. Some have shared custody; others elect to have a primary parent, but both fathers and mothers remain important and involved in their children's lives. A number of studies have found that about half the divorced parents fit into this broad category (Ahrons, 1994; Maccoby & Mnookin, 1992; Wallerstein & Kelly, 1980).

Angry associates are quite similar to cooperative colleagues in some ways; parents in these groups continue to interact and have involvement in their children's lives. The major difference between the cooperative colleagues and the angry associates is that the latter group cannot separate their parental and marital issues. When there is conflict about the children, it quickly fuses with an old marital fight. Power struggles are common to this group; their separation and divorce battles often involved custody disputes and long legal battles over financial matters.

Fiery foes are hostile and angry all the time; the ex-spouse is the mortal enemy, and they are unable to co-parent. Like conflict-habituated married couples, they are still very emotionally attached to each other, although they would be quick to deny it. Their divorces tended to have been highly litigious, involving extended family and friends, with legal battles continuing for many years after the divorce. With both angry associates and fiery foes as parents, children usually suffer from devastating loyalty conflicts and often lose significant relationships with extended kin.

In the dissolved duos, ex-spouses have no further contact with one another, and one parent assumes total responsibility for the children. Of the five groups, these families are the only ones that fit the "single-parent" category.

ESTABLISHING BOUNDARIES. While in the earlier transitions the absence of clear boundaries and the high ambiguity create most of the stress, in this reorganization transition, the clarification of the boundaries generates the distress. Boundaries are hot issues in all intimate relationships, not just divorce. They touch off unresolved conflicts or crash into opposing strongly held values. Among ex-spouses, money and new loves often are the touchiest issues, bound to set off escalating battles. Often, an old repetitious fight that the couple has engaged in for years continues, masked in the details of living separately. One major arena for these power struggles relates to the children.

All divorcing parents know how important it is to make decisions on the basis of their children's best interests. But the worst arguments can happen over what exactly these interests are. Which school Johnny should attend, although couched in an argument over his best interests, usually boils down to a pitched battle about which parent has more authority, more power, more control over Johnny's life. In reality, although "the best interests of the child" is a concept that is commonly accepted and heavily relied upon by judges, lawyers, mediators, and

therapists, there is little consensus about the criteria (Kelly, 2007).

All parents, whether married or divorced, have parenting conflicts. How they affect children is determined by how the parents resolve their conflicts. In binuclear families, it is necessary to more specifically construct firm boundaries—between households, in each parent–child relationship, and between ex-spouses.

To co-parent effectively requires a contract that sets out the rules and roles in the binuclear family. This contract—what I call a limited partnership agreement—assumes that parents are partners, but the kinds of limits that are set on that partnership are determined by their relationship. Perfect pals can have a very flexible and often unwritten type of contract because they are able to negotiate easily. Most cooperative colleagues find that they need to have a more structured agreement, outlining children's living schedules, how holidays will be spent, who goes to what meetings, who pay for what needs, and so on. Angry associates need an even more structured agreement, often stating specifics about what a parent can and cannot do with children. Fiery foes usually have everything possible written in a legal contractual form, although they are most likely to violate their contracts.

In the perfect pal and cooperative colleague families, ex-spouses often choose to spend some holidays together, attend children's events together, and share information about children's needs. In angry associate and fiery foe families, parallel parenting is the norm. They operate independently as parents, not sharing information or events.

Even midlife and later-life couples with adult children need to have some agreement about how their postdivorce family will function. Will both parents attend the child's wedding? Will they sit at the same table for the celebration dinner? Will both grandparents attend their grandchild's birthday party or graduation? Establishing clear boundaries is important across all stages of the family life cycle.

Family Redefinition: The Aftermath

A process of family redefinition frequently includes remarriage and the introduction of stepparents into the postdivorce family. Remarriage (Chapter 22) creates a series of transitions that are beyond the scope of this chapter but are part of the ongoing transitions of family redefinition. For some families, a potential remarriage partner or spouse equivalent may become part of the family system before the legal divorce and at the early phases of the reorganization transition. Some unnamed (e.g., the relationships between mothers and stepmothers) and thus unsanctioned relationships within the binuclear family structure take on the importance in the redefinition process. They are kin or quasi-kin relationships in the context of the binuclear family (Ahrons & Wallisch, 1987).

Relationships between parents and stepparents in the binuclear family provide an important emotional continuity for both parents and children. They facilitate this transition by redefining the divorced family so that the amount of relationship loss experienced by children and parents is minimized.

Family values and structures of many African American families provide a helpful model for binuclear families. The African American family is centered on the children, the family unit often being defined as including all those involved in their nurturance and support. Encouraging extended-family relationships for the benefit of the children allows for continued responsibility regardless of changes in marital relationships. Unlike the traditional family structure favored by most White American families, the African American family structure is less based on the legal relationship between spouses; hence, divorce is less likely to interfere with the child's familial ties (Boyd-Franklin, 2006; Crosbie-Burnett & Lewis, 1993). If the assumption of parental responsibility is not based on blood kin, then divorce is less likely to be as disruptive to the child's family relationships.

One important and frequently overlooked strength of many ethnic families is their bicultural socialization. Children in these families usually have to learn to live in two cultures simultaneously—that of their ethnic community and that of the wider society (Crosbie-Burnett & Lewis, 1993). This acculturation process could be a very helpful model for a child in learning to live in the two-household cultures of the binuclear family. If one parent remarries and there are children from another family (stepsiblings), being bicultural could facilitate their

being better able to accommodate the different family cultures that ordinarily create considerable stress for stepfamilies.

Although we have little research data, it is likely that gay and lesbian families, if they are not married, operate outside of the legal marital system and many have kinship structures similar to those of African American families. For children, the family structures that incorporate extended family, fictive and quasi-kin, and family relationships by choice are more likely to remain intact if the primary love relationship wanes. Because family roles are more ambiguous in gay and lesbian families, they may also prepare children better to accept the ambiguity that is inherent when families change their structure.

Lesbians, who are socialized, as most women are, to value emotional connectedness, often try to remain friends or family after the breakup of a love relationship. Their subsequent connection may take various forms: focusing on co-parenting children, celebrating holidays or taking vacations together, or remaining friends within a close circle. As with postdivorce heterosexual couples, the transformation from lovers to friends takes a lot of work, but many women are committed to the process (Shumsky, 1997). In married and divorced heterosexual relationships, women tend to be the kin keepers of the family, whether nuclear or binuclear. In the Binuclear Family Study, the findings show that the relationship between mothers and stepmothers was much more emotional and interactive than was the relationship between fathers and stepfathers (Ahrons & Wallisch, 1987).

Gay men, on the other hand, like many men, often lack the vocabulary or emotional access to their feelings of loss after a breakup. This is especially true of the sometimes ambiguous relationships that occur in gay male culture, in which open contracts may permit casual or transient affairs to coexist with long-term relationships (Shernoff, 1997).

Of course, HIV and AIDS also have a profound effect on gay male relationships, in which there may be fear of a partner's HIV-positive status, guilt if one's own status is negative, or a tendency to stay together when both partners are negative, largely because it is safe (Remien, 1997). In all of these circumstances, it is extremely important for the therapist to help those who want to break up to do so in the least destructive and most caring way, helping them to remain connected if that is desirable. The gay community, Remien reminds us, is full of stories of ex-lovers who are at their ex-partners' bedside and who maintain a bond that nourishes them both.

The struggle to define all of these relationships and transitions for themselves—coupling, parenting, and breaking up—is made both more difficult and more creative by the fact that they exist outside of society's social and legal rules. Where children are concerned, however, the nonlegal standing of a nonbiological, noncustodial parent can create devastation for someone who may for years have been a co-parent or even a primary parent of her or his partner's children (Sundquist, 1997). Interestingly, when a remarriage ends in a divorce, this same dilemma holds true for a stepparent, who has emotional but no legal, biological, or custodial ties to the child.

> **Assess your comprehension of family redefinition: the aftermath by completing this quiz.**

Clinical Overview

A model of divorce, characterizing it as a normative process rather than evidence of pathology or dysfunction, has been presented in this chapter. This is aimed at helping clinicians transcend prevalent stereotypes and myths, thereby creating clinical guidelines for treating families of divorce. Within this model, clinicians can recognize the transitions of the divorce process and help client families cope more effectively during this very painful and complex process; note differences that may be related to culture, race, and gender differences; and help client families cope more effectively during this very painful and complex process. They can then identify what differentiates divorces that are successful or "good" from those that are unsuccessful or "bad."

Quite simply, a good divorce has three major objectives: (1) The family remains a family; (2) the negative effects on children are minimized; and (3) both ex-spouses integrate the divorce into their lives in a healthy way. Although the structure of the family has been altered, parents continue to be parents who are responsible for socializing and attending to their children's emotional and economic needs. Bad divorces are those in which spouses are unable or unwilling to settle their marital conflicts without enmeshing the children in their divorce drama. Children in these divorces often lose a relationship with one parent (usually the father), are caught in painful loyalty conflicts about their parents, and suffer irreparable emotional damage (Ahrons, 1994, 2004).

By understanding the normal transitions of the divorce process, clinicians can help their clients to better understand and cope with the emotional, legal, and practical tasks they need to complete. By providing information and knowledge, clinicians can help divorcing couples to make decisions based on their children's best interests. And by learning and teaching important conflict reduction techniques, they can assist parents to make the many complex decisions that will need to be addressed.

Because divorce is a legal decision with economic repercussions, clinicians need to be aware of how the legal process works in their state. This is particularly important when working with gay and lesbian couples, especially if they were married in a state where same-sex marriage is legal but now reside in a state where it is not. It is important to seek out lawyers in your community who are experienced in the legalities of same-sex unions.

Even though all states now have no-fault legislation, many divorces continue to be adversarial. Learning which lawyers in your community are open to collaboration with a therapist and which lawyers' styles are more mediative rather than adversarial will be very helpful to the clinician's continuing work with the divorcing family. For the divorcing couple, as well as the therapist working with them, the impact of the legal system on the emotional process is complex and has the potential to be counterproductive to the therapist's goals. For same-sex couples, the confused legal context will likely lead to fear, anxiety, and stress in divorcing couples beyond that experienced by heterosexual divorcing couples (Lyness, 2012). Green and Mitchell (2002) note interesting emotional and behavioral differences between lesbian and gay and these differences are applicable to divorce.

It is best to encourage the divorcing couple to make as many decisions together as possible before engaging the legal system. As was noted earlier, mediation and collaborative divorce are very helpful ways for divorcing couples to settle their differences out of court in a mutual problem-solving approach.

The economics of divorce filter into every aspect of the process. It is important for the clinician to understand how money was managed during the marriage. In a more traditional marriage, the wife frequently knows little about the financial picture. In such cases, the husband has more power in the discussion of finances. Although a therapist should never give financial advice or try to settle the overall economic distribution (unless formally trained and acting as a divorce mediator), it is important to have an understanding of how money is used in the negotiation of the divorce. LGB relationships add more complexity to issues related to money. If they are unmarried, and had mutual agreements set forth in a committed relationship, these agreements may not hold up in court because there may be no precedents established. This situation is similar for cohabiting heterosexual couples.

In marriages with dependent children, financial issues are entwined with custody decisions. When a wife has been the primary caretaker of the children and the husband has been the primary breadwinner, the most common scenario is that the children represent power for the mother and money represents power for the father. This gets played out in the emotional terrain, often in very subtle and complex ways.

In longer-term marriages with older or adult children, women often have less power in the negotiations than men do. These midlife divorces are frequently the ones that result in women becoming "displaced homemakers." The common situation is that of the wife, who either has left a job to take care of children and home or is less educated than her husband, finding herself at midlife having to seek a job without adequate experience, education, or training. Her earning potential is often much less than that of her husband. In the next generation of mid and later-life divorces, we are likely to see more equal earning couples. The law often does not provide adequate repayment to women for the years they devoted to caring for the family. A woman of 50 may find herself without retirement and should familiarize herself with the most advantageous way to calculate Social Security benefits. Therapists need to be aware of these gender inequities and educate women about their rights.

Finally, it is important for the clinician to remember that divorce affects the entire family system. Parents and siblings of the divorcing couple usually become very involved in the process. When there are children, the grandparents, aunts, uncles, and cousins are all part of the kinship network. In good divorces, the kinship network continues satisfying relationships with the children and frequently with the divorcing in-law. In angry divorces, kin often take sides with their biological kin, creating breaches in relationships with the children as well. Clinicians would be wise to ask about extended family-relationships and be open to bringing relatives into the sessions to help them sort out their issues.

Working with divorce requires a complex multilevel approach (Ahrons, 2007). Clinicians need to be aware of their own biases and stereotypes, and they need to correct for them by gaining adequate knowledge of the emotional, legal, and economic divorce processes. They need to look through a wide-angle lens and incorporate both spouses' families of origin. Ethnic, racial, and gender differences need to enter into the therapeutic equation, as do the family's developmental life cycle transitions. A therapist who chooses to work with divorcing families will need to tolerate a high level of conflicts and cope with complex painful emotions.

Therapy with divorcing families is a challenging and difficult process for both the therapist and the family. Working with a family and taking them through the process, helping them to emerge as a healthy, functioning binuclear family is a goal worth striving for.

Assess your comprehension of clinical overview by completing this quiz.

Recall what you learned in this chapter by completing the Chapter Review.

— References —

Adams, M., & Coltrane, S. (2007). Framing divorce reform: Media, morality, and the politics of family. *Family Process, 46,* 17–34.

Ahlburg, D., & DeVita, C. (1992). New realities of the American family. *Population Bulletin, 47,* 15.

Ahrons, C. (1979). The binuclear family: Two households, one family. *Alternative Lifestyles, 2,* 499–515.

Ahrons, C. (1980a). Divorce: A crisis of family transition and change. *Family Relations, 29,* 533–540.

Ahrons, C. (1980b). Redefining the divorced family: A conceptual framework for postdivorce family systems reorganization. *Social Work, 25,* 437–441.

Ahrons, C. (1981). The continuing coparental relationship between divorced spouses. *American Journal of Orthopsychiatry, 51,* 315–328.

Ahrons, C. (1994). *The good divorce: Keeping your family together when your marriage comes apart.* New York: Harper Collins.

Ahrons, C. (1996). *Making divorce work: A clinical approach to the binuclear family* [videotape]. New York: Guilford Press.

Ahrons, C. (2004). *We're still family: What grown children have to say about their parents' divorce.* New York: Harper Collins.

Ahrons, C. (2007). Family ties after divorce: Long-term implications for children. *Family Process, 46,* 53–65.

Ahrons, C., & Rodgers, R. (1987). *Divorced families: A multidisciplinary developmental view.* New York: W. W. Norton.

Ahrons, C., & Tanner, J. (2003). Adult children and their fathers: Relationship changes 20 years after a parental divorce. *Family Relations, 52,* 340–351.

Ahrons, C., & Wallisch, L. (1986). The relationship between former spouses. In S. Duck & D. Perlman (Eds.), *Close relationships: Development, dynamics, and deterioration* (pp. 269–296). Beverly Hills, CA: Sage Publications.

Ahrons, C., & Wallisch, L. (1987). Parenting in the binuclear family: Relationships between biological and stepparents. In K. Pasley & M. Ihinger-Tallman (Eds.), *Remarriage and stepfamilies* (pp. 225–256). New York: Guilford Press.

Boss, P. (1983). Family separation and boundary ambiguity. *The International Journal of Mass Emergencies and Disasters, 1,* 63–72.

Boss, P. (1987). *Family stress.* Beverly Hills, CA: Sage.

Boss, P. (2006) Loss, trauma and resilience. New York: W. W. Norton & Co.

Boss, P., & Greenberg, J. (1984). Family boundary ambiguity: A new variable in family stress theory. *Family Process, 24,* 535–546.

Boyd-Franklin, N. (2006). *Black families in therapy: A multisystems approach.* New York: The Guilford Press.

Brown, E. (1991). *Patterns of infidelity and their treatment.* New York: Brunner/Mazel.

Bumpass, L. (1990). What's happening to the family? Interactions between demographic and institutional change. *Demography, 27,* 483–498.

Crosbie-Burnett, M., & Lewis, E. (1993). Use of African-American family structures and functioning to address the challenges of European-American postdivorce families. *Family Relations, 42,* 243–248.

Cseh-Szombathy, L., Koch-Nielsen, I., Trost, J., & Weda, I. (Eds.). (1985). *The aftermath of divorce—Coping with family change: An investigation in eight countries.* Budapest, Hungary: Akademiai Kiado.

Demo, D., & Fine, M. (2009). *Beyond the average divorce.* Los Angeles: Sage.

Glick, P. (1990). American families: As they are, and were. *Sociology and Social Research, 74,* 139–145.

Green, R.-J., & Mitchell, V. (2002). Gay and lesbian couples in therapy: Homophobia, relational ambiguity, and social support. In A. S. Gurman & N. Jacobson (Eds.), *Clinical handbook of couple therapy* (pp. 546–568). New York, NY: Guilford Press.

Hetherington, E. M. (1993). An overview of the Virginia Longitudinal Study of Divorce and Remarriage with a focus on early adolescence. *Journal of Family Psychology, 7,* 39–56.

Imber-Black, E., & Roberts, J. (1992). *Rituals of our times: Celebrating, healing, and changing our lives and our relationships.* New York: Harper Collins.

Katz, E. (2007). A family therapy perspective on mediation. *Family Process, 46,* 93–107.

Kelly, J. (2007). Children's living arrangements following separation and divorce: Insights from empirical and clinical research. *Family Process, 46,* 35–52.

Kelly, J. B. (2005). Developing beneficial parenting plan models for children following separation and divorce. *Journal of American Academy of Matrimonial Lawyers, 19*(2), 101–118.

Lamb, M., Sternberg, K., & Thompson, R. (1997). The effects of divorce and custody arrangements on children's behavior, development, and adjustment. *Family and Conciliation Courts Review, 35,* 393–404.

Lerner, H. (1993). *The dance of deception: Pretending and truth-telling in women's lives.* New York: Harper Collins.

Lyness, Kevin P. (2012). Therapeutic considerations in same-sex divorce. In J. Bigner & J. Wetchler (Eds.), *Handbook of LGBT—Affirmative couple and family* (pp. 377–391). New York: Routledge.

Maccoby, E. E., & Mnookin, R. (1992). *Dividing the child: Social and legal dilemmas of custody.* Cambridge, MA: Harvard University Press.

Mosten, F. (2009). *Collaborative divorce; Helping families without going to court.* San Francisco: Jossey-Bass.

Remien, R. (1997). Three portraits of how HIV and AIDS can complicate a break-up. *In the Family, 3*, 18–19.

Rodgers, R. (1986). Postmarital reorganization of family relationships: A prepositional theory. In S. Duck & D. Perlman (Eds.), *Close relationships: Development, dynamics, and deterioration* (pp. 239–268). Beverly Hills, CA: Sage.

Rosten, L. (1989). *The joys of Yinglish.* New York: Penguin Books.

Shernoff, M. (1997). Unexamined loss: An expanded view of gay break-ups. *In the Family,* 10–13.

Shumsky, E. (1997). Making up the rules: Lesbian ex-lover relationships. *In the Family,* 14–15.

Spring, J with Spring, M. (1996). *After the affair: Healing the pain and rebuilding trust when a partner has been unfaithful.* New York: Harper Collins.

Stewart, A., Copeland, A., Chester, N., Malley, J., & Barenbaum, N. (1997). *Separating together: How divorce transforms families.* New York: Guilford Press.

Sundquist, K. (1997). She gets the kids: Becoming an every-third-weekend and -Tuesday ex-co-mom. *In the Family, 20,* 21–27.

Trafford, A. (1982). *Crazy time.* New York: Harper & Row.

Wallerstein, J., & Kelly, J. (1980). *Surviving the breakup: How children and parents cope with divorce.* New York: Basic Books.

Webb, S., & Ousky, R. (2007). *The collaborative way to divorce.* New York: Plume.

Chapter 21

Single-Parent Families: Strengths, Vulnerabilities, and Interventions

Carol M. Anderson & Maria E. Anderson

— Learning Outcomes

- List and describe different single-parent family types.
- Compare the challenges and benefits of one-parent families and two-parent families.
- Differentiate the developmental tasks of single-parent families from those of two-parent families.
- Describe the initial phase of establishing a single-parent household.
- Discuss the increased importance of family networks for single-parent families.
- Identify the challenges that are unique to adolescent single parents.
- Examine how the dynamics of single-parent families evolve as children become older.
- Describe the difficulties single parents face when launching children.
- List and describe potential problems for single parents in the post–child-rearing phase of the life cycle.
- Explain the benefits of taking a family life cycle approach in responding to single parents who request help for their child.

When there is a commitment to living and loving together there is family.
— *The Single Mother's Book*, Joan Anderson, Peachtree Publishers.
Reprinted with permission.

Introduction

In recent decades, the prevalence of single-parent households has dramatically increased across all income groups, from the very poor to the affluent and well educated. The number of children in these homes has also increased, in fact doubling in the past 50 years, with over 29 percent of American children between birth and age 17, now being raised by single parents (Gibson-Davis 2011; Wolf, 2011). The term "single parent" is defined by the U.S. Census Bureau as a parent who cares for one or more children younger than 18 years without the assistance of another parent in the home (Ventura, 2009). However, this broad umbrella encompasses a wide range of family types. There are post divorce single parents, women who had a child before they were little more than children themselves, and an increasing

number of both women and men who purposely choose single parenthood through adoption, donor insemination, or by raising a child who has been conceived in an uncommitted relationship. These growing numbers also reflect a decrease in the traditional stigma associated with having and raising children without the benefit of marriage (Cherlin et al., 2008).

These varying pathways to becoming a single-parent household create different family characteristics that make it difficult to generalize about the issues and problems involved. All single parents and their children must find ways to deal with being founded on the loss of a person or at least a dream, the risk of emotional or task overload for the one parent doing the work usually done by two, and the need to create and nurture a network of support to make up for this absence. Beyond this, each category of single-parent family has a number of unique characteristics and needs. Low-income mothers, who remain the majority of single parents, often have little contact with their child's father and tend to struggle with finding ways to manage on public assistance (Barrett & Turner, 2005; Berger, 2007; Bratter & Damask, 2013; Cherlin, 2008, 2010). Postdivorce households, even those with adequate financial and social resources, may need to cope with ongoing conflicts with ex-partners over custody arrangements and adjusting to the need to balance work and childrearing tasks without another parent committed to their child's welfare (Bakker & Karsten, 2013; Furstenberg & Cherlin, 1994; Groze, 1991). Single parents who have had children through adoption or alternative insemination often have educational and financial resources, but may not have another parent committed to the child's welfare. (Groze, 1991). Understanding the impact of the pathways to becoming a single-parent household is complicated by the fact that this status often changes over time. Some will remain single-parent households for their entire family life cycle, while others will experience single parenthood as a transitional state, a way station between unstable serial cohabitations or longer-term committed couple relationships (Cohen & Manning, 2010; Lichter, Turner, & Sassler, 2010; Park, 2005; Sassler, 2010).

There is considerable disagreement about the impact of living in a single-parent household on the well-being of both parents and children. Studies suggest that single parents tend to work longer hours than married parents, are likely to face more stressful life changes, have more economic problems, and have less emotional support (Bakker & Karsten, 2013), all resulting in more psychological problems for these parents and children (McLanahan & Sandefur, 1994; Potter, 2010). However, these findings do not consider the comparative impact of living in a family with ongoing chronic conflict, violence, substance abuse, or poverty, all of which have a documented negative impact on child development (Afifi, Coz, & Enns, 2006; Berger, 2007; Cain & Combs-Orme, 2005; Goodnight et al., 2013; Wen, 2008). For instance, over 27 percent of single-parent households live in poverty (Cherlin, 2010), and poverty accounts for about half of the disadvantage in the lower achievement of children. When the influence of poverty is factored out, the differences in the adjustment of children in one and two-parent

families disappear (Barrett & Turner, 2005; Edin & Kissane, 2010). Unfortunately, the influence of poverty cannot be factored out for the majority of single parents who are young minority girls with little contact with their child's father (Edin & Kefalas, 2005; Hamilton, Martin, & Ventura, 2012). Their poverty is complicated by the fact that these lower-income parents also have less education and fewer resources, and live in more troubled communities, which correlate with high rates of parental depression, parenting overload, and a higher risk of child maltreatment (Berger, 2007; Butterworth, Crozier, & Rodgers, 2007; Carlson, 2001; Ceballo & McLoyd, 2002; Zahn & Pandy, 2004). But single parenthood is not the cause of these difficulties; most single-parent homes in all social classes are no more "broken" or troubled than those of comparative intact families. Single parents provide their children with structure and nurturance while finding ways to meet their own needs for intimacy, companionship, and community. They may make sacrifices, such as giving up a social life or a career to make time to provide the nurture and structure their children need, but they are not automatically dysfunctional. In fact, children in single-parent families appear to experience at least some benefits compared to those raised in two-parent households. They grow strong and make good use of their diverse experiences, assuming more responsibility, becoming more independent, and developing meaningful connections with extended family and friends. In fact, single-parent households appear to provide a better environment for some specific children, such as adopted children who have disabilities, and where their single parents describe the experience of raising them as transformative and empowering (Levine, 2009).

Surprisingly, despite the prevalence of single-parent households and the data supporting their viability, the United States continues to be one of the most ambivalent industrialized countries about accepting and supporting them (Thornton, 2009; Usdansky, 2009; Casey & Maldonado, 2012). The widely held idealized view of two-parent families seems to blind us to the strengths and accomplishments of this increasingly prevalent alternative family structure. For this reason, it is particularly important that clinicians who work with single-parent families understand their strengths and challenges and learn to use a wide-angle lens to see single parenthood in its current and historical context. In particular, clinicians should be aware of how single parenthood influences each phase of the family life cycle in order to help these families to appreciate their own viability, meet the inevitable challenges of single-parent family life, and mobilize their ties to a supportive community.

Assess your comprehension of the introduction by completing this quiz.

Single Parents and the Family Life Cycle

Some children are born into single-parent families, and some single-parent families are created mid-childhood through divorce or adoption. In fact, single-parent households can come into being at almost any stage of the family life cycle, superimposing the additional tasks of forming and maintaining a single-parent family on the usual issues of a particular family life cycle stage. All single-parent families have a shared present, but they may or may not have a shared past, and whatever structure they create may not continue if they make a future move to form a two-parent family. Single parents and their children build their families on a foundation of loss, whether the loss is that of a relationship, a two-parent family, or of their traditional ideals. There is inevitable emotional baggage related to these losses that becomes part of the single-parent family identity as it develops a blueprint for the future. The specifics of the structure created will depend on many factors, including the path taken to single parenthood, the ages of parent and child, the financial status of the family, the community/network context, and the extended-family history and culture. Different cultures may be more or less accepting of the various pathways taken to single parenthood, but whatever pathway is taken at whatever stage of the life cycle, all single parents and their children will be initially working to create a sense of home, belonging, and safety along with establishing the flexibility to change and evolve over time. All of these factors contribute to the complexity and diversity of the tasks required of single-parent families as they move through the stages of the family life cycle. In fact, single-parent family life cycle tasks will complicate and sometimes even contradict normative developmental tasks, and accomplishing them without culturally prescribed single-parent family rituals can be particularly challenging. For instance, teens who have been moving toward independence may suddenly need to sacrifice their normal time with peers when their recently divorced single parents require them to help with younger siblings; or when teens become single parents and need to give up their freedom in order to care for an infant, perhaps in the face of considerable disapproval from their family and friends.

New single-parent families with young children

The initial phase of establishing a single-parent household involves the balancing act of setting up a workable family structure that will provide children with consistent nurturance and limits, while ensuring that parental needs are at least partially met (Bakker & Karsten, 2013). Single parents with a new child must make space for that child in their work and social network, realigning their own family relationships to allow their parents to play the role of grandparents. This whole process of adjustment requires that the single parent find ways to create a family identity they can be proud of, one that will nurture the child's development within the family, maintain contact with the missing parent if possible, and facilitate kin and friendship relationships to augment missing role models and overstretched resources. During this initial phase, single adoptive parents of children from different ethnic or racial groups must not only develop a family identity that incorporates potentially rich diverse racial and ethnic themes, but also one that accommodates parent–child racial differences and sometimes the negative reactions of their community to their family (Samuels, 2009). For those who live in traditional suburban communities of predominantly two-parent households, single parenthood, not to mention racial differences, may compound the marginalization of single-parent families. Single parents will then have to work to build bridges across cultural differences for their children's sake.

Creating a new family can be a stressful experience, and single fathers and mothers can become so preoccupied with the problems in their current reality that they fail to see the broader context that might provide support, solutions, or even just another perspective. The extended-family network may be particularly important for single-parent families as they attempt to establish a necessary sense of "homeplace" and a new family identity over their formative years (Burton et al., 2004; Jones et al., 2007). An increased awareness of the extended-family life cycle context might reveal inspirational role models or other unused resources. Mobilizing the rich knowledge and possible resources from these networks is especially important for the coping of single mothers who spend more time in child care than single fathers and yet receive less support from their extended family (Goldscheider & Kaufman, 2006; Hilton & Kopera-Frye, 2007; Hook & Chalasani, 2008).

As single-parent families form, both divorced and never-married teen mothers have the added challenge of finding ways to make a place for their child's father in their lives, because children in contact with their fathers do better. A solid relationship between child and father is more likely if it can be facilitated from the onset of the single-parent family life cycle. Unfortunately, many fathers tend to lose contact with their children within a year after the divorce. Young fathers of color, many of whom become unemployed or incarcerated, are likely to fade quickly from their children's lives (Devault et al., 2008; Dudley, 2007; Dyer, 2005; Forste, Bartkowski, & Jackson, 2006; Swiss & Le Bourdais, 2009). Divorced single mothers almost always need support in allowing the father access to the child and tolerating the unfairness of those times when the father is idealized and mother is blamed for his unpredictability (Fagan et al., 2009; Laakso, 2004). Rather than complaining about being single parents, many complain that they are not quite single enough. Teen mothers and their parents may need help in promoting continued father–child involvement, especially when the parents do not approve of their grandchild's father (Cutrona et al., 1998; Roy & Dyson, 2005).

When teens begin to create their own single-parent families, they also confront the contradiction between their developmental need to move toward independence and their need for increased support from their parents to help with their child. It is not easy for a teen to maintain her credibility as her child's parent when she must defer authority to her own parents. At the same time, her own parents must continue with the developmental life cycle tasks of launching and letting go, which is more difficult if they feel their daughter seems irresponsible or needs continuing financial and emotional support.

The practical daily challenges involved in starting a single-parent family are many, and parents may need help in sorting out routines and responsibilities. Managing the day-to-day tasks and chores alone is particularly complicated for those single parents living on limited incomes. Paying for decent child care is often impossible, meaning that working single parents with young children often have inadequate arrangements if potentially helpful relatives are not available. If single-parent families are created at a time the children are slightly older, single parents have the daily pressures and stresses of maintaining a job while responding to the demands of their child's school and after-school activities, not to mention the emergencies of child illnesses and parent–teacher conferences. For those working without benefits, responding to calls from the school about the common behavioral problems of children can mean missing a day's pay or even job loss, adding additional stress to family life (Carlson, 2001; Wen, 2008). One important barrier to managing these tasks for single parents of either gender is their assumption that they must be both mother and father to their child. Clinicians can be helpful to parents by validating and supporting the good work they are doing and encouraging them to talk with their child as needed about the absence of the parent who is not there.

While most single parents are not at greater risk for mistreating their children, the relatively high percentage who are depressed are more likely to engage in poor parenting strategies unless they receive considerable support. Certainly, many single parents are well connected with family and friends, but others can easily become isolated and overwhelmed and without the time and energy to maintain relationships or reach out for support. They feel the need to collapse on the couch after a trying day, and taking the initiative to connect may seem like just one more chore. Even in African American single-mother families who reportedly are more likely to have active family networks that provide frequent contact and mutual aid, it is often the single parents most in need of help who do not receive it (Crosier, Butterworth, & Rogers, 2007; Ceballo & McLoyd, 2002; Caldwell, 1996; Thompson & Wilkins, 1992).

Some single parents attempt to gain additional support for family life by bringing a romantic partner into the household. If such a relationship can develop into a loving, supportive, and lasting one, it can benefit single mothers and single fathers, as well as their children. In fact, such support has been noted to especially protect mothers from depression in the face of stressful life events (Brown & Harris, 2001).

However, the very close relationship that often exists between single parent and child can make the inclusion of a new partner difficult, even when the relationship is not live in. Therapists must coach parents to appreciate the sense of loss for the child, when the parent whom they have had to themselves now has a new partner who takes their time and energy. The child will need reassurance that their relationship to their parent is not in jeopardy, often a slow process.

Live-in partners can be even more problematic. If there is no long-term commitment to the family, their entrances and exits can be disruptive and upsetting to children (Kamp-Dush, 2009). In addition, single parents of either gender can find themselves juggling conflicting loyalties between their children and their new partners, especially those partners who compete with children for the single parent's time and attention, undermine parental authority, or get intensely involved and then leave precipitously. Single mothers are left handling conflicts that arise when live-in boyfriends expect to be in charge, when they do not have parental credibility or a solid relationship with the child. Many mothers worry about the risk of losing the support of someone they desperately need, so they may need help and support to make it clear to that person that his or her role is not to be parent. In fact, they may need to protect their children from partners who do not have a biological bond to a child, as these children are nearly 50 times more likely to die of injuries than children living with two biological parents (Schnitzer & Ewigman, 2008; Margolin, 1992).

Single-parent families with older children and adolescents

As children in single-parent families become older, they are likely to take on and be granted more than usual authority over their younger siblings and household functioning. Getting help from parentified children is often essential for the survival of these families, only becoming a serious problem when children are encouraged to totally sacrifice their childhood to family chores and responsibilities. Most adolescents are given room to accomplish the developmental tasks of this life cycle stage, and most single parents manage to maintain their parental role during this process. The families they form have the advantages of becoming closer and less hierarchical as a result.

However, as children enter adolescence, many begin to challenge parental rules and values as they sort out their sense of self, and their parents are left tolerating their often rocky moves toward emancipation. Single parents encounter these challenges, regardless of their gender, although they are often more difficult for single mothers, who tend to be less comfortable balancing reasonable rules with allowing age-appropriate freedoms. They may need support in setting limits, particularly if they have teenage boys with behavioral problems (Autor & Wasserman, 2013).

Fortunately, over time, the payoffs of being raised in a single-parent household become more obvious for children of both genders. Many girls raised by single mothers develop social skills and relationship abilities earlier, and boys often become especially socially savvy, generous, and caring communicators, while continuing to maintain their traditional masculine interests and traits (Drexler & Gross, 2005; Kimmel, 2012). Yet the normal launching process of teens that requires changes in family structure to allow them the freedom to move out of the family and return for support as needed may be complicated by the competing needs of single parents for help with household tasks and the child-care of younger siblings.

During these years, the children of divorce may begin to question their role in the failure of their parents' marriage, and those who are adopted may begin to have questions about their biological history. Children in both of these categories may want to reconnect with the past, seeking more time with a divorced parent or seeking reunion with their birth mother (McNamara, 2009; Samuels, 2009). At the same time, single parents who have just begun to breathe a sigh of relief as their children gain increasing independence may find they need to provide care for their own parents who may be beginning to experience a number of sequential illnesses.

Single parenting in the post-childrearing years

Eventually, the children of single parents grow up and leave just as all children do. Most parents respond to their children leaving home with a sense of relief. But gracefully accomplishing this developmental task can be harder for single parents without the support or comfort of a partner to provide a continuing sense of belonging or family. The welcomed freedom, relief, and sense of accomplishment is counterbalanced by sadness that they are unable to share yet another of their child's developmental steps with a partner who cares as much as they do. Awareness of such parental anxieties can increase the child's guilt about becoming independent or stimulate anger if young adults feel smothered or constrained by the implicit demands of a parent's needs.

While most offspring eventually develop an adult–adult relationship with their parents, it helps that children of single parents tend to show an earlier appreciation of their parents as individuals with histories, strengths, and limitations of their own (Birditt et al., 2008; Fingerman et al., 2008), perhaps because of their history of an egalitarian relationship. Those with stronger adult-to-adult relationships with their children can find them a comfort and a help in later years, making it easier for single parents to appreciate the successful adulthood and accomplishments of their progeny as they alter their own priorities to create an independent life. Single parents can then discover later-life opportunities to explore new roles in their own lives and in the lives of their children, and many report great pleasure as they find ways to actively participate in their children's families, including enjoying the role of grandparent.

Yet several potential problems in the post-childrearing phase of the life cycle can create challenges for single parents of either gender. When offspring inevitably encounter the problems of adult life, single parents do not have a partner who is mutually committed to their adult child's well-being, and willing to be helpful and supportive when problems arise. This life phase can also be difficult for those single parents who have not prepared for their child's independence by developing interests and networks of their own before their child has been launched, too often finding themselves isolated and in need of developing new resources. Most single parents appear to be able to make room for new relationships and interests during this phase, but those who do not may find themselves lonely and stymied about how to develop meaning in their lives when they are no longer needed by their busy children.

In addition, a sizable subset of aging single parents have financial difficulties, particularly those single mothers who have never had a strong employment history and/or the pension of an ex-partner to provide support. Compared to married women, single mothers are 55 percent more likely to be living in poverty after the age of 65 (Johnson & Favreault, 2004). For most single parents, the eventual tasks of this life cycle stage involve finding ways to deal with health problems and possible diminishing ability to function independently without becoming a burden to their children.

> **Assess your comprehension of single parents and the family life cycle by completing this quiz.**

When Single-Parent Families Seek Help

Single-parent families are likely to seek help as they deal with the fallout from life cycle transitions, those entrances and exits from the family such as birth, death, marriage, or divorce. Managing these life cycle events can stretch the already thinly spread coping resources of many single-parent families resulting in a range of emotional or behavioral problems for parent and/or child.

Most clinicians, especially those working in public agencies, are likely to see a disproportionate number of individuals living in single-parent families, contributing to the myth that all single parents and their children are dysfunctional. But while they may use mental health services more often than two-parent families (Crosier et al., 2007; Okun, 1996; Wang, 2004; Wen, 2008), their presenting complaints are probably generated less by clinical disorders than by life cycle transitions and interweaving of multiple life stresses (Wolfe, 2009).

For instance, single parents often initially seek care for a behaviorally disruptive or emotionally distressed child, but their requests for help in managing that child may be the result of parental coping mechanisms that have been compromised by experiences of cultural and racial prejudice, chronic financial problems, unresolved past losses or abuse, and the absence of adequate support from extended family and friends. These factors no doubt contribute to the high rates of distress in single parents, and, in turn, some would say to the high rates of emotional, behavioral, and educational problems in their children (Autor & Wasserman, 2013; Broussard, 2010). Little data is available about the emotional well-being of single fathers, but there is considerable evidence that a high percentage of mothers, especially single mothers, bringing their children for care meet criteria for depression themselves (Afifi et al., 2006; Anderson et al., 2006; Downey & Coyne, 1990; Swartz et al., 2006).

Taking a family systems/life cycle approach in responding to single parents who request help for their child has several advantages. A life cycle framework can be particularly helpful as they struggle to face the myriad inevitable issues that arise at various developmental stages and times of transition. Also, it provides a way to address the needs of distressed mothers, and perhaps fathers, since they tend not to seek help for themselves despite the interrelatedness of the problems of family members. Additionally,

a contextual life cycle framework provides a wide-angle lens to locate these problems in the context of culture, time, history, and relationships, offering a view of values and patterns that help us understand single parents and their potential resources and opportunities, including the identification of possible role models from previous and current generations. Finally, it expands the concentrated and limited focus single parents often have on the current problem, a focus that can cause single parents under stress to be stuck in a present that does not provide solutions to their problems.

By definition, the formative stage of single-parent families is stressful, adding tasks to whatever stage of the family life cycle is otherwise occurring. Becoming a single-parent family almost inevitably involves the reawakening of issues from earlier times that have not been resolved, and there are always echoes of loss of one sort or another. At the most basic level during these times, it is important to define the single parent as having the right to make household rules.

Family stability and parental authority can be reinforced when the maintenance of family routines and rituals is supported. This practice helps to ensure predictability and structure. Some single parents with multiple responsibilities are so overwhelmed by day-to-day survival issues that they neglect the need for these routines and family rituals, forgetting the comfort, structure, and sense of continuity that they provide (Sassler, 2010).

The single parent's ability to be in charge can also be complicated by the need to have older children take some responsibility for their younger siblings and household chores. In some families, single parents allow children to have so much authority that their own authority is compromised; they set limits that are too arbitrary, overly permissive; or they employ an unpredictable combination of the two based on the unpredictable stresses in their own lives. Finding solutions to these relationship issues is not always easy. Helping single parents to gain credibility and power with their children is a particularly difficult task for low-income teen parents with depression and low self-esteem and divorced women, who have tended to rely on their spouses to provide discipline and limit setting.

Maternal sanity can be better maintained in the long run by encouraging consistency. Helping single parents to effectively negotiate issues of power, rules, and responsibilities with their own parents, lovers, or the children themselves is sometimes the most important task of therapy because it lays the groundwork for how everyone can live together and move through the life cycle. Therapists can help these parents to retain their status as ultimate authority and keep a direct line to each child even as they delegate more than the usual number of responsibilities to their older ones. Both parents and children should be encouraged to maintain traditional family rituals, as well as clear and predictable boundaries during the process of creating a new family structure.

At the same time, it is crucial to pay attention to the networks of both parent and child, along with the resources and stresses they might provide. Examining networks can lay the groundwork for reestablishing ties that have been weakened or disrupted by divorce, relocation, or disapproval of life choices. Some single parents lack the courage or skills to develop and maintain helpful relationships beyond the family. Their pride, fear of becoming a burden, fear of rejection, or even fear of loss of custody may make it hard to ask for help. Nurturing existing and potential contacts will facilitate a web of support, an interrelated archipelago of contacts that can provide a practical and emotional cushion for both parent and child. However, it may take a therapist, serving as a temporary cheerleader and coach, to help both parent and child to become embedded in a fabric of social support, while simultaneously sorting out the problems in existing family relationships. If possible, therapists working with divorced families should work to involve both parents and their networks as ongoing connections for their child. Even though we now know that divorce can also have positive effects, a child's social network may be painfully disrupted in a divorce. It is important to strengthen the child's network by minimizing this loss of extended family members and family friends and increasing the involvement of community supports that can minimize the impact of losses that have occurred.

CASE ILLUSTRATIONS
Single-Parent Families Seeking Help

The following narratives provide examples of single parents, with dilemmas they have encountered. Each used therapy to come to terms with common themes encountered during their life journeys as single parents.

Angela: Balancing the Need for Independence and the Need for Support

This first example is of a teen whose move toward independence became complicated by pregnancy, a cross-race relationship, and the need for help from family. She struggled to maintain her dreams and a sense of herself as a competent adult in the face of increased parental involvement, while her own parents struggled to help her and their grandchild, but simultaneously wanting to promote their child's independence and personal development. Everyone tried to balance independence and parental credibility in the face of three generational dynamics.

Angela was an 18-year-old first-generation Mexican American living on campus in her freshmen year of college and dating Michael, a 19-year-old African American student. When she discovered she was pregnant, Michael ended their relationship. She feared telling her parents not only because she did not want to give up college life but also because she knew they would be disappointed and upset that her baby would be biracial. When she eventually told them they were devastated but agreed to swallow their dreams for her success and encouraged her to move home so that they could look after her, and eventually her child. Angela, who valued her education, freedom, and the opportunity for a better life, insisted on first completing her second semester of college. When she did move home, the adjustment to her family's strict household rules/structure was a difficult one, but being pregnant with no job, no money, and no other support left her with no alternative. She was thankful for their help, but she was used to making her own decisions in the year she had been on her own, and her family's negativity about Michael upset her. Trapped in her parent's home, she feared not only that she would never be able to finish college but also that her biracial child would never be accepted by her family. Angela's family fell in love with their grandchild as soon as he was born, and they were eventually able to come to an agreement with Angela to raise him together. They developed a child care routine that allowed her to return to college at a school closer to home. Her parents struggled with just how much they should help to facilitate her participation in college life, and how much they should push her to be responsible for her child's care. Their concerns were exacerbated by requests from Michael to see his child, even though he contributed no support, had dropped out of college, and no longer had a romantic relationship with Angela. They sought counseling for help with handling the ambiguities of Angela's parenting, issues fairly easily settled. Accepting Michael as their grandchild's parent was a much more difficult task. They blamed him for their daughter's pregnancy, the interruption of her college education, and his failure to work or contribute support. However, as he and his parents continued to make efforts to be involved and provide occasional child care, they were gradually able to accept that he could play a positive role in their grandson's life. Angela, now 21, continues to hope to graduate from college and move out of her parent's home.

Daniel: A Committed Single Father against All Odds

Daniel is just one of the increasing numbers of men who want or need to be the primary parent of their child. These men tend to receive less support for taking on the responsibilities of single parenting, so they are often left to blaze their own trail. Daniel made a commitment to raise his young daughter despite the lack of support from his family and his network. He was a young African American college graduate in his early 20s, dating Pamela and leading a swinging social life when Pamela got pregnant. They married despite the disapproval of their parents, who each thought their child could have done better. Six months later, they had a daughter. A stormy 4-year marriage was followed by 4 years of conflict over child visitation. Eventually, Pamela's drug use made

it impossible for her to be an effective mother, and she offered Daniel custody. Aware that his daughter needed him, Daniel wanted to step up to the plate but was terrified of taking on sole responsibility for his daughter's well-being. Neither his single life style nor his own family history of generations of inadequate fathering had prepared him to have any idea of what it would take to be a good father, a fact that did not bode well for his chances of success. His father and grandfather, both now deceased, had failed to provide for their families either financially or emotionally. In the best of times, they had been neglectful and unavailable. Even Daniel's mother did not support his raising his child, saying men had no business raising daughters. Her opinions were, at least in part, based on the poor fathering she experienced in her own family and the lack of involvement of her husband with their four children. Paradoxically, however, she offered no help. Daniel also got little encouragement from his single friends who pointed out that becoming a full-time father would mean giving up his single life style. Determined to try, he sought counseling in hopes of gaining support for what he felt he had to do. He was coached to search for possible role models in his extended family and discovered a long-distant paternal uncle who not only expressed support and admiration for Daniel's desire to take responsibility for his child, but who was also willing to provide financial help. The sacrifices were considerable, and for several years Daniel's life was constrained by work and child care, which involved a lot of trial and error parenting. His social world gradually expanded as his daughter grew up and eventually went to college.

Mary: Divorced, Overwhelmed, and in Crisis

Some single parents live from crisis to crisis, losing sight of the impact of their culture, their extended family history, and the chance to understand and use the resources that might be available. Those who become overwhelmed and depressed may even abandon the most basic rules and important family rituals such as regular dinners, not to mention outings or birthday and other holiday celebrations (Kaplan, McLoyd, & Toyokawa, 2008). Some, like Mary, even deny the relevance of the rules and rituals they once maintained, viewing themselves as no longer a "real" family.

Mary, a 40-year-old recently divorced Polish American mother of three without much of an available network, requested help for Stephan, her 8-year-old middle son, who had been acting out since his father abruptly left and moved to another state and was now maintaining only occasional contact. Mary was not prepared to manage her children or a household without a husband. She never had enough money to meet her children's needs and could not provide them with brand of clothes which they claimed were essential for social survival. Worse yet, they blamed her for their father's absence. Frequently frazzled, exhausted, and feeling inadequate, her discipline was admittedly inconsistent, and the constant fights and chaos at home seemed to her a matter of course. Despite these stresses that dominated her life, she would not have come to the mental health center if her son's teachers had not complained that he was underperforming and acting out in class. Getting her children together to come to counseling felt like just one more major and exhausting task, one that initially made the family's attendance at treatment sporadic. The turning point came when their counselor redefined the problem as the family being trapped in mourning their old family in ways that prevented them from creating a new one. She suggested they begin by addressing the pragmatics of defining a new single-parent household structure that provided a better chance of meeting everyone's needs. Together, Mary and her children used their sessions to work out a list of rules, chores, and consequences that made everyone's life a little less unpredictable. She successfully delegated increased responsibilities to her 12-year-old daughter for a few dinnertime and after-school chores and, somewhat less successfully, delegated to her sons the chore of cleaning their own room. They created a required regular Sunday family dinnertime to reinforce their sense of family. As the chaos diminished, Mary became less depressed and her children more comfortable. In treatment, the family turned to the issues of their anger at their absent father, how they could maintain some contact with him, and how they could find ways to make up for some of the losses they experienced after he left.

Kathleen: Independent with a Vengeance

The issues that bring older single mothers by choice to treatment are quite different. Since they are usually better educated and have more resources, their daily life is usually easier to manage, and many even have hired help. But, as Kathleen's story demonstrates, their lives have their own unique set of problems.

Kathleen was a 38-year-old woman who, as she said, "had it all." An independent and successful financial advisor who owned her own home, she had a good relationship with her Irish American Catholic family of origin. She did not see herself as a woman waiting for her prince to come, having overtly rejected this message from the culture and the media. But as friend after friend married and began to have children, she increasingly felt she was a misfit. Her ticking biological clock eventually inspired her to become a single parent by donor insemination. Her family was shocked at this decision, and two of her siblings, embarrassed, cut off contact when she began to pursue this path. Without a partner, she did not have to make room for a child in a couple's relationship, but she did have to make room for a child in her very independent life. This task was not easy, but she worked hard to create a loving and predictable environment for her child. Motherhood was everything she hoped for, but she could not help feeling bad about the negative social reactions she occasionally experienced for her single parenthood. Her 38-year history of feeling accomplished and respected had not prepared her for being viewed as deviant or deficient. She struggled with coming to grips with who she was and eventually concluded she was okay. With the help of a coach, she eventually took on the task of repairing the close relationships she once had with her parents and siblings with the same determination she had always mobilized in her professional career. She began by reaching out to them in small ways, sending informal notes and photos of the baby. In search of role models, she also contacted an aunt who had successfully raised her children on her own after her husband died. Gradually, other family members responded to her efforts to be a part of her family, and by her daughter's second birthday, nearly all came to the party and subsequently included her in other family events. Today, 10 years later, both Kathleen and her daughter are thriving. Kathleen defines her life as satisfying despite the fact that she rarely dates, claiming that between her work and parenting, she just has no energy or time.

> Assess your comprehension of when single-parent families seek help by completing this quiz.

— Conclusion

The increased prevalence of single-parent families of all sorts has constituted a dramatic social change in our society in recent years. Despite worries about the demise of the traditional nuclear family, this family form has gained increased acceptance, although many single parents continue to struggle to survive in a culture that defines them as deficient and provides little formal support.

The challenges of raising children solo are real, and not surprisingly a disproportionate number of single parents eventually seek help for themselves or their children, usually in traditional mental health and social service agencies. To have any chance to work effectively with single-parent families, clinicians in community agencies must become sensitive to the challenges single parents encounter when they must raise children without the sanction of a marital relationship or in the aftermath of a marriage that was not viable. These issues may leave single parents unusually sensitive to criticism and more than a bit defensive. They are highly likely to become the treatment dropouts so frustrating to clinicians, unless they make specific efforts to engage and connect, being particularly careful to support their authority and not compete with them for their children's approval.

Engaging them in treatment is complicated by the fact that over-stretched single parents often experience the therapy they seek as just one more time-consuming burden. They also find that the narrow focus on diagnosis and pathology required in public mental health systems often minimizes their strengths and fails to acknowledge the resources or patterns of the larger family system that play a role in the child's behavior and the single parent's needs.

Clinicians can effectively employ models of individual or family intervention if they counteract these negative forces by highlighting the factors contributing to successful single-family households. Particularly important factors are the stage of the single-parent family life cycle, the relationship with their extended family and social network, and the strategies they must develop to accommodate to the many daily realities of their unique lives while developing a sense of home (Burton et al., 2004).

In addition to adapting traditional therapy models to appropriately target the needs of single-parent families, a number of creative educational and supportive programs have emerged that allow single parents to receive help without being seen in the formal mental health services system. Just a few examples of creative programs include Internet interventions for single parents (Campbell-Grossman et al., 2009), single parent by choice support groups (Ben-Daniel, Rokach, Filtzer, & Feldman, 2007), community programs in which low-income minority single mothers are paired with supportive older women (Roberts, 2006), and the Baby College that is part of the Harlem Children's Zone, helping low-income minority teen parents to become better parents, while continuing to address their own needs (Tough, 2007). All of these programs could be adapted and disseminated to other communities to address the needs of various types of single parents.

> Recall what you learned in this chapter by completing the Chapter Review.

References

Afifi, T. O., Coz, B. J., & Enns, M. W. (2006). Mental health profiles among married, never-married and separated/divorced mothers in a nationally representative sample. *Social Psychiatry and Psychiatric Epidemiology, 41,* 122–129.

Anderson, C. M., Robins, C., Cahalane, H., Greeno, C., Carr, G., Copeland V., & Andrews, R. M. (2006). Why low-income mothers do not engage with the formal mental health care system: Preliminary findings from an ethnographic study. *Qualitative Health Research, 16*(7), 926–943.

Autor, D., & Wasserman, M., (2013). Wayward sons: The emerging gender gap in labor markets and education. *Third Way: Center for Economic and Policy Research.*

Bakker, W., & Karsten, L. (2013). Balancing paid work, care and leisure in post-separation households: A comparison of single parents with co-parents. *Acta Sociologica, 56*(2), 173–187.

Barrett, A. E., & Turner, R. J. (2005). Family structure and mental health: The mediating effects of socioeconomic status, family process and social stress. *Journal of Health and Social Behavior, 46,* 156–169.

Ben-Daniel, N., Rokach, R., Filtzer L., & Feldman, R. (2007). When two are a family: Looking backward and looking forward in a group intervention with single-by-choice mothers. *Journal of Family Therapy, 29* (3), 249–266.

Berger, L. M. (2007). Socioeconomic factors and substandard parenting. *Social Service Review, 8*(3), 485–522.

Birditt, K. S., Fingerman, K. L., Lefkowitz, E. S., & Kamp Dush, C. M. (2008). Parents perceived as peers: Filial maturity in adulthood. *Journal of Adult Development, 15* (1), 1–12.

Bratter, J. L., & Damask S. (2013). Poverty at a racial crossroads: Poverty among multiracial children of single mothers. *Journal of Marriage and Family, 75*(2), 486–502.

Broussard, C. A. (2010). Research regarding low-income single mothers' mental and physical health: A decade in review. *Journal of Poverty,* 14, (4), 443–451.

Brown, G. W., & Harris, T. (2001). *Social origins of depression: A study of psychiatric disorder in women.* International Behavioral and Social Sciences Library: Classics from the Tavistock Press.

Burton, L. M., Winn, D. M., Stevenson H., & Clark S. L. (2004). Working with African American Clients: Considering the "Homeplace" in Marriage and Family Therapy Practices. *Journal of Marital and Family Therapy, 30*(4), 397–410.

Cain, D. S., & Combs-Orme, T. (2005). Family structure effects on parenting stress and practices in the African American family. *Journal of Sociology and Social Welfare, 32* (2), 19–40.

Caldwell, C. H. (1996). Predisposing, enabling and need factors related to patterns of help-seeking among African American women. In H. W. Neighbors & J. S. Jackson (Eds.), *Mental health in Black America* (pp. 146–160). Thousand Oaks. CA: Sage.

Campbell-Grossman, C. K., Hudson, D. B., Keating-Lefler, R., & Heusinkvelt, S. (2009). The provision of social support to single, low-income, African American mothers via e-mail messages. *Journal of Family Nursing, 15*(2), 220–236.

Carlson, M. J. (2001). Family structure and children's behavioral and cognitive outcomes. *Journal of Marriage and Family, 63,* 779–792.

Casey, T., & Maldonado, L. (2012). *Worse off—Single parent families in the United States: A cross national comparison of single parenthood in the U.S. and sixteen other high-income countries* (pp. 1–35). Legal Momentum: The Women's Legal Defense and Education Fund, New York.

Ceballo, R., & McLoyd, V. C. (2002). Social support and parenting in poor, dangerous neighborhoods. *Child Development, 73*(4), 1310–1321.

Cherlin, A. J. (2010) . Demographic trends in the United States.: A review of research in the 2000s. *Journal of Marriage and Family, 72,* 403–419.

Cherlin, A. J. (2008). *Public and private families: An introduction* (5th ed.). New York: McGraw-Hill.

Cherlin, A. J., Cross-Barnet, C., Burton, L. M. & Garrett-Peters, R. (2008). Promises they can keep: Low income women's attitudes toward motherhood, marriage, and divorce. *Journal of Marriage and Family, 70*(4), 919–933.

Cohen, J., & Manning, W. (2010). The relationship context of premarital serial cohabitation. *Social Science Research, 39,* 766–776.

Crosier, T., Butterworth, P., Rodgers, B. (2007). Mental health problems among single and partnered mothers: The role of financial hardship and social support. *Social Psychiatry and Psychiatric Epidemiology, 42*(1), 6–13.

Cutrona, C. E., Hessling, R. M., Bacon, P. L., & Russell, D. W. (1998). Predictors and correlates of continuing involvement with the baby's father among adolescent mothers. *Journal of Family Psychology, 12*(3), 369–387.

Devault, A., Milcent, M., Ouellet, F., Laurin, I., Jauron, M., & Lacharite, C. (2008). Life stories of young fathers in contexts of vulnerability. *Fathering, 6*(3), 226–248.

Downey, G., & Coyne, J. C. (1990). Children of depressed parents: An integrative review. *Psychological Bulletin, 108,* 50–76.

Drexler, P., & Gross, L. (2005). *Raising boys without men: How maverick moms are creating the next generation of exceptional men.* Emmaus, PA: Rodale Press.

Dudley, J. R. (2007). Helping nonresidential fathers: The case for teen and adult unmarried fathers. *Families in Society, 88*(2), 171–181.

Dyer, W. J. (2005). Prison, fathers, and identity: A theory of how incarceration affects men's paternal identity. *Fathering, 3*(3), 201–219.

Edin, K., & Kefalas, M. (2005) . *Promises I Can Keep: Why Poor Women Put Motherhood before Marriage.* Berkeley: University of California Press.

Edin, K., & Kissane, R. J. (2010). Poverty and the American Family: A Decade in Review, *Journal of Marriage and the Family, 72,* 460–479.

Fagan, J., Palkovitz, R., Roy, K., & Farrie, D. (2009). Pathways to paternal engagement: Longitudinal effects of risk and resilience on nonresident fathers. *Developmental Psychology, 45*(5), 1389–1405.

Fingerman, K. L., Pitzer, L., Lefkowitz, E. S., Birditt, K. S., & Mroczek, D. (2008). Ambivalent relationship qualities between adults and their parents: Implications for the well-being of both parties. *The Journals of Gerontology: Series B: Psychological Sciences and Social Sciences, 63B*(6), 362–371.

Forste, R., Bartkowski, J. P., & Jackson, R. A. (2009). Just be there for them: Perceptions of fathering among single, low-income men. *Fathering, 7*(1), 49–69.

Furstenberg, F. F., & Cherlin, A. J. (1994). *Divided families: What happens to children when parents part.* Cambridge, MA: Harvard University Press.

Gibson-Davis, C. (2011). Mothers but not wives: The increasing lag between nonmarital births and marriage. *Journal of Marriage and Family, 73,* 264–278.

Goldscheider, F., & Kaufman, G. (2006). Single parenthood and the double standard. *Fathering, 4*(2), 191–208.

Goodnight, J. A., D'Onofrio, B. M., Cherlin, A. J., Emery, R. E., Hulle, C. A., & Lahey, B. B. (2013). Effects of multiple maternal relationship transitions on offspring antisocial behavior in childhood and adolescence: A cousin-comparison analysis. *Journal of Abnormal Child Psychology,* 41(2), 185–198.

Groze, V. (1991). Adoption and single parents: A review. *Child Welfare, 70*(3), 321–332.

Hamilton, B. E., Martin, J. A., & Ventura, S. J. (2012). *Births: Preliminary data for 2011. National vital statistics reports* (Vol. 61, No. 5). Hyattsville, MD: National Center for Health Statistics.

Hilton, J. M., & Kopera-Frye, K. (2007). Differences in resources provided by grandparents in single and married parent families. *Journal of Divorce & Remarriage, 47*(1–2), 33–54.

Hook, J. L., & Chalasani, S. (2008). Gendered expectations? Reconsidering single fathers' child-care time. *Journal of Marriage and Family 70*(4), 978–990.

Johnson, R. W., & Favreault, M. M. (2004). Economic status in later life among women who raised children outside of marriage. *Journal of Gerontology: Series B: Psychological Sciences and Social Sciences, 59B,* 6, S315–S323.

Jones, D. J., Zalot, A. A, Foster, S. E., Sterrett, E., & Chester, C. (2007). A review of childrearing in African American single mother families: The relevance of a coparenting framework. *Journal of Child and Family Studies, 16*(5), 671–683.

Kamp-Dush, C. M. (2009). The association between family of origin structure and instability and mental health across the transition to adulthood. In H. E. Peters & C. M. Kamp-Dush (Eds.), *Marriage and family: Complexities and perspectives* (pp. 225–243). New York: Columbia University Press.

Kaplan, R., McLoyd, V. C., & Toyokawa, T. (2008). Work demands, work-family conflict, and child adjustment in African American families: The mediating role of family routines. *Journal of Family Issues, 29*(10), 1247–1267.

Kimmel, M. S. (2012). *The gendered society* (5th ed.). New York: Oxford University Press.

Laakso J. (2004). Key determinants of mothers' decisions to allow visits with non-custodial fathers. *Fathering, 2*(2), 131–145.

Levine, K. A. (2009). Against all odds: Resilience in single mothers of children with disabilities. *Social Work in Health Care, 48*(4), 402–419.

Lichter, D. , Turner, R., & Sassler, S. (2010). National estimates of the rise in serial cohabitation. *Social Science Research, 39,* 754–765.

Margolin, L. (1992). Child abuse by mothers' boyfriends: Why the overrepresentation? *Child Abuse & Neglect 16*(4), 541–551.

McLanahan, S. S., & Sandefur, G. (1994). *Growing up with a single parent.* Cambridge, MA: Harvard University Press.

McNamara P. M. (2009) Review of "In search of belonging: Reflections by transracially adopted people." *Australian Social Work, 62,* 1, 121–123.

Okun, B. F. (1996). *Understanding diverse families: What practitioners need to know*. New York: Guilford Press.

Park, J. M. (2005). The roles of living arrangements and household resources in single mothers' employment. *Journal of Social Service Research, 31*(3), 46–67.

Potter, D. (2010). Psychosocial well-being and the relationship between divorce and children's academic achievement. *Journal of Marriage and Family, 72,*(4), 933–946.

Roberts, S. (2006). Creating an intergenerational support system in an African American church. *Dissertation Abstracts International Section A: Humanities and Social Sciences, 67*(6A), 2193.

Roy, K. M., & Dyson, O. L. (2005). Gatekeeping in context: Babymama drama and the involvement of incarcerated fathers. *Fathering, 3*(3), 289–310.

Samuels, G. M. (2009). "Being raised by White people": Navigating racial difference among adopted multiracial adults. *Journal of Marriage and Family, 71*(1), 80–94.

Sassler S. (2010). Partnering across the life course: Sex, relationships, and mate selection. *Journal of Marriage and Family, 72*, 557–575.

Schnitzer, P. G., Ewigman, B. G. (2008). Household composition and fatal unintentional injuries related to child maltreatment. *Journal of Nursing Scholarship, 40*(1), 91–97.

Swartz, H. A., Shear, M. K., Wren, F. J., Greeno, C. G., Sales, E., Sullivan, B. K., & Ludewig, D. P. (2006). Depression and anxiety among mothers who bring their children to a pediatric mental health clinic. *Psychiatric Services, 56*(9), 1077–1083.

Swiss, L., & Le Bourdais, C. (2009). Father-child contact after separation: The influence of living arrangements. *Journal of Family Issues, 30*(5), 623–652.

Thompson, M. S., & Wilkins W. P. (1992). The impact of formal, informal, and societal support networks on the psychological well-being of Black adolescent mothers. *Social Work, 37*(4), 322–328.

Thornton, A. (2009). Framework for interpreting long-term trends in values and beliefs concerning single-parent families. *Journal of Marriage and Family, 71*(2), 230–234.

Tough, P. (2007). *Whatever it takes: Geoffrey Canada's quest to change Harlem and America*. New York: Houghton Mifflin.

Usdansky, M. L. (2009). A weak embrace: Popular and scholarly depictions of single-parent families 1900–1998. *Journal of Marriage and Family, 71*(2), 209–225.

Ventura, S. J. (2009). *Changing patterns of nonmarital childbearing in the United States,* NCHS data brief, 18. Hyattsville, MD: National Center for Health Statistics 2009.

Wang, J. L. (2004). The difference between single and married mothers in the 12-month prevalence of major depressive syndrome, associated factors and mental health service utilization. *Social Psychiatry and Psychiatric Epidemiology, 39*(1), 26–32.

Wen, M. (2008). Family structure and children's health and behavior. *Journal of Family Issues, 29* (11), 1492–1519.

Wolf, J. (2011). Single parents. Retrieved from www .About.com.

Wolfe, D. L. (2009). Review of single by chance, mothers by choice: How women are choosing parenthood without marriage and creating the new American family. *American Journal of Sociology, 114*(5), 1568–1570.

Zahn, M., & Pandy, S. (2004). Economic well-being of single mothers: Work first or post-secondary education? *Journal of Sociology and Social Welfare, 31*(3), 87–112.

Chapter 22

The Remarriage Cycle: Divorced, Multi-Nuclear and Recoupled Families

Monica McGoldrick & Betty Carter

Learning Outcomes

- Describe common stresses and challenges created by remarriage.
- Explain the boundary ambiguities and complexities inherent in remarried families.
- List and describe the stages of the divorce-remarriage cycle.
- Explore adjustment and family integration issues within stepfamilies.
- Discuss common emotional issues encountered during the process of remarriage.
- Examine the impact of remarriage at each phase of the family life cycle.
- Describe the most common triangles formed by members of remarried families and discuss strategies for working with each.
- List and describe general guidelines and clinical recommendations for helping remarried families.

Introduction

Divorce and remarriage have become normal life experiences in the United States, with about 43 percent of first marriages ending in divorce within 15 years and about 75 percent of spouses remarrying at least once, though the patterns depend on social class, age, race, and gender (Bramlett & Mosher, 2001, 2002). The system transformation required in divorce and remarriage is so complex in changing the status, relationships, and membership of families that we consider each transition to require an entire additional phase for families going through them. And an entirely new paradigm of family is required for conceptualizing divorced and recoupled families. This chapter will discuss the cycle of divorce and remarriage, describing families transforming and reconstituting themselves through marriage, divorce, remarriage, and re-divorce. If we visualize a family traveling the road of life, moving from stage to stage in their developmental unfolding, we can see divorce and remarriage as interruptions that put families on a new trajectory—adding additional family life cycle stages—in which the physical and emotional losses and changes must be absorbed by the multigenerational system. The family, now in two or more households, continues its forward developmental progress, though in a more complex form. When either spouse becomes involved with a new partner, a second detour occurs—requiring additional family life cycle stages—in which the family must handle the stress of absorbing two or three generations of new members into the system and redefining their roles and relationships with existing family members.

We all carry into our new relationships the emotional baggage of unresolved issues from important past relationships. This baggage makes us emotionally sensitive in the new relationships: We may put up barriers to intimacy, becoming self-protective, closed off, and afraid to make ourselves vulnerable to further hurt, or we may become expectant that the new relationships will make up for or erase past hurts. These stances complicate new relationships.

In first marriages, the baggage we bring is from our families of origin: our unresolved feelings about parents, siblings, and extended family.

In divorce and remarriage, there are at least three sets of emotional baggage:

1. From the family of origin
2. From the first marriage
3. From the process and aftermath of separation, divorce, or death and the period between marriages

To the extent that either remarried partner expects the other to relieve him or her of this baggage, the new relationship will become problematic. On the other hand, to the extent that each spouse can resolve his or her own emotional issues with significant people from the past, and manage the extremely complex structure of the present, the new relationship can proceed on its own merits.

Over the long haul, remarriage app ears more stressful than divorce (Ahrons, 2007), especially the father's remarriage, which underscores the importance of taking a family life cycle perspective when working clinically to keep focus on the longitudinal course of family life. For poor families, separating and recoupling, often without the legal protections of marriage, become even more complex. Linda Burton and her colleagues, who have been studying such families for many years have described their brittleness and the many difficulties for families living on the edge in the changing membership and structure of recoupling (Cherlin, Burton, L. M., Hurt, T., & Purvin, 2004; Burton & Hardaway, 2012; Burton & Tucker, 2009; Burton, Cherlin, Winn, Estacion, & Holder-Taylor, 2009).

As the first marriage signifies the joining of two families, so a second marriage involves the interweaving of three, four, or more families whose previous family life courses have been disrupted by death or divorce. More than half of Americans today have been, are now, or will eventually be in one or more recoupled families during their lives (Kreider, 2006). At the turn of the twenty-first century, families with stepchildren living in the household constituted about 13 percent of U.S. families (Teachman & Tedrow, 2004), although, of course, this does not begin to convey the extent of recoupled families, remarried or living together, and the number of children in multi-nuclear families who spend part of their time with stepsiblings. Indeed, stepfamilies are becoming the most common family form, and estimates are that there will soon be more multi-nuclear families than first families in the United States (CDC, 2008). Estimates are that one third of children will live with a stepparent, usually a stepfather, before adulthood (Amato & Sobolewski, 2004). Half of the marriages that occur each year are remarriages. Almost 50 percent of first marriages are expected to end in divorce and the majority of divorced individuals (more men than women) remarry (Kreider, 2006). Indeed, though stepfamily relationships have been neglected in family research and are not generally as strong as first family ties, remarriage creates an enlarged pool of potential kin who may come to have very important family bonds. These numbers do not include the frequently recoupling families of the poor who can rarely afford marriage and often have changing constellations of mothers, "othermothers" and only sometimes fathers in the picture (Burton & Hardaway, 2012).

Overall our society still does not recognize transformed and reconstituted families as part of the norm. Only recently has family research included these families and norms for forming a recoupled family are only beginning to emerge. The complexity of remarried families is reflected in our lack of positive language and kinship labels, the shifting of children's sibling positions in the new family, and society's failure to differentiate parenting from stepparenting functions. The built-in ambiguity of boundaries and membership in remarried families defies simple definition, and our culture lacks any established language patterns or rituals to help us handle the complex relationships of acquired family members. The kinship terms we do have, such as "stepmother," "stepfather," and "stepchild," have such negative connotations that they may increase the difficulties for families trying to work out these relationships. In fact, the term "step" derives from the old English word for bereavement or loss, so it is meaningful to the context in which families are reconstituted into new family constellations. Constance Ahrons calls post-divorce families "binuclear," a term that is descriptive and non-stigmatizing. We have expanded this to refer to multi-nuclear families, because in recoupling there are many times when three or four or more households must be considered at one time.

Our society offers stepfamilies two basic models, neither of which works. The media glorifies families that act like the Brady Bunch, where everybody lives together happily ever after and there are no dangling ends. The alternative narrative involves the wicked stepparents of fairy tales. Many have referred to remarried families as "blended," but, as one of Patricia Papernow's (2013) families described it, they thought they were blending but in reality it felt more like blundering. Thus, our first clinical step is to validate for stepfamilies the lack of role models and support in the paradigms of remarried families that society has offered.

We originally chose to use the term "remarried" in our work to emphasize that it is the marital bond that forms the basis for the complex rearrangement of several families in a new constellation, but increasingly reconstituted families are not actually marrying, or at least not marrying for a while. Still, it is the couple's bond that makes them take the trouble to go through the complexities of family reformation. So we sometimes refer to them as "recoupled" families or "stepfamilies" to indicate the presence of children from past relationships as part of the remarried system.

Forming a remarried family is one of the most difficult developmental transitions for a family to negotiate. Giving up forever the concept of simple and clear family membership and boundaries is no easy task. It is no wonder that the unresolved losses of the previous families so often lead to premature attempts at boundary closure in a new family. In any case, earlier losses are very likely to be reactivated by the new family formation. Indeed, Montgomery, Anderson, Hetherington, and Clingempeel, (1993) found in their longitudinal study that living together before remarriage provided a beneficial in-between stage of adjustment that reduced the trauma of remarriage, just as it can in first marriages. Much therapeutic effort must be directed toward educating families about the built-in complexities of the process so that they can work toward establishing a viable, flexible system that will allow them to get back on their developmental track for future life cycle phases.

It is easy to understand the wish for clear and quick resolution when one has been through the pain of a first family ending. But the instant intimacy that remarried families often hope for is impossible to achieve. The new relationships are harder to negotiate because they do not develop gradually, as first families do, but begin midstream, after another family's life cycle has been dislocated. Children's sibling position frequently changes, and they must cope with variable membership over several households. A child may be an only child in his mother's household, but an oldest child in his father's remarried household, where he now has two younger stepbrothers. When his mother remarries, he becomes the youngest of four with her three teenage stepchildren. Naturally, second families also carry the scars of first-marriage families. Neither parents, nor children, nor grandparents can forget the relationships that went before and that may still be more powerful than the new relationships. Children almost never give up their attachment to their first parent, no matter how negative that relationship was or is. Having the patience to tolerate the ambiguity of the situation and allowing each other the space and time for feelings about past relationships are crucial processes in forming a remarried family.

The boundary ambiguities and complexities include issues of membership, space, authority, and allocation of time. Once a remarried family is formed, it becomes forever impossible to have a clear definition (if it is ever possible anyway) of who exactly is related to you how. For example, is your stepfather's first cousin your cousin and are his nephews your cousins? In terms of space, do you get to have a room in your father's house when you are there only twice a week and his stepchildren are there every day? As a young adult, can you move back home with your mother and stepfather if he is the one paying for the house? In terms of authority, who gets to decide whether you go to private college and your stepsiblings to public college because their parents together cannot afford private college? Who gets to make the rules for you in your father and stepmother's home? And in terms of time allocation, which children get to spend more time with their father, his children or his stepchildren? An additional boundary problem arises when instant incest taboos are called for, as when several previously unrelated teenagers are suddenly expected to view each other as siblings. All these ambiguities of relationship, membership, space, authority, and time are built in and can never again be clearly defined.

In our experience, the most powerful clinical tool for helping families negotiate these complex transitions is to provide information that normalizes their experiences. Clinically useful research findings on divorced and remarried families integrated in this chapter come from the work of many authors. Duberman (1975) was one of our first role models in the exploration of these issues. The longitudinal research of Hetherington, Clingempeel, Montgomery, and their colleagues (Hetherington, Cox, & Cox, 1977, 1999, 2002, 2005, 2006; Hetherington-, Cox, & Cox, 1977; Hetherington & Clingempeel, 1992), carried out in a remarkably comprehensive longitudinal research on hundreds of families in a broad project over several decades (summarized in Hetherington & Kelly, 2002), has been extraordinarily helpful to us in conceptualizing the trajectories and complex experiences of families as they evolve over the life cycle. John and Emily Visher (1979, 1988, 1991, 1996) were among the staunchest advocates for positive thinking about stepfamilies. Connie Ahrons (Ahrons, 1981, 1994, 2005, 2007; Ahrons & Rodgers, 1987) has been expanding our understanding of divorce and remarried families for decades. Paul Glick (1984, 1989) at the Census Bureau was a generous resource to us for many years through the detailed information he had in his head about remarriage patterns. Andrew Cherlin, Frank Furstenberg, and their colleagues (Cherlin & Furstenberg, 1994; Furstenberg & Cherlin, 1994; Cherlin, 1992, 2009; Cherlin et al., 2004) have also been teaching us about the demographics of marriage, divorce, and remarriage for many years. Cliff Sager and Sager's colleagues (1983), Lillian Messinger (1978), Mary Whiteside (1978, 1982, 1989, 2006), Anne Bernstein (1989, 1994, 1999), James Bray (Bray & Easling, 2005), Pasley and Ihinger (1995), Pasley and Ihinger-Tallman (2008), and Patricia Papernow and her colleagues (2013) have been pioneers contributing for many years to the family therapy field's understanding of the clinical issues of

remarriage. And Linda Burton and her colleagues (Burton, Purvin, & Garrett-Peters, 2009; Burton & Tucker, 2009; Burton & Hardaway, 2012; Burton et al., 2009; Cherlin et al., 2004) have carried out extraordinary ethnographic research on the coupling and recoupling patterns of poor families, mostly Latinas and African Americans, for more than a decade. This chapter draws on the work of these researchers and clinicians, as well as our own clinical experience over the past four decades.

Although it is extremely hard to give up the idea of the "nuclear family" by drawing a tight loyalty boundary around household members, excluding outside parents or children who reside elsewhere is neither realistic nor appropriate. It is essential to acknowledge families' actual relationships and empower them to move forward taking those realities into consideration. In earlier times, when families lived in larger extended family and community enclaves, children had a whole network of adults who cared for them and helped to raise them. That is the model that helps here. Families need to develop a system with permeable but workable boundaries around the members of different households, allowing children to belong in multiple homes, to move flexibly between households and to have open lines of communication between ex-spouses, children, their parents, stepparents, grandparents, and other relatives. Indeed, extended family connections and outside connectedness may be even more important for children's well-being than they are in first families.

Because parent–child bonds predate the new marital bonds, often by many years, and are therefore initially stronger than the couple bond, remarried families must allow for the built-in ambiguity of roles and the differential ties based on historical connections. In particular, each parent needs to accept responsibility for his or her own children and not combat or compete with the other's parent–child attachments.

Previous experience with nontraditional gender roles may increase the flexibility necessary for stepfamily organization. Forming a remarried family requires a re-visioning of traditional gender roles. We must overturn completely the notion that the stepmother, just because she is a woman, should be in charge of the home, the children, or the emotional relationships of the system. Such a view fails to respect the family's history, that is, that the parent with the historical relationship with the child is the only one who can really be the primary parent. Traditional gender roles, requiring women to take responsibility for the emotional well-being of the family, have placed stepmothers in an untenable position, through the expectation that she can automatically be "mother" to children with whom she has no connection (Martin, 2009). This pits her against the children's mother, a contest she is bound to lose. The traditional rules that called for women to rear children and men to earn and manage the finances do not work well in first-marriage families. They have no chance at all in a system in which some of the children are strangers to the wife.

In addition, the finances of remarried families include sources of income and expenditure that are not in the husband's power to generate or control (e.g., alimony, child support, and earnings of the ex-wife or current wife). These issues, in addition to the primacy of children's bonds to their original parents, make traditional gender roles completely inappropriate for remarried families.

For poor families, there are often even more difficulties: children raised with little connection to their fathers and often living with what Burton and her colleagues refer to as "othermothers," not really stepmothers, because the roles are not that stabilized and formalized and where children may need to deal with a series of partners their parents connect with, who may or may not take on parenting roles with them (Burton & Hardaway, 2012; Burton & Tucker, 2009).

> **Assess your comprehension of the introduction by completing this quiz.**

The Divorce–Remarriage Cycle

Our concept of the divorce and post-divorce emotional process can be thought of as a roller coaster with peaks of emotional tension at all transition points:

- At the time of the decision to separate or divorce
- When this decision is announced to family and friends
- When money and custody/visitation arrangements are discussed
- When the physical separation takes place
- When the actual legal divorce takes place
- When separated spouses or ex-spouses have contacted about money or children
- As each child graduates, marries, has children, separates, remaries, moves, or becomes ill
- As each spouse forms a new couple relationship, remarries, re-divorces, moves, becomes ill, or dies

These emotional pressure points are found in all divorcing families—though, of course, not necessarily in this order—and many take place over and over again. A general depiction of the process appears in Figure 22.1.

In general, it appears to take a minimum of 2 or 3 years for a family to adjust to this transition—if there are no cutoffs and if all the adults are working at it full tilt. Families in which the emotional issues of divorce are not adequately resolved can remain stuck emotionally for years, or even for generations, although several years after the divorce, if the developmental tasks of divorcing and settling into the post-divorce transformed family are satisfactorily accomplished, there are few, if any, observable or testable differences resulting from having been part of a divorced family (Arkowitz & Lillienfeld, 2013).

The emotions released during the divorce relate primarily to the work of retrieving oneself from the marriage. Each partner must retrieve the hopes, dreams, plans, and expectations that were invested in the spouse and in the marriage. This requires mourning what is lost and dealing with hurt, anger, blame, guilt, shame, and loss in oneself, in the spouse, in the children, in the extended family, and in the friendship network.

Hetherington (1977) found that in 70 percent of divorcing couples, at least one spouse is having an affair, but only a small percent later marry, suggesting that another relationship may help you through but not beyond the divorce. Younger women tend to re-divorce more frequently than older women. About 47 percent of women who remarry before the age of age 25 divorce within the next 10 years (Bramlett & Mosher, 2001). Those who are older at first marriage are less likely to divorce or re-divorce, as are those with more education and economic resources. Men tend to remarry sooner and more often than women, and Whites sooner and more often than people of color. Although first wives are on the average

Figure 22.1 The developmental tasks for divorcing and remarrying families.

Phase	Task	Prerequisite Attitude Transition	Developmental Issues
Divorce	Decision to divorce	Acceptance of inability to resolve marital problems sufficiently to continue relationship	Acceptance of one's own part in the failure of the marriage
	Planning breakup of the system	Supporting viable arrangements for all parts of the system	a. Working cooperatively on problems of custody, visitation, and finances b. Dealing with extended family about the divorce
	Separation	a. Willingness to continue cooperative co-parental relationship and joint financial support of children b. Working on resolution of attachment to spouse	a. Mourning loss of original family b. Restructuring marital and parent–child relationships and finances; adaptation to living apart c. Realignment of relationships with extended family; staying connected with spouse's extended family
	Divorce	Working on emotional divorce: overcoming hurt, anger, guilt, etc.	a. Mourning loss of original family; giving up fantasies of reunion b. Retrieving hopes, dreams, expectations from the marriage c. Staying connected with extended families
Post-Divorce Family	Single parent (custodial household or primary residence)	Willingness to maintain financial responsibilities, continue parental contact with ex-spouse, and support contact of children with ex-spouse and his or her family	a. Making flexible visitation arrangements with ex-spouse and family b. Rebuilding own financial resources c. Rebuilding own social network
	Single parent (non-custodial)	Willingness to maintain financial responsibilities and parental contact with ex-spouse and to support custodial parent's relationship with children	a. Finding ways to continue effective parenting b. Maintaining financial responsibilities to ex-spouse and children c. Rebuilding own social network
Remarriage	Entering new relationship	Recovery from loss of first marriage (adequate emotional divorce)	Recommitment to marriage and to forming a family with readiness to deal with the complexity and ambiguity

(Continued)

Figure 22.1 The developmental tasks for divorcing and remarrying families. (*Continued*)

Phase	Task	Prerequisite Attitude Transition	Developmental Issues
	Conceptualizing and planning new marriage and family	Accepting one's own fears and those of new spouse and children about forming new family Accepting need for time and patience for adjustment to complexity and ambiguity of: 1. Multiple new roles 2. Boundaries: space, time, membership, and authority 3. Affective issues: guilt, loyalty conflicts, desire for mutuality, unresolvable past hurts	a. Working on openness in the new relationships to avoid pseudo-mutuality b. Planning for maintenance of cooperative financial and co-parental relationships with ex-spouses c. Planning to help children deal with fears, loyalty conflicts, and membership in two systems d. Realignment of relationships with extended family to include new spouse and children e. Planning maintenance of connections for children with extended family of ex-spouses
	Remarriage and reconstruction of family	Resolution of attachment to previous spouse and ideal of original family; Acceptance of different model of family with permeable boundaries	Restructuring family boundaries to allow for inclusion of new spouse-stepparent Realignment of relationships and financial arrangements to permit interweaving of several systems Making room for relationships of all children with all parents, grandparents, and other extended family Sharing memories and histories to enhance stepfamily integration
	Renegotiation of remarried family at all future life cycle transitions	Accepting evolving relationships of transformed remarried family	Changes as each child graduates, marries, dies, or becomes ill Changes as each spouse forms new couple relationship, remarries, moves, becomes ill, or dies

3 years younger than their husbands, second wives are on average 6 years younger than their husbands. The more income and education a woman has, the less likely she is to remarry. The reverse is true for men: The more income and education he has, the more likely he is to remarry, and the sooner.

In all multi-nuclear families, childrearing responsibilities must be distributed in ways that validate the bond between original parents and the children they have raised. Each spouse must take primary responsibility for raising and disciplining his or her own children. Ex-spouses are hopefully responsible adults who can learn to cooperate with each other for the sake of their children. New spouses hopefully begin as benign caretakers and build from there. Contraindications for post-divorce arrangements of joint or shared custody should obviously include the following:

- Mental illness in one or both parents
- A history of violence, child abuse, or neglect
- Alcohol or drug abuse

In those situations, the need for collaboration between parents, extended family, and community resources will even be more important to children's safety and well-being. But, assuming neither parent is abusive, mentally ill, or involved in substance abuse, children generally do better if they have regular contact with both parents. The more regularly children visit their noncustodial parent, the better their adjustment is likely to be. The more effectively custodial parents can function and the less parental conflict children are exposed to, the better the children's adjustment will be. Cordial or courteous, low-intensity relationships with the ex-spouse and the ex-spouse's new marital partner work best. It helps if therapists think of all parental figures as potentially enriching the children's support network.

The emotional issues of remarriage go back at least to the disintegration of the first marriage. The intensity of emotion unleashed by the life cycle disruption of divorce must be dealt with over and over again before the dislocated systems are restabilized. No amount of "dealing with" the emotional difficulties of divorce will finish off the process once and for all, although the more emotional work is done at each step, the less intense and disruptive the subsequent reactivations at later stages are likely to be.

The predictable peaks of emotional tension in the transition to remarriage occur at:

- The time of serious commitment to a new relationship.
- The time a plan to remarry is announced to families and friends
- The time of the actual remarriage and formation of a stepfamily, which take place as the logistics of stepfamily life are put into practice.

The emotional process at the transition to remarriage involves dealing with anxiety about investment in a new marriage and a new family; dealing with one's own fears and those of the new spouse and the children; dealing with hostile or upset reactions of the children, the extended families, and the ex-spouse; struggling with the ambiguity of the new family structure, roles, and relationships; re-arousal of parental guilt and concerns about the welfare of children; and re-arousal of the old attachment to the ex-spouse (negative or positive).

Failure to deal sufficiently with the process at each point may jam it enough to prevent remarried family stabilization from ever occurring, a problem that is reflected in the high rate of re-divorce.

The most common mistakes parents make are as follows:

1. Preoccupation with themselves and neglect of their children's experience, which follows from the conflicting life cycle tasks of parenting versus new couple relationships or couple conflict
2. Treating the remarriage as an event, rather than a complex process of family transformation, which will take years
3. Trying to get children to resolve the ambiguities of multiple loyalties by cutting off one relationship to create clarity in another.

The residue of an angry and vengeful divorce can block stepfamily integration for years or forever. The re-arousal of the old emotional attachment to an ex-spouse, which characteristically surfaces at the time of remarriage and at subsequent life cycle transitions of children, is usually not understood as a predictable process and may therefore lead to denial, misinterpretation, conflict, cutoff, and emotional reactivity. As with adjustment to new family structures after divorce, stepfamily integration requires a minimum of 2 or 3 years to create a workable new structure that allows family members to move on emotionally.

Forming a remarried family requires a different conceptual model. When there are children, they are a "package deal" with the spouse. This is, of course, always the case with in-laws as well, but not in such an immediate way, since they do not usually move in with you! At the same time, just because you fall in love with a person does not mean you automatically love their children. So how do you take on a new family in mid-journey just because they are there and part of your spouse's life? That is often the hardest part of the bargain. The first thing is to conceptualize and plan for remarriage as a long and complex process. While more advance planning would be helpful also in first marriages, it is an essential ingredient for successful remarriage, because so many family relationships must be renegotiated at the same time: these include grandparents, in-laws, former in-laws, step-grandparents and stepchildren, half-siblings, etc. (Whiteside, 2006). The presence of children from the beginning of the new relationship makes establishing an exclusive spouse-to-spouse relationship before undertaking parenthood impossible.

The prerequisite attitudes listed in Figure 22.1 are necessary for a family to be able to work on the developmental issues of the transition process. If, as clinicians, we find ourselves struggling with the family over developmental issues before the prerequisite attitudes have been adopted, we are probably wasting our efforts. For example, it is very hard for a parent to help children remain connected to ex-in-laws who were never close or supportive unless the parent has fully embraced the new model of family. Much education and discussion may be required before a client can put into effect ideas that may seem counterintuitive, aversive, or time-consuming.

The relationship of the children and stepparent can evolve only over time as their connection develops and as an extension of the child's bond with the original parent. Stepparents can only gradually assume a role, hopefully friendly, as the partner of the child's parent. Unless the children are young at the time of the remarriage, the parent-and-child paradigm may never apply to the new parent. This is a life cycle reality, not a failure on anyone's part. Indeed, in the "othermother" research of Linda Burton and her colleagues, poor women are often especially resentful of raising someone else's children unless they have a special proclivity, perhaps from family of origin experiences to be a parent figure (Burton & Hardaway, 2012).

> **Assess your comprehension of the divorce–remarriage cycle by completing this quiz.**

Predictable Issues in Remarriage

Adjustment and family integration issues with stepparents and stepchildren

The stereotypes of stepparents are deeply blaming. Most difficult of all is the role of stepmother. The problem for her is especially poignant, since she is usually the one most sensitive to the needs of others, and it will be extremely difficult for her to take a back seat while her husband struggles awkwardly in an uncomfortable situation. The fact is that she has no alternative. Women's tendency to take responsibility for family relationships, to believe that what goes wrong is their fault and that, if they just try hard enough, they can make things work out, are the major problems for them in remarried families, since the situation carries with it built-in structural ambiguities, loyalty conflicts, guilt, and membership problems. Societal expectations for stepmothers to love and care for their stepchildren are also stronger than for stepfathers. If stepfathers help out a bit financially and do a few administrative chores, they may be viewed as an asset, even though that is not a satisfactory parental role. But the expectation for stepmothers is that they will make up to children for whatever losses they have experienced, which is, of course, impossible. Clinically, it is important to relieve them of these expectations.

A stepmother's ambivalence about her parenting role tends to be particularly acute when stepchildren are young and remain in the custody of her husband's ex-wife. In this common situation, stepmothers tend to be less emotionally attached to the children and to feel disrupted and exploited during their visits. Meanwhile the husband's co-parenting partnership may appear to be conducted more with his ex-spouse than with her. Conflicting role expectations set mothers and stepmothers into competitive struggles over childrearing practices. It appears to be better for stepmothers to retain their work outside the home for their independence, emotional support, and validation. In addition to contributing needed money, it makes them less available at home for the impossible job of dealing with the husband's children.

Along with finances, stepchildren are the major contributor to remarriage adjustment problems.

Remarriage often leads to a renewal of custody difficulties in prior relationships. Families with stepchildren are much more complicated and twice as likely to divorce. Marital satisfaction is correlated with the stepparent's connection to stepchildren. Although the remarriage itself might be congenial, the presence of stepchildren often creates child-related problems that may lead the couple to separate. Some stepparents do not even consider their live-in stepchild as part of the family, and stepchildren are even more likely to discount their live-in stepparents. Stepchildren are much more likely to change residence or leave home early than biological children. Children in stepfamilies may appear to have more power than children in first families, although they experience less autonomy than in the single-parent phase, where they typically have more adult privileges and responsibilities.

Stepparents need to take a slow route to parenthood, first becoming friends with their stepchildren, and only gradually assuming an active role in parenting. It generally takes at least 2 years to become co-managers of their stepchildren with their spouses. For stepparents to compete with their stepchildren for primacy with their spouse is inappropriate, as if the couple and parent–child relationships were on the same hierarchical level, which, of course, they are not.

Stepfathers may get caught in the bind between rescuer and intruder, called upon to help discipline the stepchildren and then criticized by them and their mother for this intervention. Over-trying by the new parent is a major problem, often related to guilt about unresolved or unresolvable aspects of the system.

Overall, mothers, daughters, stepdaughters, and stepmothers experience more stress, less satisfaction, and more symptoms than fathers, sons, stepsons, and stepfathers. Stepmother–stepdaughter relationships tend to be the most difficult of all. Daughters, who are often closest to mothers in divorce, tend to have a lot of difficulty with stepfathers, no matter how hard the stepfather tries. Girls' stress probably reflects the fact that they feel more responsible for emotional relationships in a family and thus get caught between loyalty and protection of their mothers and conflicts with their stepmothers. While divorce appears to have more adverse effects for boys, remarriage is more disruptive for girls.

Boys, who are often difficult for a single mother, may settle down after the entry of a stepfather.

Different issues arise when stepfamilies are formed after the premature death of a parent than after a divorce. Gender differences are a key factor. A new stepfather may be perceived as rescuing the family from poverty after the death of the primary wage earner, whereas children tend to view their mother as completely irreplaceable and resent any efforts of another woman to function in her role. However, young children will eventually accept a stepparent, including a stepmother, if the remaining parent can help the children to grieve for their loss before confronting them with a stepmother. When the father does remarry, he needs to help the children to accept the new person in her own right rather than collude with the children in wanting the family to continue in the same way it did when their mother was alive. On the other hand, if insufficient attention is paid to the children's grief work, they may never accept a stepmother. (For a videotape with commentary on a family dealing with these issues, see McGoldrick, 1996.)

Although the fact that the ex-spouse is not around to "interfere" may be an advantage, ghosts can be even more powerful, especially given people's tendency to idealize a parent who is lost prematurely. It may be harder to recognize and deal with a triangle with a dead parent. Talking, remembering, and acknowledging the dead person's human failings and foibles help to exorcise the ghost, but none of this can be done without the active leadership of the surviving parent. Late adolescents or older children generally resist attempts to "replace" their dead parent, and the wise stepparent will honor that position.

Violence and abuse appear to be much more common in stepfamilies than in first families (Brody, 1998), probably because of the system's structural complexity and the fact that they have not had time to develop relationship bonds, and many do not withstand the early stages of family reorganization. But the instability of remarried families should not be overstated. Remarried partners do not wait as long as partners in first families to leave an unhappy situation, and those who manage the early years have no greater likelihood of divorcing than in first marriages.

The stress of money

Money is a major area of conflict in remarried families. Remarriage often leads to reopening of financial battles from the divorce and to children receiving less support from their biological fathers. Traditional gender roles run completely counter to contemporary economics and to the fact that both parents usually enter remarriage with significant financial obligations to the first family. Failure to pay or collect alimony or child support wreaks havoc in post-divorce families. A husband who is the sole wage earner in a remarried family often has to decide which set of children has top priority—his own or the stepchildren he lives with. These priorities are also influenced by his relationship with his ex-wife; if it is bad, his visits and child support payments tend to lag or even cease. A new wife may complain about the money her husband gives to his children, particularly if she does not receive the child support owed for her own children. Overall children in first families tend to receive more from their parents than children whose parents remarry. In affluent families, problems also surface around wills and how much financial assistance should be given to which adult children. Where money is concerned, blood may suddenly seem thicker than relationship.

Gays and lesbians in stepfamilies

A significant number of post-divorce families consist of a gay or lesbian couple with the children of one or both of them from a previous heterosexual marriage. These systems have all of the problems of heterosexual remarried systems in addition to the burdens of secrecy and isolation caused by the social stigma they have most likely experienced (Laird & Green, 1996). In extreme cases, the adults may feel that they have to try to remain closeted, even to their children, for fear of repercussions in custody or employment. There is almost always anxiety about the consequences of coming out to family (La Sala, 2010), the children's teachers and friends, co-workers, neighbors, and acquaintances. Therapists can be most helpful if, in addition to the usual therapy for remarried systems, they acknowledge the societal stigma that LGBT families experience and help the couple sift through their various networks to dismantle the secrecy and isolation wherever possible. Connection to supportive friends, community groups, and access to supportive literature can be extremely important.

The most complex remarried families, where both spouses bring children from previous relationships, tend to have the greatest difficulty establishing stability. All things being equal, it appears easiest if the previous spouse died, next easiest when the spouse is divorced, and hardest when the spouse has never been married, perhaps because some experience with marriage appears helpful in a second marriage. Integration is more likely when children are not left behind by either parent, or when the new couple have a child together (although having a child to save the marriage is, of course, never a good idea). The longer the new family has together as a unit, the more likely they are to have a sense of family integration. Developing a sense of belonging takes most family members 3 to 5 years, longer if there are adolescents. Remarried family integration appears more likely when extended family approves of or accepts the remarriage, next best when they disapprove or are negative, perhaps providing a "good enemy," and hardest when they are cutoff or indifferent.

Emotional issues: Anger, grief, pseudo-mutuality, loyalty conflicts, conflict and cutoff

Predictable feelings that come up in the process of remarriage are likely to include intense conflict, guilt, ambivalence, and anger about the previous spouse and children, denial of such feelings, and the wish to resolve the ambiguity. Remarried families are formed against a background of loss, hurt, and a sense of failure. Their "battle fatigue" often leads to a desire not to "rock the boat" this time, which leads partners to suppress doubt, conflict, and differences that need to be dealt with, resulting in "pseudo-mutuality" that pretends total mutuality, covering over disagreements, and making current relationships all the more fragile in the long run.

Cutoffs are more common with the paternal extended family, and connections are more often strong with maternal relatives, but extended family relationships are often difficult. While children are quite prepared to have multiple sets of grandparents, uncles, and aunts, the middle generation can get caught up in conflicts, and managing relationships with such a large network of kin is complicated. Remarriage of either spouse tends to decrease contact between fathers and their non-custodial children. Divorced fathers tend to have more contact with their children if they have not remarried and even more if the mother has not remarried either. Once both parents have remarried, children are much less likely to have weekly contact with their non-custodial fathers. Remarriage of a former spouse tends to reactivate feelings of depression, helplessness, anger, and anxiety, particularly for women. Men tend to be less upset by the remarriage of an ex-wife, possibly because it may release them from financial responsibility and because they are usually less central to the emotional system.

One of the hardest requirements for parents is to let their children express the full range of negative and positive feelings toward all of their parents, stepparents, and half- and stepsiblings. Often parents want the child's whole allegiance. Children feel caught, afraid that if they do not love a new stepparent, they will hurt and anger one parent, but if they do love the stepparent, they are disloyal and will hurt or lose the love of the other. Another loyalty conflict is the expectation for the new spouse to love the other's children as much as his or her own, which would be highly unlikely.

> **Assess your comprehension of predictable issues in remarriage by completing this quiz.**

Remarriage at Various Phases of the Family Life Cycle

In general, the wider the discrepancy in family life cycle experience between the new spouses, the greater the difficulty of the transition and the longer it will take to integrate a workable new family, especially if the partners come from very different cultural backgrounds, which always increases the bridge-building necessary for a couple. A father of late adolescent and/or young adult children with a new, young wife who was never previously married should expect a rather strenuous and lengthy period of adjustment, during which he will have to juggle

his emotional and financial responsibilities toward the new marriage and toward his (probably upset) children. His wife, looking forward to the romantic aspects of a first marriage, is likely to encounter instead the many stresses of dealing with adolescents who probably resent her, whether the children live with the couple or not.

If either spouse tries to pull the other into a life-style or attitude that denies or restricts the other spouse's family life cycle tasks or relationships with children from previous relationships, difficulties are likely to expand into serious problems. If the husband expects his new wife to undertake immediately a major role in his children's lives or to be the one who always backs down gracefully when her interests and preferences clash with those of the children, serious trouble is predictable in the new marriage, as the formation of the new couple bond is continuously given second priority.

On the other hand, if the new wife tries, overtly or covertly, to cut off or loosen the tie between father and children or to take on the role of mother to them, or if she insists that her claims always get his prior attention, forcing him to choose between them, serious trouble is also predictable. Variations in which the new wife claims to support her husband but embarks on a battle with his ex-wife as the source of the difficulties are equally dysfunctional.

Often the stepparent feels he or she knows what the other parent is doing wrong with his or her children and forcefully pushes these parenting ideas. Such efforts are very likely to jam the circuits for everyone—the new couple, the stepparent/stepchild relationships, and extended family relationships, where people get called upon to choose up sides.

Since it is not possible either to erase or to acquire emotional experience overnight, it is useful to conceptualize the joining of partners at two different life cycle phases as a process in which both spouses have to learn to function in several different life cycle phases simultaneously and out of their usual sequence. The new wife will have to struggle with the role of stepmother to teenagers before becoming an experienced wife or mother herself. Her husband will have to retraverse with her several phases that he has passed through before: the honeymoon, the new marriage with its emphasis on romance and social activities, and the birth and rearing of any new children of their own. Both need to be aware that a second passage through these phases automatically reactivates some of the intensity over issues that were problematic the first time. Attempts to "make up for" past mistakes or grievances may overload the new relationship. The focus needs to be on having the experiences again, not on undoing, redoing, or denying the past. With open discussion, mutual support, understanding, and a lot of thoughtful planning, this straddling of several phases simultaneously can provide rejuvenation for the older spouse and experience for the younger spouse that can enrich their lives. If the difficulties are not understood and dealt with, they will surface as conflict or emotional distance at each life cycle transition and for each subsystem of the remarried family.

Spouses at the same life cycle phase

When remarried spouses come together at the same phase of the family life cycle, their greatest difficulties generally relate to whether they are at a child-bearing phase. Obviously, spouses with no children from previous marriages bring the least complexity to the new situation. Families with grown children and grandchildren on both sides have long and complex histories and will require careful thought to negotiate successfully. But neither of these circumstances provides nearly the degree of strain that families with young or adolescent children are likely to experience, where the roles of active parenting and stepparenting must be included in the new family. Unfortunately, the advantage of both partners having similar tasks, responsibilities, and experiences may easily drown in a competitive struggle that stems from the overload of tasks and concerns (six children are not as easy to raise or support as three), the intense emotional investment in good parenting ("My methods are better than your methods"), and the need to include both ex-spouses in the many arrangements regarding the children ("Why do you let your ex dictate our lives?").

Stepfamilies and young children

Children's struggles with the predictable issues may surface as school or behavior problems, withdrawal from family and peers, or acting-out behavior, all of which complicate or even obstruct the process of family reorganization. Indications are that preschool children, if given some time and help in mourning their previous loss, adjust most easily to a new stepfamily, while adjustment is most difficult for stepfamilies with teenagers. Latency age children seem to have the most difficulty resolving their feelings of divided loyalty and benefit from careful attention to their need for contact with both parents. Clearly, children of all ages suffer when there is intense conflict between their parents and benefit when they maintain civil, cooperative, co-parental relationships. If parents cannot be cooperative, tightly structuring the relationships is the next best alternative.

Stepfamilies with adolescents

Since the difficulties that most American families have with adolescents are legendary, it is not surprising that early adolescence seems the most difficult time for both boys and girls to adjust to their parents' remarriage. The additional complications of this phase in stepfamilies can push the stress level beyond manageable bonds. We have found the following issues common in stepfamilies at this phase.

1. Conflict between the remarried family's need to coalesce and the normal focus of adolescents on separation: Adolescents often resent the major shifts in their customary family patterns and resist learning new roles and relating to new family members when they are concerned with growing away from the family.
2. Stepparents get stuck if they attempt to discipline an adolescent stepchild.
3. Adolescents may attempt to resolve their divided loyalties by taking sides or actively playing one side against the other.
4. Sexual attraction may develop between stepsiblings or stepparent and stepchild, along with adolescent difficulty in accepting the biological parent's sexuality.

The impact of remarriage in later life cycle phases

Although there is not the daily strain of having to live together with stepchildren and stepparents, remarriage at a post–childrearing phase of the life cycle requires significant readjustment of relationships throughout both family systems, which may now include in-laws and grandchildren. It is probable that grown children and grandchildren will accept a remarriage after a death of a parent more easily than after a late divorce. There is often great relief throughout the family if an older widowed parent finds a new partner and a new lease on life, whereas a later-life divorce usually arouses concern and dismay throughout the family, in part, perhaps, related to anxieties about who will care for the now single parents. But grown children may also surprise themselves and others with the intensity of their reactivity to an older parent's remarriage.

The strength of children's reactivity to a parent's remarriage, even after they believe that they have long ago resolved the loss or divorce of the parent(s), may overwhelm them. They may need coaching to find a way to incorporate a parent's new partner into their lives.

Adult children may fear the loss of inheritance when a parent (especially a father) remarries. They may also feel the new relationship is a betrayal of their own dead or divorced parent. Clinically, it helps to facilitate conversation about fears and expectations to avoid shut down and cutoffs between adult children and their parents. The major factor in three-generational adjustment to remarriage in late middle or older age tends to be the amount of acrimony or cooperation between the ex-spouses and the adult child's degree of resolution of the death of the other parent. When the relationship is cooperative enough to permit joint attendance at important family functions of children and grandchildren and when holiday arrangements can be jointly agreed upon, family acceptance of a new marriage tends to follow.

> Assess your comprehension of remarriage at various phases of the family life cycle by completing this quiz.

Clinical Intervention with Remarried Families

Whatever the presenting problem in a remarried family, it is essential to look laterally as well as back to previous generations and to evaluate past relationships with previous spouses to determine the degree to which the family needs help to work out the patterns required by the new structure. Ongoing conflict or cutoffs with ex-spouses, children, parents, and grandparents will tend to overload the relationships in the remarried family and make them problematic. We consider genograms particularly essential in work with remarried families, because the structural complexity so influences the predictable triangles of these situations (McGoldrick, 2011; McGoldrick, Gerson, & Petry, 2008).

We next describe several predictable triangles in remarried families. In first-marriage families, the major problematic triangles involve the parents with any or all of the children and each parent with his or her own parents and in-laws. In the more complex structures of remarried families, we have identified six of the most common triangles and interlocking triangles presenting in multi-nuclear families. In no way do we mean to suggest by this focus that the triangles with the extended family and grandparental generation are unimportant to the understanding and the therapy of remarried families. In our clinical work with remarried families, coaching of the adults on further differentiation in relation to their families of origin proceeds in tandem with work on current family problems (McGoldrick & Carter, 2001). Our experience indicates that families that are willing to work on relationships with their families of origin do better than those that are not.

Triangle between the new spouses and an ex-spouse

When a triangle focuses on conflict between new spouse and the old spouse with the partner in the middle, the usual issues are finances or sexual jealousy. Underneath, it is likely that the ex-spouses have not accomplished an emotional divorce. The first step in the tricky clinical work around this triangle is for the therapist to establish a working alliance with the new spouse, who will otherwise sabotage efforts to focus on the first marriage. Efforts to work on the resolution of the divorce by seeing either the ex-spouses alone or all three in sessions together will probably create more anxiety than the system can handle. We have found that such work goes most smoothly when a spouse is coached in the presence of the new spouse to undertake steps outside of the therapy sessions that will change his or her relationship with the ex-spouse. Along the way, the new spouse will have to learn to acknowledge the importance of that past bond to his or her spouse and to accept the fact that some degree of caring will probably always remain in the relationship, depending on the length of time the first marriage lasted and whether there were children.

Triangle involving a pseudo-mutual remarried couple, an ex-spouse, and a child or children

In this triangle, the presenting problem is usually acting out or school problems with one or more children or perhaps a child's request to have custody shifted from one parent to another. The remarried couple presents itself as having no disagreements and blames either the child or the ex-spouse (or both) for the trouble. Although the request in therapy will be for help for the child or to manage the child's behavior, the background story will usually show intense conflict between the ex-spouses, the new spouse being totally supportive of his or her spouse in conflicts with that spouse's child. The first move in sorting out this triangle is to put the management of the child's behavior temporarily in the hands of the biological parent and get the new spouse to take a neutral position, rather than siding against the child. This move will probably calm things down, but they will usually not stay calm unless the pseudo-mutuality of the remarried couple is worked on, permitting differences and disagreements to be aired and resolved and permitting the child to have a relationship with his or her original parent that does not automatically include the new spouse every step of the way. Finally, work will need to be done to end the battle with the ex-spouse and complete the emotional divorce, the lack of which is perpetuated by the intense conflict over the child or children.

Triangle involving a remarried couple in conflict over the child/children of one of them

The first of these triangles (stepmother, father, and his children), although not the most common household composition, is the most problematic because of the central role the stepmother is expected to play in the lives of live-in stepchildren. If the stepmother has never been married before, and if the children's mother is alive and has a less than ideal relationship with her ex-husband, it may be an almost impossible situation. The stepmother should be helped to pull back long enough to renegotiate with both her husband and the children regarding what her role can realistically be. Rather than leave the stepmother and children to fight it out, the father will have to participate actively in making and enforcing whatever rules are agreed upon. When their immediate household is in order, the husband will have to work on establishing a cooperative co-parental relationship with his ex-wife, or else his conflict with her will set the children off again and inevitably re-involve his new wife. If the first wife is dead, he may need to deal with his mourning for her and help his children to do the same in order to let the past go and not see his second wife as a poor replacement of his first.

When a stepmother is involved, the father needs to deliver two messages to his children:

1. Be courteous to my spouse (not "your" anything).
2. You are answering to me. You have not lost both your mother and me.

Triangle involving a pseudo-mutual remarried couple, his children, and her children

This triangle presents as a happily remarried couple with "no difficulties" except that their two sets of children fight constantly with each other. The children are usually fighting out the conflicts denied by the remarried couple either in the marriage or in the relationship with the ex-spouse(s). Since direct confrontation of the pseudo-mutuality stiffens resistance, and since the presenting request is made in regard to the children, it is wise to begin with an exploration of the triangles involving the children and ex-spouses, focusing on the welfare of the children.

Triangle involving a parent, the biological children, and the stepchildren

As in the previous situation, this triangle may present as simple household conflict with the parent caught in the middle between his or her biological children and stepchildren. It is, in fact, quite complex, always interlocking with the triangle involving the remarried couple (who may have either a pseudo-mutual or a conflictual relationship) and the triangles with both ex-spouses.

Triangle involving remarried spouses and the parents of either

This triangle features the in-laws as part of the presenting problem, but it should be remembered that relationships with the grandparents' generation are as crucial in remarried families as they are in all other families, and their exploration should be a routine part of any evaluation. The presentation of the older generation as part of the current problem is most likely to occur if they have disapproved of the divorce and remarriage or have been actively involved in caring for their grandchildren before or during the remarriage.

> Assess your comprehension of clinical intervention with remarried families by completing this quiz.

Clinical Guidelines

We recommend the following general guidelines to help remarried families think of themselves as pioneers, inventing new and workable structures:

- Give up the old model of family and accept the complexity of a new form
- Maintain flexible but workable boundaries to permit children to feel safe in shifting of household memberships
- Work for open lines of communication between all parents, grandparents, children, and grandchildren

It is surprising how often visitation decreases when either parent remarries. While the intention may be to have the child bond with the stepparent, the likelihood that strong and positive relationships will develop between children and their stepparents is diminished by a lack of relationship with the non-custodial parent. A parent's hope that the new spouse will step up and handle administrative arrangements

with the ex-spouse, serious discipline issues and visitation arrangements are misguided at best.

The original parent should always remain in charge of the relationship with the ex-spouse and should always handle the disciplining of his or her own children. This should never be given over to the new spouse. But couples who feel worn out or frustrated with the previous partner make this mistake regularly.

When there are child-focused problems, we routinely contact an ex-spouse and invite him or her to meet alone or with the children to hear our opinion of the children's problems that have been brought to our attention by the remarried family. When we inform the family of our intention to do this, we are frequently warned that the ex-spouse in question does not care, will not respond, or is crazy. Nevertheless, our phone calls frequently locate a concerned parent who is perfectly willing to come in, although warning us that our client is the one with problems. Ex-spouses can frequently be engaged in subsequent sessions alone or with the children.

Our general goal in working with remarried families is to establish an open system with workable boundaries and to revise traditional gender roles. This goal requires that the former spouses work through the emotional divorce, which we assume is not resolved if ex-spouses are not speaking or have continuous conflicts. The goal then is to create an open, working, co-parental relationship.

The following guidelines summarize our clinical recommendations:

1. Take a three-generational genogram and outline previous marriages before plunging into current household problems.
2. Educate and normalize continuously, regarding the predictable patterns and processes in remarriage, keeping in mind particular difficulties related to:
   a. Family members being at different life cycle stages
   b. The emotionally central role of women in families and their special difficulties in moving into a new system, where much is demanded of them
   c. Couples trying to maintain the myth of the intact nuclear family

3. Beware of families struggling with developmental tasks before they have adopted the prerequisite attitudes for remarriage: for example, a parent pushing a child and stepparent to be close without accepting that their relationship will take time to develop.

4. Help the family gain patience to tolerate the ambiguity and not "over-try" to make things work out. This includes accepting that family ties do not develop overnight. Encourage stepparents to understand that a child's negative reactions are not to be taken personally and help them tolerate guilt, conflicted feelings, ambivalence, divided loyalties, and so on.

5. Include the new spouse in sessions in which you coach the client to resolve his or her relationship with an ex-spouse, at least in the beginning—or you will increase the new spouse's paranoia about the old spouse—and take the frequent characterization of an ex-spouse as "crazy" with a grain of salt. The list of the ex-spouse's outrageous behaviors may reflect the client's provocations or retaliations.

6. When the remarriage ends a close single-parent/child relationship, the feelings of loss of that special closeness, especially for the child, have to be dealt with and will take time.

7. If the child is presented as the problem, try to involve all parents and stepparents as early as possible in therapy. If joint sessions are held, discussion should be directed toward cooperative work to resolve the child's difficulties, never toward marital issues. Children should never have the power to decide on remarriage, custody, or visitation. It is, of course, important to inquire from children their experiences, wishes, and preferences. But the responsibility for the ultimate decisions should always rest with the adults.

8. When problems involve child-focused uproar, put the child's original parent in charge temporarily. When the uproar subsides, coach the parent on ways to "move over" and include his or her spouse in the system—first, as a spouse only. Warn the family that the shift to active stepparenting usually takes several years and will require the active support of the biological parent. In the case of older adolescents, it may be unrealistic to expect the shift ever to occur to any great degree.

9. Work to get parents to define predictable and adequate plans for visitation and to keep up relationships with the ex-spouse's extended family, and beware of the possible "hidden agenda" in any sudden proposals to rearrange custody, visitation, or financial arrangements.

10. Include work on the spouses' families of origin as early in treatment as possible.

CASE ILLUSTRATION

Josh and Susan

The following case is meant to suggest some of the complexity of the divorce-remarriage cycle. It illustrates a therapeutic relationship, which provided a wide net of support over a long period of the family's developmental journey. See the Genogram 22.1.

When they came for marital therapy, Josh Steiner and Susan Watson had been married for 14 years. They had a 12-year-old son, Sam, and a 10-year-old daughter, Karen. Susan's complaint was that Josh was a workaholic, like his father and hers, and now that Sam was approaching his teens, "he needs his father." Josh, a surgeon, and a senior hospital administrator, worked over 60 hours a week, often more. Susan, also a physician, had, for years, kept her hours strictly part-time to allow for child care. Their relationship had veered from distance to periods of conflict "about the kids and me, not about *us*," Josh said. As marital therapy seemed to go in circles, the therapist inquired closely into their past relationship and future commitment, causing Susan to admit that she had "given up on Josh" some years ago and "could not imagine growing old with him." She agreed to "try" to help put the marriage back together, but consistently "forgot" between-session assignments, "didn't notice" Josh was coming home earlier, and had made other changes. Both she and Josh resisted the therapist's suggestions that they put some energy into their family of origin relationships.

After 6 months of stalling, Susan admitted she wanted a divorce; she acknowledged that she had

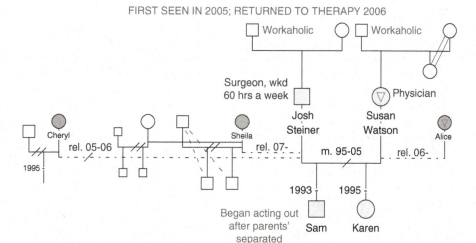

GENOGRAM 22.1 Josh and Susan's Genogram

actually decided this years ago, had hoped to be able to postpone it until the children were older, but now could not tolerate the wait. Josh flew into a rage, quit therapy, hired an aggressive divorce lawyer, and told Susan that he planned to sue for custody of the children. The therapist phoned Josh, convincing him to come back to therapy "for the sake of the children—whether it's marital or divorce therapy, they need you to rebuild or dismantle your marriage in an orderly way."

It was soon evident that it was to be divorce therapy, and in spite of his rage, Josh made several steps "for the sake of the children": he stopped threatening to sue for custody and agreed to continue divorce therapy until the family was living separately and the separation agreement was signed. On her part, Susan agreed to forego any claims of alimony and let the lawyers negotiate about child support. She was interested in the therapist's suggestion that they go to divorce mediation, but Josh refused, and she decided not to press the issue with him.

At this point, the therapist saw each of them separately for several sessions, inquiring in detail about Susan's financial plans, which she had not really thought about and Josh's plans for staying in close touch with his children ("You mean I should cancel my plan to get a studio apartment?"). For several months,

the therapist saw Josh, Susan, and their two children separately and in various combinations as the couple first planned how to tell their children ("no blaming"), then told them, then arranged for the children to help Josh move to his new two-bedroom apartment, and put some of their things there. Along this path, the therapist helped each of them resist destructive suggestions from their lawyers (e.g., Josh should refuse to move out of the house; Susan should refuse to permit Sam's bar mitzvah plan to proceed). As the early logistics were put into place and family grieving over the changes came into focus, Josh suddenly fell in love and left therapy to make a new life, in spite of the therapist's warnings about timing.

Susan remained in therapy but wanted to focus on her reactions to Josh's girlfriend and her children's reactions to the other woman, who was divorced with a daughter Karen's age. Susan made several fairly superficial moves with her family of origin, mostly making more contact with her father and brother but could not think of specific issues with them except for a global sense of being the outsider. Susan was able to follow the therapist's coaching suggestions that she not get into conflict with Josh's girlfriend but rather tell Josh that she preferred to make visitation arrangements with him directly. She felt a huge sense of relief that the marriage was over and even acknowledged that Josh had not been a bad guy at all, except for always being away, "but then, I didn't really want him around all the time anyway." She recognized but could not identify the reasons for this ambivalence. When their separation agreement was declared satisfactory and signed by both of them, Susan expressed a mixture of sadness and relief and left therapy. She said that the kids were moody, but they had all survived Sam's bar mitzvah, which Josh had "ruined" by insisting on bringing along his now live-in girlfriend, even though Sam and even Josh's mother had objected. "But now it's almost over," Susan said as she thanked the therapist and left.

Less than a year later, Susan was back because of Sam's behavior at school—fights, failing grades, and disrespecting the teachers. He was now over 14 years old. Meanwhile, Josh and his girlfriend had broken up, and Josh was angrier and less available to the children than ever. Susan now had a house-mate, an artist and writer, who "helps with the mortgage and helps with the kids. Karen loves her and Sam will too when he straightens out." After a few questions from the therapist, Susan burst into tears and acknowledged that the housemate was actually her lover. She said, "I *didn't* want to be gay; I *don't* want to be; but I never dreamed you could feel this way about someone." However, she said, no one else knew. "Can you imagine what Josh would do?" She told several stories of custody lost because of a parent's homosexuality and of gays and lesbians who had lost their careers and their families when their sexual orientation was discovered. As the discussion proceeded, she told the therapist that if this secret was behind Sam's bad behavior, she'd just have to give up her relationship with the woman she loved; she could not tell. The therapist urged her to go very slowly on any move, because society's attitude was a very big item here, and they should talk and think it through very carefully in therapy before she did anything. Susan agreed.

The first move the therapist suggested was that Susan locate a town in the area that had a legally established precedent of *not* changing custody because of a parent's homosexuality and that she keep that in mind as an "insurance policy" if Josh or anyone threatened legal moves against her. Then, when Susan decided that, more than anything, she wanted to continue her relationship with her lover, Alice, she and the therapist worked out the following plan, which Susan put into effect over the next 2 years:

Susan told Alice to back off with the kids, not discipline them or act like a parent, but to spend some separate time occasionally with each, talking or doing something fun. Susan came out to her children, who were first upset, especially Sam ("You're more disgusting than Dad and Cheryl"), but then interested. They agreed to let their mother tell anyone else she decided to.

Therapy sessions then included various combinations of Susan, Alice, and the children to process the children's reactions and to help organize their family, which had the same structure as a heterosexual remarried household. They agreed to speak to the children's teachers and to participate in gay and lesbian social groups after Josh had been told so that they would not have to live a secret life. Susan came out to Josh, who went into an uproar. Having predicted this and been coached not to react to it, Susan stayed calm and suggested that he return to therapy "for the sake of the children."

After this, Susan and Josh were seen separately—and occasionally together—for coaching in their families of origin and to review the marriage in light of their new situation. Josh had to get over his "wounded masculinity" because Susan had left him for a woman. He could not answer the therapist's question as to how it would feel better if she'd left him for another man. Slowly, their empathy for each other returned. Josh survived meeting Alice and even admitted that he rather liked her. Sam's acting out ceased, and both children became involved in their schoolwork and social activities, including those at a local center for gay and lesbian families.

Both did a little more work in their families of origin. Josh came to see that his position in his parental triangle, blaming his mother for the conflict with "poor dad," had set him up to repeat his father's pattern and be impatient with women's "demands." Susan knew that she would never be able to know whether her feeling of being left out related to her unrecognized sexual orientation or to her mother's favoritism toward her younger sister—or which came first. But she made sure she was not left out of current contact and gatherings.

Susan came out to her family, using it as an opportunity to deal differently with each member. Josh also used this revelation as an opportunity to open up to his family members and improve those relationships.

Susan told her closest associates at work and was relieved to find her colleagues supportive.

Josh requested sessions for himself and a new, serious, woman friend, Sheila, because they were thinking of getting married but were concerned about the reaction of Sheila's two teenagers. They were also concerned that her ex-husband, who was extremely distant and paid only sporadic child support, might use this opportunity to just cut off from his sons and invest his time and money in his stepsons. Josh was also concerned about Sam and Karen's reactions to another major change.

This case shows the extreme complexity of the emotional and structural issues of reconstituted families. The divorce and remarriage issues interact with issues from the families of origin, issues from the family's current life cycle stage (e.g., adolescence),

and issues created by social attitudes (e.g., homophobia). This family worked on their relationships over a period of more than 5 years before the pieces fell into place. But when they did, the results were impressive: Susan, Alice, and the children all attended Josh's wedding, mingling pleasantly with the bride, her sons, and her family. And as Sam left for an excellent college, he said that he expected "all of my parents" to write, visit, and send goodies. Two years later, Karen graduated from high school with several honors at a ceremony attended by all of them.

What is most striking about their story are the many, many opportunities along the way to fall into conflict and cutoffs, most of which, with the help of the therapist, they resisted, while setting a course, aimed always at maintaining and improving their significant relationships.

> **Assess your comprehension of clinical guidelines by completing this quiz.**

Conclusion

Many of the difficulties that families experience during remarriage can be attributed to attempts by the family or therapist to use the roles and rules of first families as their guidelines. Such attempts to replicate the original family can lead to serious problems such as making choices about who is the better parent and then ignoring the new complexities of family relationships. If recoupled families can accept that an entirely new conception of family is necessary, the complexities and ambiguities can be dealt with.

Once that happens, many transformations are possible. Where previous relationships have ended in loss and pain, families can expand their networks, invigorating and enriching their relationships in ways that expand their strengths.

> **Recall what you learned in this chapter by completing the Chapter Review.**

References

Ahrons, C. (2007). Family ties after divorce: Long-term implications for children. *Family Process, 46,* 53–65.

Ahrons, C. (2005). We're still family: What grown children have to say about their parents' divorce. New York: Harper Perennial.

Ahrons, C. (1981). The continuing coparental relationship between divorced spouses. *American Journal of Orthopsychiatry, 51,* 315–328.

Ahrons, C. (1994). The good divorce. New York: William Morrow.

Ahrons, C., & Rodgers, R. (1987). *Divorced families: A multidisciplinary developmental view.* New York: W. W. Norton.

Amato, P. R., & Sobolewski, J. M. (2004). The effects of divorce on fathers and children: Nonresidential fathers and stepfathers. In M. E. Lamb (Ed.), *The role of the father in child development* (4th ed., pp. 341–367). Hoboken, NJ: Wiley.

Arkowitz, H., & Lillienfeld, S. O. (2013). Is divorce bad for children. Scientific American, Tuesday, March 19, 2013. Retrieved July 20, 2013, from http://www.scientificamerican.com/article.cfm?id=is-divorce-bad-for-children

Bramlett, M. D., & Mosher, W. D.,(2002). Cohabitation, marriage, divorce and remarriage in the United States. CDC, National Survey of Family Growth, National Center for Health Statistics, Series 23, No. 22, pp. 1-32. Retrieved July 20, 2013, from http://www.ezjustice.com/topical_material/new%20cdc%20divorce%20study.pdf

Bramlett, M. D., & Mosher, W. D.,(2001). First marriage dissolution, divorce and remarriage in the United States. CDC, DHHS Publication No. PHS 2001-1250 01-0384, Advanced Data. Retrieved July 20, 2013, from http://www.cdc.gov/nchs/data/ad/ad323.pdf

Bernstein, A. C. (1999). Reconstructing the Brothers Grimm: New tales for stepfamily life. *Family Process, 38,* 415–429.

Bernstein, A. C. (1994). Women in stepfamilies: The fairy godmother, the wicked witch, and Cinderella reconstructed. In M. P. Mirkin (Ed.), *Women in context: Toward a feminist reconstruction of psychotherapy* (pp. 188–216). New York: Guilford Press.

Bernstein, A. C. (1989). *Yours, mine, and ours: How families change when remarried parents have a child together.* New York: Norton.

Bray, J. H., & Easling, I. (2005). Remarriage and stepfamilies. In W. M. Pinsof & J. L. Lebow (Eds.), *Family psychology: The art of the science* (pp. 267–294). New York: Oxford University Press.

Brody, J. (1998, January 28). Genetic ties may be a factor in violence in stepfamilies. *New York Times,* pp. C1, C4.

Burton, L. M., & Tucker, M. B. (2009). Romantic unions in an era of uncertainty: A post-Moynihan perspective on African American women and marriage. *Annals of the American Academy of Political and Social Science,* 621, 132–148.

Burton, L. M. & Hardaway, C. R. (2012). Low-income mothers as "othermothers" to their romantic partners' children: Women's coparenting in multiple partner fertility relationships. *Family Process, 51* (3), 343–359.

Burton, L. M., Cherlin, A., Winn, D. M., Estacion, A., & Holder-Taylor, C. (2009). The role of trust in low-income mothers' intimate unions. *Journal of Marriage and Family,* 71, 1107–1127.

Burton, L. M., Purvin, D., & Garrett-Peters, R. (2009). In G. H. Elder & J. Z. Giele,((Eds). The craft of life course research. New York: Guilford.

Centers for Disease Control. (2008). *Births, marriages, divorces and deaths: Provisional data for 2007.* National Vital Statistics Report, 56(16). Retrieved April 14, 2010, from www.cdc.gov/nchs/products/nvsr.htm

Cherlin, A. J. (1992). *Marriage, divorce, remarriage* (rev. and enlarged ed.). Cambridge, MA: Harvard University Press.

Cherlin, A. J. (2009). *The marriage-go-round: The state of marriage and family in America today.* New York: Knopf.

Cherlin, A. J., & Furstenberg, F. F. (1994). Stepfamilies in the United States: A reconsideration. *Annual Review of Sociology, 20,* 359–381.

Cherlin, A., Burton, L. M., Hurt, T., & Purvin, D. (2004). The influence of physical and sexual abuse on marriage and cohabitation. *American Sociological Review, 69,* 768–789.

Duberman, L. (1975). *The reconstituted family: A study of remarried couples and their children.* Chicago, IL: Nelson-Hall.

Furstenberg, F. F., & Cherlin, A. J. (1994). *Divided families: What happens to children when parents part.* Cambridge, MA: Harvard University Press.

Glick, P. (1989). Remarried families, stepfamilies and stepchildren: A brief demographic profile. *Family Relations,* 38, 24–38.

Glick, P. (1984). Marriage, divorce and living arrangements: Prospective Changes. *Journal of Famiy Issues,*5(1), 7–26.

Hetherington, E. M. (2006). The influence of conflict, marital problem solving and parenting on children's adjustment in nondivorced, divorced and remarried families. In A. Clarke-Stewart & J. Dunn (Eds.), *Families count: Effects on children and adolescent development* (pp. 203–237). New York: Cambridge University Press.

Hetherington, E. M. (2005). The adjustment of children in divorced and remarried families. In V. L. Bengston, A. C. Acock, K. R. Allen, P. Dilworth-Anderson, & D. M. Klein (Eds.). *Sourcebook of family theory and research* (pp. 137–139). Thousand Oaks, CA: Sage.

Hetherington, E. M., & Clingempeel, W. G. (1992). *Coping with marital transitions. Monographs of the Society for Research in Child Development, Serial No. 227, 57(2-3).*

Hetherington, E. M., & Kelly, J. (2002). *For better or for worse: Divorce reconsidered.* New York: W. W. Norton.

Hetherington, E. M. (Ed.). (1999). *Coping with divorce, single-parenting and remarriage: A risk and resiliency perspective.* Hillsdale, NJ: Lawrence Erlbaum.

Hetherington, E. M., Henderson, S. H., & Reiss, D. (1999). Adolescent siblings in stepfamilies: Family functioning and adolescent adjustment. *Monographs of the Society for Research in Child Development,* Serial no. 259, 64(4).

Hetherington, E. M., Cox, M., & Cox, R. (1977). The aftermath of divorce. In J. H. Steven & M. Matthews (Eds.). Mother-child relations. Washington, DC: NAEYC.

Kreider, R. *(2006).* Remarriage in the United States. https://www.census.gov/hhes/socdemo/marriage/data/sipp/us-remarriage-poster.pdf

Laird, J., & Green, R. J. (1996). *Lesbians and gays in couples and families.* New York: Jossey-Bass.

La Sala, M. (2010). *Coming out, coming home.* New York: Columbia University Press.

Martin, W. (2009). *Stepmonster: A new look at why real stepmothers think, feel and act the way we do.* Boston: Houghton Mifflin Harcourt.

McGoldrick, M. (1996). *The legacy of unresolved loss* [Videotape]. New York: Newbridge Communications. Available at www.psychotherapy.net

McGoldrick, M., & Carter, B. (2001). Advances in coaching: Family therapy with one person. *Journal of Marital and Family Therapy, 27*(3), 281–300.

McGoldrick, M., Gerson, R., & Petry, S. (2008). *Genograms: Assessment and intervention.* (3rd ed.). New York: W. W. Norton.

Messinger, L. (1978). Remarriage between divorced people with children from previous marriages: A proposal for preparation for remarriage. *Journal of Marital and Family Therapy, 2*(2), 193–200.

Montgomery, M. J., Anderson, E. R., Hetherington, E. M., & Clingempeel, W. G. (1993). Patterns of courtship for remarriage: Implications for child development and parent-child relationships. *Journal of Marriage and the Family, 54,* 686–698.

Papernow, P. L. (2013). *Surviving and thriving in stepfamily relationships.* Routledge.

Pasley, K., & Ihinger-Tallman, M., Eds. (1987) (2008). *Remarriage and stepparenting: Current research and theory.* New York: Guilford Press.

Pasley, K., & Ihinger-Tallman, M., Eds. (1995). *Stepparenting: Issues in theory, research and practice.* Westport, CT: Praeger.

Sager, C. J., Brown, H. S., Crohn, H., Engel, T., Rodstein, E., & Walker, L. (1983). *Treating the remarried family.* New York: Brunner/Mazel.

Teachman, J. & Tedrow, L. (2008). The demography of stepfamilies in the United States. In J. Pryor (Ed.), *The international handbook of stepfamilies* (pp. 3–29). New York: Wiley.

Visher, E. B., & Visher, J. S. (1979). *Stepfamilies: A guide to working with stepparents and stepchild.* New York: Brunner/Mazel.

Visher, E. B., & Visher, J. S. (1988). *Old loyalties, new ties: Therapeutic strategies with stepfamilies.* New York: Brunner/Mazel.

Visher, E. B., & Visher, J. (1991). *How to win as a stepfamily* (2nd edn.). New York: Brunner/Mazel.

Visher, E. B., & Visher, J. S. (1996). *Therapy with stepfamilies.* New York: Brunner/Mazel.

Whiteside, M. F. (2006). Remarried systems. In L. Combrinck-Graham, (Ed.), *Children in family contexts: Perspectives on treatment* (pp. 163–189). New York: Guilford Press.

Whiteside, M. F. (1989). Family rituals as a key to kinship connections in remarried families. *Family Relations,* 38(1), 34–39.

Whiteside, M. F. (1982). Remarriage: A developmental process. *Journal of Marital and Family Therapy, 8*(2), 59–68.

Whiteside, M. F. (1978). Can the daughter of my father's new wife be my sister? *Journal of Divorce, 1*(3), 271–283.

Chapter 23

Chronic Illness and the Life Cycle

John S. Rolland

Learning Outcomes

- Examine a family systems model of assessment and clinical intervention for families experiencing chronic illness and disability.
- Explain the importance of the dimension of time for families that are dealing with chronic conditions.
- Describe the psychosocial phases in the course of a chronic or life-threatening illness.
- Discuss the interaction of illness, individual, and family development.
- Describe how a family's multigenerational experience with illness and loss impacts their response to illness.
- Discuss how chronic mental disorders and genetic conditions interact with the family life cycle.
- Discuss how a family's culture and the health systems embedded in their culture impact their experience of illness and disability.

Introduction

Illness, disability, and death are universal experiences in families. The real question is not if we will face these issues, but when in our lives they will occur, under what kinds of conditions, how serious they will be, and for how long. With major advances in medical technology, people with formerly fatal conditions are living much longer. This means that ever-growing numbers of families are living with chronic disorders over an increasingly long time span and coping with multiple conditions simultaneously.

Over the past 30 years, family-centered, collaborative, biopsychosocial models of health care have grown and evolved (Doherty & Baird, 1983; Engel, 1977; McDaniel, Hepworth, & Doherty, 2013; Miller et al., 2006; Rolland, 1994a; Seaburn, Gunn, Mauksch, Gawinski, & Lorenz, 1996; Wood et al., 2008). There is substantial evidence for the mutual influence of family functioning, health, and physical illness (Carr & Springer, 2010; D'Onofrio & Lahey, 2010; Weihs, Fisher, & Baird, 2002) and the usefulness of family-centered interventions with chronic health conditions (Campbell, 2003; Hartmann et al., 2010; Martire et al., 2004, 2010; Shields et al., 2012).

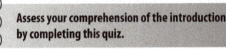

Assess your comprehension of the introduction by completing this quiz.

The Dimension of Time

When serious illness strikes, the dimension of time becomes a central reference point for families to successfully navigate the experience. The family and each of its members face the formidable challenge of focusing simultaneously on the present and future, mastering the practical and emotional tasks of the immediate situation while charting a course for dealing with the future complexities and uncertainties of their problem. Also, families draw on prior multigenerational experiences with illness and loss and core family beliefs to guide them.

Families and clinicians need an effective way to tap into the dimension of time both to comprehend issues of initial timing of an illness and to look toward the future in a more proactive manner. Placing the unfolding of chronic illness or disability into a multigenerational developmental framework facilitates this task. This requires understanding the intertwining of three evolutionary threads: illness, individual, and family development. To think systemically about the interface of these three developmental lines, we need a common language and set of concepts that can be applied to each yet permits consideration of all three simultaneously.

Two steps lay the foundation for such a model. First, we need a bridge between the biomedical and psychosocial worlds—a language that enables chronic disorders to be characterized in psychosocial and longitudinal terms, each condition having a particular personality and expected developmental life course. Second, we need to think simultaneously about the interaction of individual and family development. This is vividly demonstrated when we consider the impact of an illness on both a couple's relationship and each partner's individual development. The inherent skews that emerge between partners highlight the necessity to consider the interweaving of individual and family life cycle challenges (Rolland, 1994a, 1994b).

This chapter describes the Family Systems-Illness Model, a normative, preventive framework for psychoeducation, assessment and intervention with families facing chronic and life-threatening conditions (Rolland, 1984, 1987, 1990, 1994a, 2013, in press). This model offers a systemic view of healthy family adaptation to serious illness as a developmental process over time in relation to the complexities and diversity of contemporary family life. The goodness of fit between the psychosocial demands of the disorder and the family style of functioning and resources are prime determinants of successful versus dysfunctional coping and adaptation. The model distinguishes three dimensions (Figure 23.1).

1. Psychosocial types of disorders
2. Major phases in their natural history
3. Key family system variables

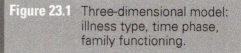

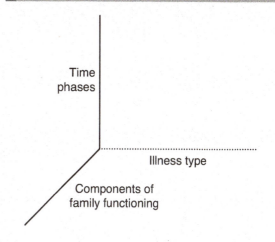

Figure 23.1 Three-dimensional model: illness type, time phase, family functioning.

Excerpted from: Rolland, J. S. (1987). Chronic illness and the life cycle: A conceptual framework. *Family Process, 26*(2), 203–221. Reprinted with permission from Family Process.

A scheme of the systemic interaction between illness and family might look like the one shown in Figure 23.2.

Family variables that are given particular emphasis include family and individual development, particularly in relation to the time phases of the disorder; multigenerational legacies related to illness and loss; and belief systems.

The chapter's first section reviews a psychosocial typology and time phases of illness framework. Chronic illnesses are grouped according to key biological similarities and differences that pose distinct psychosocial demands for the ill individual and his or her family, and the prime developmental time phases in the natural evolution of chronic disease are identified. In the following section, integrating key concepts from family and individual developmental theory, the interface of disease with the individual and family life cycles will be described. Then, multigenerational aspects of illness, loss, and crisis are considered. Finally, applications of the model are

Figure 23.2 Interface of chronic illness and the family.

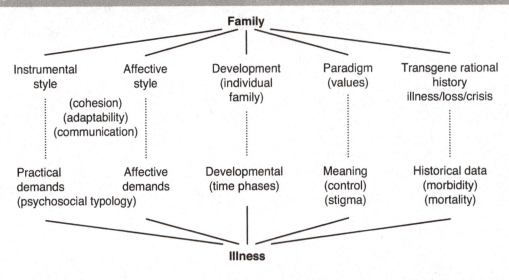

Excerpted from: Rolland, J. S. (1987). Family systems and chronic illness: A typological model. *Journal of Psychotherapy and the Family,* 2(3), 143–168. Reprinted with permission from Family Systems Medicine.

provided for serious chronic mental disorders and the new era of genetics.

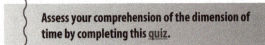

Assess your comprehension of the dimension of time by completing this quiz.

The Social Context of Illness and Disabilities

It is important to state at the outset that families' experiences of illness and disability are enormously influenced by the dominant culture and the larger health systems embedded in this prevailing culture. Families from diverse minority and ethnic backgrounds and lower socioeconomic strata are disproportionately represented among the over 48 million uninsured and the additional 60 million underinsured people in the United States (U.S. Census Bureau, 2012) (with 2013 projections by the Congressional Budget Office that roughly 31 million will remain

uninsured in 2016 after implementation of current health care reform legislation). For those with health coverage who are underinsured, a major illness often means financial ruin with 62 percent of bankruptcies currently linked to illness and medical bills (Himmelstein et al., 2009). Serious health problems represent the biggest cause of bankruptcies in the United States. For millions with disabilities, the assistance that would enable independent living is unobtainable. For these groups, a lack of access to adequate basic health care has major ramifications in terms of the incidence of illness, disease course, survival, quality of life, and a variety of forms of suffering caused by discrimination. Statistics have remained consistent: over 29 percent of Hispanics, 19 percent of African Americans, and 29 percent of those below the poverty line were uninsured in 2012. For these minority groups, chronic diseases are more prevalent, will occur earlier in the life cycle, and, when they occur, will have a worse course and prognosis because of inadequate medical care and limited access to resources. Recent data showing that African Americans' life expectancy is 7 years less than that of Whites give a glaring example of these larger societal issues.

Dedicated mental health professionals work under severe constraints in helping affected families. In recent years, most forms of health coverage have severely limited mental health benefits. For the majority of families facing illness, this means that the longstanding difficulties of integrating psychosocial services with traditional biomedical care increase.

As the population of the United States ages, the current 157 million people with chronic conditions will balloon to over 170 million by the year 2030 (Shin-Yi & Green, 2008). With advances in technology and extended survival with chronic illnesses, the strain on families to provide adequate caregiving is unprecedented. For example, in 1970, there were 21 potential caregivers for each elderly person. By 2030, there will be only six such potential caregivers for each senior citizen (U.S. Census Bureau, 2010). Many factors are involved, including decreasing birth rates; family networks that are getting smaller and more top-heavy, with more older than younger family members; geographic distance among family members; and women entering the workforce in increasing numbers and no longer being available for the traditional female role as unpaid family caregiver. These facts suggest that even the best family-centered systemic clinical models will be inadequate unless the United States develops a humane system of health care in which universal equitable care is a basic human right.

Psychosocial typology of illness

The standard disease classification is based on purely biological criteria that are clustered in ways to establish a medical diagnosis and treatment plan rather than the psychosocial demands on patients and their families. We need a schema to conceptualize chronic diseases that remains relevant to both the psychosocial and biological worlds and provides a common language that transforms our usual medical terminology. Two critical issues have hindered us. First, insufficient attention has been given to the areas of diversity and commonality that are inherent

in different chronic illnesses. Second, there has been a glossing over of the different ways in which diseases manifest themselves over the course of an illness. Understanding the evolution of chronic diseases is hindered because clinicians often become involved in the care of an individual or family coping with a chronic illness at different points in the illness. Clinicians rarely follow families through the complete life history of a disease. Chronic illnesses need to be conceptualized in a manner that organizes these similarities and differences over the disease course so that the type and degree of demands relevant to clinical practice are highlighted in a more useful way.

The goal of this typology is to define clinically meaningful and useful categories with similar psychosocial demands for a wide array of chronic conditions affecting individuals across the life span. It conceptualizes broad distinctions of the pattern of onset, course, outcome, type and degree of disability, and level of uncertainty. Although each variable is in actuality a continuum, it will be described here in a categorical manner, selecting key anchor points.

ONSET. Illnesses can be divided into those that either have an acute onset, such as strokes, or a gradual onset, such as Alzheimer's disease. For acute-onset illnesses, emotional and practical changes are compressed into a short time, requiring of the family to more rapidly mobilize their crisis management skills. Families that can tolerate highly charged affective states, exchange roles flexibly, solve problems efficiently, and utilize outside resources will have an advantage in managing acute-onset illnesses. Gradual-onset diseases, such as Parkinson's disease, allow a more gradual period of adjustment.

COURSE. The course of chronic diseases can take three general forms: progressive, constant, or relapsing/episodic. With a progressive disease such as Alzheimer's, the family is faced with a perpetually symptomatic member in whom disability worsens in a stepwise or gradual way. Periods of relief from the demands of the illness tend to be minimal. The family must live with the prospect of continual role change and adaptation as the disease progresses. Increasing strain on family caretakers is caused by exhaustion, with few periods of relief from the demands of the illness, and by new caregiving tasks over time. Family flexibility, in terms of both internal reorganization and willingness to use outside resources, is at a premium.

With a constant-course illness, the occurrence of an initial event is followed by a stable biological course. A single heart attack and spinal cord injury are examples. Typically, after an initial period of recovery, the chronic phase is characterized by some clear-cut deficit or limitation. Recurrences can occur, but the individual or family faces a semipermanent change that is stable and predictable over a considerable time span. The potential for family exhaustion exists without the strain of new role demands over time.

Relapsing or episodic course illnesses, such as disk problems and asthma, are distinguished by the alternation of stable low-symptom periods with periods of flare-up or exacerbation. Often, the family can carry on a normal routine. However, the specter of a recurrence hangs over their heads. Relapsing illnesses demand a somewhat different sort of family adaptability. Relative to progressive or constant-course illnesses, they may require less ongoing caregiving or role reallocation. The episodic nature of an illness may require a flexibility that permits movement back and forth between two forms of family organization. In a sense, the family is on call to enact a crisis structure to handle exacerbations of the illness. Families are strained by both the frequency of transitions between crisis and non-crisis and the ongoing uncertainty about when a crisis will next occur. The wide psychological discrepancy between low-symptom periods and flare-up is a particularly taxing feature unique to relapsing diseases.

OUTCOME. The extent to which an illness can be fatal or shorten one's life span has profound psychosocial impact. The most crucial factor is the initial expectation of whether a disease is likely to cause death. On one end of the continuum are illnesses that do not typically affect the life span, such as arthritis. At the other extreme are illnesses that are clearly progressive and usually fatal, such as metastatic can-

cer. An intermediate, more unpredictable category includes illnesses that shorten the life span, such as cystic fibrosis and heart disease, and those with the possibility of sudden death, such as hemophilia. A major difference between these kinds of outcome is the degree to which the family experiences anticipatory loss and its pervasive effects on family life (Rolland, 1990, 2004, 2006). The future expectation of loss can make it extremely difficult for a family to maintain a balanced perspective. Families are often caught between a desire for intimacy and a push to let go emotionally of the ill member. A torrent of emotions can distract a family from myriad practical tasks and problem solving that maintain family integrity. Also, the tendency to see the ill family member as practically in the coffin can set in motion maladaptive responses that divest the ill member of important responsibilities. The result can be the structural and emotional isolation of the ill person from family life. This kind of psychological alienation has been associated with poor medical outcome in life-threatening illness (Campbell, 2003; Weihs et al., 2002).

When loss is less imminent or certain, illnesses that may shorten life or cause sudden death provide a fertile ground for varied family perspectives. The "it could happen" nature of these illnesses creates a nidus for both overprotection by the family and powerful secondary gains for the ill member. This is particularly relevant to childhood illnesses such as hemophilia, juvenile-onset Type 1 diabetes, and asthma.

INCAPACITATION. Disability can involve impairment of cognition (e.g., Alzheimer's disease), sensation (e.g., blindness), movement (e.g., stroke with paralysis), stamina (e.g., heart disease), disfigurement (e.g., mastectomy), and conditions associated with social stigma (e.g., AIDS) (Olkin, 1999). The extent, kind, and timing of disability imply sharp differences in the degree of family stress. For instance, the combined cognitive and motor deficits caused by a stroke necessitate greater family reorganization than does a spinal cord injury that leaves cognitive abilities unaffected. For some illnesses, such as stroke, disability is often worse at the beginning. For progressive diseases, such as Alzheimer's disease, disability looms as an increasing problem in later phases of the illness, allowing the family more time to discuss and prepare for anticipated changes and an opportunity for the ill member to participate in disease-related family planning while he or she is still cognitively able (Boss, 2005).

By combining the kinds of onset, course, outcome, and incapacitation into a grid format, we generate a typology that clusters illnesses according to similarities and differences in patterns that pose differing psychosocial demands (see Figure 23.3).

UNCERTAINTY. The predictability of an illness and the degree of uncertainty about the specific way or rate at which it unfolds affects all the other variables. For highly unpredictable illnesses, such as multiple sclerosis, family coping and adaptation, especially future planning, are hindered by anticipatory anxiety and ambiguity about what the family will encounter. Families able to put long-term uncertainty into perspective and maintain hope are best prepared to avoid the risks of exhaustion and dysfunction.

Other important attributes that differentiate illnesses should be considered in a thorough,

FIGURE 23.3 Categorization of chronic illnesses by psychosocial type.

		Incapacitating		Non-incapacitating	
		Acute	**Gradual**	**Acute**	**Gradual**
Progressive	F A T A L	Pancreatic cancer Metastatic cancer (e.g., breast, liver, lung)	Lung cancer with CNS metastases Bone marrow failure Amyotrophic lateral sclerosis (ALS)		
Relapsing				Incurable cancers in remission	
Progressive	P O S S I B L Y F A T A L	S H O R T E N E D L I F E S P A N	Parkinson's disease Emphysema Alzheimer's disease Multi-infarct dementia Multiple sclerosis late Chronic alcoholism Huntington's disease Scleroderma		Type 1 diabetes* Malignant hypertension Insulin-dependent Type 2 diabetes
Relapsing			Early multiple sclerosis Episodic alcoholism	Angina — Sickle cell disease* Hemophilia*	Systemic Lupus* Inflammatory bowel disease
Constant		Stroke Moderate severe myocardial infarction	Phenlyketonuria (PKU) and other congenital errors of metabolism	Mild myocardial infarction Cardiac arrhythmia	Hemodialysis treated renal failure Hodgkin's disease

(Continued)

Figure 23.3 Categorization of chronic illnesses by psychosocial type. (*Continued*)

| | Incapacitating | | Non-incapacitating | |
	Acute	**Gradual**	**Acute**	**Gradual**
Progressive		Rheumatoid arthritis Osteoarthritis		Noninsulin-dependent Type 2 diabetes
Relapsing	Lumbosacral disc disease	Refractory recurrent depression	Kidney stones Gout Migraine Seasonal Allergy Asthma Epilepsy	Peptic ulcer Chronic bronchitis Irritable bowel syndrome Psoriasis
Constant	Congenital malformations Spinal cord injury Acute blindness Acute deafness Survived severe trauma and burns Posthypoxic syndrome Traumatic brain injury	Nonprogressive mental retardation Cerebral palsy Schizophrenia Autism spectrum	Benign arrhythmia Congenital heart disease (mild)	Malabsorption syndromes (controlled) Hyper- hypothyroidism Pernicious anemia Controlled hypertension Controlled glaucoma Controlled bipolar disorder

(NONFATAL spans the Relapsing and Constant rows)

*Early.

Source: Revised and reprinted from Rolland, J. S. (1984). Toward a psychosocial typology of chronic and life-threatening illness. *Family Systems Medicine*, 2, 245–262. Reprinted with permission of *Families, Systems, & Health*.

systemically oriented evaluation. These include the complexity, frequency, and efficacy of a treatment regimen; the amount of home versus hospital or clinic-based care required; and the frequency and intensity of symptoms, particularly those that involve pain and suffering.

Time phases of illness

Too often, discussions of "coping with cancer," managing disability, or dealing with life-threatening illness approach illness as a static state and fail to appreciate the dynamic unfolding of illness as a process over time. The concept of time phases provides a way for clinicians and families to think longitudinally and to understand chronic illness as an ongoing process with expectable landmarks, transitions, and changing demands. Each phase of an illness poses its own psychosocial demands and developmental tasks that require significantly different strengths, attitudes, or changes from a family. The core psychosocial themes in the natural history of chronic disease can be described as three major phases: initial crisis, chronic, and terminal (Figure 23.4).

The *initial crisis phase* includes any symptomatic period before diagnosis and the initial period of readjustment after a diagnosis and initial treatment plan. This period holds a number of key illness-related tasks for the affected member and family. Some are practical, while others are of a more existential nature (Moos, 1984; Rolland, 1994). These include:

1. Learn to cope with any symptoms or disability
2. Adapt to health care settings and treatments

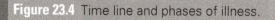

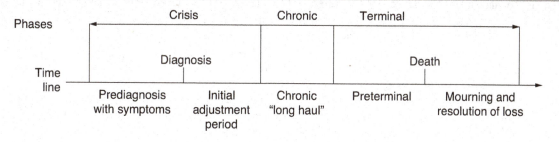

Figure 23.4 Time line and phases of illness.

From: Rolland, J. S. (1994). *Families, illness and disability: An integrative treatment model.* New York: Basic Books.

3. Establish and maintain workable relationships with the health care team:
4. Create a meaning for the illness that maximizes a sense of mastery and competency
5. Grieve for the loss of the life they knew before illness
6. Gradually accept the illness as permanent while maintaining a sense of continuity between their past and their future
7. Pull together to cope with the immediate crisis
8. Develop flexibility toward future goals in the face of uncertainty

The *chronic phase*, whether long or short, is the time span between the initial diagnosis/readjustment and the potential third phase when issues of death and terminal illness predominate. This phase can be marked by constancy, progression, or episodic change. It has been referred to as "the long haul" and "day-to-day living with chronic illness" phase. Often, the patient and family have come to grips psychologically and organizationally with permanent changes and have devised an ongoing coping strategy. The family's ability to maintain the semblance of a normal life with a chronic illness and heightened uncertainty is a key task of this period. If the illness is fatal, this is a time of living in limbo. For certain highly debilitating but not clearly fatal illnesses, such as a massive stroke or dementia, the family can feel saddled with an exhausting problem without end. Paradoxically, a family may feel that its only hope to resume a normal

life can be realized after the death of their ill member. The maintenance of maximum autonomy for all family members in the face of protracted adversity helps to offset these trapped, helpless feelings.

In the *terminal phase*, the inevitability of death becomes apparent and dominates family life. The family must cope with issues of separation, death, mourning, and beginning the reorganization process needed for resumption of "normal" family life beyond the loss (Walsh & McGoldrick, 2004). Families that adapt best to this phase are able to shift their view of mastery from controlling the illness to a successful process of "letting go." Optimal coping involves emotional openness as well as dealing with the myriad practical tasks at hand. This includes seeing this phase as an opportunity to share precious time together, to acknowledge the impending loss, to deal with unfinished business, to say good-byes, and to begin the process of family reorganization. If they have not decided beforehand, the patient and key family members need to decide about such things as a living will; the extent of medical heroics desired; preferences about dying at home, in the hospital, or at hospice; and wishes about a funeral or memorial service and burial. For illnesses such as heart disease, in which death can occur at any time, or with progressive conditions that can increasingly impair mental functioning (e.g., Alzheimer's disease), it is vital that these conversations are encouraged much earlier in the illness.

Critical *transition periods* link the three time phases. These transitions present opportunities for families to reevaluate the appropriateness of their previous life structure in the face of new illness-related demands. Unfinished business from the previous phase can complicate or block movement through the transitions. Families or individuals can become permanently frozen in an adaptive structure that has outlived its usefulness (Penn, 1983). For example, the usefulness of pulling together in the crisis phase can become maladaptive and stifling for all family members over a long chronic phase. Enmeshed families, because of their rigid and fused style, would have difficulty negotiating this delicate transition. Because high cohesion may be typical and not dysfunctional in some cultures, clinicians need to be cautious not to pathologize a normative cultural pattern. A family that is adept at handling the day-to-day practicalities of a long-term stable illness but limited in its emotional coping skills may encounter difficulty if their family member's disease becomes terminal. The relatively greater demand for affective coping skills in the terminal phase may create a crisis for a family navigating this transition.

The interaction of the time phases and typology of illness provides a framework for a normative psychosocial developmental model for chronic disease that resembles models for human development. The time phases (crisis, chronic, and terminal) can be considered broad developmental periods in the natural history of chronic disease. Each period has certain basic tasks independent of the type of illness. Each "type" of illness has specific supplementary tasks.

> Assess your comprehension of the social context of illness and disabilities by completing this quiz.

Clinical Implications

This model provides a framework for assessment and clinical intervention by facilitating an understanding of chronic illness and disability in psychosocial terms. Attention to features of onset, course, outcome, and incapacitation provides markers that focus clinical assessment and intervention with a family. For instance, acute-onset illnesses demand high levels of adaptability, problem solving, role reallocation, and balanced cohesion. In such circumstances, families' flexibility enables them to adapt more successfully.

An illness timeline delineates psychosocial developmental phases of an illness, each phase with its own unique developmental tasks. It is important for families to address phase-related tasks in sequence to optimize successful adaptation over the long haul of a chronic disorder. Attention to time allows the clinician to assess family strengths and vulnerabilities in relation to the present and future phases of the illness.

The model clarifies treatment planning. Goal setting is guided by awareness of the components of family functioning that are most relevant to particular types or phases of an illness. Sharing this information with the family and deciding upon specific goals provide a better sense of control and realistic hope to the family. This process empowers families in their journey of living with a chronic disorder. Also, this knowledge educates the family about warning signs that should prompt them to request brief, goal-oriented consultation and treatment at the appropriate times.

The framework is useful for timing family psychosocial checkups to coincide with key transition points in the illness. Preventively oriented psychoeducational or support groups for patients and their families (Gonzalez & Steinglass, 2002; Steinglass, 2011) can be designed to deal with different types of conditions (e.g., progressive, life-threatening, relapsing). Also, brief psychoeducational modules, timed for critical phases of particular types of diseases, enable families to digest manageable portions of a long-term coping process. Modules can be tailored to particular phases of the illness and family coping skills that are necessary to confront disease-related demands. This provides a cost-effective preventive service that can also identify high-risk families.

The model also informs evaluation of general functioning and illness-specific family dynamics. Other important components of an illness-oriented family assessment that are beyond the scope of this chapter include the family's belief system and process of meaning making (Rolland, 1998; Wright & Bell, 2009); medical crisis planning; capacity to perform home-based medical care; illness-oriented communication and problem solving; social support; and availability and use of community resources (see Rolland, 1994a).

Using this model, we can now address the interface of the three threads of illness, individual, and family development (see Rolland, 1994a, in press).

Interweaving of the illness, individual, and family development

To place the unfolding of chronic disease into a developmental context, it is crucial to understand the intertwining of the three evolutionary threads: illness, individual, and family development. A language is needed that bridges these developmental threads. Two overarching concepts are that of a *life cycle* and that of *life structure*.

Early life cycle frameworks assumed that there was a basic sequence and unfolding of the life course within which individual, family, or illness uniqueness occurs. Recent thinking has modified the notion of an invariant epigenetic process in light of the major influences of cultural, socioeconomic, gender, ethnic, and racial diversity. Illness, individual, and family development have in common the notion of phases, each with its own developmental tasks. Carter and McGoldrick have described six family life cycle phases, in which marker events (e.g., marriage, birth of a child, and launching children) herald the transition from one phase to the next. Illness is a significant marker event that can both color the nature of a developmental phase and be colored by its timing in the individual and family life cycle.

Life structure refers to the core elements (e.g., work, childrearing, religious affiliation, leisure, caregiving) of an individual's or family's life at any given point in the life cycle. Levinson (1986), in his description of individual adult development, describes how life structures can move between phases of transition and building/maintaining. Transition phases are sometimes the most fluid because previous individual, family, and illness life structures are reappraised in light of new developmental tasks that may require significant change. The primary goal of a life structure-building/maintaining phase is to form a life structure and enrich life within it on the basis of the key choices an individual/family made during the preceding transition.

Different phases of the family life cycle coincide with shifts between family developmental tasks that require intense bonding or an inside-the-family focus, as in the "families with young children" childrearing phase, versus phases such as "launching children and moving on" during which the external family boundary is loosened, often emphasizing personal identity and autonomy (Combrinck-Graham, 1985). In life cycle terms, this suggests a fit between family developmental tasks and the relative need for family members to direct their energies inside the family and work together to accomplish those tasks.

These unifying concepts provide a base to discuss the fit among illness, individual, and family development. Each phase in these three kinds of development poses tasks and challenges that move through periods of being more or less in sync with each other. It can be useful to distinguish:

1. Between childrearing and non–childrearing phases in the family life cycle
2. The alternation of transition and life structure-building/maintaining periods in both individual and family development
3. Periods of higher and lower psychosocial demands over the course of a chronic condition

In general, illness and disability tend to push individual and family developmental processes toward transition and increased need for cohesion. Analogous to the addition of an infant member at the beginning of the childrearing phase, the occurrence of chronic illness sets in motion an inside-the-family-focused process of socialization to illness. Symptoms, loss of function, demands of shifting or new illness-related roles, and the fear of loss through death all require a family to pull together. This inward pull of the disorder risks different normative strains depending on timing with the family's and individual members' phases of development. In clinical assessment, a basic question is "What is the fit between the psychosocial demands of a condition and family and individual life structures and developmental tasks at a particular point in time?" Also, how will this fit change as the illness unfolds in relation to the family life cycle and the development of each member?

Phases of childrearing and post-launching

If illness onset coincides with the launching or post-launching phases of the family life cycle, it can derail a family's natural momentum. Illness or disability in a young adult may require a heightened dependency and return to the family of origin for disease-related caregiving. The autonomy and individuation of parents and child are in jeopardy, and separate interests and priorities may be relinquished or put on hold. Family dynamics as well as disease severity will influence whether the family's reversion to a childrearing-like structure is a temporary detour or a permanent reversal. Since enmeshed families frequently face the transition to a more autonomous launching/post-launching phase with trepidation, a serious illness provides a sanctioned reason to return to the "safety" of the childrearing period.

When disease onset coincides with the childrearing phases in the family life cycle, such as the "families with young children" phase, it can prolong this period. At worst, the family can become enmeshed and developmentally stuck. When the inward pull of the illness and the phase of the life cycle coincide, there is a risk that they will amplify one another. In families that functioned marginally before an illness began, this kind of mutual reinforcement can trigger a runaway process leading to overt family dysfunction. This is particularly common with childhood-onset conditions (Weihs et al., 2002).

When a parent develops a chronic disease during the childrearing phase, the family's ability to stay on course is most severely taxed. For more serious, debilitating conditions, the impact of the illness is like the addition of a new member, one with special needs that will compete with those of the real children for potentially scarce family resources. In psychosocially milder health problems, efficient reallocation of roles may suffice. A recent case of a family at the "family with young children" phase illustrates this point.

Scott and his wife Molly presented for treatment 6 months after Scott had sustained a severe burn injury that required skin grafting on both hands. A year of recuperation was necessary before Scott would be able to return to his job, which required physical labor and full use of his hands. Before this injury, Molly had been home full time raising their two children, ages 3 and 5. In this case, although Scott was temporarily handicapped in terms of his career, he was physically fit to assume the role of househusband. Initially, both Scott and Molly remained at home, using his disability income to get by. When Molly expressed an interest in finding a job to lessen financial pressures, Scott resisted, and manageable marital strain caused by his injury flared into dysfunctional conflict.

Sufficient resources were available in the system to accommodate the illness and ongoing childrearing tasks. Their definition of marriage lacked the necessary role flexibility to master the problem. Treatment focused on rethinking his masculine and monolithic definition of "family provider," a definition that had, in fact, emerged in full force during this phase of the family life cycle.

If the disease affecting a parent is severely debilitating (e.g., traumatic brain injury, cervical spinal cord injury), its impact on the childrearing family is twofold: A "new" family member is added as a parent is "lost," analogous to becoming a single-parent family with an added special needs child. In acute-onset illnesses, both events can be simultaneous, in which case family resources may be inadequate to meet the combined childrearing and caregiving demands. In this situation, families commonly turn to other children and extended kin to share responsibilities. This can become maladaptive for children to the extent to which they sacrifice their own developmental needs or a developmental detour for grandparents who must relinquish newly achieved freedom from parenting to resume childcare. Yet we need to be cautious not to pathologize structural changes that may be necessary, for instance, in a single-parent household or may be culturally normative expressions of loyalty in some ethnic groups.

If we look at chronic diseases in a more refined way through the lens of the illness typology and time phases, it is apparent that the family's inward pull increases with the level of disability or risk of death. With progressive diseases, the continuous addition of new caregiving demands keeps a family's energy focused inward on the illness. In contrast, after a family develops a functional adaptation, a constant-course disease (excluding those with severe disability) permits a family greater flexibility to enter or resume life cycle planning. As the following case in the post-launching phase illustrates, the added inward pull exerted by a progressive disease increases the risk of reversing normal family disengagement or freezing a family into a permanently fused state.

Mr. L., a 54-year-old African American, had become increasingly depressed as a result of severe and progressive complications of his adult-onset Type 2 diabetes over the past 5 years, including a leg amputation and renal failure that had recently required instituting home dialysis. For 20 years, Mr. L. had had an uncomplicated constant course, allowing him to lead a full, active life. He was an excellent athlete and engaged in a number of recreational group sports. Short- and long-term family planning had never focused on his illness. This optimistic attitude was reinforced by the fact that two people in Mrs. L.'s family of origin had had diabetes without complications. Their only child, a son (age 26), had uneventfully left home after high school and had recently married. Mr. and Mrs. L. had a stable marriage, in which both maintained many outside independent interests. In short, the family had moved smoothly into the post-launching phase of the life cycle.

Mr. L.'s disease transformation to a progressive phase, coupled with the disabling and life-shortening nature of his complications, had reversed the normal post-launching process for all family members. His advancing illness required his wife to take a second job, which necessitated giving up her many involvements with their church. Their son and his wife moved back home to help his mother take care of his father and the house. Mr. L., unable to work and deprived of his athletic social network, was isolated at home and spent his days watching television. He felt that he was a burden to everyone, was blocked in his own midlife development and future plans with his wife, and foresaw a future filled only with suffering.

The goal of family treatment centered on reversing some of the system's overreaction. For Mr. L., this meant both coming to terms with his losses and fears of suffering and death and identifying the abilities and possibilities that were still available to him. This involved reworking his life structure to accommodate his real limitations while maximizing his chances of remaining independent. For instance, although Mr. L could no longer participate on the playing field, he could remain involved in sports through coaching. For Mrs. L. and her son, this meant developing realistic expectations for Mr. L. that reestablished him as an active family member with a share of family responsibilities. This helped the mother and son to resume key aspects of their autonomy within an illness-family system that could be more flexible to future life cycle transitions.

Relapsing illnesses alternate between periods of drawing a family inward and periods of release from the immediate demands of disease. However, the on-call state of preparedness that many such illnesses require keeps some part of the family in a higher cohesion mode despite medically asymptomatic periods. Again, this may impede the natural flow of phases in the family life cycle.

One can think about illness time phases as moving from an initial crisis phase requiring intensified cohesion to a chronic phase often demanding relatively less cohesion. A terminal phase forces most families back into being more inwardly focused and cohesive. In other words, the "illness life structure" that a family develops to accommodate each phase in the illness is influenced by the differing needs for cohesion dictated by each time phase. For example, in a family in which the onset of the illness has coincided with a post-launching phase of development, the transition to the chronic phase permits a family to resume more of its momentum.

Life cycle transition phases

Clinicians need to be mindful of the timing of illness onset in relation to family and individual transitions. A diagnosis may force the family into a transition in which one of the family's main tasks is to accommodate the anticipation of further loss and possibly untimely death. When disease onset coincides with an individual or family developmental transition, issues related to previous, current, and anticipated loss will often be magnified. Transition periods are often characterized by upheaval, rethinking of previous and future commitments, and openness to change. This poses a risk that the illness may become unnecessarily embedded or inappropriately ignored in plans for the next developmental phase. This can be a major precursor of family maladaptation. By adopting a longitudinal perspective, a clinician can stay attuned to future transitions, particularly overlaps in those of the illness, individual, and family development. Offering prevention-oriented family consultations at major transitions is very useful. The following example highlights this point.

In one Latino family, the father, a carpenter and primary financial provider, had a mild heart attack. He also suffered from emphysema. At first, his level of impairment was mild and stabilized. This allowed him to continue part-time work. Because their children were all teenagers, his wife was able to undertake part-time work to help maintain financial stability. The oldest son, age 15, seemed relatively unaffected. Two years later, the father experienced a second, more life-threatening heart attack and became totally disabled. His son, now 17, had dreams of going away to college. The specter of financial hardship and the perceived need for a "man in the family" created a serious dilemma of choice for the son and the family. This was additionally complicated for this family that had worked hard to move out of the housing projects and ensure that the children could get a good education for a better future.

This vignette demonstrates the potential collision between simultaneous transition periods: (1) the illness transition to a more incapacitating and progressive course, (2) the adolescent son's transition to early adulthood, and (3) the family's transition from the "living with teenagers" to "launching young adults" phase. This example also illustrates the significance of the type of illness. An illness that was relapsing or less life threatening and incapacitating

(in contrast to one with a progressive) might have interfered less with this young man's individuation. If his father had an intermittently incapacitating illness, such as disc disease, the son might have moved out but tailored his choices to remain nearby and thus be available during acute flare-ups.

It is essential to situate these developmental issues in the context of cultural values, socioeconomic considerations, availability of family or community resources, and access to health care. In many cultures, as in this Latino family, a strong emphasis on loyalty to family would normatively take priority over individual goals, especially with a major illness or disability. Also, a lack of community resources and health care benefits can severely constrain family adaptation options. It is crucial for a clinician to be aware of his/her own cultural values about the relative balance between family loyalty and pursuit of individual life goals (here in the context of illness) and its relationship to those of the client family.

Life structure-maintaining phases

Illness onset that coincides with a life structure-building/maintaining developmental phase in family or individual development presents a different challenge. These phases are characterized by living out of choices made during the preceding transition. Relative to transition phases, family members try to protect their own and the family unit's life structures. Milder conditions (nonfatal, only mildly disabling) may require some life structure revision but not a radical restructuring. A severe condition (e.g., traumatic brain injury) can force families into a more complete developmental transition at a time when individual and family inertia is geared to preserve the momentum of a stable phase. To successfully navigate this kind of crisis successfully, family adaptability often requires the ability to transform the entire life structure to a prolonged transitional state. For instance, in the previous example, the father's heart disease rapidly progressed while the oldest son was in a transition period in his own development. The nature of the strain in developmental terms would be quite different if his father's disease progression had occurred when this young man was 26, had already left home, had finished college and secured a first job, and had married and had his first child. In the latter scenario, the oldest son's life structure would be in an inwardly focused, highly cohesive, "families with young children" phase of the life cycle. Fully accommodating the needs of his family of origin could require a monumental shift of his developmental priorities, creating a potential crisis between his loyalty to his family of origin and to his new nuclear family. When this illness crisis coincided with a developmental transition phase (age 17), having made no permanent commitments, he might have felt very threatened about losing his status as a "single young adult" to a caregiving role that could become his life structure. Later, in his mid-20s, he would have made developmental choices and would have been in the process of living them out. Not only would he have made commitments, but also they would be more highly cohesive in nature, focused on his newly formed family. To serve the demands of an illness transition, the son might have needed to shift his previously stable life structure back to a transitional state. The shift would have happened out of phase with the flow of his individual and nuclear family's development. One complex way to resolve this dilemma of divided loyalties might be the merging of the two households.

This discussion raises several key clinical points. Systemically, at the time of diagnosis, it is important to know the life cycle phases of the family and of each member, not just the ill one. Illness and disability in one family member can profoundly affect the developmental goals of another member. For instance, an infant's disability can be a serious roadblock to parents' preconceived ideas about competent childrearing, or a life-threatening illness in a young, married adult can interfere with the well spouse's readiness to become a parent. Also, family members frequently adapt in varied ways, and the rate at which he or she does so is related to his or her developmental phase and role in the family. When family members are in tune with each other's developmental processes, while promoting flexibility and alternative means to satisfy developmental needs, successful long-term adaptation is maximized.

The timing of chronic illness in the life cycle can be normative (e.g., expectable in relation to chronological and social time) or non-normative (e.g., "off-time"). Chronic illness is considered a normally anticipated challenge in later adulthood, whereas its occurrence earlier is out of phase and usually developmentally more disruptive. For instance, chronic diseases that occur in the childrearing phase can be more challenging because of their potential impact on family childrearing responsibilities. The actual impact depends on the "type" of illness and pre-illness family roles. Families with flexible gender rules about financial provision and childrearing tend to adjust better.

The concept of "out-of-phase" illnesses can be refined in ways to highlights patterns of strain over time. First, because diseases exert an inward pull on most families, they can be more developmentally disruptive to families in the "families with adolescents" or "launching children" phases of development. Second, the period of transition generated by the onset of a serious illness is particularly "out of phase" if it coincides with a stable, life structure-maintaining period in individual or family development. Third, if the particular illness is progressive, relapsing, increasingly incapacitating, and/or life-threatening, then the unfolding phases of the disease will be punctuated by numerous transitions. Under these conditions, a family will need to alter their life structure more frequently to accommodate shifting and increasing demands of the disease. This level of demand and uncertainty keeps the illness in the forefront of a family's consciousness, constantly impinging upon its attempts to get back "in phase" developmentally. Finally, the transition from the crisis to the chronic phase is often the key juncture at which the intensity of the family's socialization to living with chronic disease is lessened. In this sense, it offers a window of opportunity for the family to reestablish or sometimes chart a "new normal" developmental course.

Confronted by illness and disability, a family should aim, above all, to minimize family members' sacrifice of their own or the family's development as a system over time. It is important to determine whose life plans have been or may be canceled, postponed, or altered, and when plans put on hold and future developmental issues will be addressed. Families can be helped to strike a healthier balance with life plans as a way to minimize overall family strain and relationship skews between caregivers and the ill member. Clinicians can assist families to resolve feelings of guilt, over-responsibility, and hopelessness, and to find family and external resources to enhance freedom both to pursue personal goals and to provide needed care for the ill member.

Early in the illness experience, families have particular difficulty appraising the need for temporary detours or permanent changes in life cycle plans. Once developmental plans are derailed, the inherent inertia of chronic conditions makes it more difficult to find one's original path. This underscores the importance of timely prevention-oriented psychoeducation and consultation for families. Also, the process by which life cycle decisions are reached is particularly important. Significant factors include gender-based or culturally defined beliefs about who should assume primary responsibility for caregiving. Cultures and families are quite diverse in their expectations about the relative priority of sacrifice for the family in time of need versus protecting personal goals and plans. A forward-thinking clinical philosophy that uses a developmental perspective as a way of gaining a positive sense of control and opportunity is vital for families dealing with chronic disorders.

Multigenerational experiences with illness, loss, and crisis

A family's current behavior, and therefore its response to illness, cannot be adequately comprehended apart from its history (Bowen, 1993; Byng-Hall, 1995; Walsh & McGoldrick, 2004). This is particularly germane to families that face a chronic condition. A historical inquiry may help to explain and predict the family's current style of coping, adaptation, and meaning making. A multigenerational assessment helps clarify areas of strength and vulnerability. It also identifies high-risk families, burdened by unresolved issues and dysfunctional patterns that cannot absorb the challenges presented by a serious condition.

A chronic illness-oriented genogram focuses on how a family organized itself and adapted as an evolving system around previous illnesses and unexpected crises in the current and previous generations. Patterns of coping, replications, shifts in relationships (i.e., alliances, triangles, cutoffs), and sense of

competence are noted (McGoldrick, Gerson, & Petry, 2008). These patterns are transmitted across generations as family pride, myths, taboos, catastrophic expectations, and belief systems (Seaburn, Lorenz, & Kaplan, 1992; Walsh & McGoldrick, 2004). A central goal is to bring to light areas of consensus and learned differences that are sources of resilience and potential conflict. Also, it is useful to inquire about other forms of loss (e.g., divorce, migration), crisis (e.g., lengthy unemployment; rape; a natural disaster, such as Hurricane Katrina), and protracted adversity (e.g., poverty, racism, war, political oppression). These experiences can provide transferable sources of resilience and effective coping skills in the face of a serious health problem (Walsh, 2015).

Because ethnicity, race, and religion strongly influence how families approach health and illness, any multigenerational assessment should include inquiry into these areas (McGoldrick, Giordano, & Garcia Preto, 2005). As professionals, we need to be mindful of the cultural differences among the patient, the family, and ourselves. The different ethnic backgrounds of the adults in a family or among a family, professionals, and systems of health care may be primary reasons for discrepancies in beliefs that emerge at the time of a major illness. This is especially common for minority groups (e.g., African American, Asian, and Latino) that experience discrimination or marginalization from our prevailing White Anglo culture. Significant ethnic differences, particularly health beliefs, typically emerge in such areas as:

1. Beliefs about control
2. The definition of the appropriate "sick role"
3. The kind and degree of openness in communication about the disease
4. Who should be included in the illness caregiving system (e.g., extended family, friends, and professionals)
5. Who the primary caretaker is (almost always women)
6. The kind of rituals that are viewed as normative at different phases of an illness (e.g., hospital bedside vigils, healing and funeral rituals) (Imber-Black, 2004)

Health and mental health professionals should become familiar with the belief systems of various ethnic, racial, and religious groups in their community, particularly as these translate into different behavior patterns during illness. For example, traditional Navajo culture holds that thought and language have the power to shape reality, control events (Carrese & Rhodes, 1995), and can determine reality. From the Navajo worldview, discussing the potential complications of a serious illness with a newly diagnosed Navajo patient is harmful and strongly increases the likelihood that such complications will occur. This belief system clashes dramatically with those of health professionals (backed by powerful legal imperatives) that mandate explaining possible complications or promoting advance directives regarding the limits of medical care desired by the ill family member. Carrese and Rhodes (1995), in their study of Navajo, give one example of a Navajo daughter describing how the risks of bypass surgery were explained to her father: "The surgeon told him that he may not wake up, that this is the risk of every surgery. For the surgeon it was very routine, but the way that my Dad received it, it was almost like a death sentence, and he never consented to the surgery" (p. 828).

ILLNESS TYPE AND TIME PHASE ISSUES. The illness type and time phases framework helps focus the clinician's multigenerational evaluation. Although a family may have certain standard ways of coping with any illness, there may be critical differences in their style and success in adaptation to different types of disorders. It is valuable to track prior family illnesses for sources of resilience and competence as well as areas of perceived failures or inexperience. A family may disregard the differences in demands related to different kinds of illnesses and thus may show a disparity in their level of coping with one disease versus another. Inquiry about different illness types may reveal, for instance, that a family dealt successfully with non–life-threatening illnesses but reeled under the weight of the mother's metastatic breast cancer. Such a family might be well equipped to deal with less severe conditions but may be particularly vulnerable if another life-threatening illness were to occur. Another family may have experienced only non–life-threatening illnesses and need psychoeducation to successfully cope with the

uncertainties particular to life-threatening conditions. The following case consultation highlights the importance of family history in uncovering areas of inexperience.

Joe and his wife Ann, both of British Scottish ancestry, and their three teenage children presented for a family evaluation 10 months after Joe's diagnosis with moderate-severe asthma. Joe (age 44) had been successfully employed for many years as a spray painter. Apparently, exposure to a new chemical in the paint triggered the onset of asthmatic attacks, which necessitated hospitalization and job disability. Initially, his physician told him that improvement would occur but remained noncommittal as to the level of chronicity. Although somewhat improved, Joe continued to have persistent and moderate respiratory symptoms. His continued breathing difficulties contributed to a depression, uncharacteristic angry outbursts, alcohol abuse, and family discord.

During the initial assessment, I inquired about the family's prior experience coping with chronic disease. This was the nuclear family's first encounter with chronic illness. In their families of origin, they had limited experience. Ann's father had died 7 years earlier of a sudden and unexpected heart attack. Joe's brother had died in an accidental drowning. Neither of them had experience with disease as an ongoing process. Joe had assumed that improvement meant cure. Illness for both had meant either death or recovery. The physician and family system were not attuned to the hidden risks for this family going through the transition from the crisis to chronic phase of his asthma—the juncture at which the permanency of the disease needed to be addressed.

Another crucial issue was the onset of the father's disability during their children's adolescence and the looming launching phase of the family life cycle. In these situations, adolescents may become symptomatic (e.g., exhibiting acting-out behavior, school problems, or drug abuse) as a way of coping with their fears of loss of their father or conflicts about moving ahead with personal goals if family loyalty expectations require them to assume caregiving roles.

Tracking a family's coping capabilities in the crisis, chronic, and terminal phases of previous chronic illnesses can highlight both legacies of resilience and complication in adaptation related to different points in the illness course. This can alert a clinician to potentially vulnerable periods for a family with the current illness. A family that was seen in treatment illustrates the interplay of problems coping with a current illness that are fueled by unresolved issues related to disease experiences in one's family of origin. The type of illness and unresolved complications in the terminal phase are critical features of the following case.

Angela, her husband Bill, and their 8-year-old son Mark, an Italian Catholic, working-class family, presented for treatment 4 months after Angela had been injured in a life-threatening head-on auto collision. The driver of the other vehicle was at fault. Angela had sustained a serious concussion. Initially, the medical team was concerned that she might have suffered a cerebral hemorrhage. Ultimately, it was determined that this had not occurred. Over this time, Angela became increasingly depressed and, despite strong reassurance, continued to believe that she had a life-threatening condition and would die from a brain hemorrhage.

During the initial consultation, she revealed that she was experiencing vivid dreams of meeting her deceased father. Her father, with whom she had been extremely close, had died from a cerebral hemorrhage after a 4-year history of a progressive debilitating brain tumor. His illness had been marked by progressive and uncontrolled epileptic seizures. Angela was 14 at that time and was the "baby" in the family, her two siblings being more than 10 years her senior. The family had shielded her from his illness, culminating in her mother deciding not to have Angela attend either the wake or the funeral of her father. This event galvanized her position as the child in need of protection—a dynamic that carried over into her marriage. Despite her hurt, anger, and lack of acceptance of her father's death, she had avoided dealing with her feelings with her mother for over 20 years.

Other family history revealed that Angela's mother's brother had died from a sudden stroke, and her maternal grandfather had died of a stroke when her mother was 7 years old. Her mother had experienced an open casket wake for 3 days at home.

In this situation, Angela's own life-threatening head injury triggered a catastrophic reaction and dramatic resurfacing of previous unresolved traumatic losses involving similar types of illness and injury. In particular, her father's, uncle's, and grandfather's deaths by central nervous system disorders had sensitized her to this type of problem. The fact that she had witnessed the slow, agonizing, and terrifying downhill course of her father only heightened her catastrophic fears.

Therapy focused on a series of tasks that included Angela's initiating a series of conversations with her mother about her feelings of having been excluded from her father's funeral and about the pattern of mutual protection between mother and daughter over the years. Then, Angela wrote a good-bye letter to her father, experiencing the grief that she had bypassed for so many years. It was particularly important to include her husband throughout this phase of treatment because her grief directly stimulated his own anxiety about the looming loss of his own aging parents. The final phase of treatment involved a graveside ritual in which Angela, with her family of origin and nuclear family present, read her good-bye letter to her father.

REPLICATION OF SYSTEM PATTERNS. For any major health condition in an involved adult's family of origin, a clinician should try to get a picture of how the family organized itself to handle condition-related emotional and practical tasks. It is important for a clinician to find out what role each played in handling these tasks. Whether the parents (as children) were given too much responsibility (parentified) or were shielded from involvement is particularly important. What did they learn from those experiences that influence how they think about the current illness? Whether they emerge with a strong sense of competence or failure is essential information. By collecting the above information about each adult's family of origin, one can anticipate areas of conflict and consensus.

Evaluation of the system that existed and evolved around a prior illness includes assessment of the pattern of relationships within that system. In many families, relationship patterns are adaptive, flexible, and cohesively balanced. In other families, these relationships can be dysfunctionally skewed, rigid, enmeshed, disengaged, and/or triangulated. As Penn (1983) described, unresolved issues related to illness and loss frequently remain dormant and suddenly reemerge triggered by a chronic illness in the current nuclear family. Particular coalitions that emerge in the context of a chronic illness can be isomorphs of those that existed in each adult's family of origin. The following case is an example.

Mr. and Mrs. S. had been married for 9 years when their 6-year-old son Jeff developed Type 1 diabetes. Mrs. S. became very protective of her son and made frequent calls to their pediatrician expressing persistent concerns about Jeff's condition. This occurred despite Jeff's doing well medically and emotionally and frequent reassurances from the physician. At the same time, the previously close marital relationship became more distant, characterized by Mrs. S. arguing with her husband and Mr. S. actively distancing himself from his wife and son.

Mrs. S. had grown up with a tyrannical, alcoholic father. She had witnessed intense conflict between her parents. During her childhood and adolescence, Mrs. S. had tried to "rescue" her mother. To counterbalance her victimized mother, she tried to tend to her mother's needs and cheer her up. She talked frequently to her family physician about the situation at home. However, she felt that she had failed at this, since her mother continued over the years to be stuck and depressed.

Mr. S. grew up in a family in which his father had disabling heart disease. His mother devoted a great deal of time to taking care of his father. Not to further burden his parents, he raised himself, maintaining distance from the primary caregiving relationship between his parents. He stoically viewed this strategy as having been successful. He supported his mother's caregiving efforts by mostly taking care of his own needs.

With their son's illness, Mrs. S., burdened by feelings of guilt at being a failed rescuer, had a second chance to "do it right" and assuage her guilt. The diabetes gave her this opportunity, and it is a culturally sanctioned normative role for a parent, particularly a mother, to protect an ill child. These factors, her unresolved family of origin issues, and the culturally sanctioned roles promoted the enmeshment that developed with her son.

In this situation, Mr. S., though outwardly objecting to the coalition between his wife and son, honored that relationship, as if it would make up for the one he forfeited with his own mother. Further, despite his unmet needs as a child, he believed that the structure, and his role in it, had worked. Both Mr. and Mrs. S. replicated their particular positions in triangles from their families of origin. In a complementary way, Mrs. S. was a rescuer in a coalition and Mr. S. was in the distant position in the triangle they create with their son.

The roles of each person in this triangle fit traditional cultural norms. The mother was appropriately concerned and tending to her ill child. The father was in the more distant instrumental provider position. For this reason, it can be more difficult for a clinician to ferret out a traditional pattern from the beginnings of a dysfunctional reenactment of family of origin patterns developed around prior experiences with illness, crisis, or loss. Early assessment of multigenerational patterns such as these helps to distinguish normative from problematic responses. Further, it helps to identify the source and degree of commitment to gender-defined caregiving roles. Particularly in crisis situations such as illness onset, couples may fall back on traditional divisions of labor. The climate of fear and uncertainty itself is a powerful stimulus to seek the familiar, time-tested methods of coping. This is reinforced if traditional gender-defined roles worked well in prior illness or crisis situations. Or, as this case highlights, a sense of failure around a gender-based role can act as a powerful push toward reenactment in the current situation. In this case, Mrs. S. was driven to reenact the role of emotional rescuer, a typically female role that she felt she had failed with her mother in relation to her father's chronic alcoholism. Psychoeducational guidelines can help her to distinguish what forms and degree of responsiveness are appropriate from those that are excessive and unhelpful. Also, tasks for the husband and couple jointly would be useful to increase a more balanced, shared involvement in the burdens of a chronically ill child. This would counteract the peripheral position of the father.

In this case, early referral by the pediatrician was essential to prevent entrenchment of a long-term dysfunctional relationship pattern. At this early stage, the parents were able to reflect upon the situation, recognize the connection to family of origin issues, and disengage from a destructive path.

If these kinds of cases are not detected early, they typically progress over a period of years to highly enmeshed, intractable systems. Morbidity is high and may be expressed in a poor medical course and adherence issues, divorce, or child and adolescent behavioral problems. Reenactment of previous system configurations around an illness can occur largely as an unconscious, automatic process (Byng-Hall, 1995). Further, the dysfunctional complementarity that one sees in these families can emerge specifically within the context of a chronic disease. On detailed inquiry, couples will frequently reveal a tacit unspoken understanding that if an illness occurs they will reorganize to reenact unfinished business from their families of origin. Typically, the roles that are chosen represent a repetition or reactive opposite of roles that they or the same-sex parent in their family of origin played. This process resembles the unfolding of a genetic template that is activated only under particular biological conditions. It highlights the need for a clinician to distinguish between what constitutes functional family process with and without illness or disability. For families that present in this manner, placing a primary therapeutic emphasis on the resolution of family of origin issues might be the best approach to prevent or rectify an unhealthy triangle.

Distinct from families with dormant, encapsulated illness "time bombs" are those in which illnesses become imbedded within a web of pervasive and longstanding dysfunctional patterns. In this situation, clinicians may collude with a family's resistance to addressing preexisting problems by focusing excessively on the disease itself. If this occurs, a clinician becomes involved in a detouring triangle with the family and the patient, analogous to the dysfunctional triangles formed by parents with an ill child as a way to avert unresolved marital issues (Minuchin et al., 1978). When a chronic condition reinforces preexisting family dysfunction, the differences between the family's illness and non-illness patterns are less distinct. In the traditional sense of the term "psychosomatic," this kind of family displays a greater level of baseline reactivity; when an illness enters its system, this reactivity can get expressed somatically through a poor medical course and/or treatment adherence (Griffith & Griffith, 1994). Such families lack the foundation of a functional non-illness system that can serve as the metaphorical equivalent of a healthy ego in tackling family of origin patterns around disease. The initial focus of therapeutic intervention may need to be targeted more at current nuclear family processes than at multigenerational patterns.

Many families facing chronic conditions have not had dysfunctional multigenerational patterns of adaptation. Yet any family may falter in the face of multiple disease and nondisease stressors that affect it in a relatively short time. With progressive, incapacitating diseases or the concurrence of illnesses in several family members (e.g., families with aging parents), a pragmatic approach that expands the use of resources outside the family is most productive.

Life cycle coincidences across generations

A coincidence of dates across generations is often significant. We often hear statements such as "All the men in my family died of heart attacks by the age of 55." This is a multigenerational statement of biological vulnerability and a legacy and expectation of untimely death. In one case, a man who was vulnerable to stomach ulcers began to eat indiscriminately and drink alcohol excessively, despite medical warnings, when he reached the age of 43, precipitating a crisis requiring surgery. His failure to comply with treatment created a life-threatening situation. It was only after his recovery and upon his 44th birthday that he remarked that his own father had died tragically at the age of 43, and he had felt an overpowering conflict about surviving past that age.

Knowledge of such age-related multigenerational patterns can alert a clinician to risks of undiagnosable pain syndromes and somatization, adherence issues, blatantly self-destructive behaviors, and realistic fears that may emerge at the time of an illness diagnosis or a particular life cycle phase of the ill person or a family member. A brief intervention timed with an approaching multigenerational anniversary date is very useful, preventively in this type of situation.

> Assess your comprehension of clinical
> implications by completing this quiz.

Serious Chronic Mental Disorders

Over the past 30 years, there has been a profound shift in the conceptualization of chronic mental disorders from a nature versus nurture debate to an increasingly biologically based, genetically influenced biopsychosocial model. These conditions include recurrent major depression, schizophrenia, bipolar disorder, developmental conditions such as autism spectrum disorders, and severe PTSD. In turn, the focus on families has changed from marginalizing families, who were regarded as having a pathogenic role in the etiology and course of these conditions, toward involving them as a resource and partner in collaborative models of care. There is a burgeoning research and clinical literature on families' experience and their role in chronic mental illness care. This has included how resilience-oriented family processes can mitigate the onset and severity of the conditions (Dixon et al., 2001; McFarlane, 2011; Miklowitz, 2008; Reiss et al., 2000; Solomon, 2009; Tienari, 2004). There is overwhelming evidence of the value of family psychoeducational approaches using individual family consultation and education: time-limited multifamily groups, utilizing both modules (e.g., four to six sessions), one-day skills-building workshops, and ongoing monthly groups focused on problem-solving and skills consolidation (Anderson, Reiss, & Hogarty, 1986; Lefley, 2009; Lucksted et al., 2012; McFarlane, 2002). Early collaboration with and involvement of the family is essential to establishing a functional and resilience-based caregiving team.

Chronic mental disorders can be conceptualized through the same lens and variables of the Family Systems-Illness Model provided in this chapter. For instance, conditions such as bipolar illness or recurrent depression have a relapsing course. Others, such as developmental disabilities or autism, have a more constant one. Some, such as schizophrenia, have a relapsing nature, but accompanied by persistent lower-level symptoms between exacerbations. This pattern is similar to a disease, such as multiple sclerosis. What distinguishes chronic mental illnesses is that their symptoms and disability are primarily cognitive and most often associated with stigma and shame. The illness time phases framework and associated developmental tasks of the crisis and chronic phases are applicable to these disorders.

As with medical illness, acceptance and adherence to biological treatment has enormous influence on the course of persistent mental illness. Both the cognitive symptoms themselves and the high level of onset in adolescence and early adulthood often combine to create a significant challenge regarding treatment adherence. This developmental timing can have an enormous effect on families, who may become saddled with extended caregiving and ill-member dependency that impacts and can block normative individual and family life cycle transitions—here impeding the launching and post-launching phases of the family life cycle. Although symptoms can be ameliorated through medication adherence, with conditions such as schizophrenia, residual symptoms can persist that necessitate family caregiving over the long-haul chronic phase. With autism, families can experience years of uncertainty through childrearing regarding the level of independence possible for the affected member once they will reach adulthood. The transition to early adulthood is often a major crisis point where childhood-based services end and long-term challenges of a dependent adult with disabilities confronts parents and siblings (who may complicate their own life cycle development out of guilt or the need to share in ongoing caregiving of their ill sibling). Anticipation of these major individual and family life cycle transitions can inform timely prevention-oriented consultations.

Toward the other end of the life cycle, as a mentally ill family member approaches later life, siblings and aging parents may be confronted with complex challenges. These include providing caregiving in the face of their own increasing frailty, commitments to grandparenting or caregiving their own aging parents, and expanded leisure time with increased awareness of their own mortality. The following vignette illustrates.

Jim and Sarah, a working-class retired couple in their late 60s, have cared periodically over the years for Paul, Sarah's 64 year-old brother, who has had chronic schizophrenia since his early 20s. Paul, who lives a marginal existence, has had occasional hospitalizations and lived in the local Y, homeless shelters, and occasionally for short periods with Jim and Sarah over the years. Now, Jim has developed serious heart disease that requires daily caregiving from Sarah that makes attending to her brother unfeasible. Sarah's two brothers, who live at a distance, are coping with their own financial and health issues of later life. Jim and Sarah's two adult children, who have had little contact with their mentally-ill uncle, are still raising their own children and involved in careers. The interwoven life cycle commitments and challenges of family members intersect with the ongoing issues of Paul's serious mental illness to create a crisis. With geographic spread and busy lives, the family had not discussed longer-term planning for an aging family member with serious persistent mental illness. Earlier proactive family consultation and planning would ameliorate some of these inherent, predicable challenges. The strain is magnified by the lack of adequate national long-term health care services for individuals like Paul.

As with physical disorders that compromise cognitive functioning, cause erratic behavior, or affect the ability to communicate effectively (e.g., dementia), the strain on families coping with chronic mental disorders can lead to caregiving fatigue/exhaustion, depleted resources, and adverse effects on broader family system relationship networks. Family members frequently distance themselves over time because of painful past experiences, failed rescue attempts, and anger over destructive behavior. Periodic, life cycle–informed psychoeducational consultations and brief family interventions can help support families over time. Consultation goals emphasize (1) information regarding the specific condition, limitations, retained abilities, and prognosis (especially in relation to individual and family developmental considerations); (2) concrete guidelines for caregiving, problem solving, and optimal functioning; (3) linkage to community-based services to support family caregiving efforts and maximize the affected member's functioning over time; and (4) promoting connection to consumer advocacy organization such as National Alliance for the Mentally Ill (NAMI), Child and Adolescent Bipolar Foundation, National Autism Association, and the Depression and Bipolar Support Alliance (DBSA).

Assess your comprehension of serious chronic mental disorders by completing this quiz.

The New Era of Genetics

With the mapping of the human genome, there is burgeoning scientific knowledge that is rapidly increasing our understanding of the mechanisms, treatment, and prevention of disease. This has brought increased awareness that almost all diseases and conditions have a genetic component, not only in the cause of disease, but also disease susceptibility and resistance, prognosis and progression, and responses to illness and its treatments. The impact on the family system is enormous as members move through phases of information processing, decision making, and management of genetic conditions and genomic information over the life course (Miller et al., 2006).

The emerging field of genomic health presents new challenges for living with uncertainty and threatened loss (Rolland, 2006). Acquiring and living with genetic information and possible or likely future loss will increasingly become part of the fabric of our personal and family's lives. It will expand the meaning of health risk to include not only our nuclear but also our extended families, as well as future generations. And, it will increasingly impact present and future life cycle planning.

As with actual chronic disease, coping and adaptation to genetic risk information is an ongoing process that evolves over the life cycle. Clinicians can help family members become attuned to the ongoing interplay of genetic testing and risk information with individual and family development. Four key biological characteristics can guide such discussions: (1) likelihood of development of a condition based on genetic mutations; (2) expected clinical severity; (3) timing of expected onset in the life cycle; and (4) whether there exist effective treatments or preventive life-style options to modify symptom-onset and/or clinical progression (Rolland & Williams, 2005).

For some, the emotional strain begins when predictive testing becomes available, continuing through the decision to pursue testing and the initial post-testing adaptation. For others, this phase begins as individuals reach significant developmental milestones at which testing is recommended. Still others become interested in testing to determine if having children may mean passing on a mutation. Other women receive recommendations to be tested for hereditary breast and ovarian cancer genes 10 years earlier than the age when a first-degree relative—a mother, sister, or daughter—was first diagnosed. After testing, families need to accept the permanence of the genetic information and develop meanings that preserve their sense of competency in the face of future uncertainty and loss (Rolland, 2006; Werner-Lin, 2008).

We can orient families to the value of prevention-oriented consultations at key future life cycle transitions, when the experience of genetic risk will likely be heightened. Concerns about loss may surface that family members had postponed or thought were "worked through." It is vital to prepare family members for the possibility that concerns about genetic risk and decisions about whether to pursue genetic testing may be more activated with upcoming transitions, such as (1) launching young adults, (2) marriage and partner commitments, (3) planning to have children, (4) relocation or retirement, and (5) divorce or remarriage. Also, such feelings can be reactivated by critical events such as genetic testing of another family member, diagnosis of any serious illness in immediate or extended families or friends, or death of a loved one. Clinicians can help family members decide about circumstances when further family discussion would be helpful, who would be appropriate to include, and how to discuss genetic risk with children or adolescents.

Assess your comprehension of the new era of genetics by completing this quiz.

— Conclusion

This chapter offers a conceptual base for thinking about the system created at the interface of chronic illness with family and individual development. A psychosocial typology and illness time phases framework facilitate a common language for bridging the worlds of illness, individual, and family development. This developmental landscape is marked by periods of transition, periods of living out decisions and commitments, and periods of childrearing and non-childrearing. What emerges is the notion of three intertwined lines of development in which there is continual interplay of life

structures to carry out individual, family, and illness phase-specific developmental tasks. Families' multigenerational paradigms related to chronic disease, crisis, and loss play upon these three interwoven developmental threads, adding their own texture and pattern.

Recall what you learned in this chapter by completing the Chapter Review.

— References

Anderson, C., Reiss, D., & Hogarty, G. (1986). *Schizophrenia and the family: A practitioner's guide to psychoeducation and management.* New York: Guilford Press.

Boss. P. (2005). *Ambiguous loss: Learning to live with unresolved grief.* Boston, MA: Harvard University Press.

Bowen, M. (1993). *Family therapy in clinical practice.* New York: Jason Aronson.

Byng-Hall, J. (1995). *Rewriting family scripts.* New York: Guilford Press.

Campbell, T. L. (2003). The effectiveness of family interventions for physical disorders. *Journal of Marital and Family Therapy, 29*(2), 263–281.

Carr, D., & Springer, K. W. (2010). Advances in families and health research in the 21st century. *Journal of Marriage and the Family,* 72 (3), 743–761.

Carrese, J., & Rhodes, L. (1995). Western bioethics on the Navajo reservation: Benefit or harm. *Journal of the American Medical Association, 274,* 826–829.

Combrinck-Graham, L. (1985). A developmental model for family systems. *Family Process, 24,* 139–150.

Dixon, L., McFarlane, W., Lefley, H., Lucksted, A., Cohen, M., Fallon, I., Mueser, K., Miklowitz, D., Solomon, P., Sondheimer, D. (2001). Evidence-based practices for services to families of people with psychiatric disabilities. *Psychiatric Services,* 52, 903–910.

Doherty, W., & Baird, M. (1983). *Family therapy and family medicine: Towards the primary care of families.* New York: Guilford.

D'Onofrio, B. M., & Lahey, B. B. (2010). Biosocial influences on the family: A decade review. *Journal of Marriage and the Family,* 72(3), 762–782.

Engel, G. L. (1977). The need for a new medical model: A challenge for biomedicine. *Science,* 196, 129–136.

Gonzalez, S., & Steinglass, P. (2002). Application of multifamily groups in chronic medical disorders. In W. F. McFarlane (Ed.) *Multifamily groups in the treatment of severe psychiatric disorders.* (pp. 315–341). New York: Guilford Press.

Griffith, J., & Griffith, M. (1994). *The body speaks.* New York: Basic Books.

Hartmann, M., Bazner, E, Wild, B, Eisler, I., & Herzog, W. (2010). Effects of interventions involving the family in the treatment of adult patients with chronic physical diseases: A meta-analysis. *Psychotherapeutics and Psychosomatics,* 79: 136–148.

Himmelstein, D., Thorne, D., Warren, E., & Woolhandler, S. (2009). Medical bankruptcy in the United States, 2007: Results of a national study. *The American Journal of Medicine,* 122, 741–746.

Imber-Black, E. (2004). Rituals and the healing process. In F. Walsh & M. McGoldrick (Eds.), *Living beyond loss: Death in the family.* New York: W. W. Norton.

Lefley, H. (2009). *Family psychoeducation for serious mental illness.* New York: Oxford.

Levinson, D. J. (1986). A conception of adult development. *American Psychologist, 41,* 3–13.

Lucksted, A., McFarlane, W., Downing, D., Dixon, L., & Adams, C. (2012). Recent developments in family psychoeducation as an evidence-based practice. *Journal of Marital & Family Therapy, 1,* 101–121.

Martire, L., Lustig, A., Schulz, R., Miller, G., & Helgeson, V. (2004). Is it beneficial to involve a family member? A meta-analysis of psychosocial interventions in chronic illness. *Health Psychology,* 23, 599–611.

Martire, L., Schulz, R., Helgeson, V., Small, B., Saghafi, E. (2010). Review and meta-analysis of couple-oriented interventions for chronic disease. *Annals of Behavioral Medicine,* 40(3), 325–342.

McDaniel, S., Hepworth, J., & Doherty, W. (Eds.). (2013). *Medical family therapy: A biopsychosocial approach to families with health problems* (2nd ed). New York: Basic Books.

McFarlane, W. (2002). *Multifamily groups in the treatment of severe psychiatric disorders.* New York: Guilford Press.

McFarlane, W (2011). Prevention of the first episode of psychosis. *The Psychiatric Clinics of North America,* 34(1), 95–107.

McGoldrick, M., & Gerson, R, & Petry. S. (2008). *Genograms in family assessment* (3rd ed.). New York: W. W. Norton.

McGoldrick, M., Giordano, J., & Garcia Preto. (2005). *Ethnicity and family therapy* (3rd ed.). New York: The Guilford Press.

Miklowitz, D. (2008). *Bipolar disorder: A family focused treatment approach.* New York: Guilford Press.

Miller, S., McDaniel, S., Rolland, J., & Feetham, S. (Eds.) (2006). *Individuals, families, and the new era of genetics: Biopsychosocial perspectives.* New York: W.W. Norton.

Minuchin, S., Rosman, B. L., & Baker, L. (1978). *Psychosomatic families: Anorexia nervosa in context.* Cambridge, MA: Harvard University Press.

Moos, R. (Ed.) (1984). *Coping with physical illness: Vol.2. New perspectives.* New York: Plenum Press.

Olkin, R. (1999). *What psychotherapists should know about disability.* New York: Guilford Press.

Penn, P. (1983). Coalitions and binding interactions in families with chronic illness. *Family Systems Medicine, 1*(2), 16–25.

Reiss, D., Hetherington, M., Plomin, R., & Neiderhiseer, J. (2000). *The relationship code: Deciphering genetic and social influences on adolescent development.* New York: Wiley.

Rolland, J. S. (1984). Toward a psychosocial typology of chronic and life-threatening illness. *Family Systems Medicine, 2,* 245–263.

Rolland, J. S. (1987). Chronic illness and the life cycle: A conceptual framework. *Family Process, 26*(2), 203–221.

Rolland, J. S. (1990). Anticipatory loss: A family systems developmental framework. *Family Process, 29*(3), 229–244.

Rolland, J. S. (1994a). *Families, Illness, & Disability: An Integrative Treatment Model.* New York: Basic Books.

Rolland, J. S. (1994b). In sickness and in health: The impact of illness on couples' relationships. *Journal of Marital and Family Therapy, 20*(4), 327–349.

Rolland, J. S. (1998). Beliefs and collaboration in illness: Evolution over time. *Families, Systems & Health, 16,* 7–25.

Rolland, J. S. (2004). Helping families with anticipatory loss and terminal illness. In Walsh, F., and McGoldrick, M. (Eds.) *Living beyond loss: Death in the family* (2nd ed.). New York: W. W. Norton.

Rolland, J. S., & Williams, J. K. (2005). Toward a biopsychosocial model for 21st century genetics. *Family Process, 44*(1), 3–24.

Rolland, J. S. (2006). Living with anticipatory loss in the new era of genetics: A life cycle perspective. In Miller, S., McDaniel, S., Rolland, J, & Feetham, S. (Eds.). *Individuals, families, and the new era of genetics: Biopsychosocial perspectives.* New York: W. W. Norton.

Rolland, J. S. (2013). Family adaptation to chronic medical illness. In A. Heru, A. (Ed.), *Working with families in medical settings: A multidisciplinary guide for psychiatrists and other mental health professionals.* New York: Routledge.

Rolland, J. S. (in press). *Mastering Family Challenges with Illness and Disability: An integrative model.* New York: Guilford Press.

Seaburn, D., Gunn, W., Mauksch, L., Gawinski, A., & Lorenz, A. (Eds.). (1996). *Models of collaboration: A guide for mental health professionals working with physicians and health care providers.* New York: Basic Books.

Seaburn, D., Lorenz, A., & Kaplan, D. (1992). The transgenerational development of chronic illness meanings. *Family Systems Medicine, 10*(4), 385–395.

Shields, C., Finley, M., Chawla, N., & Meadors, P. (2012). Couple and family interventions in health problems. *Journal of Marital & Family Therapy*, 38 (1), 265–281.

Shin-Yi, Wu and Green, A. (2008). Projection of Chronic Illness Prevalence and Cost Inflation. RAND Corporation.

Solomon, P. (2009). Family interventions. In P. Corrigan, K. Mueser, R. Drake, & P. Solomon (Eds.), *Principles and practice of psychiatric rehabilitation: An empirical perspective* (pp. 234–262). New York: Guilford.

Steinglass, P. (2011). Multiple family groups for adult cancer survivors and their families. *Family Process*, 50 (3), 393–410.

Tienari, P, et al. (2004). Genotype-environment interaction in schizophrenia-spectrum disorders. *British Journal of Psychiatry*, 184, 216–222.

U.S. Bureau of the Census (2010). *Statistical abstract of the United States.* Washington, DC: U.S. Government Printing Office.

U.S. Bureau of the Census (2012). *Statistical abstract of the United States.* Washington, DC: U.S. Government Printing Office.

Walsh, F. (2006). *Strengthening family resilience* (2nd ed.). New York: Guilford Press.

Walsh, F., & McGoldrick, M. (Eds.) (2015, 3rd ed.). *Living beyond loss: Death in the family.* New York: W. W. Norton.

Weihs, K., Fisher, L., & Baird, M. (2002). Families, health, and behavior (A section of the commissioned report by the Committee on Health and Behavior: Research, Practice, and Policy, Division of Neuroscience and Behavioral health and Division of Health Promotion and Disease Prevention, Institute of Medicine, National Academy of Sciences.) *Families, Systems, and Health,* 20 (1), 7–47.

Werner-Lin, A. (2008). Beating the biological clock: The compressed family life cycle of young women with BRCA gene alterations. *Social Work in Health Care, 47,* 416–437.

Wood, B. L., Lim, J., Miller, B., Cheah, P., Zwetsch, T., Ramesh, S., & Simmens, S. (2008). Testing the biobehavioral model in pediatric asthma: Pathways of effect. *Family Process*, 47 (1), 21–40.

Wright, L., & Bell, J. (2009). *Beliefs and illness: A model for healing.* Calgary, Alberta, Canada: 4th Floor Press.

Chapter 24

Alcohol Problems and the Life Cycle

Tracey A. Laszloffy

- List and describe different definitions of alcoholism.
- Identify and describe factors correlated with an increased risk of developing alcohol abuse and/or dependence.
- Describe the impact of alcoholism on a family during the launching and leaving phase of the family life cycle.
- Explain the effects of alcoholism on the establishment of a new couple relationship.
- Discuss how the alcoholism of one or both parents impacts a child's development.
- Identify the role alcoholism plays in divorce.
- Describe how alcoholism affects individuals and families in the midlife and later life phases of the family life cycle.
- Examine strategies clinicians can use when treating a family affected by alcoholism.

Introduction

Classical views of alcoholism focus on the individual who is the drinker with less attention on the family life cycle context within which alcoholism is always situated. O'Farrell (1989) pointed out the myopia of this view by explaining that alcoholism impacts at least four persons in addition to the drinker. This assessment is a serious underestimation because alcoholism affects family members well beyond the nuclear unit and across many generations. To assume a well-rounded approach to understanding and treating alcoholism, it is necessary to employ a family system perspective that illuminates how the addiction shapes the structure and functioning of families through the life cycle and how families shape the development and maintenance of the addiction (Steinglass et al., 1987). This chapter assumes that the best way to understand and address alcoholism clinically is by employing a family system perspective that focuses on how life cycle issues and sociocultural factors shape the onset, evolution, effects, and efforts to treat this addiction.

> Assess your comprehension of the introduction by completing this quiz.

Definitions of Alcoholism

Alcoholism, like other addictions, is difficult to define. A common misconception is that the quantity a person consumes determines whether she or he is an alcoholic. In fact, the quantity, regularity, and frequency of consumption culminating in alcoholism vary greatly from person to person. Mental health and substance abuse organizations tend to make a distinction between alcohol abuse and alcohol dependence. According to the DSM-IV, abuse involves repeated use despite recurrent adverse consequences, while dependence involves abuse combined with physiological tolerance, withdrawal, and an uncontrollable drive to drink (American Psychiatric Association, 2000).

Steinglass et al. (1987) expanded the definition of alcoholism to include the relationship between an individual drinker and her/his family system. They explained alcoholism as a systemic phenomenon, not just an individual one. However, they did draw a critical distinction between families that have an alcoholic member and alcoholic families where the life of the family is organized around alcohol. While Steinglass and his colleagues coined the term "alcoholic family" to underscore that families may develop patterns of interaction that revolve around alcohol and that support the alcoholic member's addiction. This is not to suggest, however, that all members share equal responsibility for the alcoholism. Ultimately, the alcoholic member is responsible for her or his behaviors and the choices she or he makes that continue to feed the addiction. For this reason, we prefer to refer to families with alcohol problems rather than alcoholic families.

In this chapter, we define alcoholism as the persistent and excessive use of alcohol that results in physiological, psychological, and/or social impairment over the course of the life cycle (Vandenbos, 2007), and this behavior is shaped by family dynamics.

Depending on factors such as age, gender, social class, cultural identity, religious background, and so forth, some individuals and families may be more vulnerable to developing addictions to substances other than alcohol including a variety of street drugs and pharmaceuticals. Although this chapter focuses on alcohol, it is important to note that many of the dynamics discussed here apply to other forms of substance addictions.

Assess your comprehension of definitions of alcoholism by completing this quiz.

Scope of the Problem

In the United States, 17.6 million people abuse alcohol or qualify as alcohol dependent each year. Men have higher rates of alcoholism than women, although rates among women have increased over the last 30 years. Young adults between the ages of 18 and 29 have the highest rate of alcohol problems, while adults who are 65 years old and older have the lowest. With respect to race and ethnicity, Whites have the highest rates of alcohol abuse in comparison

to all other racial/ethnic groups. In terms of alcohol dependence, native Americans have the highest rates, followed by Hispanics and then Whites. Mexican Americans have higher rates of alcoholism in comparison to other Hispanic groups, and acculturation to the United States is correlated with a rise in alcohol abuse. Puerto Ricans have higher rates of cocaine dependence (Chartier & Caetano, 2010). While rates of alcohol dependence are the lowest among Blacks and Asian Americans, alcohol consumption among Asian Americans is on the rise especially among Asian American women aged 18 to 29 (Johnston, O'Malley, & Bachman, 2001).

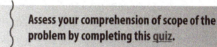

Assess your comprehension of scope of the problem by completing this quiz.

Risk Factors/Vulnerabilities

No single factor or known cluster of factor causes alcoholism. However, a variety of factors are correlated with an increased risk of developing alcohol abuse and/or dependence.

Biology and genetics

There is much controversy over the role that biology plays in the onset and progression of alcoholism, although relatively recent research provides increasingly strong evidence for the link between genetic factors and alcohol abuse. In particular, recent studies examining concordance for alcohol dependence among identical and fraternal twins, and family studies identifying overall similarity among family members sharing different proportions of their genome, "provide convergent evidence that genetic factors account for 50 to 60 percent of the total variance in the risk for alcohol dependence" (Foroud & Phillips, 2012). Recent studies have also implicated a gene (D2 dopamine receptor gene) that, when inherited in a specific form, might increase a person's chance of developing alcoholism.

A longitudinal study conducted at the University of California at San Diego also provides evidence of the biological dimension of alcoholism. The results demonstrated that resistance (or lack thereof) to the effects of alcohol is a hard-wired trait that affects the risk of alcoholism. The researchers found that those with a greater tolerance for alcohol are at a higher risk of becoming alcoholic because their resistance facilitates drinking in greater quantity and with more frequency than those with a lower tolerance (Seppa, 2009).

The Harvard Grant Study is the longest longitudinal study of human development ever undertaken and it provides invaluable data about alcohol abuse across the life cycle. Valliant's (2012) research revealed that the members of his study were twice as likely to become alcoholic if there was a history of family alcoholism. This finding remained constant even after controlling for other commonly assumed etiologies such as ethnicity, social class and multiple family problems. However, this finding was not true for those who grew up with alcoholic stepparents. Hence, Valliant asserted that the risk of becoming alcoholic has less to do with whether or not a person was raised around an alcoholic and has more to do with whether or not one has an alcoholic biological parent. Vaillant warned that the power of a genetic component does not resolve the questions about nature versus nature. While genetic history is clearly a significant factor in alcohol abuse, the complex interaction between genes and environment cannot be dismissed. For example, alcoholic parents are more likely to be separated from their children, and father absence in particular is correlated with the onset of alcoholism among adolescents, males in particular (Hoffmann, 2002).

Family of origin

Growing up in households characterized by a lack of parental support and monitoring, inconsistent and/ or harsh discipline, and parental hostility or rejection is also associated with onset of alcoholism (Conger, 1994; Enoch, 2006). Moreover, a history of physical or sexual abuse during childhood is a risk factor for developing alcoholism, especially for girls. In one study, 72 percent of women and 27 percent of men with substance abuse disorders reported physical or sexual abuse or both as children (Lown et al., 2011). Hence, it is always crucial when conducting a clinical assessment to explore family of origin experience with substance abuse and addiction to understand the potential influence of historical family patterns on the present.

Age

Age is a risk factor in several ways. First, the younger a person is when s/he begins drinking (e.g., age 14 or younger), the higher the risk of developing alcohol problems later in life compared to those who begin drinking at the age of 21 or after (Grant et al., 2004). Second, the process of aging increases the risk of alcoholism. As people grow older, alcohol affects their bodies with greater potency. Those who maintain the same drinking patterns they had at an earlier time in their lives are at increased risk of unwittingly developing alcohol dependency later in life. It takes fewer drinks to become intoxicated and older organs can be damaged by smaller amounts of alcohol (Thomas & Rockwood, 2001). Moreover, up to one half of the 100 most prescribed drugs for older people, especially those used for arthritis and pain management, react adversely with alcohol.

Attitudes and beliefs about alcohol

Personal, familial, and/or cultural beliefs that sanction the use of alcohol are a risk factor for alcoholism. Among adolescents in particular, peer acceptance of drinking and pressure to drink increase the probability of binge drinking, and teens and young adults who binge drink regularly are at a high risk of developing alcoholism (Hawkins & Fitzgibbons, 1993). Borsari and Carey (2001) reported that the influence peers exert over the decision to drink and the amount consumed is tied to the phenomenon of perceived social norms—or the belief that "everyone" is drinking, and drinking is acceptable.

Rates of alcoholism are also correlated with the extent to which specific ethnic and/or religious groups sanction or prohibit alcohol use. For example, Mormons, Orthodox Jews, and Muslims who have strong prohibitions against the use of alcohol manifest very low rates of alcoholism. The power such groups exert is observed by the fact that when members leave the group, their susceptibility to alcoholism increases exponentially.

Within various ethnic groups, beliefs about the role that alcohol serves, and attitudes toward consumption, are strongly correlated with rates of alcoholism. For example, Southern European and Mediterranean ethnic groups (e.g., Spanish, French, Portuguese, Italian, and Greek) tend to have low rates of problem drinking. Attitudes and behaviors are such that children are introduced to alcohol as part of their regular family life and learn to drink moderate amounts while still young. Alcohol is commonly drunk with meals and is considered a natural and normal beverage. Drinking alcohol in moderation is encouraged, and abuse is met with disapproval. People drink for sociability rather than a means to achieve intoxication and there are no mixed feelings or uncertainties about alcohol (Hanson, 1995). While such groups may have high rates of alcohol-related diseases, such as cirrhosis of the liver, they consistently have lower rates of alcoholism and alcohol-induced accidents, fights, and homicides.

Conversely, cultural groups that encourage drinking that is not a part of eating or ritualized behaviors, and that view alcohol primarily as a way to escape from stress, achieve an altered state of consciousness, or demonstrate one's strength, are at higher risk of developing problems related to drinking (Heath, 1982). Also, cultural groups that have ambivalent relationships with alcohol are more likely to report higher rates of both abstinence and alcoholism (Room, 1976). Within Irish culture, for instance, there is a strong dual message attached to alcohol. While drinking is deemed sinful and a sign of moral weakness, it also is strongly condoned and treated as central dimension of social and communal relating and bonding. This duality is reflected in Vaillant's (1983, 2012) finding that Irish Americans were seven times as likely to develop alcohol dependence as Italian Americans in spite of the fact that Irish Americans have a substantially higher abstinence rate.

The dual message that Irish culture transmits around alcohol is also reflected in dominant American culture. On one hand, a barrage of puritanical and restrictive messages are conveyed about alcohol, while on the other hand, drinking is portrayed as sophisticated, sexy, and cool, and often heavy drinking is regarded as a sign of strength and toughness.

In the United States, alcohol is deemed to be so dangerous that people under the age of 21 are prohibited from consuming a single drink, even under parental supervision. Moreover, one might wonder how the United States prohibits any and all access to alcohol until the age of 21, but at the age of 18 young people can legally join the military where they can both kill and be killed. The contradictions that U.S. society reflects with regard to alcohol inevitably play a role in the fact that, as in Irish society, there are high rates of both abstinence and alcoholism (Room, 1976).

Psychiatric disorders

A correlation exists between alcoholism and psychiatric disorders such as depression and anxiety. Depression is found in about one third of all cases of alcoholism. The risk for heavy drinking in women who are depressed was 2.6 times greater than the risk in women who are not depressed. However, as pointed out by Vaillant (2013), alcoholism tends to be the *cause* of co-occurring depression and anxiety rather than a response to these conditions.

Social marginalization and devaluation

Membership in socially marginalized groups often results in social devaluation and trauma that can act as a risk factor for alcoholism. For example, native Americans have the highest rate of alcoholism of all racial and ethnic groups. A study conducted by the Centers for Disease Control and Prevention between 2001 and 2005 found that nearly 12 percent of the deaths among native Americans and Alaska Natives were alcohol related compared with 3.3 percent for the United States as a whole (Szlemko et al., 2006). Genetic variation is often cited as an explanatory factor because native Americans tend to manifest the alcohol-metabolizing enzyme, alcohol dehydrogenase that increases susceptibility to alcoholism (Herrick & Herrick, 2007). Yet the influence of social marginalization and devaluation also must be considered. The loss of ancestral homes; forced relocation to reservations; poverty and unemployment; a long history of aggression and exploitation at the hands of Whites; the loss of the native American family unit as a part of a broader communal way of life; and feelings of dislocation, alienation, and hopelessness inevitably contribute to the devastating impact that alcoholism has had on native communities (Tafoya & Del Vecchio, 2005).

Bepko and Krestan (1985) pointed out that female alcoholism is often linked to gender oppression and the cultural devaluation of women. The nature of sexism is such that to be a "good woman" one is required to subjugate her needs to serve the needs of others, and to assume a pleasing, deferential posture in relation to patriarchal authority. At the same time, the role of a "good woman" is devalued by the broader culture. Women are socialized and pressured to serve and be pleasing, although they are not respected and valued for this. In response to these conditions, women sometimes turn to substances such as alcohol to help manage the frustrations and pressures. In this sense, alcoholism is an adaptive strategy, an attempt to find a way to endure the unendurable.

Assess your comprehension of risk factors/ vulnerabilities by completing this quiz.

Understanding Alcoholism From a Family Life Cycle Perspective

The expanded family life cycle framework guides us to recognize that families are not static units. Like individuals, families move through various life cycle stages characterized by the onset of developmental crises that involve exits from and entries into the family system that necessitate shifts in roles and relationships both within and between generational levels.

In healthy families, when a developmental crisis occurs (whether normative or non-normative, joyful or tragic), it creates pressure that demands the system change and adapt by shifting roles and relationships. Healthy families are able to reorganize and then restabilize themselves in response to the pressure imposed by a crisis (Laszloffy, 2000). Unhealthy systems, like those organized around alcohol, resist change, striving to maintain a dysfunctional homeostasis at all costs. Within families organized around alcohol, family development is altered by the presence of

alcoholism. "A careful review of the life history of the alcoholic family brings to light potential *distortions* in the customary life cycle introduced by the organization of family life around the alcoholic condition" (Steinglass, 1982, p. 143). In systems where alcoholism is present, families learn to organize themselves in such a way as to "blunt the destabilizing impact of alcoholism, but it also acts to blunt *any* potentially destabilizing event in family life" (Steinglass et al., 1987, p. 83). Such systems merely make a series of compromises to ensure that things stay the same and "these compromises result in compromised lives" (p. 76). Therefore, when faced with developmental pressures, families struggling with alcohol resist necessary adaptations and shifts striving instead to maintain homeostasis.

A twofold relationship exists between alcoholism and family development. First, alcoholism can develop as a response to the pressures generated by a crisis. For example, in a family where a child has died, feelings of pain, anger, loss, and grief can provoke a family member to abuse alcohol. Hence, the crisis triggers the onset of the addiction. Second, when alcoholism is already a part of a family system, it influences how families respond to developmental crises, usually in maladaptive ways. Because families with alcohol problems are organized around the addiction, most developmental demands are subjugated to the demands of the addiction. "Family regulatory behaviors are powerfully influenced by the invasion of alcohol and the shape of family growth and development may to a significant degree be responsive to the unique demands that alcoholism and alcohol related behaviors place on the family" (Steinglass et al., 1987, p. 98). Hence, families respond to developmental pressures in ways that defer to the needs of the alcohol.

The landmark seven-decade longitudinal Grant Study that followed 600 American males (who were not alcoholics at the start) from two research populations (an upper-middle-class college group and an inner-city group) is one of the best sources of data about how problem drinking changes over a lifetime. In spite of the limitation that most of the participants were White males, the study provided key insights about the way that patterns of alcohol use, abuse, and dependence can shift dramatically over the course of a lifetime and not always in a single, linear progression. The findings from this study powerfully demonstrate that alcoholism is a bio-psychosocial condition that evolves over the course of the family life cycle and within a broader social context (Vaillant, 1995, 2012).

The following section considers the various stages of the family lifecycle. It examines how developmental pressures may induce problem drinking, just as the presence of alcoholism in a family may affect the way the system negotiates changes associated with life cycle stages.

Contextual factors

Understanding alcoholism across the family life cycle requires considering the influence of sociocultural factors. Gender, race, ethnicity, religion, age, socio-economic status, sexual orientation, and mental and physical abilities can shape the onset and progression of alcoholism. For example, experiences with marginalization and oppression can create a vulnerability to addictions of all kinds. Sociocultural factors can also influence how substance abuse issues are perceived and responded to by family members and by those outside of the family. For example, "African Americans drink less than their White counterparts, but they suffer more from health problems related to alcoholism, such as cirrhosis of the liver, alcohol-withdrawal delirium, esophageal cancer, and so forth" (Herrick & Herrick, 2007, p. 143), which underscore the impact of racism. Racial minorities, African Americans in particular, as well as those who are poor, are more frequently misdiagnosed as well as being disproportionately underserved in comparison to those who are White and those who are middle or upper income (Mulia et al., 2009).

The launching and leaving phase

The transition from adolescence to young adulthood is marked by the launching/leaving home process. Children become young adults who may leave home to attend college, get married/co-habit with a partner, or simply establish their independence by moving into their own residence and supporting themselves financially. This is a stage of life that is both exciting and painful for parents and their young adult children.

In healthy families where resources permit independent development, parents derive satisfaction from watching their young adult children step into their independence when they "leave the nest." This also frees parents in their middle years to focus more on their individual interests and intimate relationships, for better or worse. When young adult children leave home, it is normal for their parents to feel anxious about having to face a partner they may have grown distant from while they were consumed with routine parenting responsibilities. It is also stressful to have to rediscover one's identity separate from the daily demands of parenting. For young adults, the leaving home process is characterized by exploration and experimentation. They are faced with making independent decisions and dealing with the consequences, struggling to succeed educationally and/or in new jobs, and striving to develop and sustain satisfying romantic and peer relationships. This exploration can be liberating and exciting, as well as overwhelming and scary.

Alcohol can exacerbate the normative stressors that arise during the launching/leaving home stage. For example, Wegsheider (1981) explained that it is not uncommon in families with alcohol problems for children to assume narrow and rigidly defined roles in response to the demands that alcoholism breeds. These roles include (1) the caretaker, who subjugates her or his personal needs to serve those of other family members; (2) the hero, who compensates for the failures represented by the alcoholism through being successful and accomplished; (3) the scapegoat, whose problems become the excuse for everything that is wrong in the family; (4) the mascot/clown, who provides the distraction of comic relief and entertainment; and (5) the lost child, who disappears from the activity of the family and makes no demands.

The role one played as a child in an alcoholic system may complicate the leaving home process. For example, an individual who played a caretaker's role in her family in response to a parent's alcoholism might feel pressures not to leave home. Alternatively, a person who served a hero role may be encouraged and feel compelled to leave but with the implicit condition that he is obligated to succeed at all costs to compensate for the family shame, and/or provide for the family financially. A person in the scapegoat role might leave in a manner that is disruptive and dramatic (e.g., running away or troubles with the law, resulting in incarceration), thereby creating a distraction from the problems caused by the alcoholism. A young adult in the mascot or clown role is likely to appear unfocused and lacking in drive and direction, thereby making leaving home unlikely. As such she or he can remain physically present and continue to provide distraction though comic relief. Finally, for a person in the lost child role, the leaving home process tends to be hard to detect. Since this role is defined by invisibility and making few demands, lost children tend to leave early and with minimal fanfare or support.

Another issue young adults may face is how much they will participate in drinking. Certainly, growing up in a family with an alcoholic parent is a risk factor. But one way or another, this stage of the life cycle is such that peers exert even a greater influence on drinking behaviors than do family. As young adults struggle to make friends in college or in new jobs, they are vulnerable to perceived pressures to drink as a way of garnering approval. Moreover, young adults who tend to be impulsive, risk-takers, manifest antisocial traits, and are highly extroverted are more likely to drink heavily during this stage of life (Vaillant, 1995).

Where young people go when they leave home also shapes their vulnerability to alcohol. Those who attend college are confronted with intense academic, social, and psychological pressures. Many turn to alcohol to manage these pressures. The altered state of consciousness that alcohol provides is a welcome temporary relief from the insecurities and self-doubts that many young people face. All too often, one of the pressures young people face is peer pressure to drink. Yet because the drinking age is 21, few parents or colleges acknowledge and address the practical realities of underage drinking. Hence, few safeguards are in place to help young people cope effectively with the temptations they encounter.

Those who directly enter the workforce tend to drink more heavily than those who go to college, and it tends to take longer for them to phase out of heavy drinking (Galanter, 2005). Those who enter young adulthood and get married, become parents, or both

tend to show the lowest rates of alcohol consumption. It may be that assuming adult roles and responsibilities is correlated with limited drinking, and it also may be that young people who have already developed a serious problem drinking are less likely to gravitate toward these roles at an early age (Arnett, 2005). Those who enter the military early are more likely to drink heavily in comparison with those who enlist at an older ago (Bray, Hourani, & Rae, 2003).

Race/ethnicity and gender also influence the extent to which alcohol will shape the launching/leaving home life cycle stage. During young adulthood, rates of heavy drinking are higher for males than for females, and higher for Whites than for racial minorities. In fact, it is during this stage of life (between the ages of 19 and 22) that drinking among Whites tends to peak, while for Hispanics and African Americans it peaks much later and persists longer into adulthood (Mulia et al., 2009). It may be that Whites see heavy drinking as part of a youthful life style, whereas Hispanics tend to see heavy drinking as a "right" they earn when they reach maturity.

> **Assess your comprehension of understanding alcoholism from a family life cycle perspective by completing this quiz.**

New Couplehood

New couplehood is thought of as a euphoric period when people are under the spell of initial love and feeling good. For those with an established pattern of heavy drinking, the euphoria of new couplehood mixes with the euphoria of intoxication. The honeymoon phase of couple formation ends on average after about 9 months at which time couples begin to transition into a more reality-based perception of each other. This transition may be so disillusioning that it results in a parting of the ways, but if not, couples end up struggling to establish the (largely implicit) rules of their relationship in terms of power, money, sex, intimacy, communication, and the execution of instrumental tasks, at least until such time that other developmental crises occur that require further renegotiation.

If one partner in a relationship is an alcoholic, and the nonalcoholic partner does not recognize and confront this person's drinking, the groundwork is laid for problematic dynamics. These include dysfunctional interaction patterns, skewed boundaries, poor communication, and imbalanced responsibilities, all of which undermine relationship quality and satisfaction over time.

Sober–intoxicated interaction patterns

When one partner is an alcoholic, couple interaction patterns shift based on whether that person is drunk or dry. This is known as the sobriety–intoxication pattern (Steinglass, 1981). Usually, these two patterns are oppositional in nature. For example, if a couple's interaction pattern in the intoxication phase is distance, it is likely to shift into greater closeness with the onset of the sobriety phase. Similarly, if a couple's intoxication pattern consists of a wife exerting high levels of authority and decision-making power while her husband is intoxicated, when he becomes sober their pattern is likely to shift in the other direction, whereby he assumes more authority and power and she relinquishes hers.

Skewed boundaries

Healthy boundaries are clear, meaning they are open enough to allow for a free flow of information, yet firm enough to distinguish the autonomy of each party. In alcoholic couple relationships, the constant cycling back and forth between the sober–intoxicated interaction pattern compromises boundaries such that spouses lean too heavily in one direction or the other. When a boundary is too rigid, partners are disconnected and do not adequately support each other. Often a crisis is required to pull them back into contact (Carruth & Mendenhall, 1989). Conversely, if the boundary is too diffuse, the nonalcoholic partner assumes too much responsibility for the relationship and for saving and "fixing" the alcoholic. In both cases, the drinking partner usually starts to drink more.

Poor communication and low problem solving

Alcoholic partners tend to use more negative communication consisting of criticizing, blaming, and contempt. They express more anger and show lower levels of warmth when trying to solve a problem than do nonalcoholic spouses. This kind of negative communication discourages the use of positive problem-solving skills such as brainstorming, open discussion, and encouragement. Nonalcoholic partners in such relationships may lose the desire to engage in problem solving and give up when alcohol is involved because they anticipate that the conversation will soon become negative.

Overfunctioning/underfunctioning

Alcoholic relationships are characterized by an overfunctioning/underfunctioning dynamic referred to as *co-dependency,* which is a habituated excessive mental and emotional attachment to a partner with an addiction. In short, the relationship revolves around the alcoholic and alcohol-based crises. The nonalcoholic partner minimizes her or his needs and desires and focuses on trying to manage or cure the drinker. When "a person unknowingly helps the alcoholic by denying the drinking problem exists and helping the alcoholic to get out of troubles caused by his drinking" (Silverstein, 1990, p. 65), this is referred to as enabling. An enabling partner might clean up the alcoholic's vomit, bail the drinker out of jail, make excuses to employers or friends, avoid bringing outsiders to the home to hide problems caused by the alcoholism, and take on a disproportionate share of functional tasks. For example, nonalcoholic partners may singlehandedly assume the burdens of household chores, managing finances, communicating (and covering up) with extending family and friends, and childrearing responsibilities. Over time, this leads to exhaustion and burnout.

Gay and lesbian couples

Gay and lesbian couples face all of the same pressures and challenges as heterosexual couples, while also having to negotiate the strains imposed by heterosexism and homophobia. Alcohol abuse is often a response to the pain of rejection from family members, social marginalization and shaming, and subtle and overt forms of prejudice and discrimination. Alcoholism rates tend to be three times higher among gays and lesbians than among heterosexuals (Hughes, 2005;

Schafer, Evans, & Coleman, 1987). For those who are struggling to accept being gay, alcohol is both a disinhibitor and an anesthetic, a way of pressing down and numbing pain (Hatzenbuehler, 2009). For gay males in particular, "The traditional patriarchal tradition of underverbalizing vulnerable feelings such as sadness, fear, and loneliness can leave men trying to 'anesthetize' these very feelings via alcohol or drugs" (Sanders, 2000, p. 249). In therapy with gay couples, Sanders recommends encouraging clients to recognize how they may be "imprisoned" by the dominant society's pressure to silence emotions and affective communication, and part of the liberation process entails giving voice to feelings rather than burying them through substance use.

Due (1995) explained that until recently, gay and lesbian couples had few places to openly socialize that did not center around alcohol (e.g., bars, nightclubs, or discotheques). Hence, a critical part of fostering non–substance-related coping strategies is by providing gays and lesbians, especially young people, with opportunities to socialize that do not revolve around alcohol.

Relationship violence

Alcohol abuse is frequently related to partner violence. Among battered wives, 40 to 60 percent reported that their husbands were heavy or problem drinkers. Among married men admitted to alcohol treatment centers, 50 to 70 percent reported participating in partner violence, with 20 to 30 percent of these men reporting having engaged in severe violence toward their spouses. Alcohol tends to make individuals more impulsive and to decrease their ability to restrain their aggression. This pattern is especially noticeable among spouses who are even more aggressive without alcohol. The more frequently men are intoxicated, the more likely they are to be verbally and physically violent toward their spouses and to inflict harm that is more severe and more likely to result in injury (Caetano, Schafer, & Cunradi, 2001).

> Assess your comprehension of new couplehood by completing this quiz.

Pregnancy and new Parenthood

Pregnancy is a life-altering developmental event. When adolescents become pregnant, often this event in unplanned and hence generates tension, anxiety, and conflict. But even when a pregnancy is planned, the transition that this event introduces is enormous. Once a person becomes pregnant, the most pressing change that is needed is the cessation of all drinking. In fact, most women stop using alcohol when they become pregnant, whether the pregnancy was planned or not and irrespective of their age (Skagerstrom, Chang, & Nilsen, 2011). Nevertheless, not all pregnant women cease drinking. In such cases, one of the most devastating consequences for the family life cycle is when the fetus suffers from the effects of alcohol exposure. Fetal alcohol syndrome (FAS) is the leading cause of birth defects resulting in craniofacial abnormalities, slow growth, nervous system impairments, and a range of learning and behavioral problems. A major factor influencing the risk of FAS is the timing of alcohol exposure during critical periods of development. Prenatal exposure to alcohol increases the risk of developing alcohol and other drug use disorder later in life.

Parenthood and young children

Becoming a parent is a major transitional event. Normal development requires that individuals and couples change and adapt in a number of key ways to accommodate the introduction of a new and totally dependent life. For those who are alcoholic prior to parenthood, a cessation of drinking is a necessary component of making a functional transition to the role of parenthood.

Teen mothers generally reduce their drinking when pregnant, yet their use of alcohol rises during the first year of parenthood in comparison with older new mothers (Kasier & Hays, 2005). Premature confrontation with the social responsibilities and pressures of early parenthood likely contributes to the rise in alcohol consumption after the parenthood transition. And, since children who grow up in alcoholic families are three times more likely to become alcoholic themselves, and because adolescent parents are more likely to abuse alcohol, adolescent parenthood is associated with a greater risk of intergenerational transmission of alcoholism (Johnson & Pickens, 2001). In comparison, those who delay parenthood until well into adulthood are more likely to manifest a decline in alcohol consumption when they become new parents, reflecting a functional adaptation to this new stage in the family life cycle.

Approaches to parenting

When couples become parents, the interaction patterns that defined their couple subsystem shape how they approach parenting. In healthy couple relationships, partners transfer functional interactional dynamics and clear boundaries to their role as parents. In relationships where alcoholism is present, "patterns of withdrawal and engagement first seen in the spousal subsystem, are conveyed to and utilized in the sibling subsystem" (Carruth & Mendenhall, 1989, p. 70). The constant cycling between sober–intoxicated interactions in the couple relationship creates an atmosphere of unpredictability and instability and a parenting style that reflects indecision and poor limit setting. When boundaries in the couple relationship lean toward too much rigidity, these tend to be mirrored in parenting, thereby placing children at risk for emotional and/or behavioral neglect. Conversely, when couple boundaries are too diffuse, this tends to be reflected in an overinvolved and smothering approach to parenting.

Gender and alcoholism interact to influence approaches to parenting as well. Mothers who are alcoholic manifest high levels of guilt less commonly found among alcoholic fathers. Guilt tends to undermine feelings of self-worth and competence stimulating depression and leading to more hostile, disruptive, and rejecting approaches to parenting. Mothers who are alcoholics are more likely to have experienced dysfunctions in their family of origin leading to unresolved issues with parents and poor models for how to parent effectively (Whipple, Fitzgerald, & Zucker, 1995), all of which increase the probability of alcoholism and dysfunctional parenting. Fathers who are alcoholics tend to interact less frequently with their children, have less positive interactions, display more negative emotions, report higher levels of irritation, and are less attuned to and

sensitive toward their children than nonalcoholic fathers (Watkins et al., 2009).

Assess your comprehension of pregnancy and new parenthood by completing this quiz.

Effect of Alcoholism on Children

In healthy families, life is child centered, but in alcoholic systems, family life is alcohol centered. Hence, children's needs often are subjugated to the demands imposed by the alcoholism. Emotional, cognitive, and behavioral problems often are symptomatic of living in an alcoholic system. In fact, children's symptoms are usually one of the first indicators of the presence of alcoholism in a family. Children of alcoholics, in contrast to children of non-alcoholics, experience more learning disabilities and lower scores on tests that measure cognitive and verbal skills. They are also more prone to psychiatric illnesses like anxiety and depression and are more likely to act out and display antisocial and aggressive behaviors (Hussong et al., 2008).

Children raised in alcoholic families are at greater risk for being abused and/or neglected, a situation that creates secondary emotional, cognitive, and behavioral problems. State child protective service agencies and state welfare records indicate that substance abuse is one of the two main problems exhibited by 81 percent of the families where child abuse has been reported. Research also suggests that alcoholism is more strongly related to child abuse than are other disorders, such as parental depression (Lung & Daro, 2006). Because of the strong association between alcoholism and violence, it is important for clinicians always to probe for one when the presence of the other has been determined.

Families with Adolescents

Adolescence is the period between the ages of 12 and 19. This is a time of dramatic physical, psychological, and social change. Families with adolescents are teeming with the tension of separation and connection. On the one hand, teenagers exhibit a strong need to separate and become independent. On the other hand, they manifest a strong pull toward security and stability. Parents are routinely mystified by the mixed messages they get from their teenagers telling them to simultaneously "go away and also stay right here."

In healthy families, parents are able to contain both of the forces of "let go" and "hold on." They provide adolescents with opportunities for appropriate role experimentation and limit testing while at the same time fostering a safe, nurturing space. In families where alcoholism is present, this kind of balanced energy is lacking. Instead, adolescents get either too much autonomy and not enough holding and nurturing, or they are held onto so tightly that they have little freedom to experiment and explore new roles and limits. Adolescents in families with alcohol problems often feel pressured to maintain the narrowly defined and rigid roles they adopted in response to the alcoholism (e.g., the caretaker, hero, mascot, scapegoat, or lost child), demonstrating how the needs of the alcoholism take precedence over normative developmental needs of individual members.

At the same time that adolescents may be grappling with a parent's alcoholism, many also find themselves struggling with the temptations of drinking. Adolescence is a life stage fraught with inner turmoil and conflict. Teens are confused about who they are and are plagued with insecurities and self-doubts. They tend to rely heavily on social approval from peers to establish a sense of meaning and worth. When all of these forces converge, the risk of using substances increases exponentially.

Whether or not teens drink, and if they do drink, how much and under what conditions, is complicated by the mixed messages society conveys about alcohol. Parents or grandparents, religious leaders, and schools may send the message that drinking is dangerous and forbidden. At the same time, movies, television, music, and advertisements communicate that alcohol is cool, sexy, and sophisticated. Moreover, laws that prohibit alcohol consumption before the age of 21 enhance the seduction of drinking. Societies where it is common for parents to allow children to have a few sips of wine with dinner promote moderate and responsible drinking reflected in lower rates of teenage alcohol abuse and dependence. Conversely, in the United States where laws and social customs make consumption taboo before the age of 21, alcohol becomes a forbidden fruit that tempts teens into drinking excessively as soon as they have a taste of independence.

Experiences with social devaluation also can make some teens vulnerable to drinking. A study by Corliss and her colleagues (2008) found that sexual minority adolescents are prone to drink earlier than their heterosexual counterparts and to develop problems that persist into young adulthood at higher rates. This pattern must be understood within the context of the alienation, isolation, and oppression that sexual minorities are subjected to and that increase the vulnerability to substance abuse (Caitlin et al., 2010).

> **Assess your comprehension of families with adolescents by completing this quiz.**

Midlife Change

The midlife is a point in the life cycle when one experiences a significant shift in focus, attention, and direction related to the course of one's life. For some, the shift is the traditional one of launching children and having to face the proverbial question: "what now?"—referred to as the "empty nest" syndrome. For others, the middle years may involve making the decision to take on parenthood for the first time, after having delayed this to establish a career. For others, the shift may involve changing career paths. And still yet, some combination of these or other issues may occur. In healthy families, whatever directional change arises, support and encouragement are present. In families with alcohol problems, since the fundamental energy is focused around staying the same, the crisis of midlife change is often met with deep resistance. For example, a man in his 40s who is struggling with alcoholism may be bored in a career and desperate for a change of direction, yet his drinking may inhibit him from taking the steps that are required to pursue a new career.

Spouses of alcoholics, women in particular, may have hung in with the alcoholism for years out of a fear of being alone. Midlife may be the point where many partners, women specifically, finally decide to take the risk of leaving the relationship and take their chances on their own. In such cases, support groups like Al Anon can play an important role in helping nonalcoholic partners find the inner resolve to free themselves from alcoholic relationships.

It is critical to bear in mind the impact that alcohol abuse in midlife has on the quality of life in the later years. For one thing, alcohol abuse in midlife diminishes the probability that one will live into older age. Moreover, for those who do live into their 70s, 80s, or beyond, alcoholism at the age of 50 predicts unhappiness in later life, in part because it damages future social supports that are essential for health and well-being, especially in the later years (Vaillant, 2012).

> Assess your comprehension of midlife change by completing this quiz.

Divorce

Divorce has become so common in the United States that it can almost be considered a normative part of the family life cycle. Roughly 50 percent of all first marriages end in divorce and the rate for second marriages is even higher at around 67 percent. The fact that alcoholism is present in one third of the relationships that end in divorce speaks to the impact that this addiction has on marital stability and satisfaction.

Alcoholism is associated with a rise in aggression and partner violence, with less warmth and more blaming and contempt, poor communication, reduced sexual intimacy and desire, depleted finances due to spending on alcohol, and less time spent together, especially if the alcoholic frequently drinks away from home. Moreover, as alcohol abuse or addiction progresses, the nondrinking spouse often grows into a compulsive caretaking role, which generates feelings of resentment, self-pity, and exhaustion. At some point, the nonalcoholic partner may reach her or his limit, leading to divorce.

Whether or not alcoholism is a factor, divorce tends to be hard on all members of a family. Even when a relationship is so deteriorated that divorce

represents a relief from suffering, this life cycle stage is characterized by anger, grief and loss, guilt, and a sense of inadequacy and failure. The presence of alcoholism can exacerbate these emotions, especially for children who tend to blame themselves when parents divorce. Divorce may also compel children to cling more desperately to narrow roles they assumed in relationship to the alcoholism. For example, a hero may attempt to save his parents' marriage. When divorce is imminent, he may blame himself and try to overcompensate by excelling at various pursuits. Parents may unwittingly target a child who has been the scapegoat by blaming him or her for the failures of the marriage rather than dealing with the impact of the alcoholism. Those in a mascot role may try to distract parents and siblings from the pain of the divorce through humor. A lost child is likely to burrow more deeply into invisibility in an effort to not exacerbate already high levels of stress.

Alcohol abuse tends to be an underlying contributor to divorce, not a reaction to it. Vaillant (2012) found that 57 percent of all divorces among Grant Study men involved alcoholism. That statistic had been artificially low until recently because although the men had spoken of their own alcohol problems, many had not been forthcoming about their wives struggles with alcohol until later in life (Powell, 2012). Other studies also confirm the link between alcohol abuse and divorce as reflected in the fact that divorced or separated men and women are three times more likely to be alcoholics or to have an alcohol problem than are married men and women (Sbarra & Nietert, 2009).

> Assess your comprehension of divorce by completing this quiz.

Aging and Later Life

As family members age, they are faced with various life cycle transitions that include retirement, a decline in physical health and mobility, the death of a partner, and their own impending mortality. In healthy families, younger generations are able to provide support to help older family members adjust to these changes. Healthy families provide care as needed, while recognizing that older family members need to feel valued and have something to contribute. Allowing older generations to assume an active role as grandparents, to whatever extent this is feasible, is important. Providing physical care, while also honoring the need for autonomy, is crucial. And it is important to offer comfort when a loved one passes.

There are a variety of ways that alcohol may affect the quality of life in the later years. For example, a significant relationship exists between alcoholism, marital quality, and happiness in later life. Vaillant (2012) explained that people who abused alcohol in midlife (around the age of 50), and who lived into their 70s and beyond, tended to have less marital happiness and this was correlated with diminished overall life satisfaction in the later years.

In families where older family members have problems with alcohol, the capacity to provide support and care for these family members is compromised in various ways. Adult children of increasingly frail and needy alcoholic parents may find it emotionally challenging to care for a parent who failed to be there for them while they were growing up. In situations where an adult child has been providing support to an alcoholic parent for a lifetime, sustaining this support when the parent is aging may be hard, especially as the parent grows increasingly dysfunctional, weak, and needy. Adult children of alcoholics may simply be so exhausted from having provided decades of care that by the time their parents are elderly, they find themselves "surrendering" to the alcoholism, rather than continuing to fight it.

As adults age, there is a risk of isolation. Reduced mobility and declining health make it hard to sustain contact with others, and if younger family members are not nearby or are otherwise estranged, the risk of isolation is heightened. As a result, some turn to alcohol for comfort and distraction from loneliness. For others, a lifetime of alcoholism may be part of the reason that younger family members avoid and isolate them. Hence, alcoholism may be a response to, as well as a reason for, isolation. In some families, an aging alcoholic member may reside with family, and yet may live in isolation, confined by physical limitations to a room, and visited only for functional purposes, which in some cases include

supplying alcohol. As one man admitted somewhat sheepishly, "My whole life I tried to get my dad to stop drinking, arguing with him, trying to protect him from himself. Now I look at him, this old man, and I think, it doesn't matter anymore. He got this far in spite of himself and he won't be here much longer. Now I just give him the damn bottle and leave him to enjoy the limited time he has left."

For most alcoholics, consumption tends to decrease with the aging process, which may help to slow down the demands placed on adult children. As the body ages, it metabolizes alcohol more slowly; as a result, alcohol remains in the body longer. They are also more likely to have health conditions that can be exacerbated by alcohol, including hypertension, strokes, memory loss, and mood disorders. Declining appetite is another challenge because the combination of alcohol with limited food intake exacerbates the effects of alcohol. And for those who take medications, there is the risk of interactions that can be dangerous or even life threatening. All of these create additional burdens for adult children who may already be exhausted from providing a lifetime of care to an alcoholic parent.

Whether or not an aging family member struggles with alcoholism, adult children who are alcoholic may struggle to provide appropriate care and support for aging parents. In some cases, the burden may fall upon the nonalcoholic partner who may have to take care of a spouse's aging parent, because the spouse's alcoholism impairs the ability to provide care for the aging parent.

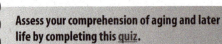

Assess your comprehension of aging and later life by completing this quiz.

Implications for Treatment

Few families come to treatment acknowledging outright that alcohol is a problem. "Common presenting complaints often mask alcoholism, such as depression, marital discord, sexual dysfunction, sexual acting out, other compulsive disorders such as overeating or prescription drugs abuse, physical violence, incest, and school or behavioral problems in one of the children" (Bepko & Krestan, 1985, p. 79).

Therefore, therapists must look closely for signs of alcoholism. When families do not acknowledge that drinking is a problem, therapists should ask diagnostic questions such as: "Tell me about the role of alcohol in your family," or "What is the history of drinking in your family?" or "Does anyone worry about anyone's drinking?" In families where alcohol is a problem, these kinds of prompts are likely to arouse the following three D's:

- Defensiveness
- Denial
- Discomfort

Once an overt understanding exists that alcohol is present in the family and contributes to some of the family's challenges, there are additional factors therapists should assess including the following:

1. Who has the drinking problem? What is the frequency and quantity of consumption? How long has this person(s) been drinking?
2. What developmental issues are occurring within the family, and in particular, what life cycle phase is the drinker in?
3. How has alcoholism been manifest across multiple generations of the family system?
4. How is the family defined in terms of contextual factors, (e.g., what is the family's identity with regard to race, ethnicity, social class, religion, nationality/immigration status, and physical/mental ability and how may these factors influence attitudes about alcohol)? What is the sexual orientation of each member? How does gender shape family dynamics?
5. What are the attitudes and beliefs about alcohol?
6. What role does each family member assume in relationship to the alcoholism?
7. What interaction patterns occur when the drinker is sober versus intoxicated?
8. What are the boundaries like?
9. What are the basic communication patterns that are employed?
10. What kinds of secrets has the alcoholism fueled?
11. Is the drinking an adaptive strategy (albeit a misguided one) in response to some other stressor? What does the family benefit as well as lose as a result of the drinking?

The answers to these questions will guide intervention. Each family is a unique case that requires interventions tailored to their specific situation that includes consideration of life cycle and contextual issues. For example, the interventions used with a single-parent family where a grandfather is an alcoholic and his adult daughter serves a caretaking role that interferes with parenting her three children would be different than those used with a new couple in their early 20s who both abuse alcohol and have just adopted a young child.

The first and most pressing clinical focus must be on sobriety. Toward that end the drinker must be willing to admit her or his problem with alcohol. Because denial is the hallmark of addictions, it is not uncommon for an alcoholic member to refuse to acknowledge dependence on alcohol. Treadway (1989) suggests that therapists use a contract to help the drinker recognize how little control she or he actually has over her or his consumption. The contract requires the individual to have exactly two drinks per day, no less and no more, for a period of 2 months. If the person is unable to comply with the terms of the contract exactly, this exposes the alcoholic's powerlessness over drinking making it easier to enlist that person in treatment.

Findings from the landmark seven-decade Grant Study revealed that there are four factors that have been shown to support abstinence over time and these are as follows: (1) substitute dependence, where drinkers find an alternative for alcohol (candy binges, benzodiazepines, marijuana, helping others, mystical belief and prayer, gambling, compulsive work or eating); (2) compulsory supervision, where an external force (e.g., probation officer, painful medical consequence) continually reminds the drinker of the unpleasant effects of the drinking; (3) new relationships with people the drinker does not have a past with who are a source of love or allow him/her to serve as a helper or giver; and (4) inspiring group membership (usually AA). Vaillant (2012) reported that successful relapse prevention was associated with those who consistently applied two of four of these factors for a period of at least a year of abstinence. The implications of this finding is that effective therapy may need to include efforts to help alcoholics to redirect their dependence into a more constructive compulsions, encouraging new love relationships or new relationships where one is able to serve others in a loving way, and encouraging active participation in an inspiring group such as AA. The benefits of regularly attending AA meetings are significant. Vaillant reported that those who "achieved stable abstinence attended about twenty times as many AA meetings as the chronically alcoholic" (p. 314).

Bepko and Krestan (1985) warn that it is not uncommon for the drinker to resist attending AA, and the reasons offered for this resistance vary widely. They encourage therapists to avoid arguing with clients and to provide information that clarifies the purpose of AA and explains what a specific client might gain related to her or his unique situation. Therapists also should encourage other family members to attend Al Anon in conjunction with attending therapy.

One factor to be considered is the "goodness of fit" between the AA model and sociocultural issues. For example, a central AA concept involves accepting one's powerlessness over alcohol. Yet feminists have critiqued the use of this term on the grounds that it merely exacerbates the disempowerment that women and other marginalized groups experience. The term "surrender" has been proposed as a more oppression-sensitive alternative. Similarly, native American communities have recognized the need to adapt AA to better fit with their values and orientation. The result has been the Wellbriety movement that adapts the 12 steps of AA to native American culture (White Bison, 2002).

While the alcoholic may refuse to acknowledge her or his problem with alcohol, the family may accept and understand the addiction. In such cases, therapists can work with the family of the alcoholic and require that they simultaneously attend Al Anon.

While specific approaches to clinical intervention vary widely, there are several guidelines therapists should follow irrespective of the family's life cycle stage. These include reorganizing the family system to achieve and sustain sobriety. Therapists strive to alter roles and interactional patterns to reduce overfunctioning/underfunctioning; increase use of clear, direct communication of thoughts and feelings; strengthen weak boundaries/soften rigid boundaries; and promote healthy skills for managing stress and conflict.

CASE ILLUSTRATION

The Burton Family ˜

The following case follows the Burton family through several phases of the family life cycle, tracking the influence of alcohol in each stage.

Peter, a White male, and Trisha, an African American female, met in their mid-20s while working as new attorneys in a New York law firm. Their relationship began passionately and they married 8 months later after Trisha became pregnant. Initially, they both drank regularly as a part of the social dimension of their careers. After Trisha became pregnant, she stopped drinking, but Peter continued to drink as an extension of his work activities, something Trisha missed. In addition to negotiating a new marriage and new baby, Amy, the Burtons faced extended-family pressures related to race and class. Peter came from an upper-middle-class Long Island family. He was the eldest child and had a sister 3 years younger. Trisha grew up in a working-class family that became a single-parent family after her father left when she was 5. She was the middle child of three daughters.

While Peter's family outwardly embraced Trisha, she felt uncomfortable that Peter's father sometimes made off-handed racially insensitive comments. Although Peter acknowledged to her that his father's comments were awkward, he nevertheless minimized Trisha's hurt by accusing her of being "overly sensitive." This fueled an underlying racial tension that the couple did not address directly but grew over the years.

Burton et al. (2004) have discussed the importance of the concept of "homeplace" as it relates to African Americans. The term refers to a location where one feels rooted, connected, and accepted, and where essential pieces of the self are reflected and valued. For many African Americans, under the best of circumstances, families provide homeplace by serving as a source of strength and a site of resistance against devaluation and oppression. Under the worst of circumstances, homeplace is an unrealized dream and a source of conflict, loss, and grief. Many African Americans experience a deep sense of yearning related to homeplace that is tied to struggles with racial devaluation and discrimination. For Trisha, certainly there was such a yearning. The lack of a warm, loving family growing up and struggles to succeed within predominately White colleges undermined her sense of homeplace. Moreover, the White, New York corporate world where she and Peter met and worked was a place where Peter felt very much "at home," but Trisha did not. Her success there both reflected and intensified her lack of homeplace. Moreover, the cultural alienation she felt in relationship to her in-laws heightened a yearning for "home."

Nearly 4 years after Trisha and Peter married, Mathew was born. At that point, the couple decided Trisha would resign from the firm and devote herself full time to parenthood. Two years later, Trisha's mother died, which had a devastating impact. After Trisha's father left when she was 5, her mother grew increasingly dependent on alcohol to cope with her heartaches. This compromised her parenting. Trisha's older sister, Yvonne, assumed a caretaker's role, while Trisha's younger sister, Lisa, became a scapegoat, frequently getting into trouble. Trisha functioned as a lost child, trying hard to be invisible and to need as little as possible. Trisha never felt close to her mother, yet upon her death she felt overwhelming grief. Shortly thereafter, she became pregnant with their third child, Rebecca. After Rebecca's birth, Trisha struggled through a bleak postpartum depression. Eventually she recovered, but like her mother, she used alcohol to manage her frustration and pain.

Had Trisha's postpartum depression driven her to seek therapy, it is likely that she would not have named alcohol as a part of her problem. This is why it is critical for therapists to ask general questions about alcohol as part of every assessment. Also, with postpartum depression defined as the problem, it would be appropriate to ask what kinds of things Trisha was doing to help manage her difficulties, which would be another way of zeroing in on the role that alcohol was playing as a coping resource. Once Trisha's drinking was flagged, an opening would exist for the therapist to explore how alcohol was shaping family patterns and to confront the dan-

gers of using alcohol as a coping strategy. It would also be important for the therapist to explore sociocultural factors, and, in particular, to consider how disruptions to Trisha's sense of homeplace contributed to her reliance on alcohol. This would inevitably lead to focus attention on how to repair her sense of homeplace (Burton et al., 2004).

Including Peter and the children in the therapy would be important as well. It would elucidate how the children's needs were being neglected by virtue of Peter's over-involvement with work and by Trisha's depression and drinking. At this point, therapy would focus on restructuring interactions to get Peter more involved in parenting and to help Trisha mourn the losses related to the death of her mother. Moreover, it would be essential for the therapist to consider how issues of race, class, and gender intersected with Trisha's personal struggles, as well as the couple and family struggles.

As a couple, Peter and Trisha were emotionally estranged. Peter worked long hours leaving Trisha to handle family responsibilities without him. The combination of Trisha's drinking and the rigid boundaries between the parental and sibling subsystems meant the children's needs were often neglected. To compensate, Amy assumed a caretaking role. One unfortunate consequence of parental neglect was that the children received minimal healthy racial socialization. Amy's physical appearance was ambiguous and she struggled greatly with how to identify herself racially. She also noted that her siblings, who were both light skinned, derived benefits from their lighter appearance that were denied to her. Unfortunately, her father lacked the racial insight to provide meaningful racial socialization, and he was rarely around, while her mother's alcoholism compromised what she had to offer. Consequently, Amy had to navigate the complexities of the racial landscape with minimal guidance.

Had the Burtons sought therapy at some point, perhaps in response to their marital estrangement, a thorough assessment would have exposed Trisha's drinking and how alcohol was shaping the couple and family dynamics. AA and Al Anon would have been encouraged in conjunction with therapy, and in addition to working with the couple it would also be important to meet with the whole family. Doing so would create an opening to challenge Amy's parentification in the face of her parents' neglect. Targeted attention would focus on both restructuring family interactions to reestablish healthier boundaries and allocation of responsibilities, as well as focusing on the couple relationship and exploring the underlying issues that had contributed to the strain and estrangement, including dynamics related to race, class, and gender, and how the strain was exacerbating Trisha's depressive symptoms and her reliance on alcohol as a coping strategy.

After their 17th anniversary, Peter revealed that he had fallen in love with another woman, who was White, and he initiated a divorce. One of the complaints he lodged against Trisha was her drinking, which infuriated her. She vehemently denied having a problem with alcohol. Trisha was crushed. Not only was her marriage ending, but to add insult to injury, her husband was leaving her for a White woman and had accused her of being an alcoholic. Peter's leaving also replicated the abandonment she had felt as a little girl when her father left. With this, Trisha's drinking grew more severe.

The divorce took almost a year and was bitter and angry. Throughout Trisha wove in and out of sobriety and intoxication. When she was drunk, Amy functioned as the adult in charge. During this period of time, Amy was also applying for colleges. She was thrilled when she was accepted into Duke University in North Carolina. Yet, the family's regulatory behaviors required Amy's presence to care for her younger siblings whose needs were being neglected in the face of Trisha's alcoholism and Peter's virtual abandonment.

Had Trisha sought therapy at this stage in the family life cycle, perhaps on the recommendation of her attorney or a good friend, as a routine part of assessment the therapist would have inquired about the role of alcohol, likely exposing Trisha's use. By including the children in the therapy, it would have been possible to better assess the impact of the divorce (and subsequently of Trisha's drinking) on interactional patterns. The therapist might help Trisha recognize the deleterious effects of alcohol on her emotional well-being and her capacity to parent and care for her children. Encouraging Trisha to attend AA meetings would be recommended, and

the therapy process would provide a space for Trisha to express feelings of hurt and anger over Peter's betrayal and abandonment, to mourn loss, and to foster more constructive ways of channeling her emotions. The therapist could also restructure boundaries in the family so that Amy could be demoted from caretaking her mother and young siblings. This would require Trisha's cooperation because she would have to agree to assume greater parental responsibility, and give Amy explicit permission to leave to go to Duke. If possible, it would also be important to reach out to Peter to assess his openness to being a more active parent. This would require explaining that while Peter and Trisha are no longer a couple, nevertheless they always will be connected by virtue of conjoint parental responsibilities.

Amy sacrificed going to Duke so that she could stay home to care for her younger siblings and mother. She attended a local community college and eventually became certified as a primary level educator, just as Rebecca was leaving home to attend college. Amy remained attached to her mother whose continued struggle with alcohol prevented her from using her middle years as an opportunity to grow in new ways. With the children grown and the divorce years behind her, she might have pursued a new career and started a new relationship. Instead, she lived in a small apartment that Amy paid for and continued to drink heavily.

At the age of 60 Trisha suffered a heart attack. At that point, Amy was married with two young children but once again, she stepped forward to offer care. She moved her mother in with her family; however, by this time Amy was exhausted from caring for her mother. Eventually, she began supplying her mother with alcohol to keep the peace. Amy also felt a lot of resentment toward her younger siblings who had never offered to share in the burdens of caring for their mother. The tension between Amy and Rebecca was especially high, which inevitably also reflected unspoken racial tensions that had existed between them for years.

At this stage in the family's life cycle, Amy might have contacted a therapist, possibly at the suggestion of a health care professional tending to Trisha after the heart attack. As part of a routine assessment, the therapist would ask about the role of alcohol in the family system. The exhaustion from years of caretaking might have helped Amy to be open about her mother's alcoholism and the strains it had created. The therapist could educate the family about the dangers of alcohol, especially for an elderly woman who had just suffered a major health crisis, and would recognize the role that family patterns had played in sustaining Trisha's alcoholism. Therefore, both AA and Al Anon would be suggested in addition to therapy.

Therapy would ideally create a place and space for family members to unpack stories of pain and struggle. Certainly, Trisha's lifetime of abusing alcohol was a reflection of her experiences with devaluation, rejection, and loneliness. Similarly, Amy also has carried decades of hurt and pain having made numerous sacrifices to care for her mother and siblings, often without acknowledgment or reward, and struggling alone with devaluation related to her racial identity. Hence, some part of the healing process would involve helping mother and daughter to speak unspoken truths, to express buried feelings of pain and rage, and to connect around shared struggles with racial and gender devaluation. At the same time, it would be critical to support Trisha in apologizing to Amy for the years she was unavailable and left her sister alone to assume the full load of caretaking responsibilities.

It would be useful to include Matt and Rebecca in the therapy to heal strains in the sibling relationships and to help more equitably distribute the burden of care for Trisha. It would also be wise for the therapist to introduce the issue of what will happen when Trisha passes away. Given her compromised health, it would benefit the family to talk about how they would like to relate as a family with the time they still have together.

As it happened, Trisha died a year after her heart attack. Her death compelled Amy to enter therapy and finally, at long last, she talked openly for the first time about their mother's alcoholism and the ways it had impacted their family, their lives, and their relationships. By breaking the silence that had defined the family for so long, Amy took a crucial step toward healing herself and transforming an intergenerational pattern that had been the basis of so much pain. Once this process was set into motion, Amy never turned back. She committed herself to naming and directly acknowledging the addiction that organized her family, she also committed herself to speaking directly about other difficult to speak truths, including the racial tensions that had been the basis of so much resentment and hurt. Amy also learned how to forgive family members who had disappointed and hurt her, and she learned to forgive herself for the ways that she had betrayed herself over the years. In other words, Amy learned how to stop overfunctioning for others and how to prioritize her own needs. She had an opportunity to assert her new stand when her father became ill and instead of jumping in to take care of him she leveled with her siblings and explained they would need to assume greater responsibility for providing care.

> Assess your comprehension of implications for treatment by completing this quiz.

— Conclusion

While alcoholism is highly treatable, it is essential for therapists to assume a systemic perspective that recognizes the salience of life cycle and contextual factors. Alcoholism is often a response to pain and hurt, and it always creates its fair share of further pain and hurt. Families need to understand the dangers that alcoholism poses while also feeling that hope and recovery are possible, at any age and stage, and no matter what the individual or family's particular circumstances and dynamics.

> Recall what you learned in this chapter by completing the **Chapter Review.**

— References —

American Psychiatric Association. (2000). *Diagnostic and statistical manual of mental disorders* (4th ed., text revision). Washington, DC: Author.

Arnett, J. J. (2005). The developmental context of substance use in emerging adulthood. *Journal of Drug Issues, 35,* 235–253.

Bepko, C., & Krestan, J. A. (1985). *The responsibility trap: A blueprint for treating alcoholic families.* New York: Free Press.

Borsari, B., & Carey, K. B. (2001). Peer influences on college drinking: A review of the research. *Journal of Substance Abuse, 1*(4), 391–424.

Bray, R. M., Hourani, L. L. & Rae, K. L. (2003). *Department of defense survey of health-related behaviors among military personnel.* Research Triangle Park, NC: RTI International.

Burton, L. M., Winn, D. M., Stevenson, H., & Clark, S. L. (2004). Working with African American clients: Considering the "homeplace" in marriage and family therapy practices. *Journal of Marital and Family Therapy, 30*(4), 397–410.

Caetano, R., Schafer, S., & Cunradi, C. B. (2001). Alcohol-related intimate partner violence among white, black, and Hispanic couples in the United States. *Alcohol and Violence 25*(1). Retrieved from http://pubs.niaaa.nih.gov/publications/arh25-1/3-4.htm.

Caitlin, R., Huebner, D., Diaz, R. M., & Sanchez, J. (2010). Family rejection as a predictor of negative health outcomes in white and Latino lesbian, gay, and bisexual young adults. *Pediatrics, 123*(1), 346–352.

Carruth, B., & Mendenhall, W. (1989). *Co-dependency: Issues in treatment and recovery.* Binghamton, NY: Haworth Press.

Chartier, K., & Caetano, R. (2010). Ethnicity and health disparities in alcohol research. *Alcohol Research and Health, 33*(1–2), 152–160.

Conger, R. D. (1994). The family context of adolescent vulnerability and resilience to alcohol use and abuse. *Sociological Studies of Children, 6,* 55–86.

Corliss, H. C., Rosario, M., Wypij, D., Fisher, L. B., & Austin, B. S. (2008). Sexual orientation disparities in longitudinal alcohol use patterns among adolescents: Findings from the growing up today study. *Archives of Pediatric Adolescent Medicine, 162*(11), 1071–1078.

Due, L. (1995). *Joining the tribe: Growing up gay & lesbian in the '90s.* New York: Anchor Books.

Enoch, M.-A. (2006). Genetic and environmental influences on the development of alcoholism. *Annals of the New York Academy of Sciences, 1094,* 193–201.

Foroud, T., & Phillips, T. J. (2012). Assessing the genetic risk for alcohol use disorders. *Alcohol Research: Current Reviews, 34*(3), 266–269.

Galanter, M. (Ed.). (2005). *Recent developments in alcoholism, Vol. 17: Alcohol problems in adolescents and young adults.* New York: Springer.

Grant, B. F., Dawson, D. A., Stinson, F. S., Chou, P. S., Dufour, M. C., & Pickering, R. P. (2004). The 12-month prevalence and trends in DSM-IV alcohol abuse and dependence: United States, 1991–1992 and 2001–2002. *Drug and Alcohol Dependence, 74*(3), 223–234.

Hanson, D. J. (1995). The United States of America. In D. B. Heath, D. B. (Ed.), *International Handbook on Alcohol and Culture* (pp. 300–315), Westport, CT: Greenwood Press.

Hatzenbuehler, M. (2009). How does sexual minority stigma "get under the skin"? A psychological mediation framework. *Psychological Bulletin, 135*(5), 707–730.

Hawkins, J. D., & Fitzgibbon, J. J. (1993). Risk factors and risk behaviors in the prevention of adolescent substance abuse. *Adolescent Medicine: State of the Art Reviews, 4,* 249–262.

Heath, D. B. (1982). Sociocultural variants in alcoholism. In E. M. Pattison & E. Kaufman (Eds.), *Encyclopedic handbook of alcoholism* (pp. 426–440). New York: Gardner Press.

Herrick, C., & Herrick, C. (2007). *100 answers and questions about alcoholism.* Indianapolis: Jones & Barrett Publishers.

Hoffmann, J. P. (2002). The community context of family structure and adolescent drug use. *Journal of Marriage and Family, 64,* 314–330.

Hughes, T. L. (2005). Alcohol use and alcohol-related problems among lesbians and gay men. *Annual Review of Nursing Research, 23,* 283–325.

Hussong, A. M., Bauer, D. J., Huang, W., Chassin, L., Sher, K. J., & Zucker, R. A. (2008). Characterizing the life stressors of children of alcoholic parents. *Journal of Family Psychology, 22,* 819–832.

Johnson, E. O., & Pickens, R. W. (2001). Familial transmission of alcoholism among nonalcoholics and mild, severe, and dyssocial subtypes of alcoholism. *Alcoholism: Clinical and Experimental Research, 25,* 661–666.

Johnston, L. D., O'Malley, P. M., & Bachman, J. G. (2001). *Monitoring the Future: National Survey Results on Drug Use, 1975–2000. Volume 1: Secondary School Students.* (NIH Pub. No. 014924). Bethesda, MD: National Institute on Drug Abuse.

Kaiser, M. M., & Hays, B. J. (2005). Health-risk behaviors in a sample of first-time pregnant adolescents. *Public Health Nursing. 22,* 483–493.

Laszloffy, T. A. (2000). The systemic model of family development. *Family Relations, 51*(3), 206–215.

Lown, E. A., Nayak, M. B., Korcha, R. A., & Greenfield, T. K. (2011). Child physical and sexual abuse: a comprehensive look at alcohol consumption patterns, consequences, and dependence from the National Alcohol Survey. *Journal of Alcohol and Clinical and Experimental Research, 35*(2), 317–325.

Lung, C. T., & Daro, D. (2006). *Current trends in child abuse reporting and fatalities: The results of the 2006 annual fifty state survey.* Chicago, IL: Prevent Child Abuse America.

Mulia, N., Ye Y., Greenfield, T., & Zemore, S. E. (2009). Disparities in alcohol-related problems among white, black, and Hispanic Americans. *Alcoholism: Clinical and Experimental Research, 33*(4), 654–662.

O'Farrell T., J. (1989). Marital and family therapy in alcoholism treatment. *Journal of Substance Abuse Treatment, 6*(1), 23–29.

Powell, A. (2012). Decoding keys to a healthy life. *Harvard Gazette.* Retrieved from http://news.harvard.edu/gazette/story/2012/02/decoding-keys-to-a-healthy-life/

Room, R. (1976). Ambivalence as a sociological explanation: The case of cultural explanations of alcohol problems. *American Sociological Review, 41,* 1047–1065.

Sanders, G. L. (2000). Men together: Working with gay male couples in contemporary times. In P. Papp (Ed.), *Couples on the fault line: New directions for therapists* (pp. 222–256). New York: Guilford Press.

Sbarra, D., & Nietert, P., (2009). Divorce and death: Forty years of the Charleston heart study. *Psychological Science, 20*(1), 107–113.

Schaefer, S., Evans, S., & Coleman, E. (1987). Sexual orientation concerns among chemically dependent individuals. *Journal of Chemical Dependency Treatment, 1,* 121–140.

Seppa, N. (2009, May 22). Sensitivity to alcohol connected with alcoholism risk: An imperviousness to alcohol's effects may not be so good. *Science News.* Retrieved from www.sciencenews.org/view/generic/id/44037/title/High_tolerance_connected_with_

Silverstein, H. (1990). *Alcoholism.* New York: Franklin Watts.

Skagerstrom, J., Chang, G., & Nilsen, P. (2011). Predictors of drinking during pregnancy: A systematic review. *Journal of Women's Health, 20,* 901–913.

Steinglass, P. (1981). The alcoholic family at home: Patterns of interaction in dry, wet, and transitional stages of alcoholism. *Archives of General Psychiatry, 38*(5), 578–584.

Steinglass, P. (1982). The role of alcohol in family systems. In J. Orford & J. Harwin (Eds.), *Alcohol and the family* (pp. 127–150). London: AEC Publishing.

Steinglass, P., Bennett, L. A., Wolin, S. J., & Reiss, D. (1987). *The alcoholic family.* New York: Basic Books.

Szlemko, W. J., Wood, J., Thurman, W. & Jumper, P. (2006). Native Americans and alcohol: Past, present, and future. *Journal of General Psychology, 133*(4), 435–451.

Tafoya, N., & Del Vecchio, A. (2005). Back to the future: An examination of the Native American holocaust experience. In M. McGoldrick, J. Giordano, & N. Garcia Preto (Eds.), *Ethnicity and family therapy* (3rd ed., pp. 55–63). New York: Guilford Press.

Thomas V. S., & Rockwood, K. J. (2001). Alcohol abuse, cognitive impairment, and mortality among older people. *Journal of American Geriatric Society, 49,* 415–20.

Treadway, D. (1989). *Before it's too late: Working with substance abuse in the family.* New York: W. W Norton.

U.S. Department of Health and Human Services and SAMHA's National Clearinghouse for Alcohol and Drug Information. Retrieved October 15, 2003, from http://www.health.org/nongovpubs/coafacts/

Vaillant, G. E. (1983). *The natural history of alcoholism.* Cambridge, MA: Harvard University Press.

Vaillant, G. E. (1995). *The natural history of alcoholism revisited: Causes, patterns, and paths to recovery.* Cambridge, MA: Harvard University Press.

Vaillant, G. E. (2012). *The triumphs of experience: The men of the Harvard Grant study.* Harvard University Press: Cambridge, MA.

Vandenbos, G. R., Ed. (2007). *APA dictionary of psychology* (1st ed.). Washington, DC: American Psychological Association.

Watkins, L. E., O'Farrell, T. J., Suvak, M. K., Murphy, C. M., & Taft, C. T. (2009). Parenting satisfaction among fathers with alcoholism. *Addictive Behaviors, 34*(6/7), 610–612.

Wegscheider, S. (1981). *Another chance.* Palo Alto: Science and Behavior Books.

Whipple, E., Fitzgerald, H., & Zucker, R. (1995). Parent-child interactions in alcoholic and nonalcoholic families. *American Journal of Orthopsychiatry, 65,* 153–159.

White Bison, Inc. (2002). *The red road to Wellbriety: In the Native American way.* Colorado Springs, CO: Coyhis Publishing.

Chapter 25

Violence and the Life Cycle

Monica McGoldrick & Mary Anne Ross

— Learning Outcomes

- Discuss the dynamics of violence as an abuse of power.
- Compare how men and women experience violence.
- Describe factors that make violence a societal issue.
- Examine the causes and effects of sexual violence on individuals.
- List and describe the forms of violence that children experience.
- Discuss strategies for assessment and intervention in cases of adolescent violence.
- Describe how patterns of violence change in families at midlife.
- List and describe factors that make older adults more vulnerable to abuse.

Introduction

When this book was first published in 1980, the Violence Against Women Act was 14 years away; only 23 states recognized marital rape as a crime and violence was a well-concealed problem in American families. Our first edition did not include a chapter on violence. Since then we have seen the devastating impact of family violence on the physical and psychological health of our clients and realized that it is a widespread occurrence throughout the life cycle. We know that rates are shockingly high, in spite of the fact that many incidents of abuse are never reported. It is ironic that while Americans' greatest fear is of strangers in the streets, the greatest danger is in one's own home at the hands of a loved one. We are more likely to be assaulted, beaten, or killed in our homes than anywhere else or by anyone else in our society. This is especially true for women and children (New York Office of the Prevention of Domestic Violence, 2011; Brodowski, 2011).

Violence is Abuse of Power

Statistics show clearly that violence operates on the basis of the strongest victimizing the weakest. It is abuse of power. Thus, the greatest volume of abuse is directed against the weakest: children under the age of 6. Violence in the form of corporal punishment against children has been the norm and sexual abuse of children tragically widespread. The most likely abuser is the more powerful parent: the father. The same is true of spouse abuse. The stronger tends to victimize the weaker (Finkelhor, 2008). Eighty-five percent of victims of battering are female (Gosselin, 2010). In families in which the woman has less power by virtue of her immigrant status or not being in the labor force, she is more isolated and at higher risk for abuse and injury (Macmillan & Kruttschnitt, 2005). Not surprisingly, the backlash against the increased awareness of violence in our society has meant some social scientists use research surveys to assert that women are, in many situations, as violent as men. Of course, some women do dominate and abuse their partners. But criminal justice records demonstrate clearly that most interpersonal violence is perpetrated by men against women or against other men (Macmillan & Kruttschnitt, 2005).

Families of color and those who are impoverished are in double jeopardy, experiencing both institutional prejudices and patriarchal oppression. Similarly, gay and lesbian relationships occur within a society that still ostracizes them and is only beginning to offer some legal protections.

Many traditional cultures and religions condone disrespect and emotional abuse of women as well as marital violence (Kimmel & Aronson, 2013). The media has recently been bringing to light the pervasive institutional abuse in our religious, educational, and athletic organizations. In America's military, women are more likely to be raped by a fellow service member than killed in enemy combat (Veterans for Peace, 2013). Yet, as a society we barely acknowledge the trauma suffered by survivors or consider the insidious consequences of having so many of our basic social structures riddled by these crimes.

The experience of violence is different for men and women

While men experience violence as well, most of it occurs outside the home (Barnett, Miller-Perrin, & Perrin, 2005). Men are more often victimized by strangers, whereas most violence against women is perpetrated by family members, boyfriends, and acquaintances. As Attorney General Eric Holder (2013) has put it: "On average 3 women are murdered every day by a boyfriend, husband or ex husband. Experts estimate that for every victim killed an additional nine nearly lose their lives." Women are also violent at times, often abusing those most dependent on them, such as their children and lashing out at intimate partners. However, the vast majority of rapes, murders, assaults, and other acts of family violence are perpetrated by men (Violence Policy Center, 2012). As Kimmel and Aronson assert: "From early childhood to old age, violence is perhaps the obdurate, intractable gender difference we have observed." (2013, p. 603).

Not just a family legacy but a social legacy

Kimmel notes that "Masculinity is often equated with the capacity for violence" (Kimmel, 2013, p. 437). Male violence is glorified in the media and intertwined with sports, such as football, boxing, and wrestling. Although violence plays out in the interior of the family, it is not an intra-familial issue. Men learn that violence is an accepted form of communication with each other and with women. Male violence is so commonplace, so deeply woven into the fabric of daily life, that we accept it as a matter of course. We need to acknowledge that it is a societal issue, not just a psychological issue, and focus on how to modify our conceptions of male development to really change the likelihood that male violence will continue to follow the current pattern throughout the life cycle.

A man is not violent primarily because his father was violent toward him, but rather because we live in a society that condones violence. Women do not invite or enjoy abuse. Nor do they suffer from masochistic tendencies that force them to stay, although these have been common psychological stereotypes. Women generally end up staying in abusive relationships because our society provides little support for them to leave. While abuse and its tolerance tend to be taught in families and transmitted from generation to generation, they are socially sanctioned issues, and their ultimate repair requires change in social values. Thus, education about the social norms that make violence acceptable is an important part of our clinical work with families.

Violence is clearly associated with isolation from community ties, friendships, and organizational affiliations (Straus & Steinmetz, 2006). It thrives in secrecy and shame. Victims often worry about what neighbors, family, or friends will think of them and their abusers. One of the primary interventions when working with victims of violence is to counter isolation by promoting connectedness to family, friends, and community resources, such as support groups where others can provide emotional support and help with practical concerns—offering a place to stay, holding on to an extra set of car keys, providing a loan and help with childcare, or giving the name of a good mechanic, lawyer, or therapist. Those comfortable with the internet can get information and share their experience while remaining anonymous. Real-life contacts are always better, but the Internet can be a good starting point.

The U.S. Government's Definition of Domestic Violence (U.S. Department of Justice, 2013) seems to capture the broad and complex ways abuse is manifested in couple relationships. Although there are numerous violence and conflict assessment forms available, clinicians may want to provide this definition to clients and review it with them to raise their consciousness about the dynamics of abuse.

The primary context for helping men at all phases of the life cycle understand and change their patterns of abuse is one that offers them the opportunity to see their behavior in societal context and understand the pressures that make change difficult (Kimmel, 2011, 2013). These pressures can be as subtle as the language we use and take for granted. Think about how the words used to describe a women's beauty reflect violence: "stunning," "ravishing," "knockout," "bombshell," "dressed to kill," "femme fatale," etc. (Kimmel, 2013; Beneke, 1982). When men are labeled "sissies," "wimps," or "fags" for not being domineering, they are being covertly pressured to undervalue their mothers, sisters, wives, and children and to treat them with disrespect. A detailed inquiry into their history and socialization is the beginning of any assessment and any intervention. They must become aware of the sexist and misogynistic influences on their lives and relationships. This awareness is empowering, challenging the attitudes they have been inculcated with to help them find the motivation to alter their behavior toward the women in their lives. We do know that when men have daughters, their consciousness of women's experience of male dominance increases (Washington, 2007).

Women as well as men need to understand the ways they have been socialized to tolerate psychological abuse and accommodate, cover up, justify, and blame themselves for men's abusive behavior. They have been taught that they are responsible for their relationships and the well-being of their families and often view tolerating abuse as a trade-off for their family well-being. They are willing to make great sacrifices for the sake of the people they love. As one client put it: "I wanted everyone to be happy—the kids, my husband. I thought we were happy most of the time and it was just when he had these mood swings that things got bad. I figured I could deal with the way he treated me, so our lives wouldn't fall apart. I thought our kids would be devastated if we split up."

Assess your comprehension of violence is abuse of power by completing this quiz.

Couples

Couples do not always report violence in therapy, especially in the early stages. There are many reasons for this. They may be afraid or ashamed and keep incidents of violence a secret. These may have happened years before and they think it is no longer an issue. Since clients may not feel comfortable sharing their experience with the therapist until well into the therapy, it is important to see couples together and separately early in the process. The clinician must inquire carefully about the dynamics of power differentials and subtle indicators of abuse, such as defensiveness or reticence to discuss how conflicts are resolved. Symptoms of psychological abuse can serve as a red flag. The therapist must be careful to examine the hidden ways in which abuse, overt, and dramatic, as well as subtle forms of intimidation and control, may be organizing family behavior (Todahl & Walter, 2011). One particularly pathological form of psychological abuse, sometimes referred to as "gaslighting," a reference to the classic movie Gaslight, in which the husband tries to drive his wife insane by telling her she is crazy any time she notices the things he is doing in their relationship to mystify her. Gaslighting is often done by husbands who deny their affairs and call their wives "paranoid" for their suspicions.

If instances of violence are uncovered or a pattern of psychological abuse becomes apparent, the therapist must be aware that the spouse can easily be "punished" for comments made in therapy, and take responsibility to be sure family members are kept safe and not asked to divulge issues that may put them in jeopardy. Once the therapist knows that abuse is occurring, family members should be seen separately until safeguards can be put in place to protect the vulnerable spouse or children. Each client should have an individualized safety plan for where to go and what to do if the spouse becomes violent, including a list of what to take and contact information for family, friends, and community services.

Mild acts can easily escalate. Women by virtue of their smaller size are at far greater risk for injury than men in any physical confrontation, even where women initiate it. Furthermore, most violence research is not designed with the subtlety to take into account that it takes a long time for most people to be able to tell the truth about traumatic experiences they view as shameful or threatening. Linda Burton, a careful ethnographer of marginalized families, found that it took years of interviews before women were able to tell the full truth about the violence they had experienced (Burton, Purvin, & Garrett-Peters, 2009; Paradis, et al., 2009). Burton's studies show that previous abuse, whether as a child or adult, has a profound impact on women's relationships. Women who had never experienced abuse were the most likely to be in a satisfying relationship. Those who were sexually abused as children tended to have unrealistic expectations about their current relationship and many of those who had been abused as adults did not want to try to have another relationship. Thus, clearly the life cycle impact of abuse is longstanding and questions must take the long range implications into account (Burton 2010).

Longitudinal research will be the key to our understanding of the cumulative effect of abuse experienced in different stages of the life cycle. We know that victims often suffer from depression, posttraumatic stress disorder, and that they are at higher risk for re-abuse.

We live in a rape-supportive culture. One out of 5 women and one out of 71 men have been raped (CDC, 2011). One of the most insidious forms of sexual assault toward women is date rape, a misnomer, because it implies a romantic relationship between the assailant and perpetrator. More accurately called "acquaintance rape," the most common assailants are male friends, boyfriends, neighbors, bosses, and fellow employees. Attitudes about domestic violence and rape have been changing, but there is still a tendency to blame the victim. Many people think that in certain circumstances, it is okay for a man to force a woman to have sex, such as, if they have been dating a long time, if they have had sex before, or if she has "led him on." Rape myths, such as that a woman "asked to be raped," liked it, or could have stopped it, are widely accepted

and are reinforced in popular pornography. Formal and informal male social groups, such as fraternities, sports teams, or even the men at the local bar, can reinforce the importance of sexual conquest and promote the objectification of women, creating an environment in which rape is acceptable for their members, as can be seen in the widespread incidents in the American military (DeKeseredy, 2011; Swartout, 2013). Societal refusal to acknowledge the abuse compounds the injury:

Stacey Dean Rambold, a 49 year old teacher in Montana, was sentenced to thirty days in jail after admitting to having sex with Cherice Moralez, a 14 year old student. The judge, G. Todd, Baugh, said the victim "seemed older than her chronological years" and "had as much control over the situation as he did." When the Moralez pressed charges, she was ostracized by the community and committed suicide a few days before her 17th birthday (Healy, 2013).

Young women often do not identify dating violence as abuse and rarely report it to the police. Indeed, women often feel that they are as responsible as their male partners. Indeed, most rapes are never reported. Women often blame themselves and feel too ashamed to make an official report, though they do frequently confide in friends (Ahrens, Cabral & Abeling, 2009). Because acquaintance rape is a betrayal by someone a woman trusts, it can be more psychologically damaging than stranger rape. Survivors frequently experience the symptoms associated with other severe traumas, which often go unrecognized by the survivor and those around her, who do not know about the rape. Understandably, rape survivors frequently have difficulty trusting men and difficulty with sexual intimacy, expressed by either a lack of interest in sex or compulsive sexual activity.

Men who are sexually victimized as children are more likely to be re-victimized later on in life, and more likely to suffer from suicidal ideation, posttraumatic stress, and depression (Aosved, Long, & Voller, 2011). Men are even less likely to report rape than women, often feeling ashamed of being overpowered, even when faced with multiple attackers. They may be disturbed at having experienced an erection or ejaculation, thinking this indicates homosexuality or perversion. Men need to understand that these physical responses are automatic and not indications of enjoyment or pleasure. Men who are raped generally experience long-term psychological damage, such as depression, anxiety, and suicidal ideation (CDC, 2011). Gay men who experience rape may blame their orientation. When orientation is the cause, the assault can be considered a hate crime.

It is important to establish an emotionally safe environment in the wake of a rape. Medical issues and legal options should be explored. It is vital that those around the survivor not reinforce societal blaming of the victim. Parents, devastated by what has happened, often close down the issue of the rape trauma. Male relatives, intimates, and friends frequently respond in a stereotypical fashion, becoming outraged and preoccupied with thoughts of revenge. Family therapy provides an opportunity for those closest to the survivor to express their feelings and provide genuine support for the victim.

Conflicts that frequently trigger violence such as jealousy, alcohol, disagreements about sexual intimacy, and verbal abuse generally reflect power inequities in couple relationships. It is important in working with young women to focus on how romantic ideals and acceptance of traditional gender roles may be influencing their tolerance of dating violence. Women with more traditional sex-role attitudes are more likely to stay in an abusive relationship. Acknowledging this can help make them conscious of the power dynamics in their relationships and the ways in which they may be controlled by their partners.

Stalking occurs more often than is commonly thought. Females are three times more likely to be stalked than males and young people have the highest rates of stalking and being stalked. The media have often portrayed stalking as romantic, but being the victim of stalking can be terrifying and lethal. Stalking can easily escalate to assault and victims suffer the same emotional trauma as other victims of sexual violence (CDC, 2011).

The term "sexual harassment" covers a wide range of behavior, from lewd remarks and dirty jokes to unwanted physical contact and rape. It takes place in the workplace, in schools, and in everyday social situations. An extremely high percentage of women will be harassed during their academic or working life. Women in traditionally male occupations suffer the most. Sexual harassment creates insecurity and a hostile, threatening work environment for women. Many are not sure how to respond and few file formal complaints. Clinical fallout includes self-blame, the loss of self-esteem, depression, and disempowerment. In practical terms, the therapist can act as a coach, rehearsing coping strategies and encouraging clients to get legal advice, learn about their companies' sexual harassment policies, and network with other women to empower themselves against the invalidation of such experiences.

A young man who had been arrested, but not convicted, for participating in a fraternity group rape of a woman at a college fraternity party, sought help in the early years of his marriage for depression and distancing from his wife. Among other interventions, he was coached to have an accountability session with his parents, his siblings, and his wife regarding his earlier participation in this behavior. His parents had initially minimized his actions and stopped discussing the assault as soon as the police backed off. He spoke to his family about his responsibility as a man to be different and to urge other men to be different so that in the future his children would grow up in a different world, where men would not commit such violence as "bravado" and women would not be vulnerable to assault. It would have been even more helpful if he could have notified his university, since we are now more aware of how commonly such experiences are a regular part of college life. It would have allowed him a specific place to be accountable, and perhaps prevented a few more such abusive experiences from happening.

Gay relationships are also plagued by courtship violence and acquaintance rape. Some studies indicate that there is an even higher rate of intimate partner violence in gay couples than in heterosexual couples (Finneran & Stephenson, 2013). This compounds the stress because it occurs within a homophobic environment that offers few resources and supports. Gay men and lesbians suffer the added insult of being victimized by hate crimes (NCAVP, 2008). The Anti-Violence Project (www.avp.org), a group that monitors such attacks, reports that there is an increase in hate crimes, mostly against young adults, whenever the media or political groups focus on the gay community.

Sexual harassment, courtship violence, and acquaintance rape are painful experiences that scar the psyches of their victims. They are experienced on a personal level but in a social environment that tolerates and even encourages their occurrence and denies the enormity of their impact. This promotes self-blame and erodes self-confidence, making it difficult for young people to accomplish the tasks intrinsic to young adulthood, such as becoming independent and developing careers and intimate relationships. Intervention to counter the posttraumatic stress of these abusive experiences can have long-range import for the life cycle of these young people.

> **Assess your comprehension of couples by completing this quiz.**

Families With Children

Childhood is a scary and dangerous phase for many American children. Every year, there are over 3.6 million reports of child abuse involving 6 million children. Every day, five children die due to maltreatment in the United States, the highest rate for any industrialized country (Brodowski, 2011). For half of American children, being hit and spanked will be a regular part of their lives from the time they are infants until they are well into their teens (Straus, 2001). Most Americans believe it is okay to spank a child. The dominant churches have strongly endorsed corporal punishment and it is legal in every state. In 19 states mostly in the north and south, hitting students with a paddle is considered an acceptable form of discipline in schools (De Nies, 2012).

The irony of corporal punishment is that it is almost invisible; it is seen as unremarkable because almost everyone has been spanked or spanks (Straus, 2001). Yet study after study has revealed the long-range negative impact of corporal punishment (Straus, Douglas, & Medeiros, 2014). Corporal punishment contributes to a sense of powerlessness, a lack of internalized moral standards, interfering with

the likelihood of graduating from college or earning a good income, and leading to more troubled and aggressive behavior on many dimensions.

Not spanking is in many ways much more conducive to the goals parents hope to attain by spanking (Straus, 2001). Non-spanking parents are less likely to ignore misbehavior and better able to maintain strong bonds with their children. It is in the home, at the hands of those who love them the most, that family members learn whether violence is morally acceptable.

In the United States, issues of childrearing have long been considered a private family matter, defined by one's culture. Parents are allowed to raise children any way they see fit. Conservative groups have always resisted the United States signing the United Nations Declaration of the Rights of the Child, fearing it would interfere with the parental right to spank children (CBS News, 2010).

We believe that children have innate rights. We urge that therapists examine their own values and help families examine theirs. The following list summarizes rights advocated by the United Nations and other child advocacy groups.

- All children have the same rights, no matter what their race, ethnicity, social class, gender, sexual orientation, religion, nationality, political status of their parents to grow up with dignity, free from exploitation, maltreatment both physical and emotional in a physically and spiritually healthy, safe environment.
- All children have the right to health care, education, housing, and other resources that ensure their well-being.
- All children have the right to special consideration because of their status as dependents, and even more care if handicapped.
- All children have the right to have their race, gender, religion, and sexual orientation accepted.

If we really believe in these rights, there are many changes we must bring about in our socialization for children and in our support for families and communities at this childrearing phase of life.

If violence has already been a dynamic in a couples' relationship, it is likely to increase when they have children. Indeed, it is quite common for men to begin abusing their wives during pregnancy (Weiss, Lawrence, & Miller, 2004). This may be because of the anticipated burdens of the child, because of the wife's new focus away from exclusive devotion to the husband, or perhaps because she is more dependent. Pregnancy also offers no protection from marital rape (Bergen, 1996; Russell, 1990). As their families grow, mothers may leave work because of the expense or lack of daycare, a situation that leaves them especially vulnerable.

Society imposes on mothers the immense task of protecting children, a responsibility impossible to fulfill, when they lack the resources or the power to do it. The effect of current legal practices is to hold battered women criminally responsible, that is, as perpetrators for their male partner's child abuse, while simultaneously classifying these women as assault victims (Barnett et al., 2005). Conversely, society rarely, if ever, holds fathers who fail to protect their children responsible. Nor are those who fail to pay child support usually charged with neglect or abandonment.

Children experiencing physical violence

It is estimated that up to 10 million children between the ages of 3 and 17 have witnessed parental violence, which is a form of child abuse as well (Straus & Steinmetz, 2006). Children growing up with violence have been found to be more aggressive with peers and may go on to abuse their own children or partners. Not surprisingly, they have fewer friends, more learning problems, and more hyperactivity and anxiety (Crosson-Tower, 2010).

Child abuse occurs in all cultures, races, and economic groups. Sadly, the highest rates are among the youngest and poorest children and those who are disabled. Perpetrators of child abuse are usually parents or stepparents who are struggling with addictions, emotional problems, poverty, and other stresses (Crosson-Tower, 2010).

The abuse of children in violent homes tends to be ongoing, commonly as frequent as several times a week (Hamby, Finkelhor, Turner, & Ormond, 2010). Sometimes, their abuse becomes the turning point for their mothers; the abuse of the children is the most

common reason battered women give for deciding to leave their abuser (Hilton, 1992). Unfortunately, not being able to support those children is also the most common reason women return to an abusing partner (Gondolf & Fisher, 1988). Even if they are not the target, children who live in violent homes are at high risk of physical and psychological injury (Crosson-Tower, 2010). They often feel impelled to try to make peace between their parents or to protect whoever they see as the victim. This puts them in the direct line of fire. The lives of children who witness a parent's violence are filled with fear (Straus, Douglas, & Medeiros, 2014). In a sense, they lose both parents. Abusive fathers are usually emotionally distant, while abused mothers tend to be depressed, anxious, ill, and focused on the behavior of the abuser, having little emotional energy left for their children.

Child sexual abuse

Child sexual abuse is defined as interaction between a child and adult or an older child with the goal of the sexual gratification or stimulation of the perpetrator. This covers a wide range of behaviors such as intercourse, fondling, viewing pornography, or posing for pornographic pictures. Because of the secretive nature of sexual abuse, it is believed that most incidents go unreported. Children are vulnerable to sexual abuse from earliest childhood. The most common abusers are family members and others known to the family. Most reports are about children between the ages of 9 and 11, but infants and toddlers are also abused. The rate for girls is at least three times higher than that for boys. Boys are even more reluctant to admit to sexual abuse than girls and are often perceived as less damaged by the experience. They are less likely to receive counseling or to be removed from their abusive homes (Masho & Anderson, 2009). Most victims of sexual abuse do not become perpetrators of sexual abuse and violence. But almost all perpetrators do have a history of having been sexually abused themselves. Men who abuse boys tend to victimize a much higher number than those who victimize girls. Children are often threatened by their abuser or made to feel that they have caused the abuse themselves. The long-term effects of sexual abuse include Post Traumatic Stress

Disorder, depression, anxiety, juvenile delinquency, aggressive behavior, substance abuse, suicide, and problems with sexual relations (Luthra et al., 2009). These problems may be exacerbated by the frequency of the abuse, the kind of sexual activity, the age at onset, the child–abuser relationship, the number of perpetrators, their gender, and whether or not the sexual abuse occurred within the context of other forms of abuse.

The role of the family at this stage in the life cycle is to provide a safe, supportive environment for the growth and nurturance of children. Violence and abuse are incongruent with these tasks. Roles are often reversed in violent homes, with children trying to protect their mother or siblings. Changes in these roles are often met with great resistance. The primary goal of therapy is to help the family create a safe environment for children by realigning and restructuring the power dynamics within the system. Mothers need to be supported and empowered to support their children and stand up for their rights.

Assessment of children's safety is not always easy and requires different skills and knowledge than those needed for work with adults. The therapist must be aware of the norms of development for young children. For example, certain behaviors, such as sexual play or victimization of other children, excessive masturbation, seductive behavior, and genital exposure, are associated with sexual abuse in both preschool and school-age children. Most mothers of incest victims take immediate steps to protect their children, often at great emotional cost to themselves. When there is sexual abuse, which is more often committed by fathers and even more by stepfathers, who play a central role in the emotional, financial, and psychological life of the family, children may feel that by seeking help, they are endangering the well-being of the entire family or even betraying someone they love. Other family members may blame the child for talking. It is essential in treating incest to acknowledge the positive aspects of the victim's and other family members' relationships with the abuser, while holding the perpetrator responsible for the abuse and its impact on the child and family. For this reason, treatment programs require that the perpetrator admit to his behavior before relationships can continue. Since protection of the child is paramount, they also require that the offending parent not have unsupervised access to the children.

Intervention begins with education

As our understanding of brain development grows, it becomes increasingly clear that abuse and trauma have a detrimental impact on the physical development of the brain (Perry, 2009). Children who are being physically abused may have learning problems, difficulty concentrating in school, or developmental delays (Barnett et al., 2005). Children who experience or witness abuse at home often exhibit aggressive behavior, which interferes with both their school and social life. Younger children may startle easily or revert to behaviors associated with an early stage of development. They may repeat events over and over again (Crosson-Tower, 2010). Attention needs to be paid to emotional issues underlying these problem behaviors. Very young children may not be able to express themselves verbally; older children often do not respond well to direct questions. Storytelling, family puppets, art and dolls can be effective in gathering information (Gil & Briere, 2006). Play therapy and group therapy help children develop their social skills and deal with their fears, anxiety, depression, and shame around issues of abuse.

Ideally, all family members, including the abuser, should be involved in treatment, although, of course, abusers should not be in discussion with their victims until they have an understanding of their behavior, so the therapy is always a several-stage process. Engagement of the perpetrator does not always happen, and participation in a program does not mean that the abuse will stop. Sometimes, it is necessary for a woman to end the relationship to keep herself or her children safe. The maintenance of a safe home, acknowledging the importance of the abuser's relationships with all family members, and the separation of the abuser from the victim until it is certain that contact will not result in the revictimization of the child are guidelines that apply to work with physically and sexually abused children and those who witness domestic violence.

Therapists should have an understanding of a family's ethnic patterns, parenting beliefs, and stress levels. They should explore support systems, including extended family and friends, who might be incorporated into treatment plans. While legal definitions of child abuse vary from state to state, all have mandatory reporting laws, requiring clinicians to notify the authorities if they suspect abuse. It is important for a clinician to understand these laws and to know what kind of services child protective agencies can offer in their area. Families with young children need to know that therapists will be required to take action if the family discloses psychological, physical, or sexual abuse.

Many parents feel that the use of physical punishment is an appropriate way of disciplining a child and are not aware of how dangerous this can be, especially with young children. Sometimes, they have unrealistic expectations about how a child should behave. The clinician can coach parents on managing problem behaviors and help them develop a sense of competency in dealing with their children. Battered women often underestimate the amount of violence their children see. When helped realize how it affects the children, they usually take steps to reduce their exposure.

Women with young children who try to leave their abuser may face seemingly insurmountable obstacles. Cultural norms pressure women not to break up the family, and the extended family, especially that of the abusive husband, may not be supportive of her decision to leave. Mothers do not always receive child support, and many are impoverished by divorce. Courts frequently refuse to consider spousal abuse an issue when considering custody. Abusive husbands often try manipulating the legal system to their advantage in custody, alimony, child support, and visitation negotiations (Hayes 2012). Finally, the woman's safety may be in great jeopardy when she separates. These times are, in fact, the periods when they are most at risk for increased violence and fatal assault. Harassment, threats, and abuse may continue in spite of divorce, separation, or restraining orders.

Bullying and cyber bullying

All children and young people are vulnerable to bullying. They may be targeted for something as arbitrary as wearing the wrong sneakers or liking the wrong band. But research indicates those most at risk are those who are different in some way, such as their looks, race, religion, ethnicity, disability, or who do not conform to gender norms or are Gay, Bisexual, Lesbian, or Transgender. Sadly those who are maltreated at home are also more likely to be victimized and to be bullies (Goldman, 2012; Georgiou & Stavrinides, 2013).

Bullying can be minor or terroristic, resulting in serious injury or death. Its impact can be devastating and long lasting. It is associated with poorer performance in school and a higher dropout rate, depression, suicide, and substance abuse (Bonanno & Hymel, 2013; Cornell, Gregory, Huang, & Fan 2013). In the age of computers and cell phones, there is no safe refuge from bullying. Young people threatened or beaten at school may find themselves under continuous psychological assault through their 24-hour Internet connection wherever they go (Jones, Mitchell, & Finkelhor, 2013).

Attitudes about bullying have changed. This may be because of the widespread publicity surrounding suicides associated with online bullying and the increasing research that demonstrates the lifelong damage it causes. Bullying is no longer seen as a painful rite of passage. It is no longer considered unpreventable. Many states now have laws against bullying and many school systems have put anti-bullying campaigns in place. These efforts seem to have met with some success. Studies indicate that children can be taught how to deal with online harassment, and to be conscientious onlookers and report bullying incidents (Fenaughty & Harre, 2013). Therapists should be aware of school policies on bullying and of available resources. Parents often also need help in dealing with a child who is being bullied. Well-meaning attempts to help can sometimes make matters worse. That is what happened in the Martin family:

Tommy, age 6, was brought to therapy by his parents, Michael and Judy, because he was being bullied at school and the school was not protecting him. He did not conform to gender norms at home or at school. His family had fairly rigid ideas about men and woman. He wanted to play with Barbie dolls and dress up in sparkly clothing. His father, Michael, was trying to help him in the best way he knew how by pressuring him to embrace "masculine" ideals, meaning playing with guns and cars, but this was getting nowhere. Viewing Tommy's interests as misbehavior, Michael's responses were getting harsher. He was thus subtly conveying to Tommy that being himself was not okay. Unintentionally Michael was reinforcing Tommy's fears about himself. The therapist helped Tommy's parents understand their part in undermining their son's sense of self. This gave them the chance to explore their own feelings about gender norms. As they considered incidents from their own lives, where they had each experienced bullying (Michael for being dyslexic and Judy as the only Jewish girl in her classes in elementary school), they began to see Tommy and their own experiences in a different light. They became more able to help him cope with the bullying in ways that did not involve physical retaliation. They also contacted the school, a strategy they had not considered previously, because they assumed they could handle the issue themselves.

> Assess your comprehension of families with children by completing this quiz.

Families With Adolescents

For many years, the primary focus on violence during adolescence was on juvenile delinquency, but teenagers have the highest risk of any age group of being victims of abuse at home and of violent crime outside their homes. One quarter of all substantiated reports of child abuse involve young people between the ages of 12 and 17 (Brodowski, 2011). As adolescents strive for independence, explore their sexuality, and begin to develop new identities, parents can no longer protect them from the world outside their family and often have more difficulty as children rebel and question their authority. In family systems where power and control are central dynamics, these conflicts easily escalate into violence. Straus (2001) reports that one third of daughters and 43 percent of sons recall being hit in their homes more than six times a year during their adolescence. Physical punishment and abuse for this age group has been

greatly underestimated, perhaps because adolescents are thought to be more able to defend themselves, or to deserve the punishments they receive. Young people from violent homes often leave home prematurely, and are likely to get into trouble.

Many teenagers also face abuse and violence at schools and in their communities, and the risk is greater for those who are poor, African American, Latino, or American Indian. The statistics are truly alarming. African American adolescents are five times more likely to be killed by a gun than White teens, and the discrepancy is even higher for American Indians (Wordes & Nunez, 2002). Children and teens are 17 times more likely to die of gun violence in the United states than in other high-income countries (Children's Defense Fund, 2013), and of these, 45 percent of teen deaths are of African Americans (though they represent only 15 percent of that age group). African Americans are actually 17 times as likely to die of gun homicide as White children of the same age (Children's Defense Fund, 2013). Teenagers who live in high-crime areas are not only more frequently victimized, but they also witness more violence, which can have severe psychological consequences. Very few inner-city families go through adolescence without personally experiencing a violent death or injury (Cruz & Taylor, 2008).

Assessment

Eliana Gil (1994) distinguishes between abuse that begins during adolescence and abuse that continues from childhood. Adolescents who have grown up in a supportive environment but experienced abuse in adolescence due to behavior problems, family crises, or parental stress can generally be helped through family and group treatment focused on communication, limit setting, parenting skills, and boundaries. Where there is a lifelong history of cumulative abuse, intervention will need to be much more extensive, involving re-socialization of the abusive family members and bringing about change in the social context for adolescents, or the pattern is unlikely to change. Such adolescents tend to suffer from depression, poor self-esteem, and anxiety and may have trouble developing social skills. In school, they are more likely to have behavioral and attention problems. Their frustration and pain are often expressed through acting-out behaviors and they are at greater risk for drug, alcohol abuse, and delinquency (Barnett et al., 2005). Joining a gang may become an appealing option. Gangs serve as a pseudo-family, providing protection, power, status, and in some cases profit. Members usually share the same racial and ethnic background. This can reinforce cultural identity, especially for minority group adolescents. Though usually thought of as an inner-city problem, gangs are expanding in suburban and rural areas, reflecting a widespread disconnection among young people, which can only be responded to by adults in every community joining forces to offer them meaningful pathways through life (Hardy & Laszloffy, 2005).

Gay and lesbian adolescents have an especially difficult time as they struggle with sexual identity. Those who do come out are sometimes ostracized and risk abandonment by their families and verbal and physical assault by their peers. Those that do not come out tend to suffer in silence.

Intervention

Adolescents can be defiant and resistant to therapy. It is important to avoid power struggles with them, give them space to discuss their many thoughts and feelings without immediate challenge, and set clear boundaries that can help them develop trusting relationships. Nonverbal forms of therapy, such as art, music, drama, as well as group therapy can be especially helpful. Family assessment is essential to ascertain the context in which the adolescent is operating and the resources that can be brought to bear. But it generally makes sense to work separately with parents and with the adolescent until parents have enough sense of control and protection to work together with their children in an exploratory discussion. Parents and other caretakers will need to be engaged in treatment to understand the role they need to play in solving the youth's problems. Until they understand this, they are likely to mistakenly get into arguments and power struggles with their adolescents, but then feel undermined if corrected in front of them, so joint sessions should be care-

fully structured and controlled. Gil (1996) recommends establishing an alliance through individual work with the adolescent before beginning conjoint family therapy, which should be undertaken cautiously and only when the teen can handle the work and the family is able to be accountable. Usually exploring family of origin patterns during their own adolescence reveals a history of previous abuse that can help parents gain perspective on their behavior. Therapists who work with adolescent clients must not make assumptions about their sexual orientation, but rather question and provide information about human sexuality in a supportive open-ended way. Clinicians should make use of community organizations available to meet the special needs of young people.

The interventions required for adolescents who have a long history of experiencing and witnessing abusive behaviors, as with serious addictions, will require changes of context: who they spend time with, what they spend their time doing, and where they socialize. In addition, as with addictions, individual interventions are not adequate for changing such socially disruptive behaviors.

 Assess your comprehension of families with adolescents by completing this quiz.

Families at Midlife

Midlife is a time of major change. As children leave home, husbands and wives need to renegotiate their relationships with each other, their adult children, and their parents. Men's careers are often at their peak. At the same time, women freed from child care responsibilities may refocus on developing their professional skills and interests. This is also a time of losses. Our culture's pairing of youth with beauty leaves little room for middle-aged women, whose attractiveness may have been a prime source of self-esteem and power. The loss of children can be painful, especially for women whose sole focus was on the home and childrearing, and who fear being left alone in an abusive relationship.

Incidents of physical abuse may decline at this phase of the life cycle, yet women are more likely to be murdered by their partners at this phase than at any other phase (Violence Policy Center, 2012). Husbands at midlife may be experiencing even more frustration than when they were younger as they see their relationships as well as their work life leading to disappointment. Overt acts of violence may no longer be needed as the abusive partner's control maybe well established. The spouse's verbal and psychological abuse, though less noticeable, may continue. Threats, continuous criticism, outbursts of rage, and jealousy can all be used to keep a wife alert and focused on the needs of her husband. Such behavior is especially effective if it is combined with occasional expressions of love and if the victim is isolated from friends, family, and other sources of support (Schwartz et al., 2000). Years of psychological abuse take their toll. Midlife women in abusive relationships often suffer from low self-esteem, feelings of powerlessness, major depression, anxiety, and posttraumatic stress. Their health is often compromised. Middle aged and older women who have been victims of domestic violence have higher overall mortality than those who have not (Baker et al., 2009).

Intervention

An important part of work with women at this stage is identifying the abuse. The most widely held image of a battered woman is that of a young mother with small children. Professionals usually do not consider domestic violence and psychological abuse when assessing a woman at this stage. Doctors do not adequately question pat explanations of bruises and injuries. Clients themselves may have become so used to the way they are treated that they do not consider the relationship abusive. Those with traditional attitudes may consider it normal for a man to "lose his temper now and then." Sharing a definition of abuse (see Figure 25.1) is useful in detecting

Figure 25.1 U.S. Government definition of domestic violence.

We define domestic violence as a pattern of abusive behavior in any relationship that is used by one partner to gain or maintain power and control over another intimate partner. Domestic violence can be physical, sexual, emotional, economic, or psychological actions or threats of actions that influence another person. This includes any behaviors that intimidate, manipulate, humiliate, isolate, frighten, terrorize, coerce, threaten, blame, hurt, injure, or wound someone.

Physical Abuse: Hitting, slapping, shoving, grabbing, pinching, biting, hair pulling, etc., are types of physical abuse. This type of abuse also includes denying a partner medical care or forcing alcohol and/or drug use upon him or her.

Sexual Abuse: Coercing or attempting to coerce any sexual contact or behavior without consent. Sexual abuse includes, but is certainly not limited to, marital rape, attacks on sexual parts of the body, forcing sex after physical violence has occurred, or treating one in a sexually demeaning manner.

Emotional Abuse: Undermining an individual's sense of self-worth and/or self-esteem is abusive. This may include, but is not limited to, constant criticism, diminishing one's abilities, name-calling, or damaging one's relationship with his or her children.

Economic Abuse: Is defined as making or attempting to make an individual financially dependent by maintaining total control over financial resources, withholding one's access to money, or forbidding one's attendance at school or employment.

Psychological Abuse: Elements of psychological abuse include, but are not limited to, causing fear by intimidation; threatening physical harm to self, partner, children, or partner's family or friends; destruction of pets and property; and forcing isolation from family, friends, or school and/or work.

more subtle types of abuse. Not all women at this stage are in long-term relationships. Sometimes, abuse starts in a second marriage. For many, though, their marriage represents an investment of 20 or 30 years. Divorce and separation can seem like a negation of everything they value. Groups are especially helpful for women struggling with these issues and for raising consciousness about the nature of psychological and physical dominance, while providing them the support and resources to confront it. Groups also combat isolation and build self-esteem.

A major concern for midlife women is finances. They may fear losing their home and health insurance if they leave. Abusive men often insist on maintaining total control of the family finances (Dunlop et al., 2005). It is not unusual for wives not to know what the couple's financial assets are or even how to manage a checkbook. The therapist should assess what skills the woman needs to develop in order to gain confidence in her ability to function independently from a husband who has fostered her dependence.

Relationships with adult children may be strained if midlife women decide to leave their marriages. Even children who have spent a lifetime watching their mother be victimized often become emotionally distant, in part fearing that she will now become dependent on them. They may feel that she deserves the abuse ("She's always nagging Dad"), or become psychologically abusive to their mother themselves. Although they may have urged their mother to leave for years, they can also have great difficulty letting her go or changing their perception of their parents' marriage. All of these issues need to be addressed to enable adult children to support their mothers' efforts and at the same time try to renegotiate their relationships with their fathers as well. Unfortunately, abusive men at this stage, as at other phases in the life cycle, often use their children to control and manipulate their wives, sometimes threatening them with emotional or financial abandonment.

Older families

Many changes occur with aging that make older adults more vulnerable to abuse. The oppression of ageism is more than an attitude or belittling images that portray older people as senile or helpless. It is the denial of employment opportunities and the cutting of pension plans. It can be seen over and over again in the lack of services and resources such as housing and appropriate medical care that enable people to maintain their independence as they age.

Although for the most part Americans are living longer and are healthier than ever before, many suffer from health problems that interfere with their ability to function independently (Werner, 2011). Their decline in physical and cognitive functioning puts them at greater risk for abuse (Dong, Simon, & Evans, 2012, 2013; Dong, Simon, Rajan, & Evans, 2011). Support networks dwindle as people age and this also increases their risk (Luo &Waite, 2011). Studies have indicated that as many as 10 percent of adults over 65 have been abused and 90 percent of their abusers are family members. The physical and psychological damage of elder abuse has far reaching consequences. Those who are abused have a higher rate of depression, medical problems, and mortality (Acierno et al., 2010).

The Administration on Aging defines elder abuse as intentional action by a caretaker, or person in a trust relationship that causes harm or serious risk to a vulnerable elder. This may take the form of physical, psychological, verbal, financial, sexual abuse, or neglect.

Elder abuse is sometimes attributed to the intense stress that caretakers experience while caring for an older adult, especially someone with dementia. Perpetrators may be a spouse/partner, adult child, or other caregiver. Education, support, respite, and coping techniques are part of the paradigm of treatment in these situations. In practice, distinguishing between long-standing domestic violence and abuse related to care giver stress can be difficult to discern, but making that distinction is vital. Treatment plans designed to reduce caregiver stress can actually end up blaming the victim and supporting the abuser ("She's so difficult to care for that I just lost my patience"). It is important to do a careful history to determine if abuse has been part of a life-long pattern or a recent occurrence.

Spousal mistreatment at earlier life cycle stages often foreshadows elder abuse, but the lack of such a history offers no guarantee. A woman may remarry into an abusive relationship and be too embarrassed to discuss the situation with friends or family. Events at this phase of life such as retirement, health problems, and decline in sexual functioning can increase tensions between long-term spouses, and make men whose identity is rooted in power and control feel threatened. Unfortunately, one of the easiest ways for them to feel empowered is by abusing family members, particularly their wives (Spangler & Brandl, 2007).

Adult children and other family members may not be good informants. Many adult children are embarrassed and ashamed of their parents' behavior or may not be aware of the abuse or really believe that their parent is in danger. After a lifetime of attempts to protect one parent from the other, they may blame the victim or be jaded and resent being asked to be a caregiver of the previously abusive parent.

For many older women, leaving their home and their abuser may not be a viable option because of their traditional/generational values. Like their midlife counterparts, older women often do not identify themselves as abused. Therapy can empower them by helping them recognize that what they are experiencing is abuse and addressing its lifelong consequences. Clinicians can help older women identify their strengths, and validate the importance of their work as wives and mothers, encouraging them when necessary to make safety plans and providing referral to local resources if they are available (Spangler & Brandl, 2007; Beaulaurier, Seff, & Newman, 2008).

Gay and Lesbian elders of this generation grew up when being Gay was a crime, and may have difficulty using services that are usually prescribed for older adults, fearing the common prejudice in traditional social support systems. They may require special legal counseling, since their relationships are often not legally recognized (Morrissey, 2010).

While battered women shelters are often willing to try to accommodate older woman, many are not set up to manage their complex care. The first shelter for older adults was started at the Hebrew Home for the Aged in 2005. It is affiliated to a nursing home and can accommodate both men and women. Since that time, a few more have opened throughout the country but nursing home placement is still the most common alternative for frail elders who can no longer live with their families. Many older adults dread the prospect of "being put away" so they will tolerate rather than report abuse. Their fear is not unrealistic. Adults in nursing home placement can, at times, also suffer physical and psychological abuse. But in reality, the greatest risk older adults face is from people who are dependent on them—such as adult children or spouses with a history of drug or alcohol abuse, mental illness, intellectual impairment, or economic problems (Lin & Giles 2013).

Mrs. Foley, an 83-year-old widow with diabetes, lived alone in her small suburban home. Her grandson Tom, 44 and recently divorced, relocated from another state and asked to live with her while he looked for a job. She welcomed him, but soon his behavior made her suspicious that he was using drugs and alcohol. He was sloppy, offered no help around the house, but resented any criticism from his grandmother and responded with a litany of complaints about how she had treated both him and his deceased mother. He continually told her she was crazy and if it wasn't for him she would be in a nursing home. By the time Mrs. Foley became aware that her grandson was stealing from her, she was too afraid and depressed to confront him, spending her time alone in her room. She began to lose weight and sometimes forgot her medication. Her plight was discovered only after she fell and was hospitalized for a broken hip. Her nurse observed how anxious she became before Tom's visits. When he showed up at the hospital drunk and was verbally abusive to his grandmother, the nurse called adult protective services. The worker interviewed Mrs. Foley, who was too fearful to admit to any problems. The worker then met with Tom, who became defensive, claiming his grandmother was senile and could not be believed. The social worker became more suspicious and interviewed Mrs. Foley's neighbors, who described Tom's comings and goings and expressed concern about Mrs. Foley. In time, once the social worker established rapport with her, Mrs. Foley began to confide her problems with Tom. She was given information about drug and alcohol addiction and made aware of her legal rights. Mrs. Foley started therapy, where she was able to deal with her feelings of guilt, depression, and powerlessness. Since she had no other children or grandchildren, the therapist encouraged her to connect with a niece and nephew, with whose support she was able to confront her grandson and threaten legal measures unless he left her home, which he did. She continued to have a warm and supportive relationship with her sister's children and became more involved with their families.

Sudden behavioral changes, including acts of physical abuse such as pushing, shoving, or lashing out, are often indicative of a medical problem that is impacting an individual's mood, cognition, and behavior. All cases of late-onset abuse require a careful medical and psychiatric assessment. The clinician should also study the dynamics of the couple. Warning signs are similar to those at other life cycle stages: verbal abuse, possessiveness, control of finances, and reluctance to allow the person to meet or speak separately. Unexplained bruises and injuries must be medically assessed, since older adults may take medications or have conditions that put them at higher risks for these signs. Those suffering from dementia are at greater risk for abuse, especially those who are aggressive toward their caregivers (Cooper et al., 2009; Wiglesworth et al., 2010).

Dementia raises particularly thorny problems in assessment, because patients may not be able to remember incidents of abuse, or they may suffer from paranoid delusions that focus on mistreatment at the hands of a family member. They may refuse to eat or bathe, putting the caregiver in the position of forcing them to cooperate or risk being charged with neglect. Episodes of sudden belligerence may require physical intervention and restraints that can result in bruises, which may give the appearance of physical abuse. Behavioral or personality changes, suspiciousness, withdrawal from previous activities, difficulty managing finances, getting lost, minor automobile accidents, neglect of personal hygiene, and other changes in daily activities may be the early signs of dementia. Often, family members do not recognize the significance of such changes and will make excuses or deny the extent of the deterioration.

Sometimes, they will interpret the older person's inability to function as willful and become angry or accuse him or her of being stubborn and spiteful. This is particularly difficult if the caregiver has previously had a conflicted relationship with the person. The professional can sometimes fall into the same trap and label an elder as uncooperative and unwilling to be helped when, in fact, the person's judgment may be too impaired to understand the need for help. A comprehensive evaluation to determine the patient's diagnosis and offering caregiver education are keys to successful work with dementia patients. An assessment and planning session with as many family members as possible is important, not only for clarifying the situation but also for supporting all family members in their shared responsibility and concern for the aging person.

The experience of caring for someone with dementia is physically and emotionally overwhelming. Husbands may not recognize their wives; mothers may not recognize their children. Basic skills such as bathing, reading, or writing are lost. Communication becomes more difficult as language skills become impaired. Piece by piece, the personality of the person with dementia seems to disappear; yet he or she is still there and requires an ever-increasing level of care. The continued decline of a family member despite the best efforts of those caring for the person causes feelings of inadequacy, helplessness, and anger. Validating the sadness, anger, frustration, and fear that caregivers often feel helps to counter their burnout and frustration. It is important to normalize and reframe the patient's behavior. For example, a patient with Alzheimer's disease repeatedly accused his 83-year-old spouse of having an affair. His wife was greatly relieved to learn that delusions of infidelity are common in people with dementia and that her husband had not secretly harbored doubts about her throughout their 50-year marriage. In family counseling, care giving tasks can be redistributed among family members. Options for the immediate situation and long-term care can be presented to everyone at the same time, and conflicts and concerns can be discussed openly. This helps the family to move forward as a whole and keeps the needs of an aging parent from becoming the point of contention among feuding relatives. Such approaches can actually help prevent abuse by relieving family and caregiver stress before it escalates. It may take time, support, and a great deal of encouragement for caregivers to utilize options.

Interventions and treatment goals with abused elders may need to include home visits and extensive telephone work. Clinicians must work with their clients' natural support systems. This may mean contacting the family doctor to understand health problems and the side effects of medication or asking a neighbor to provide respite. It may also mean advocating with community agencies, especially those that provide concrete services such as transportation or meals on wheels. Family work will focus on realigning relationships with adult children and the abuser, dealing with concerns about health and death and meeting everyday needs. Therapists must be aware of mandatory reporting laws for elder abuse and must be ready to work with agencies that investigate it.

> **Assess your comprehension of families at midlife by completing this quiz.**

— Conclusion

When we address the societal arrangements that foster violence and oppression throughout the life cycle, we are confronting norms and beliefs that are deeply rooted in the dominant culture. These inequities have been formalized in law and by religious institutions, as if they were sanctioned by God. They have become so widely accepted that they have rarely been noticed, much less questioned.

Victims of violence have more often been stigmatized than supported. They have little legal recourse, and they often receive little support or understanding even from their families and social circle. When we understand that violence is an abuse of power and recognize it in all its forms—physical, psychological, sexual, economic, political, and social oppression we become better able to contend with its distructive nature. Family therapists must focus not only on the particular emotional and psychological dynamics of individual relationships and family systems but also on the broader social forces on our clients throughout the life cycle that may encourage violence. We must enlarge our focus to support families to stop violence, develop nonviolent ways of resolving conflicts, and challenge the values that have promoted and allowed it to continue in our society.

> **Recall what you learned in this chapter by completing the Chapter Review.**

— References

Acierno, R., Hernandez, M. A., Amstadter, A. B., Resnick, H. S., Steve, K., Muzz, W. (2010). Prevalence and correlates of emotional, physical, sexual, and financial abuse and potential neglect in the United States: The National Elder Mistreatment Study. *American Journal of Public Health*, 100, 292–297.

Ahrens, C. E., Cabral, G., & Abeling, S. (2009). Healing or hurtful: Sexual assault survivors' interpretations of social reactions from support providers. *Psychology of Women Quarterly*, 33, 81–94.

Aosved, A., Long, P., & Voller, E. (2011). Sexual revictimization and adjustment of college men. *Psychology of Men and Masculinity*, 12(3), 285–296.

Baker, M., LaCroix, A., Wu, C., Cochrane, B., Wallace, R., & Woods, N. (2009). Mortality risk associated with physical and verbal abuse in women aged 50 to 79. *Journal of the American Geriatrics Society, 57*(10), 1799–1809.

Barnett, O. W., Miller-Perrin, C. L., & Perrin, R. D. (2005). *Family violence across the lifespan* (2nd ed.) Thousand Oaks, CA: Sage.

Beaulaurier, R., Seff, L., & Newman, F. (2008). Barriers to help-seeking for older women who experienced intimate partner violence: A descriptive model. *Journal of Women and Aging*, 20(3), 231–248.

Beneke, T. (1982). Men on rape: What they have to say about sexual violence. New York: St. Martin's Press.

Bergen, R. K. (1996). *Wife rape: Understanding the response of survivors and service providers.* Thousand Oaks, CA: Sage.

Bonanno, R. A., & Hymel, S . (2013). Cyber bullying and internalizing difficulties: Above and beyond the impact of traditional forms of bullying. *Journal of Youth and Adolescence*, No Pagination.

Brodowski, M. (2011). Child maltreatment, 2011. U.S. Department of Health & Human Services, Administration for Children and Families. Retrieved September 11, 2013, from http://www.acf.hhs.gov/sites/default/files/cb/cm11.pdf.

Burton, L. M. (2010). Uncovering hidden facts that matter in interpreting individuals' behaviors: An ethnographic lens. In B. J. Risman (Ed.), *Families as they really are* (pp. 20–23). New York: W. W. Norton.

Burton, L. M., Purvin, D., & Garrett-Peters, R. (2009). Longitudinal ethnography: Uncovering domestic abuse in low-income women's lives. In G. H. Elder Jr & J. Z. Giele (Eds.), The craft of life course research. New York: Guilford Press.

CBS News (2010). 31 GOP Senators oppose U.N. Children's Rights Convention. Retrieved September 11, 2013, from http://www.cbsnews.com/8301-503544_162-20014613-503544.html.

Children's Defense Fund (2013). Protect children, not guns, 2013. Retrieved October 11, 2013, from http://www.childrensdefense.org/child-research-data-publications/data/protect-children-not-guns-2013.pdf.

CDC (Centers for Disease Control and Prevention). (2011). National Intimate Partner and Sexual Violence Survey, 2010 Summary Report. Retrieved September 11, 2013, from http://www.cdc.gov/violenceprevention/pdf/cdc_nisvs_overview_insert_final-a.pdf.

Cooper, C., Selwood, A., Blanchard, M., Walker, Z., Blizard, R., & Livingston, G. (2009). Abuse of people with dementia by family carers: Representative cross sectional survey. *BMJ: British Medical Journal*, 338(7694), 1–5.

Cornell, D., Gregory, A., Huang, F., & Fan, X. (2013). Perceived prevalence of teasing and bullying predicts high school dropout rates. *Journal of Educational Psychology, 105*, 138–149. doi:10.1037/a0030416.

Crosson-Tower, C. (2010). *Understanding child abuse and neglect* (8th ed.). Boston, MA: Allyn & Bacon.

Cruz, M., & Taylor, D. (2008). Inner-city violence in the United States: What pediatricians can do to make a difference. *International Journal of Child and Adolescent Health, 2*(1), 3–12.

DeKeseredy, W. S. (2011). Violence against women: Myths fact controversy. Toronto, Canada: University of Toronto Press.

De Nies, Y. (2012). Should your child be spanked in school? In 19 states, it's legal. ABC News. Retrieved October 5, 2013, from http://abcnews.go.com/US/spanking-school-19-states-corporal-punishment-legal/story?id=15932135.

Dong, X, Simon, M., & Evans, D. (2013). Elder selfneglect is associated with increased risk for elder abuse in a community-dwelling population: Findings from the Chicago Health and Aging Project. [References]. *Journal of Aging and Health*, 25(1), 80–96.

Dong, X., Simon, M., & Evans, D. (2012). Decline in physical function and risk of elder abuse reported to social services in a community-dwelling population of older adults. *Journal of the American Geriatrics Society*, 60,1922–1928.

Dong, X., Simon, M., Rajan, K. & Evans, D. A. (2011). Association of cognitive function and risk for elder abuse in a community-dwelling population. *Dementia and Geriatric Cognitive Disorders, 32*(3), 209–215.

Dunlop, B. D., Beaulaurier, R. L., Seff, L. R., Newman, F. L., Malik, N. & Fuster, M. (2005). *Domestic violence against older women: Final technical report 212349 U.S.* Department of Justice. Retrieved /13/13 from https://www.ncjrs.gov/pdffiles1/nij/grants/212349.pdf.

Fenaughty, J., & Harre, N. (2013). Factors associated with young people's successful resolution of distressing electronic harassment. *Computers & Education*, 61, 242–250.

Finkelhor, D. (2008). *Childhood victimization: Violence: Crime and abuse in the lives of young people (Interpersonal violence).* New York: Oxford University Press.

Finneran, C., & Stephenson, R. (2013). Intimate partner violence among men who have sex with men: A Systematic review. *Trauma Violence & Abuse, 14*(2), 168–185.

Georgiou, S. N., & Stavrinides, P. (2013). Parenting at home and bullying at school. *Social Psychology of Education*. doi:10.1007/s11218-012-9209-z.

Gil, E. (1994). *Play in family therapy.* New York: Guilford.

Gil, E. (1996). *Treating abused adolescents.* New York: Guilford.

Gil, E., & Briere, J. (2006). *Helping abused and traumatized children: Integrating directive and nondirective approaches.* New York: Guilford.

Goldman, C. (2012). Bullied: What every parent, teacher and kid needs to know about ending the cycle of fear. New York: Harper Collins.

Gondolf, E. W., & Fisher, E. R. (1988). *Battered women as survivors: An alternative to treating learned helplessness.* Lexington, MA: Lexington.

Gosselin, D. K. (2010). *Heavy hands: An introduction to the crime of intimate family violence* (4th ed.). Englewood Cliffs, NJ: Prentice Hall.

Hamby, S., Finkelhor, D., Turner, H., & Ormond, R. (2010). The overlap of witnessing partner violence with child maltreatment and other victimizations in a nationally representative survey of youth. *Child Abuse & Neglect, 34*(10), 734–741.

Hardy, K. V., & Laszloffy, T. A. (2005). *Teens who hurt: Clinical interventions for breaking the cycle of adolescent violence.* New York: Guilford.

Hayes, B. (2012). Abusive men's indirect control on their partner during the process of separation. *Journal of family Violence, 27*(4), 333–334.

Healy, J. (2013). Montana legal officials step in on rape case sentence. *New York Times*, September 6, 2013. Retrieved September 17, 2013, from http://www.nytimes.com/2013/09/07/us/montana-legal-officials-step-in-on-rape-case-sentence.html?_r=1&.

Hilton, Z. (1992). Battered women's concerns about their children witnessing wife assault. *Journal of Interpersonal Violence, 7*(1), 77–86.

Holder, E. (2013). Domestic Violence Homicide Prevention Initiative Announcement. U.S. Department of Justice. Retrieved September 11, 2013, from http://www.justice.gov/iso/opa/ag/speeches/2013/ag-speech-130313.html

Jones, L. M, Mitchell, K. J., & Finkelhor, D. (2013). Online harassment in context: Trends from three Youth Internet Safety Surveys (2000, 2005, 2010). *Psychology of Violence*, 3, 53–69. doi:10.1037/a0030309.

Kimmel, M. S. (2011). *Manhood in America: A cultural history* (3rd ed.). New York: Free Press.

Kimmel, M. S. (2013). *The gendered society* (5th ed.). New York: Oxford University Press.

Kimmel, M. S., & Aronson, A. (2013). The gendered society reader (5th ed.). New York: Oxford University Press.

Lin, M., & Giles, H. (2013). The dark side of family communication: a communication model of elder abuse and neglect. *International Psychogeriatrics, 25*(8), 1275–1290.

Luo, Y., & Waite, L. J. (2011). Mistreatment and psychological well-being among older adults: Exploring the role of psychosocial resources and deficits. *The Journal of Gerontology: Series B: Psychological Sciences and Social Sciences*, 66B(2), 217–229.

Luthra, R., Abramovitz, R., Greenberg, R., Schoor, A., Newcorn, J., Schmeidl, J., Levine, P., Nomura, Y., & Chemtob, C. (2009). Relationship between type of trauma exposure and posttraumatic stress disorder among urban children and adolescents. *Journal of Interpersonal Violence, 24*(11), 1919. Retrieved December 26, 2009, from ProQuest Social Science Journals. (Document ID: 1870505741).

Macmillan, R., &Kruttschnitt, C. (2005). Patterns of violence against women: Risk factor and consequences. U.S. Department of Justice, National Institute of Justice, Document # 208346.Washington, DC. Retrieved September 9, 2013, from https://www.ncjrs.gov/pdffiles1/nij/grants/208346.pdf.

Masho, S. W., & Anderson L. (2009). Sexual assault in men: A population-based study of Virginia. *Violence and Victims, 24*(1), 98–110.

Morrissey, C. (2010). Abuse of lesbian, gay transgender and bisexual elder. In G. Gloria & S. Charmaine (Eds.), Aging, ageism and abuse: Moving from awareness to action (45-51 xv100 pp). San Diego, CA: Elsevier Academic Press.

NCAVP (National Coalition of Anti-Violence Programs). (2008). *Lesbian, gay, bisexual and transgender domestic violence in the United States in 2007.* Retrieved August 8, 2009, from www.avp.org/documents/2007NCAVPDVREPORT.pdf.

New York Office of the Prevention of Domestic Violence; National Data on Intimate Partner Violence. (2011). Retrieved September 11, 2013, from http://opdv.state.ny.us/statistics/nationaldvdata/nationaldvdata.pdf.

Paradis, A., Reinherz, H., Giaconia, R., Beardslee, W., Ward, K., & Fitzmaurice, G. (2009). Long-term impact of family arguments and physical violence on adult functioning at age 30 years: Findings from the Simmons longitudinal study. *Journal of the American Academy of Child & Adolescent Psychiatry, 48*(3), 290–298.

Perry, B. (2009) Examining child maltreatment through a neurodevelopmental lens: Clinical applications of the neurosequential model of therapeutics. *Journal of Loss and Trauma, 14*(4), 240–255.

Russell, D. E. H. (1990). *Rape in marriage.* Indianapolis, IN: Indiana University Press.

Schwartz, A., Anderson, S., Strasser, T. J., & Boulette, T. (2000). Psychological maltreatment of spouses. In M. Hersen & R. Ammerman (Eds.), *Case studies in family violence* (pp. 349–374). New York: Plenum Press.

Spangler, D., & Brandl, B. (2007). Abuse in later life: Power and control dynamics and a victim-centered response. *Journal of the American Psychiatric Nurses Association, 12*(6), 322–331.

Straus, M. A. (2001). *Beating the devil out of them: Corporal punishment in American families.* Edison, NJ: Transaction Publishers.

Straus, M. A., Douglas, E. M., & Medeiros, R. A., (2014). The primordial violence: Spanking children, psychological development, violence and crime. New York: Routledge.

Straus, M. A., & Steinmetz, S. (2006). *Behind closed doors: Violence in the American family.* Edison, NJ: Transaction Publishers.

Swartout, K. (2013). The company they keep: How peer networks influence male sexual aggression. *Psychology of Violence*, 3(2), 157–171.

Todahl, J., & Walter, E. (2011). Universal screen for intimate partner violence: A systemic review. *Journal of Marital and Family Therapy*, 37(3), 355–369.

U. S. Department of Justice. (2013). What is domestic violence? *Office of Violence Against Women,* Retrieved July 31, 2013, from http://www.ovw.usdoj.gov/domviolence.htm.

Veterans for Peace. (2013). A woman in the military is more likely to be raped than killed. Retrieved July 31, 2013, from http://vfpvc.org/a-woman-in-the-military-is-more-likely-to-be-raped-than-killed/.

Violence Policy Center. (2012). When men murder women: An analysis of 2010 homicide data. Retrieved September 9, 2013, from http://www.vpc.org/studies/wmmw2012.pdf.

Washington, E. L. (2007). Female socialization: How daughters affect their legislator fathers' voting on women's issues. *American Economic Review, 86*(3), 425–441.

Weiss, H., Lawrence B., & Miller, T. (2004). Pregnancy-associate assault hospitalizations prevalence and risk of hospitalized assaults against women during Prenancy. Washington, DC: US Department of Justice 1998—National Institute of Justice NCJ 199706.

Werner, C.A. (2011). The older population : 2010 Census Briefs, U.S. Department of Commerce, Economics and Statistics Administration, U.S. Census Bureau Nov C201BR-09. Retrieved September 10, 2013, from http://www.census.gov/prod/cen2010/briefs/c2010br-09.pdf.

Wiglesworth, A., Mosqueda, L., Mulnard, R., Liao, S., Gibbs, L., & Fitzgerald, W. (2010). Screening for abuse and neglect of people with dementia. *Journal of the American Geriatrics Society*, 58(3), 493–500.

Wordes, M., & Nunez, M. (2002). *Our vulnerable teenagers: Their victimization, its consequences, and directions for prevention and intervention.* Oakland, CA: National Council on Crime and Delinquency.

Chapter 26

Creating Meaningful Rituals for New Life Cycle Transitions

Evan Imber-Black

Learning Outcomes

- Explain the function and importance of rituals during life cycle changes.
- Describe the importance of creating rituals as a developmental task for couples.
- Examine how new or novel life cycle transitions in families can be eased with new or adapted rituals.
- Discuss how life cycle derailment can lead to the development of symptoms in family members.
- Describe the efficacy of therapeutic rituals in facilitating systemic change in families.
- Explore the use and effects of therapeutic healing rituals.
- Discuss the functions of identity redefinition rituals.
- List and describe the process of designing and implementing rituals for new life cycle transitions.

Introduction

Every culture makes rituals. Anchoring us with the past and where each of us comes from, while simultaneously moving us into the future, rituals capture and express the duality of continuity and change and constancy and transformation, required for families and cultures.

The capacity of rituals to both make and mark transitions makes them especially salient for life cycle changes. Life cycle events and transitions such as birth, marriage, and death are most frequently marked with familiar rituals. Many religious and ethnic groups also have rituals to mark young adult development (e.g., bar mitzvah, confirmation, or quincinera), or such development may be marked by secular rituals such as graduation. These rituals, while often seen as discrete events, such as *the* wedding and *the* christening or baby naming, are in actuality processes that occur over time, involving advance preparation and reflection afterward. Choices about who participates in the planning and execution of a life cycle ritual reflect family relationship patterns. Negotiations that occur during the preparation for

life cycle rituals may be opportunities to change such patterns. Thus, such rituals may be seen as the visible and condensed drama of the life cycle transitions that they mark.

Relying on symbols, metaphors, and actions that may have multiple meanings, life cycle rituals function to reduce anxiety about change. According to Schwartzman (1982), rituals make change manageable, as members experience change as part of their system rather than as a threat to it. Similarly, Wolin and Bennett (1984) suggest that rituals contribute to a family's identity and its sense of itself over time, facilitating the elaboration of roles, boundaries, and rules. Imber-Black and Roberts (1998) have delineated how rituals define family and group membership; heal losses; maintain and/or change individual, family, and cultural identity; express core beliefs; and facilitate the celebration of life. Rituals enable us to hold and express contradictions. Thus, a wedding marks the loss of particular roles in the families of origin while at the same time marking the beginnings of the new couple and in-law relationships. Since the ritual event is time and space bounded, a safe and manageable context for the expression of strong emotions is created. Rituals marking life cycle transitions function at many levels, enabling individual change (e.g., from adolescent to young adult, from single adult to married adult), relationship change (e.g., from parent–child to two adults, from dating couple to married couple), family system change (e.g., expansion through the addition of members or contraction through members leaving), and family–community change (e.g., graduation marks not only a child's leaving school but also a change in the family's relationship to larger systems; a retirement party marks not only a person's ending work but also a change in the family's relationship to the outside world). Rituals may connect a family with previous generations, providing a sense of history and rootedness, while simultaneously implying future relationships. The performance and participation in such rituals link a family to the wider community through the repetition of familiar rites.

The critical importance of rituals in our lives is evident in the responses of oppressed people when rituals are forbidden to them. African Americans held in slavery were not permitted to marry. They created their own secret wedding ceremony, "jumping the broom," to mark a committed relationship. Jewish women in Nazi concentration camps turned conversations with each other into remembering rituals and wrote out recipes for rich and delicious food in the midst of forced starvation. In so doing, they proclaimed connections to their villages, their faith, and their families (DeSilva, 1996).

Creating Rituals as a Developmental Task for Couples

Among the many developmental tasks facing any new couple is creating rituals. Coming from different families of origin, members of a couple often encounter differences in preferred and familiar rituals of everyday life, such as meals or greeting each other at the end of a busy day, family traditions such as birthdays or anniversaries, and holiday celebrations. Struggles over how to perform rituals are a lens through which couples can learn about each other's family of origin. Such struggles are particularly challenging for couples coming from different religions, ethnic groups, or social classes. While a couple may be able to create an interfaith wedding, they may discover that rituals that mark the birth of children, celebrate religious holidays, or remember the dead with an interfaith funeral become the crucible for working out loyalties to extended family and current differentiated beliefs and identities.

Gay and lesbian couples may face unique challenges where rituals are concerned. While legal marriage has begun in a few states, most gay and lesbian couples still must create innovative rituals to mark a committed relationship. Many gay and lesbian couples find that they have acceptance and support from the extended family of one partner but not from both, leading them to adopt the rituals of only one partner while the other partner's legacy gets lost. Therapy with gay and lesbian couples should include conversations about meaningful rituals starting from the premise that each is bringing an encyclopedia of rituals from which to choose ways to make new meaning together.

Jerry Corbell and Stan Best had lived together for 15 years. Since Jerry's family had rejected him, all of Stan and Jerry's holidays were celebrated only with Stan's family. Jerry felt so much pain over his family's cut off that he abandoned all familiar rituals from his own childhood, leaving him with the double loss of family relationships and family rituals. The rituals with Stan's family, while warm and caring, were at the same time a sharp reminder of his losses. In our therapy, I suggested that Jerry's parents' rejection did not mean that Jerry needed to lose meaningful rituals that belonged to him. Rather, he needed to reclaim and alter those rituals to fit his present life. Jerry began by unpacking key symbolic objects that he had hidden away—his grandmother's candlesticks from Eastern Europe, Christmas ornaments that his aunt had given him every year as a child, and a card file of recipes of his favorite dishes from his family of origin. Over time, Jerry and Stan integrated these special symbols into their ritual life together.

Many couples seeking therapy today come with multiple differences in religion, ethnicity, race, and social class. Often, the couple has not identified these differences as a source of difficulty, yet their struggles and conflicts over rituals will mirror these. Nonconfrontational conversation about each one's ritual life is often an excellent entry point, enabling couples to see the power of their own heritage in the present. Any therapy with bicultural couples must spend time helping the couple examine each one's history with rituals and negotiate meaningful rituals for their lives together.

> **Assess your comprehension of creating rituals as a developmental task for couples by completing this quiz.**

Contemporary Life Cycle Transitions

While all individuals and families experience some normative life cycle transitions and participate in rituals that facilitate these transitions, many individuals and families are faced with life cycle transitions that are new or novel. The seemingly different or unusual nature of these transitions often means they are not marked by rituals or may have rituals that simply do not fit the circumstances and need to be adapted. For instance, when Sherry and Bruce Callahan had their first baby, they planned a christening that was exactly like all such rituals, with the addition of one aspect. Their baby had been conceived through assisted insemination with donor sperm. They decided well before their baby's birth that they did not want their use of new birth technologies to be a secret that part of their family knew and others did not know. They also wanted to be able to speak about this easily with their child when the time came and not allow it to be a taboo subject. In our therapy, we talked of ways to adapt the christening ritual to include the fact of donor insemination. They decided that after the christening, Bruce would speak to all assembled, publicly thanking their anonymous donor for helping them to have the precious gift of their baby. Bruce told me later, "I was so scared to say those words, but when I did, any shame I had previously felt just lifted and flew out of the church" (Imber-Black & Roberts, 1998).

New life cycle transitions may include bicultural marriage; gay or lesbian marriage; families formed by adoption, especially when there is overt or covert nonsupport from family members; families formed by new birth technologies; the birth of a handicapped child; the birth or adoption of a child by an unmarried mother or father; pregnancy loss; forced separation through hospitalization, imprisonment, or terror; reunion after such forced separations; migration; living-together relationships; the end of nonmarried relationships; foster placement and the reunion after foster placement; sudden, unexpected, or violent death, including suicide; the leaving home of a mentally or physically handicapped young adult, especially when this leaving has not been anticipated; and chronic, incapacitating illness. This list, which is intended to be suggestive rather than exhaustive, is shaped by broad social processes that may change over time and may differ with various cultural and socioeconomic groups. For example, pregnancy outside of a legal marriage may or may not be an idiosyncratic life cycle event with all of the aspects described below attendant to it, depending on the norms of the family, the family's reference group, and the response of the wider community. While the list mentioned earlier may seem an unusual combination, all have several elements in common:

- Familiar, repetitive, and widely accepted rituals do not exist to facilitate required changes and to link individual, family, and community.
- All require complex reworking of relationships, similar to normative life cycle transitions, but lack the available maps that attend to more expected transitions.
- Contextual support from family of origin, the community, and the wider culture is often lacking. Individual and family events and processes are not confirmed by family of origin, larger systems, and the community.
- A balance of being both like others (e.g., a family with a severely handicapped member shares many features with other families) and being unlike others (e.g., a family with

a severely handicapped member has certain aspects of their functioning that are different from those of other families) is often difficult to achieve, resulting in a skewed sense of either denying the differences or maximizing them to the exclusion of a sense of connectedness with others.

- A sense of stigma is often experienced because of prejudice from the wider community. This, in turn, may lead to the emergence of secrets and conspiracies of silence that constrain relationship possibilities.

- Involvement with larger systems is often problematic. Families with handicapped members, hospitalized members, imprisoned members, or fostered members are required to deal with larger systems in ways that alter family boundaries and relationships, often over many years. Families experiencing forced migration or migration for economic necessity are often involved with intimidating larger systems. Because family identity and sense of competency include reflections from larger systems with whom they interact, families with any of the idiosyncratic life cycle events and transitions listed earlier may be at greater risk of incorporating negative images.

- The family may abandon or interrupt familiar rituals that contribute to its sense of itself, especially if these elicit painful memories. For instance, after the loss of a member through sudden death, hospitalization, or imprisonment, members may avoid family rituals. Families that are unable to accept members' gay relationships or nonmarried heterosexual relationships may restrict participation in rituals. Paradoxically, such ritual abandonment or interruption prevents healing and relationship development.

CASE ILLUSTRATION

El Salvador and the Bronx

When the Torres family arrived at Bronx from El Salvador, Mrs. Torres; her son Manuel, age 13; and her daughter Maria, age 11 were coping with the recent death of Mr. Torres in the Salvadoran Civil War and recovering from their terrifying wartime experiences. They remained very close for the first 2 years but abandoned many familiar rituals from their culture. Since most of their rituals were communal or religious and depended on people from their own country, they struggled with little success to find ways to develop meaningful rituals. Simply meeting the demands of daily life in the Bronx took precedence.

The children quickly learned English in school. Mrs. Torres became worried that they would forget Spanish and forget that they were Salvadoran. She spoke to them in Spanish at home, but they insisted on responding in English. In a fairly typical pattern among parents and adolescents who have migrated, they were soon struggling, as Mrs. Torres wanted to talk about "home," while her children insisted that home was in the Bronx.

When I met the Torres family in family therapy, I suggested that they bring symbols in our next session—symbols of El Salvador and the Bronx. Mrs. Torres was very surprised to see that Manuel and Maria brought symbols of El Salvador that showed how connected they still were to their original home. The teens brought toys and photographs that their mother did not know they had kept. They talked with their mother about their memories, letting her know that they were involved with their homeland in deeply emotional ways. Their symbols from the Bronx included a music tape and a poster from a concert. Mrs. Torres listened respectfully to them and described what this music meant to them, replacing their usual arguments about North American music. Mrs. Torres brought food for both of her symbols, including her wonderful Salvadoran cooking and a small pizza to symbolize the Bronx and the arguments they had been having when her children wanted pizza instead of her ethnic dishes. The family and I sat and ate both foods together.

Following this ritual that enabled the holding and expressing of past and present, their prior life and their current life, and their losses and their surviving, the Torres family agreed to hold a weekly storytelling session at home to include Mrs. Torres' stories of El Salvador and Manuel and Maria's stories of the Bronx. Over time, the children also shared memories of El Salvador, and Mrs. Torres began to tell stories of her daily life in the Bronx. This ritual enabled the family to express their deep sense of loss and sadness connected to their forced migration while providing healing as the ritual anchored them in a new life that could include elements of both El Salvador and the Bronx (Imber-Black & Roberts, 1998).

> Assess your comprehension of contemporary life cycle transitions by completing this quiz.

The Emergence of Symptoms

Family life cycle theorists (Carter & McGoldrick, 1980; Haley, 1973) have described the connection between life cycle derailment and the emergence of symptoms in individuals and families. Families who are experiencing idiosyncratic life cycle events and processes may be at particular risk for the development of symptoms in members. The convergence of lack of social support, intergenerational cutoffs and isolation, stigma, secrecy, sense of shame in one or more members, and frequently stressful relationships with larger systems with whom the family must interact may be mirrored by a paucity of rituals to mark developmental change. Rigid and repetitive symptoms and interactions of family members in response to symptoms metaphorically express the family's stuck position. The clinician who searches for normative life cycle issues to hypothesize about the emergence of symptoms may find that idiosyncratic and often hidden life cycle processes are salient.

CASE ILLUSTRATION

The House-Cooling Party

Candice Meyers first contacted me for therapy because she was depressed. Her family physician had prescribed antidepressant medication, but she wanted to try therapy first. In our first meeting, she told me through her tears that her husband, Brent, had left her for another woman 6 months earlier. Married for 6 years, they had been talking about

starting a family. Brent had been secretly planning to leave for over a year.

After their separation, Candace became isolated from family and friends. She stopped participating in any family rituals, giving the excuse that she was exhausted and had frequent headaches. It was clear to me that Candace was suffering from many unacknowledged and unritualized losses—of her marriage, her hoped-for first child, and all of her relationships with family and friends. Her many symptoms—sleeplessness, headaches, weight loss, hopelessness—were directly related to her unanticipated divorce.

Candace felt very ashamed that she had been left by her husband. She stopped inviting anyone to her home, since hosting people alone seemed to emphasize her abandonment. This was in marked contrast to her earlier married life when her home had been the center for all of the holidays and other rituals with her extended family and friends. She called her house her "loneliness and her memories." I suggested that she might want to begin her healing by replacing some of the familiar and jointly owned items in her home with some new things that represented her individual tastes. As Candace began to put together a house that suited her, the acute depressive symptoms abated.

But for a long while, Candace was still unable to invite anyone to her home. "I feel like a strange sort of prisoner in my own home. But I'm not locked in—other people are locked out," Candace told me.

I was intrigued with her metaphor of the lock. I wondered with Candace what effect a new lock on her door might have. Candace agreed to buy a new lock and to simply sit with it each day and ask herself, "What would it take to put this new lock on my door—a lock that I could open to my family and friends?"

During that week, Candace went through many emotions—sadness, anger, a sense of betrayal. By the end of the week, she felt ready to reclaim her life. She decided to make a special ritual, a "house-cooling party." She told me, "People usually have house-warming parties when they move to a new home, I'd like to mark my divorce with some humor and have a "house-cooling party." She designed an invitation that read: "Please come to my house-cooling party.

Please do bring gifts appropriate for the lovely home of a single woman—I need to replace the 'his and her' stuff!" Just before the party, Candace had the new lock put on her front door, symbolizing that she was now in charge of her life (Imber-Black & Roberts, 1998).

> Assess your comprehension of the emergence of symptoms by completing this quiz.

Therapeutic Rituals

Many clinicians have described the efficacy of therapeutic rituals in facilitating systemic change (Imber-Black, 1986a, 1986b, 2012; Imber-Coppersmith, 1983, 1985; O'Connor, 1984; O'Connor & Horwitz, 1984; Palazzoli, Boscolo, Cecchin, & Prata, 1977; Papp, 1984; Seltzer & Seltzer, 1983; van der Hart, 1983). Differing from simple tasks whose intent is to target the behavioral level and that the therapist expects to be performed as prescribed, rituals are intended to affect the behavioral, cognitive, and affective levels. The family or individual is expected to improvise to tailor the ritual to particular and personal circumstances. Rather than relying only on concrete instructions, rituals utilize symbols and symbolic actions that may have multiple meanings.

Therapeutic rituals draw on elements attendant to normative life cycle rituals to highlight similarities to others, while including unusual elements that are capable of affirming differences rather than hiding them. Thus, Candace's house-cooling party began with the new lock as a powerful symbol of her autonomy after divorce. Many rituals include documents. Candace's invitation became a document to announce her divorce, and the party allowed her to ask others for support. Friends and family gathered to witness and celebrate her life cycle transition, just as they would with any other life cycle ritual.

Although there are several categories of rituals that may be useful in therapy, three categories are particularly beneficial for idiosyncratic life cycle events and processes. These include transition rituals, healing rituals (Imber-Black, 2008, 2010), and identity redefinition rituals. Transition rituals have been described extensively by van der Hart (1983), primarily in reference to normative life cycle transitions. Such rituals mark and facilitate transitions of specific members and of membership in the family, altering boundaries and making new relationship options available. The transitions in idiosyncratic life cycle events and processes often have no rituals. Indeed, the family may not have anticipated the transition and all the relationship changes attendant on it.

CASE ILLUSTRATION
The Giving of Gifts

A physician referred a family to me for therapy for what was identified as depression in the mother. The family consisted of two parents, Mr. and Mrs. Berry, and two young adult children, Karen, age 22, and Andrew, age 20. Karen was diagnosed as severely mentally retarded shortly after her birth. Karen's pediatrician advised Mrs. Berry to quit her job and remain at home to care for Karen. Extended family supported this advice and visited often while Karen and Andrew were small. The parents were told that Karen would never function on her own and would always remain "like a child." Eventually, Karen went to a special school, but the parents were never counseled in ways to prepare for Karen's adolescence or adulthood. Karen developed language and self-care skills. The family functioned well during Karen and Andrew's childhood. However, as both children became teenagers, severe difficulties arose. No one in the nuclear or extended family knew how to cope with Karen as an emerging young woman. Fearful that Karen might be exploited sexually, the family became increasingly protective of her. Andrew was required to spend most of his free time taking Karen to any outside events that were scheduled by her special school, and he grew increasingly resentful and withdrawn. His own plans to go away to college seemed impossible to him. Karen became rebellious and difficult for the family to be with, and the parents felt that they had failed her and needed to try harder. At the same time, Karen's school began to push the family to put Karen in a group home. This option had not existed at the time of Karen's birth and had never been anticipated by the family. For a period of 2 years, the parents and the school struggled over Karen's future. The parents were unable to articulate their fears to the school personnel, who saw them as overinvolved with Karen. Consequently, adequate explanations of what the group home could offer Karen and her family were not forthcoming. During this time, everyone in the family deteriorated emotionally and functionally, culminating in the referral for family therapy by the mother's physician.

Through the course of a therapy in which I helped the family to anticipate the life cycle change of Karen's eventually leaving home, and that richly credited the family for their contributions to Karen, the family became able to ask for and receive adequate information from the group home about Karen's future there. As the leaving home was normalized, the parents were able to articulate expectations about visiting and holiday time together that would mark the relationship of most young adults and their families. Andrew became freer to live his own life and made plans for going away to college in 4 months, after Karen was to go to the group home. The family was preparing itself for many changes. However, as Karen began to visit the group home, first for dinners and then for brief overnights stays, conflicts began to break out between Karen and her parents. Mr. and Mrs. Berry became alarmed that Karen was not as ready to move out as they had thought. In a session alone with the therapist, they cried and said that they feared for Karen's future.

Since the family had made so many changes in the direction of Karen's leaving home and were on the verge of completing the actual leaving when the arguments emerged, the therapist decided that a ritual to mark Karen's leaving home was needed. The Berrys had stated frequently that they "didn't think we had given Karen enough in order to equip her for life in the outside community." This sense of not having given her enough was intensified by the school's criticism of the family. Their phrase "given her enough" was used to construct a leaving home ritual that would confirm Karen's young adulthood,

would promote the family's confidence in her and themselves, and would highlight ongoing connectedness among the members.

I asked the parents and Andrew each to select a gift for Karen for her to take to her new home. I suggested that they choose a gift that would remind Karen of them and would also ease her way in her new setting. Karen, in turn, was asked to select a gift for each member that would remain with them when she left. The family members were told not to buy these gifts, but rather to choose something of their own or to make something. They were asked to bring these gifts to the next session and not to tell anyone else in the family about their gift before the session.

When the family arrived, they appeared very excited and happy in a way that had not been seen before during therapy. They had not shared their gifts before the session but had decided during the 2 weeks to wrap them and put them in a large bag, which Karen carried into the meeting. Mrs. Berry began by saying that during that week, they had decided on a definite date for Karen to move out, which they had not been able to do previously. Karen had gone for several visits to the group home. She also said that there had been a lot of secretive laughter during the 2 weeks, as people prepared their gifts, and no fighting!

I suggested a format for the exchange of gifts that was simple and largely nonverbal, which involved each member giving their gift, with a brief explanation if needed, and the recipient simply saying "thank you," other discussion being reserved for after the gift exchange. This was done to highlight the family as a group together and to facilitate equal participation, since Karen often fell silent when verbal discussions became rapid. Mr. Berry began the ceremony. He reached into the bag and gave Karen an unusual-shaped package, which turned out to be his favorite frying pan. Traditionally, Mr. Berry made Sunday breakfast. Because Karen was learning some simple cooking skills in school, she always wanted to use this frying pan, but her father had been afraid that she would ruin it and so had not let her use it. Karen beamed and said, "Thank you." Mrs. Berry's package was small, and she shyly handed it to Karen. It contained an almost full bottle of perfume and a pair of earrings. Mrs. Berry related briefly that she had often scolded Karen for using her perfume and had never allowed her to wear earrings. She looked at Karen and said, "I think you're grown up enough for these—they belonged to my mother and she gave them to me and now I'm giving them to you." With tears in her eyes, Karen said, "Thank you."

The mood changed profoundly when it was Andrew's turn. He remarked that he could not bring his whole gift to the session, but that Karen would understand. She opened his package to find a partially used box of birdseed. Leaving for school meant that Andrew would have to leave his parakeet. He had been allowed various pets at home, and had been responsible for them, while Karen had not. He explained that he had called Karen's group home, and they would allow her to bring the bird. He said that he would teach her to care for it before she moved out. Karen said, "Thank you," and Mrs. Berry expressed relief that the parakeet was leaving home too.

Karen then gave her gifts. To her mother, Karen gave her favorite stuffed animal, which she had had since early childhood and with which she still slept. She said to her mother, "I can't sleep with this in my new home—please keep it." To her father, she gave a photograph of her that had been taken during one of her visits at the group home. The photograph showed her sitting with several young men and women, and she said to her father, "These are my new friends." To Andrew, she gave her clock radio. This was a prized possession that had been a Christmas present. She gave it to Andrew and said, "Don't be late for school!"

Two weeks after this session, Karen moved into the group home, and a month later, Andrew left for college. The family ended therapy. At their 1-year follow-up, the family reported that both children had adjusted well to their new settings and were visiting home for holidays. Mrs. Berry had also returned to school to train for paid employment.

Assess your comprehension of therapeutic rituals by completing this quiz.

Discussion of the Ritual

Leaving-home ritual functioned in a number of ways. Through the course of the family therapy, the family had been preparing for Karen's leaving home but seemed to get stuck just on the verge of her actual leaving. Like many normative life cycle rituals, the therapeutic ritual worked to confirm a process that was already in motion and was not simply a discrete event. The ritual symbolically affirmed and made simultaneous the contradictions of separation and ongoing connectedness that are involved when any child leaves home. The family members, in their giving of gifts, were able both to give permission for separation and affirm their ongoing but changing relationships.

The ritual was designed to introduce symmetry into a system that had been primarily marked by complementary relationships. Thus, all members participated in the giving and receiving of gifts and in the planning and thoughtfulness that went into gift selection, altering the previous pattern in the family whereby the parents and Andrew were seen to be the "givers," the "providers," the "protectors," and Karen was seen to be the recipient of care, advice, and protection.

The ritual was also designed to confirm individual boundaries, as each member was individually responsible for his or her own planning and selection of gifts. Individuation was promoted through the instruction of secret planning by each member. Dyadic relationships between Karen and every member were also confirmed, in a family that had previously operated with triads involving Karen as their primary mode of relationship. Finally, each member's contribution to the ritual was highlighted as important to the entire process, thus symbolically celebrating the whole family unit. Various aspects of the ritual functioned to introduce differences in pattern to the family system.

By asking the family to bring their gifts to the therapy session, I was able to serve as witness to the process. Witnesses are frequently a part of normative life cycle rituals. Here, the therapist also may be seen to symbolically represent an outside helping system in a celebratory stance with a family that had been used to criticism and disparagement from outside systems.

Assess your comprehension of discussion of the ritual by completing this quiz.

Healing Rituals

Every culture has rituals to mark profound losses, deal with the grief of survivors, and facilitate ongoing life after such loss. There are many creative contemporary examples of cultural healing rituals. The Vietnam War Memorial in Washington, DC, is visited by families and friends who lost men and women in the war and make pilgrimages to the memorial, during which they search for their loved one's name, perhaps leave items that have special meaning, and often make rubbings to carry back home. Public grieving for a war that held so much secrecy and shame is facilitated by this repeated ritual.

The AIDS quilt, consisting of several thousand hand-sewn patches, each memorializing a person who has died of AIDS, is displayed with a powerful ceremony in which all of the names of the dead are read aloud as the quilt is unfolded in planned, repetitive motions of connection and uplift. A quilt is often a community endeavor. The AIDS quilt connects a community of mourners with a symbol of warmth and care.

The Clothesline Project is a women's ritual devoted to recovery from abuse. A growing collection of hand-painted T-shirts is hung on a clothesline. This community ritual includes the ringing of gongs and bells and blowing of horns to symbolize how often a woman is assaulted, raped, and murdered. The marvelous contradiction of regaining power in the face of servitude is clearly contained in these hand-painted depictions of violence hung ironically on a clothesline for all to see.

Recently, we witnessed the powerful healing rituals created in the wake of 9/11. The association of Black Firefighters in New York and their wives and families—the Vulcans and Vulcanettes—created sustaining rituals to mark their losses. Beginning with the universal ritual of storytelling, they gathered to speak of those they lost. Family elders lit candles, while the youngest in each family participated in a procession to proclaim there would be a future. Since there were no images of the lost Black firefighters on television or in the newspapers, they created a special memorial flag consisting of 12 small helmets and the names of their heroes who died in 9/11 trying to save others. When New York City stated it was removing firefighters from the 9/11 site, the Vulcans created a series of emotional, spiritual, and political rituals and thereby fought the edict. In a public ceremony, surviving Black firefighters made commitments of care to the children who had lost fathers, stating, "The needs your father might have met, we will meet them" (Imber-Black, 2003).

Healing may also be necessary for losses sustained through the breakup of relationships, for the reconciliation of relationships after painful revelations such as affairs, for unresolved grief when normative healing rituals have not occurred or have not succeeded, for losses of bodily parts and functions due to illness, and for the often attendant loss of roles, life expectations, and dreams. Therapeutic healing rituals are particularly useful when normative healing rituals do not exist or are not sufficient for the magnitude of the loss.

Assess your comprehension of healing rituals by completing this quiz.

CASE ILLUSTRATION
Setting Fire to the Past

Alice Jeffers, age 35, requested therapy, saying that she was depressed and unable to live her life normally. Alice was single and lived alone. She was a trained and practicing veterinarian. In the first session, she described to me an 8-year-long relationship with a man. The relationship, which had included periods of living together, had been very stormy and had finally ended 2 years previously at his insistence. Alice's family had not approved of the relationship. They were relieved when it ended but seemed unable to extend any support to Alice for the pain she felt. Friends told her that she was well rid of him. Over the 2 years, Alice grew increasingly isolated, and by the time she came to therapy, she did not go out with any friends, spent all her free time thinking about her former lover, dreamed about him nightly, had gained a lot of weight, and felt that her work was being affected. Her family and friends' inability to confirm her pain and loss seemed to contribute to her need to do nothing else but think about him and feel sad. She said she felt that if she had been married and divorced, people would have been more supportive of her, as they had been of her sister in such circumstances.

I began with simple confirmation of Alice's loss and grief and highlighted that, indeed, there are no agreed-upon processes for the end of a nonmarried relationship. I asked Alice to perform a task that would allow her both to grieve and to begin to get on with other aspects of her life. For 1 hour a day, Alice was told to do nothing but review memories of the relationship, since this was something that obviously still needed to be completed. I suggested that she write these memories out on separate index cards and bring them to the next session. Beyond the hour a day, I urged Alice to do other things. Alice returned with a stack of index cards, which she had creatively color coded, using purple for "mellow" memories, green for "jealous" memories, and blue for "sad" memories. With laughter, she stated, "And, of course, my angry ones are RED!" As the therapy session focused on the cards and their meanings, Alice stated that she had felt much better during the 3 weeks, that she began to find that an hour a day was too much time, and that she had stopped dreaming about her former love. I asked her whether there were cards she felt ready to let go of, and she said that there were. She was asked to take the cards home and sort them out, differentiating between those she still wanted to hang on to and those she felt ready to let go of.

Alice arrived 2 weeks later, dressed more brightly than before and eager to talk. She had started to go out with friends a bit and had looked into an aerobics class. After reporting this, she took out two stacks of cards. She said she had decided she wanted to keep the purple "mellow" memories, as these were a part of her that she wanted to maintain. She felt the good parts of the relationship had changed her in positive ways, and she said she wanted to carry this into any new relationship she might have. This was the first mention of a sense of future. She also wanted to keep most of the red "anger" memories, as these helped her to remember how shabbily she had been treated many times and thus kept her from romanticizing

the past. However, she was very ready to let go of the green "jealousy" memories, which often made her feel bad about herself, and the blue "sad" memories, as she felt that she had been sad long enough. At that point, I left the room and returned with a ceramic bowl and a book of matches, which I silently offered to Alice, who smiled and said, "Oh, we should burn them!" It is important to note that she saw the burning as a joint endeavor by herself and me. I handed the cards back to Alice, who put them in a pile in the bowl and lit them. She used several matches to get a good fire going and then sat silently for several moments watching the flames. At one point, she said, "It's so final, but it's good." A few minutes later, she joked, "We should toast marshmallows—that would be the final irony," referring to the fact that her boyfriend had often criticized her body and her weight and yet brought her treats. Toward the end, she said, "This is good—my final memory is of warmth."

In sessions after the burning ritual, Alice dealt with many family-of-origin issues that had previously been unavailable because of her stuck position vis-a-vis her boyfriend. She was able to renegotiate several family relationships, began going out more with friends, and joined a scuba class. When therapy ended, she was beginning flying lessons, an apt metaphor for her new beginnings.

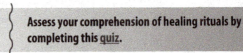

Assess your comprehension of healing rituals by completing this quiz.

Identity Redefinition Rituals

Identity redefinition rituals function to remove labels and stigma from individuals, couples, and families and often realign relationships between the family and larger systems. This is especially necessary when the larger systems have held negative points of view toward a family. A reworking of an earlier idiosyncratic life cycle transition that went awry may be accomplished. New relationship options, previously unavailable because of the constraints of labels, become available (see Imber-Coppersmith, 1983). A balance of being both similar to others and different from others becomes achievable.

CASE ILLUSTRATION

A Mutual Adoption Celebration

I met Bob Simmons, a 37-year-old single gay man, about a year and a half after he had adopted his 9-year-old son, Alan. "We're definitely a new sort of family," Bob told me in our first therapy session. "I don't have to tell you that as a gay man, I had to look all over the country to find an agency that would let me adopt a child. It took me four years, but I finally succeeded," Bob reflected proudly.

Bob had found an agency across the country that let him make a home for Alan, a biracial child with many special educational and emotional needs. Alan had been in six foster homes after his crack-addicted mother abandoned him when he was 2 years old. He had been severely abused, both in his biological family and in at least three of his foster homes. Now, living with Bob, Alan showed many of the signs of an abused and neglected child. Alan had learned to survive by drawing into himself, allowing little contact with others. Bob came to family therapy to help his son, to build their relationship, and to learn parenting strategies.

As I met with Bob and his young son, Alan refused to talk to me. No doubt, having met many professionals whose jobs had been to move him from one place to another, Alan was not about to take any risks with me. As Bob described his frustrations learning to parent, Alan sank lower and lower in his chair. My many attempts to reach him were met with shrugs and a cap pulled farther and farther over his eyes. "Tell me something," I said to Alan, "he adopted you, right?" "Right," Alan whispered in return. "Have you adopted him?" I asked. Alan's cap flew off, and his eyes grew as big as saucers. He rose up in his seat. "Oh, how could I do that?" his voice boomed. "I don't know," I replied. "How do *you* think you could do that?" "I would have to go to court and get some papers," Alan replied. "I think you've hit on something important here," Bob said.

For the rest of the session, we talked about how Bob adopted Alan. As a gay man, he was made to feel stigmatized everywhere he turned to realize his dream of being a father. When he finally adopted Alan, he did not make a celebration. There was no ritual to mark and help make this critical transition. Most of Bob's friends could not understand his decision to be a single father. His sister yelled at him over the phone that he had no right to be a parent. When Bob and Alan began to live together as father and son, Bob was unprepared for how difficult parenting a boy who had been so abused would be. He often told Alan how lucky he was to be in a nice home. Without meaning, Bob made Alan feel that he was in a very unbalanced situation. When I asked Alan whether he had adopted Bob, I struck an important chord of mutuality, one that excited Alan with its possibilities.

I met Alan alone and told him that he would not need to go to court to adopt Bob. He would just need to write out his own document on his computer at home. We agreed to keep this private between us as he worked on a "certificate to adopt my dad."

The therapy contained many other elements, including helping Bob to set appropriate limits for Alan; reconnecting Bob to his own mother, who wanted to be a loving grandmother for Alan; and aiding Bob in finding other single dads, both gay and straight. When our therapy concluded, Bob and Alan invited Bob's mother and some new and supportive friends over for a special ritual, a mutual adoption ceremony, in which Alan and Bob openly adopted one another.

 Assess your comprehension of identity redefinition rituals by completing this quiz.

Designing and Implementing Rituals for New Life Cycle Transitions

Designing and implementing rituals, such as those discussed in this chapter, is a learnable skill. Several guidelines will enhance this process.

- Just as normative rituals are processes, rather than discrete events, therapeutic rituals are part of a larger therapeutic process. Their efficacy relies on planning, careful assessment, especially regarding life cycle phases and idiosyncratic life cycle events, and respect and rapport between family and therapist. The rituals are not games or tricks, but rather rise out of a relational context that appreciates the ritualizing tendency of human beings and the need for meaning in human relationships.

- The family and therapist search for the appropriate symbols and symbolic acts of the individual, family, ethnic group, and cultural group, which represent the possibility of relationship development (Imber-Black, 2012). Such symbols and metaphorical action should connect the family with the familiar, while also being capable of leading to the unfamiliar.

- The family and therapist design the ritual with a focus on special time and special space. Thus, rituals may occur at a particular time or over time. Time may be used to draw particular distinctions or to highlight simultaneity. A sense of connection to the past, present, and future is made. The ritual may occur in the therapy session, at home, or at some other agreed-upon place, such as by a body of water, in the woods, or in a cemetery. If the ritual requires a witness, then the therapy session is often the preferred time and space, or the therapist may accompany the family to an agreed-upon place.

- The therapist attends to alternations in order to incorporate contradictions. Thus, holding on may be alternated with letting go in a single ritual, or a ritual of termination or separation may be followed by a ritual of renewal or celebration.

- The therapist looks for ways to involve the family in co-designing the ritual to facilitate imagination that may lead to problem solving and enhanced functioning. A sense of humor and playfulness are used when appropriate.

- Therapeutic rituals for idiosyncratic life cycle events borrow heavily from normative rituals, yet utilize symbols and symbolic actions that are relevant to the particular life cycle transition.

- The therapist remains open to the family's development of the ritual, including their choice not to perform the ritual. Therapeutic rituals should not be hollow events, practiced simply because someone said to do it. Rather, they are opportunities for the confirmation of existing relationships and for the beginnings of relationship change. Family readiness must be carefully gauged and respected. In successful therapeutic rituals, the ritual and its outcome ultimately belong to the family.

> **Assess your comprehension of designing and implementing rituals for new life cycle transitions by completing this quiz.**

Conclusion

New life cycle events and transitions pose particular difficulties for individuals and families. Lacking available maps that fit their situation and without wider contextual support and confirmation, complex feedback processes may be set in motion, resulting in symptoms and a high level of distress and isolation. Since rituals have the capacity to hold and express differences rather than homogenize them, they are particularly powerful resources for any life cycle transition that differs from the conventional. Therapy needs to include conversations about meaningful rituals. Creatively and sensitively crafted rituals, which both borrow richly from established life cycle rituals and are simultaneously brand new, facilitate necessary transitions and the expansion of relationship possibilities.

> **Recall what you learned in this chapter by completing the Chapter Review.**

— References —

Carter, E. A., & McGoldrick, M. (1980). The family life cycle and family therapy. In E. A. Carter & M. McGoldrick (Eds.), *The family life cycle: A framework for family therapy*. New York: Gardner Press.

DeSilva, C. (Ed.). (1996). *In memory's kitchen: A legacy from the women of Terezin*. New York: Jason Aronson.

Haley, J. (1973). *Uncommon therapy: The psychiatric techniques of Milton H. Erickson*. New York: Norton.

Imber-Black, E. (1986a). Odysseys of a learner. In D. Efron (Ed.), *Journeys: Expansion of the strategic-systemic therapies*. New York: Brunner/Mazel.

Imber-Black, E. (2010). Respectful curiosity, collaborative ritual-making, speaking the unspeakable: A multicontextual therapy of love and loss. In M. Kerman (Ed.). *Clinical pearls of wisdom: 21 leading therapists offer their key insights*. (pp. 155–168). New York: W.W. Norton Publishers.

Imber-Black, E. (2008). Rituals and spirituality in family therapy. In F. Walsh (Ed.). *Spiritual resources in family therapy* (2nd ed., pp. 229–246). New York: The Guilford Press.

Imber-Black, E. (2003). September 11th: Rituals of healing and transformation. In E. Imber-Black, J. Roberts, & R. Whiting (Eds.). *Rituals in families and family therapy, Revised edition*. New York: W.W. Norton Publishers.

Imber-Black, E. (2012). The value of family rituals. In F. Walsh (Ed.). *Normal family processes: Growing diversity and complexity* (4th ed., pp. 483–497). New York: The Guilford Press.

Imber-Black, E. (1986b). Towards a resource model in systemic family therapy. In M. Karpel (Ed.), *Family resources* (pp. 148–174). New York: The Guilford Press.

Imber-Black, E., & Roberts, J. (1998). *Rituals for our times: Celebrating, healing and changing our lives and our relationships*. New Jersey: Jason Aronson.

Imber-Coppersmith, E. (1985). We've got a secret: A non-marital marital therapy. In A. Gurman (Ed.), *Casebook of marital therapy* (pp. 369–386). New York: The Guilford Press.

Imber-Coppersmith, E. (1983). From hyperactive to normal but naughty: A multisystem partnership in delabeling. *International Journal of Family Psychiatry, 3*(2), 131–144.

O'Connor, J. (1984). The resurrection of a magical reality: Treatment of functional migraine in a child. *Family Process, 23*(4), 501–509.

O'Connor, J., & Horwitz, A. N. (1984). The bogeyman cometh: A strategic approach for difficult adolescents. *Family Process, 23*(2), 237–249.

Palazzoli, M., Boscolo, L., Cecchin, G., & Prata, G. (1977). Family rituals: A powerful tool in family therapy. *Family Process, 16*(4), 445–454.

Papp, P. (1984). The links between clinical and artistic creativity. *The Family Therapy Networker, 8*(5), 20–29.

Schwartzman, J. (1982). Symptoms and rituals: Paradoxical modes and social organization. *Ethos, 10*(1), 3–23.

Seltzer, W., & Seltzer, M. (1983). Magic, material and myth. *Family Process, 22*(1), 3–14.

van der Hart, O. (1983). *Rituals in psychotherapy: Transition and continuity*. New York: Irvington Publishers.

Wolin, S. J., & Bennett, S. A. (1984). Family rituals. *Family Process, 23*(3), 401–420.

Chapter 27

The Therapist and the Family: The Intersection of Life Cycles

Steve Lerner

— Learning Outcomes

- Discuss how a therapist's life cycle issues can intersect with those of a family in treatment.
- Explain the importance of a therapist's work in studying the dynamics of their family of origin.
- Describe why it is important for a therapist to review and modify their own family patterns.
- List and describe predictable problems that may emerge when a therapist's unresolved issues are similar to those of a family in treatment.
- Explore how a therapist's unresolved issues may result in stuck times in their clinical work.
- Examine the unique challenges therapists face when helping families with young children.
- Describe the benefits of an open-door policy that allows a family to return to a therapist during different life cycle stages.
- Discuss challenges therapists may face when helping a family process the loss of a family member.

Introduction

The family life cycle model developed by Carter and McGoldrick provides a richly contextualized, multidimensional framework for understanding the movement of the family through time. This framework helps us to locate the points at which the chronic background anxiety in a family is likely to coincide with the acute stress of navigating a current life cycle transition. These are the times when symptoms and dysfunction are most likely to emerge, in both our own and our clients' families. Although the connections may not be obvious, these crucial transitions are inextricably linked to the sociocultural context in which family life is embedded. Factors such as gender, race, class, ethnicity, and sexual orientation shape the nature of the playing field on which life cycle transitions are negotiated.

In this chapter, I focus on the intersection between the therapist's life cycle issues and those of the family in treatment—a key dimension of the fit between therapist and family as the clinical process unfolds (Simon, 1988). More specifically, I propose

that when the therapist brings unresolved issues from a past or current life cycle stage into the clinical work with a family that is struggling to navigate a similar life cycle challenge, predictable problems may emerge.

Some therapists may zoom in zealously to remake the client in the image of their own wished-for but unachieved resolution of a particular life cycle issue, overfunctioning for the client's family but not paying sufficient attention to their own. Or, when the therapist's unresolved family of origin issues come up against a presenting problem in a family (e.g., how are elderly parents cared for), the therapist may become an ineffective, fuzzy thinker, who is unable to assume leadership in the sessions and help the family move toward effective problem solving. A therapist who relies primarily on distance to manage emotional intensity in her family of origin may become overly aloof, or, if she has never extricated herself from a stuck position in a triangle in her own family, she may tend with her clients to join the camp of one family member at the expense of another. Whatever the therapist's characteristic style of managing anxiety under stress (over- and under-functioning, distancing, blaming, and triangling), it is useful to examine one's own functioning through the wide-angle lens of the family life cycle model, especially when a clinical impasse occurs.

Many therapists have studied their own families of origin as part of their professional training. They have worked to identify and modify their part in multigenerational patterns, with an eye toward navigating family relationships and life cycle transitions with greater clarity, objectivity, and calm. Those of us who have worked diligently on our own families may mistakenly believe that we have "done that" and can now focus single mindedly on problems arising at different stages in the family life cycle of the clients we work with. During stuck times in our clinical work, however, it is helpful to review our own style of managing anxiety under stress, as well as to examine how we have managed life cycle issues similar to what the client is struggling with. In this way, a therapeutic problem can serve as a signal for additional personal work that can result in renewed growth for both the therapist and the clinical family.

CASE ILLUSTRATION

Rachel

This case came up in a small supervision group that I led, in which the contract was that supervisees presented clinical cases as well as their families of origin. My theoretical framework was Bowen family systems theory, informed by feminist theory, and the family life cycle model of Carter and McGoldrick.

Rachel, a Jewish therapist in her late 20s, presented her initial work with a Mexican American couple, Fernanda and Miguel, in their 50s, both first borns, who came in with marital problems following the wife's decision to move her elderly, infirm parents into their home. Her husband, who had agreed to this arrangement, was now reacting to how much attention his wife paid to her parents, and felt very much on the outside.

In her own family, Rachel was the youngest of three siblings, in a family where achievement and professional success were highly prized, along with the individuality and separateness of family members. While family togetherness was a value, her mother's motto was "I never want my own needs to interfere with your happiness. You have to live your own life." Her father, who had died of a heart attack when Rachel was 20, was a successful businessman whom she described as a quiet man, likeable but distant and "hard to really know."

At the time Rachel began her work with Fernanda and Miguel, she was also dealing with her mother's declining health and increasing need for care. She described her older brother, Bruce, who lived across the country, as "good for nothing" as far as caretaking was concerned. Over the years, he had increasingly distanced from the family, failing to come home to attend an uncle's funeral and other family events because of his "pressing work demands" and deadlines. Rachel's sister Miriam, the middle sibling, lived several hours away, and was only marginally helpful. She visited her mother once a month, and while she frequently asked Rachel for suggestions as to how she could be helpful, she then failed to follow through on Rachel's suggestions ("It would help if you'd call Mom twice a week."). Nor did Miriam take the initiative to figure out on her own how to contribute and be a partner in caretaking with her sister.

Rachel reported feeling that she was "stuck with everything," which led her to want to do even less. In true "youngest" fashion, she was not geared toward taking responsibility for others, did not feel competent at it, and had never really examined her own core values about how to balance her responsibility toward her mother with her need to ensure the quality of her own life. She visited her mother on a fairly regular basis, but avoided becoming "too involved," or thinking ahead in terms of what might be needed as her mother's health continued to decline. Rachel took it as a given that her mother would go into an assisted living facility when the time came. While making increasing demands on Rachel as her health declined, her mother continually emphasized how she "never wants to be a burden," which she had told Rachel repeatedly since she was a teenager. As far as Rachel knew, caring for an aging parent in the home was not a family tradition, and this responsibility would certainly never fall to a youngest daughter.

Given the unresolved emotional intensity in Rachel's family surrounding the life cycle issue of caring for elderly parents, it was no surprise that she almost immediately encountered problems being helpful to Fernanda and Miguel. She perceived Fernanda's close care-taking relationship with her parents as a central problem in the marriage, and noted Miguel's "passivity" in going along with the idea of his in-laws moving in. Initially, Rachel saw the goal of her work as helping Fernanda feel less responsible for her parents, and encouraging her to increase her distance especially from her mother, which Rachel believed would lead to a better connection between Fernanda and Miguel.

In supervision, I asked Rachel how she thought her own family issues might be influencing her reactions to Fernanda and Miguel's situation. Rachel realized that her need to protect herself from feeling overwhelmed with the responsibility of caring for her mother, and going it alone in her sibling group, was getting in her way in the clinical work. While she knew intellectually that caring for aging parents in the home was a cultural imperative for Fernanda, her questioning fell heavily in the direction of suggesting Fernanda should "protect herself" from too much involvement, both for Fernanda's emotional well-being and for the sake of her marriage. Rachel observed, "I can see where I'm definitely losing objectivity with this couple. Maybe I've been trying to get more comfortable with how much I *won't* do for my own mother, or I'm mixing myself up with Fernanda in some way."

I suggested that Rachel talk with her mother about how aging parents were cared for in previous generations. She did so, and learned that her maternal grandmother, herself a youngest, who had died before Rachel's birth, had cared not only for her parents in her home but also for an older brother who had a degenerative neuromuscular disease. Rachel's grandmother thus took on an extreme caretaking burden throughout her adult life, and Rachel's mother grew up determined not to follow in her mother's footsteps, nor to have her own children do the same. Rachel's grandmother died suddenly in her 60s, as did her grandfather a few years later, so Rachel's mother did not have to confront caretaking responsibilities with them. Rachel commented that her

mother's mantra that she heard endless times growing up ("I never want to be a burden. Live your own life.") now made sense to her in a different way.

One of the supervisees suggested that Rachel might think about talking to her brother and sister about her dilemma with their mother—wanting to be responsible and do the right thing, but needing to keep her own life on track, and feeling so alone with the caretaking responsibilities. "It's not a favor to them or to yourself to assume that they can't step up to the plate with your mom," he said. I coached her to connect with her siblings, first by simply being more in touch, and then by sharing how anxious and overwhelmed she sometimes felt, especially when she pictured her mother's needs increasing in the future. I encouraged her to share her experience without telling them what to do, and without criticism or blame.

As Rachel predicted, Miriam asked (as usual) if there was anything she could do. Rachel was able to say lightly that it would help a lot if Miriam would follow through with doing what she said she'd do, because she needed her big sister on the team. In another call, she also expressed the wish that Miriam herself take more initiative to figure out how to jump in and be helpful. Again Rachel spoke to her sister in a loving rather than critical way. ("Miriam, when I watch you with your kids, you're so creative and such a great caretaker. I don't think you really need me to take the initiative to tell you how to be helpful, because you're so good at this, and my brain sometimes turns to mush under the strain of being the only one on the scene".)

Rachel told Bruce that she really needed him to plan a visit to see their mother, and that she sorely missed his presence and advice. "I just can't do this alone," she told him.

To Rachel's surprise, it was her brother who made the biggest change. Bruce flew in for a visit soon after their talk, and began more regular contacts with their mother and with her. The "good-for-nothing" brother seemed more than happy to be invited back into the family, and to be asked for his advice and perspective about their mother. He spoke to Rachel about how badly he felt about not spending more time with their father. "Dad and I always talked about doing more together when we both had time, and then there was no more time." Rachel told him how similar she felt, and how lost she had been at 20 when he died.

In her work with Fernanda and Miguel, she questioned each of them about how aging parents had been cared for in preceding generations. She learned that caring for the elderly in one's home was a long-term pattern in both of their families—one did not "hand family members over to strangers" or "put them away." Rachel let go of her notion that Miguel had been passive, instead seeing his willingness to have his in-laws move in as part of his strength and devotion to family, as well as reflecting a larger cultural pattern that he not only accepted, but valued, despite the personal costs. She also shifted away from encouraging Fernanda to distance from her mother, and instead helped Miguel to find ways to assist Fernanda in the caretaking. After a brief phase of resistance, Miguel rose to the occasion willingly. At one point, Rachel asked Miguel if there was some routine he might create with his father-in-law in which they could spend some special time together. Miguel initiated a morning ritual of coffee and a short walk around their neighborhood with Fernanda's dad before he left for work.

In questioning Miguel about his own family of origin, Rachel learned that he had left Mexico long before his younger sister began caring for their elderly parents. Miguel had always felt a deep sense of guilt for being away during the last years of their lives, which understandably made it difficult to watch his wife pour her attention into taking care of his in-laws, even as he now supported her to do so. As Rachel expressed interest in Miguel's family he began to increase his connection with living relatives in Mexico, which freed him up to move toward his in-laws more comfortably.

Rachel's challenge to navigate sibling relationships as her mother's needs increased was obviously a long-term one, with many bumps along the way. It was hard for Rachel, a youngest, to accept that she would always carry an "unfair" portion of the work, and that siblings at a distance may not consistently step up to help. What mattered is that Rachel became more thoughtful about her situation, with an eye toward navigating her sibling relationships with the least amount of reactivity and the most maturity she could muster, and, most importantly, separating out her

own anxious situation from that of her clients. This is what allowed her to be a truly helpful and empathic therapist with Fernanda and Miguel.

CASE ILLUSTRATION

Colleen

Colleen, an Irish American therapist in her early 50s, presented her own family of origin to the supervision group. Colleen's mother, Rose, died in a car wreck when Colleen was 15 years old, and the facts surrounding the accident were never discussed in the family. Colleen was an adult when she learned from a cousin that her mother, who was drunk while driving, ran a red light, and also killed a young child who was in another car. Following Rose's funeral, she was rarely mentioned again, probably because of the family's shame about her alcoholism and its terrible cost. Colleen's father quickly began dating and remarried the following year to a woman, and Colleen and her brother Joe were instructed to call the woman "Mom." Colleen had been quietly depressed through the remainder of her teenage years, and now imagined that Joe had been depressed as well. Her father and stepmother had died some years ago, without there ever being any open conversation about the traumatic loss and its impact on the family.

Subsequently in supervision, Colleen presented her beginning work with a couple, Susan and John, who were concerned about their daughter Gina, a high school student who, according to a teacher's report, seemed sad and withdrawn in class. Of particular concern was the fact that her grades were slipping badly, and Susan and John were scared that Gina was sabotaging her future chances to get into a good college. On the initial phone call, Colleen learned that Susan had been diagnosed with a serious heart condition, and that she and John were still reeling from the shock of the diagnosis. Colleen suggested that they first come in to see her together, without their daughter.

During that first session, the parents focused on their worry about Gina, who had always been a "competent and happy girl." When asked, they revealed that they had not shared any facts about Susan's illness with Gina, instead maintaining a "business as usual" stance. For example, a brief trip to the Cleveland Clinic to consult about diagnosis and treatment was described to Gina as a trip out of town to visit some old friends. Susan also tried to hide her difficulty climbing stairs from her daughter.

In supervision, Colleen told me that while she typically constructs the multigenerational family genogram in the first session (Lerner, 1983), with Susan and John she had not gotten past the nuclear family. When I asked her what got in the way of gathering more information, she said that in the session she found herself focusing in on their decision to keep Susan's illness a secret. The more she inquired about secrecy, the more they circled the wagons, insisting that "privacy" not "secrecy" was the issue, and that nothing would be served by scaring Gina with the facts before it was absolutely necessary. Colleen said, "I felt off track, like I kept getting into a struggle with them." She was surprised that they showed up for the second session, as was I.

In supervision, when we re-visited the key emotional issue in Colleen's life, she almost immediately made the connection between the secrecy surrounding her own mother's death, and the discomfort evoked in her by this couple's decision to keep Gina in the dark about Susan's illness. "The silence surrounding my mother's death cost me dearly," Colleen said. "Maybe I felt I had to rescue Gina from that."

In the second session with the couple, Colleen followed their lead, refocusing on their worries about Gina and their genuine wish to do everything possible to help her. Colleen also asked more questions about who had been told what about Susan's illness; she was careful to ask these questions in a neutral way which did not imply that Susan and John should rush in and tell all. In addition to wanting to protect Gina, Colleen learned that no one on either side of the family had been told anything. John said, "It would kill Susan's mother to know, and mine too. And Susan's mother has her own health issues." The couple readily agreed to come in for additional sessions, with the central focus

on how to help their daughter Gina get back on her academic feet.

In the next supervision session, I asked Colleen how much she and her brother, Joe, had talked about the traumatic loss of their mother, and how the lack of any open conversation had affected each of them. Colleen replied, "I brought it up a few times, but Joe always seemed so uncomfortable, so I didn't push it." I suggested she try again to open up the conversation with him, and suggested a few ways she might do this. When she approached him by communicating that his perspective would be of great help to her, he had a surprising amount to say on the subject. Most shocking to Colleen was learning that Joe did not know that their mother was drunk at the time of the accident. "I don't know why this was such a surprise though," Colleen said. "I never told him what I learned from my cousin, so why would I assume he knew? Maybe we've all been going along with the 'don't ask, don't tell' party line in our family."

Refocusing on her own family of origin allowed Colleen to more gracefully help Susan and John look at the pluses and minuses of protecting Gina and other family members from the facts of Susan's diagnosis. It was John who first ventured the idea that telling other people might make it more real to both of them, and perhaps they were protecting *themselves* by not talking about it. They were able to see that the longer they waited to tell family members, the more "out of the blue" the news would be for them, especially should Susan suddenly need major surgery, or should her condition rapidly worsen. Colleen explained to them that all families have secrets, especially between the generations, and this was normal. But sometimes a big secret can be connected to a child's symptomatic behavior, since kids tend to have radar for a "disturbance in the emotional field," and typically do better managing difficult facts than they do swimming around in anxious situations, which in turn gives rise to more frightening unconscious fantasies.

With some gentle coaching, Susan and John were able to tell their parents, and were surprised by the warmth and support that came their way. They realized that they were not alone, and that their family resources were strong. Colleen then brainstormed with Susan and John about how to open up the facts with Gina, without over-talking the subject and spilling their anxiety onto their child. When Susan and John did talk with her, Gina said, "I knew something wasn't right, Mom. I just didn't know what it was. You've been looking so tired. I'm glad it wasn't anything to do with me."

 Test your comprehension of the introduction by completing this quiz.

Families With Young Children: A Complex Intersection

A life cycle stage that is particularly challenging is that of the family with young children. With the birth of the first child, a profound realignment of family relationships occurs. The whole family diagram shifts one notch upward, and every family member gets a new name: husband and wife become father and mother; siblings become uncles or aunts; parents become grandparents; grandparents become great-grandparents.

The marital couple faces the largest challenge as they adjust to their new roles. Many equal partnerships succumb to the powerful tidal pull of the previous generation's far less equitable gender roles and expectations (Lerner, 1998). Even the most pioneering of couples will struggle with the enormous challenges of this stage and are often left with unresolved dissatisfaction stemming from the compromises and accommodations that began after the first child was born. The marital relationship can then become the crucible in which the seeds of inequality and disillusionment grow, often resulting in chronic unhappiness, early divorce, or the later dissolution of the marriage when the children are adolescents or have been launched. Therapists who have not examined the pervasive impact of gender on their own and their parents' marriages—or who deny the enormous impact of gender on every aspect of personal and work life—will be limited in helping families navigate the complexities of life with young children and the marital renegotiations that are required to make things work.

CASE ILLUSTRATION

Allan

Alan, the therapist, presented his work with Ellen, who was married with two young children. She called him up after a period of increasing distress over a possible move to another city precipitated by her husband Rob on receiving the offer of a significant promotion if he would transfer to the headquarters of his company. The prospect of leaving her circle of close women friends and her parents and sisters, who lived nearby, upset her greatly. Before having children, Ellen had worked full time, and she remembered those years with nostalgia as a time when she felt free to pursue her dreams. Currently, she has a part-time job that she enjoys, and has arranged an excellent child care situation that would be impossible to duplicate, since it included her mother caring for her children two afternoons a week. She had tentative plans to pursue more education, but had put her career goals on hold since the children arrived.

Alan empathized with her sadness and asked some good questions: What did she know about the new city? Had she visited there with Rob, and researched the work, educational opportunities, and child care options that might be available there? However relevant these questions might be as one part of helping Ellen think through her dilemma, they also conveyed the fact that in Alan's mind, the move was a given, which was precisely how his depressed client saw it. As a result, there were some significant questions Alan did not ask.

He did *not* ask the following questions: How was the decision to move being negotiated between the two of them? What impact did Rob's earning power (he earned 90 percent of the family's income) have on the decision process? How did Ellen understand the fact that she was acting as if she had no option but to reflexively go along with the move, which she called a "fait accompli"?

In supervision, I asked Alan to consider the similarities and differences between Ellen and Rob's way of navigating their current life cycle challenges and the way in which he and his wife were handling their own. Alan and his wife, Sarah, both first borns, had one 2-year-old child. Sarah had cut back from a full-time editorial position at a publishing house to do freelance work when their baby was born. At the current time, she wanted to go back to work full time, as her former employer had recently called to offer her old job back to her. Alan and Sarah were struggling to figure out how to divide household and child care responsibilities if she took the position. Before having a child, Alan believed in shared parenting, but now he did not want his child "raised by a stranger." Also, he made more than $100 an hour, while his wife would make at most $30 an hour. Alan said, "Given the high cost of child care, and the reality of her salary, I really wish she'd stay with the freelance work for a few more years." Alan admitted that he felt anxious and defensive when his wife talked about resuming full-time work.

Alan's own parents had followed a traditional path: His mother nurtured and his father earned. Their family moved four times because of his father's career, and as far as Alan knew, his mother never objected. Alan had no idea whether either of them had ever considered another arrangement or how the traditional path suited them.

In response to Alan's presentation of his clinical case, a female supervisee commented that he had quickly conveyed the underlying message that the move could not, and should not, be questioned. It was as if he were saying, "Cheer up, it won't be so bad. With a little elbow grease, you'll have almost as good a situation in the new city." I added that he also did not locate the client's depression, or the move itself, in any broader context: her marriage, her family of origin, or her life cycle stage.

I suggested that Alan's current life cycle issues (i.e., the marital tension surrounding his wife's wish to resume full-time work) were intersecting with his client's in a way that was impeding his objectivity. To move toward a clearer frame of reference on his own life cycle transition, I encouraged Alan to open up a discussion with each of his parents about the way in which decisions had been made in their own relationship, with particular reference to the four career moves.

Alan's father told him that there had never been any question but that the family would move when his job required it. Like his father before him, he had seen himself as the provider for the family.

"That's just the way life was back then," his father said. "Your mother and I never questioned it."

When Alan talked to his mother, he learned that she *had* questioned the moves—but only to herself. The moves had been extremely difficult for her. "I started to feel like a refugee, like my grandmother from Poland, but I didn't see any alternative." She revealed that she had become quite depressed when the fourth move took the family sufficiently far from her hometown that she could no longer easily visit her own parents. Her mother had also been upset to lose her close connection to her grandchildren. At that point, Alan's mother had thought of staying behind, but for a number of reasons it had seemed like an impossible choice. By the time retirement came along, she had become more assertive in the marriage. She had been working outside of the home for several years, which she continued to do after Alan's dad retired. Over time, largely as a result of her growing independence and her husband's mellowing in later life, the decision-making process between them was now much more of an equal partnership. In a later conversation, she said to Alan, "I might have considered divorce at the time of the fourth move if it had been as common then as it is today. I never really protested or fought it out with your father. Maybe he would have put me before his career—I guess I'll never really know for sure."

Alan reported that the discussions with his parents had made him think about his own marriage and whether he was putting it in jeopardy by "following in my father's footsteps where work is concerned—I never wanted to do that." I commented, "So, Alan, I guess the challenge for you is whether you want to wait until retirement to figure out how to become an equal partner with your wife, or whether you want to try to do that now." Alan smiled and wryly observed, "If I don't do it now, we won't be together at retirement—Sarah is much more outspoken than my mother." He later reported that he had started to initiate talks with his wife about how they could work together to make room for both of their careers, including the option of his cutting back some on his practice, despite the financial sacrifice, and his spending more time parenting.

In his work with Ellen, he began to ask questions about the decision-making process relating to their possible move. He suggested that she invite her husband to join her in the sessions, and through further questioning, he helped them explore the pluses and minuses of the move for each of them, their children, and their extended-family relationships. The work that Alan did in his own family permitted him to be a clearer and more effective questioner, who could help Ellen and Rob explore a wider range of options because Alan could now see similar possibilities in his own life.

> Test your comprehension of families with young children: a complex intersection by completing this quiz.

The Long-Term View: Working With One Family Over Successive Life Cycle Stages

When my own clients decide to stop therapy, I always leave the door open for them to return in the future. Each life cycle stage brings new dilemmas, and unanticipated stresses (e.g. affairs, addiction, job loss, chronic illness) can occur at any time. The family returning to therapy is comforted by the fact that they have a trusted helper who knows them well, and has the experience to help them meet a new life challenge. For the therapist, an open door policy provides a valuable opportunity to get to know different families as they move through the life cycle.

During such a long-term process, it is inevitable that an unresolved issue for the therapist will intersect with a challenge the clinical family faces. Consider one of the very first families I worked with, Jack and Sheila Vinton and their children. I saw them for eight different phases of therapy in various combinations over a period of 34 years: as a family with young children, as a family with adolescents, as a family launching children, and two phases of marital therapy, including one in which they dealt with the decline and deaths of their parents. Later, Jack came in alone to try to manage increased anxiety and depression over his work late in his career, and to figure out how to plan for his retirement. During this

time, at the age of 63, he was diagnosed with pancreatic cancer, and Sheila rejoined the therapy.

Following the diagnosis, I noticed that I was not doing my best work with them. I felt anxious during the sessions, and often talked too much, not allowing enough space for them to go at their own pace as they struggled with the issues around Jack's cancer, and their fears about his dying. I realized that I needed to take another look at my own family.

My own mother died of breast cancer when she was 49 years old, 10 years after her initial diagnosis in 1954. I was 20 at the time of her death, the second of four siblings, and my youngest brother was 12. Back then, even the word *cancer* was shrouded in stigma and silence. I heard my father mention cancer for the first time shortly before she died, and my mother never spoke the word at all. My mother was also adamant that her parents, Russian Jewish immigrants, be told nothing about her illness and impending death. My grandparents were told a week before she died.

There was more to the silence than the cultural prohibitions of the day. First I, and later my siblings, learned of a family secret 3 weeks after my mother's death that filled in the missing pieces. My father and my mother's best friend, Kathleen, had fallen in love some years earlier, and now planned to be together after she died. Both before and after my mother's death, my father's decisions were governed by this secret triangle, at the expense of considering what his children and the extended family needed to cope with the loss. For example, a month before her death, my father told me that my mother had decided not to have a funeral, an unheard of choice for a Jewish family, especially considering that my father had once been the president of our synagogue.

During the long period I worked with the Vintons, I completed psychoanalysis, and later, as my theoretical perspective shifted, did extensive work on my family of origin with a Bowen-trained therapist. I worked hard to modify my part in the silence surrounding my mother's death and its aftermath. I had separate conversations with my father, and with Kathleen (now his wife), inquiring about my mother, and about each of their relationships with her. My siblings and I spoke openly about our experience of our mother's death, and how the family had been affected by our dad and Kathleen being in love. I also reconnected with my mother's only sibling, a younger brother who had not visited her before she died, and from whom everyone in my family was cut off. In short, I felt I had "done the work." My anxious reactivity with Sheila and Jack Vinton required me to do more.

One of the additional conversations I had with my father stands out. My father and Kathleen were visiting us in Kansas, and they planned to drop me at the airport the morning of their long drive home, because I was also leaving town. The night before, I had asked my dad more questions about my mom, and then gathered my courage and said, "Dad, I don't mean this as a criticism. For me it was a real problem not having a funeral when mom died. Had there been a funeral, it would have helped me grieve her loss. I wish there had been one." My father sat quietly, and then said, "I'm sorry it was hard for you."

I learned the next day that just after he and Kathleen dropped me off at the airport, my father became acutely ill with a headache, and severe nausea. They stopped and checked into a motel just beyond the airport, and my father slept for 18 hours. This was remarkable because he was extremely healthy and stoic, and I could hardly remember the last time he had even had a cold. Although it might have just been a coincidence, his reaction reminded me of how powerful the emotional legacy of family secrets can be.

Shortly before Jack Vinton died, I received a phone call from his grown daughter who had been the original "identified patient" the very first time the family came to see me, telling me that her parents would like me to come to the hospital. I arrived at Jack's room, where his entire family was assembled, just as he died. Several weeks later, Sheila came in to work on her grief, help her children cope with the loss of their father, and figure out a new direction for her own life.

This phase of therapy lasted for 2 years of monthly sessions. Three years later, now a grandmother four times over, Sheila returned to therapy, this time to focus on her younger children's reactivity to her new live-in partner, a man she planned to marry in the coming year. Her children calmed down fairly quickly, and Sheila worked with me on finding a role for each of them in the upcoming wedding. She mentioned Jack during the ceremony, saying that the wonderful marriage she shared with him gave her strength and confidence to set out on this new path.

> Test your comprehension of the long-term view: working with one family over successive life cycle stages by completing this quiz.

Working With Loss: A Link Between Life Cycle Stages

Shortly after Jack Vinton's death, my wife Harriet's elderly parents moved to Topeka to be near us. Their move brought into focus a different impact of my mother's early death: caring for my elderly mother was a life cycle transition I had missed. Helping with my in-laws, especially my beloved mother-in-law, made me both miss my mother more and, at the same time, feel much more closely connected to her.

Perhaps it was not a coincidence that during this time I began working in a nursing home in a small Kansas town, at first to make weekly visits to an elderly client of mine who was moved there following a stroke. The administrator of the facility, impressed with my client's response to therapy, invited me to start a group for those residents—women mostly in their 80s and 90s—who were capable of conversing. I ran the group using a multiple family model and did a genogram for each member.

I vividly recall one group member, Molly, who was admitted when her husband Morris could no longer care for her at home. All of her siblings were dead, and the couple had no children. Morris was "all she had," which she repeatedly stated to everyone around her. Molly would periodically become agitated and shout, "I want to go home; I want to go home!" Two months after her admission, her husband suddenly died of a heart attack.

In the group session following Morris's death, Molly dozed off for the first part of the group, and then woke up with a start and shouted, "I have no one! I'm all alone! I have to go home!" I asked Georgia, Maxine, Violet, and Elizabeth, the other group members, what they wanted to say to Molly when she shouted that she had no one. Georgia, 90, with severe physical problems of her own, said in a clear, strong voice, "Molly, I know you miss Morris. He was a fine man. Would you like me to be your sister? I'd like to be your sister, why, we all would. You're not alone, Molly. Would you like me to be your sister?" Molly nodded. One by one, each group member voiced her willingness to be a sister to Molly. Then there was a silence, and the women all looked at me. I turned to Molly and said, "Molly, I'm only here on Thursday afternoons, and I can't be your sister. But I'd be honored to be your brother." Molly smiled, and accepted me into her newly found "family."

My investment in this work in a setting in which past, current, and impending loss is a constant might not have happened had I not revisited my own history while working with the Vintons, and not had the chance to care for my in-laws with Harriet. I mentioned to the group that they were teaching me a great deal about life. Georgia, the group member who had been there the longest, turned to me and said, "You mean we're teaching you about old age, right? If you ever need to go into a nursing home, you'll know just what to expect."

> Test your comprehension of working with loss: a link between life cycle stages by completing this quiz.

— Conclusion

The intersection between therapist and family life cycle challenges offers both pitfalls and opportunities during the conduct of family therapy. As the previous cases illustrate, it helps to revisit how we ourselves have navigated the stresses and life-cycle transitions that our clients are dealing with. This shift in focus requires a review of our own family history and the multigenerational patterns in which we participate, and a renewed effort to modify our part in unprocessed issues and triangles. An invaluable resource for such a review, and to help modify our part in stuck family patterns, is the Dance of Anger (Lerner, 2005).

Observing and modifying our part in our family of origin is the work of at least one lifetime. Many years ago, my mentor and brilliant pioneer in systems thinking, Betty Carter, agreed to collaborate on a video project about her work (Carter & Lerner, 1997a, 1997b, 1997c). This project offered me the invaluable opportunity to soak up as much as I could about her way of thinking about theory and therapy. As all who knew Betty would agree, she was a true pioneer and force of nature. As we sat in her living room in the Berkshires late one afternoon, after many hours of hard work, I became exhausted and overwhelmed: "Betty, this is too complex. There are too many things to keep in mind." With a laugh that I can still hear today, she said, "Steve, fasten your seatbelt. You have the rest of your life to figure it all out."

> Recall what you learned in this chapter by completing the Chapter Review.

— References

Carter, E. A., & Lerner, S. (1997a). *Clinical dilemmas in marriage: The search for equal partnership* [Video]. New York: Guilford Publications.

Carter, E. A., & Lerner, S. (1997b). *Addressing economic inequality in marriage: A new therapeutic approach* [Video]. New York: Guilford Publications.

Carter, E. A., & Lerner, S. (1997c). Who's in the kitchen: Helping men move toward the center of family life [Video]. New York: Guilford Publications.

Carter, E. A., & McGoldrick, M. (Eds.) (1980). *The family life cycle.* New York: Gardner Press.

Carter, E. A., & McGoldrick, M. (Eds.) (1988). *The changing family life cycle: A framework for family therapy* (2nd ed.). New York: Gardner Press.

Carter, E. A., & Peters, J. (1996). *Love, honor and negotiate: Making your marriage work.* New York: Pocket Books.

Lerner, H. (1998). *The mother dance: How children change your life.* New York: Harper Collins.

Lerner, H. (2005). *The dance of anger: A woman's guide to changing the patterns of intimate relationships.* New York: Harper Collins.

Lerner, S. (1983). *Constructing the multigenerational family genogram: Exploring a problem in context* [Video]. New York: Insight Media.

Simon, R. M. (1988). Family life cycle issues in the therapy system. In M. McGoldrick & E. A. Carter (Eds.), *The changing family life cycle: A framework for family therapy* (2nd ed.). New York: Gardner Press.

NAME INDEX

SUBJECT INDEX